BRASS ANTHOLOGY

A COMPENDIUM OF ARTICLES FROM *THE INSTRUMENTALIST* ON PLAYING THE BRASS INSTRUMENTS

The Instrumentalist Co. • 1418 Lake Street • Evanston, Illinois

I

Introduction

The 701 pages herein present just about everything that is known about brass playing and brass instruments.

Though the articles appear in chronological order (as they were initially printed in *The Instrumentalist*), the three indexes in the back of this book make it possible for the reader to find any article by either *title, subject,* or *author.* If one wishes to peruse all the articles about a particular subject, say mouthpieces, simply look up this subject in the Subject Index. Also, should one wish to read all the articles by a particular author, these can easily be found in the Author Index. A specific article title may be located in the Title Index.

The techniques of brass playing have changed little, if any, in recent decades. Thus, most articles written many years ago are just as pertinent today as when they were first printed. The writings of men like Vincent Bach, Max Pottag, and Leonard Falcone, to mention just three, must be counted as among the most valuable in the library of the brass player or teacher. Much of the content herein is not available anywhere else.

Brass specialists, band and orchestra directors, and students of brass instruments will find this Brass Anthology an invaluable reference source.

Copyright © 1980 by
THE INSTRUMENTALIST COMPANY
1418 Lake Street • Evanston, Illinois

(1946 - 1974)

Table of Contents

Index of Articles by Years

Illustrations

1946

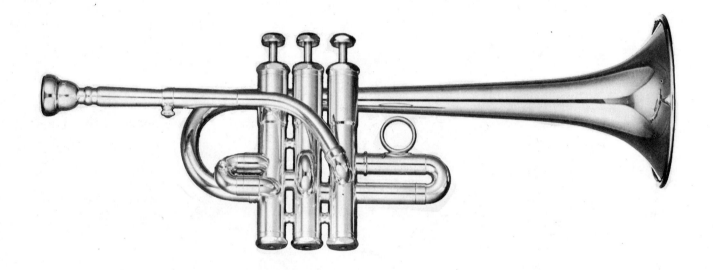

Piccolo B♭ Trumpet

TONE CONTROL

Bernard Fitzgerald

SINCE many players may have discontinued their practice during the summer months, a thorough check up on *fundamentals* is recommended. Although the problems of each player must be considered individually, the basic problems are those involved in the *development* and *coordinated control* of BREATHING, EMBOUCHURE, and ARTICULATION. In the experience of the author, the most common faults among brass players are those concerning *tone control* and *articulation*.

Practice on sustained tones is probably the best method of developing tone control through the coordination and development of both embouchure and breath control. This type of practice should, however, be used only for short practice periods since excessive practice of this type is likely to weaken rather than strengthen the lip muscles. Frequent short rest periods are recommended as an aid in keeping the lip muscles flexible and in guarding against strain and overtiring. It is recommended that the first part of each day's practice be on sustained tones in the middle register and not played louder than mezzo forte.

The first step in the development of tone control should emphasize the ability to sustain tones evenly and steadily with a clear quality and without change in pitch or dynamic level. One of the advantages of this type of practice is that the player has more opportunity to listen to his tone quality and pitch than would be possible in the playing of more rapid passages. A steady flow of breath and firmly controlled lip tension are essential to tone control. The commonly observed difficulties are: air escaping at the corners of the mouth, breathiness of tone quality due to lack of lip tension, pinched tone quality because of excessive mouthpiece pressure or too much lip tension, explosive attack resulting from striking too hard with the tongue and not supporting the tone with the breath, and poor release due to stopping the breath by means of the tongue or throat.

Dynamic Range

The beginner should develop control of tones in the middle register for a period of four to eight slow counts, while the more advanced student should be able to sustain tones for a period of twenty to thirty seconds if played mezzo forte or piano. The baritone, trombone and tuba naturally require a greater amount of breath than the trumpet or French horn, and much greater control is necessary to sustain tones for a long period of time.

It is necessary for players to do more than develop steady control of the tone in this manner and the second step is that of controlling both the crescendo and diminuendo. It is suggested that mezzo-forte be used as the starting point for this development and that the dynamic range be extended gradually until it includes a range from pianissimo to fortissimo. The following steps are suggested allowing from four to eight slow counts for each tone:

(1) $mf <\!\!= f$ (2) $f =\!\!> mf$ (3) $mf =\!\!> p$

(4) $p <\!\!= mf$ (5) $p <\!\!= f$ (6) $f =\!\!> p$

The usual difficulties in controlling the crescendo and diminuendo are uneven dynamic gradations and changes in pitch. Examples 1, 4, and 5 are frequently played using a sudden push of the breath and an abrupt stopping of the tone with the tongue or closing the throat. Continued emphasis should be placed upon the fact that the dynamic changes are to be controlled entirely by the breath by means of the diaphragm. As the player attains control of the middle and low registers in this manner, this type of practice should be gradually extended to the upper register, avoiding straining or forcing at all times.

Eventually, the experienced player should be able to control both the pitch and quality of every tone in each of the following ways:

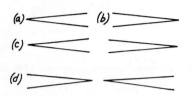

A considerable period of time will be required to acquire this control through the dynamic range from *pp* to *ff* and this development should proceed gradually with continued emphasis upon maintaining a steady pitch at all dynamic levels. All dynamic gradations should be made evenly and steadily while the tone should be resonant. The study of solos, songs, and etudes in *sostenuto* style will prove to be very valuable in the development of tonal beauty and control. The "Ave Maria" by Bach-Gounod and "Largo" by Handel are representative solos in this style.

Beauty of Tone

THE FIRST REQUIREMENT of any musical performance is beauty of tone. The great majority of brass players place much more emphasis upon technical facility than upon tone quality, and the resulting performances are frequently little more than speed demonstrations. The most common deficiencies regarding tone quality are playing too loudly, tonal distortion because of tonguing too hard, and tone quality which is not characteristic of the instrument. Undoubtedly the tone quality of young players has been influenced to a great extent by the tone quality in the field of popular music, and unfortunately this conception of tone is in many instances extremely shrill and harsh rather than the rich resonant sound which is characteristic of the brass instruments.

The increasing tendency toward shallow, small bore mouthpieces has contributed toward this idea of tone quality. These small mouthpieces were designed to aid in the playing of the high register and meet the demands of increased range and endurance required of the dance orchestra musician. The added ease of playing in the high register with this type of mouthpiece is frequently accompanied by a corresponding loss of control and quality of tone in the medium and low register. ∎

Selecting the right French Horn

MAX POTTAG

IT IS POSSIBLE to build a horn in any desired key. In fact, before the invention of valves, a horn player was able to play in the various keys only by the extensive and awkward system of changing horns or crooks as each new key was encountered. Today the problem of selecting the proper horn—single horn in F, single horn in B♭, or double horn in F and B♭, has been confused, in part at least, by a misunderstanding or a lack of information concerning these.

Eliminate E♭ Crooks and Parts

From the standpoint of the French horn there is little argument in favor of using the E♭ crook, and several good ones for eliminating it. The F horn is built to sound its best when in F, not in E♭. Second, many players fail to adjust the valve slides correctly when using the E♭ crook, thus causing many additional problems of poor intonation. In those instances where there is only an E♭ horn part the transposition involved is not difficult to learn. To the F horn player reading an E♭ part, "Read each note one whole step lower." This transposition adds two flats or takes away two sharps from the written key signature of the E♭ part. There are some alto horns and mellophones which do not have an F crook and it is these instruments which are the only drawback to the permanent elimination of all E♭ horns, including altos and mellophones, and the E♭ parts. The teacher should bear in mind that it is he who bears the expense of building two sets (F and E♭) crooks for his instruments, and the publishing of duplicate horn parts in band arrangements. Let us be practical and decide to eliminate this unnecessary expense. In a recent survey of seventy school band and orchestra directors, fifty-four agreed whole heartedly that it is high time that this simplification be effected.

Single F Horn vs. Single B♭

During the last few years there has been an increased interest in the use of the single B♭ French horn. Let us look at the advantages and disadvantages of the two horns fairly and objectively, and then, in the light of all of the available information, decide on a wise procedure.

The B♭ horn sounds an interval of a fourth higher than the F. Thus the note written as third space C will sound first space F on the F horn, and third line B♭ on the B♭ horn. Both are excellent instruments when built by an outstanding manfacturer. It stands to reason, as is the case in the entire brass family, that the larger of the two instruments is more suited to playing the lower tones while the smaller one is preferable for the higher tones. This, however, does not cover the entire subject. The professional player of the double horn is well aware of the advantages and disadvantages of each horn, as he is able to use either as desired. He does not use the B♭ horn for the notes written second line G and lower, and yet, at times, he does use the B♭ horn for the notes written around the E below middle C. Why? The B♭ horn is not as well in tune as the F for the tones from G and lower; on the other hand, the tones around low E (written) are surer and better in tune on the B♭ than on the F. The F horn has a more desirable tonal quality than the B♭ in the range below second line G. Somewhere between second line G and fourth line D (written) the professional player of the double horn changes to the B♭ horn by pushing down the thumb valve. Why? Because in this range and higher the B♭ horn has a distinct advantage over the F in ease of execution and intonation.

This is the complete picture. It is sound because the professional double horn player has no prejudices in favor of one or the other horn. He uses the one which suits him the best and which will produce superior results. There are a few first chair professionals who use the single B♭ horn and a few others who prefer the single F horn; but by and large, most of them use the double horn.

Which Horn Should I Buy?

It is quite obvious from the foregoing that each of the single horns has certain advantages and disadvantages that the other one does not have. The double horn has the marked disadvantage of costing considerably more than either single horn. The single horn in B♭ and the double horn are ideally suited to the first horn player of school bands and orchestras. For the players of the other three parts either the single F horn or the double horn are distinctly preferable to the B♭.

In making these recommendations let us remember that nearly all music for the French horn in school bands and orchestras is written within a range of two octaves—from the G below middle C and up two octaves, and that the B♭ horn has a marked advantage over the F only in the highest five or six notes of this range. Therefore, an unwarranted enthusiasm for or against either horn based on the preferences of one or two players must always be weighed carefully in the light of all the available facts. ■

November-December, 1946

ARTICULATION

Bernard Fitzgerald

THE lack of agreement among prominent teachers, performers and authors in regard to articulation (tongueing) on brass instruments is ample proof that the subject is highly controversial. According to the world famous cornetist and teacher, Herbert Clarke, this subject has caused more controversy than any other pertaining to Cornet playing. The disagreements are equally common in regard to Trombone, French Horn, Baritone, and Tuba. However, the differences of opinion are primarily in regard to the *method* of articulation rather than the *desired musical result*.

The brass instrumentalist must have complete mastery of all forms of articulation from legato to the most incisive staccato or accent and develop the ability to use the tongue to produce many varied gradations in emphasis just as the violinist must develop complete mastery of bowing techniques. Faults in articulation are a major problem to a large percentage of brass instrumentalists and often prove to be the greatest obstacle to technical development since such a handicap imposes definite limitations both in regard to rapid execution and artistic musical interpretation. Very frequently a talented student possessing all the other qualifications for becoming an outstanding performer on a brass instrument is retarded because of slow or faulty articulation. In many instances these deficiencies can be overcome since they are not due to physical disability but to the lack of proper development and coordination.

Although each player must as Herbert Clarke stated "discover the most natural and easiest way for himself", it is helpful to consider the various methods of articulation and analyze the relative merits of these methods and their application to teaching so that both the teacher and the student may be spared the necessity of depending entirely upon the trial and error method. Modern teaching techniques in a scientific age should not be in the position of having to rely upon the method of trial and error except when required as the result of the variable physical characteristics of the individual.

Lingual Habits

Racial speech characteristics and speech habits indicate a close relationship to articulation of brass instruments. Herbert Clarke believed that the Latin Race possessed the best control over all types of attack and suggested that perhaps "their language may help them to be more decisive, besides guiding them with greater certainty as to the attack for the different varieties of tongueing." This opinion is well founded, since the Latin language and those closely related to it employ a much greater variety of vowel sounds than the average American uses in his speech and requires both extreme flexibility and velocity in lingual movement, particularly in the use of the tip of the tongue. Speech correction techniques may prove to be of considerable value in teaching wind instruments, since students having poor articulation in speaking frequently encounter a similar difficulty in articulation on wind instruments.

Fundamentally, articulation on a brass instrument may be defined as "The manner in which the breath is released by the tongue, thus permitting the breath to cause the lips to vibrate." The essential elements in developing the use of the tongue in articulation are CONTROL, COORDINATION (with breath, embouchure and fingers), and VELOCITY. PRECISION should be the first objective in achieving good articulation and the student should not be concerned with velocity until a definite and clear attack has been developed.

The CONTROL OF ARTICULATION is dependent in large measure upon the following: (1) Placement of the tongue in preparation for the attack; (2) The length and direction of the tongue movement at the moment of the attack; (3) The speed with which the tongue moves; (4) The position of the tongue after the attack. Individual physical differences regarding the length, width, thickness and shape of the tongue in relation to the size and shape of the oral cavity are variable factors which must be considered in the analysis of articulation problems and in the application of remedial techniques to correct these difficulties.

Placement

The question of tongue placement is one of the most controversial points regarding articulation. Even the eminent authors Arban and St. Jacome did not agree for Arban recommended that "the tongue ought to be placed against the teeth of the upper jaw in such a way that the mouth is hermetically sealed," while St. Jacome claimed "the tongue, made thin as possible, is introduced between the teeth until it encounters the lips between which it is placed conveniently; it is pressed strongly or lightly against the upper lip (according if a loud or soft sound is desired)." Clarke agrees with Arban with the additional specific recommendation that the tongue should be placed at the base of the upper teeth.

Most authorities are agreed that the tongue should articulate the sound of the letter "T" in executing the basic type of attack but there are many conflicting ideas as to the *vowel sound* which should follow the "T". Arban and Clarke advised the use of the syllable "TU" while the method suggested by St. Jacome results in the syllable "THU". The importance of the vowel sound should not be overlooked since it has the effect of either aiding or impeding the production of tone depending upon whether or not the muscles at the *base* of the tongue are constricted. When these muscles become tensed, a corresponding sympathetic tension of the throat muscles often results and the flow of breath is then interrupted with the result that greater force of the tongue is used to start the tone with the small amount of breath which is contained in the oral cavity. This tension of the throat and tongue muscles is probably one of the greatest problems in playing for a large majority of brass instrumentalists.

It is extremely important that the vowel sound employed be conducive to the relaxation of the tongue and throat muscles and the author has found that most students obtain best results through the application of the following syllables: "TUH" (as in TUN) or TOO (as in TWO) for the middle register; "TIH" (as in TIN) for the upper register; "TEE" (as in TEA) for the extreme high register; "TAH" (as in TOP) or "TAW" (as in TALL) for the low register. The use of the syllable "TUH" seems to produce more relaxation of the muscles in the throat and at the base of the tongue than the syllable "TOO" which may cause tension in these areas.

Hammer or Valve?

In the use of all these articulations the tongue is curved downward at the tip and the movement of the tongue is as short as possible. The mastery of rapid articulation is dependent upon retaining maximum relaxation of the tongue muscles and minimum movement of the tongue. Perhaps one of the most common fallacies concerning articulation is the frequent reference to the *striking* action of the tongue. Actually, the tongue acts as a valve and the breath is released when the tongue is drawn *backward* and *down* toward the floor of the mouth.

The exact point or points of contact by the tongue against the upper teeth

will be governed to some extent by individual physical differences. Students having a short, narrow, pointed tongue usually find that best results are obtained by using the very *tip* of the tongue whereas students whose tongue is long and broad at the tip are most successful if the tip of the tongue is curved downward and the actual contact with the upper teeth being made by the upper side of the tongue, just above the tip. Most players produce best results when the tip of the tongue contact is near the lower edge of the upper teeth when using the syllable "TUH" and progresses gradually upward toward the gum lines as the syllables "TIH" and "TEE" are introduced in the higher registers.

Oral Room

It is important that the back part of the tongue be kept low and flat on the floor of the mouth to prevent its interference with the breath supply. Frequently the articulation "TOE" is recommended for French Horn students as an aid in maintaining the maximum area of resonance within the oral cavity. Trombone, Baritone and Tuba students will usually employ the broader vowel sounds of "TAH" or "TAW" with best results. Frequently players on the larger mouthpiece instruments find that the tongue touches the inner part of the upper lip in tongueing and many times the attack is hindered by the fact that the tongue disturbs the embouchure immediately preceding the attack. Tongueing between the teeth is often a defensive mechanism resulting from the inability to produce lip vibrations easily. The purpose of the tongue is that of *releasing* the breath which causes the lips to vibrate rather than forcing them into vibration by the explosive force of the tongue action.

The inability to produce a definite and clear attack can be attributed to one or more of the following reasons: too much force of the tongue movement; inadequate amount of breath to produce or sustain the tone; tongue stroke too long; tongue placement too far forward (students often place the tongue not only between the lips but into the cup of the mouthpiece which is a tremendous handicap to rapid articulation since the tongue movement for each attack must be much longer and as a result, slower by this method).

1947

High F Trumpet

The Beginning French Horn Player

MAX POTTAG

Because the French horn uses the upper partials of the harmonic series more extensively than any of the other brass instruments, it is rather important for the prospective beginner to have a "good ear" and especially a superior tonal memory. Average or slightly thinner than average lips are preferable to heavy or thick lips. Excellent players possessing thick lips are the exception rather than the rule. Reasonably straight teeth are a definite asset in the playing of any brass instrument but here too one finds some notable exceptions to the general rule.

A good mouthpiece is of inestimable importance. It is advisable to start the beginner on a medium size mouthpiece, one which is neither too deep nor too wide. If a worn dime can be placed inside of the rim one may consider the width of the cup about right. At least three of the present day symphony players use a mouthpiece which is large enough for a penny, but these also are exceptional cases. A medium size mouthpiece is also characterized by a medium size bore or throat. After the beginner is well started it may prove advisable to change to a mouthpiece which varies somewhat from the standard or medium dimensions. It should be mentioned that the very deep cup with rather straight sides may be considered obsolete today, in spite of the fact that there still are a few professional players who prefer this type.

Placing of Mouthpiece

The placement of the mouthpiece on the lips deserves some attention. A majority of the players place two-thirds of the mouthpiece on the upper lip and one-third on the lower, some prefer to place it in the exact center, while still others prefer two-thirds on the lower lip. The writer prefers the first of these three. With advanced students who have developed an excellent embouchure using either the second or the third type, it is advisable not to change. It is always an excellent rule to encourage the student to experiment somewhat in the early stages in finding the best place-ment of the mouthpiece. It may be found that an off-center placement, either to the right or to the left of center, may prove advantageous. Though the appearance of an off-center placement is not desirable, the most important thing is not the appearance but the way the horn will sound. One encounters occasional horn players, particularly those playing the low fourth part, who prefer to place the mouthpiece inside of the red part of the lower lip instead of on the outside as is the usual case in the playing of all brass instruments. This rather uncommon practice may facilitate the playing of the lowest tones of the horn, but it will also interfere with the playing of the highest tones; so at least for the beginner this method is definitely not recommended.

The left hand position for holding the instrument will vary somewhat with the type of horn used, whether it is a single or a double, or whether it has three, four or five valves. With the three valved single horn the thumb and little finger are used to hold the instrument; in fact, the horn may be held comfortably with the left hand only. With the double horn or the four valved single horn, the thumb needs to be relaxed so that it may operate the thumb valve with ease. The fingers, other than the thumb, should be relaxed also, slightly curved, and in line with the valve levers.

It is the writer's opinion that all horn playing should be done with the player seated except occasionally when long sustained tones and special breathing exercises are practiced. Even in solo playing, the slight advantage in appearance of the standing position is more than offset by the superior playing possible while seated. Obviously, the player should sit erect at all times.

Position of Hands

There is not complete agreement as to the best position of the right hand inside the bell. The most practical appears to favor placing the hand against the opposite side of the bell, away from the player. It is important that the tips of the fingers be straight. The opening of the bell is closed with the palm of the hand so that the base of the hand is about one-half inch away from the side of the bell nearest the player. Each individual has to find the most desirable exact opening to be used. The purpose of partly closing the bell is to produce a more mellow tone than is possible with an open bell. The right hand position is also altered for adjusting the intonation. This subject will be treated fully later. A definite factor in favor of the position just described over other positions is that muting or stopping is easier. It should be mentioned that a different position is desirable for the beginner and for use in playing while standing or marching with a band. This position permits the base of the right hand to rest against the side of the bell nearest the player with the first knuckle of the thumb resting against the top of the bell. With the fingers slightly cupped and apart, the tone will come through with the desired quality. This position of the right hand will be found easier for the beginner than the other one and can be used on the march. Nevertheless, before long the player should be introduced to the more preferred position. After all, the principle function of the right hand is to control the tone quality and intonation and not to hold the instrument. Care should be taken that the player using the preferred position does not let the weight of the hand and arms rest heavily against the lower side of the bell, but to have the right hand tend to support the instrument in the direction of the lips.

The player's head may bend slightly forward, but not too far. This will vary somewhat between individuals, depending upon the formation of the teeth. Under any and all circumstances the best playing position is one which is comfortable and permits a maximum of relaxation, ease in breathing and technical facility. ∎

Criteria for Selecting Students Adapted to Brass Instruments

BERNARD FITZGERALD

THE PHYSICAL CHARACTERISTICS of the lip, jaw and tooth formation of the student should be given careful analysis and consideration previous to the selection of a brass instrument. Although uniformity of length, shape and size of the teeth is not a primary prerequisite for successful performance, it is important that the outer surface contour of the front teeth (the incisors) be sufficiently even to permit the mouthpiece to rest on the lips in a comfortable position without causing the teeth to cut into the inner lip tissue.

Protruding front teeth which result in an abnormal irregularity of the outer surface of the teeth frequently interfere seriously with the placement of the mouthpiece of the cornet, trumpet, or French horn, since these mouthpieces are rather small in diameter and the rims are often narrow. The mouthpieces of the mellophone, trombone, baritone and tuba cover a greater area of the mouth, and the irregularity of the incisors does not usually prove to be detrimental. It is preferable that the upper front teeth be vertical rather than slanting either inward or outward. Extremely short upper or lower front teeth are not good.

The ability to obtain and maintain a normal occlusion of the upper and lower front teeth is one of the most important requirements (i.e., to be able to move the lower jaw either forward or backward so that the upper and lower front teeth can be closed with the cutting edges together). This is particularly important for students desiring to play the cornet, trumpet or French horn. The receding or jutting lower jaw does not seriously affect performance on the larger instruments except in cases of extreme malformation.

Physical Types

The contour of the tooth formation is frequently referred to as the jaw formation, and may be classified into three basic types: round, square, and pointed or V-shaped. The rounded type is the most common, and generally speaking, the small cup mouthpiece instruments (cornet, trumpet and French horn) are best suited to this type. The pointed or V-shaped type may prove adequate for students on the French horn, but is not usually desirable for the others. The square type is normally to be preferred for students desiring to play the trombone, baritone or tuba, since the broader frontal tooth surface provides a better base for the placement of the larger cup mouthpieces.

Although the shape, width, and thickness of the lips are factors which are frequently considered as a primary basis for selecting students for brass instrument study, the *texture and muscular flexibility* of the lips are of much greater importance. A firm, muscular lip formation is preferable for students who are to play the cornet, trumpet or French horn, since these instruments sound in a tonal register which requires higher vibrations than the trombone, baritone, or tuba. Loosely formed or flabby lip formations are not desirable for best results on any of the brass instruments. The only satisfactory method of testing lip texture and flexibility is through actual experience in producing lip vibrations either with or without the mouthpiece and through adaptability tests with the instruments. Statistics based upon some research studies indicate that tooth evenness and lip thickness have very little correlation to successful performance on the brass instruments, while *lip texture and muscular flexibility* are

much more significant considerations in making a selection.

Musical Adaptability

It is assumed that students will receive instruction and guidance in regard to breathing, posture, and correct embouchure formation in order to establish a valid basis for evaluating the following musical criteria with relation to potential success in brass instrument performance.

1. The ability to produce clear, steady vibrations with the mouthpiece at least as high in pitch as the second open tone on the instrument (fifth open tone on the French horn), without excessive pressure of the mouthpiece against the lips and without excessive tightening or stretching of the muscles at the corners of the mouth.

2. The ability to produce the second open tone (fifth open tone on the French horn) easily on the instrument, sustaining with good quality and intonation.

3. The ability to properly relax the lip muscles to produce the next lower open tone; also to contract the lips to produce the next higher open tone without straining.

4. Singing ability is a definite asset and is especially desirable for French horn students.

5. Aural sensitivity to pitch deviation is an important consideration.

The above requirements should be an adequate basis for determining adaptability to the various brass instruments.

In spite of recommendations to the contrary, it is inevitable that a certain percentage of students will prove to be exceptions to one or all of the conditions listed above as desirable physical qualifications. However, teachers should not allow these exceptions to bias judgment to the extent that instruments are assigned to students without any consideration of the various factors involved. The only genuine proof of adaptability is actual experience playing with both the mouthpiece and the instrument.

Exploratory Classes

A period of exploratory experience with mouthpieces and instruments is recommended to determine the adaptability of students for the various brass instruments. To obtain satisfactory results, these exploratory classes should be administered under the guidance of an experienced instrumental teacher. Classes may be conducted somewhat informally to encourage experimentation by the students and ample opportunity should be provided for each student to indicate his adaptability for each of the brass instruments through actual playing experience.

The three basic fundamentals of brass instrument technique (breathing, embouchure, and articulation) should be emphasized. It is recommended that classes be continued over a period of several weeks, meeting two or three times each week, to obtain conclusive evidence in regard to adaptability for the different brass instruments.

A complete record should be kept concerning the achievement of each student. This record should indicate a classification regarding the type of lip and jaw formation, and a grade for tone production, range, tone quality, and pitch control.

The exploratory classes could be organized near the end of the spring term, during the summer music school, or during the first few weeks of the winter term. Individual situations will determine the most advantageous period of the year for scheduling the classes. It is desirable that study on the assigned instruments be started as soon as possible after the conclusion of the exploratory period. The musical growth and technical progress achieved by students well adapted to the instruments will be ample justification for the time and effort expended in providing this preparatory experience. ∎

March-April 1947

THE DAILY PRACTICE ROUTINE

BERNARD FITZGERALD

IT WOULD be difficult to overestimate the value and importance of the *daily warm-up routine* for players of brass instruments. Flexibility and control in playing brass instruments is dependent upon the balanced coordination of embouchure, breathing and articulation. Embouchure development and control depends primarily upon the controlled adjustment and flexibility of the small area in the center of the lips which forms the vibrating mechanism. The flexibility and control of this delicate mechanism will be greatly impaired through uncontrolled, loud playing and it is extremely important to give *particular attention to the first few minutes of practice each day.* Many students have the mistaken idea that the "warm-up" should consist of rapid technical flourishes played as loudly as possible throughout the range of the instrument with special emphasis upon the highest possible tones. Actually, this type of playing has very little value as a warm-up drill and is usually detrimental to embouchure development and control.

Every student should evolve a daily routine designed to serve as a warm-up period and since the individual requirements of players are widely divergent, it is obviously impractical to prescribe exactly the same routine for every student. As the result of these individual differences, some players are able to obtain control and flexibility after a brief period of preliminary practice, while others may require a practice period of an hour or more to achieve the same results. Since some students are naturally endowed with a higher degree of lip flexibility than others, the warm-up routine should be planned to condition the *individual player* for the more strenuous playing of the day through a review of basic techniques.

Although the amount of practice required for each phase of the routine will vary according to the individual student, the daily warm-up routine should include studies which stress the development of the following fundamental techniques: I. Tone and Breath Control, II. Lip Flexibility, III. Coordination of Tonguing and Fingering. It is obvious that the requirements of the beginner and the advanced student are different, but the warm-up period is of equal importance to both, and its routine should be modified to suit the technical limitations of the individual. As the student progresses, drills should be included which employ a wider range and demand increased facility. Although a considerable number of books of daily technical studies for brass instruments have been published, few of them contain sufficient material which is carefully graded and adapted to the needs of beginning and intermediate students.

Tone and Breath Control

It is desirable that the first few minutes of each days practice be devoted to playing sustained tones in the middle and lower registers not louder than *mezzo-forte*. This type of practice requires the utmost concentration to be effective in maintaining and developing tone quality and breath control as well as aiding in strengthening the embouchure and developing increased endurance. (Many outstanding teachers recommend that the student begin his daily practice by "buzzing" with the mouthpiece for a brief period of time with emphasis upon producing lip vibrations without forcing or straining.) Frequent brief rest periods are recommended as a precaution against overtiring the muscles of the embouchure. Students should be cautioned to avoid excessive practice on this type of exercise, since overemphasis may weaken rather than strengthen the embouchure.

The daily practice on exercises for tone control should include two types of drill on sustained tones, (A) steady controlled tones of good quality sustained without change in volume (using the following dynamic levels: *forte, mezzo-forte, piano*), (B) sustained tones employing the various dynamic shadings within the player's ability. Although both types of drill are necessary for the experienced player, it is recommended that the less advanced student devote his attention to the mastery of the first type before attempting any extended development of the second type.

Exercises 1, 2, 3 and 4 may be applied to the trombone, baritone and tuba by playing them in the register which corresponds to that written for the cornet. Additional exercises of this type may be practiced in both the extreme low register and in the higher register in accordance with the ability of the student. Scales may be used also as long tone drills with each tone being sustained for several slow counts. There are many possible variations of this type of drill, and there is no reason for this practice to become so matter of fact that the student practices with little or no attention to the ultimate goal of tonal beauty and control.

Lip Flexibility

The flexibility and elasticity of the lip muscles must be highly developed since each tone in the range of the brass instrument requires the ability to make these changes in muscular tension accurately and rapidly. The perfection of the technique of "lip slurring" is essential and emphasis should be placed upon the precision and accuracy of the embouchure change to develop a perfect legato. Students should perfect the execution of slow moving lip slurs first and gradually increase both the tempo and the range as control and flexibility are acquired. The daily routine should include some practice of the slow, sustained type of lip

slur exercise regardless of the ability of the student to play more rapid slurs. Exercises of the type of No. 5 to No. 9 are suggested as basic drills.

Each exercise should be practiced until the player is able to play it perfectly. The range may be gradually extended upward using these same exercises starting with a higher open tone. The studies may be practiced more rapidly after good control has been established at a slow tempo. These studies may be applied to the other brass instruments by using the corresponding range of the other instruments. Extensive exercises on lip slurring will be found in Max Schlossberg's "Daily Drills and Technical Studies" published by Baron. Although this book contains some material which would challenge the virtuoso, the studies on lip slurring are graduated in difficulty to provide a considerable number of studies for the average student. The majority of the studies published for the development of lip flexi-

bility advance much too rapidly for the average player and lack sufficient studies in the middle and lower registers. In many instances, emphasis is given to the extremely rapid type of slur study before adequate control has been developed. Students should be cautioned to practice lip slurs only within the range which can be controlled.

It is recommended that interval studies of the type of No. 10 be included as a part of the daily routine. Such studies should be practised both slurred and staccato in all possible major and minor keys within the range limits determined by the embouchure development of the individual student.

Coordinating Tongue and Fingers

The coordinated control of the tongue and fingers is essential to the development of technique on brass instruments. See Herbert Clarke's "Technical Studies" (Carl Fischer). Articulation and rhythmic patterns like No. 11 will be found valuable in acquiring additional control and technique.

THE TRANSPOSING BRASS INSTRUMENTS

TRAUGOTT ROHNER

TODAY the brass instruments reading from the bass clef "sound-as-written," while those reading from the treble clef do not. Why?

Robert Hargreaves, who heads the music department at Ball State Teachers College, Muncie, Indiana, writes: "A study of the history of brass instruments and of the art of arranging music for combinations of brass instruments reveals an amazing amount of 'following the original cow-path' to the absurd and bitter end."

Chester L. Travelstead, director of instrumental music in Louisville, Kentucky, last summer asked a group of experienced band directors:

"If instruction books and band music were to be made available so that the cornet-trumpet would sound-as-written (the printed B*b* fingered open, etc.) would you use them?" Their answers were:

"Yes"—24 "No"—38

Travelstead asked also, "Do you believe that it would be advantageous to use only F slides in horns, altos and mellophones, and to use only music written in F, thereby making it unnecessary to publish E*b* parts for these instruments?" They answered:

"Yes"—54 "No"—16

In the last issue of the INSTRUMENTALIST an open letter to our readers asked similar questions and invited immediate answers and comments. Prompt replies were received from a number of college and university men whose responsibility it is to set the pattern for the future through their teacher-training connections, and other leaders of thought in executive and key positions, including:

R. C. Anderson, North Platte, Nebraska; Paul Van Bodegraven, University of Missouri, Columbia; Kenneth L. Bovee, Oxford, Michigan; Dale W. Caris (president, Iowa Bandmasters Association), Sioux City, Iowa; Gene Chenoweth, New Castle, Indiana; T. Frank Coulter (president, National School Orchestra Association), Joplin, Missouri; Clarence F. Gates, Tulsa, Oklahoma; Robert Hargreaves, Ball State Teachers College, Muncie, Indiana; James C. Harper, Lenoir, North Carolina; Dean L. Harrington, Hornell, New York; Mark H. Hindsley, University of Illinois, Urbana; David Hughes, Elkhart, Indiana; Harry A. King, State Teachers College, Fredonia, New York; William E. Knuth, Teachers College, San Francisco, California.

A. D. Lekvold (president Ohio Music Educators Association), Miami University, Oxford; Newell H. Long, Indiana University, Bloomington; Rene A. Louapre, New Orleans, Louisiana; Joseph E. Maddy, National Music Camp, Ann Arbor, Michigan; Thurber H. Madison, University of Indiana, Bloomington; David Mattern, University of Michigan, Ann Arbor; Theodore F. Normann, University of Washington, Seattle; Paul Painter, (formerly Winfield, Kansas), Chicago; Gerald R. Prescott, University of Minnesota, Minneapolis; Charles B. Righter, University of Iowa, Iowa City; M. E. Russell, State Teachers College, Cedar Falls, Iowa; Clarence Sawhill, University of Illinois, Urbana; James E. Van Peursem, Eastern Kentucky State Teachers College, Richmond; Gilbert Waller, University of Oklahoma, Norman; Walter Welke, University of Washington, Seattle; George C. Wilson, University of Missouri, Columbia; Robert Winslow, University of Minnesota, Minneapolis, and Paul Yoder, Chicago.

Our first question was, "assuming that one or more publishers could be induced to print or re-print beginning and intermediate music for the cornet-trumpet so that it would *sound as written,* would you be in favor of it?" Our correspondents listed above answered:

"Yes"—14 "No"—18

As the votes do not provide a complete picture, we desire to quote some comments. Mr. Normann, author of the excellent textbook "Instrumental Music in the Public Schools," writes: "I believe that to be effective such a move would need the support of the leading publishers. The elimination of transposition of trumpet parts would result in some intermediate saving in the printing of solo and small ensemble materials for beginners. It would lead to some confusion for several years, but to no greater extent than was formerly true of the treble clef trombone parts."

Mark Hindsley writes, "Fine, but impractical in view of music already written." Charles B. Righter is also opposed "until you find a way to eliminate all transposition." Walter Welke states that the students in his classes as well as he himself feel that "unless the matter were to be unanimous with all publishers, more confusion would result than is involved in the matter of a simple transposition." This is at least a partial picture of the written replies. More later!

Question two was, "Would you be in favor of eliminating the E*b* part and the E*b* horn?" The votes:

"Yes"—21 "No"—10

James C. Harper would "prefer to see all horns in F. If the change would eliminate the mellophone, so much the better." David Hughes commented, "If new parts coming out were to be put in F, then the manufacturers could gradually change all horns and mellophones to F." James E. Van Peursem has an idea: "Since many arrangements already have F horn parts, why do not manufacturers stop making E*b* instruments and crooks? In a matter of a few years, the problem would settle itself." Harry A. King goes one step beyond eliminating the E*b* part: "Horn parts should be put in actual pitch, using the great staff. Association of symbols with fixed sounds is a 'must' for horn players."

William E. Knuth answers the E*b* question, "Decidedly 'yes' for French horns." A. D. Lekvold writes, "Yes in concert, but not in military music." Paul Painter prefers to use the E*b* bell-front alto for the march. He adds, "In this case my boys found it quite as easy to transpose parts to the alto as to the horn." Paul Yoder voices an important consideration: "The problem of the French horn parts can be solved only by the gradual disappearance of the alto horn. As yet it is not practical to publish an arrangement with only the F parts, as there still are many E*b* alto horns in use."

We conclude that *the four to one majority definitely indicates that it is high time to eliminate the E*b* horn part as well as the E*b* instrument.* A practical solution would be for the manufacturers to cease making E*b* horns and crooks in favor of F, and

13

for the publishers to stop printing E♭ parts, starting with more difficult symphonic parts.

Tenor Clef

Question three: "Shall we eliminate the further printing of school music which uses the tenor clef for cello, trombone and bassoon?" They answered:

"Yes"—21   "No"—10

This question was not asked in Travelstead's questionnaire but has a direct bearing on the general subject of transpositions. No one who can read the tenor clef fluently understands fully that it does offer considerable difficulty for quite a while to the average school trombonist, cellist and bassoonist. Some composers and arrangers seem to use the tenor clef at the slightest provocation. Dr. Joseph E. Maddy answered this question with, "Yes, except when three or more ledger lines would be necessary." Dale W. Caris contends that "Much symphony music is written in the tenor clef, therefore it is necessary for these instruments to learn it." Newell H. Long believes that "with present tendency toward high brass parts, popular orchestrations should use tenor clef more." Van Bodegraven upholds the tenor clef pillar in the shrine of music thusly: "Don't eliminate all hocus-pocus in music! Transposition is one of those intellectual activities which can confuse even the Phi Beta Kappa. If we can be vague enough about it even the most elite of the intellectuals pay us homage." Gene Chenoweth, who is both an excellent professional musician and orchestra director, surprises us by "we should abolish the alto and tenor clef entirely, except in the case of the viola." T. Frank Coulter believes that since "pianists read two clefs" so too should the school musician.

We conclude: *Publishers should eliminate the further use of the tenor clef from school orchestrations, and that when the notes go beyond the convenient range of the bass clef that the treble clef should be used.* The flutist, violinist, and pianist thinks that it is strange that so many trombonists, cellists, and bassoonists "cannot" read beyond two or three ledger lines above the staff.

All Brasses Should Sound as Written

The question concerning the advisability of changing the cornet-trumpet music to sound as written is part of a much larger subject than appears at first sight. It is one which involves at least the entire brass family. What should be done about the treble clef baritone parts? How about the cornet players we like to transfer to the French horn or to the E♭ tuba? What should be done about the single B♭ French horn which is gaining in popularity?

Because it will be relatively simple to transfer the "sound-as-written" cornet player to the bass clef baritone (and BB♭ tuba), it will no longer be necessary to print a treble clef baritone part. We would thus not only eliminate the cost of printing an extra part but also eliminate a rather awkward transfer of a treble clef player to the baritone or BB♭ tuba.

With the foregoing, the solution for the single B♭ French horn is to write the horn part in C, the horn part in C sounding one octave lower than the written notes. The sound-as-written cornet player who is transferred to the B♭ horn would use *exactly the same* fingering. Today the cornet player transferring to the French horn in F or E♭ needs to transpose the fingered notes one octave. The simplicity with which the transfer could be made should be a real advantage to the single horn in B♭.

The solution for the single horn in F or E♭ and the double horn in F and B♭ has several possibilities: (1) the F horn part can remain as is, (2) one can add the mezzo-soprano clef to the regular F horn part and thus have the F horn part sound-as-written, or (3) the player of the F horn can read the C horn part. Without taking the time to discuss the advantages and disadvantages of each of these three possibilities, it appears that the best and most practical solution is to leave the F part as it now is. If the advocate of the E♭ mellophone or alto has become thoroughly disgusted with the opinion of the majority given earlier, let him take heart right now. The sound-as-written cornet player transferred to the mellophone or alto (or if he started on either of these instruments with a sound-as-written cornet book) could play the regular F horn part *without any transposition*. The sound-as-written cornet player who is transferred to the F horn would need to read each note one step lower with

the octave fingering transposition in effect as is the case today. Thus the horn section would be provided with two parts: a "Horn in C" for the single B♭ horn players, and a "Horn in F" for the single F or double horn players. Actually the C part would be substituted for the one in E♭, thus involving no additional expense over the present usual practice of supplying band music in both F and E♭ horn. The C part has an additional advantage in that it will never require the bass clef, for the lowest open tone is *written* B♭ below middle C.

Summary

The E♭ horn part and the treble clef baritone parts are to be dropped. The new sound-as-written cornet-trumpet parts will be substituted for the old and the new C horn parts will be added for the single B♭ French horn.

At first these ideas seem revolutionary, impractical, and certainly not worth the cost and trouble. One could discuss and argue the points pro and con at great length and in great detail, and whether or not any significant progress is made thereby would depend largely on how fairly and objectively the various issues were presented. Let us not forget that (1) human nature resists change, (2) human nature has a marked tendency to follow the road of least resistance, and (3) a prejudiced argument sheds more heat than light.

The two most significant arguments against making the suggested changes are (1) much music has already been printed in the old way, and (2) for several years we would suffer the inconvenience of having to bother with new cornet and horn parts. The two principal arguments in favor of the change are (1) the students, especially the younger ones, would benefit immensely thereby, and (2) the teacher would benefit. Let me cite just one of the many advantages. Today the teacher of a mixed string class simply says "Sound C" while the teacher of the beginning brass class has to say "Bass clef brasses sound C, cornets-trumpets and treble clef baritone play the note written D, F horns finger G while you E♭ mellophones (or altos) play A." Under the proposed new set-up the director would simply say "Sound C. Horns in F finger G." I certainly would like to give it a try. Wouldn't you?

March-April, 1947

The Use of the
TONGUE
IN
BRASS INSTRUMENTS

HOWARD W. DEYE

THE PROPER use of the tongue is of fundamental importance in the playing of all wind instruments. Poor tone quality is often the result when the attack is faulty. It is only when good tongue action is combined with correct breathing, and a well formed embouchure, that we obtain the desired results.

Skillful use of the tongue also has a great deal to do with interpretation. Methods of attack are as important to the wind instrument player as types of bowing are to the string player. A band which cannot play a light staccato or a broad legato is seriously handicapped in the performance of even the simplest music.

Not only does the action of the tongue vary for different styles, and according to what register is being played on a single instrument, but it also varies between instruments. It is essential, then, that teachers of wind instruments acquaint themselves with these fundamental differences.

Words of Experts

The numbered statements that follow were submitted to prominent brass authorities. These experts were asked to approve or disapprove these statements, and make comments on methods of tonguing. I will limit my own part in the material that follows to: (a) compilation of statistical results; (b) pointing out the most obvious conclusions.

1. The tongue should usually strike (touch) the roof of the mouth.

Twenty-six experts say, "No," and five, "Yes." Two of them say only when using the "D" or "Lu" attacks.

2. The tongue should strike at the roots of the upper teeth.

Twenty-four agree and ten disagree.

A majority of the teachers of every brass instrument favor this method.

3. The tongue should strike the tips of the upper teeth.

Cornetists favor this seven to four, trombone and baritone experts six to five, and tuba pedagogs, three to two. Horn teachers disapprove six to four.

4. The tongue should never strike the lips.

Cornet and horn teachers agree twelve to six, but the teachers of the larger instruments take the opposite viewpoint, with a score of eleven to six.

5. For low tones the tongue may come between the teeth.

Twenty-one agree and fourteen disagree.

It is only possible to draw a few rather indefinite conclusions, from the results of the above scores: all positions are used by many under certain circumstances; a majority tongue usually at the roots of the teeth; the tongue touches the lips oftener in playing the larger brasses than for cornet or horn; it is most likely to come between the teeth when playing low notes.

6. Most amateurs are inclined to tongue too hard.

This statement is substantially true, because all but one agree.

7. What syllable is best adapted for ordinary tonguing?

Twenty use "Tu" or "Too," six "Tah," six "Te" or "Tee," and two "T."

8. What syllable is best adapted for legato tonguing?

Five use "Tu" or "Too," eight "Du," seven "Dah," two "Ta," two "D," two "La," one "Ha," and one "Lu" or "Dthu" with emphasis on the "u."

Why Tongue?

The purpose of the use of the tongue

in the attack is to act as a valve. It is necessary for the breath to be released suddenly, with some pressure, else the tone has a poor start. On the violin, it is the pressure of the forefinger and the suddenness of the stroke that determines the character of the attack. On wind instruments, the action of the tongue and breath serve the same purpose.

The *consonant* with which the attack syllable begins determines the position of the tongue at the attack. The *vowel* sound used determines the position of the tongue after the attack and, to some extent, the shape of the oral cavity.

There is general agreement, in the above results, on the use of the consonant "T" for ordinary tonguing. "D" is the favorite consonant for the legato attack, but some advocate "T" and "L." I am inclined to conclude that the value of the vowel sound, used in the attack syllable, has been overestimated. The wide diversity of opinion and lack of agreement tend to strengthen this conclusion. However, it is true that the shape of the oral cavity affects the tone, possibly because of its effect on lip position.

Many of the brass teachers who answered the above questions were generous with clarifying comments. The following quotations help to clear up some of their viewpoints:

"The tongue should strike the tip of the teeth for the staccato attack on cornet. In legato tonguing, 'La' is a good syllable because it insures an open throat. 'Da' works well also."

"This method (tongue against tip of teeth) is generally best, but for certain purposes the tongue should touch the roof of the mouth or the roots of the teeth. All variations of

'T' and 'D' are possible, and vary primarily only in the amount of closure of the mouth in producing these letters."

"Use this method (tongue against lips) on low notes or for solid entrance."

"In ordinary tonguing, I don't like the use of any syllable. Simply place the tip of the tongue against the edge of the upper teeth and spit an imaginary something off the tongue."

"This question as to the position of the tongue has caused more confusion, misery, and disappointment to French horn players than anything else. I wish that not one word had ever been said about the position of the tongue against the teeth. To produce a tone we have to 'spit' into the mouthpiece, and that means just plain 'spit.' It is rather hard at first, but becomes more polished as we improve. The tongue will find its proper place."

"The tongue should be used unconsciously as in speech, and should never be stiff or tense."

"It all depends on the placement of the tone. If the tone sounds in the throat, 'De' is best to bring it forward. If the tone is nasal, 'Dah' is best to bring it out. I prefer 'D' to 'T,' as it is less likely to be windy and causes a more firm, round tone quality. 'Du' also brings the tone forward. Other syllables might be substituted, depending on where the tone needs filling out."

"If 'Da' is attempted, the tongue seems too high. 'Tda' merely softens ordinary tonguing and produces a soft attack."

"By emphasizing the time honored 'Tu' or 'Te,' there is a tendency to tighten the throat, which precludes a free flow of air, so necessary to proper tone production and relief from strain on the lips in the high register. 'Tah' or 'Dah' opens the throat and should be taught at the start. There are many systems at variance with mine which seem to function, so I would be the last to condemn any of them. However, aiding free breath control by proper use of the tongue, and the use of the lower lip to flex pitch, are two very serious matters which should be better understood by all teachers."

Herbert L. Clarke commented:

"The tongue strikes the inside of the mouth according to what register is being used. When playing loud in the low register on the cornet (especially F#) the tongue must strike the open or parted lips. Use 'Tu' in the low register as the muscles are relaxed, 'Ta' in the middle register, and 'Te' in the upper register where the muscles are contracted. For legato or singing style use 'La' when playing moderately soft, and 'D' when playing loud.

"For proper articulation, the tongue in different registers varies as in ordinary talking and the muscles of the lips move with the tongue, as in talking. It is the movement of the tongue and lips that produces proper pronunciation in all languages." ∎

May-June, 1947

Playing the French Horn

MAX POTTAG

Breath Control

IT IS THE PLAYER who controls the intensity of the air stream, the evenness with which it is propelled through the instrument, the manner in which it is started and stopped and how accurately and delicately it is controlled in keeping with the desired musical meaning. How are these controls developed?

I believe that the breath should be taken in through the mouth and not through the nose. As the air is inhaled the ribs as well as the stomach walls are extended while the diaphragm muscle is lowered to increase the capacity of the lungs. While the breath is exhaled the stomach walls remain more or less stationary while the diaphragm and ribs assist each other in expelling the the air. Tightness in the midsection will cause the tone to suffer. At all times it is necessary that the air be expelled evenly. This takes much practice.

One should bear in mind that the length of the F French horn is over twelve feet while a mellophone of the same pitch is only half as long. It is necessary to blow *through* the horn and not *at* it otherwise a good vigorous tone of true horn quality is not possible. Many cornet players who have been transferred to the French horn are especially likely to blow *at* the horn instead of *through* it. Even a beginner should be taught to produce a reasonably round and full tone instead of one that is soft and anemic in quality. It is hardly necessary to mention the need for having a good playing posture, yet many bad faults

16

can be directly attributed to a faulty posture. The shoulders should not move in the process of inhaling or exhaling.

Relaxation is a word that is often misused and yet one cannot help but use it again and again in the teaching of any skill. Though there is some tension in the lips and a certain amount of pressure is needed to expell the air, there is no need to tighten the stomach muscles unduly, nor the throat muscles. Some students who come to me have been taught to hold the stomach walls rigid while exhaling. This is incorrect. Another fault is to over-do the pulling in of the stomach wall while exhaling. The breathing process is a natural one and any artificiality or unnecessary exertion is harmful.

I also believe in more frequent breathing especially in fast music where time does not permit a deep breath. Better phrasing results thereby and greater playing facility.

Attack and Embouchure

Contrary to the opinion of many I believe it is better to place the tip of the tongue between the teeth instead of against them when starting a tone. The tongue is pulled back quickly as when saying the syllable "Ta" or

"Tu," and yet the action is similar to that when spitting away an imaginary piece of thread that has lodged on the lips. The between-the-lips attack produces a surer start of the tone than the back-of-the-teeth attack, especially is this true in the upper register of the instrument. Under no circumstances should one use the tongue to stop the tone as in saying "tut" nor should one permit the throat to be contracted to assist the stopping of the tone. All that is necessary is to cut off the air supply at the source, in the lungs. The syllable "da" used in legato tonguing should be delayed until the student has developed a good tone and a sure attack with the "ta" and "tu" syllables. As the player progresses the tongue will automatically function correctly.

The mouthpiece is placed on the center of the lips unless the teeth formation is such as to favor an off-center placement. I recommend that about two-thirds of the mouthpiece be placed on the upper lip. The corners of the mouth are firmly sealed but without pulling them back as in smiling, rather they should have a tendency to pucker just a little. This puckering tendency is highly desirous for shaping the lips as a funnel in directing the air into the mouthpiece.

It makes little difference which note is the initial starting tone for the

beginner. From whatever tone he can best produce the range is extended up and down. Contrary to what the student may think, the upper register is helped considerably by the development of a good middle and low register.

Another point of importance is for the student to avoid pulling up the face muscles when playing in the middle register but to relax the lower jaw. This will produce a mellow tone and one which is better in pitch. This relaxed playing position should be maintained even when playing high tones. It is the lips and not the pressure of the air or the muscular tensions in various parts of the body which produce the high tones. It is thus desirable to build up the higher range of the instrument while playing *piano*. One should avoid pressing the mouthpiece against the lips to assist the playing of high tones.

It is important that the beginner practice slowly so that he can concentrate on each particular task at hand.

To recapitulate: the French horn player should (1) breathe deeply but correctly, (2) blow through the horn and not at it, (3) place the tongue at the edge of the lips, and (4) adjust the lips with a slightly puckered tendency. ∎

May-June, 1947

A SUMMER STUDY PLAN

BERNARD FITZGERALD

Endurance is one of the principal factors in playing a brass instrument and every player is concerned with *developing* and *maintaining* endurance. It should be realized that failure to practice regularly during the summer months will not only affect endurance but will also result in a corresponding loss of flexibility, coordination and tone quality.

It is recommended that playing problems be analyzed and that plans for summer study be designed to remedy technical deficiencies. The following check list will serve as a basis for an analysis of strong and weak points.

	Good	Fair	Poor
1. Breath Control	___	___	___
2. Tone Quality and Control	___	___	___
3. Articulation	___	___	___
4. Flexibility	___	___	___
5. Range	___	___	___
6. Fingering	___	___	___
7. Coordination	___	___	___
8. Rhythm	___	___	___
9. Musicianship	___	___	___
10. Sight Reading	___	___	___
11. Transposition	___	___	___

PLANNING PRACTICE

The average player should find that an hour and a half practice per day will provide sufficient time for the daily practice drills, etudes, and solos. For best results, practice should be divided into three half-hour periods with frequent brief rests as a precaution against injury to the embouchure by over-fatigue.

The daily practice drills, or "warm up," should include the phases of technique outlined in Brass Clinic in the March-April issue of the INSTRUMENTALIST (See p. 11). This type of practice should be considered as the *basic daily minimum* and should not require more than a half-hour with the following apportionment of the practice period.

I. Tone and Breath Control Drills.. 5 Minutes
II. Lip Flexibility Drills...........10-15 Minutes
III. Scales and Technical Drills.....10-15 Minutes

Due to the varying factors regarding physical condition and mental attitude, it is advisable to vary this routine to provide emphasis upon the type of drill which is most needed. Each player must learn to gauge his own playing condition and ability to the extent that he will be able to determine *how*, *what* and *how long* to practice to attain maximum playing efficiency in the shortest period of practice.

Etudes, studies and solos should not be practiced in a haphazard manner and each practice period should be planned with definite objectives. Although it may be desirable to place major emphasis upon one or two technical problems, the plan for each week's study should include etudes which will emphasize various phases of playing: staccato, slurring, style, phrasing, etc.

The following lists of materials have been compiled to include etudes and studies for various stages of advancement and to provide variety and contrast in etude material. The list includes studies for style, phrasing, rhythmic problems and sightreading. The playing of duets will be particularly helpful in regard to sightreading through the challenge and stimulus provided by this type of musical experience.

Every professional brass instrumentalist is *required* to be able to transpose *at sight* and this ability should be acquired and developed simultaneously with musicianship and technique.

STUDIES FOR CORNET OR TRUMPET

ELEMENTARY

Supplementary Studies ......Endresen....Rubank
Forty Progressive Studies ......Hering....Carl Fischer
Elementary Studies ....Clarke....Carl Fischer

INTERMEDIATE

Edwards-Hovey Method, Book II..........Belwin
Thirty-two Etudes ....Hering....Carl Fischer

ADVANCED

Supplementary Studies for
  Advanced Students ....Williams....Williams
Selected Studies ....Voxman....Rubank
Twenty-four Virtuoso Studies..Paudert....Carl Fischer
Etudes Pratiques
  Vols. I, II, III............Laurent....M. Baron

TRANSPOSITION STUDIES

Transposition Method ......Williams....Williams
100 Etudes for Transposition...Sachse....M. Baron
Etudes for Trumpet..........Brandt....Leeds

DUETS

Practice Duets ....Amsden
Grand Method ....Gatti
Complete Method ....St. Jacome
Complete Method ....Arban

BAND STUDIES

Cornet Passages ....Brown...Belwin ....
Bandsman's Studio....5 Vols............Carl Fischer

DAILY PRACTICE STUDIES

Daily Drills and Technical
  Studies ....Schlossberg....M. Baron
The Secret of Technique
  Preservation ....Williams....Williams

STUDIES FOR FRENCH HORN

ELEMENTARY

Supplementary Studies ......Endresen....Rubank
Primary Studies ....Horner....Elkan-Vogel

INTERMEDIATE

70 Etudes, Book I....Maxime-Alphonse....Sansone
40 Etudes, Book II..Maxime-Alphonse....Sansone

ADVANCED

40 Medium Difficult Etudes,
  Book III ....Maxime-Alphonse....Sansone
20 Difficult Etudes,
  Book IV ....Maxime-Alphonse....Sansone
20 Very Difficult Etudes,
  Book V ....Maxime-Alphonse....Sansone
212 Selected Studies, 2 Vols.....Pottag....Andraud
Daily Exercises for French Horn.Pottag....Belwin

TRANSPOSITION AND ORCHESTRA STUDIES

Etudes, Vols. I, II.........Kopprasch....Carl Fischer
French Horn Passages,
  Books I, II, III.............Pottag....Belwin
French Horn Orchestra Studies,
  10 Vols. ....Gumbert....Sansone

DUETS

53 French Horn Duets.........Franz....Sansone
47 French Horn Duets.........Franz....Sansone
12 Duets for 2 French Horns
  Op. 2 ....Gallay....Sansone

STUDIES FOR TROMBONE OR BARITONE

ELEMENTARY

Supplementary Studies ....Endresen....Rubank
221 Progressive Studies ....Cimera....Belwin

INTERMEDIATE

Advanced Studies ....Harvey....Belwin
Advanced Method .....Gower-Voxman....Rubank

ADVANCED

Melodious Etudes,
  Vols. I, II, III.............Rochut....Carl Fischer each,
Forty Progressive Studies ......Tyrrell....Belwin ....

TRANSPOSITION AND CLEF STUDIES

Etudes, Vols. I, II.......Kopprasch....Carl Fischer each,
Twenty-six Sequences ......Blazhevich....Leeds ....

BAND STUDIES

Baritone Passages ....Brown....Belwin
Trombone Passages ....Brown....Belwin

DUETS

12 Melodious Duets ....Blume
Practice Duets ....Amsden
Concert Duets ....Blazhevich
Four Etudes in Duet Form....................Couillaud

SELECTING A MOUTHPIECE

BERNARD FITZGERALD

THE SELECTION of a mouthpiece is a perplexing problem both to teachers and players. Because of the fact that jaw and lip formations are not identical, the problem is an individual one which cannot be solved by finding a good mouthpiece and recommending it for all players. There are several factors which should be considered in selecting a mouthpiece which is suited to the individual. These factors concern both the individual measurements of the rim, cup, throat, and backbore of the mouthpiece and the numberless possible combinations of these measurements in various proportions.

At the present time several manufacturers offer an extensive variety of mouthpieces with various sizes of cup, bore and rim measurements. However, little has been done to aid the individual in selecting the mouthpiece which will prove most satisfactory. The recommendations of manufacturers are usually based upon the demand indicated by the sales records of certain models, and, not infrequently, manufacturers will admit that the best mouthpieces do not always prove popular. In the absence of scientific means to determine the best combination of mouthpiece measurements for the individual, the trial and error method must be employed and it is hoped that the following criteria will prove helpful since it is obviously impractical to attempt to try out all makes and models of brass instrument mouthpieces.

It is apparent that the beginning player will encounter difficulty in attempting to determine which mouthpiece produces best results since he will not have previous playing experience as a basis for comparison. Therefore the teacher must assume the responsibility for recommending a suitable mouthpiece on the basis of knowledge regarding the factors involved.

The Mouthpiece Rim

The selection of a mouthpiece which has a suitable rim is of prime importance. Three elements should be considered: (a) the width (thickness) of the rim; (b) the shape of the rim surface (flat, concave, or convex); (c) the inside diameter of the rim (often referred to as the width of the cup).

The principal method of deciding upon the most satisfactory rim is by the "feel" of the rim on the lips. The rim should rest comfortably on the lips without cutting into the lip tissue or restricting the muscular action of the embouchure while playing. If the rim is too wide and the inside diameter too large, the lips are likely to become fatigued after playing a very short time and tone control will become very difficult. A rim which is too narrow combined with a small inside rim diameter will tend to produce a tone which is thin and "pinched" because the lips do not have sufficient space to permit a free and unrestricted vibration.

During the past several years mouthpieces with extremely wide "cushion rims" have found favor with many professional musicians in dance orchestras. The popularity of this type of mouthpiece has been due to the ease of producing tones in the high register combined with less fatigue to the embouchure over periods of prolonged playing. This type of mouthpiece usually has a small cup and bore, the resultant tone quality being thin and penetrating but lacking depth and sonority. The wide "cushion type" rim is not recommended unless it is possible to obtain this type of rim in combination with a properly designed cup, throat, and backbore.

A medium wide rim with a rounded outside edge is recommended for players with a muscular lip formation. Players with large or unmuscular lip formations may find that the flat wide rim is more satisfactory since it will provide more support for the lips. Many players feel that mouthpieces having a slight "grip" or "edge" on the inside of the rim are preferable to those with a rounded inside edge.

Extremely narrow rims are not recommended because of the fact that this type tends to cut into the lips. With the increasing demand for greater range, flexibility, and endurance in recent years, comparatively few players use the narrow rims at the present time.

It is possible to obtain mouthpieces in which the rim is custom made to fit the jaw formation of the individual. The rims of these mouthpieces are constructed on the basis of dental impressions of the upper and lower jaw teeth formations. At present the large majority of the professional musicians use the conventional type rim, the custom made rims being used principally by players having an extreme overbite or protruding front teeth which cause the conventional type rim to be uncomfortable.

The Mouthpiece Cup

The trumpet and trombone belong to the so-called cylindrical bore type of brass instrument and are intended to produce a more brilliant and penetrating tone than the other instruments of the brass family. Technically, the mouthpieces for these instruments should be somewhat more shallow than those for the cornet, baritone, or tuba. Actually, most manufacturers make very little distinction between mouthpieces for the two types of instruments.

The trend in recent years has been toward extremely shallow cups and narrow throat diameters for the cornet, trumpet and trombone. The concept of tone quality has been altered to the extent that emphasis is likely to be placed upon tonal brilliance rather than sonority. A reasonably shallow mouthpiece may prove to be excellent providing the throat diameter and backbore taper are properly designed to compensate for the small cup. Unless the circumstances are exceptional it is usually best to choose a medium cup for the average player. Mouthpieces with large, deep cups should be recommended for players having a strong, well developed embouchure.

French horn mouthpieces are quite conical rather than cup shaped, though some models have a tendency toward a slight cup near the throat of the mouthpiece. A medium deep mouthpiece should be given a thorough trial before changing to one which is extremely deep or shallow.

Throat and Backbore

It would be impossible to specify the correct throat diameter and taper of the backbore except with relation to the diameter and depth of the cup. However, the fact that so many mouthpieces prove to have a throat diameter too small for best results indicates that it may be desirable or necessary to

have this opening enlarged. Players who find that the tone seems to choke up in the high register are often helped by this procedure.

If possible, this should be done by an expert repairman in order that the drilling be done accurately without damage to the mouthpiece. The throat should only be enlarged one drill size, and then be thoroughly tested by the player. If tone and sonority have been improved without detriment to endurance, it may be desirable to enlarge the bore another drill size. The extent of this procedure must be gauged by the effect upon the player and the relationship of the bore diameter to the other dimensions of the mouthpiece. Extremely shallow mouthpieces

frequently have a very small throat opening and may be enlarged more than the mouthpieces with deeper cups.

The mouthpiece shank must be carefully fitted into the mouthpipe of the instrument to obtain best results. Frequently the mouthpiece is not of the same make as the instrument. Since the manufacturers of brass instruments and mouthpieces do not have uniform measurements for mouthpiece shanks and the mouthpipe of the instruments it may be necessary to have the shank of the mouthpiece either built up or ground down to fit the particular make of instrument. Many mouthpiece problems are due to carelessness regarding this matter. ■

November-December, 1947

DEVELOPING
the
BRASS SECTION

HOWARD W. DEYE

No MAN can become an expert performer on all band instruments. Neither can he expect to know all the fine points, as used by artists in playing and teaching.

Then where does that leave the perplexed individual who must, without assistance, develop capable performers for his band, and possibly his orchestra also? Of course he can study the methods of successful teachers. But this process soon leads to the accumulation of a number of conflicting theories concerning the teaching of each instrument.

Consider the brass section of the beginning band. The teacher's first problem is one of guidance: how to avoid making a potentially fine tuba player into a mediocre cornetist. Once the instruments are assigned, how should he begin? Should he teach the prospective brass artist to vibrate his lips first, using only the mouthpiece, and postpone use of the tongue until a later date? Or should he give the student the instrument at once, and teach him to use the tongue at the first lesson?

Perhaps some of the answers can be found in the following statistical table. The numbered statements were submitted to prominent brass soloists, symphony performers, and directors. The scores give a composite picture of their opinions.

Questions

	Yes	No
1. Thin lips are generally best for cornet and horn, although heavier lips are not necessarily detrimental.	22	9
2. Thickness of lip is of little importance for trombone and tuba players, although heavier lips usually result in better tone quality.	27	5
3. A medium size mouthpiece with medium depth cup is best for the average high school student.	31	3
4. Heavier lips do not necessarily require a larger mouthpiece.	30	1
5. The first aim of the beginner should be to develop controlled vibration with the mouthpiece alone.	22	12
6. Much practice with mouthpiece alone is necessary for beginners and very helpful to the embouchures of advanced players. Every brass player should be able to play melodies with ease, using only the mouthpiece.	19	14
7. Use of the tongue may be entirely ignored for a few weeks, until the beginner's embouchure has been fairly well developed.	14	20
8. In development of vibration or buzz (without use of the tongue) the sound "P" may be used, but the lips should remain close together.	17	13
9. Lip slurs are essential in developing strength and flexibility of embouchure.	33	1
10. The use of long tone practice, playing with even volume and crescendo and diminuendo, is essential to embouchure development.	Yes 33	No 1
11. Number (10) should not be overdone with beginners.	34	0
12. Interval studies, scales, and chords, with a variety of articulations, have an important place in embouchure development.	33	1

Summary

The scores in the table do not tell the whole story. This article would not be complete without the following summary of the comments made by the experts who answered the questions.

1-2. Thin lips may sometimes be an advantage to cornet and horn players, but the shape of the lips is the determining factor. A freely vibrating edge is essential. Reasonably even teeth are necessary; dental attention is sometimes advisable.

E. C. Moore warns against the harelip and the upper lip with an inert pendant lobe. He says, "The edge of the lip when smiling should be straight."

Herbert L. Clarke said, "Levy had thick lips. Kryl has thick lips. One of the greatest tuba players I ever heard had thin lips. The size of their lips had little to do with their success."

3-4. The mouthpiece should fit the embouchure and the instrument bore, and the choice depends on how the instrument is to be used. A shallow cup favors the high register, but the tone suffers, especially in the low register, if the cup is too shallow.

A large mouthpiece requires greater lip strength and lung capacity; thickness of lip is not the determining factor. The rim of the mouthpiece should fit comfortably. A wide rim may be helpful for thick lips.

5-6. About 35% favor the use of the complete instrument from the start. They seem to think that mouthpiece practice is a waste of time.

The 65% majority believe that the beginner should first learn to produce a tone on the mouthpiece alone. Many would teach him to produce controlled vibration without even a mouthpiece. Some advocate mouthpiece practice for advanced students.

The "vibration" method of teaching brass beginners is based on the fact that the tone is produced by the vibrating lips; that tone control is lip-vibration control. A common practice is to start the first lesson with an explanation of breathing, embouchure formation, and mouthpiece placement. The student is not allowed to use the instrument until he can control the pitch over a limited range, and without pressure. When this is accomplished, he may use the instrument for a part of his practice period to sustain interest, but the mouthpiece practice is continued until he can produce a clear tone.

7-8. Some teachers ignore the use of the tongue for a *few days,* until lip "buzzing" has become automatic. If the student is instructed to sustain the sound of the letter "P", he usually learns to produce lip vibrations with comparative ease. He does it first without mouthpiece, and then with mouthpiece.

Use of the tongue at the start may cause complications, but when the lips are vibrating freely, addition of the tongue for the attack is a simple matter. It is sometimes easier to prevent excess pressure by this approach. This method is practical even if the instrument is used at the first lesson.

9-12. We may consider the vote unanimously in favor of these four statements. In every case, the lone dissenter approves with qualifications. Most of the comments warn against excessive use of any exercise that tires the student or causes him to lose interest, and several caution against the danger of using pressure.

The principal value of lip slurs is to develop flexibility and tone control. One teacher suggests that only wide slurs should be used, because narrow slurs encourage pressure.

Frank Young says, "Lip slurs are one of the very best ways of developing tone and control, and should be practised by everyone, no matter how well trained. Their importance cannot be overemphasized."

Long tones are mainly valuable for developing control and beauty of tone. Slow, legato melodies will, to some extent, serve the same purpose and are more interesting. Interval studies are the best exercises for developing strength. They should be played slowly and accurately, avoiding pressure.

Coda

In conclusion, a word of advice from the pen of Herbert L. Clarke.

"The foundation is the same for all: scales, intervals, and exercises to acquire control of the muscles of the lips, tongue, and fingers. Wind control is ninety-eight per cent of correct wind instrument playing from the flute to the tuba.

"As a boy, I tried to use common sense wherever it would fit, since there is a reason for everything, and experimented on all theories with little result. I found that where practicability and theory did not coincide, theory was the 'bunk'. There are no rules in cornet playing. Every cornet player I ever saw or knew played differently." ∎

November-December, 1947

SOLO LITERATURE OF THE TRUMPET

BERNARD FITZGERALD

IN GENERAL, musicians have not given serious consideration to the solo possibilities of the brass instruments. In spite of the crude instruments which existed in the seventeenth and eighteenth centuries, the art of trumpet playing was highly developed as evidenced by the concertos composed by Bach, Haydn, and Leopold Mozart. These compositions are difficult, even for soloists of the present day, notwithstanding the mechanical and acoustical improvements of the instrument which is now used.

It is unfortunate that the trumpet literature of this earlier period is limited to a very few compositions now included in the repertory. It seems probable in view of the high degree of virtuosity attained by the trumpeters of that time, other composers also may have written solos for the trumpet, and that further research may lead to the rediscovery of a considerable number of additional compositions for solo trumpet and orchestra.

Modern Repertory

Much of the modern literature in the larger forms has been written by French and Belgian composers. This is probably due, at least to some extent, to the high standard of virtuosity in brass instrument performance which developed in the conservatories of France and Belgium at the beginning of the twentieth century.

Although only a few works by Russian composers are known at the present time, the available examples indicate that composers have shown a considerable interest in writing solo works for brass instruments, and it is hoped that more information will soon be available regarding other solo compositions for brass instruments by Russian composers.

The important solo trumpet literature in the larger forms has been included in the lists which follow, although there is considerable variation in the musical merit of the music listed. Numerous other concertinos and concertos which are not musically significant have been omitted from the present list. The majority of the trumpet repertory consists of shorter solos, and these compositions are not included in the present list except in instances where orchestra accompaniment is intended.

Foreign Sources

A large percentage of the solos included in the list is not published in this country, There are a number of sources in this country through which foreign publications may be obtained. The following publishers should be the best sources of supply:

Associated Music Publishers, 609 5th Ave., N.Y., N.Y. 10017

Albert Andraud -order from Southern Music Co., Box 329, San Antonio, Texas 78206

Maurice Baron Co., Box 149, Oyster Bay, L.I., N.Y. 11771

Broude Bros., 56 W. 45th St., N.Y. 10036

Carl Fischer Inc., 56 Cooper Square, N.Y., N.Y. 10003

Leeds Music-order from MCA, 543 W. 43rd St., N.Y., N.Y. 10036

CONCERTOS FOR TRUMPET

*Barbier, Rene	Piece Symphonique (Trpt. & Pa.)	Evette-Schaeffer
*Blattermann, H.	Concertino	Oertel
Boccalari, Ed.	Fantasia di Concerto (Trpt. & Pa.; also Band Acc.)	Carl Fischer
*Bohme, Oskar	Concerto in E minor, Op. 18 (Trpt. & Pa.)	Jurgensen
Brandt, Willy	Erstes Konzertstuck in F Minor, Op. 11 (Trpt. & Pa.)	Zimmermann
Brandt, Willy	Second Concert Piece in E Flat, Op. 12 (Trpt. & Pa.)	Cundy-Bettoney
*Cahnbley, August	Concertino	Benjamin
*Carl, M.	Concerto in E-Flat Major	Benjamin
Delcroix, Leon	Concertino Op. 43 (Trpt. & Pa.)	Evette-Schaeffer
*Fitzgerald, Bernard	Concerto in A-Flat Minor (Trpt. & Pa.; Orch. parts on rental from publisher)	Carl Fischer
*Goedicke, Alexander	Concerto, Op. 41 (Trpt. & Pa.)	Leeds
*Haydn, Josef	Concerto (Trpt. & Pa.; orch. pts. pub. by Andraud)	Carl Fischer
*Herfurth, W.	Concertino in E-Flat Major	Benjamin
Lecail, Clovis	Concerto Romantique (Trpt. & Pa.; also w. Band Acc.)	Belwin
*Lecail, Clovis	Concertino (Trpt. & Pa.)	Belwin
*Liesering, Ludwig	Concertino in D Major	Benjamin
*Mozart, Leopold	Concerto for Trpt. in D and small Orch.	Kistner-Siegel
*Muller, S. W.	Concerto Grosso, Op. 50 (Trpt. & Pa.)	Eulenburg
*Pilss, Karl	Concerto (Trpt. & Pa.)	Universal Ed.
*Porrino, Ennio	Concertino (Trpt. & Pa.)	Ricordi
*Salmhofer, Franz	Concerto (Trpt. & Pa.)	Universal Ed.
*Senee, Henri	Concerto (Trpt. & Pa.)	Andraud
*Stohr, Richard	Concerto (Trpt. & Pa.)	
Strauwen, Jean	Concertino (Trpt. & Pa.)	Walpot
Vidal, Paul	Concertino (Trpt. & Pa.)	Belwin
*Wiggert, Paul	Concerto in E Flat Op. 50 (Trpt. & Pa.)	
Williams, Ernest	Concertos Nos. 1, 2, 3, 4, 5, 6 (Trpt. & Pa.)	Williams School of Music
*Wolff, Eduard	Ein Piston-Concert Op. 40 in F Minor	Ruhle & Wendling

*Indicates that the composition is for trumpet and orchestra.

OTHER SOLO WORKS WITH ORCHESTRA

Alpaerts, Flor	Concert Piece in B minor (Trpt. & Strs.)	Unpub.
Bach, Johann S.	Brandenburg Concerto No. 2 in F Major (Solo Trpt., Oboe, Flute, Violin, Strs. & Cembalo)	Associated
Bach, Vincent	Hungarian Melodies (Trpt. & Orch.; also Trpt. & Band, Trpt. & Pa.)	V. Bach
Barber, Samuel	Capricorn Concerto, Op. 21, for Fl., Ob., Trpt., Strs.	G. Schirmer
Bohme, Oskar	La Napolitaine, Tarantella, Op. 25, (Trpt. & Orch.; also Trpt. & Pa., Cundy-Bettoney)	Zimmermann
Casedesus, Francis	Hymne (Trpt. & Orch., also Trpt. & Pa.)	Choudens
Goedicke, Alexander	Etude de Concert (Trpt. & Orch.; also Trpt. & Pa.)	Leeds
Goeyens, Fernand	Morceau de Concert (Trpt. & Orch.; also Trpt. & Pa.)	Evette-Schaeffer
Jeanjean, Paul	Fantaisie Melodique (Trpt. & Orch.; also Trpt. & Pa.)	Evette-Schaeffer
Kennan, Kent	Il Campo di Fiori (Solo Trpt. & Small Orch.)	Unpub.
Maganini, Quinto	Tuolumne, Op. 2 (Trpt. & Orch.; also Trpt. & Pa.)	Edition-Musicus
Marty, Georges	Choral (Trpt. & Orch.; also Trpt. & Pa.)	Evette-Schaeffer
Riisager, K.	Concertino for Trpt. & Strings, Op. 29	Hansen
Rathaus, Karol	Little prelude for Trpt. and Strs. Op. 30	Balan
Scriabin-Stone	Etude (Trpt. & Orch.; also Trpt. & Pa. Interlude)	
Wiggert, Paul	Ungarische Rhapsodie Op. 27 No. 2 in B Flat Minor (Trpt. & Orch.)	Ruhle & Wendling

(The orchestrations for most of the above compositions are in the Edwin A. Fleisher Music Collection at the Free Library of Philadelphia, Logan Square, Philadelphia, Pa.)

SONATAS FOR TRUMPET AND PIANO

Assafiev, Boris	Sonata	Leeds
Bonnard, Giulio	Sonata	Ricordi
Emmanuel, Maurice	Sonata	Buffet-Crampon
Hansen, Thorwald	Sonata Op. 18	Hansen
Hindemith, Paul	Sonata	Schott
Schmutz, Albert	Sonatine	Ludwig
Williams, Ernest	Sonata	Williams

1948

D Trumpet

BIBLIOGRAPHY OF BOOKS PERTAINING TO BRASS INSTRUMENTS

BERNARD FITZGERALD

BIBLIOGRAPHY pertaining to the brass instruments may be divided into three categories: (1) books, (2) articles in periodicals, (3) research studies (principally unpublished theses). The research studies comprise a relatively small part of the total bibliography and unfortunately too little emphasis has been given to scientific studies pertaining to the brass instruments. Probably the most significant recent contributions to the bibliography regarding technique and the teaching of brass instruments are the articles in music periodicals by outstanding teachers and performers.

Although a complete bibliography of all three categories is highly desirable, in view of the inaccessibility of theses and back-issues of the periodicals, it seemed advisable to limit the present bibliography to books containing information about the brass instruments. To list every book in which even a brief mention of the brass instruments is given would inevitably result in much unnecessary duplication of information. The author has attempted to compile an exhaustive bibliography including all authoritative sources exclusive of the method books for the various instruments. It will be noted that many of the books are general music references or historical treatises which contain information regarding all musical instruments. It is unfortunate that a considerable number of the references are not available except in large music libraries and that some of the more exhaustive treatises are only published in French or German.

It is significant that a comparison of books by reputable authorities will reveal not only some duplication of information but, what is more important, confusing contradictions are much in evidence. For example, the disagreement among authorities in the field of orchestration with regard to the meaning and interpretation of the various terms concerning the muting of the French Horn.

In general, the existing bibliography is principally concerned with the historical background and the development of the instruments. The early publication dates of many sources emphasize the need for authoritative research to clarify contradictions in the light of current practice and interpretation.

BIBLIOGRAPHY REGARDING BRASS INSTRUMENTS

Adkins, Capt. H. E.
Treatise on the Military Band. London. Boosey and Company, 1931.

Altenburg, Johann Ernst
Versuch einer Anleitung zur Trompeter—U. Pauker-Kunst. Halle. J. C. Hendel. 1795. (Neuausgabe Verlegt von Richard Bertling. Dresden, 1911.)

Apel, Willi
Harvard Dictionary of Music. Cambridge. Harvard University Press, 1946.

Bach, Vincent
The Art of Trumpet Playing. New York. Vincent Bach, Inc. 1925.

Bartholomew, Wilmer T.
Acoustics of Music. New York. Prentice-Hall, 1945.

Berlioz, Hector
Instrumentation. London. Novello. Translated by Mary Cowden Clarke.

Blaikley, D. J.
Acoustics in Relation to Wind Instruments. London. Boosey and Co., 1890.

Brett, H.
The Cornet. London. Novello and Co., Ltd., cop. 1895.

Brucker, F.
Die Blasinstrumente in der altfranzösichen Literatur. 1926.

Bouasse, H.
Instruments à Vent. Tome I, Paris. Librairie Delagrave, 1929.

Bowles, B. F.
Technics of the Brass Musical Instrument. New York. Carl Fischer, Inc. 1915.

Buck, Perry C.
Acoustics for Musicians. London. Oxford University Press, 1918.

Buhle, E.
Die Musikalischen Instrumente in den Miniaturen des frühen Mittelalters: Die Blasinstrumente. 1903.

Carse, Adam
The History of Orchestration. New York. E. P. Dutton and Co. 1925.

Carse, Adam
Musical Wind Instruments. London. Macmillan and Co., Ltd. 1939.

Chaussier, Henry
Les Nouveaus Instruments En Ut. Paris. Paul Dupont. 1889.

Clagget, Charles
Musical Phaenomena. London. 1793.

Clappe, Arthur A.
The Wind-Band and Its Instruments. New York. Henry Holt and Co. 1911.

Clarke, Herbert L.
How I Became A Cornetist. St. Louis. Joseph L. Huber. 1934.

Coar, Birchard
The French Horn. Ann Arbor. 1947. Edwards Brothers, Inc. 98 pp.

Cobbett's Cyclopedic Survey of Chamber Music. London. Oxford University Press, 1929.

Courvoisier, Carl
Intonation. Derby: P. B. Chadfield and Son, 1892.

Culver, Charles Aaron
Musical Acoustics. Philadelphia: Blakiston, 1941.

Daubeny, Ulric
Orchestral Wind Instruments. London: New Temple Press. (n.d.)

DeLamater, E.
"Lip Science" for Brass Players. Chicago: Rubank, cop. 1923.

Eichborn, H. L.
Das (alte) Clarinblasen auf Trompeten. Leipzig: Breitkoph & Härtel, 1894.

Eichborn, H. L.
Die Dämpfung beim Horn. Leipzig: Breitkoph & Härtel, 1897.

Eichborn, H. L.
Die Trompete in alter und neuer Zeit. Leipzig: Breitkoph & Härtel, 1881.

Eichborn, H. L.
Zur Geschichte der Instrumental-Musik. Leipzig. 1885.

Euting, E.
Zur Geschichte der Blasininstrumente im 16. und 17. Jahrhundert. 1899.

Fantini
Modo per imparar a sonare di tromba. Frankfurt. 1638.

Forsyth, Cecil
    Orchestration. London: Macmillan. 1914.
Gallo, Stanislao
    The Modern Band. Boston: Birchard, 1935.
Geiringer, Karl
    Musical Instruments (Translated by Bernard Miall). New York: Oxford University Press. 1945.
Grove's Dictionary of Music and Musicians. London: Macmillan and Co., Ltd. 1940.
Hawkins, Sir John
    General History of the Science and Practice of Music. London: Payne and Sons, 1776.
Helmholtz, Hermann L. F.
    On the Sensations of Tone. Translated by Alexander J. Ellis. (a) 1875 ed.; (b) 1912 Fourth Ed.; London: Longmans, Green and Co.
Henderson, W. J.
    The Orchestra and Orchestral Music. London: John Murray. 1919.
Hipkins, A. J. and William Gibbs.
    Musical Instruments. London: A. C. Black. 1921.
Jeans, Sir James.
    Science and Music. New York: Macmillan Co., 1937.
Kappey, J. A.
    Military Music. London. Boosey and Company.
Kellog, Irwin
    Why Breathe? Los Angeles. Preeman-Matthews Music Co., 1927.
Lavignac's Encyclopdie de la Musique. Paris. Librairie Delagrave. 1924.
Lloyd, L. S.
    Music and Sound. London: Oxford University Press, 1937.
Mahillon, V. C.
    Elements D'Acoustique. Bruxelles. Imprimerie Adolphe Mertens, 1874.
Mahillon, V. C.
    Instruments á Vent. London. Mahillon and Co., 1907.
Meifred, J.
    Notice Sur La Fabrication Des Instruments De Musique En Cuivre. Paris. De Soye et Ce, Imprimeiers, 1851.
Menke, Werner
    History of the Trumpet of Bach and Handel. Translated by Gerald Abraham. London. The New Temple Press, 1934.
Miller, Dayton Clarence
    Anecdotal History of the Science of Sound. New York. The Macmillan Co., 1935.
Miller, Dayton Clarence
    The Science of Musical Sounds. New York. The Macmillan Co., 1926.
Oxford Companion of Music. Percy A. Scholes. London: Oxford University Press. 1938.
Practical Problems in Building Wind Instruments. Mimeographed pamphlet published by C. G. Conn, Ltd. 1942. Elkhart. 17 pp.
Prout, Ebenezer
    The Orchestra. London. Augener and Company. 1897.

Piersig, Fritz
    Die Einführung des Hornes in die Kunstmusik. Halle. 1927.
Raymond, William F.
    The Trombone and Its Player. Cincinnati. The Fillmore Bros. Co. 1937.
Redfield, John
    Music, A Science and An Art. New York. Alfred A. Knopf, 1930.
Revelli, William D.
    Band Technics. Ann Arbor. George Wahr. 1941.
Richardson, E. G.
    The Acoustics of Orchestral Instruments and of the Organ. London. Edward Arnold and Co. 1929.
Sachs, Curt
    The History of Musical Instruments. New York. W. W. Norton and Co., Inc., 1940.
Scherchen, Hermann
    Handbook of Conducting (Translated by M. D. Calvocoressi) London. Oxford Univ. Press. 1933. pp. 97-126.
Schlesinger, Kathleen
    The Instruments of the Orchestra and Early Records of The Precursors of the Violin Family. London. Reeves. 1910.
Schwartz, H. W.
    How Music is Made. Elkhart, Ind. C. G. Conn, Ltd., cop. 1927.
Schwartz, H. W.
    The Story of Musical Instruments. Garden City, New York. Doubleday, Doran and Co., Inc. 1938.
Seashore, Carl
    Psychology of Music. New York. McGraw-Hill Book Co., Inc., 1938.
Seashore, Carl
    The Psychology of Musical Talent. New York. Silver, Burdett and Co., cop. 1919.
Speer, Daniel
    Instruction in the Musical Art. Ulm. S. W. Kuhne. 1687.
Sweitzer, Albert
    J. S. Bach (2 volumes). London. Breitkopf and Hartel, 1911. Trans. by Ernest Newman. p. 433- ff.
Terry, Charles Sanford
    Bach's Orchestra. London. Oxford University Press. 1932.
Tovey, Sir Donald Francis
    Essays in Musical Analysis. London. Oxford University Press. 1935.
Watkins, John Goodrich, Ph.D.
    Objective Measurement of Instrumental Performance. New York. Teachers College, Columbia University. 1942. 88 pp.
Weingartner, Felix
    Beethoven Symphonies. London. Breitkopf and Hartel. 1907. Translated by Jessie Crosland.
Widor, Charles M.
    Technique of the Modern Orchestra. London. Joseph Williams, Ltd. 1906. Translated by Edward Suddard.
Young, T. Campbell
    The Making of Musical Instruments. London. Oxford University Press, 1939.

January-February, 1948

Cornet Parts in C

Transition from Bb Parts Possible

TRAUGOTT ROHNER

THE ADVISABILITY of writing Trumpet-Cornet parts in C instead of in Bb so that the music would sound as written was first presented in this magazine in May, 1947. In our last issue (November-December) Mr. Chester C. Travelstead of Louisville, Kentucky, presented the results of a questionnaire on this and kindred problems, analyzing the answers of over 600 school music directors. Meanwhile many others have written us their viewpoints either for or against the idea.

Salient Arguments Pro and Con

A. For the new C part:

1. The new C part would eliminate unnecessary confusion on the part of the beginner or the amateur cornetist.

2. Some teaching time would be saved because all the brass instruments, excepting the French horn, would now sound as written.

3. The inexperienced or young cornetist would be able to read directly from the piano music or from any other C part (oboe, flute, violin, etc.).

4. It would be easier to transfer cornet players to the trombone, baritone—bass clef, and BB♭ tuba than is now the case.

5. The present duplicate treble clef baritone part could thus be eliminated.

6. It is better ear training when the notes sound as written.

B. Against the change:

1. Too much music has already been printed in the present manner.

2. The change would cause much confusion.

3. The publishers would not print the extra parts.

4. The cost of printing the extra parts is not worth the cost of changing.

To Change or Not to Change?

Of the 600 directors questioned "If the instruction books and band music should be available so that the cornet would sound as written (written B♭ instead of C as now) would you use them?", 255 answered "YES." Because these 600 directors represent an accurate sampling of all directors, one can say that *two out of every five directors favor the change or the addition of a new C part today*. It would not take much educating to persuade a much higher proportion than this to use the new C parts.

How about the four arguments against changing which were listed? Let us number the answers the same as the arguments.

1. Since much more cornet music will be printed in the future than has already been printed, it is high time to make the change now before still much more music is printed in this old and inane manner.

2. There is absolutely no need for confusion in effecting the change as will be pointed out later.

3. The publishers will add new C parts and print new music for the cornet with two parts, B♭ and C, if YOU ask for it.

4. There are several better ways of saving money than by not printing the new C parts.

An objective analysis of all the factors involved indicates that we should make the change.

How Best Make Change?

How can the transition from B♭ parts to C parts best be made? The major task is to convince the publishers. This can be done provided *you who are interested in the new C parts* will write to the publishers of your favorite first year cornet materials, requesting them to publish an extra C part. Each publisher should thus print a C cornet part for all of his best selling first year cornet music as soon as possible, followed (within a year) with the second year cornet music. Eventually, all or nearly all cornet music would have both a B♭ and a C part, followed by a gradual elimination of the printing of B♭ parts. For those who are still skeptical, let them recall that not so many years ago we had two trombone parts (bass and treble), but that today the treble part is obsolete. The time will come when the cornet part in B♭ will be obsolete. Write to your publisher now.

March-April, 1948

PEDAL TONES on the TRUMPET and CORNET

BERNARD FITZGERALD

THE PLAYING of "pedal tones" on the brass instruments is a curious phenomenon which is rarely mentioned except as vague possibility. The infrequent references which appear in musical treatises usually associate pedal tones with the Trombone, Euphonium or French Horn rather than the Trumpet or Cornet. Although it is true that pedal tones may be produced more easily and with greater sonority on the larger instruments having a longer and wider tubing, it is nevertheless quite possible to produce pedal tones on both the Cornet and Trumpet.

The term "pedal tone" may be applied to any tone below the usual range of the instrument. Thus, tones written below F♯ (treble clef, third line below), are considered as pedal tones on the Cornet and Trumpet. In modern usage the brass instruments do not employ the fundamental tones of the instrument as a part of the normal range, although all the brass instruments are constructed on the basic principle of producing the harmonic series of overtones by overblowing. Because of the shorter and narrower tubing of the Trumpet and Cornet, pedal tones of good quality are more difficult to play on these instruments. It is difficult to explain why it is pos-

27

sible to produce not only the descending series of fundamental tones on the Trumpet and Cornet, but also the downward chromatic progression to the octave *below* the fundamental of the open tube. (See fingering chart.)

Some of the renowned cornet soloists have achieved notable success in developing the pedal tone register. Bohumir Kryl acquired a phenomenal control of this register and employed pedal tones in a spectacular manner in performing solos and cadenzas. At present, this register is rarely required for solo performance and the ability to play pedal tones is generally considered as a novel achievement of comparatively little musical value. The tubing of the cornet contains a larger number of bends than the trumpet and is generally considered to respond more easily than the trumpet. It seems probable that these factors partially explain why pedal tones on the Cornet have better tone quality and more sonority than those played on the trumpet.

Pedal Tones Necessary

There are occasional passages in the orchestral repertoire which require the use of the pedal tone register on the Trumpet. These parts were quite possible in the normal range of the longer, lower pitched trumpets in F, E♭, and D which were used formerly. The smaller, higher pitched Trumpet in B♭ is the one generally used by orchestra trumpeters at present, thus the extreme low tones required in certain passages can be played only as pedal tones on this instrument. Several musical examples are presented to illustrate the manner in which these parts may be performed on the B♭ Trumpet by employing the pedal tone register.

The notes which must be played as pedal tones are indicated by an asterisk (*). It will be noted that the pedal tone F♯ is required in the first three examples. This tone will respond more freely if the third valve slide is pulled approximately one inch. The

second measure of the example from Don Juan was incorrectly written one octave lower in the original. Apparently this error was an oversight on the part of the composer since the tone was not possible on the D Trumpets used at that time.

Embouchure and Mouthpiece

To play tones in the so called "pedal register" will require a much more relaxed formation of the embouchure, since the lips must vibrate much more slowly to produce the low pitches in this range. The control of pitch in playing pedal tones is a difficult problem requiring a careful "humoring" or "favoring" adjustment of lip tension. Special fingerings are a valuable aid. The chromatic fingering chart indicates a number of alternate fingerings. Frequently pedal tones will respond more freely when the red of the lower lip is turned outward so that the lower part of the mouthpiece rim is resting on the red portion of the lower lip tissue. This is particularly true in playing the lowest tones shown on the fingering chart.

The width and depth of the mouthpiece cup and the bore of the mouthpiece will be found to be important factors in playing pedal tones. Since a very relaxed embouchure formation is required, mouthpieces having a wide cup and a moderately large throat diameter will prove most satisfactory. It would not be desirable to attempt to develop the pedal tone register until control of the lowest tones in the normal range of the instrument has been acquired.

Relaxation

From the viewpoint of practical performance, little will be gained by the development of the pedal tone register of the Trumpet or Cornet, since present trends in trumpet performance would indicate that any extension of the range of the instrument will probably be directed to the high rather than the low register. Both the teaching and playing experience of the author, however, have indicated that pedal tones can be useful. The increasing emphasis on the development of the high register on the brass instruments may result in excessive contraction of the muscles at the corners of the mouth to the extent that flexibility is greatly impaired. The very slow rate of vibration in combination with the re-

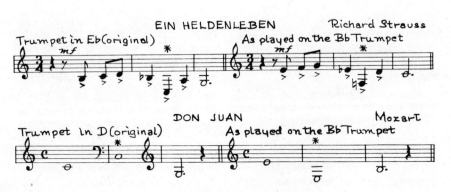

28

laxed embouchure formation required for pedal tones tends to relax the muscles of the embouchure much in the manner of a massage, so that a few minutes spent in playing pedal tones after a strenuous practice session may often prove to be more beneficial to the embouchure than complete rest.

The fingering chart which follows indicates a number of alternate fingerings, and, since it is possible to play several consecutive degrees of the scale with the same fingering, the embouchure adjustment must be very accurate.

The notation appears in the bass clef in order to simplify reading by eliminating an excessive number of ledger lines below the treble staff, and the pitch sounded will be one whole step below the notes indicated on the chart.

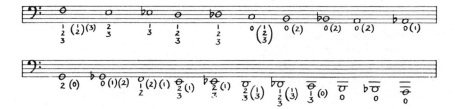

CHROMATIC FINGERING CHART FOR PLAYING
PEDAL TONES ON CORNET OR TRUMPET

Double and Triple TONGUING

LESLIE SWEENEY

THE types of articulation known as double and triple tonguing should be learned by every student who hopes to become a proficient performer. They are definitely needed in solo playing. They enable the performer to do more easily many passages which would be difficult or impossible if attempted with the single tonguing method.

It should be stressed that the foundation to the double or triple tongue is an accurate articulation of the single tongue stroke. If one can not use his tongue to produce clear and rapid tones with the single tongue, he should not attempt to do double or triple effects. The result will be indistinct pronunciation of tone, muddiness or unevenness. The tongue strokes must always be clear and even.

There are but two syllables in the alphabet which approximate the movement of the tongue when articulating tones on a brass instrument. They are the letter *T* and the letter *D*. When used in combination with other letters of the alphabet they sharpen or soften the tonal effect. They may become "too," "tah," or "tee;" or "doo," "dah," or "dee." In each inflection the tongue is used in a slightly different way. Although these are not

identical with the required movements of the tongue when pronouncing tones on the instruments, they are the nearest approximation to the necessary technique it is possible to explain. This is also true in the explanation of the creation of the "K" syllable used in double and triple tonguing. The articulation is almost the same as "kuh" or "guh," and other similar variations on the letters "k" and "g."

Double Tonguing Syllables

In double tonguing, groups of two notes, or multiples of two, are articulated by the use of the tip of the tongue for the first, followed by a syllable pronounced by the back of the tongue, as "tuh kuh," or "too koo," or "tih kih," depending on the kind of effect required, and the position of the tones in the range of the instrument. These effects may also be produced by articulating the syllables "duh guh," "doo goo," or "dih gih.'" The important thing is to make the tone produced with the back of the tongue sound exactly like the one produced with the tip. Some instructors call the second stroke a "throat" tone. This is not strictly accurate. The tone is not pro-

duced by the action of the throat, but by the back of the tongue moving up to the roof of the mouth in front of the soft palate, then releasing the required breath by a sudden downward movement, as in "kuh" or "guh."

After one can pronounce the tones alike with no escape of air to detract from the quality of tone, it is advisable to try for a more staccato effect. This is best done by moving the tongue as one would in pronouncing the syllables "tih kih," or "dih gih." The tongue is closer to the roof of the mouth, and the movement of both the tip and the back of the tongue is reduced to a minimum. A very small amount of breath is emitted with each syllable. The resulting tones should be clear, short and crisp.

The same procedure is used for triple tonguing, except that groups of three tones, or multiples of three, are used. There are two methods employed. One system is to articulate the syllables "tuh tuh kuh," or any of the variations on the basic pronunciation of T,T,K; the other is to say "tuh kuh tuh," with the K syllable in the middle of the group. The author has studied with some of the finest teachers in the country, and nearly all advise the use of the former method. The triplets

29

seem to come in a more even flow than when putting the K syllable in the middle of the group.

Make Haste Slowly

The advantage of either double or triple tonguing is in the increase in speed of articulation afforded. If one can not develop speed, neither is of much advantage. So it is important to stress the necessity of building up a firm basic reaction in the movement of the back of the tongue, along with the movement of the tip, to give a smooth even flow of tones exactly alike in character. This reaction must be built slowly. Haste will ruin any chance of accomplishing the desired result. Only after the correct articulations have been mastered should one try to increase the speed. Then the increase should never go beyond one's ability to make the tones clear and even. In the end this will result in a more rapid articulation than if one hurries and develops unevenness in the reactions of the tongue.

At first, the practice done on either double or triple tonguing should be done in the middle register of the instrument. If tones either too high or too low are attempted, the tongue will have a tendency to rise or fall in position, and impede the correct functioning of both the tip and back of the tongue. After the articulations have been learned, and clear even attacks can be produced, then it is desirable gradually to try the higher and lower tones. However, it is necessary to be careful that the precision of attack is not impaired by the change in pitch. The exercises found in Arban's Method, St. Jacome's Method, and Herbert Clarke's Method are all good for both double and triple tonguing exercise.

THE following procedure is suggested to aid in developing clarity, strength and rapidity in double and triple tonguing (most teachers advise against trying to learn both articulations at the same time, and suggest that triple tonguing be mastered before trying the double):

1. Start the pronunciation slowly (Example 3): with a clear follow-through of the breath on each tone, and careful critical analysis of the attack produced, to see that the stroke produced with the back of the tongue is as clear and precise as that with the tip. In conditioning the muscles of the tongue to produce these effects, there should be no haste. If the reactions of the muscles are developed carefully and slowly at first, their efficiency will be more dependable as one proceeds to advance in speed, range and endurance.

2. One should confine his practice to the use of only one group of triplets, ending with a stroke of the tip of the tongue. This gives a better opportunity to analyze the third tone and compare its character with the first two. After a few days, or when one is confident he has developed the correct technique, one may go on to the next stage. These first attempts should be in the middle of the range of the instrument, because of the tendency of the tongue to change position when playing high or low tones (Example 3A).

3. After assurance has been developed that the stroke with the back of the tongue has become clear and precise, increase the number of groups (Example 4). Do not try to increase the speed to the point where there is hesitation or stuttering. Stop an instant after each group or two to rest the muscles of the embouchure and tongue. Frequent rest is as important as practicing slowly and carefully.

4. Begin to try different articulations: tenuto, legato, staccato, and accents. Ultimately it will be necessary to pronounce the tones in all ways from very broad, with a full follow-through of the breath, to a sharp staccato. In producing these varieties of articulation it will be noticed that the tongue must move in minutely different ways for each. In the legato, or broad pronunciation, the tongue is relatively low in the mouth and moves with less firmness. For the staccato, the tongue (both the tip of the tongue for the first two strokes, and the back of the tongue for the third) operates closer to the roof of the mouth. And as the tones are shortened, and as the speed increases, the amount of movement of the tongue decreases.

DOUBLE AND TRIPLE TONGUING

Since the staccato stroke is the most important to develop in tripple tonguing, and since the movement of the tongue is difficult to master, great care should be exercised that in shortening the attack or increasing the speed, there will be no loss of tone quality nor unevenness in the flow of tones. All three tones in each group should remain precise, clear and even (Example 5).

5. Add more groups of triplets (Example 6). This will develop strength of the tongue muscles so it will be possible to continue such articulations without tiring and stumbling.

After assurance has been developed in accuracy and speed, one can safely try to increase the range in which the triple tonguing can be done clearly and fluently. The extreme high and low tones will be more difficult, depending to a great extent upon the development of the embouchure and proper breath control. If the high tones, especially, do not come with ease and without straining, they should be avoided. Any undue exertion on one part of the physical mechanism used in playing will weaken the other parts (Example 7).

This same procedure may be used in developing the ability to double tongue. But after mastering the triple tonguing it will be comparatively easy. In learning either, it should be remembered that one must be slow, unhurried, critical in listening to the effects produced to see that they are even and clear, and to proceed gradually from the simple to the more complex types of articulation (Example 8).

The more time one spends in this preparation the more thorough the results will be. Many of the best teachers have their students spend about six months slowly developing the ability to triple tongue, before permitting any attempt to increase the speed to more than 120 to 130 groups per minute. Then when the student needs speed or endurance to sustain triple tonguing, he has the foundation for both without stumbling, hesitating. or tiring.

September-October, 1948

TEACHING the TROMBONE

JAROSLAV CIMERA

As told to Floyd C. Ostlie

DURING the first lesson, the student should be shown how to put the horn together, how to hold it, how the slide works, and how to clean and oil it.

The instructor will then have the student put the assembled instrument to the naturally closed lips where the mouthpiece feels the best and "spit" some air into it. One should not confuse him with little details. In most cases, the students have the correct lip formation and find the best mouthpiece placement from the start. The lip formation is like that used in saying "M". The mouthpiece is placed approximately at the center of the lips, vertically and horizontally. In some cases teeth formations might not allow this and another place should be found.

In the beginning, the student should play about *mf*, wherever he produces the best tone; he must not blow too loudly. He should practice from forty-five to sixty minutes a day for the first three months. It is important that he be watched to check any bad habits. When he is in a slouching position, he will not breath properly. He should sit naturally erect, which will allow him to breath freely. His arms should be free from tension, allowing him to operate the slide freely. The cheek and lip muscles must be rather firm. The air stream is directed between the lips into the mouthpiece.

In blowing the higher tones, the lips must be tightened a little; the corners of the lips are contracted as in a faint smile. The center of the lips are brought together. The student may use a little more pressure on the high tones than on the low tones. This is permissible in the beginning. When everything seems to go along well, suggest that he use as little pressure as possible and rely more on the tension of the lip muscles. In so doing, he will eventually acquire easier attacks, clearer and richer tones, and lip flexibility. The less pressure, the better is the blood circulation in the lip and the greater is one's endurance.

It will be helpful to the student if the teacher can demonstrate some of the exercises on the trombone. He should not play along with the student to any extent, except in duets where the student is more or less on his own.

After Three Months

In addition to the material in a regular exercise book, the student can now be started on the four tone exercises in the keys of B♭, C, and E♭. For example, in the key of B♭, he will play low B♭, C, D, E♭, followed by C, D, E♭, F, and so on up to the student's top range, and then down in the same manner. These scale exercises are introduced in advance of the respective keys in the exercise book.

At this time he should also start lip slurring 4ths, starting on middle F up to B♭, and playing these slurs down in chromatics to low B♮, playing each pair of 4ths with the same position.

After A Year

Now, the student is usually able to start playing his scales softly the first time through and *mf* the second time through. These soft exercises will tend to make the lips more flexible. If the lip is inflexible, it is incapable of clean, soft, and delicate playing. Regardless whether the student has the technique for doing any delicate playing at this time, it is well to start the foundation for this type of playing. The longer one plays without doing any of the soft playing and scale work, the more inflexible the lips will become.

When the student is able to play the 3rd leger line G, he can be assigned the full scale on each step in any key. Example: In the key of A, play the scale from low A to octave up, then start

31

on low B to octave up, and so on up until he reaches his top note, and then he plays down in the same manner in which he came up. This should be played softly at two speeds. The first speed should be played in slow half notes, and the second time through should be in slow quarter notes. When the student can play high B♭, he should play his soft scales in three speeds. The third speed is faster than the slow quarter note. After two or three years of playing, the soft scales should be played in four speeds.

High Tones

When the student is able to play up to the 3rd leger line G, he can be given several aids in executing the higher tones. As he reaches the F above the staff, it can be suggested to him that if he lessens the pressure from his upper lip, transferring some of it to the lower lip by either tilting his head up a little or his horn down and saying "tee" in his articulation, these upper notes will come a little easier. Likewise with the octave slurs when playing above F, he can apply the same principle by articulating "tah-ee", and tilting back his head, or horn down a slight amount. The "ee" articulation must be at least as strong as the "tah" that precedes it. It might be a good idea to have the student say or cough out "ee" or "hee" for the sole purpose of teaching how the diaphragm works. This might not help him in the beginning, or it might not seem to him to be of any help. He must be informed that it takes time and practice before he will be able to do it exactly right. The tilting is usually overdone at first.

The Vibrato

After the student has played at least a year and can produce a good straight tone, he should start his warm up exercises with the slide vibrato on the regular scales of C, D, D♭, and E♭, going up and coming back again. These should be legato, using the natural slurs where possible. (A natural slur is where the slide is pushed out when the next note is going up and vice versa, causing a clean slur). The slide is pushed back and forth about six times a second, traveling approximately three quarters of an inch above and below the position. In the first position, one encounters difficulty. He will either have to shake the horn in first position, or tune his trombone sharp

(and thus play all positions farther out so that he will have room for the extra slide motion above the first position). Each scale should be played with eight, six, and four waves per note.

The lip vibrato may be used in the above vibrato exercises. However, the slide vibrato is easier to develop and is easier on the lip. With the slide vibrato it is possible to play a good vibrato even though the lip may be tired.

Crash Tones

After the vibrato and soft scales have been mastered, the loud or "crash" tones are introduced, using the overtone series of notes in all positions.

After this, the scale for the particular assignment should be played in full tone at a fast speed, but being careful to play every note in tune.

Lip Slurs

Next, the lip slurs in 6ths and octaves should follow. Each pair of notes is played with the same position, utilizing the alternate positions when necessary. The 6ths start from 4th line F up to D in 1st position, and follow down with all the positions, preferably repeating each slur. The octave slurs start at B natural, 7th position, up to B natural. Each slur is repeated before going up to the next position. All these slurs are to be played softly using slow half notes—the foundation for slurs of all volumes. The octave slurs should be taken to the very top of the student's range. When the lip feels tired, there should be a three to five second pause, before putting the mouthpiece to the lips again.

Another good lip slur begins on the 1st position, fourth line F, up to octave F, down to D, and B♭. Repeat continuously as far as the breath and the lip will allow. The series is repeated down a half step each time, taking in all the positions.

When the student can do the above lip slur exercise fairly well, he may start No. 1, using all positions.

No. 2 is another lip slur exercise with position changes. Here the slide moves out against the increased tension of the lip, making a slur to the over-

tone above. The student is told to tighten his lip as he moves from 2nd to 3rd position and tighten again for the top note and then reverse the procedure, coming back to F.

These exercises are taken slowly, so that the pattern of tones becomes firmly established in the student's mind. If tried too fast, notes may be left out, be out of tune, or be uneven. These lip slurs are good lip building exercises, but it must be remembered that the first one is all the student can work on for a while until he shows signs that he is ready for more.

A more difficult lip slur exercise is the two octave lip slur from low B♭ to high B♭, including all the between overtones: (F, B♭, D, F, A♭). This is repeated in all positions. The exercise must not be started until the student can play the high B♭ with reasonable ease.

Alternate Positions

Alternate positions are used in slurring and to facilitate the playing of certain rapid passages.

In songs where the notes are sustained and slurred, it is best not to go beyond the 4th position with alternate positions. The tones for which alternate positions are used most frequently are D and F above the staff, in 4th position. Fourth line F should be taken in 6th when preceded by low C and followed by notes other than those in 1st and 2nd positions. In the slur from middle C up to D, the slide moves from the 3rd to 4th position (not 1st), producing a pleasing natural sounding slur.

In General

When playing rapid passages, the student must be watched to see that he moves the slide to the correct position on time without jarring the horn and without tensing the grip of the slide. The slide action comes naturally through both the arm and the wrist, provided the student doesn't grip the slide too hard or tense his arm.

The slide must be moved quickly, without jerking, so that it is at the proper position for the whole duration of the tone. In fast passages of 16th notes and staccato passages of 8th notes, the slide should not stop for the notes, but glide smoothly past the positions, timed with the articulation of the tongue. In such case, the notes are short enough so that they will not be blurred when the slide is in motion.

REMOVING DENTS FROM BRASS INSTRUMENTS

OSMUND GIHLE

THERE have been several requests for an article on dent removal. I do not believe that this is a job for the general layman. It takes a lot of expensive equipment and experience; but you can try, and if it does not work you can always send the instrument to a repair shop.

You will need the following list of tools, and you will find them a little hard on the pocketbook.

A good strong vise, with swivel base and 4 in. wide jaws.

A pair of calipers.

A complete soldering equipment. If you do not have city gas, you should have a Presto-lite tank equipped with regulator and soldering torch.

A set of dent balls from ¼ in. to ¾ in. by .005 steps with drivers. These dent balls should be drilled with a hole lengthwise so they can be used with a new tool called the "Dentmaster."

Dentmaster with flexible shafts.
Ball holding rods.
Ball rods.
Dent hammers—several types.
Burnishing tools—several.
Mandrels—assorted.

You can easily spend $100 on the above equipment, and believe me you can have a lot of dents removed for this money by a repair man.

Removing dents from the flare of a bell is simple. Support instrument so nothing touches the dent on the concave side, and with a dent hammer, using glancing blows, lightly hammer dent out. Finish job by using a greased burnisher with a concave surface. Remember, if you are working on a concave surface use a hammer with a round face—if working on a flat or convex surface use a hammer with a flatter face.

Removing dents on tubes that are straight with an open end is also quite simple. If it is a straight tube, find a straight mandrel a little smaller than the tube—be sure that the end you insert in tube is rounded and smooth so you will not scratch the inside of the tubing. Slip tube over mandrel, which should be held firmly in the vise, and hammer it with the dent hammer. If it is a small dent the greased burnisher will do the trick. One of the ball rods may also be used.

For tubes with a taper you will have to use a suitable taper mandrel and proceed as above. If dent happens to be a little way around the curve on tubing near an opening, it is quite often possible to use the ball rods to push dent out, or hold ball rod under dent and use a dent hammer on the outside. For dents around the curve I recommend the new tool called the "Dentmaster." It is used with the dent balls, comes with full instructions, and makes this job easy.

When measuring tubing for size of dent ball, use a pair of calipers—measure the outside diameter of tubing at the point of dent and select a dent ball that is about $\frac{3}{32}$ in. smaller than the outside diameter of the tubing. If dent is very deep, use a smaller ball and select a driver smaller than the dent ball. Now, select the next size driver. This is used to drive the dent ball past the dent. The first driver selected is used to remove dent ball after it passes the dent. Be sure to grease ball and drivers. Please remember that most tubing is tapered, so be careful that you do not select ball and drivers that will mutilate tubing, for this will impair playing qualities of the instrument.

Now, first drop small driver into large end of tubing, then the dent ball and then the large driver. Work these around to a joint where dent ball becomes lodged against dents, then shake horn so that large driver hits against dent ball forcing it beyond dent. The dent ball can be helped along with a few light blows of the dent hammer. Now force ball back with small driver and repeat operation with next size ball. *Warning!—be sure you do not enlarge tubing beyond its original size as this will impair the playing qualities of instrument.*

Instruments often are so badly damaged that they have to be taken apart, and this is where your soldering technique will come in handy.

When you have done the best you can with the dent balls, finish the job with some fine emery cloth if it is a brass instrument. If it is silver plated, forget the emery cloth, as it will remove the silver plating.

For large tubes, such as baritone, basses and saxophones, you will need large dent balls to fit the tubing. These balls should be threaded so that they can be used on a dent ball holding rod. Often you can remove dents in these instruments where dents can be reached with a straight rod with a ball screwed on it, by the rebound method. Proceed as follows:

Hold rod solid in vise, support rod with a wood brace from floor to under rod near vise. Put dent on top of ball and have an assistant strike rod with sharp heavy blow with a heavy hammer a few inches away from the vise. Rod should be protected with a piece of wood. This will cause the rod to rebound carrying the ball with it, pushing the dent out. It usually takes several blows to do this. Be sure you press instrument down firmly over dent at the moment your helper strikes the blow.

All this sounds complicated, and it is not easy; but it can be done if you want to spend money for equipment.

Bernard Fitzgerald — Brass Clinic Editor 1946-1953

1949

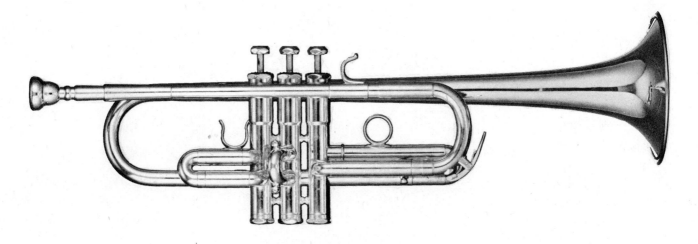

C Trumpet

TONE PRODUCTION

BERNARD FITZGERALD

THE PRINCIPLES of tone production are the same for all the brass instruments and tone is developed from the combination of the following elements: (1) the breath, a column of air generated and maintained by support from the diaphragm; (2) the lips, a sound-producing mechanism which transforms the column of air into vibration when tensed by muscular contraction; (3) the instrument, a resonator which develops and amplifies the vibration.

The player is able to produce tones throughout the entire range of the instrument by the use of various valve combinations (slide position on the trombone) in coordination with varying degrees of lip tension and breath intensity. Tones in the high register require more muscular contraction of the lips and greater intensity of the breath than is required for low tones. The three fundamentals of brass instrument technique are: *breathing, embouchure,* and *articulation,* and these elements should be introduced in that order.

Posture and Breathing

Correct breathing can only be achieved in conjunction with good posture while playing the instrument. This requires that the body be erect with the chest well arched so that the head and spinal column form a continuous vertical line. The body must be in a relaxed but easily erect position, with the arms held away from the side of the body.

Correct breathing should involve expansion of the lower chest area during inhalation. This expansion should be apparent in the entire circumference of the lower chest (front, side, and back). During exhalation, the lower chest expansion should be maintained until the depletion of the breath supply produces a natural, gradual deflation of this area. This is necessary in order to allow the diaphragm complete control of the breath during exhalation.

The gradual upward movement of the diaphragm during exhalation forms the foundation and control for tone at all times. The required wind pressure and quantity of breath are determined by the dynamic level and the register of the instrument which is being employed. Under best conditions, this variation in the speed of the breath is slight.

Nasal Inhalation

Normally, it is best to inhale through the corners of the mouth. This should be done with the least possible disturbance to the embouchure. Inhalation through the nostrils may be desirable in instances such as the following: an extended passage in the upper register wherein inhalation through the mouth may disturb the embouchure position to the extent that the attack which follows will be uncertain. Nasal inhalation may also be suggested to avoid an extreme stretched position of the lips which frequently accompanies breathing through the mouth.

The principles of correct breath support can be taught in a very short time, but breath control can only be developed over a period of time through conscientious study and practice. Tone production on the brass instruments does not require the breath to pass through the instrument under tremendous pressure except in the higher register and at the loudest dynamic level. The most efficient tone production results from the balanced coordination of breath and embouchure.

Embouchure

The term "embouchure" is used with reference to the muscle setting (position) of the lips and facial muscles used when playing. The placement of the mouthpiece on the lips is often included under the term "embouchure."

(a) Point the chin downward with the lower jaw in the position which attains a normal occlusion of the upper and lower front teeth (i.e., move the lower jaw either forward or backward so that the upper and lower front teeth can be closed with the cutting edges together.)

(b) With the jaw in this position, the teeth are slightly parted, with the throat, jaw, and chin muscles relaxed.

(c) The red part of the lips should be turned slightly inward with the lip muscles firm but not stretched or squeezed together. The lip muscles should be contracted toward the center of the mouth.

Mouthpiece Placement

Individual differences require each player to determine the exact position of the mouthpiece on the lips which produces best results. However, it is recommended that the beginning student place the mouthpiece lightly on the center of the lips with an equal amount of the mouthpiece on the upper and lower lip. Those students who are unable to achieve satisfactory results with this position because of irregularity of the front teeth or due to unusual lip formation, should vary the mouthpiece position so as to produce the most satisfactory results.

In general, players on the cornet and trumpet play with slightly more mouthpiece on the lower lip. Players on French horn, mellophone, baritone, trombone, and tuba are usually inclined to attain better results by placing more of the mouthpiece on the upper lip.

Articulation

Fundamentally, the function of the tongue in articulation is to serve as a valve which releases the breath and allows it to pass between the lips causing them to vibrate. The vibrations thus created are amplified and reenforced by the instrument which acts as a resonator.

The basic problems of articulation involve the development of *control* and *coordination* of the tongue in conjunction with the breath, the embouchure, and the fingers. The ultimate mastery of this phase of technique will require a considerable period of time during which the endurance and flexibility of the tongue muscle must be developed until the action of the tongue becomes an effortless and almost automatic response, functioning in coordination with the breath and embouchure.

Although physical characteristics of individuals vary considerably with regard to the shape and size of the tongue in relation to the oral cavity, the control of articulation is primarily dependent upon the following: (a) The position of the tongue before the attack, (b) The distance and direction of the tongue movement in releasing the breath, (c) The speed of the tongue action as the breath is released, (d) The position of the tongue during the duration of the tone.

The basic type of attack employs the use of the syllables "tah" or "too". The first step in developing the necessary accuracy and control of the tongue for the basic style of articulation demands that emphasis be given to acquiring the ability to produce the attack consistently in the same way. The release of the breath by the tongue must be achieved by a quick, definite movement which withdraws the tongue from the contact behind the upper teeth and allows the immediate flow of breath to produce and sustain a firm, clear tone.

The problem of attaining relaxation of the muscles of the throat and at the base of the tongue constitutes one of the most serious obstacles to tone production for a large percentage of players on brass instruments. Although the use of the syllables "tah" and "too" are usually most satisfactory for the middle register of the brass instruments, the various registers in the range of each instrument normally respond with best results with the gradual change from the broad vowel sounds in the low range to the bright vowel sounds in the high register. The syllables are applied to the different registers as follows: "taw" (as in tall) or "toe" for the extreme low register; "tah" (as in top) or "two" (as in two) for the middle register; "tuh" (as in tun) or "tih" (as in tin) for the upper register; "tee" (as in tea) for the extreme high register.

The legato style of articulation employs the use of the consonant "D" instead of "T" to precede the vowel sounds indicated in the previous paragraph. The softer sound of the "D" aids in controlling the release of the breath so that a legato effect is achieved. Artistic performance on brass instruments demands the control of many minute gradations and shadings of emphasis in articulation. Thus the speed of the tongue action in releasing the breath, the wind pressure and the quantity of breath which follows must be well coordinated.

In all of these articulations the tip of the tongue is curved downward and the movement of the tongue should be confined to the forward part of the tongue in so far as possible in order to develop maximum flexibility and control. The action of the tongue is actually a withdrawing from the point of contact behind the upper teeth and moving slightly away from the teeth and *down* toward the floor of the mouth.

Tongue Placement

The physical characteristics of the individual must be considered to determine the exact point or points at which the tongue contacts the upper teeth. Students having a broad tongue surface will often find it is necessary to curve the end of the tongue downward so that the actual contact of the tongue with the upper teeth is made by the upper side of the tongue just above its tip. A student whose tongue is narrow and short in comparison to the size and shape of the oral cavity may find it necessary to use the very tip of the tongue behind the upper teeth. Normally, the best results are obtained when the tip of the tongue is near the lower edge of the upper teeth when playing in the middle register and gradually moves upward toward the gum line as the brighter vowel sounds are employed for the higher register. The use of the very broad vowel sounds "Taw" and "Toe" are often more satisfactory for the larger mouthpiece brass instruments, and frequently the tongue may touch the inner part of the upper lip in playing in the low register on these instruments.

The difficulties encountered in developing control of a definite clear attack on the brass instruments can usually be attributed to the following errors in articulation: excessive movement of the tongue; lack of adequate breath support following the attack; and placing the tongue too far forward so that it interferes with the vibration of the lips. ∎

TEACHING

TONE PRODUCTION

BERNARD FITZGERALD

THE first experiences of the beginning student in playing an instrument are of the utmost importance since basic attitudes and habits are firmly established in a brief period of time. It is advisable therefore, to guide the progress of the beginner so that the fundamental problems of technique and coordination are logically presented in a manner which will enable the student to achieve the desired musical result with the minimum amount of "trial and error" experience in the process.

It is essential for the student to come to the realization that a properly produced tone responds freely, with a minimum of effort, while forcing or straining to acquire the tone will prove detrimental to progress. Too frequently insufficient time is given to the initial stages of instruction, and the student is confronted with problems of co-ordination and range which should be postponed until tone can be produced freely and easily.

Unsuccessful efforts on the part of the student usually result in one or more of the following commonly observed errors: overblowing, tonguing too forcefully, uneven flow of the breath, stretching the lips in an extreme smiling position, failure to establish and maintain the correct position and tension of the embouchure.

It is advisable for the playing experience of the student to be limited to that which can be supervised by the teacher during the instrumental class or private lesson until the basic fundamentals of tone production are well established. Unsupervised practice at home during the initial phase of instruction is frequently a hindrance to progress since the student will often practice "mistakes" unknowingly. These errors soon become habitual and the student progresses more slowly since the teacher must emphasize the correction of the "practiced errors" before new problems are presented.

Lip Vibrations

Although some controversy still exists concerning the value of exercises in buzzing with the lips, it must be admitted that the lips vibrate when tone is produced on brass instruments. Since tone production and control depend to a great extent upon flexibility and control of the lip vibrations which are amplified by the instrument, it is suggested that some experience in learning to produce lip vibrations precede playing with the complete instrument.

The ability to produce a clear, steady buzzing sound with the mouthpiece will aid the beginner in obtaining a tone on the instrument. Varying degrees of success will be noted as far as individual students are concerned, for differences in adaptability and co-ordination will have a direct effect upon the results obtained. However, there is a definite correlation apparent between the ability to produce a clear buzz with the mouthpiece and the corresponding result obtained with the instrument. This buzzing sound is produced more clearly and efficiently on the mouthpieces of the cornet, trumpet and French horn because of the smaller dimensions of the cup and bore. The larger mouthpieces of the trombone, baritone, and tuba produce pitches at lower frequencies and it is more difficult to control and focus the sound in this register.

Buzzing on the Mouthpiece

Having assumed the proper position of the embouchure with the mouthpiece resting lightly on the lips, a steady stream of breath is released through the lips and mouthpiece to produce the buzzing sound. The breath should be released gently and steadily, even though the first several attempts may fail to produce a buzzing sound. It is recommended that the tongue not be employed to release the breath at the initial stage, in order to counteract the tendency to release the breath violently and thus increase the problem of controlling the lip tension and vibration.

If the student lacks sufficient flexibility to produce this response after several attempts, the wind pressure should be increased gradually to aid the process of starting the lip vibrations. The student will soon be aware of differences in lip tension in producing various pitches. This realization is essential to the development of aural sensitivity and discrimination with respect to pitch placement, since a high degree of accuracy must be acquired in determining the necessary lip tension for different pitches.

Proper balance and coordination of breath and lip vibration is a major factor in efficient tone production. Contrary to popular misconception, lip vibrations can be produced softly and with very little wind pressure. The vibrating tissue of the lips constitutes a delicate sound producing mechanism which can easily be unbalanced by the mismanagement of the breath. Lip buzzing with the mouthpiece should be accomplished without forcing or straining in any way, and care should be exercised to avoid excessive pressure of the mouthpiece against the lips since this restricts the lip vibrations.

Although the process of describing the procedure in buzzing with the mouthpiece is both involved and prolonged, the student of average aptitude and ability should succeed in producing clear, steady, controlled vibrations with the mouthpiece rather quickly.

Having acquired the control of several pitches within the range of a perfect fifth, tone production with the complete instrument should then follow. If possible, the experience with the mouthpiece buzz should include the production of the pitch which will be used as the first tone on the complete instrument.

The procedure outlined is opposed by some teachers on the grounds that a constriction of the throat muscles is likely to occur. However, the constriction and tension of the throat muscles is a condition very commonly encountered among both students and professional musicians; and, in the majority of instances, it is the result of faulty articulation or inadequate breath control.

First Tones with the Instrument

The first tones played on the instrument should be in a register in which the student can play with ease. Variances in the aptitude and ability of individuals will be indicated by the fact that some students will be able to produce high pitches quite easily, while others will only be able to obtain the lowest tones without difficulty.

The three steps in playing a tone are as follows: *Attack, Sustain,* and *Release.* These must of necessity follow consecutively without interruption, and the techniques must be mastered to the point that the sequence is practically an automatic response. The instructions for each step are as follows: ATTACK: Form the proper embouchure and mouthpiece placement. Place the tongue in position for the attack and release the breath into the instrument by quickly withdrawing the tongue downward as in pronouncing the syllable "too" or "tah." SUSTAIN: Embouchure and breath pressure should remain steady to control tone and intonation. The chin should remain pointed, and the corners of the mouth should remain closed so that air does not escape. RELEASE: Release the tone by stopping the breath without altering the position of the tongue, throat, or lips. As the tone is released the tongue should return to the position for the next attack.

Careful attention must be given to developing control of the basic fundamentals of *Breathing, Embouchure,* and *Articulation* without the complication of problems in rhythm, technique, and rapid extension of range. If sufficient time is devoted to this phase of study, the student will progress far more rapidly and will be spared the painfully difficult and confusing handicap involved in later unlearning incorrect playing habits which should have been avoided at the outset. The principal problems of the more advanced student are usually due to failure to develop correct habits and playing technique through a mastery of the fundamentals.

Although the *slow-but-sure* method demands a much greater concentration and patience on the part of both teacher and student, the beginner would do well to adopt the motto "Make Haste Slowly." From the very beginning, emphasis should be placed upon both tone quality and a constant and consistent development of pitch consciousness and discrimination. The failure of a large majority of instrumentalists to learn to listen as they learn to play constitutes one of the principal obstacles to artistic musical performance. ∎

March-April, 1949

WHEN IS A BARITONE A *EUPHONIUM?*

HAROLD BRASCH

Is THERE a difference between the baritone and the euphonium? An old-timer recently answered this question by "I'm old-fashioned! I like to call my instrument a baritone horn." This old-timer was a bit upset when he was shown a Victor recording, "Song to the Evening Star," played by Simone Mantia, which was dated 1904, but labeled *euphonium* solo.

Some people believe it is the extra bell that transforms the baritone into the euphonium, while others think it is the addition of a fourth valve that makes the difference in nomenclature. Actually, it is the bore of the tubing that settles this question. The euphonium has a larger bore than the baritone, and it is this larger bore that produces the euphonius timbre and that definitely favors the lower tones of its range.

In the brass bands of Europe, especially in England, both instruments are used and usually a different part is written for each. Actually six different models are available in Europe: alto, tenorhorn, baritone, euphonium, E♭ and B♭ bass; each of these is successively larger. Since the American instrument is a cross between the English baritone and euphonium, it is permissible to use either name for these baritone-euphoniums.

Correcting Intonation

In the United States there are few four-valve baritones in use; and of those who do use a four-valve instrument, few know the real function of the added tubing. Some consider its sole use the extension of the range below E (below the bass clef). When it is used for this purpose, it loses its most effective function, namely, improving intonation and facilitating the fingering of certain note combinations.

It is unfortunate that this gorgeous brass instrument is so neglected by band directors and most manufacturers. Cornets and trumpets are built and played so that the third valve shank (sometimes even that of the first valve) can be moved with the fingers of the left hand to improve the intonation of some of the tones; but with the usual three-valve baritone-euphonium this is an impossibility. The trombonist, hearing a sharp tone, merely pushes the slide out a little farther. The French horn player can readily change the pitch of any tone with his right hand, but the baritone player is forced to make most of his adjustments with the lip. Only too often this adjustment is not sufficient because it is difficult to achieve. Certainly, something should be done for the baritone—one of the finest solo-brass instruments of all.

The first thing every band director should know is the exact function of the fourth valve, so that he may order such instruments for his own band; or, if he can afford it, to buy the even more desirable three-valve compensating baritone or four-valve compensating euphonium, which automatically make the desired intonation adjustments.

Function of Fourth Valve

One of the functions of the fourth valve is to extend the lowest range of the instrument as illustrated in Example 1. The scale there is very untrue, and since all the tubing is being utilized for the low C, the B is an impossibility.

Most readers are well acquainted with the fact that the first two half-steps immediately above the lowest open (B♭) tone (B and C) are noticeably sharp when played 1-2-3 and 1-3 respectively. Because the fourth valve slide can be tuned to give slightly more tubing than the sum of the tubing of valves one and three, it can be seen that the fourth valve should *always* be used as illustrated.

It can be discerned from examples 2, 3, and 4 that the tempi and strong and weak parts of the measure and of

40

the beat, may alter the choice of fingering used (in rapid passages intonational discrepancies are not as noticeable as in sustained ones, similarly it is more important that an accented note be in tune than one which is not). Regardless, the prime importance of the fourth valve is to attain the low C and B perfectly in tune.

As for the D (below middle C) the third valve is preferred to the fingering 1-2. To some experienced baritone players the use of the third and fourth valves may produce too much lowering of pitch temporarily. This is due to the fact that the good baritone player of the common three-valved instrument instinctively "lips" down these notes. Thus if he continues to do so when using the fingering given above with the third and fourth valve, he might erroneously think that this is a fault of the instrument. If this player will play up from the low Bb and use the same embouchure (without trying to "lip" the tones down) for the next four higher chromatic tones, B, C, C#, and D, he will discover that the pitch will sound true. The result is easier on the lips and more soothing to the ears for tone, and for intonation!

A number of practical examples are given here, showing the use of valves three and four.

Examples 5 to 11 show underlying functions of the third and the fourth valves. A careful study of these examples will be very helpful in deciding when these two valves should be used in other passages. In general, the usual fingerings used with the three-valved baritone are of course used; but because the ordinary baritone has such marked deficiences, its value is lessened considerably.

Try No. 12 (March and Processional of Bacchus by Delibes) with the upper fingering, then try the simpler fingering below and note the improved intonation!

(The low Bb with 1-4 is recommended only for the passage in No. 12.)

The baritone or euphonium has been a nearly-forgotten instrument, at least when we consider the importance of the great bands of yesteryear. Today, there are fewer professional jobs for baritone players; and this means, unfortunately, fewer fine performers. With fewer baritone players of profes-

sional caliber, there is less expert information and practical knowledge available concerning the instrument, and a dearth of fine music written especially for this instrument. Its usefulness to the military band cannot be overestimated. Within a four minute composition the baritone may double the bass part, be in unison with any instrument having the melody, join in the harmony of inner parts, sing out

a countermelody, or finally assume its real eminence as a solo instrument in its own right.

Let us seriously consider the merits of the four-valve baritone; or better still, the incomparable four-valve compensating euphonium. The advantages in improved intonation and technique are so great that the added cost will be considered as more than worth while.

THE DEVELOPMENT of the FRENCH HORN

WENDELL HOSS

THE FRENCH HORN is the one instrument of all the wind family rightfully entitled to the name, "horn," and in most countries is qualified by no other name. It is a direct descendant of the horn of antiquity, taken from the head of goat or ox, on which primitive people blew their calls of assembly, of ceremony or of battle.

The tone of these natural horns, the early instruments fabricated from metal, must have been coarse in quality and inexact in pitch, as well as limited in range. After centuries of outdoor life, however, during which the horn had come to be most characteristically associated with the hunt, it arrived at its present general contour: of greater length, and coiled for convenience in handling. By blowing in the upper range of the harmonic series of the instrument a greater choice of tones became available. Finally, in the time of Lully (1632-87) the horn was brought indoors from the fields and forests and became a permanent member of the orchestra, of theatre and court. No doubt the name, "French horn," derives from its early use as an accepted musical instrument by the French.

In its newer, more genteel role, however, certain modifications were called for in tone production on this rather robust instrument. The right hand was introduced into the bell primarily as a regulator of pitch, and could be adjusted to produce tones higher or lower than the natural harmonics of the instrument. This probably marked the change to the left hand in holding the horn.

Without Valves

Eventually the performers developed skill in the use of the right hand in the bell enabling them to play scales and even chromatic passages with considerable fluency. This succession of tones, some open, others of varying degree of stoppage with the hand, must perforce have been very uneven in quality.* To anyone who has studied the Mozart and Haydn concertos, written for the natural horn, it is a never ending source of amazement that these could have been performed at all without the use of valves.

In order to adapt this natural horn, with its limited selection of open tones, to the key of the composition to be played, set pieces, or crooks, were provided to effect a transposition to the desired pitch. This changing of the instrument to each new key would explain the custom, still persisting, of writing horn parts in the "key of C," or rather, with no signature.

As mechanical skill developed, however, valves, one by one, were added to the horn—as to the trumpet—until the standard quota of three was

---

*The hand in the bell extends the vibrating length of the horn, progressively flatting the pitch the farther the hand is inserted, until, on reaching the degree of almost complete stoppage of the air passage, the pitch suddenly jumps way up above that of the open bell—somewhere in the neighborhood of ½ step.

There is a conical brass mute which achieves the same effect as the hand stopping and is subject to the same transposition of pitch. Mutes are also made of different shape, of either fiber or metal, which require no transposition.

---

reached. The opening of each valve added tubing to the total length of the instrument, thus lowering the entire overtone series by so many half steps. The customary arrangement of valves is: 2nd valve, ½ step; 1st valve, 1 step; third valve, 1½ steps. These three valves can be used in combinations to lower the pitch still further. Thus by selecting overtones from the different "chords" made possible thru the use of the different valves, a complete chromatic scale of fairly uniform tone quality became available over the entire practical range of the instrument.

"But why," many ask, "is the horn fingered with the left hand, and not with the right, as are the trumpet and other brass instruments?" With the addition of valves to the natural horn coming so gradually, the practice of keeping the right hand in the bell persisted, both for its effect on tone quality as well as for pitch modulation, leaving the left hand to grasp the instrument and to perform whatever technical exercise was required on the newly introduced valves.

The Case Against Valves

As with all mechanical improvements, there was opposition to the use of keyed instruments, many arguing that the valve mechanism clouded the pure brilliance of the natural horn tone. Berlioz, for one, went on record in his treatise on instrumentation with a vigorous protest against the mechanized instruments. Even Wagner wrote for valve horns and natural horns, scored separately. The natural horn, however, eventually was completely superseded, with technical requirements increasing as composers took advantage of the greater facility of the valve horn.

Two types of valves have been generally employed on brass instruments:

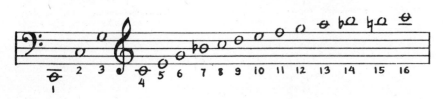

the piston valve, more commonly used by the French, which has become the accepted standard for the trumpet; and rotary valve, more closely associated with the German manufacture, and generally adopted on what we call "French" horns. The real French type instrument is of smaller bore, with bell of lesser diameter, and using piston valves. This horn has been commonly used in England, as well as in France; but it would seem, from the recent visit to this country of the Orchestre National of France, that the French too, are coming over to the German style instrument with its larger bore and rotary valves.

The horn in F, pitched in the middle of the range of transpositions to which the original instruments were subjected, has become accepted as the normal of horn pitch and quality, since the sound of the lower horns seemed too dull, and the higher horns being inclined to be too bright and thin in quality. Not content, however, with the 3-valve horn in F, mechanical ingenuity later added a further improvement consisting of a duplication of

the entire valve system of the F horn pitched in a different key—usually in B-flat, a fourth higher than the F horn. By the use of an added thumb valve, the air passage could be changed with great facility, from one horn to the other, giving the performer a selective choice of fingering most favorable for technical execution, for tone quality, or for pitch.

The Double Horn

This double horn has come to be the standard instrument of today. A few performers, however, have taken one step further—to the disapproval of many of their colleagues—and discarded the F horn altogether in favor of a single horn in B-flat. In this case some of the rich quality of the horn in F is sacrificed, for which the performer endeavors to compensate by the manner of his tone production and with the shape of his mouthpiece. The horn mouthpiece generally is deeper than that of other brass instruments and tends toward the conical shape in its inside contour: the deeper and more conical, the softer the tone; the more

shallow and cup-shaped, the brighter the tone. Greater diameter in the throat also adds to the fullness and softness of the tone.

The customary bracket of three valves is not sufficient for the single B-Flat horn, and an additional valve is necessary to compensate for the change of pitch in muting. What, by coincidence, amounts to ½ step change in stopping the bell of the F horn changes the pitch of the B-flat horn some ⅔ of a step and requires a compensating valve with a pipe of corresponding length. This actually constitutes a blessing to the performer, releasing him from further transposition when muting his instrument. Without this compensating valve the player on a double horn does not have the use of his B-flat horn in stopping, and must use the F horn, transposing the fingering one half step lower.

A popular addition to the B-flat is a fifth valve adding still greater length of tubing (usually 2½ steps) which in combination with the other valves covers the complete chromatic range of the double horn. ∎

September-October, 1949

TEACHING MATERIALS

for

Beginning Trumpet Students

BERNARD FITZGERALD

THE SELECTION of studies, etudes and solos for the beginning student should receive serious consideration in order to provide a basis for consistent and continuous musical progress and technical development. The organization and sequence of material, musical value and appeal, pedagogical approach, rate of technical and musical advancement, development of range, appearance, music theory, and cost, will constitute elements which are presented with varying emphasis and proportion in more than fifty beginning method books for the trumpet.

A large percentage of student musicians begin their musical studies

prior to the high school level; thus it is of particular importance that consideration be given to selecting teaching materials suitable for the younger age groups. The young pupil is frequently unable to recognize the importance and necessity of technical mastery of the instrument, and, because of his short attention span, will be incapable of prolonged concentration and study of purely technical problems. It is desirable to provide technical exercise and drills which are carefully graded in difficulty, so that the student will be able to achieve a feeling of accomplishment and progress through the study of new material at frequent

intervals, rather than being required to practice more difficult studies for an extended period of time.

The conservatory type methods by Arban, Gatti, and St. Jacome are used extensively, especially by teachers with a background of professional training, since these texts usually constituted the basis for their own musical training and experience. It does not necessarily follow that material of this type, designed for professional training, will prove equally adequate for the young child. This does not imply that these books are not satisfactory in providing the obviously necessary technical background which every experienced player must acquire. Neither does it imply that these materials are best suited to the interest, age, and mental development of younger children.

Enough Melodic Material?

Books of the above type provide very little material which contains melodic and rhythmic interest in keeping with the ability and interest of the young child and the development of the higher register is frequently unreasonably rapid as far as the average student is concerned. These older publications do not have the material organized so that it can be taught advantageously in a page by page sequence. The Prescott-Outlines for the Arban method constitute the only published guide to the use of this type of instruction book.

In the opinion of the author, it would be preferable to use this type of text following the completion of one of the beginning instruction books in the list which is included with this article. At that time the student should be able to realize the value and necessity of technical drill material and also be more capable of deriving the maximum benefit from this study. The skill and ingenuity of the teacher in presenting and administering technical studies and drills in accordance with the need and ability of the student are important factors which frequently determine the resulting effectiveness of technical study.

Rudiments and Notation

It is essential that beginning students be taught the rudiments of musical theory and notation. This information should either be available in the text which is selected, or it should be supplied by the teacher in the form of supplementary material. Several recent instruction books present music theory throughout the text, introducing new problems in notation, rhythm, etc., in conjunction with the musical content of the text.

Although it is desirable that technical studies, music theory, melodic interest, and solo repertory be organized and correlated so as to provide an opportunity for the student to recognize his consistent progress and thus derive the maximum satisfaction from his musical experience and accomplishment, few instruction books will contain such an ideal combination of materials. Consequently, the teacher will usually find that it is desirable and often necessary to supplement the text with additional etudes, sight-reading studies, etc. In many instances the solution to the specific problems of the individual student will be found in writing additional exercises designed especially for that purpose.

Compare and Select

The texts included in the following lists have been selected without considering the validity of the printed instructions in regard to breathing, embouchure, articulation, etc., since comparison of several books will indicate the confusing contradictions which exist concerning the techniques of tone production. No single text is likely to prove to be so definitely superior for all students as to warrant the exclusion of all other texts. Furthermore, teaching is likely to be more effective when the text employs an approach which coincides with the personal preferences of the teacher and contains material which can be readily adapted to his teaching techniques. While it may be true that a good teacher can be successful with any book, a good book is a definite aid to both student and teacher.

The materials listed below represent several different approaches with varying emphasis upon technic and music theory and appear in alphabetical order rather than in order of preference. The recommended solo materials have been limited to collections, since this serves to provide a greater amount of music in a more accessible form. These collections contain music of varying degrees of difficulty so that a rather wide choice is available to the teacher in selecting suitable solo repertory.

RECOMMENDED INSTRUCTION BOOKS FOR YOUNG BEGINNERS

Belwin Cornet Method. (Bk. I) . . . . . . *Alonzo Eidson*
  Belwin Inc., New York, N.Y. 1947, 32 pages
Belwin Cornet Method (Bk. II) . . . . . *Alonzo Eidson*
  Belwin Inc., New York, N.Y. 1947, 32 pages
Edwards-Hovey Method for Cornet (Bk. I)
. . . . *Austyn Edwards & Nilo Hovey*
  Belwin Inc., New York, N.Y. 1940, 48 pages
Freese Modern Elementary Cornet Method . . . *Harold Freese*
  Jenkins Music Co., Kansas City, Mo. 1940, 56 pages
Mills Elementary Method for Cornet or Trumpet . *Leon Ruddick*
  Mills Music Inc., New York, N. Y. 1945, 47 pages
A Tune a Day for Trumpet . . . . *Paul Herfurth*
  Boston Music Co., Boston, Mass. 1941, 52 pages
Universal's Fundamental Method for Trumpet . *Donald Pease*
  Universal Music Publishers, New York, N.Y. 1939, 52 pages

RECOMMENDED BOOKS FOR OLDER BEGINNERS
or Students Transferring from other Brass Instruments

Clifford Lillya Cornet Method (Bk. I) . . . . *Clifford Lillya*
  M. M. Cole Publishing Co., Chicago, Ill. 1937, 48 pages
Method for the Trumpet . . . . *Walter Beeler*
  Remick Music Corp., New York, N.Y. 1948, 71 pages
Modern Arban-St. Jacome . . . . *Harvey Whistler*
  Rubank Inc., Chicago, Illinois 1942, 104 pages
Music Educator's Basic Method for Cornet . *Mark Hindsley*
  Carl Fischer, Inc., New York, N.Y. 1937, 48 pages

RECOMMENDED ETUDES
AND SUPPLEMENTARY STUDIES

Dalby Trumpet Studies . . . . *Cleon Dalby*
  Belwin Inc., New York, N.Y. 1942, 32 pages

Elementary Studies for Cornet . . . . . . *Herbert Clarke*
  Carl Fischer, Inc., New York, N. Y. 1933, 53 pages
Forty Progressive Studies . . . . *Sigmund Hering*
  Carl Fischer, Inc., New York, N.Y. 1945, 42 pages
Preparatory Instructor for Trumpet . . *E. C. Moore & A. O. Sieg*
  Appleton Music Publications, Appleton, Wis. 1937, 32 pages
Supplementary Studies for Trumpet . . . . *R. M. Endresen*
  Rubank Inc., Chicago, Illinois 1934, 24 pages

RECOMMENDED SOLO COLLECTIONS

Album of Favorite Cornet Solos . . *Merle Isaac-Clifford Lillya*
  M. M. Cole Publishing Co., Chicago, Illinois
Elementary Trumpet Solos . . . . *Jay Arnold*
  Amsco Music Publishing Co., New York, N.Y.
First Solo Album . . . . *Carl Webber*
  Theodore Presser, Philadelphia, Pa.
Let Us Have Music . . . . *S. J. Price*
  Carl Fischer, Inc., New York, N.Y.

Teachers who prefer the more comprehensive conservatory type instruction books should find suitable materials among the following:

Arban-Prescott, First and Second Year . . . . *Arban-Prescott*
  Carl Fischer, Inc., New York, N.Y. 1936, 184 pages
Arban Complete Celebrated Method . . . . *Arban-Goldman*
  Carl Fischer, Inc., New York, N.Y. 1893, 347 pages
Arban Complete Method for Cornet . . . . . *Arban-Clarke*
  Cundy-Bettoney Co., Boston, Mass. 1930, 309 pages
Gatti Grand Method for Cornet . . . . . . *Gatti-Goldman*
  Carl Fischer, Inc., New York, N.Y. 1939, 250 pages
Grand Method for Cornet or Trumpet . . . . *Saint-Jacome*
  Carl Fischer, Inc., New York, N.Y. 1894, 366 pages
Modern Method for Cornet or Trumpet . . . *Ernest Williams*
  Ernest Williams School of Music,
  Brooklyn, N.Y. 1936, 325 pages ■

Trombone Problems

HERBERT E. OWEN

Use simple extension handle for young players.
Play bass trombone parts only on BASS trombones.

Having been faced with the problem of pupils who are unable to reach the sixth and seventh positions, I have rewritten—or avoided —notes involved and promised the student that some day he would grow arms long enough to play them. Or, in meeting the problem another way, I have discouraged the student from starting on the trombone and suggested another instrument.

It was not until a little ten-year old girl came to me—talented, bright, and physically normal in every way, except with no fingers on her right hand—that I decided to try to do something.

Although Mary Lou, who has a very sensitive ear, could amazingly manipulate the slide through the first five positions, it was still quite a nuisance, if not bad for her morale, to be unable to play the tones of the sixth and seventh positions.

Extension Handle

After giving this particular problem considerable thought, and after making some inquiries here and there, Mary Lou and I finally decided that some kind of a handle, long enough to reach the outer positions and yet short enough not to be awkward in the closer positions, might be a helpful solution. We made a visit to a harness company and found the personnel very helpful. After some trial and error, we decided upon the extension handle pictured.

The harness men said they used Bonna-Allen leather with number ten wire folded and sewed in to serve as a stiffener. Two "left-dot" button snaps are used. The leather is of natural color.

The gadget works for Mary Lou, and perhaps, with some minor alter-

ations if necessary, will work for others having the slide-reaching problem. In fact, I even have some university students with a perfectly normal right hand, and yet because they happen to have a rather short arm, they really have to stretch to the finger tips to play a low B-natural in tune.

I would like to list a few points about this gadget that seem to be in its favor:

1. It is simple to make—a harness maker can make one.
2. It is not expensive — around $2.00.
3. It is removable—however, by turning it between the slides it will fit in a case without being removed.
4. It is very light in weight—1½ ounces.
5. The handle makes it possible for some students to have an earlier experience with slide technique.

6. Some children might hesitate to use such an accessory, but I feel that the satisfaction of being able to handle the slide completely more than makes up for that.

Responses from Manufacturers

While we were working on this problem I contacted five of the leading instrument factories that manufacture trombones for possible help. They were asked:

1. If they made any such extension gadgets for the trombone.

2. If they manufactured any small or F alto trombones as a possible solution to the problem.

They all responded and cooperated very well. Here is a summary:

1. No such gadgets are available at present. Two of the companies have made them in the past. One stated they were not sold on the idea. Their representative felt that most players in the fifth grade could reach sixth position; if they cannot reach sixth position by that time,

---

Leather 'grip' snaps on slide. Short arms easily reach 6th and 7th positions.

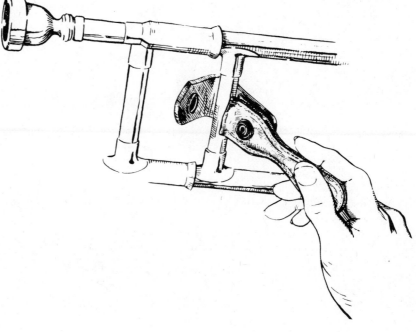

then the players should start on either baritone or E-flat alto horn until they can handle the trombone.

2. Two companies were of the opinion the beginning pupil should start on an instrument he can physically handle.

3. On the question of the F alto trombone:

(a) One company stated that on rare occasions they had made a few. However, it was considered by them a questionable investment both for the factory and the consumer.

(b) The official representative of another company stated that the F alto trombone had been considered for a number of years as a solution to the slide-reaching problem of small children, but so far they hadn't progressed far enough "to know whether a trombone of this type would be practical and musically good enough to adopt."

(c) Another company had made E-flat alto (valve) trombones in the past; stopped making them during the war; could accept a special order later on.

(d) Still another factory manufactures a "trombonium," a valve instrument which is designed similar to the baritone but having the tonal characteristics of a slide trombone. A standard stock model trombone mouthpiece is used.

The Bass Trombone

While on the subject of the trombone I have been asked to mention a few salient facts about using the bass trombone.

1. From the survey of the factories, I found that most of them manufacture bass trombones and have them available.

2. The quality of a bass trombone adds greatly to the complete balance of a good trombone section. This fine quality cannot be duplicated with tenor (regular) trombones.

3. The chief problem of using the bass trombone seems to be the need of a special large mouthpiece for best results. I have checked this problem with some noted symphony bass trombone players and also with several manufacturers. They all seem to agree the best results are obtained with the special large-size mouthpiece.

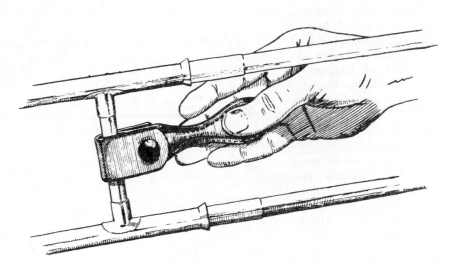

'Handle' at seventh position. Below—position of hand and 'grip' at 1st position.

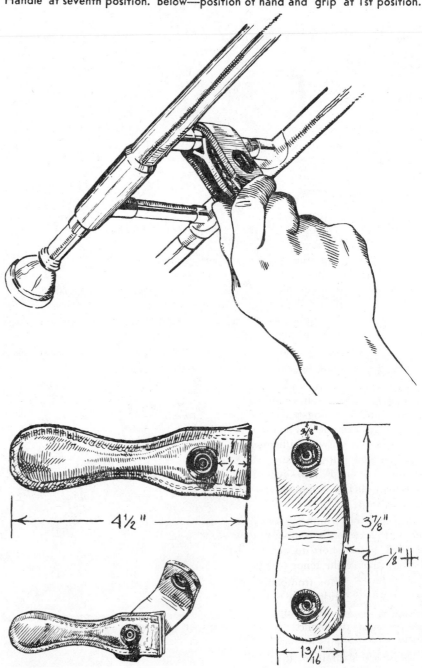

Leather extension has 2 parts. Upper left shows detail of part 4½ inches long. Right: 'snap-over' part dimensions shown in inches. Lower left: 2 parts together.

In fact, I have never seen a symphonic professional bass trombone player use anything but a bass trombone model mouthpiece. Ed Kleinhammer of the Chicago Symphony Orchestra told me he not only uses a specially built large size mouthpiece but, in the extreme lower register, practically shoves his whole face into it.

One factory, which makes an excellent bass trombone, provides an adapter (bit) which allows the use of a regular stock model tenor trombone mouthpiece. Although some

players use this method of avoiding the change of mouthpieces, yet their representative adds that the results are not as satisfactory as with the special model.

In school work this creates quite a problem. It is difficult to expect a student to specialize on the bass trombone. It is also expecting a lot to have a student, who is majoring on trombone, to be shifting mouthpieces. Yet the bass trombone should be played to produce the best quality. However, because the bass trom-

bone is so valuable an instrument to a progressive organization and because the playing of the double horn is a very worthwhile experience to a well rounded trombone player, I would venture a year or two on the instrument at its best would be very profitable.

I would also make a separate listing for bass trombone in the personnel column to add to the importance of that particular part. Except for the responsibility of a few solo parts, the bass trombone part is probably more difficult. ◼

November-December, 1949

Introducing the
F ALTO TROMBONE

TRAUGOTT ROHNER

IN THE ILLUSTRATION is an excellent likeness (right) of an F alto trombone, showing how its size compares with that of the B♭ tenor trombone. The writer and a number of trombonists have played this trombone, and all are definitely intrigued by it. A number of these instruments have been made, and they are available.

Among the major considerations concerning any new instrument is the question, does it have sufficient merit to find a lasting place among the other instruments? Though only actual use can answer with finality, there are some important arguments in favor of an F alto cylindrical brass instrument. Among them are the following:

1. The F alto trombone permits a student to learn on a trombone when his arm is too short to reach the sixth position of the tenor trombone.

2. The F alto trombone (or trumpet) can bridge the gap between the B♭ soprano trumpet and the B♭ tenor trombone.

3. The F alto trombone can be used instead of the tenor to play the ever-increasingly high first trombone parts.

1. Short Arms

Many fourth and fifth grade students would like to play the tenor trombone, but because they cannot reach the sixth position they either have to wait until they can reach this position, or use some type of an extension handle or start on some other brass instrument. Just as it is desirable for a beginning cellist to start on a cello and not on a violin, it is also desirable for a trombonist to start on a trombone and not on a valved brass instrument.

The analogy continues: just as a cellist who starts on a small-sized cello encounters little difficulty in adjusting later to a larger instrument, a student should have no greater trouble in changing from the shorter positions of the alto to the longer ones of the tenor trombone.

This matter of adjustment was also proven by several university trombonists who had been playing the tenor trombone for many years, and who seemed to be able to adjust to the shorter F alto positions very quickly.

For a beginner, one should use the regular trombone instruction

books. Thus the first position B♭ will sound a fifth higher—F. Since the same notes will be played with the same positions on both the F and the B♭ trombone, the student will not need to learn any new fingering when he transfers to the tenor trombone.

Schools which own the instruments on which the beginners are started might well consider buying one or more of the F alto trombones for the young beginners.

2. Bridging the Gap

The brass family of instruments is divided into the cylindrical and the conical bore varieties. In the cylindrical group are now only the trumpet and the trombone, while in the conical group are the cornet, horn (alto and mellophone), baritone or euphonium, and the tubas. One might call the first group the *bright* brasses and the other the *mellow* brasses. Regardless, the F alto trombone fills the gap between the trumpet and the trombone just as the horn (alto and mellophone) fills the gap between the cornet and the baritone or euphonium.

From the viewpoint of bridging the gap between the trumpet and the trombone, one should also consider the possibility of using an F alto trumpet—or it could be an F alto *valved* trombone. In either case, the tonal quality is the same. Because of the valves, technical facility would be easier than on the F alto slide trombone, but one would lose what the slide has to offer.

We could write at considerable length about the many possibilities of either the F alto trombone or F alto trumpet or valved trombone. The ensemble possibilities of four trombones, for example: 1 F alto, 2 B♭ tenor, and 1 B♭ bass (thumb valve lowering it to F); or a brass quartet having 2 B♭ trumpets, 1 F alto trumpet, and 1 B♭ tenor trombone; or a trio or quartet of trumpets with the lowest part played on the F alto trumpet. In the band and orchestra the tonal possibilities with an F alto trumpet or trombone are many. These possibilities need to be explored thoroughly.

3. High Trombone Parts

The ever increasingly high range of first trombone music, especially in dance orchestras, is discouraging to many professional trombonists. These tones on the tenor trombone (so high that many trombonists consider them "cruel or "impossible") are produced with comparative ease on the F alto trombone; and, since the tone quality of the F is practically the same as that of the B♭ in the same range, it appears to be sensible to use the F alto instead of the B♭ tenor.

When the F alto is considered as a second or doubling instrument, it seems to be of real value to *either* a trombonist or a trumpeter.

In the past, a few E♭ alto trombones have been made, but they have never found a place in the brass family. Though there is a discernible difference between the E♭ and the F, this difference is not

marked. Actually a greater difference in tone quality can be achieved within the same pitch (E♭ or F) by changing the bore and the mouthpiece. One can make either the E♭ or the F alto trombone or trumpet sound like a soprano brass or like a tenor brass, as desired. The accumulation of evidence has clearly shown ("600 Directors Can't Be Wrong," November, 1947) that the E♭ brasses (the E♭ alto-mellophone and E♭ tuba) are on their way out of the instrumentation of the band. It seems inadvisable to introduce another E♭ brass. Furthermore, an F instrument lends itself much better to playing in the orchestra and in sharp keys than one in E♭.

How To Write Parts

When a young beginner starts on the F alto trombone with a view to transferring later to the B♭ tenor, one should use the bass clef, and use the same position on both instruments for the same note. If both F and B♭ trombones are used in the same class or the same beginners band, two different parts will have to be used. Since no F alto trombone part is now printed, one will have to be written.

When one considers using the F alto trombone or the F alto trumpet as a regular instrument of the band and/or orchestra, there are several possible methods of writing the parts.

Any F alto brass will have as great a range as a brass pitched in B♭ or some other key. The first octave up from the lowest practical open tone (the second harmonic) on the F alto brass will sound from the F below middle C up one octave. By writing this octave in several different ways, one can quickly ob-

serve the advantages and disadvantages of each (bear in mind that in each example given the actual pitch and fingering are the same).

1. Actual pitch
Positions:

Valves:
2. As written for beginning trombonists (sounding a fifth higher for alto trombone)

3. Same fingering for Bb and F trumpet

4. Using mezzo-soprano clef for F alto trumpet:

From the foregoing it appears that number (2) is the best for beginners who later will play the tenor trombone. Either number (3) or (4) are preferred for the F alto trumpet or the F valved trombone because of the facility with which one can transfer to another valved brass such as the trumpet or cornet. Number (4) has the advantage that the notes will sound the pitch of the written notes; however, a poll of brass teachers would, no doubt, favor number (3). With this third example, the notes are written as they now are for the F horn. However, neither the F alto trombone nor the F alto trumpet or valved trombone should be considered as satisfactory substitutes for the French horn.

True, the tremendous force of tradition is against the F alto trombone or trumpet; but this is true simply because it never has been used and because no major composer has written for it; none of which means that the instrument is not good, nor that it might not be a very valuable addition to the brass family. ∎

November-December, 1949

Techniques for the BRASS SECTION

JAMES NEILSON

THE IMPORTANCE of the brass section to the symphonic band must not be overlooked by band directors. This being so, problems pertaining to this group's consistent performance need constant evaluation.

There are seven cardinal principles of ensemble music in performance to which the faithful conductor and ensemble give instant and constant heed. Here are the motivating factors which, being properly integrated, result in the superior performance:

1. The production of correct tone.
2. The accuracy of intonation.
3. The tautness of rhythm.
4. The faultlessness of technique.
5. The sincerity of the interpretation.
6. The artistic effect of the ensemble production.
7. The ensemble appearance.

The superior ensemble makes no attempt to evade the implications to be found within the framework of these principles.

Embouchure and Breath

The first principle of correct tone, is all important insofar as the brass section is concerned. The well-toned brass section gives to the symphonic band those over-all tonal proportions so necessary to dignified performance. Brass tone must have quality and color, freedom and naturalness, balance and blend, and controlled quantity.

Briefly stated, the release of the true inherencies of brass instruments depends upon two functional devices: lip formation or embouchure, and control of the breath through the placement of diaphragmatic pressure. The lips must be placed or set on the mouthpiece so that the upper lip will be able to vibrate freely on lower tones, and both lips will be able to vibrate freely on tones in the upper registers. Any undue pressure of the mouthpiece against the lips does not allow this free vibration and produces distortion of tonal values. This distortion is the result of a disarrangement of strength in the upper partials that are the complement of tonal totality. Higher or lower tones are produced by altering the tension across the lips. This tension is attained by the use of muscles controlling normal lip movements. Undue pressure of the mouthpiece against the lips hinders the free movement of these muscles, lack of freedom in the tone

being the result. When incorrect pressure is applied, low tones lose their sonorities, high tones become strident, and it is only in a very limited section of the middle range that anything resembling true tonal timbres is achieved.

The placement of the mouthpiece on the lips, and the proportion of the mouthpiece on each lip, is decided by the comparative size of the lips, and by the natural position of the lower jaw. In the correct mouthpiece position the burden of supporting the mouthpiece should be equally borne by the muscular part of both lips. At no time should the mouthpiece rest solely on the fleshy part of either lip. By this statement it will be seen that the position of the mouthpiece is determined by the proportionate size of the fleshy part of the lips. When the "bite" is normal (the fleshy tissue of the lower lip slightly larger than the upper), mouthpiece position is easily determined. When the "bite" is abnormal, or the fleshy tissue of the lips varies greatly in size, adjustments must be made in the position of the mouthpiece according to the necessity for having equal support on the muscular part of the lips. Any other embouchure technique than this will not allow true tonal inherencies to be released. It is both distressing and disturbing to hear the poor brass tone which is caused by maladjusted embouchures and incorrect mouthpiece pressure.

Sustained Unisons vs. Chorales

Surely, here is the place to develop careful teaching and rehearsal procedures in the interest of brass section tone. Unisonal sustained tone practice, followed by the unisonal playing of legato tongued chromatic scales and slurred intervals, seems to be the best method for achieving ensemble tonal sonority. Do you use this rehearsal device? Do you use any rehearsal device to improve tonal texture? If not, what do you do to improve the tonal output of the brass section? The playing of chorales is not the answer to this problem. The extremely narrow tessitura allotted to the brass section in band arrangements of chorales makes them impractical for the development of tonal sonority.

Furthermore, the playing of sustained tones serves two other purposes. These are: 1. The strengthening of the muscles forming the embouchure. 2. The increasing of the capacity for the intake of breath coupled with the ultimate muscular control of the diaphragm. This control is a vital necessity if the tone is to be sustained smoothly. The diaphragmatic support and response should be instantaneous and extremely flexible to varying wind pressures, able to sustain the loudest tones without faltering, yet capable of producing the easy, smooth flow of air inherent to the softer, but resonant tones. Most brass sections lose resonance in the softer passages because the performers cannot control the action of the diaphragm while playing softly.

All tone needs to be supported by breath. Normally, the diaphragm performs a subconscious action. If the brass section is to reveal the true tonal sonority at every dynamic implication noted in the music, this action needs to be moved into the conscious realm, then back to the subconscious after diligent practice on breath control. This means education at the ensemble level. The amount of breath needed to support a tone in any range, at any given dynamic, should never be a matter for guess work. It is a poor rehearsal that does not include training at this level.

Illegitimate Mouthpieces

All other things being correct, tonal values are most often maladjusted because of the poor selection of a mouthpiece, or because a mouthpiece has become dented, or misshapen. Illegitimate mouthpieces, i.e. those with broad rims and shallow cups, are illy suited to the true release of tonal inherencies. The edgy, shallow tone in evidence when this type of mouthpiece is used is due to the redistribution of strength in the upper partials. No amount of practice can overcome this faulty tone. Functionally, these mouthpieces are of wrong design. Much of the poor tone found in the upper brass of high school bands can be traced directly to this cause.

If you desire the brass section to produce the correct tone, all mouthpieces must be of the correct functional design. The type of bore, whether conical or straight, must be taken into consideration when advising about correct mouthpieces. The number of incorrect mouthpieces found in instruments of the middle brass bores is staggering. If you do not know the normal designs and measurements of mouthpieces for all sizes and types of bores, make it your business to find out. Then, in rehearsal, call attention of the brass section to deficiencies in this matter.

As previously stated, freedom of tone is the result of flexibility of lip coupled with agility in controlling diaphragmatic pressure. The brass section that does not indulge in the unisonal playing of slurred intervals both within and without the octave can have no freedom of tone. The wisdom of this type of preliminary rehearsal procedure has been long recognized by all authorities on brass instrument performance.

Balance and blend of tone are the result of certain equations correctly resolved by the conductor in rehearsal. These call for a very accurate tempering of the dynamic scale, with instruments of lesser resonating capacities being allowed more freedom in the use of the louder dynamics for the purpose of adjusting balance. The ensemble *forte* in *tutti* passages calls for a different degree of force from four BB♭ tubas than from four French horns. Frequently, I hear bands where the instruments of the secondary brass are covered in the ensemble *tutti*, and therefore unable to make their contribution to the total sonority because of a lack of ensemble balance. In the softer passages, balance and blend may be maintained by the use of a reduced instrumentation. This interpretative device could be used more often by high school bandmasters who are seemingly reluctant to cut down instrumentation in order to achieve effects of proportionate design and balance.

Naturalness of tone is the composite result of all the factors we have discussed. If these factors are considered correctly, tonal values will be produced naturally, with ease, and with correct timbres.

Sing in Tune—Play in Tune

Accuracy of intonation is yet another matter for valid rehearsal procedures. Here, I must say, and without fear of disagreement, that unless your brass section can make vocal response to all demands of pitch, it will be impossible to play in tune. I care not how carefully you tune to concert B♭; it is impossible to play within the range of brass instruments without making certain compensating adjustments of embouchure or fingering in order that all notes may be played in tune according to the demands of Pythagorean intonation. This intonation, with its sharp major scale thirds and sevenths, and its twenty-one interval relationship within the octave, is used by all good musical ensembles. The ability to make the adjustments of pitch called for when using Pythagorean intonation is utterly dependent upon the accuracy of the ear. How well does your brass section hear? Unless its members are able to make accurate vocal response to every indicated pitch stimulus, they do not hear well, they have no capacity for maintaining pitch relationships, and intonation constantly will be at fault. There is but one way to teach the brass section to play in tune, its members must be able to *sing* in tune.

There are other bad habits prevailing in the brass section that cause faulty intonation, and should have brief mention here:

1. The habit of entering the phrase with a relaxed embouchure, causing flatness of pitch; tightening the embouchure unduly in the middle of the phrase, causing pitches to become quite sharp; relaxing the embouchure preparatory to taking a breath, with flatter pitches prevailing again. A careful rehearsal technique will do much to insure improved intonation at this point.

2. The bad habit of failing to support tones in the top registers with sufficient breath, causing these tones to be quite flat.

3. The habit of pinching the embouchure on tones of the low register, causing these tones to lose timbre due to disarranged strengths in the upper partials. This type of tone sounds quite sharp.

4. The bad habit prevailing among trombonists of playing positions by sight rather than by ear.

In most high school bands the trombone section is the most out of tune.

5. The prevailing habit among the solo brass of tuning sharp.

Faulty intonation in the brass section usually can be traced to two maladjusted factors, those of embouchure and breath support. Training at these levels will result in improved intonation. The good conductor is well aware of this fact and includes this type of training in the rehearsal routine. The last thing the good conductor does is to spend time in adjusting the intonation through the moving of the tuning slides. Indeed, training in the correct placement of the embouchure plus the proper use of the diaphragm usually makes the constant adjustment of tuning slides unnecessary. Faulty intonation in performance is due largely to faulty rehearsal technique.

Attack and Release

Much more could be said about the place of the brass section in the symphonic ensemble. Manners and methods of attack and release need much explanation. Inexperienced performers are apt to have only one method of attack and release rather than the dozen that should be employed. The roughness so often heard in the brass section is due, in a large part, to the method of attack adopted by inexperienced players. In this method, every tone is played with the *subito* impact inherent only to notes marked *sfz*, and this is devastating to the development of the phrase line. Often, high school bandmasters seek to avoid this by going to the other extreme, making the brass section use constantly the legato tonguing. How insipid the total effect of the brass section when this is the case!

Although the limitations of space require that this article be concluded with much remaining to be said, the writer hopes each reader will derive some benefit from the suggestions noted. In all your work with the brass section—remember—it is the group which gives flavor and vitality to the performance of the symphonic band. ■

1950

B♭ Trumpet

THE BRASS CHOIR

BERNARD FITZGERALD

To the vast majority of musicians the Brass Choir is considered to be a musical innovation of comparatively recent origin, the scarcity of readily available information being largely responsible for this erroneous impression. Actually, original compositions for choirs of brass instruments were frequently performed during the 16th century; and, although brass instruments were used prior to this time, present available evidence does not indicate the existence of a specified instrumentation for brass ensemble music before the 16th century, except for isolated examples.

With the development of the antiphonal style among the Venetian composers of the 16th century, the brass choir achieved considerable prominence both through compositions performed with voices and other instruments, and in works for brass instruments alone. The antiphonal style of this period is particularly well suited to brass instruments, and the alternating choirs were frequently required due to the limitations of the available instruments.

Giovanni Gabrieli composed a considerable number of compositions for brass instruments which range in instrumentation from three to twenty or more instruments. His *Symphoniae Sacre* and *Canzon per Sonar* are remarkable examples of sonority and rhythmic vitality in writing which are unsurpassed by more recent compositions for brass instruments. Orlando di Lasso and Claudio Monteverdi also composed music for brass ensembles, Monteverdi employing 5 trombones and 2 cornets to perform two instrumental interludes in his opera *Orpheus.*

During the 17th century Johann Pezel and Gottfried Reiche contributed an extensive amount of brass ensemble music through the composition of *Suites* and *Tower Sonatas* which were written for four or five

brass instruments and were performed by the town musicians on various occasions. The ensembles consisted of trumpets and trombones, the pieces often being performed from the tower in the town.

The Brass Band in England

Although the interest in the brass choir is a recent development in the United States, the brass band movement enjoys a long and honored tradition in England, where contests of professional excellence are still held, and several noted English conductors have been associated with the brass band movement. The Salvation Army has sponsored and developed this activity extensively, and the musical excellence of such groups as the International Staff Band and the Chicago Staff Band are ample proof of the music potentialities inherent in the brass choir. The Salvation Army has been responsible for many original compositions for large and small brass ensembles, all of this music being published by their own organization for the exclusive use of their bands. It is unfortunate that some of these fine compositions are not available to the public.

The standard instrumentation for brass bands in England is 24 players plus drums. This number of players became the accepted standard due to the contest movement, the instrumentation numbering 16 parts being established as both adequate and most practical for the contests. Harold Hind has provided an excellent treatise on this development in England through his book "The Brass Band" which treats organization, scoring, etc., quite thoroughly.

The development of contemporary brass choir repertory is handicapped by the absence of an accepted standard instrumentation in this country. Ideally, a complete instrumentation could well be augmented to include Eb soprano cornet, flugel-

horn, tenor horn, baritone, euphonium, Eb and BBb tubas. From a practical viewpoint since neither Eb cornet, flugelhorn, nor tenor horn are commonly used in the United States at present, little would be gained by setting up such an instrumentation as required for the performance of the brass choir repertory.

The English have for many years indicated a definite distinction between the baritone and euphonium as two distinct tone qualities and sonorities, while in the United States there are only minor differences which distinguish the two instruments. The English euphonium is of large bore, the shape and taper of the bell also contributing to the mellow sonority of its tone quality.

Although the English have adopted a standard instrumentation, it must be noted that both French horns and trumpets are omitted, thus depriving the brass choir of two important tone colors. The effective use of the bright brass (trumpets and trombones) as a color contrast and the enriching sonority of the French horns are undoubtedly valuable additions to the tonal color spectrum of the brass choir.

It must be admitted that too frequently there is little or no noticeable difference in the sounds produced by players on the cornet and trumpet. This is due to both the prevalent trend toward using shallow mouthpieces on both instruments, and the lack of distinction on the part of instrument manufacturers as to the taper and bore of the respective instruments. Too frequently the length of the two instruments constitutes their principal difference. Properly used, the two tonal colors are distinctly different, although each tends to complement the other in the hands of skilled musicians.

Similarly, the Eb altos (though often more accessible than the

French horns in the average band) cannot be considered comparable to the French horn in tonal beauty or sonority, and must be acknowledged as a substitute which is inferior to the French horn in tonal refinement, and therefore not ideally suited for concert performances on the highest level of artistic accomplishment.

Recent Developments in U.S.A.

In recent years interest in music for the brass choir has been both revived and extended through the publication of new editions of many of the compositions from the 16th and 17th centuries. Much of the credit for this valuable contribution to the repertory belongs to Robert King and Richard Franko Goldman whose research and investigation have resulted in modern editions of many compositions previously unpublished or out of print. In his book, "The Band's Music," Mr. Goldman presents a comprehensive bibliography of compositions for wind ensembles, plus an excellent historical essay, "Original Wind Instrument Music." As musical editor of an eastern publishing company, he has made a notable contribution.

Robert King publishes an extensive catalog of material for brass choir and smaller ensembles entitled "Music for Brass." In addition to providing new and modern editions of the 16th and 17th century music, he has been instrumental in obtaining new compositions for brass choir by contemporary American composers.

To a large degree, experimentation and exploration of the brass choir in the United States has been done independently by a number of individuals in the colleges and universities. In some instances the resulting instrumentation has been influenced by available instrumental resources rather than an ideal combination of instruments. It is interesting to note the varying instrumentation which is employed, of which two examples are cited:

James King of Hastings College, Hastings, Nebraska, uses an instrumentation of 9 cornets and 2 trombones which are divided into sections with a cornet trio alternating on the melodic line with a cornet duet, the remaining four cornets and two trombones supplying the harmonic and rhythmic background for the ensemble. The available repertory for this instrumentation is necessarily limited to specially scored manuscript arrangements. While this type of ensemble would prove particularly advantageous in small schools, it must be admitted that a more extensive instrumentation is needed to exploit the tonal sonorities of the modern brass choir.

Robert King of Boston University omitted the French horns from much of the 16th and 17th century music both because of the lack of sufficient French horn players to provide an adequate balance, and because of his objection to the resulting blend when combined with cornets and trombones on this 4- and 5-part music. His more recent publications, however, have included French horn parts for both contemporary publications and some of the older music. These instrumentations are intended for specific music and situations rather than a complete brass choir.

The purpose of the brass choir in the schools is two-fold: (1) To expand the opportunities for ensemble training and musical experience by utilizing instrumentation which presents musical potentialities beyond those provided in present chamber music groups, and (2) To provide additional program possibilities for featuring this type of ensemble as a part of the band or orchestra concert, as the string orchestra is a part of the orchestra concert.

Instrumentation and Organization

In general there are three types of ensemble organization which can be utilized in brass choir work. (1) The multiple ensemble (i.e., the performance of quartet, quintet or sextet music with more than one player assigned to each part). The principal disadvantage of this plan is in regard to the performance of contemporary music because of the lack of dynamic and tonal contrast and the tendency toward a thick tonal texture.

Although not most effective from a musical standpoint, it is nevertheless practical for the smaller schools and it is quite possible that this approach will prove most successful in many situations. Some variety may be obtained in the multiple ensemble by the judicious use of soli and tutti passages to provide dynamic contrast. This will entail the careful marking of each individual part. The character and style of the 16th and 17th century compositions is admirably adapted to performance by multiple ensemble groups, the high tessitura and sostenuto style of this music favoring a liberal doubling on parts because of the endurance required.

(2) The augmented ensemble (i.e., one which involves 4 or 5 basic instrumental parts with additional optional parts for other brass instruments). The additional parts serve to reinforce the sonority of the smaller ensemble and also provide more dynamic contrast. Alternating soli and tutti passages will be advantageous with this type of ensemble. The principal disadvantages of this plan are (1) the meager amount of available music for this instrumentation, and (2) the inadequacy which prevents the fullest realization of the possibilities for contrasts in tonal coloring.

(3) The complete brass choir (i.e., a fully instrumented brass choir including all types employed in the modern concert band, with separate parts for each player). Only in this organization is it possible to have complete sections of *bright* and *mellow* brass which are properly balanced to permit the fullest possible musical expression. The following instrumentation is sufficiently complete to permit performance of music for all three types of ensemble instrumentation: 3 Bb cornets, 3 Bb trumpets, 4 French horns, 3 tenor trombones, 1 bass trombone, 1 baritone, 1 euphonium, 1 Eb tuba, 1 BBb tuba. It might be desirable to employ a slightly smaller instrumentation for the publication of music which is of easy to moderate difficulty in order to make these materials accessible to the small schools having a more limited instrumentation. For this purpose the following minimum instrumentation would suffice: 2 Bb cornets, 2 Bb trumpets, 2 French horns, 2 tenor trombones, 1 euphonium, and 1 BBb tuba.

Outlook for the Future

It is encouraging to note that an increasing number of composers are writing for the brass choir today. The present repertory includes compositions by the following American composers: Richard Goldman, Rudolf Ganz, Paul Pisk, Ralph Dale Miller, Paul Beckhelm, Samuel Adler, George McKay, and Wallingford Riegger. English composers who have also contributed to the repertory include John Ireland, Granville Bantock, Edward Elgar, and Gustav Holst.

Accurate predictions as to the extent of brass choir development are impossible at the present time. The realization of its possibilities are dependent upon the coordination of several elements. Composers, arrangers, teachers and directors must combine their interest and enthusiasm with an abundance of patience and perseverance in undertaking

the difficult but rewarding task of initiating this means of musical expression. Every musical medium must be subjected to a period of experimentation (referred to as the "age of the experimenters"); and, considering the present advanced mechanical development of the brass instruments, it is probable that the experimenting is likely to be concerned with new means of capitalizing upon the possibilities of the present instruments, rather than devising new instruments.

To date it appears that too little has been done in the direction of experimentation with the tonal resources of the brass choir by utilizing

the contrasting qualities of the brilliant brasses (trumpets and trombones) with the more mellow voiced instruments (cornets, French horns, baritones, tubas). A few contemporary composers have taken cognizance of these distinctions and have scored their music so that the instruments are effectively contrasted. However, many of the interesting possibilities of using various mutes, hats, and other media for tonal coloring are almost completely ignored. The potentialities of these resources are yet to be realized, and both composer and arranger have an unusual opportunity and challenge in this musical idiom. ∎

January-February, 1950

Do You Know Your Brasses?

Expert describes models and their special uses in modern symphony orchestra and band

VINCENT BACH

THE WORK of a modern symphony or opera orchestra trumpeter is highly exacting. In addition to technique, tone, and range, he must be prepared to play the various instruments indicated in the scores—brass instruments varying in pitch and bore. This is not for the purpose of avoiding the difficulties of transposition, but to facilitate the execution of difficult technical passages, to overcome problems of intonation, and to produce the particular tonal quality which the type of composition prescribes.

Not all players agree on the type of instrument that should be used for certain compositions. For instance, the D trumpet prescribed in Bach oratorios was originally played on a low D trumpet, which instrument was used with a shallow smaller mouthpiece in the extreme high register. Symphony men of today are not accustomed to playing this type of instrument and could not afford to train their embouchure just for the occasional use of these low-pitched instruments. For this reason, most Bach oratorios are today performed on a high D trum-

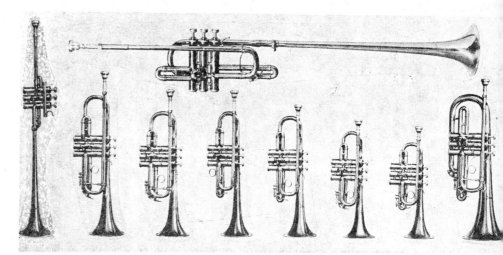

Top, Aida trumpet. Above, left to right: Piccolo trumpet in high B♭, C trumpet, high D trumpet, soprano trumpet in E♭, soprano cornet in E♭, piccolo trumpet in high F, piccolo trumpet in high G, and B♭ fluegelhorn. Not in picture, B♭ trumpet.

pet, and extremely difficult compositions, like the "Christmas Oratorio," the Bach "B Minor Mass," etc., are generally played on the piccolo trumpet in High F, or piccolo trumpet in High G, or the piccolo trumpet in High B♭.

It is a recognized fact that com-

posers do not always write the trumpet part in the proper pitch (favoring the open tones of an instrument as the old masters did to facilitate the execution of the part or to produce the right tone quality); instead they sometimes follow the road of convenience by just writing the trumpet part in the key in which the composition is written, taking it for granted that a trumpet player knows how to transpose and will select the right kind of an instrument, as he sees fit. Others take it for granted that every player uses a Bb trumpet (which is predominantly used in Germany and Russia), while other composers who lived in France or Austria where C trumpets are mostly used have written most of their trumpet parts in C.

The instruments are described as follows, with notations on how they are used by our leading symphony artists:

Piccolo Trumpet in High Bb

This instrument is not very much used but is well suited for the performance of Bach's "Brandenburg Concerto No. 2," also for the "Christmas Oratorio," and Bach "B Minor Mass." We build these instruments in two bell sizes—one on the style of the regular trumpet and the other with a comparatively large bell, resembling the fluegelhorn bell. This instrument with a large mouthpiece is used by Georges Mager, first trumpeter of the Boston Symphony Orchestra, in most of Bach's compositions.

Trumpet in C

Every symphony trumpeter must have a C trumpet available and should use it a good part of the time—if not altogether. In France, C trumpets are used exclusively in symphony orchestras, and to a great extent also in Germany and particularly in Austria. The trumpet section of the Boston Symphony Orchestra is famous for its fine performances on C trumpets. A good many modern compositions are very strenuous to play when written in the high register and a trumpeter can perform these parts with greater ease and more effectively by using a C trumpet rather than by forcing the high tones on a Bb trumpet. Our leading trumpet players are using C trumpets more and more. The instrument is particularly effective in Wagner's "Parsifal Prelude," Strauss' "Thus Spake Zarathustra," "Symphonia Domestica," Tone Poems and other compositions; Brahms' symphonies numbers 1, 2, and 4; Mendelssohn's "Italian" and "Reformation" symphonies; Dvor-

ak's "New World;" Debussy's "Festivals;" Stravinsky's "Fire Bird;" in Respighi's "Pines of Rome," and *all chamber music,* because of the light singing tone of the instrument.

Bb Trumpet

Generally built of 50% conical and 50% cylindrical bore tubing. This instrument is used for concert and dance work and because of its sure response in attack and its heroic, martial tone, is best suited for heavy fanfare music, flourishes and other staccato work. It is, therefore, the most practical instrument for all-around orchestral work. (For solo and band work, the cornet should be given preference).

The Bb trumpet is very popular in the United States, England, Germany, Italy, Russia and the German speaking part of Switzerland. In France, Austria and the French section of Switzerland, the trumpet players are accustomed to play C trumpets. In the English- and French-speaking countries, brass players prefer instruments with piston valves (Perinet valves, invented in 1839). In Germany, Russia, Austria and the German speaking part of Switzerland, the musicians use rotary valves (invented in 1813).

Modern trumpets are built in various bores and the so-called "medium" bore (.453") is recommended for dance orchestra and other strenuous work. The "medium large" (.459") or "large bore" (.462") are with some exception given preference by symphony men. The "bore" generally refers to the valve bore alone and does not indicate what tone quality or timbre is to be expected from the instrument—unless additional information is given regarding the size of the bell and the mouthpipe.

High D Trumpet

This is another "must" for the symphony trumpeter playing modern works or oratorios by Bach, Handel, etc. This instrument has a brilliant tone and is very effective in the high register in Bach's "B Minor Mass," "Christmas Oratorio," "3rd Suite in D," and most other Bach compositions; Handel's "Water Music," "Messiah;" Mozart and

Haydn symphonies are played advantageously on a D trumpet (which blends well with the strings); Beethoven's "7th" and "9th" symphonies; parts of Respighi's "Pines of Rome" (written for Bb trumpet but fits better within range of D trumpet); Purcell's "Trumpet Voluntary;" Ravel's "Bolero;" Prokofieff's "Lieutenant Kije" (written in Bb, but backstage bugle call should be played on D trumpet); Prokofieff's "Suite Scythe;" Stravinsky's "Sacre du Printemps" (for 2nd part of composition), and other modern compositions.

Soprano Trumpet in High Eb

A very important instrument for modern symphony work and which every symphony trumpeter should own and be ready to play on quick notice. The instrument is used for compositions such as William Schuman's "American Festival Overture," Stravinsky's "Sacre de Printemps" (written for D trumpet but the first part is better performed on the Eb trumpet, the second part better on D trumpet), Vincent d'Indy's "Symphony," Saint-Saens' "Jennesse d' Hercule."

Soprano Cornet in Eb

While this instrument is rarely prescribed in symphony scores, it is widely used in all European concert bands—in England, France, Italy, Germany, etc. It is a very effective instrument which deserves to be reintroduced in our American concert bands. In most of the military bands on the European continent where fluegelhorns are used instead of cornets, they also use a High Eb Fluegelhorn, which is very effective.

Piccolo Trumpet in High F

The High F Trumpet is an important instrument for a symphony musician and is used today for most of the difficult oratorio performances, for some of the very high parts in the Bach "B Minor Mass," and for Bach's "Brandenburg Concerto No. 2." It is the most popular instrument for use on these compositions. (All piccolo instruments should be used with smaller and shallower mouthpieces to do justice to both instruments and player.)

Piccolo Trumpet in High G

The High G Trumpet has been designed principally for the performance of Bach's "Brandenburg Concerto No. 2," which can be executed with greater facility on account of the high g-a trill which can be played one tone lower (f-g trill). The instrument has a very brilliant tone and is suitable for work in the extreme high register.

Bb Fluegelhorn

This instrument represents the contralto voice of opera. It has a rich, very mellow tone of lyric timbre and is well suited for song playing, especially in the middle register (contralto range). It is of exactly the same pitch and range as the Bb trumpet or cornet. It is widely used in European military bands (in Germany, France, Italy, Austria, Switzerland, etc.). If used in the proper place, the instrument is very effective and should be used much more in American military organizations. The instrument, unfortunately, is used in unison with cornets and trumpets, which gives a mixture of different tone qualities without giving each instrument a chance to display its own characteristic timbre. When fluegelhorns are used for mellow passages, trumpets and cornets should not play the same melody. In Austria and France, they also use fluegelhorns built in C.

Aida (Triumphal) Trumpet

These instruments have been designed principally for performances of the opera "Aida," but are extensively used for other triumphal affairs, processions, and martial events. If used in Bb, the instrument can be used exactly like the regular Bb trumpet, but the score in the opera "Aida" also prescribes B♮ trumpets, which should have a different timbre of tone, for which reason these instruments are built in two keys. The instruments are (including mouthpiece) about 35½ inches long.

Tenor (Bass) Trumpet in Bb

This instrument is also suitable for Wagner operas and has been designed principally for replacing the valve trombone. It is an ideal solo instrument, can be used to great advantage in dance orchestras, and is the ideal instrument for brass quartets (two trumpets, a low Eb trumpet, and a tenor trumpet in Bb). It is rather surprising that this instrument has not been adopted for general orchestra work long ago in place of slide trombones, which are the only brass instruments of two centuries ago which have survived.

Tenor (Bass) Trumpet in C

This instrument is very popular in Latin countries (Italy, Spain, Mexico) where most of the tenor instruments are played in C. This instrument has been especially designed for the performance of Wagner operas, Strauss, and other symphony compositions, and is best suited for this type of work.

Bb Cornet

This is the instrument for the solo artist. Because of its two windings and more conical bore, the instrument has more resistance and is, therefore, more flexible and better suited for coloratura work, for slurring, triple tonguing, and other technical performances. The tone is smoother and not as heroic or martial as that of the Bb trumpet. Especially the large bore cornet (having a more mellow, richer tone) is very effective for melody playing and the instrument should, therefore, be given preference for use in the concert band or by solo artists.

Low Eb and F Trumpets

These instruments are little known in the English-speaking countries, but are still very popular in Austria and other Germanic countries, as well as in Russia. In the European orchestrations they share the work of third and fourth cornet parts, also of French horn parts, playing to a great extent the afterbeat in march music. It would be very effective to use instruments of this type in American marching bands and would help to emphasize the afterbeats and thereby improve the rhythm. These instruments are also ideal for use in ensemble work (brass quartets or quintets) and in combination with the later-mentioned tenor trumpet in Bb.

Alto Trombone in Eb

The Alto Trombone is specified in symphony scores like Schumann's 3rd "Rhenish Symphony," Beethoven's "Fifth Symphony," Brahms' "Second Symphony," Mozart's "Requiem," and Mendelssohn's "Reformation Symphony." European trombone players make frequent use of it and are accustomed to playing the instrument, but the average American symphony man does not like to risk playing it on account of the shorter slide positions; however, the instrument has its proper place in the symphony orchestra and if a player has difficulty with the slide-positions, he should use an Eb valve trombone.

Tenor Trombone

These are the most popular instruments for all-round work in dance orchestras, theatres, and military bands. Generally built in medium bore, they are also well suited to solo work.

Symphony Tenor Trombone in Bb

These are the ideal instruments for the first and second trombone players in symphony or opera, also large concert and military bands. Built in a rather large bore, they produce a rich mellow tone of organ-like timbre, and are the choice of first-class musicians. The second trombone player of a symphony orchestra might use to better advantage a tenor trombone equipped with an F valve in order to be able to play the tones below E (which appear only too frequently in symphony parts).

Bass Trombone in Bb

This instrument (with F valve) is used by the third trombone player (bass trombonist) of symphony and opera orchestras, also by large military bands. Without using the F valve, the instrument is of the same pitch and range as the symphony tenor trombone. Unfortunately, it is not well enough represented in the smaller concert bands and especially not in high school and college orchestras, perhaps for the reason that players do not know how to use it. Third trombone parts written for school music are generally written in octaves, and the player using a tenor trombone plays the upper note instead of the lower one, for which a bass trombone is necessary. School band directors should insist that the bass trombone be used and that the pupils acquaint themselves with the function of the F valve.

Contrabass Trombone

This is a new instrument of ours now under construction. It is prescribed in Wagner operas, "The Ring," also in Vincent d'Indy's "A Summer Day in the Mountains." The contrabass trombone is used in the leading German opera houses. American musicians have always gotten by with using a regular bass trombone, which, however, is not the right kind of an instrument for fourth and fifth trombone parts of "The Ring," requiring a sonorous low register. The contrabass trombone is an octave lower than the regular bass-trombone and is of the same pitch as the B♭ tuba. The principal reason why the instrument is not used is because of its weight. Being twice as long as the straight length of a regular bass trombone, it is more than twice as heavy, and therefore difficult to manipulate. It could be handled more easily by the use of valves, and we are working on a new design to enable the player to use it to practical advantage.

The average trombone player, again, dislikes to use the contrabass trombone, because, since the instrument is an octave lower, a larger mouthpiece, similar to that of the tuba, must be used, which spoils his embouchure. The average tuba player, on the other hand, hesitates to tackle a contrabass trombone with a slide, as a tuba player is accustomed to valves. Therefore a happy compromise is to be worked out in the new instrument now under construction in our factory.

E♭ Alto Horn

THE UPRIGHT ALTO is a practical instrument for the marching or cavalry band. The French horn is not so practical, since the conditions in a marching band are not conducive to the playing of this instrument.

The impact on the embouchure when marching (especially on rough roads), or when riding a horse (mounted cavalry bands) makes it difficult for a French horn player to perform with surety and without risking the loss of his teeth. Since the French horn player must use both hands, it would be quite impossible for a cavalry musician to play his instrument, and at the same time hold the horse's bridle.

The necessarily brassy and more penetrating tone quality of the E♭ alto horn lends more emphasis to the rhythm of the marching band, and rhythm is the primary purpose of its existence. Also, the upright alto can be held toward the body firmly with the right arm, still permitting the free use of the right hand fingers. The alto horn should, therefore, not be overlooked, especially since symphony conductors have frequently insisted on its use for certain parts, in which the composer prescribes it, to produce a certain quality of tone.

E♭ alto horns have been built in trumpet form, which can be better heard in the marching band because the bell points forward, while in the usual style the bell points skyward.

Mellophone in E♭ or F

This instrument serves to a more limited advantage than the E♭ alto horn in the marching band. It will not serve in a cavalry band, because its balance requires the use of both hands in playing.

While "usable" in a grade school band instead of the French horn, it should not be considered an entirely satisfactory substitute, even for a talented beginner. This instrument is fingered with the right hand, and if the mellophone player changes to French horn, he not only has to change the type of mouthpiece, but he must develop his finger technique with the left hand. Therefore, any serious music student should give preference to the double horn, which will be described later.

Valve Trombone, Tenor Trumpet Trombonium, Bass Flugelhorn

These instruments belong in one class and are generally built in B♭. (In Mexico, Italy, or Austria, they are built in C). While the valve trombone is perhaps the oldest form, its antiquated design should influence one to give preference to a more modern instrument, such as the tenor trumpet (made by the Vincent Bach Corporation), or the trombonium (made by H. N. White Co.), or the bass flugel horn (made by European valve instrument manufacturers, generally with rotary valves).

The principle of our present-day slide trombone was employed 250 years ago in the early trombone models used in Spain (Sackbut), and also in slide trumpets and other brass instruments.

After the invention of the rotary valve (1813) and the piston valves (1836), the technical advantages of valve instruments were instantly recognized by all classes of brass instrumentalists, except the trombone players. They contend that a valve trombone cannot have the same tone as a slide trombone, and claim that it cannot produce glissando effects. They overlook, however, the fact that all other brass instruments have proven satisfactory in tone quality, and that the glissando effects can also be manipulated on a trumpet (and are misused only too often).

Trombone players cannot deny that in comparison with other brass instruments, the technical possibilities of a slide trombone are rather limited. A slide trombone cannot produce fast legato scales, trills, certain other intricate passages, nor a smooth legato on slow passages, or intervals without the glissando.

A further disadvantage is the inconvenience a trombonist suffers if he has to play in a crowded orchestra pit or stage, or in a marching band, where he has to be placed in the front row (where one might expect to find the smaller melody instruments) so that he will not hit the players in front of him with his slide.

There is no valid reason why a trombone could not be built with the same sonorous tone quality, either in the form of the conventional valve trombone (which, however, is also an antiquated design), or the more modern tenor trumpet or trombonium, as long as these instruments are built in the corresponding bore, and have the same proportions of bell and mouthpipe so that they will have similar resistance.

The B♭ Tenor Horn

This horn may be compared with the tenor voice of the opera. Because of its greater brilliancy, and greater flexibility (due to the smaller bell bore), it should be given preference for solo work of coloratura style, fast technical passages, and light melodies written in opera selections for the tenor voice, especially in the higher tenor range. Instruments of this type are used in England, Germany, Italy, and other countries, but are rarely heard in American bands.

The B♭ Baritone Horn

This instrument represents the baritone voice of opera, and has a more mellow, more sonorous, and less bril-liant tone than the tenor horn. On account of having a medium-large bell bore, the tone is accordingly heavier, and the instrument is, therefore, less effective for fast coloratura work, or triple tonguing perform-ances, than the tenor horn. It is well suited for playing the type of music written for baritone voice in opera. The B♭ baritone horn is featured primarily in American bands.

The Euphonium

The euphonium belongs in a similar class as the two previously mentioned instruments, but has a very large bell bore, and therefore, produces a rich, heavy, very mellow tone. It should be used in solo performances for a slow lyric melody, as written for the basso singer in opera. It is not meant for "fireworks," for the heavy tone is too clumsy, dull, and inflexible to be effective in coloratura work, and does not develop sufficient brilliancy to impress the audience.

It takes too long for the attack of each individual tone to set the big volume of air contained in such a large bell into full vibration, and it is, therefore, difficult for a euphonium player to produce fast staccato passages with a full volume of tone. Coloratura performances sound like "token" performances — even when the player possesses sufficient technical ability. Yet this rich, mellow tone is very effective for sustained tones, from which a heavy volume of tone is to be expected. Euphoniums are principally used in England.

Recommendations

For the large concert band with a complete instrumentation, I would suggest using one tenor horn, one baritone, and one euphonium. Then it can be left to the discretion of the conductor to assign the solo parts to whichever instrument has the best timbre of tone for the proper interpretation of the music. ∎

March-April, 1950

Playing The FRENCH HORN

ROBERT SCHULZE

B EFORE one decides to devote a lifetime to studying and playing the horn, it is important to consider what qualifications are necessary to become a horn player. Too many are encouraged in the beginning because they are able to produce a few tones on the horn, but any one single qualification is not sufficient to make a good player. It is a chain of attributes, such as natural talent for the instrument itself, a good musical instinct, and the necessary intelligence for practical application, all acting in conjunction, which produces outstanding horn players.

Only nature can bestow these qualifications. They can not be taught, but only cultivated and developed to the greatest extent for professional use by a competent teacher. If it were not necessary to be in possession of certain natural qualifications, we could all become great artists. All we would need would be a good teacher and the necessary ambition, but no teacher can bestow the originally deficient faculties upon a player. If he could, all of his students would be great celebrities. Not all players can become first horn players, but musically intelligent second, third and fourth horn players are just as important in a section.

If a beginner can produce a reasonably good sound on the instrument, and shows signs of musical intelligence, he may become a valuable member of the profession, for a great deal can be accomplished by conscientious study under the proper guidance. However, if the natural qualifications are lacking, the best teacher or the most scientific methods will be of no avail, and nothing but disappointment will result. Needless to say, persons physically handi-capped by signs of unusual nervousness, weak heart, twitching of the lips or poor teeth should not attempt to play the horn, since horn players must have both the physical stamina and nervous temperament to meet exacting professional standards of performance and endurance.

First or Fourth Horn?

The greater the muscular tension of the lips, the greater their elasticity and hence the greater the speed with which they can vibrate. The faster the vibration, the higher the pitch of the resultant tone. Therefore developing the lip muscles is the most important factor in producing high and low notes. Contracting and relaxing the lips to produce individual notes exercises and strengthens their muscular tension, which is so necessary for tone production, especially in a more extended range.

Many misleading claims have been made that, by certain scientific methods such as new discoveries in mouthpiece designs, new discoveries in breathing, fitting a mouthpiece to the teeth, or other fantastic means, it is possible to develop almost un-limited range in a short time. The truth is that range, though it can be developed considerably up and down, is limited to the muscular quality of the lips of the individual player. It is impossible to make a heavy-weight prizefighter out of a feather-weight; but it is possible to develop to the fullest extent those muscular qualities which nature originally bestowed on the feather-weight. Still he will never be a heavy-weight.

The same is true in horn playing. A teacher can only develop to the fullest extent those lip muscles which nature bestowed on the player, and when the limit of this development has been reached, the best teacher or the most scientific methods will not produce further development. For this reason we have many excellent second, third and fourth horn players. They are in possession of good musical instinct, but lack the natural muscular lip strength to produce extensive range. Extending the range requires time and patience and should never be attempted before the middle range has been well developed.

Conditioning the Embouchure

Literally translated, the word "Embouchure" means an "Opening." To wind instrument players it means more than just the opening of the lips. It may mean the general condition of the lips, or it may simply mean the position of the mouthpiece against the lips. When the instrument responds easily to the lips, and the player is able to produce a *pianissimo* or *fortissimo* in all registers with a good tone, he will maintain that he has a good embouchure.

The embouchure in reality, then, means nothing more than the quality of the muscular elasticity and flexibility of the lips. With some players the condition of the lips varies from day to day, while others complain of prolonged periods of poor embouchure. With careful observation on the part of the player, a poor embouchure can to a certain extent be eliminated. Of course no set rules can be given, since the physique of each player varies greatly, and some players have a more sensitive embouchure than others.

From my own experience I have found the following reasons to be responsible for sudden changes in the embouchure: lack of sleep; forcing of low or high notes; improper warming up; over-exposure to the sun or strong winds; dry lips due to smoking; sudden changes in weather; colds or temporary stomach ailments; spicy foods; a run-down physical condition; or incorrect practising. As mentioned before, by careful observation, the player may attribute a poor embouchure to some definite cause or causes, and avoid them whenever possible. When the embouchure is poor over long periods, it is advisable to consult an experienced teacher.

Selecting a Mouthpiece

Just as a prescription for eyeglasses is rarely suitable for more than one person, so one will hardly ever find two players who are able to play exactly the same model mouthpiece. Time and time again mouthpieces of outstanding players have been duplicated in every detail and widely advertised and commercialized; the result, however, was never entirely satisfactory, since the selection of a mouthpiece is a highly individual matter, depending on the amount of natural qualifications of the player. Before selecting a mouthpiece a player should have a clear understanding of the most important factors to be considered in choosing a mouthpiece, and what bearing they have on tone quality, high and low notes, intonation, endurance, attack, staccato, slurring, flexibility, and finally, on the player himself.

One of the characteristics of the horn is that it must have a funnel-shaped mouthpiece. That is to say, the horn is a cup-mouthpiece instrument. Even though trumpet, cornet, trombone, tuba, and their relative instruments also belong in the cup-mouthpiece category, the mouthpieces of these instruments differ from that of the horn in that they are shaped more like shallow cups, or bowls.

The funnel-shaped mouthpiece produces a full rich tone quality of a mellow character. To play it in its original form, that is to say with a large bore or throat, requires the highest qualifications, since the higher notes are difficult to produce, and generally require more effort in playing. Even though this type mouthpiece is still being used success-fully by some of our leading players, it is rarely used any more in its original form, since unlimited changes have been made in its design by players who had difficulty in producing higher notes. They found that by shortening the cup and narrowing the throat, they were able to extend their range and improve their staccato and flexibility.

The disadvantage of this procedure is that the more the cup is shortened and the more the throat is narrowed, the more nearly a player is approaching the trumpet or trombone type mouthpiece, which produces a harsh and brassy tone on the horn, especially in *fortissimo*. Another danger is in intonation, since a shallow mouthpiece is entirely out of proportion to the length of the horn. Therefore a player should try to play as deep a cup and as wide a bore as his natural qualifications will allow, and resort to a shallow cup only when it is absolutely necessary to improve the upper range. Of course a player must be careful not to surpass his limitations in choosing a deep cup with a wide bore, for in our times much is expected of a horn player as far as range is concerned.

The throat or bore of the mouthpiece varies in most cases from drill size No. 18 (very narrow) to No. 3 (wide). A large bore produces a bigger tone, but requires more effort in playing. A small bore produces a smaller tone of a brighter tone quality. A deep cup with a medium size bore will produce a better tone quality than a shallow mouthpiece with a wide throat, for, as mentioned before, a shallow cup mouthpiece lacks the characteristics of a French horn mouthpiece entirely and really belongs in the trumpet, trombone and tuba category.

The width of the mouthpiece (diameter across) depends to a great extent on the muscular, elastic quality of the individual player's lips, the setting of the mouthpiece, and the teeth formation. A large mouthpiece will produce a bigger tone than a small one.

In selecting a mouthpiece a player must decide whether to choose a wide, narrow, round, or flat rim. On account of the extensive range of the horn, the rim of the mouthpiece must by necessity be rather narrow. That is to say, the lips must be given full freedom to change from a relaxed position (lower notes) to a contracted position (higher notes) without being obstructed by a thick or wide rim. The setting of the mouthpiece determines to a great extent how wide a rim a player should choose. Players who set the mouthpiece "on" the lips, similar to trumpet players, may play a slightly wider rim, since the rim with this setting does not obstruct the manipulation of the lips too much; but for the players who set the mouthpiece "in" or partly so (that means into the red part of the lower lip) a thick rim will hinder lip manipulation considerably. A flat rim will set the individual notes more firmly, but also has the tendency to hinder manipulation of the lips. A round rim facilitates slurring, but the setting feels insecure with many players. A slightly rounded rim is probably the best choice for a player in the beginning, until he can determine for himself which type of rim reacts best to his playing.

A sharp inside edge on a mouthpiece has the advantage of permitting a good attack and staccato. The disadvantages are that with most players the endurance suffers, since

a sharp inside edge is inclined to cut the lips, especially when strenuous work is required. A sharp edge will also grip the lips too firmly, thereby hindering their free movement within the mouthpiece when going from lower to higher notes. A rounder inside edge may take more preparation or "warming up" before playing, but permits greater endurance and flexibility. The outside edge of the mouthpiece is not important for players who set the mouthpiece "on" or against the lips, but for players who set the mouthpiece into the red part of the lower lip (or partly so) the outside edge is a very important factor to be considered. Most of these players require a thin or sharp outside edge. It gives them freedom of lip movement, and to put it in their own words, "a grip on the mouthpiece."

The taper within the stem of the mouthpiece should gradually expand from the narrowest part of the mouthpiece (the throat) until it reaches the same width as the part of the mouthpiece where the end of the stem and mouthpipe meet. If the width of the end of the stem is smaller than the point, choking up of the tone will result. The main

factors to be considered in choosing a mouthpiece are:

*Tone Quality, Intonation, Attack,
and Range.*

Unfortunately we have no instruments to help us in the selection of a mouthpiece, and therefore the only correct procedure is to try various ones and judge only by sound and results. Any new mouthpiece usually feels good on a player's lips because he is using fresh nerves, therefore a new mouthpiece can never be judged at once. It must be played for a reasonable length of time before coming to any definite conclusion. Too many players make the same mistake over and over again in testing a new mouthpiece, by concentrating almost entirely on the higher notes only. They are constantly looking for a mouthpiece which will play "by itself." There is no such thing. A very important factor to be kept in mind is that the natural qualifications of a player can be increased by any mouthpiece, and the best mouthpiece is worthless if the player does not give it a fair chance by conscientious practice. ∎

September, 1950

The DIAPHRAGM and its AUXILIARIES
as related to
The EMBOUCHURE

*Good playing begins with good breathing,
but there is more than meets the eye!*

EDWARD MELLON

THIS SUBJECT has been fairly well discussed through the years, especially in regard to the inhalation of the breath, but not so much has been said with regard to the exhalation of the breath. The young player is still undecided sometimes about what to do with his breath after he has taken it and is ready to play. The purpose of this article is to present and discuss an aspect of the exhalation which seems to have been slighted, if not overlooked altogether. This is addressed specifically to brass

players because of their ever present embouchure difficulties.

In common with all the wind instruments, there are three factors to be dealt with:

1. *The resonation*—which is contained within the instrument. The maximum resonation hinges directly upon the maximum efficiency of

2. *The vibrating mechanism*—the sound producing agent which is the very thin membrane of the lips. The maximum vibration is attained only by the fullest cooperation of

3. *The diaphragm*—which is the foundation, the base of the whole structure.

Each of these items is dependent upon those underneath. If the diaphragm is not working properly, the others will not operate well. Obviously, the first concern is to erect a firm foundation. Although this seems clear now, the proper working of the diaphragm receives less attention than those more superficial phases which are more easily perceived. Practically all of the information on the working of the diaphragm is derived from the works written during the last couple of centuries by a few singers and singing teachers.

It may be assumed that a tone which is produced with the full co-operation of the diaphragm will be distinguished by at least one outstanding quality—a fine flexibility of tone. By this is meant a full command over the whole range of tone, from the softest sound to the most powerful. We hear and note this quality in a fine vocal or violin performance, but only in exceptional cases is it found in wind instrument performance. Rimsky-Korsakow had considerable justification when he said that wind instruments are less capable of different shades of expression.[*]

Watch that Vibrato!

Of late years it has been the custom to offer a pronounced vibrato in lieu of this quality, but too often players are unaware of the old rule that a vibrato is very good until the audience begins to be conscious of it—at that point it is overdone. The quality of flexibility is evidenced by a never ending play of nuance which vivifies the tone. There is no agency, other than the diaphragm, that can give such breath control.

The first essential for the most efficient action of the diaphragm is a low setting or placement for the breath, which must be drawn by the diaphragm to the bottom of the lungs, otherwise the diaphragm cannot maintain continuous contact with and control of the breath. The inhalation is accomplished by the action of the diaphragm, not the action of the lungs. The lungs are passive; the diaphragm active. To take a breath, the diaphragm descends, creating a vacuum which the air rushes in to fill. The expansion thus caused is centered about the entire circumference of the waist, front, back and both sides. The shoulders do not rise and the upper part of the chest is not extended by inflation.

From this point on the diaphragm becomes of vital significance. Strangely enough, our advisers fail us here, and we enter a region of misty ambiguity where one guess seems to be as good as another. The method of inhaling the breath is rather well defined, but the method of using it is not so well understood. This may

[*] Nicholas Rimsky-Korsakow, *Principles of Orchestration*, Kalmus, N. Y., p. 4.

help to explain the fact that, starting from the same point and using the same means, the results are so strikingly divergent.

The diaphragm forms the floor of the chest: at its lowest point it reaches the waist; at its highest, it has expelled all but the residual air from the lungs. It is an involuntary muscle, which means that it works continuously like the heart, night and day without rest, and has done that since we were born. Like any other muscle which is continuously in action, it is quite strong—strong enough to acquire the necessary control. It would seem that exercises designed to strengthen the diaphragm are shooting a little wide of the mark, rather we should try to harness it to what we are doing.

Diaphragm Auxiliaries

We may now consider another factor in the expulsion of the breath. There exists an ally of the diaphragm which lies altogether in the superficial area between the base of the breast-bone and the lower abdomen. The singers hold that the action of this auxiliary is helpful, and so it could be, if confined to helping the diaphragm. Too often, however, the situation is reversed and the diaphragm is reduced to helping the auxiliaries, a condition which is quite commonly found among instrumentalists. This superficial area (so called because it lies entirely on the surface, whereas the diaphragm is entirely inside the body) is the soft tissue which extends from the base of the breastbone down to the lower abdomen.

We may divide this area into two parts, one from the tip of the breastbone to the waist (the solar plexis area), and the other from the waist down (the lower abdomen). This lower area is an important one because its use is almost unconscious and unnoticed. These auxiliary muscles are again different from the diaphragm in that their use is voluntary. They are called into use only under certain circumstances. One of these circumstances is certainly the act of producing sounds from any brass or wind instrument.

The reason for objecting to the too full use of the auxiliaries, rather than to depend more upon the diaphragm is as follows: breath which is moved by a high percentage of auxiliary influence moves more rapidly than that

which is moved by the diaphragm, and this fast current of breath has a great tendency to waste. By waste is meant that not all the breath which passes through the vibrating mechanism is developed into tone. The best tones are produced with a minimum of breath, and such a column of breath can only be supported by the diaphragm.

Contrast this with a blast of air which, moving quickly, tries to find an outlet which is really microscopic. This breath forces an enlargement of the opening, the lips attempt to maintain the correct aperture for controlling the pitch, and the resulting open warfare destroys flexibility and endurance. However, let no one reading this attempt to slow down his breath consciously. It can be done gradually by transferring the seat of the tone from the auxiliary to the diaphragm by degrees. It is not a question of eradication, but of transfer.

Shakespeare and Garcia

The difficulty has been to find a practical point of attack. No one has such muscular control as to be able to effect this sort of a change immediately. However, two authorities provide a clue which seems promising. William Shakespeare (1849-1931), the English singing teacher, says to expand the back and sides without raising the shoulders. Also that considerable pressure and expansion is felt at the soft place under the breastbone; below this (below the waist) we should be slightly drawn in.[1]

Manuel Garcia[2] (1805-1906) divides the inhalation into two operations, done without pause. First, in filling the lowest part of the lungs, the lower abdomen is completely relaxed. During this partial inspiration, (abdominal) the ribs do not move, nor are the lungs completely filled. As the diaphragm continues, the stomach is drawn in and the lower ribs expand. The breathing then becomes thoracic or intercostal.

Both men agree that the lower abdomen is withdrawn and the inference is that it is kept out of the way while the tones are being produced. This certainly is not an unnatural thing to do. If we are successful in doing this, it is quite plain that we

1. Wm. Shakespeare, *The Art of Singing*, Ditson, Boston, 1898, p. 15.
2. M. Garcia, *Hints on Singing*, E. Schuberth & Co., N. Y., 1894, p. 4.

have eliminated the influence of this auxiliary.

In withdrawing the lower abdomen before beginning to play, we have to some extent, prevented it from exercising its auxiliary function. Not all of it, though. If one is accustomed to using it, the inclination will still be there, and under certain strains and moments of stress, will still attempt to move. For this reason, one should not be obliged to play louder or higher than one's method will permit at the moment. The term louder is used advisedly because one does not begin to produce a big tone (broad) until the diaphragm is fully in action. We can look forward to the time when the slowly increasing influence of the diaphragm will, in the end, obviate the strain. Any change other than this would be inadvisable on account of the possible bad effect upon the player's embouchure.

Thoracic, Intercostal

Both Garcia and Shakespeare agree in taking the breath to the lowest possible point. Garcia then tells us to withdraw the stomach midway during inhalation and only then are the lower ribs expanded while we continue the inspiration. The first part of the breath he calls abdominal, the completed breath is called thoracic or intercostal. Shakespeare evidently assumes that the stomach is withdrawn but he does not say at what point.

Upon the whole, the Garcia method appears to be the easier to acquire. We must make sure that the breath goes to the lowest possible point, by relaxing the lower abdomen. It is easy enough then to withdraw the abdomen below the waist. The lower rib expansion will, in time, take care of itself since the breath has no other place to go.

The aim is to transfer the seat of the tone from the auxiliary to the diaphragm. This is largely a question of time and it can be effected without any disarrangement of the player's embouchure.

A disturbing factor during this period would be the necessity of playing louder or higher than one's method will permit at the moment. Forced tones are of no value at any time, although they may seem exigent at the moment.

Among the characteristics directly attributable to faulty breath management, these might be mentioned:

1. A tendency to waste breath.
2. A diffuse tone which would lack both weight and carrying power.

3. An inflexible tone, which is extremely apt to be brittle in quality.
4. Warfare between the breath, the embouchure, and the tone which, in one word, is endurance.

In conclusion, how are we to know when we have reached the point where a full use of the diaphragm has been acquired? There are several things which will indicate that we are working in the right direction:

1. The seat of the tone (the sensation we experience in making a tone) is moved from the front of the body, around the waist, to the back on both sides of the backbone, below the shoulder blades and still close to the waist.

2. The tone will begin to exhibit the following characteristics:

a. It will be of maximum breadth.

b. It will be both brilliant and resonant.

c. It will have maximum carrying power.

d. It will have maximum flexibility.

e. It will be extremely easy to produce—as easy as singing a tone.

f. The embouchure will not be required to carry a double duty and will revert to its true function, that of producing vibration. ∎

October, 1950

How to make the most of PRACTICE TIME

JAMES NEILSON

A PROPER division of practice time is necessary if one is to become a competent performer. This time should be divided in the following manner:

Warm-up period	10- 15 min.
Scales	10- 15 min.
Technical exercises	30- 45 min.
Repertoire	20- 30 min.
Total	70-105 min.

The warm-up period is necessary because of the physical factors involved in playing a brass instrument. The muscular responses of the diaphragm, the muscles controlling the embouchure, and the muscles controlling the act of tonguing must be flexible and instantaneous. Muscular reaction must be brought under perfect control. Since the muscles used in playing are performing abnormal functions, there must be constant recourse to exercises designed to strengthen them, and to provide for increasing speed of the reaction time. It is best, therefore, to use the warm-up period in the following manner (sustained tones throughout the entire register):

Middle C down to low F♯ and return, chromatically, 16 counts at 72 beats per minute;

Middle C to third space C and return, chromatically, 8 counts at 72 beats per minute;

Third space C upward to G one space above the staff and return, chromatically, 4 counts at 60 beats per minute;

G space above the staff upward to high C and return, chromatically, 4 counts at 60 beats per minute (for advanced players only).

Sustained Tones Essential

There is no way to exercise the important muscles controlling diaphragmatic action other than to play sustained tones. With beginning students, this muscular reaction must be moved from the subconscious to the conscious thinking. The reaction may be a part of the subconscious domain with advanced players; constant exercise, however, is required in order that the diaphragm may be able to support tone successfully at all times. Breath control is a basic fundamental in tone production.

The playing of sustained tones serves another purpose in strengthening the muscles forming the embouchure. This, too, is important to successful performance. Sustained tones should be played at every dynamic level, changing the patterns from day to day, neglecting neither the *pp* nor the *ff* levels, and using every shade in between.

Following the practice with sustained tones, commence single tonguing on individual notes, for the second phase of the warm-up period. Use the same pattern as in sustained tones. Use combinations of three and four tones to the beat. Start at the speed of the current technique; increase the speed according to the accuracy of the muscular reaction until four notes to the beat can be played at 136 beats per minute. Advanced players should practice these exercises at varying speeds.

The Tonguing Controversy

There are two schools of thought concerning the act of tonguing. One school maintains that the tip of the tongue makes contact with the inner portion of the upper lip and teeth; the other, that the tip of the tongue contacts only the back part of the upper teeth. Unfortunately, there is no meeting of minds on this most important function of brass instrument playing.

Teachers otherwise quite friendly toward one another, constantly are at each other's throats defending their own particular views. Students who have studied with two or more teachers, and who have been forced to change their style of tonguing are often confused, and more unfortunately, very discouraged. For this reason, an attempt should be made to separate theories from facts, arriving at some definite conclusions.

Here are the facts to which both schools of thought subscribe:

1. Tonguing is an act of release. The column of air is propelled through the lips to produce the vibrations of tone only as the tongue is withdrawn from the point of contact.

2. The tongue must never go between the lips during the act of tonguing.

3. The kind of attack is determined by four factors:

(a) The speed with which the tongue is withdrawn;

(b) The size of the opening through which the air is released;

(c) The amount of breath pressure at the moment of release;

(d) The manner in which breath pressure is maintained throughout the life of the tone.

4. The tongue is not used to stop the tone during the act of single tonguing.

Beyond these few simple statements lies the method used to achieve precise attacks and releases. Here, both schools of thought are in violent disagreement. This being the case, an examination of certain physical characteristics may enable us to reach some basic conclusions. It seems to me that both schools of thought may be right, granted that we take into consideration the following characteristics:

1. The size of the upper lip from the base of the nose to the contour of the fleshy tissue of the lip. This varies in size, being as small as one-half inch, or as large as an inch and a quarter.

2. The size of the upper teeth. This size apparently is related to the size of the upper lip.

3. The placement and position of the upper teeth when the jaw is closed normally.

4. The position of the upper teeth in relation to the fleshy part of the upper lip when the lips are tensed, as in the embouchure.

A careful examination of this last

characteristic has shown me that in 60% of those examined there is a fractional part of the upper lip lower than the upper teeth, even in the very taut embouchure inherent to notes in the upper register. In the case of 25% of those examined, the fleshy part of the upper lip and teeth are even in the position of the embouchure, with the upper lip being a fraction of an inch above the teeth in the very taut embouchure. In about 15% of those examined, the upper lip was quite a bit above the teeth at every tension point of the embouchure. Usually, I advise students in this category to play some other instrument.

Vital Physical Characteristics

The position of upper teeth in relation to upper lip when lips are tensed, seems to be ignored by proponents of both styles of tonguing. I consider it the most important point of all. I am certain that the tongue must remain in approximately its normal position during the act of tonguing. There must be no curling upward of the tip to make the point of contact behind the upper teeth, nor must there be an appreciable arching of the tongue to make the contact on the upper lip alone. Surely the tongue in any other than a normal position cannot move with the rapidity necessary to produce fast single tonguing.

It becomes apparent to the thinking teacher that the point of contact will be decided by the physical characteristics already discussed. While it may be necessary to have the point of contact for one student behind the upper teeth, another student may be advised to make the point of contact against the inner part of the upper lip. There has been too much teaching of brass instruments where we have tried to make the student fit the method. We must begin to consider the possibility of making the method fit the student.

The determining factor in correct tonguing procedures seems to be the size of the upper lip. Where that size exceeds three-quarters of an inch, the point of contact should be the inner part of the upper lip, with the tongue also contacting the upper teeth. When the size is less than three-quarters of an inch, the point of contact probably will be behind the upper teeth. May I repeat, in no case does the tongue ever make the point of contact between the lips. This makes the act of tonguing quite simple, and will tend to produce uniform results in performance.

These are empirical observations. In rapid single staccato tonguing (four notes to the beat at 136-144 beats per minute), the tongue:

(a) is pointed rigidly,

(b) makes the reverse stroke from a normal position,

(c) offers only a slight surface (tip of the tongue) to the point of contact,

(d) travels approximately one-eighth inch in making the stroke,

(e) touches the point of contact very lightly,

(f) makes contact in most cases with both the upper teeth and the inner part of the upper lip (although the points of contact seem to depend upon the size of the tongue).

In marcato single tonguing, the tongue:

(a) as above,

(b) as above,

(c) offers a slightly larger surface to the point of contact,

(d) travels approximately three-sixteenths of an inch in making the stroke,

(e) touches the point of contact with more weight,

(f) seems to come less in contact with the upper teeth.

In single legato tonguing, the tongue:

(a) is pointed less rigidly (the style of address seems to determine the amount of rigidity, with tones sounding in an increasingly smoother fashion, according to the release of tension across the tip of the tongue),

(b) seems to make the reverse stroke from a position slightly lower than normal,

(c) offers a larger surface to the point of contact (this surface varies from three-eighths to five-eighths of an inch, depending upon the degree of smoothness desired—the larger the surface at the point of contact, the larger the opening through which air is propelled—this increase in size enables the air to escape with less built-up pressure),

(d) travels approximately one-fourth inch in making the stroke,

(e) touches the point of contact very lightly,

(f) does not contact the upper teeth at any time.

My observations indicate that in the less rapid single tonguing:

(a) the same qualifications hold as above,

(b) there is less tension in the tongue for all types of tonguing,

(c) this last factor seems to affect in a very slight degree the position of the embouchure, although my observations at this point are less conclusive.

Slurred Intervals

The next step in the warm-up period is practice with slurred intervals. Slurred intervals should be played in two, three, and four notes-to-the-beat combinations, according to predetermined patterns. Start at the speed of the current technique, and increase in speed until the four notes-to-the-beat combinations can be played at 112 beats per minute. Play lip slurs on the upper thirds, at 136 beats

per minute, in the following routine.

Notes given are the low note in the intervals. All exercises are to be done chromatically.

Fifths from middle C downward to low F#.

Fourths from second line G downward to middle C#, using auxiliary fingerings.

Also use combinations of the above.

Octaves from middle C downward to low F#, using auxiliary fingerings, three notes to the beat.

Tenths from middle C downward to low F#, using auxiliary fingerings, three notes to the beat.

Twelfths from middle C downward to low F#, using auxiliary fingerings, three notes to the beat.

Double octaves as above, two notes to the beat.

Fifths from 3rd space C downward to 1st space F#, auxiliary fingerings.

Thirds from 4th space E downward to 1st space F#, auxiliary fingerings.

Fourths from space above the staff G downward to 4th line D, auxiliary fingerings.

Any combination of the above.

This last section of the warm-up period provides for the attainment of muscular flexibility. There is no substitute for this type of work.

The warm-up period is a daily necessity, and must never be done carelessly. It is not a cure-all; there are other things that should receive daily consideration in order to insure competent performance. Yet, without a daily warm-up period such as the one suggested, it is impossible to become a proficient instrumentalist. ■

The Salvation Army BRASS BAND

Usual and unusual instruments blend to produce a perfect balance with specially written music.

by BERNARD SMITH

THE FIRST Salvation Army Band came into existence in 1878. A group of musicians known as the Fry family was attracted by General William Booth's preaching, and offered their services to the Army. General Booth, quick to see the value of such a group, accepted the offer and the Fry family became the first recognized Salvation Army Band. From this modest beginning has developed a musical force of some 60,000 musicians in the more than 90 countries and colonies in which The Salvation Army operates.

In the early beginning there was little or no sacred music for the heterogeneous group of players who made up the Army band. This fact probably accounts for the large number of secular tunes of the day which found their way into Salvation Army music literature. These tunes were set to religious words and used with good results to attract the people to the Gospel message.

However it soon became apparent that some further organizing was necessary if the bands were to progress. A standard instrumentation had to be established and music suitable for Army purposes provided. To accomplish this, General Booth appointed Richard Slater to head The Salvation Army music editorial department. Richard Slater was a professional musician who had recently joined the Army and was eminently fitted for his task. The first published music was a number of hymn tunes arranged for brass instruments with two clarinet parts optional. Later the clarinet parts were dropped and the scoring was done for brass instruments only.

Many people wonder why The Salvation Army has developed the brass band. The best explanation is that The Salvation Army began in England where the brass band is to the Englishman what baseball is to an American. Every village has its own town band —all brass. Most factories and mines have their own employee band— again all brass.

This enthusiasm and love for the brass band in England culminates in an annual contest to choose the National Champion Brass Band. Such bands as Foden's Motorworks, Black Dyke Mills, and St. Hilds Colliery are household names in England. With such a development among non-professional bands outside the Army it is quite natural that Salvation Army bands progressed along similar lines. Today the scoring of Army music is the same as that of the British brass bands.

Publishes Band Music

At the present time The Salvation Army publishes three different series of band music, through the International Music Department. These are designated as Festival Series, Ordinary Series and Second Series. The Festival Series is the most difficult and contains music for concert purposes including solos for various instruments. The Ordinary Series is less difficult and contains marches, devotional type selections, hymns and some solo numbers. Full scores are provided for *every* number including the marches and hymns. The instrumentation is the same for these two series and appears on the full score in the following order:

Soprano Eb	1st Baritone Bb
Solo Cornet Bb	(Bb Tenor)
1st Cornet Bb	2nd Baritone Bb
2nd Cornet Bb	(Bb Tenor)
Flugel Horn Bb	1st Trombone Bb
Solo Horn Eb	2nd Trombone Bb
(Eb Alto)	Bass Trombone G
1st Horn Eb	Solo Euphonium Bb
(Eb Alto)	Bass Eb
2nd Horn Eb	Bass Bb
(Eb Alto)	
Side and Bass Drums	

The Second Series is easier grade music and is intended for smaller bands; consequently, the instrumentation is slightly reduced. Marches, devotional type selections, transcriptions and solo numbers are contained in this series. The parts appear on the full score in the following order:

Soprano Eb	1st Trombone Bb
First Cornet Bb	2nd Trombone Bb
2nd Cornet Bb	Bass Trombone G
1st Horn Eb	Solo Euphonium
2nd Horn Eb	Bb
1st Baritone Bb	Bass Eb
2nd Baritone Bb	Bass Bb
Side & Bass Drum	

All the parts are written in Treble Clef except the G Bass Trombone and drums. This makes it possible to shift players from one part to another without the necessity of their learning a new clef. Even the shift from a valve instrument to trombone is not too difficult, if all that is required is the learning of positions in place of the fingering.

After having taught instrumental music in Public Schools in Flint, Michigan, for eleven years, I can now more fully appreciate The Salvation Army system of scoring parts in the treble clef. Many times in school bands there are too many cornets and too few trombones and basses; but the necessity of learning a new clef is enough to dissuade most youngsters from making the change. The director's task would be much simpler if all brass parts were in the same clef.

It is interesting to note the use that is made in the brass band of the less familiar brass instruments. The coloration of the brass family is the Eb Soprano Cornet. It is used to double the melody an octave higher, to play countermelody with Eb Horns or Euphonium, as an obligato instrument and often as the top note of a chord in conjunction with three or four part cornet work. It has a tone quality of its own which is unlike a Bb Cornet in the extreme upper register. No brass band is complete without a fine Soprano player.

Lesser-Known Instruments

The soft-toned Flugelhorn is another of the unusual brasses which plays an important role in brass bands. This instrument is considered as one of the Altos and is used with them. Sometimes the Flugel doubles Solo Horn, sometimes plays the upper tone of a chord when the range would place an Eb horn in the extreme high register. The Flugel is often used to advantage as a solo instrument. It is not considered as just another cornet part, as is sometimes the case in our military band arrangements.

The G Bass Trombone is probably the least familiar of the brass band instruments. It is of larger bore and played with a larger mouthpiece than the usual Bb-F bass trombone. Because it is shaped exactly like a Tenor Trombone its greater slide length requires the use of a handle, attached to the cross brace, in order to reach the fifth, sixth and seventh positions. It too has a tone quality peculiarly its own. It is used to double the bass part, in three and four part harmony with the tenor trombones, and occasionally as a solo instrument.

In brass band scoring there are three distinct baritone parts. The first and second baritone or Bb tenor parts are written for the small bore instrument.

The tone quality of this instrument is somewhere between that of the Eb alto and the euphonium. The first baritone part is similar to euphonium, having some melody, some obligato and counter-melody, sometimes doubling first trombone or first Eb alto, and often used in three part harmony with euphonium and second baritone. The second baritone part is usually a fill-in part used either in conjunction with Eb altos or with euphonium and first baritone.

The Chicago Staff of the Salvation Army Band,
Bernard Smith, Conductor

Conclusion

THE Euphonium is the cello of the brass band. The instrument used is the large bore upright with top bell. It is capable of a much heavier, more vibrant tone than the usual instrument of American design. The scoring for this instrument ranges from brilliant florid passages to soulful melody, from doubling the melody in the cornet, to supporting the bass line. It is undoubtedly the most versatile of the brass instruments in use in the brass band of today.

The Eb Horn parts are written for the Alto horn rather than French horn, mainly because the upright alto is much easier to master than the French horn. This instrument in the hands of an expert is as agile as a cornet, consequently brass band horn parts are usually more difficult than the average part scored for French horn. The Alto is capable of fine work as a solo instrument and frequently is so employed in brass band scoring.

The scoring of two bass parts is rather unusual, but here again the use of Eb and Bb basses is to secure the maximum color from the all-brass band. The part writing is generally along the usual lines with the basses either in unison or an octave part. Quite frequently, in accompanying solo instruments one or the other part is used alone. For special effects occasionally two different parts are written. Sometimes in a closing cadence the Eb bass plays the fifth of the chord above the Bb bass.

The scoring of the other parts follows the usual lines. To get the maximum range of tone-color from the brass band, however, much attention is given to the use of the sax horn family (flugelhorn, alto, baritone, euphonium and Eb and Bb bass) and the trumpet family (soprano, cornets and trombones), as units. A solo passage for cornet would be accompanied by the altos, baritones, and basses. A solo passage for euphonium would be accompanied by cornets and trombones. Every conceivable device is used to get the maximum color from the all-brass band.

In the ideal Salvation Army Band the players would be distributed on the various parts as listed in the accompanying chart.

Music for Small Bands

A band of fewer than 20 players would use the Second Series music, or publications of one of the Music Departments of the Territorial Head-quarters of the United States. Mr. Erik Leidzen has edited music for Salvation Army Bands and frequently contributed compositions of his own both for inclusion in the International Band Journals and in those produced by the Eastern Territory of The Salvation Army here in the United States.

This latter music which has become very popular with Salvation Army Bands in this country, is written for a smaller instrumentation suggested by Mr. Leidzen. It consists of 2 cornet parts, 2 alto parts, 2 trombone parts, euphonium and bass. Soprano, flugel, bass trombone, baritone and drums are optional parts which are not essential. While this music is especially designed to sound well with a small band, it is equally suited to the larger bands.

The Music Department connected with the Central Territory Headquarters in Chicago has produced another type of music designed for the very small group. As few as five brass instruments are all that are needed. The instrumentation is for first cornet, second cornet or first alto, second alto or first tenor or first trombone, euphonium and bass. Mr. Emil Soderstrom has been active in producing this publication and has edited much of the music.

The brass band as outlined here would be admirably suited to the school music program for many obvious reasons. This would be especially true in small schools where a full concert band is an impossibility. A brass choir of twenty-five, playing music written for brass instruments, is much more capable of a fine musical performance than the same number of players, some reed and some brass, attempting a military band arrangement.

There is no lack of published music for brass band. The music of The Salvation Army is restricted to its own bands, but there is a wealth of material published by such English firms as Boosey-Hawkes, R. Smith & Company, and Wright and Round.

For those who would like to hear some fine Salvation Army brass band music the following list of recordings are available either at the Eastern Headquarters, 120 West 14th Street, New York City, or Central Headquarters, 719 North State Street, Chicago, Illinois,

March, "Pressing Onward" — Erik Leidzen
   and on the reverse side
March, "Praise"—Wilfred Heaton
March, "Minneapolis"—Emil Soderstrom
   and on the reverse side
Cornet Duet, "Always Cheerful" — Albert Jakeway
Suite, "Songs of the Morning"—Eric Ball
   three sides on two records
Cornet Solo, "Tucket"—Erik Leidzen
   Two sides of a ten-inch record.
Tone Poem, "The Divine Pursuit"—Colonel Bramwell Coles
   two records—three sides
   This is based on the poem, "The Hound of Heaven" by Francis Thompson. The composer is the present head of the International Music Editorial Department.
Tone Poem, "The Bethlehem Story"—Ray Allen
Meditation, "Just As I Am"—Wilfred Heaton

These are just a few of the more than 150 titles which have been recorded by Salvation Army Bands.

We of The Salvation Army are proud of the accomplishments of our brass bands, and hope that our experience in the development of bands and band music can be useful and helpful to others.

CHART SHOWING DISTRIBUTION OF PARTS
For Various Sized Bands

Total Band Strength	20	25	30	35	40	45	50	55	60
Soprano Eb	1	1	1	1	1	*2	2	2	2
Solo Cornet Bb	2	*3	*5	5	*6	6	6	*8	*10
First Cornet Bb	1	*2	2	*3	3	*4	4	*5	5
Second Cornet Bb	1	1	*2	*3	3	*4	4	4	*5
Flugelhorn Bb	1	1	1	1	1	1	*2	2	*3
Solo Horn Eb	1	*2	2	2	*3	3	3	3	3
First Horn Eb	1	1	1	*2	2	*3	3	3	3
Second Horn Eb	1	1	1	1	*2	2	*3	3	3
First Baritone Bb	1	1	*2	2	2	2	*3	3	3
Second Baritone Bb	1	1	1	*2	2	2	2	*3	3
First Trombone Bb	1	*2	2	2	2	*3	3	3	3
Second Trombone Bb	1	1	1	*2	2	2	2	*3	3
Bass Trombone G	1	1	1	1	1	1	1	1	1
Solo Euphonium Bb	2	2	2	2	*3	3	3	3	*4
Bass Eb	1	1	*2	2	2	2	*3	3	3
Bass Bb	1	*2	2	2	*3	3	3	3	3
Side and Bass Drums	2	2	2	2	2	2	*3	3	3

*indicates parts added

CHAMBER MUSIC for TRUMPET
–with Strings or Woodwinds

BERNARD FITZGERALD

SEVERAL comprehensive lists of brass ensemble music have been published in recent years, but the meager quantity of worth-while chamber music is a cause of concern for both the teacher and the serious performer. This lack is a particular problem to teachers and students in colleges and universities, since in many instances students are required to present a recital on their major instrument before graduation.

In view of the fact that the recital repertoire for the trumpet is not particularly extensive, the problem of selecting a suitable recital program is often a difficult and perplexing one. It is difficult to provide both musical interest and variety, for several reasons. First, because the musical public is unfamiliar with the serious trumpet repertoire; second, the fact that solo recitals on brass instruments are still considered somewhat unusual; third, because of the extremely unfortunate practice of evaluating brass solo performance almost entirely upon the basis of virtuosity.

It is quite probable that teachers and performers who have not heard the trumpet in combination with string and woodwind instruments may feel skeptical as to the musical effectiveness which will result. However, those who have heard or performed compositions such as the following: *Septour*, Opus 65, by Saint-Saens, *Serenata*, by Casella, *Fantasy*, Opus 40, by Goossens, and *The Quiet City*, by Copland, will confirm the fact that the results are most gratifying.

In many respects the performance of chamber music makes greater demands upon the performer than are required for solo performance. Numerous difficulties are encountered in blending the trumpet with a small

CHAMBER MUSIC FOR TRUMPET WITH STRING OR WOODWIND INSTRUMENTS

Composer	Title	Publisher
Achron, Joseph	Suite from Theater Music to "Golem"— Trumpet, Horn, Cello, Piano	Mss. Fleischer Collection
Auric, George	Five Bagatelles on Marlborough— Clarinet, Bassoon, Trumpet, Violin, Cello & Piano	
Bach, J. S.	Brandenburg Concerto in F Major— Trumpet, Violin, Flute, Oboe & Strings	Associated
Bertini, Henri	Nonet—for Flute, Oboe, Viola, Cello, Horn, Bassoon, Trumpet & Piano	Lemoine
Beversdorf, Thomas	Concerto Grosso No. 2— Solo Trumpet and Chamber Orchestra	Mss.
Biebl, Franz	Divertimento for Trumpet, Flute, Clarinet & Strings	Voggenreiter
Busch, Adolph	Divertimento—Flute, Oboe, Clarinet, Bassoon, 2 Horns, Trumpet, Timpani, and String Quintet	
Casella, Alfredo	Serenata—Trumpet, Clarinet, Bassoon, Violin, Cello	Universal
Casella, Alfredo	Sinfonia, Op. 54—Clarinet, Trumpet, Cello, Piano	Carisch
Chavez, Carlos	Soli for Oboe, Clarinet, Bassoon, Trumpet	Mss. Fleischer Collection
Codivilla, Filippo	Octet, for Flute, Oboe, Clarinet, Bassoon, 2 Horns, Trumpet, Trombone	Pizzi
Copland, Aaron	The Quiet City—Trumpet, English Horn, Strings	Boosey-Hawkes
Delannoy, Marcel	Rapsodie, for Trumpet, Alto Saxophone, Cello & Piano	Heugel
Duvernoy, Alphonse	Serenade, Op. 24—Trumpet, Strings & Piano	Andraud
Fuleihan, Anis	Divertimento, No. 2—Trumpet, Oboe, Horn, Bassoon & String Orch.	Mss.
Gal, Hans	Divertimento, Op. 22—Flute, Oboe, 2 Clarinets, Trumpet, 2 Horns, Bassoon	Leuckart

group of string or woodwind instruments, and the trumpet, therefore, frequently must be subordinate to the other instruments in the group. This exacts a very high degree of tonal and volume control, since the trumpet is usually the instrument with the greatest tonal intensity and volume in the ensemble.

Although every fine trumpeter should develop a high degree of tonal and volume control, the absence of these more subtle shadings is all too frequently apparent, and in many instances is due to inadequate breath control. The Bach *Brandenburg Concerto No. 2* is a notable example of the necessity for acquiring control of the extreme high register. The trumpet is required to perform in this register in ensemble with three solo woodwind and string instruments: flute, oboe, and violin.

While the list which follows may appear rather meager, it should be noted that a number of outstanding composers have written music for trumpet in combination with string or woodwind instruments. By far the majority of the compositions listed are by composers of the late nineteenth or twentieth century. The list includes works by Stravinsky, Respighi, Ibert, Chavez, Martinu, Hindemith, Saint-Saens, and Shostakovitch. The instrumentation is so varied that it seems impractical to attempt to identify any one instrumental combination as being typical. Most of the compositions, however, include both woodwind and string instruments in addition to trumpet.

The author has attempted to compile a complete bibliography, but the present list is published with the realization that there are undoubtedly omissions, particularly those compositions in manuscript which are not generally known or listed.

A number of compositions were intentionally omitted, due to the fact that available information is not complete at the present time. Although the majority of the compositions included here are published, many of them are probably not obtainable now. Compositions known to be in manuscript are so indicated. In most instances they are available from the composer or the American Music Center in New York City. The remaining titles are presumed to be published, although complete details have not been obtained at this writing.

Gebhard, Ludwig	Sonatine, Op. 3—Trumpet, Horn & Piano	Bohm
Gitvotoff	Fragments, No. 2—Flute, Clarinet, Bassoon, Trumpet, String Quartet, Piano	
Goossens, Eugene	Fantasy, Op. 40—Flute, Oboe, 2 Clarinets, 2 Bassoons, 2 Horns, & Trumpet	Curwen
Grainger, Percy	The Merry King—Flute, 3Bb Clarinets, Alto Clar., Bass Clar. Contra Bassoon, Trumpet, Horn, Baritone Saxophone, Piano	Mss.
Grimm, Hugo	Byzantine Suite—Flute, Oboe, Clarinet, Horn, Bassoon, Trumpet & String Quintet	
Hahn, Reynaldo	Beatrice d'estes Ball, Suite—2 Flutes, 2 Clarinets, Oboe, 2 Bassoons, 2 Horns, Trumpet, Percussion, 2 Harps, Piano	
Hindemith, Paul	Drei Stucke—Clarinet, Trumpet, Violin, Bass, Piano	Schott
Hindemith, Paul	Concert Music No. I, Op. 36—Piccolo, Flute, Oboe, Clarinet, Bass Clarinet, Bassoon, Horn, Trumpet, Trombone, Violin, Viola, Cello, Bass	Associated
Hindemith, Paul	Septet—Flute, Oboe, Clarinet, Trumpet, Horn, Bassoon, Bass Clarinet	Associated
Holzmann, R.	Suite for Trumpet, Saxophone, Bass Clarinet, Piano	
Hummel, Johann	Military Septet, Op. 114—Trumpet, Flute, Clarinet, Violin, Cello, Bass, Piano	
Ibert, Jacques	Capriccio—Flute, Oboe, Clarinet, Bassoon, Trumpet, String Quartet, Harp	Leduc
D'Indy, Vincent	Suite in D Major, Op. 24—Trumpet, 2 Flutes, Strings	Hamelle
Krejci, Isa	Divertimento—Trumpet, Flute, Clarinet, Bassoon	
Kubik, Gail	Puck, a Christmas Score— Speaker, String Quartet, Woodwind Quartet, Trumpet	Mss.
Martinu, Bohuslav	Cuisine Parade—Clarinet, Bassoon, Trumpet, Violin, Cello, Piano	
Mirouze	Septet—Flute, Oboe, Clarinet, Trumpet, Horn, Bassoon, Piano	
Monteux, Pierre	Arietta & March—Flute, Oboe, Clarinet, Bassoon, Trumpet, Percussion	Salabert
Paz, J. C.	Second Concerto—Oboe, Trumpet, 2 Horns, Bassoon, Piano	Mss.
Persichetti, Vincent	The Hollow Men—Trumpet and String Orchestra	Elkan-Vogel
Pierne, Gabriel	Pastorale variee dans le style ancien, Op. 30— Flute, Oboe, Clarinet, Trumpet, Horn, 2 Bassoons	Durand
Popow, Gabriel	Septour, Op. 22—Flute, Clarinet, Bassoon, Trumpet, Violin, Cello, Bass	Universal
Porter, Quincy	Incidental Music for Anthony & Cleopatra— Flute, 2 Trumpets, Percussion, Strings, Piano	Mss.
Resphigi, Ottorino	Concerto for Five—Trumpet, Oboe, Violin, Bass, Piano, Strings	Ricordi
Rieti, Vittorio	Madrigal in Four Parts—Flute, Oboe, Clarinet, Bassoon, Horn, Trumpet, String Quintet, Piano	
Roland-Manuel	Suite dans le gout espagnol— Oboe, Bassoon, Trumpet, Piano	Durand
Saint-Saens, Camille	Septour, Op. 65—Trumpet, String Quintet, Piano	Durand
Salviucci, Giovanni	Serenade—Flute, Oboe, Clarinet, Bassoon, Trumpet, Piano, String Quartet	Ricordi
Scarlatti, Hasselmans	Pastorale & Capriccio—2 Flutes, 2 Oboes, 2 Clarinets, 2 Bassoons, Trumpet, & 2 Horns	Schott
Shostakovitch, Dmitri	Concerto Op. 35—Piano, Trumpet, Strings	Broude
Slonimsky, Nicolas	Orestes—Trumpet, Strings, Percussion	Mss.
Stravinsky, Igor	Histoire du Soldat—Clarinet, Bassoon, Cornet, Trombone, Violin, String Bass, Percussion	Chester
Varese, Edgar	Octandre—Flute, Clarinet, Oboe, Bassoon, Trumpet, Horn, Trombone, Bass	Curwen
Wailly, Paul de	Oktett—Flute, Oboe, 2 Clarinets, 2 Bassoons, Trumpet, Horn	Rouart
Wolpe, Stefan	Concerto—Flute, Clarinet, Oboe, Bassoon, Trumpet, Horn, Trombone, Violin, Cello, Piano	Mss.
Wood, Joseph	Incidental Music to Land of Fame Clarinet, Trumpet, Horn, Hammond Organ	Mss.

1951

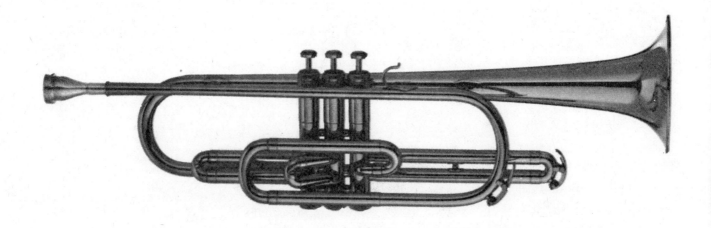

E♭ Alto Trumpet

IMPROVING SLIDE TECHNIQUE

ERNEST LYON

THE BRASS instruments that are in use today are products of comparatively recent development, with the exception of the trombone. The teaching of these instruments is still far from reaching a somewhat settled state similar to that attained by violin and piano teachers.

By "settled" I do not mean stagnant, for much progress can be attained even on these older (pedagogically speaking) instruments; but, rather, I used the term to indicate the presence of well-established schools of playing with consistent methods for their development. In the brass instruments we have had no such schools, though within the past few decades the teaching of the brasses has become so universal that the methods should soon be established.[1]

I make the foregoing remarks before taking up a discussion of the technique of the slide because this seems to be one of those obvious things about which there should be no disagreement. Yet in this discussion I want to outline and recommend a procedure that is rarely used in this country and which is considerably at variance with the accepted practices.

There are two standard grips with many variations. The one most commonly in use in this country is with the thumb on the near side of the cross bar touching the lower slide and opposite it the first two fingers (index and middle). This calls for a loose wrist to take part in moving the slide along with the action from the elbow. The theory behind this is, the two actions (wrist and elbow) complement each other to get greater speed and that the wrist action makes

---

[1] To be sure, there have been numerous teachers with great insight into how to train pupils—such as Emory Remington (trombone), Max Schlossberg (trumpet), and Wendell Hoss (horn)—but the individual development of pupils by these men has not yet developed schools of teaching.

---

for greater flexibility. My objection to this theory is very simple: it isn't so! The use of the wrist slows down the action from the elbow and the "flexibility" causes bouncing when fast action is needed.

The grip which I prefer is not as revolutionary as my preceding words may have led you to believe, nor is it so uncommon in many quarters. Two prominent method books have illustrations and one of them a good explanation: (1) *Methode Complete de Trombone a Coulisse* by LaFosse (page XV, 1928 edition); (2) *Clarke's Method for Trombone* by Ernest Clarke (p. 3, 1913 edition). The description is simple: place the thumb as in the foregoing paragraph, lay the index finger on the opposite side of the cross bar and touching the lower slide, laying the next two fingers on the slide and the little finger underneath the slide.

You will notice the difference in the wrist position. The wrist can no longer move very far and the arm is now in normal position with the palm of the hand turned down. The movement of the slide is, to quote LaFosse, "by means of the forearm alone, and not by flexure of the wrist." The wrist remains somewhat stiff in order to increase the speed and sureness of the movement from the elbow.

If you have been following by practice, holding a trombone slide as I have recommended, you probably feel that the position is very awkward. I recall the first time that I noticed the LaFosse illustration. It was pointed out to me by a pupil. I discredited the value of the position to him, but decided afterwards that LaFosse was a fine enough teacher to deserve consideration of his ideas. I tried the grip for a week and have never returned to my former method. The advantages are easily outlined: (1) more speed; (2) greater sureness of position (this is particularly valuable for beginning students); (3) less jerk or bounce (practically eliminated) when moving the slide fast and stopping suddenly.

Slide Movement

1. *In legato playing.*

I feel sure that everyone will recognize the value of learning to move the slide as fast as possible just before the next tone must begin when playing legato. By this means, each tone can be sustained to the last possible moment and a legato can be obtained without glissando. This is not the place to discuss the tongue and breath action that must be coordinated with the slide movement. Let it suffice here to remind you again that the slide must never move slowly in legato regardless of how slowly the music is moving. I am continually appalled at the number of pupils who have been moving the slide too slowly in passages marked with slurs. Some of them play such passages with glissando, others make a definite break between tones; but both are equally wrong.

2. *In detached playing.*

Again fast movement of the slide is the secret of a good slide technique, but this time the movement should be as soon as possible rather than as late as possible. To illustrate: if you are playing a series of staccato tones, as soon as you stop one tone the slide should be moved to the position for the next tone and wait in that position for the tone to be played at the proper time. This will seem awkward and unnecessary at slow speeds, but only when practiced at slow speeds can this be developed for fast work; and actually many unclear attacks in slow passages are made because the slide is still in motion when attack is made.

My first realization of the necessity for this came when I was having a very good pupil play the first exercise in the Blume *Thirty-Six Exercises for Trombone.* It is an easy exercise in eighth notes at a moderate speed, but he kept getting attacks that were bad. We worked on his tonguing with no result until finally I noticed that his slide did not stop its movement until after he attacked the note. Analysis of the problem led to the development of the above-described technique. The problem disappeared. I have since found the same trouble and the same cure for nearly every pupil I have had. Maybe you haven't noticed it; if so, it is because you have heard unclear attacks on the trombone for so long that your ear has come to take that as the expected sound from a trombone.

Cleaner Attack

If this move-as-soon-and-as-fast-as-you-can technique will be consistently developed at slow speeds (without increasing the speed of the beat) the "muddy" sound that most trombone sections get when playing fast will gradually disappear, for even when playing very fast passages the slide can stop for that very short length of time required to tongue the note. Watch even fine trombone players keep their slide in constant motion when playing fast passages and then notice how much clearer the attack is when done properly on a valve instrument (or by a trombonist using this technique!).

Have you ever read one of those fine discussions of the slide positions that gives you the exact distance from first position to each of the others? I say "fine" advisedly with my tongue in my cheek, for it is strange how wrong both from a scientific and from a practical viewpoint they generally are.

The first important point to realize is that the distance from one position to the next position increases as you get farther away from first position. When the trombone is in first position, it is a "Bb" instrument and will require a certain distance to lower the tone a half step (why I do not give the exact distance will appear later). When the trombone is in second position, it is now an "A" instrument, one of lower pitch, and more tubing will be required to lower the pitch a half step.

Putting these two facts together and adding them up down the slide and you can see that from 6th to 7th position is considerably farther than from 1st to 2nd. A simple way to see this fact is to compare the length of the third valve tubing and the second valve tubing on a valve instrument (particularly a tuba) and note that the former is much more than three times the length of the latter.

The second important point about the positions is one that drives both players and conductors insane at times — because of the imperfections of the building of instruments and because of the shifting of pitches from one key to another, the slide positions are not always the same. Let me illustrate with a few examples from the very fine horn that I own.

To play the overtone series in Bb in tune I have to sharpen first position noticeably on the tones in Figure I, and flatten on the high Bb even more noticeably. (You ask how do I sharpen first position?—I normally play the position down somewhat from a closed position). Third position is even more erratic—to play

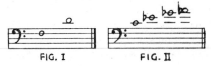

the chord in Figure II in tune I have to use four distinct distances from closed position (in case you are curious, the order of these positions from the sharpest to the flattest is Gb-Ab-C-Eb). This trouble occurs melodically, unaccompanied. The trouble mounts as you begin to favor tones in chords when playing with others.

Have you decided by this time to give up an instrument that is so difficult to play in tune? If so, then don't play any other instrument, for they have the exact same troubles, and not much can be done about it. Take your valve brass or your woodwind to a stroboscope if you doubt my word and then see how much you distort the tone trying to play in tune. Your ear has just been accustomed to hearing the out-of-tuneness so much that it sounds correct to you. That is exactly what happens to most trombone players, too, even among the top flight players.

While discussing the positions I would like to mention something that should be too elementary to need mentioning, but I find that very few high school or college players seem to understand the use of the 7th partials (6th overtones). The two most commonly used tones of this series are the high G and F# (Fig. III).

They are played in "sharp second position" and "sharp third position"

respectively. The tones are flat in the regular positions because the 6th overtone in every overtone series is acoustically flat. Horns can be built to throw these tones nearer to pitch, but in doing so other tones are thrown farther away from correct pitch. The distance sharp of the regular positions consequently varies from an inch or more down to less than a half inch. When played in tune this way, these are the primary positions for these notes. The others in the 6th overtone series are usable in a similar manner (except 1st, which may be usable if your slide has a spring in it), but they are secondary positions. The tones for these sharp 4th, 5th, 6th, and 7th positions are shown in Fig. IV.

Secondary Positions

Though they are not needed for most legitimate trombone playing, the successful trombone player needs to know the secondary positions for his instrument. They are useful in practicing lip slurs, for *legatissimo* passages, and for fast band-style solos. In concluding this short discussion of slide technique I would like to give a chart (Fig. V) that I use with my pupils in teaching the positions from the fundamentals (pedal tones) through the 7th overtones. The symbols used are these: (1) o indicates primary position; (2) ● indicates secondary position (the one with the arrow is probably the most used secondary position); (3) parenthesis indicates flat, do not use; (4) double parenthesis indicates flat, use sharp position.

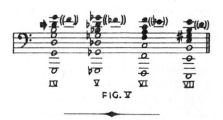

FIG. V

The finest brass instrument made will sound poor if it or the mouthpiece is not cleaned out periodically. Just a little dirt in the first few inches of tubing (including the mouthpiece) is amazingly damaging to tone and ease of blowing. ■

Which Horn Do You Prefer— *F*—or—*Bb*?

A Symposium

Editor's Note:

In any consideration of the French horn controversy, the following facts should be remembered. First. a superior wind instrument can be built in any key with equally superior intonation, ease of blowing, etc. Let us not assume erroneously that certain keys have a priority in acoustics.

Second, two like wind instruments built in different keys, keeping the physical conditions exactly comparable, will produce different tone qualities. The tone quality of one may be *preferred* to that of the other, but neither is superior or inferior. A manufacturer may have learned to build a better horn in one key than in another, but this does not mean that an equally superior horn in another key is impossible. Furthermore, two horns can be built so that they are either similar or dissimilar in tone quality, as desired.

There are three kinds of horn experts: (1) the professional hornist, the playing artist and expert, who may not be conversant with school problems; (2) the school director, who has played, taught, and listened to both horns; and (3) the "armchair expert" whose conclusions are sincere but based on hearsay and hastily drawn inferences.

A double horn player is not necessarily an expert on the single F and Bb horns. The crucial tubing of any horn is the first several inches from the mouthpiece and from the bell. Both the F and Bb sides play through identical sections; while on the single horns these crucial tubings differ.— T.R.

—FARKAS—

In the early days, before we had the luxury of valves, the composer merely indicated a horn in the same key as the composition, in order to utilize the open notes. This transposition the player accomplished by using different length crooks. (This is the reason the classics contain so many difficult horn transpositions.)

Despite the composer's need to put the horn in the same key as the composition, he could not help but be aware that some of these keys gave the horn more beauty of tone and flexibility than others. The deeper keys, such as the horn in C or Bb basso, made the tone quite thick and muddy, resulting in poor flexibility.

The high keys (horn in A or Bb alto) had a piercing, shrill quality, and the notes could not always be produced softly. Little by little, however, one of these keys began to become more popular than the others, as it was so obviously "just right." This was the horn in F.

True, we find horn parts in the band written for horn in Eb, but this is done merely for convenience as the parts are often played by the Eb alto or Eb mellophone. The modern horn player takes this transportation in his stride and certainly would not bother to use his Eb crook, if, indeed he owned one.

As the French horn becomes more and more popular in the band, we find an increasing amount of literature calling for horn in F, and one can hope for the day when the band horn parts are uniformly written for the horn in F.

Points for the Bb Horn

Considered strictly from the composer's viewpoint, it should be obvious which of the two horns, F or Bb, is the favorite. The preference goes to the F horn because of its tone. However, we are concerned not only with the composer, who, after all, does not have to play his own horn parts, but with the horn player, who does.

Unfortunately, the composer sometimes underestimates the difficulties he gives this beautiful F horn, and it is at this point that we discover it is not so easy to choose a horn key as the composer might think.

In spite of its beauty of tone, the F horn has treacherous upper notes that are much too "close together" for completely accurate playing. This difficulty results from writing in the upper register of an essentially low-pitched instrument, the harmonics coming closer and closer together as the height increases.

It didn't take horn players long to realize that if they played these higher notes on a higher keyed horn, the harmonics would then not be quite so close together. The high Bb horn did this beautifully, and the tone was as good as the F horn—perhaps better— but *only* in this high register. The lower notes did not have the veiled beauty of the F horn.

The two horns, when combined into one, however, would produce just about everything of which the horn player dreamed. Thus the double horn came into existence, and it remains the most popular model today.

Nevertheless, it was inevitable that someone should finally come along and say, "The Bb part of the horn plays so much easier than the F that I'm going to use it exclusively. I will dispense with the F part of the horn in the interests of lightness and compactness." This reasoning brought into existence the single Bb horn. It is popular with many high players, particularly those who do very strenuous work, such as opera.

The conscientious Bb player, by skillful use of the right hand, the correct mouthpiece and careful practice, can produce a beautiful, characteristic horn tone.

To sum up: the *composer* chooses the F horn for its tonal beauty and characteristic horn qualities, while the *player* who chooses the Bb horn does so because of its surer production of notes and general ease of playing.

F for the Beginner

In an organization which plays comparatively easy compositions, in which the horns rarely ascend above the written E in the top space of the staff, I believe all the horn players should use F horns. The lower horns (usually second and fourth) are in good F horn register most of the time; it is this middle-low register in which the Bb horn becomes more blatant and objectionable. Therefore I advocate that the two *low* horns *always* use the F horn.

The F horn, having an inherently "correct" horn tone, plus requiring the student to develop a really good embouchure in order to negotiate the many lip changes which produce the notes unaided by valves, invariably gives a more solid foundation to the student who intends to continue into professional playing. Because of this ability of the F horn to instill the proper tone and general approach to horn playing, I prefer to see all beginners study the F horn.

The Place for Bb

The advanced band and orchestra, which plays really difficult music, presents a different problem. During my own high school days, music in schools was on a relatively elementary plane. Today we have hundreds of fine school music organizations which play *well* the more advanced symphonic repertory. In this caliber organization the first and third horn players would definitely find themselves handicapped with single F horns.

Despite the F horn's advantages up to the written E at the top of the staff, at that point it becomes a cranky, unsure instrument. Advanced students who play high horn parts should be given the advantage of Bb horns. They will miss fewer notes, have a fuller tone in the high register, and gain in endurance and confidence.

In Conclusion

The elementary organization should use F horns exclusively. Beginners should *always* start with F horns if they intend to have a firm foundation for their advancement, and for the future of our symphony orchestras.

The moderately advanced group can use all F horns, although one or two more advanced players might get better results on the high parts with Bb horns. The very advanced band and orchestra should have at least one Bb horn for the first chair, preferably one for the other high player, also. The tone of the horn section will be better, I believe, if the low horns are F horns, no matter how difficult the music.

—MEEK—

TONE is all-important in horn playing. Our attitude toward horn tone in this country has been chiefly conditioned by the German school of playing, which in general thinks of horn tone as full, golden, and rich. From the time of Mozart there has been a trend toward the establishment of a single instrument which would best suit this conception of tone. That choice has gradually narrowed down to the single F horn, in which the golden sound is retained, and still the unusual playing range of three and a half octaves is manageable with three valves.

Present orchestral requirements of the horn player practically *prohibit* the use of a single F horn for professional use. From the teaching standpoint, however, the F horn gives the student the best foundation which can be had. It gives the proper conception of real horn tone; and the necessary series of "open" tones (harmonics), which coupled with the set of three valves, gives the complete chromatic range of the entire instrument. This range of three and a half octaves is not to be found on the single Bb horn.

Because of more harmonics being available on the F horn, playing it

is like carrying a basket of eggs without slipping and breaking one. The embouchure has a most important part in playing "sure" on the F horn. The lips must be sensitive to a very great degree in order that we avoid the unpleasantness of "splitting" a note. But within the written range of most school music this difficulty can be overcome.

The single Bb horn has a great many champions who sponsor its cause, even for beginning students. The fact that it is in a key a fourth higher than the F horn accounts for a shorter length of tubing which speaks easier and surer. But composers go right on writing for the F horn regardless of what instrument the player uses, and much of the music written for the lower register of the F horn is completely unplayable on the Bb horn with three valves.

In the latter there just aren't enough valves to open and increase the length of tubing required to produce any note below low B (great E to the ear). Even the notes requiring the fingers of valves 1-3 or 1-2-3 (in the lower register: low C and G, and low B and F♯) are always out of tune because they are too sharp. In order to overcome these difficulties on the Bb horn, the professional player uses a four-valve horn, or in some cases the five-valve Bb horn (the fifth valve giving him the "open" notes of the F horn).

The advanced player who finds himself playing first or third horn (the two "high" voices of the horn quartet) may wish to use a Bb horn for reasons of sureness. But he must be careful always to have in his own mind the tone quality of the F horn, else he is apt to produce a tone which is somewhat hard and blatant.

For a second or fourth horn player to use a single Bb instrument is to my mind taking onto himself much unnecessary trouble. For reasons of complicated fingerings and bad intonation found in the lower register, such a specialist is usually better off on the F horn.

A high horn player can make the Bb horn sound just as beautiful as the F horn, and will play surer on it. But he must be careful, because except for this one advantage of the Bb horn, the F horn has more to offer than any other instrument yet developed.

—HOSS—

THE FRENCH horn has in modern times become so thoroughly established as an F instrument that composers and arrangers often feel it unnecessary even to specify "Horn in F" in their writing. In tone quality too the F horn has been accepted as the standard. There can be no question that the F is fuller and richer in sound than the B♭. In fact, one of the chief tasks of those using the B♭ horn is to try to simulate F quality, through proper choice of mouthpiece and manner of blowing.

While tone may be the prime consideration, there are other factors to be evaluated, among which perhaps the foremost is accuracy. As compared to other brass instruments, the "middle" register is really the upper octave in relation to its fundamental. The performer, therefore, is plagued with an overabundance of "open" tones, so close together that, without a well-trained ear, he will often strike an altogether wrong tone, and may even continue playing off the pitch for several notes before discovering his mistake.

From C below the treble staff (as written for F horn) to the G above—a range of an octave and a fifth—there are nine "open" tones! Not all of these are good and usable; nevertheless they are constantly lurking just around the corner from the notes wanted, apparently lying in wait to trip the unwary performer.

The B♭ horn, on the other hand, pitched a fourth above, does not reach quite so high into the harmonic series in its working range, and has fewer open tones within any given interval. From the C to G quoted above, the B♭ horn will have only seven open tones (see chart elsewhere in this series), and will be correspondingly less treacherous in the opportunities offered for hitting the wrong notes.

In school work, therefore, the advantage would seem to lie with the B♭ horn; it is more accurate, easier and lighter to handle. Although a single F horn is in no way a heavy instrument, except for very small children, the shorter tubing (three-fourths the length of the F) makes the B♭ more easily managed and less subject to damage through careless handling.

Both types of horns have some characteristic "bad tones," for which the commonly accepted solution in professional circles is the double horn. It is naturally a more complex and heavier instrument, and considerably more expensive.

B♭ horns are made with only three conventional valves, but an additional valve is required for anything more than elementary performance. This fourth valve, usually operated with the thumb, adds tubing somewhat more than one-half step in length, and compensates for some of the more objectionable sharp fingerings, as well as making it possible to mute the horn in tune, where either the hand or the conical brass mute are used.

The change of pitch on an F horn with these methods of muting amounts to approximately one-half step, and can be taken care of by transposing. The amount of "sharping" on the B♭ horn is too great to be met in this manner however, and calls for the use of the extra valve. There is an advantage in the use of this mute valve, since no further transposition is necessary, and the notes are fingered as on the open horn.

To make the B♭ horn a really complete instrument, and a fair rival to the double horn, a fifth valve is sometimes added, which lowers the pitch a perfect fourth, making possible the entire chromatic scale from top to bottom of the instrument, with the use of substitute fingerings.

Anyone adopting the B♭ horn should learn the notes as written for the F horn, unless he is progressive enough to be willing to learn them in "concert" pitch; a procedure which can also be recommended to those playing any kind of horn. It will prove simpler to learn to transpose fingerings than to try to transpose the notes, a process which will create added confusion if the player later graduates to a double horn.

—MUELBE—

"WHY don't you play a *double-horn?*"

This question has been asked me many times during my 46 years of horn playing, especially since I came to the United States 27 years ago.

It is impossible to answer this question without arousing a heated debate, but that will not keep me from stating my objections to the use of that monster, the double horn.

The French horn is a singing instrument. It is known and appreciated for its nostalgic, melancholy, and poetic tone color. This peculiar quality is especially produced by the horn pitched in F, and is one of the reasons why the F horn became the standard horn, even after the valves had been added to it.

Everyone who is acquainted with the technical nature of the horn and the history of its development, knows this. And everyone who knows this must admit that the B♭ horn, which is the weaker half of the double horn, has a tone which is anything *but* melancholy, poetic, or nostalgic. To me, the B♭ horn sounds hollow, harsh, and offending.

The width or the bore of the tubing of the double horn is a compromise. It is neither F nor B♭, but something in between. This causes poor intonation.

Most players of double horns make the mistake of using the B♭ part of their instrument only for the higher register. Since even a first horn part doesn't always move around in the higher region, the B♭ tubing, when being used, is cold. This causes the player to pinch, in order to be in tune, which is extremely bad for the embouchure. It's lip-killing.

Many players seem to believe that the higher notes are easier to get on the B♭ horn. This is not true. Horn players are classified either as high or low horn players. A player with a naturally high embouchure will get the high notes as easily (if not more easily) on a good F horn as on a B♭ horn. The B♭ horn will not make a first horn player out of anyone who doesn't have the natural equipment.

I have never had any trouble keeping in step with my colleagues of the double horn faculty as far as the high register is concerned. And when it comes to fast passages—well! I have heard quite a few players stumble over some of them, when trying to play them with the B♭ horn. The scale in the beginning of the La Gazza Ladra Overture (to mention only one example) is comparatively easy on the F horn, but not on the B♭.

The left thumb valve is the muting valve. It is used to compensate for the approximately three-fourth step sharping caused by the right hand when muting. The muting valve may be pulled out a whole step for reading E♭ parts as if reading F parts. If one does not wish to mute by hand, but use a nontransposing mute, the 3-valve horn without the muting valve is practical.

I have heard some say, "Well, since I have a double horn, I can always play such passages on the F horn." My answer is that you can't. You are so used to playing things like that on the B♭ horn that you are scared to death to try them on the F horn. I know! I have been in the business too long not to know.

The only advantage the double horn offers is this: in case of a poor note on one horn, one can use the other part of the instrument. For example, A♭ and A♮ above the staff (D♭ and D♮ concert) are difficult to get on most F horns, but very easy to produce on the B♭.

But there is another way to solve this problem! Use false fingering. I have played those high notes on my single Schmidt with reversed fingering for the last 25 years and I think nothing of it.

My opinions are based on experience and trial. I am probably the last remaining professional single horn player. I played a double horn for two years about a decade ago, but went back to the single F horn, because I can do a better job on it, and because, most of all, it sounds to me more like a waldhorn—which is what a horn should really sound like.

—MOORE—

I HAVE USED single B♭ horns in the high school band for about 20 years; single B♭'s along with circular E♭ altos in the junior high; and double horns, single B♭s and F horns in the college band. I have had numerous opportunities to compare the effects produced by these horns with those of the horn sections of many other organizations.

From all of this I am more and more convinced that the single B♭ horn is vastly superior to any other horn as a harmony instrument for bands. I am speaking of *bands;* this entire discussion will bear upon improving the harmony section of the school band.

It seems to me that the first thing we must recognize is the fact that horns are used differently in the band than in the orchestra. Their use in the band is mainly as a bridge from the cornets to the trombones. They also act, more or less, as fillers to amalgamate the reeds and brasses, as well as lend color by solo work.

The usual range of the horns in band music of high school level is mainly between C below the staff and G above, as written in E♭ horn parts. I prefer the B♭ horns, because within that range, the lower and middle voices are clearly heard.

For example, when four horns play the four notes of the C-major chord, I want to hear the E because it gives color, and the G for resonance. The upper C will be easily heard because it is highest. This tone and the low C, since they are the fundamentals,

will be reinforced by the overtones, which are retained in our ear. The only horns that produce these chordal tones clearly, and with proper balance of volume, are the B♭s.

Another factor which, in my opinion, has much bearing on the tonal effects produced in a band using single B♭ horns, is that of the overtones of the brasses. These are uniform in series when BB♭ tubas, B♭ baritones and trombones, B♭ horns, and B♭ cornets are used. The band is brighter and more beautiful in tone color with this combination of brasses.

I have heard directors say that they do not like the tone of the B♭ horn. This statement has always been, in my opinion, rather poorly considered, to say the least. Every symphony player in America today, of whom I have heard, is using either a double horn (B♭-F) or a single B♭ with extra valve. I question whether anyone, including professional hornists, can tell when the symphony hornist changes from the F to the B♭ side or vice versa. I have seen it tested by critics with the players behind screens. The production of the true horn tone is absolutely up to the player.

(EDITOR'S NOTE: See results of other tests at conclusion of this symposium.)

I find that the ease with which the B♭ hornist handles the upper register has added years to my life. I *never* worry for fear they will "fluff" the higher notes.

For years I taught horn by the traditional method, with the F fingerings and the single F horn. The student had to learn to transpose from the E♭ parts (since no F parts were published in those days), and by the time he was a senior was doing fairly well. But what a headache! One could never rely on the notes being played accurately, especially the upper tones. The lower voices always sounded "fluffy."

I then began teaching horns for band by using a transposed fingering chart, with the F horn. Finally, I heard of men in New York and elsewhere who were using the single B♭, so I decided to discard single F's and try the single B♭s in the band.

After twenty years of this I am absolutely convinced that they are the *only logical horn for school bands.*

The veiled quality of the tone of the F horn is beautiful for solos with piano. It is also beautiful in the orchestra. However, in a band, it is rare that this type of tone is adaptable. For the most part, the horn tone in the band must speak with authority, clarity, and precision. Here the single Bb horn excels, due to its shorter length of tubing.

There are a number of reasons why I do not get double horns for students. Expense, weight, and the fact that they get out of order more quickly are some, but the main reason is that *the Bb side of a double horn is not as good as the single Bb horn.* The proportion of the bell is wrong. In the double horn the F bell is used, which is bound to cause false tones.

A little stunt that I fell into may be of use to the growing fraternity of Bb horn users. Look at the scale of C from an Eb horn part to be played on a Bb horn, and think of this as the Eb scale for a BBb tuba. Use exactly the same fingerings, and you have the Bb horn fingerings.

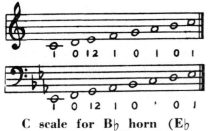

C scale for Bb horn (Eb horn part), and Eb scale for BBb tuba.

I am sure that, some day, a manufacturer will go after the Bb single horn business and do some educating on it. Smart businesses *educate* people to *want* their products. I am sure that a moderately priced single Bb horn for our young players would go over "big." It would certainly produce much better-sounding school bands!

—SCHMIDT—

THE treacherous nature of the upper range of the F horn has caused it to all but disappear from professional playing. In its place has come the double horn, a combination of the F horn with a shorter horn pitched in Bb. By virtue of its higher basic pitch, the Bb horn uses a lower set of partials for higher notes. The modern double horn in F and Bb has by far the greatest popularity among horn players everywhere.

Double horns and the 5-valve Bb horn are expensive, which makes a full section of these horns impractical in the school situation. Thus, the practical director must choose between the single F and the singe Bb for his school.

Traditionally the single F has been popular, but the Bb has been shown to be more than worthy of consideration for school purposes. To illustrate: the F and Bb horns are played alike. The same mouthpiece can be used, with a possible recommendation that the Bb use a deeper cup. The horns look alike, the only difference being a length of tubing. There is no difference in hand or lip position, or playing characteristics of any kind, unless it be the advantage of the lack of strain on both director and player where the Bb horn is used.

By all the laws of acoustics, the Bb side of a double horn is inferior to the single Bb horn. The tubing, bore, and bell of the Bb is incompatible with that of the F. Putting the two together is a compromise at best, despite the efforts of manufacturers.

For the serious student it is just as easy to shift from the single Bb horn to the double horn as it is from the single F horn to the double horn. Actually it is desirable to have experience on the usually neglected Bb side of the double horn.

The relation of the F to the Bb horn in terms of pitch and overtone series can be seen from the following:

(written in F, sounding a 6th lower):

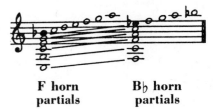

F horn partials   Bb horn partials

For all practical school purposes the ranges of the F and Bb are the same. The great bulk of horn music for school ensembles falls between the G or A below the staff and G or A above the staff. As this range does not go high enough to use the upper partials of the Bb horn, most school playing on the Bb is done in the middle register. When the upper part of the staff is used with the single F horn, the horn is playing in the difficult upper partials where the tones are close together.

In most school work the horns are muddy and out of tune; it takes an expert to control intonation and attack. The Bb horn offers solution to these major difficulties in that it retains the features characteristic of the true horn, while clearing up tonal blend and attack.

Tonguing on the Bb is easier, crisper, clearer, and can be developed to a finer degree in less time. The Bb presents much less of a problem in the early stages of teaching than the F. It is not necessary to have a pre-instrument for French horn if Bbs are used from the beginning. There is less student (and teacher) frustration. Students prefer Bbs!

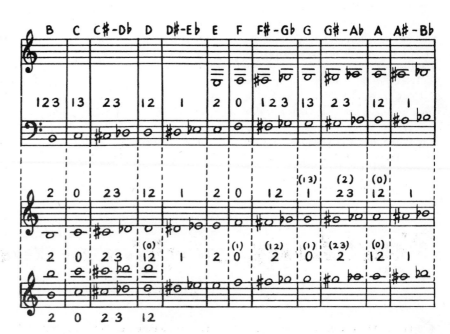

B	C	C#-Db	D	D#-Eb	E	F	F#-Gb	G	G#-Ab	A	A#-Bb
123	13	23	12	1	2	0	123	13	23	12	1
2	0	23	12	1	2	0	12	1 (13)	23 (2)	12 (0)	1
2	0	23	12	1	2	0 (0)	2 (1)	1 (12)	2 (1)	12 (23)	1 (0)
2	0	23	12								

Fingering chart for F horn parts on single Bb 3-valve horn

The Bb horn is more sure; each pitch is less variable. This is a drawback from the professional point of view, as the flexibility of the F horn makes possible more perfect intonation. This quality, however, makes it just as easy to play the F horn out of tune, a feature undesirable for school work.

The tone of both horns can match closely. With student "bell" tones especially, the qualities are very similar. Indeed the more clear Bb tone is preferable for band work, and for all work at the high school level. Though the single Bb horn cannot be stopped with the hand, it can be muted satisfactorily. A transposing mute, allowing the student to read parts as written, should be used.

The growing interest in the Bb horn, based on long experience and experiment, makes it necessary for alert educators to investigate its possibilities for their own situations. Eventually, the controversy may not be the F versus the Bb, but whether the Bb is superior to the double horn, for school use. Try it and see!

—POTTAG—

As a professional French hornist and teacher, I prefer the single F to the single Bb horn.

Only the F horn has the characteristic and beautiful tone quality. While the upper register of the Bb speaks a little easier and surer, this advantage is offset (for the professional) by the hard-sounding middle register, and the poor intonation of the lower-middle register. Properly taught, the F horn is as easy to play as the horn in Bb.

In the case of public school music, where tone quality is not as paramount as in professional playing, evaluation of the two horns may be made from a different standpoint.

Should the first chair player have difficulty with the high tones, let him use the single Bb horn. It is better to have the notes played than missed, regardless of tone quality.

This concession to the Bb horn pertains only to the first chair player. The rest should use the F horn.

An experiment was set up to determine whether the difference in quality between an F and a Bb horn is actually discernible. Here are the results.

In this experiment to determine the *noticeable* difference in quality between the F and Bb horns, four above-average university hornists played. Three double horns, one single F horn, and three single Bb horns were used. Each player, with one exception, performed the same selection various times, using the same mouthpiece on different horns.

Thirty-two seniors, all instrumental majors, judged the performances. Both players and judges were in the same room, but they could not see each other; judgments were made by sound alone.

Results of the judging are given in the accompanying chart. In the column under *Horn Used*, "Dbl." means both sides of the double horn, "F of Dbl." only the F side, and "Bb of Dbl." the Bb side only.

Conclusions

1. The judges were not able to identify which horn was used. This indicates that the players were able to make the Bb horn sound like the F.

2. Players A and D were consistently identified as the preferred players, regardless of the horn used. The less desired players were so identified consistently, also regardless of the horn used.

3. The "jury" was definitely prejudiced in favor of the double horn. Notice how consistently "good" ratings were coupled with "Dbl." ratings.

4. The highest seven ratings were given to 2 single Bb horns, 2 F of the "Dbl.," 2 Bb of the "Dbl.," and 1 "Dbl." The five lowest ratings were given as follows: 1 single F, 1 F of "Dbl.," 1 Bb of "Dbl.," and 1 "Dbl."

Although the experiment was carried out as fairly as possible, it does not show to what extent musicians could be *trained* to tell the difference between horns.

What difference there is between horns can be interpreted as of vital importance to the professional hornists, while relatively unimportant from the viewpoint of the amateur. The differences in *abilities of players*, especially in amateur ranks, remain much more significant than the difference in horns.—T.R.

Player	Horn used	Identified as:			Quality		
		Dbl.	F	Bb	Good	Fair	Poor
1. A	Single Bb	20	4	8	28	6	0
2. B	Dbl.	5	11	16	12	19	3
3. C	Single F	9	10	13	11	21	1
4. D	Single Bb	13	9	9	21	12	0
5. B	Single Bb	19	7	4	15	17	0
6. C	Single F	6	11	14	12	20	1
7. D	F of Dbl.	22	6	3	28	3	0
8. A	Dbl.	14	7	11	22	12	0
9. D	Dbl.	10	14	6	19	15	0
10. B	F of Dbl.	9	10	10	5	25	3
11. D	Single Bb	8	11	12	16	17	1
12. A	F of Dbl.	13	12	7	22	11	0
13. A	Bb of Dbl.	17	19	6	26	8	0
14. D	Bb of Dbl.	9	11	9	22	11	0
15. B	Bb of Dbl.	18	3	9	11	22	0

Teaching problems and techniques

BERNARD FITZGERALD

Effective teaching requires the ability to analyze and diagnose

the deficiencies of musical performance and to prescribe the remedies

which will ultimately correct these faults. The word ultimate is important since the remedy frequently may not produce an immediate and complete correction of the error. Just as in medical practice improvement is not always noted immediately after proper medication is applied, improvement in musical performance is often delayed until faulty habits have been supplanted by correct techniques which are repeated in practice until the correct response becomes semi-automatic.

While the experienced brass instrumentalist may frequently take these factors into account, the teacher with a limited knowledge of brass techniques will need all possible guidance and assistance to adequately understand the problems involved in teaching students to play brass instruments.

By what means, then, is the teacher able to detect faults in musical performance? The answer is brief: *audio* and *visual*, that which is *heard* and *seen*. The visible indications are of course more obvious, but frequently the audio and visual factors must both be considered, since tone production on the brass instruments involves coordinations which are not always visually apparent, and the teacher must rely upon what he hears in order to determine the source of the difficulty.

This serves to reinforce the importance and necessity of developing a concept of the tone quality which is characteristic of the instrument, a "Sound ideal," together with the awareness of those tonal defects and distortions, both subtle and obvious, which are common among brass instrumentalists. The final result is the important consideration, and in the final analysis performance must be evaluated in terms of "how it sounds." Faulty techniques are not conducive to good performance, and the predominance of incorrect playing techniques will prevent that ease and freedom of execution which is characteristically present in outstanding musical performance. Therefore, the ear must be trained to detect those flaws which exist in respect to purity of tone, accuracy in pitch, style of articulation, and the coordination of breath, embouchure, articulation and fingering.

Develop Discrimination

Unless the student develops the ability to discriminate between good and poor performance, little improvement can be expected. As a result of instruction the student must acquire the ability to analyze his own problems, since during practice periods he is actually teaching himself; otherwise the efforts of the teacher will be in vain for incorrect practice will nullify good teaching.

It is not the purpose of this article to direct attention to those performance errors due to incorrect rhythms, note values, phrasing, and dynamics. These matters should be obvious to competent music teachers regardless of specific knowledge concerning the brass instruments.

Perhaps it is desirable to consider the visual aspects first since the student may often become aware of these problems by practicing before a mirror. Visible evidence of the presence of factors which interfere with performance is apparent in the following:

1. Constricted or distended throat muscles.
2. Tenseness of the arms.
3. Tensed or hunched position of the shoulders.
4. An awkward and unnatural position of the head.
5. Gripping or clutching the instrument tightly.
6. Arms held rigidly against the body.
7. Cramped hand position on the valves or trombone slide.
8. Excessive pressure of the mouthpiece against the lips.
9. Tense facial expression.
10. Holding the instrument incorrectly: pointing instrument upward or downward at an extreme angle.
11. Poor posture.
12. Embouchure: (a) Extreme stretched position of the lips, (b) air escaping at corners of the mouth, (c) incorrect lower jaw position, (d) red of the lower lip turned outward, (e) incorrect mouthpiece placement, (f) lip formation too loosely formed, (g) lip formation too pinched.

It should be noted that the first nine items listed above involve the question of *relaxation*. This is one of the most important and most neglected aspects of brass instrument performance. Relaxation in this sense is interpreted as the elimination of conflicting, antagonistic muscular actions which interfere with musical performance. While it is recognized that muscular tension is necessary for all activity, conflicting muscular actions produce a counteracting effect which are definitely detrimental to performance.

For example, action of the diaphragm muscle is essential to provide adequate breath support to produce a steady controlled tone. If a conflicting muscular tension exists in the constriction of the muscles of the throat, or the intercostal muscles of the lower chest, the action of the diaphragm and the control of the breath will be greatly impaired. Suppose that as a further complication to the above, the player is attempting to perform an extremely rapid staccato figure in the highest register of the instrument. General nervousness, conscious or not, will add to the confusion and the player is very likely to increase the pressure of the mouthpiece against the lips until the tone is completely stopped by this combination of factors. Under such circumstances the teacher might well be grateful for the resulting silence.

What detrimental effects will result from the visible indications previously mentioned? The first seven items mentioned are interrelated to the extent that it is often extremely difficult to deal with each separately. As a matter of fact, the sympathetic muscular and nervous tension is usually unnoticed by the player, and tenseness of the arms is frequently accompanied by contraction of the muscles of the shoulders, throat and neck to the extent that the steady flow of breath is interrupted. In many instances, the origin of the difficulty can be traced to inadequate breath support.

It is recognized that mastery of correct breathing and breath support is vitally important to wind instrument performance. This problem, however, is often given only the briefest possible consideration at the time the student begins instrumental instruction, and is completely ignored during subsequent instruction. The fundamental basis for correct breathing for wind instrument performance is not difficult, but the development of breath control can only be realized over an extended period of time in which this phase of performance is *studied* and *practiced*. Practice on sustained tones provides an excellent drill for developing tone control. This type of practice should include tone studies at various dynamic levels and with varying degrees of tonal shading. Scales and etudes requiring varying wind pressures must also be studied and practiced so that the player will acquire an accurate judgment regarding the quantity and expenditure of the breath during phrases of various lengths in all registers. Players frequently develop the habit of taking a full breath for every phrase regardless of its length.

The process of achieving good performance requires the balance and coordination of all the muscular actions involved. This delicate balance may easily be disturbed by seemingly minor factors whose importance must be recognized since their effect upon performance is frequently significant. For example, poor posture and playing position often contribute to faulty tone quality and intonation by interfering with the flow and supply of the breath. Good posture for wind instrument performance does not imply a rigid position of any part of the body.

Too often, good posture or "sitting up straight" is incorrectly interpreted as being an awkward and uncomfortable position in which the body is rigidly erect and the arms held tightly against the body. While the torso must be held upright in order for the diaphragm to function effectively in controlling the breath in wind instrument performance, the position of the head, arms, and hands should be as natural as possible considering the problems of supporting the instrument in correct playing position.

An extremely stretched position of the lips will tend to produce a thin, colorless and often anemic quality of tone. Sometimes the appearance of the embouchure is deceptive and the teacher is led to suspect the student is stretching the lips, when in reality the width and shape of the lips are such as to present that impression. If the corners of the mouth do not remain completely closed, the resulting passage of air results in inefficient use of the breath and a lack of tonal solidity.

Tension and Tone

The extremely protruding or receding jaw position frequently interferes with tone production and control in both the high and low registers. In addition, the exaggerated protruding jaw formation often results in muscular tensions of the jaw and throat muscles which in turn interfere with the breath supply and control. Students may frequently resort to raising

or lowering the head of the instrument in an exaggerated manner in an attempt to play in the extreme high or low register. This tends to disturb the relative position of the upper and lower lips so that the upper lip cannot vibrate freely due to excessive pressure of the mouthpiece.

When the embouchure is too loosely formed, the lips present a flabby appearance. This condition is not conducive to firm, clear, tone quality. If the lips are pinched together too tightly, the muscles of the lips become inflexible and a free response cannot be obtained.

The apparent ease and seemingly effortless performance of outstanding instrumentalists is ample evidence of the importance of bodily relaxation. The struggles of the beginner with his instrument often convey the impression of a grudge battle in which the player is frequently the loser. The beginner too frequently believes it to be necessary to resort to the "brute force" method either because he does not understand how to play correctly, or because he is attempting to perform something he is not prepared to do at that time.

It is the responsibility of the teacher to prepare the student for each new problem so that it will be a natural step in his musical and technical advancement. The student must realize that physical strain should not be present in good performance; on the contrary, good performance is free of such strain. One of the major problems of the teacher is to gauge the capacity and development of the student so that he is not expected to meet new technical problems before being adequately prepared. This is especially true in regard to developing the extreme high register of the brass instruments. In order to meet the problems of various students successfully, the teacher must invent technique drills and exercises to fit the needs of the individual student, supplementing the assigned etudes, studies and scales.

The teacher soon discovers that it is constantly necessary to remind the student of the fundamentals of brass instrument performance; breathing, embouchure, articulation, fingering and coordination, and to re-emphasize the fact that performance defects result whenever any one of these elements does not function efficiently. Frequently the source of

difficulty may be due to several of these factors, in which case it will be necessary for the teacher to check each of the fundamentals separately before attempting to attack the problem of coordinating the elements of basic technique.

Under circumstances which combine average ability, talent, competent instruction and intelligent practice, the student should make satisfactory progress. Due to the inexperience of the beginner, undesirable tensions are frequently present and hinder performance. Under the guidance of a skillful teacher, and with careful practice on the part of the student, these tensions should disappear as skill is acquired. The student forms playing habits very quickly, and it is essential that these habits be the correct ones so that the laborious and tedious process of relearning may be avoided.

IN CONTINUING the analysis of teaching problems and techniques it should be noted that the visual evidence of factors interfering with performance is usually closely related to performance deficiencies which are obvious to the musically trained ear of the discriminating teacher. This emphasizes the importance of both the audio and the visual aspects of analyzing teaching problems and the necessity for the teacher to acquire a thorough knowledge and understanding of the desired tone quality for each brass instrument.

Ideally, a satisfactory demonstration by the teacher is the most effective means of indicating tone quality, style, phrasing, and other elements of musical performance. The student is more receptive to the imitative approach since many of the subtle nuances of musical performance are difficult to describe verbally.

In the event that the teacher is not prepared to demonstrate through performance, it is essential that he possess a thorough knowledge of the instrument and an adequate vocabulary to teach effectively, employing terminology which is understandable to the student. It is assumed that the teacher has the ability not only to analyze the reasons for faulty performance but also to impress upon the student the necessity for self-analysis.

The musical progress and development of the individual will be in direct ratio to the extent of his ability to analyze and solve his problems during daily practice. The observant student should cultivate this ability through conscientious effort and perseverance. The sincere teacher will guide the student, teaching him to analyze his performance and concentrate his efforts toward more efficient practice and consistent musical progress. Students who do not succeed in acquiring this ability are unlikely to reach musical maturity and their performance is, therefore, usually somewhat mechanical and uninspiring.

It is entirely possible for a nonperformer to teach brass instruments successfully, and it is not uncommon to find outstanding performers on brass instruments who are most successful in teaching woodwind instruments. This situation may seem rather contradictory, but it has a sound basis since outstanding performers are usually endowed with considerable native ability and adaptability for the instrument. As a result, they often attain proficiency with very little effort and consequently have not found it necessary to analyze their performance. However, the majority of students will be of average talent and ability and will need guidance in analyzing their playing problems.

The first objective is to establish an ideal with regard to tone quality. It follows that the logical source of this ideal should be the symphony orchestra, where tonal beauty is prerequisite to artistic performance. This ideal should be derived from examples in which the brass instruments perform lyric melodic passages rather than those wherein the brasses function as percussion instruments adding emphasis to the rhythmic pattern.

Numerous illustrations are to be found which represent each of the brass instruments used in the orchestra. Excellent recordings by orchestras, bands, ensembles, and soloists will provide guidance for both teacher and student. A certain amount of caution must be exercised in the selection of recordings, since commercial recordings are not a guarantee of good musical taste and discrimination.

From the audio standpoint, the following faults which are common to brass instrument performance are readily evident: Tonal Distortion, Pitch Inaccuracies, Faulty Articulation, and Lack of Coordination.

The most frequently observed Tonal Distortion is the result of playing too loudly with a resultant loss of tone and pitch control. Extremely loud playing is usually accompanied by excessive pressure of the mouthpiece against the lips and a too open position of the embouchure due to the force of the breath. Under these conditions the tone tends to spread, and the result is a loss of tonal resonance and intensity. Other tonal distortions are shrill, piercing quality in the high register and breathy quality in the low register. In the case of cornet, trumpet, trombone, French horn, and baritone, extremely shallow, small bore mouthpieces often contribute to these defects. Small bore instruments are not to be recommended; a medium bore is preferred for the average student.

Thinness of tone in the upper register also may be due to a stretched or cramped embouchure position in combination with inadequate breath support and excessive pressure of the mouthpiece. Lack of tonal focus and resonance in the low register is often caused by a too relaxed embouchure position in which the lips are turned outward and protrude into the cup of the mouthpiece.

Inability to sustain a steady tone may be due to lack of control of either breath or embouchure. A delicate balance exists in the coordination of the breath and the embouchure, and this adjustment is often disturbed by a too forceful use of the breath, which alters the embouchure position.

Intonation problems can be solved only through the development of an acute pitch sensitivity on the part of the player. These problems may be divided into three types: (1) mechanical, (2) mental, and (3) physical.

Defects in All Instruments

Mechanical difficulties arise from the fact that brass instruments are not built perfectly in tune. While more careful workmanship and better materials are factors which contribute to better intonation in instruments of high quality, it must be recognized that all the brass instruments have intonation defects, regardless of cost. For example, the trombone offers the possibility of the most perfect intonation because of the slide mechanism. However, this instrument is notably out of tune on d^1, f^1, and ab^1 when these tones are played in first position.

The teacher must be aware of the mechanical and acoustical weaknesses of each instrument in order to aid the student in solving these intonation problems. As an illustration, the tones played with the valve combinations 13 and 123 are quite sharp in pitch. The player must "humor" or "favor" the tones which are played with these valve combinations by relaxing the lip muscles or lowering the tongue position to alter the pitch downward. Some instruments require such an extreme pitch adjustment that a loss in tone quality is likely to occur as the pitch is altered.

The mechanism for extending the first or third valve slides of the cornet or trumpet is a most valuable aid to intonation; yet many students fail to take advantage of this improvement and have no idea how it should be used. Such a mechanism would be too unwieldy to be practical on the baritone, euphonium, or tuba. However, the fourth valve on these instruments serves a similar purpose, in addition to extending the downward range of the instrument. The teacher should make it a point to familiarize the student with the use of the alternate fingerings on the valve instruments and the slide positions on the trombone, stressing their value in improving intonation.

Intonation problems are also due to poor condition of the instrument. Loose fitting slides and valves, worn water key corks, or dents in the tubing (particularly in the narrow part of the bore) will have a detrimental effect upon intonation. The accumulation of food particles and saliva on the interior surfaces of the tubing is inevitable and will seriously affect both tone quality and intonation unless the instrument is cleaned frequently. The most critical points are the throat and stem of the mouthpiece, the mouthpipe, and the first several bends in the tubing.

It is extremely important that the mouthpiece shank fit into the mouthpipe properly. Some manufacturers use an unusually large bore for the mouthpipe entrance with the result that mouthpieces with average size stems are too small to fit correctly. This condition will raise the pitch of the instrument and also cause poor intonation. Frequently the mouthpiece used is not made by the manufacturer of the instrument, and since manufacturers do not use uniform dimensions for the mouthpipe and the stem of the mouthpiece, it may be necessary to grind down the mouthpiece stem, to enlarge it, or to use an extra set-piece or shank to obtain a correct fitting. Many intonation problems result from failure to correct such conditions.

Perhaps the most difficult intonation problem is that which concerns the mental attitude of the player and the teacher. A constant awareness of pitch and interval relationships is required, and the player must develop an accurate judgment enabling him to anticipate the correct pitch before the tone is produced. Thinking in tune seems to be prerequisite to playing in tune. Singing the desired pitch and matching it with the instrument is a valuable teaching device. The use of the Stroboconn, and the matching of tones by two instruments by the "beat elimination" procedure will be helpful in developing pitch sensitivity.

The physical aspects of intonation problems concern the ability to hear minute pitch differences and to develop embouchure flexibility and control which will enable the individual to make the necessary adjustments in pitch. Both of these elements must be emphasized when the student begins instruction and be continually stressed until thinking and hearing accurate pitch are automatically a part of performance at all times.

Every pitch requires a different muscular adjustment of the embouchure, and it is essential that the student develop accuracy with regard to the correct lip tension for all tones throughout the range of the instrument. It is a common tendency to contract the lip muscles too slowly in playing ascending passages and to relax the embouchure too rapidly in playing descending passages. The resultant flatting in pitch in scale passages may also be partially due to insufficient breath support.

Too frequently, brass instrumentalists appear to assume that the tone will automatically be in tune when the correct fingering or slide position is used. If this erroneous idea is not corrected early in the musical experience of the student, a careless, indifferent attitude is soon developed toward tone quality and intonation.

May-June, 1951

The Trombone Slur

—requires a legato tongue, controlled manipulation of the slide, and thorough familiarity with auxiliary positions.

JUNE PHILLIPS

DURING the early stage of his instruction, the amateur trombonist should be awakened to one of the most distinguishing features of playing his instrument—the polished rendition of the cantabile style. Executing a slurred passage is not assumed to be easy, but it can be accomplished by the young student if he understands the fundamentals in producing a legato and works diligently to experience the thrill of its mastery. It is the belief of many wind instructors that the trombone's smooth flow of consecutive tones, which is more quickly acquired on a valved or a keyed instrument, is only for the artist. Therefore, the teacher is usually reconciled to the fact that his young student will always play either detached tones or a glissando (smear) when a slurred passage is met, thereby missing the richness of full musical interpretations.

"Ritorna Vincitor" (*Aida*) Verdi

MOLTO PATHETICO

Can Your First-Year Trombonist Phrase This?

The production of a slurred phrase consists of three parts—the legato tongue, controlled manipulation of the slide, and auxiliary positions.

The first approach is to teach the legato tongue. This is most easily begun on a single tone, Bb below middle C being a wise choice. After the tone is initially attacked by pronouncing "tah," the player should continue the flow of breath while his tongue is again put into motion by saying "rah" or "dah."

TAH   DAH   TAH   DAH

At first, the player usually stops his tone at the pronunciation of the syllable because he is not used to continuing the flow of breath. It is advisable to spend six to eight weeks in becoming acquainted with the process and cultivating smoothness. At its best, the legato tongue is an audible energy impulse produced by applying the tongue and the breath to a continuous flow of tone.

Controlled manipulation of the slide is a very important factor in all phases of trombone playing and especially in this subject of discussion.

The slide is grasped solidly between the thumb and first two fingers (forefinger and middle finger). The other two fingers are left in a relaxed state. There are two fulcrum points, the wrist and the elbow, both coming into play on all positions with the elbow making the greatest compensations. The wrist should never be uncontrollably relaxed but serve only as a finer adjustment of the elbow movement, particularly in the area from 3rd position to 1st position.

When the proper slide manipulation is developed, the way is prepared for easy and efficient movement of the slide, and it is here that this point entwines with the pronunciation of "dah." Just as the tongue is starting the "dah," the slide should be directed to the next position while the "d" is being formed and should have reached its destination when "ah" is pronounced so that the full breath forms the new tone. It is easily seen that this movement has to be done in a split second, regardless of the distance to cover.

TAH...D...AH

Here is where the control of the slide is important. The player must waste no time getting there, nor should he overshoot or undershoot the new position.

Auxiliary positions (substitute positions) make it possible to shorten the slide distances between tones. This is beneficial in rapid staccato passages as well as in fulfilling one of the greatest needs in performing a polished cantabile style — the split-second movement of the slide as the "d" in "dah" is pronounced, as brought out in the preceding paragraph. Let us consider a few examples of the use of auxiliary positions:

A Partial List of Auxiliary Positions

F, below middle C, may be played on 1st or 6th positions. If the tone following F should be F♯ it is logical that the F be played on 6th position since that is closer to 5th position. The choice of the position on F, however, would also depend upon the tone that preceded it. Let us assume that the preceding tone were B♭, an octave and a second below middle C. The tone can be played on 1st position only. Since that is true, it would be logical also to play F on 1st position because the move to F♯ would be five positions, while if F were played on 6th position for the convenience of a one-position movement to F♯, the move from B♭ to F would be six positions. The following phrasings clarify the point being brought out:

TAH DAH DAH	TAH DAH DAH
1 1 5	1 6 5
Recommended	Awkward

Now, suppose the B♭ were the one immediately below middle C. This tone can be played on 1st and 5th positions. Then, the plan would be:

TAH DAH DAH
5 6 5

Auxiliary positions serve another purpose—that of giving greater opportunity for lip slur combinations. C, an octave below middle C, can be played in only one position, 6th position. Assuming that the following tone is F (a fourth above) it would be impossible to play this combination as a lip slur were it unknown to the performer that F can be played in 6th position as well as in 1st position.

TAH DAH	TAH DAH
6 1	6 6
Awkward movement if legato tongue used. Gliss. if legato tongue not used.	Excellent opportunity for both lip slur and legato tongue.

At this point, let it be said that lip slurs should never be combined with the legato tongue during a slurred passage. There are two reasons for this:

1. The legato tongue is a more dependable mechanism than the lip slur, thereby assuring greater safety in getting the tone. In other words, there are fewer chances for "fluffed" tones with the legato tongue than with the lip slur.

2. The mixture of the two is audible simply because there are two dif-ferent approaches to the production of the tone.

The general rule for the direction of slide-movement in a slurred passage is as follows: If the tone sequence goes up, the slide moves outward; if the tone sequence goes down, the slide moves inward. Therefore, a third value is found in auxiliary positions—that of giving greater opportunity to meet the above stated rule.

Tone trend is up, slide moves out. May be done with lip slur or legato tongue.	Tone trend is down, slide moves in. May be done with lip slur or legato tongue.

Now the question comes: "Should one be more concerned about the closeness-of-positions movement or be more concerned about the general rule of the direction of slide-movement and tone sequence?"

This is a matter of common sense to be decided by the judiciousness of the performer. In the following example, you will see that it is most feasible to violate the general rule and move the slide inward when the tone is going up for the sake of using adjacent positions of 5th and 6th. Example B adheres to the rule but necessitates an awkward slide movement from 1st position to 5th position.

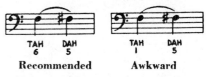

TAH DAH	TAH DAH
6 5	1 5
Recommended	Awkward

In review, the production of a slurred passage consists of three parts: the legato tongue, controlled manipulation of the slide, and auxiliary positions. Now that we have analyzed it, let us leave the smears and glissandos for use in the "special effects" department. *FINE*

May-June, 1951

ROBERT ROSEVEAR

Playing The Single

Horn

Aɴ ɪᴍᴘᴏʀᴛᴀɴᴛ development in the instrumental teaching field is the increasing adoption of the single B♭ French horn in school bands and orchestras. Only recently has this instrument been available in reasonable quantity at a moderate price. The purpose of this article is to explain how the single B♭ horn is used.

Perhaps no single factor is more

puzzling to directors than the fingering of the B♭ horn. Many have been misled by the term "single B♭," and have tried to work out fingerings similar to those of the cornet or treble clef baritone. Others have looked in vain for a special set of B♭ horn parts in band and orchestra arrangements.

The enterprising teacher can find fingering charts for the B♭ horn in a number of sources, a few of which are: The INSTRUMENTALIST, January-February (1951), p. 38; *Simplex Fingering Slide Rule for French Horn*, Mills Music, Inc.; Conductor's Manual, *Easy Steps to the Band*, p. 37 (5-valve chart, p. 120); and Roy Miller Fingering Chart in *SYB Ensemble Band Method*.

In order to read the music for horn in F on a single B♭ instrument (or the B♭ side of the double horn), the player uses "transposed fingerings." It has always seemed extremely illogical to me that a director who accepts and understands the fact that E♭ and BB♭ tuba players can play from the same part will then rebel against the parallel situation of an F and a B♭ horn player playing an F part!

The single B♭ horn, being shorter than the single F, is a perfect fourth higher in pitch. For this reason a player would be a fourth *too high* if he played F horn music using F fingering on the B♭ instrument. He could play the F part on the B♭ horn if he lowered every note a perfect fourth, but this transposition, though not impossible, is an unreasonable obstacle to place in the path of the school player, or the professional, for that matter.

Rather than transpose constantly, therefore, the B♭ horn player should learn the transposed fingering for each note; he should simply be taught to associate *sound* and *fingering* exactly as he would on any other instrument.

The teacher familiar with the F horn can quickly see the derivation of the transposed fingering by writing an extended scale of C and indicating above each note the F horn fingering of the corresponding note a fourth lower (see Fig. 1).

Two interesting points immediately become apparent: (1) the fingerings

for a, b, c′, a′, b′, c″, f″ and g″ are identical for both F and B♭ horns, and (2) the f′ and g′ fingerings are just the reverse of those used on the F horn. It should be remembered

Fig. 1.

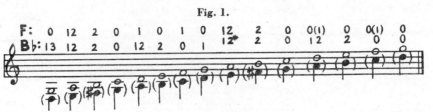

*The fingering 1-2 is generally better in tune than open.

that this system of transposed fingering is definitely used by professional players.

It is unfortunate that F horn parts are still not available for *all* school publications. While F parts are practically always published for orchestra music and for symphonic band numbers, they are sadly lacking in beginning material for the band field. We therefore face the disturbing situation that advanced players, who can cope with transposition easily, do not have to use it, while beginners, struggling with many new problems, have the added handicap of the E♭ part much of the time.

One solution to the problem of E♭ parts is the use of the E♭ crook to lower the pitch of the F horn a whole tone, or the A♭ crook now furnished with some B♭ horns. A similar effect can be obtained by lengthening the muting, or 4th, valve slide on the 4-valve B♭ horn.

I personally do not use the E♭ crook and advise against it. The constant changing between E♭ and F crooks, or from B♭ to A♭ on the B♭ horn, results in insecure attacks and faulty intonation, even when—as frequently does *not* happen—the valve slides of the instrument are properly adjusted to the changed length of the main tubing.

The preferred solution to the E♭ horn problem is to teach the student how to transpose E♭ parts. This is the relatively simple process of lowering each note a whole tone and adding two flats to the key signature, or subtracting two sharps.

Experience has confirmed that a student quickly learns this useful skill if it is carefully explained, and he has an opportunity for a bit of supervised practice in transposition. Too often it is the *teacher* rather than the student who experiences difficulty. Many teachers make the mistake of

building transposition into a psychological barrier rather than introducing it as a perfectly normal procedure. Even relative beginners can learn to transpose.

A third system is derived from the second. Here the band director frankly admits that the horn players will probably never be confronted with an F horn part, or at least there will always be E♭ parts available in the band music. He argues that it is unreasonable to expect the band player to transpose the majority of his music from E♭ parts. Rather than use E♭ or A♭ crooks with the students' acoustical and musical shortcomings, this director teaches a set of transposed fingerings similar to those described above but with the important difference that these are for use with E♭ parts.

Anyone interested in this procedure can quickly make a fingering chart by using the B♭ or F horn fingerings a whole tone below the written note. A device such as the one described by E. C. Moore in the January-February (1951) INSTRUMENTALIST will be helpful in learning these E♭ transposed fingerings. This method has much logic behind it and is used with good results by a number of teachers; nevertheless, it has always seemed to me rather a "dirty trick" to play on the student. Since nearly all solos, small ensemble parts, and orchestra compositions are published for horn in F, the student will sooner or later have to transpose anyway.

The two models of single B♭ French horns most practical for average school use are those with three and four valves. For most school purposes the 3-valve instrument is entirely adequate and a real rival to the single F horn in popularity.

It is a wonderfully light and responsive horn, a real boon to the grade school player but acceptable for any age. The 4-valve single B♭ horn adds a valve which lowers the pitch of the instrument about 3/4 of a step, and is intended primarily for use when hand muting is done. In addition to its use when muting, the "stop" valve can also serve to correct the sharpness of the low G and F♯ and the lowest C and B when used in combination with the regular valves (see Fig. 2).

Fig. 2

It might be mentioned in passing that the single B♭ French horn has been strongly criticized for faulty intonation particularly on these four low notes. While they are admittedly sharp, they can be humored into correct pitch even on a 3-valve instrument. They are no worse in this respect than the corresponding notes on *any* 3-valve instrument. Furthermore, the extremely low C and B are infrequently encountered in school horn parts.

The 4-valve instrument is often considered for the advancing player. The advantage of the 4th valve can be considerably over-rated, however, particularly in respect to its use when muting. Muted tones are not at all common in school scores and less used in band than in orchestra.

Hand muting produces a beautiful ethereal effect when properly done, but very often the effect is hidden because of poor scoring or over-zealous playing from other musicians. Notes muted by hand are difficult to attack clearly and are often badly out of tune. Young players, especially girls with small hands, have considerable difficulty stopping the horn bell properly. In other words, muting by hand, at least for most school players, is an interesting but often impractical "trick."

A more realistic approach to the problem of muted notes in school playing is the use of a good non-transposing French horn mute. The tone produced with these mutes is more "open" than when the bell is hand-stopped, but the resulting security of attack and improved intonation more than compensates.

If purchased *purely* for use with hand-stopped tones, the 4th valve might well be considered a useful luxury item when the price of the extra valve is compared to the cost of a five dollar mute. Even the professional player today uses a mechanical mute for much of his muted work—as any observant concert-goer can see!

The 5-valve single B♭ French horn has a 5th valve which lowers the instrument a perfect fourth and gives it the full range of the double horn. This valve is useful in a number of ways, such as improving intonation (using 5 instead of 1-3 and 5-2 instead of 1-2-3). The 5-valve is an excellent model for the professional but not a serious competitor to the 3 or 4-valve B♭ or F for school use.

Suggestions for improving the intonation of 1-3, and 1-2-3 fingerings have already been made. The fifth harmonic on all cup mouthpiece brass instruments tends to be flat—as, for example, the upper written E on the trumpet, the upper D on trombone, and the first space written E on the F horn.

The corresponding fifth harmonic on the single B♭ horn is the written second space A (sounding D) which, because of the flatness of this open tone, is usually played with valve 1-2. The A♭ derived from this A is thus best fingered 2-3 instead of 2.

These two fingerings have the added advantage of being the same as for F horn. The second line G may be flat on some B♭ horns when using valve 1, in which case the 1-3 combination should bring this note up to pitch. First space F♯ is generally acceptable with 1-2, but could be obtained with 1-2-3 if the former is flat.

Other suggestions on intonation include the use of 3rd valve for written D′ and D″ when 1-2 is sharp, 1st valve or O for high G; on some horns, the highest A may better be played open.

It is important that the player tune with his right hand in the *normal playing position* inside the bell. Inserting the hand farther in the bell lowers the pitch, a fact which school players should understand. French horns are built somewhat sharp to allow for this flattening effect of the right hand in the bell.

Since the tone of the single B♭ is characteristically "brighter" than that of the single F, care must be exercised to avoid harsh or blatant playing. The B♭ player, amateur or professional, usually seeks to capture the more veiled and "darker" quality of the F horn. The B♭ horn can be darkened noticeably, to simulate the F quality, by closing the bell more, sometimes simply by further cupping the fingers, carefully forming the embouchure, playing with a relaxed throat and with good breath support, avoiding excessive air pressure, and by using a larger and deeper cup mouthpiece.

The single B♭ French horn is no longer an experimental instrument either in the professional or school fields. It is a worthy rival of the single F horn, superior to the mellophone for the beginning French horn student, and in many respects a real challenge to the double horn. Its use is helping to bring the French horn section up to the technical and musical level of the other wind choirs in school bands and orchestras. ■

September 1951

Tone Color in Brasses
WARD MOORE

AS BRASS PLAYERS and teachers we often become so interested in the problems of the embouchure that we overlook some elements of tone production that are much more fundamental in nature. *I believe that body resonance is of much greater importance.*

We know that a musical tone is a regular vibration in the air caused—in the case of a wind instrument—by a vibrating column of air. Knowing this, it would seem on first thought that if we give two individuals instruments exactly alike, they should produce tones exactly alike. We know this is not the case. Why?

There is no way in which one directly changes or modifies the shape or tonal characteristics of the column of air within the horn. This modification must of necessity be indirect and is, I believe, brought about in the following way.

There are two columns of air involved in producing a tone, one within the horn and one within the body. These two columns of air vibrate sympathetically. Although the player cannot directly affect the vibration of the column of air within the horn, he can and does modify the column of air within the body, thus indirectly modifying the column of air within the horn. It follows, then, that tone is produced and colored within the body. The tone produced in the horn will be a direct reflection of that inner tone.

This conception of bodily resonance may seem to be only a matter of theory, inasmuch as it is difficult to offer concrete evidence that such a thing does exist or to give exact instructions on how to obtain it. However, here are a few of the main essentials:

1. The breath and the breathing apparatus play a most important part. The chest must be arched with the upper chest full of air *at all times*. Breathing should, of course, be diaphragmatic, with the ribs and lower part of the chest expanding as the breath is taken in. Adequate support of the tone, not only to start but to sustain it, is essential.

2. The position of the whole body is of utmost importance. Sit erect with the body slightly forward from the hips. Most of us have enough natural difficulties in producing a good tone without imposing more in the way of poor posture.

3. Absolute relaxation of the throat is necessary. It can be achieved only through adequate support from the diaphragm. Time spent in the practice of sustained tones in the low register will be helpful here.

Tone is produced very much as the singer produces it, except that the lips instead of the vocal chords are the vibrating surface. Just as the column of air within the instrument divides itself into sections to sound the overtones which make up the register of the instrument as we go higher, so does the column of air within us vibrate in sections to give resonance and color to the tone.

Tone, then, is a part of the individual; it is part of his physical make-up, if you like, and a rather intimate and personal thing.   *FINE*

How To Select
New Instruments

BERNARD FITZGERALD

THE INSTRUMENTAL teacher is frequently called upon to advise students and parents concerning the purchase of new or used instruments. This is particularly true at the beginning of the school year when instrumental classes are being organized. The well informed teacher can offer valuable assistance and guidance in aiding the student to obtain a satisfactory instrument.

The beginning student is frequently handicapped by an inferior instrument or one which is in such poor playing condition that even an experienced player would be unable to obtain satisfactory musical results. While such a situation seems absurd, it is an unfortunate circumstance which is all too common.

The understandable reluctance of parents to assume responsibility for a large investment in an expensive instrument until the child's progress indicates some evidence of continued interest and success must be taken into consideration. The trial-rental-purchase plan offered by many instrument dealers provides an opportunity for the student to use the instrument on a low-cost trial basis for a period of 60-90 days before a final decision regarding purchase is required.

TONE QUALITY, INTONATION and CONSTRUCTION are of primary importance in selecting an instrument. Tone quality is rather difficult to standardize from an objective standpoint since personal preference or prejudice may frequently be a factor in the judgment of experienced performers. Ideals regarding desirable tone quality and resonance are quite different for symphony and dance band performance. The tonal refinement which is characteristic of symphonic performance is preferred to the nasal, blatant tone quality and distortion which are commonly noted in dance band performance.

A thorough playing test by a competent and experienced performer should be considered essential. A careful check should be made with the stroboscope, testing both scalewise intonation and interval relationship, and including a check of octaves and fifths. The response and flexibility of the instrument should be tested on passages which include slurs, lip-slurs, and staccato tonguing in all registers.

The playing test should also include a check at different dynamic levels to determine whether tonal distortion or loss of resonance occurs at any point in the dynamic range. The tone quality should be full, clear, and resonant on all tones, and response should be free throughout the entire range of the instrument, with blowing resistance in general balance in all registers.

The easiest blowing instrument is

not necessarily the most satisfactory. The manufacturer can control this factor to a considerable extent, but too little blowing resistance may prove to be a handicap equally undesirable in comparison to the instrument with too much resistance. Small bore instruments should be avoided; the medium and medium-large bore instruments are preferred for the average student, while the mature player may find the large bore most satisfactory.

All brass instruments should be built in Low Pitch at A-440. Certain known intonation defects are common to all makes of brass instruments to some extent. In view of the limitations of space for this article the reader is referred to the pamphlet "Practical Problems in Building Wind Instruments" published by C. G. Conn, Ltd., for more detailed information regarding specific defects. However, a satisfactory instrument should not have these defects to the extent that a capable performer cannot correct the intonation by means of lip adjustment, tongue position, or mechanical means without sacrificing tonal resonance and clarity.

Tuning Mechanism

For example, the cornet and trumpet should be equipped with a tuning mechanism on either the 1st or 3rd valve slide (or both) which can be adjusted while the instrument is being played. The 4th valve on the Euphonium serves as a similar aid to intonation through the possible alternate fingerings, in addition to extending the range of the instrument down to the fundamental.

The type of mouthpiece and a correct fitting of the mouthpiece into the mouthpipe is an important factor in regard to both tone quality and intonation. Extremely small mouthpieces with very shallow cup and small bore are not recommended. A suitable mouthpiece is so essential for best results that second or third quality instruments will be much more satisfactory if properly fitted with a good mouthpiece. Since no single mouthpiece is equally satisfactory for all players, some experimentation with mouthpieces of different size rim, cup, and bore may be necessary to determine which is best for the individual. More detailed information regarding the selection of mouthpieces may be found in the Brass Clinic column of The INSTRU-

MENTALIST, Vol. II, No. 1, September 1947.

Strength Required

For school use, sturdy construction with strong bracing and reinforced stays and plates at points subject to most wear or damage is very important. Careful workmanship is readily apparent in the mechanical action and fittings of all moving parts of the instrument. The smoke test may be applied to check tubing, valves, slides, and water keys for leakage. The trombone slide should test well by means of the vacuum test with both slides held closed by the thumbs. All valves and trombone slides should be checked to be sure there is no side play or sluggish action. Valves should be equipped with properly fitted corks and felts for quiet action, and the mechanical action of the valves and the trombone slide should be free of any tendency to bind or stick at any point.

Piston type valves are preferable on all valve instruments except French horn, which should have rotary type valves with string action. Short-stroke, side-action valves are preferred on baritone, euphonium, and tuba. All tuning and valve slides should operate smoothly but not be loosely fitted.

Lacquered brass or silver plating with gold bell is recommended for all instruments except French horn, which is usually finished in lacquered brass. While lacquer finishes are not guaranteed, a good quality lacquer finish is an advantage over the polished brass finish as far as appearance is concerned, providing the instrument receives the proper care. The varying effects of acidity in the perspiration of the individual is a determining factor in respect to the durability of lacquer finishes. Silver plating is more durable and therefore advisable for the larger brass instruments.

Three Grades

The majority of brass instrument manufacturers producing a complete line build three different grades of instruments. First quality instruments usually have the name of the manufacturer on the bell of the instrument and represent the best in workmanship, materials, mechanism, design, and finish. In several instances a number of deluxe models

are available featuring hand-hammered, sterling silver, coprion, nickel, or german-silver bells or specially tempered alloys.

Second quality instruments do not ordinarily have the name of the maker on the instrument, are correspondingly lower in price, and rarely include the special features which are available on many first quality instruments. Other differences include lighter weight metal, less sturdy braces, thinner plating, and less satisfactory lacquer finishes. Mechanically, instruments of this quality are somewhat less satisfactory due to differences in materials and workmanship. Slides, valves, tuning slides, and other moving parts are less likely to be fitted properly for best results.

Different Name

Third quality instruments are usually sold under still another name. Poorer construction, light weight metal of less durability, unsatisfactory finishes, less careful workmanship, mechanical imperfections, and inferior tone quality and intonation are to be expected in the least expensive instruments. A used first quality instrument in good condition is usually preferable to a new third line instrument.

It should be noted that the allocation of metals for defense has resulted in the curtailment of the manufacture of brass instruments to the extent that third quality instruments are no longer available from most manufacturers.

In addition to the above three grades, a number of manufacturers build instruments for large distributors. These instruments may be obtained in two or three grades of quality and are normally issued under a "stencil" or "private" brand name rather than that of the maker. In some instances these instruments are built according to the special specifications of the distributor. The teacher should thoroughly investigate both the origin and the quality of such instruments and subject them to a careful examination before recommending them without reservation. Instruments which are sold under a "stencil" rather than a "brand" name may frequently be very good buys since the price range is often considerably below that of the "standard" lines.

Check the Pitch

The cheaper grades of imported instruments should be carefully checked to determine whether they are built in Low Pitch, A-440, since it is not uncommon to find that they are built sharp to the extent of ¼ tone.

The teacher should not be unduly influenced by the claims made through extravagant or sensational advertising which may emphasize trick gadgets of unproven value. It will be more satisfactory to depend upon manufacturers who publish specifications and provide information regarding materials and details of manufacturing processes.

In addition to the criteria mentioned for purchasing new instruments, used instruments should be thoroughly checked for dents and worn plating, especially on valves and slides. Corks, springs, and felts should be in good condition and properly adjusted; the stem of the mouthpiece should be inspected for dents and for correct fitting into the instrument. Dents in the mouthpipe or valve slides are particularly critical, for they seriously affect performance. Valves and trombone slide should be carefully checked for excessive wear and loose fitting. Be sure the trombone slide is not sprung or out of alignment. French horns, baritones and tubas should be examined carefully for cracks or holes in the mouthpipe.

Both interior and exterior surfaces of used instruments should be thoroughly cleaned before the instrument is used. This is desirable both from the standpoint of sanitation and of obtaining satisfactory musical results since the accumulation of food particles and saliva on the interior surfaces of the instrument is inevitable and will seriously affect both tone quality and intonation unless the instrument is cleaned periodically.

It is also desirable to flush the inside tubing of a new instrument before it is used since small metal particles or filings may be present and seriously damage valves or trombone slides.

It seems unnecessary to enumerate in detail the procedure for the proper care and adjustment of brass instruments since there are several excellent publications which deal with this subject and most manufacturers furnish a booklet which includes instructions for instrument care. *(How to Care For Your Instrument*, published by C. G. Conn, Ltd.)

(For detailed criteria and specifications for individual brass instruments the reader is referred to the following excellent sources: *Getting Results with School Bands* by Prescott and Chidester and *Building The Instrumental Department* by Bruce Jones. Both books are published by Carl Fischer, Inc.) ∎

October, 1951

Brass Ensembles
in Church Services

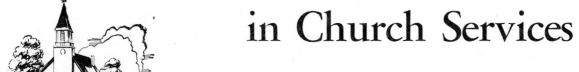

HELEN TROBIAN

TODAY MUSIC educators are fortunate to have available a number of works for brass ensembles which are very appropriate for use in worship services in schools and churches. The use of brass choirs for preludes, interludes, and postludes lends joyous dignity to the occasion. It is also a means of widening the sphere of influence of the instrumental program and thereby increasing the support of the community for the entire music program of the school.

Since early Hebrew days when Moses received instructions regarding the production of silver trumpets, brass instruments have been used to lend their unique value to church services. Gabrieli in the 16th century used brass instruments to accompany his sacred choral works and gave them interludes to play without voices or organ. Artusi, an Italian musician, commented in 1600 on the use of wind instruments in "cathedrals, churches, or chapels." In Germany during the 16th century Praetorious and Schein adopted the Venetian motet forms and used instrumental accompaniments.

That Jewitt, an Irish organist, was using wind instruments in the services of the Irish church prior to the Commonwealth is proved by the fact that in 1637 the cathedral authorities issued an act or ordinance directing the proctor to pay "to the two sackbutts and two cornetts for their service and attendance in the cathedrall the sume of twenty nobles each at or before Easter next ensuing."

The English writer, John Evelyn, says in his Diary on December 21, 1663: "Instead of the ancient, grave and solemn wind music accompanying the organ, there was introduced a concert of twenty-four violins between every pause, after the French fantastical light way, better suiting a tavern than a Church."

In Early American days the trombone choirs and the orchestras of the Moravian Church made a distinct contribution to ecclesiastical music. In present day Boston the Cathedral Church of St. Paul employs a brass quartet fifty-two Sundays in the year.

Educational Value

Because of the musical and technical advantages, many a school band and orchestra director has wished for some opportunity to interest his brass players in serious ensemble music. The performance of such music acquaints students with various phases of music history and is a powerful motivation for continued effort to produce better tone quality, to phrase carefully, and to make clean attacks and releases.

Frequently the music teacher is called upon to use his talents in the church. Sometimes he is the choir director. Occasionally he is faced with the task of leading congregational singing without the assistance of a choir or an organist. Here is an opportunity to use a brass quartet for leading congregational singing. A brass ensemble provides dynamic emotional motivation for the individual member of the congregation and for the group as a whole to take an active part in hymn singing. The congregation makes a whole-hearted response to the leadership furnished by a brass choir.

When used with the organ the brasses can play in octaves and actually lead the people in the singing of hymns while the organ supplies the harmonic background. It is preferable, if architecture permits, to place the ensemble in a position where it will not be seen by the audience. Some churches have an unused balcony at the rear of the sanctuary and others have space near the organ large enough for this purpose.

Try This in Church

Very desirable effects can be gained from using the chorus or regular mixed choir with the brass ensemble as an antiphonal choir. Another variation is having the ensemble play interludes between the verses of hymns. The use of such musical effects accompanied by appropriate remarks

on the service leaflet or bulletin will be helpful in conveying a feeling of genuine corporate worship. The members of the congregation will be able to feel that they are not onlookers at a service being presented for their passive acceptance but that they are vital participants in praise and affirmation.

The chorale harmonizations of J. S. Bach are very playable by brass quartet or small ensemble. They are not only ideal for rendition in the church but provide advantageous edu-

cational experience for young musicians. Most of the works edited by Robert King are not technically difficult and could be performed acceptably by school musicians who practice regularly and have a serious interest in their instruments.

There is an excellent body of literature available for preludes and postludes either with or without organ. A few suggestions are listed below. It is usually preferable to use more than one player on each part when possible.

LIST OF BRASS ENSEMBLES FOR CHURCH USE
With Organ

INSTRUMENTATION	COMPOSER	TITLE	PUBLISHER
Brass Quartet	Dickinson	Prelude to The Redeemer	Gray
	Glazounov	In Modo Religioso	Rubank
	Gabrieli	Pian e forte	Schott
	Kittel	Jesu Meine Freude	Breitkopf & Hartel
	Lorenz	Two Festival Preludes	Heugel
	Ravanello	Christus Resurrexit	C. Fischer
	Widor	O Lord Save Thy People	Heugel
Trumpet and organ	Krebs	Eight Chorale Preludes	Music Press
Trumpet and organ	Purcell	Trumpet Tune Voluntary	Music Press
Trumpet (or Horn) and organ	Homilius	Chorale Prelude-Adam's Fall	Music Press
Two Trumpets and organ	Purcell	Ceremonial Music	Music Press
Cornet I, Cornet II, Trombone, Baritone, Tuba	J. S. Bach	Jesu, Nun Sei Gepreistet	
	Marcello	Psalm No. XIX: First Mov't	Music for Brass
	Reich	Sonata No. 7	(Ed. by
	Brahms	O Welt ich muss dich lassen	Robt. King)
	Bach	In dulci jubilo	

Without Organ

INSTRUMENTATION	COMPOSER	TITLE	PUBLISHER
Brass Quartet	Mendelssohn	I Waited for the Lord	Bettoney
	J. S. Bach	Chorale—Christmas Oratorio	Rubank
	Verdi	There Shall be Singing	Rubank
Two Trumpets & Two Trombones	J. S. Bach	Prelude & Fugue in D Major	Marks
	J. S. Bach	Triumphant Rose the Son	Rubank
	Beethoven	Nature's Praise of God	Rubank
	Haydn	Spacious Firmament on High	Rubank
Four Trombones	Haubiel	Recessional	Composers Press
	Beethoven	Equali for Four Trombones	Breitkopf-Hartel
Three trombones, one trumpet	Beethoven	Equali for Four Trombones	Marks
Cornet, Horn, Baritone, and Trombone	J. S. Bach	Twenty-Two Chorales	Music for Brass
Cornet, Trombone, Baritone and Tuba	Reich	Sonatas No. 15 and No. 19	Music for Brass
Cornet I, II, III, IV, V, Trombone, Baritone, Tuba	Lassus	Providebam Dominum	Music for Brass
Cornet, Horn, Trombone, Baritone, Tuba	Reiche	Sonata No. 24, and No. 18	Music for Brass
	Palestrina	Three Hymns	Music for Brass
Cornet I, Cornet II, Trombone or Horn, Baritone, Tuba	Pezel	Sonatas No. 1, No. 2, No. 3	Music for Brass
	Purcell	Music for Queen Mary	
	Bach	Contrapunctus No. 1	
Horn, Trombone, Baritone, Tuba	Scheidt	Da Jesus an dem Kreuze standt	Music for Brass
Cornet I, Cornet II, Horn, Trombone, Baritone, Tuba	Purcell	Voluntary on 100th Psalm Tune	Music for Brass
	Bach	Vom Himmel hoch da komm'ich her	

October, 1951

The Small Brass Ensemble

Successful ensembles develop a nucleus of good players.
Hints on training, instruments, and repertoire.

BERNARD FITZGERALD

THE PROVEN values of small ensemble training and performance would seem to indicate that little justification is needed in support of an activity so musically rewarding to the individual. However, adjudicators and festival clinicians often observe performances by small ensembles which present meager evidence of the attainment of the musical objectives which should result from participation in this type of activity.

While a high standard of performance should be the goal of every musical group, large or small, it is quite generally recognized that playing in small ensembles is much more exacting than mass participation in band or orchestra in regard to the demand made upon each individual. Although mediocre performance is not to be condoned, it must be admitted that large groups may achieve a generally satisfactory musical result despite the shortcomings of a considerable number of performers within the group. If there is a sufficient nucleus of proficient players on each part, they maintain the musical leadership for the less capable individuals and encourage them to perform with more confidence.

It is obvious that within a small ensemble *every* part must be performed well and that each player must be both accurate and dependable throughout the entire performance. The additional responsibility which is placed upon the individual is compensated for by the opportunity for musical finesse. Unfortunately the musical result which should be realized is often lacking due to inadequate rehearsal preparation, widely divergent ability and experience among the players, and the absence of the factors of balance, blend, precision, nuance, and style which are so essential to ensemble unity and artistry.

It may be argued that realization of such goals by amateurs in public schools is not possible. However, ample evidence of both attainment and development is to be found in the superior musical performances of school bands and orchestras, whose directors attribute much of the excellence of the large organizations to the training acquired in small ensembles.

Study Necessary

Too frequently, performances by amateur ensembles present little evidence of the careful preparation and study so essential for effective results. In many instances there is little more than a mechanical rendition of notes, far short of desirable musical achievement.

Since musical and technical deficiencies are far more obvious in ensemble performance, it is important to select personnel of nearly equal ability. Then there must be regular and frequent intensive rehearsals to develop and maintain the unity and precision required for a high standard of performance. Thus, ensembles should be regarded as long-range projects, organized on a permanent basis. A spur-of-the-moment, hastily prepared group cannot possibly achieve the genuine unity that should characterize good ensemble playing.

Many performances are hampered by an unsatisfactory seating arrangement. It is not uncommon to see ensembles seated in a straight line facing the audience, making visible communication among the performers virtually impossible. Good precision in attacks and releases demands that each member of the group be seated so that he is within a direct or indirect line of vision with every other participant. Such a requirement is met by seating players in a semicircular or box arrangement.

In the interest of precision and unity, it is customary for one of the players to assume responsibility for coordinating attacks and releases. Indications may be given by a slight movement of the instrument or the head. In any case, such gestures should be as unobtrusive as possible. Ordinarily the player on the highest part is the logical one to act in this capacity since that part will usually contain the principal melodic interest under average conditions, though some other player may serve as leader. Each member should study the *entire score* in order to become familiar with it and to understand the relations of the parts to each other and to the composition as a whole.

As yet the brass ensemble has not evolved a standardized instrumentation comparable to the woodwind quintet or the string quartet. Small homogeneous groups consisting of quartets of cornets, French horns, or trombones possess the same disadvantages as quartets of four violins, cellos, or B♭ clarinets. Their limitations include restricted total range, lack of tonal contrast, and difficulty in achievement of adequate balance of the bass line. While such instrumental combinations offer excellent opportunity for ensemble training and experience, other groups are considerably more versatile as a medium for chamber music performance.

Among heterogeneous groups, the brass quartet, quintet, and sextet appear to have the greatest potentiality as standard instrumentation. At present the quartet composed of two cornets, French horn, and trombone seems to offer the most flexibility in combination with tonal balance and contrast. The baritone or euphonium might be considered as a substitute for the trombone because it possesses greater tonal sonority and is capable of more fluent technical execution. However, the trombone is likely to prove more flexible with respect to tonal shading and control, in addition to notable advantages regarding intonation.

Brass Sextet

The brass sextet of two cornets, French horn, trombone, baritone, and tuba has additional sonority and greater total range and tonal contrast, but it is quite likely to take on a massiveness not characteristic of small ensembles in which subtlety of shading and nuance are an integral element. However, some excellent repertory is available in the form of original compositions by Bohme, Busch, Simon, McKay, and others which is challenging and musically rewarding.

Perhaps the brass quintet may eventually become the standard or ideal brass ensemble. The combination of either two cornets, French horn, trombone, and baritone, or two cornets, French horn, and two trombones would be considerably more versatile than any quartet combination. This group of instruments would have the advantage of more sonority than the quartet, would alleviate the endurance problem without reducing the number of voices to less than four, and would retain more flexibility than the brass sextet. Original compositions by 17th century composers include works by Pezel, Reicha, and Gabrieli. Numerous arrangements of compositions by Handel, Corelli, Monteverdi, and Purcell, plus original contemporary works by Ingold Dahl, Robert Sanders, Carl Busch, and Albert Schmutz provide repertoire for the brass quintet.

Endurance is a major problem for players in the small brass ensemble. Little opportunity for resting the embouchure, even briefly, is provided in quartet performance. In this respect it is far more strenuous than solo performance, in which occasional piano interludes provide some rest for the soloist. The first cornet part in the quartet or quintet is usually the highest in quartet writing in the period of Joseph Haydn, but current practice is to divide the melodic interest among all members of the ensemble.

It may be necessary, in longer programs, to provide a rest from high register playing by interchanging the first and second cornet parts where this shift can be managed smoothly. Such a change makes for more interesting performance for the player of the second cornet, who is usually relegated to secondary parts devoid of melodic interest.

One unexplored area is that of combining the brass quartet or quintet with piano. In the absence of originally composed works for this combination, the writer has adapted numerous choral and instrumental compositions for brass quartet and piano with the discovery that there are many possibilities for such a group of instruments. The addition of the piano not only provides a desirable contrast to the brass sonority but is also effective in accompanying or supporting in both solos and ensemble passages. The extended range of the piano contributes both added brilliance and depth to the rich tonal texture of the brass, and thus augments color potential considerably. A further advantage is the additional available repertory which can be adapted from the larger choral works of Mendelssohn, Handel, Mozart, Brahms, and others.

Similarity in Bore

Tonal blend, balance, and sonority of the brass ensemble will be noticeably affected by the use of instruments of widely different type bore. The controversy of cornet vs. trumpet still finds many partisans on both sides. The present tendency and preference of players generally for tonal brilliance and the similarity of the mouthpieces used on these instruments serve to counteract differences in tone quality often apparent only to the trained musical ear. It may be said that, in view of the flexibility and tonal shading required for small ensemble performance, the more responsive cornet seems preferable. It is important that cornetists in the ensemble produce tone qualities that will match and blend effectively. This result can be realized more satisfactorily if players have instruments of the same bore and preferably of the same make with similar type mouthpieces.

While the bass trombone will prove cumbersome and unwieldy in rapid passages because of the very large bore and additional weight of the slide, the tenor trombone with rotary F valve attachment is a definite advantage from the standpoints of technical fluency and facility. The French horn bore is more nearly standardized among manufacturers and thus is not likely to present a problem. Never use small bore instruments. Most satisfactory results will be obtained by using medium-large or large bore instruments for cornets and trombones, with large bore recommended for baritone and tuba. In addition to the different tonal results of combining small, medium, and large bore instruments, the type and size of the mouthpieces will also affect tone quality and sonority.

Tonal deficiencies which are common in brass ensemble performance but are not necessarily caused entirely by differences in bores or mouthpieces are as follows: extreme harsh or brassy quality of tone of the cornets; brittle, too open tone on the French horn, often caused by failure of players to use the right hand in the bell correctly; thick, stuffy, and often muffled tone quality of the trombone; and heavy, inflexible tone of the baritone and tuba. In addition, there is a general tendency toward over-brilliance of the cornet, trumpet, and French horn tone, while the trombone, baritone, and tuba frequently lack tonal clarity and solidity.

Discriminating brass players are capable of modifying tone quality to match, blend, and balance with other members of an ensemble to a much greater extent than is normally achieved in performance. A high degree of sensitivity to the subtle variations in tonal shading and coloring must be developed through intensive and extensive ensemble rehearsals. Experience may often involve the use of alternate fingerings, a change from F to B♭ horn, variation of the hand position in the bell of the French horn, etc., in order to obtain the desired musical result.

Brass ensemble repertory is not particularly extensive although the situation has improved in recent years. Two comprehensive lists of graded repertory are available, the Interlochen List of Recommended Materials for Instrumental Ensembles and the list published by the National School Band and Orchestra Association.

Fine

The Euphonium—
Cello of the Band

LEONARD FALCONE

SURPRISING as it may seem, in this country the euphonium is a relatively unknown instrument though European bands have long considered it an integral part of their instrumentation. For some reason the instrument has found very little favor with our American school bands; its use is confined almost exclusively to professional musicians. Hence, it is not surprising that we are often asked, "What is the euphonium?"

It is very possible that the name, rather than the instrument itself, is what baffles the layman. The usual explanation is that the euphonium is actually a baritone horn.

"Then why don't you call it a baritone horn?" is a natural second question.

To many of us the name baritone horn, especially when seen on printed programs, does not look or sound entirely satisfactory. Therefore we just call it baritone, leaving out the word horn, although this practice sometimes leads to confusion. After a concert some years ago, a sweet old lady said to me, "I thought you were going to sing for us."

Ever since that occasion I have used the name euphonium instead of baritone on programs. People may not know what it is, but at least they will not expect me to sing!

Of course, the euphonium and the baritone are not exactly the same. As we know these instruments today, the features of the euphonium that distinguish it from the baritone are that (1) it has four valves, (2) its bore is slightly larger, and (3) it often has two bells. Currently the second smaller bell is gradually being omitted because its only effective use is to imitate the trombone, a rather unnecessary function.

Extended Range

The fourth valve serves to extend the range a fourth, from E below the staff (bass clef) down to B. It is also used for alternate fingerings to improve the intonation of certain tones, notably B and C on the staff. The larger bore of the euphonium produces a quality of tone which is deeper and richer than the baritone. The most important of these features is the larger bore, which, when combined with a deeper cup mouthpiece, produces a more sonorous tone.

In the olden days the euphonium was called a small tuba. However, its functions of the present are far removed from those of the tuba, and except for some similarity of shape, there is no parallel between the two. Rather, as I have already stated, it is more logical to consider the euphonium as a baritone because the slight differences between the two do not actually affect their basic similarity. The playing technique of the two instruments is exactly the same, and in band they play the same music. This being the case, it might be well to consider the euphonium and the baritone as one and the same instrument; therefore, whatever is said here about the playing technique of the euphonium will apply also to the baritone. It should be noted, however, that the euphonium with its deeper and richer tone is a more desirable and effective instrument than the baritone. In fact, some people consider the euphonium the most expressive of all brass instruments.

The place and function of the euphonium in the band correspond to those of the cello in the orchestra; that is, both play the same type of music. The reason for this parallel is the close affinity between the tones of the two instruments. No other band instrument can duplicate the melodies and counter melodies usually performed by the cello with the degree of warmth, expression, and power possible with the euphonium.

Disregarding certain technical characteristics of the string instruments, such as chords, double stops, harmonics, extended range, etc., the euphonium has both the agility of technic and the tonal expressiveness of the cello. Moreover, in the hands of competent performers the euphonium is capable of producing sensitive nuances and a delicate style of playing equal to the cello.

In view of these capabilities and the affinity of euphonium and cello, it would be well for the style of playing to be similar. I believe that within its own technical range, the euphonium can and should be made to sound like the cello. If it imitates the phrasing and tonal expression of the cello, we will have more effective euphonium soloists and players in our school bands. Without this approach and concept of playing, the instrument is very likely to sound insipid, weak, and devoid of warmth and expression.

Cello Style

The technique involved in developing the cello style of playing on the euphonium is basically three-fold: (1) a tone that is full, round, clear, strong, and well placed, (2) an agile and well-controlled technic, and (3) a good vibrato. The physical mechanics necessary for the production of the type of tone just described requires the proper use of the breath and breath support, a good embouchure, and a relaxed throat. These physical factors have been explained at great length in textbooks, musical periodicals, and at numerous clinics. Inasmuch as the embouchure has

94

a direct bearing on the production of the tone, it might be well to point out that the so-called "buzz system" is not entirely satisfactory for the euphonium. With as large an instrument as it is, undue stretching and pinching of the lips, along with poor breath support, produces a small and "nasal" tone. Obviously, the large amount of breath required to fill the euphonium cannot pass through the lips and into the instrument in a free, unhindered, and flowing manner if the lips are held together too tightly.

Better results can be obtained by having the corners of the mouth set firmly, not stretched, against the teeth and gums and by forming a small opening in the center of the lips in the manner of a slight pucker. The size of the opening in the center of the lips varies according to the register being played—a larger opening for low tones and a smaller one for high tones. Above all, beware of a completely loose or an overly tense and stretched embouchure. In any event, it should be kept in mind that the characteristic tone of the euphonium is big and powerful and that to produce this type of tone requires the use of full breath plus a strong breath support.

Coordination Essential

As with all brass instruments a good tone, important as it is, is not enough in itself. It must be complemented with a brilliant technic. In this respect perfect coordination of tongue and finger action is imperative. There are several ways of developing such coordination, but sometimes physical conditions make it difficult to attain. However, this writer is of the opinion that much of the bad technic we hear can be attributed to weak playing and can, therefore, be avoided.

In our anxiety to teach students not to overblow we sometimes stress soft playing too much. More often than not, missed tones are due simply to insufficient strength of attack and breath support. Attacking the tones cleanly and squarely is the most baffling problem of brass instrument playing. The nature of the problem is so elusive and intangible that the difficulty has not, and never will be completely mastered. The finest players miss notes occasionally. But we should not fear this problem. Rather

it is another reason for our proceeding to meet it in a determined and forceful manner.

"Feel" Tones

Even though the ability to "hear" the tones to be played increases the chance for clean attacks, we depend primarily on the "feel" for attacking the tones cleanly and squarely. By "feel" is meant the degree of muscular tension of the lips and the diaphragm and the pressure of the mouthpiece required to play the various tones on the instrument. The better we are able to determine and remember the association of these muscular "feelings" in relation to the various tones, the more success we will have in attacking the tones cleanly. A dependable way to learn to "feel" the tones is to attack them in a decisive and firm manner, thus getting a more definite physical sensation of the muscular reaction required to produce the various tones.

This same principle of strong and decisive attacks applies to the development of clarity and accuracy for fast playing. Daily practice of strong repeated quarter, eighth, and sixteenth notes on every tone of the chromatic scale will help to develop a firm and clean technic. Of course, in doing this, care should be taken that the tongue is not overly rigid. There should be only enough tension to retain control of the strokes of the tongue.

When the student is able to play these repeated tone exercises, he can begin practicing the chromatic scale in single notes, first in quarters and then in eighths and sixteenths. This type of daily practice will permit him to hear the tones he produces, and once he is fully aware of them, he will never be oblivious to or satisfied with playing muffled and weak tones. After the student has developed this fundamental technic, he is ready to start working on the more advanced and sensitive type of playing.

Effective Vibrato

Despite abuse and injudicious use of the vibrato, it is nonetheless one of the most important and valuable means of expression we have. Without a vibrato our range of expression would be considerably less; a good

vibrato is a necessary part of euphonium technique. Several types are used—hand, diaphragm, lip, and throat—each producing either a pitch or a dynamic type of vibrato. If not executed properly, all these methods can be unsatisfactory and dangerous.

Because of its difficulty of execution and the inherent danger of producing audible guttural sounds, the throat vibrato should be discouraged. The hand vibrato is not suitable for the euphonium because of the large size and weight of the instrument. Thus, the lip and the diaphragm vibratos, or a combination of the two, are most natural and suitable for the euphonium.

While the intensity or speed of the vibrato is a matter of personal preference, neither a very fast nor a very slow one is satisfactory. An overly fast one is likely to sound like a tremulo, while a slow and wide one sounds mechanical. Personally, I prefer a normal speed of four sixteenth notes (pulsations) to the beat at a quarter of m.m.=76, with a slightly faster speed for dramatic and emotional types of music and a slower speed for calm and lyrical music. Of course, one should not attempt to use vibrato until he is able to produce a full, solid, round, and steady tone. To superimpose the vibrato over a weak and unstable tone would only cause further distortion of the tone.

In using vibrato several factors should be kept in mind. First of all, the deviation from the pitch should be kept to a minimum and must never be so wide as to distort the center of the tone. Another point is that an effective vibrato requires continuous full and well-supported breath; otherwise, it tends to weaken the tone. Third, the vibrato should be under perfect control so that it can be used and stopped at will. Needless to say, the vibrato should be used judiciously and only for melodic phrases. Its constant use shows poor musicianship and becomes monotonous.

There are many other phases of technique necessary for good all-round playing, among which is all-important innate musicianship. But the main objective of this discussion has been to point out the fundamentals of the technique and functions of the euphonium, especially in relation to its role as the cello of the band. *Fine*

Leonard Falcone

1952

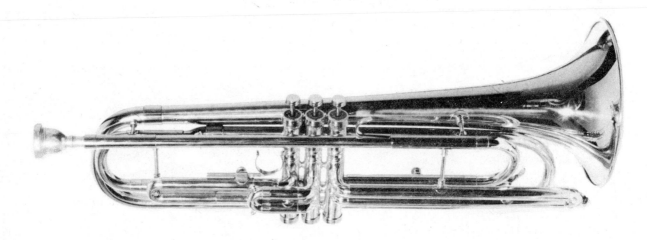

B♭ Bass Trumpet

Teaching the Cornet in Beginning Classes

Techniques include careful attention to variety of physical as well as instrumental conditions

JAMES NEILSON

TECHNIQUES of teaching the cornet in beginning classes present a number of specialized as well as general problems to the instructor who has considered the numerous factors entering into the success or failure of the pupils' efforts.

Condition of Instruments

The instrument used by the beginning student must be in good playing condition. Check for air leaks at the saliva releasing mechanisms. Make sure that the cork is in perfect condition and has an airtight sealing circumference. Check the spring; be sure that when the finger is released from the mechanism, the spring is tight enough to seal the cork firmly against the opening in the instrument.

Check the corks and pads at the top of the valves. If they are swollen, the valve ports will have reduced openings and thus will affect the purity of the tone. If they are cracked and dried out, further leakage of air from the top of the valves will result.

Make sure that all slide mechanisms move freely and that the valves are not rusted or corroded. The instrument should be cleaned inside and out.

Face Contour

In normal facial contour the teeth meet when the jaw is closed. The lower lip is slightly fuller.

Malocclusion is present when teeth do not meet when the jaw is closed. There are two types:

(1) The receding jaw. The lower teeth are back of the upper when the jaw is closed. When the distance between the upper and lower teeth is $1/8$ inch or more, a definite malocclusion is present. Excessive malocclusion occurs when the distance is $1/4$ inch or more. Often in these cases the orthodontist will advise playing a cornet for its remedial value since the lower jaw will have to be consciously thrust out to make the cornet embouchure possible.

(2) The overhanging or overshot jaw. Malocclusion is also present when the lower teeth protrude in front of the upper teeth when the jaw is closed. This type of maladjustment is much more rare than the other. It is to the interest of the student that he play some instrument other than the cornet when this type of malocclusion is found.

Following is a summary showing choice of mouthpiece:

Normal or very slight malocclusion in facial contour: with normal lips, 7B Bach mouthpiece; with larger upper lip, 7C mouthpiece; with thin upper lip, 7 mouthpiece; with normal but inherently weak lips, $8½$ B; with large but inherently weak lips, 10B, 12, 12C. (The larger the lips, the bigger the number.) Both lips fleshy but firm, 7BW.

Recessive lower jaw with normal lips, 8B; with large upper lip, 8C; with large lips, 8.

Undershot jaw with normal lips, 8B; with thin lower lip, 12; and with large lower lip, 7C.

Mouthpiece

A good mouthpiece is necessary. Inferior and second-grade instruments usually come equipped with poor mouthpieces. Fit the mouthpiece to the physical characteristics of the student.

When the facial contour and development are normal, the mouthpiece rim should rest equally upon the muscular part, not the fleshy tissue, of each lip. The fleshy tissue of each lip should be in free vibration during the production of tone. At no time will the top or bottom part of the rim rest on the fleshy tissue of the lips. When the lower lip is slightly fuller, it will appear that more of the mouthpiece is resting on the lower lip. When there is a fuller upper lip, the position of the mouthpiece will move upward a bit.

When there is a recessive jaw, the student will be likely to favor the lower lip, moving the mouthpiece downward. Make sure that the top part of the rim is not resting upon the fleshy tissue of the upper lip. The opposite will be found true when there is an undershot lower jaw.

Undue pressure of the mouthpiece against the lips must be avoided. If a red mark or impression remains on the lips after the mouthpiece has been removed, there is probably too much pressure of the mouthpiece against the lips. If the tone sounds metallic, the cause may be excessive pressure. I find it a good idea, in enabling the student to determine the correct amount of pressure, to place one hand behind the student's head and the other on the instrument and gently bring the mouthpiece into position, making sure that the student does not alter this predetermined position during the playing of the tone.

Give the student the following directions for placement of the mouthpiece:

1. Produce a buzzing sound in the lips without using the mouthpiece. Demonstrate this sound. Show how it may only be made through tense lips and with the release of sufficient breath pressure.

2. Hold the mouthpiece horizontally or at a slight downward angle. The teacher will have to determine the angle by studying the individual physical characteristics of each student.

3. With head tilted slightly backward, place the mouthpiece in position on the lower jaw. The teacher determines the correct position.

4. Tense the muscles controlling the lower lip. This will also provide some tension across the upper lip.

5. Lower the angle of the head until the mouthpiece is placed firmly on both lips.

6. Inhale, bring tongue forward to point of contact, exhale, and produce the buzzing sound through tense lips as in step 1.

7. Produce the buzzing sound for a definite number of counts.

8. Produce buzzing sounds that vary in pitch intensities. Try to play a simple three-note tune, using the mouthpiece alone.

Posture

The teacher should require good posture and should check on it consistently. Following are suggested instructions to the students:

1. Sit erect, back not touching the chair.

2. Grasp the instrument firmly in the left hand; rest the bell on the left knee. Be sure that the thumb and index finger are in the right position. Do not permit the index finger to curl over the tubing leading to the bell. Hold instrument vertically in this position.

3. Place the right hand in the proper position, tips of the fingers set carefully in the center of the valve buttons. If the instrument has a finger guard for the small finger, make the student use it since it will tend to keep the right hand in the proper position on the valve buttons.

4. Tilt the head back slightly, place the mouthpiece to the lower lip, bring head forward, and place mouthpiece to both lips as described above.

5. Make sure that arms are at about a 45-degree angle from vertical, the left arm and wrist in an unbroken line, the instrument tilted slightly from left to right. Neither arm may make contact with the body.

6. Produce a tone according to the instructions previously given. Do not begin or end the tone with a relaxed embouchure.

7. Play whole notes, followed by whole rests. Be sure not to remove the instrument from the playing position and to keep the embouchure properly tensed.

At this time a word may be said about inhaling through the corners of the lips. Be certain that the student does not relax the embouchure when taking a breath. Whole notes and whole rests may be followed, and for the same purposes of instruction, by half notes and rests, and quarter notes and rests. During the period of rests between the notes, have the student concentrate in succession upon (a) position of instrument, (b) taking breath, (c) moving the tongue to the point of contact for release, and (d) the moment to produce the tone.

8. When the facial contour is normal, the instrument will be horizontal or no more than three degrees downward from horizontal. When there is a recessive jaw, the instrument will slant downward according to the degree of recessiveness.

In this last case, be sure that students with malocclusion do not tilt the head backward to compensate for the downward angle of the instrument. When there is a protruding jaw, the instrument will slant upwards from horizontal.

Tonguing

Teach good tonguing habits. Have students say the syllables *too, tah, doo, dah,* in succession. Point out how the tongue increasingly relaxes across the tip for each syllable in succession. Start tonguing with the more relaxed *doo* or *dah,* allowing the tongue to be in a state of repose after the tone has begun. Continue to use only the legato tonguing. Save the harsher marcato and staccato tonguings until later.

Stress these suggestions:

1. The tongue must be held firmly under control during the act of tonguing.

2. The note is sounded the instant the tongue is withdrawn from the point of contact, not before or after.

3. The tongue must be in the position of release before the time for the tone to sound.

4. The tongue is never used to stop the tone. (The above four points may be checked by both instructor and student during the playing of notes followed by rests of equal value.)

5. The breath must flow smoothly through the aperture during the life of the tone; this may be done only through maintaining an equalized breath pressure. (Avoid teaching any other than the legato attack to beginners.)

6. The embouchure must remain in the same position during the life of the tone.

7. The tongue must never go between the lips during the act of tonguing.

When the distance from the top of the fleshy part of the lip to the base of the nose is ¾ inch or more, there will probably be a slight overhang of the top lip over the top teeth, even when the lips are tightly tensed. When this is so, the point of contact in tonguing should be against the inner part of the upper lip. When the opposite is true, the point of contact should be behind the upper teeth. Do not over-stress this factor. The student will probably make the initial point of contact at the place best suited to him. He will not consciously curl the tongue upward to make contact back of the upper teeth, nor will he arch it downward to make contact through to the inner part of the upper lip.

Always start to play in the middle register. The first tone the student plays is usually the one that comes easiest to him. Most often this will be second line G. Work downward to middle C from this point before working upward to third space C.

Flat intonation in the lower register is caused by a too relaxed lower lip; sharp intonation in the lower register results from a too tense upper lip. Students are inclined to play in the lower register by shifting the lower lip downward on the mouthpiece. Careful teaching will guard against this bad embouchure habit.

Sharp intonation in the upper register is usually caused by a tense lower lip; flat, by a relaxed upper lip. The student is likely to raise the position of the mouthpiece on the lips when playing in the upper registers. Guard against this tendency. Flat intonation in the upper register may be helped by increasing the intensity of the breath. This must be done before the breath is expelled through the lips; it is accomplished through elevating the tongue slightly, causing a greater concentration of breath pressure. The opposite is true when the upper intonation is sharp.

Intensity of Breath

Sharp intonation in the lower register may be corrected by decreasing the intensity of breath; flat intonation by increasing the intensity. All other things being normal, the tongue and throat should be in a state of repose for the duration of sounded tone.

You must demonstrate, or cause to have demonstrated, the true tonal aspects of the instrument. The student must hear the true singing tone of the cornet before he will have any idea of his own about tone production. When the tone is weak and anemic, cause the student to increase the in-

tensity of the breath in the manner already discussed.

When the tone is thin in the upper register, the lips are probably pressed too tightly together. This makes for a smaller vibratory surface, thereby cutting down the strength of some of the vital upper partials.

When the tone is harsh and strident, the student is probably pressing the mouthpiece too hard against the lip, causing a disarrangement of strength in the upper partials; or he may be pushing the lower jaw into the mouthpiece too much, producing the same effect.

Teach by syllabus. Make the student letter-name conscious. Be methodical in teaching scales, arpeggios, rhythmical patterns, etc.

For example, following are achievement goals for one year of class cornet instruction in fifth or sixth

grades:

The scales and tonic and dominant arpeggios of C, G, D, F, and B♭ major, two notes to the beat at 96. The minor scales and arpeggios a, d, and g minor, one note to the beat at 112.

On a given note play any of the fundamental rhythmic patterns caused through sub-dividing whole notes into halves, halves into quarters, and quarters into either eighths or sixteenths, all syncopated sub-divisions in the latter excluded.

Play any note in the middle ranges from B below the staff to G above the staff. Play tunes and band pieces based upon the above.

There is never enough instructional material of this type in the method books. You must supply the needed materials by making available original exercises and transcriptions in mimeographed form. Unless you are willing to do this, you cannot have a workable syllabus.　　　*Fine*

March-April, 1952

Criteria for Selecting Brass Solo Repertory

*Available material offers choice of numbers
musically valuable and technically appropriate*

BERNARD FITZGERALD

EACH year thousands of instrumental solos are performed by students at contests and festivals throughout the country. Discriminating adjudicators, clinicians, and teachers are frequently inclined to believe that in too many instances the educational value of this participation is open to question, both because of the music used and of the manner in which it is performed.

Two major considerations should be taken into account in the selection of solo material: (1) musical value and (2) musical and technical difficulty.

Unfortunately, many students par-

ticipating in solo contests and festivals do not perform music for which the time and effort required in study can be justified. Twenty years ago the list of available worth-while solo repertory for brass instruments was extremely limited. However, the importation of foreign publications and subsequent reprinting in this country have served to provide much additional repertory of excellent merit. Many of the solos were composed for the contests at the Paris Conservatory.

Solo repertory has been further augmented by a considerable number of significant serious compositions

by contemporary American composers, resulting in a notable change of attitude on the part of musicians in general toward the brass instruments as solo media. It should be noted here that the National Association of Schools of Music has commissioned a considerable number of sonatas and concertos for brass instruments in order to expand the existing repertory at the college level.

A considerable amount of this repertory has appeared on festival and contest lists for a number of years. However, adjudicators note that only rarely are these solos performed, in spite of the fact that the musical excellence of many of them is undoubtedly superior to the usual polka or variation type of solo. It must be acknowledged that the difficulty of the piano accompaniments may prove to be an obstacle when capable accompanists are not available, but most pianists welcome the opportunity to perform accompaniments which are musically interesting and contribute more than a token support for the soloist.

Chosen for Speed

In general, students are inclined to select solos which emphasize display of technique almost exclusively, perhaps with the belief that the adjudicator is likely to be more favorably impressed by rapid execution. Although this assumption may be valid in rare instances, the conscientious adjudicator will not be favorably influenced by mere speed in performance, particularly if this results in sacrificing clarity of execution, in producing inferior tone quality and poor intonation, or in presenting mechanical and unmusical interpretation.

It is not uncommon to receive the impression that the performer is attempting to break some speed record in a performance which at best achieves little more than "hitting the high spots." It should be remembered that technique is the means rather than the end and that the most perfect technique is that which impresses because of the apparent ease of execution rather than the frantic and laborious effort which is often accompanied by bulging cheeks, distended throat and neck muscles, and perhaps a distorted facial expression which indicates the extreme physical and mental strain of the performer.

The above does not imply that solos of a highly technical style are necessarily undesirable, but it is frequently true that this type of repertory has a very limited inherent musical value. Above all, technique should be employed as the means to the realization and achievement of the most musical performance possible.

Understanding Basic

Adjudicators are frequently disturbed by the apparent lack of musicianship indicated in student solo performances.

The contestant apparently has not realized that it is imperative for him to perform music which he is competent to understand musically and perform accurately rather than to learn a few technical tricks and execute them in a mechanical fashion which ignores musical style and interpretation. Students should be taught to realize that the worth of music is not gauged by how high it is written or how rapidly it may be performed.

Students are undoubtedly influenced by current trends in brass instrument performance by professional musicians in the popular field which emphasizes the exploitation of the extreme high register. Young players often attempt the same feats regardless of their personal limitations, both technically and musically.

Many students are handicapped in solo performance by selecting a composition which is too difficult technically or musically. In general, the grading of solo materials is likely to be based upon a consideration of the technical facility and high register required, with little or no emphasis upon the musical maturity necessary for correct style and phrasing. It has been the experience of the author to note on a contest list as being easy "Andante Cantabile" from the *Fifth Symphony* by Tschaikovsky for French horn and "Romanza Appassionata" by Weber for trombone.

Other Elements

It is unbelievable that by any stretch of the imagination the famous French horn solo by Tschaikovsky could be considered to be easy, except from the standpoints that the tempo is not fast and does not involve rapid technical execution. Such matters as tonal shading and control, phrasing, and other elements of interpretation demand considerable maturity of the soloist, a fact that can be proven by consulting a professional French hornist who is fully aware of the musical problems involved in the performance of this solo and others of the same style.

Performance difficulties of a technical nature are readily apparent, but musical difficulties which involve tone and breath control, endurance, various styles of articulation, and phrasing are frequently less obvious in a casual appraisal and evaluation in grading solo repertory. The decep-

tive appearance of the music with relation to the factors just mentioned is of particular importance regarding the solo literature assigned to inexperienced, immature players since they may be handicapped by technical or musical limitations in attempting to perform music which is too difficult.

The musical progress of the student as a soloist will often depend to a considerable extent upon the assignment of carefully graded solo materials which are well within the range of his technical and musical ability. The player who is limited technically will benefit from the study of melodic solos which emphasize the development of expressive interpretation and still do not make excessive demands in regard to range and endurance.

Although the original solo repertory of the expressive melodic style is not extensive insofar as brass instruments are concerned, ample resources are to be found in solo collections which include folk songs, hymns, art songs, lieder, and arias. Suitable repertory for all grades of difficulty is already accessible and can be utilized in providing training in expressive interpretative style.

Musical growth and discrimination are evolved only through a consistent and continuing experience with varied musical styles. It is obvious that a large percentage of high school soloists have not devoted sufficient study to the development of the *legato, cantabile* style of playing. This statement is validated by the tryouts of many college bandsmen, in which the basic principals of phrasing, style of articulation, and other aspects of interpretation are often entirely ignored. While some errors in phrasing, etc., may logically be attributed in part to nervousness under the above circumstances, careless performing habits or inadequate musical training are also indicated when interpretive markings are not given proper consideration.

It might be said that the above criticism is also valid with respect to the performance of many bands. Over-emphasis upon showmanship, even at the expense of musical integrity, would indicate the need for re-emphasizing the fact that tonal beauty and expressive interpretation are essential ingredients of every musical performance. *Fine*

The Baritone Comes of Age

*Intonation problems that have hampered
players now near to effective solution*

HUGH McMILLEN

SINCE THE MIDDLE of the nineteenth century, when the baritone horn came into general use as a solo and band instrument, players have been greatly hampered by the intonation problems inherent in its acoustical design and construction.

Many players have found that the same notes are out of tune on all makes of baritones and further that these inconsistencies in intonation follow a very definite and predictable pattern. Acoustical engineers have verified the fact that faulty pitches on all valved instruments are attributable to two factors: (a) faulty partials (modes of vibration) and (b) out-of-tune valve combinations.

Several of the most out-of-tune notes on the baritone are due to the fact that they are so-called "faulty partials" or "modes of vibration." Several notes in the overtone series of nature (bugle tones) sound either sharp or flat, and since the valved instruments are constructed on the principle of the open tube which produces this series of overtones, the partials as produced on the baritone respond in the same fashion.

Figure I shows the partials (or

Fig. I

notes) which can be produced on the open valve combination of the baritone, together with an indication as to sharpness or flatness of pitch. It should be noted that the THIRD partial is very slightly sharp—so slightly that the error is negligible on most instruments.

Figure II indicates those notes in the chromatic scale of the baritone which are sharp or flat because they are "faulty" partials.

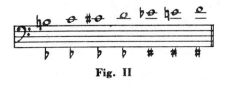

Fig. II

Other notes are faulty because of the valve combinations on which they are made. Fig. III lists these faulty valve combinations and their sharp or flat tendencies.

Valve Combination	Pitch Tendency
1-2	Moderately Sharp
1-3	Very Sharp
1-2-3	Extremely Sharp
2-3	Moderately Flat

Fig. III

Figure IV shows the chromatic scale of the baritone and all notes which blow out of tune. "V" indicates that the note is out of tune because it is produced on a faulty valve combination. "P" indicates that it is out of tune because it is a faulty partial in the overtone series of nature. *Note that only nine notes in the entire scale are actually in tune in terms of the acoustical design of the instrument.*

Acoustical engineers have experimented for years with the problem of the out-of-tune partials (Fig. II) in an effort to correct them. It was found that constrictions or expansions in bore at various places in the tube length definitely corrected the pitch on certain notes but unfortunately made other faulty partials worse in pitch. Realizing that such changes in basic design did not bring about satisfactory results, the manufacturers have produced a design which involves many compromises. What is most important, however, has been their effort to produce instruments with a maximum of flexibility so as to assist the player in his efforts to "favor" the faulty pitches.

The construction of the tubing on the valves (valve slides) has presented further acoustical problems which have been resolved by a compromise.

If the lengths of tubing on the valves (valve slides) are so constructed that the second valve lowers any open tone exactly one half-step, the first valve lowers exactly one whole step, and the third valve exactly three half-steps, then all combinations of these valves blow sharp (combinations 1-2, 2-3, 1-3, and 1-2-3). This condition exists because the total length of tubing on valve combination 1-2 (which should lower the open tone exactly one and a half steps) is not as long as it should be to lower the full one and a half steps.

Correction Devices

In other words, the combined tubing built on valves one and two as described above is not as long as would be required to lower a note a full step and a half. The error becomes increasingly greater as we progress through combinations 2-3, 1-3, and 1-2-3. The error is so great on combinations 1-3 and 1-2-3 that it has been necessary to LENGTHEN THE THIRD VALVE SLIDE so as to bring these combinations down to a pitch which could be favored nearly in tune by the player. This, of course, lowered the pitch of combination 2-3 to the point where it blows moderately flat.

Fig. IV

These compromises, then, account for the pattern of intonation difficulties illustrated in Fig. IV. It is obvious that even with a first-class instrument all but nine notes of the entire range must be favored to a greater or lesser degree in tune by the player. Several factors are very important in the production of satisfactory intonation on the instrument:

First, the player should select an instrument which is very flexible.

Second, a mouthpiece should be selected which is large enough so that it tends to minimize the sharp notes somewhat without making the flat notes flatter.

Third, the player should be aware of the devices which will help him to raise and lower the pitch of the faulty notes. Use of the syllable "TAW" to lower sharp notes and "TEE" to sharpen flat notes is important. The "TAW" opens the throat, parts the teeth, increases the resonance cavity in the mouth, and slows down the air speed slightly, resulting, of course, in flattening the pitch of a given note. The syllable "TEE" brings about just the opposite results and therefore is

effective in raising the pitch of flat notes.

It is possible that many players and teachers are unaware of these "causes" and "remedies." Perhaps there are those who know about the intonation difficulties but feel unwilling to take the time in rehearsals or in lessons to teach students these basic skills. However, if a conductor will check the intonation between baritone and piano or will cross-check pitches between the baritone and the clarinet or other instruments in the band, he will become immediately aware of the problems involved and of the necessity for concentration on this aspect of playing.

It should be understood also that "an ounce of prevention is worth a pound of cure" and that the player must be aware of the impending sharpness or flatness of notes. *A fine player must compensate as he plays the note.* It is not satisfactory to correct the pitch of a note after the note has been started. The latter practice we expect of a beginner; the former we expect of all good players.

Tone Color

At best, however, it will be found that the great amount of "favoring" which must be done to correct faulty pitches leads immediately to the next problem—that of tone color. When a player favors a flat note UP into pitch, the tone will usually become thin and strident and definitely "off-color." When the tone is favored downward, it usually becomes windy, insecure, and dull.

It would seem that the only satisfactory manner of achieving correct intonation on the baritone without sacrificing uniform tone color throughout the range must be accomplished mechanically by means of a device which will permit the player to shorten or lengthen the tubing.

About three years ago the writer designed a trigger attachment for the first valve slide of the baritone. It was developed and built by the Reynolds Band Instrument Company and was made available to the general public on the Reynolds baritone. The device proved very satisfactory in the matter of LOWERING the pitch of

BARITONE CHART by HUGH McMILLEN

(for use with the MP Tuning Slide Trigger)

INSTRUCTIONS

The instrument may be tuned in the usual manner by adjusting the lower end of the trigger rod at the point where it joins the tuning slide.

After the original tuning adjustment has been made, the trigger device permits the pitch of any note to be sharpened or flattened as needed to bring notes into good pitch.

"In" position (to sharpen notes)

"Normal position" of trigger (indicated "N")

"½ out" position (flattens slightly)

"¾ out" position (flattens considerably)

"Full out" position (flattens greatly)

*Very slightly in or out according to arrows

"In position" is approximately ½ inch shorter than "Normal"

"½ out position" is approximately ½ inch longer than "Normal"

"¾ out position" is approximately ¾ inch longer than "Normal"

"Full out position" is approximately 1 inch longer than "Normal"

These trigger positions, as far as the above described lengths are concerned, are merely guides. Individual differences in instruments, mouthpieces, and embouchures will cause these lengths to vary. The ear must be the real guide.

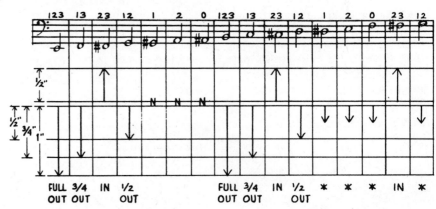

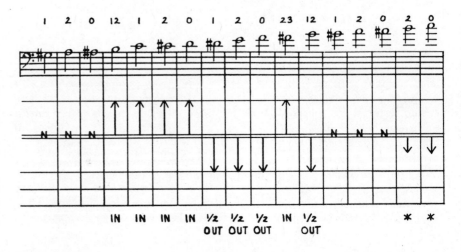

sharp notes produced on combinations involving the first valve. However, the necessity for using alternate fingerings, plus the trigger, in place of notes which blow flat on the normal fingerings left much to be desired. Experimentation with the third valve trigger indicated that it was less effective than the trigger on the first valve.

Figure V shows the notes which could not be brought into tune by means of the first valve trigger for the obvious reason that (a) the fingerings did not involve the use of the first valve or (b) the notes were flat to begin with, and since the trigger LENGTHENED the tubing, it was of no use in correcting the pitch.

Fig. V

These notes, which are among the most used on the instrument, could not be altered other than by the "favoring" methods described earlier or by the use of alternate fingerings coupled with the trigger. In the latter case the notes sounded stuffy and "off-color."

Further Experiment

Two years ago the writer began experiments with a trigger built on the tuning slide in order to permit the instrument to be tuned just as the average baritone can be tuned. The mechanism would have to be so designed that the tuning slide could be shortened so as to raise pitch, lengthened so as to lower pitch, and then automatically returned to the normal tuning position as soon as released by the hand.

After two years of research the MP Tuning Slide Mechanism was designed. A test model was demonstrated at the Mid-West Clinic in Chicago in December, 1951. The writer acknowledges the invaluable assistance of Charles Parker of Boulder, who built the first model, and Heinrich Roth of the Reynolds Company for his continuing interest and encouragement in the development and production of the mechanism commercially.

Trigger Available

The device recently became available on baritones, to be followed by application to trumpets and cornets, with recording basses and Sousaphones to follow.

Shown herewith is a chart showing the general use of the MP Tuning Slide Mechanism for baritone. It will be noted that, as in the case of the trombone slide, the trigger positions suggested are merely guides. In a final analysis *the ear must be the guide.*

September, 1952

Tips on Teaching Young Beginners

check list summarizes suggestions on getting children well started in instrumental training

BERNARD FITZGERALD

WITH THE BEGINNING of a new school year many students will be starting their training on brass instruments. The trend toward offering brass instrument classes or private lessons at the grade school level presents numerous problems for the teacher, who must take into consideration differences in the physical and mental maturity of the pupils. At this stage of development the younger pupil is much less capable of rapid advancement and must receive considerably more attention with respect to all phases of musical instruction and experience.

The suggestions which follow are not intended to represent a complete course of study or set of instructions. Rather it is hoped that they may prove helpful as a check list of problems commonly encountered in teaching young beginning students.

The Instrument

1. Instruments should be checked thoroughly to insure good mechanical operation. Valves and slides should function freely and smoothly.

2. Instruments should be checked for air leakage, especially around water key corks.

3. Both the interior and the exterior of the instrument should be thoroughly cleaned, particularly if the student has purchased a used instrument. Cleaning is desirable both from the standpoint of sanitation and for obtaining satisfactory musical results.

4. The mouthpiece should be of good design and be correctly fitted to the mouthpipe of the instrument. Avoid extremely small shallow mouthpieces which have small throat and backbore. While such a mouthpiece may aid in producing tones in the higher register, the average player is not likely to develop a full rich quality of tone using this type of mouthpiece.

5. Check the instrument for dents in the tubing. Even a rather small dent can seriously affect intonation and tone quality if the diameter of the tube is small.

6. The instrument should blow freely without excessive resistance.

Some of the common problems in this field are as follows:

1. Unsatisfactory action of valves or slides. Such a condition may be due to need for cleaning or lubrication, to weak valve springs, to trombone slides sprung out of alignment, or to damaged valves or valve casings. Oil or cold cream is usually recommended by the manufacturer. It is not advisable to use saliva as a lubricant due to the corrosion which often results from the acidity of the saliva.

2. Dented or bent stem of the mouthpiece or failure to keep the throat and backbore of the mouthpiece clean.

It is advisable for the teacher to keep a cleaning rod, a flexible cleaning brush, a mouthpiece brush, and soft clean cloths at hand for routine care and checking on the condition of the instrument. The young beginner has more than enough problems confronting him at the outset without being given the handicap of a poor instrument in unsatisfactory playing condition. It is completely unreasonable to expect a beginning student to achieve satisfactory musical results using equipment which the more mature player would condemn as being impossible.

Posture and Position

1. Emphasize the necessity of maintaining good posture, correct position of the instrument, and correct hand position.

2. Stress the importance of not moving the head or the instrument while playing since this frequently interferes with tone production.

3. Check frequently to insure that the player maintains approximately the same position of head in relation to mouthpiece position, regardless of the register which is being played.

Common problems observed in this field are as follows:

1. Failure to maintain good posture and playing position of the instrument because of fatigue. Plan for frequent short periods of rest from playing during the class to provide adequate relaxation.

2. Holding the instrument in an extreme downward or sidewise direction because of incorrect height of the music stand or incorrect height of the player's chair.

3. Faulty valve or slide action. Frequently this is due to incorrect hand position or to failure to depress the valve with a positive and vertical downward pressure, causing the valve to bind against the valve casing due to side pressure. Sidewise pressure may cause the trombone slide to bind and may eventually spring the slide out of alignment or damage it because of wear.

Basic Attitudes and Techniques

1. Establish the correct tonal concept and continue to emphasize the importance of beautiful tone.

a. Demonstrate the desired tone quality characteristic of the instrument.

b. Arrange frequent playing demonstrations by advanced students or by members of the class.

c. Supplement the above by playing good recordings which illustrate the desired tone quality of the instrument.

d. Use a tape recorder frequently as a testing device to make students aware of tonal deficiencies and errors in performance.

2. Emphasize the importance of pitch accuracy from the very beginning.

a. Use singing by the students as a means of relating pitch accuracy to instrument performance.

b. Teach students to listen constantly as they play.

c. Teach students how to listen to improve pitch.

d. Employ tonal matching between two or more players to increase awareness of differences in pitch and quality of tone.

3. Emphasize that playing a brass instrument is not difficult if done correctly.

a. Prepare the student for each new problem so that the trial and error method is eliminated as much as possible.

b. Demonstrate the relationship of a clear *buzz* produced with the mouthpiece to the sound produced with the instrument. This is more effectively achieved with cornet, trumpet, French horn, and mellophone mouthpieces.

4. Present instructions regarding embouchure, breathing, and articulation in a simple and direct manner, employing a vocabulary which is within the understanding of the child.

a. Avoid lengthy and detailed explanations which involve highly technical terminology and vocabulary.

b. Frequently re-emphasize the fundamentals of tone production.

c. Postpone detailed explanations of these elements of performance until the experience and maturity of the pupil will give genuine meaning and comprehension to details.

Common problems in this field are the following:

1. Starting on wrong tone; often due to inadequate breath support, faulty conception of the correct pitch, or incorrect embouchure tension.

2. Starting the tone below the correct pitch; due to too loose embou-

chure, tonguing between the lips.

3. Flatting pitch at end of phrase or sustained tone; usually caused by inadequate breath, lack of breath support, or relaxing the embouchure before the tone ceases.

4. Sharping the pitch at the end of a phrase or sustained tone; caused by arching the tongue in the mouth or stopping the tone with the tongue.

5. Tonal distortion; frequently due to overblowing, violent release of the breath by the tongue, faulty embouchure formation, or failure to coordinate the above factors.

6. Inaccurate intonation may be due to any of several causes but usually involves a combination of the following: failure to listen and adjust pitch of each note, insufficient breath support, and incorrect embouchure tension.

7. Tendency to flat in pitch on ascending line because of too little change in embouchure tension and insufficient breath support.

8. Tendency to relax embouchure tension too rapidly in descending passages, resulting in flatness of pitch.

Teaching Procedures

1. Teach systematic counting as a part of playing technique as soon as the basic techniques of tone production are under control.

2. "Make haste slowly" insofar as rhythm patterns and notation problems are concerned.

3. Provide extensive amounts of music which involves only simple notation and rhythm problems to encourage the pupil to gain facility in reading music of limited technical difficulty.

4. Have pupils practice under the supervision of the teacher until they have acquired adequate experience and control of the fundamentals of performance to be capable of doing constructive individual practice at home.

5. Give guidance to the student as to how and what to practice.

6. Provide creative opportunities and augment printed materials by having students use existing rhythmic vocabulary and playing range in creating pieces, etudes, and eventually duets which will be performed in class.

7. Stimulate students to achieve the best possible performance at all

times; they are usually capable of more effective performance providing goals are within their capacity.

8. Be more concerned about tone quality, pitch, rhythm, and basic musicianship than technical facility at this stage.

9. Recognize and be sympathetic to the problems resulting from fatigue, short attention span, and physical and psychological factors,

and provide musical experience which is both stimulating and rewarding to the child.

10. Make liberal use of folk songs, hymns, and easy selections by master composers to form a foundation for musical taste and understanding.

11. Provide musical experiences which will develop basic musicianship in regard to phrasing, expression, style, and articulation.

12. Develop a vocabulary of basic rhythmic patterns common to music suitable for young players.

13. Avoid overemphasis on public performance as a primary objective.

14. Stress small ensemble participation as recreation, both in school and at home.

15. Provide the basic foundation for further study in instrumental music.   FINE

October, 1952

Brass Choirs Have Educational Values

*Artistic proficiency, discipline, and satisfaction
gained in ensemble participation and training*

ERNEST GLOVER

THE BRASS ENSEMBLE, perhaps better termed the brass choir, is an organization that has a bright and useful future in this musical nation of ours.

Instrumental teachers and directors should, I believe, examine the possibility of organizing and developing such groups in their schools, not as mere side issues but as real functioning units. Under gifted direction they can provide untold training values to brass players and can become performing groups that artistically and musically will command a place of high respect among other musical organizations.

These convictions are a result of my own personal experience in this field as the founder and conductor of the Cincinnati Conservatory of Music brass ensembles. From the beginning I was fortunate in enjoying the blessing of a cooperative and understanding administration. The Brass Ensemble was properly set up as an accredited and required course of study for brass instrument players interested in a bachelor of music degree and in playing careers.

The second year that the course was offered, registration increased so much that four groups were formed.

Now, as some members of the top group are graduated each year, I can immediately replace them with equally well-trained players from other groups.

Merit System

As groups were added to the course, I made it clear that musical merit would always supersede seniority in the placement in the various groups. To this I added one proviso, the policy of never making a change in Group A, the top-ranking one, in the case of a student who had served faithfully and with musical proficiency. I am a firm believer in the policy that a player who fulfills his tasks well should never feel the unhappiness of insecurity. Of course, inefficiency is not tolerated and need not be with the competition that exists. Such a situation, I have found, makes for fine discipline.

In regard to discipline, I believe that fine musical discipline cannot be achieved without first securing disciplined conduct in the organization. Students who learn self-discipline make the most valuable players.

We must not overlook the most important phase conducive to good discipline—the music we play, good music that gives the young people

the best experience in brass performance. Fortunately, at our concerts we play to musical audiences; the desire for showmanship at the expense of musicianship is therefore easy to avoid. I do not wish to give the impression that I oppose showmanship, especially when it is governed by good musical taste. The type of showmanship that I am sure most of us abhor is that used as a subterfuge for inefficient musical performance; in other words, as a substitute for musical integrity.

Choir Type

I regard and treat the brass ensemble much more as a brass choir than as a brass band. In this attitude I am influenced by the literature we play, the style of playing, and the instrumentation. In a school like the Cincinnati Conservatory of Music I must not overlook one of the main original objects of the brass ensemble, that of preparing the more gifted players for the exacting and virtuoso type of playing required in the brass choirs of the professional symphony orchestras.

Actually, the acme of brass performance, both as to tone quality and virtuosity, is to be found in the brass sections of the world's greatest symphony orchestras. The brass ensemble is truly the finest training ground for the quality, delicacy, and tremendous dynamic range that symphony conductors demand. Such training, second only to private lessons, is extremely important because it places responsibility on each player to such an extent that any mistake, poor intonation or faulty blending can hardly escape the attention of the conductor and the other members of the group. Such exposed playing is almost indispensable, in my opinion, to the development of that sure-fire confidence that is a MUST to any player with symphonic ambitions. With the necessary exception of the baritones, I recommend that brass ensembles follow as nearly as possible the instrumentation of the symphony brass choir.

The instrumentation that I find most useful, and that I encourage composers to use in writing for the brass ensemble, is 3 trumpets (doubled because of embouchure demands), 4 French horns, 3 or 4 trombones, 2 baritones, 1 or 2 tubas, and the required timpani and percussion. Rarely are my groups composed of more than 18 or 19 brass players.

While our programs are constructed mostly with compositions that require this instrumentation, we permit ourselves to be flexible, often playing numbers calling for a lesser instrumentation. Then the character of the composition will determine whether, for purposes of greater sonority, the parts will be doubled.

Conductors should be careful not to over-instrumentate their groups. Aside from the highly important matter of balance, having too many people play the same part tends to destroy individual responsibility and the initiative and personal satisfaction that keep brass players so intrigued and enthusiastic about this medium.

The literature available to the brass ensemble is increasing quite materially. To Robert D. King, editor and publisher of "Music for Brass," North Easton, Massachusetts, I must give great credit for the building up of the finest and largest single brass library in the United States. He has done heroic research culminating in his ultimate publication of works of the sixteenth and seventeenth centuries as well as many contemporary works of excellence.

The importance of proper organization and careful training of the brass ensemble can hardly be overestimated, for in these factors lies the difference between success and mediocrity. Under no circumstances should the brass ensemble be treated as a stepchild or just an organization within an organization. Success requires concentrated effort, for the virtuoso playing required by a distinguished and extremely difficult repertoire is achieved only by tireless rehearsals and the proper esprit de corps. To be assured of this the members of the brass ensemble must feel that their group is just as important in its field as any other musical body.

Of one thing I am assured, and that is that there is a place for the brass ensemble in all schools. When the brass ensemble is brought to the state of efficiency and finesse of which it is capable, it will gain the respect of the most severe critics and will command the admiration of those sincerely interested in the greatest of all the arts, music.

SUGGESTIONS FOR BRASS ENSEMBLE LIBRARY

Composer	Title	Publisher
(For complete or fairly complete instrumentation)		
Ralph Dale Miller	Sinfonietta	Belwin, Inc.
Richard Arnell	Ceremonial and Flourish	Assoc. Music Pub.
Rudolph Ganz	Brassy Prelude	Mills, Inc.
Ulysses Kay	Suite for Brass Choir	Loan or rental Amer. Music Center
Debussy	Fanfare, Le Martyre de Saint Sebastien	Elkan Vogel
Paul Bonneau	Fanfare	United Music Pub. 1 Montague St., London, England
Paul Hindemith	Concert Music for Piano, Brass and Two Harps	Assoc. Music Pub.
(For lesser instrumentation)		
Ingolf Dahl	Music for Brass Instruments	Witmark
Jaromir Weinberger	Concerto for Timpani and Brass	B.H.B.
Nicolai Berezowsky	Brass Suite for Seven Instruments	Mills
Marcel Dupre	Poem Heroique for Organ and Brass	H. W. Gray Co.
Wallingford Riegger	Nonet for Brass	Assoc. Music Pub.
Wallingford Riegger	Music for Brass Choir	Mercury

Perhaps the most controversial piece ever written for brass; written on tone clusters for 10 trumpets, 4 horns, 10 trombones, 2 tubas, timpani, and cymbals. Score can be procured, but parts are available on rental.

British Works

(Available through Robert D. King)

Gustav Holst	Moorside Suite	R. Smith and Son, London
Cyril Jenkins	Life Divine, Tone Poem	R. Smith and Son
Mozart	Fantasia	R. Smith and Son

Composed for mechanical organ in 1791. Arranged by Sir Malcolm Sargent for British brass band competition in 1946. The above works, like all British brass band journals, are written for all instruments in the treble clef, the only exception being the bass trombone, which is in bass clef. However, these works are worth the time required for transcription. ▪

Problems Influencing Trombone Intonation

THOMAS BEVERSDORF

LIKE THE MEMBERS of the violin family, the trombone is capable of approximating perfect intonation. However, any musical instrument which produces tones that are partials of a fundamental note of the overtone series will have inherent intonation problems.

The trombone is based on the overtone series. In first position, pedal Bb is the fundamental or first partial, and each tone which can be played in first position and is above pedal Bb is an upper partial of the Bb overtone series.

When the slide is moved to second position, the instrument is no longer a Bb instrument; it becomes an A instrument. Like an open French horn in A with no valves, the pedal A is the fundamental, and each note above A which can be played in second position is an upper partial of the fundamental A.

The same principle applies to third position with pedal Ab as the fundamental. For instance, the notes in Fig. I may be played in sixth position with pedal F as the fundamental, making the trombone into an F instrument temporarily.

Fig. I

The natural French horn in F with no valves was very badly out of tune, and the notes in Fig. I are far from "true." The reason for the poor tuning is two-fold. First, and of most importance, the overtone series incurs natural, or "hunting horn," tuning, which sounds out of tune to our ears. Second, the tubing of the instrument is not in the correct proportion for a trombone in F.

Instrument manufacturers are confronted with the impossibility of making the perfectly tuned instrument. However, they are capable of altering given notes at the expense of other notes. The notes of the fifth partial of the "natural" scale of each position are the worst offenders and are excessively flat. The instrument

manufacturer can correct this, however, if he is willing to sacrifice the intonation of the upper partials.

One method of correcting the fifth partial is to sharpen the notes of the sixth partial. For instance, the fifth partial of the overtone series on pedal Bb is D¹ (above the bass clef staff). If D is tuned according to this method, F¹ (sixth partial) is slightly sharp. E¹, Eb¹, D¹ fourth position and Db¹ fifth position are also sharp and progressively worse. It is necessary to have the D of the fifth partial in tune, for one cannot sharpen first position. If F¹ sixth partial first position is sharp, it must be altered by "lipping" or even lowering the slide slightly.

It is generally accepted that D¹ sixth partial must be played in long or flat fourth position. (See Fig. II.)

Fig. II

D¹ in fourth position is the sixth partial of the overtone series of pedal G. The sixth partial has been distorted in order to correct the fifth partial. As a result, the positions of the sixth partial are actually slightly longer than the normal positions of the trombone, as indicated in Fig. III.

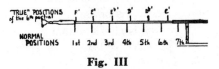

Fig. III

The sixth partial varies on each make of instrument and even between models of the same make. On certain standard instruments F¹ is sharp, and all the lower series have sharp sixth partials. On other instruments the F¹ is flat; yet, due to the fact that the sixth partial has longer positions than normal, the sixth partial positions soon overtake and pass the normal positions and are sharp in the lower reaches of the slide. (See Fig. IV.)

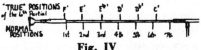

Fig. IV

Incidentally, some trombones with D¹ in tune and a sixth partial series that is flat or even in tune on F¹ play stuffy, at least in the upper range, or lack tonal resonance, probably as the result of overcorrection of intonation. Of course, overcorrection of intonation need not be the only reason for undesirable blowing or sounding features of an instrument.

The point to note regarding intonation of the sixth partial is that in some instances Eb¹ needs alteration the same as D¹ fourth position but to a less extent. In rare cases, particularly with large bore trombones, it may be necessary to alter E¹ slightly. These two alterations are never mentioned in instruction books because some trombones are relatively in tune on the E, and the Eb alteration ranges down to an almost imperceptible degree.

The seventh partial offers difficulties which are more extreme than the sixth partial. Fortunately, these difficulties, due to the extremity of their character, are more widely acknowledged. Most instruction books include the alterations to normal positions as a matter of course. This is the partial which begins in first position with an unusable Ab¹ and progresses down through G¹ second position, F#¹ third position, and F¹ fourth position, all of which must be played very short due to their inherent flatness:

A diagram of the "true" positions of the seventh partial might look like this:

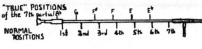

Fig. V

It may be observed that the positions of the seventh partial as illustrated in Fig. V get progressively longer. This is characteristic of the seventh partial on most trombones just as it is of the fifth partial; however, the place where the position of the seventh partial and the normal position coincide is so far down the slide that it is of little significance. The point to note is that all notes played in the seventh partial, G^1, $F\sharp^1$, F^1 fourth positions and E^1 fifth position, must be in very short positions.

Theoretically, the positions of the eighth partial or high B♭ in first position, A second position, A♭ third position, etc., are in tune. It is possible to upset this "true" partial, however, by certain methods of altering the lower partials; or if an instrument has a flat high B♭, it may be that the mouthpiece extends too far out of the horn. This will affect all the partials, particularly the upper partials; it can be remedied by thinning the mouthpiece shank or opening the mouthpiece receiver of the horn.

However, this remedy can upset and lessen the resistance of the horn and may prove a greater handicap to good tone production than the flat eighth partial would be to intonation. High B♭, if flat, can be played in third position rather than run the risk of ruining a good horn or a good mouthpiece. The other positions can be shortened as need be. However, a good horn should be in tune on the eighth partial.

The ninth partial, high C in first position, B second position, B♭ third position, A fourth position, etc., must be played slightly long. The partial is inherently sharp to a very slight degree.

The tenth partial, high D in first position, C♯ second position, C third position, B fourth position, etc., has the same characteristic weakness that its lower octave fifth partial would have if left uncorrected. High D first position is unalterably flat. C♯ should be nearly in tune, and high C in third position may be slightly sharp and may need to be altered.

There are numerous other factors which influence intonation of all brass instruments. Good intonation on the trombone is simpler when the player has an awareness of all factors.

Temperature changes, which result in contraction and expansion of the metal of the instrument, will certainly alter the intonation. Metal expands when cold and contracts when hot. A cold piece of tubing is longer than a warm one, thereby making for a lower pitch. As the trombone warms up, the metal contracts (the equivalent to closing the tuning slide), and

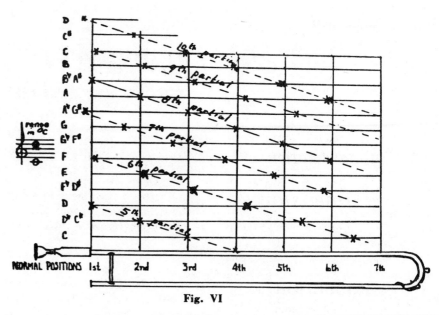

Fig. VI

the instrument becomes higher in pitch. Therefore, very warm weather will make brass instruments higher.

Strings Different

In orchestral playing the strings of the string instruments soften with heat, thereby flattening their pitch considerably. Within an orchestra, the strings will be low when the winds are high and vice versa. This situation necessitates a larger degree of compensation in tuning than one would expect.

Also, temperature affects the trombone to the point that a soloist may start a solo with a cold horn that is in tune and soon find himself playing consistently sharp. If the temperature is low and a piece of music must be started on a cold horn (which is most undesirable), it is better to tune slightly flat with the hope that the instrument will correct itself as it warms up. Perhaps one can find a convenient rest to alter the tuning during the selection.

Most trombonists find that in music some passages will move in such a line that the lip itself will alter certain notes. The trombonist's system of tone production will influence which way certain notes in a given passage will fall as to pitch. One performer will play an awkward passage with correct placement of positions, and certain notes will be flat. Another performer will play the same passage with correct placement of positions, and the same notes will be sharp. This situation necessitates thorough familiarization with the passage in question, awareness of the

tone production characteristics as applied to this passage, and, above all else, careful listening. Then the motor responses should "jell" to the point that the passage is played with exactly the same response each time.

Tuning Slide

Extreme extension of the tuning slide will alter the entire partial system of the trombone to the point that good intonation is impossible unless, of course, the trombonist habitually plays this way and his reflexes are trained to adjust accordingly. Training of this type, however, will make performance at a near normal pitch level unsatisfactory.

Many trombonists find that, according to their method of tone production, the pitch will vary considerably at different dynamic levels. Some trombonists go sharp when playing loudly and flat when playing softly. Others go flat when playing loudly and sharp when playing softly. Still other trombonists who play with relatively good intonation at medium dynamic level go either flat or sharp at both dynamic extremes. These characteristics of intonation are the result of the method or methods of tone production employed and are highly individual. Again, let it be said that the first and immediate remedy is to listen—and compensate accordingly.

In conclusion, it may be of help to give a comprehensive diagram of characteristic "normal" positions as compared to the "true" position on a "normally" tuned trombone with a caution to the trombonist to listen —listen—listen. FINE

BRASS
MOUTHPIECES

A Symposium
I

Standardization of Measurements Materials—Selections—Variations

Dimensional Characteristics of Brass Mouthpieces

RENOLD SCHILKE

INTRODUCTION

In this symposium on mouthpieces of brass instruments The INSTRU-MENTALIST presents for the first time the salient eight measurements of 213 different trumpet-cornet mouthpieces and a discussion of the purposes and functions of each part.

ANY DISCUSSION of brass mouthpieces is always of interest to players of brass instruments as well as to directors of school bands and orchestras. Invariably, a discussion among brass experts starts with an expression that such and such a mouthpiece is the best, the poorest, or the producer of best results for one particular player. The argument that follows is mainly based on conjecture. Very seldom are the opinions or "conclusions" backed by sound reality or scientific evidence.

In order to clarify the situation let us first identify the parts of a mouthpiece so that we may have a ready vocabulary. Figure A shows a trumpet mouthpiece that has been cut in half. No. 1 is the RIM, the convex*

*CONVEX—curving outward, i.e., the outside of a ball
**CONCAVE—curving inward, i.e., the inside of a ball

portion of the upper part of the mouthpiece. No. 2 is the CUP, the concave** portion as viewed from above, which is located just below the rim. No. 3 is the SHOULDER of the throat, a convex surface as viewed from above, blending the cup into the throat.

No. 4 is the THROAT, generally cylindrical in shape and having straight or almost straight sides. The throat extends in length from perhaps 1/8 inch or less to as much as 3/4 inch. No. 5 is the BACKBORE, that part of the mouthpiece which extends from the throat to the lower end of the mouthpiece.

No. 6 is the WIDTH of the cup, its diameter on the *inside* of the rim. No. 7 is the outside DIAMETER OF THE SHANK at the very bottom or end where the shank makes contact with the mouthpipe. The MOUTH-PIPE, shown in part in illustration B is the tubing inside the mouthpiece receiver pipe which abuts, or should abut, the shank end of the mouthpiece. In illustration B is shown a common deficiency in which there is an appreciable gap between the end of the shank of the mouthpiece and the beginning of the mouthpipe. The

two should meet. To correct the deficiency, the shank is turned down somewhat on a lathe so that it will be small enough to meet the end of the mouthpipe. A marked improvement in the playing of the instrument is thereby effected.

Figure L shows a cut-away section of a mouthpiece and receiver pipe. Notice the substantial overlap from the end of the shank to the mouthpipe. This is a serious defect. Though it does not show a gap between the end of the shank and the beginning of the mouthpipe as in B, it is possible that if the shortcoming of B is remedied, the present overlap as shown in L remains.

The diameter of the inside of the mouthpipe at the point where it meets the mouthpiece shank is from .325 to .345 inches on most trumpets; however, since some shanks measure only .275 to .300 there is bound to be an overlap from the shank to the mouthpipe of .030 inches. This is the shortcoming shown at L.

In the correction of this shortcoming it is not desirable to ream out the shank with a reamer as this would change the contour too far up into the backbore. It is preferable to taper the shank opening with a cutting tool only about 3/8 inch. Thus the tapering remedies the shortcoming of L

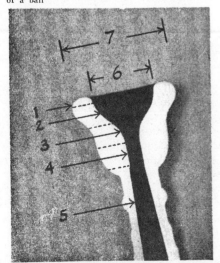

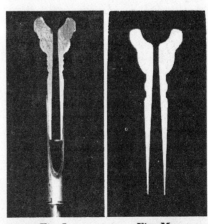

Fig. L   Fig. M

without appreciably altering the backbore of the mouthpiece.

Let us consider next the rim of the mouthpiece. Illustration A shows a mouthpiece with a desirable amount of roundness of the rim; it is especially well suited to beginners but is also used by many professional symphony players.

The narrower rim shown at C would give one more flexibility, such as demanded in playing arpeggios and intervals, than the rim shown in A. Yet flexibility is also dependent on another factor—the shape or outline of the rim curvature. Thus two mouthpieces may have an equally wide rim, but one will have a higher surface at the edge of the cup as shown in D, which produces the feeling of a narrow rim and yet has almost its flexibility, but when pressure is applied, the lips contact a relatively larger surface.

Thus this rim is a working compromise between the cushion feeling of the wide rim and the flexibility of the narrow rim. Obviously, such a mouthpiece is best suited to a player who tends to use more than ordinary pressure or who plays for long stretches of time as is the case with dance band players.

Experimental evidence and experience suggest that the higher the inner portion of the rim, as shown in D, the more accurate the attack is in both pianissimo and fortissimo playing. However, flexibility is sacrificed somewhat thereby. As the inner edge or "bite" becomes rounded, as in F, the more difficult become the attacks, but the greater is the flexibility.

Let us consider the cup next. A desirable cup for all-around performance is shown in A. If precision of attack is the major requisite, the cup shown in M is preferable. This cup produces a stridency of tone that is piercing. It is important that a cup of this shape have a high shoulder at the throat (No. 3 in A) so that

the shoulder becomes more convex and less like a second cup, or duo-cup.

Mouthpiece H is an old French Besson (there's also an English Besson); I is the famous Arban's cornet mouthpiece; J is a modern mouthpiece of the former first trumpet of the Chicago Symphony, Mr. Llewellyn; K is the cornet mouthpiece of the renowned Jules Levy. It is interesting to compare these. Note especially the varying shapes of the backbores of G and H and the varying cups of I and K as compared to the others.

The wider or more open we make the shoulder of the throat, the mellower becomes the tone. In I the throat and cup shape combine into one long cup similar to that in a French horn mouthpiece. which, if used on the trumpet, is colorless. It is possible to achieve a judicious combination with the shallow cup which aids the lip and still avoid the stridency of tone usually produced by such a mouthpiece as F. This is done by opening the shoulder somewhat as shown in E, resulting in the double-cup originally designed by L. A. Schmidt of Cologne about seventy years ago for use in the low F, E, E♭, and D trumpets used by R. Strauss. These latter instruments, incidentally but significantly, were played in the upper harmonics like a French horn. The double-cup mouthpiece makes for easier control in the difficult high passages.

As shown in the dimensions of mouthpieces by Rohner, the average throat diameter uses a 27 drill size. Small throats of 30 or even smaller and extremely large throats of 18 or 19 are used by some players, but these extremes should be avoided by the average player.

A throat made with a drill No. 27 having straight sides for as much as ¾ inch will tend to cause the player to play sharp in the higher register.

On the other hand, if the straight sides of the throat are too short, the player will tend to play flat in the high register. Thus intonational tendencies, either sharp or flat, can usually be corrected in the mouthpiece. A lot of instruments are blamed for poor intonation when the fault actually lies in the mouthpiece.

If the backbore flares out rather rapidly, the tone will be full but slightly more difficult to control. If the backbore becomes straighter, with less flaring out, the tone becomes thinner but more easily controlled; at the same time the blowing resistance is increased.

Needless to say, the shape of the outside of the mouthpiece, provided there is adequate thickness of metal in the wall, has nothing to do with its playing qualities.

None Ideal

Finally, it is a physical impossibility to provide all of the ideal features in any one mouthpiece; at best, a superior mouthpiece is an intelligent compromise of the major factors. The performer, thus, should strive for the optimum combination of factors. These will vary with the individual and the demands of the job and its playing standards. As a whole, one should favor tone quality and accurate intonation to ease of playing high notes unless the latter is a "must." No mouthpiece is perfect, and no mouthpiece will sound better than the player behind it. The player is still the major variable.

Extremes should be avoided whenever possible. This does not mean that everyone should use an average size mouthpiece, but an average size should be the most common one for beginners.

Excessive experimentation on the part of the player should be avoided; yet all players will benefit from careful thinking and trials of different mouthpieces.

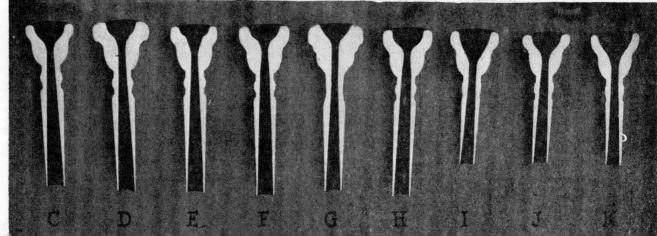

C   D   E   F   G   H   I   J   K

Standardization and Classification of Brass Mouthpieces

TRAUGOTT ROHNER

TEACHERS, MANUFACTURERS and players of brass instruments are agreed that there is an urgent need for standardization and classification of mouthpieces. It is high time, they believe, that we apply scientific measures to a subject long engulfed in surmises, inconsistencies and hocus-pocus. We need to replace fancy with facts, guessing by knowing and inexcusable inaccuracies with scientifically accurate measurements.

The numbering and lettering systems used for brass mouthpieces are almost as numerous as the number of manufacturers. Thus it is not possible to select mouthpieces intelligently. Every brass teacher tells his pupils to buy a "good" mouthpiece, but who among the experts can tell what a good mouthpiece is in terms of dimensions? None knows what an "average" mouthpiece is or in what specific ways one varies from another.

In fact, there are professional players who hang on to a certain superior mouthpiece as if it were made of platinum because they have not been able to find another like this one superior model or have not been able to have it duplicated with satisfactory closeness of tolerances. The present study purports to clarify this situation.

One must realize the importance of small variations in dimensions of a mouthpiece. The ear hears a small difference that the naked eye is not able to discern. Of the eight measurements made on each of 213 different trumpet-cornet mouthpieces in this study, not one can be made with any degree of reliability by the senses of sight or touch. Nevertheless, these minute differences are of considerable importance to the discriminating teacher and performer. A thousandth of an inch variation can probably not be discerned even by the ear, but ten-thousandths or a hundredth of an inch, as small as this is, usually can. Regardless, all of us connected with the world of brass music will benefit if we can reduce the measurements of mouthpieces to the simplicity of measurable factors. The finality of accurate and objectively determined figures will therefore come as a godsend.

Crucial Measurements

What are the crucial measurements of a brass mouthpiece? The answer is that every measurement from the rim down through the mouthpiece is vitally significant. We have selected eight measurements, two of which combine, to provide us with seven measurements for each mouthpiece. The only measurement of significance that is not included is that of the backbore, the inside of the shank below the throat of the mouthpiece. It was omitted because its variations are difficult to measure and because this is the only factor in the trumpet mouthpiece that is innately different from the cornet.

Contrary to some opinions, the same dimensions, other than backbore, can and usually are used in both trumpet and cornet mouthpieces. For example, Vincent Bach, who has the largest assortment of catalogued mouthpieces, makes cornet and trumpet mouthpieces alike from the throat up. This does not mean that a teacher or a player will use the same cup, etc., with both his trumpet and his cornet, but that he can do so if he wishes.

The seven measurements are as follows:

(1) the diameter of the throat;

(2) the volume and shape of the cup—two measurements used for this one category;

(3) the diameter of the cup near the top at a point where the curvature of the cup meets the curvature of the rim;

(4) the "bite" or inner edge of the rim;

(5) the curvature of the top of the rim;

(6) the width or thickness of the rim; and

(7) the impression width, the diameter of the high point of the rim, the part that first makes contact with the lips.

In preparation for the experiment, each mouthpiece manufacturer was asked to send one sample of each of his different kinds of trumpet-cornet mouthpieces. As a result, 213 different ones were submitted and measured. Eight are made of plastic; all the others are brass.

All are the usual round shape at the rim except for the two Cauffman hyperbolic ones sold by Selmer, which have an oblong (hyperbolic) shape. The Buescher duo-cup (two-cup) mouthpieces have the lower part of the cup into the throat enlarged to such a degree that it resembles another cup. To a lesser degree, most trumpet-cornet mouthpieces are two-cupped.

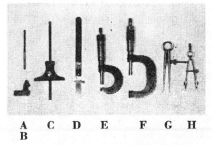

A   C   D   E   F G H
B

Left to right—left top, drill; lower left, radius gage; two depth gages; a 0-1-inch micrometer; a 1-inch to 2-inch micrometer; an inside caliper; and a compass.

Several measuring tools were used. The opening of the throat was measured by the shank end of a set of Morse Twist Drills, which were numbered from 1 to 60. Only the drills from 19 through 29 were required for the study. Vincent Bach was kind enough to lend the set of drills, one of which is shown as A. The drill numbers under T in the chart indicate the largest drill shank which will go through the throat of a mouthpiece.

To measure the volume and shape of the cup two different depth gages were used. The gage at C is made by Lufkin; it is No. 511 in the catalog and includes two differently priced tools. The rod is 3/16 inch wide. Depth gage D, ½ inch wide, is ideally suited for measuring trumpet-cornet mouthpieces. Each gage measures the depth of the cup at a specified width (3/16 and ½ inch) down from the rim. The rod goes into the cup, and the crossbar rests on the rim.

All the tools used in this study except one (the half-inch depth gage) can be purchased from any retail precision tool house. Since it is not possible to procure a depth gage which is a half-inch wide, The INSTRUMENTALIST has had it manufactured as a special service to readers. A postcard mailed to The INSTRUMENTALIST, Evanston, Ill. 60204, will bring complete information on it.

Micrometers

At E is a micrometer capable of measuring up to one inch; the micrometer at F, which measures from one to two inches, is used to measure the outside diameter of the rim. Though each of these is graded in thousandths of an inch, the measurements are recorded to the nearest hundredth of an inch. For example, a micrometer reading of .275 through .284 was rounded off to .28.

The spread of the prongs of inside caliper G and divider H were measured with micrometer E. Caliper G is used to determine the diameter of the cup just below the inside of the rim; divider H can be used for the same thing, but in this study it was used only to measure the width of the impression of the circle; this is the highest point of the mouthpiece, the part that first comes in contact with the lips.

At B is a radius gage used to measure the roundness of the top of the rim and the roundness or sharpness of the "bite," the inside edge of the rim. Set 77C by Lufkin was used in this experiment. If there is no precision tool dealer in your area, you may obtain names and addresses of suppliers by request from The INSTRUMENTALIST.

A teacher or player need not buy expensive micrometers. For the throat measurements a set of Morse Twist drills from 19 through 29 or a less expensive set will do. The depth gage being offered by The INSTRUMENTALIST not only serves as a depth gage but can be used to measure the diameter of the cup and the impression width of the rim. The half-inch rule of the depth gage has a chart printed on the back which converts sixty-fourths of an inch to hundredths of an inch so that direct comparisons can be made with the hundredths-of-an-inch measurements on the accompanying chart.

Minimum Needs

Some teachers may prefer to omit the radius gages, but there is no other way to measure curvatures accurately. The writer recommends the following sequence, based on importance and cost, in ordering the minimum measuring tools: (1) the INSTRUMENTALIST gage, (2) a divider, (3) drill Nos. 19-29; drill blanks preferred; (4) the 3/16-inch width depth gage; and (5) the radius gages. The inside caliper, about four inches in length, and two micrometers should complete the set of additional tools. A magnifying lens and a spotlight were also used in this study.

Music teachers and performers have not been in the habit of buying measuring tools for mouthpieces; yet they should buy at least a minimum set. If all mouthpieces of a certain number could be depended upon to remain the same at all times, the need would not be so acute. Furthermore, there are many mouthpieces of foreign make or of second or third line instruments that are not included in the chart and therefore will need to be measured.

As to the reliability of the results of the study, we can only say that every effort has been made to assure maximum accuracy. Each measurement was made twice at least—once by the writer and a second time by L. Cerny or William English.

Perhaps the single most important fact to remember when measuring and making comparisons is that mouthpieces of the same make and number often vary considerably over a period of time. When a shaper or other tool used in making mouthpieces is sharpened, some of the metal has to be removed, and the resultant mouthpieces from this tool will not be

the same as the ones previously made. The longer the tools are used, the oftener they will be sharpened and the greater will be the eventual differences. Molded plastic mouthpieces do not vary in this way. If people who buy mouthpieces insist, it is possible that manufacturers will maintain much closer tolerances.

Interpreting the Table

Column T in the table of statistics indicates the Throat measurements, the narrowest part of the hole. The number of the largest drill shank that will go through the throat is given in this column. One should bear in mind that the smaller the number of the drill the larger is the hole; for example, drill 19 is larger than drill 20.

V consists of three columns of figures, indicating cup depth and width and their combination into volume. The first of these three shows the number of sixty-fourths of an inch that the 3/16 depth gage can be inserted into the cup, down from the top of the rim. The second column shows the number of sixty-fourths the ½-inch depth gage can be inserted. and the third column figures equal the sum of the first two columns divided by 2. It is this third composite figure which is used for the single number indicating cup volume and which is later used in the code figure.

Column D lists the diameter of the cup at a point near its top where the curvature of the cup meets the curvature of the rim. One might call this the inside rim diameter. It is not always easy to locate the exact point where the two curves meet.

Column C shows the curvature of the rim. The numbers are in sixty-fourths; specifically, they indicate a circle whose radius is that many sixty-fourths of an inch. Similarly column B for Bite, the inside edge of the rim, is also in sixty-fourths of an inch for a circle having this radius. Obviously, the larger the number the larger is the curve and the larger is the circle.

Column R lists the rim thickness or width. These figures are secured by measuring the outside of the rim, subtracting the inside rim diameter from it, and dividing by 2. (If one did not divide by 2, the resultant figure would include two thicknesses of the rim.)

All of the mouthpieces are listed alphabetically by the name of the manufacturer. All are made in the United States except the English Besson and the French Courtois. Names of the manufacturers and suppliers are found elsewhere in the symposium.

Because the drill size numbers increase while the drill diameters decrease and because some of the figures are in sixty-fourths of an inch and others are in hundredths, it appears highly desirable to reduce all of the measurements to a common denominator through the code chart. Notice that there are ten figures to the right of each category in T-V-D C-R-I and seven to the right of B. The graphs show the range of measurements in each category. In several of these it has been necessary to reduce the listings on the code chart. For example, rim curvatures have 14 different items plus a "flat," but because the number of mouthpieces 18, 19, 20, 21, 22, and "flat" is small, these can be lumped together under column 9 in the code. In most categories, however, this did not have to be done.

On the code chart observe, for example, how the first Alexander trumpet mouthpiece was coded. Under column T this mouthpiece has a throat drill number of 23. On the code chart follow this category to the right of T to 23 and notice that the code number above it is 6. Under V go to the third column, the composite of the two previous columns, and note that the number here is 16.5. Now follow the V to the right to 16 and the code number above it is 2. Thus the first two code numbers to identify this mouthpiece are 6-2.

The other categories are coded similarly until we have the 6-2-3 9-9-0-2 code as given in the column to the far right. One should remember that any measurement smaller than the smallest number on the chart is given the 0 code number and that any number larger than the one to the farthest right is given a 9. The drill sizes are obviously the reverse of this.

With the code number of a mouthpiece one can directly compare it with any other mouthpiece. It is this code number that should be stamped on every mouthpiece.

The reason for using 0 is that from 0 through 9 there are 10 categories, while if the number 10 were used for the tenth category, we would have the nuisance of a two-digit number in the coding. By using 0 through 9 the

T-V-D C-R-I-B coding has all single-digit numbers.

Consult Bar Graphs

For a detailed analysis of any mouthpiece it is preferable to refer to the actual mouthpiece measurements. Probably the easiest manner of securing an over-all picture of the eight different measurements of 213 different mouthpieces is to consult the bar graphs showing the distribution of the mouthpieces according to each of the seven categories. These deserve considerable study.

A study of the graphs will show where the largest number of mouthpieces falls in the classification and how certain charts are skewed to one side. For example, the T or Throat graph clearly shows how the majority definitely falls under the small drill sizes, 27, 28 and 29, rather than under the three largest drills.

From these charts one arrives at the mouthpiece which can be termed the "average" or, more accurately, "median" mouthpiece. In a very real sense, out of 213 mouthpieces, the median is the 107th one, according to each of the categories. Here it is:

T-V-D C-R-I-B
2 5 6 4 3 5 4

This is an important number to memorize because it can serve as a reference number in comparing all other mouthpieces. Having learned the numbers of the median, the next important thing to know is the numbering of one's favorite mouthpiece. It should be measured and compared with the median.

It may interest the reader to observe that only 10 of the 213 mouthpieces measured come within plus or minus 1 of the seven median mouthpiece numbers: the Bach 7BW, 7C and 8C; the Besson cornet 10½C; the Harry Glantz trumpets 8M and 9M; the Olds cornet 5; the Purviance trumpet 7C3; and the Schilke trumpets H and J. One should ordinarily allow a deviation of plus or minus 1 in comparing mouthpieces.

The present study and the conclusions based on it may serve as a starting point for a number of other research studies. One that is urgently needed is an attempt to discover what the ideal mouthpiece would be for varying conditions of teeth and lips. Investigation of playing techniques

in terms of T-V-D C-R-I-B should reveal many interesting results.

Manufacturers need not fear loss of individuality, for 7,000,000 varieties of mouthpieces are possible with the ten variations of T-V-D C-R-I and the seven for B. If we add the variations in backbore, possibly ten more, the possible variations would be 70,000,000 for trumpet alone.

The salesman of mouthpieces hesitates to trade the convenience of a single number or letter name of his product for a seven-digit name. It is not possible, however, to describe a mouthpiece with any degree of accuracy without using a multiple-number system.

If a manufacturer wishes to retain his present system, he can do so, but he should designate also the code numbers mentioned above. With such help from the manufacturer and with brass teachers and band and orchestra directors measuring the mouthpieces, we should enter a new era of accuracy, clarity, understanding and progress in the mouthpiece world of brass instruments.

How To Measure

For the manufacturer as well as for the serious student a few suggestions based on several hundred hours of work with mouthpieces may be helpful.

In the photograph showing the writer measuring mouthpieces there is a spotlight in the upper left corner which assists appreciably in making accurate observations. Especially is it useful when one is using the critical radius gages. In front of the writer is a jig. It is used to hold a mouthpiece in a horizontal position, while a sliding table meets the center of the mouthpiece. A radius gage placed on the table is thus perpendicular to the rim of the mouthpiece at its center. A jig not only makes more accurate measurements possible but also saves considerable time.

T. Throat

A drill blank secures more accurate throat measurements than the shank end of a drill. Drills from the same manufacturer may vary several thousandths of an inch between the shank and drilling ends, and the variations among manufacturers is even greater. However, the Morse Twist Drills from 19 to 29 should provide measurements comparable to those on the chart.

Drill blanks are more expensive than drills, but should the present study ever be repeated, all measurements will be made with drill blanks.

V. Volume

By measuring the depth of the cup with both depth gages one achieves a fairly accurate and complete figure for cup depth and shape to combine into a volume measurement. Care should be exercised to be sure that (1) the rod or rule of the depth gage is perpendicular-straight in the cup, (2) that the end is down in and snugly touching both sides of the cup, and (3) that the crossbar is touching both sides of the rim. With the half-inch depth gage make certain that the clip is at the center of the rule.

One might suppose that a more accurate measure of volume could be secured by plugging the throat and pouring some liquid into the cup and then measuring the amount of liquid. So it would were it not for the difficulty of determining the exact spot where the cup leaves off and the throat begins. This difficulty, as well as others, is not encountered with use of the two depth gages.

D. Diameter

The major difficulty in making the diameter measurement is the determination of the exact place on the inside of the cup where the curvature of the cup ends and that of the rim begins. Care must be taken to make certain that both points of the divider or caliper are at exactly opposite places across the mouthpiece from each other. Though inside calipers of several different models can be bought, it was found easier to determine the diameter width with a caliper or a divider. The distance between the prongs can be measured with the half-inch depth gage, which has a ruler showing sixty-fourths of an inch.

C. Curvature

As mentioned previously, a jig is of considerable practical value in holding both the mouthpiece and the radius gage in a straight line with each other. The radius gage is too small if there is a slight gap between the mouthpiece and the center of the curve on the radius gage.

The rule to follow is this: Use the smallest radius gage which does not gap at the center. The eye is thus constantly focused at this spot between the radius gage and the curvature of the mouthpiece.

B. Bite

The bite requires radius gages marked 1/32 through 1/8 inch, while the rim curvature varies from 9/64 through 17/64 with a few having such a well-rounded rim as to require radius gages of 20/64 to 22/64. A rare one has actually a short flat surface on the rim.

R. Rim Thickness

The outside of the rim was measured by a micrometer (1 to 2 inch) in this study; however, a divider can be used to determine the outside rim width. Subtract the inside diameter width from the outside width and divide by 2 to secure the rim thickness, the width of the mouthpiece wall at the rim. Here, as with all other figures, even though the micrometer readings are in thousandths, the results should be rounded off to the nearest hundredth of an inch.

I. Impression

Place the rim of the mouthpiece on an ink pad, rotate the mouthpiece, place the mouthpiece on a piece of paper to blot off the excess ink and then place the rim on a clean sheet of paper. The inked rim made is the impression circle; the width of this circle is the I or impression figure. In case the inked circle is slightly wide, one can measure from the outside edge of one side to the inside edge directly across from it.

By changing the impression width it is possible to have two like mouthpieces vary considerably as to "feel" on the lips. A wider impression circle feels like a larger mouthpiece even though the cup, throat, backbore and outside width do not vary. In changing the impression width it is usually necessary to alter the rim curvature and bite somewhat.

The explanations may sound very involved and difficult, but if the reader will purchase some measuring tools and then go over the material, following the processes, he will find that many problems will be cleared up for him.

Fine

MEASUREMENTS OF TRUMPET-CORNET MOUTHPIECES

FIRM		T	V	D	C	R	I	B	Code
Alexander									
Tpt.		23	22	13	17.5	62	20	29	75	2	6-2-3-9-9-0-2
Cor.		25	26	13	19.5	64	14	28	80	5	4-4-5-5-9-4-5
Bach									
Tpt. &									
Cor.	1C	26	26	15	20.5	68	11	20	81	3	3-5-9-2-1-5-3
"	2	27	28	17	22.5	66	14	20	81	3	2-7-7-5-1-5-3
"	2½C	27	26	17	21.5	66	13	20	82	2	2-6-7-4-1-6-2
"	2¾C	27	25	17	21	67	10	19	83	2	2-6-8-1-0-7-2
"	3C	27	26	16	21	67	12	20	80	3	2-6-8-3-1-4-3
"	5A	26	29	17	23	66	11	19	82	2	3-8-7-2-0-6-2
"	5B	27	27	16	21.5	68	12	19.5	81	3	2-6-9-3-0-5-3
"	6	27	27	17	22	66	15	20.5	81	3	2-7-7-6-1-5-3
"	6B	27	26	16	21	65	10	21	82	4	2-6-6-1-2-6-4
"	6C	28	25	16	20.5	65	11	21	82	3	1-5-6-2-2-6-3
"	6½A	27	29	16	22.5	66	15	20.5	78	4	2-6-7-6-1-6-4
"	7	27	27	16	21.5	66	13	20.5	80	3	2-7-7-4-1-4-3
"	7A	26	30	18	24	67	11	20	81	2	3-9-8-2-1-5-2
"	7B	28	27	16	21.5	67	11	20	80	2	1-6-8-2-1-4-2
"	7BW	28	27	16	21.5	64	14	23	80	3	1-6-5-5-4-4-3
"	7C	28	24	15	20	65	14	21	80	4	1-5-6-5-2-4-4
"	7CW	27	26	16	21	66	10	21.5	81	2	2-6-7-1-2-5-2
"	7D	25	25	14	19.5	66	10	20	80	3	4-4-7-1-1-4-3
"	7DW	24	25	14	19.5	66	10	22	81	2	5-4-5-1-3-5-2
"	7E	25	24	13	18.5	66	11	21	80	3	4-3-7-2-2-4-3
"	7EW	25	24	14	19	64	10	22.5	81	3	4-4-5-1-3-5-3
"	8	27	28	16	22	66	12	21	82	3	2-7-7-3-2-6-3
"	8B	27	27	15	21	66	11	20.5	81	3	2-6-7-2-1-5-3

FIRM		T	V	D	C	R	I	B	Code
"	4	27	25	16	19.5	65	11	20	80	4	2-4-6-2-1-4-4
"	5	27	25	15	20	63	12	21	79	3	2-5-4-3-2-3-3
"	6	27	25	15	20	65	11	20	85	4	2-5-6-2-1-9-4
Cor.	1	27	28	15	22	66	11	19.5	82	2	2-7-7-2-0-6-2
"	2	27	27	16	21.5	66	11	19.5	82	4	2-6-7-2-0-6-4
"	3	27	26	16	21	65	10	20.5	81	2	2-6-6-1-1-5-2
"	4	27	25	16	20.5	64	10	21	82	4	2-5-5-1-2-6-4
"	5	27	25	14	19.5	63	13	21	79	2	2-4-4-4-2-3-2
"	6	27	25	15	20	67	11	19.5	84	4	2-5-8-2-0-8-4
E-Z tone									
Tpt.		19	27	16	21.5	65	13	20.5	83	5	9-6-6-4-1-7-5
Cor.		19	27	16	21.5	65	11	20	84	4	9-6-6-2-1-8-4
Courtois									
Tpt.	1	27	23	14	18.5	61	11	26.5	83	6	2-3-2-2-6-7-6
"	2	28	19	12	15.5	64	13	25	81	6	1-0-5-4-6-5-6
"	3	29	18	12	15	66	14	24.5	85	7	0-0-7-5-5-9-7
"	4	29	19	13	16	66	13	24.5	87	7	0-1-7-4-5-9-7
"	7C	29	21	13	17	64	flat	25	87	4	0-2-5-f-6-9-4
Cor.	1	29	24	14	19	63	11	19	78	5	0-4-4-2-0-2-5
"	2	29	25	15	20	62	12	22	84	5	0-5-3-3-3-8-5
"	3	28	24	15	19.5	64	11	21	84	6	1-4-5-2-2-8-6
Frank									
Tpt.	20	27	23	13	18	63	17	24.5	78	4	2-3-4-8-5-2-4
"	21	28	21	14	17.5	63	13	24	79	5	1-2-4-4-5-3-5
"	22	27	23	12	17.5	64	15	24	84	7	2-2-5-6-5-8-7
"	23	26	28	15	21.5	65	12	20.5	84	5	3-6-6-3-1-8-5
Cor.	11	28	21	13	17	62	15	25	81	4	1-2-3-6-6-5-4
"	12	26	27	16	16.5	64	15	21	78	4	3-1-5-6-2-2-4
"	13	25	26	16	16	64	14	21	80	4	4-1-5-5-2-4-4
Franklin									
Tpt.		26	24	14	19	68	16	25.5	82	2	3-4-9-7-6-6-2
Cor.		26	26	14	20	68	20	25.5	78	4	3-5-9-9-6-2-4

FIRM		T	V			D	C	R	I	B	Code
"	8C	27	24	15	19.5	66	12	21.5	80	4	2-4-7-3-2-4-4
"	8½	26	28	16	22.5	65	10	20.5	82	4	3-7-6-1-1-6-4
"	9	27	28	16	22	63	12	21.5	82	3	2-7-4-3-2-6-3
"	9A	27	29	17	23	65	11	21	82	4	2-8-6-2-2-6-4
"	9B	26	27	16	21.5	64	11	21.5	82	4	3-6-5-2-2-6-4
"	9C	27	25	15	20	66	10	19.5	80	3	2-5-7-1-0-4-3
"	9½D	27	25	15	20	65	12	20	84	4	2-5-6-3-1-8-4
"	10	27	29	16	22.5	63	11	21.5	81	4	2-7-4-2-2-5-4
"	10B	27	26	15	20.5	65	14	20.5	80	4	2-5-6-5-1-4-4
"	10C	27	25	15	20	64	11	21	80	2	2-5-5-2-2-4-2
"	10½A	27	29	16	22.5	64	11	19.5	79	2	2-7-5-2-0-3-2
"	10½C	27	25	14	19.5	64	11	21.5	82	4	2-4-5-2-2-6-4
"	10½CW	27	27	15	21	64	17	27	78	3	2-6-5-8-8-2-3
"	10½D	25	25	13	19	64	11	21.5	79	2	4-4-5-2-2-3-2
"	10½DW	26	25	13	19	66	11	21	83	3	3-4-7-2-2-7-3
"	10½E	27	25	13	19	66	10	20	82	3	2-4-7-1-1-6-3
"	10¾A	26	29	16	22.5	63	10	20.5	81	4	3-7-4-1-1-5-4
"	10¾C	28	26	15	20.5	62	14	21	82	4	1-5-3-5-2-6-4
"	10¾CW	27	26	15	20.5	63	15	22	80	3	2-5-4-1-3-4-3
"	11A	27	28	16	22	63	12	21	81	4	2-7-4-3-2-5-4
"	11B	27	27	16	21.5	65	11	19.5	81	4	2-6-6-2-0-5-4
"	11C	27	27	15	21	64	11	21.5	79	2	2-6-5-2-2-3-2
"	11D	24	25	14	19.5	65	11	21	79	3	5-4-6-2-2-3-3
"	11½A	26	28	16	22	63	10	19.5	80	4	3-7-4-1-1-4-4
"	11½C	27	27	15	21	64	15	21.5	79	3	2-6-5-1-2-3-3
"	12	27	28	16	22	61	11	22	78	3	2-7-2-2-3-2-3
"	12B	27	26	15	20.5	61	14	21.5	79	3	2-6-2-5-2-3-3
"	12C	27	24	14	19.5	62	13	21.5	78	2	2-4-3-4-2-2-2
"	17C	27	24	14	19.5	62	13	21.5	78	2	2-4-3-4-2-2-2
"	17C2	28	20	10	15	63	12	24.5	79	4	1-0-4-3-5-3-4
"	20C	27	26	14	20	60	11	22.5	78	3	2-5-1-2-3-2-3
Benge Tpt.	14	28	22	12	17	62	13	22	79	3	1-2-3-4-3-3-3
Cor.	5	29	25	16	20.5	65	13	20	80	2	0-5-6-4-1-4-2
Besson (Eng.) Cor.	10½C	27	25	14	19.5	64	13	21	80	5	2-4-5-4-2-4-5
Tpt.	6	26	25	13	19	61	9	22.5	85	3	3-4-2-0-3-9-3
Cor.	5	26	24	13	18.5	62	9	22	82	2	3-3-3-0-3-6-2
Paris Tpt.	3	26	26	13	19.5	62	11	23	82	6	3-4-3-2-4-6-6
Buescher	485	26	24	14	19	66	17	23	85	4	3-4-7-8-4-9-4
Duo Tpt.	Cup 88B	20	28	18	23	66	11	24	84	4	9-7-7-2-5-8-4
"	88C	21	30	16	23	65	11	25.5	84	2	8-8-6-2-6-8-2
"	88D	23	25	15	20	65	13	25.5	84	3	6-5-6-4-6-8-3
"	88E	28	26	14	20	63	11	25	80	2	1-5-4-2-6-4-2
Cor.	99B	22	22	18	20	67	9	23.5	82	3	7-5-8-0-4-6-3
"	99C	21	30	16	23	65	12	25.5	82	3	8-8-6-3-6-6-3
"	99D	21	26	15	20.5	64	14	26.5	82	3	8-5-5-5-7-6-3
"	99E	29	25	14	19.5	63	11	25	80	3	0-4-4-2-6-4-3
Cauffman Hyperbolic Tpt.		29	22	11	16.5	58	14	22	79	3	0-1-0-5-3-3-3
Cor.		27	22	11	16.5	58	13	22	79	3	2-1-0-4-3-3-3
Champion Tpt.		25	22	12	17	62	17	27.5	80	4	4-2-3-8-8-4-4
Cor.		25	25	14	19.5	65	11	26.5	85	5	4-4-6-2-7-9-5
Conn Tpt.	1	27	28	16	22	66	11	20	82	2	2-7-7-2-1-6-2
"	2	27	27	16	21.5	66	12	20	82	4	2-6-7-3-1-6-4
"	3	27	26	16	21	66	11	19.5	82	2	2-6-7-2-0-6-2
Purviance Tpt.	4*2	28	21	11	16	63	15	23	78	4	1-1-4-6-4-2-4
"	4*7	28	19	9	19	65	17	23.5	79	4	1-4-6-8-4-3-4
"	4*D1	28	22	12	17	63	13	21.5	80	3	1-2-4-4-2-4-3
"	4*D4	27	21	10	15.5	67	11	20	83	4	2-0-8-2-1-7-4
"	4*D4W	27	20	9	14.5	66	13	20.5	81	4	2-0-7-4-1-5-4
"	4*K4	27	20	10	15	67	12	21	83	4	2-0-8-3-2-7-4
"	4*3	27	22	10	16	66	11	21.5	85	4	2-1-7-2-2-9-4
"	6C3	27	22	9	15.5	64	14	22.5	81	4	2-0-5-5-3-5-4
"	6C6	27	23	9	16	65	13	21	81	4	2-1-6-4-2-5-4
"	5*K4	25	23	11	17	66	13	21.5	81	5	4-2-7-4-2-5-5
"	5*3	24	24	11	17.5	67	13	21	81	5	5-2-8-4-2-5-5
Cor.	7C3	27	25	13	19	65	13	22	80	3	2-4-6-4-3-4-3
Revere Tpt.	A	28	24	16	20	64	10	20.5	80	5	1-5-5-1-1-4-5
Cor.	C	28	24	16	20	64	20	27	80	4	1-5-5-9-8-4-4
Reinhardt (plastic) Tpt.	2	27	23	10	16.5	63	20	23	82	3	2-1-4-9-4-6-3
"	2A	23	23	10	16.5	63	20	23	82	3	6-1-4-9-4-6-3
"	2B	20	23	10	16.5	63	20	23	82	3	9-1-4-9-4-6-3
"	4	25	22	12	17	67	14	21	82	3	4-2-8-5-2-6-3
"	4A	25	23	13	18	67	14	20.5	82	3	4-3-8-5-1-6-3
"	6	26	26	15	20.5	71	15	17	82	3	3-5-9-6-0-6-3
"	6A	26	25	15	20	71	15	17	82	3	3-5-9-6-0-6-3
Reynolds Tpt.	7A	24	27	16	21.5	67	14	20.5	82	2	5-6-8-5-1-6-2
"	7B	26	28	16	22	65	12	21.5	80	3	3-7-6-3-2-4-3
"	Simon 5B	27	25	15	20	66	10	18.5	82	5	2-5-7-1-0-6-5
Cor.	5A	23	28	16	22	66	9	20	80	3	6-7-7-0-1-4-3
Roth Tpt.		23	27	16	21.5	68	12	19	82	2	6-6-9-3-0-6-2
Cor.		22	27	16	21.5	67	11	19	80	2	7-6-8-2-0-4-2
Glantz Tpt.	3M	29	27	15	21	67	11	20	85	4	0-6-8-2-1-9-4
"	4M	28	25	14	19.5	67	9	20	84	4	1-4-8-0-1-8-4
"	5M	26	26	16	21	66	9	20	84	5	3-6-7-0-1-8-5
"	6M	28	25	15	20	64	10	21	83	6	1-5-5-1-2-7-6
"	7M	28	25	15	20	65	10	20.5	82	5	1-5-6-1-1-6-5
"	8M	27	25	14	19.5	65	13	23	81	5	2-4-6-4-4-5-5
"	9M	28	26	14	20	65	13	21	81	4	1-5-6-4-2-5-4
Hamilton Tpt.	1	26	23	11	17	63	11	21.5	79	3	3-2-4-2-2-3-3
"	3	23	20	10	15	63	13	27.5	82	8	6-0-4-4-8-6-8
"	5	23	20	11	15.5	61	14	28.5	79	6	6-0-2-5-9-3-6
Cor.	1	24	22	12	17	63	12	27	79	4	5-2-4-3-8-3-4
"	3	24	22	11	16.5	62	14	27.5	80	6	5-1-3-5-8-4-6
"	5	23	22	12	17	63	13	27.5	79	4	6-2-4-4-8-3-4
Holton Tpt.	56	24	24	16	20	65	15	23.5	82	2	5-5-6-6-4-6-2
"	57	24	27	17	22	64	13	26	82	5	5-7-5-4-7-6-5
"	58	25	24	13	18.5	66	12	23	79	4	4-3-7-3-4-3-4
"	59	25	24	13	18.5	65	15	25.5	76	2	4-3-6-6-6-0-2
"	60	25	23	14	18.5	64	13	23.5	80	4	4-3-5-4-4-4-4
"	61	24	24	14	19	63	15	27	81	3	5-4-4-6-8-5-3
"	62	26	22	12	17	63	14	24.5	78	3	3-2-4-5-5-2-3
"	63	26	22	12	17	64	15	26.5	79	2	3-2-5-6-7-3-2
"	66	27	24	14	19	64	13	27	81	5	2-4-5-4-8-5-5
Cor.	70	25	34	19	27	63	15	24.5	85	4	4-9-4-6-5-9-4
"	71	25	34	18	26	64	15	26.5	85	4	4-9-5-6-7-9-4
"	72	25	23	14	18.5	65	15	23.5	81	2	4-4-6-6-4-5-2
"	73	24	23	14	18.5	65	13	26	81	3	5-4-6-4-7-5-3
"	74	26	22	11	16.5	64	15	24	78	4	3-2-5-6-5-2-4
"	75	26	22	12	17	65	15	26	78	4	3-2-6-6-7-2-4
"	76	27	24	14	19	65	10	23.5	80	4	2-4-6-1-4-4-4
"	Heim 12	25	23	14	18.5	64	17	20.5	80	3	4-3-5-8-1-4-3
King Tpt.	M18	25	24	14	19	63	17	21	78	4	4-4-4-8-2-2-4
Cor.	MC	23	27	16	21.5	65	9	20	79	3	6-6-6-0-1-3-3
Llewellyn Tpt.		23	27	16	21.5	65	9	21	84	4	6-6-6-0-2-8-4
Cor.		26	27	16	21.5	65	9	20.5	85	4	3-6-6-0-1-9-4
Martin Tpt.	7	26	26	16	21	65	12	20.5	82	4	3-6-6-3-1-6-4
"	10	24	21	12	16.5	62	11	22	80	6	5-1-3-2-3-4-6
Cor.	1	24	33	19	26	67	11	19	85	4	5-9-8-2-0-9-4
"	7	24	26	16	21	66	12	20	84	4	5-6-7-3-1-8-4
"	10	24	22	13	17.5	63	9	21	80	7	5-2-4-0-2-4-7
Muck Tpt.	1	24	22	11	16.5	65	17	27	80	2	5-1-6-8-8-4-2
"	2	24	24	16	20	66	18	23	82	3	5-5-7-9-4-6-3
Cor.	1	25	22	11	16.5	65	15	27	80	3	4-1-6-6-8-4-3
"	2	25	24	16	20	66	13	23	83	3	4-5-7-4-4-7-3
Olds Tpt.	1	27	26	17	21.5	64	11	21	81	4	2-6-5-2-2-5-4
"	2	27	23	12	17.5	64	15	28.5	80	3	2-2-5-6-9-4-3
"	3	27	24	13	18.5	64	13	21	79	4	2-3-5-4-2-3-4
"	4	28	26	15	20.5	64	14	24.5	82	4	1-5-5-5-5-6-4
"	5	28	22	12	17.5	63	12	21.5	78	4	1-2-4-3-2-2-4
Cor.	1	27	27	17	22	65	12	20	81	4	2-7-6-3-1-5-4
"	2	27	25	15	20	64	15	27.5	82	4	2-5-5-6-8-6-4
"	3	27	26	14	20	65	13	20.5	80	2	2-5-6-4-1-4-2
"	4	27	25	15	20	64	15	23.5	80	4	2-5-5-6-4-5-4
"	5	28	25	14	19.5	63	13	21	80	4	1-4-4-4-2-4-4
Schilke Tpt.	H	26	24	15	19.5	64	13	21.5	80	3	3-4-5-4-2-4-3
"	J	27	24	15	19.5	66	13	21.5	80	3	2-4-7-4-2-4-3
Sorkin Tpt.		29	21	12	16.5	63	12	23	82	7	0-1-4-3-4-6-7
Tilco Tpt.		24	26	13	19.5	65	15	26	82	5	5-4-6-6-7-6-5
Cor.		24	25	14	19.5	65	15	26.5	79	5	5-4-6-6-7-3-5
Tonex Tpt.	W13	27	22	12	17	65	15	22.5	76	4	2-2-6-6-3-0-4
"	X13	27	25	13	19	61	15	24	80	2	2-3-2-6-5-4-2
"	Y33	27	26	15	20.5	64	12	20	84	5	2-5-5-3-1-8-5
Cor.	W13	27	21	12	16.5	64	15	22.5	76	4	2-2-5-6-3-0-4
"	WX33	27	22	12	17	63	17	23	78	4	2-2-4-8-4-2-4
"	X13	27	25	14	19.5	61	11	24	81	2	2-4-2-2-5-5-2
"	Y33	27	26	15	20.5	65	11	18	82	5	2-5-6-2-0-6-5
Trophy (plastic) Tpt.		20	29	15	24.5	65	flat	29	82	3	9-9-6-f-9-6-3
Vega Tpt.	1	21	26	18	22	65	13	20	81	4	8-7-6-4-1-5-4
"	2	21	25	15	20	65	13	20	84	3	8-5-6-4-1-8-3
"	V1	21	28	18	23	65	12	26	81	3	8-8-6-3-7-5-3
"	V2	26	25	15	20	65	12	26.5	84	3	3-5-6-3-7-8-3
"	C3	25	20	11	15.5	64	13	27	78	4	4-1-5-4-8-2-4
"	D1	25	23	11	17	64	13	27	78	3	4-2-5-4-8-2-3
"	D2	27	20	11	20.5	63	14	27.5	80	2	2-5-4-5-8-4-2
"	D3	26	18	10	14	61	15	28.5	78	4	3-0-2-6-9-2-3
York Cor.	2L	25	28	16	22	66	13	24.5	85	5	4-7-7-4-5-9-5
"	2M	23	24	14	19	65	15	24.5	87	5	6-4-6-6-5-9-5
"	2S	24	24	15	19.5	64	13	26.5	86	6	5-4-5-4-7-9-6
"	4L	23	27	16	21.5	66	11	25.5	87	5	6-6-7-2-6-9-5
"	4M	26	23	16	19.5	65	12	23	85	5	3-4-6-3-4-9-5
"	4S	25	22	14	18	63	16	24	83	3	4-3-4-7-5-7-3

"THROAT·VOLUME·DIAMETER·CURVATURE·RIM THICKNESS·IMPRESSION·BITE"

CODE→	0	1	2	3	4	5	6	7	8	9
T· THROAT	29	28	27*	26	25	24	23	22	21	20
V· VOLUME	15	16	17	18	19*	20	21	22	23	24
D· DIAMETER	59	60	61	62	63	64	65*	66	67	68
C· CURVATURE	9	10	11	12	13*	14	15	16	17	18
R· RIM THICKNESS	19	20	21*	22	23	24	25	26	27	28
I· IMPRESSION	76	77	78	79	80	81*	82	83	84	85
B· BITE	—	—	2	3	4*	5	6	7	8	—

* Median above and below which are an equal number of mouthpieces.

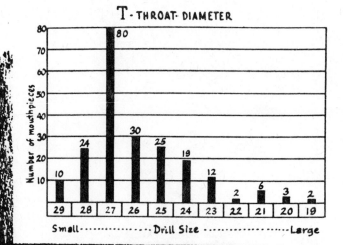

T - THROAT· DIAMETER

Small ·············· Drill Size ·············· Large

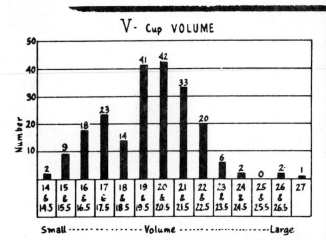

V - Cup VOLUME

Small ·········· Volume ·········· Large

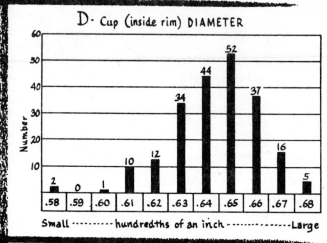

D - Cup (inside rim) DIAMETER

Small ·········· hundredths of an inch ·········· Large

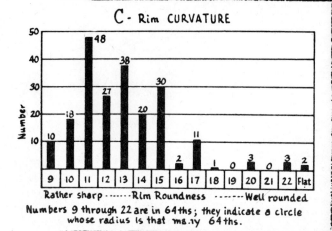

C - Rim CURVATURE

Rather sharp ······ Rim Roundness ······ Well rounded

Numbers 9 through 22 are in 64ths; they indicate a circle
whose radius is that many 64ths.

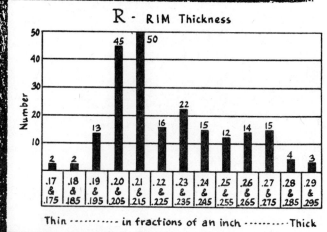

R - RIM Thickness

Thin ············ in fractions of an inch ············ Thick

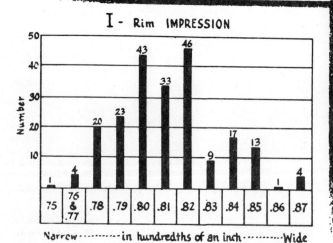

I - Rim IMPRESSION

Narrow ············ in hundredths of an inch ············ Wide

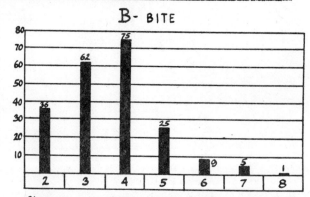

B - BITE

Sharp ·········· inside rim roundness ·········· Rounded

Numbers 2 through 8 are in 64ths; they indicate
a circle whose radius is that many 64ths.

III

Materials for Mouthpieces

TED EVANS

AT A RECENT RECORDING session I noticed that one of the trumpet players warmed up on a plastic mouthpiece but changed to a conventional brass one as soon as the actual recording started. He explained to me later that he liked to play on a plastic mouthpiece but that he thought the metal one had a better sound.

Later in the same week I found that another trumpet player on a particularly gruelling job used a plastic mouthpiece and preferred it to all others. The experience illustrates the differences of thought on this subject and presents the question of whether the material affects the performance or changes the response of the mouthpiece.

It is apparent that the metal used in making the instruments themselves has an effect on the tone quality and the ease with which the tone is produced. Instruments made exactly alike in bore and construction produce a different tone quality when made of yellow brass, red brass, or german silver. It even seems that a different sound results from the same alloy when it is smelted in different parts of the world.

Before we discuss the purely tonal aspects, however, we must consider one other very important factor, the "feel" of the mouthpiece to the performer. The surface must be of the right degree of smoothness; it must be relatively tasteless; and it must be readily warmed to the temperature of the human skin.

Some players prefer a mouthpiece that sticks exactly where it is placed, while others want one that is as slippery as possible. The musician who plays with dry lips usually prefers a surface that is not too slippery, and the one who plays "wet" likes a very smooth hard surface. The metal surface preferred by most players is that of slightly tarnished brass or soft german silver. In the case of the brass, however, it has a very unpalatable taste and a tendency to induce brass poisoning in some people. For these reasons most mouthpieces are plated with silver or gold, metals which approximate the "feel" of brass and are nearly noncorrosive. In a few instances chrome or nickel plating has been tried; both produce a very hard slippery surface. Cadmium has also been used but with little success as it turns black from the acids in saliva.

Plastic probably gives the best all-round surface although it is not very slippery. Plastic is also non-poisonous and tasteless, and since it does not tend to retain heat or cold, it warms almost immediately to the temperature of the lips. For these reasons plastic mouthpieces are popular with men who play very strenuous jobs or who must perform outdoors. It must be said, however, that plastic is not so strong as metal and that the shank end of the mouthpiece will crack if mistreated.

Wood is not successful because it is too porous. Neither wood nor hard rubber wears well at the shank end of the mouthpiece.

Most players on all instruments accuse plastic of producing a "dead" sound, but in the writer's personal experience the difference, if any, is negligible except in the French horn. It is usually impossible when blindfolded to discern between metal and plastic mouthpieces as far as sound is concerned.

Of the various metals used in the manufacture of mouthpieces, brass, sterling silver, and german silver, which is the same formula as brass with about ten per cent nickel added, are most popular. Among these, german silver is given a slight edge by most of the top French horn players in this country. One prominent player who disclaims the idea that metal affects sound will even admit that his own mouthpiece is of german silver. The consensus is that german silver gives a richer and less brassy tone.

For the rest of the brass instruments regular brass plated with silver or gold is the great favorite. Of the more seldom used metals only sterling silver has been successful. It has been, in fact, extremely good, but the expense is so great that only a very few have been made. Stainless steel, while being excellent from all other standpoints, produces a hard sound, and aluminum is quite dead sounding.

Selection and Use of Brass Mouthpieces

VINCENT BACH

SELECTION OF A SUITABLE mouthpiece which will enable the player to produce a rich volume of tone and yet give full control over the entire register has always been the greatest problem of professional musicians as well as of amateurs and beginners.

The problem is not so serious if a player uses good judgment by starting his musical career with first-class equipment—a good mouthpiece and a good instrument. However, while a properly designed mouthpiece will enable one to produce a good quality and a large volume of tone, the player still has to learn how to use the mouthpiece. He must adjust his embouchure according to the response and rim shape and then train systematically to make the lips stronger and to gain full control over the entire register.

No instructor should permit his pupil to follow the path of least resistance by using a shallow mouthpiece with a small cup diameter and a very wide rim. With such equipment he is likely to jam the high register without training his lip muscles.

Jamming the middle and high tones prevents the muscles from working freely and has a tendency toward cutting off the blood circulation. There is only one way to acquire a beautiful rich quality of tone and that is by using as little pressure as possible and by contracting or tightening the lip muscles for the high register. By using light pressure, the lip muscles can be contracted and relaxed freely. For this reason I recommend a mouthpiece with the largest possible cup. diameter so that the player cannot pinch out the high tones but will be forced to use the lip muscles correctly. A medium-wide rim offers much greater flexibility and will not cut off the blood circulation so much that the lips become paralyzed, thus making it difficult for a player to slur.

One of the secrets in developing a strong well-controlled embouchure is to relax the mouthpiece pressure as often as possible by removing the mouthpiece from the lips at every opportunity. Beginners, especially, are in the habit of keeping the mouthpiece on the lips for fear they cannot find the same place again. In so doing, they cause the lips to become numb very quickly.

When a mouthpiece rim cuts the lip, the instrumentalist is playing with a receding lower jaw so that the lips do not rest on the flat face of the rim. The correct solution is for the player to raise his instrument above horizontal without leaning his head back so that the mouthpiece will press exactly perpendicularly to the face of the upper front teeth. The lower jaw must be pushed out so that the lower teeth are in line with the upper ones; then the rim will not cut.

A mouthpiece rim that is too wide hampers the flexibility of a player's embouchure and prevents free muscular movement. Only players with very thick, fleshy, soft lips can use a wide-rimmed mouthpiece to advantage.

A correctly designed mouthpiece must have a sharp inner edge or "bite," for without such an edge the player will not have that firm grip by which he can judge what tone he is going to play. The sharp inner edge determines the lip vibrations at a fixed point, and if the rim is too rounded, the tone will be fuzzy.

Most cornet or trumpet players seem to prefer a medium-sized mouthpiece. Girls, who may have weaker embouchures, sometimes like one slightly smaller. However, a player with a normal muscular lip construction or one who really makes up his mind that he wants a large volume of tone and is willing to concentrate on hard work to strengthen his lip muscles will prefer one of the larger trumpet or cornet mouthpieces.

If a player tries different models and gets equally good results with larger and smaller sizes, he should always give preference to the larger. A bigger cup diameter will cause a larger portion of the lip to vibrate and therefore produce more column of tone; it will also give better lip control. If the lips should swell from too much playing, there will always be enough room to control the response. If a player splits too many notes, it is usually a sign that he is using a mouthpiece with too small a cup diameter.

Although the Vincent Bach Corporation makes wider rims, it does not recommend these models to the average player with normal lips but only to those with very thick soft lips. Even the latter should first try a medium-wide rim.

Avoid Strain

Another secret for obtaining a strong embouchure is never to abuse the lip muscles. For this reason a player should avoid unnecessary strain. By practicing systematically the muscles will become stronger and stronger, and the player will get more comfort from a larger mouthpiece diameter.

I also recommend that a player not use a mouthpiece that is too shallow. Great virtuosi of the past like Fritz Werner, Georg Stellwagen, Herbert Clarke, Albert Couturier, Jules Levy, Theodore Hoch, Paris Chambers, Walter Rodgers and many others have used very deep mouthpieces with large throats and large cup diameters, thus producing a rich sonorous tone of great carrying power. Yet they got the high notes just the same by training their lip muscles properly.

Many of our young people listen to so much dance music that when they play cornet, they try to imitate the brilliant tone of the trumpet by using too shallow a mouthpiece or by selecting a cornet with too small a bore. The genuine cornet tone should be of dark timbre, mellow and smooth, with a voice-like quality similar to the lyric soprano in opera. The cornetist should not try to imitate the anemic tone of certain jazz players heard on radio or in night clubs.

Some players imagine that if they use a mouthpiece with a small throat, they can get the high tones more easily, but just the reverse is true. The greatest "high-note" artists of the past as well as leading symphony musicians, who have to produce a tremendous volume of tone in some of the modern symphonies or operas, play legitimately in the extreme high register, but they all use mouthpieces with large throats.

Lips Against Teeth

The player must not permit his lips to protrude into the mouthpiece cup but should draw them back tightly against the front teeth, raising the aperture or slot between the lips a little higher so that it is exactly in line with the open space between the teeth. In other words, he should not roll the lips over the upper teeth; looking in a mirror, he should be able to see his teeth while rolling the lips in. While it is necessary to use slightly more pressure for the high tones, the additional amount of pressure is negligible; let the lip muscles do the work by contracting them or by tightening them but not by stretching them. One should not attempt to smile while playing.

A beginner should take it easy and avoid heavy strain. He should not attempt to force the high register but should start playing in the middle register between middle G, second line, and middle C. Once he controls that register, he should always use middle C as a pivot, practicing long notes, crescendo and decrescendo, starting from middle C up and then down. The mouthpiece should be removed from the lips after each tone, and the higher tones should be practiced as follows:

After a half minute's rest, start with middle C, playing the scale downward as indicated above. Practicing in this manner will eventually enable one to play the high and low registers with the same embouchure. I strongly advise against starting with the lower register, which encourages the player to let his lips protrude too far forward.

A student should practice these long notes very frequently between other technical studies so that he will not neglect his tone production. By practicing long notes without much pressure and without strain to the embouchure, by playing with a relaxed embouchure for short periods of time during the three or four sessions

daily, the embouchure will gradually become stronger and stronger.

For a beginner, 20 to 25 minutes practice at a time is sufficient, but after two or three months he should be able to play 30 to 40 minutes. He should always stop before he gets too tired, for in that way he will, after a two or three hours' recess, be able to recuperate quickly and to start again with a fresh embouchure. An advanced player may average 40 to 60

minutes or more per session if gifted with a powerful and well-trained embouchure.

One should always play with moist lips. If necessary, put cold cream or vaseline on the lips so that the mouthpiece will slip right off. One cannot play at all unless the mouthpiece is placed gently against the buzzing lips, just leaning against them so that the lip muscles can function in a natural manner. ∎

November-December, 1952

Tuning Problems of Brass Soloists

Student players show need of definite training in proper methods of practice

BERNARD FITZGERALD

SOLO PERFORMANCES of brass instrumentalists at music contests and festivals indicate that large numbers of the participants have common problems in solo performance. Although the available space does not permit an exhaustive discussion of all of these, the author hopes to be able to clarify the situation as regards one critical and fundamental problem.

It is obvious that the majority of high school soloists have not learned to adjust the tuning of their instruments properly with the piano. Their usual routine consists of having the tuning note sounded by the piano and then by the soloist, with this alternating or simultaneous repetition of the pitch continuing at an increasingly louder dynamic level in a rather haphazard manner.

The fallacy of this approach lies in the fact that the player should sound his tuning note *before* hearing the pitch played on the piano. Otherwise the soloist is very likely to make an unconscious pitch adjustment to the pitch of the piano by a change of lip tension and then proceed upon the false assumption that he has tuned to the piano. In the event that the soloist has difficulty in distinguishing whether his tuning note sounds higher or lower than the pitch of the piano, he should stop his tone as soon as the pitch is sounded by the piano since pitch differences are more readily apparent with this procedure.

It is often desirable that more than one tone be used as a check point in tuning a brass instrument. It may be

helpful to tune either to concert Bb and F or to A and E. This double check often serves to provide the player with a more accurate perspective of tonal and pitch relationships than is possible when a single tuning note is used.

It is currently the practice of instrumental manufacturers to build brass instruments so that the tuning slide must be pulled to some extent when the instrument is tuned to A-440. Many players are not aware of this fact and falsely assume that the instrument is tuned to A-440 when the tuning slide is adjusted to its shortest length.

Pull Tuning Slide

The length and size of the mouthpiece stem in relation to the receiver pipe of the instrument are factors which may also have a noticeable effect upon tuning. In view of the facts that players frequently do not use the mouthpiece provided by the manufacturer and that all instrument companies do not use the same dimensions for the mouthpiece stem and receiver pipe, the combination is often unsatisfactory and will result in the instrument being out of tune in the various registers. In instances in which the player consistently experiences difficulty in this respect, it is advisable to check the mouthpiece and the receiver pipe to determine whether they fit properly. If in doubt about this matter, it would be well to consult a competent repairman.

One problem commonly encountered by wind instrument soloists is that of attempting to tune to a piano which is pitched considerably below A-440. This situation will prove a considerable handicap to the soloist. If it is necessary to pull the tuning much more than the normal amount, it will also be necessary to pull each valve slide on a proportional basis; otherwise the tuning of the open tones will not correspond with that of the notes which require the use of valves.

Players who perform on the double French horn in F and B♭ must adjust the tuning slides on both F and B♭ if both horns are to be used, and it is frequently necessary to make further adjustments by pulling some or all of the valve slides to some extent. The amount will vary with different horns and will depend to some extent upon the player.

Tuning to Piano

The soloist will be noticeably handicapped in performance if it is necessary to tune to a piano which is considerably below the normal pitch of A-440 since he will find it necessary to make continual adjustments and compensations in pitch to an extent which will prove detrimental to tone production, tone quality and control. In these circumstances, in which accurate tuning is not feasible, the soloist may find that it is more satisfactory to compromise by not tuning below a pitch level which will result in a handicap to his performance even though his tuning will be somewhat sharp to the piano.

The practice of having another performer play the instrument to check the tuning is often entirely unsatisfactory since two players using the same instrument and mouthpiece may, and frequently do, play at a different pitch level because of individual differences in method of tone production.

Two common faults in tuning are employing an extreme dynamic level (either too loud or too soft) and using the vibrato during the tuning procedure. Since pitch deviation and tonal distortion are more likely to occur at both extremes of the dynamic range, tuning should be at the *mezzo-forte* level. Vibrato is essentially a matter of pitch deviation, and thus its use will serve to complicate the problem of identifying pitch discrepancies in tuning.

Students should be given definite instructions regarding proper tuning, learning to make pitch discriminations and adjustments under the guidance of the teacher; thus they become acutely aware of the tuning problems which must be solved with respect to their own *personal* instruments.

Continue Checking

Once a basically correct tuning has been established, most student soloists fail to consider the necessity of additional checking and tuning during the performance. This is essential since the pitch of the instrument normally becomes higher as it is played. Prolonged rests during a solo will often result in a corresponding lower pitch of the instrument except in instances in which a high room temperature prevails. The soloist must be capable of adjusting the tuning of his instrument throughout the performance, recognizing that the pitch will then normally become higher. It should be noted that the above comments refer to usual or normal performance conditions and that exceptional atmospheric and temperature variations may affect pitch adversely in a manner not consistent with the results noted above.

When in doubt about the tuning before beginning a solo it is often advisable to tune slightly sharp since a downward adjustment of the pitch can be accomplished more readily by the lips. The performer must keep in mind that under these circumstances it will usually be necessary to pull the tuning slide to some extent during the performance to compensate for the rising pitch of the instrument during performance.

The following problems are not uncommon even if the player tunes accurately before his solo performance.

1. Tendency to play extremely flat in pitch because of embouchure fatigue or inadequate breath support due to nervousness.

2. Tendency to play extremely sharp in pitch because of muscular tensions and constrictions, particularly those involving the muscles of the embouchure, throat and tongue.

Warm Up Instrument

Before tuning, the player should have ample opportunity to warm up the instrument to normal playing temperature, preferably the temperature of the room in which he will perform. He should be able to do sufficient playing to perform with normal control and flexibility.

Then he should proceed with tuning as follows:

1. The soloist sounds his tuning note at a dynamic level of *mezzo-forte* without vibrato, after which the tuning note is sounded by the piano.

2. The player must then be able to detect any discrepancy between the pitches sounded by the two instruments. If he is not certain whether he is higher or lower than the correct pitch, it is often helpful to alter the sustained pitch of the tuning note slightly by a change of lip tension. This change will result in either emphasizing the difference in pitch or in tending to eliminate it. If the adjustment is a minor one, this device will provide some indication as to the extent of the tuning slide adjustment.

3. After the tuning slide has been adjusted, tuning should be re-checked according to the above procedure and the process repeated until the tuning is accurate.

Throughout the above procedure it is imperative that the player produce the tuning note as consistently, naturally and accurately as possible, employing the same dynamic level. In the event that any considerable period of time elapses between the tuning and the performance, it will be necessary to check the tuning again because of the change of pitch caused by temperature changes.

FINE

1953

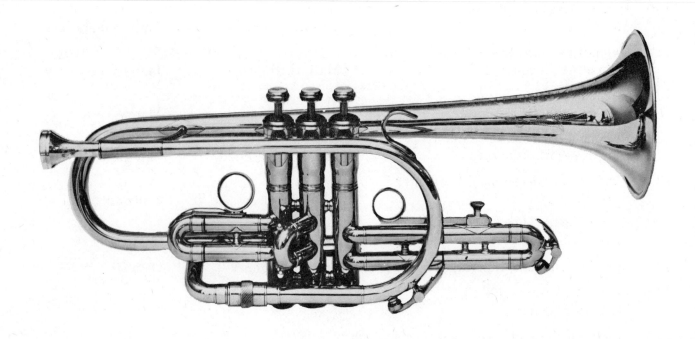

Bb Cornet

TRAUGOTT ROHNER

As FAR AS FINGERING is concerned, there is no family of band or orchestral instruments easier than the brasses. Yet there are many school band and orchestra directors who do not understand all the fingerings and who do not know how to finger a double French horn, a four-valve euphonium or a bass trombone. Many become easily confused in the various transpositions.

The difficulty cannot be blamed entirely on the directors. Rarely were they taught the basic principles by the application of which, plus a few important facts, it is possible to figure out any fingering of any brass instrument written in any key or clef. In short, the instructor should be able to throw away all brass fingering charts.

The experienced teacher learns to call off fingerings of many of the commonly used brass instruments at sight. In addition, however, he should understand and be able to teach the underlying principles so that he can figure out any fingering of any brass instrument with confidence, accuracy and speed.

To present these principles it is necessary to start from the very beginning. To some readers this material will seem repetitious; however, for the sake of completeness it is given here. Even the brass expert is encouraged not to skip it!

Partials

Each brass instrument can produce a series of harmonics (overtones or partials) without the aid of the valves. The fundamental, numbered "1," is called the pedal tone and is generally considered an impractical tone even though it can be produced. Thus the lowest practical open tone (no valves down) is the second harmonic.

The following harmonic series is the one used for the French horn. If these notes were one octave higher, they would be intended for trumpet-cornet or any of the other treble clef instruments.

THE HARMONIC SERIES

1 2 3 4 5 6 7 8 9 10 11 12 13 14 15 16

Fig. I

The quarter note heads in this series indicate notes which are badly out of tune and should be considered

unusable as such. The seventh harmonic is very flat, the eleventh is very flat when written as F♯ (very sharp when written as F♮), and the thirteenth and fourteenth are both very flat. Because of the ability of the trombone slide to make pitch adjustments easily, these "false" overtones can be used "to figure from." This fact will be explained later.

The first task of the person who wishes to master brass fingerings is to memorize the harmonic series through at least the twelfth partial.

Though the theoretically possible harmonics or overtones are many and the same for all brasses, it should be stressed that the practical possibilities are definitely limited and not the same for all brasses. The large bore (large diameter of tubing) brasses favor the lower harmonics, while the small bore brasses favor the upper ones. The euphonium, for example, is in its best range from the sixth harmonic down. The horn, on the other hand, is well suited to tones up through the tenth and twelfth harmonics.

An interesting consideration here is the important fact that both the euphonium and the B♭ horn have the same sounding harmonic series. That the notes for the euphonium are written in the bass clef and those for the B♭ horn in the treble (usually in F) does not alter the fact that both are B♭ instruments with the same sounding overtone series. (This fact will be used later to help in learning the fingerings of the B♭ horn.)

The harmonic series of open tones are marked "O" (no valves down) for the valved brasses but are marked "1" (first position) for the trombone. (Perhaps some day we will be consistent and call the trombone open notes "O" also.)

Second Harmonic Tone

Since it is the second harmonic (partial or overtone) which is the lowest one for practically all brass playing, let us list this note for each of the brasses in common use as well as for some of the less commonly used ones. Since it is possible to build superior brass instruments in any key, there are as many different harmonic series possible as there are different notes between the lowest and the highest sounding brass instrument. However, by constructing the harmonic series, starting with the second harmonic, on the notes listed in Figure II, one will have an amazingly complete repertoire of brass fingerings at his disposal.

THE 2nd HARMONIC

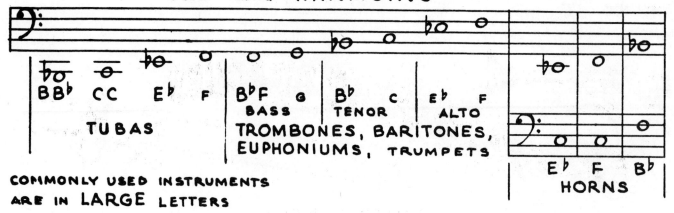

BB♭ CC E♭ F B♭F G B♭ C E♭ F

TUBAS   BASS TENOR ALTO

TROMBONES, BARITONES,
EUPHONIUMS, TRUMPETS

E♭ F B♭
HORNS

COMMONLY USED INSTRUMENTS
ARE IN LARGE LETTERS

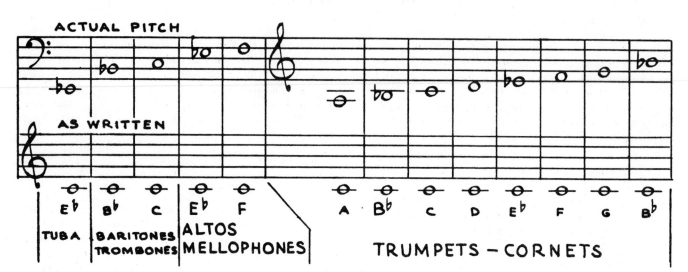

ACTUAL PITCH

AS WRITTEN

E♭ B♭ C E♭ F   A B♭ C D E♭ F G B♭

TUBA BARITONES ALTOS   TRUMPETS — CORNETS
      TROMBONES MELLOPHONES

Fig. II

A few additional comments concerning the instruments listed in Fig. II may prove helpful. Of the four tubas listed, the one in BB♭ is the most popular in bands while the CC is the one used in professional symphony orchestras. The several differing models called sousaphones, recording basses, or even the old helicon tubas have nothing to do with the pitch of the instrument. For convenience in carrying on the march, the sousaphone models are popular in bands; however, they are not used in professional symphony orchestras.

The euphonium is a larger bore instrument than the baritone. The fact that some of these instruments have two bells does not change their name.

Though E♭ instruments (tubas, altos and mellophones) are listed in large type, indicating that they are commonly used instruments, they are, as a whole, losing ground in the United States, while C brasses are gaining in popularity.

Though the trumpet in A is listed as a separate instrument, in actual practice this is usually a B♭ instrument tuned down to A. Advanced players do not tune down to A but prefer to transpose A parts.

The bass trumpet is fingered and pitched the same as the valved trombone, but there is a slight difference in tone quality between the two and a considerable difference in appearance. The "Aida" or herald trumpet has much of its tubing in a long extended bell; this model can be made in any desired key.

Function of Valves

A brass instrument consists of a closed tube extending from the mouthpiece through the bell. The purpose of the valves is to add tubing to lengthen the tubing of the "open" instrument any desired interval from one half-step to six half-steps as follows:

Valve 2 lowers the pitch of an open tone 1 half-step
Valve 1 lowers the pitch of an open tone 2 half-steps
Valve 1-2 lowers the pitch of an open tone 3 half-steps
Valve 3* lowers the pitch of an open tone 3 half-steps
Valve 2-3 lowers the pitch of an open tone 4 half-steps
Valve 1-3 lowers the pitch of an open tone 5 half-steps
Valve 1-2-3 lowers the pitch of an open tone 6 half-steps
The use of the fourth valve will be discussed later.

With the foregoing simple chart one is able to finger down chromatically from any open tone. The notes in Fig. III show the open notes in half notes, followed by the quarter notes, which are valved notes derived from the open tone(s) preceding. These fingerings are for any instrument having the second harmonic tone written as middle C.

---

*In general use 1-2 instead of 3; this statement will be explained later.

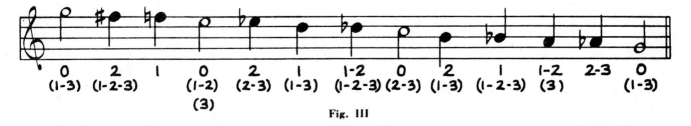

Fig. III

The parenthetical fingerings are alternate or substitute fingerings and are not preferred except in rather rare instances for purposes of tuning or for trilling. Notice that the first two parenthetical fingerings (1-3 and 1-2-3 for the G and F♯) are derived from the open C above it.

By combining the function of the valves with the harmonic series as built on the second harmonic, one can now figure out any and all fingerings of all the three-valved brasses. The procedure in finding all of the possible fingerings of any one note for a specified instrument are as follows:

(1) If the note is in the open-tone harmonic series, mark its fingering as "O";

(2) Figure down from the nearest open tone above it; if the fingering comes out as 1-2, this note automatically also has 3 as a possible alternate or substitute fingering; and

(3) Figure down from two and three (in rare cases) open tones above the given note.

Caution: Do NOT figure down from any "false" harmonic (partials 7, 11, 13, and 14).

Though the beginning brass student invariably learns to finger his instrument through the association of fingerings with certain notes through repetition, he should in time have the principles of fingering explained to him. For the teacher there is no substitute for understanding of the underlying basic principles.

WITH THE APPLICATION OF MATERIALS already presented one is able in practically all instances to figure out the fingerings of the 3-valved brasses. However, the use of valve 3 instead of 1-2, important factors of intonation, and the fingerings of both the F and B♭ horns remain to be considered, as well as the special applications of 4 and 5-valved brasses and the trombones. Foremost among these subjects is the matter of intonation as it affects fingering.

Principles of Intonation

Brass intonation and brass fingerings need not be as involved as some teachers would have us think, provided a few basic principles are thoroughly understood and applied.

1. Some tones in the harmonic series, other than the "false"[1] 7th-11th-13th-14th harmonics, are out of tune on all brasses. For example, the 5th harmonic is notably flat. Though manufacturers can correct the pitch of this harmonic, the inevitable result is that others will be put out of tune. It is a physical impossibility to manufacture a brass instrument with perfect intonation. The most prac-

tical solution is a judicious compromise.

2. The fingered notes below any out-of-tune harmonic tone are also flat or sharp in the same direction as the harmonic tone. For example, the three chromatic fingered notes between the flat 5th harmonic and the 4th harmonic are also flat. (It is to correct the flatness of the 1-2 fingering below this 5th harmonic that valve 3 is sometimes substituted.)

3. In rapid passages it is sometimes desirable to sacrifice intonation for ease of fingering. For example, in trilling G♯-A on the trumpet it is easier to finger 2-3 to 3 than 2-3 to 1-2.

4. The fourth principle, the most important one, is only too often misunderstood by even experienced brass teachers and players. It may be stated thus: The longer the tubing involved for any tone, the longer is the additional tubing required to lower this tone a desired interval.

In considering the foregoing, one should take care not to confuse length of tubing with pitch. It is the length of tubing involved in the production of a tone which determines how much more tubing is required to lower the pitch a desired interval. For example, if valve shank 2 is exactly long enough to lower an open tone a half-step, then it is too short when combined with other valves. Especially is this true and very noticeably so, when fingering 1-2-3. It is for this reason that the shank for valve 3 is pulled out farther than would be required to lower an open tone three half-steps because this valve is consistently used in combination with valves 1 and 2. The hook or ring attached to this shank 3, and sometimes to 1 also, provides a simple means for lengthening or shortening the tubing while playing.

A new special spring device for assisting the lengthening or shortening of the third and the first valve is one which may prove attractive to the discriminating musician. A unique and practical automatic compensating device found on some 4-valved baritones-euphoniums and tubas deserves more attention in the United States.

The foregoing four principles apply to all brasses; they are of particular interest with respect to the 4-valved brasses, horns and trombones.

The 4-Valved Brasses

The 4th valve on some baritones-euphoniums and tubas may be considered as having the same function as valves 1-3. Actually, the shank of valve 4 is adjusted to be slightly longer than the combined length of 1-3 so that valve 4 can be used to play the 1-3 notes perfectly in tune. Since valve 4 takes over the function of the combination valves 1-3, it is no longer necessary to pull valve shank 3 out, as is the case on the 3-valved brasses. Valve 3 can be tuned to lower the pitch of an open tone exactly three half-steps.

[1] Meaning out of tune

127

Thus on 4-valved instruments valve 3 is frequently used in place of 1-2. The foregoing is illustrated below with notes written for the 4-valved euphonium.

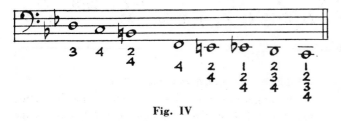

Fig. IV

The reader may be somewhat confused as to the reason that fingering 2-4 is used for the B and the low E and yet the low E♭ is fingered 1-2-4. Since the E♭ is only a half-step below the E, one can deduce that the correct fingering for this E♭ should be 1-4 and not 1-2-4. (On some instruments 1-4 may be found better in tune than 1-2-4.)

Applying intonation principle 4, given above, one discovers that the shank for valve 2 is too short to lower the pitch one half-step when valve 4 is used. Valve 4 lowers the pitch of a B♭ instrument so that it now should be considered an F instrument, and on an F instrument the 2nd shank is considerably longer than on a B♭ instrument. (Note the difference in length of the shanks on a double horn in F-B♭.) Valve shank 1, on the other hand, tends to be a little too long when used with valve 4 to lower it a half-step. However, valve shank 1 becomes quite acceptable when combined with still more tubing as in fingering 2-3-4 and 1-2-3-4. It should be noted that there is not enough tubing to play the low B♮.[2]

The fourth valve on a two-bell baritone-euphonium is used to change the air column from one bell to the other.

The three functions of the fourth valve are to improve

intonation, to improve certain technical fingering problems and to extend the range.

Horns in F and B♭

Since the French horn is not French in origin and since players consistently use the simpler term "horn" when speaking of their instrument, we shall use the single word "horn" hereafter.

The harmonic series given in Figure I (Jan.-Feb., 1953, p. 29) is written for the horn in F, sounding a fifth lower. This same series written a fourth higher would be the open tone series for the B♭ horn, also written as an F part. Thus the horn player who knows F fingerings by sight can think of the correct B♭ fingerings by thinking down a fourth.

However, for most teachers there is a simpler and sounder method for determining the fingerings of the B♭ horn. The pitch of the B♭ horn is the same as that of the B♭ baritone or trombone, and the harmonic series are identical. This places the second harmonic or open tone as B♭ (2nd line bass clef). Thus one can think of the B♭ horn fingerings as the same as those of the baritone.

In the following rather commonly used horn range, the notes on the top staff are written as they appear in an F horn part; directly below these notes are the ones showing the actual pitch. The fingerings for the F horn are given above the notes while those for the B♭ horn are given below. Notice that the fingerings for the B♭ horn are identical to those of the baritone with but minor exceptions noted.

An interesting sidelight from the horn chart and horn fingerings is that most would agree that it would be simpler if all horn parts were written to sound the written pitch (in C instead of F), that is if it would not require the use of both the treble and the bass clefs or an intermediate clef. The ideal solution is to use the 6-line staff[3] as follows:

---

[2] A 5-valved tuba in which the shank for the 5th valve is longer than that of valve 2, as is used by Arnold Jacobs, tubaist of the Chicago Symphony Orchestra, provides improved intonation for valve combinations with 4 and provides the low B♮ (actually C♯ on his CC tuba).

[3] See "Consider the 6-Line Staff," Jan.-Feb., 1951, p. 24.

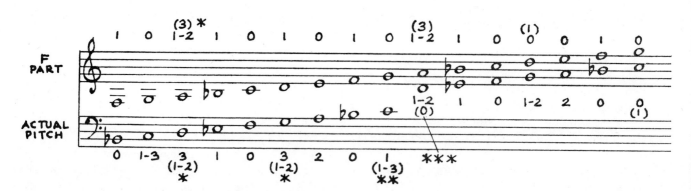

* On many horns, fingering 3 will be better in tune for these notes than 1-2, which tends to be sharp. Use the one which is better in tune on a particular horn.

** If this note is flat when fingered 1, use 1-3. One will recall that this note is figured down from the usually flat 5th harmonic. For the note one half-step lower the fingering 1-2-3 may be better in tune than 1-2, similarly as 1-3 may be better in tune than 1.

*** For purposes of better intonation this note is usually fingered as 1-2 instead of O; the note one half-step lower likewise is fingered 2-3 instead of 2. Another advantage of using 1-2 and 2-3 is that these are the same fingerings for both the F and the B♭ horn for these two notes.

Fig. V

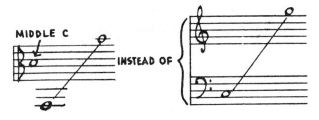

Fig. VI

On the double horn the 4th valve, operated with the left thumb, is used to change the instrument from F up to B♭. Because of intonation principle 4 a double set of valve shanks is required. When the thumb valve is depressed, the shorter valve shanks are automatically engaged instead of the longer F shank. The transition from one horn to the other is usually accomplished somewhere between G♯ on the second line and D on the fourth line. It should be noted that the fingerings for the F and B♭ horn are identical from G♯ through C above it.

Since muting affects fingering, it is necessary to cover the subject in regard to this phase. There are three ways of muting the horn: (1) by using a non-transposing mute, (2) by using a transposing mute, and (3) by hand. With a non-transposing mute it is NOT necessary to alter or transpose the fingering from that used when the horn is not muted. (From an acoustical viewpoint the non-transposing mute does the transposing, but from the player's viewpoint it is non-transposing because it requires no transposition.) The transposing mute as well as hand muting require the player to transpose the written notes down one half-step.

Hand muting the B♭ horn is not practical unless the horn is equipped with a transposing valve having a shank length of about two-thirds that of the first valve. Hand muting the B♭ horn raises the pitch about two-thirds of a whole step. However, since hand muting is not required very often in school band and orchestra music and since players with small hands find it difficult or even impossible to hand mute anyway, the extra expenditure for an additional transposing valve on the single B♭ horn is rarely warranted. The extra cost of the 5-valve horn makes it impractical for schools. On the other hand, a non-transposing mute is considered a *must* for every player of a horn section worthy of the name.

A final word of caution is in order concerning tuning the horn. It is imperative that the right hand be inserted into the bell the proper distance while tuning. At least two different harmonic tones should be used for tuning but never the fifth harmonic.

The Trombones

The harmonic open tones of the trombone (Figure VII) are played with the slide all the way in, in first position; these same notes are fingered "0" on the baritone-euphonium. If they were written one octave lower, they would be for the BB♭ tuba.

The 2nd position lowers an open tone 1 half-step
The 3rd   ”   ”   ”   ”   ”   ”   2 half-steps
The 4th   ”   ”   ”   ”   ”   ”   3   ”   ”
The 5th   ”   ”   ”   ”   ”   4   ”   ”
The 6th   ”   ”   ”   ”   ”   5   ”   ”
The 7th*   ”   ”   ”   ”   ”   6   ”   ”

*(There is no seventh position on most bass trombones.)

Fig. VII

The second position on the B♭ tenor trombone is extended about 3¼ inches, the third position is extended an additional 3½ inches, etc., through the seventh position. It should be carefully noted that due to intonation principle 4 each successive position is about ¼ inch longer than the previous position differential.

On the bass trombone, where the left thumb valve adds tubing equal to six positions of the slide, the trombone really becomes an F instrument. Applying intonation principle 4 we need a correspondingly longer tubing to lower each tone than on the B♭ trombone. This brings the 6th position (when the thumb valve is engaged) out to about where the 7th position ordinarily is. Thus, we have no seventh position, and the B♭ below the staff is not possible. It should be noted that it is possible to build a bass trombone having a slide which is long enough to produce seven positions. A bass trombone in G having seven positions without the thumb valve is also a practical reality.

The "false" harmonics (7, 11, 13, 14) are not ordinarily used on brass instruments; however, on the trombone the 7th harmonic is important to figure from. Since this harmonic is about a quarter of a whole step flat in pitch, it is necessary to shorten the slide accordingly for each lower tone derived therefrom. For example, the G below this 7th harmonic A♭ is played over an inch shorter than the usual second position, and the F♯-G♭ below it is also shortened, etc., for each of the positions below this open tone. The position numbers are usually marked as 2♯, 3♯, etc., to designate a shortened position; some prefer −2, −3, etc.

It should be mentioned that the short second and third positions for the tenor trombone notes G and F♯-G♭ are actually preferred to positions 4 and 5 for these two notes. The rule which operates here as well as in the choice of fingering on the valved brasses, when there is a choice, is that *when other things are equal, the shorter tubing is preferred.* The shorter tubing speaks easier and the notes are slightly easier to hit. It is this consideration which is also one of the arguments favoring the use of C trumpets by professional symphony orchestra players.

With a thorough understanding of the basic principles underlying the brass instruments it is possible to eliminate the need for any brass fingering charts. Furthermore, many intonational problems become simple in their solution.

FINE

How to Measure a Brass Mouthpiece

Method of Determining the T-V-D CRIB code

TRAUGOTT ROHNER

January, 1953

IN THE PRECEDING ISSUE OF *The Instrumentalist* (November 1952) measurements of 213 different trumpet-cornet mouthpieces were given, and some suggestions on measuring them were offered. However, the pictorial presentation which follows may simplify the subject considerably and encourage more readers to take up the very practical technique of measuring brass mouthpieces.

Anyone who has the necessary tools, a careful attitude and a little patience can measure a brass mouthpiece. If all brass specialists and most school band and orchestra directors start measuring mouthpieces, both they and their students will benefit much thereby.

Let us proceed to measure a Bach 8C mouthpiece.

1. **T** or Throat. Insert the shank end of the largest drill which will go into the throat as illustrated at T. Drill blanks are even more desirable than drills. The number of the drill or blank is engraved on each. For the Bach 8C we find this number to be 27.

T—Throat

V—Volume

2. **V** or Volume. Insert the 3/16-inch width depth gage, as shown at V, into the cup, making sure that the gage is perpendicular and that both sides of the arm touch the rim. The number of sixteenths on the gage for this mouthpiece is 24.

Next use the ½-inch width depth gage (not illustrated) similarly. The number of sixteenths it can be inserted is 15. Add the two together, getting 39, and divide by 2; the result is 19.5.

3. **D** or Diameter of the cup. With a caliper, as shown at D-1, or with a divider, measure the inside diameter of the cup at the point where the curvature of the cup meets the curvature of the rim. Measure the spread of the points with a rule, as in D-2. Measurement may be made with a rule such as the one which comes with the gage or with a micrometer. With the micrometer the diameter is found to be .66 inch.

D-1—Diameter

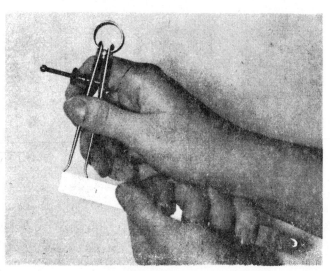

D-2—Diameter

CODE CHART

"Throat·Volume·Diameter·Curvature·Rim thickness·Impression·Bite"

CODE→	0	1	2	3	4	5	6	7	8	9
T· THROAT	29	28	27*	26	25	24	23	22	21	20
V· VOLUME	15	16	17	18	19*	20	21	22	23	24
D· DIAMETER	59	60	61	62	63	64	65*	66	67	68
C· CURVATURE	9	10	11	12	13*	14	15	16	17	18
R· RIM THICKNESS	19	20	21*	22	23	24	25	26	27	28
I· IMPRESSION	76	77	78	79	80	81*	82	83	84	85
B· BITE	—	—	2	3	4*	5	6	7	8	—

* Median above and below which are an equal number of mouthpieces.

4. **C** or Curvature of the rim. The jig shown at C is helpful for holding the mouthpiece and radius gage (curvature gage) in exactly the right position. Find the radius gage which fits exactly the Curvature of the rim. In general, select the smallest radius gage which does not

C—Curvature

gap away from the rim at the center. We find this to be the 12/64 (a circle having a radius of 12/64 of an inch); recorded as 12.

5. **R** or Rim width. Measure the outside rim width as

shown at R with a 1 to 2-inch micrometer. Subtract the cup Diameter (No. 3 above) from it and divide by 2.

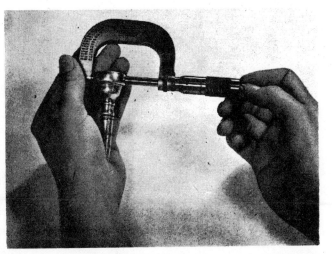

R—Rim

This Rim width is found to be 21.5 hundredths of an inch; recorded as 21.5.

6. **I** or Impression of the rim. Place the rim of the mouthpiece on an ink pad; rotate it to insure that the rim is thoroughly inked. Place the inked rim on a piece of paper. If too much ink adheres, repeat the step of placing the rim on the paper. The high point of the rim will make

a circle. Measure the diameter of this circle with the divider. If the line of the circle is rather wide, measure from the outside of the circle to the inside of the opposite side. With the aid of the micrometer we find this measurement to be .80 inch.

7. **B** or **B**ite of the inside edge of the rim. Use the small-

B—Bite

est radius gage which does not show a gap at the center when held against this inside rim edge. (See B.) The jig is helpful here again. The gage which suits this mouthpiece is marked 4/64; we record 4.

With the aid of the Code Chart we reduce the foregoing figures to a very usable and simple set of figures.

For T—27 the code figure is 2. (The "2" is found directly above the "27" on the chart.)
For V—19.5 the code figure is 4.
For D—.66 the code figure is 7.
For C—12 the code figure is 3.
For R—21.5 the code figure is 2.
For I—.80 the code figure is 4.
For B—4 the code figure is 4.

Thus the code figure, known as T-V-D CRIB, for this

Bach mouthpiece is 2-4-7-3-2-4-4. Henceforth, it can be compared with other Bach mouthpieces or with any other make of which the code figures are known. Manufacturers will place this code figure on the mouthpieces only if we, the buyers and users of mouthpieces, encourage them to do so.

Measuring Tools

For the 213 mouthpieces the writer measured, he used a set of Morse twist drills from No. 19 through 29. These can be bought at any hardware store. However, if the preferred drill blanks are desired, one needs to order them especially from a precision tool house.*

The 3/16-inch gage shown in V is a Lufkin, No. 511, available from any precision tool house.**

The ½-inch depth gage (not illustrated) had to be made especially for use on trumpet-cornet mouthpieces. It is designed somewhat differently.***

A divider (similar to a compass) can be bought at any store handling drawing equipment. If an inside caliper as illustrated in "D," is desired, though it is not absolutely essential, it also is obtainable from a precision tool house.

The radius gages, Lufkin 77A, are on the market as are also the micrometers.**** Two micrometers were used in this project, one which measures from 0 to 1 inch and another which measures from 1 to 2 inches.

If the reader or his school cannot afford to buy a complete set of tools, it is strongly urged that at least some of them be purchased. With only the drills or drill blanks, the two depth gages and a divider, four of the seven measurements can be made. If maximum accuracy is not demanded, one can get along without the micrometers or they may be bought second-hand or borrowed. It should be remembered that the tools are a life-time investment, however.

With the tools at hand anyone can measure mouthpieces and thus replace guesswork with scientific accuracy.

*Price of the blanks is about 40 cents each. Sterling Products Co., 1212 N. Jefferson St., Chicago, Ill., is one of many tool houses that can supply them.

**Lufkin No. 511 sells at $2.75. Other brands are O.K.

***Information concerning the purchase of these gages may be obtained by writing THE INSTRUMENTALIST.

****Lufkin 77A sells at $5.70; micrometers at about $15.

January-February, 1953

Valve-Brass Intonation Difficulties Conquered

*Compromising with nature's 5th harmonic
does not solve problems of correct tone*

MARK HINDSLEY

THE DESIRABLE INTONATION pattern of a wind instrument would be like that of a well-tuned piano, with basically even temperament (the octave divided into 12 equal semi-tones) and a little "stretching" on intervals in the extreme registers. Tuning a

piano and tuning a wind instrument, however, are entirely different propositions. Each tone of a piano is derived from a separate string or group of strings; most tones of a wind instrument are derived from the vibrations of a column of air used also by

several other tones.

It is this sharing of the same air column that creates the first intonation problem in a wind instrument. Nature's table of harmonics does not precisely coincide with a table of equal temperament. Of the first 12 harmonics, only the octaves 1-2-4-8 agree; 3-6-12 are about .13 per cent sharp, a very small amount which does not constitute a problem; 9 is .25 per cent sharp, still not a serious problem; 5-10 are .76 per cent flat, which *is* a problem; 7-11 are so far from a scale tone that they are not usable; we get along without them.

In the valve-brass instruments we do not seem to be able to get along without that troublesome 5th harmonic (the 10th is in the seldom-used extreme high register). It is commonly used in the "open" instrument and with the first and second valves individually and in combination, making four troublesome tones.

It should now be hurriedly said that not all brass instruments play according to nature's table of harmonics. No, indeed! Our acoustical engineers are able to change nature, and this they do to the extent that almost every make and model of instrument has a different harmonic table. It is the 5th harmonic they are usually trying to correct. However, I have not yet found any brass instrument in which the four 5th harmonic tones have been raised without compromising other tones. I, therefore, assume that it is an engineering impossibility.

Compromise in Pitch

Theoretically the valves of a brass instrument are supposed to lower the pitch of the open tones one-half, one, and one and a half steps. It is common knowledge, however, that when they are thus tuned, the valve combinations are sharp. It has been the practice to tune the individual valves a little flat so that the combinations will be only a little sharp. Here again we have compromise, slight enough to be reasonably practical on the 1-2 and 2-3 combinations, but not adequate to be effective on the 1-3 and 1-2-3 combinations. Many cornets and trumpets have a ring on the third valve slide or a trigger on the first valve slide to lengthen the tube for these latter combinations.

It is my conviction that we should not attempt to solve our valve-brass intonation problems by compromising with nature on the 5th harmonic or by compromising fixed valve slide lengths for the chromatic tones. With such compromises we are likely to end with only one tone (whichever one is tuned to) naturally in tune and

all the rest naturally out of tune.

Mechanical Adjustment

There are 31 tones in the normal register of a cornet or trumpet from low F♯ to high C. By tuning the first valve slide to lower the open tone exactly one step, the second exactly one-half step, and the third exactly one and a half steps, and by using nature's good harmonics 2-3-4-6-8 on the open instrument and with each of the three valves, we have the means of playing 20 tones naturally in tune or 19 without the E fourth space which we prefer to play open. These 19 tones have the correct tube length for their proper pitch. The remaining 12 do not have the proper tube length and will be out of tune unless an adjustment is made. Adjustments can be made by mechanical means except in complicated technical situations, and even in these situations the same mechanical means may be used to effect compromises no worse than exist in the usual instrument.

The four flat 5th harmonic tones may be raised by a movable main tuning slide held in its basic position by a spring and operated on the cornet and trumpet by the left thumb. The remaining eight tones played with valve combinations 2-3, 1-3, and 1-2-3 may be lowered by operation of the third valve slide, also controlled by a spring, with the third finger of the left hand.

These instruments and these mechanisms are not theoretical; they are real. In our studies and tests at the University of Illinois we found some cornets and trumpets—not many, but some—with nature's harmonic pattern. We found no baritones with this pattern, but there was one which came reasonably close. We have not yet found a perfect tuba, but again some have been close. We believe baritones and tubas can be made with nature's harmonic pattern.

Actual Experiment

On the cornets, trumpets and baritones we adjusted the lengths of the valve slides so that they were in tune individually. Then we worked out and applied the mechanisms referred to above. Going beyond all the theory of harmonics and tube lengths, here is the way the instruments are working in actual practice, referring for the moment to the cornet and trumpet for notation and for thumb and finger

operation.

The main tuning slide is controlled by the left thumb. It may be moved in either direction to raise or lower the pitch, springs returning it to its original position when pressure is released. It is used primarily to raise D, D♯ and E, fourth line and space. (C♯ third space is almost in tune naturally by virtue of the naturally sharp 1-2 combination.) It is also used to augment the third valve slide in lowering low C♯. It may be used further to lower 1-2 or 2-3 combinations or to raise or lower any tone which may be found faulty in the exigencies of actual playing because of embouchure condition, dynamics or the necessity of matching the pitch of another instrument. In addition to its 5th harmonic principal function, this mechanism gives to the player the feel of the violinist's left hand on the strings; any tone may be adjusted without losing tone quality or security of embouchure.

The spring on the third valve slide holds it in an "out" position in tune for low D. The player brings the slide to its closed position as part of his grip on the instrument and releases it all the way for low D. He may use either this slide or the main tuning slide to lower 2-3 combinations; he must use them both for low C♯.

Progressing upward by chromatic scale through the register from low F, here is an outline of the usual fingering and intonation situations on such an instrument:

F♯-G-G♯-A. Most players relax too much on these tones, making them flat. With the shorter valve slides in this instrument they are usually well in tune with regular fingerings, third valve slide in, no further adjustment.

B♭-B-C. Avoid the tendency to play flat on these tones. If necessary, raise the pitch with the left thumb on the main tuning slide.

C♯. Third valve slide and main tuning slide out.

D. Third valve slide out.

D♯. Lower pitch with third valve slide or tuning slide.

E. Play with 3rd valve or with 1-2 lowered with tuning slide.

F-F♯-G. Ordinarily need no adjustment.

G♯-A. Same as D♯ and E a fourth lower.

B♭-B-C. Ordinarily need no adjustment.

C♯-D-D♯-E. Raise as necessary with tuning slide.

F-F♯-G. Should not need adjustment, but watch tendency to overreach in upper register and adjust with tuning slide if necessary.

G♯-A-B♭-B-C. Same as octave lower, again watching sharpness in this register, particularly in softer playing.

It is not impossible to play in tune on an imperfect instrument. Many of our finest players have been doing it remarkably well for a long time. Most of them use mechanical aids on the first and/or third valve slides and make adjustments of the tuning slide for particular passages, accomplishing the remainder by lip flexibility and control, guided by a fine ear. Still many otherwise fine players think they play in tune while they are playing out of tune because they are accustomed to what they have always heard themselves play.

A valve-brass instrument such as has been described can never remove the extreme necessity of proper tone production with a well developed and flexible embouchure and a good ear. It has been my observation, however, that most of our young players have better ears than instruments and play out of tune mostly because it is not easy, sometimes not even possible, to play in tune with confidence and security. Brass instruments which are built as described bring every tone within reach of proper pitch, whether in "just" or "tempered" intonation.

Marked Improvement

We have used complete sections of these cornets, trumpets and baritones in our Concert Band for the entire past school year. The improvement in intonation has been most apparent. I am convinced that our remaining intonation problems in these sections are not faults of the instruments.

Cornets, trumpets and baritones with the tuning slide and third valve, slide mechanisms are now being produced by one major manufacturer, and others have indicated their intention of producing them soon. It has been gratifying to note the widespread interest and action in connection with this one phase of our common problems in wind intonation.

FINE

THE TUBA –
Foundation of the Band

BERNARD FITZGERALD

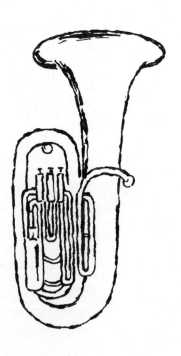

WHILE PERCUSSION PLAYERS may claim priority as the "forgotten section" of the band, the tuba section can often provide strong competition for this dubious distinction. The experience of many band adjudicators and clinicians in observing the failure of the basses to function effectively provides evidence of the truth of this judgment.

Perhaps it is desirable to consider first the responsibility of the bass section in the band. The function of bass instruments is determined to a considerable extent by both the character of the music and the harmonic principles upon which it is constructed. The overwhelming majority of the music performed by bands is constructed according to harmonic theories in which the bass line forms the foundation for the entire musical structure. In the band it is necessary for the tubas to have the major responsibility in providing this foundation, particularly in small bands, since other bass line instruments are either lacking in sufficient numbers or cannot provide comparable sonority to support the higher instruments.

The tubas normally provide the basic support for the band, having a musical importance comparable to that of the foundation as related to architecture. However, band performances too frequently convey the impression of a musical structure which is suspended in midair because its faulty or inadequate support may range from being inaudible to being unrecognizable. Such deficiencies and omissions radically alter the harmonic content, resulting in incomplete or changed harmony.

In performing marches and other music essentially rhythmic and homophonic in character, the basses serve in a somewhat dual capacity, providing a foundation that is both rhythmic and harmonic. However, it is not uncommon to hear marching bands in which the basses serve primarily as rhythm instruments with very little attention given to pitch. In fact, the bass drum and the basses frequently seem to be sounding in unison.

Instrument Care

A recent clinic involving thirty tuba players served to highlight some of the principal problems and difficulties of the section. The first very obvious problem involved the condition of the instruments. Satisfactory tuning was found to be impossible since the valve and tuning slides of at least half of the instruments were stuck and therefore could not be adjusted. Either the respective bands tuned to the pitch of the tuba section, or the bass section did not tune with the band at all!

Further observation revealed several instruments actually held together with chewing gum or adhesive tape, or both; serious dents or leaks in the mouthpipe tubing or valve slides; worn corks and broken springs on the water keys; damaged mouthpieces; and tuning bits not properly fitted to the instruments. Mechanical difficulties included poor valve action resulting from corrosion or from lack of cleaning and oiling; weak or incorrectly adjusted valve springs; corroded valve caps which prevented removal of valves for cleaning, oiling and adjusting; and worn or improperly adjusted valve corks and felts.

It is obviously illogical to expect satisfactory musical results from equipment in such poor condition. Perhaps such a situation is indicative of the extent to which the tuba section is often neglected. The sum total of handicaps results not only in impaired mechanical efficiency but also in poor pitch and tone quality. However, such problems can be remedied by proper maintenance of equipment, by teaching the player how to care for the instrument and by periodic inspections of equipment.

Listening Important

The problems of tone quality, pitch and attack were next in importance for the clinic group, and it was gratifying to observe the marked improvement even in a short period of time. The improvement was principally brought about by an increased awareness of pitch and tone quality resulting from more critical LISTENING by each individual while playing.

The general tendency to employ an explosive type of attack seriously affects both pitch and tone quality. This can be counteracted by practicing starting the tone smoothly without using the tongue, employing the syllable "hoo" or "poo." After the player has learned to use the breath properly in this way, he should then practice starting the tone, using the tongue to release the breath and continuing to avoid the explosive attack.

The major difficulties in regard to tone quality concern lack of resonance or body of tone, usually resulting from inadequate breath support and a too relaxed formation of the embouchure. It is recognized that intonation problems exist on all valve instruments, especially when valves are used in combination. However, most good tubas can be played reasonably well in tune if the instrument is in good condition and if the player will make embouchure adjustments to compensate for the out-of-tune notes. Generally speaking, the notes below the bass staff are the ones which are most troublesome. On the BB♭ tuba the low C and B♮ are sharp, and the low B♭ and A♮ are flat.

In the final analysis, good tone quality and intonation largely depend upon the attitude and aural discrimination of the player, which are the result of musical training, proper instruction and intelligent guidance.

Technique

It is difficult to obtain clarity and definition in executing rapid technical passages because of the broad tone of the tuba, the register involved, and the slow response of the instrument because of the length of tubing. Consequently, coordination of tonguing and fingering must be very accurate and precise to avoid a heavy, sluggish effect.

The lack of technical control of fingering often results in rhythmic inaccuracy in and speeding up of rapid passages. Technical drills on scales and arpeggios will aid in developing a more fluent technique, better coordination and steadier control.

Reading Problems

During the clinic previously referred to, each player was given a try-out on several passages. Not one player in the group was able to read the first four measures of "Richard III Overture" correctly, observing the rhythm, key signature, and one accidental in this passage. Such a result might not be surprising on a first reading, but the music was not played correctly even after three trials by each player.

A number of factors may contribute to such a situation.

1. Lack of experience in playing melodic parts.

2. Carelessness regarding note values due to the generally simple rhythmic character of typical bass parts.

3. Inability to recognize errors in pitch and rhythm.

4. Failure to observe key and meter signatures.

5. Lack of fluency in reading.

6. Failure to know the correct fingerings.

These factors indicate a definite need for providing etudes and study materials which will increase reading accuracy and fluency. The fact that many players fail to recognize their mistakes indicates that they did not associate the printed part with the correct sound or did not accurately identify rhythm patterns. A high percentage of technical errors is the result of carelessness, failure to analyze rhythmic patterns accurately and failure to hear correct interval relationships.

Faulty playing habits are easily developed. If the student continues to make errors without being corrected by the director, the player will assume either that he is playing correctly or that it really does not make much difference what or how he plays.

If the director regularly checks performance on assigned parts, technic or etudes, both as to individual players and as to section, tuba players will acquire a better understanding of the importance of the bass section and be better prepared to fulfill their responsibility as the foundation of the band.

FINE

Problems Involved in Standardizing Brass Mouthpieces

BERNARD FITZGERALD

THE RECENT ARTICLES on brass instrument mouthpieces (INSTRUMENTALIST, Nov., 1952) have served to focus attention upon the need for a standard system among manufacturers for. identifying the several measurements of mouthpieces. While this is an important step in aiding the teacher or player in the selection of a suitable mouthpiece, considerable research is necessary to determine which combination or combinations of throat, rim, bite, cup and backbore dimensions will produce the best results.

The answer to the question, "Which is the best mouthpiece?" can be determined only by relating the measurements of the mouthpiece to the physical characteristics of the player, the make and bore of the instrument and the type of playing for which the mouthpiece is to be used. As an illustration of the problems involved, it is obviously unreasonable to expect a trombonist to produce a tone of adequate sonority on a bass trombone if a shallow mouthpiece with a small throat is used.

Since the tone quality is affected to a considerable degree by the several dimensions of the mouthpiece, some standard as to the desired or characteristic tone quality must necessarily be determined prior to standardizing mouthpieces. This is an extremely difficult problem since the tone quality is often determined by the music being performed or by the personal preference of the player or the conductor. Research investigations in this area are currently in progress, and it is hoped that a standard basis can be established in the foreseeable future.

Other Studies Needed

In the meantime, there are several other aspects relating to the general problem which merit study and investigation. One of the important measurements in mouthpiece design was not included in the report by Rohner because of the complications involved in obtaining suitable equipment for accurate measurement.

This dimension is the backbore of the mouthpiece, which has a considerable effect upon tone quality, control and blowing resistance, depending upon the amount and length of the taper involved. It is of extreme importance that the backbore be determined in relation to the other mouthpiece dimensions and the bore of the instrument. The adjustment required to improve the backbore is often a very slight one which can be made by using a tapered reamer. However, it should be noted that even slight changes in the throat and backbore dimensions may alter the playing quality of a mouthpiece considerably since these factors are of critical importance. Therefore, alterations of the throat or backbore dimensions of the mouthpiece must be limited to adjustments which will not disturb the balance between the dimensions of the cup, throat and backbore.

The median measurement of the 213 cornet and trumpet mouthpieces reported by Rohner cannot be assumed to represent the ideal combination of these dimensions but do serve to indicate the median measurements of the mouthpieces currently available. However, since manufacturers are often influenced by public demand, competition and other considerations than ideal design, it is necessary to determine some valid conclusions as to the basic mouthpiece dimensions which will meet the playing requirements of the average player.

Physical Factors

This consideration must take into account the many variables of the individual facio-dental characteristics, the size and shape of the oral cavity and the efficiency of the embouchure and the breathing mechanism. Obviously it will be necessary to have more than one mouthpiece design if these variable physical factors are given consideration.

Another factor which affects the playing qualities of the mouthpiece is the thickness of the metal wall of the rim, cup and mouthpiece stem. Renold Schilke is at present cooperating with the author by producing experimental mouthpieces with considerably thinner walls than are normally used. Although the writer is not aware of previous experiments of this nature, the present investigation definitely indicates that the thinner mouthpieces have less blowing resistance, quicker response and a more resonant tone quality than mouthpieces of normal thickness.

Present evidence indicates that extremely thin mouthpieces may lack adequate blowing resistance, which can be detrimental to tone control at extreme dynamic levels. Further experimentation is needed to determine the thickness of metal which will achieve the desired balance between blowing resistance, tonal resonance and quickness of response.

The author has conducted performance tests for several different groups of musicians, demonstrating both the thin and the conventional type of mouthpieces. In each instance the tone quality of the thin mouthpiece has been preferred on the basis of a listening test in which the same musical examples were performed on two mouthpieces which were identical except for the thickness of the metal. While conclusive evidence is not yet available, the current experiments suggest that the mouthpieces with thin walls and shallow cups can produce a resonant full tone comparable to the tone produced on mouthpieces of conventional thickness which have deep cups.

'Feel' of Rim

One of the important factors in selecting a suitable mouthpiece concerns the "feel" of the rim to the player. This involves consideration of five of the dimensions noted by Rohner—cup diameter, rim curvature, width, impression and bite. In performance tests comparing several mouthpieces in which these dimensions were very nearly identical according to the measurements by Rohner, the author found that very slight differences in rim curvature, impression and bite were quite noticeable in regard to the "feel" of the mouthpiece on the lips. These differences affected the feel of the rim to such an extent as to create a false impression of a larger or smaller cup diameter where these differences did not actually exist.

The rims with less "bite" were very comfortable and had excellent flexibility but required more endurance and made accuracy of attack more difficult. The rims which were rounded and lower toward the outside edge increased flexibility and had a more comfortable feel on the embouchure. The minute differences in these dimensions can often be measured only in thousandths of an inch; yet the difference in the feel of the rim is quite evident to a mature player and may influence flexibility or endurance to a considerable degree.

The fact that it is extremely difficult to obtain two mouthpieces with exactly the same feel and playing response is an indication of the need for greater accuracy in maintaining close tolerances in the manufacture of brass instrument mouthpieces. One manufacturer stated that it is almost impossible to obtain exact duplicates in quantity. In part, these discrepancies are due to failure to retool frequently, but the dimensions of the throat and rim are often altered in the process of buffing prior to plating, in plating too heavily or in polishing after plating.

In view of the numerous obstacles mentioned in this article, it might appear that both standardizing and accuracy of reproduction of brass mouthpieces is not feasible. Such an assumption is far from the truth although there are numerous aspects of the problem which will require extensive investigation and research. The equipment for the accurate reproduction of mouthpieces is available, and it is simply a matter of determining what we need and of being willing to pay the necessary price to obtain mouthpieces of the accuracy and design which are most satisfactory.

September, 1953

Weaknesses Observed in Freshman Brass Players

C. B. RIGHTER

The brass clinic has been a rich source of help for the teacher of brass instruments and for the band director, whether or not he is himself a brass specialist. I regard Bernard Fitzgerald as one of the outstanding brass men, and he has been ably assisted by other specialists in the field.

What follows should be regarded strictly as the random observations of "an outsider looking in." Although the writer has played trumpet and baritone indifferently, his principal instruments have been violin and clarinet. Nevertheless, as a band and orchestra director, he has had to deal with the brasses at close range and has been forced to find a few practical solutions for some of the more pressing problems of brass instrumentalists.

The more common weaknesses found in brass players who enter the university may be summarized as follows:

1. Poor tone quality
2. Faulty intonation
3. Lack of sustaining power
4. Muddy articulation
5. Uncertainty and inflexibility of attack
6. Failure in dynamic control

We have, I fear, heard and read these categories of brass inadequacy so often that they have become more or less meaningless. We list them or discuss them, and nothing happens. Each new crop of players is characterized by the same universal weaknesses. Occasionally, by dint of great effort, we succeed in making a player conscious of what is meant in actual performance by tone quality, intonation, sostenuto, articulation, attack and dynamics. But, by and large, our failures outnumber our successes.

Is the fault in our teaching? I think the answer to this question is a definite affirmative. We do not go far enough in our analysis of each of these problems, and we do not succeed in getting across to the student the real meaning of the thing we are talking about.

Leaving the technical solutions largely to the studio experts, I should like to treat each of these categories briefly in terms of what I, as a band director, should like to hear from the players.

Tone Quality

The tone quality should be characteristic of the instrument through all dynamic levels. A trombone player who can produce only a mellow feathery tone is no trombone player. A cornet player who cannot sing a soft sustained melody with adequate lip slurring is no cornet player. A bass player who can only "pump out" a rhythmic-harmonic part is no bass player. A horn player who cannot produce a characteristic tone in his upper and lower registers is no horn player.

But quality *per se* goes beyond these points. In the simplest terms, the tone should generally be pleasing to the ear. Along with maximum resonance at the different dynamic levels we should consider the two basic ingredients of tone—velvet and sandpaper. The velvet should predominate, but there are a few spots that call for an element of sandpaper in the tone for descriptive or dramatic purposes. These extremes are the contrasting colors with which we paint our tonal picture.

Intonation

Intonation, is, of course, basic. Our failure in this department results from placing our dependence almost entirely upon the *horn* instead of upon the ear, lips and breath of the player. I would go so far as to say that one of the first things a player should be taught is how to shade the pitch of every tone on his instrument. If he cannot do this, he can never play strictly in tune either with himself or with others. Shading of pitch is not a technical device to be used occasionally; it must be a resource which is employed almost constantly, especially in all slow-moving passages.

If the reader questions the above statement, he has only to test almost any player carefully on all octaves within the playing range of the instrument. He will find very few perfect octaves!

In practical terms, the real disaster occurs when a series of octaves is played by (1) a trumpet in its high register, (2) a French horn in its middle register, and (3) a baritone in its low register. A pitch discrepancy of up to a quarter-tone would be quite usual for this test unless the players have been especially trained to anticipate and correct the difficulty. In most bands we are compelled to live with this perpetual dissonance.

The pitch shading which is needed to give all major, minor, augmented and diminished intervals their characteristic tonality must be treated as a part of the player's basic training. Two examples will serve to illustrate: (1) any harmonic minor scale with its three extra-close half-steps and its extra-wide augmented second; and (2) the melody of "Annie Laurie," especially in the key of D for the cornet or French horn or C for the baritone (bass clef) or the BB♭ bass.

But listen *carefully*; do not accept intervals that are *almost* right!

Sustaining Power

Lack of sustaining power is evident in almost every band. It arises from faulty breathing technique, lips which are too poorly trained to produce maximum tone with minimum breath, lazy musical thinking which ignores the need of sustaining melodies and phrases, and laxity on the part of directors in demanding a full sostenuto and in teaching the principle of staggered breathing within sections.

Articulation

Articulation is an almost unknown element in many bands. The concept that the phrasing should be followed precisely as it is written seems just too, too fantastic to many of our incoming freshmen. Thus we face the inevitable Babel of each player devising his own phrasing. I have tried to get the importance of phrasing across to players by saying that I would as soon hear a wrong note as a wrong articulation, but it is a constant battle with those who have never been taught the importance of correct phrasing and articulation.

In this connection, one might point out the incalculable damage that has been done by those methods which devote entire pages to single types of articulation. What we need is more etude material in which articulations, rhythmic patterns, dynamics and interval skips are widely diversified within each etude. Only then will we begin to have some players with real sight-reading ability. At present, articulation is something especially reserved for Arban, and not necessarily to be applied to the band material.

Attack

Attack is another area for the expert, but as a band director I should like to find more players who could start the first tone of a soft melody in a manner reasonably appropriate to the song-like tune which follows. Usually we hear an explosive "thump," which may or may not taper off into something resembling a melody. Woe be at the start of each new phrase! Or if there should occur a series of softly detached tones in which a slight variation in attack is suggested! Or a *pianissimo* attack in the upper register! Such are only a few of the

artistic hazards faced by the band director whose players have been trained in the "slug-em, sock-em" school. Equally disastrous are the efforts of these players to execute a series of "pin-point" attacks—say extremely short staccato tones at any or every dynamic level.

One final point in the matter of attack, one which perhaps should have been mentioned first. Can the player "pick out" a starting note—perhaps in the upper register and in an odd tonality and lacking any support—and attack this tone cleanly and clearly, with just the right emphasis and at just the right dynamic level? One such player is a priceless treasure; two in the same band would represent opulence beyond the wildest dream of the average band director.

Dynamic Control

Dynamic control, in common with most of these elements of weakness, falls in that category more from lack of attention than from lack of skill. When we begin to teach the *importance* of these basic elements, we will begin to get results. It is the "take-it-or-leave-it" attitude that causes the trouble.

The second strain of a march is marked *piano*; so what? A few players observe the dynamic change; all the others charge right through it *fortissimo*. What is the result? Naturally, the few alert players give up in disgust, or reason that the dynamic change must have been of too little importance to merit the attention of the director.

The importance of dynamics rests in the following facts: (1) A composition gains in interest if there is contrast between one portion of the piece and another; (2) The principal melody can be heard only if the accompaniment is subdued, regardless of the dynamic markings; (3) The true character of a chord is present only if the characteristic tones are heard clearly; i.e., the major or minor third, the minor seventh or a dissonant passing tone; (4) Faulty intonation can never be corrected unless the chord is heard "in balance"; and (5) Conflicting, non-blending tone color can be eliminated only when there is poised control of dynamics.

As teachers, let us try to take a new fresh look at these fundamentals and attempt to devise new ways of stressing their importance in actual performance. Sometimes a more vivid or colorful means of expressing ourselves will do the trick. Greater insistence upon accuracy or upon a *full* compliance with a high standard of performance will pay dividends. However, everything considered, no method succeeds better than that of having students themselves demonstrate in exaggerated form the *right way*, when they have achieved it, in direct contrast with an exaggerated form of the *wrong way*.

Most of the above points apply with equal force to the woodwinds and the strings, but the brasses seem to neglect many of these points with somewhat greater frequency because of their false reliance upon the *instrument*. The brass player, as a matter of fact, may often be able to play quite flashy technical passages before he learns that what passes for tone is really a most unpleasant noise.

FINE

October, 1953

A Standard Staffless Music Notation System

TRAUGOTT ROHNER

IT IS OFTEN NECESSARY to write or speak of the pitch of notes without the aid of the music staff. We all know what is meant by middle C, but here the simplicity ends, for there is no common system of calling the pitch of notes. We are bogged down by a lack of a single good method.

At least eight different systems are in use. The trouble is not that any of several of these would not serve us well but that we have not decided on any one system. It is high time that we eliminate confusion by doing so.

We don't need a national committee to weigh all the advantages and disadvantages of each system or to take a poll of all the musicians. The problem is rather simple, for there are only three major requisites of the ideal system: (1) it must be simple to understand and remember; (2) it must be easy to write and to speak; and (3) it has to be scientifically accurate and usable in both music and science.

Most systems can be eliminated by one or the other of these three requirements. Thus we come to the conclusion that there is one which deserves to be accepted as the standard system of staffless notation. The piano keyboard serves as the point of reference. The lowest C thereon is called C1; the next C, one octave higher, is C2; then C3; middle C is C4; and then follow C5, C6 and C7. The octave below C1 is C0; if one wishes to go higher than the tones on the keyboard, it is simple to proceed to C8, C9, etc.

The D above C4 (middle C) is D4, while the B below it is B3. As one can see, the notes up an octave from any C have the same number, as is the case with some other systems.

To assist in learning and establishing this system, it is desirable to establish middle C as C4 or to associate the 4's in A-440=A4. The notes up one octave from C4 are all 4's; the notes between C3 and C4 are all 3's, etc. Having established the notes in these two octaves, one can add another octave up or down with ease.

The musician might well establish first some of the important notes on his major instrument. For example, the strings of a violin are G3, D4, A4 and E5. Written C4 on the bass clarinet sounds B♭2; the lowest note on the Standard B♭ soprano clarinet is written E3. The alto oboe (English horn) when fingered C4 sounds F3. The C piccolo when fingered C4 sounds C5. If the lowest open tone (not pedal tone) of the trombone is B♭2, what is the lowest open tone of the BB♭ tuba? The lowest string of the cello is C2. What is the *pitch* of the lowest string of the bass?

Notice that the foregoing system is not only eminently well suited to music but to science as well. Furthermore, unlike some systems, this one is easy both to write and to speak. Finally, there is none which is simpler to understand or to remember.

We propose to do away with the multiplicity of differing systems and to establish one. The INSTRUMENTALIST will henceforth use this system. Gone are the days when we will say "the second B♭ below middle C"; instead we will say B♭2. Gone is the awkwardness of statements such as the E on the fourth space in the treble clef"; instead we'll write and say E5.

Some practice in using this system is highly recommended. With use and understanding will come familiarity and acceptance.

Fine

BASIS IN PIANO KEYBOARD

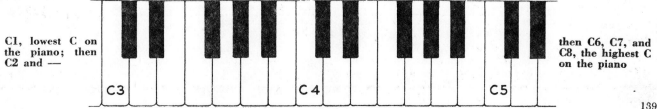

C1, lowest C on the piano; then C2 and —

then C6, C7, and C8, the highest C on the piano

C3   C4   C5

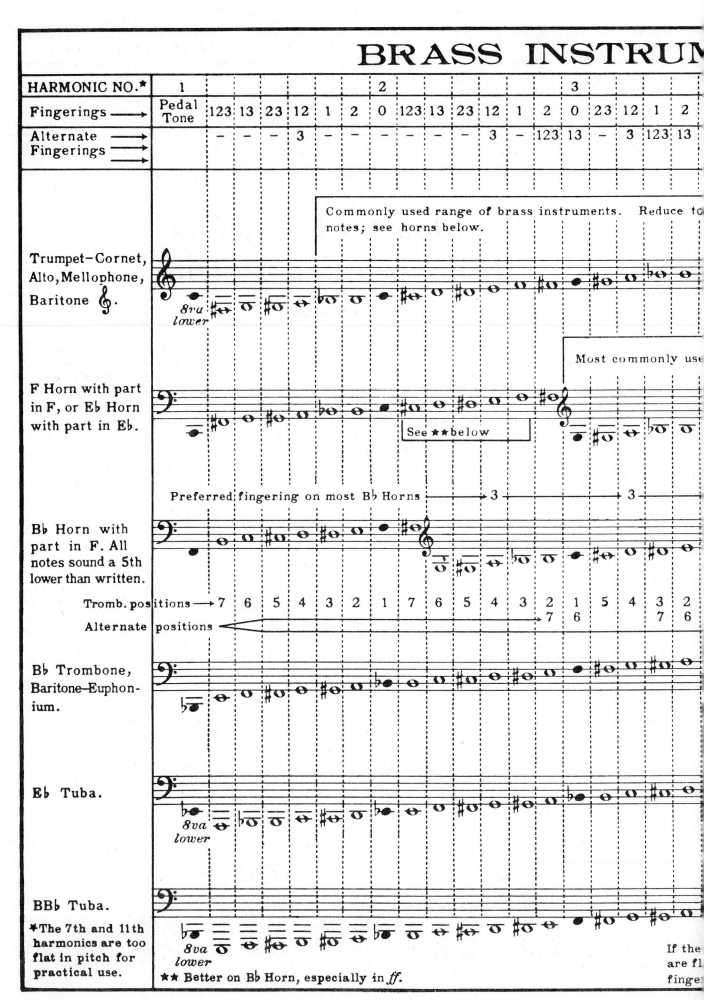

Copyright 1953 by The INSTRUMENTALIST Co.

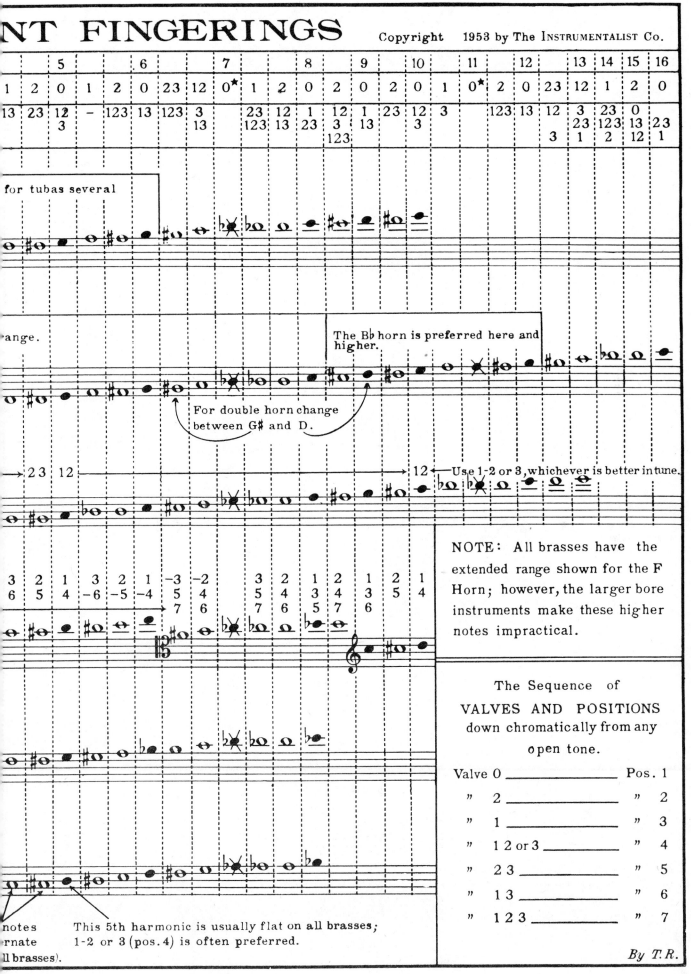

for tubas several

range.

The Bb horn is preferred here and higher.

For double horn change between G♯ and D.

Use 1-2 or 3, whichever is better in tune.

NOTE: All brasses have the extended range shown for the F Horn; however, the larger bore instruments make these higher notes impractical.

The Sequence of
VALVES AND POSITIONS
down chromatically from any open tone.

Valve 0	Pos. 1
" 2	" 2
" 1	" 3
" 1 2 or 3	" 4
" 2 3	" 5
" 1 3	" 6
" 1 2 3	" 7

By T. R.

notes
rnate
l brasses).

This 5th harmonic is usually flat on all brasses; 1-2 or 3 (pos. 4) is often preferred.

Pitch Chart for Treble Clef Brass Instruments

TRAUGOTT ROHNER

INSTRUMENTS *are listed* in descending order of pitch. In all instances where trumpet is mentioned, one should also include the cornet.

The written note for each of these instruments is C4.

Bb piccolo trumpet_____Bb4
G soprano trumpet_____G4
F soprano trumpet_____F4
Eb soprano trumpet_____Eb4
D trumpet_____D4
C trumpet_____C4
B "Aida" trumpet[1]_____B3
*Bb trumpet_____Bb3
Bb Fluegelhorn_____Bb3
A trumpet[2]_____A3
*Bb horn[3]_____F3
*F horn[3]_____F3
F alto trumpet[1]_____F3

---

*Commonly used in American bands.
[1]For photographs and description and use of these and other brasses, please see "Do You Know Your Brasses?" by Vincent Bach in the January and March, 1950, issues of The INSTRUMENTALIST.
[2]This is usually a Bb trumpet with slides pulled out to A.
[3]When the horn part is in F, the note C4 sounds F3 regardless of whether the Bb or the F horn is used; similarly for both horns if the part is in Eb.

F alto trombone _____F3
*Eb horn_____Eb3
*Eb alto, mellophone_____Eb3
Eb alto trombone[4]_____Eb3
Eb alto trumpet[1]_____Eb3
C tenor (bass) trumpet_____C3
C tenor trombone[4]_____C3

Basic to the consideration of the pitches is the fact that a superior brass instrument can be built in *any* key.

The diameter and shape of the tubing as well as the diameter and shape of the bell and mouthpiece can vary considerably within each of the above instruments. All trombones can be either slide or valved trombones. The trombonium, not listed above because it is generally considered a bass clef instrument, is a valved trombone with the tubing and bell positioned similarly to those of

---

[4]All alto and tenor trombones can also use the bass or tenor clef. In fact, all brasses can be written in treble clef as is the case in some foreign brass band music. An Eb tuba, for example, will then sound Eb2, a BBb tuba BBb1, not to mention the baritones and euphoniums, which sound Bb2.

the baritone. In view of the hard work devoted to overcoming the shortcomings of the slide, as compared to the ease with which valves are used, and in view of the fact that the music is so rarely enhanced by the peculiarities of the slide, it is amazing that more band directors do not replace the slide trombone with a valved trombone, tenor trumpet or trombonium, especially for marching bands.

Some of the more commonly used transpositions are given in the chart below.

Bb trumpet playing C part—transpose UP two half-steps
Bb trumpet playing A part—transpose DOWN one half-step
C trumpet playing Bb part—transpose DOWN two half-steps
D trumpet playing C part—transpose DOWN two half-steps
F horn, alto, mellophone playing Eb part—transpose DOWN two half-steps
CC tuba is fingered two half-steps UP from that of the BBb tuba

Fine

Fingering the Bass Trombone and 4-Valve Euphonium

TRAUGOTT ROHNER

THE FOURTH VALVE on euphoniums and tubas is equal, roughly, to valves 1-3. To be sure, the function of this valve is to lower the range of the instrument; however, it has a more important role to fill in improving intonation. (In this respect the compensating valve instruments which improve intonation automatically deserve careful attention.)

The left thumb valve on Bb-F bass trombones lowers the pitch by the same interval of a fourth as the 4th valve. Thus, if we call this thumb valve "T," we can write the formula *T=pos. 6=valve 4= valves 1-3.* This will help one to understand how

both the 4th valve and the left thumb trombone valve work.

Below is given a fingering chart showing (1) the fingering of the notes below the usual range of euphoniums and trombones and (2) the preferred fingerings for improved intonation and ease of execution. Notice how "T" replaces position 6, and valve 4 replaces 1-3.

One may ask, "How does it happen that there are three fingerings given for the euphonium for the note E2?"

The answer is that with the added tubing of valve 4, valve 2 is too short

to lower the pitch sufficiently, while valve 1 is too long, and unless valve slide 3 is pulled considerably, 1-2-3 will be very sharp.

The rule which operates here is this: *The longer the tubing that is engaged for any note, the more tubing proportionately is required to lower the pitch a desired interval.* It is the length of the tubing rather than the pitch which determines the amount of additional tubing required to lower the pitch a desired interval. Understanding the foregoing will explain why valves 1-2-3 as well as 1-3 invariably are sharp notes; it explains, too, the difficulty of playing the notes below F2 in tune on even the 4-valve euphonium.

This rule also explains why the positions on the bass trombone, when "T" is engaged, are farther apart than on the same instrument without "T." The longer positions permit only six positions with "T" while seven are possible without "T."

The 4th valve on an E♭ tuba lowers the pitch an interval of a 4th. By reconstructing the chart given above for euphonium an interval of a fifth lower, one has the correct fingerings for the 4-valve E♭ tuba.

When five valves appear on a euphonium, the fifth valve is used for directing the air into the second bell, which is smaller and gives a tone quality similar to a valved trombone.

For a more complete discussion of the use of the 4-valve euphonium with some excellent musical examples, see "When Is a Baritone a Euphonium?" by Harold Brasch in the March, 1949, issue of The INSTRUMENTALIST.

Fine

The Bb-F Bass Trombone

Preferred:	T♭7	T♯6	T♭4	T3	T2	T♯1
Alternate:	-	-	-	-	7	6

Preferred:	5	4	3	2	1	T2	T1
Alternate:	-		(T5)	(T4)	T3	7	6

The 4-valved Euphonium

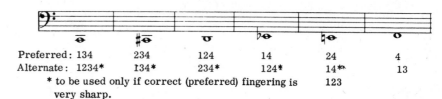

Preferred:	134	234	124	14	24	4
Alternate:	1234*	134*	234*	124*	14*	13
					123	

* to be used only if correct (preferred) fingering is very sharp.

Preferred:	23	12	1	2	0	24	4
Alternate:	-	3	(234)	(124)	14	123	13
				(34)			

October, 1953

Basic Foundations of Trumpet Playing

Excessive dependence upon systems
tends to interfere with individual skill

MAURY DEUTSCH

EVERY TRUMPET PLAYER is looking for the secret to successful trumpet playing. A multitude of special systems is on the market today, each professing to correct every difficulty the player may have, whether in range, endurance, tone, breathing or flexibility.

Yet it is a fact that the number of successful trumpet players today is not greater proportionately than twenty or thirty years ago, while the number of unsuccessful trumpet players is at its highest peak. The error seems to lie in the complexity and the inexpert approach of the different systems of playing; no two agree completely on any of the basic fundamentals.

The only correct approach to trumpet playing is making the student

rather than a pre-conceived system the starting point. Systems, instead of considering each student as an individual and adjusting the materials to his special needs, expect each to obey a set of rules.

Trumpet playing can be divided into six basic categories: (a) embouchure, (b) breathing, (c) vibrato, (d) staccato, (e) range, and (f) warming up.

Embouchure

The purpose of the embouchure is to give the lips, mouth and tongue perfect freedom during performance. Whether the mouthpiece is placed exactly in the middle of the mouth with tonguing is the prime consideration. The tongue, lips and teeth will all make their own adjustment providing

the student does not interfere with the natural functioning of the mouth.

In double and triple tonguing an important consideration is to be careful that the note produced by the "k" syllable is not flatter than when played with the regular "t" syllable. In legato tonguing the flow of air into the horn is slower; some prefer to think of the consonant "d" when playing in this manner. One serious error of many brass players is not starting the tone with the exact pitch.

Range

High tones are the result of increasing the tension of the lips. This is done in many ways by different people. Some pucker their lips forward, while others stretch their lips as in smiling. The method used is unimportant, but it should be the one giving greatest physical comfort.[1]

Many students have acquired unnecessary habits in playing high notes; e.g., closing the opening between their lips tightly, using excessive mouthpiece pressure or blowing the wind toward the upper or the lower portion to the mouthpiece cup.

[1] The editor questioned Mr. Deutsch on this statement on the basis that a large majority of trumpet players do use the pucker system. Mr. Deutsch replied: "Some of the leading trumpet players in New York, such as Harry Glantz and Harry Freistadt, use the smiling lips. This was also recommended by Max Schlossberg. High notes are easier with smiling lips because a thinner tighter lip is vibrating. More endurance is possible because the lips are firmly against the teeth."

The tightly closed lips result in a tone of lesser volume, and the excessive pressure destroys the lip flexibility. The air flow hitting the top or bottom inside the mouthpiece cup throws much of the energy into the higher partials, producing a metallic, brassy tone.

There are legitimate methods of helping the lip perform the upper register, such as (1) increasing the volume and speed of the air column into the horn, (2) using the correct amount of pressure to support the lip muscles without interfering with their flexibility, and (3) choosing the correct size of mouthpiece for your lip.

A mouthpiece should be judged with respect to the column of tone obtained in the lower register and

the ease of playing in the legitimate one half on each lip or one third on the upper lip and two thirds on the lower lip or vice versa, is of secondary importance. The mouthpiece should rest comfortably on the mouth with a sufficient area of each lip in the mouthpiece, thus producing a solid support.

A mouthpiece change should be attempted only under the close supervision of an instructor. The determination as to whether you play with a wet or a dry lip is dependent on the degree of natural oils in the lip tissues. Your personal comfort should be the only rule. In reality, the lip is actually never dry.

Following are some warm-up drills that are recommended.

(1) Play No. 1 with valves 1, 1-2, 2-3. (2) Play No. 5 as minor, diminished and augmented triads on different days. (3) Play No. 7 as harmonic and melodic minor scales on different days. Play in all keys. (4) Play No. 9 in all keys and play descending scales also as chromatic scales. In a descending line do not over-loosen the lip, or intonation will suffer.

Breathing

When you inhale the breath, the diaphragm drops, and the ribs and sternum extend out and upward. This causes a partial vacuum around the lungs, and the air rushes in from the outside. When you exhale, the reverse occurs. All motion noticed in the back, chest and stomach is always the result of correct breathing and never the cause of it.

The strength of the breath is determined by the length of the phrase. Breathing should be effortless. Only when an extraordinarily large breath is needed, does one have to concentrate on the breathing organs or process. Think of the lungs as a paper bag; the more you wish to put into the bag, the farther down into the bag you push. This process translated to the breathing mechanism results in the simple principle that the size of the breath needed is directly proportional to the depth of the intake. Stated simply, the rule is to breathe deeply.

Vibrato

Vibrato is the added warmth a musician gives to the straight tone so necessary in solo work. Experiments performed with opera singers and concert violinists have demonstrated that the vibrato speed lies within 6½ to 8 vibratos per second. The faster speeds, naturally, are used in musical excerpts of greater dynamic and emotional power; the slower speeds in subdued portions, especially in the lower register.

The best rule for the student to follow is to be sure that the vibrato does not distort the intonation of the tone, sound quivery or have a nanny goat quality. The learner should listen to recordings of great artists constantly and thus acquire good taste. The simple style of vibrato is performed with a hand motion.

Staccato

The position of the tongue in trumpet playing is different for each individual; personal comfort in fast upper register. A large and deep cup produces a greater volume and quality of tone; a shallow small cup makes for ease in high notes, but the tone is more metallic.

Warming up

The warm-up period is most important for the trumpet player. Here the lip muscles are exercised gradually and strengthened; the flexibility is improved; the scales and chords in all keys are learned; the range is extended; and the tone is improved. As a preliminary exercise place the mouthpiece in the left hand and do some light tonguing and slurring drills.

Warm-up Important for Brass Players

Muscles of embouchure, diaphragm, tongue and fingers need to be prepared for action

NORMAN DIETZ

ONE OF THE MOST IMPORTANT events in the day of a brass player is the warm-up period. A track man would never think of changing into his track suit and immediately running the hundred-yard dash. No more should a young brass player pick up his horn and begin to play vigorously in the extreme ranges of the instrument.

A brass player is, in essence, no different from a track man when it comes to warming up the muscles in preparation for action. As instrumental teachers we need to convince our players that an adequate warm-up is essential. Particularly during marching season we should require players to warm up properly before going outside to play and march vigorously.

Important Muscles

Four basic sets of muscles are used in brass playing, and all must be limbered up. They are as follows:

1. The embouchure muscles used in producing lip vibration.

2. The diaphragm and chest muscles used in breathing properly.

3. The tongue for its function in articulation.

4. The finger and arm muscles in controlling valve and slide action.

All of the muscles must be warmed up in proper relation to each other. Often players think that they have an adequate routine, but a close examination by the teacher will reveal that one or more of the basic principles has been slighted. It is our job to sell the student on the idea that there is no secret method or short cut to success. He must be made to realize that careful planning of practice routines is the only sound way to establish the fundamentals of good playing.

Each player should have a long-range goal toward which he is working. He must be convinced that day-to-day and week-to-week accomplishments are the only foundation for achieving his goal. Steady progress in the development of the basic tools should follow from day to day. Teachers must be quick to encourage the student by complimenting him on the little achievements that he makes.

With regard to specific warm-up, the writer feels that there is no set way in which to start. However, it is important to begin in the easy range of the instrument and mix the various techniques; that is, long tones, slurs, tonguing, chords and scales. Basically, warm-up is the process of limbering the muscles by slow degrees so that finally they are ready for fast action. Gradually the range should be increased until the entire playing range of each individual has been covered. An adequate warm-up could consume minutes or even an hour.

It is of utmost importance that the player keep in mind one essential fact: *If the muscle tissue is bruised or tired before or after the warm-up has been completed, check the content and the routine very carefully. Although all warm-ups should con-*

tain the same type of exercises, the amount of time spent on each may differ with individuals.

Warm-Up Procedure

A warm-up can include the following:

1. Long tones to develop facial muscles and diaphragmatic control.

2. Slurs to develop lip flexibility and general wind control.

3. All types of tonguing and attack to aid the tongue in developing a muscular or kinesthetic memory. This can come about only by practicing all types of articulation and thinking seriously as the process continues.

4. Chords and scales necessary to coordinate the mind and the fingers.

It is best to start softly so as to insure flexibility and not to bruise the lip. Before the warm-up ends, all levels of dynamics should have been covered. Since the student spends only about an hour a week under the supervision of a specialist, it is necessary for him to analyze and to think of the obstacles which confront him. The more intelligently he is able to analyze his problems, the more quickly he will progress.

Listed here are some of the points which may help the student to practice more effectively:

1. Facial muscles have control over lip vibration.

2. Excessive tiring where the mouthpiece makes contact with the lips is a result of too much pressure against the lips.

3. Since the upper lip is the primary vibrator, it cannot also serve as the main support for the mouthpiece. A careful examination of the lower lip reveals a "meaty" tissue. It, therefore, is better able to carry what little pressure is to be used against the lips.

4. Think of the mouthpiece cup as the receptacle of lip vibration. Try to eliminate the "death grip" for the higher range. Let the breath and the tongue do the work.

5. The speed with which the breath moves will determine the dynamic level.

6. Think of blowing *through* the instrument rather than into it or at it.

7. The diaphragmatic action is the same whether in playing a long tone or in tonguing a passage of 64th notes.

8. To maintain a steady tone with full resonant quality, one should feel as though he is playing a slight crescendo. In other words, the breath is continually moving throughout the duration of the sound.

9. Think of the tongue as the starter of tones only.

10. The player must be ready with the right articulation at the right time. This is not a matter of chance but the result of carefully planned practice periods which are followed faithfully.

11. The student must learn to be his own best teacher. He must think fast and practice slowly. An exercise or an etude played through once correctly is better than an hour of satisfying the ego.

Effective instrumental teaching depends largely upon methods of salesmanship used by the teacher. Players will follow a carefully planned warm-up and practice routine only if they have been thoroughly convinced that their musical skill and effectiveness will be enriched thereby.

French Horn Unique in Blending and Tone

Absence of instrument in school bands and orchestras weakens musical effect

A. D. LEKVOLD

THERE IS NO REAL SUBSTITUTE for the French horn in the concert band or orchestra. This instrument is unique in its tonal quality and blending properties.

Although mellophones and alto horns of different types can play the upper and medium range of horn music, they are really different instruments and produce a different musical result. Only in the marching band, where French horns present certain performance difficulties and become somewhat ineffective, can the use of the alto horn be recommended.

There seems to be wide acceptance of these facts regarding the value of the horn, and there has been a definite increase in their use in high school and college groups. It is still true, however, that many of the directors of the smaller school bands and orchestras have not insisted upon a pair or a quartet of horns.

What are the reasons for this hesitancy in the adoption of French horns in certain groups? Explanations usually given include the cost of the instrument; lack of knowledge of the horn on the part of the director and therefore fear of advocating and teaching it, or a failure to realize its full usefulness and potentialities; its supposed difficulty for young players; and concern regarding the advanced phases of horn performance.

Objections not Valid

It seems advisable to consider the validity of these objections, especially when we realize the extent of musical loss to organizations caused by absence of French horns.

Cost must be classified as an immaterial objection. In the first place, the single horn in F is adequate to deal with most problems of technic and range, particularly in the easier grades of music. The cost of this horn compares favorably with the cost of many other instruments which are considered common and indispensable.

Because of the instrument's wide usefulness it can be advocated for either individual or school purchase. If the director has a true belief in and an enthusiasm for the horn, his feeling will transfer to the students, and cost will not arise as a major obstacle.

Directors who do not play the French horn may have missed specific instruction regarding it in their college work. In this event it is advisable to gain the necessary information, which can be secured by taking a series of lessons from a specialist on the horn; by reading books on instrumentation and orchestration, as well as encyclopedia discussions; and by studying standard horn parts from orchestral scores made both before and after the adoption of the valve system about 1850.

Points to be especially noted in developing knowledge of the horn are as follows, though many of these points do not arise in teaching the beginning student:

1. Regular position of hand cupped in the bell;

2. The full muting principle with both hand and mechanical mute;

3. Length of the horn, twice the normal, causing it to be played an octave higher in its harmonic series;

4. Transposition problems;

5. Use of low register;

6. Use of double horn.

In teaching horn to beginners no attempt should be made to explain the advanced phases any more than is done, for instance, in the case of the clarinet. The tone is more easily produced on the horn than on the trumpet. It can be successfully started with most beginners at the fifth grade level. Although it is advisable for the teacher to have a complete knowledge of the horn, it is important at the beginning stage to teach only what is necessary to the beginner.

The pupil should have an average, or better, sense of pitch. He will have fewer embouchure problems if he has fairly even teeth and if his lips are medium to fine in thickness.

Normal Position

The hand cupped in the bell is the normal position and must be taught as such in the first lesson. If this procedure is not used, the horn is sharp and the tone quality is affected. Beginning notes usually center around G on the second line. The pupil should be instructed to remain seated while he is practicing.

For later study such advanced fea-

tures as the following may be emphasized:

1. Transposition. In band work the transposition from E♭ parts will be the first taught. It is better to transpose these parts than to use the E♭ slides. In orchestra work other transpositions will be needed for advanced work.

2. Full muting principle for echo effect. The mechanical mute is recommended. If hand muting is used, the player must adjust his fingering a half tone to compensate in pitch.

3. Development of low register when needed.

4. Use of double horn.

The idea of using mellophones and alto horns instead of French horns because they are easier to play carries with it the assumption that they will be played better. Judges of musical events have not been impressed by this point. Even if we admit that the mellophone and the alto horn are easier to play, we cannot avoid the observation that they are more often played poorly than well.

It might be added that if publishers and composers could depend upon the presence of French horns in all school groups, they would make more complete use of the horn range in low register. As it is, easy school arrangements are pointed at the alto horn range, and the low horn range is not used as it is in symphonic writing.

FINE

Varied Uses of Mute
in Tone and Volume

Recent added popularity of 'sordino'
conducive to special musical effects

AUGUST SCHAEFER

I N ITALIAN *sordino* is mute. The French call it "sourdine," the Germans say "Dämpfer," and we know

it as "mute." No matter what the term used, the function of the mute is the same—to dampen or reduce

sound, volume or tone, to lessen vibration or to serve as a muffler.

When a musical composition has

the word "mute" indicated and does not specify which one is desired, it is taken for granted that the composer wishes the "straight" mute to be employed. For band, concert or symphonic purposes the straight mute is used unless otherwise designated. It is constructed of metal, paper, leather, aluminum or fibre and is usually cone shaped.

Until the early part of the twentieth century the purpose of the mute was to lessen the tone of the brass so that it would blend into the color and balance of the small string orchestra or ensemble. It also was used to give an effect of distance or to suggest an echo.

Nowadays, if the music is of modern design, has a flavor of dance rhythm and has notes marked with a dot over or under them (staccato), then the intent of the composer could be interpreted as wishing the notes to be played ultra short or snapped. This can be accomplished by pulling the tongue backward very rapidly from the vibratory area, the portion of the lips which span across the cup of the mouthpiece.

In the last decade the mute has been more extensively used. I distinctly remember when a well-known Broadway musical show conductor requested the entire brass section to play several complete acts with mutes. When we remonstrated, saying that if he did not want to hear us, we might as well just rest, he explained that it was a new trend. He said that he wanted us to play very loud as he wanted a special effect. This style required a mute which was of easy response and played very freely. A mute

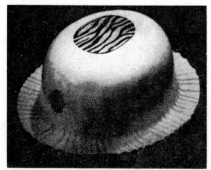

Photo courtesy Harmon Mute Co.
The picturesque Derby Mute

can be made to play easier if layers of new cork are cemented on the old ones.

The new trend also brought forth the use of the wa-wa, solo tone, megaphone, tonal color and various other

kinds of mutes, including the derby hat. All of them were created to give a variation of tonal color or musical sound and to gain special effects. Leopold Stokowski once had the trumpeters place felt bags over the bells for a certain effect he wanted in the Debussy "Fetes." Even the plumber's rubber suction plunger has now become an honored musical device.

Mutes for Brass

Mutes are available for all brass instruments. The horn player may mute his instrument by placing his hand far beyond its usual position, thus sharpening the tone a half step. Then he is required to transpose each tone down one half step. Paradoxically, on some horns it may be more effective to transpose a half step up. Muted notes on the horn parts are indicated by a plus sign and open notes by an O. A stopped horn is often called for; it means just that. Non-transposing horn mutes are available.

Daily practice with a mute is highly recommended because there is a certain hindrance of tone response, mute resistance, which must be overcome. When we have mastered this knack, we can then play freely and reliably with or without the mute. As there is a differential in pitch, we should strive to humor downward all tones which require it, as all mutes have a tendency to sharpen pitch. With practice, the tendency will be automatically corrected.

It is not uncommon to see entire brass sections playing professional engagements week after week with everything muted. When this occurs, it is usually because the auditorium is too small or because the director wants a certain tone color.

Playing Softly

Brass players should not overlook the importance of playing open horn by practicing very softly. *Pianissimo* playing is the most difficult accomplishment; it must be under perfect control. Its mastery is indispensable to every player. Especially must the symphony player be prepared to play extremely loud, having sure control of the loud tones as well as of his *pianissimo* attacks and releases.

In practicing open horn, we should try to play as softly as is humanly possible. Liberati, one of the world's greatest cornet soloists and bandmasters, would practice so *pianissimo* in his hotel room that I once complained that I could hardly hear him. He replied: "Anybody can play loud; it takes an artist to play softly and musically."

Many fine artists condemn use of the mute while practicing on the ground that the tone will suffer to some extent. However, if the player will be alert and become "tone conscious," playing for tone instead of

Photo courtesy Harmon Mute Co.
Plunger for Trumpet or Trombone

sound, he will benefit from the practice. He will soon discover that it is more difficult to produce a round full tone on the muted horn as he must use more effort to follow the tone

Photo courtesy Harmon Mute Co.
Tripl-Play can be used as Straight, Plunger or Cup Mute

through the horn. Of course, this kind of practicing is more laborious than playing open horn.

A round full tone may be developed by dropping the base of the tongue downward as when saying "ah." This action enlarges the throat cavity; then the player should take a deep breath and use it. This exercise will develop the various muscles which are involved with the production of a tone which has quantity and quality.

Fine

1954

Bb Flügelhorn

Repertoire for the Tuba Student

*Scarcity of interesting materials that
provide training in desired techniques*

MARY RASMUSSEN

ONE OF THE BIGGEST obstacles in interesting music students in studying the tuba is the almost complete absence of musically interesting and challenging study and solo material for the instrument. Musical tuba players are just as necessary as musical players on any other wind instrument, for the tuba is an important part of the harmonic and rhythmic bass of the band and provides much of the harmonic foundation of the brass choir, either alone or as a section of the orchestra.

Modern works for band, orchestra and brass choir often contain tuba parts which demand a high degree of technique and musicianship. Where is the player to find solo and study material that will enable him to acquire such technique and musicianship? . Where is the talented student to find music that is sufficiently appealing to maintain his interest? Unfortunately, the published literature for tuba is insufficient at all levels from beginning to virtuoso; hence, the teacher and the student must be resourceful in gathering suitable material from other sources.

For the beginning student there are several standard methods which can be used in teaching basic technique, but easy solo material to add interest and develop musicianship must be supplied by the teacher. Folk songs, classic and baroque music and original tunes provide three possible sources of easy solos. Among the folk songs, work songs and sea chanteys are "The Countersigns" and "The Dreadnaught" from

Janet Colcord: Songs of American Sailormen (Norton)

which seem to be especially adaptable and appealing to young players.

From classic and baroque composers, transcriptions of simple sara-

bandes, gavottes, minuets, etc., can provide many beautiful pieces. A very nice collection of such transcriptions is available in

Moffat: Old Masters for Young Players (AMP)

published for young cellists but easily adaptable to the tuba by reading the solo line down an octave.

For the intermediate student, published literature includes

66 Etudes of Slama (C. Fischer)
50 Etudes (Russian text) of Gregoriev (Leeds)

and a number of solos of the

Asleep in the Deep

variety. Here again most of the repertoire must come from outside sources.

For study material the fairly simple process of learning to transpose down an octave opens up almost all of the trombone literature, including

Bordogni-Rochut: Melodious Etudes (3 vols., C. Fischer)

which are fine for teaching legato style and phrasing,

Bleger 31: Brilliant Studies (Cundy-Bettoney; separately or in the back of the Cornette Method)

excellent for teaching clean staccato tonguing, the

Arban Method
Kopprasch: 60 Studies

and many others.

For solo literature we are again faced with having to transcribe works from other instruments to augment the tuba's limited repertoire. Even the tuba solos from the

Paris Conservatory Repertoire

which forms a large part of the solo repertoire for the other brass instruments, must be virtually transcribed because they are written for French style tubas, which are more what we would consider very large bore 5-

valve baritones, pitched an octave higher than our BB♭ tubas. As a result, the high register is extreme for most E♭ and BB♭ tuba players. A couple of such solos are

J. E. Barat: Introduction and Serenade (Baron)
J. E. Barat: Reminiscences de Navarre (Baron)

The works of the baroque period include a number of solos suitable for transcription, of which a random selection might contain

Teleman: Bassoon Concerto in F Minor
Corelli: Cello Sonato in D Minor
Luigi Merci: Bassoon Sonata in G Minor

Borrowing from more modern works depends somewhat on the taste and inclination of the player. Among the many available solos, two which have proved suitable are

Barat: Andante and Allegro (Andraud)
Blazhevitch: Concert Sketch No. 5 (Leeds)

For advanced players there are published

Paul Bernard: 40 Etudes apres Forestier (M. Baron)
Paul Bernard: 12 Pieces Melodiques (M. Baron)
Lakedes: Concerto (Leeds)
Leonard Bernstein: Waltz for Mippy III (G. Schirmer)
E. F. Goldman: 12-Tone Duo for Two Tubas (Mercury)
Bigot: Carillon at Bourdon (Leduc)
R. Clerisse: Idylle (Leduc)
Leclerc: Concertino (Leduc)

The last three named are from the Paris Conservatory Repertoire and subject to the revision noted above. Several books of orchestral excerpts are published by International,

Peters, M. Baron and others.

Studies from other brass instruments might include

Gaetke: School of Etudes for Trombone (Zimmerman)
Blazhevitch: 26 Sequences, in bass, tenor, and alto clef (C. Fischer)

both excellent training in modern intervals and rhythms for those interested in going into orchestral playing;

St. Jacombe: Method, 2 vols.,

treble clef (C. Fischer)
with the Bousquet studies at the back, especially valuable in their frequent use of low register;

Walter Smith: Top Tones for the Trumpeter (C. Fischer)
Blazhevitch: Concert Duets for Two Trombones, tenor, alto and bass clef (Leeds).

Transcriptions of solo literature might range from the

Bach-Lafosse: Suites (Leduc)
and the other baroque works to

Hindemith: Sonatas for Trombone and String Bass (AMP).

An especially interesting and rewarding way of augmenting the solo repertoire is through original compositions especially written by friends and teachers with a flair for composing. Every now and then one turns out to be very fine.

In the long run, the repertoire of the tuba is only as limited as the resourcefulness of the teacher and the student.   FINE

Brass Ensembles
Foster Permanent
Interest in Music

Achievement not dependent on technical mastery alone but on future enjoyment

JOHN RICHARDS

WHEN WE READ the title "Brass Clinic," we most often think of the technical problems dealing with various members of the brass family. It is natural for us to assume that we must take care of the problems of breathing, tonguing, fitting of the mouthpiece and the other mechanics of playing brass instruments.

Assuming that we have some understanding of these basic problems, we are still confronted with several larger problems. One of these is the method of making personal contact with each and every member of the brass sections in large organizations. How do we promote better musicianship? How do we stimulate interest in the formation of bands in schools which have had no instrumental program? How do we keep the brass players practicing? Even a student who understands the problems of playing his chosen brass instrument does not sound well after a period of inactivity.

Another problem which confronts all music educators is that of making teaching meaningful enough so that

contact with playing is not lost upon graduation. One answer to these problems can be found in the formation of small brass ensembles.

Little has been written about the value of brass ensembles in music education; yet they are a phase of musical activity which, if promoted, can be of the utmost value to the instructor, the individual student and the group. The brass ensemble can be the common ground upon which the student and the teacher can meet to promote better social understanding and more precise musicianship. It can be a device to aid in the formation of a band or orchestra in a school which has no organized music. It can be the means of stimulating practice, not only during the regular school year but also during the summer months. It can also be a means of musical outlet for those thousands of brass players who are graduated from our schools each year who do not wish to become professional instrumentalists and would normally join that vast group who could have for

their slogan, "I used to play, but . . ."

New Atmosphere

Participation in a brass ensemble is of special value to those players who are seldom given a solo or melodic part to execute in band or orchestra. For example, the tuba or horn often plays nothing but a rather dry series of "um-pah's." It is only natural, therefore, that such a player seldom formulates any concept of the music as a whole. He is usually so engrossed in making himself heard that he is oblivious to any melodic or counter-melodic part which he may be covering at the moment.

When this same type of student is initiated into a brass ensemble, he has an entirely different musical atmosphere in which to adjust himself. He is seldom required to play a part which is uninteresting. He finds that he must learn to adjust his intonation dynamic level and phrasing to the group. Other players, in turn, develop an appreciation of the contribution which these often unappreciated instruments make.

The tuba or horn player becomes acutely aware of tone matching and learns that in ascending or descending passages, he must often act, not as tuba or horn, but as an extension to the range of the cornet, trombone or baritone. In order to do this, he must adjust not only pitch but also tonal quality and dynamic level. In this matching process, the students are quick to emulate the qualities of the better member of the group, thus raising the standard of the entire group.

Feeling of Importance

Students who play second or third parts in the band or orchestra usually have great difficulty in identifying their position in the group and often lose interest because they feel that their performance is of little importance. By playing in the ensemble they learn the beauties of harmonic balance and phrasing. They build up a sense of pride in being able to control the balance of the entire harmonic structure of a composition.

Every member of a brass ensemble is given an opportunity to execute solo and contrapuntal passages. This leads to greater confidence on the part of those players who do not carry on that function in the band or orchestra. On the other hand, those instrumentalists who usually play the more prominent parts learn to subordinate themselves to the other instruments. The entire endeavor is one of cooperation and fraternal feeling.

Group Incentive

Every September there are many school band and orchestra directors who are confronted by brass students who have "lost their lips" during the summer months. A few players join summer organizations in which they can play, but too many do not have an opportunity for group participation, and they find that individual practice has little of the appeal that is found in group playing. The number of existing groups is often inadequate to supply an outlet for every child who needs it. It is important, therefore, that we supply some means of self-motivated home participation which can function throughout the summer vacation period. The brass ensemble program can accomplish this.

Some music educators may be reluctant to investigate the values of such a program simply because it appears on the surface to be an extra load for the teacher to carry. There are many methods of ensemble inauguration and presentation, which, if used, require a minimum of teacher time but effect a maximum in teaching efficiency. The brass ensemble can, and should, be formed by a group of compatible students who will carry on the ensemble program outside of school hours.

The smaller the ensemble the greater is the need for care in selecting the personnel of the group, for each individual is solely responsible for a definite part and must be dependable. The teacher should act in a highly advisory capacity in selecting personnel, for if this process is left entirely to the pupils, cliques and personal friendships often become the deciding issues.

If the instructor plans his program of brass ensemble playing wisely, he will form not only sextets but also duets, trios, quartets and quintets. These should be organized with compatibility of students and geographic location of the students' homes in mind so that members can "get together" after school hours. In the writer's own teaching experience, it was found that if ensembles were organized with these circumstances present, the students often carried on ensemble rehearsals in their own homes with the same spirit and spontaneous enthusiasm which mark the voluntary "jam-sessions" common to many high school musicians.

The student is not the only one to benefit from these home ensemble groups, for it brings music into the family circle and stimulates parent and community interest in the school program. The teacher directly benefits because the enthusiasm and technical advancement of the members of the ensemble are carried over into the band and orchestra.

The benefit to the band and orchestra is great, for the students who are ensemble-trained have a better feeling for form and balance in music. They are more sensitive to dynamic levels because they learn that only by playing in the proper level can one hear the other members of the group with any accuracy.

One result of any intelligently organized brass ensemble is the creation of such an attitude among students that they will concern themselves more with the formation of proper playing habits than with the mere execution of notes. The individual who has a background in brass ensemble playing will be exposed to an intimate style of playing, facilitating his transference to the more serious types of music.

In a school which has never had organized instrumental music of any kind the brass ensemble can be the means of promoting and stimulating interest. Easy material is available for every type of brass ensemble so that a teacher can launch an instrumental plan if only two or three players are available. The beginning student can be admitted immediately into an ensemble group. It takes but a short time to prepare the small brass group well enough so that it can play two or three simple but full-sounding numbers. Even at this early stage of development, it can be a real aid in launching a full instrumental program. Presentation of any neophite group at student body meetings, home room programs, P. T. A. or civic organizations can be the needed stimulus to promote interest in instrumental education.

After several groups have been organized, for instance a brass sextet, a woodwind quintet, a saxophone trio, a brass quartet, a clarinet quartet and a percussion trio, there are enough trained musicians to launch a small but musically effective band program. In essence—bands can be built from ensembles, and the small brass ensemble can be the "trigger."

Fundamental Weakness

Perhaps one of the greatest weaknesses of our school band program is that, for the majority of students, active participation in music ceases upon the day of graduation from high school. It is certainly not intended that every instrumental student should enter the field of music as a profession, but there are countless numbers who would like to maintain contact with a playing group.

In the average city, there is little opportunity for the continuation of participation in a band or orchestra. It is not feasible for any city to maintain enough musical organizations to accommodate all who would enjoy playing. Then, too, there are those who do not wish to be tied down to a regularly scheduled rehearsal with a local band or orchestra and yet would like to join a group occasionally. The ensemble is the logical answer to their problems because the brass-ensemble-trained person is capable of organizing and playing with musicians who fall into his own category.

When the instrumental student's only contact with music is through the band or orchestra, he is in a position to receive but limited training.

Every brass player needs the type of training and the socializing influence which can be obtained only through participation in a small and intimate group such as the brass ensemble.

FINE

The Tuba — As a Solo Instrument

Factors influencing effectiveness of pitch and tone quality of much-maligned 'Tubby'

REX A. CONNER

THE FIRST PREREQUISITE to a good tuba solo is, of course, a good instrument.

Without taking time to discuss the budget problems we all have, let's face the fact that usually when a tuba, or any valued brass instrument, is overhauled, the leakage around the valves becomes greater. The reason is that corrosion and rust are taken off in an acid bath and the valves are polished down, leaving a greater play between them and the valve casing.

If we can't get our school boards to purchase new instruments, then let's add at least a few more dollars to have the valves re-plated. The writer once had the valves of a Conn tuba over fifty years old re-plated as an experiment, and the tone was marvelous. Another fact to be considered is that an estimate of an overhaul job with the price of re-plating included might convince the board that it should buy a new tuba rather than overhaul the old one.

Which do you prefer, the recording bass or the sousaphone? This is a common question. The recording bass is more difficult to use on the march than is the sousaphone; however,

when it comes to concert work, we must keep in mind that thinking artistically is extremely difficult when one's shoulders are burdened with approximately thirty pounds of instrument. It is the writer's opinion that much of the laborious and forced playing we hear from sousaphone players is conditioned by the pain to which the player is subjected during a long rehearsal or concert. The sousaphone chair or stand is well worth the money to any band director who uses sousaphones.

Upright Bell

We have often wondered why major symphony orchestras employ the upright bell rather than the bell-front tuba. This question was answered quite adequately by Bruce Jones, director of the Louisiana State University Band, at a recent clinic in Missouri. When we listen to a string bass section in an orchestra, regardless of where the players are standing, the tone is non-directional. It comes from all over the orchestra and supports the entire orchestral tone.

Not so with the bell-front tubas. The tones, good or bad, smack the

listener right in the face, usually quite blatantly. Mr. Jones told us how he had his sousaphone players turn their bells toward the wall in a demonstration that gave a very fine effect. A recent picture of the Louisiana State University Band reveals that it is now using bell-up sousaphones just as Sousa originally designed them. It now has two sets of bells for sousaphones, one for marching and one for concert work.

For solo work the bell-front recording tuba is the best* because any rapid execution by the performer will have a run-together sound if played up into the ceiling.

The second prerequisite for a good tuba solo is a good solo to play. Unfortunately very few have been written. Composers for the instrument don't understand it, or don't realize the ability of a student once he is given a decent chance, or insist on having a piano accompaniment.

In the first place, a tuba solo, to be easy for a young student, need not

---

*Editor's note: Most professional tuba players in symphony orchestras prefer the upright tuba for both orchestra and solo work.

be written as low in the instrument range as a solo for trumpet or cornet. The tones of a tuba from Bb 2 (2nd line) up to Bb 3 are beautiful solo tones and are not difficult to reach if a student is ever challenged to play them. Solos written below Bb 2 are usually unappetizing for the listener as well as for the performer.

Many solos written for Eb tuba before the BBb became so popular sound better on the BBb instrument. For the advanced player some of the horn sonatas played an octave lower than sounded by the horn make excellent solo material.

Principles of Playing

It seems to be a very popular misconception to speak of the tuba as being sluggish, lumbering, slow in response and clumsy. Of course, we have some very popular records for children in which the tuba is affectionately known as "Tubby." Such characterizations are simply not true. The fault lies primarily in the way the instrument is played rather than in the instrument itself.

The tip of the tongue in making attacks should be placed on the roof of the mouth in exactly the same manner it is when one pronounces the letter "t," or even farther back for the extreme lower register. It should never get forward far enough to touch the upper teeth. Tonguing through the lips is generally unacceptable for all brass instruments.

Tuba players should practice enough so that the tongue muscle is strongly developed. The tongue should be placed rather tightly so that no air is released before the tone is started. Too often, what we hear is a "tsaa" instead of "taa." By the time there is an air column big enough to make the lips vibrate fully at the desired low speed for the tuba, the breath is mostly gone, and there is no support for the tone. One director once called this type of playing, "walrus-mouthed tuba playing," an excellent description.

Improper Breathing

Another type of very objectionable playing, which is all too familiar, is the explosive, cracked, raspy tone quality. The trouble here is that the tongue is arched high in the middle so that there is not a full air column to support the tone. In this kind of poor playing the jaws are clamped shut too tightly, and there is no follow-through with the breath. The player bites every tone.

Again, the instrument is not slow in responding. The player is simply breathing when he should be blowing because those who play this way waste a whole breath on every explosion. The offender is often also behind the beat.

The correction for this kind of playing is to have the player breathe only with the rest of the band even though there is a short rest between notes. He is then prepared to attack the correct pitch; he is better in tune, in time, and in quality.

After the student has developed a good tongue, change him from the "tah, tuh and tu" tonguing to a "dah, duh and du" type of tonguing. Why? What is the difference? A "t" is a breath consonant and "d" is a voiced consonant. There will be no air preceding the tone, the throat will be more open, and the breath will be allowed to follow through enough to produce a sonorous tone. Following this idea, let an advanced player change triple tonguing from "tu-tu-ku" to "du-du-gu" and the tones can be as smooth as those that are sustained. The tongue, then, will truly serve only as a valve and not as a percussive hindrance.

Jaw Position

Correctly manipulating the jaw has much to do with correct pitch and tone quality. A recent article in The INSTRUMENTALIST states that low Bb (Bb 1) on the tuba is out of tune. But this Bb need not be out of tune. It is a peculiar fact that the more one opens the jaw, the sharper these low notes become. The reason is that when the jaw is wide open, the lips are allowed to turn inward more, allowing for a faster vibration. Most of the lip muscle is in the white of the lips. When the jaws are too close together, the red of the lips protrudes, slowing the vibration and causing the notes to be flat; but, again, this is not the fault of the tuba.

To play Bb 1 properly in tune, the jaws should be open wide enough to stick the index finger between the teeth up to the first knuckle. To play a good round F 1 the jaw should be open even wider. The jaw should also be pulled back some.

Breath Control

Volumes have been written about correct breathing, but let us say here that high chest breathing has as much to do with the blasted tones one hears on a tuba as any of the above mentioned factors. For those who insist on playing too loud, make them take a low note and attempt to maintain the loudness for four or more slow counts. They will then realize the necessity of conserving breath. Let them compete with other wind players to see who can sustain a tone the longest. The deeper the breath the more organ-like or sonorous the tone.

The handling of the embouchure for the tuba is similar to that of other brass. However, the embouchure is naturally more relaxed for the tuba in the lower range.

To avoid shifting and having several embouchures the corners of the lips should be brought slightly forward so that they may act as an anchor or hinge for the lips. Then one can play from F 1 to Bb 3 without a shift. Never puff the cheeks but hold them tightly against the teeth. The player should feel as though they freeze in their normal position.

Another difference is that the lips must protrude farther into the mouthpiece, especially from Bb 1 on down. Sometimes thinking of the long *o* vowel will form the embouchure more correctly for the lower notes. To attack and get a good tone say *dough*.

Much has been written concerning the trumpet and the manipulation of the back of the tongue in forming certain vowels to aid in range and tone quality. These principles apply to the tuba as well; however, we would like to bring out the fact that on the tuba these qualities are magnified. Many tuba players get a tone quality that has the essence of singing through the nose. A demonstration showing how a singer gets more mouth resonance and less nasal resonance will usually do the trick. Keep the throat open and relaxed.

In general, with the exception of the low Bb (Bb 1) and Ab as mentioned, the tuba is out of tune at the same points as other brass instruments, and these notes have to be corrected in much the same way. One make of tuba on the market has compensating connecting tubing which is automatically engaged to play well in tune on all notes using the third valve and its combinations. ∎

Vibrato for Brasses

Methods of producing different types

IRA D. LEE

VIBRATO IN VOCAL OR INSTRUMEN-TAL music is one of the most useful ornaments at the disposal of the performer, for it gives life and sparkle to the tone and causes a spinning quality that gives direction to the tone.

There are those, of course, who feel that it causes flaws or is a defect in tone production. These criticisms may come as a result of hearing someone play with a tremolo or quaver or lack of control in the basic tone quality. The vibrato should be a controlled process, not to be confused with an underlying bad tone quality.

Some teachers of brass instruments have felt that vibrato is a natural phenomenon which "comes" to the player or is a part of his general ability. Too many times no effort is made to show the student a more desirable manner of producing vibrato than to let it "just come." Violinists were probably the first to get away from letting it "happen" and to follow very decided methods in teaching a suitable vibrato. Brass teachers should also try for a better system of teaching vibrato which will give as much beauty of tone and regularity of rate as possible.

Rate Variation

The rate of vibrato has been found to vary in singers and instrumentalists in performance as much as 4.5 cycles per second to 9.5 cycles per second. The large variance can be largely attributed to the types of music being sung or played. A very brilliant work will probably demand a more intense speed of vibrato, whereas a very lyric, smooth melody will suggest a slower, smoother rate. The rate of 6 cycles per second is the usual speed and probably is the most usable for the majority of players.

After the 6 cycles per second speed has become very even and regular, then the music being played can and will be the guide to frequency of pulsation.

Change of pitch is a very important factor in establishing a good vibrato. It has been said that the pitch should rise and lower at least 1/10 of a step in order for the vibrato to be recognizable. Be that as it may, the change in pitch should not be excessive or a wobble will result and the frequency will probably be so slow that it will be unmusical. The too-small variation in pitch is usually not a problem.

The methods used in producing vibrato on brass instruments are diaphragm, throat, hand, and lip or jaw. The diaphragm and throat vibratos are not so prevalent today due to the fact that these two particular areas are used for much more important tasks than producing vibrato. The diaphragm should keep a good steady stream of air going, and the throat should remain as open and relaxed as possible. There are exponents of these two types of vibrato who are very capable and who produce a splendid effect; however, these two types are difficult to do and are likely to produce adverse effects.

Hand Vibrato

The hand vibrato is very popular now and is gaining impetus all the time from dance band musicians. Some teachers think of this type as the simplest to use and to teach. Some say that high notes can be played better without the danger of "falling off the tone" or missing high notes, as is sometimes reported in lip vibrato. However, when this happens,

it is not due so much to type of vibrato as it is to lack of control in the upper register. The technique involved is a movement of the right hand forward and backward, pressing and releasing pressure on the lip, thereby raising and lowering the pitch of the tone. The movement should be rapid enough to get the proper frequency and small enough not to wobble the tone too much. One danger in this type of vibrato is that the movement of the hand may be too large for a musical vibrato. The hand movement can be a great disturbance to the embouchure and can cause a certain tension in the lips which can be a detriment to flexibility.

On the trombone, the slide is moved in and out rapidly to get the proper frequency. Many players hold the slide with the fingers and use a wrist motion, but possibly a more satisfactory vibrato may be obtained by keeping the wrist firm and bouncing the slide between the holding fingers. A faster motion may result by not gripping the slide too tightly. The fingers should be firm and insure keeping the slide as close to the original position as possible and still getting a noticeable vibrato. Sometimes this insecurity of never being quite on the correct position will result in bad intonation problems, particularly in young players.

This type of vibrato on the trombone goes against some players' principle of correct manipulation of the slide—that is, that a firm arm position with a straight wrist should be maintained at all times. This way, the whole arm locates the correct position rather than the fingers or the wrist. There again, the hand and arm have a more important duty than producing vibrato. The slide must be as close to the correct position as possible if good intonation is to result.

Lip or jaw vibrato has long been one of the more acceptable types for many reasons. The vibrato comes from the place where the sound is being produced and can lend itself to the emotional qualities that the player may have to express. Lip vibrato is an aid in intonation in that it is a rapid lipping up and down of any note. Many times a director will tell a brass player to lip up or down with not a great deal of explanation as to how this is done. Two things can be obtained with one vibrato exercise: first, a good vibrato, and second, a flexibility for intonation which will offset many of the shortcomings of this type.

Use of lip vibrato is also a safeguard against excessive pressure. A player will not be able to squeeze the embouchure too hard and still use this type of vibrato. It is also a very good exercise for the lips in gaining strength and endurance, the idea being that movement in exercise builds muscle rather than strains muscle. Strain deteriorates rather than builds. While working on vibrato, it is necessary to keep in mind that a straight tone is still essential and that both straight and vibrato tone must be practiced.

Time Required

Vibrato takes time to learn properly; the time element should not be the chief worry in learning a satisfactory vibrato. If some players find after an adequately long trial period that it is too difficult to learn lip vibrato, then a switch to hand vibrato would be advisable. Conversely, if hand vibrato is found to be impracticable, the student should try lip vibrato instead. Even if lip vibrato is never used publicly by the player, it is a good exercise in developing control of the embouchure.

In starting a young player on vibrato the teacher should observe first that a good basic straight tone is apparent and that the range is adequate enough to be no longer a major problem. In lip vibrato, start the student moving the lip (actually the jaw) as if saying the vowels, "oo-ah-oo-ah," in an exaggerated manner at first and very slowly so that as nearly as can be determined, the vibrato is going over and under the note in equal proportion. The student should count six complete cycles (oo-ah) for each note. Long notes, simple scales and intervals can be used at first so that full concentration can be given to the sound that is being produced.

Control Essential

A slow speed should be maintained for sufficient time to give adequate control and then gradual speeding up until a rate of 6 cycles per second is reached. This can be incorporated in a daily warm-up routine which will insure that the student begins slowly and carefully in the first stages of starting his daily practice.

Vibrato is used generally on cornet, trumpet, trombone and baritone. Some players use it on horn to good advantage, and it is gaining in popularity for that instrument. When vibrato is used on baritone and tuba, lip vibrato is practically a necessity unless diaphragm or throat vibrato is used. Some directors of bands experiment and debate on a general over-all use of vibrato by the entire band. This practice is, as yet, very limited, but who can say what may come up next?

There are many exponents of each of these different types of vibrato, each with his own reasons for his preference. Most players use the one they were taught to use in their first contact with playing and the one with which they have had success. The important thing is that vibrato should not degenerate to a mannerism opposed to good taste and common sense. Rules of this good taste and musical expression are difficult, if not impossible, to impart. Observing fine players and seeking a model may be helpful. A singer or violinist or the tone of a fine organ can be excellent models from which to draw conclusions.

One rule that my teacher had was: "Vibrato should be 'in the tone'; it should not 'be the tone.' " ■

Professional Brass Tone

KENNETH SNAPP

Only when the tone is well-supported and projected and can be produced **freely over a wide dynamic range** can the brass be really effective in **powerful passages. It is not the vol**ume alone which makes a fine brass climax thrilling to the listener but also the ease and intensity with which the tone is projected.

Many weak-sounding young brass players never work for this quality because they are so concerned with how their tone sounds up close that they forget that the important thing is to get it over the footlights to the audience. If the teacher is able to prescribe effective steps which will help the student to experience such a tone just once, the problem is half solved. Some of the more common causes of inadequate tone are therefore listed here, with suggested remedies which have proven helpful in remedying this deficiency.

1. *Sub-standard, damaged, or dirty (inside) instrument.* Have a good player try out each instrument periodically.

2. *Mouthpiece too narrow, shallow, small throat, thick rim.* The

157

mouthpiece is the heart of the instrument. An expert should be consulted if at all possible.

Muscular Control

3. *Insufficient or improper use of the abdominal muscles and diaphragm.* We all seem to talk about this, but somehow we don't always really see that it is understood and applied. Try having the student lean forward from the waist (not the hips) like a rag doll so that his abdominal muscles are completely free. Now have him relax his throat and puff like a dog panting. Note the almost whip-like inward and upward motion of the abdominal muscles as the breath is expelled. Next put the lips together as though saying "poo, poo," and blow them apart with each unvocalized breath, with identical waistline motion.

Finally, go through the same process with the instrument pointed toward the floor, starting each tone with a relaxed flip of the abdominal muscles without using the tongue. This establishes the feeling that each tone is lifted from below the rib cage. Try for complete relaxation from abdomen to embouchure.

4. *Tight chest or throat, or tongue too high in the mouth.* A real troublemaker, often tipped off by a grunting sound while playing. Ask the student to inhale as quickly as possible without making any sound as he does so. When he is able to do it almost instantaneously, have him notice how open his throat feels, and that the tongue flattens somewhat almost like yawning. Then have him exhale while retaining the same "inhaling" feeling in throat, mouth and chest. Finally, put it all together with the untongued exercise suggested in 3 above.

5. *Lips too far apart.* Another way of saying not enough lip is inside the mouthpiece. One of the

requirements for big vibrant tone is sufficient lip in motion. Starting the tone with lips touching insures plenty of lip available for vibrating. Spend some time daily starting tones with a "boo" or "poo" sound without using the tongue.

6. *Teeth too close together.* It is of little use to have sufficient lip in the mouthpiece if the teeth won't let it vibrate and if the area inside the mouth is not large enough. For a starter try dropping the jaw as far as possible with the lips still together. The size of the tone when produced in this way may surprise the student. Later, close the teeth as far as is necessary for control. Herbert Clarke used to say that his teeth were parted a distance about equal to the diameter of a nickel.

7. *Too much pressure on mouthpiece.* Try balancing the instrument on the thumbs so that little pull can be exerted. If a student can't get three to five open tones in this manner, he's probably using too much force and killing valuable lip vibration. A few minutes of this exercise daily is excellent, not so much to teach non-pressure as to combat unnecessary force.

8. *Only one lip vibrating effectively.* A rather controversial point, but most of my students seem to get their best and easiest tones when conscious of both lips vibrating about equally. For most people this means being sure that the lower lip does not roll back over the lower teeth, particularly in the high register.

Smile System

9. *Lips drawn tight across teeth in smile.* The smile system is still a "hot potato" in some brass circles, but it seems to be rapidly losing ground. The "lips together, teeth apart" suggestion given above tends to counteract any tendency to stretch

excessively. The feeling that one reaches toward the mouthpiece with the lips rather than pulling the mouthpiece in toward the lips frequently helps.

10. *Constant use of vibrato to mask tone.* While vibrato has a very definite place in the playing of all brass instruments with the possible exception of the horn, most practicing should be done without it so that the basic, unadorned tone can be critically heard.

One other way in which we can put the tone "under a microscope" and often dramatically strengthen it is by using the mouthpiece alone. In much the same way that an oboist checks a new reed by seeing whether it will "crow" with a rather harsh and unpleasant sound before he puts it on the instrument, the brass player can check whether he is getting enough lip vibration by blowing into his mouthpiece. The student whose tone is small and pinched usually has practically no mouthpiece sound at all, while even a nasal mouthpiece tone which is clear and strong is often beautifully refined by the addition of the instrument. Sustaining a penetrating open tone on the mouthpiece and gently sliding the instrument on and then off the mouthpiece serves as a check on whether any "choking up" takes place. If the pitch remains steady, then the instrumental tone will usually be strong and free.

Finally, it should be understood that many of the procedures described above are exaggerated initial steps in developing fullness and body in brass tone. Individual modification will be necessary in every case, but as starting points these have proven most helpful to the author.

FINE

Evaluation of Solo Brass Literature

Report shows contest material needs improvement

ELMER MAGNELL

A COMPETENT ADJUDICATOR at a recent state music contest be-

moaned the fact that he had just listened to five renditions of the popular

trumpet solo "The Carnival of Venice."

Every band director and brass instructor is well acquainted with the technical display possible in this selection, and with the ovation an audience exhibits after a favorable execution of such a solo. What troubled this particular judge most was not the monotony of listening to five similar renditions but rather his necessity of having to assign ratings to the performances on the basis of musicianship when little more than technical skill was involved. The concept of musicianship of both performers and listeners was based primarily upon competency in technical display with little concern for all the other factors that contribute to the musical worth of a performance.

Slow Rate Difficult

Most musicians who have had occasion to play in a reputable symphony orchestra will agree that a player in that organization who has not had previous professional orchestral experience has more difficulty with a slow-moving passage of music than with technical passages which are generally thought of as being more difficult. The ultimate goal of most amateur performers seems to be the attainment of a "certain number of notes per inch of music" rather than the achievement of an acceptable tone, style of performance, expressiveness and other factors which constitute good musicianship.

At a certain contest held in one of the North Central states, this writer listened to approximately thirty-five brass soloists in the course of a day. All except five of the selections chosen by these performers terminated with a polka strain. Even more distressing was the fact that the music used was included in the state contest listing.

It probably should be admitted that polka literature does have its place in stimulating adolescents to greater activity in practice and enjoyment. The younger students are prone to rebel when asked to perform music of a song-like nature even though they may be convinced of the value of such literature in achieving good tone production.

Neglect of Quality

Must music appreciation cease after reaching this level of understanding?

Are not music educators, who usually suggest literature to be performed, adequately acquainted with the better brass solo literature and sensitive to the significance that a keener appreciation of this literature will have on human living?

So as not to sound arbitrary in the condemnation of certain literature, this writer conducted a study on evaluation of selected solo brass literature to ascertain whether other competent music educators felt as he did concerning the musical worth of selected literature.

Data for this investigation were collected by the use of questionnaires in which the opinions of qualified judges were obtained as to the relative value of certain musical criteria. Twenty-six selected brass solos were rated on an over-all general impression or "snap judgment" appraisal and a separate rating on the basis of each of five criteria. The jurors also gave their reactions as to the quality of solo brass literature used at state music contests.

Since a critical judgment was desired in the evalution, a specialized group of thirty music experts, all teaching at the college level, was obtained to comprise a jury panel. This group was composed of ten band directors, ten music theory instructors and ten brass instructors, chosen from three different fields of music specialization in order that significant information might be obtained as to variations in evaluation and consistency in rating results.

Literature Used

The selected brass literature used in the evalution consisted of twenty-six solos, varied in style, representative of different periods of music, and diversified in interest and expressive qualities. Most of the literature selected had musical value, but at least one mediocre solo composition (in the writer's opinion) for each brass instrument was included to sample the juries' opinions as to consistency of rating results.

Agreement among the three juries in their rating of the selected solos was fairly high. Although the music theory instructors were more conservative in their ratings of the solos

than the other juries, the general ranking of the literature remained much the same. The music theory jury as a group functioned more efficiently in evaluating the literature than either the band directors or the brass instructors, who were more acquainted with the selected literature. One might infer that a concentrated study of theory assists one in performing a better evaluation of music in general.

Acquaintanceship with the music literature appeared to have a positive effect on its rating. Selections by the recognized classical and romantic composers were given the highest ratings although those of competent contemporary composers were rated high as well.

Conclusions

It was disclosed that accompaniments must be well integrated with the solo in order to have musical worth. The common chording type of accompaniment has proven undesirable.

Selections stressing a cantabile and legato style of playing are preferred by the jurors to compositions stressing technique. The three selections included by the writer as having less musical value were classified by the combined juries as being the least acceptable. Two of the selections used a chording type accompaniment with variations. The third utilized predominantly tonic, sub-dominant and dominant harmonies.

Improvement Needed

Undoubtedly there is need for improving the solo brass literature used for teaching purposes and contest use. The music educators should initiate this change. Contest lists in many states need revision. It is a generally accepted fact that much of the solo brass literature performed at state music contests is not musically sound.

Attention should be directed toward the use of more discerning musical criteria in the appraisal of solo literature by the average musician. Music educators, who are in an advantageous position to influence music students in developing their musical tastes, should become better acquainted with existing solo brass literature.

FINE

Teaching of Double and Triple Tonguing

Mastery of single tongue and correct breathing
should precede more complicated articulations

ROBERT GROCOCK

I HAVE LONG FELT THAT THE POOR TONE, uneven rhythm and indistinct articulation that occur so often when students attempt to triple or double tongue passages are directly attributable to a misunderstanding of the correct production of the articulations.

In the first place, double and triple tonguing should not be attempted until the student has mastered a clean, light (as opposed to hard) single tongue based upon the concept of articulation ON a stream of air, much like running the hand back and forth under an open faucet. He must never lose sight of the fact that the tone is instigated by the breath mechanism and not by the tongue. For instance, if the student performs single tonguing correctly, then his tonguing will not become harder when he plays louder. He will realize that the increase in volume is caused by the emission of more air from the breath mechanism rather than by a harder stroke of the tongue, which only tends to tighten up the throat muscles and make the tone harsh and strident.

It is not necessary that the single tongue be very fast before the other articulations are studied. If it is clean and consistent in all registers and produced without noticeable tension in the throat, then the "K" articulation can be started.

At the beginning, and many times after, it should be made clear to the student that the closer together in location the "te" and the "ke" can be, the more consistent will be the tone quality and rhythmic accuracy. The use of the syllable "ku" (koo) tends to throw the tone back in the throat and to alter the quality of tone from that when the "te" is used. "Ke" is more forward. While "ku" can be enunciated forward in the mouth, it is much more prone to fall back in the throat than is the "ke."

Tongue Position

Much difficulty also arises from thinking of the "ke" as a stoppage with the middle of the tongue. This also tends to throw the tone back in the mouth and impart tightness. If the "ke" is produced with a minimum of tension and as far forward in the mouth as possible, it will be found that the tongue is relatively dormant while the "ke" is being used.

A good way of finding this position is to have the student whisper or say in a high voice, "kitty" over and over in the same way we call a kitten when we want its attention. Upon slowing this word down and analyzing its production, the student will find that the tongue movement is almost entirely on the "te" and that the "ke," while close in point of articulation to the "te," actually calls for little motion of the tongue. In fact, the production of "ke," in relation to the movement of the tongue, is closer to that of "hee" than of "te." This can be experienced in another way by reversing "kitty" to say "tih-kee."

The student should practice producing tones with "ke" by itself until he can play eighth notes in slow tempo with it. In this beginning stage a full unforced tone should be aimed for so that the student is conscious of his breath production and of keeping a stream of air going upon which to articulate. After a consistency here has been acquired, I have found it valuable to have the student take a passage such as the following and

te te te te te te te te   te
ke ke ke ke ke ke ke ke   ke
te ke te ke te ke te ke   te

play it three times: first, with "te";

second, with "ke"; and third, with "te ke." Each of the three times the results should be the same in tone quality and clearness of attack. This process can be carried out with repeated tones, scales and then arpeggios.

Triple Approach

The same approach is used for triple tonguing. I have found that once the student has acquired some mastery of the "teke" relationship, triple tonguing offers no particular problem, and, by beginning its study in the same way as was that of double tonguing, the student has an opportunity to review the fundamentals of the articulations again. A problem which often arises when starting the student with triple tonguing rather than double tonguing is that of playing a triplet correctly as far as rhythm is concerned, regardless of the articulation used. This, coupled with the learning of the new articulation, often makes progress exceedingly slow. In view of these factors, beginning with double tonguing seems to offer fewer problems, both technically and rhythmically.

When working for greater speed the syllables "tih kah" are useful; however, the student must be cautioned against trying his "speed wings" too soon. Two to four weeks of slow to moderate tempos with careful observance of good tone quality, even rhythm and clear articulation will result in a strong correct foundation for adding speed GRADUALLY.

Even after considerable skill has been acquired, the student should include some slow practice each day, using passages in many different tempos so that he does not become a "one-speed" double or triple tongue performer. This applies also to dynamics, so that neither his articulation nor his tone will suffer from changes in dynamic level.

Double and triple tonguing are not SPECIAL articulations in the sense that they are to be employed only in sections of solos specifically so marked. They should also be used in playing the standard band and orchestra repertory, especially by those students who do not have a very fast single tongue. There are many passages, in marches for example, that would be more brilliant and have better ensemble if some of the players were to use the appropriate articulation.

FINE

May, 1954

What Is a Good Cornet or Trumpet Mouthpiece?

VINCENT MALEK

ALTHOUGH A GREAT RANGE of mouthpieces varying in dimensional characteristics has been made available to the trumpet player or cornetist, very little has been done to aid him in selecting a model with which he will best be able to develop his musical possibilities. Most of the literature concerning both embouchure and mouthpiece measurements has been of dubious value because it has consisted of generalities, ambiguities and even contradictions.

In an attempt to aid the player who is contemplating selection of a mouthpiece, a study was made to determine the best range of dimensions for each of seven different mouthpiece characteristics. This study was the follow-up to the Brass Mouthpiece Symposium which appeared in the November-December, 1952, issue of The INSTRUMENTALIST. In those articles Renold Schilke discussed dimensional aspects, Traugott Rohner presented his measurements for 213 standard model trumpet-cornet mouthpieces, Ted Evans considered the materials from which mouthpieces are made and Vincent Bach offered advice about the selection and use of mouthpieces.

Mouthpiece Code

Mr. Rohner identified each mouthpiece according to his T-V-D C-R-I-B code, the letters representing Throat diameter, cup Volume, cup Diameter, rim Curvature, Rim thickness, diameter of rim Impression, and Bite curvature. To supply documentary evidence concerning the best range of measurements for each of these seven constructional characteristics, the present study was made.

The procedure consisted of interviewing a sample of expert professionals to determine the specific dimensions of their mouthpieces and to record the physical features of their lips, teeth and lower jaws. The measurements were made exactly as were those by Mr. Rohner in his study; in fact, the identical tools were used in both studies. The embouchure classifications were made in accordance with previously determined standards that were established on the basis of dental and orthodontic considerations. To assure as much consistency as possible, the writer personally interviewed each subject in the sample.

Basis of Study

Analysis of the data would show whether or not specific ranges of dimensions had been favored for each of the seven mouthpiece characteristics. The outstanding professionals selected were assumed to have mouthpieces whose construction was well adapted to their embouchures; otherwise, it was felt that they would have been unable to achieve their eminent status. Each subject had to be a professional expert whose principal occupation was trumpet-cornet playing and who was occupying, or who had occupied, a prominent position in the symphonic, concert band, teaching or radio-television-theater fields.

The dance band field was excluded because some performers in it employ the use of unorthodox equipment to obtain novel effects. However, many of the subjects in the sample were active in this field to some degree.

Cooperating Artists

The fifty-two performers who graciously co-operated in the study were:

William Adam, trumpet instructor, Indiana U; Bernard Adelstein, Minneapolis Symphony; Charles Alberti, trumpet instructor, Cosmopolitan School of Music, Chicago; Frank Anglund, trumpet instructor and mouthpiece manufacturer, Chicago;

William T. Babcock, Jr., Chicago Symphony; Edward D. Ballantine, conductor, ABC, Chicago; Byron Baxter, Staff of ABC, Chicago; Leslie Beigel, Chicago Theater House Orchestra; Alvin Belknap, MUSN, principal, Great Lakes Naval Training Center Band; Elden Benge, trumpet manufacturer, and staff of Mutual Broadcasting Co., Chicago;

Vincent Cichowicz, Chicago Symphony; Frank Clark, Boston Pops Tour Orchestra; Joseph Contursi, staff of Mutual Broadcasting Co., Chicago; Thomas Crown, Boston Pops Tour Orchestra;

Austyn R. Edwards, trumpet instructor, VanderCook College of Music, Chicago; Dom Geraci, staff of NBC, Chicago; James Greco, Minneapolis Symphony; Robert G. Grocock, trumpet instructor, DePauw U;

Robert J. Hanson, trumpet instructor, State U. of Iowa; Leslie Harkness, Chief Warrant Officer and director 5th Army Band, Ft. Sheridan, Ill.; Adolph S. Herseth, Chicago Symphony; Mark H. Hindsley, director, U. of Illinois Bands; Don Jacoby, staff of ABC, Chicago; David H. Jandorf, Boston Pops Tour Orchestra; Seymour Kalmikoff, Chicago Theater House Orchestra; Elmer Kaniuk, staff of ABC, Chicago; Hans Kelter, trumpet instructor, Sherwood School of Music, Chicago; Warren Kime, formerly of Bad Nauheim Symphony, Germany; Norman Kingsley, trumpet instructor, Madison, Wis.; Ted Kukulewicz, Chicago Civic Orchestra;

Ralph Larson, formerly Chicago Theater House Orchestra; Donald Lindley, staff of ABC, Chicago; Rudolph Nashan, Chicago Symphony; Turner Nearing, formerly of Scotch Highlander Band; Vincent Neff, trumpet instructor, Northwestern U; Marvin Nelson, Boston Pops Tour Orchestra; Forrest Nicola, trumpet instructor, Midwestern Conservatory of Music, Chicago;

Frank Panico, staff of CBS, Chicago; Sheldon Rockler, Minneapolis Symphony; Renold O. Schilke, trumpet instructor, Northwestern U; Haskell Sexton, trumpet instructor, U. of Illinois; Alfred Spriester, PFC, principal, 5th Army Band; Joseph Summerhill, trumpet instructor, Chicago Conservatory of Music;

Charles Tamburino, staff of ABC, Chicago; David B. Tetzlaff, Minneapolis Symphony; Alfred Vernon, trumpet instructor, North Park College, Chicago; Richard Wang, trumpet instructor, Cosmopolitan School of Music, Chicago; Edwin W. Webb, trumpet instructor, Madison, Wis.; Donald Whitaker, trumpet instructor, Wheaton College Conservatory of Music, Wheaton, Ill.; Stan Wild, staff of ABC, Chicago; John Wolf, staff of NBC, Chicago; Richard Zelek, trumpet instructor, Mundelein College, Chicago.

Many of these performers, of course, are active in other fields as well as in the ones indicated. Also, the positions listed were those held by the players at the time they were interviewed between January 19 and March 31, 1953.

Thirty of the subjects used custom mouthpieces, six used a Bach 7C, two used a Bach 7B, and one each used a Bach 2½C, Bach 6, Bach 7, Bach 9C, Bach 10½C, Bach 12, Anglund 2B, Benge 9, Holton-Heim 1, Olds 3, Parduba 4*, Parduba 5*, Purviance 5*K4 and Vega Cornet 2.

Conclusions

The conclusions of the study were as follows:

1. No mouthpiece in the sample had any of the following extreme dimensions:

a. A throat smaller than size 28 or larger than size 21.

b. A cup diameter of less than .61 inch or more than .67 inch.

c. A rim curvature of more than 15/64 inch radius.

d. A rim thickness of greater than .255 inch.

e. A bite curvature of more than 6/64 inch radius.

2. Very large percentages of the sample avoided the following extreme dimensions:

a. A throat smaller than size 28 or larger than size 24.

b. Cup volume of less than 18 or more than 21.5. (These numbers are the result of the averaging of two depth gauge measurements (3/16 inch and ½ inch) and are given in sixty-fourths of an inch.)

c. A cup diameter of less than .63 inch or more than .66 inch.

d. A rim curvature of less than 10/64 inch radius or greater than 14/64 inch radius.

e. A rim thickness of less than .20 inch or more than .235 inch.

f. A rim impression diameter of less than .80 inch or more than .84 inch.

g. A bite curvature of less than 2/64 inch radius or more than 4/64 inch radius.

3. The mouthpiece dimensions which have proved themselves most satisfactory to a large number of expert players are those given above. It is reasonable to assume that these measurements, therefore, are the ones which are most compatible with artistic performance. However, it is not necessarily suggested that the beginner, or even the advanced amateur, be given a mouthpiece embodying these dimensions only; the demands made of experts are not those made of amateurs. Rather, these dimensions can probably be used to greatest advantage as a goal toward which the student progresses as he matures both physically and musically.

4. Translating the information in No. 2 into the Rohner T-V-D C-R-I-B code, we see in Figure I that the code numbers represent the "preferred" mouthpiece dimensions.

5. The median mouthpiece of the sample is coded 2552254; the model mouthpiece is 2552244. The closest standard model is the Olds Trumpet 1, whose code number is 2652254;

its cup volume is slightly greater. (*Median* is a statistical term indicating the item in the center of a distribution that has been arranged in order of size. Thus, the median measurement for each of the seven constructional features was taken to compose the median mouthpiece. *Mode* is a statistical term meaning the single item in a distribution that has the greatest frequency of occurrence.)

6. From the Rohner study of 213 standard model mouthpieces, it appears that manufacturers tend to fa-

Fig. I

vor the dimensions found most desirable by the players in the sample; but they do not incorporate all, or most, of them into the same mouthpieces. 176 or 82.6% of the 213 standard mouthpieces have dimensions exceeding the ranges indicated in No. 4.

7. The measurements of the custom models in the sample were in no case exactly duplicated by any of the 213 standard models. Many expert performers, apparently, cannot find a suitable standard model.

8. The data are inconclusive concerning specific dimensions for different embouchure categories. Further refinement of the ranges given in No. 4 is probably impractical, because they are already quite small.

9. The player can guide his choice of a mouthpiece by consulting these ranges. Experimentation is necessary to discover the precise dimensions and the proper backbore.

10. Contoured mouthpieces, those with rims curved to fit the arch of the teeth, were not found to be necessary or desirable by the players in the sample. Not a single mouthpiece of that type was encountered during the study.

11. Most of the subjects use but a single mouthpiece for all of their playing.

FINE

Embouchures of Professional Trumpet-Cornet Players

VINCENT MALEK

THE TERM *embouchure* means a variety of things to different people; here it will be taken to signify the structure of the lips, the teeth and the lower jaw of the player. Fifty-two* expert professional trumpet-cornet performers were classified on these points to determine whether or not certain characteristics are common to those who achieve eminence in this field.

Twenty-seven embouchure types were classified by different combinations of lip thickness, evenness of teeth and rest position of lower jaw. The incidence or frequency of specific embouchure types cannot be taken as an index of adaptability to cup-mouthpiece instruments because the portions of the general population having similar embouchures are not known. The musculature of the lips was not made a factor in the identification of embouchure types since there was no feasible method of ratng it.

Embouchure classifications of the fifty-two players are as follows:

Lips

8 thinner than average
36 average thickness
8 thicker than average

Teeth

20 even
27 slightly uneven
5 quite uneven

Jaw

5 receding
43 average
4 protruding

In classifying the teeth only the three or four center ones in the upper and lower jaws were considered. Regarding rest position of the lower jaw, it should be noted that slight recession—approximately 1/8 to 3/16 inch is normal. Any thing greater than this was termed "receding." Any upper-lower arch relationship that did not have this slight recession was termed "protruding."

Only two specific embouchure categories had more than four cases. These were: 18 slightly uneven teeth and 12 even teeth.

The remaining 22 players were thinly distributed among eleven other embouchure categories.

Playing embouchures exhibited were as follows:
51 contracted lip
1 stretched lip
10 dry lip
38 moist
1 wet
3 dry or moist

"Stretched" was the designation given to anyone who tried to keep his lips as thin as possible while playing; "contracted" included all other types of lip formations.

Mouthpiece placement was as follows:
Approximate center of lips 26
Slightly off center: Right 12; Left 13
Considerably off center: Right 1; Left 0

Approximate even distribution on each lip 24
More on upper: Slightly 14; Considerably 6
More on lower: Slightly 2; Considerably 6

All of these designations were made on the basis of visual inspection. "Slightly" was indicated for those variations that would not be noticeable except upon close inspection; "considerably" was given to those that were easily noticeable.

Lip conditions, clean shaven vs. mustache, were as follows:
37 clean shaven
11 mustache, upper lip
1 mustache, lower lip
3 mustache, both lips

The conclusions of the study may be summarized as follows:

1. Thinner than average lips appear to be no more desirable than thicker ones, and neither type appears to be particularly detrimental.

2. Mildly irregular front teeth seem to be unimportant.

3. Extreme recessions and protrusions of the lower jaw tend to be incompatible with fine performance. Lack of such conditions among the players in the sample strongly suggests this conclusion. Although five cases of "receding" jaw and four of "protruding" were recorded, none was of such magnitude that it could be detected by other than close inspection; in no case were the contours of the face distorted. Regarding the four protrusions, three happened to be perfect occlusions which, however, had to be clasified as protrusions since a slight recession is the norm.

4. Contracted lip formations were found to be more desirable than stretched ones by just about the whole of the sample.

5. Moistening of the lips or keeping them dry prior to setting the mouthpiece in place appears to be merely a matter of preference, with a majority preferring wet lips.

6. Placement of the mouthpiece in relation to the center of the mouth seems to be a matter of preference as long as extreme positions are avoided.

7. Although the half-and-half distribution of the mouthpiece on the lips was favored, any distribution appears to be acceptable as long as not more than two-thirds is concentrated on either lip.

8. Shaving, evidently, does not irritate the lips of expert performers; it does not, at least, hinder performance.

FINE

*The fifty-two players were listed in "What Is a Good Cornet or Trumpet Mouthpiece?" See May, 1954.

Toward a Professional Sound

DANIEL TETZLAFF

TONE

IN THE MARCH 1954 ISSUE, Ken Snapp of Indiana University gave readers of The INSTRUMENTALIST an outstanding article on "Professional Brass Tone." This has since become required reading for all my pupils. Have you given it similar attention and importance? If not, I recommend you review it to aid in putting this article to its intended use, which is to show that it is *not always* necessary to hear someone else in order to hear brass instruments played well. You can develop your tone if you care enough. You can duplicate the sound you hear a professional player use at a concert if you coordinate knowledge with listening, concentration and practice. When you improve your own tone you can then better help your pupils improve their tonal quality. Observe here a subtle point. These magazine articles can at the most help you only one-fourth of the way. They can increase your knowledge and they can remind you "how to" and "what to." But the listening and concentration and practice which are at least three-fourths of the battle are your responsibility. Hence, *you* are the largest factor in *your* progress.

It will not be the good fortune of every interested brass player to receive advanced instruction this fall. Many communities do not have a brass instructor of extensive training and experience; in other places such a teacher is so swamped that he doesn't have time for all those who wish and need his help. Some students can't afford the price of lessons, and others cannot travel the distance necessary to study with a good teacher. Even so, there is help providing there is interest. For no matter where you live or what your circumstances are, you should be able to read and to think and to remember. And to practice. These articles are being written for those with the interest and the courage to try to *help themselves.*

More—Just More

The first requirement of musical maturity is *more tone.* Thinking back over the past two years or so, I cannot recall a single student who came to my studio who exhibited *sufficient* tone during his first lessons. Tone is not inherited, you acquire it! Along the line of encouragement, however, I hasten to add that I also cannot recall a single student who did not make progress immediately upon understanding the cause of tone deficiency and the cure for it.

More tone comes from using more air. In order to send more air through the instrument, more air must be taken into the body. So the first step is to inhale more. Here are some suggestions to try:

1. If the music is in 4-4, take one whole measure's time value, four counts, to inhale slowly, steadily, deeply. These four beats will give you sufficient inhalation and the pulsation of the music you are about to play. Apply the same formula to music in 3-4 or 2-4 time, making sure to inhale the same full amount of air in the shorter time. After experiencing a full inhalation it is necessary to learn to "refill" completely in the time of only one-half beat as is required between phrases where no rest occurs.

2. You can get a clearer picture of your efforts by using a toy balloon. Notice that it is easier to fill the balloon with three or four puffs than to fill it with one quick one. It takes more concentration and effort to produce equally full inflation, doesn't it? You can easily see the parallel between balloon and your lungs. Notice how the balloon swells out *in all directions.* After a full inhalation are you conscious of a similar expansion? You should be. Air is "for free"; don't cheat yourself (or other listeners). Take in your share. That means all you can get.

3. Your greater inhalation means greater exhalation. To get more tone, use more air; keep the instrument filled with air; pack the tubing from sidewall to sidewall with air. This brings out the solidity of the tone. Keep the air moving on out the bell, ever towards your listeners. It is not necessary to be stingy and saving; use up the air, get rid of it. There is plenty more just for the gasping. You will not run out too soon if you plan to blow steadily for a *full phrase at a time*, not just for the first note.

Like Whistling

Try these steps. They are important clues that will help you to a clearer realization of the necessary ingredients of the fuller tone.

1. Produce a whistled sound. Use the pitch F4 (a fourth above middle C). How long can you sustain this sound *without diminuendo?* Listen carefully. Try again. Take a bigger breath this time, produce more tone. Don't be so surprised that more blowing means more work. The extra effort hasn't killed anything yet except puny tone.

2. Again whistle (or blow a steady stream of air through a small opening between the lips, as if playing a flute). This time hold the back of your hand about an inch from your mouth so you can *feel* the air coming out steadily. Does it weaken and die down? If it does, so will the tone. Your efforts must produce a steady exhalation with no weakening, no

lessening and no diminuendo.

3. Now with the mouthpiece only, do the same; play a long steady tone on the pitch concert F4 (like you whistled) in the octave most suited to your instrument. This time hold the back of your hand one-half inch from the end of the stem of your mouthpiece. You can prove to yourself in a minute that if your ears hear a steady, full tone, the back of your hand will feel a steady, constant stream of air moving out the end of the stem. Likewise, if the air weakens, so does the tone.

4. Place the mouthpiece on the instrument, take a deep breath, and sound a tone. It will be the fullest, most sonorous tone you have ever played. It has been so for many other players and it can be for you. The thrill of hearing yourself play a fully developed, mature tone should even exceed the lift that comes from hearing a professional play a beautiful composition.

Do you have access to back copies of The INSTRUMENTALIST? In the September 1950 issue there is an article on breathing by Ed Mellon of the University of Texas that I believe can do more to help you in a few minutes than any other article I have seen recently. This would be a good time and place to stop and review this article and see how much of that discussion you can master and apply to this lesson.

Carry On

You can learn to apply the knowledge of the ingredients that produce "one golden tone" to the production of *all tones*. Lessons II to IV in this series will offer you more guides in that direction. In the meantime, from this beginning see how far you can develop your tone. Remember your goal is to play a whole phrase, a whole etude, with all notes just as rich and full as possible. To do this you must think, listen, and remember. It's not easy, but it certainly isn't an impossible goal. Try it.

Within my sphere of activities I have found that a discussion as above constitutes the most practical and the most needed first lesson for *almost all students*, even youngsters. Few first chair high school or col-

lege students exhibit a sufficient acquaintance with these fundamentals unless they have had the advantage of considerable advanced instruction. One of the largest contributing factors to poor tone is that most of the players have little experience playing alone and under scrutiny. If their playing is mostly with a large group where they can "hide" and take almost no share of responsibility (either in tone or in mental effort), it is a long step to advanced work which asks for unaided solo performance with all tones solid and true.

Now would be the time to test yourself. How is your sound? You would be amazed at the improvement possible in your tone with just one hour of concentration and application of the above suggestions. This magazine should now be on the edge of your music rack, your etude book on the other, your instrument up to your lips and *more air going through it*. That is what will give you more tone and more listening pleasure to yourself and to your audience.

Evenness of Tone to Achieve Matched Quality

THE NEXT TIME YOU LISTEN TO your favorite instrumentalist at a concert or on records note the evenness and equality of each note and phrase. *No note is slighted.* Equal care and attention are given each sound, especially to the "little notes" like eighths and sixteenths. There is no smearing, no blurring, no faking. As the "boys" say, "Every note a pearl". This is the product of long hours of self-discipline in care and concentration. There is hardly a more worthy objective in playing. Most important of all, the practice of this control is the most reliable method for avoiding the various pitfalls that can obstruct a brass man's progress.

A tone without diminuendo could be depicted thus:

Just imagine a long piece of adhesive tape that is straight and true on both sides. This is the way our long tone on G should be. Try it. Is it? To make sure, try it on the mouthpiece. Does the tone gurgle? Does it have waves and wobbles? Listen!

Should we graph your tone thus?

It is absolutely necessary that players learn to sustain a straight, true tone to achieve (1) accurate intonation, and (2) the blending of tones between various instruments of the band.

The "wobbles" and the unevenness are removed by combining the following:

(1) Holding the embouchure *absolutely firm and motionless* throughout the duration of the tone. Use a mirror to check for the slightest twitch.

(2) Hold the tongue, after the attack, absolutely motionless inside the mouth. Watch the neck and throat in the mirror.

(3) Hold a steady, unfaltering pressure on the "exhale mechanism" as practiced in Lesson I.

Give yourself a week of good practice to clear up any deficiencies in this. Listen carefully to your progress.

A good G4 should facilitate a good C5 (third space). Check to make sure. Then try the descending C scale. Most of us think this the easiest thing in the book. But is it? Try for eight absolutely evenly matched tones like eight perfectly moulded bricks piled one on top of another.

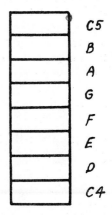

The low C4 should sound the exact equal of the higher one. The average player will change the quality around E or before and from there on downward do poorer. The main cause will be over-relaxation. *Almost no change in embouchure* is necessary. The minute amount of change comes automatically to most players while descending if they think *no change*. Actually, the valves lower the pitch; the lips do not have to help much. No relaxation of breath support should occur. Lower tones take *more* air and more work to fill out the tone, and for many of the notes the tubing involved is longer, so again use plenty of air! Be sparing only in letting it out! *Keep the air support.* Play all tones with the same feeling as near as possible.

A Test

One of the purposes of these lessons is to encourage more ear training, more thinking, and to point out what to listen for. To free the mental processes for more listening we should avoid too much note reading. *Practice by ear.* Take all cues from the sound that comes out the bell. By the time the C scale sounds perfect you may be tired of it. With the mouthpiece alone, try the national anthem. Can you play it with correct pitch and rhythm? (Are you sure?) Can you play it with every tone absolutely equal in volume and in quality? It is quite an accomplishment and a test for control and mastery of the points discussed so far. Success will depend on your care and practice of each and every step. Remember that although the tones go up and down in the melody, the breathing must come absolutely evenly like the long piece of tape and that first long tone. To prevent any diminuendo, counteract with effort by playing a slight crescendo. *Keep the air moving toward the next note.* ∎

Tone Production

VINCENT MALEK

FOR ALL BRASS instrumentalists, the function of the breath is to set the lips of the performer into vibration. The lips, in turn, transmit the vibrations to the air column which is formed by the brass tubing of the instrument. Tone begins the instant the air column begins to vibrate. By increasing the length of the initial air column, either by depressing valves as on the trumpet, or by extending a slide as on the trombone, variations in pitch can be achieved.

Tone Carrying Breath Theory

Many brass players subscribe to the fallacious theory that the breath they blow through the instrument carries the tone. This notion must be dispelled before any consideration can be given to the association between breath and tone production. The exact function of each must be clearly understood before an insight into the relationship between the two can be gained.

If the breath which is forced into the instrument actually created and carried tone along with it, as so many believe, the conclusion would have to be accepted that before any sound could be heard, the air within the instrument would have to be forced out and replaced with the tone-carrying breath. This process, especially for a large instrument such as the tuba, would require several seconds and many breaths; but every brass player knows that the production of sound is an almost instantaneous reaction. What actually occurs is quite different from this tone-carrying theory of the breath.

What Science Tells Us

Psychophysics, the scientific study of the relations between mental and physical processes, informs us that sound is a sensation due to the stimulation of the auditory nerves and the auditory centers of the brain, the stimulation being achieved through vibrations transmitted through the atmosphere. These longitudinal vibratory disturbances are called sound waves.

Since we have scientific proof that sound is produced through vibrations and that the breath blown into a brass instrument does not carry tone with it, simple logic compels us to arrive at the conclusion that the tone must be produced by vibrations of the air column within the instrument. On the trumpet, or on any three-valved brass instrument, there are seven fundamental air columns. Six are formed by adding tubing to the first or open fundamental length, the additions being made by depressing the valves. By fingering from low C down to low F-sharp and tapping the palm of the hand against the mouthpiece in every position, each of the seven fundamental tones can be heard distinctly. This is still further proof that the tone is produced by a vibration of the air column within the instrument.

Effecting Lip Vibration

The next area of consideration concerns the method through which the vibration is effected. Preliminarily, it must be realized that the breath which is blown into the instrument could never, by itself, produce tone. Passage of breath into the instrument and vibration of the air column are not synonymous. Anyone who doubts this should immediately convince himself otherwise before pursuing the theory of brass tone production any further. The simplest proof is merely

166

to place the lips over the mouthpiece and blow through the instrument. By removing them from the position against the mouthpiece in which the passage of breath can bring about their easy vibration, any possibility of producing a tone is precluded.

Experimental Evidence

An experiment suggested by William Thieck demonstrates the belief that the main purpose to be served by the breath is the vibration of the lips.[1] He suggests playing a tone and then attempting to play it again immediately after pouring a small quantity of gasoline through the instrument. Of course, no sound can be achieved, since the air within the instrument has been rarefied by the gasoline.

Another experiment, suggested by O. A. Peterson, demonstrates that tone does not require breath for its production.[2] In order to transmit lip vibrations to the air column without allowing the passage of breath into the instrument, two preparatory steps are necessary: place a very thin membrane about halfway down in the cup of the mouthpiece; drill a small hole in the side of the mouthpiece just above this membrane. Breath going into the mouthpiece would transmit vibrations through the membrane and would escape through the hole. Tone would be produced without a particle of breath passing the membrane and entering the instrument.

Undoubtedly, other experiments could be devised to prove in still other ways, or in more convincing fashion, the basic hypothesis underlying the question. Probably the best proof would feature an electrical or mechanical impulse to set the air column into vibration. This would be ideal since it would eliminate the use of breath or air in the experiment itself, with the exception, of course, of the air within the instrument. Nevertheless, there is sufficient evidence already to make the statement, without fear of contradiction, that the principal function of the breath in brass instrument playing is to force the lips into vibration. Without this there could be no sound.

With the lips vibrating properly and with the correct fingering, each of the seven fundamental tones of the

[1]Thieck, William A., *Common Sense Lip & Tone Development*, Milwaukee, Wisconsin, 1928, p. 5
[2]Peterson, O. A., *The Cornet*, Concord, Massachusetts, 1924, p. 14

three-valve or slide brass instrument can be produced. The reason that these instruments are capable of playing other notes to form a two and one-half octave, or even greater, chromatic scale is that an overtone series exists for each of the fundamental tones; and all the overtones or harmonics can be sounded without changing the fingering, if the lips are properly adjusted to cause subdivisions of the fundamental length as it vibrates. The series exists in exactly the same ratios no matter what fundamental tone it is built upon, the intervals between each two successive tones being a perfect octave, perfect fifth, perfect fourth, major third, minor third, etc. Theoretically, the harmonics can never be exhausted.

Because there are seven fundamental tones for brass instruments and because the overtone series exists for each of them, a full chromatic scale can be played. Many tones are common to more than one harmonic series, and this is the reason that alternate fingerings or positions can be employed to produce these tones.

Controlling Frequency of Vibration

Since a tone is produced by a vibration of the air column, different tones calling for the same fingering, that is, being in the same harmonic series, can be played only if the frequency of vibration is changed. This task falls to the lips. *They cannot generate a vibration but they can and must control it.* The control is effected through the facial muscles which relax and contract the lips, and through the slight movement of the lower jaw which aids in governing the size of the aperture.

Besides controlling the frequency of vibration, the lips must also humor any tones which are out of tune. The trombonist can play in perfect tune without "lipping," since he has direct control over the length of the air column; but the player of a valved brass instrument faces the problem of faulty intonation due to mechanical imperfections in the instrument itself.

We now have three basic facts about the production of tone on a brass instrument. First, the air column within the instrument produces sound whenever it is set into vibration. Second, the frequency of vibration, which determines pitch, is controlled directly by the lips from which

the vibrations are transmitted to the air column, causing it to oscillate from the lips to the bell. And third, the generating force through which the lips are set into vibration is the controlled passage of breath between them, which carries the vibrations out through the instrument.

Air Column Divisions & Subdivisions

We know that pitch is determined by the number of segments in which the air column is vibrating. The more segments there are, which become shorter in direct proportion to their increasing number, the higher the tone. The long segments are produced through a slow vibration of the lips; and as the lips vibrate with increasing rapidity, the segments become shorter and higher tones result.

The slow lip vibration necessary to produce low tones is achieved by a combination of two elements. First, the lips are relaxed; and second, the aperture is made wider, causing the vibrations between the lips to travel a greater distance—thus slowing down the frequency. As the player ascends into the upper range, his lip contracts and the aperture becomes smaller, thus increasing the frequency of vibration.

A question which may logically pose itself at this point is: *How does the combined action of the breath and the lips produce specific or individual tones?* The easiest approach to a solution is probably working back from the tone itself.

When the air column within the instrument is vibrating as a whole, the fundamental tone of the harmonic series is sounded. For example, on a trumpet with no valves depressed, the vibration of the air column as a whole would produce pedal C. By depressing the second valve, pedal B-natural would be obtained; and so on down through all seven positions to pedal F-sharp.

The upper tones of the harmonic series are produced, not by a vibration of the air column as a whole, but by its vibration in an ever-increasing number of segments. For instance, on the trumpet the second tone of the overtone series, of which pedal C is the fundamental, is low C one octave higher. It is the second tone of the series, and correspondingly, the air column vibrates in two segments to produce it. The third tone is second line G, a perfect fifth above low C, and it is produced by an air column vibrating in three segments.

The pattern is consistent throughout. For example, high C is the eighth harmonic, and the air column vibrates in eight segments to produce it. Besides following this specific pattern for all the tones in a particular series, the patterns of all seven overtone series, which are built on the seven fundamentals, are identical. Although the harmonics can never be exhausted in theory, each player has his own limitations.

Tone Development

To make low notes sound, a large amount of breath of limited intensity is necessary; and the lips, though in a state of comparative relaxation, must still maintain firmness. In the middle register the contraction of the lips is comfortable, and a free easy-flowing breath is all that is necessary to produce a good tone. In the upper register the lips are fully contracted, and the mouthpiece must be held against them with a reasonable degree of firmness to assure security.

There is no such thing as a non-pressure system. Advocates of such systems are laboring under a semantic difficulty. What they actually favor is limiting the amount of pressure as much as possible, since whenever two surfaces come into contact pressure or friction is unavoidable. The reason that pressure is not necessarily harmful is that properly contracted lips can withstand a considerable amount of force without being injured in any way. Injury results only when pressure is applied to relaxed lips.

Thus, we find the embouchure in a peculiar situation for the playing of high notes. The aperature in the lips is very small, and the increased pressure of the mouthpiece against them further impedes their easy vibration. To balance this condition the breath passing through the lips must flow with enough force to make them vibrate at the necessary high frequency. The conditions are exactly opposite from those needed for the production of low notes. Low notes require a large amount of breath with limited pressure behind it; high notes require a large amount of pressure behind a lesser quantity of breath.

The term, *pressure*, in its usage here should not be confused with *mouthpiece pressure*. The latter designates the amount of force with which the mouthpiece is held against the lips, while the former denotes the bodily support employed in the controlled expulsion of breath from the lungs.

Besides needing more air pressure for the production of high notes, increased air pressure is necessary in all registers to develop the tone in magnitude or loudness. Just as pitch is determined by the frequency of vibration, amplitude of tone is determined by the intensity of vibration. This means, simply, that to play louder the lips must vibrate at the same frequency but over a wider range. This is accomplished by forcing more breath through the lips, thus spreading the aperture. By playing a tone and increasing the flow of breath, the aperture is forced farther apart; and this, automatically, makes the vibrations travel the greater distance between the upper and lower lips.

A Conclusion

The whole question of tone production on a brass instrument can be reduced to this conclusion: *The ability of the performer to balance amplitude and frequency of lip vibration with breath pressure to produce a tone of desired pitch and intensity is the principal determinant of the character of that tone.*

Thus, the brass player finds himself in a unique situation. The playing breath he uses is only indirectly responsible for the production of tone, but it, nevertheless, is perhaps the most important single concomitant of artistic performance. Articulation, fingering, slurring, intonation, accuracy of attack, smoothness in playing and musical discrimination are all important aspects in the conglomeration of requirements for fine musical performance upon a brass instrument; but, without being accompanied by a highly developed ability to control the breath, they can never operate to their best advantage.

Put Emphasis on Breath Control

Since in music the *whole* is greater than the sum of its component parts, poor tone quality or inability to distribute the breath properly always detracts, immeasurably, from an otherwise commendable showing. For instance, a player may develop his tongue muscles to enable him to produce rapid and exacting articulations, but if they are accompanied by a thin or strained tonal quality, the result will almost inevitably sound poor and unmusical.

Whereas the combination of technical ability and poor breath control cannot result in anything but an unsatisfactory performance, the reverse situation does not have the same chaotic consequence. Good tone quality, achieved through proper breath management, combined with limited technical ability can produce a musically satisfying result. Simple music well-played is infinitely more desireable for all concerned than a struggle through a difficult composition. Of course, for truly artistic performance every aspect of playing ability must be developed to its utmost level.

Only a few individuals can ever achieve the status of *artist*, but every player is capable, by intelligent and persevering application, to perform up to his ultimate ability. Unfortunately, most players work tirelessly on the development of technique but give relatively little attention to breath control. In light of the usual results obtained, this is the wrong approach. In the great majority of individual cases, the development of the ability to manage the breath will not be automatic; *it must be learned.* Ignoring it in the hope that, eventually, it will work itself out is, in all likelihood, merely allowing a bad habit to engrain itself deeper and deeper.

By allowing himself to by-pass serious consideration of the control of the breath, the student dooms himself to musical incompetency—unless he happens to be that lucky and unique individual who acquires breath control automatically. If progress is to be made, faulty breathing habits must be corrected; but the longer correction is delayed, the more difficult the process becomes.

If the beginner works on technique only and neglects breathing, the further development of technique becomes more and more difficult as the gap between the two begins to widen. And as the gap widens, closing it becomes increasingly difficult. The reason for this is that an additional procedure must be employed. Prior to the development of proper breath control and support, the student must first unlearn all of the undesirable breathing habits he has acquired.

FINE

1955

Single French Horn

How to Acquire Evenness in Tonguing

DANIEL TETZLAFF

ONE OF THE EARMARKS OF A schooled brass player is clear, clean tonguing. Untrained players seldom have the control and flexibility of the tongue necessary to perform, distinctly, the rhythms found in all serious music. Tonguing facility is acquired through careful training and practice.

As an aid to those who desire further progress in this direction, here are some suggestions.

Before practicing today, review two articles on tonguing by James Nielson; the first appeared on page 20 of the October, 1950 issue of The Instrumentalist and the second on page 21 of the January, 1952 issue. Both articles contain discussion of other matters, but at this time concentrate only on the sections explaining tonguing. These articles, in my opinion, are among the most enlightening and informative text materials available. Since they explain *how to tongue* so well, I will be concerned mainly with a discussion of what good tonguing should *sound like*.

When you are warmed up and ready for serious practice, open your *Arban Method* to page 44, exercise #22. Play the first G4 (G above middle C) as a long tone, thus setting a pattern for *sustained even blowing*. The last note on the line must still equal the first in volume, quality, intonation. Now, slightly alter what is written. Change each B4 to a G4, thus giving a single pitch to the whole line; also, omit the 5th bar containing the sextuplets. Playing the exercise in this manner will produce the effect of a measured accelerando on a single note.

Although the notes come faster and faster and get shorter and shorter, *they must not get weaker or thinner*. Allow no diminuendo, no irregularity, no unevenness. This can be accomplished only by steady air pressure, steady lips and a relaxed throat and back tongue—the same components required to produce good tone. Sustaining a tone and tonguing on a single tone should feel almost identical. The only difference is that in the latter the tip of the tongue makes interruptions in the desired rhythmic pattern. The following illustration is a graphic representation of this idea:

□□ □ □ □ □ □ □ □ □ □ □ □ ▯▯▮▮▮ ▭▭▭▭▭▭

Further Considerations

Attack. In the illustration you will notice that each tone is depicted as starting in an identical manner. Careful practice and critical listening are required to duplicate this control in sound. First, the tip of the tongue must touch the identical place in the mouth for each and every note. It must not be allowed to wander about sideways or up and down. Secondly, there must be concentration on making the stroke of the tongue identical for all the notes. Finally, only the tip of the tongue should move in performing this exercise, *nothing else.* Make sure!

Use of a Mirror. Since action at the tip of the tongue is invisible when tonguing, you should see no movement of any sort when playing this exercise in front of a mirror. The cheeks, lips, jaws and throat must show no movement—just as they do not during a sustained, steady tone. *Flops, wiggles* and *swallows* can be seen easily; worse still, they can be heard. They give tonguing an unmusical, scooping sound. No clean execution or speed can be developed until they are eliminated.

Rhythm. A majority of students will *fake the rhythm* when first attempting the revised Arban exercise as explained above, especially commencing with the bar of triplets. This is a good opportunity to insist upon the elimination of guessing. There is no guessing in fractions, and rhythms are merely accurate divisions of the beat. Insist upon accuracy; use a metronome, or, if foot tapping is used, make certain that it is steady. *Style.* Purposely, no mention has yet been made concerning the type of tonguing to be used. At first, it does not matter; just try for evenness of sound and evenness of rhythm. After perfecting this in one style of tonguing, review again Mr. Nielson's articles for tips on producing at least three variations: smooth legato tonguing, crisp staccato, one halfway between. The differences will be twofold: first, in the attack or the start of the tone; secondly, in the space between the tones. Remember, staccato does not mean *short*; it means *separated.*

Spacing. The most overlooked detail in performing rhythmic passages is the attention to *the spaces.* Of course the notes must be even, but so must be the spacing. Care must be given to maintain the rhythm of the spaces.

Tempo. The correct tempo for practicing the recommended studies is the maximum speed at which the most difficult bar can still be played accurately. That means that the quarter notes should start out at a moderate pace.

Volume. Since one of our aims is the pursuit of the solid professional tone, all the recommended exercises should me done between *mf* and *f*—closer to the latter, so that a full tone becomes the habit.

To gain the maximum amount of benefit, each of the first eight lines on page 44 of the *Arban Method* should be played three different ways, until the same attack and the same tone quality are present in every note.

During the third time through,

change the third tone in each group to a higher harmonic. On the first line, that would give the *do, mi, sol* triad in the key of G. Treat the other lines similarly.

Attention to Intervals

All the factors of evenness acquired while practicing reiterated notes on a single pitch, No. 1 in the above illustration, must be transferred to intervals. In No. 2 a new process is introduced; the lips must change for the higher note. Make sure by playing in front of a mirror and observing the change. You should be able to see small muscular contractions each time the upper note is played. They, too, must be in strict rhythm and coordinated exactly with the rhythm of the tongue. The top tone *must not* be louder; the pitch goes up and down, not the volume.

No. 3 in the illustration is an extension of problem No. 2. The lips must now feel a definite third position—three different notes, three different positions. A vague tightening or loosening of the lips must be supplanted by a delicate feel for each position, for only then will it be possible for the lips to change the pitch accurately from one tone to the other —in any interval pattern—with the same rapidity as the tongue. That is the trick, to develop the lips to move as fast and as flexibly as the tongue.

FINE

Matching Tonguing and Slurring

DANIEL TETZLAFF

IT IS FOLLY TO BLUNDER ON AND stumble through to the back of an exercise book before acquiring balance and control on the fundamental exercises found in the first few pages. Advanced etudes all abound in passages that continually alternate between tonguing and slurring. It is impossible to play these etudes, or the solo literature to which they lead, in a musical manner until the instrumentalist develops an equal control and evenness in both skills. It comes from applying the *same fundamentals* to each of the two processes. It is illogical to attempt tongued intervals one way and slurred intervals another. Rapid and accurate shifting from one process to the other at any tempo and in any register would then be impossible.

It matters not which of the two problems are studied first. I have observed that no player starts out with *the gift* of equal facility at tonguing and slurring an identical pattern of notes. Practice and concentration alone produce this *professional touch*. Younger players seem to be able to acquire tongue control easier; however, older players, many of whom have for years played only the smooth melodic style demanded in the performance of popular music, have more control of the legato. They, then, can best start from that vantage point and proceed to acquire equal tonguing ability, always using the evenness of sound of one as a check on the other.

How and What to Practice

Turn again to the exercises in *Arban's*, page 44 or *St. Jacome's*, page 19. First play a long sustained G4. Then play the first measure of the page over and over again, for the duration of a full breath. Alternate tonguing and slurring continually. Over and over again *until every note has absolutely the same tone quality and the same volume.*

What to Listen For

The ear should hear but one difference from measure to measure; in one the notes are separated, in the other they are connected. Do each successive measure of the first line in this manner, making an *exercise in matching* out of each bar.

Next, play the whole line as written (the 5th bar can be omitted in *Arban*). Play the line through twice, once tongued and once slurred. Use full tone. Catch a quick breath after the second bar without delaying the rhythm.

Proceed through the entire series in like manner. If using the *Arban Method*, proceed to page 142 and play the first line three different ways as a test of evenness: 1. all tongued; 2. all slurred; 3. as written.

If you hear a good quality *on all tones*, high or low, tongued or slurred, then only are you ready for advanced etudes. But listen carefully! Do you detect any of these common flaws?

1. The top notes *must not be louder*. A heavy push from the diaphragm is not a substitute for the necessary small lip contraction. Crescendos, bumps and honked out high notes are not a part of smooth playing.

2. The top notes *must not be thinner* in slurring than in tonguing. Check this carefully. The opening in the throat must stay the same during both processes. The front of the tongue, also, must always move or rest at about the same level.

3. When a student fails to sound the upper note at all, the trouble can usually be traced to:

   a. not starting with enough lip flesh *in the mouthpiece;*
   b. no *muscular contraction* of the lips for the higher tone;
   c. no *maintenance of steady blowing* of the air against the lips while going from one note to another.

Two-Fold Purpose

Practicing the exercises in this

172

series to achieve the results here emphasized will:

1. Develop the instrumentalist's control of matched tone quality and intonation so that at any speed tonguing and slurring will have the same size tone.

2. It will provide a "do it yourself" checkup for deficiencies in previously acquired processes of either teacher or pupil. Younger players can be guided away from bad habits; older

players can experience a beneficial "straightening out" or "refresher course."

Accent Ear Training

Although there are many different approaches to playing the brass instruments, in the long run they prove to be of *unequal* merit and *unequal* possibilities. How can you tell if your way is a good way? Only by constant listening and checking up on results! Every player should be alert for new

information, or different explanations of old material, that can result in more direct and more efficient progress. Many of the finest players have found success only after trying several approaches. Many have changed or modified their procedures several times in the light of new information from many sources. No one person has all the answers. The search is continuous.

FINE

To "Ah-ee" or not to "Ah-ee"!

JODY HALL

TRUMPET TEACHERS HAVE LONG been in disagreement concerning the manner in which the tongue and the mouth cavity are employed to aid the lips in changing register. Some teachers have stated that the tongue is never used as such an aid, while others have said that the proper shaping of the tongue into various vowel formations is all important. Still others maintain that the tongue and mouth are used not for register changes but for variation in tonal quality. The use of a particular mouth formation after attack is implied through the syllable used in articulation, as in "tu", "du", "tah", "tee", "dee".

In order to determine if there really were many different ways of playing trumpet, the writer examined by X-ray the playing techniques of nine outstanding trumpet performers. The players had studied with different prominent teachers and were advocates of different methods of teaching. Some aspects of the study are presented here.

The three vowels most often referred to by trumpet teachers are

"a" (ah), "i" (ee), and "u" (oo). These three vowels are referred to by phoneticians as the extreme vowels. The vowel "i" has maximum front elevation of the tongue, "u" has maximum back elevation of the tongue, and "ah" has minimum elevation in either area.

The performers who play or teach without reference to vowel formation may not be conscious of these positions, but the tongue is assuming one of these positions (or a position intermediate between them) after the attack. The problem of articulation involves the placement of the tongue before the attack, the movement of the tongue during attack, and the placement of the tongue after attack. It is with the last factor that we are concerned here.

The Experiment

Each trumpeter played Bb4, Bb3 and Bb5 on his own instrument, using his own mouthpiece. As he played these tones, a radiograph (X-ray picture) was made and the sound produced was recorded.

Then each performer played the same three notes with a control

trumpet and mouthpiece (used by all subjects). Once again simultaneous radiographs and recordings were made.

For purposes of orientation, each player then said the vowels "ah", "oo", and "ee". Radiographs were made of these positions.

Detailed measurements were made of the positions of the various portions of the mouth and throat for all registers and for the three vowel formations. These measurements were compared to discover what changes had taken place.

Results and Conclusions

In answer to the question, "What physical and anatomical changes occur when a trumpet performer changes from one register to another?", the following conclusions were made (based only on the results of these nine players):

1. *Trumpet players tend to assume their own individual physiological formations.* The most common formation used was that of "ah". However, some players used the "oo" formation or intermediate formations

between the extreme vowels.

2. *Trumpet performers tend to use the same basic formation in every register.* Variations in formation between different registers were small. In nearly every case, the changes were not as great as the changes between vowels.

3. In changing from middle register to low register, three different patterns of physical change were used, each of which was identified with a particular movement of the tongue. The most common pattern was that of lowering the tongue.

4. The method of changing from middle to high register varies greatly with individuals. The most frequent tendencies were the following:

a. Raising of the lower jaw.

b. Moving the high point of the tongue forward and/or downward.

c. Enlarging of the pharynx (throat cavity).

d. Moving the larynx (voice box) forward and upward.

5. When the lips were widely stretched, no particular vowel formation accompanied such stretching.

6. Most trumpet players move the mouthpiece closer to the teeth for the high register, even to the extent of having the teeth actually protrude into the mouthpiece! However, some players reverse this procedure.

Evaluation

During the preliminary stages of the study, the writer believed that as a player moved into a higher register, the natural tendency was to move the tongue upward and forward to the roof of the mouth as in saying "ee". The writer believed that in the effort to control tone quality, some players retarded, or delayed, the tendency to raise the tongue. Consequently, he was hardly prepared for the reversal of this pattern, i.e., lowering of the tongue for the high register.

It was a personal belief that there was a common basis of adjustment for all playing. Such a basic procedure has not been shown. However, there are some indications that the original supposition has some foundation. In a preliminary experiment, a relatively inexperienced subject showed a much greater tendency to shift from vowel to vowel than did the trumpet players participating in the study itself. Also, in an additional high tone experiment, the three players tested all shifted toward the

X-rays of "ah", "oo" and "ee" tongue formations as produced by one player.

"ee" formation in playing E6 regardless of their previous technique in playing lower tones. It is the opinion of the writer that somewhere in the extremely high register, placement of the tongue in an "ee" position becomes necessary. The point of transition probably varies from player to player.

One subject, who attempted to play all tones with an "ah" formation, actually did so, but in changing to a higher register, he lowered the tongue more radically than did the other players. In spite of this situation, he deliberately teaches the "ah-ee" system[1] because "it gets quicker results".

Tone Quality

Since different procedures were used by different performers, it was assumed that those differences might result in differences in the sound produced. Accordingly, analyses were made of the harmonic structure of all tones. This was done by means of the Kay Sound Spectrograph, which gives a permanent record of the acoustical pattern of a tone.

A difference was found to exist between those tones which were played with an "ah" formation, and those that were played with an "oo" or an intermediate position. The peak of the formant[2] was found to be at 1260 c.p.s. when an "ah" formation was used. When the "oo" or intermediate positions were used that peak tended to become lower (1050 c.p.s.) and in addition became stronger in relation to the fundamental. Those tones produced with the "ah" formation tended to have added strength present in the higher harmonics (above 2100 c.p.s.).

A similar relationship between "ah" and "oo" has been found to exist in speech. The principal difference between these vowels is in the location of the 1st formant, which is lower for "oo" than for "ah".

One might well ask, "How much different are these sounds?" It is the

writer's opinion that the difference is readily discernible. By the time the last subject was examined, both the sound technician and myself, after hearing the sound, could predict with considerable accuracy the position of the tongue which would be shown by the X-ray negative. One subject requested that the recording of his E6 be erased because it was not the type of sound which he tried to produce. In practice, he had been playing a *matched* tone quality up to Bb6, but under the conditions of the study he was unable to do so. The change from the "oo" formation to the "ee" formation for that tone is quite pronounced.

As a result of the information which has been obtained, the writer has developed several personal concepts for his own guidance in teaching. Those concepts are presented for consideration by the reader.

1. A tone quality which is consistent in all registers should be the controlling factor in determining basic tongue position.

2. In order to develop a consistent tone quality in all registers, emphasis should be placed on changing register by use of the embouchure and breath support alone (without aid from the tongue).

3. If the "ah-ee" change is ever used with inexperienced students as a device to aid in register change, it should be done with an awareness that eventually that method will be altered or abandoned.

4. After advanced students have learned to play in all registers with one basic tongue position and tone quality, they can learn to produce different qualities of tone, as demanded by the music, by varying the tongue position.

Fine

[1]Ah-ee system: Use of "ah" vowel in lower registers and "ee" vowel in higher register.
[2]Formant: A concentration of energy in a frequency area. All harmonics lying within that area are of greater intensity. The peak of the formant is the point of greatest intensity.

Right Hand in Horn Playing

JAMES WINTER

MOST PEOPLE who are interested in the horn are aware that the player inserts his right hand into the bell of his instrument so as to create a more beautiful and more characteristic tone quality. Still, some misconceptions remain; perhaps they can be corrected by a brief explanation.

The first of these misconceptions is that the hand in the bell is sufficient in itself, and that once the student has been shown the *magic spot* his tone will be beautiful. Unfortunately, this is not true; the right hand in the bell is only an additional and final *coloring* agent for a tone that is already fundamentally acceptable. If the student has a thin, bright tone, using a trumpet embouchure, the tone will remain thin and uninteresting regardless of proper hand position. Embouchure and the manner of blowing falls outside the scope of this discussion, so let us assume that in this respect, all is well. Now, what of the right hand?

The right hand serves three basic purposes: (1) it helps to *darken* the tone for normal playing; (2) it helps to control intonation; (3) it is used for special muted effects. Unfortunately, there are no precise rules as to where the hand belongs for these three functions, because no two hands are the same size and shape, and because there is some variation in bell size in horns.

We can follow certain principles, however. To begin with, the hand is somewhat cupped, just as it is cupped in swimming. It is important that there be no *leaks* through the hand, and that the thumb be placed so as to give the hand maximum breadth, again as in swimming. See Figure 1.

Figure 1
The hand cupped, as in swimming.

In order to permit maximum freedom of the right hand, there is no harm in permitting the bell of the horn to rest on the right thigh, preferably near the hip, provided that the bell does not become buried in the lap. Burying the bell is a particularly

Figure 2
Bell buried in player's lap, smothering the tone.

insidious fault, since it tends to make the tone sound very dark and solid to the player, but actually muffles the tone so that it lacks carrying power. See Figure 2.

First Position

For normal playing there are two common positions of the right hand, both of which do essentially the same thing, darken the tone. In the first position, the hand is placed in the bell with the backs of the fingers against the far side of the bell, away from the player. The hand is thus at approximately right angles to the floor, and the tone is deflected—by the soft inner palm—toward the player. The extent to which the heel of the hand is closed toward the op-

Figure 3a
Side view of "first position".

Figure 3b
"First position" shown from behind the bell.

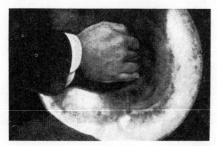

Figure 3c
Modified "first position" for playing while standing or marching.

posite side of the bell, toward the player, will vary with the individual, but it must not close the bell completely. Figure 3a shows a position about level with the bell of the horn, looking from the player's right; Figure 3b was taken from behind and slightly above the bell, and shows a normal degree of closure. Figure 3c illustrates a slight modification of the first basic position. Here the weight of the bell is permitted to fall along the thumb and forefinger. Note that there is a good opening below the hand. This position is useful when playing while standing or marching.

Second Position

The second position differs only in that the hand is placed, palm up, against the bottom of the bell. The hand is about at a thirty degree angle with the floor, and the tone is deflected upward. See Figures 4a and 4b. The degree of closure is determined by the extent to which the heel of the hand is brought upwards, toward the upper side of the bell, and will vary with the individual. In general, this second position seems to produce a somewhat darker tone than the first.

The writer's hand is about average

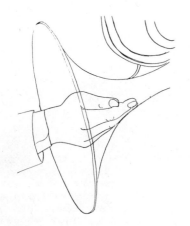

Figure 4a
Side view of "second position".

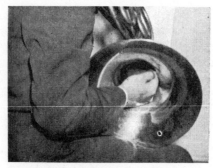

Figure 4b
"Second position" shown from behind the bell.

in size, and the photographs show an average placement. A smaller hand may be placed farther into the bell, so as to effect a comparable degree of closure. A larger hand will remain further out and may have to be cupped slightly more. It is important to note that the palm of the hand is *never* permitted to lie at right angles to the bore of the bell. This is a fairly common fault, resulting from excessive cupping of the hand. In *piano* and *mezzo-forte* passages no ill effects will be noted, but in *forte* the tone will acquire a brassy sound. This is not to say that horns must never sound brassy; occasionally it is musically desirable that they do, but this is normally in very heavy *fortissimo* passages, far more powerful than those one ordinarily plays.

A more open position of the hand will brighten the tone, and raise the pitch a little; a more closed position will do the opposite. Therefore, for a student with a conspicuously too-bright tone, the teacher should recommend closing the heel of the hand more; if the tone sounds too muffled, try opening the heel of the hand. Similarly, a flat note may be raised by opening the hand, and a sharp one may be lowered by closing the hand; the amount of motion required in this case is very slight, as the student will find by experimenting.

Muted Effects

All of the various muted effects are produced in the same basic way; the hand is simply placed further into the bell, so as to close it entirely. The heel of the hand is brought forward, so that the palm *almost* forms a right angle with the bore of the bell. Unless the hand is very small, the fingers and thumb will have to be overlapped somewhat to permit them to slide up into the bell. With the hand in this position, a line drawn around the out-

side of the palm, up the back of the thumb, across the backs of the fingers between the first and second knuckles, and down the outside of the little finger, will be found to approximate a circle. Contact with the bell is made on this circle. Figure 5a looks down over the player's right shoulder; Figure 5b was taken from directly behind the bell.

Closing the bell in this manner also shortens the tube, so that the player must now transpose DOWN a semitone. A very small hand will slide too far into the bell, and the student will tend to play sharp even after transposing. A student with a very large hand may tend to play a little flat. Since the tubing is shorter, the single Bb horn and the Bb side of the double horn will be raised about three-quarters of a step, and cannot be used for normal hand-stopping unless the horn is equipped with a special muting valve.

Figure 5a
Muted position, shown from above, over the player's right shoulder.

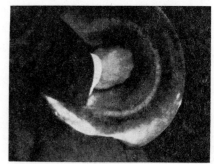

Figure 5b
Muted position shown from behind the bell.

Suggestions

The more firmly the bell is closed, the more nasal the tone; if a *crash* sound is desired, close the bell tightly, and blow very firmly. If a true echo is desired, with little or no nasality, close the bell less firmly, and blow as dark a tone as possible. It will be found that this effect is nearly impossible to achieve in the lower register, as the tone loses focus when

Natural Hunting Horn

loosely stopped.

If the hand is smaller than average, make it as broad as possible, by placing the thumb alongside the first finger, and flattening the arch of the knuckles. Close the bell firmly, so that the tone has a distinct nasal whine when you blow solidly. Now, leaving the heel of the hand in place, try to lower the pitch by backing the fingers out of the bell as far as possible without losing contact. If the hand is extremely small, you may be able to use the Bb side of the double horn and transpose down a WHOLE step. In this case, of course, close the bell

tightly.

If the hand is larger than average, try to make it as small as possible by overlapping the thumb and fingers. Be particularly careful to keep the heel of the hand flattened against the bell, as overlapping the fingers will tend to cause a crease, through which air may leak.

If the hand is very bony, there will probably be serious difficulties, since the tone will leak around the knuckles. Try to use the fleshiest part of the fingers, avoiding direct contact between the knuckles and the bell.

If you must play in the low register

—hand-stopped—and find it difficult to focus the tone, try closing the hand more firmly, look for leaks past a knuckle or a finger, blow very solidly. If you have a good closure, it will be possible to play to the lowest (fingered) tone of the F horn, hand-stopped with regular transposition DOWN one semitone. If this doesn't work, try transposing the wrong direction, UP a semitone, in the register in which the tone loses focus. I know of no logical acoustical explanation for this phenomenon, but it will definitely work for some individuals.

FINE

September, 1955

Blowing with Ease and Freedom

William Cramer

ONE OF THE GREATEST problems which every beginning instrumentalist must solve is that of acquiring the habit of blowing with the greatest of ease and freedom. In some manner, the breath in the lungs must be forced through a windpipe filled with various obstructions which either choke off the air stream or deflect it in such a way that it fails to reach the lips with its greatest force and vitality.

These obstructions in the windpipe include the vocal cords, the glottis, the uvula, the tongue, the teeth and the lips.

When a tone is being well sounded the air passes freely from the lungs through the lips, setting the lips in vibration. Any of the above-mentioned obstructions may be used unconsciously by the unsuspecting student either for articulation, for controlling the air stream in adjusting the dynamic level, or in adjusting the pressure necessary to help change the pitch. There is a certain amount of security in feeling the air column working against something, and it is

therefore natural for the beginning student to create these points of resistance in his windpipe, which the breath must then overcome

Any obstruction results in a choked tone quality and style of playing which sounds "muscle-bound." A better understanding of these obstructions and their misuse may be of some help in teaching the student to blow more freely.

Vocal Cords

The vocal cords are often drawn together and allowed to sound immediately before an attack. Sometimes they sound on each note that the student plays while he is executing a legato passage. The effect may go completely unnoticed if the teacher stands any distance away from the student. The great harm that it can cause can be shown by sounding a middle F on a trombone, for instance, and trying to sing the same pitch at the same time. The least out-of-tuneness will produce a very disagreeable wave in the tone. Rarely does a student know that he does this.

The Glottis

The glottis is a "flapper" valve in the windpipe which prevents food from entering the lungs. Some students will use the glottis as an articulative device, holding back the air under pressure and then releasing it as an attack. In this case the "follow-through" in tone production is rarely satisfactory. Other students will use the glottis as a means of building up the air pressure as an aid to playing high tones. It can usually be detected in an ascending passage, and less often in a descending passage. In this instance a good slur or trombone legato is practically impossible because the air stream is constantly being broken or pinched off.

The Uvula

The uvula is the appendage at the back of the mouth which hangs down from the soft palate. It is often misused in the same way as the glottis but results in a slightly different sound. Students who attack with the uvula will have a sound like a cough. Others who do not keep the uvula raised sufficiently will find air leaking out the nose because the windpipe opening at that point is not large enough to permit the air to pass through the mouth freely. Occasionally, the air which is held back by the uvula is forced into the stomach.

Articulation

The tongue is properly used as an articulative device, a means for marking off the air stream into lengths we know as half, quarter, and eighth notes, and as a means for defining the style of attack. This articulation is always done with the tip of the tongue except when double or triple tonguing, and then the tip alternates with the middle of the tongue. If this latter articulation moves too far to the rear of the tongue then the uvula is brought into play and the attack becomes indistinct largely because the windpipe is closed too much. Some students may get into the habit of keeping the middle of the tongue arched in such a way as to close off a free flow of air, thus producing a thinner sounding tone.

The teeth provide a point of contact for the tongue in the articulative process. Further, they provide a support to the embouchure when the mouthpiece is placed to the lips. But there are occasional instances where a student will hold the teeth—or more correctly, the jaws—too close together, again preventing the free flow of air through the windpipe. Students who inhale through the nose are generally holding the teeth and jaws too tightly together.

The Lips

When properly positioned, the lips set the pitch. Changes of pitch are made by adjusting the muscles of the embouchure which in turn control the lips. The sensation of tone production should be as simple as that of allowing the lips to vibrate freely in the breeze that is passing through the windpipe.

Some students use the lips for the attack or for articulation, holding back the air until the correct air pressure is reached or until the moment for attack arrives, and then releasing it either by blowing the lips open or by dropping the chin to open the lips. This latter habit is relatively easy to detect because the chin goes up and down with each attack.

Remedial Measures

The correction of any of the above-mentioned faults may be accomplished simply by sounding long tones in the most comfortable register, using *no attack whatsoever*. The sensation should be similar to that of gently but firmly blowing out several lighted candles, one right after the other, with a single breath. It would be better if a teacher or some other interested instrumentalist could stand by and watch as well as listen for tell-tale sounds and signs. So often the undesirable habits are so firmly set that the student does not know that he uses them.

When the student knows exactly what it feels like to blow one tone freely, then he should progress to simple diatonic slurs, ascending and descending, but still with no initial attack. Diatonic scales in various forms may be added, leading to chromatic scales covering the entire register of the instrument.

The end result should be a much larger tone with a feeling of greater security, greater strength, greater endurance and greater flexibility.

FINE

October, 1955

The Initial Attack

A good start sets the pattern.

William Cramer

THE FIRST NOTE played by the instrumentalist may well be the most important one in the entire composition. Once he has begun to play, it is rather difficult for the inexperienced performer to correct his faults in the middle of a phrase. That first note can set the pattern for success in performing the whole piece as well as the first phrase.

A capable teacher will have a good start in forming an opinion of a student's ability by the time the student has played the first few notes.

In that short space of time the teacher will have had an opportunity to observe the breath intake, the body attitude for playing—including the placement of the fingers on the valves or slide, the amount of opening in the windpipe and the mouth cavity, the style of articulation, and the embouchure formation.

Breath Intake

The breath intake should be in tempo, smooth and quiet. The tempo of the composition should be set in mind so that the student will, generally, take his breath in the full beat just before he begins to play. A quiet breath indicates that the mouth and throat are open wide enough to allow the breath to enter without rasping or sucking noises. The teacher should notice that the sound of the breath is low in pitch when the mouth and throat are open wide, and that the sound is high in pitch when the throat and mouth are somewhat closed.

Posture

The proper body attitude is one of alertness, a state of being ready to do the most efficient job at the right instant. All the forces that go into tone production should be brought to bear in a finely co-ordinated motion. The student should be able to call upon almost unlimited power, with smooth and instant conversion into tone production. The end result should be the making of music without being distracted by the mechanical or physical processes. It is therefore quite impossible to be in the highest state of readiness if one's posture is poor.

Carelessness in certain kinds of attacks can be traced directly to carelessness in placing the fingers on the valves or slide. The result may be a valve pushed only part way down with a peculiarly out-of-focus pitch. Again the slide may be only an inch off the correct position but the pitch suffers. In the latter instance the tone quality may suffer too when the student tries to force one pitch through the instrument and the slide is in position for another.

The hand is made for grasping, so the thumb should assume a position of opposing the fingers. The greatest sensitivity is in the fingertips, so it is better that the student learn from the beginning to make contact with his instrument through the fingertips.

Oral Cavity

The largest possible opening in the windpipe and the mouth cavity will assist greatly in tone production. A large opening allows for a free flow of air from the breathing mechanism, resulting in a buoyant sound rather than a forced sound. Any closure in the windpipe or throat may bring the vocal cords or other membranes close enough so that they will vibrate, resulting in distasteful rasping or humming noises. Some students will even use this throat closure instead of the tongue as an articulative device.

Experimentation will show that a fuller tone is produced when the mouth cavity is kept as large as possible. Further, it aids in a freer passage of air from the breathing mechanism to the lips. Control of the breath ought to be felt at the source of power, the breathing and blowing muscles. The throat or windpipe should not be used to choke off the breath when the student wishes to play softly.

Articulation

The act of articulation on a brass instrument is similar to articulation in singing, yet uniquely different. In singing, one articulates with the tongue, lips and teeth, sounds which have been made by the vocal cords; while on a brass instrument, the air stream itself is articulated with the tongue before it reaches the lips. The lips in turn convert the air stream into sound. In either case there must be a continuous flow of air for the duration of the phrase in order to make that phrase coherent as well as unified. At the same time it must be suitably articulated in order to convey style and meaning to the phrase. Use of the throat, the glottis, or the lips for articulation is to be avoided for they cause disagreeable sounds, lowered efficiency, and poor tone quality.

Embouchure

The embouchure formation should be such that the lips respond instantly to the flow of breath, resulting in the correct pitch and tone quality. This is the essence of flexibility. The discriminating teacher will know at once if the muscle tension within the embouchure is either too little or too much, causing pitch variation which is too low or too high. He will know when either too much or too little flesh is inside the mouthpiece for the tone will be either too thick or too thin.

Teacher Guidance

It now becomes apparent that the approach to performing music on a brass instrument presents a problem of very great complexity. The young student cannot hope to master the problem by himself. Though he may read and understand, he still needs the guidance of a teacher who will pass judgment on the degree of progress. The position of the teacher is of utmost importance. He must judge what the student cannot see and what he does not hear.

FINE

Materials for Tuba

Methods and etudes, solos and solo collections.

Leon Brown

THE FOLLOWING list of tuba materials was intended to be as comprehensive as possible. No attempt was made to evaluate; every listing, regardless of quality, was included:

Methods and Etudes

Arban-Prescott — CF
First and Second Year (E♭ or BB♭)
Beeler, Walter — Rem
Method for Tuba
Bell, William — CF
Foundation to Tuba and Sousaphone Playing (E♭, CC, BB♭)
Bernard, P. — Baro
Douze Pieces Melodiques (F. E.)
Bernard, P. — Baro
Quarante Etudes (F. E.)
Bernard, P. — Baro
Traits Difficiles in Four Books (F. E.)
Blasewitsch, V. — imported
Schule Fur Bass Tuba (F. E.)
Blasewitsch, V. — imported
Seventy Etudes for Tuba (F. E.)
Brown, T. C. — B&H
Tuba Passages (English Band Music)
Buck — Kjos
Elementary Method
Caton — Volk
Progressive Instructor
Cheyette, I. — Pro
Elements of Sight Reading
Cheyette-Salzman — Lee
Three-Way Method (Band, Class, Ind.)
Clarke, H. F. — Mil
Mills Elementary Method for E♭ and BB♭ Bass
Collins, F. — Bost.
Daily Embouchure Drills (Bass Clef)
Dippolito-Thompson — Volk
Modern Way Method
Eby, Walter — Jac
Scientific Method for Tuba (E♭ or BB♭) (in two volumes)
Eidson, A. D. — Bel
Brass Bass Method (Books I, II, III)
Endresen, R. M. — Cole
Method for E♭ or BB♭ Tuba
Endresen, R. M. — Rub
Supplementary Studies
Fischer (edition) — CF
Eclipse Self-Instructor for E♭-BB♭ Tuba
Geib, F. — CF
Method for Tuba
Goldman, E. F. — CF
Daily Embouchure Studies (E♭)
Gornston, David — Schu
The Very First E♭ or BB♭ Bass Method
Gower-Voxman — Rub
Advanced Method for Bass (E♭, BB♭)
Gregoriev — imported
Fifty Studies for Tuba (F. E.)
Hawkes — B&H
Simplicity Tutor
Herfurth — Bost
Tune-A-Day for Bass
Hindsley, Mark — CF
Carl Fischer Basic Methhod for E♭ Sousaphone
Hindsley, Mark — CF
Carl Fischer Basic Method for BB♭ Sousaphone

Hovey, Nilo W. — Rub
Elementary Method for Bass (E♭, BB♭)
Hovey, Nilo W. — Volk
Universal Fundamental Method
Johnson, H. M. — Fitz
Aeolian Method
Kuhn-Cimera — Bel
Method for Tuba
Langey — CF
Tutor for BB♭ Bass

Langey — CF
Tutor for Bass Tuba
Langey — B&H
Practical Tutor
Little, L. — Pro
Embouchure Builder (Bass Clef)

Lorenz — ?
Imperial Method
——— — CB
Military Band Studies (Tuba)
Moore and Seig — CF
Preparatory Instructor for Bass (E♭, BB♭)
——— — Int
Orchestral Studies of Symphonic Works (Trombone and Tuba)
Paisner, B. — Gorn
B. O. E. Trainers (Rhythmic)
Pares, G. — CF
Scale Studies for BB♭ Tuba
Rollinson — Big 3
Method for E♭ or BB♭ Bass
Ronka — CF
Daily Lip Drills and Studies for Tuba
Skornicka-Boltz — Rub
Intermediate Method for E♭ or BB♭ Bass
Slama, A. — CF
66 Etudes in All Major and Minor Keys
Stretton — B&H
Unison Scale Studies
——— — CF
Tuba Players Studio (Vade Mecum) (Collection of difficult passages)
Tyrrell, H. W. — B&H
Advanced Studies for Tuba (E♭)
Tyrrell, H. W. — B&H
Advanced Studies for Tuba (BB♭)
Vandercook — Rub
Etudes for Tuba (E♭ and BB♭)
Whistler, H. S. — Rub
Modern Pares for BB♭ Bass
Whistler, H. S. — Rub
Modern Pares for E♭ Bass

Solos and Solo Collections

Adam — B&H
Aria from "Giralda"
Alletter-Knight — CF
Deep Sea Stories
Ameller, A. — AMP
Concerto, op. 69, for Tuba and Orchestra
Bach-Bell — CF
Air and Bourree
Bach, E. — CF
Spring's Awakening
Barat, J. E. — Baro
Introduction and Dance (F. E.)
Barat, J. E. — Baro
Introduction and Serenade (F. E.)
Barat, J. E. — Baro
Morceau de Concours (F. E.)
Barat, J. E. — Baro
Reminiscences de Navarre (F. E.)
Barnhouse — Barn
Barbarossa
Baseler, J. — CF
Happy Thoughts
Beethoven-Bell — CF
Variations on a Theme of Judas Maccabeus
Belwin (edition) — Bel
Three Favorites:
Massa's in de Cold, Cold Ground;
My Grandfather's Clock;
Marine Hymn
Bell, William — CF
Gavotte
Bell, William — CF
Jig Elephantine
Bell, William — CF
Low Down Bass
Bell, William — CF
Nautical John (medley)
Bell, William — CF
Nocturne, op. 6
Bennett, David — CF
Voice of the Viking

Bernstein, L. — Sch
Waltz for Mippy III
Bigot — Baro
Carillon et Bourdon (F. E.)
Blemant, L. — Baro
Andante et Allegro (F. E.)
Blemant, L. — Baro
Vulcain (F. E.)
Brahmstedt — Rub
Stupendo (polka)
Bratton-McLean — Wit
Teddy Bear's Picnic
Briegel, G. F. — Brie
Basso Profundo
Buchtel, F. — Mil
Apollo
Buchtel, F. — Mil
Hermes
Buchtel, F. — Fil
Il Penseroso e L'allegro
Buchtel, F. — Barn
Introduction and Rondo
Buchtel, F. — Mil
Jolly Sailor
Buchtel, F. — Fil
King Mydas
Buchtel, F. — Mil
Reluctant Clown
Buchtel, F. — Barn
Salamander
Buchtel, F. — Kjos
Song of the Sea
Buchtel, F — Cole
Young Artist's First Book of Solos
Buchtel, F. — Kjos
Achievement Series:
Peony;
Lily;
Hyacinthe
Buchtel, F. — Kjos
Progress Series:
Tulip;
Marigold;
Message

Buchtel, F. — Kjos
Superior Series:
Morning Glory;
Wild Rose;
Magnolia
Buchtel, F. — Kjos
Peerless Series:
Atilia;
Wotan;
Hercules
Buchtel, F. — Kjos
Success Series:
Ajax;
Adonis
Catozzi-Seredy — CF
Beelzebub
Clerisse, R. — Baro
Idylle (F. E.)
Cleresse, R. — Baro
Romance (F. E.)

Cohen, Sol — Bel
Romance and Scherzo
Danks — CB
"Silver Threads Among the Gold" and "Deep River"
DeLamater, E. — Rub
Auld Lang Syne (air and varie)
DeLamater, E. — Rub
Rocked in the Cradle of the Deep (air and varie)

DeLamater, E. — Rub
Tramp, Tramp, Tramp (air and varie)
Del Negro — Brie
Polka Grazioso
Del Negro — Brie
Sousaphone Polka
Demersseman-Wilson — B&H
Cavatina, op. 47
Desmond — Bel
The Sea Song
DeVille, Paul — CF
Happy Be Thy Dreams

DeWitt, L. O. — CF
  Pride of America
Dowling — Bel
  His Majesty the Tuba
Fillmore, H. — Fil
  Deep Bass
Frangkiser, C. — B&H
  A Cavern Impression
Frangkiser, C. — Bel
  The Sea Song
Geib, F. — Mil
  Caprice in B♭ Minor
Geib-Forst — Mil
  Cavatina, op. 6
Geib, F. — CF
  A Heroic Tale
Geib, F. — Brie
  In the Deep Forest
Geib, F. — Mil
  A Joyous Dialogue
Geib, F. — Brie
  Lightfoot Polka
Geib, F. — CF
  Melody, Theme and Variations
Geib-Forst — Mil
  Nocturne, op. 7
Geib, F. — Mil
  Polka Piquante
Geib-Forst — Mil
  Serenade
Geib, F. — CF
  Song Without Words
Godfrey, F. — CB
  Lucy Long (air and varie)
Golterman-Bell — CF
  Excerpts from Concerto No. 4
Grieg-Holmes — Rub
  In the Hall of the Mountain King
Guentzel, G. — Mil
  Mastadon
Guy, E. — Rub
  Carry Me Back to Ole Virginny

Handel-Harvey — Sch
  Honor and Arms from "Samson"
Harris, A. E. — Lud
  The King's Jester
Harris, A. E. — Lud
  Little Fiesta
Harris, A. E. — CF
  Tempesta
Hayes, Al — Fil
  Solo Pomposo
Holmes, G. E. — Rub
  Carnival of Venice
Holmes, G. E. — Rub
  Emmett's Lullaby
Huber, A. — CF
  Theme from Concertino #4
Hume — B&H
  In the Deep, Deep Depths
Hume — B&H
  A Soliloquy
Hume — B&H
  Te Anau Fantasia
Hume — B&H
  Wakatipu
Hume — B&H
  Whangaroo
Hupfield-McLean — Har
  When Yuba Play the Rumba on the Tuba
Irons, E. D. — Fil
  Cedarvale Polka
Isaac, M. — CF
  The Jolly Dutchman
Jenkins — B&H
  Rondelay
Jude — CF
  The Mighty Deep
Kappey — B&H
  Introduction and Allegro
King — Barn
  Octopus and the Mermaid
Kottaun — CF
  Billy Blowhard
Kroepsch — CF
  Down in the Deep Cellar

LaFont — B&H
  The Challenge
LeClercq, E. — Baro
  Concertino (F. E.)
McQuaide — Lee
  Samsonian Polka
Martin, C. — CF
  Aeola
Martin, C. — CF
  Pompoia
Merle — CF
  Demetrius
Merle — CF
  Mummers
Merle — CF
  Quintero
Monroe-Isaac — CF
  In the Garden
Moquin — Fil
  King of the Deep
Moquin — Fil
  Sailing the Mighty Deep
Moquin — Fil
  Sousaphonium
Nevin, E. — Bost
  The Rosary
Newton — B&H
  Modern Lullaby
O'Neill, Charles — CF
  Spring Fancy
Ostrander, A. — Fil
  Concert Album for Tuba and Piano;
  Andante — Handel;
  Nature's Adoration — Beethoven;
  Ancient Greek Melody — Maganini;
  Gigue — Corelli;
  Adagietto — Bizet;
  Plaisir d'Amour — Martini;
  Air from "Orpheus" — Gluck;
  Siciliano — Bach;
  Bourree — Handel;
  Berceuse — Strauinsky;
  Menuet — Beethoven;
  Song of the East — R. Korsakoff;
  Rigaudon — Rameau;
  Etude — Concone;
  Veni Creatur — Meyerbeer
Painpare-Voxman — Rub
  Concert Piece
Panseron — B&H
  Qui Tolli
Petrie-Teague — Wit
  Asleep in the Deep
Petrie-Walters — Rub
  Asleep in the Deep
Pierre-Petit — Baro
  Grave (F. E.)
Prokofieff — EMI
  Romance and Scherzo
Ringleben — CF
  Storm King
Rollinson, T. — CB
  Rocked in the Cradle of the Deep
Rossini — B&H
  Una Voca M'ha Colpito
Rubank (edition) — Rub
  Soloist Folio:
  Bedouin Love Song — Pinsuti;
  Forget Me Not — Macbeth;
  In the Hall of the Mountain King — Grieg;
  Out of the Deep — Lohr;
  Rocked in the Cradle — DeLamater;
  Bombasto-Vandercook;
  The Jolly Peasant — Schuman;
  Marine's March — Phillips;
  Stupendo — Brahmstedt;
  Toreador's Song — Bizet
Sabathil-Wilson — B&H
  Divertissement
Scarmolin — Barn
  Polka Giocoso
Scarmolin — Pro
  Pomp and Dignity
Schaefer — Fil
  Gay Caballero
Schlemuller, H. — CF
  "A Prayer" and "Cradle Song"

Schroen-Spencer — CF
  Fantasie
Schumann-Bell — CF
  The Jolly Farmer Goes to Town
Southwell — Volk
  My Tuba Solo
Sowerby, Leo — CF
  Chaconne
Storm — Volk
  Bouquet for Basses
Troje-Miller — Bel
  Sonatina Classica
Vandercook — Rub
  Behemoth
Vandercook — Rub
  Bombasto
Vandercook — Rub
  Colussus
Vandercook-Buchtel — Kjos
  Magnolia
Volkwein — Volk
  Soloist Folio:
  Admiration — St. Clair;
  Andante Maestoso — Suppe-Long;
  Chant d'Amour — Buchtel;
  Dream Time — St. Clair;
  Golden Days — St. Clair;
  Home, Sweet Home — Long;
  Rocked in the Cradle — Knight;
  Romance — Rubinstein;
  Silvertone Polka — Clement;
  Stand Up for Jesus — Webb;
  Valse Romantique — Buchtel
Wallace — B&H
  The Bell Ringer
Walters, H. — Rub
  Forty Fathoms
Walters, H. — Lud
  Tarantella
Weber, F. — Bel
  Big Boy
Weber, F. — Bel
  The Elephant Dance
Weiss — CB
  The Village Blacksmith
Williams, E. — Mor
  Concerto #2
Williams, Vaughn — Ox
  Concerto for Bass Tuba and Orchestra (Rental only.)
Worth, G. — Rub.
  Serpent of the Brass

Key to Publishers

FINE

The Fingering Relationship of Brass Instruments

Traugott Rohner

ALL BRASS INSTRUMENTS are capable of producing a fundamental tone and several overtones without the use of the valves or slide. The bugle playing bugle calls is an example of this principal.

Treble Clef Instruments

The open tones of the *cornet, trumpet, fluegelhorn, Eb alto, mellophone,* and *baritone* (treble clef) are:

All brass instruments overblow in this manner — the open tone intervals above the fundamental an octave, being a perfect 5th, a perfect 4th, a major 3rd, a minor 3rd, etc.[2]

On all valved brass instruments

the 2nd valve lowers any open tone (no valves down) one half-step;

the 1st valve lowers any open tone (no valves down) one whole step;

the 3rd valve lowers any open tone (no valves down) a step and one-half.

With the various combinations of these three valves, all the half-steps can be produced — down through six half-steps below any open tone. Hence, the 2½ octave chromatic scale for the instruments listed above is as follows:

The open tones of the *French horn* and its chromatic scale are as follows:

Notice that the fingering of the French horn is identical to that of the trumpet one octave higher.

Though the *Eb bass* uses the bass clef, it is convenient to know that the fingering may be regarded as if the notes were written in the treble clef, less three flats in the key signature.

NOTICE THAT THE FINGERING OF ALL THE ABOVE LISTED INSTRUMENTS IS RELATED TO *ONE* BASIC FINGERING. The pitch or sound of these instruments will be discussed later.

Bass Clef Instruments

The open tones of the *trombone, baritone,* and *BBb bass* are:

The slide of the trombone has the same function as the valves of the valved instruments. The 1st position of the trombone is with the slide "in", corresponding to no valves down on the valved instruments. Notice that the open tones of the trombone are marked "1" while the open tones of the valved instruments are marked "0".

The 2nd position of the trombone is with the slide out about 3¼ inches — corresponding to the 2nd valve down on the valved instruments — lowering any open tone one half-step. There are seven positions in all. Hence, with the seven positions on the trombone, any open tone can be lowered as much as six half-steps — the same as with the three valves on the valved instruments. Notice the following relationship:

On the trombone,

1st position corresponds to 0 valves down on a baritone.

2nd position corresponds to 2nd valve down

3rd position corresponds to 1st valve down

4th position corresponds to 1-2 valves down

5th position corresponds to 2-3 valves down

6th position corresponds to 1-3 valves down

7th position corresponds to 1-2-3 valves down

The following two octave chromatic scale illustrates this relationship. The trombone positions are marked *above* the notes and the baritone valves are indicated *below* the notes.

The baritone sounds the same whether using the treble or the bass clef, but the notes read look entirely different.

An easy means of transposition is not possible. It is simpler to learn anew the fingering of the baritone in the other clef.

The BB♭ bass (tuba or sousaphone) chromatic fingering for two and one-half octaves is given below. Notice that the fingering of the BB♭ bass is identical to baritone fingering one octave higher.

NOTICE THAT THE FINGERING FOR ALL OF THE ABOVE LISTED INSTRUMENTS IS RELATED TO ONE BASIC FINGERING.

Sound or Pitch of Brass Instruments

Two rules for remembering the sound or pitch of the brass instruments are:

1. The notes played by the instruments using the bass clef *sound as written.* There is but one minor exception to this rule; occasionally, some of the low notes of the French horn are written in the bass clef and will sound a 5th lower than written.

2. For instruments using the treble clef, *an instrument playing the note written "C" will sound the note that designates its name.* For example a C instrument will sound C, a B♭ instrument will sound B♭, an F instrument will sound F when playing the note written "C".

It is a simple matter to determine what octave is represented by any of these instruments.

1. All of the bass clef instruments sound exactly as written.

2. All of the treble clef brasses in B♭, F, and E♭ *sound lower* than the written note by intervals of a major 2nd, a perfect 5th, and a major 6th respectively.

Baritone and trombone players should be taught to read from the bass clef as soon as possible, even though they may have been transferred from some treble clef instrument; however, when these two instruments are playing from the treble clef, they sound a major 9th lower than the written notes. The other possible exception is in the case of the rarely used E♭ trumpet, which sounds a minor 3rd higher than the written notes.

Duplicate Fingerings

The major purposes of duplicate (alternate) fingerings are:

1. To check the intonation of the valve slides.

2. To facilitate the execution of some otherwise awkward technical passages.

3. To secure better intonation.

In order to check the distance that the valve slides are to be pulled, first tune the instrument as a whole, using at least two of the open tones such as C5 and G4 on the cornet. Usually, if the tuning slide had to be pulled, it is necessary to pull each of the valve slides a little. Bear in mind that the valve slides need to be pulled in the proportion of 2 to 1 to 3 for valves 1, 2, and 3 respectively. The 1st valve slide should be pulled twice as far as that of the 2nd valve, etc.

Using the trumpet as an example to be followed by the other valved brass instruments, use the following tuning notes to check the valve slides:

Now pull the 2nd valve slide half the distance of the 1st valve slide.

It is not possible in this short treatment of duplicate fingerings to present all of the special fingering patterns and duplicate slide positions that facilitate the playing of awkward passages, or those that will improve intonation. However, a few generalizations will make it possible for one to work out most of these problems.

1. All of the open notes above the lowest one can be played by one or more combinations of valves or slide positions.

2. Remember that the low notes using the valve combinations of 1-3 and 1-2-3 are sharp on valved brass instruments. A lip adjustment is usually not adequate, so;

3. Many players pull the 3rd valve slide out a little extra. Bear in mind that the 3rd valve is the equivalent of valves 1 and 2; but in this case, when the 3rd valve is pulled out a little extra to improve the intonation of notes fingered 1-2 or 1-2-3, it is more than the equivalent of valves 1-2. This device is particularly useful for those players who play "inside" or low parts, such as 3rd or 4th trumpet (cornet) parts.

4. Duplicate slide positions should be used frequently on the trombone to facilitate the playing of awkward passages, for example:

The possible combinations of these alternate positions are very many. The trombone student must learn the alternate slide positions and then follow the general rule of "economy of motion."

With the aid of duplicate slide positions, including those positions which are a little "short" or a little "long" to improve the intonation of certain notes, the trombone can be played in better tune than any other brass instrument. For example:

The F♯ and G must be played short to be in tune. The D played just a little short in 4th position is better in tune here than if played in 1st position because this D, being the 5th harmonic, is usually a little flat.

FINE

1 Notes marked "false" are out of tune; they should be played with the first valve, never open.

2 A low pedal open tone and several high notes not given are possible but are seldom used by school instrumentalists.

1956

F French Horn

What about Brass Embouchure?

An analysis of the physical structure of the lips, teeth,
and jaw as it pertains to cup mouthpiece adaptation.

Vincent Malek

THE AIR COLUMN of a brass instrument is excited and produces
sound by the vibratory motion of the
player's lips held against the mouthpiece. The manner in which the lips
vibrate determines the sound spectrum which, in turn, determines the
spectra for the mouthpiece and the
instrument.

Therefore, the main factors which
fix the shape of the embouchure are
of vital concern, since the shape conditions vibration. These factors are
lip thickness and musculature, regularity or irregularity of the teeth, and
shape and position of the mandible or
jaw.

Apart from conditioning lip vibration, the structure of the embouchure
is also relevant to the adaptability of
the individual to cup mouthpiece instruments. Thus, the lips, teeth, and
jaw may not be the only physical
characteristics important to lip vibration and flexibility on brass instruments, but they are certainly the main
ones.

Definitive Connotations

Embouchure means a variety of
things to various individuals. To a
highly professional brass instrument
performer, "Embouchure is ability to
produce all tones within one's compass or range flawlessly. The lips
must ·respond to the softest pp and
must not lose tonal quality in ff, infallible in legato and sureness of attack in pp or ff."[1]

To a teacher, "The term 'embouchure' is used with reference to the
muscle setting (position) of the lips
and facial muscles used when playing.
The placement of the mouthpiece on
the lips is often included under the
term 'embouchure'."[2]

To a dentist interested in the problems of the musician, "Embouchure

is a technique of using the lips, teeth,
jaws, and related structures against
the mouthpiece of a musical instrument to produce a tone. In this activity, physical adaptation is dependent both on the dentofacial form and
on the shape of the mouthpiece used.
In view of the knowledge about the
differences in facial form, it is reasonable to expect that some individuals will make better adjustment than
others."[3]

Most definitions of embouchure
are alike in that they refer to the
mouth formation in playing. The differences occur in explaining the function of the formation. For our purposes here, embouchure will be taken
to mean the setting of the lips, teeth,
and lower jaw just prior to playing.

Classification of Lip Formations

In order to be able to classify the
physical features of the embouchure,
standards of reference must be deter
mined.

A search of medical and dental
literature will reveal that averages for
lip thickness and musculature are unavailable. The only feasible alternative seems to be to set standards of
thickness that will be consistent with
general opinion among brass players.
On this basis, the individual may be
identified as having lips of average
thickness, of less than average, or of
greater than average.

The Teeth

The standards for evenness of the
teeth may be determined in similar
manner. In orthodontia, which is the
dental science of treating irregular
formations of the teeth, satistics are
available as to the incidence of various degrees of tooth irregularity
among the general population. However, these figures are determined by

counting the number of teeth that are
out of alignment wherever they happen to be in the mouth, back or front.
Yet, in playing a cup mouthpiece instrument, only a few of the front
teeth are directly involved. Thus, the
evenness or unevenness of perhaps
seven or eight front teeth only is relevant.

If the few teeth — which support
the portion of the lips against which
the mouthpiece is placed — are even,
then the individual should be identified as having even teeth, no matter
how irregular or uneven other teeth
may be.

As to the incidence in the general
population of people having even,
mildly uneven, or very uneven front
teeth, no statistics are available. However, an orthodontist and dental
school faculty member is of the opinion that a large majority of the general population has relatively even
front teeth.[4] He feels, also, that brass
players as a group — especially those
using small cup mouthpieces — probably have front teeth of greater regularity than does the general population, due to the straightening effect of
mouthpiece pressure against the lips
and teeth. In fact, instead of braces,
trumpet or cornet playing is often
recommended for children with mildly irregular front teeth.

Occlusions of the Teeth

The third consideration in evaluating embouchure structures is the type
of lower jaw. Its position when relaxed determines the occlusion or
malocclusion of the teeth. In dental
terminology there are several classes
of jaw-tooth formations. Mainly, they
are:

1. Normal: normal jaw recession,
   regular teeth.
2. Class I, Neutroclusion: normal jaw

recession, irregular teeth.

3. Class II, Distoclusion: marked jaw recession.

4. Class III, Mesioclusion: protrusion of the jaw.

With regard to the portions of the general population which are affected by malocclusion of the teeth, relatively little is known. "A search of the literature for information concerning the prevalence and incidence of malocclusion revealed the fact that while such studies have been carried out sporadically since 1889, the figures obtained show little agreement with each other."[5]

Although recessions and protrusions of the mandible are determined with great accuracy in orthodontic work, a much simpler procedure can be utilized by the brass teacher. The scientific manner requires an X-ray of the head; recession or protrusion is indicated by the number of degrees in an arc made by drawing lines on certain plains on the X-ray.

The simple but effective procedure that we may use is based upon the fact that a slight recession of the lower jaw is normal and that it is just about the thickness of the teeth, approximately 1/8 to 3/16 inch. Thus, when the jaws are completely closed, if the top portion of the lower teeth in the center of the mouth is in contact, or just about so, with the back of the upper teeth, then the recession can be termed normal or average. The large majority of the population has this type of lower jaw; only relatively small percentages have marked recessions or protrusions.

Thus, the standard is set for normal recession. Any recession greater than the approximate thickness of the teeth can be termed *receding jaw*. On the other hand, if the lower teeth do not fall behind the upper when the jaw is closed, the proper description is *protruding jaw*.

From the dental standpoint, even a perfect occlusion — upper and lower teeth exactly aligned — falls into this category, since a slight recession is the norm. However, *perfect occlusion* should not carry any undesirable connotations of protruding jaw for the brass player, because in his case such an arch relationship of the teeth is a distinct advantage. He does not have to push the lower jaw forward to achieve the necessary alignment of the teeth, which is needed for a secure positioning of the mouthpiece against the lips.

Musculature of the Lips

The musculature of the lips is an important consideration in embouchure, study, but we are hindered by inability to rate it on any basis other than one of subjectivity. Many different muscles are involved, and those which are used primarily, vary according to the schooling of the player. At least thirteen separate facial muscles may be called into action by the player, resulting in the possibility of creating muscular activity horizontally, vertically, diagonally, etc.

Players who tend to favor "stretched" embouchure (fewer and fewer brass players are advocating this technique) probably employ the horizontal muscles mostly, in order to pull back the corners of the mouth. Others, undoubtedly, create lip tension or contraction through antagonistic action of various muscles.

Since these muscles cannot be observed accurately while a player is performing, and since different players achieve lip tension in a variety of ways, it is impossible to state which muscles should be activated and with what strengths. Suffice it to say that the lips are surrounded by a network of muscular tissue which, by working co-operatively or antagonistically, can exert tension in any direction or in different directions at the same time.

Contributions of Dental Science

Dental science could undoubtedly tell us much about embouchure, but, unfortunately, not too much research has been done in this area. However, a step was taken in this direction by Edward A. Cheney, D.D.S., M.S., who studied embouchure problems of wind instrumentalists. The portions of his work pertaining to brass playing go a long way in suggesting possible answers to embouchure questions that have long troubled teachers and players.

An experiment in which one hundred players of various brass and woodwind instruments participated was conducted under the direction of this orthodontist. Of the group, thirty-six represented the small brass instruments.

Dr. Cheney accumulated evidence which caused him to conclude that, "Difficulties in adaptation occur most frequently among small brass instrumentalists . . . Embouchure difficulties attain their greatest frequency among small brass instrumentalists with Class II malocclusion (marked jaw recession) . . . Often mesial relationships of the mandible associated with lower anterior irregularity (protruding jaw and uneven lower teeth) are disturbing to both large and small mouthpiece brass players . . . In addition to functional inefficiencies arising from basic jaw discrepancies, there are many problems associated with irregularities of the teeth and lips . . ."[3]

Survey of Expert Performers

In attempting to elucidate the results of experiments such as Dr. Cheney's and to clarify what brass teachers and players thought about embouchure, viz. that irregularities of the lips, teeth, and jaw either are or are not of significant importance, part of a Ph. D. dissertation which I did a few years ago included a survey of trumpet-cornet performers.[6]

This personal interview survey of fifty-two expert professionals — trumpet and cornet players who had achieved great distinction in legitimate performance — revealed the following information concerning embouchure formations from the physical standpoint:

As far as lip thickness is concerned, just as many players in the sample had thick lips as had thin ones — with the vast majority having lips of average thickness. This certainly suggests that the old belief that thin lips for trumpet-cornet are best is *not necessarily true*. If it were, natural selection would have favored thin lips in the study.

The data on evenness of the teeth, coupled with the fact that relatively few people in the general population have serious irregularities, tend to corroborate the findings of experiments in the field of orthodontia and dental orthopedics. Irregularity of the teeth, especially if it is not serious seems to be of *minor importance* to the development of aptitude on the trumpet or cornet.

Regarding recession and protrusion of the lower jaw, the data suggest that serious malformations *are incompatible*, in general, with fine performance on trumpet or cornet. Only five of the fifty-two players in the sample had even a suggestion of a receding jaw. And only one had a protrusion, this being very, very slight.

Since the embouchure is so vital to adaptation to the small cup mouthpiece, and since it plays such an important role in conditioning lip vibration, it would seem desirable to question, seriously, the advisability of suggesting small cup mouthpiece instruments for students exhibiting marked irregularities of the lips, teeth, or jaw. Contrariwise, we should

remember that slight irregularities did not hinder the players so afflicted in the sample from achieving eminent status.

1 Thieck, William A., *Common Sense*, Milwaukee, H. Bechler, 1928, p. 10
2 Fitzgerald, Bernard, "Tone Production," *The Instrumentalist*, Vol. III, No. 3, p. 15
3 Cheney, Edward A., D.D.S., M.S., "Adaptation to Embouchure as a Function of Dentofacial Complex," *American Journal Of Orthodontics*, Vol. XXXV, No. 6, June, 1949, p. 440
4 Robert J. Donovan, D.D.S., Ph. D., Orthodontic Department, School of Dentistry, Northwestern University
5 Massler, Maury, D.D.S., M.S., & John M. Frankel, D.D.S., M.S., "Prevalence of Malocclusion in Children Aged 14 to 18 Years," *American Journal of Orthodontics*, Vol. XXXVII, No. 10 p. 751
6 Malek, Vincent F., *A Study of Embouchure and Trumpet-Cornet Mouthpiece Measurements*, Ph. D. dissertation, Northwestern University, May 1953

FINE

February, 1956

The B♭ Horn — *Try It And See*

Paul B. Moore

"To use or not to use," that is the question most band directors are asking about the single B♭ French horn. I would like to add my bit to the discussion by telling about my own experience with them in professional playing and in school band work. In the Model High School Band of Minot State Teachers College we are using five single B♭ horns at the present time. This band was started from scratch four years ago, so I was able to introduce the single B♭ horn without having to overcome any previous prejudice in favor of the F horn.

My own experience with the B♭ horn started when I was playing professional symphony work. I picked up a B♭ horn one day and blew it a bit. The sound was poor. However, curiosity got the better of me and I tried one for a couple of months just to see if it could be made to sound well. I became quite satisfied with it and have used this type of horn for my own playing ever since.

Why the Prejudice?

In all fairness to the single B♭ horn, the question should be raised as to why the initial reaction to this instrument is almost invariably unfavorable. Incidentally, too many horn players and band directors allow this first reaction to be their last, without further investigation. I think that, primarily, this reaction comes be-

cause the B♭ horn is compared to the F horn on the basis of blowing the two horns in the same manner and with the same mouthpiece. This comparison is fostered by the use of the double horn, which attempts to incorporate the two horns into one. The B♭ horn requires less forcing of air pressure, but more control of velocity of air. It should be played with a somewhat more shallow mouthpiece.

Difference in Construction

The physical difference between the two horns is a matter of measurable distance in brass tubing. That distance can be visualized, if you like, by adding the tubing of the first and third valves of the B♭ horn to the open tones of that horn — that is, with the first and third valves down, the single B♭ horn becomes an F horn. As you can see, the actual difference is slight; but it is enough to make a great deal of difference in response between the two horns.

After playing the F horn for some time, the B♭ horn seems to be wide-open and brassy. But after playing the B♭ horn for a comparable period, the F horn then seems stuffy, sluggish, and quite unresponsive. Unfortunately, it is that wide-open brassy tone by which the B♭ horn is judged, possibly because those who do the judging are too often confirmed slaves of the F horn. They take a slight sample of the B♭ horn

freedom and it frightens them back to the supposed security of their F horn prison.

Double Horn

Going back to the double horn, there are very few horn players who can make the transition from the F horn to the B♭ horn from note to note without changing the quality of tone. The character of each instrument is too different, as explained before. So they never enjoy the true tonal possibilities of the B♭ horn, using it only as a means of gaining security in the high register. A matter of physical construction enters into the picture when comparing the B♭ and F sides of a double horn.

It is safe to say, I believe, that every double horn on the market is built as an F horn. That is, on the F side of the horn the tubing is continuously conical from mouthpiece to bell. When the B♭ valve is opened, a section of this tubing is by-passed to shorten the total length to that required for the pitch of B♭. This also means that on the B♭ side of the double horn the tubing is *not* continuously conical; there is a definite jump from small to large, like a stair step. This factor of continuous conical tubing is very important to tone production on the French horn. On the single B♭ horn this factor is present; on the B♭ side of the double horn it is *not* present.

Tuning the Double Horn

Another factor of physical construction that should be mentioned in connection with the double horn has to do with tuning. I do not know of any double horn that has adequate tuning facilities for the B♭ side of the horn. They all have one woefully small slide that tunes both sides of the horn and then one or more large slides for tuning only the F side of the horn. The single B♭ horns have slides adequate for tuning even to the pitch of the average school piano.

True Horn Tone

The old argument used by professional horn players is that only the F horn can produce the true French horn tone. This argument was very effectively punctured in the test reported in *The Instrumentalist* (January-February, 1951) wherein college music majors were asked to tell which of the three types of horn was being played behind a screen.

The results showed plainly that a good horn player will make any type of horn sound good, and a poor horn player will sound poor no matter which type horn he plays. With an equally good performer on each type of instrument, the only one who can distinguish the difference is a fine horn player. We are not performing for audiences of fine horn players, however, so the tone argument just doesn't make sense.

After nearly four years of using the single B♭ horns in the band here at the Model High School, I am even more satisfied with them. The horn section compares very well with other sections of the band, although in a beginning band, this section usually lags behind. While it is a comparatively young group, our horn players carry their parts very capably. It relieves me for other details because I do not have to help the "hunting horns" find their notes, and the tone they produce has satisfied some very capable contest judges.

I am convinced that any director who gives the single B♭ horn an honest trial in school band work will be more than satisfied with the results.

Fine

Let's Stress Fundamentals

Daniel Tetzlaff

THE NEED FOR highlighting the fundamentals of brass playing was again impressed upon me during my last summer's experiences at the Bemidji State Teachers College Music Camp, where I had the chance to hear and work with a large representation of Midwestern brass students. Solos and advanced etudes were brought by all the students; but since I was completely unfamiliar with their backgrounds, I always asked them to start the lesson by playing a scale and then the very first tone in their methods books (usually the *Arban*). In all but a few cases, I found there was plenty to work on right there.

Honestly, we must admit that there is a constant pressure to press ahead and go faster than allows for *care* and *accuracy* and *understanding*, and we must admit that we all succumb in some degree to this pressure. Then also, we must admit that the success we all seek in music depends on a recapitulation of what was once hurried over, or even left out.

Why Long Tones?

My teaching experiences have convinced me that "the forgotten fundamental" is the long tone; and my playing experience has taught me that long notes, once thought "the easiest," are really the hardest ones *to sound* with real excellence. I am not surprised that hardly 5% of the young players I hear can hold a *steady* and *clear* and *full* sound for 16 counts. No one told me, either, when I was a beginning student why or how long tones should be practiced.

Now I am concerned, for I cannot force myself to accept a philosophy of nonchalance, like some amateur bricklayer who might think, "I'll put in my first row of bricks any old haphazard way, and then straighten out the wall *as I go along.*" Oh??? You've never seen it done with bricks. How about with music? If the "first row" is not in solid and true, is there much chance for subsequent rows? If the fundamentals are not solid, the etudes won't be either.

There comes a time when you have to play more of the instrument before you can play more sheets of music. The millions of unsuccessful instrumentalists who have tried it the other way, backwards, will do better if they start over with that "first row," this time with more attention.

Suggestions for Improvement

I believe all teachers can quickly improve their brass sections through a program along the following lines. First, hear your brass section a stand (2 players) at a time. Second, have the players sustain their C5 for 4 counts. About 98% of the time several discrepancies will be heard. As soon as these are eliminated we will have our first real progress toward a better sounding brass section.

Somehow the teacher must find time to explain orally all of the following points to the players, so that they too can hear inaccuracies which then can be corrected to beautiful sounds:

1. Dynamics. Long tones should be played a solid rich mf so that later they can be doubled in volume to a *fortissimo,* or "halved" *to a piano* (that is still secure and mellow). When two players play together, the weaker sound is the useless one. It should immediately be "blown up" to a level equal to the stronger. Also, the weaker tone will sound flat usually.

2. Intonation. Most growing players do not sound their tuning note at sufficient strength to know what it really sounds like. Two players must play equally—and at full tone—in order to determine whether faulty pitch is a matter of the tuning slide or a lack of expelling enough breath. Half of "flat playing" problems will be corrected just by blowing more.

3. After the two instruments are tuned and balanced, ask the players to inhale deeply and sustain the tuning note solid and steady for 16 counts, no wavering, no weakening toward the end.

How many pairs of players in your band can do this? A wager says but few. However, if you will point out what is wrong and why, within a day or two the majority of *interested* students will accomplish miracles.

The teacher must make it clear to the students that the band's improvement in intonation starts with two players learning to play as one — same volume, same straight tone. If the tone of either one or the other wobbles, we again hear *two* players and are back where we started. If two players cannot play together, how can 22, or 62, or 92?

4. The students can then proceed to play the rest of the descending C scale in long tones. On the successive

seven tones some will sound better; some will get even worse. A safe bet is that never will the two players match each and every tone of the scale. But they can improve greatly.

As soon as interested students *hear* the problem, they are usually eager to conquer first things first. This is the time "to sell" the two-fold benefits of learning to play long tones correctly, and practicing in pairs: the band needs this skill for better intonation, blend, and balance; the individual needs the muscular control that is built by long tone practice for every single facet of playing that is a part of instrumental progress.

Where to Look

As soon as the teacher hears an unsteady long tone he can check two places. First, the lips. If they wobble and quiver they show lack of strength and development. This can be brought to the student's awareness quickly and easily with a mirror. He hears, then he sees. Now let him *feel!* Holding the instrument with the left hand alone, the student can play G4 or C5. The 2nd and 3rd finger of the unoccupied right hand then can be gently placed on each side of the mouth to feel if the muscles are steady or if they are twitching.

For every wiggle that is felt or seen, a wiggle in the long tone will be heard. Once the student understands his problem, he can steady and strengthen his lips in a short time by practicing some long tones with care, with a listening ear, and with a mirror.

Belly Flops

The second place to check is the front stomach wall. The teacher will notice some players whose lips are steady, yet whose long tones bubble and weaken. Now if the teacher will gently place his hand on the student's abdomen, fingers spread wide to cover a large area, he will feel a bump of the stomach muscles for every bump he hears in the tone; and as he feels the stomach wall collapse inward, he will *hear* the tone collapse downward in volume and in pitch. Then the teacher merely has to ask the student to play again C5 or G4 and place his own right hand on his abdomen so that he, too, *feels* the same bumping that has already been pointed out to him "by ear."

Curing this stomach wiggling and jerking is not easy. The student must learn to steady his front wall from the inside, with much air and with a gentle steady leaning or bracing feeling.

This brings us right back to the subject of breathing, which seems the most elusive thing of all, the most unknown, the most misunderstood and misapplied, yet the most basic of all helps to better playing. By now the teacher has consumed far more of his time than planned and yet he is just now on the threshold of the cure. Somehow, more time must be found for breath control work.

Individual Progress

When stressing individual progress we should emphasize again, in plain loud words, that the long tone is the foundation for all of instrumental playing. Good tonguing is simply an interrupted long tone. If the long tone wavers or weakens, so will the tonguing passages. Good slurring is simply a long tone moving from one pitch to another. Unsteadiness or weakening of the long tone results in bumpy, broken slurs. Smooth, connected lip slurs depend greatly on the same steady blowing used for the long tone. Also, the ascent into the high register is dependent always on more air, never less, as is indicated by an ever-weakening and bumpy simple long tone.

My approach to helping a large group of young players during the week of their summer clinic lessons was as described above, for I quickly found out that hardly any of them had heard these things before. Have your students heard and understood? Have they heard themselves play, not lost in a sea of sound of 50 uncontrolled tones, not home alone where there is no one to match with or blend to, but in pairs where the sound simply is or isn't matched.

One of my students was a teacher. He asked for some general advice that could perhaps apply to large numbers of students. My answer was that we best teach like a doctor prescribes. He does no business by mail; you come in for an examination. Only after this can he prescribe what *you* need. The same applies to the music student. Individual problems must be treated individually.

FINE

191

Preparing for Solo Contest

An article for students who want to help themselves.

Daniel Tetzlaff

BAND DIRECTORS are busy, busy men. I know; I'm one, too—teaching in 10 schools. Every day I wish I had a brief case chock full of printed materials I could just hand the student and explain, "We can answer only so many questions in class. But you can take this home and read it, and learn the fun of figuring out extra things for yourself." So that is the idea behind what follows:

Last summer I wrote an article *after* judging at a state contest. An alert college brass instructor from Florida wrote in suggesting some of the information be presented this year *before* contest time, so that students would have a guide enabling them to do a better job of preparation.

Various Aspects

The youthful soloist should be aware of the most impressive aspects of performance. The first and most important is the tone or sound that is produced. It is always a pleasant surprise for the judge to hear the sound that is characteristic of the instrument. This is the solid, mature, full tone quality that is usually associated only with seasoned performers. It comes naturally to a few players, but most of them have to acquire it through study and careful practice.

The second factor for which the judge looks is the performer's ability to command attention, the way he projects what he has to say. Not many players sound as though they are confident about how the music should go. The player must sell himself to the audience, but first he must sell himself on his own confidence.

Although there are many reasons for lacking a positive approach to playing—insufficient preparation, not enough coaching, lack of talent, fear—too many students have prepared simply *not to make mistakes*. This is a negative approach. Errors might be avoided, but the player won't really make the music *sound* either!

Look Ahead

If you desire efficient instrumental progress, it is necessary to have a definite program in mind. The first step is to *become aware* of deficiencies and accept suggestions for improvement. These are the main helps that can come from entering a contest.

Students, be sure you realize that improving your tone will require serious work. Better brass instrument playing comes with "learning how to blow."

Improving the preparation of a solo requires long careful study, adequate coaching, selection of a number fitting your capabilities and musical understanding, plus—*as much previous experience as possible playing alone in front of strangers.*

Read

If you want to better yourself refer to the articles which appeared in March, 1954; October, 1954; and September, 1950 and are reprinted in this book. After reading these articles you will be much more conscious of *why* you must inhale more air, *how* the sound is "fattened out" by exhaling more air through the lips, *what* to do to develop these all-important techniques, "Deep Breathing" requires no "extra time," only extra thought. It can be practiced every day so easily, while walking to and from school, while falling to sleep at night.

Remember, everyone gets a bit nervous when playing. This involuntary reaction can reduce breathing ef-ficiency 50%. So, concentrate on developing yourself so that even "your half-best" is still *very good*. Some of the best diagrams and the best condensed explanations of "good breathing are found in vocal method books. See *Vocal Technique*, pp. 2-6, and *Vocal Artistry*, pp. 2-5 by Peter K. Tkach, published by Kjos.

Listen

I would suggest starting the second phase of your solo preparation by listening to outstanding examples of solo trumpeting. Perhaps you have listened carefully to some already, but be sure your list has included:

Louis Menardi—THE TRUMPET (Vol. II)—London ffrr; Raymond Sabrich—THE TRUMPET (Vol. I)—London ffrr; Bobby Hackett—with strings—Capitol; Raphael Mendez—with orchestra—Coast or Decca.

Do not try to duplicate the range, technique, super perfection, or spectacular feats of the performers. Save all that for later. Remember, you are not listening to youth, or the "first experiences." *Do* try to imitate their "expression," their spirit, their "give." This is possible for you or anyone who will take the time to listen and to feel.

Next, arrange for the use of a tape recorder. Make three recordings, one each week. Listen for things to improve each time. Place the microphone at the rear of the room, where the "back row" is. That is where to aim your sound.

On the playback, keep your eye glued to your solo part. Listen. Can you *hear* each and every note you see there on the page as you follow along? Did you slight some? If so, you know where to review. Work out these spots by going over them at a slower tempo. Also, can you count *exact time* and keep with "the fellow on the tape," or did he leave out a beat or two here, and add a couple there? Such inaccuracies can be eliminated with more care and attention, and will vastly improve the performance by making it more comfortable for the accompanist.

Lastly, try to arrange at least two playings of the solo *before* going to contest, one at school in front of the band or in front of your room, and one at a big church or club meeting. Your accompanist needs this experience with you, too. And remember, the piano part should be played *at equal volume to the trumpe*t. Think of a duet. It is trumpet *with* piano, not trumpet (and piano).

In a realistic picture of progress there is no overnight accomplishment, no miracle, no magic. There is no substitute for the satisfactions and security that come from study, practice, rehearsal, and conditioning by experience.

FINE

May, 1956

The Bass Trombone

George Kizer

I HAVE BEEN pleased to see an increasing number of bass trombones in use in our school bands during the past few years. This is certainly a step in the right direction, and one which may eventually lead to the widespread acceptance of the instrument as an integral part of our brass family instrumentation.

The bass trombone is probably as important to the brass choir of the band or orchestra as many instruments of the woodwind family which have found widespread acceptance in our modern concept of instrumentation. The tenor trombone, the baritone, or the tuba can certainly produce any *pitch* that might be written for the bass trombone; but it is impossible for these instruments to reproduce the quality of tone of the bass trombone.

What Is a Bass Trombone?

Does the presence of the additional tubing operated by a thumb valve and commonly called an F attachment identify a trombone as a BASS trombone? The answer is an emphatic NO! The factors that really determine a true bass trombone are those affecting *quality* of tone (bore, bell size, proportion, etc.) rather than the lower pitch afforded by the F attachment.

Since most brass instrument manufacturers make a regular tenor trombone with F attachment, let us not confuse this with the true bass trombone which is of different construction proportions and delivers a full, sonorous, bass sound which is impossible to duplicate on the tenor trombone.

In selecting a bass trombone, if you are not adept on the instrument I would suggest that you get a good trombonist to check it for you, much as we brass players might do in the case of purchasing an oboe or bassoon. Check particularly for the playing qualities of the F attachment, since the mere presence of the extra tubing is no guarantee against a "stuffy" and unsatisfactory response. The instrument should respond well and produce the characteristic quality when the F tubing is used. The thumb trigger, called "T" henceforth, should be located so that a person with a hand of normal size can operate it with ease. I have seen triggers located in such a position that one had to shift the grip of the left hand in order to activate the F tubing!

Slide Positions

In regard to the use of the added lower range afforded by the F attachment, keep in mind that the slide positions do not coincide with the regular positions.

The reason for the different positions in the lower register is that the trombone with F attachment engaged is no longer a B♭ instrument, but is an instrument pitched a perfect 4th lower in F. This fact is easily illustrated by comparing the relative lengths of tubing of the valves on an E♭ tuba with those on a BB♭, which is pitched a perfect 4th lower.

There is room on the slide for only 6 positions when the longer tubing of the F attachment is used (instead of the usual 7 positions for the regular B♭ trombone); this eliminates low

Location of regular B♭ trombone slide positions.

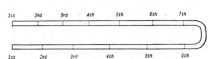

Location of the 6 longer positions on the same slide when F attachment is used.

B2 above pedal B♭2 unless the F tuning slide is pulled to an extreme length, which actually pitches the instrument in approximately E, and involves a different approach to the slide positions in the lower range.

I think it will be found that the most practical tuning for the F attachment tuning slide with the slide in 1st position will be equal to the regular slide in 6th position. In this way C3 played with "T" alone will match the same note when played in the usual 6th position. With this tuning, it can readily be seen that the slide technic requirements can be greatly lessened by the use of "T" for 6th position C3, and T-2 (flatted) for B2, as shown in the following example. The use of T1 and T2 for 6th and 7th positions is especially helpful in playing the larger trombones with the heavier slides, but will be found of great value on any trombone with F attachment.

Need for Bass Trombone

At the present time, very few American band arrangements call for the 3rd trombone range to go below E2 because regular tenor trombones are generally used to play these parts. Many British arrangements however, call for the real bass trombone lower range quite often, as this instrument seems to be much more widely used in Europe. When we encounter one of these situations when playing a tenor trombone, we simply have to transpose those tones an octave higher, which is an obviously unsatisfactory solution since it upsets the concept of voicing and chord position.

Probably the most important reason, however, for wishing to see a more widespread use of the bass trombone is that we need an instrument of real bass quality at the bottom of the trombone section. The use of this instrument will not only improve the balance of the trombone section, but will improve the sound of the brass choir and of the complete ensemble of which it is a part. Both bands and orchestras can benefit by the bass trombone.

FINE

Quality in Tone Production

Robert Rada

A PREREQUISITE for any trombonist, or any brass player, is the ability to produce a good tone. Nothing, in my estimation, is more displeasing to hear than a poor tone coming from a trombone.

From an instrument whose natural sound is of a noble quality and which is capable of producing a beautiful tone, I have heard some of the most horrible sounds that can be imagined. It is highly inconceivable that an instrument would produce such awful noises if the player had any conception of the capabilities that the trombone really possesses. Every note that is produced, whether it is in a loud passage from a Wagner opera, a velocity exercise, or a lyrical melody, should be pleasing to the ear.

The tone should be pure and free from distortion. I realize, certainly, that the same type of tone is not acceptable both to a dance band and to a symphony orchestra, but this is a matter of adapting oneself to the organization. The same approach to producing a good tone should prevail whatever type of music one is playing. Any notes that come from the trombone, or any other instrument, are completely meaningless unless they are accompanied by a good tone.

Essential Factor

First of all, a player must establish an aural image of the tone quality he wants to achieve. It is this mental picture rather than any type of study or etude that should serve as his guide. By listening to established trombone artists the student can get an idea of what constitutes good tone and musicianship. And, certainly, there are many opportunities for this in concerts, on the radio, on television, and through the record medium.

Once this conception of good tone quality has been established, the player has a basis on which he can judge for himself whether or not he is producing physical sounds in keeping with his mental picture. Developing this conception of tone quality within ourselves rests upon the player alone; no amount of reading or discussion is an effective substitute.

Overtone Structure

A good tone possesses many overtones; that is, on a fundamental pitch many more overtones have been detected coming from a tone of good quality than from one of poor quality. Perhaps that is why we often hear a desirable tone being described as one possessing substance, resonance, or richness.

Another distinguishing factor of a good tone is the ability of the player to establish a definite pitch on each note that is produced. A note being played could hardly possess good quality if the player were unaware of the pitch of the note. This is especially important to the trombonist who has to guide the pitch of his instrument by his ear, more so than other brass players.

Breath Support

The breath also plays a very important part in producing a good tone. If the embouchure is properly supplied with breath and supported by the air column, a better tone will be produced.

The player must feel that the air is going *through* the instrument and not just to the lips. He must create a sensation of a solid column of air passing across the vibrating lips, through the instrument, and out of the bell. The "carrying quality" of a tone is dependent upon the air column going through the instrument.

The more slowly the air passes along the vibrating surface of the lips, the softer the tone; the more rapidly the air passes over these sur-

194

faces, the louder the tone becomes. Hence, volume is controlled entirely by the column of air and not by distortion of the embouchure.

Too many players are misled into thinking that the embouchure must take a different shape for every dynamic range. This is one reason why their tone quality changes when they change volume. The tone quality should remain constant at all dynamic levels.

Additional Factors

Certainly, there are many factors that relate directly to tone quality. Differences in instruments, mouthpieces, and embouchures may give the tone a character all its own; but, basically, the quality will remain the same as long as the same conception of tone is maintained. A fine player can produce a good tone on a completely foreign mouthpiece and instrument. Of course, there is no substitute for good equipment and every player should take great care in choosing a suitable mouthpiece and instrument. Too often, though, we tend to place the blame for a poor tone on our tools instead of on ourselves.

We must also consider the various factors of musicianship and technical proficiency in relation to tone quality. If we assembled ten trombonists, for example, and had each produce only one note, the actual difference in tone quality might be very slight. And yet, if each were to play a page from the same composition, we could immediately distinguish ten completely different variations of tone quality. Therefore, we must assume that the variation of each was determined not only by the ability to produce good tone but also by breath control, attack, phrasing, range, accuracy, endurance, and, in general, the musicianship and technical skill that are required to make a piece of music "sound well."

Thus, tone is dependent upon our general technical capabilities based upon a definite concept of desirable quality. Whatever we play, no matter how difficult, we should always strive to play it correctly with good quality and intonation.

FINE

September, 1956

CONTROLLED BREATHING

Leonard Smith

MUCH OF WHAT has been said about breathing and breath control seems to me to have been handed down like "Old Wives' Tales." You hear that you shouldn't raise your shoulders when you breathe; you hear that you *should* raise them slightly. You are told to push your stomach muscles down; you are told to push your stomach muscles out; you are told to pull your stomach muscles in. Is it little wonder, therefore, that there are so many conflicting ideas and theories about breathing, when so much of it is founded on hearsay and so little on fact?

Regrettably, there are too many people willing to *tell* you how to do it and too few to *show* you how to do it.

Naturally, the more involved breathing becomes, insofar as the presentation of its application to the playing of the brass instruments is concerned, the deeper one gets into a labyrinth of confusion.

Types of Breathing

There are two types of respiration. One is called COSTAL RESPIRATION, which is produced chiefly by the movements of the ribs; the other is called DIAPHRAGMATIC RESPIRATION which is produced chiefly by movements of the diaphragm. They are so inextricably blended that it is often impossible to draw a line of demarcation between them. However, it is the latter type of breathing which we invoke, for it is of the greatest concern to us in the playing of the brass instruments.

Actually, the diaphragm is a partition composed of muscles and sinews and it separates the cavity of the chest from that of the abdomen. Its position is oblique and it is lower in back than in front. It extends from the six or seven lower ribs and their cartilages to the lumbar vertebrae. In shape, it is convex, upward, and when it contracts as it does in breathing, it flattens and thus increases the capacity of the thorax. It is the most important muscle in breathing.

You and I have both been using the diaphragm in breathing since time began for us!

Every time you shout or cough, you use this muscle and you don't read a book to find out how to use it! You don't think about your abdominal muscles being pushed or pulled in, or up, or out. You know the air must be present in the lungs in order to produce the tone for the shout or the sound of the cough.

Stopping the Breath

The breath passage can be stopped in any of four ways:
1. By the raised velum (soft palate).
2. By the lips.
3. By the tongue.
4. By the closed glottis. (The Glottis is the name given to the *structures* surrounding the vocal fold or true vocal cord.)

It can also be stopped by a combination of the lips and the tongue and it is in this manner that we, as brass instrument players, stop the breath passage. Later it will be shown that the raised velum also is used to close off the breath passage as in double and triple tonguing.

When we cough or shout, the action which takes place is this: The air is sucked in by the contraction of the diaphragm when it flattens and increases the thoracic cavity. A momentary action of the glottis occurs and it closes. The air in the lungs, at this point, is compressed between the closed glottis and the diaphragm. The action of the diaphragm *supported* by the abdominal muscles tends to push and return the diaphragm *back to its normal position.* Since it is being forced in this manner, and with the sudden damming up of the air by the closed glottis, there occurs a consequent compression of the air which in reality, is nothing more than *air pressure.* Opening of the glottis results in a rush of air and production of the cough or shout.

It is this same air pressure which

195

is required in the playing of your instrument or my instrument. The only difference is that instead of the breath passage being stopped by the glottis, *it is stopped by the lips*, with the tongue at the aperture or opening of the lips.

An effect not unlike that to which I allude may be achieved by making the various consonant sounds: *p, b, t, d, k, g*. Do not pronounce the letter itself, but rather, say the *sound* of the letter that it has in speech. Observe, then, that the breath passage is stopped by the lips for the *p* and *b*. It is stopped by the tongue for the *t* and *d*. It is stopped by the raised velum (soft palate) for the *k* and *g*.

I'm sure you realize now that this is why we choose to adopt the *t* and *d* as the consonant sounds most closely illustrating the attack or start of a tone on a brass instrument. Likewise, through this same simple logic, we see that the *k* and *g* are illustrative of the stroke of the tongue when articulating double or triple tonguing.

Faulty Breath Stopping

It will be found that most of the breathing difficulties arising in the playing of the brass instruments do not stem from incorrect support of the breath, **as is commonly supposed,** but from the *improper stopping of the breath passage*. The player who closes the breath passage *to any degree* with the glottis shows one or more of the following symptoms:

1. His neck becomes tense.

2. His neck swells.

3. His tone, while perhaps at its best in the middle register, is of little volume in the low register and is pinched in the upper register.

4. He has great difficulty with passages which require slurring upwards.

5. He has great difficulty in developing rapid single tonguing.

Closure of the glottis in the playing of the brass instruments also restricts the complete use of the back of the tongue. Freedom of movement of the back of the tongue is essential if the player is to have a full and natural sound throughout the entire tonal range of the instrument. A raised or lowered position of the back of the tongue should be available to every player. The raised position of the tongue is employed in the upper register and may be

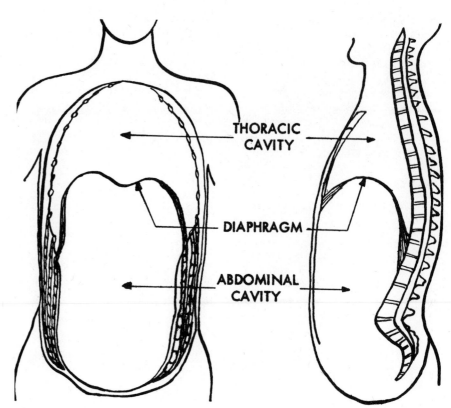

Position of the diaphragm. Notice that it is well up in the thorax, not near the waistline—a common misconception.

simulated by saying the vowel sound *e* (as in EAT). The lowered position of the back of the tongue is employed in the lower register and may be simulated by saying the vowel sound *o* as in ODD. Changing from one to the other will readily convey the sensation to be experienced.

Posture

Correct breathing begins with correct posture. There is no tone without air. Every tone we play is the direct result of vibration of the lips by the breath. The lungs, which contain the air used in respiration, are normally suspended freely in and occupy the entire lateral parts of the thorax. Each lung has a broad base which rests upon the diaphragm.

If we sit or stand in a slumped or slouched position, the lungs, of a consequence, will be stretched into an abnormal position. Instead of assuming their normal shape, which is slightly conical, they will be stretched and forced into a slight kidney shape. The act of inspiration, that of taking in the air, therefore will accentuate this buckling action and it will become more pronounced. The diaphragm is thus affected in that it cannot perform its task with its *natural* ease. The result is that we gain little use of the tidal air, that air which passes in and out of the

lungs in ordinary respiration. We are obliged to rely upon and exert the supplemental air, which can be expelled from the lungs after an ordinary expiration. All of this is unnecessary and can be circumvented if correct posture is established without delay.

The most direct means of acquiring correct posture is to raise and stretch up that part of the head which is the extension of the spinal column. Young boys will immediately recognize it as that place on the top of the head where the hair never seems to lay down just right after combing. (I choose to describe it in this manner so that the forehead is not the only part of the head to be raised. Raising of the forehead would imply thrusting out and raising the chin, which would not be correct.)

The greater the exertion of the diaphragm to return to its normal convex position, the greater the breath or air pressure developed in the breath passage. The aperture or opening of the lips determines the volume of air which will be allowed to escape into the mouthpiece. Obviously, it is seen then, that great muscular control of the lips is necessary in order to hold back and control the onrush of air.

FINE

196

Singing Approach to the Brasses

William Whybrew

THE IMPORTANCE of a good method of tone production cannot be overemphasized. It is the foundation upon which all phases of brass instrument playing rest. Beauty of tone, technical facility, range, and even expressiveness are all largely dependent upon good tone production.

If the brass player is to develop the ability to move quickly about his instrument over a wide range with accuracy and delicacy, if he is to play musically with expressiveness, he must be able to produce a sound which is light and free in quality, a sound which flows unhesitatingly from his instrument and which, consequently, can be freely manipulated.

Other factors cannot, of course, be disregarded, especially the speed and agility of tongue and fingers and the maturity of the performer's musical taste. Yet, high degrees of ability in these respects go for naught if the sound is tight and stiff, if it comes from the instrument reluctantly and only thru the expenditure of great physical effort by the player. Many apparent deficiencies in tonguing can, indeed, be traced to faulty tone production rather than directly to inability of the tongue itself.

Awareness of the importance of a good method of tone production, however, is only a first small step along the road toward solving the problem which confronts us. It is more to the point at the moment to consider some of the common deficiencies in this respect and to find ways of remedying these.

Breath Support

The first essential of good tone production on any wind instrument is, of course, adequate breath support. Increasing attention has been called to this factor in recent years, and it seems that awareness of its importance has spread accordingly.

Diaphragmatic support of the tone is indeed an essential of good tone production, and it is one in which a great many school players seem deficient. Actually, however, it is only *one* important aspect in the proper use of the breath. Of equal importance is the *flow* of breath.

Conceivably, one may have adequate support and still not be free of the pernicious habit of blowing a separate puff of breath for each note. Indeed, it is possible, by emphasizing support in a narrow and superficial manner, to induce in the student a mechanistic concept of tone production which may be as erroneous as lack of support.

It is often difficult, too, for the fifth or sixth grader to grasp the concept of proper diaphragm support, when it is couched in terms more or less technical. Yet it is important that the groundwork for developing a good method of production be laid in the early months of the child's playing career.

Flow of Sound

In listening to hundreds of young brass players over a period of years I have been sadly impressed by the large number who fail to maintain a *flow* of sound, who puff or blow at individual notes in succession. Many of these same players, if asked to sing the melodies which they puff out so laboriously on their instruments, would not respond with a series of disconnected sounds, each emitted with a separate puff of breath. Even more surely they would not, in speaking, deliver their sentences word by word in the same disjointed manner in which they play.

It is this concept of *flow* which must be transferred to the playing of the brass instrument, and one way in which this can be done is by the analogy to singing. Emphasis on "singing the tone" is perhaps the most inclusive and effective way of developing good habits of tone production.

In playing a brass instrument the performer should experience all of the sensations in the mouth, the throat, the chest, and the diaphragm that he would if he were singing the same line, with one exception: notes must be articulated by the tongue when playing instead of by the lips as in singing and, consequently,

there should be no movement of the jaw when articulating on the brass instrument.

The "singing approach" subsumes the use of adequate support. However, support is not emphasized in an isolated fashion but is included in a more comprehensive concept, thus lessening the chances of a mechanistic concept of support and providing a more effective means of attaining this end with younger players.

Developing Flowing Breath

To establish the flow of breath it is, perhaps, best to start with a note of moderate duration, four counts at a moderate tempo. This should be done as soon as the student produces a sound on the instrument. Then, as soon as possible, the student should be asked to play on the same pitch two notes of two counts each, *keeping the continuous flow of breath as in playing the single long note.*

No concern need be given to the termination of the first note, only to the beginning or initiation of each note. The next step is to play four equal notes using the same procedure. The essential point is the transfer of the flow of breath from the single long tone to the succession of shorter tones.

With each of these steps the teacher should illustrate what he wishes the students to do. Actually singing the notes, articulating with the tongue, using a "tah" syllable, and sustaining the "ah" is desirable. Having the students sing the notes in the same manner, then play them is frequently helpful.

The concept of *flowing tone* should be carried over to all playing which the student does. Phrasewise playing should be emphasized from the beginning lessons. If the student is unable to play thru complete phrases, then he should at least think and play groups of notes with the constant effort to extend these groups into complete phrases. The essential point here is to avoid playing note by note.

It is frequently helpful, with students who lapse into notewise playing, to have them sing a phrase and then repeat it with the proper articulation. The device of singing a phrase before playing it is another which can be used advantageously at all levels of advancement. To be of help, of course, the vocalized rendition must be free in character, although it need not be an example of beautiful singing.

Staccato

It may seem to some that such heavy emphasis on a flowing tone completely neglects the staccato. This is not so. It must be understood that flow of breath and sustained support are basic to all phases of brass instrument playing. Until this has been established a really good, light staccato is impossible. Thus, I feel that staccato should not be emphasized too early, as is so often the case. Furthermore, the staccato may well be best approached by beginning with a fairly rapid reiteration of notes rather than with an attempt to play detached notes rather slowly. Too often the more conventional approach of emphasizing shortness of rather slow, spaced notes leads to, or confirms, the notewise concept of playing which results in the "blowing at notes" found in so many school brass players.

At a moderate or moderately slow tempo, alternate beats should be divided into four equal notes, the other beats serving as terminals for the groupings. Emphasis should be placed on the flow of breath and the articulation with a well pointed "T". Termination of each note is best ignored.

Similar devices may be employed as remedial techniques with students who have difficulty in developing a light, free, well-controlled tongue. In many such cases, the fault lies with the breath rather than with the tongue.

Tonguing difficulties, particularly heaviness and stiffness, can frequently be aided in more advanced players by reverting to the slur. Thus, in using a scale exercise, the student might first slur it. Then, *keeping the same feeling of flow of breath,* he might tongue the same scale using a light, but pointed "T" articulation. Thinking the total pattern instead of individual notes will also help.

Singing Style

The singing style is developed most effectively thru extensive legato playing, including both slurred and tongued legato. Printed material in considerable quantity is available for this purpose. Familiar songs are suitable at various levels of advancement, according to the other difficulties involved.

For players in the various stages beyond the beginning level, vocalises—such as those by Concone and, for the lower brasses, those of Bordogni transcribed by Rochut—provide excellent material for work on this important element of brass technique. Chorale and song material also serves well with ensembles of various sizes.

It must be remembered, however, that no material can by itself develop any phase of instrumental playing. The material merely provides exercises in the use of a particular procedure or technique. The proper concept must first be grasped and passed from teacher to student.

Flow of breath and maintenance of support provide no easy formula for quick success on a brass instrument. Performance on any music instrument is a highly complex affair composed of many co-ordinated elements. Deficiency of the tongue, of the fingers, of the lips, or of the ear, and immaturity of musical taste all can and do inhibit success in wind instrument performance. Yet, basic to all of these is the proper use of the breath. It is in this respect, more than in any other, that the majority of school players are deficient. The singing approach, relating the strange to the familiar, the unnatural to the instinctive, offers a hope that this circumstance may yet be relieved.

FINE

November, 1956

Warm-Up Procedures for the Cornetist

James Nielson

TECHNICAL COMPETENCE is achieved only thru adequate preparation. When young players are asked to negotiate difficulties beyond their comprehension, the results tend to prove distressing and ineffectual. Much of the difficulty experienced by younger players is caused by their inability to control muscular responses with the resultant slow reaction time. These adverse factors introduce unwonted tension into the act of performance. Since muscular responses are involved, the warm-up routine must provide basic exercises designed to bring these under control.

Sustained Tones

The warm-up period should begin with sustained tones. As the student concentrates on such factors as intensity, pitch, etc, the action of the diaphragm moves from the subconscious to the conscious. True, with the artist this action has become instinctive; however, during the initial development there must be concentration on these points. To co-ordinate the action of the diaphragm with the act of producing tone at all dynamic levels throughout the entire register of the instrument is one of the reasons for practicing long tones. The other, equally important, is to strengthen the muscles which form the embouchure. Some factors deserve brief mention:

1. Sustained tones must be played throughout the entire register, with emphasis placed upon the lower tones.
2. There is no merit in playing long tones unless there is concentration on intensity of tone (which affects the beauty of tone), pitch (which

is affected adversely by lack of breath support and unstable embouchure), and varying degrees of dynamics (long tones should be played at every degree of intensity).

3. The following routine may be employed profitably, the quarter note pulse equaling 72 beats per minute:

Chromatically downward and return. Each tone 16 counts.

Chromatically upward and return. Each tone 8 counts.

Chromatically upward and return. Each tone 8 counts.

Chromatically upward and return. Each tone 4 counts. For advanced players only.

Tonguing

Tone is produced when the tongue is removed from the point of contact. The speed of the release and return, the tension across the tip of the tongue at the point of contact, all are controllable factors which can be maintained with astonishing accuracy. The point of contact, whether behind the upper teeth or thru to the inner part of the inner lip, is not a topic for discussion here. Nor is the validity of the staccato exercise to the legato of great importance. The important thing is the movement of the tongue which must be exercised until a speed of four notes to the beat at varying tempi (60-146 MM) can be maintained with accuracy. This refers to single tonguing only. Factors to be considered are these:

1. The release should be made rapidly and to the same place, the withdrawal distance depending upon the rapidity of action and the degree of staccato or legato.

2. The tongue should touch the point of contact lightly. Exceptions occur for special effects such as explosive accents or abrupt cut-offs.

3. Accurate response must be attained and maintained at all speeds from very slow to very fast. It is difficult when four notes to the beat are played at speeds of MM 60, 70, 80, etc. Indeed, all things being considered, it is easier to be accurate at the higher speeds.

4. All dynamics and shadings except the very loud should be used.

5. Tonguing exercises should be played throughout the entire register, with special emphasis given to the low register.

I have found the following to be helpful:

Chromatically downward and return (MM 60-126).

Chromatically upward and return (MM 60-132).

Chromatically upward and return (MM 60-142).

Chromatically upward and return (MM 60-142). For advanced players only.

For advanced players, interesting variations may be introduced, some of which follow:

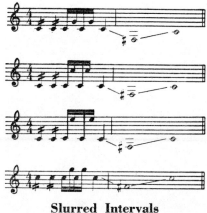

Slurred Intervals

The art of making simultaneously the precise and minute adjustments of embouchure and diaphragm which must be effected when playing in extended ranges should be developed thru constant practice on slurred intervals. Lip slurs have a place in this routine, but only as an end product.

First, flexibility should be developed across the registers as suggested in the following exercises. This accomplished, lip slurs can be played with comparative ease. The following routines will be found helpful. Concentrate on these factors:

1. Use all dynamic levels, but maintain an equal level throughout each exercise.

2. Start at slow speeds. Concentrate on a smooth transition from register to register. Master all of the technical difficulties at the slower speeds before increasing the range of tempi.

3. Make the transition from register to register without the use of the portamento.

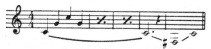

Chromatically downward and return (MM 60-182).

Chromatically downward and return (MM 48-112).

The following exercises are for advanced players only:

Chromatically downward and return (MM 48-106).

Chromatically downward and return (MM 48-106).

Chromatically downward and return (MM 72-120).

These are the basic groups. Combinations of these may be introduced to meet the demands made upon the performer's competence. It will take approximately 20 minutes to complete the warm-up routine, which should be done each day if the performer is to derive the maximum benefit.

FINE

Getting a C Trumpet?

Clifford Lillya

WHEN YOU FIRST play your C trumpet, you may be disappointed in its intonation. Of course, no trumpet is 100% in tune, and it is futile to expect perfection. However, to the confirmed Bb trumpet player, some C trumpets seem to have more than their share of shortcomings.

Don't Be Hasty

Before deciding that the new trumpet is hopeless, give it a chance. Your whole sensory system is geared to the feel of the Bb instrument, and this conditioning is the cause of some of your difficulties with the C trumpet. You are relating the C to the Bb instrument in two ways. First, in the association of pitch and fingering. When you play concert C on the Bb trumpet, you are accustomed to using the first valve. On the C trumpet this tone is "open." But more significant than this, you are subconsciously trying to duplicate the *feeling* associated with producing this pitch on the Bb trumpet or cornet.

The second area in which you may believe your new trumpet to be unsatisfactory is in timbre, or sound. First trials of the C trumpet are apt to produce a tone which may be somewhat strained and hollow. This happens because you have not yet discovered the centering place of the tone.

You must play an instrument long enough to let the tone find its proper placement before judging it. This can be compared to letting a pendulum swing freely until gravity brings it to a stop. If you want the pendulum to stop in any other than a perpendicular position, you must hold it there. The off-perpendicular position

of pendulum is somewhat analagous to a tone which is not in proper focus. This will be a sound which is lacking in resonance and conviction, a tone with a forced or affected quality.

Difficult Notes

You will probably find yourself fighting the tones E5 and D#5 (4th space E and 4th line D#). As you try to squeeze these tones up to what you consider the correct pitch, they will become even poorer in quality, and maybe even lower in pitch. Do not try to correct these tones in this strong-arm manner. Realize that the Bb instrument invariably produces too large a major third between concert C5 and E5. This is also true of the interval between Bb and D#.

Because your ear has become accustomed to these intervals on the Bb trumpet, you are dissatisfied with the C trumpet because it will not do likewise. On the C trumpet, these intervals are inherently a trifle too small. Play the following tones on your C trumpet:

Notice how flat the tones indicated "x" sound. Now play the following tones:

Notice that the 3rd of the chord (again marked "x") does not sound nearly as flat as it did in the first two chords. This is partly because you are used to hearing these tones as part of a sequence produced by a

Top: C trumpet. Note shorter tuning slide section than that on Bb trumpet (bottom).

single length of tubing on the Bb trumpet (open and second). You

have learned to accept these tones.

Common Sense Approach

Here are some suggestions for Bb trumpet players to follow when starting to play the C trumpet:

1. Play only the C trumpet for *at least* a week.
2. Play mainly in the middle and lower registers.
3. Play in an effortless dynamic range—about mf to f.
4. Do not become pre-occupied with intonation. Rather, try for maximum sonority.
5. Give priority to the phrasing and content of the music.

If you follow the suggestions given above, your C trumpet will seem to improve. For example, the major 3rd between C and E will no longer seem to pull together, as tho the tones were connected by a rubber band.

The reasons for this apparent improvement are two-fold. First, you will have relaxed, and will be getting into the trumpet more properly so that C5 will have settled down, and E5 will have come up a very little. Second, your ear will not be demanding so wide an interval, because you will have, for the time being, "forgotten" the conditioning received from playing Bb trumpet on these tones. You will have begun to play the C trumpet directly, instead of thru a Bb trumpet scrim.

It's Worth The Effort

Intonation is apt to be a relative thing, and there are times when different fingerings must be used. Slide alterations and lip adjustments must also be made on all trumpets and cornets. However, each trumpet has its advantages, and trumpet students will do well to get acquainted with both the Bb and C. When a player feels equally at home with the Bb and the C trumpet, he can base his choice of instruments on musical and technical considerations. Even if you reject the C trumpet (after a reasonable trial) as being incompatible with your aims and tastes, playing the new instrument can be a valuable part of your experience.

Ed. Note: Adolph S. Herseth, 1st trumpet with the Chicago Symphony Orchestra, uses the C trumpet on all parts, even tho the parts may be for Bb or D trumpet.

FINE

1957

E♭ Alto Horn

The E-Flat Horn Crook
IS a Crook

Lloyd Schmidt

SOONER OR LATER every instrumental director faces the problems arising from E♭ and F parts for French horn. Most directors solve the dilemma by using an E♭ crook, or by requiring the student to transpose.

The continued and frequent use of crooks seems to testify that many directors still feel the practice to be necessary; on the other hand, the very idea of using a crook makes the professional horn player wince! Leading horn players and brass authorities condemn the practice of using crooks for French horn playing.

Historically Significant

Historically, the crook was an ingenious and useful invention for making different overtone series available to the natural (no valves) horn player without the necessity of changing horns. A player of a natural horn in "F," for instance, playing only the open tones of that horn, could follow a modulation in a composition to "C" horn by inserting a crook instead of changing horns. The advent of the valved horn in the mid-19th century, however, made the use of crooks obsolete.

Early band literature was often written for an alto saxhorn in E♭ (members of this family are cornets, alto horns, baritones, tubas). Modern symphonic band concepts brought the French horn as a replacement for the alto. This caused the phenomenon of E♭ and F parts to be played on the French horn in F. It was at this point that the expedient of using a crook was introduced.

E♭ Crook Abuses

On the surface this seems to be an excellent and efficient solution. However, we can soon see by the results that, tho it *is* easier to read an E♭ part with the E♭ crook than it is to transpose, we are soon led into abuses and shortcomings which far outweigh any immediate advantages.

The crook lowers the F horn one whole tone, making the basic length E♭ in pitch. The ideal taper and bore have been violated. Furthermore, it immediately becomes apparent that valve slides *must be pulled* to maintain a proper ratio for the lower pitch of the horn. I am convinced that fully 75% of crook users neglect to pull valve slides, and perhaps less than 10% pull them the correct distances. Assuming, however, that the E♭ crook is in place and that the slides are properly pulled, what further problem?

It is generally accepted that the somewhat treacherous nature of the horn makes lip "feel" and ear "memory" of prime importance. Our E♭ crook very effectively (1) robs the lip of its proper "feel" for the pitch, and (2) upsets ear-eye training and co-ordination so dearly gained throughout past experience (unless one visualizes the true pitch one step lower). In effect, the student must master *two* very similar lip-ear-eye techniques which, consequently hurt accuracy to a considerable extent. The reader who feels this to be exaggerated should please make the experiment!

Transposing the E♭ Part

Further argument could be developed; however, it might be more profitable to examine the other alternative, transposition. Here, in exact contrast to using a crook, difficulties are met immediately. This accounts for the fact that some directors hesitate to teach transposition. The transposition that must be learned by the F player reading an E♭ part is: transpose one whole step down, or, add two flats and read one staff degree downward.

While this may seem complicated for the student, it is nonetheless much easier in the long run. Students can learn to transpose within a couple of days, and can be reading like veterans within a week or two. Thousands of alert band and orchestra members all over the country do transpose; it is basic horn technique. Transposition, as a matter of fact, comes much more quickly than might be imagined; it very soon becomes automatic. Furthermore, the process, like pulling teeth, is much better faced quickly by throwing away all E♭ crooks.

The "crook" is aptly named; it leads a crooked path, forms a crutch with all of the attendant evils of most musical crutches, and like most crutches, it betrays the user. It is a crook! The player soon becomes a slave to it. The transposing player, on the other hand, may falter a little at first, but soon develops an independence which enables him to run ahead while his companion with a crook limps along behind.

In the interest of better bands and orchestras, and especially of better horn players, let's do away with crooks! Publishers might well save their money and that of the schools by printing *all* horn parts in F!

FINE

The Brass Choir

Leon Brown

IN THE PAST decade our nation has witnessed the phenomenal growth of the brass choir movement. A large number of university and college music departments maintain opportunities for brass choir programs, and many recognize this phase as a part of the regular curriculum for brass players. The movement has expanded to include many high school instrumental programs which foster opportunity for brass choir participation. A large amount of interest has been shown by school instrumental leaders in determining the size of a brass choir, and to what extent literature is available and adaptable for high school performance.

At first the term "brass choir" referred to that group which comprised the brass section of the symphony orchestra, this designation having been made to set apart the brass as a section from the woodwinds and strings. The brass choir, patterned after the orchestral brass section, tho sometimes enlarged to include two or three performers on each part, can and does function as a separate entity capable of concert performance. More recently the terminology has referred to the brass section of the concert band.

In school instrumental programs it is recommended that the brass choir be offered as a stimulus to enjoyment of the brass players of the band or orchestra, thus limiting the opportunity to those who serve faithfully in the larger organizations. Its work, therefore, is supplemental and offers a splendid opportunity for enriching and improving the musicianship of its players. This same incentive should also serve in instituting the woodwind choir or string orchestra.

Historical Background

The immediate predecessors of the brass choir may be found in the British and the Salvation Army Brass Bands. Brass bands were instituted about the same time social reforms were taking place in Britain, which in turn afforded more leisure time to the working classes. Employers of labor were keenly alive to the value of bands as a social adjunct to their factories, mines, etc., and encouraged their formation.

Temperance societies and similar bodies were all cognizant of the attraction that a band presented, with the result that bands sprang up all over Britain. At the height of the movement around the beginning of the present century there were an estimated 20,000 bands in existence. They were employed to lead processions, to play at outdoor meetings and to be present at flower shows, sports events, etc. These bands from the outset were amateur organizations, their membership comprising personnel of the factories, mines, or societies in which they were employed.

Oddly enough, one of the factors that led to the institution of the movement a century ago has caused the reduction in the number of brass bands today, i.e., increased opportunity for the employment of leisure time. However, there still are approximately 3,000 brass bands in existence at the present time, numbering some 60,000 players.

The Salvation Army Brass Band is a direct descendant of the British Brass Band movement. The size of the bands varies from twenty members to as many as sixty in the larger bands. Both types are limited, however, to twenty-four players when participating in contests.

In order to show a comparison of the standard instrumentation of the two organizations, the following table is given:

BRITISH BRASS BAND

Solo B♭ Cornet
Soprano E♭ Cornet
Ripiano B♭ Cornet
B♭ Flügelhorn
Second B♭ Cornet
Third B♭ Cornet
Solo E♭ Tenor horn
First E♭ Tenor horn
Second E♭ Tenor horn
First B♭ Baritone
Second B♭ Baritone
First B♭ Trombone
Second B♭ Trombone
Bass Trombone
B♭ Euphonium
E♭ Bass
B♭ Bass
Drums, cymbals, bells
  (no timpani)

SALVATION ARMY BRASS BAND

Solo B♭ Cornet
Soprano E♭ Cornet
First B♭ Cornet
Second B♭ Cornet
B♭ Flügelhorn
Solo E♭ Alto horn
First E♭ Alto horn
Second E♭ Alto horn
First B♭ Baritone
Second B♭ Baritone
First B♭ Trombone
Second B♭ Trombone
G Trombone (Bass)
B♭ Euphonium
E♭ Bass
B♭ Bass
Drums, cymbals, bells
  (no timpani)

It is interesting to note that the individual parts of both British and Salvation Army Brass Band scores are written in treble clef with the exception of bass trombone, which is scored in bass clef. Since all the players are amateurs, it is often necessary for them to switch from one instrument to another on a moments' notice, therefore simplicity of the reading is of paramount importance. This practice makes it possible for the valve-brass players to learn only one fingering that may be adaptable for *all* treble clef notation. The modern school band program makes use of this practice in the transfer of cornet and trumpet players to E♭ horn, B♭ treble clef baritone, and E♭ Bass.

The success of the brass bands has largely been attributed to contests. Annual brass band contests have been held without a break since 1853. Area elimination contests are held at centrally located places, and the "finals" in London's famed Albert Hall. The adjudicators of these contests are selected from the leading English conductors and composers. These contests have lent incentive for well-known composers to write music for brass band. Sir Edward Elgar, Gustav Holst, John Ireland, and Granville Bantock are among the most prominent.

Brass band activities are kept before the bandsmen and public by several publication agencies. Three periodicals are devoted exclusively to British Brass Bands and three publishers' entire output consists of music for brass bands. Other publishers, as well, have brass band items in their catalogs. Music for the Salvation Army Bands is still published. Because of the nature of Salvation Army work, its music is based upon religious context.

The Literature

In organizing a brass choir it is very important to consider the literature that is available, using this medium as a factor in determining the size of the group desired. The rapid growth of the brass choir movement has been made possible by the publication of a considerable amount of quality literature, good music of the past as well as important contemporary pieces and well-arranged transcriptions. Since there has been no move made to standard-ize the size or instrumentation of a group, much care should be taken when organizing to prevent over-balance or weakness in the sections comprising the group.

There are many compositions scored for small brass ensembles such as quintets or sextets, a majority of which may be used effectively with brass choirs. An equal number of players on each instrumental part is therefore recommended, when such music is used. This procedure may require the use of two, three, four, or five performers on each part, depending upon the sonority desired by the director. The size of the group is thus determined.

Many compositions are specifically written for an orchestral brass section. Since this music requires approximately twelve to fifteen individual parts, it is recommended that one, or no more than two, players be maintained on each individual part, and only one on each percussion part. Certain other compositions may call for an entirely different instrumentation. If it is a very unusual combination of instruments, perhaps the "one to a part" designation would be the best recommendation.

There is a substantial amount of good music scored for the previously mentioned British and Salvation Army Brass Bands which may be adapted for brass choir. Usually the substitution of the modern French horn for the E♭ Alto and Tenor horns of the brass bands readily renders most of the music for performance.

The Instrumentation

Most of the music scored for brass choir can be performed within the framework of the three following suggestions on instrumentation:

(1) A recommended small brass choir would include four trumpets (cornets), four horns, three trombones, one baritone, one tuba, and the necessary percussion required of the music (15-18 performers).

(2) A recommended medium-sized brass choir would comprise six trumpets (cornets), six horns, four or five trombones, two baritones, two tubas, and the percussion necessary for performance of the music (22-25 performers).

(3) A recommended large brass choir would include eight trumpets (cornets), eight horns, six trombones, three baritones, three tubas and the necessary percussion (30-33 performers).

In the event that the full brass section of a large band is used, some rescoring of music may be necessary to prevent an overbalance of parts. Usually this can be taken care of by discriminate rehearsal on the part of the director. It is my opinion, however, that when a group becomes much larger than the above recommendation for large brass choir, the results will furnish diminishing returns for the performers as well as listeners. Since the criteria are placed upon efficient performance, any effort to the direction of an unwieldy or overbalanced group is to be avoided. A group of thirty to thirty-three competent brass players can upon demand supply adequate volume for any occasion.

Brass Choir Uses

The brass choir may be effectively utilized as a performing organization in many ways. It would be possible to designate a portion of a band or orchestra concert to the brass choir on occasion. A number of choral pieces have been written which effectively use the brass choir as an accompanying medium. It is a very desirable group to employ for professional music at commencement exercises, and a very effective and impressive unit to render some of the great sacred music of the past as a part of church worship services. The brass choir is also very effective as a touring organization; its size and the ease by which it can be transported will not involve a large expense, as do the larger organizations.

Finally, the satisfaction derived from performance of brass choir music is excellent for the performers and the listeners. The quality of the music being composed and published is greatly improving. Such established music as the well-adapted instrumental church music of the Italian Renaissance and the German Tower music of the Baroque era has been revived, and contemporary music is being composed in abundance.

FINE

Why So Many Cornet-Trumpet Misfits?

Howard Deming

THE NUMBER of students of brass instruments who would have been much more successful on some other instrument is appalling. Why or how they started on a brass instrument is usually a forgotten or inconsequential thing. Too many public school music teachers have misinterpreted the slogan, "Music for every child and every child for music" to mean, "A cornet for every child and every child for a cornet."

Right at this point I want to dispel any fears that I am about to suggest a musical aptitude test. I am speaking mainly of purely physical differences which make performance on a cup-shaped mouthpiece very difficult. I firmly believe in "music for every child" in the basic meaning of the phrase, but the term *music* embodies a wide variety of experiences. Performance on a music instrument is only one of these.

Lips and Teeth

In instructing brass instrument students, the teacher must first accept one undebatable fact; each individual is given only one set of teeth and one pair of lips. The lips are the property of this individual for life and cannot be discarded when worn, chipped, or broken like a reed.

These lips are the vibrating surfaces by which the tone is produced on all cup mouthpieces. The lips to the brass instrument player are what the reed is to the woodwind performer. If a reed does not produce a tone or respond the way the

woodwind performer wishes, it is discarded; the brass player has no such alternative.

If the lips are unable to produce a healthy, sustained buzzing sound because of extreme malocclusion, shape or size of lips, or irregular teeth, the player is not physically adapted to the instrument. These simple things are too often overlooked.

In young students, physical correction can sometimes be made. Dentists are able to straighten irregular teeth with the aid of braces and have at times recommended the playing of brass instruments for teeth straightening purposes. Some brass methods have advocated protruding the lower jaw in cases of extreme recession. However, a few minutes experimentation with this method usually develpos a muscular ache at the hinges of the jaw. Wouldn't it be better for students with extreme malocclusions to be encouraged to play some other instrument?

Off-Center Playing

Playing a considerable amount on one side of the mouth is generally not successful. The problem here is one of unequal distribution of muscular control, improper position of the tonuge for articulations, and an uneven vibrating surface. A less common problem is the "cupid's bow" which consists of overhanging tissue in the center of the upper lip. This often hangs loosely and seemingly without muscular control.

A few simple tests will, generally, dispel all fears as to whether or not the student is capable of trumpet-cornet performance. First, the prospective trumpeter should be asked to whistle. If the aperture when whistling is in the center of the lips and the teeth are relatively even, the student should be able to place the mouthpiece in the center of the lips. Second, ask the student to produce a buzzing tone with the lips alone; have him imitate the sound after you have demonstrated.

If after a few minutes' work the student is able to produce a sustained buzzing sound, he has the basic physical attributes for the production of a tone on a cup mouthpiece instrument. If the music teacher will remember that the tone of a cup-shaped mouthpiece instrument is simply the amplification of this buzz, he will find that it is much easier to determine the adaptability of his prospective brass students.

Certain things can be done for some minor physical irregularities; however, the more problems one is able to eliminate before study is begun on an instrument, the better are the chances for musical success and enjoyment. Generally speaking, the size of lips is not too important. The size of the mouthpiece and its placement can help such things, but there is little that can be done for the would-be cornetist with extremely irregular teeth or an extreme malocclusion.

FINE

March, 1957

Improving Brass Instrument Performance

DeForest Chase

THE BRASS MUSICIAN must develop fully his musical ability in order to perform with technical facility, tonal beauty, and musical taste. All factors that enter into tone production and technical execution should be considered in every daily practice routine. The practice time should be divided so that old problems may be reviewed and new ones attacked intelligently.

The main problems of brass playing are: 1. posture, 2. breath control, 3. tone production, 4. finger (slide) technique, 5. lip flexibility, 6. dynamics, 7. range, and 8. intonation. Careful thought concerning these will aid in the steady improvement of the performer.

Posture

1. Stand straight, but relaxed, with weight on balls of feet.
2. Sit straight, but relaxed.
3. Keep head up.
4. Practice exercises which tend to strengthen the back and stomach muscles and which relax the spine and neck.

Breath Control

1. Yawn several times to relax thoroughly.
2. Breathe deeply several times. Check diaphragmatic breathing by placing hands on bottom of ribs; there should be expansion and contraction in the back, front, and sides.
3. Open throat and relax jaw.
4. Inhale *only* amount of air needed to play desired tone or phrase, leaving just a small amount in reserve.
5. Do not force air out with stomach muscles, chest, or ribs. The diaphragm should expel the air. (An exception to this is when a tone is to be accented and a sudden push of air is necessary.)
6. Think of breathing wind into the instrument rather than blowing air thru it.

Tone Production

1. Get a clear conception of a good tone by listening to performing artists.
2. Listen to tone quality and use tape recorder, stroboscope, and oscillograph.
3. Use following drill to obtain resonant tone:
   a. Find the center of the tone by humoring the pitch to the most resonant sound.
   b. Sing the tone.
   c. Buzz the tone on mouthpiece.
   d. Play the center of the tone again on the instrument.
4. Use the following drill to improve intervals:
   a. Sing scales, arpeggios, intervals, exercises, and solos.
   b. Buzz them on the mouthpiece.
   c. Play them on the instrument.
   d. Sing, buzz, and play octave intervals.
5. Attack each tone using the tongue correctly.
   a. Place tip of tongue high on front teeth.
   b. Seal off all air with the tongue.
   c. Keep a steady flow of air to the mouthpiece at all times.
   d. Start the tone by lowering the tongue quickly and releasing the air.
   e. Practice single, double, and triple tonguing.
   f. Do not stop tone with the tongue; stop breath with diaphragm.
6. Form embouchure correctly.
   a. Place the lips together naturally.
   b. Place mouthpiece on fleshy part of lips.
   c. Check lip vibration by buzzing the mouthpiece.
   d. Do not use excessive mouthpiece pressure.
   e. Place mouthpiece near center of mouth; comfort and satisfactory results govern exact location.
   f. Moisten the lips.
   g. Develop lip flexibility by practicing lip slurs and rapid interval changes.
7. Produce tones of several seconds' duration with no change in pitch or quality.
8. Produce tones of several sec-

onds' duration using a controlled vibrato.

9. Shape the mouth to different vowel sounds in order to secure desired quality.

10. Use suitable equipment, instrument and mouthpiece. Have an expert help you, if necessary.

11. Keep equipment in good playing condition. Keep it clean and check it regularly for leaks.

Finger (Slide) Technique

1. Memorize scales — major, all three forms of minor, chromatic, and whole tone—and execute them as rapidly as precision will allow. Play two octaves if practical, both slurred and tongued.

2. Follow above procedure for arpeggios, also intervals.

3. Practice any series of tones that present difficulty in fingering or slide technique.

Lip Flexibility

1. All of the suggestions for developing finger or slide technique are applicable here.

2. Practice lip slurs, starting slowly and gradually increasing the speed.

3. Practice octave intervals, slurred and tongued.

Dynamics

1. Produce the following effects, in sequence, on a single tone: pp-p-mp-mf-f-ff; ff-f-mf-mp-p-pp; ff-pp; pp-ff.

2. Produce the following effects, holding any one tone several seconds and maintaining a steady pitch: p to f; f to p; pp to ff to pp; ff to pp to ff; f to p (diminish quickly from the f to the p and hold the tone); and p to f (hold the soft tone and then push quickly with the breath just before releasing the tone.)

3. Use various dynamic ranges when practicing scales and arpeggios.

Range

1. Be conscious of a matched tone quality throughout the entire range.

2. Improve the high range by—
a. Maintaining breath support.
b. Opening jaw and throat.
c. Keeping a cushion of lips between mouthpiece and teeth.
d. Avoiding excessive mouthpiece pressure.
e. Raising the tongue slightly to form the vowel sound of "too" or "doo."

f. Beginning the tone precisely thru the valve action of the tongue in releasing the air.
g. Tonguing and slurring all scales, arpeggios, and intervals.
h. Thinking of attacking tones from above.
i. Forming the lips close together.

3. Improve the low range by—
a. Extending the jaw.
b. Pushing the embouchure forward.
c. Opening the lips more.
d. Using very little mouthpiece pressure.
e. Using a "tah" or "dah" sylla-ble.
f. Beginning the tone precisely thru the valve action of the tongue in releasing the air.

Intonation

1. Practice hearing the tone mentally before producing it.

2. Sing and buzz on the mouthpiece new music before playing it.

3. Use the stroboscope and check tones carefully.

4. Discover the tones which are out of tune on the instrument and make necessary adjustments as automatic as possible.

FINE

Brass Tone Improvement Chart

If the tone is →

Then check possible causes ↓	Weak (stuffy)	Light (shrill)	Dark (dull)	Loud	Forced	Weak in High Range	Weak in Low Range	Flat	Sharp	Pitch, Quality Variations	Slow Response	Breathy
Too Little Air	X					X	X	X	X	X	X	
Tonguing Faults										X	X	X
Pinched Lips	X					X	X		X			
Closed or Receded Jaw	X					X	X	X	X	X	X	
Closed Throat	X					X	X	X	X	X	X	
Lack of Diaphragm Support	X					X	X	X	X	X	X	
Shallow Cup Mouthpiece		X				X	X					
Small Bore Instrument	X	X				X	X					
Leak in Instrument	X					X	X	X				
Small Bore Mouthpiece	X					X	X		X			
Valve Height not Adjusted	X											
Instrument not Clean Inside	X					X	X					
Large Cup Mouthpiece			X			X						
Vowel-Shaped Mouth (tee)		X					X		X			
Vowel-Shaped Mouth (tow)			X			X		X				
Too Much Air				X	X				X	X		X
Forcing Air with Chest or Ribs				X	X	X	X		X	X		X
Excessive Mouthpiece Pressure	X					X	X	X		X	X	
Lips not Vibrating Correctly	X					X	X	X	X			
Correct Pitch not Heard	X					X	X	X	X	X		
Optional Fingering								X	X	X		
1st & 3rd Valve Slides Extended							X			X	X	
Poor Quality Instrument	X	X	X			X	X	X	X		X	
Improper Conception of Good Tone	X	X	X	X	X	X	X			X		
Poor Mouthpiece Placement	X					X	X	X	X	X	X	
Mouthpiece Does Not Fit Inst.	X							X	X			
Lips too Far Apart				X	X			X			X	X
Change in Vowel Shape of Mouth										X		

Cornets and Trumpets

How many can hear the difference?

George Kyme

MOST SUCCESSFUL band directors today prefer to use cornets in their bands rather than trumpets. The assumption is that there is a tone-quality difference between these two instruments that makes one suitable for melodic and harmonic parts but delegates the other to the realm of a "pitch-controlled" percussion section, to be used only when brilliant and piercing noises are demanded of the band.

The question arises "Is this *quality* concept a product of the tonal imagery of the performer and thus obtainable on cornet and trumpet alike; or, is there something in the conical shape of the bore of the instruments that renders one aesthetically more acceptable for bands and men for the all-conference groups of the California — Western Division Meeting of M.E.N.C. Mark Hindsley of the University of Illinois acted as conductor of the all-conference band.

In setting up the instrumentation of the band, Mr. Hindsley requested that we provide twelve cornets and four trumpets—*the instruments not to be interchangeable.* Ray Dvorak requested a similar proportion for the M.E.N.C. Golden Jubilee Band at St. Louis last April.

In California, most of our fine teachers play trumpets, and naturally their best pupils play trumpets also. In fulfilling Mr. Hindsley's request, we found ourselves in the position of the other more acceptable for orchestras?"

In 1955, it was my privilege to serve as one of the organizing chairaccepting cornet players decidedly less superior than some trumpet applicants — merely because they played cornets. This dilemma led me into a serious discussion as to whether the *tone quality* differences between cornet and trumpet warranted making the selection of personnel on this basis. We decided, with Mr. Hindsley's permission, to test this assumption of the cornet's superior tone quality as a part of an adjudication clinic.

Procedure

The plan of the experiment was quite orthodox. A local band, the Oakland Technical High School Band, performed several "festival" compositions, each in three different ways, and six competent adjudicators, concealed behind a screen, were asked to decide which of the three performances was the most pleasing and why.

In the first performance, first-grade borrowed cornets were used by all members of the cornet and trumpet section of the band. In the second performance, the 1st, 3rd, 5th, 7th, and 9th players used trumpets, while the even-numbered players used cornets. All trumpets were used in the third performance.

The judges, Ralph Rush, Clarence Sawhill, Russell Howland, Edwin Kruth, Fred Westphal, and Harold Cain agreed, five to six, that the second performance—one-half cornets and one-half trumpets — was the more satisfying, tho none made *tone quality* the distinguishing factor. Indeed intonation was the most evident differentiating element.

Second Experiment

This experiment, admittedly, is open to severe criticism. Too many factors were uncontrolled. In the first place, clarinets were interchanged as well as cornets; and the intonation was not stable when the players changed from their accustomed instruments to "all cornets" or "all trumpets." Furthermore, the judges were not aware that the important differences would be in terms of tone quality and perhaps were not listening for minute tone quality differences.

The logical follow-up of this exploratory experiment, therefore, required that we design an experiment that would control the variables better. This second experiment was carried out at the brass clinic of the California Music Educators' Association Conference in Santa Rosa, last year. It attempted to determine whether trained musicians, i.e., music teachers, could distinguish between the tone qualities of cornets and trumpets when each instrument was played by the same player using the same mouthpiece. The question also was presented as to whether one could estimate the monetary value of an instrument just by hearing it played.

The experiment was two-fold in nature. One part was concerned with whether the 103 music teachers could determine differences in qualities between the two instruments, and the other part was concerned with the ability of the professional player to make distinctions between cornets and trumpets and to estimate their monetary values.

Twenty-two paired instruments were borrowed from the exhibitors present. These instruments ranged in price from $139.00 to $315.00. Each instrument was played by the same professional musician behind a screen. He used the same large bore mouthpiece for each horn. The player was blindfolded and wore gloves to disguise to feel of the instrument. He was asked to designate the trumpets and the cornets and their costs, using intonation, response, and ease of playing as criteria.

Results

The musicians present could not tell beyond the level of pure chance which instruments were trumpets and which were cornets. In the 103 cases tabulated, the highest correct response for any instrument was 62 correct and 41 wrong. In one instance, the score was reversed, and only 37 were correct while 66 missed describing the proper instrument. The mean number of correct responses was 54. Moreover, every instrument was classed as the most expensive by at least two persons, and also rated the least expensive by even a greater number.

This report was not true of the performer, however. He was almost entirely correct in determining the type of instrument played, and he had a good conception of its cost.

It is interesting to note here that manufacturers are not in complete agreement as to what constitutes a trumpet or a cornet. Vincent Bach, a manufacturer of symphony brass instruments, states that there are no arbitrary laws describing the design of a trumpet or cornet. He further states that he has 73 different bell mandrils which can be used for either trumpet or cornet, and any one of them might be better adapted to producing the tone quality expected from one or the other of these two instruments.

Both the cornet and trumpet are made in a variety of different bores and bell shapes, resulting in a more mellow or more brilliant tone quality, but in certain orchestras, preference is generally given to a rich, mellow tone of larger volume. This quality our symphony conductors call a "Teutonic tone."

Mr. Bach believes that the two major factors distinguishing a trumpet from a cornet are: that a trumpet has about 50% conical bore, and *the entire tubing of a trumpet has only one winding*. His cornet, however, has about 90% conical bore and only 10% cylindrical bore, and *the tubing has two windings*.

If there is a fast growing taper of the mouthpiece and if the tubing is bent only once, a heroic, martial, brilliant tone quality and a firm response results. If an instrument, however, has a slower growing taper extending over a considerably longer stretch of tubing (such as does the Bach *cornet*), much more resistance is presented to the player, which is further increased if the tubing has two bends. This type of an instrument offers greater resistance and flexibility, and makes it easier to slur from one tone to another. This attribute renders the instrument more suitable for Coloratura work in solo playing.

Apparently, there is a greater difference between the tone qualities of the several makes of cornets than there is between trumpets and cornets of the same make, if size of bore and mouthpiece is held constant.   FINE

The CLOSED Throat

Shuts the Door on Musical Performance

Vincent Malek

ONE OF THE MOST objectionable conditions, as far as *musical* performance on brass instruments is concerned, is the partially closed throat. If the player is lacking in ability to control his breath he is likely, either consciously or unconsciously, to constrict the muscles in the throat in an effort to compensate.

Teachers frequently attempt to correct this fault in their students by employing imagery of various types. This is, of course, desirable—provided it works!

However, judging by the large numbers of brass players exhibiting this fault at district and state solo contests (and these are supposed to be our better players), the problem of the closed throat cannot easily be dismissed. Misconceptions, on the part of the teacher, of the physical construction of the throat may be responsible for lack of success in overcoming this irksome habit in their students. After all, it is difficult to prescribe a remedy for a little understood situation. If we are going to solve this problem, it is imperative that we familiarize ourselves with the area in which the trouble arises. Understanding the physical construction of the throat, we will have a much sounder basis for employing imagery with our students.

Throat Construction

The opening in the back of the mouth (see illustration) leads into the top part of the throat, which is called the pharynx. This passageway in the throat also leads to the nasal cavity. The roof of the mouth is called the palate and is divided into two portions. The fore part has a bony base and, consequently, is called the *hard* palate. The rear section has no bone and is therefore termed the *soft* palate. Since there is nothing to constrict it, it drapes down over the opening into the throat. From its center hangs the uvula, a small mass of tissue which further covers the opening.

Each of the two sides of the soft palate consists of two folds of muscular tissue. Since the technical name for the opening in the throat is the *fauces*, these muscular folds are termed *pillars of the fauces*. The front pillar is attached at its bottom to the back of the tongue, the tongue occupying the floor of the mouth. The bottom attachment of the rear pillar is to the wall of the pharynx.

Throat Constriction

If the pharyngeal muscles in the pillars of the fauces are contracted, the pillars are drawn together, resulting in a constriction in the size of the opening. This is one way in which the throat may become partially closed. There is also a second manner.

This second method is effected when the back portion of the tongue is pulled upward and when the soft palate is allowed to continue to hang downward. The soft palate should, during exhalation thru the mouth, be drawn upward, in which position it blocks the opening of the pharynx into the nasal cavity.

For brass players, the inordinate raising of the rear section of the tongue is most likely to occur during the execution of high tones. The syllable "ee" is usually employed to

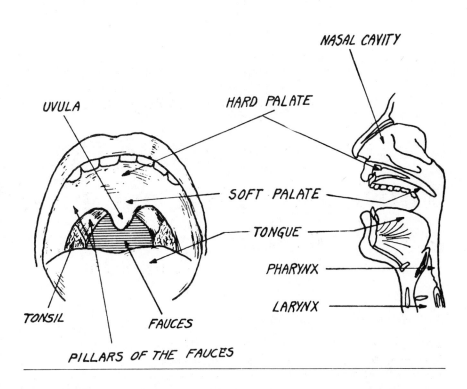

The open mouth and throat. A knowledge of the physical structure of the throat and the manner in which it constricts and relaxes is most beneficial in helping teachers aid their students in overcoming the problem of the closed throat in playing.

facilitate their production, but this also arches the tongue. Many teachers feel that the arch is desirable and necessary, but if it is overdone —especially at the extreme rear portion of the tongue—the throat opening will become partially closed.

Whereas contraction of the pharyngeal muscles results in a sidewise constriction of the opening into the throat, the second method causes a constriction from top to bottom. It is also more of a valve-type action.

Double Problem

Just how independent these two processes are, or can be, is problematical. In all likelihood the player afflicted with a closed throat is suffering from a combination of both. The air passageway is therefore made smaller in all directions, from top to

bottom as well as from side to side. Under these circumstances it is conceivable to close the throat so completely that no breath is able to pass.

Perhaps the reason that so many players of brass instruments are burdened with a closed throat is that

they tried to progress too rapidly at the beginning of their instruction. They probably attempted to play the upper tones before they should have. Not having had developed, as yet, sufficient ability to control the breath for the production of high tones, they reverted to the highly unmusical process of "squeezing" them out thru a partially closed throat. Such a practice develops very rapidly into a habit from which extrication becomes increasingly difficult as time passes.

About the only way to break the habit is to concentrate on breathing.

Effective management of the breath will eliminate the closed throat for most persons who are afflicted with it. For relieving momentary tenseness in the throat and to broaden the opening, simulating a yawn may prove helpful.

Since the breathing process, especially as employed in performing on a wind instrument, is a complicated thing, future articles will deal with it in detail.

FINE

211

Improving Intonation
with the
Third Valve Slide and First Valve Trigger

Clifford Lillya

CORNET AND TRUMPET students should learn to adjust the third valve slide while playing. Early use of this slide need consist only of extension when playing low D (D4) or C♯ (C♯4).

When a student first tries to adjust the slide while in playing position, he may find that he jars the instrument. Therefore, it is best to start with situations which permit adjustment during a rest or breath rather than while sustaining a tone.

The D major and D♭ major arpeggios also constitute good exercises for learning to use the third valve slide. The slide is left extended for the former; for the latter, it must be brought back in for the A♭'s.

Lipping

Some teachers regard the movement of the slide as a complicating rather than simplifying technique. These teachers prefer to have the student "favor" the pitch by adjusting the embouchure.

This can be done, and all players use this quality of adaptability, mostly without being aware of doing so. Some who have learned to play D4 in tune come to feel that they have "blown the instrument in tune." However this may be, we know that by moving the slide we can make it easier to play in tune without impairing the sound.

Movable Slides Not New

Since the invention of valves (1813) players and instrument makers have recognized that perfect intonation could not be an inherent characteristic of the cornet or trumpet. J. B. Arban, in his *Complete Conservatory Method* (published in 1864) said:

"A well constructed cornet ought to be so mounted that the thumb of the left hand should be able to enter the ring of the tuning slide, and open and shut it at pleasure, without the help of the right hand. It is then possible to regulate the pitch of the instrument while playing . . . The slide is also used for the purpose of equalizing all those notes which, in the course of natural production, are rendered too high. Each valve is tuned for separate use, and the natural consequence is that when several are employed simultaneously the slides get too short and the precision of tone is inevitably affected."

Experimentation has gone on continually, and while the idea of the *movable tuning slide* is still with us, a majority of players seem to have gravitated to the *mobile third valve slide.*

Other Possible Corrections

A player who is willing to use the third valve slide may safely have his slide made a trifle shorter than the standard (fixed position) length. This tuning not only corrects E♭4 and all A♭'s, which on many instruments are too low, but makes possible the more frequent use of the third valve alone, as an alternate for the combination of first and second.

The student who understands this much about the theory of tuning is in a position to choose fingerings appropriate to a given musical passage and situation, rather than to think of fingerings as being arbitrarily "real" or "false."

The use of the mobile third valve slide may begin on an elementary level, and become more complex as the player matures. If the teacher chooses materials and does not demand achievements that are beyond the student's level of proficiency, the slide manipulation will be learned without confusion.

The movable third valve slide is not the only device that players use to aid intonation and tone quality, although it is perhaps the most common one. Some players prefer to alter the length of the first valve slide, usually by means of a "trigger." Others like to have *both* the first and third valve slides adjustable.

1st Valve Trigger

What can be accomplished with a first valve trigger? Obviously, we can control (within limits) the intonation of any note which requires use of the first valve slide. However, if the instrument is constructed by the manufacturer with the first valve slide a trifle short (to bring C♯ and D5 in tune), we are apt to find that certain tones requiring the first and second valves in combination are too sharp for comfort in some situations. Therefore, when we play sustained tones on E4, A4, E5, and A5 we must often count on using the extension device, or on having recourse to the third valve alone.

Complex Picture

To use the third valve alone is often the best solution, but one which is not always feasible. When the student begins to weigh the factors governing the use of the first valve trigger he soon discovers that its area of function is not so clearly defined as that of the movable third valve slide. Sometimes, solving one problem creates another, and a choice can best be made in terms of a particular musical context.

There are four general categories of tuning problems which involve the manipulation of the first valve trigger. The first category includes those situations which can be handled with either the first or the third valve slide (1-3 and 1-2-3).

In many instances pitch may be controlled equally well with either slide, but there are times when altering the first valve slide is easier than altering the third. For example:

A second type of circumstance stems from the aforementioned tendency of the first and second valve combination to be sharp. The outlines of this problem are difficult to clarify. They vary with individual instruments and players, sometimes from day to day. However, the following quotations may be considered as being typical of the second kind of intonation which can be alleviated by adjusting the first valve slide:

From top to bottom: 3rd valve slide retracted (normal position); 3rd valve slide extended, by pushing the ring outward; 1st valve slide retracted (normal position); 1st valve slide extended, by pushing the trigger with thumb.

An especially effective use of the first valve trigger is found in the rapid alternation of two tones. Trills are generally more secure and distinct if the longer tubing is on the lower note. The student will find that in the following examples, the fingering is smooth, and can be perfectly in tune if the first valve slide is slightly elongated:

Ensemble Playing

The category of band and orchestra playing embraces all of the previously mentioned species of intonation adjustments, but they take on a little different cast. Here the emphasis is on pitch in relation to the tonal center of a group.

Happily, there is often more time to use the adjustment devices in orchestral music than in solo literature. Often, after a number of measures of rest, the music calls for a sustained tone which must fit into a chord structure. In passages of this kind the mechanism on the first valve can become very valuable.

A case in point is the following brief quotation from the *Symphony in D Minor* by Cesar Franck:

Notice that if the player uses the third valve slide he must move it when going from 1-3 to 2-3. But if he lengthens the first valve slide he can leave it in the extended position throughout the passage.

For Advanced Students

There is no pat formula covering the use of the first valve slide trigger. Learning to use it should be a gradual thing, arising out of the need of the student, rather than the teacher's decree. Since this implies mature judgment, and since the actual working of the mechanism requires some skill, this had best not be forced on the student before he is ready for it.

The movable slides, then, are plainly not a panacea but a supplement to the natural flexibility of the instrument. Of the two, the first valve slide is in the more sensitive position. At least an elementary understanding of the slide lengths, in relation to the open series and to each other, is necessary for intelligent adjustment. Use the movable slides, but do not expect miracles!

FINE

Discriminating

Use of the Tongue

Harold Brasch

STUDENTS OF BRASS instruments often seem more concerned with tonguing problems than with difficulties arising over tone, intonation, interpretation, or endurance. Tonguing is a very important factor in good brass playing, and it should receive its proper share of attention.

To the average student, however, tonguing is something involved in technical displays, something that suggests the execution of a difficult passage, something that requires speed as in triple-tongue variations. On the other hand, to a *discriminating* player "attack" is what the word implies.

Styles of Tonguing

Good attack is the secret of the symphony trumpeter's ability to play extremely high or low tones either "pp" or "ff". Proper attack also implies the ability to play a song with good taste. The problem of what is good or proper in each instance is a difficult one because there are no hard and fast rules. The musicianship of the player tells him how to perform.

From the mechanical standpoint of being able to produce the various tonguing styles, what is difficult for one performer often comes easily to another. Then, too, since no two players are physically identical, it follows that different bone structure of the face and the teeth and differences in the gums and the lips may well alter circumstances a little.

Inadequacy of Method Books

Method books have very little to say as to the *use* of the various methods of tonguing. Most seem limited to the directions of using *ta* and *la*, the syllables used for staccato and legato styles. What about the use of *da* in the legato attack? The results often seem more effective, and this syllable is an easier function for the tongue to perform.

What is our aim for the legato? It is to play a song or lyrical passage exactly as it would be sung by a competent vocalist. Strange as it may seem, most of us can sing, whistle, or hum a well-known song in quite a natural fashion. Then we pick up an instrument and proceed to mutilate the same song. *Ta-ta-ta-taaa* is the chief fault; *ta-ta-ta-daaa* would be far better. We should learn to interpret a song on our instruments as well as we hum or whistle. This will require neither expensive tutoring nor method books; only thoughtful consideration is needed while in your practice room.

Vary the Tongue Syllable

It should be noted that *ta* and *da* are used in the middle register only. *Tee* and *dee* are correct syllables for higher notes, and *too* and *doo* should be used for low tones. An ascending tongued interval is produced more easily if *ta* is used for the first tone and *tee* for the second; the same notes are slurred *ta—ee*. In descending intervals the syllables would be *tee—ta* when tonguing and *tee—aa* when slurring. Tonguing has a direct bearing on producing intervals, whether large or small, whether detached or slurred. Even what is normally called a lip trill is an exercise for the tongue as well.

Experiment Intelligently

As to the *exact* position and motion of the tongue, we can generalize only. One player's individual needs and peculiarities may differ greatly from those of another. A bit of experimentation can be very beneficial; if confined to the tongue (embouchure experimentation is not advisable), it should cause no harm.

Usually when playing loud more of the tongue is used than when playing softly. Most brass players form the attack directly behind the upper teeth—some heavily, others lightly. For a few, the tongue touches both upper and lower teeth; or it may even be slightly between the teeth, touching the lower lip. This is the position I prefer on baritone, although it might not be best for others.

In any case, better results are obtained when the tongue is loose and relaxed; this can be achieved by practicing softly at first.

Let careful observation be our greatest teacher.

FINE—

Breath Support and Tone Placement Considerations

Robert Grocock

ONE OF THE MOST difficult problems in teaching the brasses is that of keeping the stroke of the tongue the same, in hardness or lightness, throughout dynamic or register changes. The student's tendency is to strike harder with the tongue when playing louder or when entering the upper register of the instrument, with a resultant variation in tone quality. I have found the following steps helpful in overcoming this:

Maintain Breath Support

The student will not be able to articulate correctly unless his breath support is constant and sufficient. Therefore, it is important that the student be required to demonstrate easy production and good tone throughout the playing of a passage without recourse to the tongue. For example, a scale passage should be practiced quite slowly, first *piano* and then *forte*. The tone quality in both instances should be open and (in the case of *piano*) not squeezed nor (in the case of *forte*) forced.

It should be made clear to the student that breath support is not dependent upon the dynamic level; proper support from the breathing muscles is just as important in soft playing as in loud playing, for *piano* is not synonymous with weak, nor *forte* with strong. Whereas to achieve proper support, a conscious physical movement has to be experienced, in the case of dynamic change the process is largely mental and the physical adjustments unconscious or involuntary.

Start Tone with Breath

In articulating the scale the stu-
dent should never lose sight of the fact that the tone is instigated by the breath mechanism, not by the tongue. If he will apply this knowledge correctly, his tonguing will not become harder when he plays louder, for he will realize that the increase in volume is caused by the emission of more air—not by a harder stroke of the tongue, which will tend only to tense the throat muscles and make the tone harsh or strident. The aim should be to have a clean, consistently light tongue stroke in all registers and with a tone quality equal to that of legato passages.

If the student is required to play passages slurred, then tongued, he can check for himself if his quality, breath support, and ease of production remain equal.

Place Tone in Mouth

The basis of proper articulation lies in proper breath support coupled with correct placement of the tone within the mouth. The latter is often neglected in teaching and is very often the basic cause of a pinched tone quality or improper use of the tongue. All tones should be placed forward in the mouth. This is especially important in the upper register.

If in ascending a scale the tone quality becomes thinner, the embouchure pinched, and the throat tighter (a very common threesome!), ask the student to sing the scale with *tee* and to notice where the tones go as he ascends, back toward the throat or toward the front of his mouth. If they go back, demonstrate for him (in singing and playing) how tone production is affected by incorrect, then correct, placement. It should be mentioned here that it
is most useful from a teaching standpoint to be able to demonstrate incorrect procedures as well as correct ones. The feeling of "forwardness" can be acquired, generally, in one of three ways:

1. By a vocal approach, having the student change to falsetto instead of straining his voice as he ascends the scale, and then applying this sensation to the instrument.

2. By thinking of blowing all tones toward the mouthpiece.

3. By projecting each ascending tone farther away (for example, aim F5 at the music stand and keep projecting the tone away as you ascend so that by the time F6 is reached you are aiming for the far end of the room). Once this technique is acquired the pinched embouchure and tight throat will clear up, and the tongue will not have to work harder in tonguing to compensate for poor tone placement.

This is the reason for having the student play the scale passage at a *piano* level at first. The tones will not speak unless they are properly placed, whereas at a *forte* level forcing can often disguise to the student (if not the teacher) that the tone is not being produced correctly.

By having the student play the passage slurred, then tongued, with emphasis on ease of identical production, correct placement, and breath support, he will be enabled to gain a concept of articulation ON a stream of air (much like running the hand back and forth under an open faucet) which will result ultimately in a clean, light articulation in all registers and at all dynamic levels.

FINE.

Concerning Attack and Release

William Whybrew

ATTACK IS A BASIC factor in brass instrument performance and many advanced players as well as young students find themselves confronted with problems in this respect. These problems vary in degree of subtlety, perhaps, but many stem from a common basis. An analysis of the attack, leading to a clearer understanding of the functions of the various elements involved, can be of great help in overcoming these difficulties.

The elements actively involved in making the attack on a brass instrument are the breath and the tongue. The lips, although a very important factor in producing the tone, play no active part in making the attack. Failure of the lips to respond to the breath with free and even vibrations admittedly constitutes a cause of poor attacks, but the fault then is one of basic tone production rather than specifically of attack.

Function of the Tongue

The role of the tongue in making the attack is that which is, perhaps, understood least clearly. In preparation for the attack the tongue is placed forward in the mouth with the tip against the upper teeth or even against the upper gum in the roof of the mouth. It then functions as a kind of valve, holding back the breath until the instant when the tone is to begin. Then it is drawn back and down in the mouth allowing the breath to pass between the lips, causing them to vibrate.

Some players and teachers may prefer slightly different preparatory positions of the tongue, but its function is the same no matter what the preparatory position. We might compare the tongue to a floodgate holding back a mass of water which pushes against the gate seeking to escape. When the floodgate is withdrawn from its path, the water bursts forth.

Cause of Poor Attacks

This brings us to the cause of many poor attacks, failure to prepare the breath. Many young players attempt to start the air stream at the same instant that the tongue is moved back away from the teeth. This results in "blowing at the horn" and in missed or unclean attacks. It frequently is the cause of the undesirable jaw movement of which some players are guilty, largely because they try to *project*, rather than *release,* the breath into the instrument.

The original impetus for the air stream, the pushing action of the diaphragm, must *precede* the withdrawing movement of the tongue so that the breath is ready behind the tongue before the latter is moved away from the teeth.

In actual performance this sequence of preparation and execution of attack occurs so quickly that the performer attends to it automatically; and when notes occur in close succession, steady diaphragm support ensures preparation for all attacks except the first. It is the initial note of a phrase which is so often poorly attacked and for which special care must be taken to prepare the breath. For purposes of illustration and practice it is possible to separate the steps of the attack consciously and thus to exaggerate the preparation of the breath.

Another undesirable consequence of failing to prepare the breath adequately for the attack is the "wah" or, even when the tongue functions correctly, the "t-wah" effect which is heard all too frequently. This spreading of notes results when the flow of breath is suddenly increased in volume immediately after the attack.

Sharpness of Attack

Not infrequently one hears the term "staccato attack." It would be more accurate to speak only of degrees of sharpness of attack, or of

sharp and soft attacks, since staccato is really a matter of release rather than of attack.

Sharpness of attack is determined by the speed with which the tongue is drawn back from its forward position. For a sharp *tee* attack the tongue is snapped back with a very fast and vigorous motion, allowing the breath to escape suddenly. Softer attacks are accomplished by more gentle movements of the tongue such as *da* or *du.*

Weight of attack, on the other hand, is determined by the degree of diaphragmatic pressure and consequent volume of breath. For accented or heavy attacks, strong diaphragm pressure and a quick snap of the tongue are required. When a sharp accent with less weight is desired, the same snap of the tongue may be used but accompanied by less diaphragm pressure and less volume of breath. The diaphragm pressure mentioned here is, of course, in addition to the steady support which must be constantly maintained in all brass playing.

Some players attempt to give a separate impulse of the diaphragm for each attack. This is to be avoided. When notes are separated by time intervals sufficient to give each the character of a fresh beginning, the diaphragm may indeed be relaxed between notes and the breath prepared afresh for each attack. However, when notes occur more closely together, even tho separated by brief rests, the diaphragm should remain firm throughout the phrase, thus keeping the breath constantly in preparation for the attacks.

Releasing Notes

The release of notes presents another problem to brass players and teachers. *In teaching it is a difficult problem to solve through positive means. Most readers are probably familiar with the usual incorrect methods of terminating tones on brass instruments.* The most common error is the cutting off of the air stream by returning the tongue to the attack position, causing an abrupt, chopped effect and robbing the note of resonance and quality— the "tat" effect. A somewhat similar effect is attained by cutting off the air stream by closing the aperture in the lips. These two faulty methods of terminating notes also frequently inhibit development of light, fast tonguing since the former causes the tongue to become tight and stiff and the latter involves excess movement.

A note is properly released by turning off the flow of breath at its source rather than by re-imposing the tongue as a block or by clamping the lips together. This does *not* mean,

however, that the flow of breath is stopped by relaxing the diaphragm. If the diaphragm is relaxed *before* the termination of the sound, even by an instant, the result will be a flatting in pitch at the end of the note.

It is much easier to explain how the sound should not be stopped than it is to explain just how the flow of breath is turned off. Fortunately, however, it is not too difficult to illustrate the proper release. Sing a short "ha" syllable, being sure to hold the diaphragm firm even after the sound stops and being sure to terminate the sound with the vowel. Now, just how was the flow of breath turned off? Certainly not by relaxing the diaphragm, since it was held firm after the sound had stopped. And neither tongue nor lips cut off the

breath if the sound was terminated with the vowel. But we have the desired effect—a note with quality and resonance and with a nicely rounded release.

Performance on any music instrument is a unified act, the elements of which must be so closely co-ordinated as to defy conscious analysis during execution. An overly analytical approach to performance can, indeed, result in a self-conscious and stilted style and at times even impede progress. However, for the teacher, who must guide the development of his students and who must be prepared to diagnose problems and to suggest solutions, the clarity of understanding attained thru analysis is indispensable.

FINE

October, 1957

Brass Teaching for String Players

Daniel Tetzlaff

THERE ARE MANY similarities in the playing of string instruments as compared with the playing of the brasses. It is to the teacher's advantage to have these similarities clearly in mind. None of us can really claim an *equal* knowledge of all instruments; hence, it is logical to transfer, whenever possible, something from your strong side over to a weaker side. I'm thinking especially now of string teachers who would like to fill in some on their lesser acquaintance with the brasses.

Starting Beginners

The number one problem with most beginners is their lack of "know-how" to guide them. It is clearly the teacher's job to instill confidence by providing the information and instruction that will enable the beginners to produce some "healthy sounds."

We know that this will take a few weeks, but it certainly need not take years and years! However, it may take many repeated tellings. There just cannot be too many ways of explaining things in group teaching.

Brass beginners usually have no tone. With strings it is caused by "no bow," with brasses it is "no blow." Even in grade schools this

can be explained and the children can grasp it in just a little time. Students can quickly demonstrate to themselves and to others that to get a better tone it is necessary to use more bow (strings), or to blow more (brasses). When this light dawns on them, it continues to burn bright and clear in their memory. It is a simple matter then to stop the class when there is insufficient tone, and ask why. Each group will be only too glad to point out the other's faults— "not enough bow," or, "you are running out of breath and forgetting to blow."

Surprisingly mature results will come if the teacher constantly demands of the brasses, "take in more air, take a *big* breath now, fill up all you can. Now, use more gas to drive that machine." And for the strings, "please, not just little two inch strokes in the middle of the bow; loosen up that elbow and get that lower arm swinging like a hinge to keep the bow moving—longer, swifter, right on out to the tip."

Holding the String

When string beginners first put their fingers to the fingerboard in an attempt to go up the scale, they often fail to hold the fingers down firmly. Also, the dull thud of blurred and foggy pitch that is the first pizzicato is quite disappointing. But what fun it is to hear this clear up as soon as the student is reminded to hold the finger hard to the fingerboard. This stops the string at a definite place, and now a definite pitch comes out good and clear.

Watch the brasses for similar lack of firmness, *in the face muscles*. The muscles of the cheeks and lips must be held firmly inward toward the teeth and gums for the support and strength necessary for (1) a clear tone, (2) ascent into the higher register, and (3) control of pitch.

Brass players who have weak or flabby lips (with air pockets under them) or cheeks that puff out will *never* be able to demonstrate any control of a clear tone or accurate intonation in any register. Lips supported correctly and firmly show dimples in the corners of the mouth. Look for them, and have the students look for them by practicing occasionally in front of a mirror.

Going Higher

A second problem on brass instruments, especially the cornet, trumpet, and French Horn, is going into the high register. To make a string sound a higher pitch, one of two things can be done. It can be stretched tighter, or its length can be made shorter. The brass player's lips are his string. Which shall it be, stretch or shorten?

In the old days the smiling (stretch) system was advocated for brass players, and—to a degree—it was successful. It seemed tho that one could stretch only so far; then that was the end of it. Seldom were

trumpet parts ever written above G5 (G above the staff). Anyone who could go higher was said to have a "freak lip." Maybe these players were just those who first discovered you could go higher and with greater ease and better tone if you *shortened* the vibrator rather than *stretched* it (like any string player does). Also, as any string player well knows, the tighter a string is stretched, the sooner it is injured or worn out.

To play the high register on the brasses, first the vibrating length of the "string" (the mouth) is shortened by buttoning down the corners of the mouth. This acts just like the nut and the bridge do to confine the vibrating length of a violin string to its middle portion. This part of the "string" is then tensed by holding the lip flesh sufficiently firm against the teeth and gums to give this "string" its characteristic tone, which is naturally brighter and clearer the higher it is to sound. Thus, more tension is required for the trumpet embouchure than for the French Horn or the trombone, because (1) the instrument is higher in pitch and (2) a brighter tone color is one of its true characteristics.

The high register of the trumpet definitely does not depend upon hope. Rather, it depends upon the player's development of muscular strength enough (1) to *set* and *hold* the lip muscles for quite a long time and at quite high tension, and (2) to contract the muscles more and more in order to go higher and higher.

Tone and Resonance

A cigar box violin is hardly a string performer's idea of the ideal music instrument. String players would like to own a fine instrument that has as rich and as ringing a sound as possible. This means an instrument that vibrates profusely, one that emanates all overtones possible.

It is one of the most incongruous and fantastic paradoxes of this hi-fi age that there is such a love in the schools for *lo-fi brass.* Beware of muffled tubas, giant bell trombones that sound like fog horns, French Horns stuffed up to the hilt with fists, cornets played *peep-peep-peep* and into the racks yet. And trumpets? Stop! That's a dirty word. We don't even use them!!! Oh well, maybe if this is pushed just a little more, orches-

tras will come back sooner than you think—automatically. For who will want to sit in the graveyard with all those dead brasses?

Knowing that the tone and resonance of the violin family is very much in the hands of the instrument maker, I would still like to compare some parts of the body of a good string instrument to the body of a brass instrument *performer*.

1. Lips (and strings) held more taut sound more brilliant.
2. Lips (and strings) that are thinner (by nature) sound more brilliant.
3. Lips (and strings) that are thicker have more low overtones.
4. Lips (and strings) that are held loosely give off low (but few high) overtones.

The body of the violin being—in reality—a sound box is, then, the instrument's main resonator. No string instrument maker would think of trying to increase resonance by *squeezing it together.* On the contrary, and especially with some violas and basses, there is often the attempt to "open up the tone" by increasing the instrument size almost to "oversize."

For similar resonance and added richness, the brass player must get rid of the idea of squeezing out the tone, not only from the instrument but mostly from *within himself.* For full resonance the brass player must have a well-supported air column (diaphragm support) without any tightening in the throat. There is no rich sound from a collapsed sound post, nor from a collapsed air column in a performer's body.

A common brass fault is that of trying to ascend to a higher note in an interval jump mainly with a heavy push of air. When this causes a noticeable bumping of the sound, it destroys the smoothness all slurs should have. The mistake is in trying to assign "an auxiliary helper" more than his fair share of the load. Steady air is needed for all smooth slurs. The heavy push is a poor-sounding substitute for genuine lip flexibility which will change the notes smoothly and with accurate (instead of approximate) intonation. When the violinist plays slurred intervals, his bow just keeps moving steadily and the fingers of the left hand take care of the note changes. Let the brass student take his cue from this principle.

FINE

Materials for Mouthpieces

Francis Wilcox

IT HAS BEEN about five years since *The Instrumentalist* published the "Symposium on Brass Mouthpieces" (November-December, 1952). Recently I completed some research which should be appended to the symposium. The effects of making trumpet mouthpieces from materials other than brass were investigated.

Why?

Many persons have asked "Why do this research? Nearly everyone uses brass mouthpieces. Haven't they been proved to be the best?" Yes, nearly everyone uses brass mouthpieces, but as far as could be determined no systematic controlled study of other materials had ever been made. With modern technology it is hazardous to say that brass is the best material just because it has been doing a good job for many years. Any contention of this sort needs to be established scientifically.

13 Materials Selected

A questionnaire, asking for information about materials other than brass, was sent to 27 instrument and mouthpiece manufacturers. Results were compiled from 26 replies. This information plus historical research was used to aid in selecting the materials for the study: Aluminum Alloy, Leaded Phosphor Bronze, Tellurium Copper, 444 Bronze, Heat-Treatable Steel, Teflon, Nylon, Rexolite, Lucite, Dirilyte, Coin Silver, and Sterling Silver. Free Cutting Brass was included as the standard material.

20 Mouthpieces Made

Regular trumpet mouthpieces were made from all of the materials, and skeletonized (thinned walls of cup and throat) mouthpieces were made from each of the metals except coin silver and sterling silver. They were made by Renold O. Schilke (whose "Dimensional Characteristics of Brass Mouthpieces" was Part I of the original symposium). Without his skill and personally designed equip-

ment the dimensional stability of the mouthpieces could not have been maintained. The greatest variation in dimensions from the brass mouthpiece was within plus or minus .004 inch, and most of the mouthpieces were within plus or minus .001 inch.

It is probably apparent that the reasoning behind the experiments was this: If the mouthpieces have the same shape and the experimental conditions are controlled, then any difference in results would be due to the materials and or skeletonization.

Mechanical Testing

The mechanical testing was done in an acoustically constructed room, using tones produced by a mechanical embouchure, and controlled in such a way that air pressure ratings—as well as tone qualities—could be compared. A vibralizer, which shows the strength of the overtones, was used to compare tone qualities. The mechanical testing was done at C. G. Conn, Ltd., in the only laboratory equipped for this kind of experimentation.

Player Testing

Player testing was done by three groups of testers: ten college students who had had beginning instruction on trumpet, ten college students who were trumpet majors, and ten professional performers on trumpet. The testers used rating sheets to rate the experimental mouthpieces as compared to the standard brass mouthpiece. After the tester had completed the rating sheets, he was asked to choose the mouthpieces which he preferred as first and second choices—by a process of elimination.

Results

1. Plastics were the only materials which displayed a measurable difference in tone quality.

2. The only mouthpieces which had a definite and consistently different feel were the plastics. Usually, this *feel* was not preferred by the testers.

3. Plastic and aluminum mouthpieces used less air pressure than the brass mouthpiece. Aluminum skeletonized used less than the regular aluminum. The skeletonized steel mouthpiece used more air pressure than the brass mouthpiece.

4. The mouthpieces most often chosen as the ones preferred were: skeletonized aluminum—7 times, regular brass—6 times, regular aluminum—3 times, and skeletonized steel —3 times. None of the others were chosen more than twice. The four mouthpieces mentioned accounted for 19 of the 30 tests, an impressive number considering there were 20 mouthpieces from which to choose.

These are some of the major results of the testing. They are not necessarily true for any other conditions than those of the testing procedures, but would it be safe now to say that brass is the best material for trumpet mouthpieces?

Possibilities for Improvement

Judging from the results of the experiments, lightness of weight is a critical factor in ease of response. This presents many possibilities for improvement, not only for the experienced performer but also for the student. During the course of the experiments there was evidence that the students with *excess tension* and *squeezed tone* would choose mouthpieces with less resistance, and students who had a tendency to overblow would choose mouthpieces with more resistance. It seems probable that differences in response could be an invaluable aid to teachers.

A mouthpiece which would not need plating would be a definite advantage. Not only would dimensional stability in manufacture be improved, but the cost and nuisance of plating and replating would be eliminated. Solid silver is very good, but it is extremely expensive. Two other materials stood up well during the tests. Dirilyte, a type of aluminum bronze produced commercially for tableware, responded in much the same manner as brass as far as tone quality, etc., were concerned. It did not corrode or discolor nearly as fast as most of the other metals in the test. This material is comparable to brass in price, but it is somewhat more difficult to machine.

Aluminum had been reported by mouthpiece manufacturers to be unsatisfactory because it would corrode, but the aluminum alloy mouthpieces in this experiment have not shown signs of corrosion. There are many types of aluminum alloy, and further research would show which ones are the most satisfactory for mouthpiece use. Most aluminum alloys machine readily and are about half the price of brass. Besides being economical, there is also the possibility of differences in ease of response with aluminum alloys.

Research Needed

These experiments have only scratched the surface of mouthpiece research. There is still much to be done, not only with mouthpieces but in many phases of music instruments. Teachers and performers should insist upon answers backed by research when asking questions about instruments. When systematic research has been applied to any area of human knowledge it has moved forward by leaps and bounds. Instrument builders would be more than repayed for additional investment in research.

FINE

Middle and Low Registers on French Horn

Joseph Schmoll

THE DOUBLE HORN is the most popular French horn today because it combines the advantages of the F horn and of the B♭ horn. The tonal color of the F horn is considered to have greater beauty, especially in the middle and low range; but it is more difficult to play in the high register. The timbre of the B♭ horn is considered to be just as beautiful as the quality of tone of the F horn in the high register, but it is thought to be rough and out of tune in the middle and low register. For this reason, most horn players use the F horn in the range of

![musical notation] to around ![musical notation]

Above these pitches (G4 to D5). or even E5 or F5, depending upon the individual preference of the performer, the thumb key is depressed and the remaining higher notes are played on the B♭ horn.

There are a number of advantages in using the B♭ horn occasionally in the middle and low registers, however, and I would like to point them out.

Low Notes on B♭ Horn

A close proximity to the characteristic F horn quality can be achieved in the middle and low ranges by closing the bell slightly with the right hand, by exercising restraint in blowing *piano* to *mezzo forte* passages, and by a conscious effort to match the tonal color of the F horn. There is a tendency for the pitch of the B♭ horn to be sharp in the lower range. Partially closing the bell with the right hand will produce the correct adjustment, after some experimentation. When this technique is mastered, even the most experienced observer will have difficulty in discerning which horn is being used.

Most performers play practically all the pitches of the middle and low registers on the B♭ horn with the exception of the following notes which are played on the F horn. However, some players may prefer to add or subtract some notes:

When playing in an ensemble and making an entry in the low or middle register after a rest, the performer will find that if he plays the first note or two on the B♭ horn his entry will be more secure. If he prefers, he can play the remainder

220

of the passage on the F horn. For example, the following two excerpts

from *The Flying Dutchman* by Richard Wagner can be played more securely, if the E4's and E♭4's are played on the B♭ horn.

An isolated sustained note or a group of repeated notes will be easier to attack on the B♭ horn. The third movement of the Mozart *Concerto No. 2 for Horn* contains an example of this:

After a seven measure rest, the horn enters playing repeated notes. If performed on the B♭ horn there is less chance of breaking the first note, and in addition the group of notes will sound with a clearer and crisper staccato.

Another advantage of using the B♭ horn in these registers, is that the performer can play louder with ease. When executing a solo passage, part of which lies in the middle register, the use of the B♭ horn will help to make the solo heard above the rest of the orchestra. The following passage from the *Concerto No. 1 for Piano and Orchestra* by Franz Liszt is an illustration:

In fast passages it is much easier to use the B♭ horn entirely and avoid the awkward fingering which results from constantly changing from horn to horn. This passage from Wagner's *Lohengrin* is an example:

Since this is written for horn in

G, transposition is involved. The first four notes of the first horn part are F♯, A, D, F♯. By depressing the first and second valves and playing on the B♭ horn, the need for further valve change for these notes is eliminated. This passage is played at a fast tempo. When the second horn part is transposed, the first four notes are D, F♯, A, D. Again the first and second valves on the B♭ horn can be used for all four notes.

Overtone Series

With no valves depressed the following notes can be sounded on the B♭ horn:

Therefore, when performing an F major arpeggio, the performer can take advantage of the overtone series. He will not have to use the valves, except for the A3 which requires the use of the first and second valves:

With one valve pressed down the following notes will sound:

The E♭ major arpeggio then can be played with one valve depressed.

When pressing down the second valve, the following notes are yielded:

It is apparent that the E major arpeggio can be played on the B♭ horn with only the second valve depressed.

With the first and second valves pressed down the following notes are possible:

We have a D major arpeggio.

The depression of the second and third valves will produce the following notes:

The C♯ major arpeggio can easily be played with this valve combination.

It is apparent, then, that the preceding arpeggios can be played in their entirety on the B♭ horn. Clumsy fingerings, which result when the performer constantly changes from F horn to B♭ horn, are eliminated. The reason for this simplicity of fingering is, of course, that the pitches fit into the overtone series for each valve combination.

Avoiding Awkward Changes

This passage from Haydn's *Oxford Symphony*, if performed on the F horn, would require constant valve changes. Since this is for G horn, the performer plays the D's an octave apart, alternately. By using the B♭ horn, the first and second valves can be depressed for both D's. This not only simplifies the fingering, but the pitches will be sounded more clearly with less effort:

In the third movement of the *Concerto No. 3* by Mozart, there is this melody for the horn near the close of the composition:

This is written for E♭ horn, and the transposition downward of a major second has to be considered. The whole passage, if played on the B♭ horn will be more secure and easier to finger. The pickup note and first complete measure can be played: open, first valve, first and second valves, open, and so forth. It is true that it can be played entirely on the F horn with the first valve depressed, but the performer does not enjoy the security and sureness which the B♭ horn affords.

The fifth complete measure can be executed more easily on the B♭ horn since it involves, except for D (which requires the first and second valve), an alteration between first valve and open. This is an easy fingering for a horn player.

Other Advantages

The final three measures of the Mozart *Concerto No. 3 for Horn* when played on the B♭ horn can be played louder with ease:

There is a tendency for the orchestra to overpower the horn here, so additional volume and brilliance is desirable.

In the first movement of the *Trio for Piano, Violin, and Horn* by Brahms, at the end of the first theme, there is a tendency on the part of the performer not to give the third note of the quoted example equal prominence with the other notes:

By playing this pitch on the B♭ horn, it will sound clearer with less effort. If this is done, it is advisable to play the preceding two notes on the B♭ horn as well.

In the second movement of the same work by Brahms, the opening horn melody is easier to play if executed entirely on the B♭ horn. Again the music is written for E♭ horn:

The octave leaps do not require any change of fingering, for the D's can be played with first and second valves depressed, and the octave leap of F to F can be played with no valves at all. The use of the B♭ horn on the low notes makes it easier for them to be played louder and more distinctly.

In the following etude by Gallay the use of the B♭ horn for the entire quoted excerpt eliminates the continual use of the thumb key:

Later this figure is encountered:

If one were to alternate horns, especially in the second half of each measure, the timing of the fingering would become a very difficult problem. By playing all notes on the B♭ horn the passage sounds smoother and is easier to play.

Large leaps from the middle register to the high register can be played more easily if the last note or notes of the middle range are executed on the B♭ horn. The following example taken from a study by Belloli is an instance:

If the D4 is played on the F horn and the following A♭5 is played on the B♭ horn, there is a possibility that a break will occur on one of these notes. By playing the D on the B♭ horn, this possibility is minimized.

Another example of this same kind of problem is in a study by Gugel, from which the following excerpt is taken:

In the first complete measure, the first note can be played on the B♭ horn, or if the performer prefers, all four notes of the preceding incomplete measure can be played on the B♭ horn. The last four notes of this example again present the same problem. The use of the B♭ horn on the low note, as well as the high note on the large leap, will make it much easier to perform and with less chance of a break.

When a trill feels awkward on the F horn, it is worth-while to try it on the B♭ horn. The following trill

if played on the F horn, can be executed by playing the G with no valves depressed, and the A with the third valve. It is awkward for some performers to operate the third valve rapidly. If the trill is played on the B♭ horn, the G is played with the first valve pressed down and the A with no valves. An alternation between first valve and "open," is much easier for most performers.

The advantages of using the B♭ horn in the middle and low ranges are the lessening of the tendency to break notes, the elimination of complicated fingerings in fast passages, greater sureness in negotiating large leaps at fast tempi, the achievement of *forte* and *fortissimo* dynamic levels with greater ease, and less difficulty in the execution of some trills.

In spite of the advantages enumerated for using the B♭ horn, the F horn is the one usually best suited to low and middle register playing. However, the performer should not think there is any inflexible rule governing the use of the thumb valve. Instead, he should approach each problem with the intent of solving it in the simplest way.

A thorough knowledge of the fingering of the B♭ horn is essential and this can be gained by daily practice. Since many of the fingerings of the B♭ horn are the same as those of the F horn, this should not be difficult. Part of the daily *warmup* exercises can be practiced on the B♭ horn, especially scales and arpeggios, until the fingering becomes automatic and can be interspersed with F horn fingering at will.

EDITOR'S NOTE: Non-horn majors can easily determine B♭ horn fingerings by thinking of the actual concert pitch of the notes and applying baritone (bass clef) fingerings. Occasionally valve 3 sounds better in tune than 1-2. On the double horn, finger G♯3 with 2-3 and A4 with 1-2 on BOTH horns. This plus the material in this article will give you a complete understanding of fingering. The B♭ horn is not hand muted, so there are no additional fingering problems.

FINE

1958

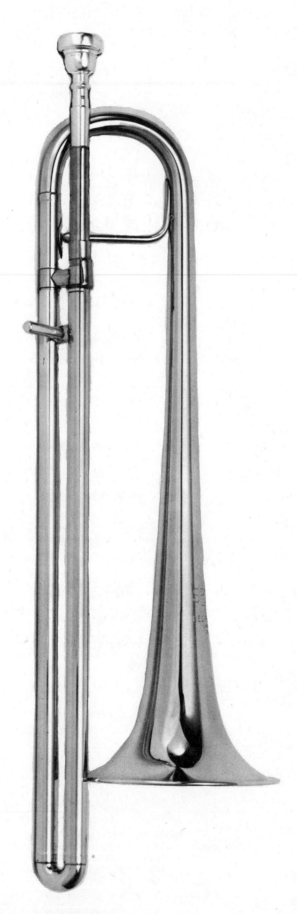

B♭ Slide Trumpet (Soprano Trombone)

Valve Brass Intonation

Can brass instruments be blown out of tune?

Vincent Bach

THIS QUESTION cannot be called controversial because anyone who is familiar with the construction and acoustics of brass instruments will know that the intonation of the open tones (harmonics) and the relation of the pitch of the overtones to the fundamental tone depend entirely upon the proportions of the conical bore of the instrument. This, of course, includes the bore of the mouthpiece.

There is no music instrument with absolutely perfect intonation, and there never will be one because the natural scale is not in tune. If a piano is tuned correctly to the pitch of C major, when it is played in the key of D — or any other key — a number of the white keys will require different vibrations than those obtained in the key of C. For this reason alone, it is impossible to construct any kind of brass or woodwind instrument with perfect intonation in every key.

It is possible, however, to have a brass instrument adjusted to the open tones to such a degree that a player, using the right kind of mouthpiece and having a reasonably good ear, *can* play well in tune. Even C♯4 and D4, also F♯3 and G3, may be played in tune by extending the mobile third slide.

Playing in Tune

It is therefore, not a question of whether an instrument *is* in tune but *whether it can be played in tune*. And this depends on the proportions of the conical bore and on the proper length of the valve slides, which must also be tempered to compensate for the deficiencies caused by using two or three valves at the same time. A player possessing a well-trained embouchure should be able to control fully the intonation of a good brass instrument by compensating for slight mechanical deficiencies.

It must be taken into consideration that a newly made instrument with a hand-hammered bell responds rather stiffly. There is a certain tension which changes after a while. The changes are caused by atmospheric conditions, temperature variations, oxidation and other chemical effects produced by acid in the saliva, and thru the billions of vibrations which occur while playing. Thus, the instrument loosens up and responds more flexibly. However, the conical bore of the instrument is not changed, nor is its inherent intonation.

The acid of the saliva causes the brass to corrode and form verdigris; and after a number of years the metal becomes thinner, which causes the instrument to respond more easily and the intonation to become easier to control. After using an instrument for a long time, the player's embouchure also adjusts itself to the response and the setting of each individual tone so that he has little difficulty playing in tune.

Keep Instrument Clean

Some players believe that they have an instrument on which certain tones were originally badly out of tune, but by forcing them continually up or down as necessary, they corrected the deficient tones. This is an erroneous conclusion, for one cannot change the bore of the instrument in that manner; he can merely adjust his embouchure. If such an instrument with bad intonation is given to a different player, he will find it to be just as much out of tune as it ever was. It does happen, however, that an instrument can become *out of tune* after even a comparatively short period of time. The reason is that the inside of the tubing (especially on the mouthpipe and tuning slide) becomes incrusted with foreign matter.

As verdigris forms inside of the tubing, these accumulations become heavier and heavier and cause a serious change in the bore of the instrument which, therefore, changes the intonation. Much of this difficulty is found in the mouthpiece which a player carries in his pocket and which at times is so full of foreign matter that one cannot look thru it. To avoid this a player should use a mouthpiece brush and clean the mouthpiece frequently.

For cleaning the mouthpipe and the rest of the tubing of a trumpet, a player should use a flexible cleaning brush. By taking the instrument apart, he can brush the mouthpipe, tuning slide, and all valve slides, thereby removing all loose accumulations. Some players have the kind of saliva which actually petrifies the inside of the mouthpiece and the instrument tubing. They should go to a reliable instrument repairman and have him clean the instrument thoroughly with a solution of Oakite.

Proportions of Bore

The reason why certain tones of brass instruments respond on one instrument better and firmer than on others depends entirely on the proportions of the bore. These proportions must be such that each individual tone which is a composite of the fundamental tone and overtones is tempered so that the overtones are principally intense harmonics. This is a formidable problem!

Risky tones called "wolf tones" cannot be corrected no matter how long a player may try to blow them in tune — unless they are caused by leakage in the pistons or tubing. He can merely adjust and strengthen

Vincent Bach

his embouchure so that the fault is not quite as severe.

On a brand new instrument which is absolutely clean both outside and inside and which is very air-tight, each individual tone holds the pitch firmly and it is not easy to "humor" the tones either up or down. When playing for the first time on such an instrument, a player will naturally complain that it responds too stiffly, that it is not flexible enough, and that he has difficulty slurring up and down. Such an instrument, however, loses its airtightness after many years of constant use. (Poorly made instruments might have loose slides and pistons even when they are new.) That can easily be judged when one

tries to play the very low tones such as low F♯3 and G3, which will sound muffled.

Many players have the peculiar idea that an instrument which is perfectly clean on the inside responds with difficulty, while one which is dirty on the inside responds more easily. Actually this is only a matter of becoming accustomed to the instrument. If a brass instrumentalist from the very beginning plays an instrument which is perfectly clean and maintains it in that condition by letting warm water run thru the bell at least twice a week so as to wash out the loose dirt and neutralize the acid of the saliva, he will then be accustomed to playing on a clean instru-

ment and will find the response easier.

Another player, however, who never cleans his instrument and permits foreign matter to accumulate on the inside until he can hardly play, and then finally decides to have it cleaned, will suddenly find that his instrument has a larger bore than that to which he is accustomed and he will have his difficulties. It is best, therefore, to keep the instrument clean.

If an instrument has bad intonation from the very beginning or if the pistons are loose, it would be a waste of money to try to have it repaired in the attempt to bring it into pitch.

FINE

February, 1958

Producing Vibrato

Harold Brasch

HOW IS VIBRATO PRODUCED on brass instruments? This is a question that is asked at all brass clinics, and one that should be answered at each of them. Other frequent and related queries are: Should all brass players be taught vibrato? Is the vibrato for advanced performers only? Do all professional players use vibrato? What method books teach proper use? And should the players of one section attempt to produce similar vibratos?

It is true that this undulation in the tone is produced by various means on the instruments in common use. With the string instruments of the orchestra the effect is produced by motion of the left hand, or fingering hand. The pipe organ stop-knob labeled "tremolo" causes a shaking of the bellows, or in rare instances an actual fanning of the air over the pipes. The vibraphone has an electronically operated disc which revolves within each tube. With the human voice this rapid wavering, which so beautifies the tone, seems to be an endowment of nature, as it is evident

even in untrained voices. On the other hand, our most commonplace instrument, the piano, cannot effect a vibrato by any means.

Vibrato on Brass

There are two principal means in common practice and these are effected by the HAND and by the JAW. We should consider both systems as applied to each member of the brass family. All other systems—diaphragm, throat, lungs, and tongue—should be relegated to the third-choice basket.

Cornetists (trumpeters) use either means of production. The hand vibrato is accomplished by a motion of the right forearm, thus shaking the hand that is over the valves. There are players of note who advocate this method, and others recommend using the jaw. Excellent results are observed in both cases.

Players of alto horns (mellowphonists) have the same choice as cornetists. French horn players, however, are not taught vibrato; neither is it

generally advocated by players, teachers, or conductors.

Trombone and Baritone

Trombonists can be recommended either of the two methods. In our school bands we notice many users of the hand (slide) vibrato. This trend can be traced to its universal use by trombonists in modern dance bands; a young player can be expected to mimic those whom he sees in action. Certainly this system cannot be criticized when we consider the tone quality of the late Tommy Dorsey. On the other hand, a newspaper reporter interviewing the late Arthur Pryor asked him to what single item he attributed his beautiful sound. The famous soloist and composer answered without hesitation, "the jaw vibrato."

There are a few trombone virtuosos who employ both means. They use the slide in lyric passages and the jaw on notes of sufficient duration occurring in technical passages.

Baritonists (euphoniumists) and bass players must take a different view. Their instruments offer no choice. The jaw vibrato is to be accepted as the simplest and most effective way to improve the tone. These instruments are too large to attempt shaking with the right hand. The resulting pounding and pressure on the embouchure would cause swelling of the lips and loosening of the teeth. More important, the appearance of the performer would not be enhanced by such a motion. Indeed, viewed from the audience, a section of shaking basses might cause undue concern from parents and doctors alike.

Additional Considerations

It can be safely affirmed that a slight up and down motion of the jaw is far less damaging to the young player's embouchure than forearm motion. With normal advancement, a player of two years' experience should be encouraged to try this easy step on the road to fine playing. The motion need not exceed one-sixteenth of an inch for the small brass, nor should the length of stroke exceed one-eight of an inch for the large brass.

The speed of this motion should always be moderate—slightly quicker for the top register tones and slightly slower for the lowest register tones. Both the width and speed of the vibrato can be easily overdone. Observation of accepted instrumentalists should determine the usage.

It is a simple matter to vary the vibrato, depending upon the style of the music. Thus, a hymn tune is rendered in a subdued tone, a Verdi aria much more intensely. A player within a section can use less than the soloist. And those using vibrato will always be playing better in tune than those playing straight, since vibrato helps to eliminate *beats* between two like tones. It is for this reason that conductors usually insist on straight tones when tuning up their groups.

In the 2,500 competing brass bands of England all players use vibrato simultaneously. These groups can be compared with a vocal chorus. In symphony orchestras the brass choir performs with straight tones. These groups can be compared with the classical concept of organ playing.

In summary, it is true that a brass player who has good control can alter his tone quality with various degrees of vibrato, or with none. The choice is dictated by the expression terms on the music and by the conductor. As brass performers, let us follow the example put before us by the vocalists and the string players—a discriminating use of vibrato to improve our capabilities and to lift brass playing students to a higher plane.   FINE

The "F" Attachment Tenor Trombone
Reginald Fink

WHY WOULD A tenor trombonist need an "f" attachment on his instrument? Even if most or all of his playing is confined to the middle and upper range of the instrument, can he find a practical use for the valve? Where and to what extent is the thumb valve used in tenor trombone literature?

History

Historically, a tenor trombone was pitched in Bb, while the bass trombone was pitched in F, or occasionally in G. Neither had a valve and the bass trombone's design differed from the tenor's only in that it had larger dimensions. The extreme positions on the bass were difficult to reach, and the player's reach was extended by means of a handle.

With the introduction of the rotary valve, around 1812, it was possible to engage or disengage a section of tubing added to the Bb tenor trombone which increased its lower range without increasing its slide length. Thus, with a large bore Bb tenor trombone with a large bell and a rotary valve "F" attachment, it was possible to obtain the same pitches and nearly the same tone quality as that of a "straight" bass trombone. Although these instruments are more correctly called *tenor-bass-trombones*, they have become known in America as bass trombones.

Correct Name

Not every trombone that has an "F" attachment can be called a bass trombone. Turning to the major symphony orchestras and large concert bands as a reference, it will be found that most bass trombonists are using an instrument which has at least a bore of .560 inch and a bell diameter of 9½ inches.

Instruments smaller than these can produce the same tones, but their overall tone quality is smaller and they tend to be more stuffy and/or more raspy in the lower register. These smaller trombones should not be called *bass* nor *tenor-bass trombones*, but *tenor trombones with "F" attachments*.

Because of many differences of opinion it is impossible to define the "proper" bell joint bore and bell diameter. I would set the *minimum limits* as .500 inch for the bore and 8 inches for the bell diameter; although for all talented students above 6th grade level, these dimensions should be increased .020 inch and ½ inch, respectively.

Sounds Produced

Many people have difficulty understanding what note is sounded when the "F" attachment is used. The attachment lowers 1st position notes a perfect 4th, but it lowers 7th position notes only a major 3rd. This means the slide is divided into 6 positions when the valve is used, rather than the 7 positions of a regular tenor trombone. For this reason it is not possible to match exactly the slide positions when using the valve with the slide positions without the valve.

In the following illustration, the notes given are the 1st and 2nd overtones produced when the "F" attachment is used. The numbers below the notes represent tenor slide positions.

The 1st overtones of the valve in terms of regular tenor trombone positions, are: F2—1st position; E2—2nd position, flatted very slightly; E♭2—3rd position, flatted slightly; D2—4th position, flatted considerably; D♭2—6th position, approximately; and C2—7th position, flatted slightly.

If the valve slide is changed, the positions will vary accordingly. When the valve slide is extended so that the 1st position overtone is E2 rather than F2, the whole slide position chart above is shifted downward one semitone.

It must be noted that the use of the valve when playing tenor trombone music is not limited to C's and F's (valve and 1st position) and B's and E's (valve and 2nd position). The 2nd overtones can be played in all of the positions and usually fall exactly at the point on the slide that

the first overtones do.

If the tenor trombonist fails to take advantage of these possibilities, he will not be using his instrument at its best. For example, in the following illustration the slide sequence *should be* 5th, 6th, flatted 3rd with valve, and 3rd, *rather than* 5th, 1st with valve, 1st, and 3rd.

Not this   This

Using the valve for B♭ makes the longest change in slide 3 positions, rather than 5 positions. In non-scalic passages the possibilities of using the 2nd overtones of the valve are too complicated to enumerate here. Many of the technical difficulties in the tenor trombone etudes of Blume, Slama, Kopprasch, Mueller, Rochut, and Mantia are greatly eased by the proper use of the valve.

Higher Overtones

Some recent material has greatly over-rated the 3rd, 4th, 5th, and 6th overtones on the "F" attachment. True, they are available and should be practiced, since their development tends to enhance the tone quality of the lower overtones, but their use in a concert situation is highly questionable.

Since each extension of the slide increases the distortion of the trombone's basic proportion of 2/3rds cylindrical and 1/3rd conical bore, the intonation discrepancies become more and more magnified as addi-

tional cylindrical tubing is added. Also, the tone quality is not as pure.

Of course, the tuning can be adjusted and the tone quality improved with practice, but these notes are never as stable and clear as the notes in the regular positions. Highly technical solos like *Willow Echoes* and many trills and turns can be almost impossible without a valve, but the occurrence of these exceptions is relatively rare.

Special Advantage

One advantage of the "F" attachment on a tenor trombone, which tends to be overlooked, is the high register benefits the player achieves from practicing the 1st, 2nd, and 3rd overtones on the valve. These notes tend to expose the player's production faults. They will not tolerate being bitten, chewed, pinched, or forced.

The steps in correcting or improving these high register tones are: (1) learn to produce correctly the lower notes, and then (2) carry this basic "feeling" into the upper register. This second step can be accomplished by practicing slow lip slurs from the 1st overtone up thru the overtone series.

This whole approach to high register development, besides correcting faulty production, tends to modify the embouchure into its best and most natural setting.

In summary, I consider both the technical and the tone building advantages of the "F" attachment a warranted and very useful addition to the tenor trombone.   FINE

Embouchure Control and Development

William Cramer

THE ACT OF PERFORMING on a brasswind instrument is essentially that of properly manipulating muscles of the body in such a way that air is directed to the lips which are then set in vibration, and they in turn cause the air in the instrument to vibrate and produce musical

sound. Tone production is accomplished by the human body in motion. The instrument itself acts as a resonator and amplifier only. The instrument and the body must be in sympathy with each other to achieve maximum results.

But what does one mean when he

says, for instance, that he takes *trombone* lessons? The trombone, tho being the product of extensive scientific research, can do nothing by itself; it needs no lessons. Thus, it must be the *student* who needs lessons in the proper way to control the musculature of the body in order to produce musical sound on the trombone.

Muscles Involved

One set of muscles is used for inhaling the breath and then expelling it thru the windpipe to the lips. Another set of muscles (the tongue) is used for articulating that air stream into appropriate rhythmic patterns and styles of attack. A third set (the embouchure) operates the vibrating medium (the lips) to control the tension and set the proper pitch. And yet a fourth set of muscles is necessary to operate the valves or slide which assist in setting the pitch.

The lips may be compared to a violin string as a medium of vibration. In order to change the pitch of the vibrating string, the violinist has the choice of (1) adjusting the tension with the tuning peg, (2) shortening the string with the fingers of the left hand, or (3) changing the string to one of different weight or thickness. The brass instrumentalist can make similar adjustments by (1) flexing the muscles of the embouchure, (2) changing the size of the mouthpiece, or (3) adjusting the amount of lip flesh within the mouthpiece.

It is somewhat impractical to change mouthpieces in order to change pitch, and adjusting the weight of the flesh inside the mouthpiece also changes the tone quality, so the instrumentalist is left with only the possibility of adjusting the muscle tension while trying to keep the other two constant.

Smiling and Puckering

Two well-known systems of embouchure control have been used over the years, *smiling* and *puckering*. The smiling technique seeks to stretch the lips horizontally, exactly as one would stretch a rubber band over the mouthpiece. The tighter the band is drawn the higher is the pitch. There is no tension in the lip itself but there is tension in the muscles that are stretching the lips.

Unfortunately, there is a limit to which the lips can be stretched, and because the lips are drawn thinner the tone quality also tends to become "thinner." Having reached his top limits by smiling, the instrumentalist is then forced to jam the mouthpiece against his lips in order to stretch them further in exactly the same manner that a drum head is tightened to produce a more lively tone or higher pitch.

Puckering seeks to control the pitch by contracting and tensing the lip itself. It appears to have two disadvantages: (1) the "puckering" can be carried to the point that the aperture thru which the air must pass is gradually closed off till there is little or no sound, or the lips do not vibrate freely, and (2) the increased amount of flesh within the mouthpiece changes the tone quality, usually to a kind of thick, tubby sound.

Ideal Formation

Ideally, it would seem that the best embouchure formation is one which allows for changes in muscular tension with no other movement which would alter the tone quality or the placement of the mouthpiece.

The lips are a single ring of muscle which, when contracted, gives the pursed or puckered appearance. Observe how wrinkled the lip tissue becomes when the lips are puckered. This wrinkling of tissue can be the cause of poor tone quality.

Attached to the lip muscle are those muscles with which we smile. When the "smiling" muscles contract they merely stretch the lip muscle.

There are similar muscles on either side of the nose, which—when contracted—cause the upper lip to curl up as tho in the act of snarling.

In the chin is a third set of muscles which, when contracted, pull the lower lip down. This is the contraction that takes place when a man shaves his chin.

Now if the lip muscle can be made to contract at the same time that these other muscles contract there will be a change in tension (and a change in pitch) with little outward facial motion or change in tone quality. The situation will be one of muscles opposing each other.

The instrumentalist should now try buzzing on the mouthpiece, rapidly changing the pitch up and down, all the while noting results in a mirror. Then the same procedure should be tried on the instrument while slurring diatonic and chromatic scales without even an initial attack. Great care should be taken that only the facial muscles are being used, and that the instrument is not being jammed against the lips with the arm muscles.

Development of strength and endurance, as well as range, now follows exactly the same pattern as that which an athlete follows in getting himself into shape. The muscles must be exercised deliberately and gradually made to take on greater loads that will lead to extended range and endurance. Hurrying this process can however, cause injury to the lips. FINE

The Tongue and the Tuba

Rex Conner

Dᴵᴰ ʏᴏᴜ ᴇᴠᴇʀ try to whistle a range of three octaves and pay particular attention to what the tongue does? It is interesting to note that the tongue is responsible almost entirely for the pitch change.

When one whistles high notes the tongue crawls forward, the middle section of it arches high as if pronouncing an "ee" sound, and the tip comes up against the teeth. Whistling a real low sound causes the tongue to do just the opposite. It draws back down the throat as if one were pronouncing the word "oh" down in the throat. There is also a feeling as if the throat were opening up.

Let's carry this analysis a little further. Let's try to tongue all of those notes we are trying to whistle. What happens now to the tip of the tongue? Taking the lowest note one can get, it will be noticed that the tip of the tongue is way up in the middle of the roof of the mouth, behind the rim back of the teeth as the "oh" sound is pronounced; then, as we come up about an octave it is discovered that the tip is coming further forward. We are now pronouncing a "tu" instead of a "toh". Continue on up and we are now blending into a "tee" sound with the tongue extremely arched, and with the tongue striking against the teeth.

These principles can be very helpful when it comes to playing, not only the tuba, but all wind instruments. First of all, vowel formations are just as important in making good tone quality on the wind instruments as they are in making good vocal sounds. There are some who will doubt this statement, saying, "It doesn't make any difference where the middle or the back of the tongue is as long as the tip of the tongue is in the right place."

This can easily be tested. Take any wind instrument, blow a long sustained tone, and while blowing, articulate rapidly from the "o" to the "ee" sound. In other words articulate as tho you were saying "to-ee-o-ee-o." It will sound as tho two instruments are playing out of tune with each other.

Most trumpet players recommend that the tongue should strike at the edge of the upper teeth, and a trombonist will advise that we tongue about where the upper teeth and gums meet. This follows thru very nicely. Now how about the tuba? I have found that much better results in attack and tone quality are achieved by tonguing on the roof of the mouth for the greater part of the tuba range. Place the tongue exactly where you would if you were pronouncing the letter "t" and the results will be quite rewarding, providing one works at it.

When we wish to play from Bb2 on down to E2 it will help to tongue even further back and pronounce the syllable "do". We have now changed to a "d" attack in our discussion instead of the usual "t"; however, we will deal with that more in detail later.

How Not to Tongue

We might now consider several ways not to tongue. These methods of tonguing cause a teacher much trouble because it is sometimes difficult to know just what is happening inside the mouth to produce such an ugly sound.

The worst possible way to tongue, of course, is against or thru the lips. This sort of attack is usually not used on any of the brasses, except, perhaps, for special effects; but, on the tuba, it is atrocious. The tuba embouchure is too relaxed to allow for any solidity of attack, the embouchure set is disturbed, the tongue moves forward and backward instead of up and down, and the tone is very thuddy.

There is another type of attack that is sometimes difficult to diagnose, yet which gives poor results. When a student is told to attack against the teeth as trumpeters usually do, he sometimes fails to get that little sharp bend in the very tip of the tongue. The majority of us do it without thinking about it; however, if not, instead of a "t" sound, one produces a "th" sound.

There is still another type of attack quite common to all the lower brasses. This is the attack which is just not firm enough. It can be caused by allowing a greater portion of the tongue to press against the attacking surface or by just not pressing the tip of the tongue tight enough. When this happens each tone starts with a hissing or "ts" sound.

When attacking a note either piano or forte, the tongue should press firmly against the roof of the mouth (for tuba) and be released, not slowly, but quickly. Bear in mind, we are not talking about accents here. Press the tongue as hard as you wish against the roof of the mouth and there will be no accent or even tone unless the air stream is pressed against the tongue by the diaphragm. *Accents are made with the breath.*

Syllables for Attack

I mentioned, previously, the syllable "do" instead of "to". "tuh", "tah", or "tee". There was a reason for this. Did you ever stop to ask yourself the difference between the consonants "t" and "d"? It's a rather perplexing question when one starts thinking about it.

The tip of the tongue goes to the same place in pronouncing both letters, but each has a distinct sound. What real difference is there in producing these two sounds?

First of all we find that voice teachers call the letter "t" a *breath consonant* and the letter "d" a *voiced consonant*. Pronounce the letter "t" slowly and you will hear air before you hear the voice. Pronounce the letter "d" and you will hear the voice immediately. Two other things happen that are worth noting. First, we find that the throat is more relaxed; and secondly, we find that the diaphragm tends to pull up and in more intensely when pronouncing the "d" than it does with the "t". The "t" attack, in contrast to the "d" attack, has a tendency to give an explosive beginning to notes.

Advantages of "d" Syllable

For a number of years I have been favoring the "d" tongue more and more for practically all purposes on the tuba. It gets faster, surer responses, especially in the lower register. It eliminates the "cracking sound" tuba players often get while playing marches fortissimo. Above all, it greatly enhances the tone quality.

If you want a big organ-like tone attacked fortissimo on a half or whole note, then use the "d" attack. The beginning of the tone will sound more like the middle and end of it, and the breath follows thru more surely and solidly.

If your tuba players are quite advanced and do triple tonguing it will be found that "du-du-gu" is more relaxed, faster, and obtains more tone quality than the usually recommended "tu-tu-ku." Incidentally, why is triple tonguing on the tuba considered so difficult and novel? Perhaps it's for the same reason that few tuba players know much about the notes above F3. The literature seldom calls for it.

I know of only one tuba solo, *Billy Blowhard*, which calls for triple tonguing. The fact is, however, that triple tonguing from Bb2 on up is just as easy, if not easier, on the tuba than it is on a cornet or trumpet—providing the player has developed a good embouchure for the instrument.

Firm Tongue and Breath Support

Before leaving our discussion of the tip of the tongue we might leave one word of caution. It might be better to allow beginners to tongue the traditional "tu" for awhile simply because it will tend to develop stronger tongue muscles which the tuba player needs.

Slowness of response is not due to the length of tubing. It is due to lack of resistance to the diaphragm and weak tonguing. Anticipating the beat merely gets that indecisive attack there sooner. It's still no attack. One just hears tone sooner that finally got going after a poor start.

At the beginning of this discussion it was suggested that vowel formations have considerable bearing on tone quality. Many times bad sounds produced with the wrong manipulation of the tongue will be attributed to the embouchure and lack of breath support.

Vowel formation affects pitch as well as quality. Take a BB♭ Bass and play low B♭ 2, articulating "toh" or "do," and then play E♭2, articulating a "tuh" or "duh." Now reverse the process; articulate "tuh" on B♭2 and "toh" on E♭2. Both tones will lose quality and be out of tune. Chances are the B♭ will sound nasal.

No set vowel can be given for individual notes. Each person possesses a mouth and tongue of different size and shape; therefore, his resonating chamber is different in size than another's would be while pronouncing the same vowel.

Additional Suggestions

Quite often when we ask a student to play a scale for us we hear each note scooped; the pitch is changed and the quality is changed on each note. Chances are that the pupil is articulating "to-ee" instead of "tu" on each note and the action of the tongue is forward and backward in-

stead of more up and down. This can be even worse. Articulating the sound "ta-ree" not only causes one to scoop the tones, but it adds raspiness. The faster the notes are played the worse the tones are.

If any of the above suggestions fail to help the tone of your tuba players, try to get them to open the jaw more. Still another suggestion might be helpful. Try having the player tilt the head slightly upward into the mouthpiece. Sometimes a tall tuba player may play a recording bass which sits on the chair between his legs. If he has to reach down into the mouthpiece with an extended jaw the sound can be very objectionable.

June, 1958

Playing the French Horn

Jack Bourdess

THE FRENCH HORN section is now an accepted part of most school bands all over the country. This may range from one horn and a mellophone in the smaller schools up to ten or twelve double horns. But no matter what the size of the section, the *sound* is what counts. And this, to a large degree, depends on the director.

Many times the director may be plagued with a large trumpet section and no horns, so he lays down the law: either the last stand of trumpets play horn or they don't play in the band. This is sure to solve the overload of trumpets but it doesn't make a good horn sound. Such a horn section will sound like trumpet players playing horn.

Who Should Play Horn?

The French horn player should have a little better than average musical ability. He has a difficult instrument to control, he will have pitch problems that others don't have, and he will have to transpose, to name a few of the difficulties. He should not be started on the horn too early, although a good-sized boy or girl in the 5th or 6th grade would be all right.

The horn player should be started *on the horn,* not on the trumpet. The

embouchures for the two instruments are different. If a student is going to be a horn player, let him be one from the very beginning. In many orchestras there will be dead wood, and many times these weak players will be covered up in a big section like the strings. However, this is not the case with the horns. There are *four horn* parts and *four* horn players; there is no one to cover up the player. The part must be played, and one person must do it. So the mental strain can be difficult. The student need not be an extrovert, but he should have confidence and be able to produce when the chips are down.

Horns and Mouthpieces

Horn playing is a very personal thing, since what may work well for one person may not be the best thing for another. The student should do much listening to fine performers to decide what kind of horn sound is desirable. Then he should experiment and practice until he gets that sound: *then stop experimenting.* Changing horns, mouthpieces, and embouchures have been the downfall of many good horn players.

There is no such thing as a perfect mouthpiece. Rim cushion, cup width, throat, and bore will affect the tone and ease of playing; but when you

get a mouthpiece that plays well in the high register, it may give a thin tone. A mouthpiece that gives a dark rich tone may make it hard to fill the horn. Again this is a personal matter. Everyone has different lip and teeth formations which make mouthpiece selection an individual thing.

It is true that the mouthpiece, leader pipe, bore, throat of the horn, embouchure, etc., will affect the tone color of the horn. So you must experiment until you get the equipment that will do the job.

F Horn, B♭ Horn, Double Horn

For school bands I like the F single horn because of the sound it produces. The B♭ horn, to some directors, may have advantages—easier control and less difficulty in switching trumpet players to horn—but the B♭ horn in the middle register just doesn't have the *horn* sound.

The best answer is to combine the good points of both horns, and of course this brings up the double horn. The double horn is expensive, and many schools have one double horn for the first horn player and single horns for the rest of the section. The double horn is really two horns in one, pitched in F and B♭. The player can go from one horn to the other by using the thumb valve. One big problem is to get the horn in tune with itself. Play C5 on the F horn, then very quickly push the Bb valve—still playing the same note. If the second note is sharp or flat adjust the Bb slides, then try it again. The Bb valve must move quickly so that you will not automatically correct the pitch with your lip. Of course, this is only one note, but this will tune the F and Bb sides of the horn to each other.

Another question is where to switch to the Bb horn while playing. Some teachers say from G#4 on up, others say C#5 and up. I like the sound of the F horn in this middle register; and if I have a solo or soli, I stay on the F horn until D5, then I switch to the Bb horn. But if I am playing with the other brasses or am playing a heavy, loud passage, I switch to the Bb horn at G#4. The Bb horn is used in the extreme high register because its tubing is shorter and produces higher notes more easily.

Embouchure

Horn players should use a pucker form of embouchure rather than tight, thinly drawn lips. They should play on the damp inner part of the lip and not the outside edge. Then as the range goes higher the corners of the mouth contract drawing the lips tighter and thinner. When playing in the extreme low register use a relaxed embouchure with a larger opening in the lips. The old idea

that first horn players should play only the high register and fourth horn players the low register is no longer true. A good horn player has command of the full range of the horn.

A good embouchure comes from practice and a teacher who will watch for bad habits. This is most important because without a good embouchure you cannot get a good high or low register and you will tire quickly.

The Right Hand

The horn bell is at the player's right side for a definite purpose. The right hand must be cupped in the bell, as if the player were going to catch the tones. The horn is constructed sharp to allow for the right hand; and if it isn't there, it will play out of tune. Pictures and diagrams of hand positions can be found in method books on horn playing. In *The Art of French Horn Playing* by Philip Farkas, good hand position is illustrated on page 13. But again, there are different hand positions. Horn bells are different and all right hands are not the same size, so the player must find a hand position that suits him.

Transposition

When I first started to play the horn, most of the horn parts were in Eb; and the band director took the Eb slides out of our cases and wouldn't let us use them. At the time I thought he was just trying to make life difficult for us, but he knew that horn players must learn to

transpose. Using Eb slides puts the horn out of tune and moves everything down a step for the player's ear.

Most of the music for band published today has parts in F, and even the American publications for the major classical works will give the original notation and the same part in F. This is certainly a step in the right direction. Still the horn player in the band should be able to transpose Eb parts, and the orchestral player should be able to transpose parts in E, C, D, and G. Transposition may be by interval or clef. Both methods are good.

The School Horn Player

After the horn player has played in high school for four years and, perhaps, college for four years, then what? He shouldn't put his instrument up in the attic and leave it there till his child is ready to play in the school band or orchestra. There are town bands and civic orchestras that are always in need of horn players. If you want to play, there is some group in the vicinity that will welcome you. A relatively new field for horn players is the dance band. Claude Thornhill started the idea and Mitch Miller, Xavier Cugat, and Stan Kenton now use horns with their bands.

There is also a wealth of chamber music that includes horn. In addition, there are solos. Playing the horn is something one can do all his life.   FINE

Supplemental Techniques For Beginning Brasses

Helen Trobian

STUDENTS IN BEGINNING brass groups are getting acquainted with instruments as tools for making music. They are developing skills and attitudes which may eventually equip them for membership in a musical ensemble. Learning to play a brass instrument involves such techniques as tone production, articulation, and

music reading; but to be a valuable member of an ensemble a student must, in addition, be capable of such experiences as listening for the tones of a chord in order to harmonize accurately, and following the interpretations expressed by the conductor's gestures.

For the beginning brass group the

instructor may find it helpful to use exercises which will give students an opportunity to concentrate on the sound produced, without the added difficulty of attention to the printed page. The following items are a few brief illustrations which I have found to produce good results in a relatively short period of time. These exercises are best accomplished as brief inserts during the rehearsal period at whatever moments they may seem most pertinent.

The instructor gives the class a pattern orally, which is then played and repeated in unison on concert B♭. As the class progresses the rhythms gradually become more difficult and different notes and time signatures are used. They are still presented orally. Later the class is asked to play four tones of the B♭ or E♭ major scales, and eventually complete scales using various tonguing patterns. In each instance the instructor tells the students which notes to play and repeats the rhythm twice with distinct tonguing.

At first, rhythmic cues are given with the hands; later the class is asked to follow the baton. For following the beat of the baton the instructor first states the pattern, then explains it. Students are asked to make up their own tonguing patterns and to practice them at home on all notes within their range.

The instructor names a tone, giving both low brasses and trumpets notes well within present playing range. Explanation is made about "preparatory beat," "hold," and "cut-off." Effort is made to establish group precision in starting the tone with an alert tongue and stopping exactly at the "cut-off." Later students take turns directing the group in these procedures.

Each section is told a tone to play, e.g. basses and baritones play B♭, trombones and horns play D, and trumpets play F (G). The chord is built up by intervals first. Then while holding the tones of the chord the class works on attack and release or tonguing patterns. After major triads, dominant 7ths are introduced and then minor chords.

Each section gets a chance to play all tones of the chord. At first the tones are sounded by individual sections, then sounded together. The second phase of the chord practice is to sound the chord with trumpets only, or trombones only, assigning the higher tones to the students having greatest range. The class pays particular attention to tuning and blending.

The instructor announces a tone for each section and states how many beats, 8, 10, or 12. The tone is repeated with short intervals of rest until the signal to stop is given. Three or more tones are played in succession. When the group has advanced sufficiently, the C, F, B♭, E♭, and A♭ scales are played, holding each tone for at least 8 counts without rest between tones.

These are done using major flat scales, first using only the first four tones, then the next four. The first articulation is usually four quarter notes with the first two slurred. Then three notes slurred, one tongued; four notes slurred; one tongued, two slurred, one tongued; etc.

The instructor announces a tone, then calls on several individuals in turn to play it, asking each to compare intonation. As the class progresses requests for individual performance may be an arpeggio or a scale, a particular tonguing pattern or articulation, dynamic change from pp to ff, or other technique the student may wish to demonstrate.

After these exercises have been developed students are asked to *read* rhythm patterns and chords from staves on the blackboard. Then the instructor chooses a time-signature and key. Bar lines for four measures are marked on a three stave score (trumpets, horn, and bass clef instruments).

Students are then asked to present a rhythm pattern and a melody is gradually evolved by asking different sections which notes they wish to play. This original four measure composition is played by the group. If it does not sound good, students decide where to make changes. By this method elementary harmony is introduced.

When the beginning student is ready to audition for a chair in the band he should also know how to interpret the movements of the baton. Some time is spent using scales (or simple reading materials) following the baton for changes in tempo, changes in time-signatures, coming to a fermata, a sudden stop, a new start, and changes in dynamics.

After the class has made progress, the baton is used while performing such exercises as mentioned on attack and release, tonguing, chords, articulations, and long tones. The instructor endeavors to develop ability to change both tempo and dynamics without prior knowledge by students.

In actual use any one of these exercises is interspersed informally and spontaneously into the regular class work at any time. The teacher may occasionally demonstrate on any instrument. A typing table just behind the conductor's stand is helpful to hold instruments. Perhaps these few illustrations will suggest ideas for your own supplemental techniques.

FINE

October, 1958

Tuning and Intonation on- - -

The Double French Horn

Cutler Silliman

THE DOUBLE FRENCH HORN in F and B♭ is the most complex brass instrument in regular use today. The tenor-bass trombone has some similar problems, but it is not as complicated.

The double horn is built so that a thumb valve shortens the length of tubing of the lower F horn to the proper length for the B♭ instrument. (It is possible to build a horn so that the thumb valve either cuts off some of the tubing of the F horn, or adds tubing to the B♭ horn. The former is most common, but the basic problems of tuning and intonation are the same, either way the instrument is constructed.)

Tuning the Open Horn

All double horns have at least one tuning slide that affects both instruments. In addition, there must be another slide (frequently two) for the longer F horn.

To make an equal change of interval on two instruments of different length requires a greater change in tube length on the longer instrument than on the smaller. Perhaps this can best be seen on the tenor-bass trombone on which the positions of the slide are farther apart on the bass than on the tenor trombone, although in each case the change in pitch is the same. Therefore, a change in the main tuning slide of the double horn will have a greater effect on the shorter B♭ horn than on the F horn, and this explains the necessity for an additional tuning slide for the F horn.

When tuning a double horn that has no separate slide for the B♭ horn (the most common type), the B♭ horn should be tuned first, adjusting the main tuning slide as necessary. Then the F horn should be tuned to match the B♭ horn, making any necessary changes on the F horn slide. Any large change on the main tuning slide that is made after this will necessitate a corresponding adjustment of the F horn slide.

A word of admonition is pertinent here. When tuning a horn the right hand must always be in its normal position in the bell. It is far too common to see a high school player adjust-

ing the tuning slides with his right hand at the same time that he is sounding the tuning note. Naturally, he will then be flat when he begins to play with his hand in place in the bell.

Tuning the Valve Slides

Once the horn is in agreement with the tuning note, it is necessary to synchronize the tuning of both the F and B♭ sides of the instrument. The best way to do this is to start with open C5, (third space) and play down chromatically, checking each finger combination on both instruments. These notes down thru G♯4 are usually fingered identically on both horns, and by matching the pitches the proper adjustment of the valve slides can be made.

After the horn has been tuned to a fixed pitch and the two instruments synchronized, most players still have difficulty playing with correct intonation throughout the range of the horn. The player is able to make small adjustments sharp or flat with his hand and lips. Of course, he must recognize the need for an adjustment and further understand which way to make it. This is a matter of training and experience, and no mechanical adjustment of tuning and valve slides will completely solve the problem of intonation. However, an understanding of some of the acoustical problems involved and some principles of valve construction will aid in showing why certain adjustments must be made.

The fingering system provides some of the difficulties in intonation on brass instruments. The valves add the tubing necessary to alter the basic pitch (open tone) a specified amount. The second valve lowers any open tone one half step, the first valve

makes a whole step change, and the third valve (equivalent of one and two together) a step and a half. In effect, the F horn becomes an E horn when its second valve is added, an E♭ horn with its first valve, and a D horn with its third valve. Similarly, the B♭ horn becomes an A, A♭, and G horn successively.

Since it takes a greater change of tubing to make an equal change of interval on a longer instrument than on a shorter one, it will be seen that if a second valve is built to lower an open horn (F or B♭) one half step, it will be too short to lower the horn with its first valve down (E♭ or A♭) an additional half step. When valves are used in combination, the tones, although lower in pitch than the open tones from which they are derived, are sharper in intonation than they should be. This becomes progressively more aggravated the farther one is from the simple fingerings (open, first, and second valves). For this reason most players of brass instruments avoid whenever possible the finger combinations of 2-3, 1-3, and 1-2-3.

Although the third valve is theoretically the same as the combination of first and second, it is usually drawn out somewhat to compensate for the sharpness of valve combinations. It is therefore not always the best fingering for the tones which are a minor third below an open tone. These are usually played with first and second valves together, with the sharpness compensated for by the player with his lips or right hand.

Out-of-Tune Open Tones

Another factor that affects intonation concerns the open tones themselves. In some cases, the natural partials vary considerably from tempered tuning. The natural partials for both F and B♭ horns in the simpler valve combinations are shown in Fig. 1.

Fig. 1—The natural partials for the F and B♭ Horn for the open and some of the simpler fingerings. The whole notes are reasonably close to tempered tuning, the half notes are a little flat, and the quarter notes are to be avoided whenever possible.

The notes shown in whole note values are reasonably close to agreement with tempered tuning. Most players avoid the notes shown in quarter note values, numbers 7, 11, 13, and 14. Partials 5 and 10, indicated with half notes tend to be a little flat so that the player must exercise care when using them.

The flatness of partials 5 and 10 seems to be more exaggerated on the B♭ horn than on the F horn; because of this, A4 (second space) is usually played with the first and second valves rather than as an open tone. On the other hand, G4, when played on the B♭ horn, is usually played with the first valve, the first and third combination being both awkward and sharp.

With a double horn, a player is able to select fingerings for partials that are closer in agreement with good tuning than on a single horn. The G4 is difficult to tune on the B♭ horn, but it is one of the easiest tones on the F horn when fingered open. E3 and D3 (below the treble staff) tend to be sharp on the F horn (fingered 1-2 and 1-3); they not only tune better on the B♭ horn (2 and 1-2) but are often easier to attack. The D5 (4th line) is usually quite

sharp on the B♭ horn; this is particularly noticeable when the interval of a perfect fifth from G4 to D4 is played. In this case the intonation is frequently improved by playing the D open on the F horn. Other examples could be enumerated, but this list gives the more common ways the double horn can be utilized to improve intonation.

There is no fixed place in the horn register where an advanced player should shift from one horn to the other. It is important that the player know both instruments over the entire range, and it is valuable practice to play passages where one would normally be on the F horn on the B♭ horn and to use the F horn where one would normally use the B♭. Thus, the player can decide for himself how he can best utilize the full possibilities of the double horn.

Summary

The following list summarizes the suggestions for better tuning and intonation on the double horn:

1. Be sure that the two parts of the double horn are in tune together;

2. keep the hand in the bell while tuning;

3. play as low in the harmonic series of either horn as is possible but using only the partials which are closely in agreement with tempered tuning;

4. avoid the partials 7, 11, 13, and 14;

5. use care with partials 5 and 10;

6. adjust valve slides so that they counteract the sharpness of combination fingerings;

7. master both F and B♭ horns so that alternate fingerings can be used to improve intonation.

No horn can be built that is perfectly in tune with tempered tuning throughout its range. Each player must adjust his instrument to suit his own playing, adjusting some tones by changing the slides, others with his hand or lips. However, reputable manufacturers build horns as well in tune as is physically possible, and a careful player can play *any* good horn in tune.

Editor's note: Much of the above discussion is equally adaptable to other brass instruments.　　　　Fine

November, 1958

Determinants of Tone Quality

William Cramer

THE PROBLEMS OF building a fine ensemble must be handled as they arise, and handled with care relative to the importance of the problem. The band director's primary problems usually have to do with matters of getting his ensemble to play with rhythmic accuracy, with good phrasing, with careful attention to intonation, and with good dynamic balance among the sections. Ultimately, he must face the problem of insuring that each of the different instruments of the band sounds as it was intended to sound. More important, he must try to achieve a tonal consistency within each section so that one player with poor tone quality will not detract from the total effect.

The description of tone quality is difficult at best. More often we asso-

ciate color words such as *bright* and *dark* with tone qualities. While these will suffice to carry on an informal discussion, they are at best only relative.

Tone quality is a product of a single pitch, together with its component overtones, being sounded in certain proportions of dynamic level. A change in that proportion causes the instrument being sounded to assume the tone quality of some other instrument. Scientific instruments have been developed to illustrate and prove the point. Listening to high fidelity recording equipment will show this difference. We say that hi-fi tones seem fuller or more alive simply because we can hear the fundamentals of each instrument and all their overtones in their proper dynamic proportions.

When we say a tone quality is thin we mean that the low overtones are too weak. When the tone quality is dark the low overtones are dominant. When the tone quality is very full then all the overtones and the fundamental are present in their best proportions. Other relative tone qualities may be described in the same manner.

The Mouthpiece

The first determinant of tone quality on a brass instrument is the mouthpiece. If pressed for time and money, the band director can most quickly improve the tonal consistency of each section by having the players match mouthpieces. The choice of mouthpiece will, of course, depend upon the tone quality the band director finds most desirable.

In general, it may be said that a shallow cup will enhance the production of the upper overtones and a deep cup will enhance the production of the lower overtones. Another way to describe this is to say the first will produce a bright tone and the second will produce a dark tone. Carried to extremes, this can become a thin tone or a dull tone.

Exactly the same things may be said of a small throat opening and a large throat opening. The first enhances the production of the upper overtones and the second enhances the production of the lower overtones.

The shape of the backbore is also a determinant of tone quality but need not be considered here. The backbore is already proportioned to the cup and throat, and is rarely described by the manufacturer in such a way that a band director can use the information.

Instrument Bore

The second determinant of tone quality is the bore of the instrument. The length of the instrument is a factor in determining its pitch, but the shape of the bore of the instrument is a strong factor in determining its tone quality. Where it is possible, the band director can further improve the tonal consistency of each section by having the players match their instruments.

In general, the brass instruments of the band may be placed into three categories according to the shape of the bore, and consequently the tone quality that is produced. (Actually, this is over-simplification, but it is done merely to provide a guide in improving the tonal consistency within the ensemble).

The first category is the trumpet family which has a bore shape that is roughly two-thirds cylindrical and one-third conical. Trumpets and trombones properly belong in this family.

The second category is the cornet family which has a bore shape that is aproximately one-third cylindrical and two-thirds conical. This family includes the cornets, the alto horns or mellophones, the baritones. and probably a great many tubas.

The third category is the fluegel-horn family which has a bore shape that is entirely conical. The fluegel-horn, French horn, euphonium. and the true tubas belong in this family.

In general, it may be said that the cylindrical shape enhances the pro-

duction of the higher partials, and the conical shape enhances the production of the fundamental and the lower overtones. Unfortunately, there is such a diversity of opinion and design among manufacturers that no instrument will fall neatly and precisely into any one category. The band director will probably come closest to his goal of achieving tonal consistency if he has all his players in the section use the same make and model of instrument.

Concept of Quality

The third determinant of tone quality is the student's own conception of what constitutes a characteristic sound for his instrument. In most instances. the beginning student is interested in these problems and in this order: production of mere sound. change in pitch, mechanical manipulation, change in dynamic level, speed in performance, and rhythmic accuracy. The subtleties of producing good tone quality need not be delayed until after these other problems are met, but the traditional pattern of public school music teaching is difficult to change.

The band director who seeks to improve the tonal consistency of his ensemble through a direct approach to the students' conceptions might keep these things in mind:

(1) The idea of tone quality and discrimination among tone qualities can be taught. To create an awareness within the student that good tone quality is important is a fine beginning.

(2) The student's conception of tone quality can be developed and improved. Much of teaching follows the principles of observation, comparison. and conclusion, and the band director can use these same principles by leading his students to listen. compare. and discriminate.

(3) The student will work best if his environmental influence is consistent. That is to say, he will make faster progress if others around him are trying for the same goal. A teacher-pupil relationship is not enough. It is better that the student share his experiences with his classmates so that they may compare and discriminate.

(4) The student needs a standard or goal toward which he can work. Mere talking and reading are not enough. The student must hear good tone quality frequently for compari-

son with his own. Phonograph records will help but the live sound would be better. The band director should be able to produce at least *one* good solid tone on each instrument. The student can quickly take care of pitch changes after he can produce a satisfactory sound.

The student has control of two things within his own physical being which will directly influence tone quality. These are the embouchure and the wind chamber. In speaking of the embouchure we are more directly concerned with the lip tissues which vibrate than we are with the muscles which bring about the changes in the embouchure.

In general, it may be said that a thin embouchure will enhance the production of the upper overtones, and this is what happens with those who use the "smiling" embouchure. Conversely, a thick embouchure will enhance the production of the fundamental and the lower overtones, and this is what happens with those who use the "pucker" embouchure. An analogy might be made with the open strings on the violin and viola sounding the same "A." The difference in tone quality is largely due to the thickness of the string.

In speaking of the wind chamber, reference is made to the opening inside the mouth, the throat, and the lungs. It has not yet been proved scientifically, but there is a feeling among teachers that the larger the wind chamber the easier it is to produce the lower overtones, and the smaller the wind chamber the easier it is to produce the upper overtones. The use of the syllables "ah-ee" in slurring is an illustration of this principle.

Place Emphasis Correctly

Now, while it is useful to know that mouthpieces, instruments, and student conception are determinants of tone quality, this does not solve the problem as to what constitutes good tone quality for a particular instrument. Two references may be of some help: (a) high fidelity equipment has made us aware of the fact that we have never really heard the outward extremes of the tonal spectrum; (b) when talking of poor tone quality we invariably say the tone is too thin, and rarely do we say the tone is too dark. Therefore, it would seem that the band director should concentrate his efforts on having the students produce the **lower** overtones and let the tonal spectrum develop upward from there.

Experience has probably already indicated to most band directors that the students conception is of far greater importance than either the mouthpiece or the instrument. You will recall many students who were forever seeking the mouthpiece or the instrument which would do the job for them. Every time they found the perfect mouthpiece or instrument, results were very satisfying for about two weeks and then followed a return to the same old frustrations. Occasionally one finds a student who seeks to improve his tonal conception and the choice of mouthpiece or instrument is made to fit that conception. In most cases, it is not even necessary to change either the mouthpiece or the instrument.

Developing and improving the student's tonal conception will produce more positive and lasting results. It is the student who must be taught and not the instrument. The student who is receiving instruction and learning will advance more rapidly than the student who buys the finest instrument and then sits in the high school band for four years playing "more" music.   FINE

December, 1958

Relationship between

Breath Support and Lip Tension

Robert Weast

MOST OF OUR beliefs and teaching methods are based on personal observation and experience over the years with many students. It is not often that our field can produce scientifically valid data either to disprove, substantiate, or refine our methods of playing or teaching. With this as a partial incentive, we constructed an air-membrane instrument for the purpose of measuring quantitatively the relationship between the two basic components of brass performance: (1) air pressure, and (2) membrane (lip) tension.

This type of research instrument is not entirely new. Several have been constructed previously by both instrument manufacturing firms and individual investigators. Their primary purpose was to get away from human variability in testing horns, mouthpieces, and other such factors.

With our apparatus, air gauges and a spring scale are mounted with appropriate tubing and valves to secure actual measurements of a simulated playing situation. Air flow and compression, as well as membrane tension, are altered mechanically to determine their effects on one another.

Examination of the accompanying chart substantiates the long held theory of "breath support." The operation of the apparatus and the manner in which a brass player produces sound are identical, viz., tonal frequencies are the result of the action of the air on the vibrating membrane. Air and membrane tension operate in ratio to each other. Should one be reduced, the other must be increased in order to maintain the same pitch.

In the player, air compression within the mouth induces involuntary action of the embouchure muscles, producing higher frequencies thru the direct action of the air compression and velocity on the lip tissue. Contrast this with low air compression, or stated otherwise, inadequate breath support. In order to compensate for the reduced air support, the embouchure "over tenses" producing an inferior tone. Such superfluous contracting restricts the free vibration of the lip, resulting in a cramped, choked tone. This excessive muscle contraction, often referred to as "pinching" greatly impairs endurance. The sooner one transfers the work load from the embouchure to the air, the sooner will his endurance increase.

The results of the experiment are recorded on the accompanying graph. Tonal frequencies resulted from the action of the air on the membrane. Notice that as the air is increased the membrane tension can be reduced and still produce the same pitch. Conversely, as the air is reduced the membrane tension must be increased. D5 for example, can be sounded at 14 oz. air pressure and 1 oz. of membrane tension. As the air is reduced the membrane tension must gradually be increased, arriving finally at 5 oz. air to 8 oz. membrane tension. Note that E♭5 and E5 first occur at higher membrane tensions and that A♭4 and A4 are lost at 7 and 8 oz. of membrane tension respectively.

It should not be deduced from the foregoing that softer notes require more "lip tension." This would be an erroneous and incomplete conclusion. The soft volume note should be performed with the embouchure as relaxed as possible. Thus, the slightest amount of air flow will activate the membrane. While the quantity of air will be reduced for soft notes, the amount of air compression and velocity should still be maximum for any given pitch. Air intensity is not synonymous with degrees of volume.

Many persons misinterpret the change in aperture size for added lip tension. As they unconsciously reduce the lip opening during a diminuendo they feel they are adding lip tension. If this were true, pianissimo would require extremely high tension and fortissimo would be a relaxed, low tension state. Such a situation cannot successfully occur, since soft notes with their lesser quantities of air could not activate a rigid, highly contracted lip. Furthermore, loud, high air compression notes impose a great work load on the embouchure.

The interpretation of data is just as important as securing it. This can be a difficult thing, especially when applied to a playing situation. FINE

1959

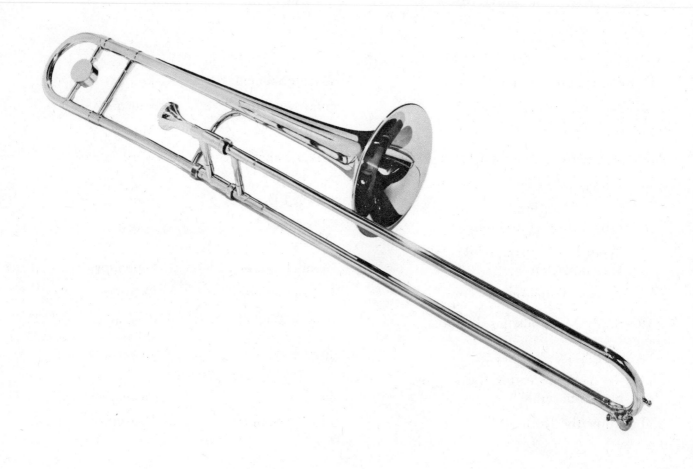

Tenor Trombone

Playing the French Horn

Joseph Schmoll

THE MOST IMPORTANT requisites for horn playing are a good ear, innate musical ability, and a desire to master the instrument. The size of the lips is relatively unimportant. A number of well-known teachers of the horn agree that thin lips are not necessary to play the instrument well. The shape of the teeth and jaw are important only if there are glaring malformations present.

It is helpful for the student to have played another brass instrument before taking up the study of the horn. The trumpet, or cornet, or mellophone are instruments that will provide a background of basic musical knowledge, fingering, and familiarity with a mouthpiece. It is a mistake, however, to transfer the poorest trumpet students to the horn.

Types of Horns

The three most popular kinds of horns today are the horn in F, the horn in $B\flat$, and the double horn in F and $B\flat$. The horn in F is found in many of our school systems today but is played by few professionals. Its advantage is its rich tone which is preferred by most musicians. Its disadvantage is its inability to speak clearly in the high register. In comparison to the $B\flat$ horn it feels "stuffy" to the performer, and it is easier to miss notes when playing the F horn.

Most instrument makers supply an $E\flat$ slide with the F horn. This slide is inserted when playing an $E\flat$ horn part. Many students fail to extend the valve slides when the $E\flat$ tuning slide is used and this results in unsatisfactory intonation. It is best to purchase music with F horn parts or else teach the student how to transpose $E\flat$ music on the F horn. When playing an F horn and reading music written for the $E\flat$ horn, transpose all pitches down a major second.

The $B\flat$ horn is pitched a perfect fourth higher than the F horn, therefore sounds the high notes with less effort from the performer than does the F horn. On the $B\flat$ horn there is also less chance of missing notes. One disadvantage, however, is its inability to play the notes from low $B\natural2$ down to low $F\sharp2$. A fourth valve, however, added to the horn will enable the player to sound these notes. This valve was pioneered by a well known American horn manufacturer. Other manufacturers would perhaps add the valve upon request.

A thumb valve, in addition to the finger valves, is necessary for muting because muting raises the pitch 3/4 of a step on the $B\flat$ horn and the thumb valve compensates for this.

If the student, or teacher, knows what a characteristic horn tone is, there is no reason why the $B\flat$ horn cannot produce a beautiful tone. By listening to accomplished performers one can quickly ascertain the qualities of distinctive horn tone. Good tone on the $B\flat$ horn can be aided by slightly closing the bell with the right hand. The $B\flat$ horn is the easiest horn to play of the three kinds of horns and a school system might well supply the players who play the low parts with $B\flat$ horns which have the fourth finger valve. These performers then could play all of the low notes. Most professionals who play a single horn prefer the single $B\flat$ horn.

The double horn is the popular horn today because its combines the advantages of the F and $B\flat$ horns. A thumb valve allows the performer to select the F or $B\flat$ side of the horn. The F horn side is used for the middle and low registers and the $B\flat$ side for the upper range. The change in horns is usually made between G4 and D5.

A horn which is manufactured by an instrument maker noted for the quality of his French horns is usually a good buy. A compromise mouthpiece ordinarily is supplied with the horn by the leading American horn manufacturers. These mouthpieces, and those which bear the name of leading American players and teachers, are suitable ones.

Playing Position

The horn is most often played in a seated position. Sometimes a performer is called upon to play standing up or while marching. If this is necessary, some practice in those positions would be helpful. Most of the time, however, it is best to practice while seated.

A chair similar to those furnished for performing organizations is best. The performer should sit in a comfortable position with the bell of the horn resting on the thigh. The bell should point away from the body or else the tone will be muffled. Pointing the bell towards the body is sometimes called "hugging the bell" and is practiced because a great deal of the sound reaches the performer's ear. The result sounds impressive to the player but not to the listener.

The legs of the performer should be slightly to the right of the music stand. This allows the mouthpiece to come directly to the mouth. The head and shoulders face the music stand directly. The correct height of the horn can be adjusted by moving the right leg forward or backward.

The head should neither be tilted to one side nor slightly backward. Such positions of the head increase the problems of playing and fill the onlooker with wonder as to how the player can play at all.

Mouthpiece Placement

The mouthpiece should be placed in the center of the mouth with approximately two-thirds touching the upper lip and one-third the lower lip. There may be slight individual differences among performers, depending upon what each finds most comfortable.

Placing one-half of the mouthpiece on the upper lip and one-half on the

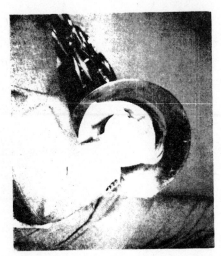

Correct position of hand in bell. Sharp pitches are adjusted by closing the hand, while flat pitches are compensated for by opening the hand.

lower lip is not encouraged. There is no proof that this method will not produce results but most successful horn players place more of the mouthpiece on the upper lip, and for this reason this procedure is recommended.

Hand Position

When the hand is put in the bell, the thumb and fingers are placed together in the same manner as they are when saluting. Experimentation will reveal how far the hand should be placed in the bell. If it is placed too far in the bell, the tone will be muffled. The wrist should be free and relaxed for the sake of comfort and so that pitches which are a trifle sharp can be lowered by slightly closing the hand. If the pitch is flat the hand should be opened as far as possible. See acompanying illustration.

Non-transposing mutes should be used whenever possible. They are relatively inexpensive and easy to procure, except for horns having a larger bell opening, in which case it is more difficult to find a mute which will produce muted notes in tune. Hand muting raises the pitch one half-step, so transposition down of one half-step is necessary to compensate for this change of pitch.

Embouchure and Tonguing

The correct embouchure is formed by slightly puckering the lips as if to whistle. Buzzing the lips makes the instrument speak and it is very important to press the lips against the mouthpiece with a minimum of pressure. The attack is also very important and if properly executed can be one of the most beautiful features of horn playing. It is undesirable to hear a breathy stream of air or any other unpleasant sound when a note is attacked. Good horn tone should begin immediately and this is accomplished by an action of the lips resembling spitting. The student should be encouraged to spit rather vigorously into the horn at first until he has mastered the technique.

The tongue can be placed between the upper and lower teeth or behind the upper teeth. Both of these methods have been used with success by leading horn players. With either method the tongue is drawn toward the back of the mouth at the same time the lips spit. Before the attack, the tongue blocks the air stream. By withdrawing it quickly the air is free to pass into the horn.

Conclusion

Good horn tone is aided by concentrating on blowing thru the horn, rather than just blowing into the mouthpiece. The tone should be big and free, neither forced and brassy, nor, on the other hand, small and anemic. Daily practice is essential to produce a good tone. In fact, mastery of the horn is impossible without daily practice.

Most horns are built slightly sharp so the tuning slide is usually pulled out a little to compensate. The valve slides are also pulled out to compensate for the sharpness of the horn. Experimentation will produce the correct adjustment.   FINE

Beginning Brass Class

John Kinyon

MOST INSTRUMENTAL music teachers reluctantly agree that the class method of teaching is here to stay. Because of the number of beginners and the multitude of scheduling difficulties, this method is usually the only solution to the problem of when to meet with the youngsters at all. Any possible private lesson time is given to the more advanced students, although at the same time we remind ourselves that it is the beginners who most need individual attention. Against this difficult situation the instrumental music teacher must turn his skill and ingenuity, hoping to turn this musical Tower of Babel into an efficient teaching set-up.

Grouping

Classroom teachers have long recognized the inefficiencies incumbent upon teaching large classes and have attempted by various means to group their students according to mental capabilities. The instrumental music teacher has the same problems, but they are carried to a further degree by the fact that he has within his classes physical as well as mental differences. This is obvious from the very first lesson. Nowhere are these differences more acute than in the brass class where tone production is so directly related to embouchure.

The first lessons are the most important, but, when the elements of time and excitement are against us, they are often not as constructive as they should be. Johnny wants to "take the next lesson," Johnny's parents want to hear a tune, and Johnny's teacher needs him in junior band as soon as possible.

Poor Johnny! He is often the victim of this impetuous triumvirate before he is able to produce a legitimate tone. If ever a slogan were apropos to the first year of musical training, it would be "SLOW DOWN—CHILDREN AT WORK." Any time *lost* in getting across to the young student the fundamentals of tone production will be more than repaid at the other end of the line.

Concentrate on Tone

The usual problems of young brass players (tight throat, pinched lip, too little upper and/or too much lower lip in the mouthpiece, clenched teeth, tongue held too high and forward, puffed cheeks, chewing action when tonguing, weak and faulty attack, ad infinitum) unless detected and remedied in the early lessons will, in all predictable probability, never be conquered. This is especially true in the brass class where the teacher is caught in the predicament of a man watching a seven-ring circus.

While it is not the purpose of this article to examine each of these problems, in general it may be said that the development of a natural and relaxed manner of tone production is essential to good tone. In turn this relaxation is contingent on building range slowly, i.e. not squeezing and pinching for high tones before the embouchure is sufficiently set. *Tone* is of primary importance; range will develop as a natural by-product.

Establish Routine

The class lesson itself, no matter how brief or under what frantic conditions, should set a pattern for home practice. Since it is customary to meet our students at least once per week, it is important that we impart (if only into their subconscious) the IDEA of routine in home practice. After students have achieved to some extent the ability to produce a tone correctly and are launched into their instruction book, the lessons should develop into a definite routine. First of all there should be a warm-up, even as rudimentary as a half-dozen long tones in the easiest register. Gradually, in keeping with the students' progress, placement studies (intervals), scales, song playing, lip slurs, and technical exercises will be added.

One of the blessings of any class lesson is that the experience of ensemble playing carries over into band performance. The class may even be conducted by the teacher to give the students the experience of following a visible beat. Simple exercises in counterpoint, such as easy contrapuntal duets, should be introduced almost from the very first. A conception of independence in reading is basic to all ensemble performance.

Tuba and French Horn

Ordinarily the beginning brass class will include only cornets, trumpets, trombones, and baritones. Although it is very possible to begin grade school youngsters on tuba, there is the natural disadvantage of handling an instrument of such proportions and lugging it home for practice. It is suggested that future BB♭ tuba players be started on baritone, reading from a BB♭ tuba instruction book. It is of no matter that the part will sound an octave above the actual written pitch. When the time is right for a switch-over to the larger instrument any problems inherent in the change will be small ones.

It is the French horn players who "get the short end" when it comes to heterogeneous groupings in the early stages. Because of discrepancies in the beginning ranges and difficulties in tone placement, it is not usually desirable to include horns in mixed classes of beginners. The most efficient way is to start the future horn players on trumpet or cornet, letting them mature and prove themselves musically before making the switch-over to the more difficult instrument.

It is possible, however, to use B♭ horns in the brass class, letting these students play from a modified (a few changes of fingering) trumpet book. When these same players perform the regular F horn parts in band they can either switch to F horn (thus keeping the same fingerings but "hearing" a fourth lower), or they can stick with the B♭ horn (by transposing down a fourth). Neither system is particularly desirable for young, easily-discouraged students.

Conclusion

It may be well to remind ourselves that we must constantly ask perfection of our students and patience of ourselves. It is so easy to lower our standards when the pressure is on; it is so tempting to "go to the next lesson" before today's assignment is really accomplished. My recipe for brass players: begin with TONE . . . add range slowly . . . mix thoroughly with rhythm . . . season well with patience.

FINE

Brass Players Need a —

Daily Practice Routine

James Hoffren

A DAILY PRACTICE routine is a facet of brass pedagogy often neglected. Many instructors mention it to their students but fail to instigate an intelligent plan, nor do they follow thru in helping the student thru the initial stages of establishing a carefully thought-out practice routine.

What is even more surprising is that so many instructors minimize or completely ignore a daily practice routine. All athletes, for example weight lifters, have certain prescribed exercises which must be done each day for maximum improvement. Ambitious athletes allow nothing to interfere with their daily routine of exercises. And what is more significant is that they usually do the same series of exercises, continually endeavoring to increase *gradually* the number of repetitions.

Yet, not enough brass teachers make use of this well-known fact in their own teaching. Are we not also dealing with muscles? The musculature of the embouchure, the diaphragm, the fingers, and the tongue will all respond to a daily routine as surely as will the biceps.

Need for Emphasis

Most students have inefficient and haphazard practice habits. They practice as the mood strikes them—two hours one day, half hour the next, and probably none the following day. Or their mood may dictate working on solos one day, perhaps emphasizing high register the next day, and transposition will be studied the following day. Or they concentrate one solid hour one day and daydream thru half their practice session the next day. Also many students spend most of their time on that aspect of their technique on which they already excel. Isn't it obvious that under these conditions the embouchure will not manifest maximum improvement. There must be regularity and consistency.

Keys to Success

Regularity, perseverance, and variety are the key words in the development of brass endurance and technique. The student who conscientiously uses the following *Daily Practice Routine* will reap dividends of progressive improvement. The emphasis must be on a regular daily routine, preferably at the same hour each day. Some will benefit more from two or three practice sessions each day with the most extensive warm-up during the first session.

In the beginning the student will spend a very short period of practice time on each item in the daily routine. Very gradually he should increase the minutes on each item as his embouchure strengthens and his technical facility improves. Remember that practice with excessive pressure upon the mouthpiece *or* when the lip is tired can do more harm than good.

The strength of the embouchure limits the time available for practice; therefore, the best possible use must be made of the practice time. The student must learn what to practice, when, and for how long. The content of the practice session is more important than the length of time. Also, half the secret of improvement is knowing when to *quit* practicing and how long a period of rest and recuperation is needed until the next practice session.

Endurance will improve from practicing when the embouchure is tired *only up to a point*. Excessive practice beyond this point will tear down the lip. Every individual must discover this limit for himself.

Why So Important?

Of paramount importance is regularity and daily study without exception. The student must adhere religiously to the systematic practice schedule. One day of not practicing may eliminate the beneficial results of several days of practicing. There is one exception to this. If the lip has been abused from a lengthy concert or other difficult playing situation, I believe many individuals should not play the next day.

Give the embouchure a day to recuperate. Also, the embouchure must be very carefully warmed-up in the practice session following the abuse. Some individuals should do *only* the soft warm-up after abuse, omitting the more ambitious exercises—thus not taxing the recuperating muscles.

Perseverance is absolutely necessary since progress is slow and difficult to observe over short periods of time. No system or method will work unless given a sincere, faithful opportunity over an extended period of time. Do not expect miraculous results in a few weeks.

Variety is required for the progressive development of the embouchure. A common mistake is to practice one type of technique, such as high tones, at the exclusion of the other facets of performance. For example, if the student can comfortably practice approximately two half-hour sessions each day without overtiring, then he will spend from 10 to 20 minutes on the all-important warm-up and five minutes on *each* of the other ten items in the *Daily Practice Routine*. Students with weaker embouchures may do several minutes only on each item. However, each item should be studied

each day.

As the endurance increases, the allotted time on each item should gradually increase always avoiding overfatigue. The value of this routine lies in accurately measuring the time. I do not agree with some brass authorities who maintain that it is possible to increase the practice time five minutes each day. Muscles do not build that quickly. Most students must increase the time more gradually. It may take a month before the embouchure can handle an increased allotment of time on each category in the daily routine.

Suggested Routine

1. *Warm-up*—must be in the low register, of a slow tempo, and *piano*.
   a. Mouthpiece buzzing—scales and slurs.
   b. Sustained tones—also with crescendo and decrescendo.
   c. Low lip slurs—as *pianissimo* as possible for better control and less pressure upon the mouthpiece.
   d. Tonguing—not too rapidly in the warm-up.
2. *Major and Minor Scales*—use numerous articulations.
3. *Chromatic Scales*
4. *Lip Slurs*—very important to the development of endurance and flexibility. Try to play more in one breath each week to develop the diaphragm.
5. *Internal Exercises (including arpeggios)*—slurred and tongued.
6. *Single Tonguing*—legato and staccato, more ambitious than the warm-up tonguing.
7. *Double and Triple Tonguing*—repeated notes and scalewise—also in musical context.
8. *Songs*—for the development of expressive playing and *cantabile*.
9. *Etudes*—for work on individual rhythmic problems and so forth.
10. *Solos*—covering all styles and periods of music.
11. *Transposition* (optional)—this category could include chord improvisation for those interested in jazz or dance work.
12. *Sight Reading*—do not stop for mistakes nor slow down during difficult passages. Use a metronome. Move the eyes ahead of the actual sound.

FINE

Starting Beginners on French Horn

Milan Yancich

MOST OF US in the teaching profession have a certain *approach* or *presentation* to the new student, and I believe that the initial lessons can in most instances set the standards for all the lessons to follow. Of primary importance is the ability to set the new student at ease. With judicious care the rapport between student and teacher can be established in the first lessons.

For the student who has had some training in blowing a brass instrument, ask first for an ascending scale beginning on C4. When he reaches a "point of no sound," then have him begin on C4 and descend the scale to the best of his ability. Sometimes the novice is unable to begin on C4; in that case have him start higher, wherever he can produce a sound. Thus, in a few notes, his range can be determined.

For the recruit who has never held a horn or blown into the instrument, ask him to buzz his lips and then have him try buzzing into the mouthpiece. When this is successfully accomplished, have him strike any note on which he can produce a sound. After he is able to create a sound on the instrument, then direct his attention to stance, posture, and the holding position of the French horn.

The buzzing episode is of great importance in determining the possibilities of brass students. If they cannot buzz in the first lessons due to malformation of teeth or a peculiarity of lip, their chances for any degree of proficiency on the instrument are limited.

Position

Demonstrate the proper sitting posture, placement of the feet on the floor, and holding of the horn. Stand in front of a chair, feet together, holding the horn in front of yourself, left hand fingers on the keys and the right hand placed in the bell. Then sit down without moving the feet. The horn rests on the knee feet on the floor, back straight.

Placement of the horn becomes a real problem to the young child, for it seems larger than the student. It is sometimes physically impossible for a player to hold the instrument in playing position and hold the bell on the knee. Then the teacher should make adjustments in the position of the horn so as to achieve a maximum of comfort.

At this point show the pupil the *approximate* hand position. The right hand is inserted into the bell of the horn, fingers together on the far side of the bell away from the body. The thumb is placed either alongside or on top of the forefinger; and, if held off the knee, the horn is supported along the forefinger and thumb.

Because each person's hand varies in size and because horn bells differ in dimensions, there is no "one" place to insert the hand. To find the approximate hand position have the student place his hand in the bell in a manner so that the bell is wide open; then ask the student to sustain a tone, and as he plays have him cup his right hand slowly until the tone sounds muffled. At that moment of muffled sound tell the student to open his hand slightly—and that is his *approximate* hand position for playing.

Warm-Ups

At this point in the lesson have the student take his mouthpiece and press it tightly against the palm or back of his hand. After a minute have him remove the mouthpiece and see the ring imprint. This demonstration of pressure is to remind the player that the lip is a sensitive structure of nerves and tissues and must be treated with care, especially by the beginner.

Then ask the pupil to press the mouthpiece on another area of skin and remove it, several times. He sees by this action that the blood has a chance to return to the affected area of the skin after each withdrawal, thereby avoiding the heavy ring imprint.

This example leads to my first warm-up exercise which I recommend to all students. Basically it amounts to this: the student plays a whole note tied to a quarter (five counts and then rests three counts). On the rest, the mouthpiece is removed from the lips, and—in tempo—he plays again on the first note of the next bar. This warm-up exercise is played as quietly and in as relaxed a manner as possible. If the student is a beginner and can play only a few notes, I have him repeat them; otherwise, he warms up on a one octave C scale.

For his second warm-up exercise, I have the student play a few notes in the scale as long and as softly as possible. His goal should be about thirty seconds. This is primarily to help him control the breath, sustain his pitch, and to listen to his tonal quality.

The third warm-up exercise is for the purpose of securing a big breath and playing with a large tone. Have the student play a few notes as long and as loudly as possible. The problem here is to be able to strike a note immediately at a fortissimo level and not attack the note and then expand on it.

These three warm-up exercises are a *must* for my beginning horn students. They are to be done daily.

Attack

Care must be taken to impart to every note the same degree of force so as to insure perfect quality. The note should be started with the tongue and the pupil cautioned to avoid squeezing out the tone from his throat.

Describe the attack by the tongue as being similar to the action of pulling a plug from the bottom of a tub full of water. When the plug is withdrawn, the water in the tub rushes out. Assuming there is air in the lungs providing pressure behind the tongue, the same action occurs here. With the withdrawal of the tongue the air rushes out creating an attack on the horn.

During the demonstration of the attack make a distinction among the various types. There has always been a great deal of controversy about the placement of the tongue, and I must admit, that I do not use "one" attack exclusively, but several, depending upon the desired result. I do believe, however, that the beginning horn player must make a definite attack so that he acquires assurance and confidence in striking the notes accurately.

The French horn by nature does not respond as quickly to an attack as do the other brass instruments and one can easily prove this to himself by triple or double tonguing on a trumpet or trombone and then trying the same thing on a French horn. Because of this "delayed response" one must try for a more pointed attack than on the other brass instruments.

Breathing

Have the student stand so that he can take a complete and full breath. Although we hornists do sit while performing, I believe that in a standing position we are more apt to breathe in a natural manner. I like to think of a breath as being produced in three stages: starting from the lower part of the abdomen, going thru the middle or rib part, to the high or upper chest. Sometimes this is called abdominal breathing, low breathing, deep breathing, or diaphragmatic breathing. Whatever the terminology, the important thing is to know the importance of breath control in one's playing.

Have the student place his hands on your waist and back so that when you take a breath he can feel the expansion. Then he should imitate the same action. If this is unsuccessful, ask him to yawn. A yawn demands the filling of every air space in the lungs, and I cannot think of anything more allied to a perfect intake of air than a yawn.

Then demonstrate how to blow air thru the French horn, and explain the function of the diaphragm in controlling breathing. Also point out the importance of keeping the chest from collapsing and the problem of controlling the throat in playing.

I have my students play the C scale in quarter notes up and down in one breath. This they must do with a fine attack and ho mistakes. I then have them play an arpeggio pattern in quarter notes. With the same degree of perfection, they then learn to play the scale twice up and down in eighth notes, all in one breath. Finally, they learn to play the scale three times up and down, also in one breath, but now in triplets; the same applies to chord patterns.

In this manner the student develops his technique simultaneously with his development of breath control. The speed of development and success of any musician is dependent upon his ability to grasp the technique of "how to practice."

FINE

Trumpet/Cornet Intonation Problems

Slide Mechanisms—Their Need, Desirability, and Use

Howard Deming

To DATE, satisfactory slide mechanisms have been devised for only the first and third valves.

We all know that certain tones are out of tune on trumpets, but perhaps we have never stopped actually to catalog them, or reason why. There is not a trumpet made that has all notes in tune without adjustment and there never will be one. This is a physical impossibility as long as we use the *tempered scale* of the keyboard instruments along with the natural or *just* scale derived from the harmonic series produced on the trumpet.

Just vs. Tempered

The comparative frequencies of the open tones on the trumpet and the concert pitches of the tempered scale are as follows:

TRUMPET	TEMPERED
C4—233.08	233.08
G4—349.62	349.23
C5—466.16	466.16
E5—582.70	587.33
G5—699.24	698.46

It will be noted that G4 (second line G) is 0.39 vibration sharp on the trumpet, while E5 (4th space E) is 4.63 vibrations flat, and G5 is 0.78 vibration sharp. This leads one to the conclusion that G4 and G5 for the trumpet are *naturally* sharp pitches with G5 being more out of tune than G4, while E5 has a great tendency—over four vibrations—to be flat.

Now, should the valve slides be made the exact length to lower the tone (1) one-half step (2nd valve), then (2) a whole step (1st valve), and finally (3) a step and a half (3rd valve), each harmonic series would show the same relative tones to have similar discrepancies.

Complications

When valves are used in combination, we have additional problems. The second valve lowers the pitch one-half step, exactly as the old quick change to "A" did. In the so-called "quick change to A" trumpet models, it was necessary to lengthen the valve slides: the 2nd valve about 1/16 inch, the first valve 1/8 inch, and the third 3/16 inch. When the 3rd valve is used alone, by lowering the instrument 1½ steps, it makes the instrument a G trumpet so that now the 1st slide should be lengthened approximately 5/16 inch, while the second should be pulled 5/32 inch. If all three valves are used, the resultant note is, of course, extremely sharp.

Perhaps this compound "out-of-tuneness" can be understood more readily by thinking in terms of a graph. Suppose, for the sake of convenience, we let 24 squares represent the basic tube length of the trumpet and two squares the additional length necessary to lower this basic length ½ step (2nd valve), and 4 squares one whole step (1st valve), while 6 squares would represent 1½ steps (3rd valve). I think you will readily see that if it takes the ratio of 2 squares to 24 to lower the tone ½ step, then

it will take more than 2 squares to lower the pitch one-half step when the basic length is combined with, say, the 1st valve which would cause a ratio of 2 to 28.

So, added to the original problem of two conflicting scales, we find this additional problem which at best brings about a compromise—one which Vincent Bach calls "The Golden Middleway." This compromise varies from one manufacturer to the other. Basically, however, it usually involves proportionate lengthening of all three valve slides. They lengthen the 2nd valve slide a small amount making it possible still to play the written B♮4 in tune by lipping up. The same treatment is afforded the 1st valve. The length of the 3rd valve is usually extended to the point that, on most models, it is too flat in pitch to be used alone for lowering the pitch 1½ steps.

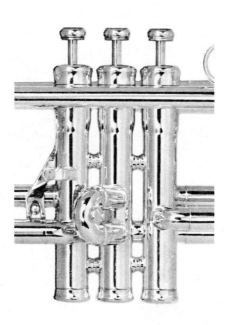

The tendency is for written G♭5 and F5—2nd, and 1st valves, respectively—to be sharp. Lengthening the valve slide has a tendency to alleviate this problem, but one must also note that E♭5 and D5 are flat originally, which problem is now increased with the lengthened valve slides. At any rate a compromise is used causing multiple valve notes to be sharp and single valve notes to be flat.

Solution

By now, it should be fairly clear as to the need and desirability of the sliding mechanisms. It is true that the proficient performer can lip the pitch up or down (more easily on a cornet

than trumpet) to a degree but always at the risk of security, accuracy, and tone.

With the slide mechanisms available on both 1st and 3rd valve slides, the manufacturer is faced with much less of a need for compromise. Valve slides will not have to be lengthened so much to compensate for sharpness in valve combinations. First valve can be left short enough so that D5 can be played in tune and then lengthened for the F5 if sharp or for any valve combination using it. Similarly, the 3rd valve slide will not have to be lengthened to the degree that makes 2nd and 3rd combined-valves so flat.

First and second valves can sometimes be used to play E5. However, this usually makes the pitch as much too sharp as the open E5 is flat. The mechanism on the first valve can, however, help solve this problem.

In fast moving passages the use of these mechanisms is many times impractical, but there is no excuse for playing exposed tones of any duration out of tune, with the possible exception of open tones and tones played with the second valve alone. The fifth and sixth overtones for the valves will be naturally flat and sharp, respectively. Until a practical slide mechanism is developed that will work on all tones, we will still have to lip these tones in tune at the sacrifice of tone and accuracy.

For the critics who say that 1st and 3rd valve triggers are complicated and unnecessary, I can reply only that there are probably some who still refuse to change from the Albert to the Boehm System on clarinet. A third-valve slide mechanism on a trumpet is a *necessity* and, if playing in tune is to be considered, the 1st valve mechanism can hardly be considered a *luxury*.

One last word of warning might be given concerning the condition of the instrument. The saying that an instrument that is continually blown out of tune develops those characteristics is entirely false, but it is true that the instrument that is not kept clean inside can very quickly become an out-of-tune instrument.

The knowledge of imperfections in the manufacture of the instrument should not deter the brass performer, but should encourage him always to strive to play more nearly in tune and at the same time with better quality.

FINE

Reflections on the history of the ——

French Horn Ensemble

Max Pottag

MY FIRST EXPERIENCE with French horn ensemble playing goes back to my youth. When I was 16, I joined a group of fellow students, and we formed an ensemble of three horns and a trombone. We received encouragement and took every opportunity to perfect ourselves and to acquaint the public with this new combination. In addition, we found much pleasure in searching for and arranging suitable music.

During the period when I was studying at the Royal Conservatory of Leipzig, we were requested to serenade my teacher, Frederick Gumbert, on his 62nd birthday. He was so pleased with the horn ensemble music that he resumed playing in quartets after not having done so for years. He even reorganized his own group for regular performances. With six horn players available in the famous Leipzig Gewandhaus Orchestra, two were always at liberty; the retired Mr. Gumbert and these two orchestra members chose me to complete their quartet, a privilege I have never forgotten. We concertized and played for our own pleasure.

During my engagement with the Hamburg Symphony, while on tour we stayed at the famous German spa, Bad Ems. In spite of three concerts a day, our horn quartet found time to float down the river in a boat performing ensemble music, to the delight of those walking or sunning themselves along the banks.

Revival

In 1947, as a faculty member of Northwestern University with a horn class of 25 students I revived the idea of ensemble work and produced a program of music by Beethoven, Wagner, and Brahms. Criticisms were so encouraging that the ensemble became permanent, giving two or three programs every year and making four appearances at the Mid-West National Band Clinic in Chicago.

In 1951 twenty-three of Hollywood's finest professional hornists gave a program which I directed. This resulted in the birth of the world-famous Los Angeles Horn Club, developing the most unbelievable versatility under the guiding spirit of Wendell Hoss. The recordings which they plan should be a welcome addition to the libraries of those who enjoy horn ensemble performances.

Horn ensembles have developed in many localities in the United States: 50 players in Gunnison, Colorado; 36 in Joliet, Illinois; 34 in Boulder, Colorado; 18 in Miami, Florida; 42 in Tallahassee, Florida; 42 in Memphis, Tennessee; 50 in Enid, Oklahoma; 20 in Dallas, Texas; 20 in Toledo, Ohio; and finally, 72 under my direction at the last Mid-West National Band Clinic in Chicago.

Music Available

There is much material available today for ensembles, some difficult and some easy, including: *Scherzo and Funeral March* by Mendelssohn-Steiner; *Adagio Pathetique* by Beethoven-Arne Oldberg; Ronald LoPresti's *Suite* for eight parts; Rudolf Mayer's *Festmusik* for eight parts and *Capriccio and Praeludium* for 12 parts; and Paul Nelson's three songs for soprano and eight horns.

The great range of the French horn produces an unusually full, rich, and fascinating sound. It is almost unbelievable that this one instrument can produce such a variety of color. For special effects with a large group, players might raise the bells up for the last few *fff* chords, keeping hands in the bell for the sake of intonation. I hope the French horn ensemble can continue to grow and demonstrate just how fascinating the instrument is.

FINE

Avoid Lip Injuries While Marching

Samuel Mages

WATCH THOSE BRASS players during the coming outdoor marching activities! Overblowing and strain resulting in overtired lips, changes in mouthpiece position, faulty intonation, and bad tonguing habits, all can creep into the brass player's performance. This is especially true of the cornet and trumpet players.

Outdoor Sound

Most experienced players realize that when playing out-of-doors, the "sound" leaves the player immediately and seems to be very small in contrast to his usual "sound" indoors. A reminder to all young brass instrument players is necessary, calling attention to this trap for overblowing and unnecessary strain.

The natural tendency for the player is to blow harder as soon as he misses the usual fuller sound with reverberation that he is accustomed to hearing in a room. With overblowing, the tone quality and intonation suffer immediately, lips are apt to become bruised rather than tired, the important mouthpiece position may shift, and faulty tonguing habits may develop.

Several simple procedures by directors would enable their brass instrument players to cope better with these problems of performing out-of-doors. Begin with rehearsing the music indoors, enabling the players to be familiar with their parts and routines before attempting them on the football field.

By assigning more players to the first parts, the individual brass player would be able to take short and frequent rests without the pressure of having to play continuously. Be considerate of your brass sections by conducting your rehearsals so as to avoid too much continuous playing. It is often advantageous to rehearse routines without music.

Advice to Players

Every individual player would find it very worthwhile to get into the habit of a set short warmup routine before each marching rehearsal. Remembering that you are dealing with small delicate muscles in the playing of a brass instrument, you should start your daily playing with easy warmups. A few soft long tones and several short scale passages in the middle register are usually good for this purpose.

Avoid the abuse given to your lips by plunging into a march selection or "blasting away" before the rehearsal as so many players foolishly do. In rehearsal, endurance, intonation, and better tone quality will be maintained by frequent and short pauses in your playing. These pauses need not be very long and when taken during less important phrases you are able to be stronger on the more important spots.

If you are playing the higher and more demanding parts, do not be too proud to drop your part one octave if you have to repeat it or if the rehearsal runs long. This applies especially to the many endings used in football shows.

If, in spite of cautions, a player finds that his lips are overtired, possibly bruised, and not rested by the following day, then the only remedy is to take a complete rest by not playing at all for a day or two. Following this rest, he should begin to play again in easy stages for the next several days, avoiding unnecessary strain.

Practice on tired lips rarely produces good results. Many players find that as a result of straining for upper notes or achieving staccato effects, they begin to stop notes with their tongue. Other players may find themselves keeping their tongue too far forward in their mouth, causing their ease of blowing to become more difficult due to this obstruction of the tongue.

Players finding themselves in this predicament should avoid excessive strain and overblowing. Review the fundamentals of attack and release of notes. If you find your mouthpiece position changing, you had better check the basic mouthpiece position carefully and practice easy material in order to strengthen the proper embouchure position. The mouthpiece change, which is usually a "slipping down" on the lips, could be the source of real potential trouble to the player.

So, watch those brass players during the outdoor marching activities! Help your brass players to keep their best tone quality, endurance, and intonation in their performance. Your band will sound better as a result of it.

FINE

Playing Trombone in Tune

Gabriel Kosakoff

IN READING THRU the forewords of most trombone method books, be they beginning or advanced, one is very likely to find much attention paid to breathing, attack, release, phrasing, rhythm, style, arpeggios, slide technique, scales, tonguing, etc. However, rarely, if ever is much attention given to the trombonist's most important problem, intonation.

Not only are the method books at fault, but many of our teachers are lax in their approach to playing in tune, and students are content to play with faulty pitch. There is too much of a rush to play a song or to fill in an empty place in the marching band, and a neglect of fundamental problems results.

Developing a Good Ear

The delicacies of intonation are assimilated only after long exposure to correct pitch which must be stressed from the very first lesson. Although perfect intonation depends upon specifically gifted ears, good ears can be developed, and students—when capably guided—can recognize loss of pitch, false notes, and imperfect semitones.

Why must we always stop the student and tell him he is sharp or flat? Let him hear for himself. He must be taught to know when and in which way he is out of tune, particularly in relation to group playing. For this reason ensemble experience is important right from the start as it teaches the student how to blend with and listen to others. Isn't ensemble playing the objective of most wind instrumentalists?

True, beginning embouchures are inclined to play flat and tire quickly. This should serve not as an excuse, but as an excellent teaching situation in the development of careful listening on the part of the student. The enterprising teacher can seek out good ensemble literature on this level. Good intonation and blending in the ensemble depends on the relative position of the note one is playing within the chord being played.

The Trombonist's Prerogative

Of all the wind instruments, the trombone has the most natural means of adjusting the pitch of notes. By shortening or lengthening the slide, any desired pitch can be obtained, even quarter tones or less. Therefore, any note can be sharpened or flattened to meet the exact demands of the highly developed ear. What seems to be the trombonist's biggest problem—how far to push out the slide—can prove his greatest asset. Instead of having seven rigid positions on the instrument, let the student put his slide where the intonation is truest. Rather than relying on an eye-hand-lip co-ordination, make it an eye-ear-hand-lip co-ordination.

As on the other wind instruments, many trombonists are satisfied to lip or "humor" the notes in tune, and achieve success thereby. Why should we have to depend solely on this "crutch" when we have a much more natural means at our disposal? Take advantage of the ability to play any desired pitch. Don't be afraid to move the slide. Thru its use we can achieve perfection even with the natural scales that are not based on the compromising scale of equal temperament that is found on the keyboard instruments.

Overtone Series and Intonation

Let us examine the overtone series from the first nine partials which comprise the notes normally playable in each position of the trombone. Wm. F. Raymond, in his book, *The Trombone and Its Player*,[1] shows the pitch discrepancies between the overtone series and the scale of equal temperament. Using 58.27 vibrations as pedal Bb, he constructs the notes in first position. (The frequency of any partial in the overtone series can be found by multiplying the frequency of the fundamental by the number of the partial.)

In the comparison with the tempered scale (which is not the scale of the band or orchestra), the 5th and 7th partials are noticeably flat. A 5th partial on most brass instruments is usually lipped in tune, although once the trombonist leaves the 1st position, he can raise the slide.

The 7th partials are rarely if ever used on the other brass instruments, because they are so noticeably flat. The trombonist, however, can and does take full advantage of these notes (once he leaves 1st position) by pulling in his slide approximately 1¼ to 1½ inches. The best examples of this are the high G4 which is almost always played in the short 2nd position, and the high F#4 which is almost always played in the short 3rd position.

An excellent example of the trombonist's unique advantage of playing in tune is cited by J. C. Deagan of the Deagan Bell Company, in his chart *Fundamentals in A=440 Pitch*.[2]

When the note G4 (he could have chosen any other note) is played as a minor 3rd in the chord of E minor, the diatonic pitch differs in frequency from the G that appears as a major 3rd in the chord of Eb major:

395.55 cycles per second, diatonic scale of E; 391.99 cycles per second, tempered scale; 388.90 cycles per second, diatonic scale of Eb.

Notice that the tempered scale frequency is a happy medium between the other two, and that this note can vary as much as 6.65 c.p.s. Guided by his ear, and using proper slide control, the skillful trombonist plays them differently.

Must a trombonist be a mathematician in order to play in tune? Of course not. Most trombonists have no knowledge of these figures, and some don't even realize that they are playing these notes differently, but they do.

Other Considerations

There are many factors affecting correct intonation other than those referred to above. The temperature of the room, condition and cleanliness of the instrument, mouthpiece, posture, embouchure, diaphragmatic support of the tone, etc. However, I feel the desire to play in tune is the most essential. Only thru correct conditioning, awareness, and experience with good pitch can students play accurately in tune.

Conclusions

1. Intonation must be foremost in the mind of the beginner from the first lesson.

2. Use alternate positions advantageously.

3. Vibrato can't hide faulty pitch.

4. Try to hear the desired tone before you play it (some sight singing will help master this problem).

5. Devote more effort to blending than to being heard.

6. There are no exact places for the seven positions. Get there by your *ear*, not your eye.

FINE

1. Wm. F. Raymond, *The Trombone and its Player*, page 20, Fillmore Music House, Cincinnati, Ohio, 1937.
2. J. C. Deagan, *Fundamentals of A=440 Pitch*, Deagan Bell Company, Chicago, Ill. 1916.

Study Materials for Trumpet

Daniel Tetzlaff

IN RESPONSE TO inquiries about good trumpet and cornet literature for study, for recreation, and for development, following is a list of materials which I have used and found so helpful that I keep them in my personal library. No trumpet player should be content with any single method.

I would also recommend the list to anyone desiring to build a music library for school or city use. Perhaps only a few readers would care to have all these items among their own materials, but at least one or two from each group would be a good idea.

Books with Helpful Explanatory Material

Farkas	*Art of French Horn Playing**	Summy-Birchard
Reger	*The Talking Trumpet**	Lawson-Gould
Thieck	*Common Sense Lip and Tone Development**	Bechler (Milwaukee)

Foundation Exercises

Colin	*Lip Flexibilities*	Colin
Schlossberg	*Daily Drills*	Baron
Shuebruk	*Graded Lip and Tongue Trainers*	C. Fischer

Studies for Melody Playing

Duhem	*24 Melodic Studies*	Cundy-Bettoney
Lavignac	*Solfege Exercises for Soprano Voice*	Lemoine (Paris)
Pottag	*Preparatory Melodies*	Belwin
Reinhardt	*Selection of Concone Studies*	Elkan-Vogel

Studies for Finger Dexterity

Clarke	*Technical Studies*	C. Fischer
Klosé	*209 Tone and Finger Exercises*	Gornston

Large, Complete Methods

Arban	*Complete Method*	C. Fischer
Gatti	*World Method*	Ricordi
Gower-Voxman	*Advanced Method, Vols. I, II*	Rubank
St. Jacome	*Grand Method, Vols. I, II**	C. Fischer
Williams	*Modern Method, Vols. I, II, III*	Colin

Books to Develop Musicianship

Chavanne	*25 Etudes*	Leduc (Paris)
Clarke	*Characteristic Studies (and Solos)*	C. Fischer
Donderer	*Little Etudes in All Keys*	Rahter (Leipzig)
Duhem	*24 Melodic Etudes and 20 Etudes for D Trumpet*	Walpot (Brussels)
Fontana	*16 Studies*	Cundy-Bettoney
Goldman	*28 Practical Studies*	C. Fischer
Hering	*32 Etudes*	C. Fischer
Kopprasch	*60 Selected Etudes*	C. Fischer
Paisner	*Beethoven Sonatas Transcribed*	Gornston
Paudert	*24 Studies*	C. Fischer

Shuebruk	*Daily Technical Exercises and Drills*	C. Fischer
Voxman	*Selected Studies**	Rubank
Wurm	*20 Etudes*	Cundy-Bettoney

Books for Studying Transposition

Bordogni	*24 Vocalises*	Leduc (Paris)
Brandt	*Orchestra Studies and Last Etudes**	Leeds
Liesering	*Transposition School*	Benjamin (Leipzig)
Sachse	*100 Etudes*	International
Williams	*Modern Method for Transposition**	Morris

For Style and Versatility

Balasanyan	*20 Studies*	International
Bozza	*16 Etudes*	Leduc (Paris)
Charlier	*36 Etudes**	Leduc (Paris)
Faulx	*20 Etudes from Bach*	Brogneaux (Brussels)
Freitag	*22 Modern Studies*	Gornston
Glantz	*48 Advanced Studies**	Witmark
Gornston	*Weird Etudes*	Gornston
Harris	*Advanced Studies*	Harris
Huffnagle	*Unusual Studies*	Gornston
Kaucky	*Heroicke Etudy*	Hedebri (Prague)
Mancini	*Etudes, Caprices, Divertissements*	A.G.M. (Hollywood)
Mancini	*Modernistic Rhythms**	Mills
Maxime-Alphonse	*Etudes in 6 Graded Volumes*	Sansone
Pietzsch	*22 Virtuoso Studies*	Cundy-Bettoney
Porret	*24 Manuscript Etudes*	Chant du Monde
Smith	*Top Tunes*	C. Fischer
Williams	*Supplementary Studies*	Morris

Duets

Applebaum	*Kiddin' Around*	Colin
Carnaud	*30 Progressive Duets*	Cundy-Bettoney
Clodomir	*12 Duets*	Leduc (Paris)
Franz	*100 Duets for French Horn*	Sansone
Gatti	*33 Duets*	C. Fischer
Huffnagle	*Streamlined Duets*	Gornston
Kling	*15 Classical Duets*	Sansone
Koenig	*6 Operatic Duets*	Cundy-Bettoney
Kuffner	*20 Selected Duets*	Sansone
Marie	*30 Easy Duets*	Cundy-Bettoney
Mazas	*Duets for Manuscript Reading*	Gornston
Mozart	*12 Duos for French Horn*	Marx
Paudert	*6 Duets*	Cundy-Bettoney
Pottag	*60 French Horn Duets, Vols. I & II*	Belwin
Saro	*Studies in Canon Form*	Cundy-Bettoney
Schubert	*5 Little Duets*	Mercury
Sylvius. C.	*20 Original Duets**	Fox
Vanasek	*New Arban Duets*	Mills
Voxman	*Selected Duets, Vols. I & II*	Rubank
Williams	*114 Cornet Duets*	Colin

Note: The large method books by St. Jacome, E. S. Williams, Gower-Voxman, and Arban all contain many very interesting and helpful duets, as well as etudes.

*Volumes of unusual excellence that would make an ideal "core collection" for the aspiring trumpeter.

FINE

Graded Solos

John Haynie

IT IS NOT SURPRISING that many young trumpet and cornet players become bored with practice and at the first opportunity quit playing altogether. With all due respect to the *Arban* and *St. Jacome Methods* and the half dozen other commonly known books used the world over, these materials are not musically attractive enough to warrant spending a lifetime learning to play them. In the case of solo literature for trumpet (cornet) some people still feel there isn't anything written other than the virtuoso polka-type solos so wonderfully well received some thirty to forty years ago.

Contrary to this belief, there is more good to excellent music written for trumpet than any one player is likely to perform in a lifetime. As partial evidence of the great volume of available literature the following is a graded list of the more seldom played solos.

Grade II

Bach, J. S.	*If Thou Be Near*	Ricordi
Baines	*Pastorale*	Schott
Bakaleinikoff	*Legend*	Belwin
Bakaleinikoff	*Serenade*	Belwin
Barat	*Orientale*	Andraud
Bernstein	*Rondo for Lifey*	Schirmer
Cirri-Forst	*Arioso*	Edition Musicus
Galajikian	*Allegro Marziale*	Belwin
Gaminerie	*Friboulet*	Andraud
Defossez	*Les Gammes en Vacances*	Andraud
Fitzgerald	*Call*	C. Fischer
Fitzgerald	*English Suite*	Presser
Fitzgerald	*Legend*	C. Fischer
Klein	*Lament*	Boosey & Hawkes
Krieger	*Allegro*	Presser
Langue	*Impromptu*	Baron
Legrand	*Adoree*	Baron
Maleqieux	*Melodie Religieuse*	Andraud
Maniet	*Petit Morceau de Concours*	Baron
Montbrun	*March*	Andraud
Montbrun	*Scherzo*	Andraud
Montbrun	*Lied*	Andraud
Porret	*Concertino I, II, III, IV*	Baron
Poulain	*Melodie*	Baron
Ruetter	*Fanfares*	Andraud
Robbins	*Mont Saint-Michel*	Andraud

Grade III

Alary	*Morceau de Concours*	Cundy-Bettoney
Arnell	*Trumpet Allegro*	Schott
Balay	*Andante et Allegro*	Andraud
Balay	*Petite Piece Concertante*	Andraud
Balay	*Prelude et Ballade*	Andraud
Barat	*Fantaisie in Eb*	Andraud
Bloch, Andre	*Meou-Tan Yin*	Andraud
Chaplaevsky	*Valse Caprice*	Leeds
Cole	*Hammersmith Galop*	Schott
Cools	*Solo de Concours*	Andraud
Delmas	*Choral and Variations*	Alfred
Damase	*Hymne*	Elkan-Vogel
Fiocco	*Allegro*	Presser
Fitzgerald	*Frolic*	C. Fischer
Gibbons-Cruft	*Suite*	Mills
Goeyens, A.	*All'Antica*	Andraud
Goeyens, A.	*Introduction and Scherzo*	C. Fischer
Guillaume	*Andante et Allegro*	Baron
Hue	*First Solo de Concert*	Remick
JeanJean	*Capriccioso*	Alfred
Karsev	*Two Pieces*	International
Mouquet	*Impromptu*	Andraud
Persichetti	*Hollow Men*	Elkan-Vogel

Porret	*Six Esquisses*	Baron
Rathaus	*Allegro Concertante*	Boosey & Hawkes
Ropartz	*Andante et Allegro*	International
Smith, arr.	*Suite Classique*	Edition Musicus
Tuthill	*Scherzo*	Remick
Trowbridge	*Alla Marcia*	Composers Press
Vento	*Sonata*	Edition Musicus
Vidal	*Aria and Fanfare*	Andraud
Young	*Contempora Suite*	Bandland
Wormser	*Theme and Variations*	Baron

Grade IV

Asafiev	*Sonata*	Leeds
Bach-Deherve	*Preludes*	Andraud
Barat	*Andante et Scherzo*	Andraud
Barat	*Lento et Scherzo*	Baron
Bitsch	*Fantaisetta*	Andraud
Bonneau	*Fantaisie Concertante*	Andraud
Bonneau	*Suite*	Andraud
Boutry	*Trompetunia*	Andraud
Bozza	*Badinage*	Andraud
Busser	*Variations in Eb*	Cundy-Bettoney
Chapuis	*Solo de Trompette en Fa*	Andraud
Clergue	*Sarabande et Rigaudon*	Andraud
Contemporary French	*Recital Pieces*	International
Corelli	*Sonata VIII*	Ricordi
DeBoeck	*Allegro*	C. Fischer
Douliez	*Piece Concertante*	Baron
Emmanuel	*Sonate*	Andraud
Fiala	*Concertino*	International
Fitzgerald	*Concerto in Ab Minor*	C. Fischer
Fitzgerald	*Introduction and Fantasy*	Belwin
Francaix	*Sonatine*	Baron
Gabaye	*Boutade*	Andraud
Goeb	*Lyric Piece*	Mercury
Goedicke	*Concert Etude*	Leeds
Goeyens, F.	*Suite Romantique*	Peters
Hamilton	*Capriccio*	Schott
Handel	*Adagio and Allegro*	Presser
Handel	*Aria Con Variazioni*	Ricordi
Hubeau	*Sonata*	Andraud
Martelli	*Sonatine*	Baron
Martinu	*Sonatine*	Andraud
Mozart	*Concerto*	C. Fischer
Purcell	*Sonata*	Edition Musicus
Saint-Saens	*Fantaisie en Mi Bemol*	Baron
Schmitt	*Andantino*	Andraud
Thome	*Fantaisie*	Andraud
Torelli	*Concerto*	International
Tournemire	*Fantaisie*	Andraud
Vidal	*Concertino*	Belwin
Wagner, J.	*Introduction and Rondo*	Chappell
Williams, E.	*Sonata*	Morris

Grade V

Addison	*Concerto*	Mills
Ahlgrimm	*Concerto*	Peters
Bitsch	*Quatre Variations sur un Theme de Domenico Scarlatti*	Andraud
Bohrnstedt	*Concerto*	Remick
Bonnard	*Sonata*	Ricordi
Bozza	*Caprice*	Baron
Bozza	*Concertino*	Baron
Bozza	*Rustiques*	Andraud
Brandt	*First Concert Piece, Op. II*	Cundy-Bettoney
Casterede	*Sonatine*	Andraud
Charlier	*Solo de Concours*	Baron
Chaynes	*Concerto*	Andraud
Darcy	*Rhapsodie*	Baron
Defay	*Sonatine*	Andraud
Delerue	*Concertino*	Andraud
Desenclos	*Incantation-Threne-Danse*	Andraud
Desportes	*Concerto*	Andraud
Enesco	*Legende*	Andraud
Giannini	*Concerto*	Remick

Goedicke	Concerto	Leeds
Grimm	Concertino	Andraud
Haydn	Concerto	Boosey & Hawkes
Hindemith	Sonata	Associated
Honegger	Intrada	Baron
Ibert	Impromptu	Andraud
Jolivet	Concertino	Andraud
Jongen	Cadence and Rigodon	Baron
Kaminski	Concertino	Leeds
Kanitz	Concert Piece	Affiliated
Kennan	Sonata	Remick
Lantier	Concert en trois parties	Elkan-Vogel
Latham	Suite	Presser
Lewis	Concerto	Mills
Montbrun	Sarabande and Finale	Andraud
Poot	Etude de Concert	Andraud
Porrino	Concertino	Ricordi
Riisager	Concertino	Schirmer
Rueff	Fantaisie Concertante	Andraud
Sowerby	Sonata	Remick
Tomasi	Concerto	Baron
Tuthill	Sonata	Remick
Wal-Berg	Concerto	Leeds

So often the comment is made that "the European type literature is too difficult for young students." Possibly this is true from the musical standpoint; however in regard to technique, range, flexibility, tonguing, and endurance the polka-type solos that so many youngsters attempt to play are far more difficult than the general run of European solos. It is indeed unfortunate that we have to refer to the more musical literature as that belonging to the European composers.

Some progress has been made thru the efforts of the NASM and its commissioned trumpet solos; however, these works are primarily intended for very advanced players capable of playing complete concertos or sonatas. We have a great potential market for single movement solos of about five minutes duration that would be suitable for the high school and college trumpet students. Until more first-rate American composers answer this call, we will have to rely upon the European composers to supply us with the greatest variety and best quality of trumpet literature.

The problem rests with the school band directors and others of us who teach trumpet who have not seen fit to encourage publishers to produce more first-class materials.

FINE

Are You —

November, 1959

Neglecting the Brass Ensemble?

Jay Zorn

TODAY WITH THE prominence of show bands, festivals, and large instrumental organizations, there is a vital need to balance this emphasis with significant small-group activities. In our large instrumental programs the individual rarely is given an opportunity to utilize his talents fully. It is obvious that these large, popular organizations are here to stay, even tho quality of music and performance are sometimes sacrificed. How, then, can we expose our students to quality sensitivity and encourage their individual growth? The *brass ensemble*, I have found, is an excellent solution to the problem, well within the possibilities of every instrumental program.

Advantages

The brass ensemble affords our brass players an opportunity to perform high quality chamber music. Parts are rarely doubled, except in some of the larger works, and each part becomes equally important in the closely knit framework of the ensemble. In contrast to band and orchestra brass parts, these parts are not written in "skyscraper" fashion.

Generally, in the band and orchestra brass parts, the melody or lead is assigned to the first part in the section and the rest of the parts merely fill in and support. In the brass ensemble each player gets a chance to play a lead part, as the melody gets passed around among them. For example, in *Two Ayres for Cornetts and Sagbuts* (trombone) by John Adson, an original composition for five brass instruments from the 17th century, the theme is passed from one instrument to the other until all have played it twice. In *Sonata No. 19* by Bach's famous trumpet soloist, Gottfried Reiche, each of the four instruments plays the four-bar theme as a solo. The theme started by the trumpet goes to the horn (or 2nd trumpet substitute), to the trombone, and finally to the tuba. Examples of this kind are endless in these fine brass works.

Careful Listening

When it comes to careful listening, nothing can improve on the small ensemble for this valuable experience. Correct intonation becomes essential, perhaps for the first time in the brass player's experience. I have had many brass players—bothered about faulty intonation during an ensemble rehearsal—raise the inviting questions: "What tones are out of tune on our brass instruments?" "How can we correct them to play better in tune?" The interest and enthusiasm that arises out of subsequent discussions are truly exciting.

In the brass ensemble the player can hear and feel the power of the most basic harmonies and interval relationships that are only vaguely sensed in larger groups. This is a fine opportunity to integrate ear training and a bit of theory into the experience of the performers. Just have a group of brass players produce a simple major chord, adjust for fine intonation

253

and balance, and a whole new world of sound is opened to these players.

Replace Sectional Rehearsals

Few band and orchestra directors realize the possibilities of the brass ensemble for improving the brass section of their organizations. One of the standard practices of most directors has been the "sectional" rehearsal. In the sectional rehearsal, the hollow-sounding brass parts of the band and orchestra are picked-at out of context and overplayed. Bits and pieces are polished up but are rarely improved when put back into the band or orchestra.

Just as an experiment to prove the capabilities of the brass ensemble for promoting musical growth, at your next brass sectional rehearsal pass out some brass ensemble music instead of the regular band or orchestra parts. Use a piece like Bach's *Contrapunctus I* from *The Art of the Fugue*. The Robert King edition calls for Trumpets 1 and 2, Horns, Trombones, Baritones, and Tuba. The fugal subject gets handled by all players, providing a workout in ear training, tone, balance, and reading. The ending of this piece is very dramatic and a large organ effect can be achieved.

Another fine work for the entire brass section is Johann Pezel's *Sonata No. 2* for five-part brass. Parts of these larger works may occasionally be doubled if you have additional players to include. The editions supply substitute parts for additional flexibility of instrumentation. For instance, a 2nd trumpet part may be substituted by horn, or a horn part by trombone, etc. Since all these instruments are closely related members of the brass family, very little is changed by substitutions.

If your brass section takes to these works well enough, you might reward the players with the thrilling experience of reading a two-choir composition of the 16th century Venetian master, Giovanni Gabrieli. The *Sonata pian'e forte* can be handled by most high school as well as college, brass players. Since the piece was originally written to be performed antiphonally from the opposing choir lofts in San Marco Church, Venice, you should try placing the two choirs at opposite ends of the rehearsal hall. The players must bring out their solo parts, blend within their choir, and blend and balance with the combined choirs. Performing such a work is a special thrill that can revive even the weariest of sophisticated professionals.

To complete this experiment with the brass section, after a couple of these brass ensemble sessions, listen to the players carefully during the next full band or orchestra rehearsal and you will be amazed at the progress that they have made in real musicianship in a short time.

Don't neglect the performance capabilities of brass ensembles. They are ideal for Christmas and Easter programs; find a nice balcony in which to perch them and they will be the highlight of the evening. Christmas and Easter carols in the hallways, if once used, will become a tradition. Find a place for them in your regular band or orchestra concerts, a fine way to spotlight the brass section of the larger organization.

In conclusion, give the brass ensemble a chance to prove itself within your program and, I assure you, you will have introduced an extremely useful and popular organization.

FINE

Know the Horns!

Lloyd Schmidt

THO FRENCH HORNS are now commonplace in school music, the old fears for the instrument seem to persist. Even the experienced director may occasionally be baffled by an unusual shape, valve system, or pitch, but clear understanding of a few basic horn facts should enable any director to recognize and teach even the most unusual specimens.

The two sides of the double horn (F and B♭), their single counterparts, and the alto horn in E♭ are fundamental types; once these basic types are thoroughly understood, the usual problems involving crooks, extra valves, and fingerings should give little difficulty.

The horns to be encountered may be listed as follows:

1. Double horn in F and B♭; four or more valves.
   a. Single horn in F; three valves, with or without E♭ crook.
   b. Single horn in B♭; three, four, or five valves.
2. Alto horn (mellophone, altonium, tenor saxhorn) in E♭ or F, upright or traditional form.
3. Unusual specimens: descant horn, Wagner tubas, hunting horns, unusual extra valves.

French Horn and Alto Horn

It is easy to distinguish between the French horns and the alto horns; the two instruments have divergent backgrounds, function completely differently, and are nearly an octave different in basic pitch.

The French horns, enjoying the prestige of a long orchestral history, are really bass instruments performing in treble range on the upper partials by means of the small and deep mouthpiece. French horn tubing is narrow in bore and the metal is thin so as to produce the characteristically mellow and flexible tone.

The alto horn is more recent, of course, being a modified saxhorn and cornet type which appeared after mid-nineteenth century. It has been the traditional alto voice in military and brass bands, tho recent changes toward symphonic band concepts have brought a preference for the more versatile French horn. The alto horn is pitched below the B♭ cornet and above the B♭ baritone of the modified saxhorn choir. The following example shows the concert and written differences between the playing ranges of the French horns and the alto horn:

General Features

Tho French horns in America reflect the German preference for rotary valves, the alto horns and many English and French models of French horns have piston valves. German brass makers generally tend to the use of rotary valves, the piston valve trumpet being described by German players as a "Jazz Trompete"!

German silver is sometimes used in the construction of the better French horns which are to be distinguished from cheaper models of plated brass. The alto horns, in common with other brass instruments, appear normally in plated or brass models. Occasional experiments with sterling silver, bronze alloys, or other metals for French horns have given way to brass or German silver in the quality instruments. Bell direction may vary; horns and alto horns exist which reverse normal directions (bell right for French horn and bell left for alto horn).

Some enterprising makers have introduced mouthpiece shanks for alto horns to accommodate French horn mouthpieces, a convenience which fails to achieve its effect since the advantages of both alto and French horns disappear while the difficulties of marching with French horn mouthpieces remain.

Tho there are exponents of the E♭ alto horn as a necessary member of the band's brass choir (matching the range and pitch of the B♭ and E♭ saxhorn choir) the alto horn has come into ill-repute somewhat.

The usual alto horn seems to pose few problems for the director; indeed, it is often ignored once basic fingerings have been taught! The practice of switching frustrated trumpet players to alto horn explains the misery of many alto horn sections and seems to be tacit admittance that the instrument is unworthy of better players. A limited instrument at best, it takes special attention if results are to be expected. The usual section improves immensely if the instruments are played with hand in bell, using a French horn style as far as is possible; traditional rather than upright models are, therefore, to be preferred for concert use. Simple trumpet techniques are ill-suited to the instrument.

Crooks

Caution must be taken in the use of crooks. Obviously valve lengths must be changed to match the new instrumental length. It cannot be over-emphasized that the best pitch of any instrument is its basic pitch; to add tubing arbitrarily, without changes in valve slides, is an unthinkable and makeshift alteration. To add crooks merely for ease of fingering is preposterous. The director with feeling for quality in instruments, who seeks good intonation and accuracy, will avoid using crooks at any time.

Some recent alto horns are pitched in F for ease in reading the now standard F parts. If an E♭ crook is added to an alto or French horn in F, valve slides *must* be pulled to maintain intonation. Valve slides are often marked for this purpose.

The E♭ alto horn performs the E♭ part with normal (same as trumpet) fingerings, the part being transposed from concert exactly as the E♭ alto saxophone part.

Double Horn

The advent of valves gradually caused the horn in F to dominate as a middle-pitched compromise suitable for playing in all keys. Modern styles in composition and earlier music intended for horns of higher pitch, have worked real hardship on professionals who consequently have adopted the double horn which offers the advantages of both the standard horn in F and the higher horn in B♭. More frequent use of the B♭ horn has brought increased interest in single horns of that pitch.

The double horn is, in a sense, a compromise between the F and B♭ requirements; it might be said that a single F or single B♭ horn would each be superior to its counterpart on a double horn.

Normally, each valve of the double horn has a double set of valve slides, the shorter set for the B♭ horn and the longer set for the F horn. When the thumb-valve is depressed it shortens the main tubing while coupling the shorter valve slides; conversely, when the thumb valve is raised it adds tubing and couples the longer valve slides for the F horn. In some rare instances, the thumb-valve action is reversed. In effect, the player has two instruments in one with separate tubing lengths and appropriate valve slides for complete F and B♭ horns.

Some double horns have a basic set of B♭ valve slides to which another shorter set of slides can be added, thus reaching F proportions in combination. Such a horn can be viewed as emphasizing the B♭ side and is especially suitable for "high" horn players who customarily play upper parts.

A simple method of remembering the function of the double horn is to realize that most fourth valves on brass instruments have a relationship of a fourth. In the case of the double horn this fourth valve has an extra set of individual valve slides to make the change complete.

A few double horns have the shorter B♭ valve slides stacked above the longer F slides, tho the reverse is far more common.

Use of the Double Horn

The quality school program owes the better student an opportunity to experience the double horn; to insure results on this instrument, however, the director must insist on the use of both sides, the horn having no merit, of course, if played like a single horn. Even for the average student, full use of the double will produce a real improvement in general playing; this is its function. The use of the double is not so complex that it cannot be learned in rehearsal; normal playing facility should not be affected during the process.

Fingerings for the B♭ side frighten many directors unnecessarily. To find fingerings the director need only reduce the horn part to concert and then use baritone fingerings (the B♭ horn is exactly the length of the baritone and trombone). If preferred, fingerings can be obtained by comparison with trumpet or F horn. The fingering of a given note on an F part for B♭ horn is the same as the fingering on F horn a fourth below or on trumpet a fifth above. A few minutes of study can make this quite clear and useful. The student, of course, learns a set of fingerings for B♭ horn on F parts, no playing transposition being involved.

In practice, the switch from F to B♭ on the double is generally made between G♯4 and C5 (on the staff), fingerings being alike on both horns and on trumpet between these pitches, the F horn being used below G♯ and the B♭ horn being used for C♯ and above. An expert player uses both horns to advantage throughout the full range.

Single F Horn

The single French horn in F is the traditional instrument and the type of horn most frequently encountered. It can easily be distinguished by its long valve slides and its open overtone series on concert F. Comparison with a single horn in B♭ or between the valve slides of a double horn will make the relationship between F and B♭ horns obvious.

A crook, either straight or coiled, may be present in the single F horn making it difficult to determine its real pitch at sight. A horn with an E♭ crook would, of course, produce an open overtone series on concert E♭, or simply a whole tone lower than an open horn in F. Again, crooks are avoided by professionals; if used, valve slides must be pulled.

A far better procedure is to transpose. The process is simple: lower the E♭ part a whole step; lowering the signature a whole tone may simplify the process. Conversely, an E♭ alto horn must read F parts a whole tone higher than written. Fingerings for French horn in F may be derived from trumpet, if care is taken to use the trumpet fingerings an octave above the written notes.

Single B♭ Horn

A more recent arrival on the scene, being shorter and higher in pitch than the single F horn, the single B♭ horn has gradually assumed a significant role in school and professional ensembles. The numerous and excellent reasons for this have been stated often and need not be repeated here. The director's concern is simple: double horns are expensive, most schools finding it necessary to purchase at least some single horns.

The choice, after the double, is between the single F and the single B♭. The professional never attempts the single F, yet it is the common beginner's instrument! On the other hand, the professional uses a great deal of B♭, a large part of horn parts lying in this range of the double. Tho for many reasons the single B♭ becomes a logical choice after the double, the instrument is still poorly understood, unfortunately, and the single F often becomes the unthinking director's choice.

The B♭ horn looks much like the F horn, but once a comparison is made it should not be difficult to distinguish between them, particularly if notice is made of the shorter B♭ valve tubing. The open overtone series of the B♭ horn matches that of other B♭ instruments on concert B♭.

Fingerings, as discussed above, can be determined by any director from baritone, trumpet, or F horn. It should be noted that the acoustically proper fingerings for G♯4 and A4 are "second valve" and "open," respectively; in practice these may be used, but trumpet or F horn fingerings (2-3 and 1-2) are much more commonly used for these pitches.

Extra Valves

A common horn, tho baffling to many, is the four-valve B♭ horn. The fourth valve is merely a transposing valve for hand muting since it is impossible to hand mute a B♭ horn, the pitch altering somewhere near ¾ of a tone. This fourth valve generally does *not* act as a crook to produce a lower horn for E♭ parts. In some cases the fourth valve is identical with the second valve and can be used to lower the horn a half step for "horn in A"; valve slides can be pulled to match this horn, but in modern practice the valve is practically worthless. If such a half-tone valve is present, it must be pulled half its length for hand muting. Commercial mutes which transpose for the student make fourth valves on B♭ horns totally unnecessary for school use.

The five-valve B♭ horn has caused many a director to throw up his hands, but the instrument is really not so complicated. A fifth valve for the little finger is added to the four-valve B♭ just described. This fifth valve is a direct counterpart to the usual extra valve on most brass instruments, and as such, it lowers the B♭ horn a perfect fourth to a basic F horn. This is

not a double horn, extra valve slides not being present. The real purpose of the five-valve B♭ horn is to equal the full range of the double while retaining the advantages of the single B♭ horn. For orchestral purposes the hand muting valve is essential, and the open F horn (fifth valve) and the possible open "A" or "E" horns (fourth valve "in" or pulled slightly) are extremely useful.

The presence of a fifth valve on the double horn is unusual but does occur. In this case it may operate as a transposing valve for hand muting both B♭ and F horns, or it may operate as the fourth valve on the single B♭ horn mentioned above.

Unusual Specimens

Early Classic or Baroque scores occasionally call for smaller instruments for extremely high parts. For these parts a small descant horn may be used which is usually pitched in F an octave above the horn in F. The small shape and easily tested overtone series of these horns make them easy to recognize. Even smaller, tightly coiled natural horns are still used for hunting signals in England and on the continent; these, however, should never find their way to school ensembles to perplex the school director.

In Wagner's *Ring* one encounters the so-called Wagner tubas, the composer's own invention to add lower voices to horn harmony. These tenor and bass instruments are built on horn principles, but are more likely to be confused with baritones rather than with French horns. They are built in B♭ and in F just as the horns and are often played by horn players, however, they are of large bore and of different shape and cannot really be included in the modern horn section. It might be added that the more recent "Wagner tubas" are somewhat different and depart even further from their horn counterparts.

Thus, in spite of the verbal complexities to be encountered in any description of French horns and their idiosyncrasies, a small effort to study the basic F horns, the B♭ horns, and the alto horns, will show the horn section to be quite understandable. Problems can usually be reduced to extra valves or crooks once basic pitch is established, the complexity not being so great as to warrant ignorance on the part of music directors. It is time for directors to know the French horns!   FINE

1960

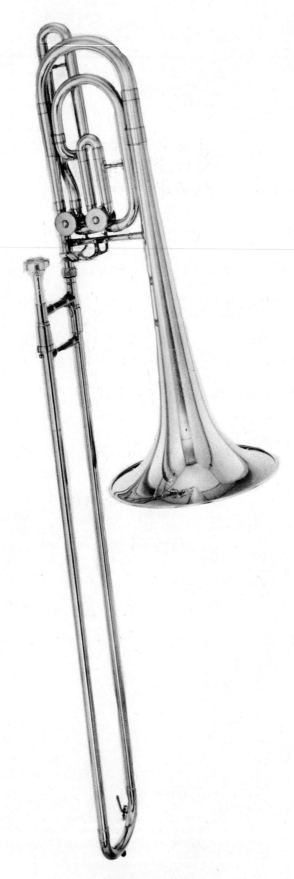

Bass Trombone

Development and meaning of—

Breath Support

Robert Weast

As all fine brass players know, a well developed use of air is vital to the success of performance. Only thru correct blowing procedures can tone, range, accuracy, and endurance be attained.

To develop—as well as to demonstrate visually—the blowing process, we constructed a glass tube. Three different weights are dropped thru the open top, first singly and later in combination. These are to be blown right out of the top of the tube.

Results Visible

Results are immediately evident. Persons using the correct, most efficient muscles can blow the entire stack of three weights several inches out of the tube. Other persons, not blowing correctly, cannot get the lightest of the weights off the bottom. Such individuals are working every bit as hard as the apparently stronger people but they are demanding work from muscles incapable of the job.

The abdominal muscles, those muscles surrounding the waist area, are capable of powerful contractions. During the inhalation they expand outwardly. Work with the air tube indicates that if they are contracted in place, or better yet, pushed farther out against the belt while the contraction is being made, maximum air compression can be attained. The internal body pressure from this type contrac-tion causes the diaphragm to move upward more strongly against the lungs, compressing the air.

Thoracic Contraction Inadequate

Players who have difficulty getting the lightest weight to rise in the tube usually are attempting to get air compression by contracting rib and chest muscles. At the same time, they hold their chests expanded, thus causing their lungs to remain in a partial state of suspension. This is an impossible situation. It can easily be remedied by allowing the waist to swell as the lungs fill with air, instead of expanding the chest and raising the shoulders.

It is one thing to develop good breath support and another to utilize it correctly. Too often, players will choke off as much as 50% or more of their efforts with a constricted throat, a tensed embouchure, or with their lips too close together. Air is effective only at the embouchure and at the point of lip vibration.

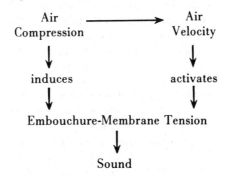

Air Compression ⟶ Air Velocity

Air Compression induces Air Velocity activates

Embouchure-Membrane Tension

Sound

Formula

The effect of air on the embouchure can be expressed by the preceding:

Air compression (breath support) inducing embouchure tension is an adaptation of the "Valsalva Effect," in which the air is held internally under pressure. Air pressure forcing against the inner side of the embouchure causes it to tense itself *proportionately*. This is in direct contrast to players who hold independent "lip tightness," above that induced by proper air support. Their tone is thin and shallow with their range and endurance greatly impaired.

Lip muscles naturally tense more against high air pressure than low. For example, high air compression induces high embouchure tension and this, in turn, produces a high lip surface tension.* This in turn is activated by a projected air velocity, producing a sound frequency. Great and subtle control of the air can be achieved by fluctuations of the arched tongue and lip aperature principles.

When breath support and controls are utilized to their maximum potential, the work load of the embouchure becomes reduced and endurance, tone quality, accuracy, and high register work appear. This is what we are striving for.

*It is conclusively proved that the membrane of the upper lip is the sole vibrator, not both lips as commonly believed.
Fine

Polishing the Trumpet Player

Wesley Lindskoog

Two aspects of the technique of trumpet playing which most readi-ly distinguish the polished player from the amateur are the attack and the slur. Students are sometimes hampered in their ability to develop these facets of technique properly because of their lack of a proper conception or idea of what should actually be the sound of a *good* attack or a *good* slur.

Those students are fortunate who have a teacher who can and will demonstrate to them, lesson after lesson, until proper concepts become engrained in their playing. The fact that no two players have exactly the same physical equipment with which to play, i. e., dental structure, jaw structure, shape of lips, and interior mouth structure, precludes the possibility of obtaining optimum results by telling the student that he must place the tongue in *exactly* this or that position. There is the exception, however, that the attack is made higher in the mouth when playing in the high register and lower in the mouth in the low register. Nor can the student be forced to hold the instrument at exactly a certain angle relative to his head, except that basic and general instructions of this type must be given to the beginner. But if a student knows what the sound should be, he will—with proper guidance—make the adjustments necessary to produce this sound.

Slurring

First, let us consider the slur. The common fault of less advanced players is to neglect the slur or to treat it with indifference. A slur between two notes should be construed to indicate that the sound does not stop or change quality between the two notes. There is, therefore, an actual sound on the slur itself. Could we visualize, graphically, the sound of the trumpet slurring from one long note to another, we might see two straight parallel lines which encompass the sound of the first note connected by lines, still parallel but curved, to two straight parallel lines encompassing the sound of a note of a different pitch. The lines are always equidistant from one another, indicating that the sound *on the slur* does not change in quality. There is no break or extraneous sound between the notes. Instead, the two notes actually become one continuous sound changing in pitch.

An exercise that has proved effective in aiding students to develop the slur is shown in Example 1. The objective should be to play each line in one breath so that it sounds like one long note changing in pitch—no breaks or changes of quality between notes and no breath accents on notes.

It will be noticed that there is a natural "break" in the trumpet scale somewhat similar to that occurring between the registers of the clarinet. This break occurs between C5 and D5 in the staff. By giving this part of the scale additional attention as it is played this break may be eliminated and the quality of the slur maintained as it is in the rest of the scale.

The player must give a little more air at this point and try not to constrict the lips so as to permit a free flow of this air. Repetition of this area of the exercise will help the player to achieve comfort on the slurs.

At the end of each line where the comma appears a breath should be taken but the mouthpiece should not leave the lips until the end of the fourth line. At this point the mouthpiece sould be taken from the lips for a period of about five seconds before repeating the first line to the *fine*. The tempo of the exercise should be 88 quarter notes per minute. When the player finds that he can complete the exercise with *every* slur intact, he is ready to repeat it using the key signature of six sharps, this time beginning each line *mp* and making a steady crescendo to *mf* at the end of the line. The tempo should now be increased to approximately 96 beats per minute to enable the player to complete each line in one breath.

If the intonation of the low C♯4 necessitates the extension of the third valve slide, another unwieldy slur will occur between the E♯ and D♯ in the fourth line of the exercise. The player should compensate for this in the same manner as he dealt with the slur on the break between C5 and D5 in the staff—by giving more air and relaxing the lips so that the sound does not stop or change in quality.

After the exercise becomes comfortable in the key of F♯ it should be repeated in the key of G major. This time each line should be started *mp* and the crescendo made to *ff*. The tempo should now be increased to 116 beats per minute. Finally, the three scales in thirds should be memorized so that the player's concentration will not be hampered by reading notes, and so he can devote his full attention to the sound he is producing.

Attack

In striving for perfection in the preceding exercises the player is likely to have improved his attack. For it is in this careful approach to the symphonic style of trumpet playing that the attack achieves its full importance. A good attack, of course, embodies accuracy, for a clean attack has no extraneous sound. We cannot expect a note to sound well if it is not begun properly.

There are certain preparations necessary in starting the tone which become automatic with practice. First, since a dry lip does not vibrate readily, before the initial attack of a passage we should moisten the lips. This does not mean to moisten the entire embouchure on which the rim of the mouthpiece rests unless the player uses a "wet" embouchure.

The breath may be taken before or after the lips are moistened, whichever is more comfortable for the player. If the breath is taken after the lips are moistened, the inrush of air is apt to dry the lips somewhat if care is not taken to drop the jaw instead of pulling back the corners of the mouth in taking the breath. The lips may still retain their playing position on the mouthpiece while the jaw is dropped to take the breath.

The tip of the tongue now acts as a valve to release the air into the trumpet. Ideally, the air is brought up with pressure from the diaphragm at the exact moment the tongue releases the air. If the pressure is built up against the tongue and there is a lapse of time before the tongue releases it, the resulting tension that is built up will be communicated to other parts of the body and make the attack increasingly difficult. The entire operation of moistening the lips, taking the breath, and making the attack should not consume more than about one second.

The attack should first be practiced softly on long notes in the middle register. The goal should be to produce

Example No. 1

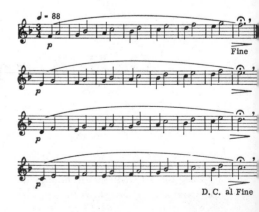

D. C. al Fine

a *clean* attack completely free of extraneous sound. There should be no little sounds coming thru the instrument, no "fuzz", and no "pop" to start the tone. The first thing that should be heard is the actual pure tone with a precise beginning, and attacked squarely in the center. Again, if we could visualize graphically the attack as it is related to the tone, we might see a long, narrow rectangle with one end removed. The closed end represents the attack and the long sides of the rectangle encompass within them the sustained sound. The sound is in no way distorted at the beginning—it just begins.

When the player has experimented with and listened to the sound of his own attack until it is comfortable and pure and clean he is ready for a staccato exercise to combine with the slurring exercise. Now he should follow the scale in thirds in the key of F major with the staccato style illustrated in Example 2. He should insist that each note is attacked cleanly with a beginning as if it were a long note given careful attention and preparation. Of utmost importance is the equality and uniformity of the sound of each attack. Do not tolerate an occasional bad attack or allow any note to disappear.

Example No. 2

Each note must sound exactly the same as the one preceding it in quality and amount of attack. The tempo of this exercise should be 96 quarter notes per minute. After this scale is completed to the best of the player's ability, he should play the slurred scale in the key of F♯ major. This should be followed by the staccato scale in thirds, this time with the key signature of six sharps at a dynamic level of *mf* and at the same tempo as the first staccato scale in thirds. Then the slurred scale in thirds in G major, followed by the staccato scale in thirds in G major at a dynamic level of *f* with a crescendo to the end of each line.

To increase the facility of the single-tongue it is advisable to play the staccato scales with an accelerando to the end of each line. The speed should be increased to the maximum tempo that the player can accommodate with absolutely no sacrifice of cleanliness or quality. Common sense tells us that the less the tongue moves the faster it can move. So to increase the speed of articulation the player should be conscious of shortening the stroke of the tongue on each attack.

These exercises should all be memorized so that the player can devote his full attention to the quality of his playing. They will be found excellent for use in the first part of the warm-up period.   FINE

March, 1960

The Voice in Brass Playing

Victor Kress

THE RESONANCE OF THE human voice is due to the reinforcement of the sounds produced by the vocal cords. These sounds are augmented by the sympathetic vibration of the air in the larynx, throat, and mouth. In like manner, the resonance of a brass instrument is due to all of the components of the human voice, plus the sympathetic vibration of the player's lips. The player's lips vibrate in sympathy with the vibrations of the vocal cords, just as a piano does when someone sings a note into it while the damper pedal is depressed. One hears chiefly the response of the string which is in tune with the voice. Similarly, the lips of the player vibrate in tune with the voice; the instrument acts as a megaphone or resonator which, in turn, vibrates in tune or in sympathy with the lips.

Sing Into Instrument

The principle of sympathetic vibration as applied to brass playing can be further illustrated. Sing any of the vowel sounds in a deep, resonant voice. Now close the lips, leaving a slight aperture; in other words, set the embouchure. Notice that the lips are vibrating enough to make the vibration perceptible upon being touched with the fingertips. As the player sings into the instrument, the volume of the sympathetic vibrations of his lips are increased by the instrument. In addition, the instrument reduces any loss of sound due to the spreading of the vibrating sound waves.

The player should never hum into the instrument. This type of sound production utilizes the nasal cavity as a resonance chamber; hence, not all of the vibrations are available to be picked up by the lips. The resulting sound is commonly known as "jazz tone."

The ear hears the pitch before the note is played. The workings of the diaphragm, vocal muscles, and tongue muscles should be immediately synchronized by tensing or relaxing in proportion to the pitch desired. This co-ordinated support both guides and regulates the voice so that in its completion the voice sound is thrown thru the instrument by the vibrating lips. Thus, the sound is created before it leaves the lips of the player.

Adequate Breath Support

The voice in brass instrument playing, just as in singing, requires a tone founded on adequate breath support. Correct breathing should involve expansion of the lower chest area during inhalation. This expansion should be apparent in the entire circumference of the lower chest. During exhalation, the lower chest expansion should be maintained until the depletion of the breath supply produces a natural, gradual deflation of this area. The purpose is to allow the diaphragm complete control of the voice during exhalation.

The principles of correct breath support can be learned in a very short time if the student will relax and think of himself as a barrel being filled with water as he takes in air. Breath control, on the other hand, can be developed only thru conscientious study and practice over a period of time.

Overblowing

Singing into the instrument provides immediate results, for it removes all unnecessary pressure and shifts responsibility to muscles which can easily accept it—diaphragm, larynx, etc. In a like manner, one of the greatest problems of the brass player, the tendency to "overblow," is very impressively reduced. Since overblowing is caused by exhaling too much air, the problem can be virtually eliminated by using no more air than is used in speaking or singing.

Contrast the length of a musical phrase that it is possible to sing with the comparative shortness of phrase the average brass player is capable of. Certainly the singer can sustain the tone longer than the player. In addition, the more modest exhalation will remedy short, chopped phrasing. Thus, voice application in brass playing offers a solution for two major problems: undue fatigue and its attendant "sour notes," and poor phrasing.

The voice must be so flexible that it can be applied to an attack of even a 64th note. The student must separate himself from the mechanics of the instrument. Rather than "push behind the instrument," he should drop his voice down deep, open his throat wide, and sing the notes in tune. He must realize that all brass instruments, with the exception of the trombone, are nothing more than glorified bugles with three, four, or five valves, as the case may be. Technique is not all-important. It is not the pushing down of the valves that brings about the important change, for that merely makes possible the playing of chromatics. It is the singing of each note, regardless of the slightness of the change in interval. Thru this medium perfect intonation can be acquired. If we sing in perfect tune, the result will be in-tune playing. When one ceases to struggle and begins singing into the instrument, he will be near the perfection that the greatest artists have spent a lifetime achieving.

Desirable Tone Quality

The character of any brass instrument is boldness and initiative. Its purpose is to add weight, brilliance, aggressiveness, accent, and color to the performance of the ensemble. A student should always bear in mind that even when we play for ourselves, we have an audience in mind. Therefore, we should never use a "conversational" tone even, or especially, in practicing.

Many students place all their attention on mastering technique and developing smooth and fast playing, overlooking the main point: "How will it sound to an audience?" Picture a fine opera singer doing all of his practicing *sotto voce*, and then trying to sing a fine performance. Or imagine someone talking to a friend in a conversational voice. The sound of his voice would be adequate. Now picture the same speaker on a stage talking to an audience. His voice would not even carry over the footlights unless he changes his tone. The tone of voice for an audience is entirely different from that of a conversational voice. This doesn't mean that it must be very loud. It must have depth and resonance so that everyone in the audience will hear every word.

Many musicians who have spent years studying find their playing isn't adequate. They have become so set in their manner of playing that it is practically impossible to change. They get along well enough when playing in a very small group, but they fail in an orchestra or band where dynamics are required. When a *fortissimo* is required, their only recourse is to blow harder, and the result is a harsh, disagreeable sound and poor intonation. When *pianissimo* is required, they partly close either the throat or lips, or both, and the result is a dead or pinched tone with practically no resonance. In the upper register the tone is usually thin and shrill and often sharp in pitch.

A fine player, on the other hand, would hold back the air pressure to avoid overblowing and distortion. He would enlarge the depth and resonance of the voice in *fortissimo* passages, thereby producing a much fuller *fortissimo*, with far more sonority and control of intonation and with half the effort. In *pianissimo* passages he would maintain the same deep, resonant voice, but he would sing softly, thereby keeping full control of intonation and a fine resonant quality in all registers.

One should remember to do all of his practicing with the quality of voice he will use when playing before the public. It is difficult to maintain this quality when practicing in a very small room or a crowded space, but one must be persistent. Loudness isn't necessary, but the voice must have resonance so that every note will be heard in every part of the auditorium, even in *pianissimo* passages.

Analyzing the Problem

Most brass players produce a rather forced sound and have considerable difficulty attaining a good register, mastering difficult articulations, and maintaining quality of sound in their complete register. A few outstanding players, however, seem to have a "natural" ability to produce a fine resonant quality of sound in every register and to have little difficulty with articulation. After studying with several fine artists on brass instruments, and after hearing a great many of the finest vocal artists, I find an exact parallel. I conclude that most brass teachers and most vocal teachers advocate a rather mechanical approach to playing. Brass teachers usually tell

their students to:
- buzz the lips,
- tighten the cheeks,
- pivot the lips,
- direct the air column down for one register,
- direct the air column upward for another register,
- pucker the lips for high notes,
- pronounce syllables "oo-ee" for slurs,
- move the diaphragm this way or that.

Vocal teachers, too, have a long list of "do's and don'ts." The fact is that any change in the position of the throat, lips, tongue, teeth, or mouth alters the tone or voice. Any movement of any of these parts should be kept at an absolute minimum. No more air is required to play a brass instrument than is required for singing.

Both the voice and a music instrument are primarily means of expression. If we would express ourselves most satisfactorily, either vocally or instrumentally, we would eliminate many of the mechanical "do's and don'ts" that actually detract from fine playing and singing.

The first and most important thing necessary for good expression is a clear, distinct, resonant voice. Such a voice would be almost impossible if the throat were constricted or held rigid, even if it were open. It would also be practically impossible if the lips or teeth were held too close together, or if the tongue arched so it would obstruct or cramp the full vibration of the voice. FINE

April, 1960

Use That Fourth Valve

A discussion of the uses for the extra valve on low

brass instruments.

Carson Johnson

Is a FOURTH valve really necessary on euphoniums and tubas? Since the majority of low brass instruments are purchased by schools, this is a question which confronts many directors. For the sake of economy this *extra* valve is often not requested on a new instrument, because many feel its sole purpose is to extend the range of the instrument downward into a register seldom used by school bands and orchestras. This extension of range is of course an important function, but it is only one of the many uses for the fourth valve. If used properly it will be an aid to intonation and a valuable tool to facilitate fingering in certain difficult passages.

Aid to Intonation

First, let us examine a few of the ways the fourth valve may be used to improve intonation. With the exception of a few makes and models of instruments, the fourth valve lowers the pitch a perfect fourth. This means the length of the tubing added is equal

to the combined length of valves 1 and 3. Since the valve combinations of 1-3 and 1-2-3 are notoriously sharp, especially on low brass instruments, this affords the player another choice of fingering for these notes.

By pulling out the fourth valve slide until it is slightly flat of the note normally played 1-3, the player may now use valve 4 instead of 1-3, and 2-4 instead of 1-2-3. The reasons for tuning the fourth valve slightly flat of the note played 1-3 are, first, the intonation is better when valves 2-4 are used, and secondly this extra length will be needed when using valve 4 to play downward to the pedal tone.

Using the BBb tuba as an example of what has been discussed, the player should tune his fourth valve slightly flat on C2 (normally 1-3). This note can easily be "lipped up" in tune and will enable B1 (1-2-3) to be played in tune using valves 2-4. This also applies to F1 (played 4 instead of 1-3) and to E1 (played 2-4 instead of 1-2-3).

To Facilitate Fingering

Almost every director has been plagued from time to time with a "muddy" sounding bass section, when the low brasses are called upon to perform certain fast passages. On a three-valve instrument these passages usually include fast changes from 2 to 1-3, or occur where two or three valves must be depressed and released quickly. The majority of these passages occur when the player must perform music not written especially for his instrument. In orchestra transcriptions for band the tubas are usually required to play the string bass part, and in the case of older music they often perform the serpent or ophicleide part. By employing the use of the fourth valve many of these awkward fingerings may be eliminated, and the fingering in certain passages greatly simplified.

Here are two examples of passages that may be played more easily and with more clarity by using the fourth valve. These examples refer to the BBb tuba, but will apply to the euphonium one octave higher, and to the Eb tuba a fourth higher.

The first example is from *Concerto No. 4, Op. 65,* Goltermann-Bell.

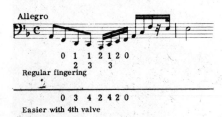

In the second example, by using valve 4 and valve 2 instead of 1-3 to 1-2-3, the player will avoid a lip change upward in this fast passage and will eliminate an intonational problem by playing E2 with 1-2-3.

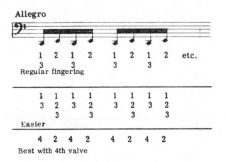

In certain passages the player may employ harmonic fingerings and leave the fourth valve depressed to simplify difficult fast passages. Here are two examples of such passages. The first applies to the BBb tuba (and to euphonium one octave higher).

The next example shows simplified fingerings for the Eb tuba. It is from the *Bartered Bride Overture* by Smetana.

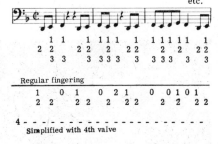

Use in the Low Register

The fact most generally thought of concerning the use of the fourth valve is that it enables the performer to play chromatically all notes down to the pedal tone. Its use in this respect is often misunderstood. The *false* rule generally followed is that when the fourth valve is depressed all notes are fingered on the remaining three valves the same as they are one octave higher. Unfortunately, this is not true of all notes in the extremely low register.

The length of tubing on valves 1, 2, and 3 is designed to function on a Bb instrument. When the fourth valve is depressed the pitch of the tuba is lowered and it actually becomes an F tuba, which would require longer additions of tubing on each of the remaining three valves. This is comparable to the double French horn which is provided with two sets of valve tubing, one for use when the thumb has engaged the Bb horn and another for use when the regular F horn is played.

Because the euphonium and the tubas are not provided with these two sets of valves, the player must listen closely and do a considerable amount of adjustment with the lip in the low register while using the fourth valve. Here are a few fingerings for the extreme low range; the player should experiment with each and choose the fingering that suits him and his instrument best.

Suggested fingerings for the Bb Euphonium:

Suggested fingerings for the Eb Tuba:

Suggested fingerings for the BBb Tuba:

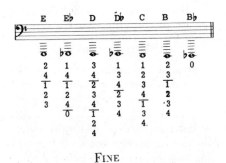

FINE

TRUMPET TRANSPOSITIONS

Norbert Carnovale

A STANDARD PART OF the study for serious trumpet students is the development of the ability to transpose at sight while playing on the Bb trumpet those parts written for trumpets in other keys. This is certainly a demanding endeavor, requiring concentration, patience, and background in music theory.

A mistake some of us make in presenting transposition study is failing to provide enough incentive for the student. The usual approach is to explain that as orchestral trumpet parts are written in several pitches, transposition is a prime requisite for orchestral trumpet playing. While this is certainly true, I wish to attempt to show that there are additional benefits to be obtained from the study of trumpet transposition, which in turn provide incentive for the study. In order to appreciate these additional benefits, we must review the fundamentals of trumpet transposition study.

What Are the Transpositions?

Transpositions must be thought of in relation to the instrument on which

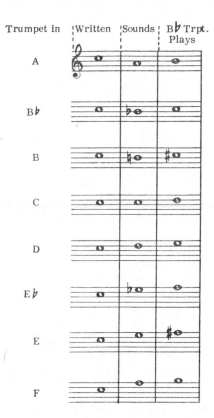

Trumpet in	Written	Sounds	Bb Trpt. Plays
A			
Bb			
B			
C			
D			
Eb			
E			
F			

we play (which is usually the Bb trumpet).

The accompanying chart shows the manner in which orchestral parts may be written. When playing on a trumpet in any pitch, it is up to the individual to make the appropriate transposition.

Learning Transposition

In order to tranpose, the player must first be aware of the key in which the transposition places him. With the key in mind, the student then transposes the part by interval up or down as need be. Here is an example: Assuming that the student is playing on the Bb trumpet, if he wishes to play a C trumpet part written in the key of C major, he must play a major second higher in D major (notice No. 4 in the chart).

Harry Glantz recommends practicing the actual intervals to be used in the transposition. For example, the interval involved in playing D trumpet parts is a major third up from the written note. By practicing by ear an exercise such as follows, the student develops a feeling for the interval. The lower note is the written note and the upper note the transposition pitch played.

Incidentally, this exercise also works well for the French horn (pitched in F). Assuming that the F horn player is going to play a D horn part, where the transposition is down a minor third, this exercise is helpful:

The popular approach in learning trumpet transposition, once a method is decided upon, is to start with easy melodies such as those in the Arban "Art of Phrasing" studies, and progress to the Sachse "100 Etudes for Transposition," Ernest Williams' "Transposition Studies," and finally orchestral excerpts books.

Other Values

Aside from the necessity of transposition for the potential orchestral trumpet player, there are other advantages for band directors whose major instrument is trumpet.

Having thoroughly mastered trumpet transpositions, the band director can think of concert pitch condensed scores merely as C trumpet parts and thereby ascertain correct pitches. Trumpet players may be called upon to read solos written for C trumpet, solo parts from the non-transposed piano accompaniment part, as well as reading melodies from sheet music.

The trumpet player who is reading bass clef music may use the C trumpet technique here, e.g. the Bb just above the bass clef (Bb3) may be read by a trumpet player a major second higher as treble clef middle C (C4). All of the preceding are applications of C trumpet transposition.

A further application in instrumental teaching regards hearing pitches of instruments in Eb or F. The trumpet player well schooled in transposition may think of Eb alto saxophone or Eb horn parts as trumpet parts (played on Bb trumpet) written in Eb. While this method gives the trumpet pitch one octave higher, it still provides the auditor with the correct pitch and the ability to hear students playing wrong notes and to read transposed parts with proper pitch.

Here are two examples of how this works:

A) Eb instruments

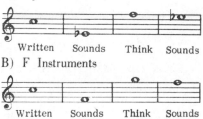

B) F Instruments

I submit these ideas in hope that they will provide a broader incentive for the study of transposition, as well as a broader application of the technique, once learned.

FINE

How to Increase...

Diaphragmatic Control

Peter Ciurczak

ONE OF THE MOST important fundamentals of brass playing is gaining command of the diaphragm and using it to its fullest extent in affording breath support to the tone. The student should always feel that each note he plays rides freely upon a strong column of air while the embouchure remains relaxed and relatively free of mouthpiece pressure. It is the job of the air stream, controlled by the diaphragm, to support pitches in all registers.

Lip Adjustments

The player who depends upon his lip muscles—exaggerated puckering, stretching, and/or pressure—drastically reduces his endurance, limits his range, and inhibits his tone. As a result of such methods, the tone has the tendency to change quality with each change of register. This is, of course, as undesirable on cornet or trumpet as on any music instrument. Yet we have all had experiences with the student who gets good quality from C4 to C5, but whose tone begins to thin in the upper register limiting his practical playing range to A5 or B♭5.

The logic of using more pucker, stretch, smile, or pressure to increase range is very definitely open to question. Reducing the size of the aperture with any of these practices is basically wrong. It is not logical to expect an ever smaller aperture to produce the same quality of tone that a larger one produced a 5th or a 4th lower. Reducing aperture size will, however, facilitate higher pitches to some extent, but the tone quality will be thin; furthermore, there is a definite limitation as to how much one can pucker, smile, etc.

The answer lies in concentrating on the utilization of the embouchure to the utmost in its most comfortable and most productive position, that register where it feels most comfortable and produces the best sound. The player should attempt to use as little lip motion as possible, allowing the air stream—not lip movement—to change pitches. The feeling should be one of keeping the aperture as constant as possible—in direct opposition to puckering toward the center or pulling the corners of the mouth up in a smile—and allowing an increase in air pressure to cause the pitches to flow one into another.

Diaphragmatic Control

This demands diaphragmatic control and much breath capacity. Fortunately, these things can be developed. First the student must realize where his diaphragm is and just how it works. Then, using the exercises on pages 26 and 27 of the *Arban Complete Method* at 84 quarters per minute, the player should take a breath after each dotted 8th—the exercises consist of the dotted 8th followed by a 16th—and play until he has consumed too much air to continue. Beginners can intone the rhythms and, by breathing in the same manner, acquire this experience. Whenever the player takes a breath in normal playing, he should attempt to take in as much air as he had when forced to stop playing the above exercises.

Learning to control such large quantities of air with the diaphragm is a little more difficult, and the best way to facilitate this is by playing slowly slurred scales up and down thru one octave. When these can be done successfully at a very slow tempo,

extend the scales to two octaves.

The student should inhale air until he feels exactly as he did when forced to stop playing the dotted 8th and 16th exercise. Then he should play the scale, increasing the air pressure with each ascending tone. He should keep the aperture constant and relaxed (using a mirror will help), allowing each pitch to flow into the next. The starting speed of the scale should be the tempo at which the player can complete one octave, ascending and descending, in one breath.

Upon successful completion of all major scales, lower the metronome one notch for the next day's practice. Finally, when the tempo becomes such as to make one octave scales impractical, continue this routine with scales of two octaves. These will bring the pitches into the upper register, where the player must concentrate on increasing the air pressure with each ascending pitch instead of puckering or using pressure. No vibrato should be used.

This tempo will facilitate listening for sameness of quality of sound throughout the registers. Also, the playing of a two octave scale at 63 quarters per minute, for instance, will really force the student to breathe deeply and control the air properly.

When practicing, remember:
1. Embouchure relaxed.
2. Aperture as constant as possible.
3. Increase air pressure with every rise in pitch.
4. Keep the tone quality the same with each pitch.
5. Take a deep enough breath to complete a two octave scale successfully, ascending and descending.

FINE

Bach's "Brandenburg Concerto No. 2"

Vincent Bach

ANYONE UNDERTAKING the performance of the trumpet part to Johann Sebastian Bach's *Brandenburg Concerto No. 2* exposes himself to severe embouchure punishment—a fact not readily considered by many symphony conductors. They frequently schedule difficult symphonies requiring numerous rehearsals and then expect the first trumpeter to have enough reserve power for this *Brandenburg Concerto*.

To accomplish this one needs a supernatural embouchure. Such a player not only needs a robust physique and unusually powerful lip muscles, but he must be prepared for this type of playing during his early training.

The best symphony orchestra trumpeters have different qualifications or strong points. Some of them concentrate primarily on developing a beautiful Teutonic tone, so necessary for symphony work, others work for a light, flexible embouchure suitable for solo playing, and others take particular interest in the performance problems of Baroque music. Seldom does one hear a trumpeter who is "tops" in all respects.

Bach's Trumpeter

Johann Sebastian Bach had at least one fine trumpeter, Gottfried Reiche, who specialized in performing Bach's music. Reiche was a physically powerful musician. During concert tours he traveled in open air on horseback, and since he did not have to practice finger technique or transposition, he was able to concentrate entirely on

developing his embouchure—becoming the outstanding trumpet soloist of his time. However, Reiche is believed to have died of over-exertion following the performance of one of Bach's compositions containing a typically difficult trumpet part! Thus, a reasonable symphony conductor will not insist that his first trumpeter perform the *Brandenburg Concerto* unless the player feels that he is gifted with an embouchure and physical strength well beyond normal capacities.

Those performers who feel that they are overstraining themselves can suggest the use of the Mottl arrangement of this work, which is somewhat simplified and calls for an assistant trumpet player to change off with.

To perform the strenuous parts in the *Brandenburg Concerto, B Minor Mass, Christmas Oratorio,* the *Magnificat,* or in the cantatas a player must have an ability to recuperate quickly from excessive strain. A young player can be expected to do this more easily, but only if he included this type of Baroque music in his early training and refrains from overstraining his embouchure.

The Problem

Some ambitious music students make the mistake of spending their conservatory years playing B♭ trumpet exclusively, giving their lip muscles a one-sided training. When, later, they join symphony orchestras, their problems begin. They quickly discover that they also must play a C trumpet as well as the D or E♭ trumpet. Not only are they bothered by

the different range of these instruments, but they need to develop their embouchure muscles and to adjust themselves to the strain, the response, and the control of intonation required by the variety of instruments in different keys.

These problems become more acute when the trumpet player is called upon to play the *Second Brandenburg Concerto,* originally written for natural contralto trumpet in low F and played in an octave higher range and the low pitch of A-423. This type of instrument is not used today, and no performer could be expected to devote months of practice in order to master it.

How Can It Be Done?

Mel Broiles (associate first trumpet, Metropolitan Opera Orchestra) played the part repeatedly on a Bach sopranino trumpet in high F (curled). Others having success with Bach trumpets for performances of the *Second Brandenburg* include William Vacchiano, first trumpet, New York Philharmonic, with a sopranino G trumpet; and Gilbert Johnson, associate first trumpet, Philadelphia Orchestra, with a piccolo trumpet in high B♭ (playing the same part several times in one week).

Each of these three instruments has advantages and disadvantages that the artist learned to control thru diligent practice and the proper selection of a mouthpiece. The sopranino trumpet in F has the most solid tone (the greater the length of tubing attached to the mouthpiece, the more control and amplification of the tone the instrument will have), but the instrument must be used in the upper register up to the high D6. Therefore, the trill of G5-A5 is difficult to perform.

The soprano trumpet in G requires slightly more strength, but this is compensated for by transposing the *Brandenburg* one tone lower, playing the G-A trill on F-G and making the highest tone in the part C6. The piccolo trumpet in high Bb requires the greatest lip control (because the short length of tubing attached to the mouthpiece), but the *Brandenburg* is played a fourth lower in the middle register; the trill D-E is relatively easy to perform and the highest tone is A5.

Mouthpieces

Tho most of these artists use their regular mouthpiece rim and cup diameter but a shallower cup, it is reasonable to assume that a player specializing in the performance of Baroque music would use a smaller, shallow-cupped mouthpiece. The piccolo trumpet, being an octave higher than the regular mezzo-soprano Bb trumpet, requires the use of a proportionally smaller and shallower mouthpiece. A trumpet player would not think of using a trombone mouthpiece, his trumpet being an octave higher than a trombone. But "where there is a will, there is a way," and the previously cited top trumpeters, thru diligent practice have developed a "Superhuman" embouchure, and accomplish the impossible.

Nevertheless, an a s p i r i n g symphony trumpeter would do well to practice d u r i n g his conservatory years at least several months on a C trumpet, followed by a similar period on soprano D and Eb trumpet, then a sopranino trumpet in F, and finally a piccolo trumpet in high Bb. During that time he should start working on each instrument in the middle register (between the staves) and gradually build up the high and low registers with a relaxed embouchure, avoiding too much lip pressure and strain. He will then be able to manage any of these high-pitched instruments.

The big mistake being made by s o m e symphony trumpeters who never played these high-pitched instruments previously is attempting to perform the *Brandenburg* or Bach oratorios and cantatas on short notice.   FINE

October, 1960

Start right by teaching the —

Fundamentals of French Horn Playing

Joseph Schmoll

HOLDING THE INSTRUMENT correctly is one of the first problems a student encounters in the study of the French horn.

The horn is usually played in a sitting position. The performer should sit up straight in the chair but only touching the back of the chair in the area from the waist downward. The upper part of the back should be leaned slightly forward. This gives a feeling of alertness and allows the ribs and muscles in the back to expand freely when inhaling. The head should be kept comfortably erect and not tilted forward or backward, or to either side. The performer should feel that he is bringing the horn to his mouth and not his mouth and head to the horn. This attitude will help to prevent tilting of the head to awkward and uncomfortable positions.

The rim of the bell should rest on the outward edge of the right thigh. In instruction books of an earlier date, occasionally there are pictures of the horn being held above the thigh with the right hand. This position is impractical today because the modern horn is heavier than its predecessors.

The right hand is placed in the bell on the side away from the body. The hand is approximately vertical to the floor. The fingers and thumb are placed together in much the same way as saluting except that they are not tense. The ear dictates as to how far the hand is placed in the bell. The wrist should be relaxed sufficiently so that the hand can partially close the ‚opening of the bell to adjust sharp pitches. Flat pitches can be adjusted by opening the hand. It is important to remember that when adjusting for a sharp pitch the hand is not pushed farther into the bell.

The bell should point away from the performer or the tone will be muffled. Pointing the bell toward the body is sometimes called "hugging the bell." This practice is to be avoided because the body will absorb the sound. Sometimes after a student is asked to point the bell away from the body, he will comment that the tone is not as rich as before. This is because the sound is now being directed to the listener's ear instead of to the performer's.

It is a mistake to attempt to place the mouthpipe of the horn parallel with the floor. This position points the bell downward and the body absorbs the sound. A 180 degree angle of the mouthpiece on the lips also makes playing difficult for most people. Some performers attempt to tilt the head backward as a compensation, but this is not desirable. Apparently those students who prefer to hold the horn in this manner do so because they feel that they should approximate the position of the trumpet or trombone. Of course, this is a mistake. As a matter of fact, few good trumpet or trombone players hold their instruments in exactly a horizontal position.

For most players, the legs should be slightly to the right of the music stand. This allows the mouthpiece to come directly to the mouth. If the legs point straight ahead, the head has to be turned to the left in order to play the horn.

After repeated practice, the correct way to hold the horn will appear to be the natural way. The performer can play for long periods of time without tiring. An uncomfortable performer cannot be expected to play well.

Mouthpiece Placement

As a general rule, the mouthpiece should be placed in the center of mouth with approximately two-thirds touching the upper lip and one-third on the lower lip. If a student has deviated slightly from this position but is playing well, there is no reason for him to change. On the other hand, a student should not place the mouthpiece on the lips in a haphazard position.

Placing one-half of the mouthpiece on the upper lip and one-half on the lower lip is not encouraged. Often students who have played another brass instrument will attempt this placement on the horn. If they make a determined effort to put more of the mouthpiece on the upper lip, using a small mirror to check regularly, the adjustment will soon be accomplished. It is best to experiment a little for no two players will place the mouthpiece in exactly the same position.

Often good performers play with the mouthpiece a little off the center of the mouth. Each person has a slightly different structure of the jaw and teeth and must make adjustments accordingly. However, the rule of placing the mouthpiece in the center of the mouth with approximately two-thirds touching the upper lip and one-third on the lower lip is the guiding principle.

No one has demonstrated that small lips are an advantage in horn playing. It has been thought that if the mouthpiece can be seated on the outer skin around the mouth, mastery of the horn will be accomplished more easily; but it is doubtful that the size of the lips or minor malformations of the jaw or teeth have any bearing on good horn playing.

Good Ear Necessary

The important qualities in the prospective horn player are innate musical ability and a good ear. Without a discriminating ear a student cannot be expected to progress very far. The harmonics are very close on the French horn and the valves do not determine the pitch as easily as on other brass instruments. The ear must dictate the correct adjustment of the embouchure to sound each pitch. It is for these reasons that often the correct pitch is obtained with the wrong fingering.

Many students possess a good ear but lack the musical background to make this apparent to the instructor. Drill in sight singing and dictation will aid the development of a horn player or any other instrumentalist. Relating melodic figures to scales and the various kinds of chords is helpful. It is also helpful for the student to sing an exercise before he plays it. This will aid him in realizing the nature of his difficulty. A student must know the sound of the various intervals, chords, and scales before he can relate melodic fragments to them. Even a small amount of instruction of this kind would be very valuable if it were provided somewhere in the program. It is easy to demonstrate the sound of intervals and chords, first with the piano and later with other instruments. A few minutes a day of this kind of instruction would improve any instrumental group. Since in most band training programs the young performer often has an opportunity to play the different kinds of scales, special attention should be given in this situation to intervals and chords.

Embouchure

The correct embouchure is formed by shaping the lips as if to whistle. The corners of the mouth should be held firmly together, however. Surrounding muscles will be made tense if the corners of the mouth are held together. This is highly desirable because effective use of these muscles will eliminate excessive mouthpiece pressure and make playing more effective.

The smile setting is not recommended for the reasons that the tone is usually unsatisfactory, the high and low notes are very difficult to produce, and there is danger of injuring the lips and teeth. Sometimes students mistake the use of the muscles at the corners of the mouth for a smile setting. A real smile setting results, however, only when the corners of the mouth are drawn back, causing the lips to stretch. This procedure is the opposite of a slight pucker of the lips.

The vibration of the lips produces the sound on the horn in the same manner as on any other brass instrument. Breathy tones and unpleasant sounds usually can be traced to lack of efficient lip vibration. The lips must vibrate more vigorously than most beginners imagine. Many students attempt to press the mouthpiece against the lips as a compensation for improper lip vibration. This makes matters even worse.

It is impossible to play the horn using no pressure against the lips. Some pressure is needed for normal playing and slightly more is needed for notes in the high register and those with a *forte* marking. On the other hand, as little pressure as possible should be used. Tired and aching lips are a sign of too much pressure. The best antidote for this is to keep the corners of the mouth firmly together and to use the surrounding muscles on each side of the face. When these muscles become tired the student then has assurance that he is using them. If they never become tired he can conclude that he is not using them. A beginner should take frequent rests, for the point of playing certainly is not tired facial muscles.

The chin should be pointed downward. Occasionally a student points the chin downward but somehow manages to keep the upper and lower lips pressed firmly together. The reason for dropping the chin is to allow an opening in the lips for the emission of air into the mouthpiece. One of the reasons a student might not be able to play the extreme high notes successfully is because he raises his jaw. This shuts the opening between the lips almost entirely. If he were to play in his middle register in this manner, he would have the same difficulty. The chin should be dropped even more to play the low notes. If the chin is not dropped, the low notes will continue to be difficult or impossible to play. When this point is digested by a student, he will often add another octave to his range in a few minutes.

The corners of the mouth should not spread outward under any circumstances. The performer should be aware of the position of the corners of his mouth when playing in the middle register at a *mezzo piano* dynamic level. If his performance in this register is satisfactory, then the corners of the mouth should remain in the same position when playing in the low register, the high register, and at a *fortissimo* level. Spreading of the corners of the mouth in the low register will make the notes very insecure or entirely impossible to sound.

Puffing the cheeks is an indication that the facial muscles are not being used properly. It is for this reason that such a practice is undesirable. Often constant reminding over a period of time is necessary before this disappears.

Protruding the lower lip away from the teeth is another fault that will cause a great deal of trouble. If the high notes are difficult and the tone lacks resonance, this could be the difficulty.

Managing the Breath

Expansion of the rib cage and the abdominal area is necessary in order for the lungs to fill up with air. It is possible to get air into the lungs by raising the shoulders but not enough air to play a music instrument effectively.

The diaphragm is a muscle that lies horizontally across the body. Its function is to separate the lungs from the lower organs. At the moment of inhalation it drops downward and creates a vacuum in the chest cavity. Air rushes into the lungs to fill this vacuum. The lungs, therefore, expand into the space that the lowered diaphragm created.

A great deal of air has to be blown thru the horn in order to play it well. The amount of air that is inhaled for normal conversation is not enough. The greater the expansion of the rib cage and abdominal area, the more air will enter the lungs. It follows then that deep breathing is the general rule for horn playing whether performing in the high or low register or at a *forte* or *piano* level.

The rib cage and muscles in the back also expand when inhaling. This is highly desirable. A good exercise to enable the student to feel this expansion is for him to bend forward in a sitting position and touch the floor with his hands. In this position, he should inhale. Only the muscles and ribs in the back will expand. He then should remember this feeling and try to approximate it under normal playing conditions.

The air is inhaled thru the corners of the mouth without taking the lips from the mouthpiece. Inhaling in this manner allows the lungs to fill up more rapidly than when the air is taken in thru the nose. No sound should result from inhaling. Occasionally there is a student who inhales by sucking the air thru the horn. For both sanitary and aesthetic reasons this is not desirable.

Expelling the air thru the horn is the next important step. It should be expelled at a rate of speed that will bend the flame of a candle without blowing it out. The muscles of the abdomen and rib cage contract while the air is being expelled thru the horn. This contraction is steady and constant. Slightly more pressure is needed for high notes and *forte* passages. On the other hand, it is a serious mistake to release the pressure entirely when playing at a *piano* level or in the low register.

Although this may sound contradictory, the tendency to contract the rib cage and abdominal area must be resisted. Some contraction will take place but the collapse of this area will result in lack of proper breath support. When it is time to inhale for a succeeding breath, the rib cage and abdominal area should not be collapsed first but immediately expanded.

Attack

The attack is achieved by a spitting action of the lips. The student should imagine that he has a particle of paper on the tip of the tongue. A spitting action starts the lips vibrating efficiently immediately. For this reason it produces a clean attack on the horn. It helps to eliminate breathy sounds and other undesirable effects. At first the student should spit rather vigorously until he has mastered the technique. Later he can restrain the action, especially in slow singing passages. This spitting action is the basis for all attacks and should not be abandoned when playing *piano* or employing legato-style tonguing.

A fine horn player not only uses this spitting action to achieve a clear attack but also to create a beautiful musical effect. For this reason a sustained note or an ordinary scale becomes a beautiful musical experience when played by an accomplished performer. It is possible, however, for even the most mediocre secondary school student to produce clear definite attacks if he practices this technique.

The tongue acts as a valve that controls the passage of air into the horn. When it is forward in the mouth, it stops the stream of air from entering the horn. When it is withdrawn to the back of the mouth the air is free to enter. Whether the tongue is placed behind the upper teeth or between the upper and lower teeth is not important. The student should choose one of these methods and stay with it until it is mastered.

A clear attack is accomplished by withdrawing the tongue quickly from either of these two positions while the lips perform the spitting action.

Legato

The legato technique does not involve the use of the tongue. A change in pitch is effected by flexing the muscles of the lips and face while keeping a constant flow of air into the instrument. The important thing to remember is that the stream of air does not stop. At first, when slurring larger intervals, a *glissando* effect will result. This should not disturb the performer. He should strive to remove it eventually and at the same time to keep the flow of air constant. If the air flow is interrupted, in an attempt to remove the *glissando*, progress will not result.

If the enunciation of syllables or

vowels is an aid to good legato technique, it should be used. However, students have learned to slur effectively without this.

Conclusion

Unpleasant tone quality is not the natural product of a French horn. This can easily be established by listening to the French horns in a professional symphony orchestra. Satisfactory tone quality is also within the reach of the average student. The requisites are proper breath support, correct embouchure, the right posture in holding the horn, and an idea of how a characteristic horn tone should sound.

Whether the tone quality should be bright, dark, or somewhere in between is a matter each student will partially decide for himself. The most sensible advice is to avoid the extremes of brightness or darkness.

Although the F horn is extremely popular in the public schools, it is not necessarily the best kind of horn for the beginner. I have changed students of modest playing accomplishments from the F horn to the Bb horn. Their playing immediately improved and this improvement was apparent to even the most casual observer. Bb French horn parts are not necessary even tho members of the horn section may play Bb horns. The

fingering chart supplied by the music dealer, or that found in any instruction book, enables the Bb horn player to read an F horn part.

One tuba part is supplied to all tuba players regardless of the pitch of their instrument. Each player, whether he knows it or not, has already been taught a fingering which makes the necessary adjustments. There is exactly the same situation in the use of F and Bb horns. All read from an F horn part. Also, the director does not have a problem of securing extra parts when using Bb horns in his organization.

FINE

Orchestral literature requires —

November, 1960

Development of Brass Tone

Glen Law

WITH PROPER ADVANTAGE, the performance of orchestral literature can be selected to serve as a criterion of excellence in brass technique. It appears to be generally assumed that symphonic performers must acquire exacting techniques, and this type of performance seems to be the most difficult. It is not unusual for conductors of major symphony orchestras to expect almost flawless performances from their musicians. These stringent demands necessitate a high quality of control, delicacy, flexibility, and sensitivity to style, as well as mastery of skills. Thru the study of orchestral music and orchestral playing, brass players, students, and teachers can **concentrate on tone development.**

The foundation of brass playing is the important activity of tone production. Almost every technical aspect of brass performance, including facility throughout the range, accuracy, delicacy, and expressive control is dependent upon proper tone production. The similarity of brass performing to singing can be utilized to strong advantage. In order to convey musical meaning to the listener, the instrumentalist should conceive of his playing as being related to the expressive qualities of the human voice. The sound emitted by the brass player should be comparable to the freedom of tone projected by an excellent singer, otherwise the performance becomes over-technical and impersonal. **Tone** on brass instruments should be

executed with a communicative force that emulates fine singing.

The lips of the brass player serve as the vibrating agents, the counterpart of the vocal chords of the singer. The concept of tone production in brass playing can be thought of as phrase patterns that have musical continuity, rather than music "note for note." Orchestral passages and solos should be expressed as musical thoughts. The flow of tone cannot be utilized efficiently if it is hampered by constriction and tension. The loss of energy would hinder the player's technique. A lack of ease in tone production is a symptom of technical deficiencies, an assertion that makes it necessary to examine the mechanisms that contribute to and affect tone production.

Tone Producing Mechanisms

Playing a brass instrument, as with singing, depends upon a regular column of breath that starts from the lungs. The music instrument can be considered as an attachment to the tone producing mechanism that originates with diaphragmatic movement and the other muscles of respiration. Pressure, exerted on the lungs by the diaphragm moving upward, will cause the air to pass up the trachea, thru the larynx and glottis, over the tongue, and thru the lips, causing them to vibrate, and to produce tone. The instrument amplifies the vibrations of the lips, causing the air column within the instrument to vibrate.

Use of Diaphragm

The essence of good tone production is sufficient breath support that is evoked by the correct and extensive use of the diaphragm. The diaphragm, a musculofibrous partition that divides the thoracic cavity from the abdominal cavity, is extremely important in brass playing. Diaphragmatic movement is a natural phenomenon during involuntary breathing. Voluntary diaphragmatic contraction is exerted in activities other than playing a wind instrument, such as in shouting, coughing, lifting, and panting. When the diaphragm is used correctly, it is vital in the support and projection of tone, e.g., saying the syllable "ta-a-a," sustained for a long duration, sets the diaphragm in action. The degree to which all the functional muscles of the breathing mechanism control air pressure is the crux of the matter.

The proper use of the diaphragm is needed to control and sustain the emitting air. The diaphragm is situated at the floor of the thoracic cavity and is dome shaped. When an inhalation occurs, the diaphragm contracts, tends to flatten, and afterward helps to control the breath. This control is aided by the abdominal muscles. The intercostal muscles that control the upward and downward—as well as the outward and inward—motion of the ribs in breathing are part of this activity. When playing brass instruments there is a combination of thoracic or costal breathing with abdominal or diaphragmatic breathing.

The component parts that are essential in tone production are the throat, tongue, teeth, lips, and the muscles surrounding and controlling the lips. If there is obstruction or improper control of the muscles and tissues involving the above items, tension and harmful pressures appear to result, possibly inhibiting tone production.

Role of the Throat

An essential component of tone production is the concept of the open throat. The throat should be kept open for free air passage because during times of physical stress excessive muscular contraction produces a small and pinched tone, resulting in fatigue and limited power and range. Since playing in the middle and low registers requires less muscular contraction, the stopping of the tone, even in staccato parts, can be controlled more easily. But in the upper register more muscular contraction is exerted, especially for short notes.

The tendency in high, staccato passages is to close the throat. This tightening prevents the breath from passing freely. Players should try to eliminate constriction by concentrating on the control of the breathing muscles. In this problem the important consideration is the avoidance of the use of certain muscles, such as tensing the laryngeal and pharyngeal muscles, thereby choking the tone. The old trick of placing two fingers vertically between the teeth and whispering the words "he" or "who" produces the feeling of an open throat. This type of freedom is needed when projecting the air thru the throat. All resistance seems to be magnified when the dynamic level increases and/or the registration rises.

Function of the Tongue

The position of the tongue affects tone production. When vocalizing, the singer employs vowels for resonance and quality in various registers. Adjustments are also necessary for different qualities throughout the range of brass instruments. In brass playing many teachers advocate the syllables "ah" for the low register, "oo" for the middle register, and "ee" for the high register. The sound chamber formed in the mouth should be as large as possible if a free and resonant tone is desired. The tongue does arch higher when the player approaches the upper register, but this action may not be as pronounced as many teachers claim and certain theories advocate.

Breath Control

Effective breath control injects vitality into the brass player's tone. It is not a natural process to adapt the muscles of the breathing mechanism to produce tone on a brass instrument. The muscles are developed for a physical activity that is different from their intended function. Therefore, constant review of fundamental playing reactions must be practiced in order to retain the instantaneous muscular response. Subtle conditioned physical responses seem to disappear with relatively little activity and review. However, a precise measurement of all muscular activity in playing brass instruments has not as yet been defined.

It is apparent, nevertheless, in controlled breathing that there are muscular and counter-muscular tensions. The muscles that control inhalation are in counteraction, so to speak, against the muscles that control exhalation. This delicate balance is what contributes to breath control. The amount of muscular contraction is in proportion to the volume of sound required and the registration of the music. Different types of passages call for a variance in the expenditure of physical energy. This concept is formed by perceptive judgment on the part of the performer who discovers and gauges rather closely how much pressure is needed in a forthcoming phrase.

Controlling the breath depends upon the practical consideration and the intelligent analysis of the technical and musical implications concerned therein. In the process of producing louder notes, the muscles used in breathing exert more pressure on the lungs, thereby forcing more air thru the lips which opens the aperture. However, the embouchure muscles must maintain the correct frequency of vibrations while at the same time there is an increase of intensity. Tone is controlled by an intricate relationship between the amount of breath and the muscles of the embouchure. In this way the performer produces various combinations of dynamics and frequencies of vibrations.

A full tone depends upon deep inhalation. Air should be expended so that enough remains to play the last note of a phrase as fully as the first. More breath is naturally going to be used in loud passages. To maintain an even, full tone, the air should be emitted steadily by constant diaphragmatic support. It is this constant process of tone-building by proper utilization of breath that produces tremendous power by skilled performers.

Care should be taken to achieve the most extended loud tone quality with the least flow of breath. Controlling the breath is very beneficial in developing evenness of tone throughout the brass player's range. The goal of the brass player should be to achieve the same bigness of tone in the upper register that is prevalent in the lower range. This process can be promoted by retaining as much of the open tone production as possible in approaching the high register. The concept is to progress upward a tone at a time, extending this free production without excessive tension. Of course, each player has his own limitations, but this open range can be developed, extended, and maintained.

Sostenuto Style

The sostenuto style is an important concept in symphonic playing and is executed by projecting a constant stream of air. Too little air produces an anemic tone, while frequent inhalations produce a choked and breathy tone. Unnecessary and forceful tonguing can destroy tone quality. In the sostenuto style the air constantly flows into the instrument, and the tongue rises when necessary in the correct manner to sound the next note. If this style is not developed, a short, choppy effect appears, resulting in a style that is musically undesirable. Except where indicated by expression marks, tones should be sustained their complete value, and there should be no diminuendo. If this does not occur, the tone becomes weak at the end of each note, causing too much separation.

Conservation of Muscular Action

To conceive of the desirable conservation of energy and muscular activity, it is helpful to observe certain beginning or intermediate students who use excessive energy and exaggerate muscular movement. The absence of physical control makes the beginner unable to eliminate unnecessary movements. In the process of forming and manipulating the embouchure, there seem to be contractions of facial muscles. These relatively weak muscles need careful development and maintenance. With the beginning student, the muscles controlling the lips have not as yet been developed.

To help solve the problem the student should try to utilize muscular activity, thereby excluding restrictive motion that interferes with fluency. The player should realize that it is best to conserve his potential strength and power until an extremely difficult part presents itself. If the performer uses excessive energy and motion in the lower parts, there is not enough reserve strength for the maximum effort. The procedure is equivalent to the string player who uses most of the bow on the first two beats of a whole note, with not enough remaining to finish with a solid tone.

Faulty Tone Production

The brass teacher should remain alert for faulty habits in the playing of students who frequently adopt styles of production that are unmusical. One of these happens when the tones are squeezed out. This result is the consequence of not allowing the tone to flow freely, with proper attack, and the tone is stopped with the tongue and/or throat. The teacher might also notice that students, in faulty tone production, frequently use syllables such as "tawg" or "tawck"; consequently the tones sound choked off.

This happens to the inexperienced brass student who has not acquired the correct orchestral style of sustained playing. The experienced brassman will display resonance, tone projection, power, and brilliance. Musical understanding should be expanded for the purpose of giving meaning to techniques. Experiences of students should give them cognizance that unmusical sounds are not compatible with the performance of excellent literature.

Dynamic Range

The dynamic range of brass instruments can extend from very soft passages to extremely loud playing. When power is denoted, the full tonal characteristics of the instruments can produce a ringing brass effect. It is almost impossible to overblow an instrument of reputable quality if there is correct tone projection.

Good tone projection can be noted in the following comparative observation: If one listens to the playing of an inexperienced brass player in a relatively small room or at a short distance, the impression is that the sound is very loud. However, when comparing this tone with one by a proficient symphony musician, in a very large concert hall it would appear weak and strident, because the student does not have the brilliant intensity which projects tone. The unskilled performer's tone diffuses too quickly.

Each day students should cover the entire dynamic possibilities of the instrument, without sacrificing quality. Probably one of the most difficult techniques is to maintain a loud, full tone without destroying the clear quality. Playing *fortissimo* is just as important as playing *piano*. Loud playing, if executed properly, is not only beneficial but essential in the development of a strong embouchure.

Symphonic Tone

A clear tone seems to be the most desirable for symphonic playing, and many composers have employed this characteristic. There are isolated effects and styles that appear in orchestral literature that require unique tonal characteristics, e.g., the flutter tongue. The use of different composers and styles necessitates adjustments of quality and concept of tone. Adaptibility to various styles of tone and interpretation has a common focal point, for the pleasing tone has timbre, resonance, and a beautiful texture. When a player injects a sound into an ensemble he should make a confident entry, and this should be pleasing and convincing to his fellow players and listeners.

The symphonic brass performer must retain the unique qualities of his instrument and is often called upon to display these characteristics, but there are many times when he should blend with the entire group to produce the orchestral sound, i.e., where each instrument loses its identifying qualities. A beautiful, rich tone seems to fit into this mass of tone quality, blending with the sounds of strings and woodwinds. This technique can be accomplished by players with flexible tones of warmth and sensitivity. Such tones combine with a total expression of sound.

After the basic control of tone is achieved, the player should add the flexibility necessary to adjust to the subleties of artistic expression and the finesse that enhances performance. The demands of the symphonic ensemble permit only judicious divergence from the clear, solid tone expected. It is left to the performer to embellish this basic quality by phrasing, elegant interpretation, and sensitive adjustment to style.

FINE

November, 1960

Some Brass Tacks About Brass Bands

Erik Leidzen

THE FIRST "tack" to be driven home is the fact, that a brass band is a BRASS band. This is important, since quite often the term brass band is used—loosely and erroneously—to describe any band of any size using any instrumentation. The persistent use of this nomenclature may have been caused, partly at least, by the fact that in the period following the Civil War there actually were real brass bands here in America. This is not generally known, and the writer of this article was totally unaware of this defunct brass band movement until Major Holz of The Salvation Army showed him an antiquated volume on *How to Write for Brass Band*, published in this country during the abovementioned period. Even a cursory glance at the contents of this method shows why the movement soon died out, and also from where stems much of the prejudice against all bands, so rampant in many quarters even in our day.

Our opinions are far too often influenced by our prejudices, and anything which is different is often considered wrong. We should realize, that as the string orchestra is not a symphony orchestra minus wind instruments, a male chorus not a mixed choir without women's voices, nor a women's chorus a mixed choir without male voices, so a brass band is not a concert band without wood-winds. All these various aggregations are simply different media of musical expression, personalized by their respective characteristics and idiosyncrasies. Whatever our personal bias may be, the acceptance of this mode of reasoning will always have a widening and enriching influence on our true enjoyment of music. So let us consider the brass band in this light and at its best.

The Movement in England

In Great Britain, where this particular medium of musical expression has reached a very high peak of artistry, the pure-brass idea is adhered to even to the exclusion of all percussion—at least at contest time —tho there are those who advocate the inclusion of whatever percussion instruments the composer might consider suitable for the immediate purpose.

The contests just referred to have gone on continuously, in peace and in war, for over a century and have brought the playing techniques of the better bands to an almost unbelievably high level, although these bands are all composed of amateur players —"amateur" being taken in its basic and best sense. Every town, yes, almost every village has its own band. There are Salvation Army bands, church bands, and factory bands. It has been said, facetiously, that the three most popular sports in Britain are: cricket, soccer, and brass banding.

Twenty-four men, no more no less, make up the contesting complement of each band, tho additional players are sometimes used on other occasions. Each year a new piece, composed especially for the annual contest, is published six weeks prior to this event; and the writer of this article has the distinction of being the only composer, not British born, commissioned to write such a work. This taxing number, called *Sinfonietta*, was played at Manchester in September, 1955, with varying taste, but always with consummate skill by 16 of the top bands of Britain; and it was also played at the contest held in connection with the Edinboro Festival later the same month.

The instrumentation of the British Brass Band is—with very slight variations—as follows:

Eb Cornet (called Soprano) and several Bb Cornets (called, respectively, Solo, Repiano, 1st, 2nd, etc.)

Bb Flügelhorn and three Eb Horns (called Solo, 1st, and 2nd).

1st and 2nd Baritones ("Baritone" indicating the smaller-bore "Bb Tenor," as we Americans used to call it).

Three Trombone parts (two tenors and a bass).
Euphonium
Basses (E♭ and B♭)

This instrumentation insures wide and unbroken registers of the two distinct colors, namely:

1) The sharper-toned or more trumpet-like timbre, from the topmost notes of the E♭ Cornet to the lowest register of the Bass Trombone: and

2) The rounder-toned or more mellow sound of the complete Saxhorn group, from Flügelhorn to B♭ Bass.

It should be pointed out that by E♭ horn is meant alto, which goes for homogeneity in the Saxhorn group. The widespread American objection to this particular instrument is traceable to the fact that so many American-made altos are of poor quality. However, the same objection could be raised where clarinets or even violins are concerned. There is also some criticism of the baritone (B♭ tenor), notably this: that it is not an euphonium. One might as well say that the viola is no good because it is not as big as a cello. Where well-made instruments are available the prejudice is not so common.

In at least one of his symphonies Anton Bruckner, who certainly had an ear for color, whatever else he lacked, prescribes a set of Saxhorns in addition to the usual complement of brasses; and the larger Italian (and even other) bands employ a set of altos in addition to the French horns, as well as a section of B♭ tenors in addition to the trombones and/or the euphoniums. Merely to lift the brass section out of the symphony orchestra is not to create a brass band. For instance, the usual grouping of three trombones and a tuba—so frequently scored for in orchestra—works well enough in piano-passages, but where *forte* is required the different timbres of trombone and tuba become more pronounced, so it is no wonder that Wagner—who also had an ear for color—had that contrabass-trombone made.

All this about timbre and color has been dwelt on in order to stress the finer nuance possibilities of the true brass band. Anyone who has heard good British Band recordings, for instance the *Men of Brass Series* or the better Salvation Army discs, must have been struck not only by the sonority but also by the flexibility and pianissimo possibilities of the

brass band.

Salvation Army Bands

When Dr. Williamson heard the accompaniments furnished by the New York Staff Band of The Salvation Army for his Westminster Choir, he immediately said that, as advisor to the U. S. Navy in matters of sacred music, he would recommend the use of pure brass. Unfortunately, his suggestion was not heeded: and when one considers the usual 21-piece Naval band, which has to struggle with music scored for a much larger instrumentation, one wonders if Dr. Williamson's suggestion might not—and with profit—have been stretched to include all the small bands of the Navy. Many British Army bands are brass bands.

Considering the eventual future of a more widespread American brass band movement we are faced by problems similar to those Major Holz had to solve when he, about a decade ago, was made Music Director of all Salvation Army Music in the Eastern part of our country. Many of his bands did not have all the instruments typical of the British set-up, so in conjunction with the present writer he decided on a practical instrumentation that would meet the most common needs. It consists of:

Two B♭ Cornets (of which the 1st may at times be divided).
Two E♭ Horns
Two Trombones
Euphonium and Bass (plus Percussion).

To this were added four optional parts, namely, E♭ Cornet, Flügelhorn, Baritone, and Bass Trombone, for use by the larger bands which already had these instruments. Basically, however, nine players can render the music completely.

The artistry as well as the practicality of this procedure is borne out by the fact that the music thus published in New York has become in the best sense popular all over the globe wherever Salvation Army Bands are active.

By the initiative of Ralph Satz the Chappell-group published four marches for brass band as a beginning to a *Brass Band Repertory Series*. As it was for American use it had the benefit of being able to adopt the instrumentation already proven practical by The Salvation Army. However, only one optional part (E♭

Cornet) was issued, but, on the other hand, three Trombones were considered standard. Three of these four marches have been recorded by the Ohio State Brass Band. Moreover, the popular Goldman march *Kentucky* was actually premiered by a favorite brass band of the composer and under his baton, namely by a picked group of skillful Salvation Army bandmasters. If all the brass parts are used and the cues in the trumpet parts played, anyone may use this march as a means to get to know what a brass band can be like. It will be found that it has all the sonority of the bugle corps PLUS a much wider range and all possible harmonic and contrapuntal possibilities.

Activity in the U. S.

During a visit to the University of Louisville this writer was invited to one of the high schools of that city. At 7:30 a.m. the brass band met. It played British music, and when the writer—knowing that all the parts were written in treble clef—wondered how the players of the larger instruments got along, Mr. Griffith, the leader, proudly proclaimed: "All my trombone players read four clefs!", which gladdened the heart of the visitor, being—as he is—strongly in favor of musical literacy.

In passing it may be said that if we cultivated that kind of reading ability, not only would the whole British Brass Band literature be within our reach, but also that vast treasure house of French band music, which now remains unplayed here in the United States since the cost of reprinting the material in other clefs and keys is prohibitive. Learning to read a few clefs is not expensive financially speaking. All it costs is a little consistent mental application. The opposition to other clefs than the bass clef for the larger instruments is quite widespread. Richard Goldman even ran into it among the players at Juilliard, tho he managed to overcome it. This objection to the use of the treble clef is not logical, as long as we print all our saxophone parts in treble clef. "What is sauce for the goose," etc.

It is evident from what has been said that there already is an active American brass band movement, and in as widely different areas as, among

Erik W. G. Leidzen

others—the university. the high school. and The Salvation Army fields. That this movement has reached summits of the highest standards in proficiency was shown last summer when the New York Staff Band of The Salvation Army toured Great Britain and there. in the very hotbed of brass band activities. received eulogies and raves from the enthusiasts in all sections and on all levels of the brass band movement.

That the brass band lends itself well to the American idioms was likewise shown, inasmuch as the most popular number on the tour was the *Post Bellum Rhapsody*, based on Civil War songs, not particularly well-known in Britain. A recording entitled *Star Spangled Band Music* was released in connection with the tour and shows what a good American brass band can do. The disc includes the *Post Bellum* (a concert band version of which is being published by Bandland, Inc.).

Since history has already shown, that a brass band movement on a low level proved abortive and died, it is to be hoped that if the brass band again gets under way in our land it will be on a deservedly high level. It should not be a mere off-shoot of the bugle corps. but an effective and truly artistic expression of the best in music, and not merely be—in the stinging words of the Apostle—"a sounding brass and a tinkling cymbal." FINE

December, 1960

The Tuba Section

Gerald Meyer
Montpelier, Ohio

A MUSICALLY ALERT tuba section is a great asset to any large wind ensemble. It is capable of playing a full rich legato bass line as well as one that is rhythmically accurate and a part of the rhythmic accompaniment of the group.

Since we are dealing with more than one tuba, it is necessary to come to some decision on how many should be in the section. As with other instruments, the problems of ensemble are increased in proportion to the number of players. This is especially true with the tuba. The acoustical problems caused by the extreme length of tubing and the lowness of the pitch of the instrument, make it very difficult for several tubas to play together as accurately and cleanly as an equal number of cornets or trombones.

How Many Tubas?

In deciding how many tubas can best be used effectively as a section, we must compromise between these two considerations:

1. The section must be large enough to provide a solid bass line for the fortissimo passages of the full ensemble.

2. The section should be kept small enough to avoid a thick and heavy sound and to enable the players to play together accurately and easily.

With these considerations in mind, the following is recommended: 3 tubas for a group of 60-75 players; 4 tubas for 75-90 players; and 5 tubas for the ensemble numbering 90-110. The section should consist of a minimum of three players, and for all practical purposes, not more than five. The availability of instruments and players may change these numbers either way, however, for best ensemble balance and clarity they should be followed.

Type of Instruments

Along with determining the size of the section, deciding the type of instruments is equally important. In bands today, the BBb tuba has become the most popular. This popularity has risen from its extensive low register while maintaining a high register that is adequate for playing the entire band repertoire.

Unfortunately, even tho there are many of them available, the Eb tuba has become relegated to the role of a beginner's instrument because it is smaller than the BBb and more easily handled. However, the Eb tuba is not merely a beginner's instrument. One Eb should be used in each section to double the BBb tubas one octave higher wherever possible. Because the Eb tuba has a higher range than the BBb, it is much easier for the Eb to articulate clearly in this register.

This one tuba playing an octave higher has a tendency to clear up and avoid the muddiness that often occurs in a section during the performance of passages lying in the low register of the BBb tuba.

Inevitably, the question of whether to use sousaphones, recording basses, or upright tubas arises. The sousaphone is still the most practical instrument for schools that cannot afford two sets of tubas. It is indispensable for the marching band and serves adequately in the concert band. However, wherever possible, the sousaphone is best replaced by either the upright or recording models for concert use.

Upright or Bell-Front Tubas?

While necessity often dictates whether or not to use sousaphones in the large ensemble, the question of upright or bell-front recording models is not so easily answered. This is determined only after considering the type of sound desired and the acoustics of the areas in which they are to be used. Generally speaking, the upright bell tends to give the instrument a brighter sound and a bit more clarity to the articulation. The bell-front models are obviously more directional and tend to have a more "spread" or less brilliant sound, and the articulation does not seem to be as crisp as it is on the upright tuba.

While the upright tuba sounds good in many halls, there are places where it is not able to be heard properly because the sound is being lost as it is sent upward. This is true in buildings where the ceilings are extremely high or on stages where the curtains overhead swallow the sound before it can reach the conductor or the audience.

The solution to this problem is to have detachable bells that may be changed from upright to bell-front models as the acoustics dictate. Where it is financially impossible to secure detachable bells, it would probably be best to purchase the bell-front models unless you are sure that the acoustical conditions permit the use of upright tubas. This decision is best reached by trying out both types to determine whether you prefer the performance of the upright or bell-front tuba in your particular situation.

Music

After determining the number of players as well as the key and model of the instruments, the next item for consideration is the music to be played . . . the tuba parts themselves. Because composers and arrangers are often not aware of the special problems of the tuba, the players are frequently asked to perform passages that do not sound clear. For this reason it is necessary to edit tuba parts very carefully in order to keep the tuba section from sounding heavy and cumbersome. In general, it is advisable to look over and edit the parts before passing them out.

Because the tuba tone is by nature quite heavy, it is often necessary to cut down the number of players during soft and delicate passages. This can be done by checking the dynamics of the score and indicating how many tubas should play the part.

Parts may be registered up or down an octave. Slurred passages occurring downward from $Eb2$ often do not sound clear; the section im-

proves in sound when such passages are put up an octave. It may also be desirable to register the notes down an octave on some of the parts during a sustained passage. These lower pitches are often desirable on the fundamental tone of the chord being played.

All Eb parts that descend into the low register of the Eb tuba should be raised an octave so that they can be played more easily. Invariably when the Eb tuba is given a BBb part, it must first be edited and put into the proper range for the Eb tuba.

Rapid slurred passages are rarely, if ever, acceptable when played by more than one tuba. The effect is usually cumbersome and heavy and tends to lack clarity and definition. This problem may be eliminated by any one of the following ways:

1. If the passage is soft, the part may be played as written by one tuba, or by one tuba doubled by a contrabass clarinet.

2. The sound of the section is often clarified and the original slurred idea of the composer maintained by having the passage tongued by all of the players except the first chair performer who plays the original slurred part.

3. Rapid slurred passages may be clarified by slurring only a few notes rather than many. For example, slurring two and tonguing two notes is usually better than slurring all four of a group. Triplet figures are often better if the first two notes only are slurred and the third is tongued rather than slurring all three.

In editing the parts it is important to check orchestral transcriptions very closely. In these works the tuba parts are usually the string bass line that has been registered within the tuba range. As a result they often contain many technically difficult sections that are quite acceptable when bowed or plucked on the double bass, but are very awkward and difficult for one tuba and nearly impossible for an entire section. Here it is often necessary to simplify the parts and have the tubas play fewer notes for the sake of clarity and accuracy. A good solution is to play only the notes occurring on the beats, or to play every other note of a 16th note passage. Since these parts are often doubled with the low woodwinds and euphoniums, the musical idea is not lost or hindered but improved by greater clarity and precision.

Special Problems

There are some basic rules of style that are important in making the tuba section sound as well as possible. The first to consider is spacing notes properly. This is extremely important in tuba sectional playing.

Quarter and half notes that are not spaced sound like whole notes for lack of definition. This spacing is not to be extreme, but just enough to have the notes sound with definition and to keep the pulse of the meter in the bass line.

With experience the tuba player should acquire the ability to anticipate each beat. There is a slight time lag in getting the large air column within the tuba to vibrate. The player must compensate for this by anticipating the beat.

Because the tuba section is so important in playing a march correctly, it is important to understand the correct style for playing the bass line. The so called "oom-pah" quarter note beats of most marches are often dull and contribute little to the ensemble because they are played incorrectly. In order to sound they must be played short and in tempo with the first note of each measure getting more stress than the second. The idea of heavy-light, heavy-light, heavy-light, etc., should be kept in mind in order to make the bass line light and characteristic rather than dull and uninteresting.

In discussing the capabilities of the tuba section, mention should be made of the use of the pedal tones of the instrument. They are highly effective for putting a real foundation to the full sonority of the ensemble. The effect they give is often compared to the very low pitches of a pipe organ. Unfortunately, however, they are rarely used since most players do not know how to produce them. In order to allow the lip to vibrate the player should use approximately one-fourth upper lip and three-fourths lower. Relaxation and breath control are required.

The Bb is the first pedal tone to develop, and then the range may be extended downward by half-steps, using the regular fingerings. These tones become especially valuable in filling out the sonority of the ensemble on full chords, especially at cadence points where this sound is very effective. FINE

1961

B♭ Valve Trombone

Teaching Lip Vibrato

Lorin Richtmeyer

How often do we hear young brass students, some quite advanced technically, with either "nanny goat" vibratos, slow, jazz vibratos, or none at all? The answer—if our solo and ensemble festivals in the midwest are any criteria—must be, all too often. Why is this so? Are we to believe that vibrato is so difficult to teach? Or do we go on hoping that our brass players will develop a vibrato naturally—that "it will come in time, as soon as the tone matures"?

Occasionally players do develop natural vibratos, either instinctively or by unconscious imitation; but on the whole, the great majority of brass students must be taught its mechanics and spend part of their practice time in developing it.

Lip versus Hand

Generally speaking, there are only two types of vibrato commonly used on brass instruments: the hand, or slide; and a combination of lip and jaw, which I will refer to for the sake of brevity as "lip" vibrato. Although I have used and taught both, and acknowledge the fact that many fine players use the hand and slide vibrato very successfully, I greatly prefer the lip vibrato.

My reasons are: first, the hand or slide movement (particularly that of the slide) is objectionable visually; second, it too often consists of a weak or thin tone disguised by a mechanical shaking of the instrument; third, since the lip vibrato is not possible without embouchure control and a minimum use of pressure, its study thereby enhances the quality of the straight tone; and fourth, the lip vibrato, thru its origin with the embouchure, seems (perhaps partly psychologically) to become more an integral part of the tone, not a mechanical device superimposed on it. Lip vibrato is more difficult to teach, but the results justify the added time and effort.

When to Start

The study of vibrato should begin as soon as the student is able to produce a free sounding tone up thru a medium-high register. This, of course, presupposes a proper foundation of correct breathing so as to avoid pinching and excessive pressure for the higher tones. It is not possible to develop a good lip vibrato without good breath support, and since most embouchure ailments can be traced back to lack of breath support, this part of the student's training must receive careful attention.

First Steps

Assuming, then, that the student has reached this stage in his development, we are ready to begin the vibrato. If the player has had some experience with lip slurs it is easier to get across the principle of the lip vibrato. Start by having him "bend" his tone (say G4 for cornet and T.C. baritone, F3 for trombone and B.C. baritone, and Bb3 for bass) down and up as far as he can without breaking into the next open tone. He can produce this sensation by saying "yah—ee—yah—ee," dropping the jaw and relaxing the corners of the embouchure on "yah" and closing the jaw and tightening the embouchure on "ee."

As soon as he is able to do this, the next step is to have him regulate it by producing one wave (yah—ee) per beat at a metronomic marking of 60. When this becomes even and relaxed, strive for two waves per beat, then three, and finally, four.

Do not let the student go any faster than he is able to control smoothly and evenly. There must be a feeling and sound of continuity in the wave, not a series of broken pulsations. This latter is usually the result of not having a steady flow of breath thru the horn at all times. Also, insist that he exaggerate the width of the vibrato at first even tho it does not sound musical. As its speed is increased, the width will automatically decrease.

In Tuneness

At this point, just a few words concerning the relationship of the wave or vibrato to the true pitch. According to many brass performers and teachers, when the bottom of the wave represents the true pitch of the straight tone, the tone sounds sharp to our ears. When the top of the wave is the true pitch, it sounds flat. And when it is evenly divided above and below, it sounds in tune.

Others have maintained that the ear hears only the top of the wave, thus the second pattern would be most apt to sound in tune.

Without entering into this discussion, let me merely point out that it is very unlikely that any student will use a vibrato based on the first pattern, as this is most difficult to do. As to whether the second or third is correct, it has been my experience that as soon as the player can produce this wave in a relaxed manner no problem of "in tuneness" exists, again assuming that the student can blow a straight tone in tune and in a relaxed manner. However, should intonation enter the picture, the instructor should compare the student's straight tone with his vibrato, and if the latter sounds sharp or flat in comparison, he should adjust the wave to correct this. So far, this phenomenon has never occurred in my presence unless the student was pinching or did not have a sufficiently developed embouchure to begin with.

(*Ed. note: Most acoustics experts and music psychologists term the vibrato an "aural illusion" in which the listener hears a mean or average pitch. Only when a vibrato gets too wide are the crests and troughs of the wave discernible as pitch fluctuations.*)

Speed of Vibrato

When the student can produce four waves at a metronomic marking of 60. gradually increase the tempo until 80 is reached. Generally speaking, this speed is the most pleasing to the ear. The player will find in use, however, that he will tend to speed up the vibrato to impart excitement to his tone or for higher notes, and to slow it somewhat in the lower register. This later becomes a matter of personal taste.

Aids in Using Vibrato

Many times, at this stage of development, the player is able to adapt the lip vibrato to the music on his own. More often, however, he finds that articulations and different note values disrupt the vibrato, and he is in need of further assistance. I have found the following procedure very helpful in making it possible for the player to use vibrato in lyric passages:

First, warm up the muscular action by playing vibrato on whole notes up and down the scale, keeping in a medium range and using a metronomic marking of 80, with four waves to a beat.

Next, while staying in this medium range, play the rhythm patterns (♩ ♪ ♪ — ♩ ♪ ♪ ♪ — ♩ ♩. ♪) with vibrato on each scale degree. These should be done evenly and smoothly at M.M. 80, being careful not to let the vibrato stop as the tongue articulates.

By the time the student is able to do this in a free and relaxed manner, using different tempos in the vicinity of M.M. 80, he should be able to apply his vibrato to simple songs. For this study, any slow, melodic type of music will do, as long as it is kept fairly simple rhythmically at first. I have found that the "Classic and Popular Melodies" in the *Arban Method* are excellent material to use for this.

One other point should be brought out. At the beginning, the student must rely upon his instructor's judgment as to what constitutes a pleasing vibrato. However, as he practices and progresses, he should begin making judgments on his own.   FINE

February, 1961

The Larger Trumpet Sound

Willard Musser

FOR QUITE A number of years many trumpet players have been aspiring, asking, and working for a larger sound. Besides the trend toward a bigger sound, contemporary composers and arrangers are writing brass parts ever higher. This is progress. The outstanding trumpet player is the one who develops his range, plays with consistency in the entire register, has the new larger sound, and possesses fine endurance.

Instruments and Mouthpieces

In working for a larger sound, we often find the player first looking over the various makes of instruments for a bigger bore horn. Several surveys have been made that point up the fact that the demand is for larger bores, and manufacturers have been continually building trumpets with a greater bore.

The trumpet player's second thought toward acquiring a larger sound will probably be the securing of a bigger mouthpiece. It is here that the player might find the improvement in tone quality is accompanied by greater problems of range, intonation, and endurance.

In recent years most studio musicians, symphony orchestra men, and serious trumpet students, seem to be using larger mouthpieces. Especially is this true if these individuals are using a medium large or large bore instrument. The larger size cup allows a larger portion of the lips to vibrate. However, it should be pointed out that to control these larger mouthpieces, it is necessary to have a well-trained, well-developed, strong embouchure.

There are general conditions in regard to intonation that we might well remember when trying to develop a larger sound and an extended range by means of changing mouthpieces. If a mouthpiece has too deep a cup or too open a throat, the tendency will be to play on the flat side of the tone. If the mouthpiece has a very shallow cup or too small a throat opening, the tendency will be to play on the upper side of the pitch.

The Fluegelhorn

The demand for an instrument that will produce a rounder, fuller, more mellow sound has recently brought increased popularity to the fluegelhorn . . . not to replace the trumpet but as an addition to it.

The fluegelhorn, originally a member of the keyed-bugle family, is a tapered-bore instrument usually with piston valves. Because its mouthpiece is more funnel shaped and its bore is considerably more conical than that of the cornet or trumpet, the fluegelhorn produces a broader, mellower tone. This instrument can and should be considered the mezzo-soprano voice of the brass family.

The fluegelhorn is not a new instrument. Its ancestor, much like our common bugle in bore, can be traced back many centuries. According to Curt Sachs, the instrument was first constructed in Austria between 1820 and 1830 and its original German name has ever since been preserved in the English-speaking countries. There is much evidence that these instruments were very popular in European bands throughout the remainder of the 19th century and have continued to maintain their prominence up to the present day.

In America, the fluegelhorn has not always been included in our regular instrumentation. To most listeners, even to many professionals, it was only a name. But many famous composers are now writing for the fluegelhorn, including it in their original compositions for band. Among these is Heitor Villa-Lobos who scored for fluegelhorn in his recent *Fantasy in Three Movements for Wind Orchestra*. And it has just recently made an entrance into the symphony orchestra. Ralph Vaughan Williams, with his acute sense of color, heard or had the fluegelhorn's ideal mezzo-soprano brass quality in mind when he recently wrote his *Ninth Symphony*, creating for it several very lovely solo passages.

FINE

Teaching the Bass Trombone

John Christie

THE BASS TROMBONE, one of the oldest orchestral brass instruments, is being used in much the same form today as it was in 1500. Tho the other members of the family of trombones have become obsolete, the tenor and bass trombones are still in use.

It has become common for composers to write three trombone parts, two parts intended for tenor trombones, and a third part for the bass trombone. This distribution of parts has been in use since the days of Gabrieli. At one time, the first part was intended for the alto trombone, and the second for the tenor, but the lowest of the trombone parts has always been intended for the bass trombone.

Considering the great amount of literature that calls for a bass trombone, it is surprising that the instrument is so seldom found in high school orchestras and bands. There are even some college bands and orchestras that do not have a bass trombone.

The range of the bass trombone, as far as practical usage is concerned, can be compared to that of the bass voice. It extends from C2 to F4. The bass trombone is the only bass instrument that covers the bass range in its normal playing range.

As compared to the tenor trombone, the sound of the bass trombone should be heavier, darker, and richer. The bass trombone is intended to play the bass line, while the tenor trombone is intended for the baritone or tenor parts. Just as the range of the tenor, baritone, and bass voices overlap, so the range of the tenor and bass trombones overlap. This does not mean that they can be used interchangeably on the trombone parts. The tenor trombone should not play the bass trombone parts even if the range makes this possible.

This is no more correct than having tenors singing the bass part in a choir. The quality of tone is different, and cannot be matched by any other brass instrument, regardless of the range in which the instruments are playing.

A musician of high standards cannot accept the substitution of a tenor trombone for a bass trombone, except as a temporary measure until a bass trombone can be had.

Different Types

Several types of bass trombones are in use today. There are single bass trombones without a valve section. These are pitched in G and F and are used in Europe, as well as by the Salvation Army brass bands, and by the Moravian trombone choirs in America. The instrument generally used in this country, however, is the combination Bb-F bass trombone, with a valve. This is the instrument intended when a bass trombone is specified in the score or for the lowest of the trombone parts in a piece of music, unless there is a specific indication to the contrary, such as *Tenor Trombone III* or *Trombone IV (Contrabass)*.

The Bb-F bass trombone is in Bb until the valve is pressed, and then is lowered a perfect fourth to F. When in Bb the instrument is a large bore instrument pitched the same as the tenor trombone. It is designed, however, with a much larger bore and bell, and for richness and greater power in the lower register. The difference is often noticeable at sight. Bass trombones have a bore between .560″ and .565″ and a bell that measures 9½″ to 10½″.

Often there is a problem for some people in telling a bass trombone from a large bore tenor trombone with an F attachment. The presence of the F attachment has absolutely no bearing on whether a trombone is a tenor or a bass trombone. Bore, bell size, and proportions are the sole guide. If the bore size is not known or available, the best procedure is to get a bass trombone and compare sizes, or to try a bass trombone mouthpiece for fit. This does not always work as there are large tenor trombones in which a bass trombone size mouthpiece can be used. The surest test is the size of the bore.

There are several types of rotary valves in use today on bass trombones. One is a string valve, as used on French horns. A second is a mechanical action as used on tubas.

Staveless pitch identification is used throughout this article, as well as in other *Instrumentalist* articles. This basis of the system is that middle C is identified as C4, the reason being that there are approximately four octaves of audible sound below this tone. The C's below C4 are C3, C2, C1, while the tones above are C5, C6, C7, and C8. Thus, any tone is identified by its letter name (plus a ♯, ♭, or ♮ as necessary) and takes its number for octave identification from the C below. A-440 is A4. This system is accurate, simple, and easy to speak or write.

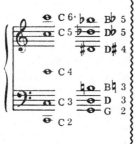

The third is a ball and socket arrangement peculiar to bass trombone valves.

The main tuning slide may be in the bell or, on older models, in the slide. This tunes both sides of the instrument. There is a separate tuning slide for the F attachment. As there is no water key on the F attachment, the player must empty the water out in the same manner as the horn player. Pull the F attachment slide out entirely, and turn the instrument upside down. The valve should be held down before the slide is pulled and left down until the slide is replaced. Care should be taken to replace the F slide to the same tuning.

Mouthpieces

A tenor trombone mouthpiece can never be used successfully on a bass trombone. Even with an adapter shank, a tenor trombone mouthpiece will not be satisfactory.

A proper bass trombone mouthpiece is much larger in cup size, much deeper, and has a much larger throat opening than that of a tenor trombone. By measuring mouthpieces with a quarter, you can get a quick and quite accurate idea about the comparative sizes. Lay a quarter flat in the mouthpiece, and you will see that in a tenor trombone mouthpiece it lies flush with the rim, or possibly just a little further in. In a bass trombone mouthpiece the quarter should be about half an inch down in the cup. This measures the width of the cup.

To measure the depth, place the edge of the quarter in the cup, holding the other edge perpendicular to the rim, so you can sight across. About one half of the quarter will show above the rim in the tenor mouthpiece, but it will be completely covered—or at least just even with the rim—in a bass trombone mouthpiece. The size of the throat opening should be so much larger on the bass trombone mouthpiece that difference is easily visible to the eye without any kind of measurement. A mouthpiece such as a Bach 1½G would be appropriate for the bass trombonist.

Using a mouthpiece that is too small, especially a tenor trombone mouthpiece, will not only produce a thin tone, make the low register very difficult to produce, and cut down on volume and richness, but it will also affect the proportions of the instrument, producing faulty intonation.

Deep Breathing Necessary

The bass trombone requires more wind than the tenor. This is due to the larger mouthpiece and the bore of the instrument, and to the amount of playing done in the low register. The student will find that he cannot play a whole phrase in one breath at first, but must often break phrases to provide additional places to breathe. Deep breathing must be practiced. The student should use as much of his lung capacity as possible. Even with full capacity the bass trombonist cannot play as long in a given register, at a given volume level, as can the tenor trombonist.

The bass trombone should possess a tone darker, richer, and larger than that of the tenor trombone. There should be less brilliance; in fact, the player should have to work hard to produce a brilliant sound in any register. A tone that is not properly supported by breath will often sound "tubby" and dull. This is not to be confused with the desirable qualities listed above.

The bass trombone belongs to the bright brass family and should sound brighter than the mellow brass instruments. It should never sound like a euphonium or a baritone.

The range most frequently used is that from middle C4 downward two octaves. This must be cultivated as the middle register of playing, working upward and downward from these two octaves. It is common practice today, and it has been since the time of Mozart and Beethoven, to write down to the low C1.

The student will also notice that the notes on the F attachment are slower speaking and less clear than those of the Bb side. Conscious effort must be made to balance the sound between the two sides of the instrument. More breath support, and a slightly firmer embouchure must be used. In addition, the student should be trained to listen for this difference in sound, and to note it whenever it occurs. This can also be checked by matching notes on the F side with those on the Bb side, where duplications occur.

The embouchure should *look* about the same as that for the tenor trombone, but the jaw should be opened or dropped considerably more, and the corners of the mouth should be kept firm. More embouchure support than usual should be given to the notes of the low register. Contrary to what might be assumed, playing the low notes does not require a flabby or loose embouchure. Firmness is very important, just as it is in tuba playing. The most important item is opening the jaw. More bass trombonists get a poor sound as a result of this than of any other embouchure defect.

The slide of the bass trombone is slightly larger and slightly heavier than the tenor trombone slide. This will make the player hold it more securely, and will require little more effort to move it. This may decrease the student's technical facility at first.

In lubricating the slide, cold cream and water seems best. It is generally thought to give better action with less effort. However, this method requires much attention and regular cleaning. The slide should be wiped clean and re-lubricated about once a week under normal playing conditions.

Intonation and Positions

Intonation on the bass trombone will be somewhat different than that on the tenor. In general, it could be said that any intonation trouble found on the tenor will be exaggerated on the bass. Flat notes will be more flat, sharp notes more sharp. Often these notes that were a little out of tune on the tenor, become unusable in exposed passages on the bass trombone.

The first position D4 is quite flat and is best played the majority of the time in a slightly flat 4th position.

The most difficult technical problem on the bass trombone concerns what happens to the positions when the valve is pressed down. The amount of tubing necessary to lower an instrument in Bb one half-step is not enough to lower an instrument in F, a 4th lower, a half-step. The lower the pitch of the instrument, the more length of tubing it takes to lower it one-half step. This may be seen by comparing the length of the second valve slide on a cornet, with that on an alto horn, with that of a euphonium, with that of a tuba.

This means that on the bass trombone, a slide that is long enough to lower the Bb side seven half-steps, down to low E2, is not long enough to lower an instrument a perfect 4th lower this same distance. On the F attachment, only six positions are possible, lowering the low F2 in 1st position with the valve down, to low C2, in extended 7th position, also with valve down. The notes between the F2 and the C2 will not correspond in position exactly with those an octave above on the B♭ side. This means that a new set of positions must be learned for the F attachment notes.

Low F2 will be in 1st position, and little flat at that. E2 will be in 2nd position or possibly a little below. E♭2 will be in low 3rd position. D2 will be in a very low 4th position. D♭2 will be in sharp 6th position. Low C2 will be in extended 7th position, as far out as the slide will safely go, and definitely out beyond the sleeves by an inch or two.

The best way for a student to accustom himself to these new positions is to practice octaves. Start on 1st position F3. Play this tone and then push down the valve and play the octave below. Check intonation. It will probably be flat, and possibly not usable at all, except in fast passages, or for short notes. Then check E3, 2nd position; push the valve down and check the E2 below, possibly moving the slide out just a little. Then play E♭3; push the valve and check the octave below, this time moving the slide out an appreciable amount. Then check 4th position D3, push the valve, move the slide out halfway to 5th position, and check the low D2. Check D♭3, push the valve down, and then check both of these against low C2 in extended 7th position with the valve down.

The student must eventually learn where these positions are without any additional thought. It must be automatic. This will come only thru serious practice and listening. An electronic tuning device can be extremely helpful in this process.

As there are not set pitches on the trombone caused by valves, keys, or holes, intonation can be adjusted just as on the string instruments to meet the needs of each separate key, and sometimes, even individual chords.

It is good practice to tell all your students always to play A♯3 below middle C4 in sharp 5th position, and the A♯2 in sharp 3rd position with the valve. To check this play a B major scale using B♭, 1st position, as the leading tone. Then substitute the A♯'s, in sharp 5th and sharp 3rd

position with the valve, and listen to the improvement. The same thing applies to E♯'s. The high E♯4 should always be played in sharp 4th position; the middle E♯3 always in sharp 6th position, never as F in 1st position; and the low E♯2 should always be sharp 6th position, never 1st position with the valve. Check these on the F♯ major scale.

To generalize these enharmonic changes, we could say that you never play any notes in 1st position that are notated as sharps, A♯, E♯, or C double sharp. They are always played in another position so that they can be raised slightly in pitch. They should be raised more than a 1st position spring can provide, as this is a safety measure not to be used in the normal playing of a note.

A student must be taught to pick positions not only by the ease of execution, but also on the basis of tone quality, intonation, and control of the note. In certain difficult technical passages, this rule obviously will be put aside in favor of fluency.

The low F2 in 1st position is very often flat, due to the fact that the tuning slide of the F attachment has to be pulled out some to get the low C2 in tune in a flat 7th position. This F2 should most frequently be played in 6th position on the B♭ side of the instrument for the best sound and intonation.

F Attachment Usage

For those who are not familiar with the use of the valve, perhaps it would be wise to mention those notes

most commonly used on the F attachment. The valve is seldom, if ever, used on any notes above C3, which is played in 1st position with the valve down. B♭2 is played in 2nd position with the valve down. A♯2 is always played in sharp 3rd position with the valve down, and B♭2 is occasionally played in normal or slightly flat 3rd position with valve down. The A2, A♭2, and G2 are seldom played with the valve. The next note is F2 played in 1st position with the valve, and then down chromatically, as described before to C2.

It is good to remember that when the valve is down, any note normally played in 6th position is now playable in 1st position. Any note normally played in 7th position on the tenor trombone is available in 2nd position on the bass trombone.

The valve is particularly valuable in simplying technical passages involving C3, B2, B♭2, and A2. Where the tenor trombonist must work between the farthest positions and the closest positions, the bass trombonist can work solely in the close positions, coupled with the use of the valve. As the notes mentioned above are in the lower register in terms of most trombone parts, these notes are most apt to fall in the lowest, or bass trombone part.

Careful practice is necessary for the student to perfect co-ordination of slide, tongue, and valve. The valve will often bother the transfer student. He will forget to push it down, or forget to lift it up. Slow practice of technical exercises in this register will

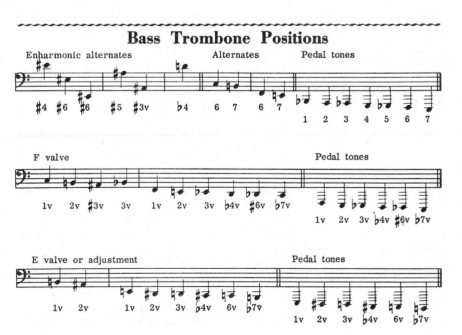

Bass Trombone Positions

help to correct this. No. 5 in Tyrrell (see bibliography following article for this and subsequent references) is excellent for this purpose when played down an octave, and not too fast.

Some trills are made possible by the use of the valve, but they are of little value because they sound somewhat labored, and are not called for except in playing music not originally intended for the trombone.

Some of the notes in the low valve register, notably D♭2 and C2, are slow to speak and hard to articulate cleanly at first. A somewhat broader tongue stroke should be used, and a good deal of mental preparation is necessary. The student who attacks these notes carelessly is apt to miss them.

Tonguing rapidly and cleanly in the low register is a problem. Try to find technical exercises that can be played an octave lower, putting them in this range. Look at Vanesek-Klose, Tyrell, and Cornetti. These books all contain good material for low register study, when played down an octave.

Legato Playing

The legato style is very important to a bass trombonist. Since a good deal of the ensemble music played will be of the opposite style, it is necessary for the teacher to encourage the development of a fine legato style. This requires much work and careful guidance as to the music to be studied. The *Bordogni Vocalises*, transcribed for trombone by Rochut are excellent for this purpose. They should be played down an octave, and also in the original octave. Due to breathing problems, the phrases will have to be broken into two parts many times. Knowledge of how to taper off the end of a passage, take a breath, and go on smoothly, are essential to an effective legato style.

The use of vocal music to achieve a fine legato cannot be too highly stressed. It is better to play fine music in the legato style, taken from another medium, than to play no legato material at all. Those who reject the playing of music on the bass trombone intended for another instrument often do not produce trombonists who can play a cantabile style that is convincing.

For personal satisfaction and musical enjoyment, nothing is more valuable to a brass trombonist than the ability to play lyric solos and melodic material. Also, solos of this type are always popular on recital programs. Such music requires good breath control, musicianship, and a beautiful sound that can satisfy without depending on virtuoso technique or a phenomenal range.

With the mention of solo playing, and especially legato solo playing, we must face the problem of vibrato. First of all, it should be stated that a trombone vibrato is not to be used in orchestra, and very seldom in band. Only on music of a lighter nature or in a real solo should the bass trombonist use a vibrato in ensemble playing.

The type of vibrato to be used by trombonists is always under discussion. The important considerations are these: Can it be turned off easily and completely when not wanted (the majority of the time)? Can the speed and intensity of the vibrato be controlled effectively in various registers and at various dynamic levels? Is it being produced in a manner that does not impair the other vital functions of playing, namely breathing, and lip control? To accomplish these ends, only one type of vibrato would seem to fill the need — that is the slide vibrato. Some directors claim that a slide vibrato can be seen, hence should be avoided. It seems strange that no cellist has ever heard this comment, if sight of the vibrato is bothersome to some people.

Missing Chromatic

Now we come to the most unusual technical problem of the bass trombone. It is not a fully chromatic instrument. As you recall, the slide of the B♭ trombone is not long enough to lower the F side of the horn seven half-steps. It lowers the F side only six half-steps. That means that the F2 in 1st position with the valve, is lowered to C2 in extended 7th position. The next lower note is pedal B♭1, in 1st position on the B♭ side. This is the fundamental of the B♭ side of the instrument. However, between the C2 and the pedal B♭1 there is no B♮1. This note is not possible on the B♭-F bass trombone as it is now adjusted. Since this note is called for from time to time, it is necessary to find some way to play it.

There are two possible solutions to this problem. The first is the use of a long F attachment tuning slide.

This slide is pulled out as far as it will go, or as far as indicated by the manufacturer. This lowers the F attachment to E, down a half-step. This permits the playing of a low B♮1 in extended 7th position, where previously, on the F attachment, we had C2. There are two problems with this solution. First, the F attachment must in reality often be lowered a little below E, to provide a good B♮1. This means that the E2 and B2 available in 1st position with the valve are not usable, and must be played in 7th position.

Secondly, the positions of all notes on the valve side of the horn are now different. F2 and C3 are no longer playable anywhere but in 6th position. E2 and B2 may not be playable in 1st position, if it is necessary to lower the valve to a flat E adjustment. This means that only the notes below E2, down to B♮1 are available on the valve side, with the single exception of a A♯2, which is now in 2nd position with the valve. This is not easy to understand, but must be given careful study and thought. The positions on the E valve then become as follows: E2 may be possible in 1st position, not always; E♭2 is in 2nd position; D2 is in 3rd position, possibly a little lower; C♯2 is in flat 4th position; C2 is in very nearly normal 6th position; and B♮1 is in an extended 7th position.

This adjustment of the F valve to E, or a flat E, is the most common solution of the problem. It requires no extra equipment on the instrument, and takes only a few seconds for the experienced player to complete the change.

Additional Valve

The second solution of this problem to complete the chromatic range of the bass trombone is the addition of another valve. The second rotary valve gives an additional half-step of tubing to the F attachment, lowering the valve section to E or a flat E, depending on the individual instrument or player. This eliminates the need for the manual change, and makes the instrument both convenient and fully chromatic at all times.

There are, however, some drawbacks with this solution. The extra weight of the additional valve and tubing is considerable. Since this low B♮1 is not too common, most of the time this extra valve is excess weight not in use. Also, this necessitates the learning of a new thumb technique on the part of the player. This consideration, however, is not too important. If the student has mastered the F valve, and the adjustment to E, he will not have any difficulty learning to combine the two with two valves.

The proper tuning of the two valves is as follows: Tune the F side so that you have a good usable F2 in 1st position with the F valve. Then tune the E valve so that C2 on the E valve corresponds with normal 6th position on the B♭ side. Then F2, E2, E♭2, D2, and D♭2 would always be played on the F valve, and C2 and B♮1 on the E valve. This is a very convenient arrangement, as it minimizes the number of notes in new positions.

If you have any doubts as to exactly how this works, I would recommend study of the accompanying chart of notes and positions. If a good bass trombonist is available, it would be worth your while to ask him to demonstrate some of these technical points for you.

Playing Range

It should not be thought that the range mentioned earlier, from C2 to F4, is the entire range that may be called for in bass trombone literature. Really, the literature covers a range from D1 (five lines below the bass clef) to C5. Certainly a good bass trombonist will want a range that is larger that that required of him. This gives him a margin of safety in that he never, or rarely, has to play his highest or lowest notes possible. Therefore, I would set as a goal a range from high F5 (top line treble clef) down four and a half octaves to pedal C1 (six spaces beneath the bass staff). This gives a margin of five notes in the upper register above the highest note needed. In the lower register a margin of only two notes is provided, as the upper register is apt to be less certain than the lower.

The bass trombonist should not have trouble playing in the upper register of his instrument, providing he plays up there only a reasonable amount of time and properly approaches the playing of high notes. Because the mouthpiece is larger and the bore is larger, there will not be the resistance felt as there would be on a smaller instrument. More breath support is needed, and it is definitely hard work to play in the upper register properly. There is no easy shortcut method. A firm diaphragm, and great amounts of air are needed.

The work in playing in the upper register must not be done with the lip. The embouchure will soon get very tired under this type of strain. The upper register must be developed with the breath doing the majority of the work. If this procedure is followed, the high notes will be dependable and have a good sound.

It should be mentioned here that the student should not try to make the upper register of the bass trombone sound like a tenor trombone. He may try to do this by pulling his jaw up and squeezing out the notes without proper support. The upper register on the bass trombone starts on C4 and goes upward from there.

When a student plays above this point a great deal of the time, as in a dance band using only one or two trombones, both the embouchure and the sound are bound to suffer.

On the other end of the range are the pedal tones. On the bass trombone, pedal tones are playable from B♭1 down to C1, or with the E valve or adjustment down to low B♮0, (six lines below the bass clef). Some modification on the embouchure may be needed for these notes. This may mean shifting weight more to the upper lip, using more upper lip in the mouthpiece, or something else.

Articulation of the pedal tones will need practice. Slurring from one to another and from the valve register down to pedal tones is very difficult. This requires a great deal of breath control, coupled with lightning fast slide movement, and a well disciplined tongue stroke. The student should practice slurring from pedal B♭1 to C2 and back. If this slur can be mastered, the student is in good shape. This necessitates moving the slide from 1st position to extended 7th position and back. Also, the lip change from the low valve register to the pedal tones is difficult at first. Again it should be said that the embouchure needed in the low register and for the pedal tones is not flabby. It is not a loose, completely relaxed embouchure. There must be firmness and control at all times. The student must learn to tighten the corners of the mouth without tightening the vibrating part of the lips. As the low register is the main-stay of a bass trombonist's sound, it must be solid and dependable.

Selecting Players

What type of student should you pick for a bass trombonist? First of all, a person who already has a fairly good low register on tenor trombone, and who can play as many pedal tones, if not more, than other students of the same level. Secondly, a person with at least normally long arms. This means that for most purposes, a girl would not be the best choice for a bass trombonist, due to the length of reach needed, as well as the physical demands in breath. Thirdly, a rather intelligent student is needed, who can see the importance of the instrument, even tho it does not play a solo, or first, or melodic type of part. Fourth, this must be a student who already has a strong full sound. It should not be a weak student.

One good way to interest a bass trombonist, and make him feel important, is to have a strong small ensemble program. Especially desirable is a good trombone quartet. Here the bass trombonist has a real chance to see what his instrument can do. There are many quartets on the market, some of which are quite good. Be sure to get quartets that call for a bass trombone on the fourth part, or which could be edited to use a bass trombone to advantage. A trombone quartet made up of four tenor trombones is just as limited as a male quartet made up of four tenors.

The bass trombonist will need to be able to read music written in the tenor, alto, and treble clefs — as well as bass clef. While music written in these clefs is not common, they do occur often enough to make fluent reading ability essential.

A good bass trombonist is an asset to any group, as is any fine player; but the director must work harder to achieve a good bass trombonist, since there is very little information available on teaching the instrument, and because there often is need for only one player in a band. This means there is little competition for the position. The motivation must come from the director, the teacher, the student, and from the music put before the student.

FINE

Music For Bass Trombone

John M. Christie

Methods, Studies, Instructional Material

Arban-Randell-Mantia, *Complete Method for Trombone*, Fischer. Contains some very good material for tonguing, scales, and technique. Grade III-V.

Bernard, Paul, ed., *Traits Difficiles Vols. I-IV*, McGinnis & Marx. For bass trombone. Grade IV-V.

Blazevich, Vladislav, *Advanced Method for Trombone, Parts I, II*, Leeds. Excellent material to develop reading ability, facility, slurring, and precision. Alto, tenor, and bass clefs. Challenging. Grade III-V.

Blazevich, Vladislav, *Clef Studies for Trombone*, Leeds. Excellent material in alto, tenor, and bass clef. Covers all keys, meters, and many complex rhythms. Grade IV-V.

Blazevich, Vladislav, *Twenty-Six Sequences*, Leeds. Melodic studies in varied rhythms and keys. Excellent, difficult material. All clefs, many problems. Grade V.

Blume, O., *36 Studies for Trombone, Bks. I,II,III*, Fischer. Good technical studies as printed. Number 31 is also good an octave lower. Grade IV-V.

Bordogni, Marco., *Vocalises, Bks. I, II, III*, Fischer. Transcribed for Trombone by Joannes Rochut. Some of the best melodic material available anywhere. Vol. I will last most students as long as needed. Almost all exercises can be played an octave lower, as well as where written. Especially valuable for bass trombone are Nos. 5, 6, 31, and 38. Number 48 is good for the E valve adjustment. Highly recommended. Grade III-V.

Cornetti, *Complete Method for Trombone*, Cundy-Bettoney. Some of the longer studies and etudes are excellent played an octave lower. A good addition to the school's library. Grade III-V.

Delgiudice, M., *12 Rhythmic and Melodic Studies*, Associated. For bass trombone. Grade IV-V.

LaFosse, Andre, *Methode Complete de Trombone a Coulisse*, Leduc. A good general method. Has a short section on pages 275 to 280 dealing specifically with the Bb-E adjustment of the bass trombone. Grade III-V.

Ostrander, Alan, *The Bass Trombone*, M. Baron. This is the only bass trombone method available in this country. It is comprehensive and covers most of the problems thoroughly. Written by the bass trombonist of the New York Philharmonic. This book should be the basis around which all other study centers. Well worth the price of $10.00. In manuscript. Grade III-V.

Tyrrell, H. W., *40 Progressive Studies for Trombone in Bass Clef*, Boosey & Hawkes. One of the best books of its kind. Many of the studies are good played an octave lower, especially Nos. 5 and 9. Be sure to get the bass clef edition. The entire book is excellent in the original octave. Grade IV.

Vanasek-Klose, *270 Tone and Technic Exercises for Trombone, Baritone or Tuba*, David Gornston. Contains short repeated patterns. Played down an octave, they are the best material available for improving low register tonguing. Grade III-V.

Weissenborn, Julius, *Method for Bassoon*, Cundy-Bettoney. Some of the studies are excellent for bass trombone. Good duets also. Some tenor clef. Grade III-V.

Orchestral Studies and Excerpts

LaFosse, Andre, *Methode Complete de Trombone a Coulisse*, Leduc. Contains some good excerpts near the end. Mostly French music, most of which is not found in the other collections. All three clefs. Grade IV-V.

Menken, Julian, ed., *Anthology of Symphonic and Operatic Excerpts for Bass Trombone, Vols. I, II*. An excellent collection of prominent or difficult bass trombone parts from orchestral and operatic literature. Grade III-V.

Stöneberg, Alfred, ed., *Moderne Orchesterstudien fuer Posaune und Basstuba Vols. I-VII.*, Hans Gerig—Cologne. Comprehensive material, including many modern German works. All three clefs. Grade IV-V.

Straub, Richard, *Orchestral Studies from Operas and Concert Works for Trombone*, International. All three trombone parts. Excellent work for the orchestral trombone section. Alto, tenor, and bass clefs. Grade IV-V.

Wagner, Richard, *Orchestral Studies from Operas and Concert Works for Trombone*, International. All three, or in some cases, four trombone parts. Same comment as for the collection above. Grade IV-V.

Bass Trombone Solos Original

Barat, J. Ed., *Reminescences de Navarre*, Leduc. A conservatory contest piece. Demands technical agility. Range down to pedal F1. Grade V.

Hume, J. Ord., *The Majestic*, Boosey & Hawkes. A British contest solo. Not too difficult. In G and C major. Good for a first contest number after transferring to bass trombone. Grade III.

Martelli, H., *Suite, Op. 83, for Bass Trombone*, Associated. Modern. Somewhat hard to hear. Deserves attention. Grade V.

Müller, J. I., *Praeludium, Chorale, Variations, and Fugue*, McGinnis & Marx. One of the few pieces written in the 19th century for bass trombone. Well worth playing. Grade IV.

Petit, Pierre, *Wagenia*, McGinnis & Marx. Conservatory contest piece in 1956. Rather showy. Grade V.

Tcherepnin, Nicolai, *Une Oraison*, G. Schirmer. Not too difficult, and good music. Slow and sustained. Demands good breath control. Grade III.

Standard Trombone Literature Playable on Bass Trombone

Berlioz, H., *Recitative and Prayer*, Mercury. From the *Grand Symphony for Band*. Very musical. Has a published band accompaniment. Grade IV.

Blazevich, Vladislav, *Concert Piece No. 5*, Leeds. Grade IV.

David, *Concertino for Trombone*, Cundy-Bettoney. Grade V.

Gräfe, F., *Grand Concerto*, Cundy-Bettoney. Grade V.

Guillmant, *Morceau Symphonique*, Remick. Grade IV.

Hindemith, Paul, *Sonata for Trombone and Piano*, Schott. Grade IV.

Jacob, Gordon, *Trombone Concerto*, Williams. For trombone and piano or orchestra. Grade V.

Laube, P.X., Ed., *Concert Album for Trombone, Vol. 2*, Cundy-Bettoney. A collection of the old standbys. Not expensive and contains many good solos. Grade IV-V.

Pryor, Arthur, *Selected Solos*, Fischer. Some of these are very effective on bass trombone, especially if the cadenzas are edited to exploit the low register. Grade IV-V.

Rimsky-Korsakoff, N., *Concerto for Trombone and Band*, Leeds. Excellent for bass trombone if played in the octave intended by the composer, not heeding the 8va markings, except in the cadenza. Grade V.

Adaptations and Transcriptions

Galliard, J. E., *Six Sonatas for Bassoon and Piano*, McGinnis & Marx. Be sure to get the bassoon edition, not that for trombone. Excellent music, some of which is not too difficult. Grade III-V.

Mozart, W. A., *O Isis und Osiris, from Die Zauberflœte*. There are many editions of this aria available for bass voice and piano in the original key of F Major. It is not difficult technically, but very effective. Must be slurred throughout. Highly recommended. Grade III.

Mozart, W. A., *In diesen Heil'gen Hallen, from Die Zauberflœte*. There are many editions of this aria available in the original key of E major for bass voice and piano. More technical difficulty than the previous aria due to the key. Must be slurred throughout. Highly recommended. Grade IV.

Northcote, S., Ed., *Bass Songs, New Imperial Edition*, Boosey & Hawkes. Interesting recital literature including art songs and folk songs. For bass voice and piano. Grade III-IV.

Oratorio Songs, Vol. IV for Bass, John Church Co. Good selections, including bass numbers from *The Messiah*. Grade IV.

Spicker, Max, ed., *Operatic Anthology—Vol. V for Bass*, G. Schirmer. Some excellent arias, well suited for bass trombone. Grade IV.

Trombone Ensemble Music

Blume. O. *12 Melodic Duets*, Fischer. Long, four-movement duets. Mostly technical, but good also for musicianship and balance. Grade IV.

Blazevich, Vladislav, *Concert Duets*, Leeds. Difficult, especially in fitting together the rhythms of the two parts. Alto, tenor, and bass clefs. Good for student-teacher work. Grade V.

Müller, P., *35 Duets for Tenor and Bass Trombone*, Jack Spratt. Good material,
but the manuscript is very difficult to read. Only duets available for this combination. Grade IV-V.

Shostakovich, D., *Four Preludes for Two Trombones*, McGinnis & Marx. Grade IV.

Uber, David, *10 Concert Studies for Two Trombones*, McGinnis & Marx. Grade IV.

Bassett, Leslie, *Quartet for Trombones*, Manuscript. Available from the Composition Department of the University of Michigan School of Music. An excellent quartet in the contemporary style. Requires four mature players. Grade V.

Beethoven, L., *Suite from the Mount of Olives*, McGinnis & Marx. For three trombones. Arranged by Alan Ostrander. Good music. Excellent bass trombone parts. Grade IV.

Handel, G. F., *Suite of Six Pieces*, McGinnis & Marx. For three trombones. Same as above. Grade IV.

Mozart, W. A., *Suite for Three Trombones*, McGinnis & Marx. For three trombones. Same as above. Grade IV.

Uber, David, *Modern Trios*, McGinnis & Marx. Interesting program music in the modern idiom. Grade III-IV.

Beethoven, L., *Three Equali*, Music for Brass. For four trombones. Original—not an arrangement. Not difficult. Slow, sustained. Grade III-IV.

Colby, *Allegro con brio*, Remick. One of the better of the published American quartets. Grade IV.

Defay, J. M., *Quatre Pieces pour Quator de Trombones*, Leduc. Excellent contemporary French music. All parts are difficult. The Finale is particularly fine. All ranges are high. Tenor clef in all parts. Outstanding music. Grade V.

Maas, *Zwei grosse Quartette*, Cundy-Bettoney. This is the Tallmadge arrangement of this quartet, eliminating the need for a bass trombone on the fourth part. In the old style, but excellent material and challenging. Grade V.

Mendelssohn, F., *Three Equali*, Witmark. A quartet, in three movements, each published separately. Originally did not specify instruments. For similar bass clef instruments. Excellent. Grade IV-V.

Peeters, Flor, *Suite for Four Trombones*, Peters. An excellent suite, the best to be published in recent years. Very interesting and varied. Requires a good bass trombonist. The *Lied* is particularly beautiful. One of the best quartets available. Grade V.

Phillips, B., *Piece for Six Trombones*, McGinnis & Marx. Interesting and rather modern in style. Calls for four tenor trombones and two bass trombones. Grade IV.

King, Robert, Ed., *Chorales for Four-Part Trombone Choir*, Music for Brass. Published in two volumes, each in score form. Excellent for quartets or larger combinations. Not difficult. The fourth part can be edited for bass trombone. These are scored rather low. Grade III-IV.

Manuscript Quartet Arrangements

Arrangements by John Christie available from the University Music House, Ann Arbor, Michigan. For three tenor trombones, one bass trombone. First two parts are in tenor clef throughout. Mostly for college or professional trombonists. Grade IV-V.

25 Christmas Carols for Trombone Quartet. Scored to sound brilliant and clear.

10 Chorales for Trombone Quartet. Straightforward arrangements for clarity and brilliance.

Four selections for Trombone Quartet. Somewhat longer pieces containing:
1. Bortniansky-Tschaikovsky, *Cherubic Hymn*.
2. Handel, *Blessing and Honor*.
3. Lully, *Bois Epais*.
4. Welch Folk Song, *Ash Grove*.

Beethoven, L., *Three Equali*.

Mendelssohn, F., *Three Equali*.
FINE

March, 1961

Vibrato And Style

Robert Nagel

MUSIC IS AN EXPRESSIVE and creative art. Its techniques are merely the tools of creativity. But all too frequently, in discussions of brass playing with students and teachers, we are so concerned about these various means of instrumental training that we often lose sight of the ultimate goals that should be achieved. Too often we become so engrossed in the technical development of the performer that we are somewhat unmindful of the real aims of artistic expression for which he should ever be striving.

One facet of musicianship in which this failing is particularly self-evident is the use (and misuse) of the vibrato. It is the intent of this article to discuss, in a general way, the application of the technique of vibrato to more expressive performance, enhanced tone, and personal style. Proper use of the vibrato can be a very important element of instrumental individuality. A well-controlled and tastefully employed vibrato lends a refinement and a subtlety to performance that is unmistakable.

The term vibrato, as applied to musical sound, may be defined as a regular or measured pulsation of tone. More specifically, the vibrato is the result of fairly rapid but slight alterations of pitch, fluctuating above and below the mean tone.

Recent Development

Although the vibrato has been employed by string players for several centuries, its common usage among the brass and woodwind instruments is a relatively modern phenomenon. Therefore, it is not very surprising that there still persists a good deal of misconception and misinformation concerning the vibrato. For instance, in the 1946 edition of the well-known orchestration treatise by Cecil Forsyth, we read that, "On the unmuted brass there is no way of making the vibrato. The instruments have to be muted . . . with a specially-bored mute that has a fine airway pierced through it. Over this the player flip-flaps his closed fingers so as to interrupt the air-stream." Speaking of the woodwinds, he says, "vibrato is made by lightly beating the air, with a disengaged finger, at an open tone hole."

To say the least, these are certainly very misleading statements in the light of current musical practices. Even the *Harvard Dictionary* (1947 edition) article on vibrato neglects to mention anything about woodwind or brass vibrato, as tho it did not exist. Nevertheless, we know today that skillful, controlled use of the vibrato is definitely possible on all of the brass and wind instruments. Admittedly, however, it is sometimes avoided in cases where the combination of vibrato with the timbre (or tone quality) of some instruments produces results which are not in keeping with the prevailing concepts of kinds of music. For example, this is generally true of the clarinet and the French horn in regard to most symphonic music.

Two Methods

Vibrato is produced on the brass instruments by slightly increasing and decreasing the embouchure tension. This in turn causes a corresponding set of fluctuations in pitch. It must be immediately pointed out and emphasized, however, that such tension changes are *not* accomplished directly by the embouchure muscles. To do this would be extremely fatiguing to these lip muscles. Instead, we must use other forces to act upon the embouchure. We have at our disposal two commonly used methods. One is usually called the "jaw vibrato," sometimes erroneously referred to as the "lip vibrato." This is done by a barely preceptible raising and lowering of the jaw. This type of vibrato production is very effective on the lower brass instruments: trombone, baritone, and tuba. It can also be used to good effect on the French horn and the trumpet. But it is a little more difficult because of the smaller mouthpieces and the more highly critical problem of embouchure control.

Another popular method is known as the "hand vibrato." This is executed by a sidewise motion of the hand thru the fingers in contact with the valves. This serves to increase and decrease the pressure of the mouthpiece on the lips just enough to vary slightly the embouchure tension. Incidentally, if the hand vibrato is executed with enough force, it is possible to emit a lip trill in this manner.

The French horn player and the trombonist can make a hand vibrato in differing ways. The trombonist merely moves the slide back and forth, above and below the true pitch. On the horn, some players get a vibrato by oscillating the right hand in the bell of the instrument. In making any comparison of these two methods of vibrato, it must be made clear that, in the final analysis, preference for one or the other depends upon personal musical taste, since both can be developed to a very high degree of control and flexibility thru diligent practice. As a matter of fact, many professional musicians employ both kinds of vibrato, using them as they see fit. For the novice, perhaps the hand vibrato is somewhat easier to master.

When to Start

A question frequently encountered is, "When should the student begin to learn to use the vibrato?" Before commencing to practice to acquire vibrato, the teacher should be perfectly assured that the student is quite capable of producing a good, well-rounded tone throughout the range of his instrument. He should also be able to play with reasonably consistent intonation. And he should possess fairly advanced finger dexterity and reliable lip control. These are all quite necessary.

It should be remembered that the vibrato must never be used in an attempt to conceal poor tone production. It is not a panacea for faulty intonation. And it is most certainly not a substitute or a disguise for a lack of real musical feeling. The discriminating use of vibrato demands a high degree of musical taste and sensitivity, traits that the teacher should make every effort to cultivate in the student.

A student is advised not to attempt to learn vibrato without the aid of competent instruction. A wrong approach may prove harmful. Although it is not the purpose of this article to discuss the mechanical details of teaching vibrato, it is worth mentioning that it is of paramount importance to master first a very slow and moderately wide vibrato. Four pulsations per beat at approximately M.M.72 is recommended. Then the speed should be gradually increased, and the width of the vibrato should be narrowed by lessening the amount of movement. Naturally, the vibrato is more difficult to control at the very soft or very loud dynamic extremes. A simple way to practice for vibrato control over the entire dynamic range is to practice long tones beginning pianissimo with a crescendo to fortissimo, and then a diminuendo back to pianissimo again. Ideally speaking, an expert player should be able to produce any speed of vibrato combined with all gradations from narrow to wide.

When to Use

Now, once the basic technique of vibrato is assimilated, the student should study how and when to apply it to actual musical performance. Here we can indeed learn much from listening to the performances of accomplished musicians. This pertains not only to hearing fine brass players, but also to observing the use of vibrato by great woodwind and string artists as well as singers. As a matter of fact, since vibrato seems to be a fairly natural and intimate part of the human voice, great vocal artistry can teach us much about the use of vibrato to good effect.

Generally speaking, vibrato heightens the human qualities of sound. A perfectly straight tone tends to sound almost mechanical in its purity, whereas a tone which carries an intense vibrato creates a very impassioned effect. These characteristics are to be utilized according to the intent of the music. This is where musical discernment and a sense of style become crucial. Sometimes whole phrases or sections of a piece will seem most effective without vibrato or with a constant vibrato. In other instances certain individual notes may require more or less vibrato depending upon their relation in the phrase. And once in awhile it may be effective to alter the vibrato throughout the duration of a single note.

Special Problem

Once the student has had some experience and success with vibrato in his etudes and solo pieces, he may then venture on to apply it to ensemble playing. This is more difficult. The blending of vibrato among the various sections of the band or orchestra is an added problem. Within each section the players' vibratos should be similar enough to sound matched. Otherwise there will be a lack of tonal balance or unity.

Another factor that enters into the picture in this electronic age is the effect that the recording and broadcasting media have on vibrato. Depending on recording conditions and engineering, the subtleties of vibrato tend to fluctuate from being almost completely lost, due to inadequate "pick-up," to being magnified and exaggerated beyond intended proportions, due to overly-sensitive "pick-up." For this reason, in view of the problems of recording, it is recommended that, although tape-recording of the student's playing is often helpful in many respects, it cannot be relied upon to any great extent as regards vibrato.

In conclusion, let it be noted that, while it is quite natural in the early stages for a student to imitate the style and vibrato of some well-known artist whom he admires, his eventual goal should be to adapt the technique of vibrato to the development of his own musical personality. Whenever we hear a unique musical artist, we can be sure that much of his artistic individuality, which we so readily recognize, can be attributed to the intelligent cultivation of an expressive vibrato.   FINE

April, 1961

Tuba: A Word of Many Meanings

Roger Bobo

WHEN THE WORD "tuba" is seen on a piece of orchestral music, it is only a hint to what instrument the composer had in mind for the part. It is up to the artist to decipher exactly what the composer did intend and to apply it to its best advantage in the modern American symphony orchestra. To do this it is necessary not only to understand the history of the instrument, but also to know the differences in the concept of the tuba in various parts of the world today. The difference between the effect needed in a contrabass tuba part in one of the Wagner *Ring Cycle* operas and the works of Berlioz, which were originally written for ophicleide, is so great that it would seem almost impossible to do both composers justice on one instrument. The tuba player, then, should train himself to become sensitive not only to such extreme differences, but also to the many subtle variations, and to choose an instrument that will lend itself to the best advantage of the music.

Serpent and Ophicleide

The parts to be considered first are those that were not written for the tuba, but for the tuba's predecessors, the serpent and the ophicleide. The serpent was used in the symphony orchestra by very few composers. Handel's oratorio *Israel in Egypt* uses the instrument. Although the original orchestration was for a relatively small group, most orchestras today play the version that was re-orchestrated by Mendelssohn.

In this version the serpent part was used as the bass to the woodwind section, and it demands a very light, veiled sound and style. Although most symphony tuba players could play this part on a large CC tuba, the instrument that is usually used in this country, the effect would be lost because this type of instrument would be very much out of character playing with pianissimo woodwinds in its higher register.

The best way to achieve the needed feeling for serpent parts is to play them on a smaller tuba. Usually an F tuba, pitched a 4th above the customary CC tuba, will lend itself much more appropriately.

Another example of the use of the serpent is Mendelssohn's oratorio *Saint Paul*. Since Mendelssohn had used the ophicleide ten years earlier in his *Midsummer-Night's Dream* overture, it is curious that he reverted to the serpent. The serpent was used mostly in church music to play the bass line along with the voices, and Mendelssohn most likely thought, because of its religious background, it would be more fitting in a religious oratorio than the ophicleide.

The serpent was very unpopular with some composers especially after the ophicleide came into acceptance. Berlioz, in the short section on the serpent found in his *Treatise on Instrumentation*, says: "The truly barbaric tone of this instrument would be much better suited for the bloody cult of the Druids than for that of the Catholic Church where it is still in use." If this was the typical conception of the way the serpent usually sounded, this is the point to stop trying to play in the style of the serpent and remember that discretion and good taste are the most important aspects in the interpretation of music.

The serpent was a wooden, leather-covered instrument that used a cup-mouthpiece. It derived its name from its shape, which was similar to the sinuous movements of a snake. Because of the awkwardness of this shape, the instrument makers began building it in an upright position similar to that of the bassoon. Later, brass was used and keys replaced the original fingering holes. This last development was no longer a serpent but an ophicleide.

It is very simple to see that the ophicleide is nothing more than a serpent in its most advanced stage of development. Both the serpent and the ophicleide have the same range, B1 to C5. It can be seen that the register of these instruments is more what would be required for the trombone than the tuba. Unlike the serpent, the ophicleide was often scored with the trombones, as well as with the woodwinds because its sound was much clearer and stronger than that of the serpent. However, its sound still was a long way from the sound of the large-bore CC tuba.

When playing an ophicleide part, a player should treat it the same way as a serpent part and play it on a smaller tuba. Many ophicleide passages, especially in the works of Berlioz, are scored in unison with fortissimo trombones in their medium-high register. Although this is much different from playing with pianissimo woodwinds like the serpent, the sound of the instrument should be homogeneous with the trombones. Usually the best instrument to accomplish this effect is the

same F tuba that would be used to play serpent parts.

Contrabass Trombone Parts

Although the contrabass trombone is not related to the tuba, it is sometimes necessary, because of the scarcity of both contrabass trombones and their players, to play the part on the tuba. This instrument was developed by Wagner for use in the *Ring Cycle* operas. It has exactly twice the length of tubing of the Bb tenor trombone, and the slide is doubled so that the positions are the same as for the tenor trombone. In the *Ring Cycle*, Wagner's uses of the contrabass trombone are probably the greatest in the repertoire, but since these operas call for contrabass tuba, the tuba player is not able to cover the contrabass trombone part.

Usually in this country, when a real contrabass trombone is not available, the parts are assigned to a bass trombone player with a good low register. Most other composers, when writing for this instrument, used no tuba but a lower brass section consisting of four trombones. This type of scoring is found mostly among Italian opera composers such as Puccini and Verdi. In the cases where no tuba is needed, the tuba player will usually be called on to play the contrabass trombone parts. Any tuba which blends well with trombones would be satisfactory to play these parts. The best effect is usually achieved with a small-bore CC tuba or any F tuba.

If a real contrabass trombone is available it is a very useful instrument for the tuba player to learn, besides being a logical double for tuba players, just as most good trombone players can double on baritone. There are some composers living today who write for contrabass trombone, such as Stravinsky and Gianinni. Gianinni maintains that for most purposes the contrabass trombone is a far better orchestral instrument than the tuba. Of course, Gianinni realizes the rarity of this instrument and notes in his scores, "tuba acceptable if contrabass trombone is not available."

Different Tubas

The real problems for the tuba, however, do not come from parts that were written for other instruments, but from parts written for the tuba itself. The concept of the tuba differs throughout the world. Most

French music is written for a tuba in C but pitched a whole octave above the CC tuba used in America. This instrument would be one step higher than the baritone horn or euphonium, which are so widely used in bands.

Because of the six valves that these French tubas have, they can play all the way down to D1, but the quality in this register of the instrument is much weaker than that of the CC tuba or even the F tuba. Most European composers, other than the French, write for the F tuba and in Europe the F tuba is almost the only tuba that is used in the symphony orchestra.

Wagner, who was the first man to write for the tuba as it is known today, called the F tuba the bass tuba. This is the instrument with which all his operas, except the four operas in his *Ring Cycle* were scored. The *Ring Cycle* uses contrabass tuba, which is the largest CC tuba. Some German composers follow Wagner's example and specify on which tuba, bass or contrabass, they want the part to be played. Most of them, however, just indicate "tuba."

America's tuba is just beginning to get over the influences of the band. The BBb bell-front tuba, which fits so well in bands, is somewhat of a misfit in an orchestra. Although the band concept has not been broken away from completely, the upright CC tuba, because of its more compact sound, fits better than the bell front BBb.

Because of the tuba's many different uses in the orchestra it cannot be said that just the F tuba or just the CC tuba is the answer. When it is apparent that the music calls for the F tuba or the CC tuba, of course the correct instrument should be used. Many works, however, have passages that need both the light blending sound of the F tuba and the heavy, powerful sound of the large bore CC tuba. For this type of work it is best to have a tuba that will serve as a compromise. This can be achieved by a smaller bore CC tuba.

There are many works in which the tuba part would be acceptable on the F, small CC, or the large CC tubas. In this type of situation making the choice of which instrument to use can be a difficult problem. Usually in this country the choice should be confined to the large and small CC tubas because the F tuba, except under the circumstances already mentioned, is not large enough to match the power of the typical American symphony orchestra brass section.

The brass instruments, especially the trombones, which are used by most symphony players in this country, have a very large bore giving them a very big and full sound. The best way to judge which one of the CC tubas to select is by whether it is used to fill out the sound of the bass instruments at louder dynamics or whether it is used as the bass in the quartet consisting of three trombones and tuba. Two examples which demonstrate both these uses of tuba are the *Fourth* and *Sixth Symphonies* of Tchaikovsky.

The *Fourth Symphony* would be a typical piece in which to use the large CC tuba. In the first and last movements, the only movements that use tuba, the instrument is used entirely as a support for the bass sound of the orchestra. The softest dynamic in the whole work for tuba is *mf* which appears only twice. One of these *mf's* is only a means to make a greater contrast for a crescendo to fortissimo that comes three measures later. Throughout both these movements the tuba has melodies in unison with the string basses and some-

times in octaves with the trombones which should be very powerful and heavy.

In the *Sixth Symphony* it is almost as if Tchaikovsky had a different instrument in mind. Almost every note the tuba has is connected in some way with the trombone section. There are many passages that start with tuba in an ascending melody line that must blend into the trombones, which take over the ascending passage and, in turn, blend into the trumpet section. The opposite situation also occurs where the first trumpet starts descending and dove-tails with the second which dove-tails with the first trombone, and so on thru the section until the tuba takes over from the bass trombone. The changes must be made so that the whole section sounds like one beautiful brass instrument with an extremely large range.

The last passage for trombones and tuba in this symphony is a chorale in which they are the only instruments in the orchestra that are playing. The chorale ends on a chord that is marked *ppppp*. In this type of orchestrating where the tuba really is nothing more than a fourth trombone, the small CC tuba would definitely be superior. Instead

of sounding like two trumpets, three trombones and tuba, this tuba will help to sound like one section of brass instruments.

In addition to being familiar with different composers' conceptions of the tuba, it is necessary for the tuba player to be very versatile. It is preferable to have more than just one instrument to play in varied styles. An F tuba for the serpent and ophicleide parts, a small CC tuba for the best blend with other brass instruments and for smaller chamber orchestra work, and a large CC tuba for a very full and powerful sound. Of course not all tuba players are able to have all these instruments at their disposal. In this case the instrument that will serve best as an "all purpose" tuba is the smaller bore CC tuba. This instrument can be used with good effect in both bands and orchestras; and with a good player, it could be used on serpent and ophicleide parts, although the F tuba would always be preferable. Whether the player performs all parts on one instrument or uses different instruments for different purposes, the most important thing for all musicians to remember is to play in the manner that best suits the style of the music.

FINE

Expression
Thru Articulative Techniques

Glen C. Law

ONE OF THE MOST important devices of expression on brass instruments is the articulative use of the tongue in dealing with musical interpretation. Therefore, this discussion will concern the problem of how to articulate the well-produced tone.

After students have the correct concept of free, easy tone production, the development of the tongue for articulation is necessary. The lack of articulative ability is an insurmountable obstacle in the rapid execution of much musical literature and the finesse of musical interpre-

tation. Articulation in brass playing can be compared to the bowing technique of the string player. Students should strive for control in the execution of the most incisive staccato to the most flowing legato. There is a wide variance in articulations that the tongue is capable of producing.

Position and Movement
of Tongue

The tongue rests on the bottom of the mouth when it is inactive, and the tip of the tongue lies behind

the lower front teeth. Since there are various muscles that compose and control the movements of the tongue, it is advantageous to concentrate on the use of this important organ. The first attack of a passage seems to be the most crucial. For instance, the cracking of the first note of a phrase destroys the entire musical effect. The urgency of an accurate entrance demands that brass players develop surety of attack. The first entrance of a brass instrument has a formidable psychological impact on the listener, consequently it

293

is highly desirable that there be an instantaneous flow of tone.

Preceding an entrance, the tongue should remain at rest at the bottom of the oral cavity while the player inhales. At the height of the inhalation, the tongue should rise and strike behind the upper teeth as when saying the syllables "too" or "tah." It is quite significant whether the tongue is placed on or strikes the teeth, and how fast and far the tongue moves. The position and movement of the tongue before, during, and after the attack appears to be relative to the characteristics of the music being performed. It would seem that in most instances the tongue should not be set behind the upper teeth for the first attack. The proper action can be illustrated by the following figure:

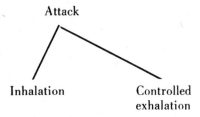

Attack

Inhalation   Controlled
                    exhalation

The use of the tongue in this manner, at the peak of the inhalation, should give the student more control of attack and subtle manipulation of articulative effects.

The tongue serves as a valve, and students should practice getting the tongue out of the path of a steady flow of controlled breath. But it is neither possible nor desirable to get the tongue out of the way when executing rapid attacks. In this process the tongue should employ short strokes with little movement, so as not to interfere with the tone. All excessive movement in the performing of a music instrument should be eliminated or minimized. The muscles affecting the lips and the jaw also should be controlled, so they do not move needlessly when tonguing various rhythmic patterns.

On the other hand, setting the tongue behind the upper teeth might make it more difficult to produce delicate articulations. Setting the tongue seems to operate more effectively in *sforzando* articulations or when an explosive effect is wanted. The habit of setting the tongue can also produce hesitancy and might result in restraining the air pressure that the muscles of breathing should be producing. This restraint could

easily induce tightness in the throat and constriction at the back part of the tongue.

Many teachers feel that tonguing between the teeth has a tendency to produce a larger aperture between the lips than necessary. The result of this practice seems to cause fatigue and insecurity in the upper range. This action also flattens the lips on the teeth and the player consequently is unable to utilize the full potentialities of the muscles forming the embouchure. The method of attacking the notes behind the upper teeth seems to promote a smoother transition from one register to another. Moreover, it requires less movement and minimal change, resulting in faster and cleaner articulation. The tongue should be controlled effectively or it will unnecessarily stimulate and involve other muscles. Brass players should try to avoid muscular activities of the tongue that involve processes that interfere with proper attacks.

The starting of a tone is the exact co-ordination of timed inspiration, breath control, and striking the teeth with the tongue at the precise instant. The movement of the tongue should co-ordinate with the muscles that control breathing and the embouchure, and the problem of co-ordinating articulation with valve and slide action is important.

Marks of Articulation

Composers place a variety of symbols over or under notes to designate how the music should be articulated. The marks help indicate expression, i.e. some interpretation of the composer's style. Signs in Greek and Latin literature indicated inflections for the voice. These symbols were the *accentus*, *gravis*, and the *circumflex*. Some theorists today consider that *neumes*, musical notation of the middle ages, grew out of these early symbols. Therefore, with the origin of Western music, various symbols were used to designate inflections, phrasing, interpretation, and accent. In past periods of music, especially the Baroque era, there were traditional methods of interpretation. Frequently very little concerning expression was included, so the articulations were left to the interpretive skill of the performers.

Styles of performance have fluctuated throughout the history of music. As the marks of articulation de-

veloped, the concepts of composers differed. It is possible to find different expression marks by different composers who desire the same sound. Beethoven made it quite clear that a definite difference be made between the performing of the dash and the dot. Many composers are not this decisive, consequently the instrumentalist must interpret within the general atmosphere of style and tempo.

In relation to the arbitrary symbols of expression and articulation used by composers, the player must realize that there is no absolute criterion in interpreting expression marks for a web of indecisiveness and minor confusion surrounds the subject. The best method appears to be an interpretation within the composer's style and the period of the composition. When there is no sharply defined method, performers by instinct and experience interpret, thru sensitivity to style, what the composer desired concerning articulation, and their fellow players, also skilled in interpretation, help establish a common consent. The inexperienced player cannot feel these subtle nuances; consequently this is where the role of teacher becomes vital, and the acquaintance of students with orchestral literature is indispensable in this process.

Thru the extensive study of orchestral literature it is possible to find many variations in articulation and interpretation that are not covered well in method books.

Gradated Articulation

Unless the articulation of music is designated by expression marks, notes in moderate and slow tempos are played in a smooth manner. Music not containing articulative indications would frequently be subject to such flowing production, ordinarily considered *legato*. Under legato style, *sostenuto* and *tenuto* would be included because a fluent effect is produced simply because the notes are sustained fully. The space of time between notes is what indicates that the music is not legato style. Spaces should be placed between notes according to the marks of articulation. This procedure results in shorter notes that fall into the category of *staccato* style.

Staccato

Several marks are employed to indicate staccato articulation. While there is an extensive range of style among composers, and there are disagreements in the interpretation of marks, certain general practices can be noted. This discussion starts with the shortest articulation.

Dash (**I**).—When this is placed over or under notes, it indicates that the notes should be played as short as possible. This mark is usually applied for heavy staccato passages and a quarter note would be shortened about three-fourths of its value and played as a 16th note. The dash seems to appear where a loud, sharp attack should be employed. This requires a thick, broad, forceful stroke of the tongue. It is a percussive effect and is executed by short, powerful strokes of the tongue using the syllables "tawt" or "toot." The quick stoppage of air at each note helps produce the articulation. The traditional interpretation of many passages in orchestral works requires that notes be articulated in this manner, even tho there may be no marks of articulation.

If the brass player gets acquainted with traditional performances of certain brass passages marked with accents or dots the effect is practically identical with the performance of the dash. The speed and dynamics of certain parts often determine the possibilities of tongue movement. Frequently the performer has so little time to execute a passage that he can articulate in only one specific way.

Dot.—The dot appears to indicate a slightly longer staccato than the dash. This symbol shortens a note by approximately one-half its written value. The dot is more often associated with light, crisp attacks. The tongue is more pointed and applied with a lighter stroke when playing the dot. However, as was mentioned above, not all passages marked with the dot are light and crisp. Many fortissimo parts that require forceful staccato tonguing, similar to the dash, are prevalent.

In addition to producing staccato articulations using the syllable "toot," short notes can also be produced by controlling the breathing mechanism. The stream of air is stopped after each attack, producing an effect that is very desirable in certain passages. The tone is not stopped by the tip of the tongue; therefore, the short notes contain more resonance, giving

the listener an impression quite like the pizzicato of string instruments. The effect is very pleasing when a ringing sound is desired after a staccato chord by the brass section. The preceding staccato effect is limited when short notes must be sounded in very rapid succession for it is not feasible to stop each note with the breathing mechanism.

When studying certain excerpts with fast tempos, it is essential to recognize another technique involving articulation. To facilitate articulation, situations arise where the player should not stop the flow of breath with either the tongue or the breathing mechanism. Actually, the tongue must move so rapidly in certain passages that it is not possible or advisable to stop each note. The notes are articulated so quickly that the listener cannot discern if they are produced by staccato techniques. The musical impression is that of a quick succession of notes that sound meticulously distinct. In this process the performer should realize that the tonguing is secondary to a steady flow of air. The tip of the tongue functions like a waving hand in front of an electric fan, and the fastest type of single articulation seems to be executed with this technique. When the player concentrates on producing sharp, separated, staccato notes, music cannot be articulated as fast.

Marcato

The marcato articulation denotes that the tones should be emphasized, marked, and accented. There should be a slight decrescendo in sustaining the notes the entire value.

This occurs because the tongue strikes the teeth in a deliberate manner to sound the accent. The action is similar to that of a clapper striking a bell and producing a ringing quality. In orchestral literature there are many passages in all registers that require this accentuation.

Vertical marks of accentuation (ΛΛΛΛ) are abundant in brass parts. Such vertical marks seem to occur in music that should be tongued in a very emphatic manner. They appear in passages where the heaviest and most powerful articulation is in order.

Sforzando

The *sforzado*, also known as *forzando* and *sforzato*, is executed in a manner similar to the vertical accent except that the effect should sound

more explosive. Setting the tongue behind the upper teeth seems fitting in this process. The sound is produced by drawing the tongue back exceedingly fast, thereby releasing great air pressure built up by the breathing mechanism. This sudden accent should be executed when the marks *sf*, *fz*, *sfz* are present. Any note produced with such sudden stress seems to lower in volume after the accent. To emphasize this effect, composers add another expression mark to the sforzando, indicating sudden *piano*, in this manner: *sfp* or *fp*. These attacks are found in **various** works.

Portato

The *portato* type of articulation is about half way between legato and staccato. It is designated by the combination of a dot above the note as well as a slur. Since the slur indicates a partial legato expression, the tongue strikes the teeth more lightly, using a softer syllable, *du*, to articulate. The dots indicate a separation, consequently quarter notes would not be held their entire value.

The portato is commonly employed in slow and soft passages, e.g. the brass chorales written by Johannes Brahms. It is interesting to note the difference in interpretations of these chorales. In some recorded performances the chorales are articulated in a legato style, where the notes are connected smoothly. But in others a separation of notes is noticeable. It appears very helpful to students to listen to recorded and actual performances for the purpose of identifying various techniques. Where different recordings of the same composition are available, extensive study should develop discriminating judgment. Preferential selection as to style and technique is necessary since two excellent performances may vary in respect to articulation, tone, and phrasing.

The "Long" or "Strong" of Prosody

The "long" or "strong" style of articulation is designated by horizontal lines (————) that are placed either over or under the notes.

Authorities seem to disagree as to the execution of the symbol. One well-known reference states that the notes should be separated slightly and are not completely legato, while another source of information describes that this symbol means the notes should be tenaciously sustained. From observation of style, it appears that many brass parts that contain this symbol are performed very broadly and sustained completely. This type of articulation is known as soft tonguing, and the effect is produced by gently brushing the back of the upper teeth with the tongue. The term *leggiero* is also occasionally associated with this mark of articulation that might imply a light use of the tongue when articulating. The effect is quite similar to legato, except that stress is placed on each note, an expression sometimes called the *agogic accent*.

FINE

Selected Bibliography of — Music for Brass Choir

James Hoffren

COMPOSER-ARRANGER	TITLE	PUBLISHER

Grade II

Anderson, Leroy — *Suite of Carols* — Mills

1. While by My Sheep; 2. In dulci jubilo; 3. Lo, How a Rose E'er Blooming; 4. I Saw Three Ships; 5. From Heaven High I Came to You; 6. We Three Kings of Orient Are; 7. March of the Kings. Scored for 4t, 4h, 4tb, bar, tu.

Bach, J. S.—Gordon — *Five Pieces for Brass Choir* — Witmark
2t, 2h, tb or tu, tim, perc.

DeLassus, Orlande — *Providebam Dominum* — King
Choir I: 3t; Choir II: t, h, tb, bar, tu.

Elgar, Edward — *Theme from Pomp and Circumstance No. 1* — B & H
4t, 3 tb, tb (tu).

Gabrieli, G. — *Canzon duodecimi toni* — King
4t, 2h, 2tb, 2bar, 2tu (in two equal choirs). Organ optional.

Gabrieli, G. — *Canzon noni toni* — King
Eight parts.

Gabrieli, G. — *Canzon quarti toni* — King
For three choirs. I: t, t (h), tb, bar, tu; II: 4tb, tu; III: t, t(h), 2bar, tu.

Gabrieli, G. — *Canzon septimi toni* — Baron
4t, 2h, 4 tb (two equal choirs).

Gabrieli, G. — *Canzon septimi toni No. 2* — King
Choir I: 2t, h, bar; Choir II: h, bar.

Gabrieli, G. — *Sonata octavi toni* — King
Choir I: 2t, 2tb, bar, tu; Choir II: tb, bar, tu.

Ludwig, Carl — *Three Chorales for Brass Choir or Ensemble* — Ludwig
One arrangement of J. S. Bach, one of J. C. Bach, and one original composition.

Palestrina, Giovanni — *Ricercar del primo tono* — King
2t, 2h, 2tb, bar, 3tb, tu.

Schumann, R. — *Northern Song* — Gamble
2t, 2h, 2tb, tu.

Schumann, R. — *Rustic Song* — Gamble
2t, 2h, 2tb, tu.

Grade III

Adler, Samuel — *Praeludium* — King
2t, 2h, 2tb, bar, tu, tim.

Bach, J. S. — *O Jesu Christ, mein's Lebens Licht* — King
Ten parts.

Bach, J. S. — *Ricercar from Musical Offering* — King
Seven parts.

Bantock, Granville — *Two Irish Melodies* — Paxton (Mills)
British brass band (E♭ cornet, B♭ cornets, flugelhorn, E♭ horns, B♭ treble clef baritones and trombones, euphonium, basses) and percussion.

Buonamente, Giovanni — *Sonata et canzoni* — King
2t, 2h, tb, bar, tu.

Buxtehude, Dietrich — *Fanfare and Chorus* — King
Eight parts.

Canning, Thomas — *Four Christmas Pieces* — American Composers Alliance
Brass ensemble.

Cesti, P. A. — *Prelude to the Opera, Il pomo d'oro* — Fitzgerald
6t, 4h, 3tb, bar, tu. Published by Bernard Fitzgerald, University of Kentucky, Lexington.

Chopin—Dawson — *Les Sylphides (selections)* — Paxton (Mills)
British brass band plus percussion.

Cohn — *Music for Brass Instruments* — Southern Publishing
3t, 2tb, Btb, t (h).

Corelli, A. — *Concerto grosso, Op. 6, No. XI* — King
4t, h, 2bar, tu.

Corelli, A. — *Pastorale* — King
Six parts.

Cortes, Ramiro — *Introduction and Dirge* — American Composers Alliance
Brass and percussion.

Cowell, Henry — *This Is America* — American Composers Alliance
A fanfare. 4t, 3tb, tu.

Cui, Cesar—Wilson — *Petite March* — MPH
4t, 4tb.

Cundell—Wright — *Blackfriars* — Paxton (Mills)
Symphonic prelude. For British brass band plus percussion.

Dietz, Norman — *Modern Moods* — AMP
2t, h, tb, bar, tu.

Gabrieli, G.—King — *Sonata pian'e forte* — King
Choir I: 2t, h, bar, 2tb; Choir II: tb, bar, tu.

Gabrieli, G.—Harvey — *Sonata pian'e forte* — Elkan-Vogel
2t, 2h, 3tb, tu or bass tb.

Goldman, R. F. — *Hymn for Brass Choir* — American Music Center
Sixteen instruments.

Handel, G. F. — *Three Pieces from the Water Music* — King
Six parts.

Hanna — *Song of the Redwood Tree* — King
Six parts.

Hartmeyer, John — *Negev, Tone Poem* — King
3t, 3h, 3tb, bar, tu, tim.

Ireland, John — *The Holy Boy* — B & H
3t, 2h, 2tb, bar, tu.

Jacob, Gordon — *Prelude to Revelry* — Paxton (Mills)
British brass band and percussion.

King, Robert D. — *Seven Conversation Pieces* — King
4t, 3tb, 2bar, tu.

COMPOSER-ARRANGER	TITLE	PUBLISHER
Lange, Gustave–Cafarella	*Hunting Party*	Witmark

2t, 2h, 2tb, tu.

Locke, Matthew — *Music for King Charles II* — King
3t, h(tb), tb, bar, tu.

Lully, Jean Baptiste — *Overture to Cadmus et Hermione* — King
2t, h, tb, bar, tu.

Mascagni, Pietro — *Cathedral Scene and Intermezzo* — Belwin
From *Cavalleria Rusticana*. 2t, h, tb, bar, tu.

McKay, George F. — *Bravura Prelude* — AMP
4t, 4h, 2bar, 4tb, tu.

Mendelssohn, F. — *Excerpts from the Oratorio Elijah* — Fitzgerald
6t, 4h, 4tb, 2bar, tu.

Mendelssohn–Cafarella — *Songs Without Words* — MPH
2t, 2h, 2tb, bar.

Miller, Ralph Dale — *Sinfonietta* — Belwin
3fl, 2t, 4h, 3tb, 2bar, tu.

Monteverdi, Claudio — *Sonata* — King
4t, 2tb, 2bar, tu.

Mozart, W. A. — *Eine kleine Nachtmusik: Allegro* — King
2t, 2h, tb, bar, tu.

Osborne, Willson — *Prelude* — King
3t, 2tb, bar, tu.

Osborne, Willson — *Two Ricercari* — King
2t, 2h, tb, bar or tb, tu.

Pachelbel, Johann — *Allein Gott in Höh' sei Ehr* — King
Four part brass choir with organ.

Paynter, John — *Fanfaronade* — Kjos
4t, 3tb, tu.

Purcell, Henry — *Symphony from The Fairy Queen* — King
Twelve parts plus timpani.

Purcell, Henry — *Voluntary on 100th Psalm Tune* — King
2t, h, tb, bar, tu. Another arrangement of this number is available from Summy-Birchard.

Rubinstein, Anton — *Kamennoi Ostrow* — Belwin
2t, h, tb, bar, tu.

Ruggles, Carl — *Angels, from Men and Angels* — American Music Center
4t, 3tb.

Saint–Martin — *In Memoriam* — Elkan-Vogel
3t, 3tb, organ.

Schmid, H. K. — *Turm-Musik, Op. 105* — B & H
6t, 2 perc.

Schubert–E. Leidzen — *Melodies* — Baron
2t, h, tb, bar, tu.

Seeboth — *Suite* — Heinrichshafer (AMP)
4t, 3tb.

Stewart, W. — *Trumpet Tune* — Paxton (Mills)
In 17th century style. British brass band plus percussion.

Tchaikovsky, P. — *Romance, Op. 5* — King
4t, 3tb, 2bar, tu, tim, perc.

Wagner, R. — *Prelude to Parsifal* — Fitzgerald
5t, 4h, 3tb, 2bar, tu. Published by Bernard Fitzgerald, University of Kentucky, Lexington.

Wagner, R. — *Vorspiel and Chorale from Act I, Die Meistersinger* — Fitzgerald
6t, 4h, 4tb, 2bar, 2tu.

Weinberger, Jaromir — *Concerto for the Timpani* — AMP
4t, 4tb, tim.

Wurz, Richard — *Tower Music No. I* — AMP
Intrade, Chorale, and Finale. For 4t in F, 2tb, 2Btb or tu.

Wurz, Richard — *Tower Music No. II* — AMP
Reveille and Chorale. Instrumentation as above.

Wurz, Richard — *Tower Music No. III* — AMP
Morning Music and Chorale. 3t, 2tb, Btb or tu.

Wurz, Richard — *Tower Music No. IV* — AMP
Evening Music and Chorale. Same instrumentation as No. III.

Grade IV

Adler, Samuel — *Concert Piece* — King
3t, 2h, 3tb, 2bar, tu, tim.

Adler, Samuel — *Divertimento* — King
3t, 3h, 3tb, 2bar, tu.

Altenburg, Johann Ernst — *Concerto for Clarini and Timpani* — King
7t, tim.

Arnell, Richard — *Ceremonial and Flourish* — AMP
3t, 4h, 3tb.

Bach, J. S. — *Contrapunctus No. I* — King
t, h, tb, bar, tu.

Bach, J. S. — *Contrapunctus No. III, from the Art of the Fugue* — King
2t, h, tb, bar, tu.

Bach–Wilson — *Prelude and Fugue in D Minor* — Fitzgerald
5t, 4h, 2tb, 2bar, tu.

Bantock, Granville — *Dramatic Overture —Orion* — Paxton (Mills)
British brass band plus percussion.

Bassett, Leslie — *Designs in Brass* — American Composers Alliance
4t, 4h, 3tb, 2bar, tu, tim, perc.

Beaver–Wright — *Sovereign Heritage* — Paxton (Mills)
Symphonic overture. For British brass band plus percussion.

Becker, Arthur — *Romance* — Remick
2t, h, bar, tb, tu.

Beethoven, L. — *Allegretto from Symphony No. 7* — King
3t, 2h, 3tb, bar, tu, tim.

Beyer — *Suite for Brass Instruments* — King
Ten parts.

Bonelli, A. — *Toccata* — King
2t, 2h (t), 2tb, 2bar, 2tu.

Bonneau, P. — *Fanfare* — Leduc
3t, 3h, 2tb, tu, 4tim.

Boyd — *Four Pieces for Brass Choir* — Witmark
2t, 2h, 3tb, tu.

Brabec — *Blaser Musi Ken* — Ullman ((AMP)
2t, 3h, 2tb.

Bradley — *Honeysuckle and Clover* — American Music Center
Brass choir.

Brant, Henry — *Millenium II* — American Composers Alliance
Brass and percussion.

Canning, Thomas — *Rondo for Percussion and Brass* — American Composers Alliance

Cazden, Norman — *Suite, Opus 55* — American Composers Alliance
2t, h, tb, bar, tu.

Clapp, Philip Greeley — *Circus Day* — B & H
2t, h, tb, bar, tu.

Cowell, Henry — *Grinnell Fanfare* — American Composers Alliance
Brass and organ.

David, Johann Nepomuk — *Introitus, Choral and Fugue* — B & H
On a theme of Bruckner. 2t in C, 4h, 3tb, organ.

Ewald, Victor — *Symphony for Brass Choir* — King
Six parts.

Francisque, A. — *Suite from Le Trésor d'Orphée* — King
Seven parts.

Franco, Johan — *Fanfare for Brasses* — American Composers Alliance

Franck, Melchoir — *Intrada for Brass* — B & H
3t, 3tb.

Ganz, Rudolph — *Brassy Prelude* — Mills
4h, 3t, 3tb, tu.

Goeb, Roger — *Septet* — American Composers Alliance
2t, 2h, 2tb, tu.

COMPOSER-ARRANGER	TITLE	PUBLISHER
Greb, Benedictus	*Paduana*	King
2t, h, tb, bar, tu.		
Guentzel, Gus	*La Fiesta*	Barnhouse
2t, h, tb, bar, tu.		
Haubiel, Charles	*Ballade for Brass Sextet*	The Composers Press
2t, h, bar, tb, tu.		
Haufrecht, Herbert	*Symphony for Brass and Timpani*	American Composers Alliance
Hovhaness, Alan	*Khaldis*	American Composers Alliance
4t, perc, piano.		
Jenni, Donald	*Allegro for Brass Choir*	American Composers Alliance
Jesson	*Variations and Scherzo*	King
Twelve parts.		
Kessel	*Sonata mit blasenden Instrumenten*	King
2t, h, tb, bar, tu.		
King, Robert D.	*Prelude and Fugue*	King
2t, 2h, 2tb, bar, tu.		
Komma	*Musik*	Ullman (AMP)
Seven parts.		
Lecail	*Septet for Brass*	Evette & Schaefer
4t, 3tb.		
Liadov, A.	*Slavlania*	Belaiev (AMP)
No. 1, 2, and 4. For 3t, 4h, 3tb, tim.		
Lockwood, Normand	*Concerto for Organ and Brasses*	AMP
Organ, 2t, 2tb.		
Macero, Teo	*In Retrospect*	American Composers Alliance
Brass choir and percussion.		
Meyers, C.	*Rhapsodie for Brass*	AMP
2t, h, tb, bar, tu.		
Parris, Herman	*Four Rhapsodies for Brass Ensemble*	Elkan-Vogel
3t, 4h, 3tb, tu.		
Parris, Robert	*Sonatina for Brass*	American Composers Alliance
2t, 3tb, tu.		
Pinkham, Daniel	*Sonata for Organ and Brasses*	American Composers Alliance
Pisk, Paul	*Cortege, Op. 536*	American Composers Alliance
Brass choir.		
Pisk, Paul	*Variations on an Old Trumpet Hymn Tune*	American Composers Alliance
Brass choir.		
Price, R. Maldwyn	*A Welsh Fantasy*	Paxton (Mills)
British brass band plus percussion.		
Roy	*Tripartita*	King
3t, 2h, 3tb, 2bar, tu.		
Schmidt, G. Fr.	*Heldenehrung*	B & H
2t, 3tb, tu, 2 perc.		
Schmutz, A. D.	*Fantasy Sketch*	Fischer
2t, h, bar, tb, tu.		
Scott, Wayne	*Rondo Gioioso*	King
Thirteen parts.		
Shahan	*Spectrums*	King
Fourteen parts.		
Stewart, W.	*Britain on Parade, March Patrol*	Paxton (Mills)
British brass band plus percussion.		
Sullivan	*Overture to the Mikado*	King
3t, 3tb, 2h, bar, tu, perc.		
Tchaikovsky, P.	*Capriccio Italien*	Belwin
2t, h, tb, bar, tu, marimba.		
Tchaikovsky, P.	*Lake of the Swans*	Belwin
2t, h, bar, tb, tu, marimba.		
Vitali, A.	*Capriccio*	Fitzgerald
4t, h, bar, 2tb, tu.		

Wagner, Richard	*Excerpts from Tannhäuser*	Pro-Art
2t, 2h, tb, tu.		
Wagner, Richard	*Siegfried's Funeral March*	King
3t, 2h, 3tb, bar, tu, tim, perc.		
Wagner, Richard	*Introduction to Act III, Die Meistersinger*	King
6t, 4h, 4tb, 2bar, 2tu.		
Wagner, Richard	*Prize Song and Finale*	Fitzgerald
From *Die Meistersinger*. 6t, 4h, 4tb, 2bar, 2tu.		
Weber, Ben	*Colloquy*	American Composers Alliance
2t, 2h, 2tb, tu.		
Weiss, Adolph	*Tone Poem for Brass and Percussion*	American Composers Alliance
4t, 4h, 3tb, 2bar, tu, 2tim, perc.		
Wood, Thomas	*The Lilliburlero March*	Paxton (Mills)
British brass band plus percussion.		
Wright, Denis	*Overture Glastonbury*	Paxton (Mills)
British brass band plus percussion.		

Grade V

Beadell	*Introduction and Allegro*	King
3t, 3h, 3tb, bar, tu, tim.		
Beckhelm, Paul	*Tragic March*	King
4t, 4h, 3tb, bar, tu, tim, perc.		
Berezowsky, N.	*Brass Suite for 7 Instruments*	Mills
2t, 2h, 2tb, tu.		
Bozza, E.	*Fanfare héroique*	Leduc
3t in C, 4h, 3tb, tu, 4tim, perc.		
Cobine, A.	*Vermont Suite*	King
4t, 3h, 4tb, bar, tu.		
Dahl, Ingolf	*Music for Brass Instruments*	Witmark
2t, h, 2tb or tu.		
DeYoung, Lynden	*Divertissement*	King
4t, 4h, 3tb, bar, tu, tim, perc.		
Grant, Parks	*Prelude and Dance, Op. 39*	American Composers Alliance
3t, 4h, 3tb, tu.		
Hindemith, Paul	*Plöner Musiktag: Morning Music*	AMP
2t, 2tb, or brass choir.		
Hogg, Merle	*Concerto for Brass*	King
3t, 3h, 3tb, bar, tu, tim.		
Kay, Ulysses	*Suite for Brass Choir*	American Composers Alliance
4t, 4h, 3tb, tu.		
Marks, James	*Introduction and Passacaglia*	King
3t, 3h, 3tb, bar, tu, tim.		
Marks, James	*Music for Brass and Timpani*	King
Twelve parts.		
Merriman, Thomas	*Theme and Four Variations*	AMP
4t, 2h, 3tb, bar, tu.		
Rautavaara, Eino	*A Requiem in Our Time*	King
4t, 4h, 3tb, bar, tu, tim, perc.		
Read, Gardner	*Chorale and Fughetta*	King
4t, 4h, 3tb, bar, 2tu.		
Read, Gardner	*Sound Piece*	King
4t, 4h, 3tb, bar, 2tu, tim, perc.		
Reynolds, Verne	*Theme and Variations*	King
3t, 3h, 3tb, bar, tu, tim.		
Riegger, Wallingford	*Nonet for Brass*	AMP
3t, 2h, 3tb, tu.		
Riegger, Wallingford	*Music for Brass Choir, Op. 45*	Mercury
10t, 8h, 10tb, 2tu, perc.		
Shulman, Alan	*Top Brass*	Shawnee
4t, 4h, 3tb, tu.		
Tomasi	*Liturgical Fanfares*	Leduc
3t in C, 4h, 4tb, tu, tim.		
Uber, David	*Gettysburg*	Edition Musicus
3t, h, 3tb, tu.		
Zindars, Earl	*The Brass Square*	King
4t, 4h, 3tb, 1tu, tim, perc.		

FINE

Diagnosing Embouchure Problems

Maurice Faulkner

AFTER MANY years of research and experience with a great variety of players I have attempted to classify the various types of embouchures that I have come across. But first of all, a definition of the term *embouchure* should be attempted. The word is taken from the French verb *emboucher* which means "to put into the mouth, to discharge by a mouth or outlet." It is derived from the combination of *em,* meaning *in* or *into,* and *bouche* meaning *mouth.* The French dictionary defines it as dealing with mouthpieces of wind instruments or as concerning the tonguing of wind instruments. We have changed the latter concept as having to do with the adjustment of the player's mouth to the mouthpiece of a wind instrument. And to carry the modern connotation one step further, many brass players and teachers use the term *embouchure* to concern all phases of the lips and teeth that have to do with the tone-producing vibrations on a brass instrument.

In this article I do not propose to consider the various problems of occlusion or malocclusion of the teeth. That is the subject for a treatise in itself. We will deal here with the several methods by which the lip muscles can produce the vibrations that are then amplified by the instrument into the sounds of the trumpet.

Harry Glantz, the great first trumpeter of the NBC Symphony under Toscanini once told me when he was asked to describe his concepts on embouchure: "I just screw up my lips and blow!" And what came out of the end of his horn were some of the finest trumpet tones this side of Gabriel's Heaven.

That doesn't give us much to go on to help young musicians, but it does indicate the attitude that many artists have about the physical aspects of their technique. Somewhere, either by accident or thru astute teaching, they have learned to produce beautiful musical results without apparent concern for the methods. Nevertheless, for those less fortunate performers, it is important that the ills that beset them be analyzed and corrected, just as a medical doctor diagnoses the ills of a sick body.

All brass players are interested in developing a high range with flexibility and ease. And after the beginner has learned the fingerings of his first notes, he attempts to soar beyond his level. There are a number of ways in which he can do this, but all of them have to do with getting those two membranes, the lips, vibrating more rapidly. The following listing catalogs the various devices of developing lip vibrations. I do not recommend all of them and list them only to establish a clear-cut point of view.

Pressure

This is usually the first type of vibration attempted by the youthful player. It is nothing more than forcing the metal of the mouthpiece more and more powerfully against the lips, which in turn press against the teeth squeezing the lips into ever smaller and tighter areas. Thru the smaller and tighter opening, the player then blows with additional wind pressure. Under these conditions it is difficult to play with a good tone, for the sensitive lips are being mauled unmercifully.

Furthermore, it is difficult to play with a variety of soft dynamics, for the wind pressure needed to aid in the production of the tone must be powerful enough to force itself thru the squeezed and battered lip opening. This method of embouchure is a common error and a fatal one if the player expects to achieve virtuoso capacities.

Wind Wedging

If the player hasn't used the arm pressure of the previous category, sometimes he attempts to develop his range by creating pockets of air in the cheeks of upper and lower lips—thus tightening the   at the lips and making the pitch go up.

What actually happens here is that the addition of air in the cheeks and lips stretches the lips more tightly at the center. This is a faulty embouchure although some jazz musicians use it, for it never gives the player the security of a direct flow of air from the diaphragm. There is always the uncertainty of the wind pressure in the cheeks and lips; it can change at the slightest movement and cause a bubble in the tone.

This method is something like playing on a balloon where the opening is held tightly in order to make pitch changes while the balloon varies according to the pressures on its surface. I have had a student whose inner cheek tissues were pulled apart because he used so much wind pressure to produce his high notes. He had literally been blowing a hole in his face from the inside. For a legitimate player who wishes to develop accuracy and brilliance of sound, we recommend that he correct this type of embouchure as early as possible.

Rolling Lower Lip Wedge

This is another device that creates a wedging of one lip against the other in order to close up the opening and make the pitches go up. By the wedge-like opening, the musician can push the breath thru at greater speed. It is difficult to describe this pattern; it must be seen to be recognized.

What happens is that the student rolls his lower lip back over his teeth with so much concentrated pressure against the upper lip that this upper lip becomes tense and tight enough to change pitch. Sometimes this lower lip wedging is caused by a wind pocket in it. Usually it is caused by a muscular puckering or rolling that pushes the lip up.

A teacher who takes the time to examine the facial muscular action can see this happening. One of the drawbacks of this type of playing is that so much of the lower lip is pushed up into the path of the air stream that it is difficult to blow around the flesh that is in the way. This causes a small tone, especially as the player goes higher and higher. And quite often the tonguing is thick and inaccurate.

To remedy this fault, the player must concentrate upon the flattening out of the lower lip, and he must maintain it in a firm position. The muscles of the lower lip must be tensed slightly in order to keep them from rolling or puckering upward toward the opening where the air is vibrating the lips.

Smile or Stretch

This type of embouchure uses the several facial muscles that stretch the upper and lower lips across the opening, thus tightening the vibrating edges so that they will change pitch accordingly.

The smile is not always the most effective manner of tightening the opening thru which the wind goes in order to raise the pitch. One of the drawbacks is that these muscles can be drawn only slightly backward and upward to their maximum resiliency. When that maximum has been reached the performer can tighten no further, and his range ceases to develop unless he uses pressure or wind wedges or some other method of going beyond the maximum pull of his facial muscular system.

I have had a number of students with small mouths who have been able to use this style of embouchure effectively. Those with long upper lips tend to find themselves stymied at a relatively low top range. The tone color of the player who produces all of his register with a smile tends to be somewhat thin and brittle in the upper reaches.

Tongue Wedge

This is a device that has to combine with one of the other embouchure styles in order to be utilized by the player. It is an unfortunate device for it requires a forward position of the tongue in order to produce the higher pitches, and this makes fine legato, as well as pianissimo, playing almost impossible. What happens here is that the student presses his tongue against the lower edge of the upper lip so that

the membrane is thinned out from behind rather than from in front as is the case with the mouthpiece pressing against the lip.

Usually the tongue wedge is used in conjunction with the pressure system, and the three pressures—(1) the mouthpiece against the lips, (2) the extreme wind pressure from the lungs, and (3) the pressure of the tongue against the upper lip from behind—push the lips into a narrow orifice with tremendous forces working to get the pitches to rise.

This is a very faulty embouchure development and one that can be corrected only by long and arduous exercises of diaphragmatic attacks. Use the syllable "hoo," somewhat like the breath attack used when one whistles. By consistent daily practice with this device one can overcome the tongue wedge that has produced a faulty embouchure with the most unmusical results.

The So-called "Pucker" System

Pucker is a misnomer here for it doesn't actually happen. When the average student thinks of puckering he immediately conceives of the kiss pucker. The movements involved tend to push the lips away from the firm foundation of the teeth and create fleshy cushions at the opening where the vibrations must occur.

In French horn playing a severe pucker of this type tends to develop a more "lush" tone quality and, if it is combined with the "setting-into the lip technique" of the European school, it can become effective in producing superior tone quality with range. But for a trumpeter to use an overdone pucker of the kiss variety brings a mass of flesh to the point where he needs precise vibrations of great flexibility.

In describing the pucker style, I talk about the use of the smile to flatten the lips out against the teeth and bones of the mouth and jaw. When that position is achieved the student then should compress the muscles at the center of the lips toward the opening, thus developing a firmness in the center that takes on the concept of being able to hold a pencil with the lips alone. Try it and see if you can do it! The tighter you grip the pencil, or the tighter you firm up the opening at the center, the smaller the opening and the higher the pitch.

This has a drawback for the tone

also tends to become smaller. Furthermore if the opening is compressed too tightly without proper lip control the center redness of the lip tends to close up the opening and the player cannot blow thru it. Thus it is essential that the player thin out his upper lip. It may be necessary at first to tuck the red of the upper lip under with the fingers before the student has the feeling for controlling the muscles independently. This thinning-out process will clear out the unnecessary red section of the lip and permit the white area to vibrate more clearly and precisely. It is never possible or desirable to eliminate all of the red of the lip for it must vibrate in order to insure a fuller, rounder tone.

To summarize this technique: Draw the lips across the teeth with a smile so that the lips are flattened out in a position of relaxed firmness. Thin out the red part of the upper lip if there is too much of it in the way of the air column. Firm up the center of the lips by bringing the muscles together as if you were going to hold a pencil with the lips alone. Buzz softly without using the tongue; any pitch will be satisfactory to start. Then tighten the muscles toward the center opening and slur your buzz higher. After the lips can buzz easily intervals of a 5th or more, bring the mouthpiece up to this opening as you buzz and slur upward and downward with the mouthpiece in place. Next, add the instrument without permitting its pressure to change the lips.

It is difficult to diagnose every lip situation in a short article. The principles are similar for good tone production and range on most brass instruments, with variations for the specifics of the instruments and individual differences of the players.

One must recognize that there are many ways of "squeezing the lips together" to make them play a brass instrument, and some experts use one as opposed to another. There will always be the need for adequate pressure of the mouthpiece against the lips to seal off the potential leaks around the opening. Herbert Clarke told me one time that it was essential to develop the finest control of the left hand so that a light flick of the left hand wrist could insure the success of finding F6, when the lack of such control would result in a bubble.   FINE

The British Brass Band

Herbert Hazelman

THE BRITISH BRASS band has a long and proud tradition of serving as the most important means of expression for the amateur bandsman in the British Isles. School, college, university, and civic concert bands, as we know them in the United States, are completely foreign to the residents of Britain. British military bands, which are somewhat akin to the American concert band in instrumentation and repertoire, are almost exclusively professional. Hence it is to the town, factory, church, or neighborhood brass band that the Englishman, Scotsman, Welshman, or Irishman looks when the urge to join with his fellow citizen in the production of band music becomes irresistible.

Tradition is worshiped by the Briton with much the same passion with which the American worships change. In the last 60 years the American concert band has evolved from a relatively small group of brass and woodwind instruments into a highly complex group capable of an almost plethora of instrumental colors. During the same 60 years, the British brass band has not changed one instrument. The traditional instrumentation of 1 E♭ cornet, 4 solo B♭ cornets, 1 ripiano B♭ cornet, 2 second B♭ cornets, 2 third B♭ cornets, 1 flügelhorn, 1 solo E♭ alto horn (sax horn) 1 first E♭ alto horn, 1 second E♭ alto horn, 1 first B♭ baritone, 1 second B♭ baritone, 2 B♭ euphoniums, 2 first B♭ tenor trombones, 1 second B♭ tenor trombone, 1 bass trombone in G, 2 E♭ tubas (sax horns), and 2 B♭ tubas is still the accepted make-up of the brass band just as it was six decades ago. All of the parts are written in treble clef except the G bass trombone that is in bass clef.

Purists among us wince at the idea of having tenor, baritone, and bass instruments play in the treble clef. To the British brass bandsman, however, the practice is completely logical since it enables any player of a valve brass instrument to change from one instrument to another with only the problem of adjusting to the new mouthpiece. This is a great boon to the British brass band movement since it makes it possible for 22 valve brass instrument players to join forces with 4 trombonists to form themselves into a band with a minimum of new learning. We should not underestimate the value of this practical arrangement to the British brass band. Unlike the United States, where almost all band instrument players are taught by professional teachers and where almost all bands are directed by professional conductors, the great majority of the teaching and directing in Britain is in the hands of amateurs. These dedicated men have a minimum of energy to devote to developing bands since their main means of earning a living is usually in a job of an artisan nature that is demanding of both time and energy. They almost all work at other jobs for a living. Work with the band is a labor of love.

Since instrumental music is not taught in the British state-supported lower schools, a great deal of the instruction in the playing of brass instruments is in the hands of the parents. The parent-taught player is the rule, not the exception. After observing the skill which results from this perfectly logical arrangement, it seems that careful consideration should be given to encouraging the same practice in America.

British Class Lines

This last point raises some interesting comparisons between the amateur bands of Britain and those of the United States. The overwhelming majority of amateur bands in the United States is composed of students from our schools and colleges, and a high percentage of the students who people our bands are from homes in the professional and management classes. In Britain, on the other hand, most amateur brass bands are adult groups with personnel drawn almost exclusively from the semi-skilled and artisan classes.

Class lines are much more rigidly drawn in Britain than in the United States, and it is much more difficult to cross these lines there than here. While it is the rule rather than the exception to find young people from all classes of society in the community high school band in America, it is rare indeed to find children from the manor joining with children from the cottage in a British band. It would not be too much of an over-simplification to say that the orchestra is the means of instrumental musical expression for the upper classes in Britain, the military band for the middle classes, and the brass band for the working classes.

This is not to say that the brass band holds an inferior position in Britain. While class lines are more rigidly adhered to in the British Isles than here, it is also true that the upper classes feel more responsibility for the well being of those of lower station, especially in matters dealing with culture. The National Brass Band Club is an organization of middle and upper class Britons dedicated to helping preserve the brass band tradition. Thru the Empire Memorial Fund, raised and administered by the Executive committee representing over 1,100 members, many fine projects that contribute to the continuation of brass bands in Britain are helped.

Brass Band Club

One noteworthy project sponsored by the National Brass Band Club is the National Youth Brass Band that was organized in 1952 by Denis Wright, well-known conductor, composer, and authority on brass bands. Over 100 young players of brass instruments from all over the British Isles are brought together twice yearly—during Easter vacation and in August—for a week at each session of intensive training culminating in a public concert under the direction of some outstanding conductor. The top age accepted is 18, and many youngsters return year after year (until the cut-off age is reached) for this experience that is designed to widen the musical experience of the players. Music that would be beyond the abilities of the individual young band is learned and performed. The 1960 spring concert that was presented in the city of Bradford consisted of the following program:

March, Pomp and
   Circumstance No. 4 .... Elgar
Overture, The Thievish
   Magpie .... Rossini
Solemn Melody .... Davies
Suite, English
   Folk Songs .... Vaughan Williams
Prelude, Act I, La Traviata ... Verdi

Excerpts from
   Sheherazade ... Rimsky-Korsakov
Grand March, Aida .... Verdi
Overture, Patience .... Sullivan
Octet: Gay Air .... Purcell
   Fugue in D Minor .... Bach
Mock Morris .... Grainger
Suite from the Mastersingers
   (Prelude, Act 3; Dance
   of the Apprentices;
   Entry of the Masters) .... Wagner

The quality of performance achieved by the individual brass bands is very high indeed, but the quality achieved when four or five of these bands are massed for a festival, which happens frequently, is amazing. It is not at all unusual for world renowned British symphony conductors such as Sir Adrian Boult, Sir John Barbirolli, or Sir Malcolm Sargent to appear as conductor of one of these festivals. Almost all of the front-rank British composers have composed test pieces for the annual brass band competitions. These contests for both bands and soloists are very serious affairs, and the winners who are crowned at the end are champions of champions.

There is none of the group rating system that is used almost exclusively in American band contests today. In Britain there is only one winner, and be it a soloist or be it a band, when the dust of battle settles (and some of the contests have become real and not figurative battles), a true champion stands out. This system often promotes ill feelings, but it produces playing of high quality.

Industrial Brass Bands

Almost every large industrial plant in Britain has a company sponsored brass band. The conductor and all of the players work a full day for a day's wage, and playing in the band is purely recreational. The players do not expect or receive preferential treatment. The company may supply some instruments and music and an occasional hour off to prepare for a competition, but this is about the limit of support proffered by the company other than moral encouragement which is highly regarded by the players. The feeling of pride that these men feel for the band is fierce and exciting to behold. The aura of sophistication that is so apparent among many American industrial recreation groups (bowling, softball teams, and the like) is missing among the industrial brass bandsmen of Britain. They are very serious about the band.

Church and Civic Bands

There are many church and mission brass bands whose primary object is to further the work of the church in saving souls and the mission in rescuing derelicts. The quality of playing and the pride in the calling here is also high.

Almost every town that has a town hall also has a brass band,

and the competition among these town bands is no less fierce than the competition among the town cricket and soccer teams. The venerable BBC, source of most home entertainment in Britain, recognizes the worth of the band as both entertainment and cultural lifter. Harry Mortimer, one of the great authorities on British bands and band music is producer in charge of band activities for the BBC and is charged with producing eight hours of programs per week of brass and military band music. Many of these programs are live. Others depend on records and tape, but all of them have millions of loyal listeners among all classes of Britons.

The brass band is a true folk tradition in Britain that reaches into every corner of the islands. Groups such as the National Brass Band Club are dedicated to keeping this fine tradition alive.

In Conclusion

Tho Britain has extensive governmental subsidies for professional orchestras, bands, ballet, and opera there is little school instrumental music. America, on the other hand, can learn much from the British brass band movement. If we can develop and encourage a generation of players to teach the skills of playing instruments to their offspring and make them willing and eager to take the time to sit down with their children and neighbors to play music together, we will have overcome one of the most damning criticisms leveled at our school instrumental music program—the lack of carry-over into adult life of these skills developed at such expense in time and money.

FINE

Tuba Talk

Rex Conner

C ONSIDERING THE PRICE of tubas in comparison to other instru-

ments, one should expect an instrument built with care, but this is not

usually the case. Rarely, can one pick up a new tuba, first or second line, and find that the valve action is quiet. They sound worn out before they are played. It is discouraging to try out a new instrument, run thru a chromatic scale and to hear the valves clatter simply because too much play exists between the valve guide keys and the channel in the cylinder wall. Some manufacturers will say the noise is not noticeable. Perhaps it isn't in a band concert, but it certainly is to the player who hears the clatter during his daily practice.

Valve noise is also quite noticeable to a judge listening to tuba solos and on a tape or disc when recordings are made. Anyone who has had the experience of conducting a large tuba section in a fast technical passage will certainly agree on this point; and we should not have to tolerate more extraneous noise from a tuba than we do from a clarinet. Of course, one reason for this noise is the quantity of brass in the instrument that magnifies the sound much more than on a cornet or trumpet.

A Remedy

To correct this noise ask the manufacturer for a new set of valve guide keys. The old ones screw out and new ones can be easily installed. New ones will need to be fitted, but it can be done with a small point file. In making a good fitting one should first consider that the channel in the cylinder has worn in a concave manner while the very top has hardly worn at all.

To do an effective job, open the cylinder's channel a little at the very top. Use a file without a cutting edge on the side. After the bottleneck is eliminated, determine the width of the channel down inside the valve; then dress the guide key down to fit it snuggly. There are two ways to fit the keys in. One is to caliper the channel; and the other is to grasp the threads on the guide key very lightly with a pair of small pliers and by reaching down inside the valve, check until the fit in the channel is perfect. The top of the guide key must also be dressed down because it will usually be too thick. Use the old guide key as a guide. Calipers make the job certain.

Once the guide key is properly fitted, screwed on the valve, and set exactly horizontal with the valve, one can use a little force (not too much)

to work the valve until it frees up. and it will be as snug as a trombone slide.
Then the valve action will be silent.

Springs

Speaking of valves, we should also mention valve springs, for they too can be troublesome. It is rather irritating to practice long sustained tones and have one of the springs decide to sing sympathetically along with the tone of the instrument. Since springs are made of various thicknesses, strengths, and materials, it is well to experiment a little. They are not expensive.

Providing the valves are in good working condition, E♭ tuba valve springs will often work fine on a BB♭ tuba causing much less effort and fatigue to the student. It is certainly difficult to develop good rapid finger technique when springs are too stiff or of unequal stiffness. Usually the middle valve spring tends to weaken sooner than the others because it is used more often. When this happens, it helps to move the third valve spring to the middle position.

Finger Techniques

It is well known that a good tone quality cannot be produced until the valves are completely depressed or completely up. (Why do composers write glissandos for any brass instrument except trombone if they want good sound?) If one plays a chromatic scale *staccatissimo*, slowly and well spaced, tonguing exactly at the same time the valve is snapped down, it might sound clean to the ear. If one tries to put the valve down first and then tongue, he will notice that the tone sounds even cleaner. When tonguing a rapid passage, one should feel that the fingers lead the tongue. Imagine that the tongue is tied to the fingers and when the latter move they cause the tongue to articulate. Quite often students complain because they are unable to tongue cleanly. In reality the trouble lies with the fingers that are moving slower than the tongue.

Perhaps because the valves are longer and heavier than those of a trumpet, the tuba player has more trouble in fingering than those who play higher brass instruments. If a passage calls for a 2-3 combination followed by a 1-2 combination the 3rd valve must be all the way up

when the first is down. The ring finger is sometimes quite damaging to clean articulation on any wind instrument. Snap it up at the same time the first finger is snapped down; do not allow just the spring to push it up.

Keep the fingers curved and keep the finger tips touching the valve buttons. There is a strong tendency to tongue at the instant the finger starts to move. Students who have the faults mentioned above may find that they are actually tonguing notes before the finger even touches the valve that is supposed to be all the way down. This occurs most frequently when playing fast passages. Sluggish, imprecise fingering accounts for much of what is called "muddy tuba playing." Playing softer and more staccato in ensemble usually does not clean up muddy spots, but it merely makes them less conspicuous. If the middle of the fingers are placed on the buttons the root joints of the fingers must move about twice as far as they would if the tips of the fingers were used.

Legato Playing

We have already mentioned legato playing. If slurred eighth notes are played at 100 beats per minute the valves should be snapped into position. Move the valves quickly, if the speed is much slower, then the legato effect would be better if the player would press the valves decisively but not necessarily with a snap. Allow each note to melt into the other, and try to keep the air stream moving steadily thru one porthole to the other. A little added support just on the change will sometimes do the trick. This is a subtle technique but very effective and musical.

Mouthpiece Angle

The angle of contact between mouthpiece and embouchure is a very important factor in producing a good tone; yet it is something that is rarely considered. Tall students who play short upright tubas by tipping their heads downward to reach the mouthpiece frequently sound terrible. A student sometimes improves his tone quality greatly by simply placing the instrument on his leg. This, in time, becomes quite uncomfortable, but it is good for a quick check.

A short player trying to reach a mouthpiece that is located too high on the instrument for him also will have problems. The curved mouthpiece is not the answer. The mouthpiece may reach the embouchure but it will not be at the right angle for the best tone production. In such cases either the player or the instrument must be elevated.

Literature

There is not nearly enough good literature for the instrument. Unfortunately, the few good publications that are available are not used enough. Two very excellent solos that are quite playable by ambitious high school tuba players are the *Sonatina* by Walter Hartley and *Concertpiece No. 1* by Roger Vaughn (publications of The Interlochen Press). *The Brass Teacher's Catalog* published by Robert King Music Company, North Easton, Massachusetts, lists most of the good tuba literature available.

Fine

November, 1961

The Development of the Upper Register

Robert Weast

THE DEVELOPMENT OF RANGE on a brass instrument presents a problem to most beginners and consistency and ease of performance constantly confronts many experienced players. Although there exist many variations for playing high notes, certain factors can be listed that adversely affect most brass players. Ironically, these detrimental methods are available to almost everyone and usually are used in preference to the positive, more correct methods. Even though one may use correct playing habits when he is fresh, he is likely to slip into the negative methods as fatigue or nervousness sets in.

Negative Methods

1. *Excessive mouthpiece pressure.* This tends to mash the lips, causing swelling and loss of sensitivity. Mouthpiece contact over and above that needed to maintain an air seal and to support the embouchure against the internal air compression may be defined as excessive.

2. *Lip corner stretching.* This thins the muscles making them vulnerable to mouthpiece pressure. A thinner tone is usually produced.

3. *Dry lip distortion.* When the lips and the mouthpiece rim are wiped dry, the player can then tilt or twist the horn, thus pinching and twisting the lips into extra duty.

4. *Binding the embouchure muscles together.* By clamping the jaws shut or by using excessive pucker, the embouchure is wadded together against the rim. The tone is usually thick and dull.

5. *Tightening the embouchure.* This is an incomplete concept, since range is primarily achieved through proper action of the air on the embouchure. When thinking is limited to the concept of tightening the lips to ascend, air is usually neglected. The embouchure then becomes hard, and the vibrating lip is virtually "frozen" from this over-tension. The air will not activate this rigid membrane.

6. *Changing mouthpiece position.* Exhausting strength in one mouthpiece setting and then moving to another place on the lips does not permit the development of range, but leads rather, to inaccurate notes and to a chronically weak embouchure.

Positive Methods

1. *Breath support.* Waist expansion or diaphragmatic inhale is the first step for range development. Contraction of the abdominal muscles produces the most efficient exhale. There is bound to be embouchure strain when there is inadequate air support. Tone quality and pitch are two good ways to determine if there is sufficient support.

2. *A projected air stream.* By actually blowing at imaginary points from the bell of the horn, air velocity is created. The higher the note the further one should project the air. High air velocity produces high vibrations. Slow air produces low vibrations.

3. *A correctly formed embouchure.* While ascending, the embouchure must assume a more contracted, puckered state. This is the position of strength comparable to flexing the biceps when lifting weights. Air compression within the mouth will quite naturally induce the proper flexing and contraction. The lip corners should be stabilized into the teeth and the lower lip should not be permitted to collapse into the mouth over the lower teeth or behind the upper lip. A real contribution to embouchure strength can be provided by the lower lip if it is permitted to develop in an aligned position with the upper lip.

4. *Correct aperture setting.* High notes demand a smaller lip opening. To attempt high notes with a wide setting causes undue embouchure strain and mouthpiece pressure.

5. *Embouchure strength.* Weak embouchures cannot withstand the higher air pressures and consequently the lips within the cup tend to blow open, rather than hold their position. The result is a lower but louder harmonic.

6. *A relaxed embouchure.* The more one can maintain a relaxed embouchure and yet retain the correct position the higher he can play, provided of course, air velocity is what it should be.

7. *The arched tongue.* When the frontal area of the tongue is raised and the aperture is reduced, the air column is thereby intensified. This focusing of the air column to a jet air stream produces maximum air

velocity.

The reason some players are quite successful with the negative methods of playing is that such factors as excessive mouthpiece pressure do not seriously affect them. For example, most players experience a swelling and deadening of the lips when heavy pressure constantly is applied. Consequently their endurance and range is very limited. On the other hand some players can take much lip abuse without the fatal swelling and can continue to play quite well. They are in the minority.

Embouchure Strength Necessary

Because of the control and embouchure strength required for correct playing, a person not in top shape must always use judgment and a degree of caution when playing for an extended time in the upper register. Moreover, strength can easily be sapped in a moment's time by foolish playing. Conversely, with periodic rests and thoughtful application, endurance can be extended for several hours.

In the development process, one will find that he can play up to a certain note correctly without undue strain or distortion. It is precisely here that his attention should be directed. A lesser volume of tone should be used in this area of difficulty, since the work load of the embouchure will be less. As strength is gained, this register can be played at a louder volume and the immediate notes above it should be attempted at the piano volume.

It becomes obvious that the upper register does not become available merely by playing in it. The act of blowing high notes is no guarantee that they will become strong and consistent. Long tones, shorter at first and lengthened as progress is made, arpeggiated figures, and careful attention to the air and embouchure are features that develop range and endurance. The key to the inclusion of positive factors is the broken practice time and the rest of a few beats or measures in actual performing situations. This allows the player to maintain the correct controls and permits him to retain his strength indefinitely.

FINE

Brass Warm-Up

Walter Moeck

A GOOD WARM-UP ROUTINE is one of the brass player's most valuable assets. Since so much of brass performance is physical it is vitally important that the player have a common sense warm-up procedure that will insure free lips for good tone quality, control, flexibility, and endurance.

The lips will tend to be stiff after long intervals of not playing and it is the function of the warm-up to stimulate blood circulation in the lips and to allow the flexibility required for the lips to vibrate at any desired frequency. Muscles receive their strength and nourishment from the blood. An organized warm-up will help to get the needed circulation to its maximum.

Suggested Procedure

The following warm-up routine has been used successfully by the writer and is suggested as a daily procedure.

The first part of the routine (Example 1) starts on G4, where the lip is about in its normal position. The exercise works down to the lower register *slowly* and *softly*. This will help the lips to become loose and to free them from their natural stiffness. After completing the exercise it is helpful to play it backward, returning to the starting note.

After a few moments rest the next part of the routine (Example 2) starts with the slurring of a fourth, using the seventh partial fingering combinations. By using the false fingerings the lips are allowed to do all the work, thereby allowing for better flexibility. In slurring the intervals it is wise to use the syllable *tow* in the low register, *ta* in the middle register, and *tee* in the high register. These variations of syllables vary the size of the mouth cavity and help to produce a smoother slur.

The third part of the warm-up routine (Example 3) is a soft staccato exercise. This starts to get the tongue limber so that there can be better co-ordination between the tongue and the response of the lip to the attack. The exercise should be started very softly and slowly. It can be taken faster as the scale descends and as the tongue begins to feel more limber.

In the next exercise (Example 4) the range is extended to the interval of a sixth. Again the partial fingerings are used to allow the lip to do most of the work. After a short rest this exercise should be played from end to beginning, as in Example 1.

In Example 5 the range is now extended to G5, again using the false fingerings. Playing in the high register too soon will cause the, lips to tighten and stiffness will occur. After completion of this part of the routine it is a good idea to rest for approximately five minutes to allow the circulation of the blood to strengthen the lip muscles. Flexibility is taxing on the lip muscles but when it is done with common sense it will strengthen rather than weaken. For this reason frequent resting is necessary.

Covers Complete Range

The final part of the warm-up routine (Example 6) includes full octave skips and goes all the way to C6 (or the top note of the players range). A short rest after reaching G5 is suggested, after which the octave study should be completed.

This complete warm-up procedure should take no more than twenty-five minutes, including frequent rest periods, and it will be found that it is time well spent. A conscientious application of such a routine each day will result in more control and consistency in performance.

Frequent resting is always wise in brass performance. The lip is being pressed between the mouthpiece and the teeth and frequent resting will remove the pressure and let the blood circulate to strengthen the relaxed muscles.

If the brass player will treat his lip with care and respect he can expect the same from it during performance.

FINE

The Flügelhorn

Lucien Cailliet

The Flügelhorn (called in French: *bugle*) belongs to the mellow brass family known as the Saxhorns after the name of the inventor Adolph Sax, who created this group of instruments in 1843. The family of saxhorns comprises: The Eb and Bb flügelhorns (soprano register), the Eb alto horn (alto register), the euphonium or baritone (tenor register), the Bb bass (bass register), and the Eb and BBb tubas (contrabass register).

To illustrate the difference between the saxhorns and the clear brasses—the cornet, trumpet, and trombone—we can say that the flügelhorn compares with the trumpet or cornet the same as the baritone compares with the trombone. It should be pointed out that a primary difference is that increasing the blowing in a trumpet or trombone will cause the tone to become brassy while the flügelhorn and baritone will retain their characteristic mellowness at any volume.

Accordingly, the saxhorn family constitutes an added brass section in the band which the orchestra does not have. In band arranging either brass section can be used separately or together at the option of the composer or arranger. A good illustration of a contrasting effect between two sections is at the beginning of the march *Father of Victory*, by Gannes.

The combining of both sections produces a more full and less brassy effect somewhat similar to an imaginary great organ. These effects can provide interesting variety to the band.

The saxhorn family constitutes a bridge between the clear brasses and the reed sections.

Obviously, by eliminating the flügelhorn from the band, as we often do in this country, we deprive this instrumental family of its soprano instrument which is an incredible and most detrimental omission.

Directors Often Cue Part

Band arrangers, being fearful of the absence of the instrument, cue into the solo cornet part important figures assigned to the flügelhorns; while this compromise might save the day, it is nevertheless inferior to the intended effect.

For example, the introduction to *Father of Victory March* is intended as a contrast between two complete brass sections. If the 1st flügelhorn is absent and replaced by a cornet, the latter instrument is more brilliant and prominent than the alto horns (or French horns) and baritones, thus resulting in this passage sounding like a cornet solo with saxhorns accompaniment, which is far different from what Mr. Gannes created; this substitution could even be termed unethical.

In the French and Italian bands, the 1st flügelhorn is as important as the solo cornet. The instrument is softer, more lyric, and more flexible than the cornet, with easier emission throughout its entire compass.

It is imperative that the flügelhorn be played with a flügelhorn mouthpiece, as either a cornet or trumpet mouthpiece will alter the nature of the flügelhorn sound and cause bad intonation.

In closing, I wish to mention that the Eb flügelhorn—named in French: *petit bugle*—pitched a fourth above the Bb flügelhorn, would contribute power and brilliancy to the high register together with the Eb cornet. Let us hope that these instruments will soon receive due recognition as an integral part of the band and with adequate parts published for them.

We know that pioneering towards musical progress is ever interesting and good for the soul, even if the road is somewhat rough.

FINE

1962

B♭ Baritone

From Tenor to Bass Trombone

Reginald Fink

TWO SEVENTH GRADE BOYS, just beginning their adolescent growth, were finishing their weekly semi-private trombone lesson. Tho one was equipped with a medium bore tenor trombone with an F attachment and the other with a 9½" bell, .564" bore bass trombone, their complaints were identical. Try as they may they could not make the low notes on the F attachment speak.

The teacher took the larger instrument. He pulled the valve. Then extending the slide to a flat 7th position, played a C2.

The result was the familiar example, common to all teachers, of the students imitating the teacher. Within a few minutes, they both had played a C2 also, and opened up the whole lower register of their playing. This serves to illustrate once again that an example is better than a thousand words, and that children's accomplishments surmount their physical immaturity when the proper motivation has been found.

Additional Tubing Causes Difficulty

Almost everyone who transfers from a tenor trombone to a tenor trombone with F attachment or to a bass trombone experiences the same problems. They either get the same tone they got on the old instrument, with quite a bit more labor, or they get a foggy sound commonly termed "not filling the horn." Either sound is accompanied with an inability to make the notes on the valve speak.

Part of the difficulty with the valve notes stems from the additional tubing which is engaged. The instrument then becomes about 14 feet long, approximately the length of a French Horn and nearly the length of an Eb tuba. At first the student may be unable to feel the low resistance of the instrument, and the breath flow and pressure which was correct to play the tenor trombone is not correct for a larger bore instrument or the increased length of tubing. In addition, the ear must be trained not only to anticipate the

pitch of the lower notes but to imagine accurately the tone quality of the valve register.

During the first critical period of the change from small trombone to large trombone the student should relax as much as possible. He can evolve a new embouchure by starting in the middle register where he is accustomed to playing and then working down into the valve register. Later he can work from the middle register up into the high register.

As he starts developing the tone he should relax the embouchure to the point where he is just about to fall off the note down to the next note of the overtone series. As he lets the note down the tone probably will become dull. At this point the breath flow must be increased. He should imagine blowing large quantities of warm air into the instrument, relax the embouchure as much as possible, and open the jaw slightly.

Use Proper Mouthpiece

The biggest problem at this period is the desire on the student's part to find an embouchure that works in the low register regardless of whether it is useable in the middle and high register. The mouthpiece that comes with the new instrument or a larger one should be used, even if the manufacturer has provided adapter shanks which supposedly make it possible to play the new trombone with the student's old mouthpiece. The use of the old mouthpiece with the adapter shank is rarely satisfactory. Using the new, larger mouthpiece and the student's normal embouchure it is possible to change trombones and develop the new tone without much difficulty.

Applying what has been mentioned before, the student should work scales and lip slurs down chromatically to and thru the valve register. As the notes get lower he will have to give more air to get the same amount of tone. Pivoting up, shifting the mouthpiece weight more to the upper lip plus extending the jaw a little, also will help the tone on

the low notes.

The embouchure theoretically remains the same throughout the entire range of the instrument. Generally this means that the mouthpiece does not slide up, down, or sideways on the lips when changing from high to low or vice versa, but the pivoting which tends to change the looks or shape of the embouchure is considered permissible and not classified as an embouchure change.

Develop Good High Register

The high register may be momentarily unstable and indefinite when the student changes to the larger mouthpiece and trombone, but usually he has a better high register, at least in regards to getting the notes, on the larger instrument. The larger mouthpiece gives the embouchure less of a crutch and there is less resistance from the bore, hence the student is less able to cheat in the high register. As a result he produces the tone correctly or else not at all. The tone is never the same, yet a brilliant high register can be developed.

Since the instrument is larger the volume must be considerably greater before the distortion, or brilliance of the tone occurs. Thru correct tone production and more volume a brilliant tone can be produced in time.

Recordings of good bass trombonists, or better yet a live example of good playing is necessary for the student's concept, but this alone will not develop a good tone. The physical requirements for playing a large bore trombone or bass trombone are no more than those required for other trombones.

The high register is not seriously impaired if correctly produced and the breath necessary to play a larger instrument is available from all normal trombonists of junior high school age or older. Pinched embouchure and shallow breath are the two major problems to be overcome. This can be done with methodical work and examples of how it is supposed to sound when it is correct.

FINE

Sound That "Tah"

ELMER MAGNELL

STUDENTS RECEIVING their initial instruction on a brass instrument often experience difficulty in properly attacking a tone. Some fail to use their tongue at all; most are delayed in the attack; tongue placement is faulty with some; few support the tone with sufficient air; and the throat cavity often becomes constricted.

Just as correct habits improve and become spontaneous with systematic repetition, so faulty habits become more implanted with continued practice. *The first few lessons become the basic pattern for continued study.* Once an imperfection in tone production appears, its correction becomes doubly difficult. The adage, "An ounce of prevention is worth a pound of cure," is applicable.

Gomer Pound says, "A good tone begins and ends with a good tongue." An exploration of a few tonguing techniques appears in order.

Background Material Concerning Tonguing

The famed Herbert Clarke, in his famous *Arban Method*, recommended the use of the syllable *tu*.[2] Also he advocated using the tongue as in spitting away a small piece of paper which had been placed between the lips. Few people today suggest this procedure of tonguing but who would be brazen enough to say that this great performer-teacher was incorrect?

John F. Victor in his excellent instruction book, *The Victor Method*, said:

"We agree with the celebrated cornetist, Gatti, that the best method of articulation is the pronouncing of the syllable, *Ta-ta-ta*. This syllable is an open vowel and is musical, whereas, *Tu*, the syllable usually employed, is not."[3]

M. E. Hall presents an interesting and educational treatise in three parts on problems of articulation in the article, *Stage Bands*, with illustrated exercises advocating tongued syllables, *dah*, *da*, and *daht*, for varying

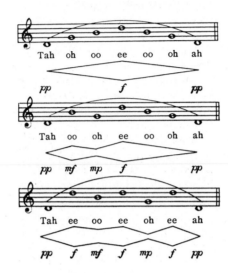

articulated effects.[4]

Vincent Bach, teacher and instrument manufacturer, says: "Do not tongue between the lips but touch the upper front teeth with the tip of the tongue. For the low notes attack at the lower edge of the teeth, near the gum line. For double and triple tonguing articulate also with the front part of the tongue by pronouncing the K a short distance behind the tip of the tongue saying *Kee* (not *Kaa* at the back of the tongue) as follows: *Ti-Ki-Ti-Ki* or *Ti-Ti-Ki-Ti-Ti-Ki*."[5]

Articulate With Tah

Psychologically speaking, the greater the number of rules a young student has to follow in wind instruction, the more chance he has to err in performance. Rather than expound on an involved explanation of correct tonguing and breathing procedures, this writer advocates the student tongue using the syllable *tah*. Since the student learns more rapidly by imitation, it might be advisable for the instructor to sing along in the early stages using the *tah* syllable. It should be made clear that although the teacher, to be heard, makes a *vocal utterance* of the sound, the student uses only the tongue and breath support.

Analysis of the Syllable Tah

To clarify for the reader the choice of this particular tonguing syllable, *tah*, let us divide it into component parts for analysis. "T" is a consonant assuring an instantaneous attack, assuming the air is expelled simultaneously with the tonguing. Sluggishness of attack accounts for much of an ensemble's lack of precision. In addition, the consonant "T" enables a student (without burdening him with lengthy explanation) to place the tongue in a favorable position behind the upper teeth. It is difficult to verbalize on actual tongue positions. Simply say, "Tongue with Tah."

The second part of the syllable is a, pronounced ah. On this vowel the tongue takes a position at the bottom of the mouth out of the way. This is an open vowel, causing little restriction in the air column. It is an easy syllable to enunciate as many vocalists will verify.

The last sound in the syllable, "h," is the most neglected and yet probably the most important. An "h" consonant assures diaphragmatic action proportionate to the extent sounded and amount of air following. It is possible to tongue on the syllables *ta* and *tu* without the sensation of using air from the lower regions but not with *tah*, if the "h" is stressed. Many teachers recommend, even for more mature performers, starting tones employing only air to assure an open throat. This procedure might be advantageous the first month of beginning instruction but even the value of this teaching method is debatable if the student is introduced to the correct use of the syllable *tah* and its implications. The use of this syllable also aids in the termination of the tone, preventing an abrupt stop as is often found in a *tat* attack where the tongue stops the tone.

Adequate Breathing Necessary

Tone production is dependent upon adequate breathing and expiration of air. Try an exercise inhaling and exhaling using the "h" sound alone (comparable to a dog's panting). The muscles of the diaphragm are active in achieving deep breathing.

In rapid passages notes are attacked with little or no thought of release. *Staccato* tones in a slow tempo are given a correct release by an expulsion of air through the "h" sound of the syllable *tah* while maintaining a firm embouchure. Such *staccato* tones have character since they are produced by the tongue and air simultaneously rather than by the tongue and insufficient breath support, often experienced in tonguing with *tu*.

The transfer from marcato to legato articulation and style involves a change to the *dah* syllable attack with the maintenance of a continuous flow of air for a cantabile performance. Some authorities recommend *lah* or *rah* attacks for legato playing but such articulation styles tend to be rather indefinite and uncertain.

Increased Range Thru Use of Syllables

For more advanced students a consideration of the placement of the back of the tongue in the mouth cavity is important in its effect on the quality and pitch of a tone. This position can be changed from low to high in the roof of the mouth by enunciating syllables through these stages: *tah, oh, oo, e*, for four pitch levels. This action results in change to a smaller mouth cavity, facilitating the production of higher tones. A smaller cavity also tends to effect a thinner tone which is the reason instructors hesitate to use this tonguing technique. William Cramer says, "The largest possible opening in the windpipe and the mouth cavity will assist greatly in tone production. A large opening allows for a free flow of air from the breathing mechanism, resulting in a buoyant sound rather than a forced sound."[6]

An open throat is important, however, if the performer uses *proportionately more air pressure the higher the tone*. This will compensate for the smaller mouth cavity formed in progressing from *tah* to *ee*. This sounds complicated but actually if one listens discriminately to the sound produced and tries conscientiously to match tone quality and sound in all registers, adjustments in air pressure will become automatic.

Below are a few cornet lip slurring exercises to promote proper tongue placement and to encourage air pressure adjustments:

1-3 fingerings throughout, followed by 2-3, 1-2, etc., chromatically. Remove the mouthpiece from the lips and rest after each double bar.

Recapitulation

Sensitivity to conducting can be taught in the initial stages of wind instruction by having students attack tones precisely. Clarity is achieved by using an open vowel in tone production. The tongue starts the tone but the flow of air supports the sound and gives the tone character. Employ, in tonguing, the syllable, *tah*, directing attention to the "h" sound in its activating diaphragmatic action in controlling air flow. It helps to prevent the disagreeable "tongue without tone" technique so often heard. It is amazing how simplified one's instruction can become by a simple reference to an apparently simple illustration of the tonguing syllable, *tah*.

---

[1]Gomer Pound, "A Good Tone Begins and Ends With a Good Tongue," *Selmer Bandwagon*, Vol. 9, No. 2 (April 1961), p. 14.
[2]Herbert Clarke, *Arban Method* (New York: Carl Fischer), Preface.
[3]John F. Victor, *The Victor Method* (Dallas Texas. Bk. 1, Revised Edition), Preface.
[4]M. E. Hall, "Teacher's Guide to the High School Stage Band," *Selmer Bandwagon*, Vol. 9, No. 2 (April 1961), p. 19.
[5]Vincent Bach, *Embouchure and Mouthpiece Manual* (Mount Vernon, New York: Vincent Bach Corporation), pp. 20-21.
[6]William Cramer, "The Initial Attack," *The Instrumentalist*, Vol. X, No. 2 (Oct. 1955), p. 53.

FINE

Brass Instrument Beginners

Daniel Tetzlaff

IF YOU STARTED BEGINNERS last fall, are you satisfied with their progress in playing into the high register? Or, if you are teaching at a higher level, do you think the incoming cornet-trumpet section will be able to handle the first parts of the music you would really like to play next year? What help can we offer the less than outstanding players? Perhaps this discussion will help the beginner as well as those who have played long enough to desire a new idea or two.

Two Embouchure Aids

1. *High placement of the mouthpiece on the upper lip.*

Advantages. The upper rim rests mostly (or even entirely) above the red flesh, the soft mucous membrane. This reduces swelling and fatigue of the tissues, allows more muscles inside the mouthpiece cup to control pitch and tone quality, and increases endurance and strength. (*The top of the mouthpiece will come quite close to the nose of trombone and tuba players.*)

For beginners, this placement should be made by the teacher, either in the classroom or in the studio. The largest factor contributing to poor trumpet embouchures is the unguided first day of instrument playing.

Too often the student, or the parent, or the music store owner is too eager. In the anxiety and hurry-up to make that first sputter and prove "We can do it," a large percentage of beginners get doomed to years and years of more sputtering.

It is true that out-of-school starts are sometimes difficult for the teacher to control, but it can be worked out if advance announcements are made, and aspirants are asked to wait, for instance, until the end of a semester of pre-instrument training in reading and listening.

Here is why. The rim of the mouthpiece quickly "digs a trench" into the lip flesh, a kind of trough wherein it tends to settle and feel comfortable. Once it is formed it is difficult to change, or get out of, as the ruts in a muddy or snow-covered road hold the wheels of a car. The rim of the mouthpiece also acts as a clamp. If it helps hold together enough lip flesh, the vibrations come easily as soon as even a gentle breath is blown. Conversely, if the rim holds a scanty amount of muscle in the cup and if the lips are apart, response is difficult, and the struggle begins—and often never ends! So be aware of the importance of the very first lesson.

Correction Not Easy

For intermediate or advanced players, correction is possible, but it is not easy. Ideally, it is undertaken after a vacation or lay-off period, when possibly the lips have forgotten just exactly where the mouthpiece should rest, and thus could accommodate a carefully determined and deliberate higher placement.

The mouthpiece will tend to slip back to its familiar resting place if one uses "wet lip"—which is recommended as a plus factor in lip flexibility, necessary for control of pitch, intonation, and tone quality, or it will tend to drop from the simple action of gravity. For example, the instrument seems quite heavy to some beginners, and some girls; when played on the march the mouthpiece tends to slide off the upper lip; proper position becomes a problem after the player becomes fatigued.

A Moving Lower Lip

2. *The lower lip tucked slightly under the upper.*

Advantages. As the lower jaw is advanced slightly to even up the teeth, and to open the jaws and throat to allow a free and unrestricted flow of air, so also are the vibrating lips touched to each other without force, insuring an easy and

instantaneous response to even a small amount of exhaled breath. These are among the considerations necessary for both soft playing and high register playing, two of the big problems in trumpeting.

Many brass instrument players, either consciously or unconsciously, use a mouth formation that relies upon a moving lower lip, wherein more lower lip is drawn in and up for the high register, and then conversely, is lowered for the low register. This can be accomplished by the smallest possible movements of the lower jaw.

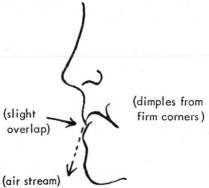

(slight overlap)

(dimples from firm corners)

(air stream)

Why tuck under? To compensate for the fact that when the mouthpiece is placed on the lips, the jaws are opened to facilitate maximum resonance, and breathing out starts, the natural tendency will be for the lower lip to fall forward and down a bit. We just want to be sure that even so, it will meet readily with the upper lip and vibrate easily against it. We wish to prevent a falling away that will miss the contact and result in a blurred sound, no sound at all, or a forced tone as a reaction to sensing these results.

Start High—End High

Most of the method books start the beginner on rather low notes. This is perhaps the safest way if guidance is absent, or at a minimum. But this also is why many players cannot successfully play in the upper register even years later. It could be that what is advocated as an ideal embouchure for the large mouthpiece instruments does not produce equal results on the small mouthpiece.

Keep an open mind. Do not shut the door to trial of what possibly is an opposite approach to what you were first told many years ago. Experiment with these two ideas. Also, ask the student to produce a buzz of the lips alone before putting the

mouthpiece to the lips. Practicing on the mouthpiece alone for at least one week is another shortcut to a more immediate control of the instrument. Student results with these efforts help the teacher discover who has the aptitude for playing high (trumpet) and who should play low (trombone, baritone). Instead of starting beginning trumpets on C4 start them on C5.

The conception of starting each day's lip limbering up with a tucked in formation that produces the highest possible note without strain, can easily set up C5 or E5 as the player's immediate middle and not his eventual high. Relaxing down from this is no trick if lip points and jaws are not rigidly locked. All further muscle control and strength acquired thru subsequent exercise serves to carry this start up an octave. Instead of starting at C4 and going up to G5, the player can start at C5, relax to G3, and eventually finish at C6 or even E6 or G6!

High Register for All Brasses

Do not be amazed if suddenly there is a large crop of high-note trombone, baritone, and tuba players. They will get the low notes, too, as they learn to open the jaws more. It is easier to learn to relax than to acquire the strength to tighten up a too-loose start.

Should you hear pinched tones, check for clenched jaws shutting off the breath supply. Check also to see that the upper lip covers the edge of the upper teeth. The overhanging part must vibrate against the lower lip in order to produce a tone both full and smooth.

Some advanced players have quickly added up to a fifth to their range by using these two suggestions. Make a test. On the mouthpiece alone, play the highest tone possible with your present mouth formation. Take a full breath, play the note loudly and try to hold it for 12 counts without diminuendo. Try a second time, but now with lower lip tucked under. If the high notes seem easier perhaps you will be encouraged to seek further information. See *The Art of French Horn Playing* by Philip Farkas (pub. by Summy-Birchard) and this writer's article, *Should I Change My Embouchure?* in the June, 1958, issue of *International Musician.*

USING SYLLABLES

William McKee

THE USE OF VOCAL SYLLABLES in teaching a beginning student to produce a tone on a brass instrument is well known. We have all heard of the use of the syllables *too* or sometimes *tuh* in giving the beginning student something concrete to do which will help him form the proper embouchure and attack.

The next step in utilizing syllables as a brass teaching aid, and specifically as an aid in teaching the French horn, is to use different syllables for the attack and tone production in the three basic registers of the Horn. These registers, of course, are the low, middle, and upper, and the syllables associated with each are *taw* for the lower, *too* for the middle, and *tee* for the upper.

These particular syllables are exceptionally well adapted to the tongue and embouchure formations needed in these three registers of the horn. Many horn methods give the syllable *too* (sometimes spelled *tu*) for the first middle register notes which a beginner must learn. (See Farkas, Howe, Pottag-Hovey *et al.*) With this syllable the embouchure muscles are fairly relaxed, the lip aperture is somewhat open, the teeth even, and the tongue is back of the opening between the teeth or even slightly between the teeth, and everything is in readiness to produce a pitch between C4 and C5 as written for the F horn. All that remains is for the player to release the tongue and allow the air to escape at the proper pressure and continue the vibration of the lips which have been jarred into motion by the pronunciation of the syllable. The force of the air escaping combined with lip-tension should produce the desired pitch.

Resonant Low Register

For the notes of the Horn below C4 the syllable *taw* seems to be eminently suited for the proper embouchure formation and tongue position. When this syllable is pronounced the embouchure muscles are quite relaxed, the lip aperture is opened more and rounded, and the lower jaw may be thrust forward a little so the lower teeth are slightly ahead of the upper. More of the tongue may be between the teeth than in the other registers, and the mouth cavity will be larger and the throat more open to accommodate the large amount of air at low pressure needed to produce a full, resonant tone in the low register of the horn.

The syllable *tee* admirably arranges the circumstances needed for a vibrant and forceful attack and rich tone in the upper to extreme upper register of the horn. This is the area from D5 to as high as one can play. When *tee* is said into the horn the embouchure is firm, the lip aperture small, the teeth are even, the tongue is back of the upper teeth ready to release a jet of air at high pressure, and the mouth cavity is now small to restrict the air stream and help produce the high air pressure needed to produce the upper register.

At this point the reader may wonder what happened to the C#5 as we gave the syllables and their registers. Arcady Yegudkin of the Eastman School of Music faculty (fondly called the "General" by his many students) says, "Dot note is between *too* und *tee* und eet's a keeler." Players of the Bb horn in this register put down the second and third valves, tongue very lightly, and hope for the best.

Help to Locate Pitches

The vocal syllables used in this way are also then a help in rather generally locating pitches—always a problem with the Horn.

Another use for syllables is in helping the player to produce a smooth slur within and between the registers. This difficult facet of horn technique needs constant attention to keep a high level of skill since much of the appeal of fine French horn playing comes from a smooth legato style.

The important point in a smooth slur occurs in the fraction of a second between the notes. When the slurred tones are close in pitch the problem is minimized since no great changes are needed in embouchure or air pressure. The easier slurs lie in the intervals of the major third and smaller. It is the intervals of the perfect fourth and larger which cause the trouble although usually the descending intervals are easier to negotiate than the ascending.

The earlier mentioned fraction of a second between the notes of the wide upward slur can be used to make the proper adjustments in embouchure and air pressure to facilitate the slur. One of the best ways to make this adjustment is to pronounce the syllables coinciding with the registers desired and, most importantly, prefacing the syllable of the note toward which the slur moves by an "h" sound. For example, a slur from a written B4 (middle register) to E5 (high register) would be made by pronouncing the syllables *too-hee*. The slur from A3 (low register) to F4 (middle register) would use the syllables *taw-hoo*. Slurs made within registers as from C4 (middle) to B4 (middle) would use the same syllable for both notes.

Fast Diaphragm Movement

The "h" sound for the beginning of the second syllable is the important point in this system of playing wide interval slurs and helps change the physical arrangement of the player in that fraction of a second between the notes. This "h" sound, when done with some energy, causes the diaphragm to make a fast movement (usually outward) and quickly compress the air within the lungs, sending it upward with a very fast rise in pressure. This rise in pressure, from the bottom of the air column, coupled with the thinning of the air stream and greater lip tension caused by the syllable pronunciation, should help the slur to be made more quickly and smoothly.

Establish a Pattern

Using this system, slurs of very large intervals can at least be attempted with a concrete plan of attack upon the problem. For an extreme example: G3 (low register) to E5 (high register) would be played by saying *taw-hee*. One cannot over-emphasize the importance of the energetic, quick pronunciation of the "h" for the note at the peak of the slur. The "h" sound can,

of course, be used in a succession of notes within a slurred passage if the contour of the passage demands such activity. Usually downward slurs do not need the "h" sound since the diaphragm generally is relaxing as the pitches descend but the syllables should still be utilized since the embouchure and air stream will need the pattern to establish their positions and dimensions.

Many exercises for working with syllables may be easily devised. An excellent one is:

taw - haw taw - haw taw - hoo taw - hoo

taw - hoo taw - hoo - taw - hoo

The same pattern can then be repeated starting on A3, and continuing up the scale as high as one desires to go. The process can then be reversed, working from the highest note and slurring downward. Often, as mentioned earlier, the "h" sound can be omitted from the downward slur. This downward exercise is also valuable since it requires many attacks in the high register—an area of Horn-playing which can always stand practice. Also, if one is ambitious, he can make these exercises chromatic instead of diatonic thus almost doubling the benefits.

Training and practice in the use of syllables for both tonguing and slurring can start with the first lesson and continue with profit throughout one's performing career.   FINE

May, 1962

Helpful Hints for Tuba Players

David Kuehn

THE MATERIAL PRESENTED here is intended primarily for the tuba player, but can be applied to performance on other members of the family of low brass instruments. The three basic areas covered are presented without unnecessary technical language. Perhaps other tuba players and teachers will have other methods and techniques, but these have been successful for the writer.

Slurring

It is very important that the young tuba player be taught to slur correctly from the very beginning of his study. When slurring upward the player must be aware of the pitch for which he is aiming and must adjust his embouchure immediately for the new note. For ascending intervals the player should think the syllables *ta-ee* for the two notes. The opposite is true when playing descending intervals, and the player should think *tee-ah* for the two

notes. The player cannot depend upon the diaphragm to do all the work, or he will get a rough slur, and perhaps unconsciously accent the note to which he slurs. Curling of the lower lip for high notes is not recommended for fear that the student will use it as the main focus of his slurring. The tongue should rise as the pitches ascend. To illustrate the effect of the rising tongue the teacher should have the student whistle a low note and then slur to a higher one. The tongue will lift in the same manner as it will when slurring on the instrument. In slurring downward the student must be able to hear the pitch of the lower note before it is played. The back of the tongue and the jaw will drop slightly, but only enough to reach the desired note.

The Pivot System

There are two methods helpful in teaching the pivot system. The

first is to have the student think of raising his forehead slightly as the pitches ascend and to think of lowering it as the pitches descend. Care must be taken that the student does not wrinkle his forehead and that he makes certain that the head is actually moving so that the mouthpiece will rest more on one lip than the other. The second method is to teach the student to tilt the instrument backward gradually as the pitches descend to allow the lower lip to be less firm against the mouthpiece, thus allowing more freedom for the jaw to drop. As the pitches ascend the tilting is forward to achieve the opposite effect. This is more practical in playing the upright tuba than the sousaphone. Since all brass instruments are somewhat awkward it is difficult to have complete flexibility with the pivot system. However, these two approaches to the system will help to improve flexibility.

Tonguing

There are essentially three positions of the tongue: behind the upper teeth (or gum); between the teeth; and behind the lower teeth. If the student is having trouble with placement of the tongue have him tongue where it seems most natural. This natural placement solves many problems because the tongue is not having to fight itself, so to speak. It is free to do what it naturally wants to do. Often it is helpful to suggest positioning the tongue around the gum line of the upper teeth. In rapid tonguing the tongue does not go to the back of the mouth and come all the way to the front to strike the teeth or gum each time a note is attacked. Instead, the tongue moves very little and strikes the teeth or gum softer than when one is tonguing slower, and a smaller area of the front of the tongue touches the teeth. The tongue cannot move fast enough if it has to move a great distance between each attack. Rapid tonguing done by strongly striking the back of the teeth or gum will produce a very choppy, and in most cases, a very uneven flow of notes.

Phrasing

Because a person plays tuba does not mean he is allowed to take a breath after every note or whenever he feels like it. The tuba player must be as conscious of phrasing, attacking, and releasing as any other player. Practicing melodies and etudes will help in overcoming choppy phrasing.

Tuba literature in the form of etudes is very difficult to find. This lack of literature is probably one of the main reasons for the lack of an abundance of good tuba players. For advanced players it is important to find other material. There are several trombone etude books that can be used by the advanced tuba player, and some trombone material useful to the beginner. In order for the material to be used to the fullest advantage, it is necessary to play the exercises down one octave. All phrasing and other markings must be observed in order for the player to develop the musical aspects of his playing.   FINE

The Sound of a Bass Trombone
Reginald Fink

Have you purchased one, two, or more bass clarinets and a contrabass clarinet for your band? Have you considered adding an additional baritone saxophone? Do the cellos and basses of your orchestra become far too indefinite in the low register, especially above a *mezzo forte*? Have all the low clarinets, saxophones and E♭ sousaphones or tubas you have bought failed to properly outline the bass line of your band? Maybe it is the sound of a bass trombone that you have spent hundreds of dollars and several good players trying to imitate.

A 3rd or bass trombone part in most cases is doubled in at least one and probably several other parts, and while the notes are the same the sound is not. In marches the E♭ bass and the 3rd trombone part are often exactly the same. The baritone saxophone and the bass clarinet parts usually closely coincide with the 3rd trombone part. In most current orchestra and band compositions this lower trombone part rarely goes lower than F2, and this note is within the compass of the tenor trombone without an F attachment.

Why, then, should you consider the purchase of a bass trombone or a large bore tenor trombone with an F attachment?

The bass trombone sound will add a "bottom" to the trombone section, bridge the difference in tone quality between the tenor trombones and bass section (brass or string), and will outline, without being obtrusive, the bass line whether it is played by sousaphones, string basses, baritones, or cellos.

Player Carefully Chosen

The player chosen should be one of the better trombonists. By usual tryout and seating procedures he would be seated fairly close to the top of the section. This means that he would be eligible to play the 1st or 2nd part and may not welcome a move to 3rd or "down to the end of the line" without a convincing explanation.

Therefore it will be necessary for you to make arrangements for him to retain his status while playing this lower part. Once this transfer to the lower part has been made and the student has experienced the importance and satisfaction in playing these lower notes with the larger, more mellow bass trombone sound

Therefore it will be necessary for you to make arrangements for him to retain his status while playing this lower part. Once this transfer to the lower part has been made and the student has experienced the importance and satisfaction in playing these lower notes with the larger, more mellow bass trombone sound he often will be reluctant to move back to the top of the section.

The adjustment to the larger mouthpiece, bore and bell, and the accompanying sound is not immediate. The best instruction is, of course, the live example. In communities where the music staff cannot play trombone well enough to demonstrate and there are no local bass trombonists or teachers, recent recordings should be sufficient help. A few dance bands and some commercial arrangers and their orchestras have recently recorded many arrangements where the bass trombone is quite prominent.

Worth the Price

Consider the cost of this sound. In money, up to $400. In talent, one good trombonist. On the other hand, an attempt to imitate it will cost several hundred dollars in clarinets and if they are to be of value to the organization it will cost a few, if not several good clarinetists, which most directors do not have to spare in the first place.

This is not to belittle the bass and contra bass clarinets. They are certainly a necessary part of the instrumentation, but using several in an attempt to reinforce and define the bass line of an ensemble is usually not as successful as using one well-played bass trombone.

FINE

Selected Solo and Ensemble Literature
for the French Horn

Gary Thomason

This alphabetical listing of French horn literature was examined by the writer and selected, studied, analyzed, and classified according to educational purpose and validity. Both American and foreign publications are listed.

It is hardly necessary to say that it is impossible to list all the good music available. Such a task is almost beyond human resources. Consult catalogs of the various publishers for further lists.

The titles are grouped under Grades I through V. While there may be some overlapping, in general these designators represent this gradation:

Grade I - mainly for first year instrumentalists.

Grade II - for those definitely beyond the beginning stages.

Grade III - for those who have acquired some technique.

Grade IV - for advanced instrumentalists.

Grade V - mostly for college or professional players.

A breakdown of the classifications according to school levels would be:

Grades I and II - Elementary School.

Grades II and III - Junior High School.

Grades III and IV - Senior High School.

Grade V - College, Conservatory, and professional performers.

Divisions are made in the following manner: The first two groupings are *Instructional Materials and Methods and Etudes and Orchestral Studies for the French Horn.* They are graded for beginning, intermediate, and advanced students. Group three is composed of solos for the French horn. Group four is made up of homogeneous horn duets. Group five is composed of homogeneous horn trios. Group six is made up of homogeneous horn quartets.

The compositions are listed according to composer and/or arranger, title, publisher, key, and range. They are alphabetized by composer.

Definitions

Composer and/or arranger. The original composer is given first. The second name is that of the arranger. The arranger is anyone who has edited, arranged, scored, or transcribed the composition or parts of it in any way. In the case of songs, the lyricists' name is omitted.

Title. Only the original title is given, as found on the composition.

Publisher. At the end of the listing will be found the publisher's key. If the original copyright has been transferred to another company, the latter name is given. In the case of foreign publications, the American distributor is listed. Where there is no American distributor of a foreign publication, the foreign publisher is listed.

Key. Major keys are indicated with a capital letter, minor keys with a small letter.

Derivation. By this is meant the source, other than original, from which the composition has come. For example: the *Andante Cantabile* from Tchaikovsky's 5th Symphony.

Bass clef notation. When the bass clef is used for the horn the notes are by custom written an octave lower than they sound. Modern composers have tried to correct this illogical notation by writing notes in the bass clef in their proper octave. In this evaluation of horn literature the modern notation for writing notes in the bass clef in their proper octave was observed. All bass-clef notes were considered as they sound, not as they were written. For example, horns in the bass clef were considered sounding a perfect fifth lower than written, just as they do in the treble clef by modern notation. This is noted with the hope that there be no misunderstanding of the ranges indicated in this evaluation.

INSTRUCTIONAL MATERIALS AND METHODS

Composer-Arranger	Title	Publisher
Beginners		
Charlier, B.	Complete Method for French Horn	EV
Devemy, J.	A Modern French Horn Method / 3 Parts and Orchestral studies.	Le
Eidson, A.-Hovey, N.	French Horn Methods / Three Volumes	Be
Franz, O.	Complete Method for the French Horn	Fi
Guerrera, A.	French Horn Method I	Co
Hauser, E.	Foundation to French Horn Playing	Fi
Howe, M.	Method for French Horn	Re
Lambert, A.	Method for Horn	EV
Manus, M.	The Beginners Band Musician	Al
Penable, A.	Grand Method for Valve Horn / With a supplement of orchestra studies.	Ba
Pottag, M.-Hovey, N.	Pottag-Hovey Method for the French Horn, Volume I	Be
Prescott, G.	Outlines of Technic for French Horn	Fi
Schantl, J.	School for the Horn / Three Volumes	Fi
Thevet, L.	Methode Complete de Cor, Vol I.	Le
Intermediate		
Devemy, J.	A Modern French Horn Method / Three Parts and Orchestral Studies.	Le
Eidson, A.-Hovey,	French Horn Methods, / Vol. I, II, III.	Be
Manus, M.	The Intermediate Band Musician	Al
Pottag, M.	French Horn Passages / Solo parts of Symphonic and Standard literature, / Three Volumes.	Be
Schantl, J.	School for the Horn, Vol. I, II, III.	Sc
Thevet, L.	Methode Complete de Cor, Vol. II.	Le
Advanced		
Devemy, J.	A Modern French Horn Method / 3 Parts and orchestral studies.	Le
Eidson, A.-Hovey, N.	French Horn Methods / Three Volumes	Be
Farkas, P.	The Art of French Horn Playing	Su
Guerrera, A	French Horn Method II	Co
Pottag, M.	Daily Exercises for French Horn	Be
Pottag, M.	French Horn Passages / Solo parts of symphonic and standard literature.	Be
Pottag, M.	Trio Album for French Horns	Be
Singer, J.	Embouchure Building for French Horn	Be
Thevet, L.	Methode Complete de Cor, Vol. II.	Le

ETUDES AND ORCHESTRAL STUDIES

Composer-Arranger	Title	Publisher
Beginners		
Alphonse, M.	70 Easy and Very Easy Etudes for Horn	EV
Buchtel, F.	The Young Artists First Book of Solos for French Horn in F	Co
Ceccarossi, D.	Ecole Complete du Cor. / Six Volumes	Le
Getchell, R.	1st and 2nd Book of Practical Studies	Be
Gumbert, W.	Orchestral Studies / Ten Volumes	So
Horner, C.	Primary Studies for French Horn	CB
Kopprasch, C.	Sixty Studies for French Horn	CB
Maxime-Alphonse	70 Easy Etudes	SA
Mueller, B.	12 Etudes for French Horn, Op. 64.	SA
Sansone, L.	A Modern Method for the French Horn	SA
Skornicka, J.	Rubank Elementary Method for French Horn	Ru
Intermediate		
Alphonse, M.	40 Etudes of Medium Difficulty	EV
Bitsch, M.	Douze Etudes	Le
Cugnot, A.	30 Melodic Studies for Valve Horn	So
Ceccarossi, D.	Ecole Complete du Cor / Six Volumes	Le
Gallay-Thevet	28 Etudes, Op. 13 / 29 Preludes, Op. 57	EV
Getchell, R.	First and Second Book of Practical Studies for French Horn / Two Volumes	Be
Gower, W.-Voxman, H.	Rubank Advanced Method for French Horn / Two Volumes	Ru
Howe, M.	Two Dozen Horn Quartets	Mo
Kopprasch, C.	Sixty Studies for French Horn	CB
Maxime-Alphonse	40 Medium-Difficult Etudes	SA
Pease, A.	Universal Fundamental Method	CB
Pottag-Andraud	Three Hundred and Thirty-Five Melodious, Progressive and Technical Studies / Two Volumes	So
Pottag, M.	Sixty French Horn Duets	Be
Pottag, M.	Quartet Album for French Horns	Be
Ranieri, V.	Thirty Instructive and Melodic Exercises	CB
Skornicka, J.-Erdman, R.	Rubank Intermediate Method for French Horn	Ru
Sansone, L.	A Modern Method for the French Horn	SA
Voxman, H.	Selected Duets for French Horn / Two Volumes	Ru
Advanced		
Alphonse, M.	20 Difficult Etudes / 20 Very Difficult Etudes / 10 Grand New Etudes	EV
Bach, J.-Faulx	20 Studies of Virtuosity	So
Bajeux-Bernard-Couillaud, et al.	Traits Difficiles Du Repertiore Du Conservatoire National De Musique De Paris / The most difficult exercises in the repertory of the National Music Conservatory of Paris.	Le
Chaynes, C.	Quinze Etudes	Le
Ceccarossi, D.	Ecole Complete du Cor / Six Volumes	Le

Cosia, S.	The Modern French Horn Player Studies	Bar.
Cugnot, A.	30 Melodic Studies for Valve Horn	So
Devemy, J.	21 Reading Studies and 9 Studies of Examination	So
Fontana, C.	Studies from the Works of Gallay	CB
Gallay	12 Grand Caprices 24 Exercises, Op. 37 12 Grand Etudes Brillantes, Op. 43 Etudes for Second Horn, Op. 43	EV
Gebhardt, W.	Orchestral Studies: Book I, Richard Wagner Book II, L. Van Beethoven Book III, W. A. Mozart Book IV, Richard Wagner Book V, Richard Wagner Orchestra Studies of Richard Strauss	CB
Gower, W.-Voxman, H.	Rubank Advanced Method for French Horn Two Volumes	Ru
Gumbert, W.	Orchestra Studies Ten Volumes	So
Howe, M.	Two Dozen Horn Quartets	Mo
Irons, C.	Horn Exercises and Duets	So
Kopprasch-Franz	50 Etudes	So
Kling, C.	Wagner Orchestral Studies	Br
Maxime-Alphonse	20 Difficult Etudes 20 Very Difficult Etudes 10 Virtuoso Studies	SA
Mueller, B	22 Etudes for French Horn	Be
Pares, G.	Pares Scales for French Horn	Ru
Pottag,-Andraud	Three Hundred and Thirty-Five Melodious, Progressive, and Technical Studies Two Volumes	So
Raphline, E.	Concert Studies for Horn	EM
Schmutzig-Goldstein	Complete Method fur der Waldhorn oder der Ventilhorn (A real side splitter!)	Arthur Goldstein 96 Hemenway Street, Boston, Mass.
Voxman, H.	Selected Duets Two Volumes	Ru
Vuillermoz, E.	Les Classiques Du Cor	Le
Vuillermoz, E.	Dix Pieces Melodiques	Le
Weber, A.	Treize Etudes	Le
White, W.	Unisonal Scales, Chords, and Rhythmic Studies	Fi
Wipperich, W.	Richard Strauss Orchestral Studies	In

SOLOS AND ENSEMBLES

Comp.-Arr.	Title	Pub.	Key	Range
	SOLOS			
Grade I				
Bakaleinikoff, V.	Cavatina	Be	C	D4-D5
Brahe-Woude	Bless This House	Cl	G	C3-F5
Buchtel, F.	Arcadia	Kj	C	C4-B4
Buchtel, F.	My Buddy	Kj	F	C4-C5
Buchtel, F.	Prince Rupert	Kj	C	C4-D5
Buchtel, F.	Solitude	Kj	F	C4-C5
Elgar-Akers	Pomp and Circumstance	Fi	C	C4-F5
Hauser, E.	At the Fair	Fi	F	C4-C5
Hauser, E.	Soldier Song	Fi	G	D4-D5
Hauser, E.	Twilight Thoughts	Fi	C	C4-C5
Hauser, E.	Woodland Memories	Fi	G	Bb3-E5
Kaplan, D.	Serenade	Be	Eb	C4-C5
Lake, M.	On the Bandwagon	Fi	C	E4-D5
Lake, M.	Song at Twilight	Fi	C	D4-C5
Lortzing, A.	Air	Fi	C	C4-D5
Lotzenhiser, G.	Autumn Dream	Be	C	B3-C5
Morra, G.	Romantique	Fi	Eb	B3-E5
Nyquist, M.	Melody for Horn	Be	C	C4-C5
Pelz, W.	Ballad	Be	C	C4-E5
Pelz, W.	Lady in Blue	Be	F	C4-F5
Sousa-Buchtel	Stars and Stripes Forever	Be	F	Bb3-Bb4
Weber, F.	Above the Clouds	Be	F	C4-A4
Weber, F.	The Mighty Major	Be	F	G3-C4
Grade II				
Abbott, F.	Parting	Fi	Bb	C4-F5
Auchert, P.	Lied	LD	C	E3-C4
Bach-Gallo	Canzona	Be	C	E4-F5
Bakaleinikoff	Canzona	Be	C	E3-F4
Ballatore-Sansone	Serenata	GS	F	Bb3-F5
Beethoven-Sansone	Little Rondo	GS	Bb	F3-G5
Benson, W.	Soliloquy	Ma	Eb	A3-F5
Brahms-Hauser	Lullaby	Fi	F	F4-F5
Buchtel, F.	Cielito Lindo	Kj	Bb	Bb3-Eb5
Buchtel, F.	Elegy	Kj	G	D4-E5
Adams-Buchtel	Holy City	Kj	Eb	Bb3-Bb4
Buchtel, F.	Meditation	Kj	D	C4-E5
Mendelssohn-Buchtel	On Wings of Song	Kj	C	G3-B4
Buchtel, F.	Reverie	Kj	Eb	C3-C5
Buchtel, F.	The Hunter	Kj	Eb	Bb3-C5
Buchtel, F.	Valse Romantique	Vo	F	E4-F5
Chambers, A.	Cavatina	Wa	G	D4-E5
Cohen, S.	Pastorale	Be	F	F4-F5
Fibich-Holmes	Poem	Ru	C	C# 4-E5
Flotow-Holmes	Cavatina	Ru	G	D# 4-E5
Fournier, H.	Brown and Gold	Wa	G	E4-E5
Fournier, H.	Melodie Chant Du Matin	Wa	F	C4-F5
Franck, C.	Panis Angelicus	Wi	F	E4-D5
Godard, B.	Berceuse from Jocelyn	CB	G	E4-E5
Grieg-Wilson	I Love Thee	Re	C	D4-Eb5
Grieg, E.	Northern Ballade	Wi	Bb	G4-F5
Harris, F.	A Short Suite	Lu	F	C4-F5
Herbert, V.	Gypsy Love Song	Wi	Eb	C4-E5
Holmes, G.	Home on the Range	Ru	Ab	Eb4-Eb5
Howard, J.	Still Waters	EM	C	B3-E5
Kaplan, D.	Soliloquy	Be	Eb	D4-Eb5
Lake, M.	Valse Lente	Fi	C	C4-D5
Liebe, L.	To Meet Again	Fi	G	G3-C5

Composer	Title	Pub	Key	Range
Liszt-Holmes	Liebestraum	Ru	F	C4-D5
Maganini, Q.	An Ancient Greek	EM	G	G3-Eb5
Martini, P.	Plaisir d'Amour	EM	C	G3-F5
Mascagni-Painter	Siciliana	Re	Eb	E4-E5
Mendelssohn-Holmes	Andante	Ru	F	C4-F5
Meyerbeer, G.	Veni Creator	EM	F	C4-D5
Nevin-Woude	The Rosary	Cl	F	D4-Eb5
Nyquist, M.	Golden Summer	Be	G	D4-D5
Nyquist, M.	Mazurka in A Minor	Be	e	E4-E5
Ostrander, A.	Concert Album for Horn and Piano	EM	C, F, Bb, D	F3-A5
Pergolesi-Vuillermoz	Sicilienne	Le	G	C4-E5
Poot, M.	Arabande	Le	C	B3-E5
Ranger, A.	The Old Refrain	Fi	F	C4-A5
Saint-Saëns, C.	My Heart at Thy Sweet Voice	CB	C	A3-F5
Scheurer, R.	Elegie	Be	Eb	Eb4-Db5
Schubert-Eger	Die liebe Farbe	AM	A	C#4-C#5
Schumann, R.	Abendlied	CB	Eb	Eb4-Eb5
Schumann-Klemoke	Abendlied	Fi	F	G3-F5
Schumann, R.	Traumerei	CB	Bb	F4-Eb5
Scriabin, A.	Romance	Ld	C	B3-E5
Taubert, W.	Cradle Song	Fi	C	C4-E5
Tomasi, H.	Chant Corse	Le	C	C3-F5
Tchaikovsky, P.	Chanson Triste	SA	F	G3-F5
Tchaikovsky-Weber	March Slav	Be	Bb	Bb3-D5
VanderCook, A.	Lyra	Ru	C	C4-D5
Walters, H.	Christmas Vespers	Ru	Bb	A3-Bb5
Weber-Holmes	Adagio	Ru	Eb	Eb4-Eb5
Warren, D.	Meditation	Lu	F	Eb4-F5

Grade III

Composer	Title	Pub	Key	Range
Abinenko, F.	Melody	Le	C	G#3-A5
Andersen, A.	Nocturne	Fi	C	C4-G5
Bach	Spring's Awakening	CB	C	C4-G5
Balfe-Holmes	Bohemian Girl	Ru	Bb	B3-D5
Beethoven, L.	Adelaide	CB	G	C4-F5
Beethoven, L.	Menuet	EM	Bb	G3-Bb5
Berg-Sansone	The Shepherd	SA	Bb	D4-A5
Brehm-Leidzen	Horns A-Hunting	PI	C	E4-A5
Chopin, F.	Cavatina	Kj	C	B3-E5
Corelli, A.	Gigue	EM	F	F3-F5
Cohen, S.	Legend of the Hills	Be	Bb	Bb3-F5
Cox, P.	Lullaby	SP	C	Eb3-G5
Cleriose, R.	Chant Sans Paroles	Le	C	B3-E5
Cleriose, R.	L'Absent	Le	Bb	Bb3-D5
Damase, J.	Berceuse	Le	C	E3-D5
De Lamarter, E.	Ballade	Wi	G	C4-G5
Douane, J.	En foret d'Oleonne	Le	C	B3-F#5
Endresen, R.	The Victor	Ru	F	Bb3-E5
Faure, J.	The Palms	CB	F	E4-A5
Francaix, J.	Canon in Octave	In	C	C4-F#5
Frangkiser, C.	Melodie Importune	BH	F	C4-F5
Gabaye, P.	Serenade De Printemps	Le	C	C4-A5
Garfield, B.	Soliloquy	EM	C	E4-F#5
Godard-Hauser	Berceuse from Jocelyn	Fi	G	C4-E5
Godard-Buchtel	Berceuse from Jocelyn	Kj	G	C4-E5
Goltermann, G.	Andante	CB	B	B3-F#5
Gottwald-Sansone	Friendship	SA	F	F3-F5
Gounod, C.	Ave Maria	CB	C	C4-G5
Gounod-Hauser	Ave Maria	Fi	D	D4-F#5
Gounod, C.	Dio Possente	CB	Bb	G3-D4
Gounod-Holmes	Sing, Smile, Slumber	Ru	Eb	Bb3-F5
Gliere, R.	Intermezzo	Le	C	F3-G5
Gluck, C.	Air	EM	C	B3-G5
Gluck, C.	O del mio dolce Ardor	HE	Bb	A3-E5
Grieg, E.	Northern Ballade	Wi	Bb	G4-F5
Harris, F.	Vesper Moods	Lu	F	E4-F5
Harvey, W.	Menuetto	Wa	D	A3-G5
Hondy, P.	Lamento	Le	C	G3-Ab5
Hubay-Buchtel	Traumerei	Kj	F	B3-F5
Haugland, A.	Suite of Two Pieces	Be	F	D4-G5
Ilyinsky-Buchtel	Lullaby	Kj	C	A3-E5
Ketelbey-MacLean	In A Monastery Garden	Ha	F	C4-F5
Klein, J.	A French Waltz	EV	D	A3-Eb5
Lamarter, E.	Poem	Wi	C	F3-A5
Levermann, W.	Serenade Espagnole	SA	Eb	Bb3-G5
Maganini, Q.	Peaceful Land	EM	D	A3-G5
Mascagni, P.	Siciliana	Fi	Eb	Eb4-Eb5
Massenet-Wilson	Elegy	Re	Eb	G3 Db5
Mason, J.	Tenuto	Co	G	Ab3-G5
McKay, G	Three Pastoral Scenes	Sc	E	B3-F#5
Mendelssohn-Vuillermoz	Romance Sans Paroles	Le	F	C4-F#5
Mendelssohn-Vuillermoz	Romance Sans Paroles	Le	A	C#4-F#5
Mendelssohn-Vuillermoz	Romance Sans Paroles	Le	F	C4-F5
Mendelssohn-Vuillermoz	Romance Sans Paroles	Le	D	C4-D5
Mendelssohn-Hauser	Nocturno	Fi	Bb	G3-G5
Montbrun, R.	Ballade	Le	C	G3-G5
Mozart, W.	Andante	Be	F	C4-F5
Mozart, W.	Aria	CB	C	C#4-F5
Mozart, W.-O'Neil	Aria	Wa	Bb	C4-Eb5
Orr, R.	Serenade	SC	Bb	C3-F#5
Pergolesi, G.	Se tu m' Ami	HE	F	G3-D5
Pergolesi-Maganini	Sicilian Air	EM	E	D3-C5
Piantori, L.	Air De Chasse	Le	C	G3-F5
Poot, M.	Legende	Le	C	G3-G5
Pottag, M.	In the Country	Fi	Bb	D4-G5
Pugno, R.	Solo	Le	C	E4-G5
Read, G.	Poem	Fi	C	Eb4-Ab5
Reissiger, K.	Riccordanza	Fi	Bb	E4-F5
Rimsky-Korsakoff, N.	Song of the East	EM	C	D4-D5
Rousseau, M.	Romance	Le	C	G3-G5
Rubinstein-Cheyette	Romance	Fo	Bb	B3-A5
Saint-Saëns—Smim	Romance	EM	C	E4-F5
Saint-Saëns, C.	Romance	In	C	E4-F#5
Schaefer, A.	Spring in the Forest	Fi	C	C3-F5
Scriabin-Singer	Romance	Le	C	B3-E5
Schubert-Vuillermoz	Ave Maria	Le	Bb	Bb3-F5
Schubert-Vuillermoz	Serenade	Le	F	D4-F5

Schumann-Vuillermoz	Chant Du Soir	Le	G	A3-A5
Schumann, R.	Traumerei	Fi	C	G3-F5
Schumann-Painter	The Horseman	GH	C	B3-E5
Schumann, R.	The Voice of Love	Fi	C	A3-F#5
Schweden, K.	Dream of the Rose	Fi	F	C3-F5
Sitt, H.	Reverie	Bs	G	A3-B5
Stravinsky, I.	Berceuse from the Firebird	EM	D	B3-E5
Sylvius, C.	Romanza	Bar	F	A3-F5
Tenaglia-Maganini	Aria Antica	EM	Eb	C4-G5
Titl-Roberts	Serenade	Fi	C	C4-E5.
Tchaikovsky-Holmes	Andante	Ru	F	F3-D5
Tchaikovsky-Seredy	Andante Cantabile	Fi	A	A3-F#5
VanderCook, A.	Vega	Ru	F	C4-D5
Vidal, P.	Piece De Concert	BC	Db	F3-Bb5
Villa, H.	Song of the Black Swan	Ma	C	E3-G5
Vuillermoz, E.	Les Classiques Dur Cor	Le	G	D4-G5
Waldsee, J.	Romance	Bs	C	B3-G5
Wagner-Holmes	Introduction to Third Act of Lohengrin	Ru	Eb	Bb3-G5
Wagner, R.	Walther's Prize Song	Fi	G	B3-E5
Weber, A.	Improvisation	Le	C	Bb3-Eb5
Whear, P.	Pastorale Lament	Ip	C	E4-A5
Wiedemann-Pottag	Nocturno	Be	G	C4-G5
Wittmann, R.	Barcarole	Fi	C	G3-G5

Grade IV and V solos are listed in the complete compilation Selected Solo and Ensemble Literature for the French Horn by Gary Thomason, available from The Instrumentalist Company, 1418 Lake Street, Evanston, Illinois.

DUETS

Grade I

Buchtel, F.	Waltz "Iris"	Kj	Bb	G3-Bb5
Sarada, L.	Mists of Morning	Wa	C	B3-E5
Tallmadge, I.	56 Progressive Duets	Be	G-C-Ab	G3-G5
Voxman, H.	Selected Duets	Ru	G-C-Bb	C3-C6
Williams, C.	24 Duo-Studies	Sw	B-C-Eb	E3-Bb5

Grade II

Buchtel, F.	Mexican Clapping Song	Kj	Bb	G#3-Bb4
Brahms-Buchtel	Slumber Song	Kj	Eb	G3-C5
Buchtel, F.	The Hunter	Kj	Eb	G3-C5
Buchtel, F.	Two Friends	Kj	C	B3-C4
Buchtel, F.	Two Tooters	Kj	D	A3-Bb4
Harris, F.	A Short Suite	Lu	F	C4-F5
Henning-Sansone	59 Duets for Two French Horns	SA	G-C-Bb	C3-G5
Sarada, L.	Winsome Frolic	Wa	G	A3-D5
Voxman, H.	Selected Duets	Ru	A-C-Bb	C3-C6
Cobb, S.	Sonatina for Two Horns	Fi	G	G3-G5
Cobb, S.	Sonatina for Two Horns	Fi	G	D4-G5
Francois, C.	Six Duets for Two Horns	In	C-F-Bb-G	Bb3-G5
Franz-Sansone	100 Duets for French Horn	SA	C-F-Bb-G	C3-C6
Harris, F.	A Short Suite	Lu	F	A3-F5
Harris, F.	Vesper Moods	Lu	F	C4-F5
Kreisler, F.	Rondino on a Theme of Beethoven	Fo	Bb	A3-G5

Lassus-Maganini	Two Motets	EM	C	G3-F#5.
Rimsky-Korsakov	Two Duets	MR	C	C3-G5

TRIOS

Grade I

Bach-Whistler-Hummel	The Light of all Our Seeing	Ru	G	G3-C6
Massie-Whistler-Hummel	One and All Rejoice	Ru	D	G#3-D5
Verdi-Whistler-Hummel	Operatic Air	Ru	D	A3-B5
Whistler-Hummel	Blow the Man Down	Ru	D	B3-B4

Grade II

Flemming-Whistler-Hummel	Integer Vitae	Ru	D	B3-D5
Sullivan-Whistler-Hummel	Wand'ring One	Ru	C	C4-D5
Whistler-Hummel	God Rest You Merry, Gentlemen	Ru	D	B3-B4
Weber-Whistler-Hummel	Concert Waltz	Ru	C	B3-C5
Work-Whistler-Hummel	Grandfather's Clock	Ru	C	A3-D5

Grade III

Brehm-Leidzen	Horns A-Hunting	Pl	C	G3-A5
Cowell, H.	Hymn and Fuguing Tune No. 12	AM	C	B3-A5
Foster-Whistler-Hummel	Plantation Favorites	Ru	C	A3-D5
Gabrieli-Clark	Seincento	EM	C	G4-A5
Kling, H.	30 Selected Pieces	AM	D-C-Bb	C3-A5
Lehar-Whistler-Hummel	Vilia Song	Ru	C	A3-C5
Mendelssohn-Whistler-Hummel	On Wings of Song	Ru	D	A3-D5
Pottag, M.	Pottag Trio Album	Be	C-Eb	C3-Bb5
Reicha, A.	Six Trios	In	C-Bb	G3-G5
Reicha-Sansone	Six Trios	SA	C-Eb	C3-A5
Schubert-Whistler-Hummel	The Parting Hour	Ru	C	C4-D5
VanderCook	Whip-Poor-Wills	Ru		Bb3-G5
Whistler-Hummel	The Miller of the Dee	Ru	G	D4-D5
Whistler-Hummel	Viennese Melody	Ru	C	Bb3-C5

QUARTETS

Grade II

McKay, G.	Fiesta Mexicana	Fi	F	A3-G5
Lorenz-Pottag	Adagio Religioso	Be	Eb	Eb4-G5
Weber-Pottag	Hunting Chorus	Be	G	D4-F#5
Vecchi-Maganini	The Cricket	EM	Bb	B3-G5

Grade III

Bach-Treat	Fugue	Wi	Bb	F3-G5
Bennett, D.	The Four Hornsmen	Fi	Bb	F4-G5
Bizet-Zamecnik	Agnus Dei	SF	Eb	F4-G5
Clark, F.	St. Hubert's Hunting Song	EM	G	C4-G5
Cofield, F.	Winter Sunset	Ru	Bb	Bb3-Eb5
Frangkiser, C.	Gage D'Amour	Be	G	G3-G5
Godard-Holmes	Adagio Pathetique	Ba	Bb	Bb3-Eb5
Graham, W.	Minaret	Po	C	B3-F5
Harris, F.	Vesper Moods	Lu	F	F4-F5
Koepke, P.	Introduction and Scherzo	Ru	Eb	F4-G5
Lorenz, L.	Cantabile-Donzona	Po	G	G4-G5
Johnson, W.	Nocturne	Fi	F	F4-G5
McKay, G.	American Panorama	Fi	F	G4-A5

McKay, F.	Marche	Fi	C	G# 4-E5
McKay, F.	Moderato E Cantabile	Fi	C	F4-A5
McKay, F.	Nocturne	Fi	C	E4-F5
McKay, F.	Prelude No. 1	Fi	C	G4-G5
Mendelssohn-Zamecnik	Nocturno	SF	Bb	F4-F5
Ostransky, L.	Aeolian Suite	Ru	C	G4-F5

Ostransky, L.	Velvet and Tweed	Ru	Bb	G4-G5
Scarmolin, A.	Lento	Fi	C	C4-G5
Tcherepnin, N.	Six Pieces for Four Horns	EM	C	C4-A5
Wagner, R.	Pilgrims Chorus	CB	C	C4-E5
Wagner-Zamecnik	Pilgrims Chorus	SF	Eb	F4-F5
Weber-Pottag	Hunting Chorus	Be	G	D4-F# 5

Publisher

Key	Publisher						
Al	Alfred Music Co.	BV	Bergman-Vocco & Conn	Ha	Harms, Inc.	Re	Remick Music Corp.
AM	Associated Pusic Pub.	CB	Cundy-Bettoney, Inc.	HE	Henri Elkan Music Pub.	Ri	G. Ricordi & Co.
An	Andraud, A. J.	CF	Carl Fisher, Inc	He	Heugel Co.	RK	Robert King Music Co.
Ba	C. L. Barnhouse Co.	CI	Classic Pub. Co.	In	International Music Co.	Ru	Rubank, Inc.
Bar	Baron Co., M.	Co	Composers Press	Ip	Interlochen Press	SA	Sansone Music Co.
BA	Band Associates, Inc.	Eb	Educational Music Bureau	Ki	Karl King Music House	Sc	Schmitt, Hall & McCreary.
BC	Buffet Crampon, et., Cie.	EM	Edition Musicus, Inc.	Kj	Neil Kjos Music Co.	SC	B. Schott & Sons
Be	Belwin, Inc.	Em	Educational Music Ser.	LD	Alphonse Leduc	Sf	Staff Music Co.
Bh	Breitkopf & Hartel	Ev	Evette & Schaefer	Le	Leeds Music Corp.	Sc	Southern Music Co.
BH	Boosey & Hawkes, Inc.	EV	Elkan-Vogel Co.	Lu	Ludwig Music Pub. Co.	SP	Jack Spratt Music Co.
Bn	Besson & Co.	Fi	Fillmore Music House	Ma	Edward Marks Music Co.	SU	Summy-Birchard Pub. Co.
Bo	Bourne, Inc.	Fo	Sam Fox Pub. Co	Mi	Mills Music, Inc.	SW	H. Swain Music House
Br	George F. Briegel, Inc.	Fs	H. T. FitzSimons Co.	MO	Edwin H. Morris & Co.	Vo	Volkwein Brothers, Inc.
Bs	Bosworth & Co.	GH	Gamble Hinged Music Co.	PI	Pleasant Music Co., Inc.	Wa	Waterloo Music Co.
		GS	G. Schirmer Co.	Po	Pro Art Music Co.	Wi	M. Witmark & Sons

September, 1962

Extended Trumpet Range

R. Dale Olson

THE RANGE OF THE MODERN B♭ trumpet varies from two-and-a-half octaves to approximately five octaves, depending on the ability of the individual performer. Due to the fact that the lower limit of the trumpet is somewhat standardized, the general trend has been to extend the upper register to indefinite heights. Considering the relatively few pedagogical writings which provide instruction for this extreme register, trumpet students of today are faced with the problem of seeking alternate methods of developing this aspect of performance. Although the existence of various methods which include notes in the vicinity of the eleventh harmonic is acknowledged, the lack of reliable instructional material concerning the development of this range is the fact which is stressed. Of considerable consterna-

tion also, is the lack of competent teachers who offer scientific courses of study with regard to these extended ranges.

Scholars of the trumpet will hasten to remind us of the many historical instances which indicate that range is not a new problem for the trumpeter.

The potential of the trumpet as an instrument possessing a wide range of frequencies was noted by Mersenne in 1636: "As to the compass of the trumpet, it is marvelously great if one takes all its tones from the gravest to the highest, for it supplies a thirty-second, so that it surpasses all the keyboards of spinets and of organs, it is sufficient to give it the compass of a twenty-ninth, that is to say of the four octaves which form the compass of keyboards."[1]

An eminent performer of the era, Girolamo Fantini, took a somewhat more practical view of the extreme limits suggested by Mersenne when he suggested C6 as the upper limit of the trumpet.

Over one hundred years later, Altenburg wrote: "We understand by Clarin, . . . a certain melody played mostly in the octave from treble C to C in alto . . . to sound high and clearly. The right embouchure for the production of this sound is uncommonly difficult to acquire and is not to be defined by fixed rules. Practice must here do the best it can, although a great deal depends on the formation of the lips, etc."[2]

Menke recalls an anonymous trumpeter of approximately the same era who possessed range capabilities of an octave higher: "Johann Walther

321

tells us of a member of the Erfurt Council Band, whom he had gotten to know, was able to warble on the trumpet up to C in altissimo and beyond . . ."[3]

Despite the antiquity of range as a problem for the trumpets, the style of performance and frequency of usage of the high register has definitely changed in recent years. The stage of evolution which these two factors have reached presently presents an almost insurmountable hardship to many instructors who are forced to direct students interests toward other aspects of trumpet performance due to their own lack of knowledge concerning the successful teaching of high register development. While it is not the contention of this writer that range, as such, is the most important aspect of trumpet playing, it is emphasized that brass instructors should consider the requirements of potential professional musicians presently under their tutelage in an effort to develop specific pedagogical methods which would properly prepare these ambitious students.

Reliable information concerning range development is nearly nonexistent in written form. This void is largely the fault of the few instructors who, despite the fact that they alone are in a position to add to the general store of knowledge in this area, fail to perpetuate the development of their specialty.

The fear of being misunderstood, lack of time and/or writing ability, and, in some cases, secrecy are the reasons usually given by the experts in this field for not writing articles, books, or papers. It must be remembered that, although a theory may not be properly presented by one authority, it may, nevertheless, form the basis upon which a more talented writer-pedagogue may eventually formulate a writing which is worthwhile. Unless the few theories and methods of range development which presently exist are preserved in writing, no foundation can be laid upon which to base future work by other teachers.

Writing Needed

The few teachers who have concentrated their practice on the areas presently under consideration are invariably located in the major professional music locations of the United States. This situation precludes the possibility of study by students in other geographical locations and accentuates the need for more written material by these instructors.

Considering the lack of proper instruction and training with regard to high register performance, many young or immature performers are often unduly impressed by professional trumpeters who utilize the extreme registers of the instrument without proper regard for retaining the basic trumpet tone. Students unfortunately look to such players as the exemplification of correct upper register technique. With many "high note" artists, the basic trumpet sound degenerates into a piercing "whistle" in the extreme upper register and thereby becomes representative of an entirely different approach to trumpet performance rather than a simple extension of the basic range.

Various musical styles occasionally dictate the range requirements imposed on the professional trumpeter. The unmusical "whistling" tone referred to above has become idiomatic in many modern dance and recording orchestras. Since many modern fields of performance demand proficiency in the extreme upper register, some players subject themselves to concentration on this register at the sacrifice of all other aspects of trumpet techniques.

The performance of the extreme high register, demanded by various professional situations, is often injurious to the trumpeter who forces the development of the high register merely to retain a particular position. A parallel may be drawn by using the example of the junior or senior high school student, active in school musical organizations, who is expected to perform in registers beyond his level of development simply in an effort to retain "first chair," etc.

Without digressing into a résumé of embouchure theory, it will be mentioned that the development of this type of performance is possible if the player is not adverse to subjecting his embouchure to abuse by employing the aforementioned "short-cuts" to range.

Ironically, alternate methods, or "short-cuts" require as much practice time to fully develop as correct methods. By employing a slower, more methodical approach, it is entirely possible to develop this same high range without sacrificing flexibility and tonal quality.

The first logical aid (or short-cut) to increased high register is a change to a smaller mouthpiece. Often the mouthpiece chosen has as its characteristics, (a) a wide rim to prevent cutting into the lip when using excessive embouchure-mouthpiece pressure, (b) a shallow cup which facilitates the emission of the upper partials, and (c) a pronounced "bite" to afford accuracy of attacks.

The physical dangers inherent in the utilization of such a mouthpiece are well known. Musically, however, the tonal quality of the middle and lower register is adversely affected by the shallow cup. Flexibility is undermined by the wide rim, and physical embouchure damage is often incurred by the sharp "bite" or inner-rim of the mouthpiece. Rather than being encouraged to take necessary time to develop the proper physical apparatus which gives the high register, the student, and many times the professional player, resort to "strong-arm" methods and excessive embouchure-mouthpiece pressure.

Basically, four reasons exist for the employment of these various "short-cuts" to high register development: (1) A near total absence of qualified instructors on the subject. (2) Lack of available information concerning proper development of range. (3) Impatience on the part of the students. (4) Professional requirements and demands.

The writer personally has known several performers who have developed the extreme registers of the instrument without the aid of an instructor. In nearly all cases, however, the gaining of this particular phase of playing has resulted in ignoring many others. Of the many who have attempted the self-teaching of range, comparatively few have succeeded.

Range Important

Consultation with numerous professional trumpeters active in all musical idioms has brought out the undeniable fact that range today is more important than ever before in recent years. Composers, who have become aware of the extraordinary range of a few isolated players, are prompted to write new music which includes the extreme high register in an effort to obtain new tonal colors and musical excitement. The performance of these compositions is then attempted by other musicians who possibly do not possess the extraordinary range of the aforementioned artist. As previously discussed, the change of mouthpiece, as well as the employment of "strong-arm" trumpet performance, is too often the answer to the situation.

The fact that such occurrences exist in many school bands is disturbing. The over-stressing of range and the complications incurred in attempting to adjust to these newly-found notes will very possibly lead to an underdevelopment of musicianship and a rather distorted conception of logical, musically-acceptable trumpet technique.

Improper Methods

The answer to this situation is not simply to ignore the range problem with the belief that it will someday revert back to the conception of C being the uppermost limit of the trumpet. The answer lies in counteracting improper methods, devised by impatient students, with pedagogical processes developed by competent instructors. Considering the degree of specialization so obvious in the medical and other professions, it is definitely not premature to consider the possibility of specialized trumpet or brass instructors who restrict their private teaching to the practice of developing range, power, endurance, tone, and flexibility. It is entirely feasible that such a specialist could function in accord with a "general practitioner" who is capable of instructing theory, literature, interpretation, etc., but who

has not seen fit to specialize in the development of any one specific aspect of performance.

The evolution of an era of specialization could be built upon the proven theories of range development, as offered by the precious few experts in the field. These theories or methods must, however, be analytically explored and presented in a logical presentation which may ultimately contribute to the advancement of trumpet performance.

1. Pere Mersene, "Harmonie universelle, Traite des instruments," 1636.
   Girolamo Fantini, "Modoper imparai a sonare di tomba," 1638.

2. Johann Ernest Altenburg, "Attempt at an Introduction to the herois—musical Art of the Trumpeter and Kettle-Drummer," Halle, 1795.

3. Werner Menke, "History of the Trumpet of Bach and Handel," London, 1934.

FINE

October, 1962

The question is—

Horn in F or B-flat?

Elmer P. Magnell

A FEW YEARS AGO *The Instrumentalist* published a series of articles extolling the merits of both the F and B♭ horns for use in school bands. It was a most interesting controversy, with professional musicians generally favoring the F horn, many music educators the B♭ horn.

Advantages of Certain Horns

Most hornists agree that the tone quality of the F horn is superior to that of the B♭, especially in the written register from C4 (middle C) up an octave. The competent performer on the B♭ horn, with an adequate conception of the F horn tone quality, can closely approximate this sound. With reference to tone quality it makes little difference which horn is used in the register above C5.

Most performers will admit that the B♭ horn responds with greater accuracy than the F. Since a high

register of the harmonic series of overtones is used when playing F horn music on the F horn, there is naturally a great chance for error, due to the close proximity of the tones.

An interesting experiment is to ask a mediocre performer to play written A4 fortissimo on his F instrument. Unless he has an excellent sense of pitch he may sound G, A, or B, and any of these tones may be played in tune.

Using the B♭ horn, and fingering the same note 1 and 2 (not open), accuracy is increased many times. With this fingering the next possible

tone above written A is C and the closest below is F♯. In the upper register of the F horn problems are further complicated by intervals being still closer.

The B♭ horn, as played by most students, tends to sound more resonant, approaching a baritone quality, especially in the low register. Horn teachers striving for a characteristic French horn quality are disturbed by this phenomenon and strive to brighten the sound produced by these students. However, with the anemic tone quality one generally hears in a horn ensemble where F horns are the more popular, the additional resonance of the B♭ horns would be welcomed, even at a slight sacrifice in quality.

Horn Preference

This writer's first preference would be to use all double horns

(F and Bb): F for quality; Bb for accuracy; Bb especially for high and some low register notes; and a combination of the two horns for better intonation in adjusting to questionable tones (found on any horn). Many technical passages become easier by utilizing both horns. A double horn has no advantage, of course, if only one portion of the horn is used.

The second choice would be: a double horn for the first chair player, since he is to provide the ideal sound for the others to emulate; the second, third, and fourth chair performers playing Bb horns for increased accuracy, confidence, and resonance. Most amateur organizations would find their horn sections playing with a better balance of tone throughout, and with greater technical accuracy, using Bb horns in the second, third, and fourth parts.

One will not find the tone quality appreciably impaired providing the first chair player is a competent musician. This writer will concede that the ultimate in tone quality and resonance (at least theoretically) is achieved with a section of F horns, but amateurs cannot attain this. With limited time and talent at one's disposal for adequate instruction, fine results should be had sooner if Bb horns are used with F music.

FINE

Important but Often Neglected —

The Low Register of the French Horn

Cutler Silliman

THE LOW REGISTER of the French horn is an important aspect of horn playing often neglected in the instruction of younger players. This is particularly true with regard to the lower half of the octave C3 to C4 (middle C). (All pitches in this article are given in F notation.) For professionals, of course, this is merely the lower part of the middle range. Below this point, students are usually able to reach the notes thru the use of an exaggerated or false embouchure.

For the good high school player, a comfortable range would probably be G3 to G5. The purpose of this article is to point out the importance of extending this "comfortable" or average range downward, to indicate why it is a problem, and to make some suggestions for developing it.

It has always been a basic tenet of brass instruction that the way to develop a high register is to practice in the low. The lower register of a brass instrument is the foundation of a good tone and an extended range. This is probably more pertinent to the French horn than to the other brasses by virtue of the horn's greater range. A beginner on the French horn starts relatively higher on his instrument than do beginners on the other brasses, making it essential that he be given special instruction and help in extending his range downward.

The basic reason for the importance of the lower register, particularly the octave C3 to C4, is that it can be played well only with a good breath support and a relaxed, but firm embouchure. These two factors must be achieved before a satisfactory facility over the entire range of the horn can be attained, and the best way to achieve them is to work in this particular area.

Ease of Playing

The "relaxed but firm" embouchure means that the lips are slightly puckered with the corners held in and down, but with a rounded opening. There must be some tension in order to produce the proper vibrations, but the total effort must be aimed at ease of playing. It should be felt that the cheek muscles are supporting the lips and not pulling them into a thin line over the teeth.

As has already been pointed out, the extreme low notes can be produced with an exaggerated or false embouchure; the upper range can be produced with a tight embouchure and excess pressure. None of these practices is good, and none of them will work in this particular range of the horn. Working primarily in the upper register it is possible to develop a proper embouchure and support, but there is a much better chance of superior development of these thru work in the octave below middle C. Once the proper breath support and embouchure have been developed, it is relatively easy to extend the range upward without undue tightening and pressure, and downward without exaggerating the embouchure, and without sacrificing a full, rich tone.

Changing the embouchure for the extreme low notes is usually to an exaggerated "setting-in" embouchure or to an off-center mouthpiece place-

324

ment. It is not recommended for student players at all. It is an expedient to which a player should resort only when absolutely necessary, and it should not become a regular practice until the player has exhausted all possibility of extending his range thru these notes with his regular embouchure. Young players are impatient, and do not want to go thru the months, and even years of tedious practice usually necessary to produce the complete range without any drastic changes of the embouchure; these are the players who need most to be cautioned against seeking a short-cut such as that just described.

Not Enough Players

Many young players also are pushed too fast in their development in the high register. Most instruction books give too little attention to the lower range. One reason that players do not have sufficient experience on the lower register is that most schools do not have enough horn players, so that a student does not work his way up to the higher parts in a section gradually, as is the usual case with other brass instruments. Too frequently, a talented player is asked to play the top horn part early in his high school career instead of playing second, third, and fourth parts and allowing his embouchure to develop more

naturally. Another factor is that even these "lower" parts in many school band and orchestra arrangements do not use the true low register in a satisfactory manner.

The lower register is a particular problem for students who transfer to the horn from trumpet. These players are accustomed to vibrating their lips for higher pitches than they use on the horn, and they need special practice and exercises in the lower range of the instrument.

In order to provide adequate practice material in the lower register, it will usually be necessary for the instructor to write out special exercises to supplement the instruction books. Models for this type of exercise can be found on the last page of the Pottag-Hovey *French Horn Method, Book One* (Belwin), pages 60-61 of Philip Farkas' *The Art of French Horn Playing* (Clayton F. Summy, Co.), and in Marvin Howe's *Method for French Horn* (Remick). Howe introduces the bass clef on page 25 of his book and thereafter has frequent exercises for the lower register.

Practice Attacks

Clear attacks are especially difficult to produce in the lower register. Several exercises will help, such as playing repeated notes in scale and chord figures, and slurring down to a note and then repeating it with a firm attack. Long tones and arpeggio

studies will help to build breath support and a good tone.

Orchestral horn players currently meet two practices in the use of bass clef—the "old" notation in which middle C is on the second space, and "modern" notation in which it is on the first leger line above the staff in accord with piano notation and the practice of all other instruments. Both practices are used by contemporary composers and publishers so that it has become necessary to indicate on the part which notation is being used. As recent a book as Gunther Schuller's *Horn Technique* (Oxford University Press, 1962), page 78, advocates the use of the old notation. The Howe method mentioned earlier uses modern notation, which seems to this writer to be the most logical choice.

In summary, it can be said that the octave below middle C is almost the most important part of a horn player's range for proper development of embouchure and breath support. It is also the most neglected part of a student's range, because it is so often thin and weak. It is important because a player must develop control of breath and embouchure in order to correct these deficiencies. Once they have been developed properly they can easily be applied to the remainder of the horn range, making a free, full, and easy tone possible throughout the horn's compass.

FINE

A Selected List of TUBA LITERATURE

David Kuehn

MANY FINE TUBA ARTISTS are encouraging students to approach their study of the instrument as would a violinist or vocalist, using the best quality music available.

Following is a selected list of tuba literature. By including many of the recently published contemporary works for the instrument, the list

contains literature comparable to the type of music available for other brass instruments. The list contains original tuba literature and several adapted vocal works, but does not include any of the trombone, horn, etc. music which has been transcribed for the instrument.

Certain French literature included

requires transposition down an octave for use on the standard BB♭ tubas (recording basses, sousaphones, etc.) in use. The solos listed have been considered and graded on the basis of both their technical and musical requirements. While admittedly not complete, this list presents a nucleus of material for the interested teacher and student.

Composer	Title	Pub.

Grade I

Composer	Title	Pub.
Adams-Buchtel	Holy City	Kjos
Bonheur-Walters	The Lancer	Ru
Grieg-Holmes	In the Hall of the Mountain King	Ru
Mattei-Walters	The Mariner	Ru
Petrie-Walters	Asleep in the Deep	Ru

Grade II

Composer	Title	Pub.
Clarke-Lillya-Isaac	Trumpet Voluntary (Purcell)	CF
Clerisse	Idylle	SMC
Handel-Ostrander	Arm, Arm, Ye Brave	Ed.M
Martin	Aeola	CF
Vandercook	Behemoth	Ru
Vandercook	Colossus	Ru
Verdi-Ostrander	Aria from "Don Carlos"	Ed.M

Grade III

Composer	Title	Pub.
Adam, A.	Aria from "Giralda"	BH
Bach-Bell	Air and Bouree	CF
Barat	Introduction and Serenade	SMC
Beaucamp	Cortége	SMC
Bennett	Voice of the Viking	CF
Briegel	Basso Profundo	GFB
Clerisse	Romance	SMC
Cohen	Romance and Scherzo	Bel.
Desmond	The Sea Gong	Bel.
Geib	Cavatina, Op. 6	Mills
Geib	Nocturne, Op. 7	Mills
Geib	Song Without Words	CF
Geib-Forst	Serenade	Mills
Handel-Harvey	Honor and Arms from "Sampson"	GS
Huber	Theme from Concertino #4	CF
Kesnar	Prelude	CB
Painpare-Voxman	Concert Piece	Ru
Petit	Grave	SMC
Stradella-Felix	Pieta, Signore!	Ed.M
Vaughan	Concertpiece No. 1	IP

Grade IV

Composer	Title	Pub.
Baseler	Happy Thought	CF
Beethoven-Bell	Variations on a Theme of Judas Maccabeus	CF
Bozza	Allegro et Finale	SMC
Bozza	Prelude et Allegro	SMC
Castellucci	Intermezzo Capriccioso	Mills
Catozzi-Seredy	Beelzebub	CF
Del Negro	Polka Graziosa	GFB
deVille (arr.)	Happy be Thy Dreams	CF
deVille (arr.)	Atlas	CF
Dowling	His Majesty the Tuba	Bel.
Gabaye	Tubabillage	SMC
Geib	In the Deep Forest	GFB
Guy (arr.)	Carry Me Back to Old Virginny	Ru
Harris	Tempesta	CF
Hartley	Suite for Unaccompanied Tuba	E-V
Hartley	Sonatina	IP
Holmes (arr.)	Emmett's Lullaby	Ru
Hume	"Te Anau" Fantasia	BH
Lebedev-Ostrander	Concerto in One Movement	Ed.M
Mozart	Iris and Osiris from "Magic Flute"	Col
Muller-Ostrander	Praeludium, Chorale, Variations and Fugue	Ed.M
McKay	Suite for Bass Clef Instruments (Two movements only)	UMP
Purcell-Ostrander	Arise Ye Subterranean Winds	Ed.M
Rossini-Hume	Una Voce M'ha Colpito	BH
Scarmolin	Introduction and Dance	Lud
Schaefer	Gay Caballero	Fil (CF)
Schoen-Spencer	Fantasie	CB
Schumann-Bell	The Jolly Farmer Goes to Town	CF
Semler-Collery	Barcarolle et Chanson Bachnique	SMC
Sowerby	Chaconne	CF
Tcherepnine	Andance	BH
Walters	Concertante	Ru

Grade V

Composer	Title	Pub.
Ameller	Concerto, Op. 69, for Tuba and Orchestra	Esc
Barat	Introduction and Dance	SMC
Barat	Morceau De Concours	SMC
Barat	Reminiscences De Navarre	SMC
Bernstein	Waltz for Mippy III	GS
Beversdorf	Sonata for Bass Tuba	IP
Bigot	Carillon et Bourdon	SMC
Boutry	Tubacchanale	SMC
Dubois	Piccolo Suite	SMC
Geib-Morse	Melody, Theme, and Variations	CF
Golterman-Bell	Excerpts from Concerto No. 4	CF
Hindemith	Sonate	B.SS
Holmes (arr.)	Carnival of Venice	Ru
Lebedev	Concert Allegro	UMP
Leclercq	Concertino	SMC
Mueller	Concert Music for Bass Tuba	UMP
Poot	Impromptu	Esc.
Spillman	Concerto	Ed.M
Swann	Two Moods for Tuba	SF
Vaughan-Williams	Concerto for Bass Tuba and Orchestra	Ox.P
Williams	Second Concerto	Col

Key to Publishers and Distributors

AMP	Associated Music Publishers
Bel.	Belwin, Inc.
B.SS	B. Schott's Söhne
BH	Boosey and Hawkes, Ltd.
CB	Cundy-Bettoney, Inc.
CF	Carl Fischer, Inc.
Col.	Charles Colin
EHM	Edwin H. Morris, Inc.
Ed.M	Edition Musicus, Inc.
E-V	Elkan-Vogel Co.
Esc.	Eschig
Fil.	Fillmore (owned by Carl Fischer)
GFB	George F. Briegel
GS	G. Schirmer, Inc.
IP	Interlochen Press
Kjos	Neil A. Kjos Music Co.
Lud.	Ludwig Music Publishing Co.
Mills	Mills Music, Inc.
Ox.P.	Oxford Press (London)
Ri.	Ricordi
Ru.	Rubank, Inc.
SF	Sam Fox Publishing Co.
SMC	Southern Music Co.
UMP	University Music Press

FINE

1963

4-Valve Euphonium

Brass Instrument Bore

R. Dale Olson

Performance characteristics of brass wind instruments are determined by numerous variable factors. The "bore" of such instruments is possibly one of the most widely discussed and misunderstood of these factors.

To the average brass performer, an instrument having a minimum of "resistance" is presumed to have a large bore, while considerable resistance is thought to be peculiar to a small bore instrument. These abstract, unscientific terms are even more confusing and alarming when one considers their widespread recognition by many performers and educators in an effort to describe the performance characteristics of a given instrument.

Tapers and Curves

By examining the drawing in Figure 1 it is possible to comprehend the complex of tapers, curves, and cylindrical sections which constitute the make-up of an instrument. The standard American-produced trumpet, for example, is comprised of approximately 10 inches of tapered tubing normally referred to as the "leaderpipe" or "mouthpipe," a straight cylindrical section of approximately 19 inches in which the valve section is usually placed, and a remaining tapered section of 22 inches which terminates in a "bell," the shape of which can be described as an imperfect exponential curve. The term "bore" refers to the valve bore, the only purely cylindrical section of the instrument. Due to their complex nature, the remaining tapered sections are not possible to categorize by one term. Therefore, the term presently under consideration refers to only approximately 37% of the entire instrument.

The placement of this cylindrical section along the taper is the determinant of the size of the valve bore.

Due to the fact that all tapered sections generally are in a state of constant expansion, the following illustration will show that various placements of the cylindrical section will change the bore size. For example, should a cylindrical section be placed at letter a . . . . a in Figure 2 the degree of expansion at that point would be four hundred and sixty thousandths of an inch (.460) thereby necessitating the use of a cylindrical section of the same size. Should it be inserted further along the taper, however, at letter b . . . . b in Figure 3 the diameter at that point may be four hundred and seventy six thousandths of an inch (.476).

Bore Dimensions

Well known and accepted by acousticians and instrument designers is the fact that the tapered sections can and do exert considerably more influence on the performance characteristics of an instrument than does a slight variation in the valve bore. It is possible, by altering the design of the various tapered sections, to construct a B♭ trumpet having a four hundred and fifty-three thousandths of an inch (.453) bore (considered to be comparatively small), and yet retain the basic performance characteristics of a large bore instrument. Obviously, the opposite also is true.

Of general agreement among performers is the fact that the B♭ flügelhorn is a large bore instrument as evidenced by its distinctive tonal characteristics. A recently completed flügelhorn, designed by Mr. Zigmant J. Kanstul and the author in the F. E. Olds and Son, Inc. Research Laboratory has a bore size of only four

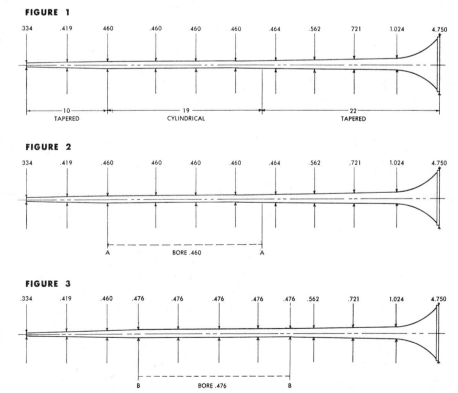

FIGURE 1

| .334 | .419 | 460 | .460 | 460 | 460 | .464 | .562 | 721 | 1.024 | 4.750 |

10 TAPERED · 19 CYLINDRICAL · 22 TAPERED

FIGURE 2

| 334 | .419 | .460 | 460 | 460 | .460 | .464 | .562 | .721 | 1.024 | 4.750 |

A · BORE .460 · A

FIGURE 3

| .334 | .419 | .460 | .476 | .476 | .476 | .476 | .476 | .562 | .721 | 1.024 | 4.750 |

B · BORE .476 · B

hundred and thirty-seven thousandths of an inch (.437). Most readers will note that this is twenty-three thousandths of an inch (.023) smaller than the standard trumpet, yet the instrument possesses a tone quality more closely related to the French horn than to the trumpet. This phenomenon is the result of the placement of the valve section relatively close to the beginning of the taper.

After years of experimentation, both empirical and scientific, manufacturers have arrived at a norm which is most suitable for present-day performance. This norm of bore size for Bb trumpets, for example, includes a range of inside diameters from approximately four hundred and forty-eight thousandths of an inch (.448) to four hundred and sixty-eight thousandths of an inch (.468). Although various experimentors have occasionally ventured as far as to construct a four hundred and eighty thousandths of an inch (.480) bore, most of their attempts have proven comparatively unsuccessful.

Psychological Effect

More than the actual differences between the bores of various instruments is the psychological effect upon the average performer. Particularly among young students the phrase "large bore" is impressive. In reality, the number of professional performers actually using a true large bore instrument is small. Although possibly a regional phenomenon, the majority of professional trumpeters in the Los Angeles area employ an instrument of approximately four hundred and sixty thousandths of an inch (.460) bore. A recent article by another writer indicates that 70% of the trumpet performers in his area (Minneapolis-St. Paul) also indicate a tendency to this same bore size and only 22% prefer a large bore instrument.[1] Even from this extremely cursory survey, it is logical to assume that four hundred and sixty thousandths of an inch (.460) is accepted generally as the standard bore for Bb trumpets.

The common comparison of bore between two different instruments made by removing the second valve slide from one horn and attempting to fit it into another is grossly misleading. When one considers the variances of metal thickness from one brand to another, such a test is shown to be totally inconclusive. For example, if instrument "A" has a valve bore of four hundred and sixty thousandths of an inch (.460) and is constructed using twenty-two thousandths of an inch (.022) brass, we find that the total outside diameter of the second valve slide is .460 plus .044 (the combined total of two wall thicknesses) or five hundred and four thousandths of an inch (.504). If instrument "B" is constructed using a valve bore of four hundred and sixty-eight thousandths of an inch (.468) but has been made from eighteen thousandths of an inch (.018) brass the total inside diameter of the second valve slide of instrument "B" would be .468 plus .036 (the combined total of two wall thicknesses) or .504. It is easily seen that the slide from instrument "A" will fit perfectly (theoretically speaking) into instrument "B" although the actual bore varies by .008. This discrepancy is attributed to the variation of metal thickness and is sufficient evidence to discredit this method of comparison.

An accurate scientific measurement of the valve bore and interior dimensions of an instrument can only be accomplished with precise measuring devices such as small hole gauges and/or micrometers. To facilitate inspection of these dimensions they must be projected graphically for visual representation.

The basic misconception that style or musical idiom dictates the size of the bore is perpetuated by the unfounded theory that symphonic performers use instruments of large bore while dance orchestra players prefer those of smaller bore. In the choice of bore, as in every other aspect of instrument-performer relationship, it is the individual performer's psychological and physiological make-up that requires a specific bore, not the idiom in which one performs.

It is the contention of this writer that the majority of performers do not place the problem of bore in its proper perspective. Although a usable alternate point of reference other than "bore" has never been offered, the brass performer should be fully aware of the inaccuracy of allowing this term to completely describe performance characteristics of an instrument.

FINE

[1]Tetzlaff, Daniel B. "Bore Details are not Boring", *International Musician*, Feb., 1960.

The Large Brass Class

Marceau Myers

THE POPULATION EXPANSION, which has been to a large extent the number one problem of school administrators and school boards for several years, is fast becoming a problem of major concern for many teachers of instrumental music. Coupled with the population expansion problem is the one arising from the fact that greater percentages of students are participating in the instrumental music programs of our public schools. Hence, the instrumental music teacher—often without the benefit of additional staff or improved scheduling—has had to devise methods for teaching more students. In most instances larger classes have been the only workable solution to the existing problem. However, if the larger classes are taught effectively, the results can be just as satisfactory as with the smaller classes, and they can serve as an excellent supplement to the private lessons which students may be taking concurrently with their work in school.

Heterogeneous and Homogeneous Classes

Large brass classes can be taught effectively either heterogeneously or homogeneously. Each, however, has distinct advantages, and hence the ideal schedule would be to meet a group of brass students one day per week in homogeneous classes, and then one day per week in a large heterogeneous class. This would permit the teacher to take advantage of the unique potential inherent in each type of grouping. However, where the scheduling does not permit this type of arrangement the teacher must then determine which type of grouping will enable him to accomplish the best results.

There are many factors involved in playing a brass instrument which relate to all of the brasses, and students can learn much from other students regardless of whether they are playing like or unlike instruments. In the heterogeneous class the student can learn to better balance and blend his instrument with the other instruments of the brass family, and by playing music which utilizes the entire brass choir the musical results can be very gratifying to both the student and teacher.

In a homogeneous class the problems which are unique to a given instrument can be given more concentrated attention: the problem of slurring on the trombone, or stopping and muting the horn.

If a large number of the enrolled students are studying privately perhaps the large heterogeneous class will better serve the needs of the students. On the other hand if the majority of students are not studying privately the class will benefit more from a schedule which places them in classes of like instruments.

Helpful Procedures for Beginning Classes

Intensive work with just the mouthpiece of the instrument will help to establish many of the important principles of brass playing, and thereby minimize a great number of the problems often encountered later.

After explaining the embouchure formation to the class, the teacher should buzz several long tones on the mouthpiece in the pitch vicinity of F4 on a trumpet mouthpiece or F3 on a trombone mouthpiece. The students should then endeavor to imitate this sound. If the presentation is clear the students will produce a sound similar to that which has been demonstrated. At this point the embouchure formations should be carefully scrutinized and special attention should be given to those beginners who have encountered difficulty. After the students can buzz a few tones on the mouthpiece successfully, tone production on the instrument may be attempted. Posture and proper playing position should be presented at this time.

Flexibility Drills

Use the mouthpiece to teach the students how to alter the pitch in order to ascend or descend at will. Have the student imitate glissandos buzzed on the mouthpiece with attention given to the necessary breath support and embouchure adjustments to be made. The students may buzz glissandos from the very lowest tone they can sound up to the highest and back down again. Apply this flexibility by playing various scales on the mouthpiece in simple rhythmic patterns. Four quarter notes followed by a dotted half note is a good starter. Explain the function of the tongue prior to this part of the exercise and give an adequate demonstration.

If careful attention has been given to the important playing fundamentals and those students who need individual help have been given the necessary special attention, the class should be able to perform the drills

with some degree of facility and the transfer from mouthpiece to instrument should be quite smooth. However, mouthpiece drills should be carried on at each meeting of the class so that the teacher may continue to stress proper playing fundamentals and at the same time check individual development. These mouthpiece drills are also excellent for class warm-up, and eliminate the cacophony produced by twenty or thirty young brass students playing ad lib warm-ups.

Sustaining a Full Tone

Proper breathing techniques may be emphasized in several ways. Students may practice a sustained hissing sound to get the feeling of proper support. The relaxed feeling of blowing thru the instrument can be assimilated by having the students remove the mouthpiece and tuning slide from their instruments and place their lips around the leadpipe, and blow a steady stream of air thru the instrument for a count of four or five without attempting to produce a tone. After blowing thru the open pipe several times add the mouthpiece and blow several sustained tones with the tuning slide still removed. Finally, add the tuning slide and play several sustained tones. In most cases the student will blow in a much freer manner than previously, and will begin to relax considerably after this procedure. This drill can serve as a change of pace during each meeting of the class.

Importance of the Teacher

Not only must the teacher serve as a model, but he must also be an astute diagnostician who is alert to the individual differences inherent in the large class. However, there must be some vehicle provided to give the additional help to those students who do not progress as rapidly as the majority of the class. Often the more advanced students are willing and able to give special help to them. Also, wherever and whenever possible the teacher should encourage all students to study privately. Private lessons are seldom in conflict with the overall objectives of the brass class, and they do enable the student to realize his objectives more rapidly. Both teachers strive for this result: To have students play as musically and as technically proficiently as possible.

FINE

THE
DOUBLE
HORN

Cutler Silliman

THE CONVENTIONAL DOUBLE French horn in use today is pitched in F and B♭. It has two complete valve slide systems operated by one set of valves. The change from one horn to the other is made thru a thumb valve. The same mouthpiece, mouthpipe, and bell are used for both horns.

The valve slide system is constructed in two ways: 1. Two independent sets of slides; 2. A set of slides for the B♭ horn with additional short lengths of tubing used in conjunction with the B♭ horn slides for the longer F horn slides. The latter system is generally the less satisfactory, probably because it involves more sharp bends in the tubing. It seems to lack the resonance of a system having independent sets of slides for each horn.

The single B♭ horn with an F attachment is not a true double horn as the F horn must use the valve

Ex. 1
F Horn

Partial:
1 2 3 4 5 6 7 8 9 10 11 12 13 14 15 16

B♭ Horn

slides of the B♭ horn, which are too short. This F horn is serviceable only on open tones and in the extreme low register where it is relatively easy for the performer to make large adjustments in intonation with his lips.

The harmonic series for the F and B♭ horns of the double horn are shown in Example 1. These are both given in "F" notation, a perfect fifth higher than actual sound, as are all other examples in this article. It should be noted that this instrument has the same fundamental tones as the tenor-bass trombone in B♭ and F. Historically, the B♭ horn of the double horn would be called a high B♭ horn as it is an octave higher than the B♭ horn in common use before valves were introduced.

Because of the narrowness of the tube in relation to its length, the fundamental tone of the F horn is difficult to produce. The fundamental tone of the B♭ horn is easy, therefore the theoretically higher B♭ horn may be used for lower pitches than the F horn.

A mature player should be able to control his tone, intonation, and accuracy on both F and B♭ horns so that in most circumstances the listener cannot tell which horn is being used. A player usually has a concept of sound which he attempts to produce regardless of the instrument in his hands. What determines his choice of horn is the relative ease of performing a particular note or passage in the most satisfactory manner. Obviously, before a player can make a valid choice of instrument, he must first have a mastery of both horns over their complete ranges. Once this is accomplished, he should be able to change back and forth from one horn to the other with complete freedom. Then he no

longer thinks of F or B♭ horn, but of the best fingering, with or without the thumb valve.

For younger players, it is best to establish definite points at which to change from one horn to the other. The selection of these points will differ with various players and with various makes of instruments. Example 2 shows a satisfactory pattern, one which is in common use. The use of the two horns overlaps on the tones from A♭ to C.

In an article in the October, 1958, issue of *The Instrumentalist* we discussed in detail the use of the double horn in improving intonation. The suggestions made in that article for better tuning and intonation were:

1. Be sure the two parts of the double horn are tuned together.

2. Keep the hand in the bell while tuning.

3. Play as low in the harmonic series on either horn as is possible using only the partials which are closely in agreement with the tempered scale.

4. Avoid partials seven, eleven, thirteen and fourteen.

5. Use care with partials five and ten.

6. Adjust valve slides so they counteract the sharpness of combination fingerings.

7. Master both F and B♭ horns so that alternate fingerings can be used to improve intonation.

Exceptional Use

The four requisites of good playing—tone, intonation, accuracy, and ease of fingering—are normally satisfied by following the pattern given in Example 2. At times these requisites are not balanced and one or more are sacrificed in favor of the others.

The five notes in Example 3 have a simpler fingering and are easier to attack on the Bb horn than on the F horn, but they have a superior tone and better intonation on the F horn. Therefore, a sudden attack or a rapid passage using these notes will usually be taken on the Bb, while a slower, melodic passage will be taken on the F horn.

Ex. 2

Bb Horn   F Horn   Bb Horn

Ex. 3

Ex. 4
(Kopprasch)

Ex. 5 (Dvorak, Symphony No. 5)
Allegro

Ex. 6
F Horn

Ex. 7

F Horn

F Horn   Bb Horn P4   M3

Bb Horn   F Horn

The F horn would be more satisfactory for the lowest four notes in Example 4 if they appeared in isolation, but in the context given, it is easier to remain on the Bb rather than to shift back and forth between the two.

For hand muting, it is necessary to play all the notes on the F horn. When the hand is in the proper position, the pitch of the F horn is raised one half step which may be compensated for by transposing the notes a half step down. With the hand in the same position, the pitch on the Bb horn is raised about three quarters of a step. There are some single Bb horns built with a small bell so that it is possible to mute them with the hand, but the bell on the double horn is too large for this.

Example 5 contains a passage in which the fingering is much simplified thru the use of the F horn in the higher register. This implies an application of the old natural horn principles to the modern double horn. Each finger combination provides the player with a complete natural horn: on the F horn, open is an F horn; 2, E; 1, Eb; 1-2, D; 2-3, Db; 1-3, C; 1-2-3, B. On the Bb horn, open is a Bb horn; 2, A; 1, Ab; 1-2, G; 2-3, F#; 1-3, F; 1-2-3, E. This can be practiced by playing natural horn exercises such as those in the Oscar Franz *Method for Horn* and transposing them to the various keys. Understanding the hand horn is also a great aid in transposition.

Special Practice Procedures

Special exercises taking advantage of the double horn can be used to improve technique. The use of the natural horn principles described earlier is one. Another is playing high notes on the F horn to improve accuracy.

A common misconception about the F horn is that it cannot be played as high as the Bb horn. It is the speed of the vibrations of the lips in the mouthpiece that determines pitch and since both F and Bb horns on the double horn are played with the same mouthpiece, neither horn is capable of playing higher than the other. The small advantage (and in a range of four octaves a "small" advantage can be important) the Bb horn has in the high register is that its notes are slightly more widely spaced in the harmonic series so there is a little more margin for error. Being lower in its harmonic series, the tone of the Bb horn will not thin out quite as much as the tone of F horn in the high register. But if the lips are set correctly for the pitch before striking the tone, either horn can produce it readily. Practicing on the F horn will sharpen the ability to set the lips correctly.

Arpeggio exercises are frequently given for the F horn but rarely for the Bb horn. A typical pattern is that shown in Example 6. In this type of exercise, students often experience difficulty in playing the lower octave. Reading this (lower) pattern a perfect fourth higher, it can be played on the Bb horn with the same finger pattern. These Bb horn arpeggios can be used to fill in and strengthen the range between the two octaves of Example 6.

In a similar manner, the two horns can be used to supplement each other in practice to increase the high register. Arpeggios are ideal for this as they enable the student to approach the high notes from a middle or low point which will help to prevent undue tightening of the lips and excess pressure. Several patterns on the double horn will give different intervals for approaching the high note. In some of these patterns, the wider intervals at the top will be on the F horn while in others they will be on the Bb horn. Example 7 provides a few of the possibilities for this type of pattern.

Summary

It has been shown that a thorough knowledge of both F and Bb horns is basic to a full use of the double horn. Neither should be used to the exclusion of the other, nor should it be assumed that either is always better for certain registers. Example 7 showed that the F horn can be of value in extending the high register; Example 6 illustrated the use of the Bb horn to strengthen the middle and low registers.

One approach to the understanding of the double horn is to revert to natural or hand horn practice. An application of this was shown in Example 5.

Using the double horn in the manner discussed will greatly add to the student's understanding of his instrument and to his skill and enjoyment in playing it.

FINE

ANTIPHONAL MUSIC

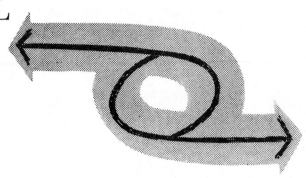

FOR BRASS CHOIRS

David Uber

DURING THE PAST FIFTEEN YEARS a great amount of music has been composed, edited, adapted, and arranged for various combinations of brass instruments. Renewed interest has been seen, particularly in the antiphonal music of the Italian and German masters of the sixteenth and seventeenth centuries. Very little music, however, has been composed for antiphonal brass choirs in the twentieth century idiom.

The thrilling sound of alternating choirs of brasses becomes even more magnificent and colorful when the new streams of harmonies, the new linear concepts, compound rhythms and special effects are employed. The contemporary style of writing for brasses bearing the influence of Ravel, Debussy, Hindemith, Stravinsky, Bartok, and Dahl is both intriguing and challenging to the young brass player. Melodic, harmonic, and rhythmic innovations, skillfully applied to the great Venetian tradition of antiphonal writing make for exciting listening and new compositions in this idiom are guaranteed to provide the audience with a memorable experience.

Ancient Technique

Antiphonal music, although not an invention of the Venetian school, reached its greatest heights from approximately 1580-1630 in the polychoral works of Giovanni Gabrieli (c. 1554-1612). The whole idea behind antiphonal music, that of alternating choirs of singers or instrumentalists, is an ancient one, dating back to the very dawn of music history. The principle was embraced by early religious leaders and became a vital part of the Christian liturgy.

By definition, the word antiphonal or antiphony denotes a response of one choir to another when an anthem, psalm, or instrumental work is sung or played by two choirs. With the development of new musical resources, both the number of alternating choirs and the number of performers were expanded considerably. Even to this day, the ideal habitat of antiphonal performance is the church or cathedral.

The glory and splendor of St. Marks Cathedral in Venice inspired the greatest and most sonorous antiphonal music the world has ever known. At the time of the Gabrielis, St. Marks had become a treasure house of beauty and decoration. Its very architecture cried out for spacious music—music that would resound from its ornamental walls and ceilings. Great alternating choirs of voices and brasses adorned the spacious interior and performed music of such splendor and magnificence that it has never been equalled anywhere else in the world.

Giovanni Gabrieli (c. 1554-1612), nephew of Andrea Gabrieli (c. 1520-1586), was destined to write the glorious music that became intertwined with the fame of St. Marks Cathedral. His music brought the brass instruments out of the dark ages to a prominence never before attained and it had a far reaching influence on his Italian contemporaries as well as his German pupils.

Antiphonal Contrast

Most of Gabrieli's works were based on the old chanson style expanded to a polychoral and polyinstrumental type of piece. He was obsessed with the tone color of the instruments of his day and employed them skillfully to obtain great contrast thru antiphonal treatment. The instruments available to him were most probably cornetts, violins, violas, trombones, bassoons, and, of course, the organ. When the alternating choirs "skip and play" with one another in an almost teasing style and then are brought together in a full climatic tutti, we can only sit back and praise the great technical skill of this master of three centuries ago.

It is indeed a pity that the polychoral style of writing reached its true glory for only a brief period of about fifty years and then fell into comparative obscurity. We are grateful for the works of the Italian and German masters that have been preserved and handed down to us but, with the renewed interest in great brass music, it seems the right time to crusade for a renaissance of antiphonal music. To work within the framework of the noble examples of our sixteenth century pioneers and create new compositions utilizing the twentieth century tonal and technical resources would be a worthy project indeed.

Unlimited Scope

Today's composers have an unlimited creative scope in writing for antiphonal brass choirs. The use of seventh, ninth, eleventh, and thirteenth chords adds a piquant seasoning to the interplay of the alternating groups. Then, too, chords constructed in fourths supporting contrapuntal lines that weave and skip in irregular patterns and intervals can create tension and excitement as well as sonority. Remember that sharp dissonances are considerably softened and "tamed" when the choirs are placed twenty-five to fifty feet apart.

A wonderful idea in antiphonal writing is to score for three brass choirs and one vocal choir, using the brass to punctuate the voices and the voices to soften the overwhelming effect of the brasses. Here, too, the distance between the choirs permits the listener to hear with clarity and distinction. We have real living stereophonic music, borrowing our format from creative musicians who lived centuries ago.

Vigorous Rhythms

The influence of American jazz on contemporary music throughout the world has been staggering. Composers have become obsessed with the vigorous, healthy rhythms of the jazz movement and certainly these rhythms have a place in antiphonal brass music. It must be remembered that the city of Venice in the sixteenth century made no bones about mixing the sacred and the secular. The Cathedral of St. Marks became headquarters for many public musical festivals. Festive antiphonal music in our time, joyful and full of rhythmic movement, can be every bit as majestic and glorious as the secular works performed in the golden age of the Gabrielis.

There are numerous special effects available to the dedicated composer of brass music and skillful use of these devices can do much to add color and contrast to antiphonal writing. The use of mutes to soften and change the color of the brass sonority creates an exciting effect. The raging torrent of three brass choirs playing tutti can be transformed to a gentle, distant whisper. Extensive use of various dynamic levels, and effects of sforzando, crescendo and decrescendo are recommended.

The trumpets have great resilience and agility in their extreme registers as well as the techniques of double and triple tonguing. The horns contribute great sonority, hand muting effects, and a most astounding compass of approximately three and one-half octaves. The trombones have a bagful of tricks, including the loose sounding pedal tones (introduced by Berlioz), the glissando, and, above all, a noble, resonant sound. Bell tones are effective for all the instruments, including the tubas; and trills, flutter-tonguing, and shakes may be used, with discretion, for various effects.

Ensemble Important

Above all, it must be remembered that antiphonal writing creates problems of keeping the different performing groups together, so it is best to avoid extremely complex rhythms or difficult alternating passages. At the same time, there is the advantage of frequent rest intervals for the players, since one choir characteristically takes the theme away from the other just as in a musical relay race. In the great tutti passages the players need not play as loudly as in the orchestra, band, or small brass ensemble.

The instrumentation of the various brass choirs in antiphonal music can be as flexible as the style of the music itself. A work by this writer, *Twentieth Century Antiphonal for Three Brass Choirs* has the following distribution of instruments as well as alternates:

Choir I
Trumpet I
Trumpet II
Horn (Trombone)
Trombone
Tuba

Choir II
Trumpet
Horn (Trombone)
Trombone
Bass Trombone (Tuba)

Choir III
Trumpet
Horn I
Horn II (Trombone)
Baritone
Tuba

Notice that Choirs I and III are quintets and that Choir II is a quartet. As in all large brass choir music, the parts may be doubled with excellent results.

There are many advantages and benefits to be derived from the playing of brass antiphonal music. Since the players are spaced in small groups some distance from one another, it is paramount that they listen intently, not only to their own part but to all of the other sounds around them. Each player must strive for musical perfection within his own individual choir as well as when the choirs are combined in tutti passages. Here is a golden opportunity to develop a keen sense of musicianship, accurate intonation, clean attacks and releases, and a good conception of balance. From my own personal experience, there is no greater musical or aesthetic satisfaction than the playing of antiphonal brass choir music.

Let us begin a crusade for a rebirth of the golden sounds of the Venetian antiphonal school, garnished with the harmonic, melodic, twentieth century.

FINE

How to develop

UPPER BRASS RANGE

Howard Liva

THE PROBLEM OF GETTING THE students in a high school, or for that matter a college band to play the complete, practical range of their instruments is a universal one. For most of us, only the top chairs in the several brass sections can produce the top and bottom tones on their instruments with some measure of security.

Directors are cautioned not to attempt to make radical changes in the playing techniques of their players without the opportunity of close supervision by a brass specialist. The suggestions should merely be used as guides and then with discretion.

Physical Factors

The range problems in the brasses stem, in most cases, from an imbalance of several physical factors. The following aspects of brass playing should be watched carefully:

1. *Inhalation.*

a. Throat is relaxed and open.

b. Embouchure is not disturbed.

c. Chest is held high by muscles in area of clavicles.

d. Abdomen and lower back swell like rain barrel.

2. *Exhalation.*

a. Throat remains relaxed and open (not used for compression).

b. Vocal chords rest apart and "Adams apple" does not bob.

c. Embouchure is set before exhalation.

d. Chest does not collapse.

e. Abdomen pulls inward as tho to meet spine.

f. Diaphragm pushes upward.

g. Buttocks are pressed together.

3. *Tongue placement.*

a. Tongue rests in relaxed position for low register.

b. Edges of tongue line inner sides of bottom jaw teeth.

c. Tip of tongue touches back edge of bottom teeth.

d. As pitch ascends, the center of the tongue raises from "ah" to "ee" position.

4. *Embouchure.*

a. The vibrating surface at the center of the lips moves from the soft inner side toward the lip line (red to white) as the pitch ascends.

b. The lower, flexible jaw accommodates the lips by adjusting to desired positions. The jaw generally drops forward for low notes.

c. The corners of the mouth hug the teeth and, in normal position, turn downward.

The Air Column

The balances of respiration, oral cavity, and embouchure may be described in terms of their effects. Air is controlled by voluntary muscles and is directed upward, in contrast to the downward forcing of the grunt. The air column is directed over the tongue in somewhat· the same manner as when one whistles. The sound produced is clear and full, independent of the pitch. High notes are neither choked nor shrill, and low notes are neither insecure nor muddy.

Now let us examine these several factors and their consequences more closely. Inhalation and exhalation must be accomplished by the use of voluntary muscles. The body expands and the air, equalizing the pressure, rushes into the lungs. The lungs are expanded in a direction most easily affected by the controllable muscles across the abdomen. Compression (hence air velocity) is consequently controllable regardless of the air volume.

As the lips close in nozzle fashion, the compression must be sufficient to keep the lips slightly apart. Teachers frequently demonstrate correct breathing by yelling "Hey!" The importance is in *how* the word is produced. When the student shouts "Hey!" in the way he might prepare his stomach for a swift kick, he is blowing downward instead of upward.

More obviously related to the range problem, the word "Hey" is often used to describe the feeling one has in reaching for a high note. This tends to imply a natural confinement to the staff and, at the same time, may bring with it the undulating collapse and recovery of support as the pitch descends and ascends.

Intensity Important

Youngsters are able to understand that intensity of the support may be held above a minimum level despite the relaxation of the embouchure center. Even beginners notice how the artist performer leans into a piano passage with an intensity which is obviously not required for the pitch he produces, but which is required for the sound he demands.

It is true that pitch changes may be achieved by forming vowel positions with the tongue. It is by this technique that so-called lip trills are executed. However, over-emphasis of this single element in the production of low to high notes (especially for beginners) frequently allows the embouchure to become inflexible. In this case, the vibrating surface of each lip remains in constant relative position to the other.

Sometimes accompanying this inflexible "pointed jaw" position is the "rubber band" technique of pulling the corners back, hence stretching the lips across the teeth. The aperture (hole blown open) is consequently laterally oblong instead of round. The sound produced also thins as the aperture narrows. However, this is not to assume a simple cause-effect relationship discounting the withdrawal of flesh from the cup and other peculiarities of the smile technique.

A somewhat rarer malady in experienced players is the exaggerated "kiss" embouchure. One can easily effect the sound by saying the word "poo," pressing the lips together very tightly, and forcing air between them. The strained sound becomes pronounced as the pitch ascends. Luckily, the young player usually is graduated from this particular ear-taxing practice as he strives to cease fighting the instrument and begins to emulate the clear sound of experienced players.

The Lips Roll

In the correct embouchure, the lips roll, very slightly, in and out to assist in the adjustment of pitch. For the lowest notes, the vibrating surface of the lips is the softer inside that one can feel with his tongue without parting his lips. As the pitch ascends, the lips roll inward toward the teeth but not between the teeth, so that the vibrating surface moves from the soft inside toward the harder lip line where the red of the lips meets the white.

The centers of the lips do not actually roll against one another, but they roll against the air stream which is forced between them. The rolling action, noticeable at the corners, must not be exaggerated beyond what is necessary for good sound with maximum flexibility. Over-emphasis of the rolling can cause undesireable results.

The beauty of correct embouchure is that a higher note is not the result of brute strength in the muscles that surround the mouth. The higher note is the result of an embouchure (including the oral cavity) which is intended for that note. When a student repeatedly hits E5 while trying for G5, the likelihood is that, if his breath support is sufficient, the embouchure is one to be used for E5—not for G5.

Remember that facility in the upper register is the result of controlled air compression, slightly arched tongue, and lips which have found the most satisfactory position for higher pitches without compromising clarity of sound.

Mouthpiece Choice

Any discussion of range inevitably includes mouthpieces. A small cup and narrow diameter make the upper register easier to obtain for a student who depends more upon his arm than upon his orbicular muscles. An extremely small mouthpiece causes the tone to become thin in all registers, most noticeably so in the middle and low registers. However, neither is there virtue in using a soupbowl mouthpiece, in quest of a bigger sound, if the performer cannot handle it. It is most important that the student select the mouthpiece suitable for his particular physical characteristics, and for the type and amount of playing he does. This critical part of the instrument deserves the attention of a specialist.

Insecurity in the extreme upper register is often the result of inadequate ear training. The partials in the third and fourth octaves are so close that poor relative pitch discrimination may be the primary fault rather than physical incompetence. The problem may be alleviated by practicing sight singing and by practicing intervals with the mouthpiece alone.

Remove Impediments

The instruction for young experienced students often consists of the removal of impediments. Many widespread faulty habits are due to several teacher-oriented problems. Overrated early execution of the ascending major scale and familiar melodies prior to adequate technical development is responsible for much of the poor sound in schools. This is not to minimize the usefulness of scales and tunes for student proficiency and interest, but their greatest value is in correct execution.

Also common is unreasonable dependence upon assignments of graduated difficulty. Technical tasks (including high notes) which are not quickly accomplished despite super-

vision and instruction will likely not be accomplished correctly in home practice thru mere repetition.

Not long ago, the formidable high C was an impressive grasp at the stratosphere. Today, dance band music is common which demands sustained passages in the trumpet's fourth octave. Methodical study of the trumpet's altissimo register will provide more than screech effect in the school stage band. Hardly any of even the most difficult concert band arrangements demand higher than written F6 of the cornets. Yet, cornet sections which are capable of controlled playing in that range evidence an assuring feeling of horsepower in reserve when performing in the third octave.

Directions on the "how" of performance is conspicuously absent from most method books. While brass teachers' instructions may differ in semantics, the teachers are generally in accord regarding the essentials of artistic performance. The non-brass public school teacher should search for the brass technique publications which do exist, be acquainted with trends and discoveries, and so keep in his own music department *top brass*. FINE

June, 1963

A Stroboscopic Analysis of Lip Function

Robert D. Weast

A THOROUGH INVESTIGATION to ascertain the function of brass players' lip activity was undertaken during playing conditions. Common reference to "the vibrating lips," "getting both lips to vibrate equally," and that "the lips are comparable to a double-reed instrument," prompted the study so as to secure valid data based on several tests. In light of the tests it is not difficult to see why there is so much misconception and contradiction. What the brass player *feels* is not necessarily what *happens*. Opinions stated as

fact without any scientific evidence may lead to confusion and inaccuracy. Since a certain amount of our teaching method can and does rely on how our lips react in performance, it seems imperative that a clear-cut study should be made.

There are several simple tests that have been used for several years to indicate the tone producing importance of the upper lip. Tissue paper, when placed over the lower lip, allows the upper lip to continue to vibrate. When the upper lip is thus covered, no sound at all emanates.

The lower lip can be placed behind the upper slightly into the mouth and a good tone still can be produced. The tongue can be rolled over the lower lip and the upper lip will vibrate against this substitute with an excellent tone resulting. The lower lip can be held at different tensions from the upper, it can be moved sideways, in, out, or down, being almost out of the mouthpiece and yet the tone remains virtually the same. In spite of these simple but revealing tests, there is persistence in referring to both lips being tone

337

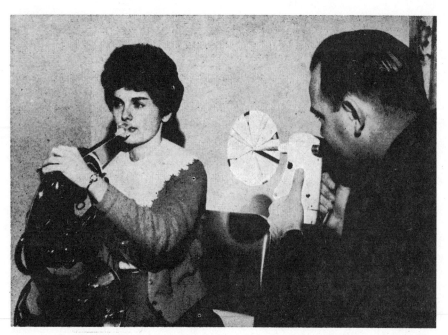

Example 1. Examining lip activity with the stroboscope disk.

producing vibrators.

The Stroboscope Disk

A visual study of the lips under playing conditions had to be made. The curved, transparent plastic mouthpieces on the market distort vision and only with some difficulty can vibrating action be seen and then it is only a vague blur. Square, plexiglas mouthpieces were made for trumpet, French horn, trombone, and tuba. These permitted excellent viewing. A stroboscope disk was used which permits the viewer to witness an oscillating object in slow motion (Example 1). A disk with a hole in its periphery was attached to the shaft of a variable speed motor. When the speed of the revolving disk was synchronized with the speed of vibrations, all visual activity, as seen thru the hole on the disk, was brought to a standstill. When the speed of the disk was slightly changed, lip motion became apparent. The lips then could be held in any position or moved at the will of the operator of the disk.

In slow motion the action of the lips is a remarkable phenomenon. The air column causes the lips, especially the upper, to blow outward. The resiliency of the membrane causes it to spring back in place, thereby completely closing the aperture for a split instant. Without this lip contact there is no vibration. The lip vibration is then a rapidly occurring sequence of the lips blowing apart, springing back, striking each other and then repeating the

process a given number of times per second. It will be pointed out that it is the *upper* lip that consistently goes thru this process, the lower lip reacting in a number of ways, usually irrelevant to tone production.

Upper Lip Consistent

It became apparent early in the study that a large number of players would have to be examined, since the activity of the lower lip was highly erratic. To use the lower lip activity of any given individual as the norm for all brass players would be misleading and erroneous. By contrast, the upper lip activity of any brass player could be used as the norm, so consistent is it in its behavior. A total of forty-two trumpet, French horn, trombone and tuba

players were studied and the results were graphed (Example 2). In every case the upper lip was consistent in its activity. The lower lip had extremes of no activity to free activity. The majority of time there was some degree of activity, but considerably reduced from that of the upper lip. Occasionally, it would be out of time with the upper lip. Most, but not all players have a more active lower lip in the low register, where it is relaxed and most susceptible to the beatings of the upper lip. As the tones ascend the lower lip becomes more rigid and thus less active.

Is the lower lip truly vibrating independently or is it merely reacting to the beatings of the upper lip? This was answered by inserting a probe thru a hole drilled in the mouthpiece and placing the plate of this probe on each lip during performance. When the plate of the probe covers the lower lip the upper lip continues to vibrate against it, but when the plate covers the upper lip, all lower lip activity ceases immediately. Clearly now, a case of the lower reacting to the upper. Another test to determine the effect of the upper on the lower was to place the rim of the mouthpiece on the red of the upper lip, thereby inhibiting its full amplitude of vibration. Even tho the lower lip has more than enough room to freely vibrate, its activity is proportionally reduced to that of the upper lip.

Lower Lip Independent

It should be pointed out that certain individuals can vibrate the lower lip independently from the upper by protruding the lower lip,

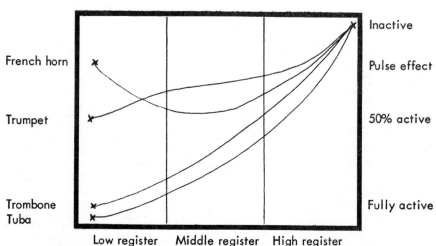

Example 2. The lower lip activity of 42 brass players was studied and graphed. The upper lip is consistent and fully active. The lower lip is erratic and varies from player to player. There is no correlation between its activity and tone quality.

thus exposing the softer tissue of the inner lip. This is most easily done in the low register. Such players can then play two notes at once, producing the familiar "split" or "cracked" tone. When the lower lip is thus vibrated it assumes the full vibrating status of the upper, with an interference of lip activity ensuing, causing a disturbance in the tone. Beginners correct this difficulty unconsciously by tightening the lower lip, shutting it off so to speak. The double or split sound is also produced from the upper lip containing two vibrations at once, *i.e.*, the normal vibration area contained within a larger vibrating area. These phenomena can easily be seen with the stroboscope disk.

Study of the graph reveals that most trombone and tuba players have an active lower lip in their low register. As they ascend, this lip becomes proportionately inactive, and many times ceases to move at all in the upper register. The French horn curve is most interesting. Whether or not they realize it, one

Example 3. The probe covering the lower lip. The upper lip continues to vibrate against this probe. When the probe covers the upper lip all lower lip activity ceases immediately.

reason French horn players use the higher mouthpiece placement on the upper lip is to enable this lip to fully vibrate at maximum amplitude for the low register. Their lower lip is almost out of the mouthpiece cup in their low register, and thus it can hardly react to the beatings of the upper lip. As they ascend it becomes more susceptible to the vibrating upper lip and in the higher register it again becomes more inactive. The lower lip of trumpet players reacts as a slight pulsating effect, usually less than fifty per cent of the upper lip's activity. This instrument does

not have the low register of the first three, hence the fairly consistent pulse effect.

Even Lip Alignment

The even lip alignment or the protruding lower lip formation are the most susceptible positions for an active lower lip. The inactive lower lip is most often associated with the overlapping upper lip formation. Nevertheless, a beautiful tone can be produced with this malformation, further indicating the insignificance of the lower lip. Beginners and players with tired embouchures revert to the overlap because lip contact and response are easier to attain. The deficiency of the overlap occurs in the upper register where the lips are squeezed together by mouthpiece pressure, thereby thinning out the tone. One can play past his controlled endurance and perhaps higher but he is on borrowed time. It is more difficult at first to play high notes and to get immediate response with the aligned lips, but the tone will remain full and additional strength is gained by the lower lip when it is held even and not allowed to chronically collapse into the mouth. The even lip alignment is good then, because it avoids binding the lips together, and not because it permits the lower lip more activity.

The question presents itself, "Why is it always the upper lip that is the prime vibrator and not the lower?" This, I believe, is due to a combination of circumstances. First, most beginning players have a normal overbite and thus the upper lip is naturally in position for vibration, the lower lip being held back and frequently overlapped by the upper to a degree. Second, it is easier to get a tone with the overlap formation as the upper lip can easily make contact with the lower lip. Third, it would be difficult to get both lips at the exact tension required of all notes. Oboe and bassoon reeds are made in balance so that response from both reeds is identical. This is not necessarily true with lips. Fourth, and this is speculative, it appears that the upper lip is more sensitive to vibrating control than the lower lip. Theoretically, individuals might exist that have the process reserved, the lower lip being the vibrator and the upper lip the erratic, less respon-

sive lip. I have never seen such an individual.

Aside from purely factual interest, this study yielded practical applications. Lip vibrating amplitude, lip contact during vibration, and the all important specific functions of the upper and lower lips were the valuable data secured on a valid basis. These have been taken out of the realm of opinion and placed on established factual status.

Lip Amplitude

Lip vibrating amplitude, or the distance the lip travels during a vibration is in accordance with volume and register. Loud volume or low register playing is produced with great lip amplitude. The upper lip moves its greatest distance in these circumstances and must have a large aperture to accommodate such movement. When there is insufficient aperture, the tone is choked and stuffy; the low register is difficult to secure. Soft volume or high register playing is produced with minimum lip amplitude. The aperture must be reduced so that the upper lip can easily make contact with the lower. An aperture spread too far causes an airy, frequently flat tone. The upper lip must beat against something as it will not vibrate in open air. Delayed attacks are frequent. Most players can move the lower lip up and down to produce the necessary aperture changes. Players instinctively learn to gauge the right distance with their ear and by feel. As long as the mouthpiece remains in a fixed position on the upper lip, accuracy is retained. The lower lip can and should freely move up and down. Certain individuals that do not have independent lower lip control must pucker and smile to make lip opening changes. The latter method can sometimes have deleterious limitations.

Conclusion

Evidence of the vibrating action of the lips as herewith presented according to several cross-checked methods produces overwhelming evidence of the upper lip being the prime vibrating mechanism. The activity, or usually lack of activity, of the lower lip is irrelevant to tone production. To refer to the "vibrating lips" is quite inaccurate and gives a status and function to the lower lip that is highly misleading. FINE

A Graded List of Trumpet Solos

John Haynie

Much has been said and written concerning *how* to play; it is this writer's opinion that *what* to play is of equal importance. If the student's musical development is to mature along with his technical advancement there must be some attention to the quality of music performed.

The following list of trumpet literature is chosen from the vast amount of material available. Conspicuously missing are the polka-type and training solos that are always popular with young students in their musically formative years. This omission is not to down-grade such solos or to belittle their importance. The intent of this selected bibliography is to introduce to teachers and students trumpet solos that probably are not well known.

Examination of the material will show that the piano accompaniments are interesting and usually difficult. In most cases the piano part is of equal importance to the solo part, and the trumpeter will find much more pleasure in practicing with the piano than alone.

COMPOSER-ARRANGER	TITLE	PUBLISHER
	GRADE II	
Anderson	A Glad Tune	C. Fischer
Bach	Arioso	C. Fischer
Bach	If Thou Be Near	Ricordi
Baines	Pastorale	Schott
Bakaleinikoff	Legend	Belwin
Bakaleinikoff	Serenade	Belwin
Barat	Orientale	Penders
Benson	Prologue	Marks
Bernstein	Rondo for Lifey	Schirmer
Bond	Concerto	Boosey-Hawkes
Burke	Amourette	C. Fischer
Clerisse	Theme Varie	Penders
Cords	Romanze	Cundy-Bettoney
Defossez	Les Gammes en Vacances	Penders
Donaudy	Aria and Allegro	Ricordi
Donaudy	Arioso and Canzone	Ricordi
Donaudy	Two Arias	Ricordi
Douane	Diptyque	Penders
Ellis	Mark 1-0	Penders
Fitzgerald	Call	C. Fischer
Fitzgerald	English Suite	Presser
Fitzgerald	Legend	C. Fischer
Friboulet	Gaminerie	Penders
Friboulet	Introduction et Marche	R.D. King
Galajikian	Allegro Marziale	Belwin
Glinka	Romance Melody	Spratt
Grundman	Conversation for Cornet	Boosey-Hawkes
Handel	Largo	Cundy-Bettoney
Hartley	Sonatine	Rochester
Klein	English March for an American Trumpet	Marks
Klein	Lament	Boosey-Hawkes
Langue	Impromptu	Baron
Legrand	Adoree	Baron
Malequieux	Melodie Religieuse	Southern Music
Maniet	Petit Morceau de Concours	Baron
Mihalovici	Meditation	Penders
Montbrun	Lied	Southern Music
Montbrun	March	Southern Music
Montbrun	Promenade	Penders
Montbrun	Scherzo	Southern Music
Poot	Humoresque	Penders
Porret	Concertino I, II, III, IV	Baron
Poulain	Melodie	Baron
Purcell	Trumpet Voluntary	C. Fischer
Purcell	Two Airs from Bonduca	Mercury
Reger	Romanze	Southern Music
Robbins	Mont Saint-Michel	Penders
Ruetter	Fanfares	Southern Music
Sibelius	The Swan of Tuonela	Baron
Strauss	Zueignung	Editions-Musicus
Tenaglia-Krieger	Aria and Allegro	Presser

	GRADE III	
Alary	Morceau de Concours	Cundy-Bettoney
Albrespic	Lied et Scherzo	Penders
Andrieu	Contest Solos I, II, III, IV, V	Alfred
Arnell	Trumpet Allegro	Schott
Aubain	Marche et Scherzo	Penders
Bakalienikoff	Polonaise	Belwin
Balay	Andante et Allegro	Penders
Balay	Piece de Concours	Penders
Balay	Petite Piece Concertante	Penders
Balay	Prelude et Ballade	Penders
Barat	Fantaisie in Eb	Penders
Barraine	Aria	Southern Music
Beaucamp	Arlequinade	Penders
Berghmans	La Chenille	Penders
Bloch, A.	Meou-Tan Yin	Southern Music
Busser	Andante et Scherzo	Penders
Busser	Fantaisie sur des Themes Ecossais	Southern Music
Casadesus	Hymne	Southern Music
Chailleux	Morceau de Concert	Penders
Chaplaevsky	Valse Caprice	Leeds
Cole	Hammersmith Galop	Schott
Cools	Solo de Concours	Penders
Corelli	Air and Dance	Editions Musicus
Cowell	Triad	Peer International
Dallier	Fete Joyeuse	Southern Music
Damase	Hymne	Elkan-Vogel
Deherve	Allergo de Concours	Baron
Delmas	Choral and Variations	Alfred
Donato	Prelude et Allegro	Penders
Fiocco	Allegro	Presser
Fitzgerald	Frolic	C. Fischer
Fitzgerald	Rondo Capriccioso	C. Fischer

Foret	Deux Pieces	Penders
Gaubert	Cantabile et Scherzetto	Cundy-Bettoney
Gedalge	Piece	Penders
Gibbons-Cruft	Suite	Mills
Goeyens, A.	All' Antica	Penders
Goeyens, A.	Fantaisie Dramatique	Southern Music
Goeyens, A.	Introduction and Scherzo	C. Fischer
Goeyens, A.	Morceau de Concert	Southern Music
Goeyens, F.	Fantaisie Caprice	Penders
Goeyens, F.	Morceau de Concert	Penders
Guilbert	Impromptu	Penders
Guillaume	Andante et Allegro	Baron
Houdy	Sarabande	Penders
Hue	First Solo de Concert	Remick
Jean-Jean	Capriccioso	Alfred
Jolivet	Air de Bravoure	International
Karsev	Two Pieces	International
LeBoucher	Scherzo Appassionato	Southern Music
Levine	Scherzo	International
Malipiero	Le Fanfaron de la Fanfare	Penders
Mihalovici	Scherzo-Valse	Penders
Mouquet	Impromptu	Penders
Mouquet	Legende Heroique	Southern Music
Persichetti	Hollow Men	Elkan-Vogel
Porret	Six Esquisses	Baron
Purcell (Lillya)	Sonata	C. Fischer
Raphael	Marche	Penders
Rathaus	Allegro Concertante	Boosey-Hawkes
Reed	Ode for Trumpet	Hansen
Rohlig	Eight Intradas and Chorales for Trumpet and Organ	Concordia
Ropartz	Andante et Allegro	International
Rossini	Cujus Animam	C. Fischer
Rossini	Inflamatus	C. Fischer
Sanders	Square Dance	Galaxy
Silver	Scherzo	Penders
Smith	Suite Classique	Edition Musicus
Tchemberdjy	Pioneer Suite	Rochester
Teleman	Presto	Southern Music
Trowbridge	Alla Marcia	Composers Press
Tuthill	Scherzo	Remick
Vento	Sonata	Edition Musicus
Vidal	Aria and Fanfare	Southern Music
Vidal	Piece de Concert	Penders
Vivaldi	Allegro	Ricordi
Young	Contempora Suite	Bandland
Whitney	Concertino	Schirmer
Wormser	Theme and Variations	Baron

GRADE IV

Antufeyev	Variations	International
Asafiev	Sonata	Leeds
Bach-Deherve	Preludes	Southern Music
Barat	Andante et Scherzo	Penders
Barat	Lento et Scherzo	Penders
Bariller	Citoyen Mardi-Gras	Penders
Barraine	Fanfares de Printemps	R. D. King
Beriot	Scene de Ballet	Southern Music
Bitsch	Fantaisetta	Penders
Bloch, E.	Proclamation	Broude
Bonneau	Fantaisie Concertante	Penders
Bonneau	Suite	Penders
Boutry	Trumpetunia	Penders
Bozza	Badinage	Penders
Bozza	Rhapsodie	Penders
Brandt	Concertpiece, Opus 12	International
Burke	Danza Alegre	C. Fischer
Busser	Variations in Eb	Cundy-Bettoney
Cellier	Chevauchee	Southern Music

Challan	Variations	Penders
Chapuis	Solo de Trompette en Fa	Penders
Clergue	Sarabande et Rigaudon	Penders
Contemporary French	Recital Pieces	International
Corelli	Sonata VIII	Ricordi
DeBoeck	Allegro	C. Fischer
Douliez	Piece Concertante	Baron
Ellis	8771-W	Penders
Emmanuel	Sonate	Penders
Fiala	Concertino	International
Fitzgerald	Concerto in Ab minor	C. Fischer
Fitzgerald	Introduction and Fantasy	Belwin
Francaix	Sonatine	Baron
Gabaye	Boutade	Penders
Geehl	Concertstuck	Boosey-Hawkes
Goeb	Lyric Piece	Mercury
Goedicke	Concert Etude	Leeds
Goeyens, A.	Andante et Scherzando	Southern Music
Goeyens, F.	Suite Romantique	Peters
Hamilton	Capriccio	Schott
Handel	Adagio and Allegro	Presser
Handel	Aria Con Variazioni	Ricordi
Holmes	Sonata	Shawnee
Hubeau	Sonata	Southern Music
Kreb-Biggs	Eight Chorale Preludes for Trumpet and Organ	Music Press
Martelli	Sonatine	Baron
Martinu	Sonatine	Penders
Mozart	Concerto	C. Fischer
Porrino	Preludio, Aria, et Scherzo	Southern Music
Purcell	Sonata	Edition Musicus
Saint-Saens	Fantasie en Mi Bemol	Baron
Schmitt	Andantino	Southern Music
Shinohara	Trois Pieces Concertantes	Penders
Simeone	Trumpet in the Night	Shawnee
Strauwen	Piece Herioque	Baron
Thome	Fantaisie	Penders
Torelli	Concerto	International
Torelli	Sinfonia con Tromba, Organ	R. D. King
Tournemire	Fantaisie	Southern Music
Vidal	Concertino	Belwin
Wagner	Introduction and Rondo	Chappell
Webber	Suite in F Major	Mills
Williams	Prelude and Scherzo	Colin
Williams	Sonata	Colin
Zbinden	Concertino	Schott

GRADE V

Addison	Concerto	Mills
Ahlgrimm	Concerto	Peters
Bennett	Rose Variations	Chappell
Bitsch	Quatre Variations sur un Theme de Domenico Scarlatti	Penders
Bohrnstedt	Concerto	Remick
Bonnard	Sonata	Ricordi
Boutry	Trumpeldor	Penders
Bozza	Caprice	Baron
Bozza	Concertino	Baron
Bozza	Rustiques	Penders
Brandt	First Concert Piece, opus 11	Cundy-Bettoney
Brenta	Concertino	Penders
Casterede	Sonatine	Penders
Charlier	Solo de Concours	Baron
Chaynes	Concerto	Penders
Clostre	Concerto	R. D. King
Constant	Trois Mouvements	Penders
Darcy	Rhapsodie	Baron
Defay	Sonatine	Penders
Delerue	Concertino	Penders
Desenclos	Incantation-Theme-Danse	Penders

Desportes	Concerto	Southern Music	Mayer	Concert Piece	Boosey-Hawkes
Dubois	Concertino	Penders	Montbrun	Sarabande and Finale	Penders
Enesco	Legende	Southern Music	Pilss	Concerto	Universal
Gartenlaub	Trois Pieces Breves	R. D. King	Poot	Etude de Concert	Southern Music
Giannini	Concerto	Remick	Porrino	Concertino	Ricordi
Goedicke	Concerto	Leeds	Riisager	Concertino	Schirmer
Grimm	Concertino	Southern Music	Rueff	Fantaisie Concertante	Penders
Haydn	Concerto	Southern Music	Rueff	Sonatine	Penders
Hindemith	Sonata	Associated	Schmitt	Suite	R. D. King
Honegger	Intrada	Baron	Shapero	Sonata	Southern-N. Y.
Ibert	Impromptu	Penders	Sowerby	Sonata	Remick
Jolivet	Concertino	Southern Music	Stevens	Sonata	Peters
Jongen	Cadence and Rigodon	Baron	Tomasi	Concerto	Penders
Kaminski	Concertino	Leeds	Tomasi	Triptyque	Penders
Kanitz	Concert Piece	Affiliated	Tuthill	Sonata	Remick
Kennan	Sonata	Remick	Wal-Berg	Concerto	Leeds
Lantier	Concert en Trois Parties	Elkan-Vogel	Weber	Sonatine Breve	Penders
Latham	Suite	Presser	Williams	Concertos I, II, III, IV, V, VI	Colin
Lewis	Concerto	Mills			

September, 1963

HOW HIGH IS HIGH?

Harry Jenkins

ENDURANCE IS ONE OF THE TRUM-peter's biggest problems. The development and maintenance of the higher register is one of the phases of playing that most affects it. (The higher register is here defined as those notes above high C.) This extreme register is more difficult to develop than the others; it is more unpredictable and treacherous; it tires the embouchure more than other registers, and is the most exposed in performance.

The player should ask himself, "How high can I go without impairing the quality of my tone or my other registers and endurance?" Ex-cessive strain in the higher register has an unpleasant effect and is detrimental to overall development.

When one has full command of a high note: He can attack it cleanly, piano and forte; he can slur to and from it with comparative ease; intonation presents only a minor problem.

The written high D is the perfect note to aim for. With this note under good control he can "coax" his way upwards. Merely by adding a little "muscle" he can hit a high F. At this point it would be a good idea for him to stop, unless he is prepared to sacrifice some of his more stable assets. To illustrate: Suppose we take a rubber band and stretch it. As we do so, more and more tension is created and the band, thru excessive overwork, gradually becomes thinner and weaker. This is the effect on the lip when the tone becomes thinner and the lip weaker.

What to Practice

Certain exercises help to develop the higher register. These exercises can be improvised or they can be found in books dealing with the high notes. Some of these books are:

Top Tones by Walter Smith; *Tech-*

342

nical Studies by Herbert Clarke; *Daily Drills* by Max Schlossberg; *Daily Technical Studies* by Aaron Harris; and *Daily Technical Exercises for Advanced Players* by Richard Shuebruk. It is interesting to note that many such exercises deal with chromatic scales (still, in my opinion, the most gradual and effective way to approach high notes).

Here are some improvised exercises. They can be altered or varied according to the individual player's needs.

In Conclusion

I mentioned the high F as the top note for the player to attain, and that to be able to do this he must be able to control a D easily. It is quite possible to go much higher. In fact, there is practically no limit as to how high one can go, but the player who wants to go higher must be prepared to make sacrifices in tone, intonation, etc.

Here are some suggestions for maintaining and improving the higher register:

1. Practice the high notes only after the warmup—after the first twenty minutes of playing.

2. Practice them only on a fresh lip and not on one which has suffered excessive abuse from the day before. In that case leave them alone for the day.

3. Do not make the high register an end in itself in the daily practice routine. Work on other things as well.

4. Do not spend more than fifteen minutes on the high register. Better too little work than too much.

5. Practice the high notes softly. Coax them, do not force them.

Now to return to the original question. How high is "high"? As a note to have, hold, control, and to provide a solid base for higher notes to follow, high D is, indeed, "high"!

October, 1963

STYLE IN BRASS PLAYING

Maurice Faulkner

A NUMBER OF YEARS AGO WHEN Toscanini was conductor of the New York Philharmonic Orchestra and Harry Glantz was the highly respected first trumpeter, this writer was invited to attend a rehearsal of the orchestra by that master of the trumpet. It was during the warm summertime in New York, and the orchestra was playing its concerts each evening at the Lewisohn Stadium. Toscanini did not conduct the summer series, and a lesser man was on the podium that morning when I walked thru the gates at the rear of the stage. Glantz greeted me and showed me to one of the shaded tables in front of the stage. The program for that day was one of those national celebrations saluting the music of Switzerland. Much of the music of the program had never been performed before in this country, and the orchestra was sight-reading it at rehearsal. The two-hour session represented all the time that would be devoted to getting the music ready for that evening's concert, so the morning had to be an efficient one.

The conductor greeted the men jovially and the rehearsal started off with a light-heartedness which might have had an effect upon the efficiency of the orchestra if the men had not been virtuosos on their instruments. The music covered a span of several hundred years, and the style variations had to be apparent the first time it was played, for there was not enough time to re-work it extensively. I had come to hear Glantz play the trumpet, and I sat there in great awe as I heard him play the baroque, classic, romantic, and contemporary Swiss scores with ease and a variety of style concepts. This marvelous musician interpreted each work in just the right manner so that his playing became a harmonious blend with that of the strings and woodwinds. All were recreating the original style concepts as they rehearsed one piece after another.

After the rehearsal, I asked Harry how he felt the music and how he produced such results. His answer was a classic of understatement; it might have squelched a more contrite man. "I just screw up my lips and blow," was his answer. Perhaps this is the only answer one can give to a question of that sort, and perhaps it is the answer which comes to a man who has the inherent musical qualities as displayed by the great masters of brass, string, and woodwind instruments when they are at their finest. A word or two about these items to the neophyte player might ease the learner's burden and guide him into paths which would make him grow more rapidly and more musically.

Tongue and Style

There are many factors which need to be considered in this question of style. We will consider here only one: the element of tonguing. The concept of the tongue as a valve which interrupts the flow of the air from the lungs to the lips is one which has developed over the past century of brass playing. The older concept, which proposed that the tongue was the driver of air into the lips and the instrument, is still in vogue and has some merit in certain types of playing. However, it usually results in a rougher tone production and will not suffice in careful stylistic playing. The musical brass man must be able to recapture the essence of baroque, classic, romantic, and contemporary music at a moment's notice. He needs the technical know-how to accomplish this without placing a strain on the other factors of his tone production. Above all, he must introduce these stylistic techniques at the appropriate moment and in the appropriate music. Thus, the study of a brass instrument requires something more than learning to blow it easily.

If the tongue is thought of as a valve which interrupts the air flow, then it is possible to develop a number of different types of interruption. The usual tongue syllable taught to young players is *too*, which produces a fairly sharp attack without too great an explosion. When the player switches from the middle register to the high register, some teachers have him use the syllable *tee*, thus taking advantage of the smaller column of air of the higher tongue position which that syllable develops, making the higher tones come more easily. Of course, when this is used, the smaller column of air creates a smaller quality of tone; this may change the color of the melodic pattern as the player moves from one octave to another. The syllable *tah* is often used to help the player produce broader and heavier low tones. This also counteracts the smooth quality of range which should be carried from the low to the high octaves.

Foreign Languages and Tonguing

This early learning experience continues with the addition of the legato tongue syllables, *doo, dee, dah*, which result in smoother articulations for more lyric passages. The Germans have used a slightly different combination in some of their tongue exercises: they vary these ideas with *tü, dü*, using the umlaut (or combination of eu) to bring the tongue forward, with the resulting tongue position creating a different sound. Try it. See if it has an effect on the quality of tone. In fact, an interesting study should be undertaken some day in which the researcher examines, by means of tape, the effect of different language backgrounds on the tonal quality of the brass instruments. The Italian, French, German, and English vowel and consonant sounds could be analyzed for their effect upon the trumpet tone. We all are aware of the variety of accents in spoken communication among various peoples. Does this variety of accent have an effect upon the tone quality of those instruments which use vowel and consonant sounds in the production of tone?

Double and Triple Tonguing

After the neophyte has learned to tongue with the *too* and *doo* positions, he usually is taught to double-tongue and triple-tongue. There are interesting variations of this technique from country to country. Teachers teach a double tongue based upon the syllables *ti, ki, tee, kee, tü, kü*, or *ta, ka*. If many syllable variations are possible, would it not be wise for each player to learn all forms of the variations and thus develop the flexibility of his tongue as well as a variety of control devices? Triple tonguing, also, is taught in different ways with various vowel sounds. Some teach *tu, tu, ku*; others *tee, tee, kee, tü, tü, kü, ti, ti, ki*, etc. An interesting triple tongue technique is the one which uses double tongue as a basis. The syllables are placed in triplet patterns: *tu, ku, tu; tee, kee, tee; tü, kü, tü*; or *ti, ki, ti*. Again, it seems plausible and simple for any student who expects to become a specialist on the trumpet—or other brass instrument—to develop as many of these syllables as possible. For with these tongued syllables comes variety in the control and facility of the tongue.

These are the usual syllables taught in basic tongue techniques. But in order to create a style consciousness, we must go further and teach other control devices. There

Maurice Faulkner — Brass Clinic Editor since 1965

must be a smooth and flexible speed which does not build up percussive sounds in tonguing. This type of flexibility is used in the running baroque figures often found in band transcriptions of Bach chorale preludes, fugues, etc. Rapid and smooth tongue style can be achieved by practicing the tongue syllables *loo, lee, lü, li, lah*, etc. The *loo* position is one of the most relaxed positions. When it is done well, it articulates the air column with a beautiful roll which separates the tones without percussive explosions.

Breath Attack

Another tongue position which eliminates the usual percussive attack of careless brass playing so common to amateur performance is that of the breath attack, or diaphragm attack, as it is called. This is use by woodwind players and has now come to be one of the best devices for brass players when they have to match woodwind passages. It is an exhaled breath-push which is best done by using the syllables *hoo, hee, hü, hah, hi*. The spurt of air is started from the abdominal or diaphragmatic area and is breathed into the lips with those syllables. It results in an imperceptible start without noise and can be done at the most pianissimo passages. When this is done by woodwind and brass sections together, it is one of the most delightful wind techniques.

Practice tongue syllables with the tongue high and low in the mouth. Work at them with the back of the tongue low and the front high. Produce the tone with the back of the tongue high and the front low. Develop new concepts of tongue control. Teach the tongue muscles to control all parts of the tongue. Herbert Clarke used to have his students anchor the front end of the tongue against the bottom teeth and practice fast articulations with the middle of the tongue coming up rapidly. Try this, and see what it does to eliminate the percussive attack in fast passages.

Rapid Tonguing

This writer has found that many brass players have difficulty in speeding up their staccato tongue. Usually this comes about because they are using too much of the tongue in a driving pattern. Rapid tongue

exercises by the student to maintain a relaxed position of the tongue in the mouth with the syllable *loo* seem effective. When the player can control this in regular sixteenth-note patterns, he is advised to place the tip of the tongue slightly forward with the syllable *thoo*, maintaining the relaxed position as far as possible. Then a syllable pattern of *loo, loo, loo, loo, thoo, thoo, thoo, thoo*, is repeated over and over again to combine the relaxed *loo* position with the more articulate *thoo* position. When the *thoo* pattern becomes flexible and easy, more of a point is brought in to the tongue so that the articulation becomes more precise. With time and effort, this exercise pattern develops a speed which can almost double the rate of the usual single tongue. This writer has kept a clocking on students who work on this pattern, and in some instances single tongue speeds have increased from 340 per minute to 760 per minute.

WHEN TONGUE FLEXIBILITY AND variety have been developed, the player is then technically equipped to use these abilities for his interpretive ideas. In order to perform convincingly, a brass player must be aware of evolving styles. He should undergo a careful study of the literature for keyboard, string, and woodwind instruments, in various historical periods, to help bring about this awareness. Such study will strengthen his concept of the performance practices of music from a given historical period.

Brass playing has a long history stretching back to ancient times. The actual performance styles, techniques, and practices of ancient cultures are not known to the modern brass musician, but the more recent periods of history have yielded substantial documentation of their stylistic idiosyncrasies. By studying reliable scores (made available largely thru the work of musicologists, and other scholars, who have carefully edited old scores and manuscripts into practical editions for modern performance) and music history, performers have the opportunity of learning important details which will affect their musical outlook. Certain vexing questions about style can be faced more securely. How should the trumpeter play the brilliant passages in Bach's Brandenburg Concerto

No. 2, or his part in a Gabrieli brass work, or the motifs in Wagner's "Ring"?

Baroque Trumpet

There is a world of difference between the music Bach wrote for trumpet and that written by Wagner. Each requires a specific sound, for each represents a different style. Since styles change with each musical epoch, the musician's interpretive approach to dissimilar styles likewise must change.

What is the special sound necessary for Bach's trumpet passages? How is it achieved? One ideal way to find out is to examine one of the original Baroque trumpets in D or F and try to play a passage written for it. The 18th century trumpet, when we examine it, has a tubing which curls back twice on its entire length. It is pitched lower than our modern version of the D trumpet. One plays in the upper partials on this trumpet as the modern French hornist does on his instrument. Therefore, the higher octaves were achieved, in Bach's time, with flexibility of lip and tongue and not with finger exercises. A heavy attack quite often overblows a Baroque trumpet. The process of being accurate and maintaining balance requires a tongue position that will not interrupt the lip vibrations and yet is far enough forward to speak cleanly and readily. In this way, fanfare-like arpeggios can be played with brilliance. For running diatonic passages, the player's tongue retires slightly to give the close intervals less of a chance to break or sputter. The Baroque trumpeter, therefore, needed to have two tongue positions for the passages in Bach's Brandenburg No. 2: the forward tongue and the syllable *tü*, for fanfare, and a syllable of *thü* for rollicking technique passages.

The Baroque sound is difficult to produce on modern instruments. The importance of each contrapuntal line can be altered by the modern instrument unless tonal balance is maintained in ensemble. In 1957, this writer had the opportunity to hear the famous Cologne Baroque Chamber Orchestra playing modern instruments built on the principles of the Baroque originals: short-necked violins, which copied earlier designs, *flutes à bec*, oboes, bassoons, horns, trumpets, etc. The tone

An 18th century *trompeta clarina*, the trumpet used in Bach's scores. The round pommel often bore ornate carvings.

quality of the ensemble was sonorous, and less brilliant than would have been the case had contemporary instruments been used, but each instrument could be distinctly heard in the glorious counterpoint. The modern French horn can be heavy for the inner parts of Baroque counterpoint, but the smaller-bore Baroque horn does not overpower the winds and strings. The brilliant modern trumpet pierces today's performances of Baroque music with its forceful tone quality. The Bach-era trumpet, on the other hand, had a more mellow sonority, which, when played with facility, had a virtuoso-like quality that made it a fit companion to the delightful string roulades and arpeggios.

The Classic Era

The Classic Period offers a different concept to the brass specialist. Let us isolate the case of the trumpet, in particular. The Classic composers utilized the trumpet as a kind of percussive instrument. In this music, the precise details of harmonic clarity require the trumpeter to reduce the breadth of tone in order to blend with strings and woodwinds. The sonorous, spinning contrapuntal lines of the earlier period gave way, in the era of classicism, to rhythmic precision and melodic clarity. Melody in the upper instrumental parts predominates in this music. All else must balance with it. In ensemble, the sound of two trumpets in 5ths, 4ths, and 3rds, reinforcing the harmonies in tutti passages, must be

contained below the dynamic level of other instruments.

There are two ways to do this. One way is to consistently maintain the volume at one or two dynamic levels below that of the other instruments. (This, however, may sometimes interfere with the vitality of tone.) The other technique is to attack the tone on the dynamic level indicated in the score, but drop off immediately to a softer level. (This technique is sometimes carried to the point where the note is not held for its full duration. Thus, for a fraction of a second, the trumpet may sound like an echo of itself, while the other instruments are fully sustaining their notes.) This device, of course, should be varied according to the tempo and mood of a work. Allegro movements will require more of it, whereas andantes and largos may call for an elimination of the technique altogether. Some conductors call this device "lightening the tone."

Wagner and the Romantics

The Classic trumpet style is found in the early symphonies of Beethoven as well as in certain passages of his later works. There are times, however, when Beethoven foreshadows the Romanticism of Wagner, Berlioz, Liszt, Tchaikovsky, and others. Where the Classical trumpet requires precise, clear attacks with a slight dropping off, the Wagnerian scores, by contrast, demand a heavier initial sound, broadly sustained to the end of its duration. This can be achieved by a broader position of the tongue's point. The *too* syllable is desirable for Mozart's inner trumpet parts, but for Wagner, the *tü* or *thü* is needed to create a more rounded air column striking the lips, which, in turn, vibrate creating a thicker and more lush sound. In producing legato tonguing, the same technique must be developed. The syllables *dü* and *dah* will produce a full sound for a broad legato passage in Wagner.

The problem of attack varies somewhat in each national school of the Romantic period. The Russians looked to both the French and the Germans for their orchestral inspiration. For this reason, we should not overlook the fact that, quite often, in a Tchaikovsky symphony, for example, a smaller French sound is desirable. This can be made by using

the syllable *thi* rather than *thü*.

French Impressionism

The Impressionists reacted to the lush sensuality of the typical Wagnerian sound. For the orchestra, they scored with transparency and delicacy. This, in turn, typified the French sound of the era, and it influenced a number of composers in other countries, notably in England and Italy. A trumpet line in an impressionistic score calls for a thin tone with precise, unwavering pitch—one that will blend well with woodwinds and strings. A fat, unyielding tone is quite out of place in the orchestral color palette of Impressionism. The tonal requirement calls upon some of the techniques developed in the Classic idiom but molded anew.

The syllable *hoo* (produced diaphramatically) affords the best results of this woodwind-like attack. Brass writing in Impressionistic music is often blended with woodwinds and strings: trumpet and oboe, trumpet and flute, horn and viola or cello, etc., to produce coloristic effects in great favor with the Impressionists. If the trumpeter is not to overshadow his colleagues in the woodwind or string section of the orchestra, he must develop an attack of considerable subtlety. The player should also try to sustain the line without vibrato or pitch deviations in order to maintain the clarity of color. One should try to hear the finest French orchestras play the music of Debussy, Ravel, Dukas, and other Impressionistic composers for superior examples of their tonal qualities produced by their matched brasses and woodwinds.

Modern Music

Contemporary composers have utilized some of the color of the Impressionists. Among our own American composers, we find this somewhat more discernible in those composers who have been influenced directly by French musical thought and training, as in the case of those who have studied with Nadia Boulanger. Generally speaking, the dissonant harmonies of modern idioms require the player to be extremely conscious of pitch discrepancies. He must produce a precise, bright tone which will blend with pitches and qualities of the other instruments. Of course, not all modern music needs this kind of tone. Hindemith's music, for example. represents a diversity of stylistic demands. When pitted against the weighty contrapuntal scoring of other instruments, the trumpeter might well use a broad Wagnerian tone. On the other hand, some passages by this composer seem to ask for a reversion to the flexible Bach-style tongue and tone techniques but with the addition of considerable body and support to the sound. Hindemith is only one example, of course: the brass player must be prepared to seek out the special quality of tone needed for each of the important contemporary composers.

Modern brass styles are sometimes governed by national considerations. Although the Italians seem to demonstrate no particular idiosyncrasies in their music today (other than, perhaps, their allegiance to cantabile lines), the French brass tone seems to conflict less in dissonant harmonies than, by comparison, the German sound; while the English trumpeter can produce a sound of both tonal depth and precision. In our own country, the considerable emphasis on band cornet tone over the past 50 years has produced a penchant, in brass players, for broad, sonorous tone qualities which fit nicely into the Romantic concept of sound but do not correspond to the tonal requirements of other styles. This quality, however, seems to suit most American music.

This writer still likes to remember the outdoor rehearsal of the New York Philharmonic when Harry Glantz played Baroque, Classic, Romantic, and contemporary styles with exquisite grace and with a firm grasp of style without the slightest trace of effort. Such ability is representative of the greatest virtuosi and makes a fine trumpeter comparable to the greatest violinists.

FINE

Practicing With the Mouthpiece

Harry Jenkins

IS PRACTICE WITH THE MOUTHpiece an indispensable part of the daily routine? When should it take place—and for how long? Is it always beneficial, or can it be harmful? What is the real value of this oft-discussed exercise?

Potential Benefits

For the beginner who has difficulty in starting a tone properly, time spent with the mouthpiece before the taking of the instrument quickly provides the ability to make the lips vibrate freely. Commonly, the beginner will puff out his cheeks, blow air through the mouthpiece, and make no contact. However, once he tucks in the corners of his mouth, moistens his lips, and attacks *tu*, he is amazed at the simplicity of the act when a sound ensues where previously nothing happened. Now, putting the mouthpiece into the instrument mouthpiece receiver, he attacks properly and starts the tone without any difficulty. He must be cautioned, though, to hold the mouthpiece against his lips with a minimum amount of pressure, for too much pressure chokes off the vibrations needed to produce the sound.

For the advanced player, too, mouthpiece practice has its advantages. A few minutes of staccato and lip slur practice before the taking of the instrument has the effect of quickly stimulating the lips. But beneficial practice in sustained tones, especially in the low register, is hardly possible with the mouthpiece alone.

Possible Harm

Mouthpiece practice executed incorrectly can do more harm than good. Unfortunately, this is what happens in many cases.

Many players, deceived by the puny mouthpiece tone, unwittingly attempt to duplicate in volume the sound of the instrument. Thus, their practice on the mouthpiece amounts to what (on the instrument) would be fortissimo playing in the middle and high register—something they would never sanction, especially in the prewarmup stage. Is it any wonder that their lips afterwards are slow to respond properly, that their practice session proves so unrewarding? In effect, they have abused their lips and robbed them of some of their sensitivity.

In order to practice correctly with the mouthpiece, players must be able to judge how their efforts will sound coming out of the bells of their instruments—AMPLIFIED. Until they are able to do so, they should omit practice with the mouthpiece.

In Conclusion

1. Practice with the mouthpiece is not a substitute for instrument practice; it is only an aid.

2. It should occur before the instrument is taken; it is of little benefit afterwards.

3. It should not exceed five minutes in duration.

4. It is not indispensable. If the player is in doubt as to how to proceed, he should omit mouthpiece practice and add five minutes of practice of the instrument itself to compensate.

The player need not guess in order to determine what he is doing when he practices with the mouthpiece. He need only start practicing immediately with the instrument, and he will KNOW.

FINE

1964

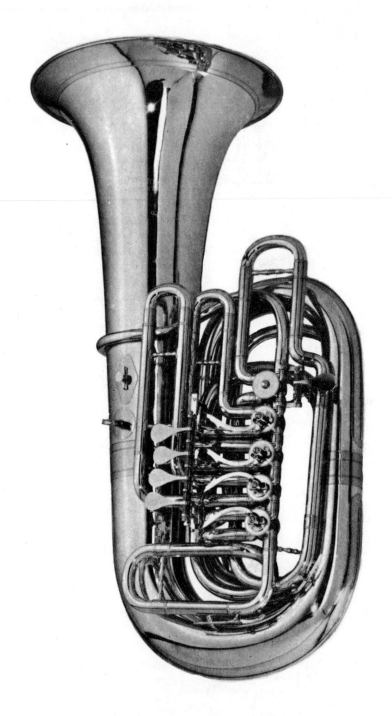

5-Valve CC Tuba

Technical Problems on the Double Horn

A. Cutler Silliman

FULLNESS OF TONE AND CORRECT intonation are of such paramount importance in horn playing that other basic technical skills are often neglected in the training of young players. This is unfortunate, as composers and arrangers today are demanding almost the same degree of technical proficiency from the horn as that commonly expected from the trumpet. Rapid single tonguing, double and triple tonguing, and fast legato passages are now common in horn parts. Students must be given the necessary technical studies to enable them to master these problems.

Accuracy of attack and endurance are two other difficult aspects of horn playing. That they are related will be shown in the discussion of how to improve them. Some special effects, such as valve and lip trills, glissandos, and hand stopping, must also be mastered by the hornist. These, too, will be discussed.

Rapid Articulation

Since most method books in regular use for horn instruction do not adequately cover the technique of rapid articulations, it is necessary to find supplementary material. Trumpet methods, such as Arban's and St. Jacome's, can be used for this purpose, as the written ranges of the articulation exercises usually do not go too high for the horn. For younger horn players, trumpet exercises may have too high a tessitura. It will be necessary to edit them, either eliminating sections or transposing them down. It should be borne in mind that, even for advanced players, trumpet books are strictly supplements to horn study;

the development of the horn's low register will be neglected if they are the primary material.

Trills

Fingered tone trills are practical only in the range in which adjacent notes of the harmonic series are more than a whole tone apart. This would be below F♯4 on the F horn (with middle C as C4 and the octave above as C5) and below B4 on the B♭ horn. (All pitches and notation given in this article are written a perfect fifth above the actual sound.) Above these notes, a fingered whole tone trill will usually result in a repeated single pitch instead of two alternating pitches. To avoid this "door-bell" effect, the lips must make the changes of pitch in exact coordination with the fingers. Since this is the same lip movement necessary for a lip trill, it is easier to use the lip trill and eliminate the problem of coordinating the lips and the fingers. Charts of trill fingerings can be found on pages 76 and 78 of Farkas' *The Art of French Horn Playing*, published by Summy-Birchard.

Endurance and Accuracy

One of the secrets of endurance is to relieve the pressure of the mouthpiece against the lips at every opportunity. Whenever possible, the mouthpiece should be removed from the lips entirely. It is a great temptation to maintain pressure—and the embouchure setting—through rests for fear of losing the setting and missing the next attack. This is an understandable fear, but maintaining mouthpiece pressure through

rests greatly increases the muscular strain in the lips.

Breaking the embouchure during short rests means that all notes immediately following the rests become like first notes—the most difficult single problem of French horn playing. Nevertheless, the instrument is not really mastered until initial attacks are as accurate as those within a passage. The problem is actually one of tonal memory, because the lips should respond automatically with the proper embouchure setting if the player thinks the correct pitch.

Listen, Play, Sing

Singing and dictation drills are excellent means for improving accuracy; both require the student to think consciously of the pitch. The student should be asked to sing phrases and single pitches. One good drill for the student would be to have him play part of a phrase and sing the continuation. Another would require that he sing the first note of a new phrase or composition, relating it to the music just completed. Singing also helps to improve intonation.

Dictation drills can be related to the horn if the student plays the material on his instrument instead of writing it. He can repeat phrases, intervals, or single notes after the instructor or another player. Playing by ear is also good practice.

Accuracy of attack can be improved by playing isolated tones in an unrelated sequence. An example of this type of exercise can be found on page 69 of Farkas' *The Art of French Horn Playing*. The *Méthode*

Complète de Cor by Lucien Thévet, published by Alphonse Leduc, incorporates this type of exercise throughout its two volumes, beginning with simple ones and progressing to a quite difficult level.

Another approach to the problem of accuracy is to play an exercise such as the following in a very exaggerated manner: slowly, with extremely harsh fortissimo attacks and with a definite break for a breath between groups of four tones. The sound of this is quite unpleasant and unmusical, but a little of this type of practice each day will improve the sharpness of the attack.

Kopprasch, *Sixty Selected Studies for French Horn*, No. 6, Carl Fischer. Reprinted by permission of Carl Fischer, Inc.

Bell Up

A unique problem in horn playing is the direction for "bell up." In normal playing, the hand in the bell modifies the basic tone slightly by taking a little of the rough "edge" off the tone and by flatting the pitch. When raising the bell for bell up, it is difficult to keep the hand in the correct position with the result that the pitch usually becomes quite sharp. Since this effect is played fortissimo, the sharpness of intonation becomes even worse. If there is sufficient time before and after

such playing, the intonation change can be compensated for by pulling out the tuning slide.

An advantage in the double horn is that one side of the horn can be tuned flat and then used only for the bell up passage, while the side of the instrument tuned normally is used for the remainder of the music until there is time to adjust the tuning again. Care must be taken not to raise the bell so high that the right hand is no longer effective in the bell when later there is no adjustment of the tuning to be made.

Glissando

A special effect now quite common in horn parts is the glissando. This is usually achieved by a "scooping-up" of adjacent tones of the harmonic series in a rapid lip slur. It can be made easier by starting on the F horn and shifting to the B-flat horn for the top note. Occasionally, a rapid, ascending scale passage is effective as a glissando, as in Saint-Saens' *Morceau de Concert*.

Saint-Saens, *Morceau de Concert*, Op. 94, from Selected Studies for Horn, Southern Music Co. Reprinted by permission of Southern Music Co.

With a thorough knowledge of the harmonic series for both F and B-flat horns, it is possible to find a convenient fingering for a glissando. Composers' notations are not always in accord with the best fingerings, and since, in a glissando, the

pitches themselves are blurred and indistinct, it is permissible usually just to approximate the intermediate tones of an indicated glissando.

Hand Stopping

In normal practice, hand stopping *raises* the pitch of the instrument. On the F horn, this change of pitch can be controlled easily to obtain one half-tone, but the same hand position in the B-flat horn will raise the pitch about three-quarters of a tone. This necessitates playing stopped passages, regardless of register, on the F horn. Two distinct qualities of tone can be produced with this kind of hand stopping—a very soft, "distant" sound and a harsh, piercing, "brassy" sound—depending on the force of the breath and the tightness of the embouchure.

A pitch change of a half step *down* can be made by closing the bell with the hand but not completely stopping it. This tone is muffled and of use only in soft passages.

From *Serenade*, Op. 31, by Benjamin Britten. Copyright 1944, Hawkes & Son (London) Ltd. Reprinted by permission of Boosey & Hawkes, Inc.

The glissando between the final two notes in the example by Britten is possible only with this type of hand stopping. It is a special effect and should never be used for normal muted playing.

FINE

February, 1964

The Brass Choir
What and Why?

Kenneth Bloomquist

WHETHER CALLED A LARGE BRASS ensemble, a brass band, an orchestral brass section, or a brass choir, a group of brass instruments such as the following—4 trumpets, 4 French horns, 3 trombones, 1 baritone, 1 tuba, 1 percussion—when molded into a unified ensemble, can

be one of the finest outlets for brass performance at any level of proficiency.

Though the size of the group naturally varies with the composition, this instrumentation forms a sound nucleus which seems to meet

with most composers' desires. Additional percussion and perhaps string bass and piano sometimes are needed to satisfy a composer's wishes. For touring purposes, another trumpet, French horn, and trombone (if the baritone player cannot double on trombone) may be desirable.

Why Have a Brass Choir?

Certainly, as performing groups, the symphony orchestra and the concert band have stood the test of time in the development of instrumentalists. Yet, in the public schools and at the university level, in many cases, the development of individual performance technique is lost in the doubling and redoubling of parts in concert band or in the lack of challenging material in certain orchestral literature, particularly that of the Classical Period. To be sure, the skills required of players in large sections are vast; but it is doubtful whether in such a situation the individual development of the performer adequately reflects his potential ability. While orchestral brass work lends itself to a most reliable performer analysis, it just does not provide enough to do, particularly in public school literature and oftentimes in college level work. In other words, the literature frequently does not tax the technique, range, or endurance of the performer. This void of performance experience the brass choir fills in every way.

In the perfection of tone, intonation, technique, blend, balance, phrasing, expression, and rhythm—constant goals of the music educator and conductor—the brass choir can prove itself faster and sometimes better than most other performance media.

In matters of tone production, the performer must strive not only for a clear tone but also for one that can be brilliant or dark, piercing or subdued, straight or with vibrato. Consequently, he must be able to hear himself at all dynamic levels and in all styles and in all ranges of his instrument. He must develop the ability to project his tone without over-blowing or blasting. In brass choir playing, where he can always hear himself clearly and often is shocked with this very experience, the performer comes to appreciate the difficulty of matching a tone as to timbre, or of projecting a phrase over twelve or thirteen other brasses without distorting the sound. The natural statement here is that the band and orchestra provide these very challenges, and certainly this is so; but, in this writer's opinion, they do not provide them as often as does a brass ensemble.

Intonation presents probably the most constant problem of all public school music educators and one that certainly is not ignored at any level. Obviously, to play in tune, the performer must know when he is not in tune. Rather than place the blame for poor intonation on instrument construction—an excuse used by all and many times justifiably—he quite often should recognize his lack of ability to hear unisons, octaves, fourths, fifths, and so on.

Again, to properly tune, the individual must hear himself in relation to the ensemble. Brass instrument tuning is difficult since it varies with register and interval. The brass player must go beyond the tuning of unisons or the good old concert B♭ to achieve good intonation and provide the learning experience of proper tuning. His tuning must include fourths, fifths, and octaves, as well as unisons.

In addition, the register of the particular instrument in the particular composition is a factor to be considered in tuning, as is the way in which the performer produces a tuning note. How often have we listened to a trumpet section play pianissimo in tuning and then render the composition before them at nothing less than forte?

Though the art of tuning could be discussed at great length here, let it suffice to say that the brass player when tuning must give attention to intervals, registers, tone, and dynamics, and that the brass choir affords almost constant opportunity for this attention.

Blend and balance are factors that sometimes seem to be on the fringe of the intangible—that happen almost mystically as an ensemble performs together for a long, indefinite period of time. However, while length of association of the performers is important, blend and balance certainly are not intangible or mystical or a happenstance. Here again, the brass choir proves to be an invaluable training medium. The performer suddenly is compelled to fit his individual part within a group of individual parts and hear not only himself but also the total product. This very consciousness of one's own positioning within a chord, phrase, or melodic line is the essence of all types of ensemble playing from orchestra to band to dance band and so forth.

Repertoire

Mention should be made of the literature for the large brass ensemble and of the great strides which have been taken in recent years to increase and improve it. Many good compositions are being written, published, or adapted by publishing firms for the brass choir.

The repertoire of The University of Kansas Brass Choir is necessarily varied for its forthcoming tour of the Far East. It includes music from the 16th and 17th centuries—the period often referred to as the golden age of brass—as well as contemporary European and American works, marches for brass, folk songs, and national anthems. Jazz, too, is represented, for, since this music plays a vital part on the American musical scene, the State Department encourages its inclusion on programs presented to foreign audiences.

The following sampling of K.U. Brass Choir repertoire all is published and available.

Giovanni Gabrieli—Canzona per Sonare No. 2; Canzona per Sonare No. 4
Johann Pezel—Three Pieces
Henry Purcell—Allegro and Air from King Arthur
Gottfried Reiche—Sonata No. 24
Johann Altenburg—Concerto for Clarini and Timpani
Claudio Monteverdi—Sancta Maria Ora Pro Nobis
John Adson—Two Ayres for Cornetts and Sagbuts
Ingolf Dahl—Music for Brass Instruments
Leonard Lebow—Suite for Brass
Aaron Copland—Fanfare for the Common Man
Leroy Anderson—Suite of Carols
Thomas Canning—Rondo for Percussion and Brass
Quinto Maganini—Shenandoah
Eugene Bozza—Sonatine
Robert Parris—Sontina for Brass
John Lewis—Three Little Feelings; Fanfare II and The Golden Striker
J. J. Johnson—Poem for Brass

The brass choir, in this article considered a performance medium all its own, obviously also can serve and should serve as a means of sectional rehearsal for the band or the orchestral repertoire class, and as a general clinic nucleus for brass pedagogy. Properly orientated and maintained, the brass choir thus becomes a most valuable tool for improving brass performance—and at the same time an extremely rewarding performance group.

FINE

1. The New York Brass Quintet

2. The Brass Choir of the Cincinnati College-Conservatory
of Music, Ernest Glover, Conductor

A virtuoso discusses his instrument —

Euphonium—Well Sounding

Raymond Young

THE WORD EUPHONIUM IS DERIVED from the Latin *euphonia*, which means "well sounding." Thus, with this definition in mind, the performer on the euphonium recognizes his obligation to strive toward the sound characteristic of the instrument— to be, in effect, "well sounding."

Unfortunately, most euphonium players have been transferred to the euphonium from the cornet or trumpet. As a result of such transfers, which are often a necessity, these players usually have developed the wrong concept of how the instrument should sound.

The sound of the euphonium should not be bright, as is usually the case with the trumpet and trombone. Instead, it should be dark in color and rich in texture—vibrant, smooth, flexible, and full. If sound can be visualized, we may see the sound of the euphonium as a large tapestry of velvet, which is royal blue in color. In this writer's opinion, the main objective of a performer on the euphonium is to project a sound of beauty to the listeners; and, even though unlimited technical virtuosity can be obtained on the euphonium, this phase of performance must never be allowed to overbalance that of beauty and musical expression.

By no means is the achievement of beautiful tone an easy task. The true tone is produced only after the student has mastered the basic fundamentals of tone production and then has continued to develop his tone with the same care with which he would work on a very difficult etude.

To achieve a vibrant and full tone, the student must develop a fast breath line. That is, he must inhale a large amount of air and have the sensation that the air is moving rapidly past the embouchure and through the horn. We may use the analogy of water going through a garden hose with the faucet at the house wide open, but the water controlled by the nozzle at the end of the hose. The water in the hose represents the player's breath, and the nozzle, his embouchure.

For a tone which is smooth and flexible—one which responds in all registers with equal ease—the player must learn to control the instrument in all ranges by the amount of breath control and embouchure control he uses within his complete range. Long tones throughout the entire range bring control and accuracy, but the development of lip slurs to encompass his range with facility results in control which is smooth and flexible.

To develop a tone which is dark in color, the player must have the proper embouchure and concept. The lips are held in a slight pucker, giving the contrary feeling of being relaxed but firm. They are not pulled as in smiling, for this produces a tone which is bright and thin. The upper lip is formed slightly over the lower lip with the lower jaw held in a natural position. The air is directed not straight toward the center of the mouthpiece but rather in a downward direction.

However, as accurate as all the physical adjustments may be, a student cannot obtain the proper sound unless he realizes the proper concept. This he can form by attending concerts and clinics where an accomplished euphonium performer is appearing and by listening to recordings displaying proper euphonium sound. Two recordings may be recommended: the fine disk which can be purchased from Harold Brasch[1] and the one which the author recently completed.[2] Both provide a good representation of proper concepts of euphonium playing.

When the euphonium student is well on his way to mastering the proper sound, he should begin to work on the vibrato. Probably the strongest asset in developing the final polish of a beautiful tone, the vibrato should be of a natural type, originating from the breath line— the type used by vocalist, flutist, and oboist. It is obtained by developing a pulsation of the breath through the use of the muscles at the bottom of the rib cage. The student should begin by blowing on his hand and developing the feeling of obtaining a very slow forte, piano, forte, piano with the breath. After he has obtained the correct feeling of his breath line, he should try the same method with his instrument, keeping the pulsations large, controlled, and even. He should gradually increase in speed, thus causing the pulsation to decrease in size. After a period of about two months, he should have mastered this method of the vibrato, its use having become involuntary and natural.

Again, a student of the euphonium has a specific duty to strive for beauty of tone. He must not defeat his purpose as musician and performer by being satisfied with a tone that is not characteristic of the instrument. Always, he must work carefully and diligently toward a tone which is *euphonia*.

1. Harold Brasch, 2707 South June Street, Arlington, Virginia. $3.50.
2. Raymond G. Young, Southern Station, Box 142, Hattiesburg, Mississippi. $4.50.
FINE

A professional tuba player examines the evolution of
his instrument and reflects on registers, repertory,
and recent developments . . .

TUBA TRENDS

Abe Torchinsky

OF ALL THE INSTRUMENTS IN THE modern symphony orchestra, probably the tuba alone lacks standardization. Indeed, the very name of the instrument—stemming from the word used by the Romans for their short military trumpet—is a misnomer since the tuba from its inception has been intended for use as the bass voice of the brass family.

Prior to its invention, Handel, Mendelssohn, and other composers employed on occasion such instruments as the serpent and the ophicleide—both very unsatisfactory in tone and intonation. Though in the modern orchestra the tuba player, by accepted procedure, plays any part written for these instruments, both were totally dissimilar to the present-day tuba except for their cup mouthpieces, and both usually called for a register much higher than the normal tuba range.

About 1820, a Mr. Stolzel of Berlin, co-pioneer of the valve, issued a price list of "chromatic brass instruments of my own inventions" which included a bass horn or bass trumpet in F or E♭ and a tenor horn or tenor trumpet in B♭. Neither can be identified positively, but they probably may be correctly regarded as the prototype of the tuba.

The tuba in its familiar style and shape appeared around 1835, when Wilhelm Wieprecht, working with Berlin instrument makers Greissling and Schott, introduced a price list which contained the first mention of the bass tuba in F, jointly patented under this name by himself and another Berlin maker, Moritz. However, both this instrument and their subsequent invention, the bombardon in F—the name of which previously had been given to a variety of valved trombones—proved unsuccessful due to inferior tone. And instrument makers and composers alike continued to search for the sonority unobtainable in the forerunners to the modern tuba.

Many countries participated in the further development of the tuba. In Russia there appeared the Helicon or circular bass, precursor of our modern sousaphone. Czerveny of Bohemia, long-famous instrument maker whose factory is still in existence, developed the fourth valve that today's tuba players, at least at the symphony orchestra level, regard as a must. Presently, there are in existence tubas with as many as seven valves. Invariably, these are F models since the F tuba player, experiencing less difficulty with his upper tones, constantly seeks ways to improve his lower registers.

Wagner, who probably knew more than anyone else of his time about the instrument and certainly was the first to exploit it to fullest advantage, wrote for a variety of tubas from the contrabass to the very small French model still being used in France today. All of the smaller tubas, of course, lack the one important feature that American conductors expect from their tuba players—sonority. Yet, these instruments possess some highly desirable features—for instance, extremely easy high registers that greatly simplify a part such as the *Bydlo* solo in the Moussorgsky-Ravel *Pictures at an Exhibition*. This particular composition, written with the French tuba in mind, naturally becomes more difficult as the instruments become progressively larger; and to even attempt such a part with our tubas seems almost ridiculous. In this country and even in some of the European countries where the F tuba is used all the time, parts written as high as or even higher than the *Bydlo* commonly are given to a baritone player, the baritone being approximately the same size as the French tuba.

Of the many solos written for the tuba, probably the most important works are the Paul Hindemith sonata, which is quite comfortable on the larger tubas, and the Ralph Vaughan Williams concerto. The latter work, written specifically for the F tuba, the one most commonly used in the English symphony orchestras, presents quite a challenge for players of larger models, although many of our professional players and even some students have performed it magnificently.

While in Russia with the Philadelphia orchestra, I had the opportunity to meet several tuba players and was not too surprised to find them all using BB♭ tubas, which are more common in bands. If the reader is familiar with the scores of Prokofieff, Shostokovitch, and other contemporary Russian composers, he can understand my lack of surprise, for practically all of their writing for the tuba is in a register for which Wagner scored his contrabass tuba parts. One "old-timer" playing in the ballet orchestra in Leningrad told me that he would much prefer playing the F tuba, the instrument of the old days no longer used in Russia.

As a result of the great strides America has taken in the development of the tuba, the CC tuba today emerges as the model preferred by most of our tuba players for orchestral use. With its multiple valves—four and preferably five—it enables the competent performer to play rather comfortably in all registers and to realize the various colors required by composers and conductors of different countries.

Actually, confronted with music written over a period of many years, by various composers, and perhaps with now obsolete instruments in mind, tuba players face this choice: either to use several variously pitched instruments or to make the attempt —which sometimes can be very foolhardy—to play everything on one tuba. Personally, I prefer using differently pitched tubas when I think the work calls for it or when a conductor requests it, as has often been my experience.

As a rule, modern composers write in sensible proportions for the tuba. But, aware of the proficiency tuba players have attained, they also on occasion write, as we say, "all over the instrument." Of this I approve wholeheartedly. Tuba playing has come a long way in a rather short time; so, I say, let them write it and we will play it.

In chamber music, popular music, and in the Broadway musical, too, the tuba has found a welcome. Popular dance bands and even jazz bands now employ the tuba in its rightful place, as a part of the brass section and not merely a rhythm instrument,

and give it solos and melodic lines to play.

In closing, I would make this suggestion to young people studying the tuba. Since tuba players will continue to play music that calls for a variety of models, and since probably no single instrument will meet all demands in the near future, young students of the tuba would do well to learn to play as many of the variously pitched instruments as possible. Among these young tuba players are tomorrow's professionals, for whom such early training will be of great value.

FINE

May, 1964

Developing
the
TRUMPET EMBOUCHURE

Thomas Miller

OF ALL THE PROBLEMS ENCOUNtered in teaching trumpet, the most frequent and usually the most acute is that of the embouchure. Because it bears directly on not only the troublesome matter of changing registers but also the very production of acceptable tone—a primary factor in any discussion of brass playing—it must be regarded, too, as the most basic problem, taking precedence even over breath control.

To succeed in properly developing the embouchure, the trumpet player must make use of the natural function of the muscles by which it is controlled, those located on each side of the mouth at the corners of the lips. If he will smile and then pucker, he will see that the muscles are used to their maximum in either case. Setting the lips in a semismile and gradually tightening these muscles, he will produce a sort of

semi-pucker, the lips pushed slightly forward and definitely not stretched as in the smile. On this semi-pucker, the embouchure must be based.

Too often, in the matter of proper vertical and horizontal setting of the mouthpiece, the trumpet teacher does not allow enough latitude for individual differences. He should check the prospective student for teeth formation, size of lips, and jaw structure, not with the intent of disqualifying for trumpet or cornet study the student with large lips, crooked teeth, or protruding or receding jaw formations, but rather that these factors and their relation to the placement of the mouthpiece may be considered from the very start of the student's career.

Determining Correct Embouchure

Basically, the teacher will encoun-

ter two types of players as regards embouchure formation. The first is the individual who has an overbite, however slight—i.e., whose front teeth do not meet squarely when the back teeth are placed together. To utilize his overbite in the embouchure development, this player should blow the air *down* at the mouthpiece.

The deflection of the air column as it passes through the lips directly affects the ability to change registers. Normally, in playing any instrument which makes use of a cup mouthpiece, the player directs the air into the throat of the mouthpiece only in the extreme low register, the air at other times being deflected by the cup of the mouthpiece into the throat. However, the type of player now under consideration aims the air stream at the lower rim to ascend into the higher register and brings it back to the throat again to descend. The higher the note, the more the angle of the air stream is lowered and, consequently, the closer to the rim it strikes.

The teacher must realize that it is quite natural for such an individual to hold the instrument on a slightly downward angle. To expect him to hold the trumpet perfectly parallel to the floor is to disregard his inability to play in this position without discomfort.

The teacher will also observe that the angle becomes more acute as the player ascends in the high register. This, too, is perfectly natural. However, the player's head must be kept in a straight line with the spine, and the chin must not be allowed to drop. In this position, the upper lip acts as an anchor point for the mouthpiece. and the lower lip controls the deflection of the air as it passes between the lips.

The muscles of the lip now act on the top lip, causing a slight pucker, which in turn forms a cushion for the mouthpiece and alleviates much of the pressure that some students find necessary in order to ascend. The lower lip pulls in and upward as the player ascends and then rolls downward and out as he descends. The top lip remains in the original position.

The jaw is also an important factor. It recedes to ascend, and protrudes in a forward and downward direction to descend, thus tightening and relaxing the bottom lip. The lower jaw and lip assume most of the pressure required to ascend. The upper lip gradually assumes more pressure in descending. It must be stressed that an undue amount of pressure on either lip is neither necessary nor advisable. There should be only enough pressure to maintain a seal between the lips and the mouthpiece.

For most players, the method outlined above proves the most satisfactory, the majority of people possessing a slight overbite. Modified to fit the individual, the procedure assures a maximum of control with a minimum of pressure. The tone produced is clear and in tune, with a slight edge which enables it to penetrate the woodwind and string tone. And, since tone and pitch are inseparably related, the player is constantly on top of the pitch,

achieving increased flexibility and control. Not playing on the bottom of every pitch, he is less troubled by a "spread" tone quality which lacks a center, by difficulty in doing lip slurs, and by the frequent production of overtones, growls, and rattles.

Another Method

The second type of player makes use of a naturally protruding lower jaw formation by blowing the air *upward* to the mouthpiece. Few people are able to master this method; only the occasional player whose jaw protrudes, or whose front teeth meet squarely when the back ones are placed together, can successfully make the air pass between the lips in an upward direction.

For this type of individual, all procedures are the reverse of those described above. As the player ascends, the air is deflected more toward the upper rim of the mouthpiece. As he descends, it is blown directly toward the throat of the mouthpiece. The player holds the instrument parallel with the floor or at a slight upward angle, though never so extreme as to cause an undue amount of pressure on the top lip. He must not drop his head so that the chin forces the throat to close, a common fault, but must keep the head in a straight line with the spine.

In this type of embouchure, the upper lip pulls in, controlling the direction of the air and, consequently, the pitch produced; and the lower lip becomes the anchor lip, assuming the function of forming a cushion rest for the mouthpiece. The jaw now protrudes to ascend and recedes to descend. Most of the pressure necessary in playing is assumed by the upper lip as the player ascends, the lower lip as he descends. However, once again, it is never necessary to have an undue amount of pressure on either lip. The player must take care that he does not create tension in the jaw and throat muscles as he ascends.

As described above, this method can best be utilized by players whose lower jaw protrudes or who possess a slight underbite. As is the case with the first type, the player should be able to produce a clear tone which is on top of the pitch, the same considerations stated above applying to the tone.

There is one problem unique to this type of player: though usually able to produce much stronger high tones, he frequently suffers from a lack of accuracy in the middle register. Many dance band trumpet players make use of this method for the added range it gives them above the staff. However, anyone whose facial characteristics do not fit this type will tend to produce a fuzzy tone or one which has a prominent "buzz" or, in extreme cases, noticeable rattles or overtones.

IN ORDER TO ACHIEVE A BALANCED embouchure, which should be the first consideration of the trumpet player, the individual should be able to place the mouthpiece and change registers with accuracy and comfort without resetting the mouthpiece for each register. He should set the embouchure for the middle of his register, determining this by blowing a stream of air through the instrument without the use of the tongue and then allowing the tone to start on its own. In most cases, the tone produced is the second line G. Beginning from this point, the air then is deflected in the manner previously described for either type of embouchure formation, producing a lip slur up to the next closest harmonic—in this case, C. This slur usually produces a "pop" if the player does it correctly. It proves difficult, however, if the tone is not correct or if the pitch is flat, and almost impossible if the individual tries to use the wrong method for his type.

In order to get the player to feel this change, it is most helpful to allow him to raise or lower the bell slightly, depending on his type. However, he should never be allowed to wave the trumpet freely up and down. As he becomes more skilled with the method, the motion of the instrument will tend to lessen and be taken up by the embouchure. The player with a weak or undeveloped embouchure cannot be expected to be able to do this without moving the trumpet; even experienced players find it necessary to move the instrument slightly to change registers. The setting of the mouthpiece on the lips, however, never changes.

Slurring Exercise

The exercise most helpful in developing this technique is partly explained above. After slurring to the C, the player should return to the G and then slur down to low C and return to G. This may be repeated using the various fingerings, each producing a fundamental one-half step below the last. After the player is able to do this, he should add the E above the C in the following manner—G-C-E-C-G-low C-G—and then repeat, using the various valve combinations down to 1-2-3. As the individual progresses and is able to do this with more accuracy and flexibility, he should be able to shift his starting note to C on the third space and add more of the higher harmonics.

As he adds notes above the last, he should take certain precautions: (1) he must not attempt to add the note above until the one he is working on is mastered and the top note sounds free and relaxed; (2) he must not break the slur at any time; and (3) he should rest a sufficient amount of time after practicing this drill, for it is very taxing.

This method is an attempt to make use of natural lip movements in playing the trumpet. In most cases, the individual does naturally exactly as the above description states for either type.

Faults Related to Embouchure

Certain inconsistencies in tone production, endurance, and range result directly from a faulty embouchure —for instance, the very common "smile" embouchure. The player who sets his lips in an extreme smile invites excessive pressure to the lips, usually the top lip, thus creating a difficulty in reaching the high register and causing the tone to be thin and frequently "spread" or lacking in center, and the pitch flat. Usually, he also lacks endurance. He must endeavor to get more lip in the mouthpiece in the manner discussed above.

The extreme "pucker" is another frequently encountered embouchure difficulty, often found in the player with large, fleshy lips. In this fault, the player turns his lips out when setting the embouchure; that is, he puts too much lip in the mouthpiece, allowing the mouthpiece to rest on the pink rather than, as is customary, anchoring it to the white of the lip. Consequently, the tone quality is "mushy," lacks a center, and has little or no "edge"; the

pitch is extremely sharp; and difficulty in the low register is common. The player must learn to set the lips in a semi-smile, thus turning the fleshy part in as far as is feasible. The procedure in this case is most often the first one described.

Air pockets around the embouchure create still another problem. A word of clarification should be added here. Air pockets under the cheek bones, which some players find advantageous, have no bearing on the current discussion; these pockets have little or no effect on the embouchure if the player's muscles can control them. The type considered here are those which are under the top and/or bottom lip and which cause the embouchure to "float." As a result of these air pockets, the embouchure lacks stability, and the player's accuracy and consistency suffer. Though he is capable of producing good tone, the quality of his tone varies. He also encounters great difficulty in changing registers and in doing the simplest of lip flexibility studies, especially if the air pocket is under only one lip, causing excessive pressure on the remaining one.

Wet or Dry Embouchure?

Many players question whether the embouchure should be wet or dry. No ground rule can be applied in this matter; the individual must determine the best solution for himself.

There are several variations which may be tried by the player who is having difficulties. First, the face of both lips may be moistened to see if flexibility can be increased without causing the tone to suffer. There will be a temporary loss of control if the player has been accustomed to a dry embouchure. Young players may find this procedure best.

Second, the player may try wetting the lip opposite the one which is used to anchor the mouthpiece. This is the lower lip in the case of the player who blows downward, the upper one being the anchor. It is the top lip in the case of the other type of player, who blows upward, the bottom lip or anchor being kept dry. Usually, the player can use this most common method without too much immediate loss of control and finds that it does the most to promote flexibility while holding the tone firm.

Third, the player may dry both lips, wetting only the vibrating point. As a rule, only experienced players with a strong embouchure can do this successfully. Though the tone may seem to be more firm, the loss of flexibility produces a severe handicap in most cases.

As was previously stated, there is no set procedure. With guidance from his teacher along the lines suggested above, the individual will adapt to that which is best for him. However, it should be pointed out that, whereas one method at first may seem better than another, the question can be settled only over a period of time.

Buzzing the Lips

Regarding the controversial matter of buzzing the lips, in the opinion of this writer, the disadvantages outweigh the advantages. Particularly in young players, lip buzzing causes a contraction of the throat and possibly a closed throat when finally applied to the trumpet. To result in any good, it demands a strong embouchure, thus negating its value to beginning or intermediate players.

The inexperienced player should approach the trumpet by blowing a fine stream of air through the center of the lips in the manner described for his jaw and lip formation. Then, by slightly increasing the pressure of the mouthpiece, and by applying a gentle push from the diaphragm to give more intensity to the air, he will achieve a free and relaxed tone with none of the strained sound produced by buzzing.

In Conclusion

How disconcerting it is to discuss these problems—and countless others which could be explored in this area—with trumpet students and band directors, only to discover that very little emphasis has been placed on proper development of the embouchure, whereas a great deal of time has been spent on breath control and even more on mastery of finger technique. Many players would benefit considerably by paying more attention to matters of embouchure at the outset of their careers, rather than mastering technical skills without the ability to produce an acceptable tone with good intonation.

FINE

Trumpet Pedal Register Unveiled

R. Dale Olson

MANY INVARIABLES ARE PRESENT in trumpet performance. The pedal register, however, is classified purely as a variable. Its mastery is certainly not necessary to insure a high level of ability, nor is its existence even acknowledged by all pedagogues and performers with any degree of seriousness. This register can nevertheless be developed to a fine degree when used as an instructional technique to relax the embouchure after strenuous playing or as an adjunct to flexibility and muscular development exercises.

This article will neither defend nor attack the use of this register in trumpet performance. Rather, information will be offered which, after digestion by the reader, can be used as a basis upon which his personal judgment may be founded. In an effort to negate the possibility of divergent terminology, the term *pedal register* will refer to all notes below the standard range of the Bb trumpet.

Although the production of the pedal register is rather simple on the trombone[1], it becomes increasingly more difficult on the higher brass instruments. Experimentally, one will find that the interior dimensions of an instrument exert a great influence on their production. For example, the Fluegelhorn will readily emit the pedal C3, [C3 is an octave below middle C. A4 is A-440]; the cornet, however, inhibits its production considerably; the trumpet all but forbids it.

Acoustically, the pedal register has proven to be somewhat controversial. The pedal note of an instrument has been presumed by many writers to be the *fundamental* (usually thought to be written C3).[2] As will be mentioned later, the *fundamental,* in this sense, is extremely difficult to produce. One prominent writer, Dr. F. J. Young, offers mathematical and musical evidence that C3 is not the true fundamental of the Bb trumpet. He further states:

Most musical authorities state dogmatically that the frequencies of the open tones of brass instruments are integral multiples of the frequency of the "fundamental" . . . . from the experiences of countless brass instrumentalists it can be said that such a statement is not true. Contrary to many musical acoustics books, the players of trumpets . . . . *can* play tones in the general vicinity of the fundamental pitch of those instruments. However, most players of Bb trumpets . . . . attempt to produce Bb-116.5 [written C3] as their fundamental. This can only be accomplished through a drastic adjustment of the internal impedence of the musician. The resulting tone is poor in quality, strains the musicians lip and is a very unreliable note. However, the same musicians can produce a good tone close to Ab-103.8 [written Bb] with little effort.[3]

The writer has spoken to other acousticians who concur with Dr. Young's conception of the fundamental being Bb2, not C3, and that the Bb2 is an isolated fundamental. That is, it does not bear the relationship to the regular series normally thought to exist.

Dr. Arthur Benade of Case Institute acknowledges the existence of a *privileged* note close to the fundamental of C3 and writes:

The "pedal note" on most modern brass instruments is *not* associated with the lowest mode of the horn![4]

Regardless of scientific terminology the pedal register (referring to our aforementioned term of reference) has been accorded at least a mention by numerous less-scientific authors in the past. Of general agreement is the fact that these notes are rather difficult to obtain and offer somewhat questionable aesthetic rewards.

Pedagogically, however, this set of notes has served many instructors as the basis for exercises regarding relaxation of the facial muscles, range development, flexibility, and muscular development of the embouchure. Herbert L. Clarke, according to ex-students, employed the pedal register in his teachings. Although no specific mention of this range is made in the text of his books, he provides a set of fingerings to employ:[5]

Apparently the production of pedal notes was developed by a few of the more prominent cornet soloists during the first part of this century when highly developed technique was in vogue. A well-known cornetist of this era, Bohmuir Kryl, was known to have possessed skill in the execution of the pedal register. Glenn Bridges states:

Kryl's exceptional embouchure made him one of the few cornetists able to play below the fundamental range of the instrument, and in this feat he was peerless.[6]

Obviously, however, Clarke was equally capable as evidenced by the same author's statement that ". . . Clarke possessed a full tone range of six C's."

Approximately three decades passed before August H. Schaefer offered this somewhat vague description of the physiological process in the production of pedals:

Pedal tones can be more easily produced when you place the mouthpiece "into" the mucous membrane (red) of the lower lip and hold the lips quite relaxed. Mouthpieces with deeper cups will be more responsive.[7]

Schaefer's suggested fingerings do not totally agree with those of Clarke, although neither writer offers an explanation or defense of his particular choice.

More recently, Albert Mancini offered a set of fingerings which differ in no way from their counterparts an octave higher.[8]

Mancini Fingerings

Exercise No. 2

Although the same fingerings proposed by Mancini are probably the most widely used, the present author proposes the following:

Pedal Tones Fingering

Exercise No. 3

As the reader will note, these are approximately the same as those proposed by Clarke. At least partial explanation of these fingerings may be offered thusly: Considering the fact that the length of valve slides is determined by the overall length of an instrument, we may then assume that a lower mode of vibration, such as the pedal register, would demand proportionately longer slides. Although this phenomenon has always been accepted as working in exact ratio, other evidence has been offered indicating that such is not necessarily the case.[9]

Lacking somewhat in mathematical precision, the use of the fingerings associated with the *major seventh* above a given pedal note usually permits a greater resonance for this register than simply employing the customary fingerings of the octave higher. (Example: Pedal F3, vibrating at a lower mode than the F4 an octave higher, requires longer valve slide length to afford better resonance. Utilizing the first and second pistons, the same as the major seventh above, will give that extra length whereas the first piston alone would not suffice.)

Several variances from this formula will be noted, however, upon examining the suggested chart. These

discrepancies may be explained as representing experimentation which has brought out the fact that the theoretical fingerings do not always offer the best musical results.

As partially mentioned by Schaefer, and as is commonly agreed, the mouthpiece and individual instrument exerts considerable influence on the facility with which pedal notes can be produced. This fact will therefore necessitate experimentation on the part of each performer in an effort to determine his optimum fingering possibilities.

Discrepancies between authorities with regards to fingerings can be attributed simply to the fact that the lip exerts more influence upon the pitch of a note in the pedal register than do the resonance characteristics of the instrument. Therefore, any given note in this range may be performed with a variety of valves or combinations thereof. Obviously, some will be found to be more suitable than others.

Actual performance of this elusive register may be approached by using several techniques. The author personally recommends that the instrumentalist simply *lip* down to them. As shown below, the tone C4 may be forced down a minor, or possibly a major, third to A3 or Ab3. While not instantly at the disposal of every player, this technique may be easily developed. The lower the register, the wider the interval may be forced. Between C4 and F#3, for example, this interval is a major third, or perhaps occasionally a fourth. It is upon this principle that this approach to the pedal register is built.

Approach to Pedal Tones

Exercise No. 5

Assuming that the C4, and each lower note, is being forced down a major third, it will be found that,

upon reaching A3 the major third lower is F3, the first pedal note. The fingering for A3 being first and second valves, and the suggested fingering for F3 the same, the production of this pedal note is simply a matter of extreme lipping.

By employing this approach to the pedal register, the performer will find that notes down to and including D3 may be obtained with a reasonable amount of practice. Upon learning this technique the production of the remainder of the range is greatly facilitated. The problem areas have been found to be the first pedal (F3) and C3. The notes intervening and lower are comparatively easy to produce and control.

Following are five self-explanatory exercises which employ the pedal register.

In the writer's experience, no adverse effects have been observed which were prompted by the moderate employment of pedal notes in practice. Certainly, the approach prescribed above (extreme lipping) cannot be accomplished if excessive embouchure-mouthpiece pressure is present. In that respect, an excellent pedagogical technique presents itself regarding the lessening of such pressure.

The final result all mature musicians seek is the ultimate improvement of performance and a general raising of musical and technical skills and abilities. The pedal register, however, contributes only to a small part of these goals. If employed primarily as a teaching tool and as a practice device, its full potential may be realized and possibly expanded.

[1]Henri Bouasse, *Instruments a Vent*, Vol. I (Paris: Librarie Delegrave, 1929).

[2]D. J. Blaikley, "Pedal Notes," Grove's *Dictionary of Music and Musicians*, Fifth Edition (New York: St. Martin's Press, 1962).

[3]F. J. Young, "The Natural Frequencies of Musical Horns," *Acustica*, Vol. 10, 1960.

[4]Arthur Benade, *Horns, Strings, and Harmony*, (New York: Anchor Books, 1960).

[5]H. J. Clarke, *Elementary Studies for the Cornet*, (New York: Carl Fischer, 1909).

[6]Glenn Bridges, "The Virtuosos," *Selmer Bandwagon*, Vol. II, No. 2, May, 1963.

[7]A. H. Schaefer, *The Stratosphere*, (Cleveland, Fillmore Music Co., 1941).

[8]Albert Mancini, *Daily Studies for Trumpet*, Vol. I (Los Angeles, A. G. M. Publishers, 1955).

[9]R. W. Young, "Optimum Lengths of Valve Tubes for Brass Wind Instruments," *Journal of the Acoustical Society of America*, Vol. 34, No. 5, May, 1962.

FINE

The Voice of the Trombone

GEORGE DUERKSEN

IN COMBINATION WITH THE TONE quality peculiar to the trombone, the trombone slide makes it the wind instrument most capable of performance in a style like that of the human voice. The trombone has the same advantages as the unfretted string instruments. It is capable of the most minute discriminations and alterations in pitch without impairing its tone quality, and it can slur in vocal style. Although this is a disadvantage in some styles of music, a survey of the history of trombone usage will show the ways in which musicians through the ages have taken advantage of this peculiarity.

Of all music instruments, with the exception of the human voice and possibly the drum, the trombone probably has the longest continuous history of evolution. The modern trombone is very much like the first trombone in construction. The major changes have been refinements of construction such as the improvement of rigidity, the addition of the tuning slide, the development of the stocking or sleeve on the slide which makes the slide action more flexible, and an increase of the flare of the bell.

One of the earliest pictorial representations of the trombone is in a painting by Matteo di Giovanni, who died in 1495. The picture hangs in the National Gallery of London. In 1495 the inventory of the band of King Henry VII listed four sackbuts (trombones). Accounts of the Great Council of Constance in 1414 report that large groups of Posaunen (trombone players) and Pfeiffen (pipers) paraded through the streets prior to the investiture of Frederick of Neurenberg as Elector of Brandenburg. One of the first discussions of the trombone in a theoretical work appeared in *Musica Getutscht*, which was written by Sebastian Virdung in about 1511.

The trombone in this period was often used as the bass voice of the tower band. The tower bands functioned as community musical organizations in that they provided all of the instrumental music (other than that of the organ) for the church, for civic festivals, and for processions and dances. At this time, instrumental music had not yet drawn away from vocal music. Thus most of the music performed was vocal in style. Indications on scores specified only that the music could be sung or played by a group of instruments, either wind or string.

Indications of various occasions upon which the trombone was used include the performance in Venice in 1495 of a five-voice motet by Obrecht, accompanied by two trombones. At the wedding of the Duke of Tuscany with Elanor of Toledo in 1493, the bride was met at the gates of Florence by twenty-four singers with four zink and four trombones and a ballet accompanied by five-part choir and four trombones. In these instances, the trombone was associated with the human voice.

Used in Church

The use of the trombone to support vocal music in the church may be traced through the music of Josquin, Lassus, Palestrina, the Gabrielis, and Luther. Josquin was probably one of the first composers to use the trombone in church music. Lassus used a choir of three trombones and one zink in some of his sacred music. The Gabrielis represented the Venetian polychoral style of sacred composition. In this style, two choirs of instruments or voices were used. In performance the groups were often located at opposite sides of the church. They played separately and together, thus producing a multitude of effects. One of the first compositions in which instrumentation was specified was the *Sonata Pian'e Forte* by G. Gabrieli. It required two groups of instruments—one group of a zink and three trombones, and the other a viol and three trombones.

The music of the Reformation varied greatly from sect to sect, though the Lutheran group probably made the greatest use of music. Their emphasis upon the chorale sung in the vernacular by the congregation brought into focus what was to become the prime function of the trombone in the church music of the following century—the accompaniment or reinforcement of the vocal line. This use again required a vocal style of instrumental performance.

During the Baroque. the trombone was given new duties. It was used to double the keyboard bass in the thorough-bass style. Instrumental music began to gain some independence from vocal music. In the opera *Orfeo*, Monteverdi used the trombone and other instruments for mood and other special effects rather than limiting it to the function of "played voice parts."

Yet in the music of the church, the trombone remained a vocal style instrument. Bach used choirs of trombones to duplicate and support choral lines in some of his cantatas, but gave them no independent orchestral function or obligato roles.

Trombone and Vocal Music

During the Classical era, the trombone fell into disuse in the music of the people, but it was retained as an adjunct to vocal and choral music. Gluck standardized the use of the trombone trio in his opera orchestra. Mozart used the trombone in operas such as *Don Giovanni* and the *Magic Flute*. In the *Requiem*, Mozart used the trombone as a solo instrument. The first part of the "Tuba Mirium" section is an interplay of the solo trombone and the bass vocalist. The trombone plays the vocal line in anticipation of the singer, and later it provides a fluid accompaniment for the voice melody. In this period, the trombone was not admitted to the symphony orchestra. This may have been because there was no treble counterpart capable of facile chromatic performance with which it could join to form an orchestral brass choir.

In the Romantic era—probably the "golden age" in the development of the trombone—it was admitted to the symphony orchestra. Composers often assigned it prominent solo roles. In the *Grand Symphony for Band* by Berlioz, the entire second movement is a solo—for trombone with band accompaniment. Berlioz titled this movement of the program symphony "Recitative and Prayer" and assigned the trombone the function of an orator. This obviously demands performance in a vocal style.

Although Wagner is thought of as a titan of the school of "spectacular" brass writing, his use of the trombone was often vocal in style. He used the trombone section in the *Prelude to The Meistersinger* to play independent voice lines in chorale fashion. In the *Overture 1812*, Tchaikovsky used the trombones for a unison performance of the Russian National Hymn, a type of song in which vocal connotations are necessarily present. Rimsky-Korsakoff, in the *Russian Easter Overture*, used the trombones to perform a chant of the Orthodox Church. In this function, the trombone imitates the voice used in the actual church service. In the *First Symphony* of Brahms, the trombones were assigned a solo statement of the chorale in the final movement. In the fourteenth variation of the final movement of his *Fourth Symphony*, they were assigned a long-note chordal variation of the theme. In the *German Requiem*, Brahms used the trombone to reinforce vocal lines.

In the present era, the trombone is still used in the vocal style. In the symphony *Mathis der Mahler*, Hindemith assigned cantabile melodic passages to the trombone section. Even in recent works such as Stravinsky's *In Memorium, Dylan Thomas*, which is scored for tenor, string quartet, and four trombones, the trombone is closely associated with vocal style performance. A cursory examination of the style of many popular and jazz trombonists shows the predominance of vocal style and idioms in the trombone performance of "people's music" of today.

Of course, not everything written for the trombone is vocal in concept. It would be less than correct, for instance, to claim that the trombone parts of *"Semper Fidelis"* are vocal in style. Nevertheless, it is important that instrumental directors be aware of this trend in the history of the usage of the trombone. Knowledge of this should give conductors a more valid basis for their decisions concerning the interpretation of various trombone idioms that occur in ensemble scores. A knowledge of this usage should also be valuable for the student trombonist. Every bit of information the student can acquire concerning the history, development, and function of his instrument should lead him toward the development of more adequate concepts of his ultimate goals in performance ability.

FINE

NOVEMBER 1964

Alternate Fingerings for Results

DONALD BULLOCK

In approaching the topic of alternate fingerings the pitfall of stressing theory rather than results becomes a problem. This discusion of alternate fingerings shall proceed with the avoidance of this pitfall continuously in mind. Examples have been prepared to reveal possible alternate-fingering situations in order that the trumpet player, or the non-trumpet-playing teacher, may examine them and explore similar situations in the literature with which he comes into contact. The reader is asked to keep in mind that in each case the example came first. The theories were not formulated with examples to support them, but rather evaluations were made by the author concerning the reason for the choice of an alternate fingering in each case and the advantage it has over other fingerings. This study does not encompass the entire realm of alternate fingerings, nor do the examples reveal the only types of situations in which alternate fingerings should be used. The wide variables in embouchures, instruments, and even in desired results prohibits a definitive study into this topic. The main departure taken in this study is in the direction of stimulating the reader to consider the utilization of alternate fingerings in situations where he perhaps had not considered them before and, through

f#³‑gb³	g³	g#³‑ab³	a³	a#³‑bb³	b³	c⁴	c#⁴‑db⁴
1 2 3	1 3	2 3	1 2-3	1	2	0	1 2 3

d⁴	d#⁴‑eb⁴	e⁴	f⁴	f#⁴‑gb⁴	g⁴	g#⁴‑ab⁴	a⁴	a#⁴‑bb⁴
1 3	2 3	1 2-3	1	2 - 1 2 3	0 - 1 3	2 3	1 2-3	1 - 1 2 3

b⁴	c⁵	c#⁵‑db⁵	d⁵	d#⁵‑eb⁵	e⁵	f⁵
2-1 3	0-2 3	1-2-3-1 2	1-1 3	2-2 3	0-1-2-3-1 2 3	1-1 3

f#⁵‑gb⁵	g⁵	g#⁵‑ab⁵	a⁵	a#⁵‑bb⁵	b⁵	c⁶
2-2 3-1 2 3	0-1-1-2 3 3	2 3 - 1 - 1 2 3	1 2-3-2-1 3	1-0-1 2 3	2-1 3-1 2-3	0-2 3-1

these considerations, build a repertoire of ideas in solving problems with alternate fingerings.

In the following chart, the fingerings given first are the ones used under normal circumstances of playing. Any other fingerings given will be considered alternate fingerings, though certain ones may be used so frequently that for some players and some instruments they have become regular fingerings. The notes a5(3) and e5($\frac{1}{2}$) are examples of alternate fingerings which have come to be used regularly for some players because faulty intonation results from the use of the normal fingerings on their particular instrument. On some C trumpets third valve (3) is used as a common method for playing e5 because the normal alternate choice ($\frac{1}{2}$) does not adequately accommodate the intonation problem.

Musical Examples

At this point the discussion turns to the musical examples in which alternate fingerings could, and perhaps should, be used. The discussion will first consider those situations in which the need of an alternate fingering is somewhat obvious and the choice of the valve combination to replace the regular fingering is common.

WILLOW ECHOES by Frank Simon
Fillmore Brothers
(meas. 13-14 in final Allegro)

The common fingering for the pattern e4($\frac{1}{2}$)-d#4($\frac{2}{3}$)-e4($\frac{1}{2}$) above would involve the awkward change of two fingers, whereas the alternate choice given here would eliminate the use of the first finger, requiring only the second finger to make a shift as the notes change. The same would be true of the common a4-g#4-a4 pattern.

C⁴(0)-a4 (3) C4 (0) - db⁴(3)

In example 2 the cumbersome movement of two fingers is exchanged for the cleaner movement of only the third finger. Of course, if the player has difficulty with the mobility of his third finger nothing has been gained, but the above-average player has usually overcome this difficulty. Note that a g#4 trill to a4 would also be done best by playing a4(3).

ARIA CON VARIAZIONI by Handel/Fitzgerald
Ricordi & Co.
(Var. IV—meas. 7)

Perhaps the most awkward fingering combinations involve those patterns which call for the second and third fingers to move simultaneously in opposite directions. In the example above a solution to this fingering problem is found by playing e4(3), therefore confining the finger movement to only the first finger.

(M.M ♩=c.88)

Oftentimes the trumpeter or cornetist finds himself faced with a passage in which only one note requires a valve change. If the passage is slow enough the special problems are minimal, but as speed becomes a factor the performer finds that his finger response may not coordinate with the rhythmic demands of the passage. Example 4 presents a problem of this type. The immobility of the fingers during the first two notes gives rise to difficulties on the change of valves for the third note of the triplet. At a rapid tempo it is difficult to lift the two fingers precisely on the rapidly passing e5. The alternate choice seems much more logical in this case. If, on the other hand, the note in such a passage were sustained, the performer must consider the properties of intonation and tonal color before applying an alternate fingering.

In connection with example 4, mention should be made of the written notes in the G major arpeggio, all of which can be played ($\frac{1}{3}$). Any performer who has played Sousa's familiar "Semper Fidelis" is acquainted with the bugle passage which calls for this fingering throughout the entire sixteen bars. While the alternate fingerings create the special bugle effect desired, other passages using the notes of the G major arpeggio are best-played with the normal fingerings due to the excessive problems of intonation which are characteristic of this alternate possibility.

Before proceeding with the discussion of less common alternate fingering situations, mention should be made of the g5-a5 trill which is commonly played ($\frac{1}{2}$) as a lip trill or a hand shake, depending upon the desired sound. The bb5-c6 trill with (0) fingering is also a common lip trill. The lower note in both of these trills is the one receiving the alternate fingering. The trills are considered here because both situations constitute the utilization of common alternate fingerings. Further mention of trills shall be made later in this discussion.

The topic then turns toward alternate fingerings that are not commonly used and situations that do not commonly call for their use. From the foregoing information, one can already begin to see possible situations where alternate fingerings may produce better results than the regular fingerings. These suggestions should not be used indiscriminately. In each case the player and teacher must weigh the results of the alternate choice against the regular fingering with regard to finger facility, intonation, quality of sound, and other criteria which may apply to the given circumstances. The reader must be cautioned concerning this matter of applying the information found in the examples without first giving his fullest evaluation of each case in light of his own personal demands in playing. If these samples only make the reader curious enough to realize the possibility of alternate fingerings in situations where the normal fingerings do not produce satisfying results, then the discussion has accomplished its purpose.

Greatest Use

In general, the greatest use of alternate fingerings occurs in passages where intonation or technical facility is mediocre with the use of regular fingerings. By this, the writer does not mean to imply that if a mediocre player gets mediocre results using regular fingerings in a given musical passage, that his problems will be over if he uses different fingerings. On the contrary, before attempting an alternate method, the player must have achieved a certain amount of success with the written fingerings. Then, through the use of an alternate valve combination, his problem may be eased and chances of playing the passage correctly every time may be greatened.

ANDANTE ET SCHERZO by J. Ed. Barat
A. Leduc Co.
(meas. 6-7)

Alternating (3) for ($\frac{1}{2}$) is commonplace for the trumpet player, especially on the note a5, but the ex-

change oftentimes goes no further. On instruments that have no first-valve compensating device, e4 should be played (3) in exposed situations in order that the note be brought down to the correct pitch. Example 5 shows the type of musical circumstance under which a sharp e4($\frac{1}{2}$) can be most damaging to the effectiveness of the passage. Third valve easily rectifies this problem.

CONCERTINO by Riisager
Wilhelm Hansen
(1st movement—meas. 36-37)

In the above example, the upper g♯5 has a tendency toward sharpness, due to the ascension into the upper range coupled with the *piano* dynamic level. The intonation in such a passage is very critical because of the comparative lower g♯4. In this case the trumpet plays both notes unaccompanied, which poses the added problem of exposure. The writer has found the first-valve alternate fingering an effective solution to this predicament.

QUATRE VARIATIONS SUR UN
THÈME DE DOMENICO SCARLATTI
by Marcel Bitsch
A. Leduc Co.
(Var. III—meas. 19-20)

The slow tempo and the forte dynamic level present critical intonation problems in this example, especially as the *tessitura* rises to the high c6 at the climax. The writer uses the ($\frac{2}{3}$) fingering for the c6 to keep the pitch from rising and the tone quality from becoming too bright.

SONATA by Maurice Emmanuel
A. Leduc Co.
(Gigue—meas. 16-17)

The g5 in passages such as example 8 would rarely be played ($\frac{1}{2}$), but in this particular case the author experienced difficulty in maintaining an ultra-smoothness of line when he had to concern himself with altering the sharpness of the pitch with his embouchure. The alternate fingering rectifies the problem of intonation without causing the tenseness that is inherent in sounds which require em-

bouchure change for correction of pitch.

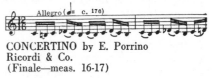

CONCERTO by Vittorio Giannini
Gamble Hinged Music Co.
(2nd movement—last four meas.)

The above musical situation could call for one of two possible alternate fingerings, depending upon individual players and instruments. That the normal fingering could be employed here is seriously doubted. An interesting combination of factors contribute to this dilemma. The dynamics and mute, both of which cause tendencies to sharpness, combined with a note that is notably high on all instruments presents a problem too great to be handled by lip alteration. The music allows only one count for insertion of the mute, which may mean that with some mutes, such as the harmon which is often used for such passages, the left hand may be forced to hold the mute in place for the entire passage. If so, the right hand may be placed in such a position that it may be unable to operate the first-valve compensating device. The author has found himself in just such a predicament in this music, finding a solution in the playing of a 5 with the second (2) valve. Other players may be better satisfied with the alternate choice of third (3) valve.

Perhaps a greater need for alternate fingerings arises for reasons of technical facility than for any other reason, though the player and teacher are urged to be careful not to overlook their use in correcting problems of intonation, as suggested in the previous examples. Technical facility is meant to include various aspects of facility in this discussion. The following examples may provide thought-provoking situations concerning the application of alternate fingerings to problems in finger facility, lip flexibility, and combinations of both.

CONCERTINO by E. Porrino
Ricordi & Co.
(Finale—meas. 16-17)

In the scale pattern d4-e4-f4 the alternate fingering (3) for e4 is often very effective. In example 10 the c4 scale, which includes the cited pattern, occurs after several repeated c4-b3-c4-d♭4-c4-b3 figurations in triplets. At the rapid tempo indicated the clean break between the second and third fingers in the d4($\frac{1}{3}$)-e4($\frac{1}{2}$) pattern becomes a problem in finger facility, especially considering the repeated use of the third finger for the many d4-flats preceding the pattern in question. The e4(3) eliminates the problem by transferring the difficult finger shift from the third to the second finger in the d4($\frac{1}{3}$)-e4($\frac{1}{2}$) pattern to a much easier shift from the third to the first finger in the e4(3)-f4(1) pattern. The problem pattern naturally occurs in countless numbers throughout the literature because it is found in the common c4 scale. It can be assumed that the key of F would also include the c4-d4-e4 pattern quite often.

QUATRE VARIATIONS SUR UN
THÈME DE DOMENICO SCARLATTI
by Marcel Bitsch
A. Leduc Co.
(Var. II—meas. 16-17)

In order to facilitate rapid passages alternate fingerings may be utilized for the purpose of propelling finger rhythm. For instance, example 11 presents a situation in which the e4 and a4 would normally be executed with the first and second fingers. Even if an alternate fingering were deemed necessary it would be most likely that the third valve would be used for both the e4 and the a4, coming after the g♯($\frac{2}{3}$). However, after reaching the point of the e4(3), the rhythmic action of the fingers continuing on to the a4 with the first and second valves facilitates the movement of the notes in the passage.

Example 11a presents another case in the same category as that discussed in example 11. It would seem that if finger rhythm were needed the normal alternate fingering would be d♯5($\frac{2}{3}$), but a better finger action is created with the f♯5($\frac{2}{3}$) because an additional finger is being depressed at each note change. The common alternate method (utilizing the second and third fingers on the d♯5) would necessitate the irregular finger movement of two fingers down followed by the movement of one finger up, which is not the most effective choice of finger action. A lip slur is just as easy here but it will not achieve the smoothness of which

the alternate version is capable.

CONCERTO by Hummel
Robert King Music Co.
(1st movement—12 meas. after [J])

Rather than simultaneously lifting the second and third fingers while depressing the first in the shift from a♭4($\frac{2}{3}$) to b♭4(1) and then reversing the change as the b♭4 returns to the a♭4, it becomes much easier to play the pattern here by keeping the second and third valves down and merely adding the first valve for the b♭4($\frac{1}{3}$). The required smoothness of the turn is then achieved.

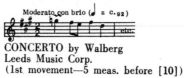

CONCERTO by Walberg
Leeds Music Corp.
(1st movement—5 meas. before [10])

The concept of smoothness brings up a point which may be of value in this discussion. There are times when an alternate fingering may help the performer to achieve the smoothness desired in a given composition, such as in example 12. On the other hand, in passages such as example 13 the alternate fingering is avoided in order that the desired brilliancy may be achieved. This brilliancy would be lessened by playing a5(3), because the firmness of the third valve action alone is not equal to the firmness of the first two fingers. The finger action inherent in the regular fingering is needed to maintain the *con brio* concept here.

The matter of trills has been only briefly mentioned thus far. Examples 14, 15, and 16 have been prepared to demonstrate some principles governing the use of alternate fingerings in trills. The first example seeks a solution to a finger trill. The e5, when played with the first and second valves, belongs to the same partial in the overtone series as the f5(1), which is the upper note of the trill. The e5($\frac{1}{2}$) and f5(1) belong to the fifth partial above the unsounded fundamental. If e5 is played open (0) it belongs to the fourth partial above the unsounded fundamental. By keeping both notes of the trill on the same partial, the break between the notes is not so great.

Note that the information given in

the foregoing paragraph may be applied directly to a trill from e5 to f♯5. The author personally feels that the application of the alternate fingering in this trill is even more important than in the preceding example due to the fact that the trill encompasses a whole step rather than a half step, as in example 14.

CONCERTO by Hummel
Robert King Music Co.
(2nd movement—meas. 3-4 after [D])

In example 15 the choice of a method to use in trilling the f5 hinges upon that method used on the g5 trill found in the following measure. The writer is of the opinion that a lip trill captures the clean, crisp, classic concept better than a finger trill. If the g5 trill is to be executed by the lip, the f5 trill should match it. A lip trill on the first and third valve combination matches the f5 trill to the g5 lip trill on valves one and two.

TRUMPET VOLUNTARY
by Jeremiah Clarke

A final example on trills appears in the famous Trumpet Voluntary. The normal fingering for b5 in this trill would be second valve. The utilization of the normal fingering would mean that the performer would have to coordinate the movement of two fingers in the change between b5(2) and a♯5(1). For a trill in this precarious range, the least possible amount of roughness is needed for clarity of the embellishment. The common fingering creates some roughness because of the rapid simultaneous movement of both the first and second fingers. An alternate method is needed to reduce the finger movement to only one finger. Two possible choices come to mind, the first being a♯5(0)-b5(2) and the second being a♯5(1)-b5($\frac{1}{2}$). Each alternate method for playing the trill requires the same simple movement of the second finger, but the a♯5(0), being slightly flat, brought about the author's choice of the trill employing b5($\frac{1}{2}$).

That an infinite number of examples in the use of alternate fingerings could be prepared is perhaps fast becoming evident to the reader. While realizing that even a substantial percentage of possibilities cannot be presented, the author has attempted to outline enough different types of situations wherein alternate valve combinations could be utilized to bring about an awareness of this technic in the trumpet performer, teacher, and student. The examples may appear to be somewhat unusual, but the reader may be assured that each of them has been tested under performing conditions by the author and,

in some instances, by students. The examples represent situations wherein the author experienced better results than those derived from the common fingerings and were not devised merely for the sake of providing material for this discussion.

The student is cautioned against pursuing this technique for any other reason than that of improving performing results. To accept these samples completely without doubt is to accept them without thought and

without trial. Rather, the reader is again asked to evaluate each example critically. Perhaps even one example may suggest a situation which calls for an alternate fingering of which the reader had not given previous thought. In the final analysis, no two performers would agree whole-heartedly on the employment of alternate fingerings, but the purpose of the study will have been realized if the reader only takes a second look into the utilization of this technique.

Discussing the Tuba

REX CONNER

Last year a young high school boy performed a tuba solo at the district contest. He was very frightened, as most contestants are, but he had little reason for confidence. His tone, phrasing, intonation, and the composition he was attempting to play were anything but musical. In addition to this, one of the valves made a very noisy click, clack, every time it went up and down.

When the ordeal was over the judge asked him about the clicking noise. He said, "Ah, somebody busted the button off of it." It's true, the first valve button was gone, and, as the young fellow leaned over to show the judge, there was a swishing, scratchy noise inside the tubing of the sousaphone. "What's inside the horn." "Oh, everybody thinks he has to throw rocks and gravel in it." As the boy unwound the horn a couple of small rocks and a candy bar wrapper fell on the floor; along with them fell a solder laden mouthpipe section.

Whatever possessed a teacher with four years of training in a music school to allow such a thing to happen at what we commonly know as a music festival remains a mystery. This, of course, is an extreme example of what can happen under the event known as a tuba solo contest, but the general idea is by no means rare.

The writer of this article began playing an E♭ upright tuba at the

age of eleven. It needed a little chewing gum well placed over a few tiny holes in the mouthpipe, but he loved it. In those days bell-front sousaphones were quite new and something to really stare at. So, when at the age of 13 a brand new silver plated sousaphone with a gold plated bell was lowered onto his shoulder by his director he loved that, too. To this day, his difficulty in going to sleep any way but on the left side isn't compatible with the ache in the left shoulder.

As you may have guessed by now, the writer is prejudiced in favor of the upright tuba. The sousaphone is a monster, whether it is all brass, partly fiberglass, red or gold. Anyone who sits or stands by the hour with fifteen to thirty pounds hanging on his shoulder while trying to play beautiful music can certainly testify to this. Fighting this weight undoubtedly conditions high school sousaphone players to overblow. At least players of upright basses do not seem to have as much tendency to do so. The sousaphone is an instrument that has a way of sticking out in front, behind, and up above. After about five or six years of experience, the player can usually guide it thru a door without damaging anything up front; however, if a good dent isn't well placed behind or up above, it's a miracle. Now, if the player does make it thru the door without any mishaps with that

instrument that you just spent a good percentage of your budget for this year, and, if you don't have a nice place to hang it on the wall, he'll set it down hurriedly, resting it on the bell and the curve in the mouthpipe which is fairly soft brass.

That little thump made on the mouthpipe will probably lower a whole series of overtones about a quarter step. The director and player probably won't notice it immediately unless they check with a stroboscope because the human ear isn't as sensitive in this range. Of course, the player may have thought about this or have been trained differently, so he may lay it down carefully on its side. By the time the bass drummer gets in the area and pushes the bell aside, the mouthpiece and one of the bits are jarred loose and they fall on the first valve tubing. Now, the intonation for all the first valve notes has been affected.

There is another problem that is detrimental to a sousaphone. If the student uses a sousaphone stand beside his chair, he usually won't bother to loosen the nut that holds the mouthpipe section securely before he swings it around to reach his mouth. In time, it's loose, even when the nut is tight and it has to be held to the mouth. It also leaks. So, we wrap a piece of paper around it, or maybe adhesive tape, and get it fixed next summer when the repairman is two months behind in repairs.

Quality Instruments

Manufacturers of quality instruments tell us that in order to have an instrument play its best it must have a perfectly smooth, graduated surface inside the instrument and the mouthpiece must fit the inner mouthpipe tubing perfectly. They have also told us that in order to get the overtone series well in tune on their new trumpets and cornets, they have incorporated about six individual microscopic tapers in the mouthpipe section. Must we accept less for the tubas? How would they accomplish this on a sousaphone with two or three bits? Incidentally, it is always quite surprising to say the least, to find sousaphone players using from one to three bits just for the comfort of it without ever questioning whether it will affect the intonation of the instrument or not.

Tuning the Tubas

As we have mentioned before, bass intonation is much more difficult to hear than intonation in the higher register instruments, but all band and orchestra directors should be well aware of the fact that bass instruments playing one vibration per second flat or sharp at the bottom of the staff will require a soprano instrument three octaves higher to be eight vibrations per second flatter or sharper in order to play in tune with it.

A good tuba tone is rich with overtones. In order to tune the tubas well with the other instruments it is best to check with a soprano instrument. The beats created by the overtones of the tuba sounding against the tone of the higher instrument are easily discernible. Don't check with a baritone or another tuba and expect to come out perfectly in tune unless you have an exceptionally fine ear for the lower tones and your tuba player can hold a perfectly steady tone without variation for a period of five or six seconds. String bass players tune with harmonics, but this technique isn't possible with tubas. The players could conceivably tune with high B♭; however, it is the lower tones that are the least possible to lip in tune. Tuba players who play well in tune listen to the instruments playing above them. If the rest of the band is out of tune, then the tubas will probably be, too. If the tubas are out of tune, the whole band will sound out of tune no matter how much time you waste tuning the rest.

It is quite common to watch a band director tuning his band before a concert or contest and find that each individual instrument is checked carefully until he gets to the tubas. Then, there begins to be uncertainty. Perhaps the 1st tuba is checked with a baritone and the rest are checked with him. When the succeeding instruments are checked it is not uncommon for those with a good pitch sense, in general, to ask for the slides to be moved the wrong way. Bass tones have a way of sounding sharp when they are in tune. Any piano tuner knows this. For this reason many of them stretch the lower octaves slightly flat just to avoid complaints.

Marching Upright Tubas

Most directors argue that they must have sousaphones instead of upright tubas for their bands because they have to have them for marching season. Some manufacturers are now making lightweight upright tubas that are well in tune and sound amazingly full in tone quality. Junior high students can carry them more comfortably with a strap than they can a sousaphone. They can't slump with them either. They keep those backs straight in order to equalize the weight. These small model tubas will be much superior in sound than the best sousaphones after a year or so of the punishment that sousaphones invariably take. The audience has seen those great big bells up above the band for a good many years now and they hardly add to the show any more. They are quite effective in keeping the back rank from seeing the drum major, though. Who can doubt that the tubas in the fine English bands which visit this country sound better than our sousaphone sections.

Bell Front vs. Bell Up

One summer, at the National Music Camp, it was our privilege to have eight tuba players in the National High School Band all playing instruments with upright bells and eight tuba players in the All-State group playing bell-front tubas. All sixteen of these musicians were outstanding, selected players; however, the upright bells produced much the finest ensemble sound. Upright bells are non-directional in sound and provide a bass for all of the band much the same as a string bass section does for the orchestra. The sound seems to come from every direction. Many of the harsh overtones, some due to poor embouchures, are lost to the ears of the audience, and this is good.

Perhaps a vast majority of directors still prefer tubas with large bells pointing forward. There might be a good reason for this with young players who lack the breath support to project the tone and rhythmic precision needed for a young group of players, but imagine yourself going to hear the Boston Symphony Orchestra and discovering the tuba player sitting there with a sousaphone on his shoulder and that big bell pointing at you like a huge washtub suspended in mid air. Immediately, your past experiences would tell you that the brass ensemble would produce something short of that heavenly sound you had been used to hearing.

Strictly Business

Manufacturers will continue to build monstrosities with gaudy appeal as long as directors favor and buy them. The good tuba player doesn't favor them for his personal instrument. When we start insisting on good compact instruments that have a beautiful sound throughout the range, that can be played in tune without losing tone quality, and that can respond to the technique of a good player without springs buzzing and valves clattering the ingenuity and energies of the manufacturers will be guided in this direction. They would be more than happy to be able to manufacture the same kind of an instrument for the schools as they would for the professional tuba player. Both would benefit financially. When we show the parents of a prospective tuba player something that compares a little more favorably with what they see and hear in the best symphony orchestras, perhaps they can imagine their son or daughter playing something besides oom-pah in the daily band rehearsal for the next six years. It would be better for the parent to think of a tuba standing neatly in the corner of the living room over the week end than a sousaphone in the middle of the floor.

1965

4-Valve BB♭ Tuba

Brass Tone Color

MAURICE FAULKNER

Electronic reproducing devices seldom capture the essence of brass tone quality, whatever its origin. The specialist in brass instruments is reluctant to offer a recording as an illustration of his sound. He doesn't mind such a substitute depicting his technical facility or range, and, possibly, style; but to base judgment upon quality of sound is something that the true artist will not leave to a recording.

We have enjoyed the discs which emanate from European countries at prices often below those of our own recording companies. They have given us musical literature that adds to our libraries with seldom-played works of quality. We have always discounted the tone qualities of such recordings though, because of our past association with the actual, live performances of the same orchestras.

As a result of these experiences with the concert hall sounds and the recorded sounds of the major European symphony orchestras, we have felt that a subjective description of the brass tone of such organizations might be of interest to the instrumental specialists of America. The writer must confess that these are purely personal judgments and experiences which are based upon eight European review tours at summer festivals. In many instances we have conferred with the musicians and joined some of them in post-concert jamborees where talk supplemented the sound which they had so recently provided.

The orchestras which offer us excellent examples of a more or less representation of national taste and style in the manner of br. tone quality are the Vienna Philharmon-

ic, the Concertgebouw of Amsterdam, the Philharmonia of London, the Prague/National Orchestra, the Berlin Philharmonic Orchestra, the Turin Radio Symphony, and the French National Radio Orchestra.

Concert Halls

One of the most important factors in judging an orchestra's basic tone quality is finding an opportunity to hear that group in its native habitat: the concert hall where it rehearses and performs the majority of its concerts. A brass specialist learns to judge the reverberation time of his concert home in order to create the style of attack and duration of tone according to the dictates of his own creative personality as well as that of his conductors. For instance, when playing a Wagnerian overture in the new home of the Berlin Philharmonic, the brasses must counteract the brilliant edge of the hall in order to reproduce the sonority associated with the Wagnerian atmosphere. Too brilliant or forward a position of the tongue attack will drive the tone into the woodwork almost as if a hammer had been struck upon a nail.

Each concert hall has its idiosyncracies, and if one speaks with the performers about those idiosyncracies, he will learn that they vary from section to section within the same orchestra. The Musikvereinsaal in Vienna, where many of the Vienna Philharmonic concerts are presented, has a long rectangular design which serves the brasses effectively when they are placed at the rear of the platform and upon risers. When they play across the orchestra from right to left, on the

other hand, their reverberation time is speeded up and their techniques must be changed to accommodate such a position. As a matter of fact, this orchestra seldom places its brasses on the side in the concerts which we have attended. The same orchestra performing on the broader stage of the Konzerthalle has a different problem of balance and attack. And, when they are moved to the recently renovated Theater an der Wien where a number of Festival concerts are performed, the orchestra has to readjust its balance, all of which affects the brass section more importantly than the others because of its ability for greater sonority and power.

The famous old Concertgebouw Hall in Amsterdam is probably as ideal a music listening auditorium as the world has to offer. When the strings are at their best in this orchestra, there is a vibrant, precise sound that takes advantage of the clean reverberation of the hall and is a delight in Haydn and Mozart symphonies. The brasses therefore have to adjust their tongue attacks and tone duration to such a hall, with finesse. It is a delight to hear the accuracy of the strings in such a place when the brasses and woodwinds provide a clear-cut intonation and don't color the ensemble quality with overly extended notes held for a duration that resounds and clutters the beautiful, white string tone.

London offers the new Festival Hall and the arena-like Albert Hall as two of the sites for the Philharmonia. The grandiose Albert is too large for concerts of quality, and one has to discount the problems found there and enjoy the usual fare of the English brasses with their broad but accurate tones from virtuosi of the finest quality. The Philharmonia is at its best in Usher Hall at the Edinburgh Festival although the London Festival Hall is mellowing as the players and conductors learn of its finest points.

The Prague Symphony and the Turin Orchestra have not been judged in their native halls, and our experiences with them have been gained in the Viennese concert palaces mentioned above. The French National Radio Broadcasting Orchestra has not been experienced in its natural home of the studio but in various concert halls where it has performed while on tour. So these latter groups have not been heard under the most ideal of conditions, and the reader will have to judge the following assessments with that in mind.

Points of Analysis

In reporting upon the quality of brass tone, it is important that the judge organize his concepts along technical lines which make for more objective judgments. We will discuss the qualities of the several brass sections upon the following basis:

1) *Basic tone quality:* a) Breadth or sonority of sound. b) Preciseness of color, i.e. is the line of the tone clear, or does it spread over a fairly wide area?

2) *Pitch of the tone:* a) Does the pitch vary from beginning to end of tone? b) Does the pitch of the section blend easily? c) Is the general intonation of the brass group well-adjusted to that of the other sections?

3) *Duration of tone:* a) Does the tone fill up the reverberation of the orchestra and thus dominate the total sound? b) Does the brass section interpret a variety of styles appropriately by controlling the duration of tones in various compositions effectively?

4) *Range of tone:* a) Does the brass section as a whole, and do individual players, produce a similar quality of tone from their lowest to their highest tessituras? 2) Does the pitch of the section vary from range to range and from trumpets, to horns, to trombones when ranges change?

5) *Attack in producing tone:* a) Does the brass section as a total group use the same style of articulation in interpreting various styles and composers? b) How does the attack style affect the quality of the tone production?

6) *Instruments used:* a) Do the type of instruments and the sizes of the bores affect the tone quality? b) Are the instruments of the section well-matched for the best tonal results?

The French National Radio Broadcasting Orchestra

When the French National Radio Broadcasting Orchestra toured the United States a number of years ago, American instrumentalists were intrigued by the type of brass color which the orchestra produced. For those of us who had spent time in concert halls in France however, there was very little mystery about this sound because we had become accustomed to the small bore C trumpets, tenor trombones, and small tubas. The piquant tone which blended so efficiently with the delectable woodwinds had become a trademark of French orchestral color and had been as indigenous to that nation as the fish and vegetable soup known as "bouillabaisse," which graces almost every French restaurant's menu.

Remember that the following description of the brass sound will be a personal, subjective one from the writer's recollection of that tone, and every reader will have the privilege to disagree and set up his own concept in words: a difficult chore for the best of literary giants. The French brass tone of this orchestra has a basic, precise color that, first of all, emphasizes the accuracy of the orchestral pitch as set up for it by the woodwinds and strings. Then the line of the tone holds firmly to that pitch and the precise, "white" sound without any variance. The pitch is the most important and valuable aspect of the brass tone for it must be identical with that of its complementing sections. There are moments with this orchestra when one hears a sound that has never been produced in American organizations, because the pitch is so exact a match between oboe and trumpet, for instance, that a new color is developed. The pitches of the brasses, because of the smallness of the bore of the instruments and because of the higher pitches of the same, blend so efficiently with the woodwinds that sometimes the brasses sound like a new type of woodwind instrument. The small bore trombones have some of the quality of the bassoon at its best moments. Since the duration of the tone affects the style interpretation of various works, it has become an especial factor in the production of brass tone. For Wagnerian sounds in the French idiom, there is not enough duration to fill in the spaces between notes, but the shorter duration of the sound from this orchestra is especially effective for Haydn, Mozart, and the coloristic backgrounds for Debussy, Ravel, Stravinsky, and others.

When the French musicians are at their best, they can control the quality of tone with a sameness that carries from the low register to the highest notes necessary. There are moments though, that the high pitches tend to be slightly pinched and do not flow as freely as the middle octave tones. These inadequacies show up more in the demanding scores where volume of sound at high octaves is most essential.

The French have probably perfected the ability to attack a tone in the greatest variety of styles of any of the European groups. They have followed their magnificent woodwind specialists' abilities to create a style by the use of the tongue and its variety. And, when the orchestra is at its peak, every musician in the brass section follows the patterns of the woodwinds and strings in developing interpretive ideas as an ensemble.

The French were the developers of the piston style instrument after the Germans, Stölzel and Blühmel, had invented the valve instrument in 1815. Adolph Sax and Francois Perinet improved the earlier valve about 1840 which has continued, with minor modifications, to the present day in France. These are the choice of the French performers, and the instruments give them the keen, sharp, and stimulating tone which they enjoy. Since most French musicians are products of the well-organized French conservatory system, their matching instruments have become a part of their heritage and, as a result, their basic ensemble tone.

The Vienna Philharmonic Orchestra

One of the world's great organizations, the Vienna Philharmonic Orchestra, is a versatile group of musicians whose duties include operatic accompaniment as well as symphonic concerts. The brass instrumentalists must be prepared to play anything from the symphonies of Beethoven, Mozart, and Haydn to the latest contemporary opera or ballet. As we write this article, we have before us the October, 1964 program of the Vienna Staatsoper where this orchestra performs the accompaniment chores, and it lists a variety of operas which include Mozart's "The Marriage of Figaro," Strauss's "Der Rosenkavalier," Wagner's "The Flying Dutchman," and Britten's "A Midsummer Night's Dream" among others over the two-week period represented by the publication.

When a brass specialist receives his weekly assignment with this group, he not only prepares himself technically for the variety of styles ahead, but he also has to adjust his concepts to the variety of conductors who will grace the podium on that week's performances. Upon Monday he will need to perform Wagner with the sonorous tone so common to the Austrian and German ideal of these works. He produces a rather thick, full-bodied sound with a lowered tongue position that offers a large column of air to the lips as they vibrate it. It is difficult for him to change this type of sound because he has been ingrained with its quality from his earliest student days. Even in the lighter styles of Mozart and Haydn, he achieves a broadness of tone that, although almost weightless in character, still has a wide spectrum of volume and color.

The Austrian is not as careful about his basic pitch as his French counterpart. Quite often he will produce a pitch variance from the first attack to the end of the tone. Sometimes this is the result of carelessness, but at other times it is the result of the tongue style which he desires. As the broad tone varies over the duration of the tone, the pitch of the orchestra will not change with it, and the brasses may sound out of tune. One can hear this on some of the poorer recordings of this orchestra. The pitches do not blend as evenly as in the French group because the players are not as careful. Part of this pitch problem stems from the fact that the responsibility for the section's pitch varies as the first-chair players move around in the section. This is essential for an orchestra as overworked as this one, and as a result the first desks are occupied by a variety of players over the period of a week's services.

The Viennese are astute when it comes to achieving style concepts by varying the duration of the tone. With their heavier sonority for the Mozart and Haydn interpretations, they have to shorten the notes in order to create the lively, delicate style which is essential. Perhaps the Viennese concept is the proper approach to these classical masters because the composers were Austrian in their origins, or at least most of their first performances were Austrian. We personally favor the French and Amsterdam achievements in this way because they blend so effectively with the virtuosic string sections, but that is a private matter.

The brass tone quality of the Vienna Philharmonic carries especially well from the bottom to the top of the range. The broad cantilena is even in color wherever they need it. And it matches from section to section almost as if it were a great river of brass sound that continues to flow unimpeded through the wilderness of other orchestral textures.

The paragraphs above have described some of the attack devices used by the Vienna aggregation. Since breadth of tone is a personality characteristic of this group, the tongue devices carry out this concept even in the more delicate passages. This creates a broadness of sonority in such works that enhances the total orchestral tone with a resonance that is picked up and amplified by the Musikvereinsaal where the concerts are presented. At the State Opera House too, the wooden walls of the pit reinforce this quality and provide that unique auditorium with a sonorous accompaniment sound that is delightful in overtures, but sometimes obscures the delicate voices on the stage.

Perhaps the most important factor in developing the special Viennese tone quality is the use of rotary valve trumpets to match the French horns. The effect of the rotary valve construction on the bore of the tubing and the bending of the lead pipe will require a special article at another time. But it is important to recognize the fact that the trumpets of the Germans and Austrians as well as the Czechs and other eastern European groups have a solidifying effect upon brass quality and perhaps present a more even scale throughout the whole range. Because of this matching of trumpets and horns as well as trombones and tubas with similar construction, the total brass section has a homogeneity that is lacking sometimes in American orchestras with their individual variations of bore and and length of tubing.

The Berlin Philharmonic Orchestra

Like its counterpart in Vienna, the Berlin Philharmonic Orchestra has many of the same characteristics. Its permanent musical director, Herbert von Karajan, in an exclusive interview with this reporter, described the differences between these two groups when asked to compare the two orchestras: "They are two completely different ensembles. The Berlin Philharmonic Orchestra performs symphonic music only. If it ever does operatic music at all, it does such works as concert performances and without the problems of staging and dramatic action. The Vienna Philharmonic, on the other hand, is primarily an opera orchestra with the majority of its duties concerned with opera accompaniment. Its symphonic concerts are rehearsed and performed as adjuncts to its regular repertoire accompaniments at the Vienna State Opera. Its players have become the finest routined opera musicians in the world. They have also produced some of the finest of symphonic concerts as well, but their basic job is that of opera accompaniment."

This difference, as pointed out by the maestro who has led both ensembles probably more than any other living conductor, is notable in the symphonic programs which they produce. The Berlin brasses are especially gifted in developing the broad German tone so that it fits with whatever section requires matching at that moment. Since a brass specialist is usually an auxiliary who must compromise his judgment with more important strings and woodwind sections, he must learn to adjust everything that comes to his mind and out of the bell of his instrument to the taste, style, and knowledge of his confreres in those other sections. And the Berlin men are specialists at achieving this compromise. In the Philharmonic Hall at Berlin, the strings are so placed upon the polished hardwood platform that their tone reverberates and rings out in the unusual hall. At times the strings become even strident on certain pitches because of this brilliance. The brasses with their broad sound fill in the chinks of this brilliance and add to the organization's sonority with the German characteristics of an ample, sweeping, and vast tone that can be tempered by changed tongue positions and varied volumes of breath.

They are masters at matching all sections, and they fit together their brass pitches into a careful matrix of quality intonation. They use the duration of tone as a value in producing style contrasts. Their Debussy is as entrancing as their Wagner, and part of the reason for this is the manner in which they handle the lengths of the notes.

They have fine embouchures and are able to produce the same quality of tone from the lowest notes to their highest pitches. This was especially true of the tuba who carried his magnificent low register quality into the altissimo. And for the tenor tuba roles in the Wagner and Strauss tone-poems, the able performers bring this expert brass concept to this rather maligned instrument.

The brass instrumentalists in this orchestra can develop a variety of attacks for whatever purposes necessary, but they are especially versatile in producing the hammer tongue devices essential to much of the German repertoire. As these broad sonorous tones emerge from the larger bore German instruments, they have a weightiness about their beginnings that create in the listener the massive concept of Germanic ponderousness and gravity. The tongues use the syllable *thoo* for this effect, and the wind pressure is increased as the tone begins to give the result without a pointed, edgy sound.

The Germans also use the rotary valves with some of the results mentioned in the discussion of the Vien-

na group. In East Berlin, we spent many hours in the opera house listening to rehearsals of the opera orchestra preparing ballet and other works. Here we found that these rotary valve instruments are the pride of the state factories, and the players speak highly of them.

The Prague Philharmonic Orchestra

One of the finest homogeneous brass tones we have heard anywhere is that of the Prague Philharmonic Orchestra whose instrumentalists astonished our ears with their beauty of tone and accuracy of pitch. We have heard them in the Musikvereinsaal of Vienna and can compare them only to the other orchestras which have performed there, but we were amazed at their versatility and quality. We spent some time with the members of the trumpet section backstage and discussed the unusualness of this orchestral brass tone with them as well as with members of the Vienna Philharmonic. The result of our research made us realize that these men are not only well-trained virtuosos on their instruments, but that the instruments are also objects of intense, artistic construction. They are built in state-owned factories and are all similar in quality.

The Viennese brass players told us that the Czechs have held the reputation as being the finest brass instrumentalists in Europe for more than a century. Before World War II, many of them emigrated to other European nations and held first desk positions at the major opera houses. They have a "national gift" for the brasses according to one foreign observer. And their training program has developed them into a homogeneous group as to tone quality pitch, and technique. Like the French in developing woodwind players, the Czechs have evolved a school of brass playing that probably surpasses the others of Europe, if our ears are any criteria.

The tone quality has elements of the broadness and sonority of the German and Austrian, especially in those works requiring volume of sound and massiveness. But these players can shift their color concepts, probably by tongue positions and air direction, to develop the piquant color of the more delicate

scores. An instance of this was apparent this past summer when a contemporary Czech score using the eclectic idioms of the Impressionists, the Austrian Expressionists, and elements of Wagnerian romanticism tested the brass musicians' versatility. Breadth of tone in one section was changed to the precise and colorless sound essential to backing up delicate and figured woodwind or string passages of another style.

Part of this is achieved by the varied attack styles essential to performance of a wide repertoire; part was due to the changing concept of note duration; and part was the result of an ability to blend the individual characteristics of tone quality into an unified sectional sound that modified everyone's special personality. There were seldom any discrepancies in pitch for the brasses compromised with the woods and strings to adjust to the latter section's requirements.

We were especially impressed by the solo horn's use of vibrato along with matching woodwind solo bits. For the first time we heard a colorful transference of woodwind solo passages where the oboe and bassoon used a pleasant vibrato which was picked up by the clarinet and the French horn with similar vibrato, and carried out the original line with good taste and appropriate character throughout. We had always been opposed to vibrato in the horn, either for solo or ensemble performance, but after this experience we could recognize its advantages.

Probably the greatest factor in the homogeneity of tone in this orchestra was due to their use of the same rotary-valve trumpets, French horns, and tubas made from the same engineering patterns and by the same workmen. The *Amati* instruments have an evenness of scale that is hard to find on our American instruments, in this writer's experience. We were so impressed after we had heard this group that we made a special trip into Czechoslovakia to purchase an Amati rotary valve trumpet. We have been pleased with our experiences in playing on this instrument.

The Turin Radio Symphony Orchestra

We were pleasantly surprised when we first encountered the Turin Radio Symphony Orchestra which serves northern Italy with its broadcasts and concert performances for our experiences with the orchestras of Rome, Naples, Florence, Milan. and Venice had left us with a lack of respect for many of their brass specialists. But the Turin group reflected an expert conductor who had trained his personnel in the techniques necessary to participate in respectable interpretations of quality.

The brass tone of this group is smaller than its German counterpart. It is not as precise in color as the French sound, but it has some of the edge of the brilliant French tone with more of the warmth of the Italian *bel canto* vocal character in its make-up. The pitch of the tone varies a little from the beginning to the end yet it is not noticeable enough to carry the section badly out-of-tune. And this carelessness in pitch tends to depend upon the quality of the performer. The Italian temperament places emphasis upon a slight shortening of the tonal duration regardless of the style and the interpretations. For instance, in the music of Verdi a half-note is seldom carried out to its fullest value in rapid tempos. It is more apt to be shortened to the value of a dotted quarter or a double dotted quarter so that the player can prepare his attack for the next tone.

The Italians do not always have control of the total range of their instrument with similar tone colors. They may broaden the tone at the lowest range while pinching the sound for the altissimo tones. These are not characteristic of the Turin musicians as much as some of the others because these men have been trained to care for pitch and tone quality at the extremes as well as in the middle of their register.

The Italian brass specialist has a versatile facility when it comes to developing tongue attacks in connection with tone quality, and he uses varied tongue positions for a variety of styles. The tone quality seldom suffers from his use of the tongue except in heavily accented bravura passages when he does not have time to prepare each successive attack properly. Then he over-explodes with the tongue too far forward on fortissimo, and the tone may splatter a little.

The Italian instruments are more like our own and the French in structure. Pistons are more common then in Austria, and they lend a brilliance and edge to the sound that is characteristic of the trumpets and trombones, and, to some extent, the French horns. But the instruments do not provide the same small tone associated with the French production.

The Concertgebouw Orchestra of Amsterdam

Willem Mengelberg, so the authorities insist, was responsible for the great ensemble tone of the Concertgebouw Orchestra of Amsterdam. His long tenure as conductor there, from 1895 until 1941, created a versatile group whose major concern was ensemble unity in tone and pitch. The stories that old hands who played under him relate describe his rigid attitude during rehearsals. One of them told us of his experiences when Mengelberg would stop the orchestra and ask each member to play a difficult section which was hindering the development of the work. He even would pass out assignments to the sections before the rehearsal ended, and the players would be confronted with a playing examination at the next rehearsal. And, as certain as they were alive, Mengelberg never failed to call upon them to prove that their practice period had been carried out.

Therefore, little was left to chance or carelessness in that great instrumental ensemble when Mengelberg was conductor. It has not maintained that great status since his demise, but his assistant, Eduard van Beinum, continued in the Mengelberg tradition and carried on the ensemble concept which the latter had generated. We heard the orchestra for the first time in those years following Mengelberg's tenure, and the brasses still had the sheen of tone that was characteristic of the whole orchestra. A mixture of French precision with Germanic sonority permitted the musicians to produce the most effective brass ensemble of any of the great orchestras. The carefulness of matching pitches throughout the orchestra gave the brasses a homogeneity of tone that was not cluttered with beat tones due to poor intonation or even fair intonation.

The players of the section used every facet at their command to equal the sparkling luster of the strings. Where the latter achieved such a clarity of pitch that the total section sounded as if it were one person, the brasses copied this concept and agreed upon color, pitch, attack style, and duration with the same rigid submergence of personal ideas to the good of the ensemble.

They worked long hours to achieve a smooth transition from their lower and middle tone colors to similar results in the high octaves. The instruments were selected and matched with similar care. The results of such attention to detail provided the total orchestra with the reputation at one time of being "Europe's greatest orchestra." In our experience we can say that it achieved that reputation at only one occasion when it performed a Haydn symphony in its own concert hall at Amsterdam. At other performances in Vienna, at Edinburgh, and in America it fell short of the Mengelberg-Van Beinum standards.

The Philharmonic Orchestra of London

We don't reserve the Philharmonia Orchestra of London until last because it is the poorest of these groups, because that is not the case. It is a virtuoso orchestra in its own right and measures up to the others in so far as the brass section is concerned, with the maturity and responsibility accorded them. We hold it for the end because, to our ears, it characterizes the sounds which are most apparent in our American orchestras. Its solo desk men are some of the world's greatest brass specialists, and their solos have been recorded for posterity by major companies.

The Philharmonia is not the only London orchestra of quality either. There are at least three other good ones that might be compared in a variety of ways. But the Philharmonia is one of the finest for our survey. Its brass tone provides a median of sonority with the versatility that makes it possible to lean on either side of a rather solid tone quality, for the purposes of interpretive concepts. It can handle Wagner and Strauss with the solidity, if not the massiveness, of the Germans and Austrians, and it can quickly exchange that for the piquancy necessary for the French and contemporary idioms. But the English concept requires its musicians to be able to play a graceful, flexible tone with a slight vibrancy that gives it lift and carrying power as opposed to ponderosity.

The British brasses often have been schooled with two backgrounds, one of which is in the English brass band mode that carries out the full-bodied continuum of breathed-out phrases which call for complete duration of notation as well as for a broad spectrum of pitch. Therefore, the men often form pitch concepts which do not always jell with the more versatile and flexible woodwinds. This is not due to carelessness but to the breadth of sound which has not been confined precisely upon a central core of pitch.

British brasses can achieve a powerful sound without overblowing. They are very versatile in developing an attack that satisfies the conductor's interpretive ideas. Broad tongue strokes with accompanying breathed accents vie with delicate pianissimo precision strokes that create lace-like figurations. The instruments are usually of solid and sturdy British manufacture of first-rate quality designed to give service comparable to similar American instruments. They are not necessarily matched in pairs or groups and thus tone and pitch suffer when some of them develop idiosyncracies that create diversity rather than homogeneity.

Conclusion

The fact that individual orchestras have personalized brass sections which reflect the orchestral egos as well as that of the individual conductors is not a new aspect of musical understanding. The author has not attempted to present a new attitude about such aspects, but has tried to make a comparative analysis of one special phase of the European orchestras: the brass tone color.

We continue to emphasize that this is a personal matter, based upon our personal prejudices and background and should not be accepted as a final categorization of this subject. One would need a large number of specialists in brass tone, putting down their individual concepts and then tallying the results, to arrive at a more comprehensive analysis of the brass tone color of European orchestras. And the reader must remember that the time of day, the amount of rehearsal, the concert hall, the conductor, as well as the personal health of the musicians are extraordinary factors that affect the total results.

In brief we can suggest that the Germans and Austrians will settle for a broad sensitive tone that uses carefully prepared breath and tongue coordination to achieve this broadness in their attacks. The French, and less so the Italians, will emphasize a precise, small tone with very careful pitch concentration that blends effectively with the piquant woodwinds. The Czechs have many of the characteristics of the Germans but with more versatility in changing character and an expert superiority in blending within the section. The Hollanders and the English favor the compromise between the Germans and French with a variety of effects contributing to the German sonority but without the weightiness of tone.

At best the discussion above can only serve as a starting point for intelligent excursions into the why and wherefore of brass tone and technique. The writer hopes that many of his readers will use this article as a stimulus for an occasion to travel to the European summer festivals in order to hear these orchestras in their musical homes.

Fine

Part II

The first survey of the brass sections which appears above, attracted a number of letters from brass specialists throughout the nation. They encouraged us to undertake another survey in several different climes which more or less dealt with similar patterns of the previous experiences. Scandinavian orchestras in Denmark, Sweden, and Finland were included as well as those in Balkan countries. In this most recent tour our point of view has not changed considerably from that previously expressed. The Scandinavian and Balkan nations reflect other European influences in the type of instrument used, and style of technique and interpretation, with some national derivations to suit idiosyncracies of the national concepts.

Vienna has always set a pattern for so much of musical interpretation in these areas because guest conductors as well as permanent ones have been trained in the Vienna Academy or in professional orchestras in the Austrian capital or hinterland. And as the guest directors move from one nation to another they set patterns of brass playing to which they have become accustomed elsewhere. Some of the musicians reflect French influence, especially in Rumania where France was an important political entity following World War I. One finds Germanic or Austrian strains of style in Scandinavia with broad, sonorous brass tone and tongue concepts. As the French influence enters in the Balkans there is a piquancy of tongue style and delicacy of shading which is such a delight when it is applied to the proper works. When it is used indiscriminately, however, it becomes tedious and fails to balance the interpretations which are evolving in the other instrumental sections.

One of the highlights of this present survey of brass performance in Europe has occured at the Dubrovnik Summer Festival in a superior presentation of Bach's *B Minor Mass*. Any trumpeter who has worked out the difficulties of the three parts of this complicated work will recognize the problems which confront the performers. First of all, the altissimo range overwhelms the usual Bb or C trumpet used in modern sections. Secondly, the problem of matching refined pitches at such registers with flutes, oboes, violins, and voices calls for unusual accuracy and excellent ear training. Third, there are moments when endurance must carry the player beyond his usual capacities and, if a conductor has a flare for demanding a powerful sound at the end of long phrases of altissimo playing, the performer may not be able to carry it out.

The Zagreb Philharmonic Or-

376

chestra and the Slovenian Choir offered an intelligent and artistic interpretation of this work of superior quality. But in order to be assured of the finest of trumpets in these difficult parts, Maestro Milan Horvat, conductor, had imported three specialists from that center of great brass players, Prague, Czechoslovakia, to carry out his demands

with superlative capacities. We can't remember when we have heard three better matched trumpeters or instruments which have handled these parts so effectively, and our most recent experience was a fine professional presentation on the West Coast this spring.

We inquired into the background of the musicians and their instru-

ments after the performance and learned that the first man was using a piccolo B♭ trumpet, the second was using the small D trumpet for which the three parts are written, and the third played his music upon a C trumpet. Since the pitch accuracies were so refined we were particularly impressed with the instruments used. ∎

Muting the French Horn

MERTON JOHNSON

A prime color resource in instrumental music is the variety of muted brass sounds. For French horn this tremendous potential has often been neglected or misinterpreted partly because of overlapping terminology and partly because of uncertainties in technique. We will try to clear away at least part of the debris.

When the horn was first introduced into the orchestra, about 1639, it was little more than a hunting horn, capable of playing only the overtone series for the key in which it was built. About 1718 the idea of providing interchangeable coils of tubing (crooks) made it possible to use one or two basic instruments in several keys. However, because of the spacing of the overtone series, parts were still most generally of a hunting horn flavor or else placed high in the horn's register where the notes of the natural horn lie closer together.

Sometime between 1750 and 1760 a Dresden horn player, A. J. Hampel, codified the technique of using the hand to partially or wholly stop the bell of the horn, the principle being that the degree to which the opening is sealed determines how much a particular overtone is lowered in pitch. (Of course, sealing the bell completely produces an overtone series one half step higher than that natural to the instrument.) The result of Hampel's study was a whole new school of hand-horn play-

ing boasting a more covered sound and capable of playing chromatically passages *written* above the fourth harmonic (C4). Mozart's four concertos, the Beethoven Sonata, Op. 17, and even the Brahms Trio, Op. 40, for horn, violin, and piano were all originally conceived with the hand horn in mind.

Hand-Stopping

It was almost inevitable that the stopped sound which occurred as part of hand-horn playing would develop into a special effect. With the development of a *practical* valve about 1835 the horn became truly chromatic, capable of correcting the half step rise in pitch which hand-stopping causes. Beethoven may very well have been the first important composer to use stopped horn as a special effect in an extended passage. Anyone wanting to follow up the idea would enjoy reading Blandford's articles on the fourth horn part to the Ninth Symphony.[1]

In the Berlioz-Strauss *Treatise on Instrumentation* there is rather early mention of the use of hand-stopping for echo effects. A particularly apt illustration of this use is the passage in Rimsky-Korsakov's *Capriccio espagnol*. The *plus* signs over the notes indicate stopped horn—the small o's are for open notes. The stopped sections are played by most hornists by firmly sealing the bell with the

palm of the right hand and transposing *down* a half step. Trouble with centering the stopped sounds sometimes occurs if the player does not keep the backs of the fingers firmly pressed against the far side of the bell to complete the seal made by the palm of the hand.

One means of achieving the effect of distance (lontano) without asking the horn player to leave the stage is to play hand-stopped at a soft dynamic level, thus minimizing the biting quality of the loud stopped sound. There is a very effective passage of this sort in *Villanelle* by Dukas.

Bending the Sound

Two other interesting possibilities for using the hand-stopped effect are based on the pitch change it causes. One means of putting this to advantage is by "bending" a note flat gradually, a sort of *portamento*. This is done by gradually closing the bell with the hand while allowing the lip to relax slightly. Britten's *Serenade* for tenor, horn, and strings uses this device briefly.

The other possibility is to start with the bell fully stopped and the lip firmly holding the pitch to the half step above. Then, as the hand is opened, the pitch will descend a half step if the lip is relaxed slightly. Borodin used this effect in the *Polovtzian Dances* from *Prince Igor*.

♩. = 100

Later, **3rd** and 4th horns have a similar passage beginning an octave lower. It is much more difficult to make this come off in the lower register, because the notes tend to lose focus and intonation becomes doubtful.

Advantages and Disadvantages

From a mechanical standpoint, the chief advantage of hand-stopping rather than muting is that the change can be made almost instantaneously. However, composers such as Ravel and Debussy were very specific when indicating which they wanted because of the slight variances in color.

There are two important limitations to the use of hand-stopping. 1. If the B♭ half of the double horn is used, hand-stopping raises the pitch by about ¾'s of a step which means that a complicated system of alternate fingerings has to be worked out for each passage, or else the player must trust himself to the single F horn, and that can be risky in exposed high register passages. 2. The low register can be very fuzzy when played hand-stopped, as in the 3rd and 4th entry from *Polovtzian Dances* above.

The Bouché Mute

One solution exists to both of the above problems—the brass transposing mute—often referred to as the *bouché* mute. This mute is effective even below written C4 for F horn (middle C) and is not affected by switching from the F to the B♭ side of the horn. It does, however, require the player to transpose down a half step just as with hand-stopping.

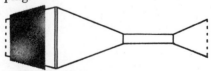

Fig. 1
Brass BOUCHÉ mute
(transposing)

For an extremely nasty biting sound the player can cup the right hand and hold it an inch or so be-hind the opening in the small end of the *bouché* mute to deflect the sound. The cutting effect of this sound can be a great equalizer where the stopped horn is covered by heavy orchestration.

Cuivré

Perhaps the most ambiguous, disputed term in the whole horn vocabulary is *cuivré*. Translated in its most likely form it means *brassy*. There seems to be no reason why it could not apply equally well to hand-stopped, open, or muted notes, and contemporary composers (as well as the Impressionists) use it all three ways. Unfortunately, a number of texts take the term *cuivré* to be interchangeable with bouché. To most present day horn players, *cuivré* means brassy and can be produced any of the three ways just mentioned. Of course any passage played extremely loudly will begin to have a brassy quality, and many composers use only dynamic marks to ask for *cuivré*.

Echo Horn

Echo horn has been variously called *half-muting*, *half-stopping*, and *echo horn*. Calling it *half-muting* could be misleading since horn players often insert the standard mute only part way to veil the sound without giving it the bite of fully muted sound. *Half-stopping* comes nearer to describing what happens. This particular echo technique is accomplished by making an almost imperceptible passage between the palm and the curve of the thumb, which allows freer vibration and permits a sweeter sound comparable to an echo of the normal tone. It is still necessary to transpose down a half step. Another means of obtaining this same sound is to draw the fingers inward slightly after a hand-stopped position has been reached. Either method when taken at a relatively soft dynamic level produces a quiet echo with a minimum of the biting quality of completely hand-stopped horn tone. It

should be pointed out that neither of these hand positions will retain the half step higher pitch if they become too open.

The Standard Mute

The history of muting the horn has not been very thoroughly documented. It appears that players of the valveless orchestral horn in the first half of the 17th Century used a mute quite similar to the standard mute in use today. By Beethoven's time hand-horn was well established, and use of any such simple mute would have prevented using the hand in the bell. Yet, if editions can be trusted, Beethoven calls for mutes in an early *Rondino* for wind instruments, in the *Violin Concerto*, and a few other places. Morley-Pegge's interesting book *The French Horn*[6] . . . suggests that a mute did exist for the hand horn. It was made of paper maché in the shape of a ball with an inner ball which could be drawn into the neck of the mute by pulling an external cord. This made it possible to more or less full seal the bell as with the hand, but presumably the tone would also be different for varying degrees of occlusion. With the advent of practical valves, horn players were able to revert to the simpler types used earlier.

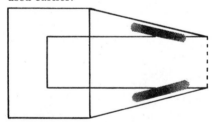

Fig. 2
Standard mute
(non-transposing)

Figure 2 shows the mute which made of cardboard or fibre material and DOES NOT require the player to transpose. One commercially available mute of this type is lined; another type is made of aluminum and features an adjustable inner tube to aid in tuning the mute. Both types have a somewhat *brighter* sound than the regular cardboard variety.

Color Variation

A player using just a basic mute has at his disposal quite a range of tone color, and the more color-conscious composers have done a great deal to exploit the possibilities.

Debussy's *La Mer,* for example,

calls for the *dolce* quality of horn muting. Most often this occurs at a *piano* dynamic level which relieves some of the edginess. To make the sound even smoother, the player often inserts the mute only part way instead of pressing it in firmly. This, of course, depends partly on the thickness of the spacing corks which can greatly affect the tone of a mute.

For contrast, consider the sweeping muted *fortissimo* passage at the opening of Strauss' *Don Quixote*. Later passages add even more bite through use of accented tonguing.

For the composer who has a particularly keen sense of color, it must be a real frustration to describe accurately what he expects in hand-stopped and muted sounds from a horn section. Terminology has not always been carefully used; more often than not the horn section will have several makes of mute; and there will always be differences in the shapes of their hands. Additionally, factors such as thickness of a mute's corks, shape of a horn's bell, and especially the concept of muted sound which each player has, will vary. In spite of all this, the composer must indicate his intentions just as clearly as terminology will allow, and it's the job of the horn player to follow these indications just as closely as he possibly can. The terminology list accompanying this article is one effort in this direction.   *Fine*

Commonly Used Terms for Hand-Stopping and Muting the Horn

HAND-STOPPING:

English	Italian	French	German
hand-stopped	*chiuso*	*bouché*	*gestopft*
stopped			
sound	*suono chiuso*	*sons bouchés*	
+	+	+	+

OPEN (after hand-stopping):

English	Italian	French	German
open	*aperto*	*ouvert*	*offen*
o	o	o	o

BRASSY (whether open, stopped, or muted):

English	Italian	French	German
brassy	(fff)	*cuivré*	*schmetternd*
		sons cuivrés	*blechern*

ECHO (terminology is least certain here):

English	Italian	French	German
echo	*eco*	*en écho*	*Echoton*
	come un eco	*sons d'écho*	
(veiled)		*sons voilés*	
(distant)	*(lontano)*		
stopped,			
not brassy		*bouché, non-cuivré*	
half-stopped			*halbgestopft*
half-muted			
(misnomer)			

MUTED:

English	Italian	French	German
muted	*con sordino*	*avec sourdine*	*gedämpft*
take mute	*mette il sordino*	*mettez la sourdine*	*Dämpfer nehmen*
mute	*sordino*	*sourdine*	*(mit) Dämpfer*

OPEN (after muting):

English	Italian	French	German
open	*aperto*	*ouvert*	*offen*
mutes off		*enlevez la sourdine*	*Dämpfer weg*
(or out)	*senza sordino*	*ôtez la sourdine*	*ohne Dämpfer*
remove		*sans sourdine*	
mute, etc.	*via sordino*		

1. W. F. H. Blandford, "The Fourth Horn in the 'Choral Symphony'," *Musical Times*, V66, Nos. 1,2,3 (Jan., Feb., March, 1925) 29-32, 124-29, 221-23.

2. Domenico Ceccarossi, *Il Corno*. Milan: G. Ricordi & C., 1957, 71 pp.

3. Birchard Coar, *The French Horn*. Dekalb, Ill.: Birchard Coar, 1947, 102 pp.

4. Phillip Farkas, *The Art of French Horn Playing*. Evanston, Ill.: Summy-Birchard, 1956, 95 pp.

5. Robin Gregory, *The Horn: A Guide to the Modern Instrument*. London: Faber and Faber, 1961, 250 pp.

6. R. Morley-Pegge, *The French Horn: Some Notes on the Evolution of the Instrument and of its Technique*. New York: Philosophical Library, 1960, 222 pp.

7. "The Orchestral French Horn: Its Origin and Evolution," in *Waits, Wind Band, Horn*. London: Peters Edition (Hinrichsen Ed.), 1952, pp. 195-219.

8. Gardner Read, *Thesaurus of Orchestral Devices*. New York: Pitman Publishing Corp., 1953, 631 pp.

9. Gunther Schuller, *Horn Technique*. London: Oxford University Press, 1962, 118 pp.

The Pre-Rehearsal Warm-Up

JAY ZORN

A problem that plagues band and orchestra directors as well as brass players is the matter of warming up before a rehearsal. Many directors, in desperation, trying to avoid the screeching and honking that usually occurs, forbid any warming up before the conductor mounts the podium. Some allow only a tuning note, others attempt to warm up all instruments together with a few scales or chords. I even know of some directors who pride themselves in a unique solution, they say, "I always warm up my band with a march."

None of these solutions is adequate, nor is the, "Turn 'em loose—free for all—jam it up" solution. Much rehearsal time is lost and what is more the brass players still remain in poor condition for a strenous rehearsal. Without proper warm up they will tire physically after five or ten minutes and play badly the rest of the rehearsal and possibly the rest of the day.

The First Five Minutes are Critical

Why do they tire and play poorly? Mainly because they did not wake up their embouchure gradually—they did not loosen their tongues and find the correct position for tongueing—they did not form a center or core of sound for a good tone—then starting in on a band or orchestra piece they overplay and force every note.

It should be obvious that the solution to a good functioning brass section lies in the proper warming up of these players, but in 3 or 4 minutes before a rehearsal starts can a brass player warm up sufficiently to perform well in a rigorous rehearsal? Yes, it *can* be done. 3 or 4 minutes of careful, concentrated playing is all that is needed. At the end of this article is a suggested warm up written in the treble clef, but may also be written in bass clef for trombones and baritones. This warm up can be accomplished easily in under 4 minutes and may be used to warm up for any type of brass playing: concert band, marching band, orchestra, stage band, combo, brass ensemble or before regular daily practice. Indeed, it should be used every. time the instrument comes out of the case for playing.

If you examine the suggested warm up you will find it to be very simple.

Bear in mind that it was created to be memorized by *every* brass player in the section and to be used by second year elementary school players on up through college. This warm up has many advantages. It is always in the players head, being easily memorized. Before a rehearsal you can't pull out all sorts of books hunting for warm up material. Besides, any player should begin playing with "sound and and ear" without the distraction of the

printed page. Another advantage of using this set warm up is that it can be used as sort of a gauge, measuring the player's physical condition at the time, thus giving him a clue as to his weaknesses and what his problems are going to be in rehearsal. Remember this is a *suggested* warm up. With a positive philosophy any teacher or student can create his own warm up or piece one together from several books. (The suggested sequence is very important).

The General Formula

1. *Buzzing*—start with a buzz without the mouthpiece to get the lips to vibrate.
2. *Middle register slurring*—remain on the staff, scale and interval slurring.
3. *Lip slurs*—using overtone series. Starting on the staff then move higher.
4. *Low register*—push to the low register, mainly scalewise.
5. *Tongueing*—mostly legato playing, single, double and triple. Remain on staff. Repeat staccato if desired.
6. *Upper register*—mostly scale slurs —as high as possible. At this point no harm will occur in playing high. (There are few books or studies for the high range, yet I have found most brass players after a year of playing capable of warming up to high "D" on trumpet or high "B♭" on trombone).
7. *Solo excerpt*—if there is time in the warm up have the student test his playing on some short passage of a solo or band or orchestra excerpt that he likes to play and keep that in the warm up.

The Warm Up

1. *Buzzing:*
Directions: Corners of the mouth firm. Concentrated tone.

2. *Middle Register Slurring:*

Directions:
1. Take a long, slow breath.
2. Clear, centered tone—corners of mouth firm.
3. Keep lip pressure at minimum —back off in lower register.
4. Hold back on breath—don't relax diaphram.

b.

3. *Lip Slurs:*

a.

Repeat using each valve combination 2,1,12,23, etc.

10 Second Rest

b.

Repeat using each valve combination 2,1,12,23, etc.

Directions:
1. Let the back of the tongue and breath do the work.
2. A little more lower lip pressure going to high notes, relax lip pressure going down.

4. *Low Register:*

Directions: This exercise is good to loosen up after high notes or anytime the embrochure is stiff.

5. *Tongueing:*

a.

Da Ga Da Ga   Da Ga Da Ga   etc.

Directions:
1. Play first time single tongue.
2. Repeat double tongue.
3. Keep it legato.

b.

Da Da Ga   Da Da Ga

Directions:
1. Legato playing.
2. Start slowly—repeat fast.

6. *Upper Register:*

a.

Directions:
Breathe higher, shorter air column.
Play lowest note as relaxed as possible, holding back on breath—let higher notes have more air and lower lip pressure.

b.

c.

d.

e.

f.

g.

h.

Directions: Breathe high—fill up with a great deal of air.

i.

Directions: Alternate **fingering** may also be used—same as lower octave—often in better tune.

j.

Directions: **Advanced students** should not stop here, but move as high as possible.

k.

7. *Solo Excerpt:*

Directions: Write above your favorite solo passage or create your own new material—keep this as part of your regular daily warm up.

Fine

FEBRUARY 1965

The Character of the French Horn

BURTON HARDIN

Although Jean-Baptiste Lully introduced the horn to the orchestra in *Princess d'Elide* in 1664, the instrument did not become a regular orchestra member until the beginning of the eighteenth century, and even then it was delegated its ancestral role of lending an atmosphere of the hunt. The horn was common in Germany by 1713, and Handel included two horns in his *Water Music* in 1715.

It is interesting to note that in most of the early orchestral literature which includes horns, the horns usually play alone in imitation or in contrast with the orchestra, as in Handel's *Water Music*. They are almost never sustained long, due to the fact that the early instrument had no provision for adjustment of intonation; it was literally tuned at the factory.

The high tessitura of early horn music is due to two factors: first, the horn could more nearly complete a diatonic scale in the high register, being limited to the notes of the overtone series, and secondly, the instruments of the time had such small bores that the lower partials were stuffy and hard to produce. (It should be noted that on the horn, as with other brass instruments, the seventh and eleventh partials always sound out of tune because they are out of phase with our tempered scale. In the tempered scale, often referred to as "equal temperament," all pitches are adjusted to even spacing within the octave so that intervals will sound the same in all keys.)

Horns were pitched in many keys, the most popular of which were the F horn and the D horn. The player played by reference point to the overtone series, rather than transposing separately. The modern French hornist, when confronted with a part which calls for a horn pitched in a key other than the standard F, is conscious of the fact that he is transposing: all transpositions

381

are in reference to the F horn. In contrast, the ancient horn player was conscious only of the horn upon which he was playing at a given time: tone eight was always in the same position on the staff whether the score called for horn in C, D, E, or whatever it might be, although the system of numbering these tones was not used at the time.

A standard method of notation was not known for the early horn, but each composer devised his own. The most practical of these methods involved clefs and was devised and used by Gluck. The composer arranged the clefs in such a way that the overtone series would always be in the same position on the staff; the position of the clef would change to correspond with the transposition of each instrument. The key signature of the concert pitch was included. This method benefited both hornist and score reader, making horn notation easily decipherable to each. The hornist followed the position on the staff, disregarding, for all practical purposes, the key signature; the score reader could tell immediately what the true pitch of the horn line was because of the clef and the key signature. The four notes in the following example are each tone eight of each respective instrument, but sound F, D, A and G respectively.

The technique of the time called for holding the bell high with the hand outside of the bell. This brought forth a raucous sound which had been meant to carry through the woods to signal stages of the hunt.

Handel was one of the first to use four horns in any one work, although one authority credits the later Mozart in *Idomeneo* and Cherubini in *Lodoiska* with originating the method. Handel used two horns in D and two in A in his *Guilio Cesare*. Using horns pitched in opposing keys gave composers the advantage of additional notes to assign to the horns. Horns were also more adaptable to minor keys if one horn (of a pair) was pitched in the tonic of the minor and the other in the relative major. Among other advantages, this made possible the use of the minor third.

Originally, for each key the composer required, a complete and separate horn would have to be used. Needless to say, this posed a physical as well as financial handicap for the horn player. However, about 1718 the crook and the tuning slide were invented in Vienna, making possible a more economical and portable instrument. For each desired key, there was a slide or crook, which when inserted into an instrument, lengthened the instrument sufficiently to cause that instrument to sound a series on the note which the crook was designed to produce.

Pitch	Length tubing required
B♭	9'2½"
A	9'9"
A♭	10'4"
G	10'11"
F♯	11'7"
F	12'3½"
E	13'
E♭	13'9½"
D	14'7¼"
D♭	15'5½"
C	16'4" (Basso)
B	17'4" (Basso)
B♭	18'5" (Basso)

The Second Half of the Century

Up to the middle of the eighteenth century, composers had only the basic partials of the overtone series to write for the horn. This was a serious limitation of the instrument, and little of any real value was written for the horn during this early period. However, in 1754 in Dresden, a horn player named Joseph Hampel began experimenting with the horn, with the desire of creating a method of attaining a more acceptable tone quality. The basis of his experimentation was the custom of oboists of the time of placing cotton wool in the bell of the instrument to soften the sound. In the early stages of his experimentation, Hampel found that the presence of the hand in the bell of the horn not only performed the function of softening the tone, but also could be made to alter the pitch of the instrument. He distinguished three positions: quarter stopping (¼), half stopping (½), and whole stopping (+). Certain notes achieved in this manner are difficult to play or have a very dull, muffled sound. The lower register tends to sound

muddy, whereas the upper register rings bright and clear.

A traveler and historian, Sir John Hawkins, leaves us with this description of the performance of a horn concerto:

> In the beginning of the year 1773, a foreigner named Spandau played in a concert at the Opera-house a concerto, part whereof was in the key of C with a minor third, in the performance whereof all the intervals seemed to be as perfect as in any wind-instrument; this improvement was effected by putting his right hand into the bottom or bell of the instrument, and attempering the sounds by the application of his fingers to different parts of the tube.

This hand stopping technique involves a phenomenon of physics: as the right hand is slowly inserted into the bell, the pitch falls in a gentle portamento until, with the hand entirely stopping the horn, one suddenly finds that he is sounding a series which is a semi-tone higher than the original open series. The latter can easily be explained as being due to the fact that with the hand entirely inserted, the vibrating length of the tube has been shortened, thereby causing a higher note to be sounded. The only satisfactory explanation to the gradual portamento is that the pitch of the open horn descends to the next partial below in the higher series as seen in the following example. Tone five in the open series would then be lowered to tone four of the stopped series.

Because certain notes were in varying degrees of stoppage and others were open, there was a great deal of unevenness of quality between the notes. Composers recognised this and avoided these notes to a certain degree. Mozart and Haydn rarely used stopped tones other than the 11th partial, which could be humored with a little stoppage, in their symphonies, but their horn concertos are filled with examples which may be noted by comparing the works with the basic overtone series on "C."

Further experimentation brought about the existence of two separate categories of hornists, the *corno-alto* and the *corno-basso*, the former being basically the executant of the type of playing which had been done up to the time, and the latter being the use of a horn with a larger bore and a more uniform taper and larger mouthpiece. This larger (not necessarily longer) instrument had a darker, more mellow tone quality, and was not expected to play as high as the *corno-alto*. However, the *corno-basso* was not considered inferior to the *corno-alto* as the second horn of today is considered lesser than the first, but because of its pleasing sound, was assigned the majority of the solo passages.

A most confusing method of notation came about when the horn began use of the low register. Composers notated an octave too low in the bass clef; middle C was written as the second space in the bass clef. Its origin, which probably had to do with the overtone series, has been lost in time, but its long lasting confusion can still be observed in modern works, where the composer must stipulate that his is "new" notation.

Because of the advent of the *corno-basso*, a Bohemian hornist named Dauprat in 1760 began using and advocating a new embouchure in which the upper lip is covered by about three-fourths of the mouthpiece and the bottom lip by one-fourth. This embouchure made possible more accuracy and flexibility in the lower register, as well as the facility of changing registers without shifting the entire embouchure.

In addition to the notes made possible by hand technique, and in conjunction with the *corno-basso*, several false notes below tone two were used. It must be noted that these notes were not members of the natural harmonic series, nor were they brought about through the application of the hand; rather, they were the result of an extremely loose embouchure. Although the notes want for stability, they can be and were developed to a point where they could be used as well as any other notes in the low register, as the entire low register was sluggish. All such notes were termed "facticious" notes, and all were lowered from tone two. Beethoven uses the low G in the adagio of his ninth symphony, in the famous fourth horn solo.

Berlioz quotes one more facticious note, the E natural between tones two and three, but terms it a "detestable note."

About 1770 a third type of horn player made his appearance in the orchestra: the *corno mixte*, who concentrated on the two best octaves of the horn, and made up with technical facility what he lacked in range. About the same time, the more mature Haydn and Mozart began limiting the range of the horn parts in their compositions. Haydn, as a young man, had taken a position in charge of the music of Prince Esterhazy, and had virtuosos of all instruments at his disposal, not only for concerts, but for experimentation as well. Consequently, he was prompted to write to the limits of the virtuosos' capacities. Later, however, in traveling, Haydn discovered that the calibre of musicians was not high, particularly outside of Germany, so he reduced the range required of the instrument. He and Mozart, in their later symphonies, wrote horn parts which encompassed from the second through the twelfth tones.

The Modern Horn

Realizing the limitations of all natural brass instruments, inventors began seeking a more practical instrument as early as 1760, when the keyed horn was invented by Koebel of the Russian Imperial Orchestra. The instrument was basically the same as the natural horn, except that along its length were openings which were covered with padded keys similar to those found on the modern Saxophone. Haydn wrote for keyed trumpet in 1796. In 1801, an instrument maker named Weidlinger, of Vienna, put a chromatic keyed bugle on the market, but it, like Koebel's horn, was defective in sound due to its construction. Only on the lowest note was the sound carried through the entire instrument, causing an unevenness in tone quality which was even more pronounced than that of the hand French horn.

A large version of the keyed bugle, the Ophicleide, was used with some success for several years as the bass of the brass section, but was replaced by the Bombardon or Bass Tuba soon after 1835.

Another interesting invention was a mechanical mute, made by Carl Thuerschmidt. This was so constructed that chromatic passages could be played with it, the muted effect being preserved throughout. Beethoven must have written for this or a similar device in the *Rondino* for eight wind instruments.

Although there are several types of valves, most are variations of two basic types: the piston valve, a cylindrical piece of metal with holes drilled to control the direction of the passage of air, and the rotary valve, a disc drilled to perform the same function. As their names imply, the former moves up and down in its casing; the latter turns. The function of the valve is to channel the passage of air so that it may be directed through extra tubing, lengthening the instrument, thereby making a different series of notes possible.

The originator of the valve was Bluemel of Silesia, who sold his rights to Heinrich Stoezel of Pless in 1815. The first valves made by Stoezel were square blocks of brass which worked like two piston valves in a brass box. A trumpet having two valves made by Stoezel is preserved in the museum of the Brussels Conservatory. In 1825 Stoezel improved the valve, making it tubular and calling it *Schub-Ventil*; it was a lighter, more rapid acting valve.

The valve horn made its orchestral debut in Halevy's opera, *La Juive*. Schumann used the valve horn extensively, notably in his *Adagio and Allegro*, opus 70 in A flat, for Horn and Piano, and *Konzertstuck*, opus 86, for four horns and orchestra.

Wagner used both the hand and the valve horn in combination, but abandoned the valve horn in favor of the hand horn in *Lohengrin* in 1848. He also wrote for eight horns.

The valve was originally intended to be used only to change the key of the horn quickly, but even in Berlioz' time, hornists were beginning to use the instrument chromatically, and by doing so, in his opinion, they were damaging the works of older masters.

Brahms, however, accepted the valve horn early and wrote to good effect with such works as the famous *Trio*, op. 40, for piano, violin and horn.

The use of three valves produced an imperfect scale. When a length of tubing which was designed to lower the pitch of an F horn a semitone was used in conjunction with one which was meant to lower the pitch of the same F horn a whole tone, it did not lower the pitch precisely the desired tone and one half. This was true with each of the possible combinations, the length of tubing being further from being long enough with each valve addition. About 1920 a band instrument manufacturing company put on the market for the Euphonium a compensating valve which would automatically add the amount of tubing necessary to produce the correct pitch when more than one valve was used at a time. This invention as yet has not been applied to the French horn, but most hornists have been able to compensate with subtle movements of the hand within the bell.

The single B flat horn, which is often used by first horn players, is shorter in length than the F horn, and in hand muting it is difficult to achieve the right position to raise the pitch exactly one semi-tone. The hand must cover so much area that a hornist with other than an extremely large hand will find it im-

possible. To make muting with the B flat horn possible, several companies employ a mute valve which lowers the pitch slightly more than a semi-tone. The hornist employing the mute valve and stopping with the hand will find transposition unnecessary.

In the late nineteenth and early twentieth centuries, composers were inclined to give the horn no key signature, but provide accidentals, since it was felt that hornists were accustomed to reading natural horn parts and could not be expected to read key signatures. This was found to bring about confusion, and most composers since 1930 have provided key signatures when necessary. Forsyth recommended the use of key signatures in his orchestration book.

There is no reason nowdays why the Horns should not have a correct key-signature . . . whether they key-signature is on the paper in front of him or not, the play-

er who is transposing is compelled to have it in his head. The brain that can master such a difficult instrument up to symphony standard is not likely to be worried by seeing the sharps and flats on the left hand top corner of his music.

All professional hornists can testify to the fact that even in music where signatures have been avoided, some enterprising hornist with a pencil has usually provided them to clarify the situation!

There are several names for each of the horn instruments. Cor, Cor d'harmonie, Corsimple, cor a main, Waldhorn, Naturhorn and Corno all properly refer to the natural or hand horn. Cor de chasse, Trompe de chasse, Jagdhorn and Corno di Caccia refer to the hunting horn. Cor a Pistons, Ventilhorn and Corno a Macchina refer to the valve horn. In recent music composers refer to the Cor, the Horn, or the Corno, all meaning the valve horn.

Fine

Problems of FRENCH HORN Playing

JOSEPH SCHMOLL

There are a variety of problems among student horn players. One of the most common is indefinite attacks. Attacks such as these discourage the performer and teacher and encourage the other students to believe that the French horn is not on a level musically with the other band instruments. The cause of poor attacks is that the student says "too" and moves the tongue with about the same amount of energy as he would playing another brass instrument. More energy is required for horn attacks, as well as a spitting action of the lips. To someone who has transferred from the trumpet to the horn, increased effort to make each attack at first will seem to be unnecessary. Such a student requires constant encouragement from the teacher until he masters the technique a few months later.

Before the attack begins, the tongue is placed against the upper

teeth and barely touches the inside part of the upper lip. As the attack begins, it is withdrawn quickly to the rear and bottom of the mouth. As the tongue is being withdrawn the lips commence a spitting action. This spitting action is similar to when one ejects a particle of food from the lips. It is best for the student to tongue vigorously at first. Later he can make less strenuous attacks and attempt legato style tonguing. When the attack is mastered it is one of the most beautiful features of horn playing.

Dropping the Jaw

Another common error among students is attempting to play with a high jaw. A high jaw partially closes the opening between the lips and causes the tone to lack resonance. The high notes sound pinched or are impossible to play at all. The remedy is to drop the jaw. This is

easily accomplished by most beginners but is difficult to accomplish by some students who have already played for a few years. Dropping the jaw for the more advanced student will seem to be unnatural, and his playing will suffer temporarily. If he is aware of this and if he is convinced that further progress is impossible he will probably drop the jaw. Many students protest that they are doing all they can to drop the jaw but that it will not come down. Perhaps the real reason is that they are not convinced that the effort to drop the jaw is worthwhile. A suggestion that they should consider taking up another musical instrument has achieved good results in every instance where it has been tried. A real effort is then made to drop the jaw. Such a suggestion should be made only as a last resort, however. It is helpful for some students to refrain from playing the horn for two or three months. After a period of inactivity it may be easier to drop the jaw.

The mouthpipe of the horn should be at an 180° angle with the mouth. The lower teeth should be directly under the upper teeth. If the lower teeth are withdrawn behind the upper teeth, the mouthpipe will then point at an angle to the floor. Many students try to compensate for this by tilting the head to the rear. They are not correcting the problem but merely deceiving themselves.

The low register of the horn will sound if the jaw is dropped even lower than when playing in the middle or upper register by loosening their lips but with a high jaw. The notes are insecure or do not sound at all. Often students must be told to tighten the lips slightly in the low register if their jaw has already been dropped sufficiently. This will make the low notes sound as part of the true range of the horn rather than as if they were pedal tones.

Important Qualities

It is a mistake to select students only with thin lips to play the horn. The author has never noticed a relation of the size of the lips and ease of horn playing. Far more important qualities are a good ear, average or above average intelligence, and musical talent. Since the horn is one of the most difficult instruments to play, it is logical to assume that the more gifted students should play it. Good horn players in a band will attract talented beginners on that instrument. The best horn player can play a solo with band accompaniment. This helps to create interest in the instrument. Playing only background harmony notes and rhythmic patterns in marches will discourage above average horn players. It is essential to choose compositions and arrangements that allow the horns to be heard. A composition which features the horn section in unison in exposed places is safe and effective.

The Double Horn

The double horn is the best instrument for most playing, however, directors operating on limited budgets can get more instruments for their money by purchasing single horns.

The F horn is the most popular single horn but not necessarily the best. Most beginners will make more rapid progress playing the B♭ horn. A short experiment will help to determine which horn is easier to play. Have a student play both the F and B♭ horns, listen to the results and ask the student which horn he prefers. In most cases the B♭ horn will be chosen by teacher and student. The author has had beginners on the double horn play almost exclusively on the B♭ side of the horn for the first few months. Gradually notes on the F side of the horn are introduced for the middle and low registers.

It is not necessary to transpose when playing a B♭ horn. A fingering chart which can be obtained from most any music dealer already makes the adjustment for the performer to read from a F horn part.

There is no reason why a characteristic tone cannot be produced on the B♭ horn. If the student hears accomplished horn players and listens to phonograph records he should be able to produce a good tone on the B♭ horn.

Fine

The Trumpet's Day

EDGAR TURRENTINE

When "The ides of March are come," and Cassius with the "Lean and hungry look," and Brutus, "Noble Brutus," plunged their daggers into "The most high, most mighty" Julius Caesar, all the city of Rome was in the midst of a twenty-four day festival-ceremony. This festival-ceremony heralded the beginning of the campaigning season for the army and began on the first day of March. A group of young men from patrician families, Marc Antony was one of these in his time, formed a procession and paraded through the streets. They carried the holy war shields and were preceded by trumpeters blowing "clarion calls" and "brazen blasts." The procession stopped at all the altars and temples along the line of march and danced a war-dance, from whence the participants became known as *Salii*—"dancers." The young men, or *Salii*, continued parading with pauses for special games, feasts, and rituals until March 24. On the eleventh day there was a chariot race in honor of Mars, the god of war. On the nineteenth day, the procession paused to "cleanse"—"purify"—"bless" the holy shields. Four days later, March 23—"the day belongs to Vulcan; they call it Tubilustria (Ovid, *Fasti*, V.726)"—the procession halted, again, to "purify" and to sound the holy trumpets *(tubae)* belonging to the priests of the cult *(tubilustrium)*. The 23rd of March also was the second day of the spring festival of Cybele and Attis and the chief ceremony of the day was the felling of the sacred tree and the blowing of trumpets (Julian, *Orations*, V.168.c). Indeed, ancient Rome must have been a musical-sounding city on March 23.

According to Krohmeyer and Veith *(Heerwesen und Kriegführung der Griechen und Römer)*, there were four types of trumpets in use by the Roman legions—the *tuba*, *cornu*, *lituus*, and *bucina*. The *tuba* was a long, straight instrument, 20 inches to 5 feet in length, which the army used in battle to give signals of a tactical nature. The *cornu* was in the form of a G, the length of the tube sometimes as long as seven or eight feet. This instrument was used to give signals within the army camps. The *bucina* was a shorter instrument, slightly curved as an animal's horn. It, too, was used by the army inside the camps. The *lituus*, shaped like the shepherd's crook, about six feet in tube-length, was considered a cavalry signaling instrument. Gellius (*The Attic Nights*, XX.ii) lists another type of trumpet. He says it was used exclusively for funerals, however, iconographic investigation shows that the *tuba* and *cornu* were used in the funeral ceremonies and processions and no other types of trumpets have been "pictured."

Roman legend has it that the trumpet was invented by Tyrrehenus, son of Hercules. Tyrrehenus, leading his people from the east, colonized Etruria (present-day Tuscany) shortly after the Trojan Wars, hence many of the early Greek and Roman writers called the trumpet an Etruscan invention. The story of Tyrrehenus inventing the trumpet was so well-known that many of these early authors referred to any trumpeter as "Tyrrehenus" and the sound of the trumpet as the "Tyrrehenian melody." Just exactly what was the quality of the sound of the Roman trumpet is not known but Aelian (Book X.28) and Plutarch (*Isis and Osiris*, 362.30) comment that the good citizens of Busiris and Lycopolis disliked the trumpet because its sound reminded them of the braying of a donkey! However, the most interesting description of the sound of the Roman trumpet comes from Ennius (*Annals*, 143): *At tuba terribili sonitu taratantara dixit*—And

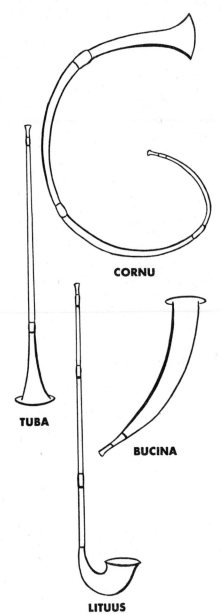

CORNU

TUBA

BUCINA

LITUUS

the trumpet spoke forth, taratantara, in terrible tones.

The Roman armies not only used the trumpet as a signaling instrument but also as an instrument of psychological warfare. At the beginning of a Roman attack all the trumpets were blown at once to create a loud and terrifying noise so as to frighten the adversaries. It was also used in all types of processions—martial, civic, and religious—lending "pomp and circumstance" to the occasion. The instrument was also used at festivals and games to start the races and contests; indeed, it had its own contest, one of endurance—to determine who could blow the loudest blast, in the ancient Olympics, beginning in the 76th Olympiad and continuing until Theodosius discontinued the games. Guests at Roman banquets were entertained with trumpet blasts. Varro (*On Farming*, Book II.iv) reports a rustic use of the instrument. He writes that Roman farmers blew the trumpet to call the livestock to be fed!

So, in this month of March, when the trumpeter is reading his *Julius Caesar* and comes to Shakespeare's stage directions, "Sennet," after the Soothsayer's warning, "Beware the ides of March," he may pause in his reading, take his trumpet in hand, and sound a trumpet call. If it happens to be on the 23rd day of March, may it be an extra loud and long flourish—for it is the trumpet's day.

Fine

The Bass Trumpet: From Wagner Until Today

DONALD HUNSBERGER

When we consider the subject of the bass trumpet, the first thoughts that occur are: Where does one begin? What sources are available? Who has written for the bass trumpet? Is it a real bass voice or does it really belong in a different voice register? Of what value is it today? Does it warrant consideration for inclusion in the instrumental ensembles of today and tomorrow?

To be more fully equipped to answer some of the above questions and to provide some food for thought concerning the future of the bass trumpet, the author turned to the music containing parts for the instrument, to the texts which review the immediate history of the bass trumpet, and to those manufacturers who are presently engaged in research on and testing of auxil-

iary brass instruments such as this. Just as it is impossible to review every word or note written for the bass trumpet, it is likewise impossible to interview every person who has some individual ideas concerning the subject.

To begin, let us first examine the bass trumpet and observe the development of this distinctive tone color which Wagner conceived over

110 years ago. In his essay *Oper und Drama* (1851), Wagner established the role of the orchestra in the music drama as a musical counterpart of the sub-concious, thus containing the various colorings of the emotional spectrum—the blacks, the whites, the intermediate grays, as well as the brilliant and subtle shadings. To achieve this the orchestra was enlarged from the classical instrumentation which had prevailed with little change even through the early and middle years of Berlioz. The brass section was considered standard with 2 to 4 soprano trumpets (natural and/or valve), 4 valve), 3 trombones, and 1 tuba. From this basic grouping Wagner expanded the brass choir until it reached a total of seventeen individual parts!

In the Preface to the four music dramas of the *Ring of the Nibelung* Wagner lists the instrumentation and doubling he desires (the latter being a consideration which composers today seem to have lost with our massive bands and orchestras). The listing included:

1st violin . . . . .16 players
2nd violin . . . . .16 players
viola . . . . .12 players
cello . . . . .12 players
bass . . . . 8 players

3 flutes; 1 piccolo (or 2-2)
3 oboes; 1 English horn (or 4 oboes)
3 clarinets; 1 bass clarinet
3 bassoons (Contra if necessary)

8 horns (4 of which are to take alternately the nearest four tuben [Bayreuth tubas] parts.

3 trumpets
1 bass trumpet
3 tenor and bass trombones
1 contrabass trombone
1 contrabass tuba

6 harps

Timpani, triangle, cymbals, side drum, 1 carillon

In a careful consideration of the above listing, the complete balancing of each individual family stands out as a musically sound principle. The number of strings is perfect for divisi up to four parts; the woodwinds are grouped in fours with the basic colors predominating and with fringe colorations in the piccolos, English horn, and bass clarinet. It would seem that Wagner continued his predilection for fours in the brasses as well, for the eight horns are occasionally divided into four

horns and four tuben; the trombones have a balanced four-voice choir with the three tenor/bass and the one contrabass trombone, while the trumpets appear equally balanced with three soprano and one bass trumpet. But, as will soon be illustrated, this latter quartet was little used in actual musical practice. To further explain this last statement, it is necessary to digress for a moment and examine the original instrument and see why it developed as it did.

In the period from November 1848 to December 1852, Wagner wrote the dramas which were the poetic basis for the *Ring* cycle. He composed the music from 1854 through 1874 with the final touches placed on *Die Götterdämmerung* in the latter year. To achieve the expanded brass colors which he desired (over and above the natural and valve trumpets and horns, trombones and tuba) he had instruments constructed which pushed aside the existing tonal and range barriers: the tuben (those strange instruments with a fantastically long tubing, small bore and mouthpiece, usually played by French horn performers—an interesting study in themselves); the bass trumpet; and a revised model of the Baroque contrabass trombone, pitched an octave below the standard B-flat tenor-bass trombone.

Two very interesting and informative sources on the early history of the bass trumpet have been Cecil Forsyth in his book, *Orchestration*, and Mr. Vincent Bach, long known for his deep interest in the development of brass instruments. To quote Forsyth, at one time the orchestrator's *basic manual*, on the bass trumpet:

This trumpet, as imagined by Richard Wagner for the *Ring*, was to be an instrument of Brobdingnagian [giant, enormous, from Swift's *Gulliver's Travels*] length and Brobdingnagian tone-colour, with a compass which extended from the bottom notes of the tenor trombone to the topmost notes of the French horn . . . It was to be played with three crooks, C, D, and E♭, transposing downwards an octave, a minor seventh, and a major sixth respectively . . . But, . . . it was found that, with a narrow-bore instrument of such enormous length—viz. 23 ft., nearly the size of a double-bass-trombone—the two lowest harmonics (Nos. 3 and 4) were poor in quality, while the four top harmonics (Nos. 16, 17, 18, and 19) were unplayable by human lips.[1]

This combination of crooks and the

recently installed valve mechanism on an instrument of such length and bore proved to be more of a paper advantage than a practical one; thus, the original instrument was discarded and another one was made with a harmonic series pitched one whole tone above that of our modern-day tenor trombone in B-flat. This instrument had a much shorter tubing and thus was able to combine the valve mechanism and the crooking system (again in C, D, and E-flat) more successfully.

The first major problem now arises—that of pitch and register location of the contemporary bass trumpet in the complete trumpet family. It would seem that this instrument is in reality more of a tenor trumpet than a true bass trumpet; and, when the instrument is played with an E-flat crook or is pitched in E-flat (as its open harmonic series) it falls more into the classification of an alto trumpet. These assumptions are based on the comparative vocal registers plus the proximity of the tenor trombone harmonic series to that of the bass (or tenor) trumpet. To be a true bass instrument it would have to have the fundamental of its open harmonic series located at least a perfect fourth lower, as in the case of the bass trombone in G, F, or E-flat. Other than the fact that the original instrument was to have such a fundamental location (and thus the misnomer of the title was carried through the years) there is really no reason for our present day instrument in B-flat to carry the name of "bass" trumpet.

The primary source in research of this type is the music containing parts for the "bass" trumpet.[2] In this respect it is interesting to speculate about the possible changes and alterations which took place in Wagner's mind concerning the brass family during the extremely long period during which he composed the total *Ring* cycle. As was previously mentioned, the music dramas were composed between 1854 and 1874; during this time *Das Rheingold Die Walküre*, and Acts I and II of *Siegfried* were composed in that order, Act II of *Siegfried* and the complete *Die Götterdämmerung*

[1] Cecil Forsyth. *Orchestration*. Second Edition. (New York 1949). pp. 101-102.
[2] To avoid any possible confusion at this point, the term "bass" trumpet will be continued throughout the article.

were composed between March 1869 and November 1874. During the twelve year period between Acts II and III of *Siegfried*, Wagner composed *Tristan und Isolde* (1864-65) and *Die Meistersinger* (1867). Neither of these latter operas contain any of the auxiliary brasses: the tuben, the bass trumpet, or the contrabass trombone. The interesting question now posed is: Did brasses change during this twelve year period or was he able to maintain an equal and even usage despite the fact that he composed two major works in the interim without using them?

An examination of the orchestral score of the *Ring* indicates that *Die Walküre* has the most consistent employment of the bass trumpet during the first period while Acts II and III of *Die Götterdämmerung* have the greatest during the second period. A detailed analysis of these two works reveals the following doublings and solo entrances (as will be quickly noticed, not all the instrumental combinations used are listed, as many occur but once and have little statistical value):

Bass Trumpet with:	Walküre	Götterdäm- merung
4 trbn., and tuba)*. as Voice 1	40	8
4 trbn. as Voice 2 or 3	0	3
4 horns	11	2**
4 horns and 1 trumpet	7	1
2 horns	7	0
Trpt. 1 or 3 (in uni- son or octaves)	13	4
2 trumpets	6	4
1 trpt., 4 trbn., as Voice 2	8	6
3 trpts., as Voice 4	2	0
Solo capacity	16	8

*Tuba plus 4 trombones occurs 9 times.
**Once with 4 horns and 1 bassoon; once plus Trombone 2.
Die Walküre—134 entrances total.
Die Götterdämmerung—49 entrances total.

A quick analysis reveals that the predominant employment was as the soprano member of the bass trumpet-trombone group. Secondly, the solo capabilities of the instrument were utilized fully plus its ability to blend with the horns. In converting the chart into percentages it becomes apparent that the use of the bass trumpet as the fourth voice of the trumpet family would rank very low in comparison to the usage as a member of the trombone choir. A slight, although significant, alteration which occurs between the two

columns is the new writing for the bass trumpet as a harmonic filler in the middle of the trombones in the last two acts of *Die Götterdämmerung*. Also noted in the score of this drama is the tendency to score many of the solo entrances usually given to the bass trumpet in earlier works now for the solo trombone.

Following the *Ring* the bass trumpet led a rather checkered career. Among those compositions which contain parts for the bass trumpet, the following are the most prominent:

Macbeth, a tone poem (1889-1890) Richard Strauss

Guntram, a three act opera (1894) Richard Strauss

Gürre-Lieder, a vocal/orchestral composition (1901) Arnold Schoenberg

Le Sacre du Printemps (1913) Igor Stravinsky

Sinfonietta (1926) Leos Janecek

The Strauss parts range from a rather mediocre ensemble and solo writing in *Macbeth* to a rich, full part in *Guntram* which recalls pages of the best of Wagner's brass writing. Strauss does not use the bass trumpet as a fourth trumpet. The Stravinsky scoring is actually an E-flat alto trumpet part in range as well as being included as part of the 4th trumpet part (to be doubled by the 4th trumpet player). The Janecek score calls for a massive trumpet section using two bass trumpets, the latter's parts usually doubling the timpani part (recalling the Altenburg Trumpet and Drum Method!).

The consideration now is one of adapting ideas from the past to an instrument of today which bears little or no resemblance to the original instrument which Wagner had in mind. Our present-day bass trumpet is an instrument pitched in B-flat with a 7″ bell, a venturi of approximately .410-.425″, and with a valve cylinder measurement of .484-.485″. The valves have practically the same dimensions as those of the soprano B-flat trumpet (large bore), a consideration which possibly has some effect on the intonation difficulties found in most modern bass trumpets. Another consideration which must be faced is that of available mouthpieces in varying cup depths and rim sizes; at present only a very few mouthpieces will render a reasonably

satisfactory harmonic series.

In the event that a more perfected instrument is manufactured, what might we expect from the inclusion of the bass trumpet in our ensembles? First of all, the recent fantastic growth of the Woodwind Choir must be recognized: the addition of the bass flute and the alto flute, the contrabass clarinet, the sopranino flute and clarinet, the *complete* saxophone family (from soprano through bass). This type of growth has not been equalled in the brasses; rather, some composers, arrangers, and conductors are attempting to return the brass section to the dimensions of the post-Classical orchestra. Consider the present-day brass ensemble: 3-4 trumpets, baritone, and 1 tuba. In all, we have just five basic colors before muting and doubling takes place.

We have been steadily losing the battle of the 4th horn recently just as we have almost completely lost the cornet sound. Fortunately the bass trombone has earned itself a rightful place along-side the tenor trombone, but in doing so has merely filled the gap left by the loss of the euphonium voice in the gradual switch to the smaller bore baritone horn. The fluegelhorn, used by a courageous few, has so much to contribute, especially in offering a mellow, rounded sound in contrast to the brilliant sound of the trumpet. The consideration of the mellow brass versus the brilliant brass has been one of the most healthy and progressive movements in recent years.

Why not try a bass trumpet in a brass quartet with two soprano trumpets and a trombone? This offers a more homogenous sound than that of the French horn attempting to blend with three cylindrical instruments. Or, why not try trumpet quartets with three soprano trumpets and one bass trumpet? (Likewise, why not experiment with baritone or euphonium trios or quartets using music from the ever-growing trombone ensemble repertoire?) The number of combinations which could utilize bass trumpets is limitless, all that is needed is a spark of imagination and a desire to further the somewhat stagnant level of brass ensembles in our present organizations.

Even the field of jazz has utilized the bass trumpet more than the

Richard Wagner

concert stage or the educational institution. Witness the fine solo playing of men like Cy Touff, Johnny Mandell, and Dave Wells who have forwarded the position of the bass trumpet by incorporating its individual sound into contemporary jazz ensembles.

In an effort to condense some of the above thoughts into some workable ideas the author wishes to offer these proposals concerning the present and future status of the bass trumpet:

I. The name "bass trumpet" should be discarded and the more correct title of "tenor" trumpet should be adapted for our present-day B-flat instrument.

II. This instrument should be adaptable for use with a variety of

Figure 1. B♭ Flügelhorn, B♭ Soprano Trumpet, and B♭ Tenor Trumpet (Photo by Louis Ouzer)

mouthpieces of varying cup depths and rims, this without detriment to an inherent intonation balance.

III. The tenor trumpet should be written in the bass clef and the tenor clef as a non-transposing instrument; to retain the present treble clef writing with its downward transposition of a major 9th is senseless and merely adds confusion to the bass and tenor clef performers for whom the instrument is manufactured.

IV. The tenor trumpet, along with the alto trumpet and the fluegelhorn, rightfully deserves an opportunity for inclusion in ensembles of all sizes and functions.

Fine

The Legato Style of the Trombone

JAMES GRAHAM

One of the most serious problems confronting the student trombonist (and his teacher) is the correct execution of the beautiful, flowing, singing legato style of performance so peculiar to the trombone. Simulating the fluid, faultless slur between notes characteristic of piston or rotary valved instruments, but without the inherent advantage of the almost instantaneous change between notes provided by the valve, is indeed a formidable task for the student. A beautiful legato style is essential to the complete technique of any trombonist and possibly the most difficult aspect of performance he will ever be called upon to master.

Not only are there many problems relating to the legato style for the student to overcome, but his teachers can not seem to agree on "The" proper method for instruction and execution of the legato style. In this article, the author will attempt to discuss the most effective means of producing the legato style encountered in experiences as student, performer, and teacher.

First though, both as refresher to some and as explanation to the uninitiated, *legato* can be defined as follows: "To be performed without any perceptible interruption between

notes." (*The Harvard Dictionary of Music*) When found in the literature, this particular phrasing will be indicated:

Preferably

legato or leg.

or Possibly

these indications are not to be misinterpreted as a *glissando* or *smear*, usually indicated:

Preferably

or Possibly

gliss.

The *glissando* is used occasionally for an effect. The latter indication of glissando can sometimes create obvious problems as it is quite similar to the proper indication of legato. One must be continually attentive to detail to insure that students do not make this error in performance.

The essential difference between *legato* and *glissando* is that *legato* imitates the slur of the valved instrument, while the *glissando* is a continuous movement across the scale. It is usually of wide enough interval that the full effect of the *rip* or *smear* can be gotten. To properly execute the *legato* style, and eliminate the *glissando* effect between notes is not an easy task for either

the pupil or his teacher. Essentially, the teaching of the *legato* style can be broken down into four categories:

1. The *tongue* and its proper usage
2. The *breath* and its control
3. The manipulation of the *slide* (the right hand and wrist)
4. The *embouchure* and its function

Certain exercises and study materials will also be suggested.

The Tongue

Proper use of the tongue is of utmost importance to the correct execution of the legato style, as it must take the place of the valve in defining the attack. Syllables are of a great help to the student in solving tonguing problems. For detached playing, it is generally agreed that the syllable "Tah" or other open "T" syllable such as "Too" gives the desired precision and definition of for the separated attack. For best execution of the legato style, the softer syllable "Dah" is ideal. Not "Lah," "Loo," "Rah" or "Roo," etc., but *"Dah"* This is quite important for several reasons:

Even though the legato style is much more flowing than the detached style, each attack must be executed with a maximum amount of control on the part of the performer. Any extra movement of the tongue such as the rolling motion that is required to produce such syllables as "Lah," "Loo," "Rah" or "Roo," etc., produces a vague, inconsistent movement between notes. These four syllables and others like them are definitely a hindrance to the production of an acceptable legato technique.

The tongue must move quickly and precisely away from the teeth in much the same manner as the detached tongue to produce the proper attack in the legato style. This is most important because as mentioned before, the tongue actually takes the place of the valve. It must momentarily impede the flow of air so that the moving slide may be changed without any perceptible glissando or natural slur being noticed by the listener. For this task, the tongue must be precise, not a vague, rolling blur.

Repeat to yourself, "Tah," "Tah," "Tah," Then "Dah" "Dah" "Dah." After this experimentation it becomes quite apparent that the "Dah" syllable is much more even and fluid than the detached "Tah" syllable, but yet it still retains the necessary precision and definition that is needed.

For both detached and legato attacks, the tongue should move from exactly the same place in the mouth. In the author's opinion this ideal spot should be from the center of the upper teeth—not consciously being able to detect the gum line. This spot should not be on the gum line or between the teeth, etc., but *directly behind the upper teeth*. There will be variations to this placement as all individuals are of different physical construction, but it is an ideal starting point to begin with. The important rule to remember concerning legato tonguing is as follows: *Tongue in the same place and in the same manner, but think "Dah" instead of "Tah."* This will produce the softer, more desirable attack required.

In actual practice, the student must be taught very carefully to produce this "Dah" syllable quite definitely. Many times a rather vague, hazy legato will be produced not because the student is tonguing incorrectly, but because the tongue is not heavy enough. In most cases, too much, rather than too little tongue is probably best. One must listen very carefully to one's play-

ing to determine the exact amount of tongue required to best articulate a particular interval.

The legato phrase gives rise to some controversy as to just what constitutes the proper style of execution. Some authorities say to tongue each note of the legato phrase. Others differ in that they would advocate tonguing only those notes that if not tongued would allow a glissando to be produced. The slide moving outward and the pitch descending:

or the slide moving inward and the pitch ascending:

they would make complete usage of the natural slur or break created by the slide moving in the following ways. The slide moving outward and the pitch ascending:

the slide moving inward as the pitch descends:

the slide moving inward and the pitch ascending to a higher partial, necessitating a change of embouchure:

the slide moving outward and the pitch falling to a lower partial:

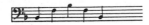

or the most obvious of all, those from partial to partial in the same slide position:

When and where this natural break occurs in the phrase, they would execute it in the same manner as one would slur on a valved instrument. That is by allowing no tongue

to be utilized allowing the movement of the valve (slide in this particular case) to create the necessary definition of attack.

In theory perhaps this is all fine and good, but it must be remembered that all slurs can be produced in this manner on the valved instrument, but not on the trombone. Therefore, the valved instrumentalist can produce consistent phrases by utilization of this method, but *not the trombonist!*

The utilization of two methods of articulation to produce a consistent legato phrase is virtually impossible. The author has been exposed to both methods of instruction and has reached the conclusion that no matter how skilled the performer is, a difference of attack between the legato tongue and the natural slur can easily be detected by the ear. For the sake of a consistency of phrasing alone, the student should be taught to tongue each note in the legato phrase in the following manner:

Tah dah dah dah dah, etc.

This can be a great teaching aid as well. The student only has to learn the one method of producing the legato phrase; not "do not tongue here, but some there," etc. In summary, the only way to produce the acceptable legato phrase is by the previously described method of consistent articulation. After some experimentation, the more advanced student will discover that perhaps not quite so much tongue is needed to produce certain intervals or natural slurs, but again, one will find it to his advantage to produce the consistent phrase by varying the amount of tongue employed on certain intervals rather than eliminating its usage all together.

The importance of the ability to sing the melody should be mentioned at this point. If the student can not sight sing the melody he is working to perfect on the instrument, how can he ever hope to perform it correctly? The ability to follow the line and a complete awareness of the pitch at all times is of absolute necessity to the trombonist. Having the student sing the melody with the proper "Tah," "Dah," "Dah," "Dah" articulation can also be of great help in solving articulation problems.

The following tonguing exercises can be of great value to the development of the legato style:

Tah dah dah dah dah dah dah dah, etc.

Utilize the same articulation as above

Please remember: Play both exercises through all positions and
1. Tongue in the same place but softly.
2. Think "Dah" instead of "Tah."
3. Keep the breath flowing.

The Breath

The proper support and control of the breathing apparatus is much more important to the brass player than is realized by many people. As the conditioning of a baseball pitcher's legs determines his endurance on the mound, so it is that proper breath support determines the endurance and control of the brass player. This is especially true of the legato style.

The flow of the breath for the proper execution of the legato style must be very even and above all, constant, as must be the breath of the performer on the valved instrument when playing a slurred passage. The breath must not cease flowing from the first note of the phrase until the final release has been concluded. Unlike the detached style calling for a complete stoppage of the breath between notes, in legato the tongue merely interrupts the air column long enough for the slide to change positions.

A word should be said here concerning the release in legato or in any phrase. Many a fine legato phrase has been spoiled by a faulty release, either done by cutting off the final note too quickly or allowing it to go flat in pitch as the breath diminishes. The final note of the phrase must have as much support behind it as the first note. It must be held out for its full value to insure a singing and full sounding phrase. In order for all of this to be achieved, the tone must be fully supported until the release is completed. A legato phrase must have a singing quality in its entirety, not 99% or 99½% of its length, but 100%, or the entire effort will have little or no pleasing effect on the listener.

All the mechanics of deep breathing must be carefully reemphasized to the student. It is most important that the throat be kept open at all times, and control of the breath with the support of the muscles of the diaphragm area is critical to this success. To take in the maximum amount of air, with the minimum amount of extra noise, it is best for the trombonist to keep the upper lip anchored to the mouthpiece in normal playing position and to quickly drop the lower jaw. This wide opening of the mouth will insure the large quantity of air needed if one breathes fully, deeply and quickly. By keeping the upper lip in place, dropping the lower jaw presents no placement problem. This technique of breathing will improve not only the quality and control of legato, but of all performance.

A good exercise demonstrating this necessary flow of the breath during the legato to the student can be accomplished in the following manner: Have him play an entire legato phrase without the tongue, allowing all of the natural slurs and glissandi to sound. This will be beneficial for two reasons:
1. By this the teacher can be certain that the student gets the feel of the proper breath support required to produce the legato phrase. The student should also become acutely aware of the continuous flow of air necessary for the legato technique. After he has experienced this feeling, ask him to play the legato phrase correctly by adding the "Dah" syllable articulation. In many cases, this relatively simple illustration can save much wasted time spent in long involved discussions of how to properly execute a legato phrase.
2. Slide technique can also be checked by utilization of the above demonstration. Any sloppy or careless manipulation of the slide will be instantly noticed as all movements of the slide are made audible by the continuous sound being produced. Suggestions can then be made to improve this aspect of legato technique.

The Slide

When discussing the slide technique, it should be first pointed out that *the entire weight of the instrument is to be supported by the left hand alone!* Any support of the weight of the instrument by the right hand will hinder slide technique. The increased friction resulting from supporting any part of the weight of the instrument with the slide will also cause much excess wear to the plating. The slide should be kept free of small nicks and dents as they can also cause undue wear and serve to slow this vital, quick technique. The slide must be completely free to be moved as quickly, smoothly and precisely as possible at all times.

The manner in which the slide is held is of great importance to the legato technique. The slide should be gripped with the thumb and first two fingers at the base of the slide brace next to the lower tube as shown in photograph A. Notice the position of the wrist. A relaxed and freely moving wrist is essential to the legato slide technique. It must be held in a position relatively parallel to the brace to achieve this freedom of motion and flexibility that is desired. If placed in a flat or other similar position, as in photograph B, this will result in a rigid, stiff, fore-arm movement of the slide originating at the elbow.

You can experiment with this yourself without the benefit of the instrument if you like. Place your hand and wrist in a similar position to the correct photograph. They should be in a relatively vertical position. Now move the hand and arm back and forth as if manipulating the slide. Feel how relaxed a motion this is? The wrist bends easily to give you the added ease of longer and more flexible reach with a very fluid, "hinge" type of a motion.

A. CORRECT. The wrist is parallel to the brace. Slide is controlled by the thumb and first two fingers.

B. INCORRECT. Notice the flat, rigid wrist.

Now, try the same exercise with the wrist and hand in a more flat, horizontal position. Move in the same manner as before and notice that the hand, wrist and arm form a straight, rigid line from the elbow. This becomes much more of an arm motion producing a rigid, stiff, unnatural movement of the slide. This very stiff, rigid, mechanical slide movement can be detected easily in legato phrasing by the ear, as a somewhat "frantic" quality will be imparted into the sound by any slide movement of this sort. It is usually quite noticeable to the eye as well, making it rather easy to spot offenders when teaching either the ensemble class or private lessons.

Even though this legato slide technique is accomplished with a relaxed and free wrist, this can be somewhat misleading to the student as far as to the speed and precision with which the slide must be manipulated. This fast, precise, but yet relaxed slide movement is essential to the production of singing, smooth legato phrases. This rather lazy, floating sound can be assimilated by the student into a slowing down of the speed by which the slide is moved between positions. The tongue in the legato, as mentioned, is producing no more than an interruption between notes, and this relaxed, precise slide motion is of utmost importance to insure no "smear" or "drag" becoming audible between notes. Though the sound is of a flowing nature, the slide must retain both precise movement and accurate placement.

Another problem of the slide is that encountered in a phrase containing intervals causing the distance between positions to vary a great deal. If going from first to second, then first to fifth to second

to fourth, etc. the notes must still be played with the same interval of time lapsing between notes. Therefore, the slide must not only be moved quickly and precisely between positions, but sometimes at greatly varying speeds depending upon the distance traveled. Much practice should be devoted to these areas of slide technique in the legato style.

The following exercises can be most helpful in developing the relaxed wrist and smooth, precise slide motion between positions:

For the Wrist:

Tah dah dah dah dah dah dah dah dah dah dah dah dah, etc.

For Varying Reaches and Intervals:

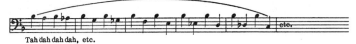
Tah dah dah dah, etc.

For Longer Reaches and Matching Intonation:

I VI I VI   II VI I   II VII II VII II VII II,   etc.

The embouchure, being directly related to all phases of brass performance, is very clearly related to the production of a fluid legato style. The tone quality of the legato must be very singing and full. A good basic embouchure formation combined with the proper breath support will do much to insure this quality of sound. However, the embouchure will also affect articulation in the legato, particularly if the intervals are sufficiently distant as to cross the partials of the overtone series. Any change in register will facilitate an adjustment in the embouchure to produce the vibrations sounding the particular pitch desired.

Teachers will find that the "smile," or stretch system embouchure, is quite detrimental to a good legato style as there will be much excessive back and forth movement of the embouchure as the muscles are drawn and then released. This excessive movement will cause breaks or cracks in the otherwise smooth transition between notes of the legato phrase. The "smile" embouchure is a stretch system of control created by pulling the corners of the mouth upward and out as the pitch ascends, thus stretching the embouchure like a rubber band. To descend in pitch one must relax this embouchure, particularly the cor-

ners. One can only stretch so far and relax so much. A very thin, pinched high register and tubby, dull lower register will result from application of this system of control. Flexibility suffers terribly whenever the "smile" embouchure is employed.

Perhaps the ideal embouchure, if there is such, should be more of a "pucker," but yet still retaining a proper and sensible amount of firmness, particularly in the corners. The corners should have more of a feeling of controlling the central vibrating area of the embouchure inside the mouthpiece. A feeling of consciously pressing down at the center of the embouchure should also be avoided as much as possible. The concept described above is sometimes referred to as being "relaxed but firm." That is tension in the corners of the embouchure, at all times and in all registers, controlling the more relaxed, vibrating area to produce the desired pitch. To produce higher pitches, the aperture or opening between the lips must be reduced in proportion to the pitch level desired. This firming of the corners should help control the size of the opening rather than overly stretching to achieve it. As opposed to the "smile" system's relaxation of the corners to produce the lower register, the "tense pucker" system retains this basic tension in the corners to facilitate a full even vibration, which in turn produces the full vibrant tone quality of the trombone's lower register.

Look carefully at the photographs of the embouchure. As we slur up the overtone series, notice that relatively the same amount of tension is retained in the corners at all times, from the low Bb up to the F above the staff. Although it can not be seen in these photographs, the center of the embouchure adjusts somewhat. It moves from a

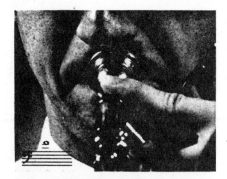

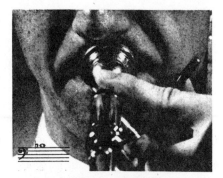

Notice the almost uniform firmness of the corners, even in the lower octave. Also the less perceptible adjustment of the corners as the intervals become progressively closer in the upper partials.

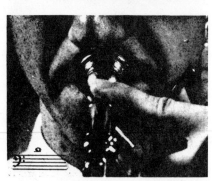

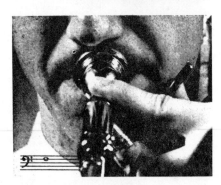

more relaxed wider aperture for the low B♭ to a smaller, more tense opening for the higher F. To produce this, notice the manner in which the corners move as the slur goes upward. The corners must have the feeling of going in and down as the pitch ascends. By adjusting the embouchure in this manner, the basic modified "pucker" is retained, rather than being stretched by the fatiguing smile. Also, due to the evenness of control of this embouchure, the movement over the overtone series is much more even and constant, thus helping produce the necessary faultless and effortless slur. This ability is quite closely linked to the production of the flowing legato phrase as previously mentioned. As we ascend, the embouchure assumes a continually smaller aperture, but the basic "pucker" is retained. This has several advantages: It provides a "cushion" for the embouchure. The "smile" system tends to pull so

tightly that the thickness of the embouchure is considerably thinned until the mouthpiece pressure is almost directly against the teeth through the lips, thus cutting off the circulation so vital to endurance. Also, by retaining this fullness of embouchure, vibrating capabilities are kept at a maximum, particularly in the upper register, producing a very clear and full quality of sound.

For additional information of considerable value pertaining to the embouchure and other facets of brass performance, one should consult the two excellent books by Philip Farkas. *The Art of Brass Playing* and *The Art of French Horn Playing* represent a wealth of well thought-out ideas concerning the many problems confronting brass players. These two books should be in every brass teacher's library.

Many solos can be utilized to contribute to the development of this essential style of trombone perform-

ance. Works of a more melodic nature should be selected for this purpose. The Walter Beeler *Method for Trombone* is most helpful and logical in its approach to the legato technique, especially for the younger, more inexperienced pupil.

The Bordogni-Rochut *Melodious Etudes for Trombone*, Vols. I, II, and III, should be basic study utilized in all trombone practice routines, student or professional. They represent the best single body of melodic material to be found for the development of the legato style of trombone performance. They can also be of great value in the teaching of the sometimes difficult art of proper phrasing.

By emphasis of the ideas discussed above, and other materials, the teacher can be of great help to his student trombonists. This essential legato technique and style is often misunderstood or neglected. It deserves some careful thought and study; then practical application. Many instruments have a much more spectacular and brilliant technique than the trombone, but none are capable of producing a more beautiful and flowing legato style, so characteristic of the instrument. □

Stresses in Playing the French Horn

WENDELL HOSS

Ignoring for the present the mental and emotional stress involved in controlling so treacherous an instrument, let us concentrate on the stresses, or accents, which are necessary to good phrasing in general, with particular application to music written for the horn. Essential as are the goals of developing a beautiful tone and acquiring a dependable technique, these stresses should not monopolize the student's attention to the exclusion of some consideration being given to phrasing. Otherwise we may miss completely the chief objective: an understanding interpretation of the composer's intent in writing for this instrument, be it in orchestra, band, chamber music, or solo works.

Since rhythm is the most basic element in music making, this article will confine itself to the rhythmic phase of expression, with especial emphasis on the accents involved. Primary accents are metrical, falling on the downbeat of the measure and giving a feeling of regularity and stability to the movement. Secondary accents may be called for on subsequent beats within the measure, particularly on a strong beat such as the third quarter in 4/4 time. In faster movements it may be sufficient to place the strong accent only on the beginning of alternate measures, thus creating what might be called a "downbeat measure" and an "upbeat measure." Where measures are short and the tempo swift moving, one accent to every four measures may suffice, producing a smoother flow of line than if each bar is strongly marked.

Accents may be achieved in three different ways: *strength*, *length*, and—perhaps the most effective—*delay*; or through a combination of two or all three of these. Strength (just playing louder) is the most obvious, and is a means we all employ almost instinctively on encountering an accent mark. But many times accents are implied where no indication exists, and where a choice must be made as to the manner and degree of stress needed. Perhaps the most insistent in demanding accents are the syncopes—in fact one could safely state that any syncopated note should receive an accent, of one sort or another. Whereas, in the rhythm

there is only one strong accent to each measure, on the downbeat; in

there will be, in addition to the metrical accent on the beginning of the measure, a still stronger one on the following, syncopated note. Here the effectiveness of the performance will be heightened by a delay, ever so slight, before the attack on this

note—along with the added strength one will naturally give.

From the above comment on syncopes one may conclude, and rightly, that any deviation from the normal, rhythmic or otherwise, constitutes an accent and should be recognized as such. (A black marble in a bunch of white ones, or a white chicken in a black flock, may be considered accents.) Thus a longer note in a sequence of uniformly short ones will be accented. The second note, the dotted eighth, in the "Seigfried Call" will receive the strongest attack. A lift before striking this note will also add to its effectiveness. (Example 1)

Another famous example with a natural stress on the long note of the group, which in this case happens also to be an appoggiatura note, thus with a double claim to an accent—is the opening theme from Strauss' "Till Eulenspiegel." A little lift before the note in question (written D♯) will add piquancy to the taunting character of the phrase. This holds true especially in the first statement where more latitude in interpretation is suggested.

The music of Mozart is full of the use of the appoggiatura (delaying the resolution of a non-chordal note) a device which adds immeasurably to the expressiveness of his melodic line. As an example, the composition most familiar to all horn players would no doubt be the *Third Horn Concerto*, with its copious use of the appoggiatura. Take the opening phrase where the strongest accent falls on the beginning of the second full measure, the "downbeat measure," which therefore is preceded by the "upbeat measure."

Extending the length of this note on the strong beat will help to emphasize its importance as an appoggiatura, and will increase the effectiveness of the phrase. A similar situation occurs on the downbeat two measures later.

Now turn to the opening of the last movement, and again you will find the major accent falling on the beginning of the second full meas-

ure, also a "downbeat measure." This is preceded by a measure of repeated eighth notes on one pitch, which can sound quite colorless unless played with a certain amount of crescendo leading into the strong downbeat to follow.

The accent will be accomplished much as in the first movement example: with a tenuto on the quarter note in question, together with a natural additional strength of tone. The two subsequent measures are an exact rhythmic repetition (sequence) and should be treated in the same manner.

An extremely effective employment of the appoggiatura is to be found in that most popular of horn solos, the Andante Cantabile from Tschaikowsky's *Fifth Symphony*.

As in Mozart the stress called for will be largely one of length, and in this case, occurs on the downbeat of both the first and second full measures of the solo part. A suggestion of delay can also be added by sustaining almost imperceptibly the last of the eighth notes just before the appoggiatura. An interesting sidelight is thrown on the construction of this theme by observing the multiple repetition of this motive of a descending second, not only in the solo horn part, but in the answering voices of clarinet and oboe; and following further, in woodwinds and lower strings, carrying into the second statement of the principal melody by the cellos. Then finally comes the answering call in the third horn, with further repetition of the two descending notes at the end of the first measure of the cellos.

Before dropping completely the subject of accents, a word should be put in for the smaller members of the musical fraternity, the eighth and sixteenth notes, so often slighted in favor of their larger brethren, but which have a dignity and importance of their own. In the rhythm

the second of the two sixteenths should—but seldom does—receive as strong and positive an attack as the first one. In a dotted eighth-sixteenth sequence, the short note is the one which suffers, by being played either too short or too weak —sometimes both; and the passage loses in strength thereby. The opening declamation in the Strauss *Concerto No. 1* is a case in point.

In general it should be borne in mind that the sixteenth and similar notes are not just "short notes"; but that they have definite time value which must be respected. It is true that in a lively tempo such notes may be shortened to add brightness to the movement, but in slower, more expressive passages it is a good rule to sustain all the shorter notes as long as possible.

Bearing in mind the above suggestions for rhythmic emphasis, the student can profitably check thru the musical material he may be studying with a view toward applying, at every opportunity, these principles of accent. Inevitably his playing will gain in interest, both to himself and to the listener. ■

SEPTEMBER, 1965

The Brass Choir in the Band

William Schaefer

Blending the brass choir in the band involves a constant concern for the matching of styles and dynamics of unequal instruments where appropriate, and the projecting of the brass colors where the music calls for this.

The first approach to balance within the brass choir is the proper assignment of parts. Though some flexibility is possible in instrumentation with the everchanging available players in most school situations, there are two basic concepts which should be kept in mind: first, that the available strength be distributed throughout each section so that all parts are played as equally as possible, and second, that the top parts in each section be not overly doubled. Perhaps it is more fun to play first cornet, but if the part is covered by too many strong players, in addition to being in the brilliant register of the instrument and the highest voice of its color, balance throughout the section is nearly impossible. Also, I encourage the recognition that in full brass scoring, the third trombone is usually more important than the first.

The following chart suggests workable proportions between the voices of brass choirs of various sizes. It will be noted that top parts are doubled in the smaller units, in recognition of the problem of endurance in performance, but that in larger sections the greater doubling tends toward the lower parts of sections.

Cornet I	2	2	2	2	2	2
Cornet II	1	1	2	2	3	4
Cornet III	1	2	2	2	3	4
Trumpet I	(1)	1	1	2	2	2
Trumpet II	(1)	1	1	2	2	2
Horn I	1	2	2	2	2	3
Horn II	1	1	2	2	3	3
Horn III	1	1	1	2	2	3
Horn IV	(1)	1	2	2	3	3
Trombone I	1	1	2	2	3	3
Trombone II	1	1	2	2	3	3
Trombone III	1	2	2	3	3	4
Baritone	1	2	2	3	3	3
Tuba	1	2	2	3	3	4

The next problem of dynamics comes from the indefinite and varying meanings of musical terminology. The inexperienced player tends to have absolute meanings in mind for *forte, piano, fz, fp,* etc., usually based on some limited association with those terms in a particular usage. The mature player, however, has come to realize that these are highly subjective terms that must be adjusted to the music of the moment. What conductor, upon seeking to bring out an important part, has not heard the argument expressed either musically or verbally "But it is marked *piano*."

Of all musical instructions, the only specific ones other than notation, concern tempo, when expressed in *metronomic* markings. All others are subjective. Thus the conductor in his study of a score, and the player in rehearsal, should analyze each moment of music to supplement, in his thinking, and in additional editing in parts, the subjective factors that control dynamics and balance. There are two basic approaches to assignment of markings on the part of composers and arrangers. The most common tends to use the same marking for all players at any given moment, with no adjustment for the melody *vs* accompaniment, the strong instrument *vs* the weak, etc. The other manner is to attempt to cope with these problems, but never completely, and with liberal supplementary usage of such terms as solo, dolce, cantabile, espressivo—each of which is inclined to affect the dynamic situation.

The basic dilemma of the individual player can be easily illustrated by the horn player as he functions in three forms of chamber music. As the weakest instrument of the brass sextet, he must constantly strive to balance the other stronger instruments; hence, all dynamics are louder. In the woodwind quintet, he is the strongest instrument; hence, all dynamics tend to be softer. In the Brahms

Trio for Violin, Horn, and Piano he must play even more delicately to balance the violin.

In other words, a musician must be chameleon-like, constantly changing his color to suit the surroundings in which he finds himself. In the band, one must not assume that a single adjustment is sufficient, for a varying segment of the band may be playing, and each change in instrumentation affects all who are playing. Here are *some* of the items that affect dynamics which should be considered in performing any work:

1. The level of dynamics at any given moment must be determined by the weakest instrument playing. Hence the trumpet in unison with clarinet, flute or oboe must play delicately. The basses, in particular, being so often used with the woodwinds in older scores, should take on the delicacy appropriate to such surroundings when necessary. With modern instrumentation, the conductor may elect to have such parts played by fewer basses or delete them entirely and add the lower woodwinds now available.

2. Solos in the brasses, which are not doubled in woodwinds, must be projected more.

3. The brass choir in the full tutti must play with some restraint, so that the balance of the entire band is achieved. Yet when playing as a choir without doubling of woodwinds, a similar passage must be played more fully.

4. When muted, brasses are naturally softer, and compensation is necessary.

5. Maintain logical balance between the melody and the accompaniment. Many first cornet players perform as if they were always supposed to be soloists, and many horn players as if they never were.

Neither can be held to be true.

6. In contrapuntal music, generally the moving voice should prevail, though careful consideration of possible conflict with thematic material must be considered.

7. Height of bells within the section is important, for the highest bell will project, particularly among cornets, trumpets and trombones. Height of bells should be considered adjustable, and raising of bells for brilliant effect, such as in a fanfare, is most effective.

8. General musical inflection, such as rising line tending toward crescendo and falling line to decrescendo and the natural tendency of a phrase to swell should be given due consideration.

9. In general, assess the number playing at any given moment so that the hall is kept filled with music. A chamber ensemble playing for the moment can not function as if the rest of the band were still playing, for this would result in weakness.

The second matter of concern for this article is the problem of matching of styles between the brass instruments and the rest of the band. Audiences are frequently subjected to hearing the same melody passed around the various voices of the band with each instrument "doing what comes naturally." The lyric beauty of the flute's initial statement of the theme culminates in the blatting of trombones and grunting of tubas. It is perfectly possible for any wind instrument to play with a beautiful legato singing style, though players of some instruments may find it requires more effort and concern than others. The conductor must constantly coax low brass players to play smoothly where appropriate, not to attack

too hard, not to let notes decay too rapidly, to break phrases or shorten final notes of figures. Many have found that orchestral tubas used in the band help this situation, being considerably easier to play musically than the typical marching instrument.

I am not suggesting that the woodwinds always set the style, for they have their moments of imitating the brasses too. The fanfares which are more typical of the brasses must be played in a matching style by the woodwinds, as in Debussy's *Fêtes*. Nor am I suggesting that natural contrast is not desirable, providing that is the musical intention of the composer. However, in general, the same musical material must be played in a compatible manner by the various instruments employed.

There is a pronounced tendency to over-attack among many brass players. This becomes more evident with appearance of accents of various types, and there must be concern for matching throughout the choirs and throughout the band. How frequently I tell brass players to play accents with their breath, not their tongues.

So, playing a brass instrument, or any instrument, in a band or any ensemble involves a constant analysis of the music in order to achieve balance and the musical effect which, to the best of our ability to determine, the composer was seeking.

In conclusion, I am reminded again of an oft-repeated tale about Brahms. It is reported that a friend once asked him why he didn't give more specific instructions for the performance of his music. His answer is classic. "If I am talking to a fine musician, additional instructions are unnecessary; if I'm not, they won't help." ∎

False Security

MAURICE FAULKNER

Teachers of brass instruments quite often find, in their daily schedule, problems concerning embouchure

that cannot be solved with the usual attention to lip-building exercises. These problems stem from

the youthful or inexperienced player whose high octave depends upon the support of the tongue in order to get the notes to speak easily. In a description of a variety of embouchure types which this writer has listed in earlier issues of this publication he has called this a tongue-wagging embouchure.

This type of trumpeter places the tip of his tongue immediately behind the upper lip at the lower edge and, with a certain amount of wind pressure from the lungs, a limited amount of arm pressure against the lips, and the forceful tip of the tongue; is able to squirt out a high tone with some vigor and accuracy. It also has a great amount of percussiveness in its production, and this is one of its detrimental factors, because he seldom can produce this type of a note with lovely pianissimo sound in delicate passages.

Furthermore, an embouchure of this type usually lacks the flexibility so essential to fine tone quality and ease of maneuverability on the instrument. Seldom can this performer produce anything in his upper octave that does not need this close tongue position as a crutch to producing accuracy. If the style of the work calls for delicacy in tongue control, light accentuation or no

accentuation, care in developing lip control of difficult pitches, etc., he will not be able to function well.

We have found that one way to overcome this problem, and an aid in building a finer lip strength and control, is the development of what some musicians call a diaphragmatic attack. This is a purely breathed tone, thinking the syllable "boo" as one does when he whistles. Take a simple scale and breathe each note without any movement of the tongue whatsoever. Arban's Method or St. Jacome's are filled with exercises which can be adapted to this type of practice. If the player uses a heavy amount of pressure as he climbs the scale, it would be wiser for him to practice the usual lip slur exercises without slurring, but with breath attacks, as he goes from one overtone to another. Consistent work on this diaphragmatic attack will produce a tone that begins immediately as the breath passes through the lips and will clear up much of the wind that now escapes through the center of the lips without vibrating.

Furthermore, as the student progresses to higher and higher octaves he will be able to count upon

tone production at these ranges without such a need for loud playing because his lips will form the tone easily and without the crutch of the close tongue position. In addition to the ease of range he will find that much of his tonguing technique will improve because he can then use the tongue for a variety of styles without having to think of it first as a necessity in the production of range.

As a matter of fact, if the trumpet or horn player's embouchure is perfect in its formation it should be possible to breathe quietly through the lips and produce the sound that they have formed with their muscular tension. This program of exercising is as valuable to the baritone, trombone, and tuba students as it is to the trumpet and French horn specialists. All brass players should be able to produce a quiet or loud tone without the use of the tongue if that is demanded by the astute musical conductor. European conductors have demanded this type of control for many years. Herman Scherchen is noted for his requirements in this idiom and his orchestras reflect the finesse which such brass techniques produce. ■

Problems of Brass Intonation

MAURICE FAULKNER

The brass specialist probably has the greatest problem of any musician when he must fit his pitches into the web of the instrumental organization with which he performs. From hours of performing in, listening to, and conducting a variety of musical units over the past quarter of a century, this writer has come to the conclusion that the youthful musician might appreciate a description of some of the problems which have been encountered, and thus alert himself to some of the aspects of professional performance which might be anticipated.

Why does the brass instrumentalist have more trouble with in-

tonation than the others? In the symphony orchestra he must face the tendency of string players to tune in a subdued form of mean temperament. In addition to this major situation with the strings he must also adapt himself to the individual idiosyncracies of the woodwinds, all of which have been adjusted to an equal temperament from a natural temperament of just intonation which is common to their structure in its primitive state. And each specific woodwind family type has a different situation in its original, or just intonation, state. For instance, the conical bore of the oboe differs considerably from the cylindrical bore of the

clarinet or the flute, with its parabolic headjoint. And these problems multiply when one deals with the instruments of alto range or bass sonority in the woodwind family.

Furthermore, if a keyboard instrument is used in the orchestra, the brass musician must adjust to its equal temperament whenever that tuning becomes predominant. The manufacturers of these brass instruments have attempted to adapt the original just intonation of the brass overtone series of the various instruments to the equal temperament of our modern

system. These adaptations have

necessitated a variety of concessions to the system which have changed certain pitches and been unable to change others.

Recently, at the Edinburgh Festival of 1965, we heard the first trumpet of one of the fine British orchestras enter on a long solo phrase, performing flat with the rest of the orchestra, and it was especially noticeable for he was combining in unison with the first oboe and the first violins. He had been sitting idle for several minutes, waiting for the cue, and had to enter cold and match instantaneously the pitches of the other sections with precision and blend. He failed to achieve this satisfactory result and the moments of his performance were disconcerting to the musicians in the audience.

Space does not permit a discussion of the historical backgrounds of these systems of intonation: just intonation, mean temperament, and equal temperament. If the young scholar is interested he can search this out as an interesting challenge to his intelligence. He should begin with the Pythagorean experimentation, look into Aristoxenus's *Harmonics* (of about 330 B.C.) which has been translated and discussed in a British publication, spend considerable time with Helmholtz's *Sensations of Tone*, pp. 430-441, and examine the *Harvard Dictionary of Music's* section on mean temperament where the historical background of such a tuning is described briefly.

What we hope to do here is to point up some of the practical solutions to the problems presented. First of all, each family of brass instruments has its own peculiarities. The trumpets differ from the trombones, French horns, etc. And each instrument within each family has its peculiarities too. The manufacturers have attempted to solve these problems, in so far as they can, before the instruments leave the factories. But perfection is difficult to achieve, and the musician who picks up the instrument must bring his talent and ear training to bear upon its acoustical advantages and disadvantages.

The orchestral brass player, when he tunes his instrument, must organize his ear to work from the sharp keys based upon the A

which is normally used. His *B♭* trumpet will not be adequately tuned if he adjusts only his second valve B natural. He needs to obtain, either by actual pitch from the oboe or by his own native ability to hear the *B♭*, the true *B♭* which will fit the *A* to which the other instruments are tuning. Then he must adjust his valve slides to accommodate the equal temperament that the other instruments will attempt to reach in their performances. He also must be able to find a good sharp concert *D* (his *E* on a *B♭* trumpet) to match the violins tuned to a fifth below the *A*, a flatted *F♯* to match the violins open string *E* tuned to a fifth above the *A* and a sharper 2nd space treble clef *A* to match the *G* string of the violins tuned a fifth below the *D* string.

If he is a first trumpeter he will be more concerned with tuning the intervals in his upper octave so that they will blend in unisons and chords with the higher strings and woodwinds. If he is a second or third player in the section he will be more concerned with tuning the lower octave carefully so that those notes will match the lower strings. Since our natural instruments in the brass families are not in tune with themselves in octaves he has to adjust with his own friends within his section and other brass sections as well.

The first hornist has a different problem from that of the trumpeter or even that of his colleagues, the second and fourth hornists. His instrument in *F* or *B♭* will have to be tuned so that his overtone series will match the mean temperament of the strings and the just intonation-equal tempered woodwinds. His *E (F* horn's tuning to the orchestral *A)* needs to be adjusted for the one at the top of the treble staff as well as for the one at the bottom. The latter is usually flat because of the just intonation of the harmonic series. The first and solo horn will be using his upper octave consistently, and he will probably be moving back and forth from the *F* to the *B♭* horn note by note. Thus he complicates his tuning problems. And every individual instrument presents its own difficulties.

It is not enough for the brass specialist to know where the dif-

ferences lie in his own instrument. He must recognize the problems of every man in his section so that he can anticipate the intonation as music develops. If the solo hornist is aware of the flatness of his second horn's fifth partial he can help the latter lip it up to reach a careful unison, third, fifth, or other interval with his changes in range. Each section leader has to become a teacher of intonation for his fellows so that their ears improve as well as their ability to correct the problems.

If we could have our way in the training of brass specialists, we would require all of them to study the string instruments at the same time that they are learning their techniques in brass performance. We would want them to have some facility upon the violin and cello, for these instruments will enhance their ears and intonation awareness. Examine the reputations of the leading bandmasters and you will find that those who have the most sonorous sounding groups with careful intonation have usually studied string instruments at some time in their lives.

It is even more difficult in the orchestra and the concert band to blend the brasses with the woodwinds. The trumpeter who must match tones with the first oboist, the hornist who must fit into the woodwind section as an integral part, the trombonist and tubist who must provide the tenor and fundamental to woodwind chords and at the same time flourish effectively in unison with the bassoons, saxophones, and bass clarinets, have their troubles.

Most brass specialists of any quality recognize the bad intervals upon their instruments: The flat fifth partials, the sharp second partials, the sharp sixth partials, etc. What they need to learn are the idiosyncracies of each of the woodwinds that combine with them to produce the sonorities of the orchestra and band. We do not have space to go into them here, and each instrument differs according to the embouchure and facility of the performer, as well as according to its own construction.

The band brass instrumentalist can eliminate one of his problems, that of the mean temperament of strings, but he is still faced with the just intonation-equal temperament of the woodwinds. Manufacturers have had to create a hybrid instrument in attempting to make all of our band instruments equal tempered within the realm of just intonation. The fact that they have succeeded so well in this modern era is a tribute to their intelligent research and ingenuity. But the manufacturers or their research specialists cannot play every instrument for us in our organizations. They have put in our hands the best that can be developed under the circumstances of modern music. We must be thankful and attempt to adapt their genius to our needs and our failings.

Every brass specialist should be able to produce at least two, and possibly three, good pitches on every tone. These should not be fuzzy sounds but full-fledged tones with all the warmth and strength of the best production possible. Thus, with three pitches for every fingering in his scale, the player can adjust to the idiosyncracies of the string and woodwind tunings more easily. If he has only one good sound for each fingering he is limited in his adjustment to auxiliary fingerings, which also may be off the mark in combination with woodwinds or strings. And with this capacity for several pitches he can perform more easily with that bane of our existence, the equal-tempered piano or keyboard instruments.

How do we achieve three pitches with each fingering and still obtain a full bodied, sonorous tone? This requires experience, but some hints may help the youthful talent. The position of the back of the tongue makes a difference in the column of air which reaches the lips and thus changes the pitch accordingly. If the tongue is high, the column will be more thin and the consequent sound will tend to be sharper. If the tongue is lower and the column of air thus larger as it strikes the lips, the pitch tends to be slightly flatter.

The tension of the lips is an obvious method for changing pitch of the instrument. But embouchures differ considerably, and one cannot advise about this phase of tuning without observing each individual player. Some musicians change the type of pitch of the

tone by pivoting the mouthpiece against the lips. Others change the mouthpiece cups for situations in which they have to match woodwinds or strings of difficult intonation.

To practice this capacity to produce three good pitches on each fingering the neophyte must learn to strike the tone with a broad flow of air at *mezzo forte*, at different tongue positions. He then works to *forte* and *fortissimo* as well as to *piano* and *pianissimo* with these pitches. In doing this type of exercise he will enhance his own ear training. But to be sure that he can control these three pitches he would find it wise to practice with a stroboscope which will give him eye-vision of the differences of pitch until his ear becomes astute enough to hear the differences.

Every tone within his range must be developed in this manner. Then he must find unisons and match them with different fingerings, such as the first-and-second valve trumpet A against the third valve A, etc. Then he works for octaves at three different pitches: the trumpet low C to the middle C to the high C; the low D to the middle D to the high D, etc. Then he works out fifths and fourths and finally the smaller intervals. This takes patient practice, and the young man in a hurry won't spend the time upon it. But he will be found wanting when he reaches the peak of real professionalism, for he will fail to qualify with expert ear training when he is playing with the wizards of the strings and woodwinds.

American brass specialists have some of the finest techniques in the world. They can play higher, faster, with more style, and with better tone than most other musicians of similar background, but their knowledge of pitch and its blending in professional organizations is below the par of the well-trained Europeans. I have discussed this situation with great conductors of major orchestras and they are amazed at the difference. They often assign this fact to the idea that in Europe the members of the major orchestras have all studied in the same conservatories with the same teachers or their assistants, and thus they have a

homogeneous concept of pitch and tuning. They even believe that much of the success of the best-tuned brass sections is due to the fact that the players all used matched sets of instruments from the same manufacturer.

This writer has examined the performances of numerous bands and orchestras throughout the world and cannot agree that the musicians must have studied with the same teacher or must perform upon matched sets of instruments in order to achieve superior pitch controls. I believe that it is possible for a brass musician to develop as fine an ear as the string or woodwind specialist. The fact that the brass player does not always have this qualification is due to the lack of concentration upon superior ear concepts. In band music much of his material is organized around the flat keys natural to his instrument, and, therefore, his problems are not multiplied. When he moves into the orchestral sphere he finds himself thrown into the keys which are most effective for strings, predominantly the sharp keys based upon, A, E, D, G major and their relative minors, and moving out from there. If he will analyze his own keys in relation to those of the strings he will recognize that he is bogged down with B, F♯, E, A major and their relative minors before he moves on into the more agreeable natural keys to his B♭, F, or other instruments in flat keys. The fact that his fingering, in these sharp keys, must deal with notes using his

valve tubings, rather than only using his open or natural pipe, should alert him to the complexities that will plague him in so far as pitch is concerned.

At the Edinburgh Festival another fine orchestra used two trumpets, doubling the first part in order to develop power and to relieve the solo performer. One of the instruments was a C trumpet and the other a B♭. Imagine the problems inherent in this situation when the two men played in unison on the parts, especially in fortissimo, where they had to blend a C and a B♭ and at the same time match with the woodwinds and strings. The fact that they did not achieve a blend in the type of tone necessary for the unisons was not as important as the lack of coherence in unison intonation. Their ears were not keen enough, nor were their techniques facile enough, to cover the differences which the two bores of instruments gave to their section.

Intonation and temperament require a vast study, and we have not spent enough time in understanding it in our musical studies. The talented young brass instrumentalist who wishes to go far in his profession or avocation will

want to examine all the aspects of the three temperaments: just intonation, mean temperament, and equal temperament.*

A fine ensemble tone can be achieved by careful attention to precise intonation relationships even when the individual tone qualities of the various brass musicians are not sufficient or even pleasant. The blend of several players upon unisons and doublings can make a better tone when the intonation is exact and equable. ∎

*Just Intonation: A system of intonation and tuning in which all the intervals are derived from the natural (pure) fifth and the natural (pure) third. *Harvard Dictionary of Music* p. 384

Mean Temperament: A system (of tuning) which is based on a fifth which is one-fourth of the syntonic comma (c. 20 cents) smaller than the perfect fifth (697, instead of 702 cents), the result being that four such fifths, if taken in succession (c^4-g^4-d^5-a^6-e^6), lead to a perfect third. *Harvard Dictionary of Music* p. 735

Equal Temperament: A system of intonation in which the octave is divided into twelve equal semitones. *Harvard Dictionary of Music,* p. 735

DECEMBER, 1965

Contemporary Concepts of Trombone Playing

PAUL TANNER

The better trombone players and the better trombone teachers are constantly alert to changing theories concerning the techniques of playing the instrument. It seems unfortunate that some of these thoughts seldom reach print. It appears to me that there should be a continuous flow of contributions by these players and teachers for the general improvement of trombone playing and that this knowledge should be disseminated as thoroughly as possible over the entire world. Sometimes during a clinic, I will explain a given situation that I consider common knowledge, and yet I will find that this particular point is an entirely new concept to my audience.

The competition among trombonists in the studios here in Los Angeles is extremely keen. Yet, we are all quite close friends, and as a result we learn from one another constantly. We are in an atmosphere where survival depends on the consistency of our very best performance. As a result of this situation, we not only use every standard tactic to improve ourselves, but also we search for new methods of improving old solutions. All good trombonists are not ana-

lytical; so of these few items I mention here some come from fine teachers of the instrument who do not actually perform in this competitive field. Also, all of the thoughts are not really new. We have known of certain improvements in techniques for some time, and yet research proves that there is a usual set of issues that keeps reaching publication.

First let me mention the syllables used for starting notes; in the past, there have been several suggested that have become fairly standard, "tu," "tah," "tee," etc. Today, the most acceptable sound on the trombone is a more full and more open sound than ever before. We seem to be headed toward a French horn sound but with the clarity and brilliance of a cylindrical instrument. I find that I use, as much as possible, the syllable "teau" (sounding rather like "toe" or "tow"—but with a French accent). My good friend, Clarence Sawhill of UCLA, has been recommending this for years. This sound has its corresponding approaches— "deau" and "leau." The advantage of this syllable over previous concepts is that it keeps the throat, the mouth, the entire resonance chamber as open as possible. It

tends to keep the tongue down out of the way too so that there will be no restriction to a free flow of air. One item that may seem revolutionary to some people is that many of us are attempting to use that same syllable all over the horn; we try to avoid the older "ah-ee" approach to upward skips. In the past, many players even intentionally thinned out their sounds in the upper register. It made them sound higher and control was a little easier. Today, we attempt to play the upper register with just as big a sound as the lower and to match our tone all over the horn. The prices we pay for this are twofold: flexibility seems a trifle harder with a full sound, and listeners do not realize that we are playing as high as we actually are, so often we are working harder than we are getting credit for.

The next item is related to the first one in that it concerns tongue activity. I have seen some very surprised teachers when I explain that I try to keep my tongue down and not move it at all when slurring upward. The reason for doing this is that if I raise or arch the tongue when slurring upward, I must diminish the size of the reso-

401

nance chamber, and I would rather keep my mouth just as open as possible. Therefore, I try to do my slurring by a combination of subtle alterations in the tension of the aperture and changes of air speed.

This next item is pertinent only to trombone playing. It is important, but I have seldom heard it mentioned. The present attitude by outstanding trombonists is to develop better speed and technique with the slide by avoiding stopping the slide at given spots in fast passages. For example, if you play C,D,E,F, in the staff as eighth notes or less, there would be no stopping of the slide at 4th position for the D or 2nd for the E. The problem with this approach is to make sure that the tongue acts at exactly the precise moment when the slide passes the correct spot. Intonation could only be insured by a great deal of practice of diatonic and chromatic scales and portions of scales, but if this technique is perfected, greater facility must result. I do not say that players have not been doing this; I am simply saying that it is too seldom mentioned.

I am amazed whenever teachers ask me what is the real top of the trombone range, and they are just as amazed when I say that there is none. Too many people take our standard reference books literally and believe that somewhere around C above middle C is the top of the instrument. It is up to the individual. Many of us, including some of my best students, have a workable G above that that can be actually written for us, and we practice up to the Bb or so above that. Now there are a couple of important points about playing that high. The tone in the middle and low registers must not be made to suffer in order to play high. It is a true fact that the fine studio musicians who are capable of playing the highest notes also seem to have the best extreme low registers. I must state that a usable G an octave and a fifth above middle C is not at all essential; but, the C above middle C must be an easy note to play at all times. It just stands to reason that if you can handle the G, the C will be quite easy and most dependable. I must hasten to suggest that the extreme upper register should be devel-

oped slowly and never at the sacrifice of any other register.

There are new concepts concerning the extreme low registers. Up until recently, it had been considered that because of the overtone arrangement, the trombone could not play between low E and pedal Bb. We are now playing in this register on the standard tenor trombone without the F attachment. There are trombonists in the Los Angeles area who are capable of sforzandos or anything else on these notes. I am often asked, "Why use this register, why not leave it solely for bass trombones or tubas?" These tones are hard to play with a true sound; it takes a great deal of practice. Their biggest value comes from practicing them. It takes great strength and finesse to control relaxation. I also find that players who have control over this area have strong embouchures (aiding upper register and endurance) and fine open sounds. We are also playing pedal notes below pedal E, I practice down to double pedal Bb. Once again, this is an exercise in the control of relaxation. One more thing to be said for playing in this unusual register is that the more we can do, the more valuable we become. My big question then is this: if we now consider these notes as playable, does this mean that the first overtone skip of an octave is wrong, or is the basic note for nine feet of tubing much lower than we used to think it was?

I think more should be discussed and written about the problems especially pertinent to the bass trombone. This particular instrument has really come into its own. While working in movies, television, and recordings there is hardly ever a session where three trombones are used when one of them is not a bass trombone; and I suspect that soon when two trombones are used, one will be a bass trombone. When players switch from tenor trombone to bass trombone, there are many transferal problems. I restrict my performance activities to tenor trombone, but I have teamed with the finest of bass trombone players, George Roberts, and have written a method book to try to help solve these problems. Not many people conceive the instrument as being melodic or flexible;

in fact, Roberts is one of the few musicians who really understands the potentiality of the bass trombone.

In past literature, not nearly enough has been said about developing relative pitch. This really must be one of the most essential techniques to be acquired. The player must know the difference between the sound of a fourth from a sixth, etc. Also, an extremely fine sense of "feel" for each note available to a player must be developed. For example, he must know how an F above middle C "feels," so he can start a tone there without any aid in locating the correct pitch. It would help to practice extremely angular lines like possibly some twelve tone compositions.

Another item that seems to be baffling trombonists is the cold cream problem. I do not know of any professional trombone player who still uses oil. Ever since Pond's changed their formula many things have been tried, and there has been a great deal of frustration and exasperation. I must pass along information which is working most satisfactorily for me. A druggist made up a jar of pure cold cream for me, with no lanolin of course, and it solved this difficulty.

One more point that I seldom see in print is the matter of physical condition. We are given fine breathing advice, suggestions for coordination of the hand and tongue, sight-reading aids, etc. None of this is going to be of much help if the player is not in top physical form. I have heard many stories about the late Dennis Brain and other extremely exceptional players who almost trained to play. You can develop air capacity by swimming, strength in your back and stomach muscles by exercises, and your reading and general alertness, as well as stamina, will be improved by keeping in the best possible health. This suggestion is not secret or classified material, but why take it for granted?

All of the items that I mention in this article are as important as the more standard issues, yet they are so seldom discussed. I want to urge other players and teachers to share their valuable experience with the rest of the world.

1966

BB♭ Recording Bass

Making the French Horn Articulate

WENDELL HOSS

Articulation seems more accurately to describe the start of a tone on the horn, or for that matter on any wind instrument, rather than the usual term, "attack," which implies a certain violence which is by no means always desirable. The tongue, which points the attack (articulation), acts as a valve, releasing the breath into the instrument and, without in any sense pushing the air, simply gets out of the way to let it pass. Essentially a negative action, it can, however, be thought of in a positive manner: as the eminent James Stagliano once suggested, "Try to think of throwing the tongue forward together with the breath." Impractical as it may sound, this is an excellent concept, for it will encourage a forward—and necessarily downward—motion, as opposed to drawing the tongue back and clogging up the throat; and it will bring about a full-bodied "follow through" to the tone.

Various placements for the tip of the tongue may be used to fit the style of articulation desired. For an explosive "sfz," or for any attack requiring a sharp definition, or accent, the customary placement behind the upper teeth is probably the best choice. This position seems to be the most generally preferred and may be regarded as basic. Some may move the tongue farther up—perhaps just for the higher register—so that the tip touches the gum (hard palate) just above the teeth. On the other hand, something may be said for reducing the distance between the point of release of the breath (the tip of tongue) and the spot where the tone actually starts (in the vibrations of the lip).

To acquire a clear but gentle articulation, practice resting the tip of the tongue against the lower lip and leaving it there while breathing "tah" into the instrument. The area immediately back of the tip will automatically take care of the necessary valve action to produce the attack, resulting in an ideal legato tonguing with the closest connection between notes and yet with a complete clarity of enunciation. One might think of the articulations in a phrase as the consonants in a line of poetry and the sustained tones as the vowels.

Regardless of the type of attack, one can think of the tongue and breath as being released simultaneously, thus not banking up an excess of breath before the attack. An accumulation of pressure of any kind tends to build up tensions that can mitigate against a free and natural production.

At this stage a warning should be given as to the dangers of starting the tone with the tongue between the lips. While some good players may employ this method on occasion, its use requires especial care to avoid an overly bulky beginning of the tone, with the added hazard of a possible variance in pitch or quality when the tongue is removed from the lip aperture. A further caution: one should be very careful not to change the position of the jaw during the attack, as any motion will almost inevitably cause a deviation of pitch—a sort of "wow" in the tone.

Above all, avoid allowing the tone to develop after the initial attack, which should in all normal instances be at the maximum volume for that particular note. The tone may be sustained at an even level, or it may taper off or drop suddenly in loudness; but, excepting where a crescendo is indicated or suggested for purposes of expressiveness, the tone should receive no additional boost following the attack. An involuntary push of breath after once establishing the tone seems to be one of the most common and flagrant misdemeanors among younger students, who are often unaware of this fault.

Another practice to be heartily condemned is that of performing crisp staccato passages with a dull, soggy attack, suggesting nothing so much as wading through thick mud in a pair of heavy bots. Try at all times to refine the tone and to point up the attack with the tip of the tongue, allowing one note to finish before starting the next. Except in very fast pasages and in extreme cases where a hardness of sound may be desired, let each tone round off at the end with the breath alone; then place the tongue back into position for the next attack.

For those who have advanced to the point of being interested in accuracy of attack, i.e., of hitting the right note cleanly the first time and not depending on a second and third try, the most important fundamental is cultivating the ability to hear the note mentally before attempting the attack. Try to remember the pitch of that tone from having played or heard it earlier, or by recalling some other closely related note. A good practice for acquiring pitch sense, together with an improved accuracy in attack, would be to sing the note before trying to play it. In order to develop the ability to remember and identify a given pitch, select a note which seems easy to locate and try to sing that note at various times during the day, checking immediately afterward with an instrument for correctness. A few weeks of this practice will show a gratifying improvement in pitch retention which will build the player's confidence and constitute a direct aid in the surety of attack. ∎

51 + 2 = INTONATION

MARK McDUNN

"The crowning fortune of a man is to be born with a bias to some pursuit which finds him in employment and happiness."

It is hoped that you enjoy Emerson's "crowning fortune" and have found such employment and happiness, as I have, in a most gratifying profession, teaching music. There is much to be said for an occupation that allows one to help grade school students learn to enjoy music, to see them become good high school musicians, to watch some enter college in pursuit of music education degrees, and to experience the thrill of having some of these students become professional, performing musicians.

But for all its joys, music education has its frustrating moments. One such moment occurred to me some years back. The incident began when a student of mine, whose primary interest was mathematics and the study of music a hobby, brought up the fact that the trombone is a scientific instrument. This student's simple question, asked by countless others before him, started it all.

"Mr. McDunn, where is second position on a slide trombone?" he asked.

And in the same manner as I had answered the question many times before, I picked up my trombone and demonstrated second position for him.

"That sounds fine, Mr. McDunn," he said. "You've played an excellent A-220, but I want to know exactly and specifically where on the slide trombone is second position. Please pinpoint it with a measurement of some kind."

I was both embarrassed and frustrated at not being able to provide an immediate answer, but this young mathematician unwittingly sent me searching for that answer.

Not too long ago I watched somebody else attempt to field my student's question. The query was put to a symphony trombonist who was appearing on an educational television program directed at young children. His reply to the question was that there is no specific point on the slide for any position. He mentioned that there were too many forces at work against any possibility of having specific positions. His answer was correct, inasmuch as he did state the presence of these forces, i.e., air capacity, tonguing, and lip surfacing. These are all obstacles manufactured by the individual playing the trombone. But how would a mathematician look at this problem? He would probably answer the question of locating specific positions by equalizing the deterrrent factors. That is what shall be done in this article. Assuming the factors of air, tonguing, and embouchure to be in perfect harmony, we will point out the exact spot on the slide for each position.

It has been said that no rule exists if there is one exception to that rule, and music has so many exceptions the existence of hard and fast rules is an impossibility. Therefore, in discussing rules for intonation on the slide trombone we must also be concerned with a few of the exceptions to those rules.

In the playing of a slide trombone, to lower a tone one semitone the player must add 5.95% to the original tubing. Thus, a pitch in B♭ needs a total length of 110″. When this is lowered one semitone an additional 6¹⁰⁄₁₆″ of tubing is needed. To lower it yet another semitone we must increase our now 116¹⁰⁄₁₆″ by another 5.95%. It can be seen that our distances between positions becomes progressively greater. Figure 1 shows the specific inch measurements between each position. Note the distance between positions 6 and 7 is 4⁷⁄₁₆″ or 1⅛⁄₁₆″ greater than the distance between positions 1 and 2. Remember, these measurements are valid only when the afore-mentioned factors are in harmony.

Figure 1

Note	Measurement	Position	Distance Between Positions
B♭	O	1	
A	3⁵⁄₁₆″	2	3⁵⁄₁₆″
A♭	6¹³⁄₁₆	3	3⅛⁄₁₆
G	10⅝⁄₁₆	4	3¹¹⁄₁₆
G♭	14⁷⁄₁₆	5	3⅝⁄₁₆
F	18¹⁰⁄₁₆	6	4³⁄₁₆
E	23¹⁄₁₆	7	4⁷⁄₁₆

It is necessary for us to synchronize the slide length with air flow, tonguing, and the proper lip settings. It must be done by every student and instructor, for if the tubing length is wrong of necessity the note is wrong. For example, if the player has a fatigued lip and his lip surface is vibrating flat he may still hear the pitch very well and thus sharpen his slide position to compensate. The tone will be distorted, and it will bring the slide to a position unlike any shown on the chart.

To help the student appreciate the importance of tubing length we sometimes call upon an instrument which measures pitch to ¹⁄₁₀₀th of a equal-tempered semitone. Known as the stroboscope, this instrument has the distance between two semitones calibrated into units, each one called a cent. The stroboscope works in the following manner: Using a B♭ as our note, should the instrument indicate the note is being played 50 cents flat it means the note is a quarter tone flat; this is because the distance between B♭ and A is one semitone or 100 cents.

Figure 2

The 51 Positions of the Slide Trombone

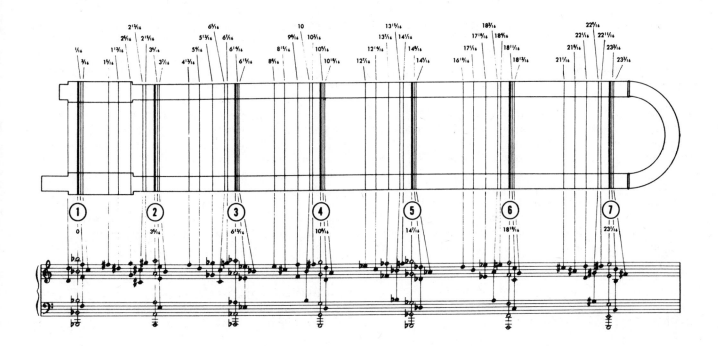

Now, let's take a look at Figure 2. It represents the slide portion of the trombone and shows its seven fundamental positions, plus the various slide positions through 16 overtones.

These basic fundamentals and their octaves are the only notes possible in these positions. They would then be the fundamental, 2nd, 4th, 8th, and 16th overtones. And since in acoustics every odd overtone and its *octaves* over a given basic fundamental is a different discrepancy of being out of tune, any discrepancies will occur at the 3rd (6th & 12th), 5th (10th), 7th (14th), 9th, 11th, 13th, and 15th overtones.

Referring to the slide chart again, let us look under the second position and read from the bottom up. We note that the 3rd overtone is only 2 cents sharp or ⅟₅₀th of a semitone. It is a slight discrepancy to be sure, but a discrepancy it is, so it must be mentioned here. To properly play this note the slide should be extended ⅟₁₆″. By reading across the chart in the 3rd channel, or series of overtones, you will note that all notes in this same channel require the slide to be lengthened this same ⅟₁₆″.

Continuing up the series under the second position we can see the 5th overtone is 14 cents flat, necessitating raising the slide ³⁄₁₆″. The 7th overtone is 31 cents flat requiring a 1″ reduction. The 9th is 4 cents sharp calling for a lengthening of ²⁄₁₆″. The 11th is 49 cents flat, the 13th is 60 cents flat, and the 15th is 12 cents flat, requiring respective shortenings of the tubing length by 1⅝₁₆″, 2″, and ⁹⁄₁₆″. It is well to repeat at this point that these measurements are the distance from the nearest fundamental or its octave.

Just how did we arrive at a total of 51 positions for the slide trombone? This number is formed on the basic fundamentals through 16 overtones. Glancing again at the chart, it can be seen that there is a fundamental and 2 pitch discrepancies in the 1st position

of the slide and that each of the other fundamentals to be counted in addition to itself has seven discrepancies, adding up to 51 positions. The 1st position has a lesser amount because from this position the slide cannot be shortened but only extended. Here is one of the exceptions to the rule. Some of the flat overtones could be lipped sharp, distorting the tone but enabling the player to play some flat overtones in the 1st position by lip surfacing high. D the second space above bass clef staff is one of the flat overtones.

And here is how some exceptions to the rule develop. Different manufacturers of slide trombones deal with many of these overtones by different types of styles of tubing tapers. This can change some of the overtone difficulties such as the D we just mentioned.

Our goal with the student is perfect slide length. Admittedly, this is a difficult goal to reach because of the many factors working against it. The student is faced with such obstacles as the temperature of the room and its effects on the metal of the instrument, the quality of the instrument itself, or the player's lipping the notes. One or all of these factors prevents even the stroboscope from calibrating the tones in terms of less than ⅟₁₆″.

The chart indicating the 51 positions of the slide trombone goes with me in my travels about the country to various band and music clinics. This chart is 9 feet wide and is done in 8 different colors. For a brief time I felt proud of my accomplishment in so graphically and so beautifully presenting this discovery of the 51 positions, but one evening whatever illusion I may have had about it disappeared.

Shortly after completing the chart I was fortunate to have as a guest in my home a famous trombonist, probably the highest paid trombonist to be found. None too cleverly I brought the conversation around to the intonation technique which applied to our instrument.

"I'd like to show you a project I've been working on in regard to intonation, but first tell me, did you know there are 51 positions on the slide trombone?"

"Can't say that I did," he replied, with something less than the curiosity I expected him to show.

While leading him into the McDunn music room I filled him in briefly on the history of this discovery. He listened with what amounted to polite interest. Then in the music room I enthusiastically opened out the chart, all 9 feet of it, all 8 colors bright and vivid. I stood there beaming. He stood there silently musing. After an eternity of perhaps 10 seconds duration he shrugged his shoulders and said, "Who needs it?"

Obviously, my guest has not needed this chart or the information it contains. He is one of those extremely rare musicians who, when he picks up the slide trombone, breaks every mathematical, scientific, and musical rule and in spite of this makes beautiful music pour forth from his instrument. He could use the information presented here, but because of his great talent he can compensate with fine ear and lipping manipulations to reach his end result, even with his unorthodox methods.

But you and I as teachers need it. We need it to become better players, to become better teachers. We need it to pass on to our students, to be able to answer those inevitable questions about specific slide positions. But in making use of this information one thing must be kept in mind—any factor that is malfunctioning, be it air, tonguing, or lip surfacing, does not alter the relative position of the measurements shown on the chart. Their relative position remains constant when all other factors are being perfectly performed.

Equipped with the knowledge of tubing length, the student's road to better intonation is wide open. Any instructor should do his best to see that the youngster is set upon this road as early in his musical education as is possible. The combination of these 51 positions, *plus* an eager student, *plus* a diligent teacher can't help but add up to improved intonation. What remains to be done is to integrate this intonation with techniques of air flow, embouchure, tonguing, and rhythm. And as before, this can only be done by constant practice in coordinating these five parts. Who knows, we might someday cause some young student of mathematics to decide that the beauty of music and the flexibility of and exceptions to its rules is just too much to resist. ∎

February, 1966

Performing Original Brass Music

MAURICE FAULKNER

As a conductor of bands, orchestras, and brass choirs of various hues and abilities it always terrifies me that someone in my audience, following a production of a work by Giovanni Gabrieli, Heinrich Schuetz, Johann Pezel, and others, will come up and take me apart because I have transgressed upon musical authenticity. There is very little possibility that modern groups can perform the works with the colors which were intended originally. We don't have the instruments available in their original patterns outside of museums, with the exception of a few institutions in some American and European professional centers.

It has been my good fortune to have had the opportunity to use the original instruments for experimentation, both in America and Europe, but such experimentation was hasty at the best, and I was never able to take them away from their refined museum premises for performance in ensembles made up of competent professionals. Thus it is with great trepidation that I approach a forthcoming performance of Giovanni Gabrieli's "Jubilate Deo" which will use the usual brasses available on the modern college campus.

The superb volumes of Giovanni Gabrieli's *Opera Omnia* which are coming off the presses of the American Institute of Musicology regularly, as the illustrious editor, Denis Arnold, finds the time to complete them, offer the interpreters and instrumentators of these works for school and university groups suggestions which should not be ignored. One such suggestion which bothers this conductor no end is contained in the following quotation from page v, Volume I, of Giovanni Gabrieli's *Opera Omnia*, (Editor, Denis Arnold):

As probably all these motets were performed with instrumental participation, it is important wherever possible to augment voices with instruments . . . Here it might be said that the principle should be to give strong contrast between the choirs. The choirs of upper range can often be realized by three string parts with the lowest line sung by a tenor or baritone. The choir of lower range is often effective with the uppermost part sung by tenor or alto, and the three lower parts played by trombones. In each choir at least one voice is necessary to ensure the continuity of the words. Any attempt to imitate the use of *cornetti*, the favorite instruments of the Venetian wind band, on modern instruments is difficult if not impossible, and therefore the issue should be avoided as much as possible. For parts specifically marked for this instrument, clarinets are perhaps the best substitute, and on no account should any brass instrument be used. Any choir marked 'capella' should be sung without instrumental accompaniment. However, it must be emphasized that the freedom of a conductor was always considerable in the 17th century, and any effective method of contrast is justifiable, and many will sound exciting in performance.

The only justification I have for substituting modern trumpets for the Gabrieli cornetti is the last statement which permits the conductor a certain amount of musical freedom in order that the contemporary public may be able to hear some sort of version of this exciting music which represented a revolution in musical color and a peak of musical history.

This writer longs for the day when our manufacturers of instruments will find the time to reproduce, with exactitude, the dimensions and qualities of the cornetti (actually an instrument made of wood, or, as the German term, "Zink," and the French term, "cornet à bouquin," indicate, these were probably made from tusks or goathorns by early shepherds in their first versions).

But think how delightful a contrast to modern sonorities the music of Gabrieli would sound if performed with the original cornetti, with their bright and clear tones, somewhat like well-trained choristers' voices, and with the small-bore but thick-walled 16th century trombones which had a less-flared bell than our modern instruments and a more appropriate softer sound for accompanying voices and performing in small ensembles, as well as with the viol family of stringed instruments. Curt Sachs in his expert volume of description of these instruments describes three of these: the alto, tenor, and bass which were used to double choral groups as well as to play in the tower bands which were part of the municipalities' responsibilities to their taxpayers for musical alarms and entertainments. ∎

March, 1966

The Diaphragm: Teacher's Pedagogical Pet

DOUGLAS SMITH

A student recently gave this reply when asked about his short-windedness: "I guess maybe I'm not using my diaphragm enough." He then proceeded to explain that for maximum use of the breath a wind player or singer must keep pushing from the diaphragm until the end of the phrase to insure a steady tone. Another player seemed a little sheepish in admitting that even though he had been taught to use his diaphragm, he was still breathing with his chest. One rather talented young performer seemed reasonably self-assured in his explanation: "In normal breathing a person uses only his lungs, but in singing or playing an instrument he must fill up the diaphragm instead of the lungs." Then, after reconsidering, he admitted pensively, "I guess the lungs are filled . . . but not until the diaphragm is entirely full!"

Everybody seems to have great respect for the diaphragm's role in breathing, but those who understand this role and are capable of explaining it to their students are relatively few, if the explanations above indicate the average student's knowledge of the subject.

It is easy to find causes for this almost universal misconception as we witness a dispersion of paradoxical concepts by instrumental and vocal breath experts. The following insights, gleaned from the writings of several such authorities, will be an effective indication of how the layman could easily be led astray:

The diaphragm is a muscle described as "flat," "tense," "full," and even "protruded." One writer speaks of the lower region of the diaphragm located in the cavity below the rib cage—implying that there is also an upper region, possibly contained inside the rib cage. Certain authorities say that the diaphragm pulls the air in; others, with equal conviction, dwell verbosely on the fact that it forces the air out in a steady, "straight line." One vocal treatise advises the student to place his hand on his diaphragm as he exhales—it even shows a drawing of a student patting his stomach! A brass authority reminds his readers that "improper breathing comes from improper use of the diaphragm, or the failure to use the diaphragm at all."

Not at all satisfied with our knowledge of this respiratory vehicle, a group of high school band directors and college brass teachers, all part of a graduate seminar in brass pedagogy held on the North Texas State University campus, set out a few months ago to discover its true nature. Painfully aware of the discrepancies of musical authorities, we were obliged to search through the writings of those whose job it was to know such things—the physiologists.

The findings were remarkable to us and quite contradictory to the time-revered theories to which we had been subjected. Our research led us to an understanding which, despite the "unlearning" it necessitated, proved very helpful in later study. The simplified definition reads as follows: The diaphragm is a dome-shaped muscle, roughly similar to the plane of an open umbrella, the outer edge of which is attached to the bottom of the rib cage. When it functions it contracts downward, thus pulling the floor of the lungs with it and causing air to enter the body by creating a negative atmospheric pressure. If the diaphragm continues to be contracted, the air stays in the lungs; if it relaxes, it ascends passively to its normal arched position as the exhaled air permits.

In short, the diaphragm can do two things by contraction—and only two: (1) it can bring air into the body, and (2) it can keep it there. By relaxing (a muscle's only alternative to contracting), it lets the air out of the body. Here is where the problem begins for the musician, because if the air stream meets with resistance, such as the constricted aperture of the vocal folds, or a trumpet mouthpiece orifice, it must be propelled by physical energy. Since the diaphragm definitely relaxes during expiration, we have no choice but to find another muscle, or combination of muscles to use for the desired tone; we must content ourselves with the **diaphragm's inability to help in any** way once the air is in the body.

Preaching this "new" doctrine proved most difficult for the group of crusaders. Those outside the group came with accusations of heresy, charlatanism, even disloyalty. One boy was so distraught that he called a doctor 300 miles away and talked a full 30 minutes before he was convinced that "only in the *absence* of diaphragmatic contraction can air be dispelled from the lungs."

Bent on a full understanding, our little group of "physiological revolutionaries"—many of whom had actually used the theories we were out to disprove—made our way to a radiology laboratory. Using the powerful fluoroscope we devised crude experiments to see for ourselves what we had come to accept as scientific fact.

We first observed the diaphragm's motion during natural respiration. Needless to say, during inhalation it moved down; during exhalation it moved up, etc.

Having heard teachers say, "Don't breathe to the chest; breathe to the diaphragm!" we raised shoulders, arms, even eyebrows, but try as we could, the diaphragm acted exactly as it did during normal breathing.

"Keep the diaphragm firm when you play," was our next target. The subjects took turns, all trying to keep the diaphragm tensed, but not one could prevent it from ascending—just as in any respiratory motion, voluntary or involuntary.

Finally, we wanted to make sure that the diaphragm's downward motion was caused by its own contraction, rather than by the force of atmospheric pressure acting upon it. The subjects exhaled, then held their mouths and noses. When they tried to inhale, the diaphragm contracted violently, but the semi-vacuum in the lungs forced the retaining of its familiar dome shape. Had the atmospheric pressure theory been correct, the diaphragm would have moved only as a result of the encroaching air.

Essentially, what the four observations showed us was that no matter what you say or do, the diaphragm's action will be the same—so why even mention it?

"But," we rationalize, "I teach for results, and my methods have proven successful for many years. What does it matter whether I say one certain muscle pushes or pulls, tightens or relaxes?"

Sad but true! If mentioning the diaphragm had never brought forth a correct response, we might have been spared all reference to it. As it is, this "king of old wives' tales" has become an integral part of our very philosophy, supported by thousands of misinformed triumphs—fortunate mistakes. Surely results can be just as rewarding when founded on scientific fact as with hand-me-down theories which are unwittingly filled with anatomical inaccuracies. "Support from the diaphragm" (positively a physiological impossibility) might be better stated, "Support from the hips." At least the student knows what and where the hips are, and we *know* that contraction of the pelvic muscles gives support to the air stream. "Breathe with the diaphragm" (what chances are there of breathing *without* the diaphragm?) could be more effectively directed, "fill the lungs quickly and easily." What could be simpler or more correct?

It would appear that a teacher of the "breath-propelled" arts such as singing or playing wind instruments, would be alert to more efficient modes of communication. By using this term, "diaphragm," the connotations of which have a time-proven nebulosity, the student finds a new perplexity to further complicate his already garbled understanding of the simplest of all physiological phenomena—breathing. Certainly the music teacher owes himself the satisfaction of understanding the diaphragm and its function, but he should refer to it (if he must) only after he and his students know for sure what it is and what it does. Ideally we could even follow the examples of several professional artists who have completely eliminated the word from their pedagogical jargon. They feel that such words as "deep," "full," "rich," or "free," solicit just as correct a response as "diaphragm," and their students perform in such a way as to back up this feeling. It might be worth a try. ∎

Playing in First Position

ALBERT STOUTAMIRE

A phenomenon frequently heard is that of the student trombonist playing less well in tune in first position than in other positions. This occurrence may sound illogical to those who reason that the first position is "fixed" (the slide is all the way closed), and therefore "finding the pitch" is less problematical when playing a tone in first position than when playing in other positions. This is certainly true during the very early stages of learning to play the trombone. But as the trombone student becomes more proficient on his instrument he may erroneously come to believe that if he "tunes up" on a tone played in first position, he then needs to listen very carefully and adjust the location of the slide in all other positions, but in first position he is "safe." In other words, he learns to locate positions two through seven more efficiently, he listens carefully and adjusts the slide according to judgments based on newly acquired listening and performing skills, but the beginning student may not utilize these same techniques for improving intonation when he plays in first position. He may develop a false sense of security concerning the intonation of pitches played in first position.

It is recommended that the trombone student be taught, from the very beginning, *that first position on the trombone is played with the slide extended ½" from the closed position.* The remainder of this article offers ideas relative to this recommendation.

The trombonist can manipulate his instrument so that the correct length of tubing can be utilized in producing each tone he plays. No other wind instrument is constructed in such a manner, but unfretted string instruments do have this feature. During the first few years of instruction this physical asset of being able to select the correct length of pipe or string for each note performed is frequently spoken of as a liability. A teacher will say, "Pick the students with the best ears to play strings and trombone." The implication is that trombonists and string players should be taught to listen and make adjustments in intonation sooner than performers on other non-pretuned instruments. Whether or not that practice is sound, it is true that certain wind instruments can be and are played with little attention given to precise pitch adjustment in the beginning stages, but this is not true of trombone playing, except for the closed first position.

The beginning trombonist learns that positions two through seven are "out there somewhere," and he may know that each position is slightly longer than the one closer to the "closed" position of the slide

—that is, the distance from second to third position is slightly longer than the distance from first to second, and so on, with each successive position being longer than the preceding one.

The successful beginner on trombone learns to make physical adjustments rather quickly according to what he hears, and he may locate positions two through seven by "ear and feel" fairly accurately soon after he starts playing. Continual improvement in speed and accuracy in locating these positions usually follows.

As the embouchure, breath support, and other aspects of tone production develop, intonation improves, and positions two through seven are located more accurately. But first position may erroneously become a fixed position, all the way closed, for all notes played in that position. As a result, *players can become conditioned to listen less critically to tones played in first position than to tones played in other positions.* In other words, the trombonist can learn to "turn off his ears" when playing a tone in first position and "turn on his ears" while playing tones in other positions.

I have heard intermediate level trombonists play poorer intonation in first position than in other positions so frequently that I consider it a major pitfall in learning to perform on the instrument. To avoid or solve the problem, the performer must concentrate on: (1) listening critically to all tones produced, including those played in first position; (2) being prepared to adjust the slide for intonation correction in first position as well as in other positions; and (3) being especially attentive to the *F*, third space above the bass clef staff, which is likely to be sharp. Also the *D*, second space above the bass clef staff, and the *B♭* and *C* above that may be flat, and for these tones the player will find that he has to close the slide slightly to produce the desired pitch.

The subject of variation in pitch of instruments playing in ensemble will not be attempted here except to indicate that an advanced trombonist playing in ensemble with other wind instruments and/or with string instruments may find

that he wishes to use a variety of slight deviations from the norm (equal tempered scale at *A*, 440 v.p.s.) during the course of one composition. These variations are regulated through a combination of slide movement, embouchure adjustment, and possibly by other means. Consequently the trombonist may wish to play a tone, *D* above middle *C* for example, with the slide above the "normal" first position in one instance but play the same tone in a new context below the "normal" first position.

There is a second reason for not closing the slide all the way when playing in first position. Simply stated, it is that rapid playing does not permit one to close the slide all the way without risking a "bump" on the lip or at least the extraneous noise of the slide hitting the cork or spring—depending on the type of instrument being played. In Figure 1, for example, closing the slide all the way each time the *B♭* is played would be, in my opinion, an undesirable practice.

Figure 1

Closing the slide all the way is also impractical when a slide vibrato is utilized because a series of bumps would be produced—one bump each time the slide arrived in first position at the top of a vibrato cycle. Further discussion of the vibrato is beyond the scope of this article because one immediately must ask: Does the vibrato cycle go above the mean pitch? Studies of voice and violin vibratos indicate that the top of the vibrato could go as much as a quarter of a tone above the mean pitch. The player using such a vibrato might find it necessary to play first position in an even further extended first position than the person who does not utilize the slide vibrato.

Tuning an instrument without a fixed slide position is somewhat of a problem for persons who were trained to play and tune first position all the way closed, but for the person who is taught from the beginning to "find" first position just as he "finds" the other positions, playing the "tuning note" presents no more of a problem than playing any other tone. This becomes apparent when one considers that orchestral trombonists tune to the tone A, played in second position. If the "tuning note" for band is B♭, the trombonist merely holds the slide where he normally plays B♭, as he produces the tone. It is recommended that if the ensemble is tuning to B♭, the director should instruct the trombonists to play the notes given in Figure 2 (a), (b), or (c) and listen to *all* of the tones in checking intonation. Similar groups of notes can be devised for tuning to A, F, or whatever pitch may be chosen for tuning.

Figure 2

When tuning in this manner, the trombonist should be instructed to place the slide where he normally locates each tone to be checked, without making further adjustments. If he plays all "check tones" flat or all of them sharp, the appropriate tuning slide adjustment is made. If the various tones are played neither consistently flat or sharp, but some flat and others sharp, the intonation problem will not be solved by adjusting the tuning slide, but further tone

matching and ear training is called for.

In summation, I suggest that teachers—band and orchestra directors—check the routine playing intonation of their trombonists and determine whether or not they may play more out of tone in first position than in other positions. It is recommended that all trombonists be taught to play first position slightly extended from the closed position. I believe that improved intonation and more facility of slide movement by student trombonists may result from following the recommendations presented here. ∎

Some Solutions for Brass Problems

CHARLES D. WHITEHILL

Most high school and college brass players exhibit an abundance of playing problems. Solutions to these problems can be found through application of the fundamentals of brass playing which must be stressed in private lessons, section practice, and full group rehearsals. The following statements represent brass playing problems this writer has encountered and the cause and cure for these deficiencies.

1. *Brass players are unable to play tongued passages legato, and they produce a very explosive sound when trying to play staccato passages.*

In most cases, the students are actually tonguing through and between the teeth and lips into the mouthpiece. This opens the vibrating points of the lips and delays the sound until the tongue is brought back into the mouth cavity, permitting the air to get through the instrument. Consequently, the tone quality suffers and tonguing facility is inhibited. The cure is to tongue behind the upper teeth and bring the tongue back quickly for maximum tone.

One should attempt to produce a "ta" or "la" sound against the back of the teeth, depending upon the staccato or legato effect desired. To insure a good attack in any playing style, the mouth corners, the tongue, and the diaphragm must be synchronized (i.e., when the tongue is moved back from the teeth, the mouth corners snap forward and the stomach muscles contract simultaneously).

2. *When tones are released, they usually stop very suddenly and with some accent which is musically and mechanically faulty.*

This type of sound is produced when the tone is stopped by placing the tongue against the back of the upper teeth or by protruding the tongue against the back of the upper teeth or by protruding the tongue between the teeth and lips in preparation for the next attack. Many times in brass teaching attack is stressed, but the release of tones is ignored. Brass players must learn to stop the tone with the breath rather than the tongue. The tone should stop an instant before the tongue goes up to the back of the teeth to begin the next tone.

This requires much practice to perfect it in faster passages. The result is more tone and a musically satisfying release of tones.

3. *Trombone players generally have difficulty playing legato passages. Slurred passages are frequently either disconnected or glissed chromatically.*

This basic problem stems from the lack of knowledge about legato tonguing and the lack of knowledge about the mechanics of the trombone in relation to slurring. Legato tonguing must be employed to avoid a gliss (smear), which results when slurring from one partial to a like numbered partial of the harmonic series. To state the matter more simply, for younger students, the legato tongue is employed when notes and slide move in the same direction, (i.e., when the notes ascend and the slide moves up or the reverse). Natural slurs result when playing between unlike numbered partials. In this case the tongue need not be employed. Again to simplify, natural slurs result when the slide and notes move in opposite directions. Correct use of legato tonguing (a light tonguing action high on the upper teeth using the syllable "la" producing an almost imperceptible interruption of the tone) and knowledge of the harmonic series coupled with fast slide action will produce legato playing.

4. *When playing passages containing both valve slurs (natural slurs on trombone) and lip slurs, the notes are often rhythmically and tonally uneven.*

This is caused by an undeveloped embouchure and an unawareness of the difference between the two types of slur. Good results can be obtained by practicing lip slurs to strengthen the embouchure and by learning to read ahead enough to be ready mentally and physically for the lip slur.

5. *Students find it very difficult to change registers when tonguing and have difficulty tonguing intervals from fourths to octaves or more.*

The cause for this problem is a multiple one. Considering that the student attacks and releases tones correctly as described earlier, the cause may be a failure to read ahead or to hear the pitches correctly. The trouble may also be the position of the tongue behind the upper teeth in relation to the register in which the tone lies. The tongue, as well as the embouchure, must be flexible, striking lower on the upper teeth for the low register and higher for the high register. For the extremely low notes the player may have to articulate behind the upper teeth at the lower edge and bring the tongue down, rather than tongue between the teeth. The use of the syllables "toe" for the low register, "ta" for the middle register, and "tee" for the upper notes may aid the player's accuracy. Also one should be conscious of using syllables to aid in slurring up and down: "Toe-hee" or "ta-hee" to slur up; "tee-ha" or "ta-ha" to slur down. This technique helps to change the size and shape of the oral cavity and the direction and intensity of the air stream, making slurring easier and smoother.

6. *Most students have very little endurance on a brass instrument.*

Twenty to thirty minutes is the limit of peak performance for most students this writer has encountered. The embouchure simply gets

tired, the tone becomes fuzzy, and intonation suffers. Again, there may be several reasons for this. Lack of muscular strength in the embouchure is perhaps the most obvious reason for lack of endurance. As mentioned earlier, lip slurs are excellent to strengthen the lip muscles and acquire flexibility. But the way in which the lip muscles are built up is just as important as the materials used to do the job. One can exhaust the embouchure on the very best exercise material. It is the practice-rest, practice-rest theory that must be stressed. Some brass teachers emphasize that one should practice five minutes and rest five minutes before resuming; therefore, two hours must be spent to complete one hour of practice. When one finishes practicing, he should not be completely exhausted. The desire to master a difficult passage should not dictate all practice habits. Of course, a student may depend upon his embouchure alone for his playing strength and depend very little upon the support available from the abdominal muscles. Any embouchure will soon tire without proper breath support. If proper breath support is substituted for excessive mouthpiece pressure, the player will certainly develop more endurance.

The awareness of the need and practicability of a warm-up routine must be impressed upon students. This will greatly increase one's endurance and will enhance the tone quality and all the finer points of brass playing. Lip muscles become slightly stiff and swollen a few hours after playing. To begin practicing on long tones in an easy register is very wise. One should gradually increase the range and the technical difficulty during the warm-up. Long tones, lip slurs, scales, arpeggios, and breath support and breath endurance exercises should be included in a warm-up routine. Such a procedure should not tire the player but prepare him for the practice period ahead. For best results one should warm-up in the morning and practice in the afternoon if possible. In case of an impending performance, one should not practice extensively the day before.

7. *Brass students generally have difficulty playing in tune.*

Again, the reasons for this are varied. Students must be encouraged to listen carefully to themselves and to others to be able to play in tune. On all brass instruments many out-of-tune notes can be traced to poor equipment or improper use of equipment. For example, most trumpet players do not know how to manipulate the third valve slide in order to tune written D and $C\sharp$. In many cases the third valve slide will not function properly because of lack of use or neglect in upkeep. Also, worn valves and slides, valve ports that do not line up with the tubing, and leaks may cause an instrument to play out of tune.

Brass instruments cannot be built acoustically perfect. Certain partials of the harmonic series, such as the sixth and ninth are sharp. The fifth and tenth are flat. Students must learn to adjust these notes mechanically (by using alternate fingerings and first and third valve slides) and with the lip, to be able to play in tune.

8. *Use of vibrato is absent in most brass players.*

Most students do not know how to use vibrato or may use a type injurious to the embouchure and the tone. Jaw vibrato (like that used by many saxophone players), lip vibrato, head vibrato (produced by moving the head), and throat vibrato may be detrimental to the player's embouchure and tone quality. Diaphragm vibrato sounds well if done correctly. It is produced by tightening and releasing the diaphragm, causing vibrations in the air column. This type becomes a very integral part of the player's sound. The hand or slide vibrato is effective for most players. It can be matched by an entire section and can be terminated or resumed at will. The embouchure, breathing, and the openness of the throat are not affected by this type of vibrato, and the tone and general style of playing are enhanced immeasurably by its judicious use.

Many problems of brass playing can be solved through careful application of the fundamentals as outlined herein. These fundamentals can be exposed in a short period of time, but must be repeated many times to become playing habits. ∎

413

Brass Recordings

DONALD WHITAKER

A vital adjunct to music education is the exposure of students to the performances of the finest artists, either in live concerts or on records. There has been a tremendous increase in the recorded literature available, and the following compilation is offered as a guide to enrich the aural experience in the classroom.

Trumpet and Cornet

Kapp 9062. Voisin. Tartini-Fanfare, chiamata no. 3. Purcell-Symphony from "Fairy Queen." Stradella-Sonata for trumpet and string orchestra. Lully-Carousel music. Tartini-Fanfare, chiamata no. 6. Monteverdi-Fanfare, sinfonia da Guerra. Fischer-Le journal de printemps, suite no. 8. Petzold-10 O'clock, sonata no. 3.

Kapp 9033. Voisin, Rhea. Vivaldi-Concerto, E♭ major. Manfredini-Concerto for two trumpets. Torelli-Sinfonia con tromba. Biber-Sonata no. 6 for trumpet. Telemann-Concerto in D major for trumpet.

Kapp 9050. Voisin, Rhea. Stanley-Trumpet tune. Purcell-Yorkshire feast song. C.P.E. Bach-March for three trumpets and timpani. Telemann-Concerto for trumpet, D major. Altenburg-Concerto for seven trumpets and timpani. Legrenzi-Sonata "La Buscha." Daquin, Noel Suisse.

Westminster 18931. Buxtehude-Fanfare and chorus. Schein-Paduana and galliard. Fux-Serenades. Altenburg-Concerto for clarini and timpani. Shahan-Leipzig towers.

Archive 3151. Lind, Scherbaum. Haydn-Concerto for horn and strings no. 2, D major, Haydn-Concerto for trumpet and orchestra, E♭ major.

Anard 103. Burke. Goldman-Introduction and tarantella. Demonstration performance.

Westminster 18954. Delmotte, Haneuse. Haydn-Concerto for trumpet and orchestra, E♭ major. Torelli-Concerto for trumpet and orchestra, E major. Vivaldi-Concerto for 2 trumpets and orchestra, C major. Handel-Concerto for trumpet and orchestra, D major.

EMS 4. Wilson, Smith, Garfield. Hindemith-Sonatas for trumpet, trombone, and bassoon.

Guide Records. 11417. Masters. Bach-Bist du bei mir. Balay-Petite piece Shelukov-Two pieces for trumpet and piano. Bernald-English suite Buchtel-Impromptu. Balay-Prelude et ballade. Gaubert-Cantabile et scherzetto. Fitzgerald-Call. Latham-Suite for trumpet and orchestra. Barnt-Andante et scherzo. Kennan-Sonata for trumpet and piano.

VOX Album 300. Spotlight on Brass. Demonstrations of the trumpet, clarino, cornett, herald by Voisin; demonstration of the hunting horn, post horn, French horn, Wagner tuba by Meek; demonstration of the serpent, bass trumpet, trombone, tuba, baritone, euphonium by Orosz.

Golden Crest 7004. Reynolds. Hue-Solo de concert. Saint-Saens-Amour viens aide. Hummel-Rondo. Senee-Concertino. Senee-Ballet. Fitzgerald-Call. Gliere-Two pieces op. 34, no. 21 Porret and Baron-6 Exquisses. Barrow-Scherzo. Paisner-Prelude to a mood.

Decca 8869. Mendez. Body and Soul. Memories of You. Sleepy Lagoon. On the Sunny side of the Street. I Surrender, Dear. I

Don't Stand a Ghost of a Chance with You. El Gitano. One Fine Day. Les Filles de Cadiz. Waltz. Intermezzo. Canto moro.

SPA Records 12. Wobish. Kaufmann-Music for trumpet and string orchestra in three movements.

Golden Crest 7008. Haynie. Handel-Aria con variazioni. Fitzgerald-Polly Oliver. Arne-Rule Britannia. Niles-Black is the Color of My True Love's Hair. Goedicke-Concert etude. Klein-Lament. Poot-Etude de concert. Tenaglia-Aria. Krieger-Allegro. Munro-My Lovely Celia. Fitzgtrald-Begone Dull Care. Bakaleinikoff-Serenade. Bozza-Rustiques. Robbins-Mont Saint-Michel. Gabaye-Boutade.

Golden Crest 4012. Smith. Dark Eyes. Barsoti-Tally Ho. Come Back to Sorrento. Parish-Starduct. Brown-Temptation. Greene-Sing Me to Sleep. Neopolitan Fantasy. Bond-Perfect Day. Trumpet voluntary.

Grand Award 33-344. Margulis. La Macarena. Fandango. Andalusian Skies. Linda Rosa. Night and Day. Begin the Beguine. In the Still of the Night. Embraceable You. La Paloma. La Golondrina. Yearning. I Surrender, Dear

Monitor 2030. Shapiro. Afanasiev, Starozhilov, Krivnetsky. Schumann-For four horns, F major, op. 86.

London 3020. Longinotti, Pepin, Leloir. Haydn-Concerto for trumpet and orchestra. Mozart-Concerto for flute and orchestra, K. 314. Schumann-Adagio and allegro for horn.

Kapp 9017. Voisin, Ghitalla. Haydn-Concerto in E flat Vivaldi-Concerto in C major Purcell-

Tune and Air for trumpet and orchestra Purcell-Voluntary *C* major. Purcell-Voluntary, *D* major. Purcell-Sonata for trumpet and strings, *D* major.

RCA Victor 1906. Fiedler. Verdi-Aida. Rossini-Barber of Seville. Offenbach-Tales of Hoffman. Bizet-Carmen. Verdi-Il Trovatore. Massenet-Thais. Verdi-Rigoletto.

Decca 8427. Mendez and sons Robert and Ralph. The Brave Matador. A Trumpeter's Lullaby Chunca. The Tre-Mendez Polka. Chiapanecas. Cara Nome. Polka in the Box. Flight of the Bumblebee. Hefre Kati. Estrellita. Dark Eyes. Hora Staccato. Valse Bluette.

Decca 8489. Burke. The volunteer. Foneta. Spring is Never Ending. Carnival of Venice. Deuxieme grand solo. Jolene. Deuxieme fantasie brillante. Aida.

Decca 8624. Mendez. Borodin-Danse Polovtsienne. Puccini-Munsetta. Black-Paper Doll. Brahms-Hungarian dance no. 5. Bizet-Habanera. Mendez-Scherzo, *D* minor. Mendez-Jota no. 2. Rodgers and Hart-Betwitched. Mendez-Hungarian Chant. Raskin and Mercer-Laura. Smetana-Dance of the Comedians. Arlen and Harburg-Over the Rainbow.

CRI 122. Blee, Krell, Marcellus, Kilburn. Nagel-Concerto for trumpet and strings, op. 8. Lessard-Concerto for flute, clarinet, bassoon, string quartet, and string orchestra.

Columbia 4629. Krauss, Kincaid, Tabuteau, Schoenbach, Monroe, Jones, Krachmalnick, Gigliotti. Purcell-A trumpet voluntary, *D* major. Griffes-Poem for flute and orchestra. Handel-Concerto for oboe and strings, no. 3, *G* minor. Phillips-Concert piece for bassoon and strings. Weber-Adagio and Rondo for cello and orchestra. Chabrier-Larghetto for horn and orchestra. Beethoven-Romance no. 2 in *F* major for violin and orchestra op. 50. Weber-Concertino for clarinet and orchestra.

Bach Guild 6256. Wobisch. Clarke-Trumpet voluntary. Vivaldi-Concerto *C* major for 2 trumpets, strings and continuo. Perti-Sonata for trumpets, strings and continuo. Tovelli-Sonato no. 5 for trumpet, strings and continuo. Purcell-Sonata for trumpet, strings and continuo. Purcell-Trumpet overture from Indian Queen. Torelli-Sinfonia for 4 trumpets, oboes, strings, timpani and continuo. Gabrielli-Sonata for trumpet, strings and continuo. Corelli-Sonata for trumpet, violins and continuo. Stanley-Trumpet tune.

Olseau Lyre 60019. Pirot André, Suzan, Arque, Verdier, Callot. Simpson-Intrada. Harding-Almande. Holborne-The Fairy Round. Leetherland-Pavan. Guy-Almande No. 13. Holborne-The Choice. Bassano-Fantasia. Farnaby-Almande. Holborne-Galliard. Johnson-Almande no. 7. Holborne-As It Fell on a Holy Eve. Coperario-Fantasia no. 76. Ferrabosco II-Almande no. 5. Dering-Fantasie. Lupo-Almande. Bassano-Pavan no. 16. Holborne-The Fruit of Love. Ferrabosco II-Pavan. Ferrabosco II-Alman.

Award 701. Smith Corelli-Sonata 8. Smith-Vignette. Simon-Willow echoes. Bach-Prelude. Clarke-Carnival of Venice. Clarke-Maid of the Mist. Barat-Fantasia in *E♭*. Fitzgerald-Concerto in *A♭* minor, 2nd movement. Llewellyn-My Regards. Goedicke-Concert etude.

Archive 3009. Scarlatti, Wobisch. Scarlatti-Su le sponde del Tebro.

French Horn

Angel 35092. Brain. Mozart-Concertos for horn, nos. 1, 2, 3, 4.

Archive 3151. Lind, Scherbaum. Haydn-Concerto for horn and strings no. 2 in *D* major, and Concerto for trumpet and orchestra *E♭* major.

Vox 300. Spotlight on Brass. [See listing under trumpet.]

Vanguard 1069. Linder. Mozart-Concertos for horn, nos. 1, 2, 3, 4.

Westminster 18931. Poeschl. Buxtehude-Fanfare and chorus. Schein-Paduana and Gaillard. Fux-Serenade; Marche, Guigue, Menuet and Aria. Fux-Serenade; Overture, Menuet, Guigue, Aria, Bouree 1 and 2, Intrada, Rigadon, Ciacona, Guigue, Menuet-Finale. Altenburg-Concerto for clarini and timpani. Shahan-Leibzig towers.

Angel 60227. Brain. Hindemith-Concerto for horn and orchestra.

Golden Crest 4014. Fitzpatrick. Music for hunting horn. Beethoven-Sonata op. 17. Mouret-Five divertissements pour un comedie Italienne.

Boston 401. Stagliano. Mozart-Concerti for horn no. 1, *D* major, K. 412; no. 2, *E♭*, K. 417; no. 3, *E♭*, K 447; no. 4 *E♭*, K. 495.

Golden Crest 7002. Barrows. Wilder-Sonata no. 1, Wilder-Suite for horn and piano. Wilder-Sonata no. 2.

Award 704. Chambers. Corelli-Sonata, *F* major. Mozart-Concerto. Bradford-Anderson. March, in canon. Poot-Sarabande. Hermann-Concerto for horn. Clerisse-Chant sans paroles. Piatoni-Air de chasse. Bakaleinikoff-Cavatina. Heiden-Sonata for horn and piano.

RCA 2146. Eger. Mozart-Horn concerto no. 3, *E♭*, K. 447. Haydn-Trio, *E♭*. Rossini-Prelude, theme and variations. Schubert-Serenade and Die Forelle. Bartok-For children nos. 17 and 33. Bernstein-Elegy for Mippy 1. Gershwin-Prelude no. 2.

Audiophile 70. Leuba, Binstook. Mozart-Horn duos, K. 487. Beethoven-Sextet for horns and strings.

Capitol 7175. Brain. Mozart-Quintet *E♭* major, K. 452 Berkeley-Trio, op. 44.

Boston 212. Stagliano. Gliere-Nocturne op. 35, no 10 Gretchaninov-Lullaby op. 1, no. 5. Cui-Moment musical op. 51, no. 1.

Gliere-Intermezzo op. 35, no. 11. Glazounov-Reverie op. 24. Tchaikowsky-Autumn Song op. 37a, no. 10. Scriabin-Romance. Kalinnikov-Elegy. Scriabin-Prelude op. 11, no. 4. Akimenko-Melody op. 18. Dukas-Villanelle Fauré-After a Dream op. 7, no. 3. Poulenc-Elegie. Vuillermoz-Etude.

RCA 2420. Eger. Brahms-Trip, $E\flat$, op. 40. Beethoven-Sonata, F major, op. 17.

Angel 45030. Marchi, Cecearossi. Vivaldi-Concerto in F major, p. 320. Vivaldi-Concerto in F major, p. 321.

Kapp 9053. Berv, Stagliano. Telemann-Concerto D major. Telemann-Suite F major. Handel-Concerto F major. Barsanti-Concerto D major. Opus 3, no. 4. Steinmetz-Concerto D major.

EMS 4. Wilson, Smith, Garfield, Lettvin. Hindemith-Trumpet, bassoon and trombone sonatas.

Boston 201. Stagliano. Mozart-Quintet in $E\flat$ major, K. 407.

Classic Editions 6. Polekh Gliere-Concerto for horn, op. 91. Prokofieff—Gypsy fantasy. Glinka-Jota Aragonesa. Amirov-Azerbaijan Mugam.

Trombone

EMS 4. Wilson, Smith, Garfield. Hindemith-Trumpet, bassoon and trombone sonatas.

Classic Editions 1041. Schuman. Rimsky-Korsakov-Concerto for trombone and military band. Beethoven-Three equali for four trombones. Hindemith-Trauermusik for trombone and strings, morning music for brass. Starer-Five miniatures for brass.

Audio Fidelity 1811. Schuman. Serly-Concerto for trombone and orchestra. Serly-Miniature suite for 12 wind instruments. Trombone encores.

Epic 601015. Suzan. Milhaud-Concertino D'Hiver from the four seasons.

Golden Crest 62183. Schuman. Martin-Ballade. Hindemith-Sonata. Goch-Concertino.

Baritone and Euphonium

Golden Crest 7001. Falcone. Clarke-From the shores of the mighty Pacific. Ponce-Estrellita. J. S. Bach-Bourees from cello suite no. 3. DeLuca-Beautiful Colorado. Simons-Atlantic Zephyrs. Ravel-Piece en forme de Habanera. Senaille-Allegro spiritoso. Guilmant-Morceau symphonique.

Brasch 11485. Brasch. Manning-Carnival of Venice. Davis-Concert Polka, Jenny Wren. Bellstedt-La couquette. Romberg-

Serenade. Schmidt-The devil's tongue. Brahe-Bless This House. Bellstedt-La Mandolinata. Brasch-Weber's last waltz fantasie.

Gunnison Music Camp 13018. Jacobs, Bell, Louder, Waller. Strauss-The swan. Weber-Concerto for clarinet, no. 1, F minor, op. 73.

Tuba

Golden Crest 7006. Phillips. Wilder-Sonata. Bach-Komm, susser Tod., Bourree. Handel-Andante Flute sonata no. 9. Corelli-Gigue. Mozart-O Isis und Osiris. Swann-Two moods for tuba.

Golden Crest 3015. Bell. When Yuba Plays the Rumba on the Tuba. Asleep in the Deep. In the Hall of the Mountain King (Peer Gynt). Tuba Man. The Elephant's Tango. Mummers. Carnival of Venice. Osis and Osiris. Variations on a Theme of Judas Maccabeus. The Jolly Farmer Goes to Town.

Gunnison Music Camp 13018. Jacobs (Strauss-Concerto).

Brass Ensemble

Audiophile 32. Chicago Brass Ensemble. Handy-St. Louis Blues. Lebow-Suite for brass. Lebow-Brass quintette.

Golden Crest 4003. New York Philharmonic Brass Ensemble. Ewald-Symphony for five part brass choir. Starer-Five miniatures. Sanders-Quintet for brass instruments, $B\flat$ major.

Golden Crest 4017. New York Brass Quintet. Wilder-Suite for brass quintet. Hammond-Quintet for brass.

Cantate 452. Hessen Sextett. Nun lob, mein Seel, den Herren. Nun preiset alle Grottes Barmherzigkeit. Ist gott für mich, so trete. Kommt her zu mir, spricht gottes sohn.

Cantate 453. Hessen Sextett. Reiche-Fuga no. 19. Reiche-Sonatina no. 10. Pezel-Turmsonate no. 1, Intrade no. 1, Intrade no. 76.

Cantate 451. Chor der Posaunenmission Bethel. Lobe den Herren, den mächtigen König. Nun danket alle Gott. Wie schönleuchtet der Morgenstern. Wachet auf, ruft uns die Stimme.

Cantate 455. Chor der Posaunenmission Bethel. Aus tiefer Not schrei ich zu dir. Vater unser im Himmelreich. Allein zu dir, Herr Jesu Christ. Erhalt uns Herr bei deinem Wort.

Lehigh University. 1103. Lehigh Instrumental Ensemble and Brass Choir. Riegger-Music for brass choir. Ruggles-Angels. Brant-Millenium II.

Cantate 454. Bläser der Westfälischen Kantorei. Sollt ich meinem Gott nicht singen. Jesu, meine Freude.

Period 515. Koch. Hindemith-Concert music for brass and strings. Hindemith-Horn concertino.

Period 734. New York Brass Ensemble. Gabrieli-Symphoniae Sacrae 1597, nos. 1, 2, 5, 7, 8, 10, 13 ,14.

Classic Editions 1039. The Chamber Brass Players. Adson-Two ayres for cornett and sagbuts. Gabrieli-Conzona per sonare no. 1 and no. 2. Holborne-Honie-Suckle, Night watch. Pezel-Sonata no. 2 and no. 22, suite. Purcell-2 trumpet tunes and ayre. Reiche-Sonata no. 19. Schein-Paduana, Gaillard. Storl-Sonata no. 1. Susato-Three dances. Anonymous-Sonata from die Bänkelsängerleider.

Monitor 2023. Shapiro, Afanasirv, Starozhilov, Krivnetsky. Schumann-Concerto for four horns, *F* major, op. 86.

Decca 9969. Hindemith-Concert Music for Piano, brass and 2 harps op. 49 (1930).

Westminster 18664. Vaillant, Dupisson. Alberli-Sonata for two trumpets, *D* major. Bononcini-Sinfonia No. 8, op. 3, *D* major. Sinfonia No. 10, *D* major. Jacchini-Sonata no. 5, *D* major. Torelli-Sinfonia, *C* major, Sinfonia for two trumpets, *D* major, Sinfonia, *A* minor.

Period 526. Schuman Brass Choir. Gabrieli-Canzoni, Ricercari and chori Pezel-Four sonatas for five voiced brass choir.

Kapp 9020. Voisin. Dahl-Music for brass instruments. Hindemith-Morgen Musik. Berezowski-Brass suite. Sanders-Quintet in *B♭*.

Stradivari 605. Glanz, Sklar, Pulis, Berv. Saint-Saens-Septet, *E♭* major, op. 65. Poulenc-Sonata for trumpet, trombone and horn.

Unicorn 1003. The Brass Ensemble. Italian brass music, English brass music, German brass music.

Morgram 817. Music Hall Brass Ensemble. Holborne-Three pieces. Monteverdi-Orfeo music, Questi Vaghi, Tempro la cetra. Schein-Intrada and paduana. Pezel-Gigue, intrada, sarabande, Sonata no. 3. Banchieri-Two fantasias.

Columbia 941. The Brass Ensemble of the Jazz and Classical Music Society. Schuller-Symphony for brass and percussion. Johnson-Poem for brass. Lewis-Three little feelings. Giuffre-Pharaoh.

Golden Crest 4023. New York Brass Quintet. Holborne-3 pieces. Gabrieli-Canzona per sonare no. 1. Glasel-16th century carmina. Harris-4 moods for brass quintet. Haines-Toccata. Bozza-Sonatine for brass.

Capitol. 8525. Horn Club of Los Angeles. Mendelssohn-Tarantella. Garcia-Variations on a 5 note theme. Palestrina-Stabat mater. Lasso-Echo song. Hyde-Color contrasts. Lo Presti-Suite for 8 horns. Raksin-Morning revisited.

Columbia 5443. Biggs, Boston Brass Ensemble. Gabrieli-Canzon prima, Canzon seconda, canzon terza, canzon quarta, Fantasia in the sixth tone. Frescobaldi-Canzona prima, seconda, terza, quarta, quinta. Toccata, *D* minor. Toccata *G* major.

Golden Crest. 4008. Chamber Brass Players. Tower Music of Pezel, Scheidt, Bach, Reiche, Hassler.

Esoteric 503. New York Brass Ensemble. Gabrieli-Canzonas for single and double brass choirs.

CRI 144. New York Brass Quintet. Schuller-Music for brass quintet. Blackwood-Chamber symphony for 14 wind instruments.

CRI 125. New York Brass Ensemble. Franchetti-Three Italian masques. Johnson-Trio for flute, oboe and piano.

Toward Better Tuba Players

DAVID KUEHN

"We expect less from tuba players —and we get it." This saying, borrowed from a well-known oil company, is much too true. The reason is a simple one: the average tuba player is usually not regarded as a musician in the same sense as a violinist or pianist. In many cases a tuba student's ability is overshadowed by the burden of an instrument that for no substantial reason has taken the "back seat" in many public school music programs. This author is constantly amazed at the comparatively poor quality of tuba students in many high school music organizations.

It is hoped that you are now reading with some interest, for the idea behind this article can be condensed into a single statement: we must start immediately to train the average tuba student as if he were a musician in his own right, and not a transplanted player from another instrument who could not meet the competition.

With the idea of assisting the tuba player to attain higher standards of performance the remainder of this article is devoted to basic suggestions that may be of help to the instructor of the average public school tuba student.

Breathing

It is not good enough that a sound is made on an instrument, but one must have sufficient breath to control this sound and the shape of notes and musical phrases. The practice of taking large, deep breaths can help to open the sound (and open the throat if inhalation and exhalation are relaxed) and project the improved tone. There are several satisfactory approaches to sufficient inhalation that can be used in connection with young students. The idea of "inhaling to the bottom of one's feet" is a strange but often helpful approach. In doing this a student concentrates on taking a low, relaxed, full breath. The fact that the lower ribs move out and up when one takes a proper breath is often helpful for the student to realize, *providing* he does not simply thrust out his ribs with the thought that through this procedure alone air will automatically be brought into his lungs. The theory of "deep breathing" can be shown quite easily to the student in several ways; two such ways are explained below. First, as the student sits in a straight chair have him bend forward from the waist until his head is near his knees. At this point have him take a large breath; the result will be a low, deep breath that the student should immediately recognize. (The formation of the mouth as if saying the vowel "O" helps direct the air for proper inhalation). This aids in pointing out that high chest breathing cannot be the basis of good inhalation in wind playing. Secondly, as the student rests in a reclining position he is able to observe the proper function of normal inhalation; this same occurance is amplified when one takes a breath to play an instrument.

The feeling that the instrument is an extension of the player is a tremendously important concept. Too many young musicians blow 'against' or 'at' the tuba. The concept of air projecting through the instrument, out the bell, and, if you will, "across the room", is indeed an important one. Having the student hold a sheet of paper against a wall strictly with his breath can illustrate the power of a projected and steady stream of air. Setting one's embouchure and blowing (with some force) against the back of one's hand (placed 6 to 8 inches from the mouth) also strengthens this same concept. A personally successful approach to correct exhalation is to imagine a series of difficult notes (such as a musical phrase) being played "off" a steady, quick-moving column of air. In this way a low brass instrumentalist does not feel "bogged down" going from note to note, but tends to see beyond individual notes to the end (or the climax) of the particular phrase, thereby shaping the total concept of the group of notes played. Once this idea of projected air is established, a player can take his basic sound and refine it; without this concept of projection the air can easily become stagnant. What a wonderful feeling it is when a young musician knows that his instrument is a partner and not an obstacle in music making.

Embouchure

Puffed cheeks do not help control a tone—not even on tuba and certainly not in the low register. The corners of the mouth should be firm (the word "tight" is often misleading). If a student is in the habit of puffing his cheeks he should be made to realize that certain facial muscles are not functioning to control the embouchure. Without the use of an instrument or mouthpiece, instruct the player to set the corners of his mouth (holding the corners gently against the gums); he will find it a difficult task to puff his cheeks. Now the student can apply the same principle when buzzing the mouthpiece and finally when placing the mouthpiece into the instrument. Under no circumstances should a player pull the corners of his mouth back to set for a particular pitch. In fact, one will often find it helpful to let the corners of the mouth come in toward the mouthpiece (the corners still remaining in a firm position). It must be stated that the student may regress the moment he goes to the instrument, but the idea and feeling are established and now can be approached with understanding.

The vertical opening between the teeth must be enough that a full sound is possible. This amount of openess while playing the tuba is often hard to explain, since the idea of "relaxation" and "openess" must be adjusted if the player has been changed from an instrument with a smaller cupped mouthpiece. Compared to the player on a small cupped mouthpiece, the aperture of a tuba student must be in a more open position vertically. If one could visualize the aperture of a fine tuba player on the following notes,

he undoubtedly would find that in playing #1 the aperture would be to the point where the vertical opening in the center of the lips is close to ¼ of an inch. The vertical aperture opening of #2 would be less than half as large, and the vertical aperture opening of #3 would be about ½ the size of #2. A portion of the lips under the rim of a cornet player's mouthpiece is part of the vibrating surface in a tuba student's mouthpiece.

Another common problem is that of locking the jaw when the embouchure becomes fatigued. The firmness in this situation is shifted from the corners of the mouth to the jaw and, consequently, much trouble results in controlling the tone, particularly when it involves the low register. The jaw must remain free enough to drop open gradually, as the student plays toward the extreme low notes. Overcoming the bunched chin is an important step to free movement of the lower jaw on brass instruments. The verbal illustration of a student with a brick or weight tied to his chin provides a good description to young (and often older) students.

Phrasing, Tone, and Technique

It is certainly unnecessary for the tuba player to breathe after every note in any piece of music—even a march. Several measures in one breath (while teaching the idea of phrasing) is not too much to expect of any instrumentalist. Shallow inhalations during a march or similar passage have direct effects on the student's ability to take and conserve air in a melodic passage. The student should be expected to do some individual practice with long tones (for development of tone quality) and scales and lip slurs (for more facility). Strengthening the muscles of the embouchure for greater endurance is a very important function of regular practice. This author finds that one way of beginning the practice of long-tone exercises is, first, to find the point, in terms of counts, when the pupil normally runs out of air. By starting just on the conservative side of this point in setting the duration of each long tone, the student immediately has a personal goal for which to aim. The following three ways are examples of how long tones can be treated:

The student must be reminded to remain relaxed in the shoulders,

throat, and chest. Encouraging the instrumentalist to take some time every day to practice fundamentals can be of great value towards a general improvement in the student's playing ability. It is of more value to practice some each day than to have larger blocks of practice time on a less regular basis.

Centering the pitch on a low brass instrument is of extreme importance. Each tone must have a "core" or "center" which a student can constantly strive to find. Without this "center" to every note, a young musician has little concept of what good tone production really means. "Mouthing" (opening up into a note after the attack) is a common problem with beginning players, particularly in the low register. A successful teaching aid in helping to overcome these "squeezed" attacks is, first, to have the student hold a long tone. In the middle of this tone (presumably when the sound is comparatively open), have the student stop the air and, without consciously moving the embouchure, reattack the same pitch. The embouchure change which some

students instinctively make to restart the note is easily identifiable by both student and instructor.

The shortage of training material for the tuba player still exists, but many fine exercises can be found in intermediate trombone methods. A tuba student is capable of learning the octave transposition with a minimum amount of effort, with invaluable results. An entirely new world of literature is unfolded, and the instructor is able to select exercises to help overcome some of the abovementioned problems.

As time goes on, the tuba is attracting more followers because of its increasing status as a musical instrument. There are many fine professional tuba players and teachers, but alas, for one reason or another these specialized instructors are not available to the average student. Basic instrumental fundamentals should be taught in the public schools to all young musicians, regardless of instrument size or shape. It is high time we change the slogan to read: "We expect more from tuba players—and we get it." ∎

So You Play the Euphonium?

E. J. Robbins

In recent years a great deal of ignominy has been heaped upon the instrument I am going to discuss. Every euphonium player has heard his beloved instrument called a raincatcher or fire hydrant, and when you consider the mediocrity of some of the euphonium's exponents, perhaps these epithets are well-deserved.

Contrary to the opinion of some that it should suffer the same fate as its forerunner, the ophicleide, the euphonium is a legitimate instrument, having been used by many composers of contemporary classical music, though for these occasions it was re-classified as a

tenor tuba. The euphonium part in "Mars" from Gustav Holst's suite, *The Planets*, is one of the most challenging pieces in the euphonium repertoire. Maurice Ravel used the euphonium for the solo line in his arrangement of "Bydlo" in Moussourgsky's *Pictures at an Exhibition*. Leo Janáček has written a very prominent part in his *Sinfonietta* which is quite taxing for the best instrumentalist. These examples of classical literature give some indication of the euphonium's place in serious music.

However, even the most stalwart defender of the euphonium would have to admit that this role is small,

and, in any case, I am concerned with the euphonium primarily as applied to the concert band. I would like to state a case for the euphonium by pointing out the advantages that could be realized if an effort were made to reinstate it to its rightful place in the concert band.

Firstly, it can be used as a melodic instrument in octaves with the solo clarinet to add sonority, depth, and warmth of tone to a clarinet melody line. Secondly, because of the similarity of euphonium tone to the tenor saxophone it can be used with saxophone sections. Thirdly, since in orchestral transcriptions

419

for band, especially older arrangements, the B♭ clarinet section, replacing delicate string tone, often tends to overpower the reed bass line, the euphonium can be used to remedy this imbalance. Fourthly, the euphonium can be used effectively to increase the quality and power of the French horn section. If there is a particular horn part you would like strengthened the euphonium is at your disposal. Fifthly, if you desire a solid bass line with the bass family but not quite the preponderance of the tuba, once again the euphonium is useful. Sixthly, because of the facility and range of the euphonium, it is really the only suitable brass instrument to take over the cello parts in a transcription from orchestral work. This is closely allied to its present role, as the cello very often does double the bass line.

And, finally, it is a beautiful solo instrument in its own right. It is assumed, of course, that in each case stated above the euphonium player has reached a high degree of development both as a technician and musician, for this is a firm requirement in order to accomplish these tasks.

It would appear that in the last decade or so the euphonium has suffered an extreme loss of status, possibly because arrangers lack understanding of its potentialities. Certainly, in many modern arrangements, it does no more than reiterate the bass line in octaves. Let us briefly consider the probable causes of this development. Since the euphonium is low on commercial appeal most beginners would rather play the glamorous trumpet or saxophone, and a vicious circle ensues; a lack of interest leads to no development, hence there is no demand, hence poor parts which brings us back to a lack of interest. Unfortunately, it is true that there has been little challenge offered by composers because they do not understand the instrument. Or, because of the mediocrity with which it is played, they have shied away from issuing a challenge, thus furthering the circle outlined above. In addition, the emergence of the saxophone section to respectability as a solo ensemble in contemporary American band music, as used by Paul Creston in his "Celebration" and "Zanoni" overtures, has provided an additional alternative to euphonium tone colour. In fact, quite recently some American educators have recommended the complete doubling of the saxophone section, i.e., two of each first altos, second altos, tenors, and baritone. Moreover, our concept of trombone tone has entirely changed since the adoption by bands of the large bore trombones used extensively in the symphonic field. This tone, which is much larger and softer than the small bore trombone, compares favorably with the tone of the light American baritone and hence tends to replace the euphonium. This is all the more the case when we consider the vast improvements in trombone technique which have possibly resulted from the challenging parts written for the instrument by composers.

We should also remember that the development of the balanced clarinet choir and the increased use of, bass and contrabass clarinets, bassoons, and contrabassoon have changed the concepts of band scoring. It is no longer necessary to use the euphonium and tuba to double the bass line when no other brasses or only the horns are playing; this was the case in the past. The woodwinds are quite capable of playing independently of the brasses, and the addition of the horns and the saxophones, especially with the baritone and bass saxophones, gives a full sound without the addition of any heavy brass.

Having pointed out the role and advantages of the euphonium, we might discuss briefly the techniques used to achieve these aims.

Euphonium Sound

A firm principle in regard to the sound of an instrument is that a person must be able to hear and recognize good sound before he can hope to produce it. Of course this is difficult in the case of the euphonium as there are very few recorded exponents of the art that can be used for reference. So we will have to fall back on description and definition.

A Good Euphonium Tone

A good euphonium tone will approximate the sound of the cello section of an orchestra or the bass-baritone human voice. It will avoid many of the common faults which have possibly contributed to its decline. It should not be syrupy-sweet but rather should have a fairly robust core of sound without fuzziness. It should not be thin and it should not be hard in timbre. It should not have a consistent, wide vibrato. When the euphonium is used as suggested earlier one special problem develops for the player; he must have the chameleon-like quality to adapt to the tone colours of the moment.

Embouchure

There are many schools of thought on this subject, but as I consider this a very personal thing, no hard and fast rule can be applied. However, I would suggest to beginners that the mouthpiece be placed with the lip line slightly below centre, if this is comfortable.

Blowing the Euphonium

Contrary to some opinion, you must blow *through* a euphonium rather than blow *into* it. There must be a free flow of air from the lungs right through the instrument, supported by the diaphragm as in other wind instruments. There should be no restriction of the throat, a frequent fault resulting in a choked sound. The only restriction the column of air should encounter is the opening of the embouchure and the tongue acting in its capacity as a valve to activate the speaking of sounds. There should be as much freedom of the throat as there is in normal breathing or in the singing of the vowels "oo" or "ah."

Tongueing

As great a variety of attacks is required as on any instrument and for this purpose different syllables are advocated. For a sharp attack use "tu" and for a soft attack use "du." For legato tongueing use a stroking of the upper palate of the mouth by the tip of the tongue much as the movement of the tongue in a soft pronunciation of the word "the."

Vibrato

The vibrato has recently been rehabilitated in school circles after having been renounced, but as far as professional circles are concerned it was never abandoned. A vibrato used with discretion is a very desirable and colourful tool in producing notes that require musical warmth, in contrast to a straight flat sound which can also be very effective in its place. Once a vibrato has been developed one must learn how to use it. It must be controlled to the point where it can be turned on or off, at will. For example, it should never be used when playing with horns or brasses. On the other hand, when the euphonium is playing with a single trumpet or trombone it can be used, conditional upon a unity of thought between the players involved. When used, as suggested earlier, to give sonority to the clarinet line, vibrato would be quite desirable. Perhaps most demanding, however, is its use when the euphonium is playing as a solo instrument for it is here that tasteful discrimination is essential. Certainly some long tones will call for vibrato but some notes or parts of notes in a melodic line can be most effective when played straight. The whole art of vibrato cannot be dictated in cold terms on sheet music. Rather, it has to be applied in the final analysis with feeling and musicianship, which can only come about by studying style and listening to the experts.

Intonation

The extent of and reason for the errors of intonation in valve brass instruments are not generally realized. The principal sources of error are as follows:

1. certain inherent errors of pitch due to the difference of natural harmonic scale and scale of equal temperament;

2. errors due to faulty construction, mainly in the graduation of the bore;

3. errors in pitch from the use of more than one valve in combination.

Of the three reasons listed above, the third is the most serious and, in fact, can cause a note to be as much as half a semitone sharp. It is much harder for a euphonium player to force the note into tune against the natural frequency dictated by the dimensions of the instrument because of the large column of vibrating air. This has been compromised by some manufacturers by lengthening the third valve slide tubing, but the effects of this compromise are as follows:

1. No note involving the use of two or more valves is naturally in tune, and it requires lipping by the player to make it correct.

2. Notes which should be played on third valve for natural intonation have to be played on first and second valves in combination, resulting in a natural error of one-tenth of a semitone sharp which again has to be corrected by the player.

3. The third valve cannot be used alone except in rapid chromatic passages or trills where errors in pitch are not as noticeable.

4. The tone quality of notes played with valves in combination is impaired by this correction or "lipping in."

5. The reduction of the natural error of .52 of a semitone to .2 by compromising the length of third valve tubing is obtained at the expense of spreading a smaller error more widely over the range of the instrument.

These errors have been corrected in one way by an instrument manufacturer who has patented the system and calls it "compensating valves." Correction of these errors by compensation is achieved by adding the appropriate length of tube into the air column whenever two or more valves are used together, controlled from the third valve compensating system. This extra tubing connected to each valve gives us, in effect, a total of 3.85″ to correct the natural error of .52 of a semitone sharp to considerably less.

If the euphonium player has a four valve compensating system he has a great many more advantages at his disposal for intonation, range, and alternate fingerings. The fourth valve, in effect, lowers the fundamentals a fourth from B♭ to F, so in this sense with the fourth valve you have a double horn, thus opening up a whole new series of harmonies, as in the F attachment on a bass trombone. In addition to the ability to play all notes reasonably in tune from the lowest note of E natural down chromatically to the pedal B♭ and the advantage of alternate fingerings in difficult passages, perhaps the best feature of a fourth valve is the fact that the F fundamentals includes the C in its harmonic series which can be played in tune with the fourth valve as an alternate to valves one and three on a B♭ non-compensating instrument. Furthermore, the worst note on B♭ brass instruments, B natural, can be played by a combination of fourth valve (replacing first and third) and second valve, bringing it into tune without any correction on the part of the player. ■

TEACHING THE BRASS

WILLIAM CRAMER

The beginning of each semester brings many young students with newly acquired instruments and a desire to learn how to play them. Unfortunately, too many of these instruments soon begin gathering dust on family shelves, or are sold after a brief, unsuccessful trial. Getting the young people started with correct habits so playing becomes a joy rather than a chore is a constant challenge to instrumental music teachers.

The author once gave a clinical demonstration over a six-day period using six boys who had never before played any wind instrument. The boys were all from the fourth, fifth, and sixth grades. The results of this demonstration were so successful that the methods of the approach are presented.

Free Flow of Air

The students were placed in a single line with ample space for walking between them. They sat erect, away from the backs of their chairs, and were constantly checked for good posture. A handkerchief was held about two feet in front of each student; they were then, in turn, encouraged to blow at the handkerchief vigorously. The idea here was to fix the attention outside the student and prevent him from setting up certain internal constrictions (particularly in the throat) which would prevent a free flow of air.

Cornet mouthpieces were introduced and the boys were asked to blow at the handkerchief through the wrong end of the mouthpiece. The mouthpieces were compared to bean-shooters. The wrong end of the mouthpiece was used because it offered less resistance and also because it gave a feeling of forming an open embouchure. The handkerchief remained in evidence to focus the attention outside the body and to remind them that the breath does the work.

Open Throat

At this point the boys were instructed to breathe so the teacher could not see them do it. This eliminated breathing by elevating the shoulders. They were also instructed to inhale so that it could not be heard. This caused them to open their throats wider.

The blowing at the handkerchief was then continued with the students using the proper end of the mouthpiece. Further references were made to good posture and quiet breathing.

The mouthpieces were placed in the cornets and the tuning slides removed. Blowing at the handkerchief continued—the bean-shooter was just a little longer. Sounds were permitted when the buzzing came by accident, but discouraged when intentionally made by pursing the lips. The emphasis at this point was still on getting a free, uninhibited blow through the instrument and showing that the breath was doing the work.

The boys were told that they had neither nose nor tongue; that is, they were not permitted to breathe through their noses, nor to articulate with the tongue. Each boy's nose was held to encourage him to inhale more deeply through the mouth and to find out if he were allowing air to escape through his nose. If air were leaking through the nose he would complain of an uncomfortable sensation in the nose or ears.

Psychological Motivation

Tuning slides were replaced and the boys encouraged to blow vigorously at will. Loud full sounds were forthcoming. It is much easier to keep the throat open and the tongue down when blowing loudly. The handkerchief was draped on the bell of each instrument in turn. It is almost impossible to move the handkerchief with the breath, but the psychological motivation is evident and even dramatic.

This first operation takes no more than ten minutes.

The instructor is constantly moving back and forth, working with each boy in turn, so that they try to outdo each other no matter what the momentary operation might be.

They were encouraged to do everything they could to keep their cheeks from puffing, but not by the teacher's insisting or demanding. At this age, they may not have sufficient muscle strength to keep the cheeks from puffing. The neuromuscular structure is still developing toward maturity and this common fault is usually due to immaturity rather than lack of practice.

Value Numbers

Having successfully sounded their first fully resonant tones, the boys were shown how to remove the second, the first, and then the third slide valves. They were instructed to sound the horn with the matching valve depressed so they could see that depressing the valve allowed for the addition of tubing. After the slides were replaced, the numbers 0, 2, 1, 3, were placed on the blackboard and the students asked to make one long sound while they depressed the valves in that order. This was then changed to 0, 2, 1, 12, 23, 13, 123, to show how the valves changed the pitch with a minimum adjustment in the embouchure. Correct right hand position was achieved by telling the boys to shape the hand as though they were holding a ball.

Practically no mention was made of embouchure formation. On previous occasions where this procedure had been followed, it was found that the student's embouchure always aligned itself correctly while he was focusing his attention on blowing. The lips assumed a position which would allow the freest vibration in response to the generated air column. There was no fumbling around for the right groove. The same thing held true with this demonstration.

Avoiding Notation

Having followed the principle of forming the embouchure around the moving airstream, we were reasonably sure that the immediate playing range would be from low C to middle G, and up to middle C at the most. Fingerings for the tune "Mary Had a Little Lamb" were then placed on the board in the following manner:
12, 13, 0, 13, 12, 12, 12,—13, 13, 13,—12, 0, 0, etc.

The boys played it straight off with no difficulty. They had had a successful experience on the first try with the instrument. They knew the melody and the rhythm and the fingerings as written had immediate meaning. To demonstrate to those assembled for the clinic just how much of the beginning problem involves reading and translation of the symbols into doing, the entire tune was then transposed to C# without telling the boys: 1, 23, 123, 23, 1, 1, 1,—23, 23, 23,—1, 23, 23, etc. Again the performance went off well.

The boys then copied the fingerings for this tune in C, C#, and D, and were sent home with instructions to play whatever they wished before the next session, but to remember what they had been taught.

Checking Students

The second session began with a review of the work done the day before. Each student was checked in turn to make sure that he was getting a full, resonant sound according to the previous instructions.

The boys were aware from the repeated notes in the first tune they had learned, that they had to have some means of articulation other than just taking a breath and blowing each note in turn. Accordingly, they were asked to play several long G's in a row to again establish the feel of blowing freely. Then they were instructed to use the syllable *tah* when sounding each note. This was prefaced by several trials without the instrument, and then on the instrument. Several simple rote rhythmic patterns were then tried on G, F, E, D, and C. The trials were successful insofar as each boy produced a well-resonated sound with a decisive attack and there seemed to be no closure of the throat. If any difficulty in articulating with the tongue had occurred, it could have been helped by playing the rhythmic patterns without articulating the first note and articulating all the other notes according to the instructions.

Questioning indicated that the boys had some idea of scales, so the fingerings for an ascending C scale were placed on the board. After playing this through several times, the rote rhythmic patterns were played on each degree of the scale.

Articulation

The fingerings for "Twinkle, Twinkle, Little Star" were placed on the board and the same procedure followed in playing this tune as the day before, with the exception that each note was articulated. The tune was then written in C, C#, and D.

Succeeding days were spent in carefully re-establishing each of the techniques, and then combining them in all their possible variations. Slurred diatonic passages were alternated with articulated rhythmic patterns. Simple tunes which the boys knew well were written out (by fingerings alone) and played in all the keys which would keep the playing range between low Bb and fourth-line D.

Rote to Note

Under normal circumstances, where the class meets daily, this procedure would have been continued for about four weeks or until the students had run out of tunes which they knew by ear or expressed a desire to read music. The transition from rote to note would be made by first notating on the board certain rhythmic patterns they had used. They would then play them on each degree of the scale. When it became apparent that the students had a fair grasp of note values whole melodies would be presented in notation. These melodies would be those they had already played, so that this symbolism would represent sounds they had previously produced. The fingerings can be written under each note and gradually erased as the associations are established. The student learns that each note on the staff has many different meanings such as a letter name, a syllable name, a sounded pitch, a duration, a fingering on the instrument, etc.

It is of primary importance that the young student acquire a feel for the instrument before he tries to read complicated directions from the printed page. The instrument and student must become a single unit, each working for and with the other.

Summary

In summary, the following principles are those used in developing teaching techniques necessary for working with young beginners on wind instruments:

1. The breath is the motivating force. Establish its forceful presence and then bring it under control at its source. The breath is something to be *used*, not something to be bottled up under pressure inside the body.

2. Good posture is a means for improving the efficiency of breathing and blowing but is not an end in itself. An erect position will elevate the rib-cage so the diaphragm and abdominal muscles can do their work properly. It will also aid in opening up the windpipe.

3. The windpipe is a means for conveying the air from the lungs to the lips. The passage must not be unnecessarily constricted by the vocal cords, glottis, uvula, tongue, teeth, or lips.

4. The embouchure is formed around the moving airstream. The lips vibrate freely in response to this airstream. Forming the embouchure before blowing may lead to using the lips for articulation and necessitate either blowing or pulling the lips apart before the tone can be produced.

5. The natural function of the hand is grasping. The greatest sensitivity is in the fingertips. *Hold* the instrument in the left hand and *operate* it with the right hand. *Feel* it through the fingertips. Place the right thumb between the first and second valve casings so that it will *balance* the fingers in their work.

6. The tongue is an articulative device and cannot initiate sound. The tongue must articulate something and the only thing it can articulate is the airstream. Blowing must precede tonguing in the early stages. Reversal of the process leads to throat closures which may be used either to control the free flow of breath or for articulation.

7. At this age, the playing range is directly related to the player's age or level of maturity. Range cannot be extended materially by practice alone. Practice for the sake of increasing muscle strength, playing range, or dexterity is most successful when started about the middle of the seventh grade.

8. Reading and the translation of new symbols is a problem so complex that it may prevent the young student from forming good physical habits for playing an instrument. Where possible, reduce the problems of performance to single basic principles and develop them firmly before combining them into more complex problems. Reading should be avoided until the student has a fair control over the mechanics of blowing and operating the instrument.

9. A rhythmic pattern is a single unit in the experience of the student. Introduce these patterns as units, rather than building up the pattern from note values.

10. At this age, practice and playing are done for the purpose of widening the student's musical experiences and understanding, within the limits of his immediate physical potential for performance, and for enjoyment. Keep his interest alive by showing him how to make music. ■

A TRUMPET PHILOSOPHY

Donald Whitaker

I shall start by outlining my philosophy of teaching the trumpet or cornet. I make no distinction between them when I am teaching, as the fundamentals of breathing, tonguing, embouchure, etc. apply to both equally well. Both of them are usually pitched in B♭, as this is by far the most common key. Some orchestral trumpeters use C instruments as a general rule, possibly also having B and D, or even higher pitched instruments for certain works.

As on all brass instruments, one has to take in air and then expel it in a controlled manner to start the lips vibrating, which in turn starts the air column outlined by the instrument vibrating. There are only seven combinations possible, since there are only three valves on the trumpet. Each combination can produce at least seven different notes, so it is up to the player to select which of those seven notes he is going to play with the proper combination of embouchure setting and breath speed. This he usually learns to do rather quickly but with quite a percentage of error. Then we spend the rest of our lives reducing that percentage to a satisfactory minimum! It's rather like the garden hose when you are watering the garden—to go farther out (or higher), you can increase the water pressure by turning the faucet on more, thereby getting more velocity from the same size opening in the hose; or, you can put your thumb on the end of the hose and reduce the size of the opening, getting more velocity from the same water pressure. In playing, I think we do both—we reduce the size of the embouchure opening somewhat and increase the air pressure to get more velocity from the air; this causes the lips and the air column to vibrate faster and produce a higher note. An important thing to remember is that there is always a certain minimum air pressure necessary to

sustain a tone, even when coming down in register or dynamics or both. A reasonably erect posture is necessary to make full use of the abdominal muscles in controlling the air flow, but the most important thing here is not to get tight. West Point posture can be just as bad as a slouch. If the posture from the waist up is good, it should make no difference in playing whether a student stands or sits. Of course, clothing should be comfortable—a tight collar or waist can inhibit the best player. The throat should stay relaxed and the tongue down as much as possible.

Moving to the embouchure, the mouthpiece should usually be close to centered, up and down and side to side. Slight variations are not important and it is only when the embouchure is considerably off center that it might cause more problems than it would solve.

Evenness of teeth is nice to look at but not particularly important —one of my best students has teeth that look like they were put in by a shotgun at ten paces. Thickness of the lips is usually not too important either. Dental-facial structure is also not too important unless there is a serious lower jaw problem—either receding or protruding. I believe in the pucker system for changing register, with as little additional pressure in the left hand as possible. (Sometimes at the end of a concert there has to be more than when the lip is fresh.) This system merely reduces the size of the tone hole by bringing the lips in toward the center slightly. This is the only motion that one should see in the embouchure at any time, except for the possible exception of a slight dropping of the lower jaw for the very low register. When working on this with students, I find a cutaway mouthpiece a big help. I think that it reproduces actual playing conditions more exactly than the usual visualizer.

The tongue is the third link in the chain of events and it acts as a valve to meter the air flow into longer or shorter notes, add variety to the music by legato or accented attack, and occasionally add a slur. Usually it should be placed back of the upper teeth, on or near the gumline, depending on the length of the tongue and dental arch. The important thing here is to get a good seal and be able to stop the air completely. The actual act of tonguing, of course, is in the release of the air, and any reasonably long note is stopped by the action of the abdominal muscles. In rapid tonguing, for all practical purposes, the start of the second note is the end of the first. The placement of the tongue should not change at any time, for high or low register, slow or fast notes, legato or staccato attack. It should move as little as possible, especially on rapid tonguing passages.

I favor the hand vibrato for trumpet over any other method because I think it is more reliable and controllable. If properly used, it can add a great deal to the beauty of a tone and to the performer's versatility. Usually it should not exceed a fourth of a tone in breadth and it should oscillate about six times a second. A skillful player can shade this, however, to brighten the effect of a crescendo or accelerando, etc. I would usually not teach it until the basic tone is solid and pure, perhaps two or three years after a person has started the instrument.

There are many fine instruments on the market today and the choice a person has to make is largely confined to the tone color and the response one likes. For the beginner, the teacher will probably pick the instrument, so I would advise a medium bore (about .460) and one that has an easy response. Check to make sure everything works, especially the 3rd valve slide, as the use of this in tuning the low D and $D\flat$ should be taught early. I usually do not use anything smaller than a 7C *mouth-piece*, and I like to see a student have as big a mouthpiece as he can handle. I think this gives him greater possibility for dynamic response and he *has* to blow to get the upper register!

I think that a player should be versatile and know how to play in a band, orchestra, ensemble, etc. and have as much experience with styles as possible. However, if I had to pin down the basic style of playing that I use, prefer, and teach, I would have to say that it

would be basically a lyric, or sing-ing, approach to the instrument. With young students, a little theory goes a long way and you have to go about this concept business gradually. On the other end of the scale, college students in a tech-nique class or minoring in an instrument shouldn't try to become virtuosos, but should concentrate on comparing stylistic approaches and forming a solid concept of their own. I think it is important to have a concept of how they want their trumpets or cornets to sound and then work to get it.

To help in hearing and forming

concepts of trumpet and cornet styles, there are a number of recordings available. One of the best is by Armando Ghitalla, from the Boston Symphony, playing the Hummel *Concerto in E*, with the late Pierre Monteux conducting. Others from the orchestral field include Roger Voisin, Helmut Wobisch, Paulo Longinotti, Eugene Blee, Adolph Scherbaum, and George Eskdale. Others who play on both cornet and trumpet are John Haynie, Leonard Smith, and Jimmy Burke. In the more popular vein are Raphael Mendez, Bram Smith, and Charles Margulis. ∎

December, 1966

THE ROLE OF THE GLOTTIS

IN

BRASS PLAYING

William Carter

The field of brass teaching is full of old arguments relating to such subjects as the proper way to achieve maximum breath support, whether or not to use a variable tongue level for changes of register, whether or not the diaphragm should change position for changes of register, and others.

Such questions, being of a phys-iological nature, are not likely to be properly answered by musicians. In fact, they aren't likely to be answered by the physiologists ei-ther, for physiologists have had no reason to direct their research toward problems of this sort. The intention of the writer in under-taking this research project has been to thoroughly investigate just one of these often misunderstood areas in hopes of dispelling some of the mystery shrouding breathing

and breath control problems. As is often the case, however, more ques-tions have been *raised* by this in-vestigation than have been an-swered. It is the *answers* with which this article is concerned, however. To fully discuss the ques-tions raised by this project would require another article of some length.

A major controversy centers about the methods to be used in controlling the air stream as it leaves the lungs and eventually passes through the vibrating lips of the brass player. This area is generally placed under the large heading, "breath control."

"Breath control" in brass play-ing becomes especially critical at low loudness levels. In this type of playing the player is called upon

to maintain an extremely fine de-gree of control over the airstream.

Some authorities believe that this control can be achieved by means of the simplest possible relation-ship between the player's dia-phragm and his vibrating embou-chure, while others just as strongly state that the base of the tongue should be used as an additional point of resistance.

By far the most controversial stand on this subject has been that first stated by Philip Farkas in his book "The Art of French Horn Playing,"[1] and again, in more detail, in "The Art of Brass Playing".[2] He set forth a theory which stated that the first point of resistance is found in the throat, at a point called the glottis.

His description of the glottis as

425

the opening that exists between the vocal folds (cords) is consistent with those found in standard physiological sources.

Farkas led up to his theory by discussing the importance of *resistance* during exhalation, and illustrated the function of resistance in brass playing by pointing out that ". . . resistance is what gives *steadiness* to the hissing sound of a "slow leak" in an automobile tire; tire "blow-out" is the result of all resistance giving way."[3] He stated that,

> The real danger of blowing a brass instrument incorrectly occurs during soft passages. At such times, the player has the choice of simply pushing very lightly with the diaphragm and letting the air *drift* through an open, unresisting passage, or of pushing *quite firmly* with the diaphragm, but *holding back* this stronger air-column to the desired volume by resisting the air somewhere. I do not believe that a large, strong muscle like the diaphragm has enough finesse to *float* a very soft pianissimo through the instrument with a great degree of steadiness. On the other hand, the moderately heavy push which I advocate . . . . can be converted to an extremely steady *pianissimo* by holding it back with resistance.[4]

Farkas further clarified his concept of resistance by the use of the following analogy:

> If one wished to trickle a tiny stream of cold water into his too hot cup of coffee, he could phone the pumping station and request it to slow down the pumps, then proceed to turn the faucet on full force. This would possibly result in the desired trickle. But, with the pumps slowed down or stopped, the trickle would be anything but steady. However, the thing that amuses us with this idea is the incongruity of doing a simple act the "hard way." How much easier and simpler to let the pumps go ahead in their efficient way and simply "crackopen" the faucet a tiny bit, until the desired trickle appears. Not only is it easier and faster, but the trickle has an entirely different character. It does not dribble, flood and drip by turns, but forms a little rod of water, firm and steady. Even its diameter is completely controllable.
>
> In just the same way, the steady diaphragm pressure against a "cracked-open" air column lets through a firm steady rod of air of any diameter desired.[5]

The logic of Farkas' argument is extremely powerful and his theory commands even more respect through his fine reputation as performer, teacher, and writer. All that remains to make Farkas' theory a definitive contribution to the art-science of brass teaching is *proof* based upon systematic research.

Extensive reading of both musical and physiological sources encouraged the writer to pursue the subject further, for the physiology references showed the glottis to have a very active role in the regulation of respiration by exerting an obstructive influence on the air current.

It was decided, on the basis of this evidence, to undertake systematic proof of Farkas' theory and to explore its implications.

The Method

The problem, of course, was to find some practical way to observe the glottis during the process of playing a brass instrument. Laryngoscopic examination was impossible because the laryngoscope is introduced through the open mouth.

The search for a practical method of observing the glottis began with a discussion with Dr. Atis Friemanis of the radiology department of the Ohio State University Hospital.

Preliminary X-ray photos, taken under Dr. Freimanis's supervision, of the writer's throat area while playing trombone showed dramatic evidence of glottis size variation in changes of dynamic level from loud to soft.

This led to the development of a method in which X-ray photos were taken of brass player's glottis areas under *four* different playing conditions: (1) a loud high note, (2) a soft high note, (3) a loud low note, and (4) a soft low note.

Pictures were taken of four players on each of three orchestral brass instruments; trombone, French horn, and trumpet. X-ray photos could not be taken of tuba players, because the tubing crosses directly in front of the throat area.

Measurements were then made from the X-ray films by the use of a divider. The glottis was measured at its narrowest point, and the trachea (windpipe) was measured at its widest point. The ratio of *glottis opening* to *trachea width* was the comparative measure used in this investigation. This method was used in order to eliminate a variable magnification factor caused by small differences of distance between the X-ray plate and the throat area, and to allow comparisons from one player to another.

Other variable factors were controlled by the following means:

Pitch extremes were very conservative (see Fig. 1) in order to avoid the use of any unusual physical techniques by the players.

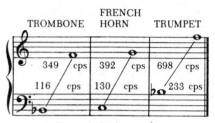

Figure 1. Pitches used.

Variable resistance factors were minimized by having all players play on large-bore instruments with large mouthpieces. All tones to be played were chosen because of their availability on the open harmonic series of the instruments.

Pitch level was carefully controlled by the use of a Strobo-tuner.

Loudness level was controlled by the use of a Conn Dynalevel loudness level meter.

The subjects chosen for this study were outstanding brass players in the Ohio State University School of Music. They were chosen mainly on the basis of their ability to produce and control a good legitimate tone quality. Prior to the X-ray sessions, they were told only that their throat area was being observed.

Conclusions

The Glottis and Dynamic Level—Visual examination of the X-ray photos indicated a definite pattern of glottis size variation. Out of 24 comparisons (two per subject) there were only three (involving two players) which were contrary to this pattern. Twenty-one out of 24 comparisons showed a smaller glottis opening for soft tones than for loud tones.

Statistical analysis of the measured data (see Figs. 2 and 3) shows that the findings reported here, although based upon observations of only 12 players, bear a high degree of statistical significance. In other words, the possibility of the pattern observed here being *chance* is extremely small.

In summary, the data compiled show that in the playing of brass instruments, the size of the glottis opening varies with loudness level, being small for soft playing and large for loud playing.

The Glottis and Pitch—The data show that there is no practical difference in glottis opening from the high to the low register, indicating that *pitch control, within the normal playing register, can be discarded as a possible function of the variable glottis aperture.*

Differences in Glottis Use Within the Orchestral Brasses—(See Fig. 2) The marked differences, along the vertical axis, apparent among the different brass instruments, show, in brief, that the trombonists tested used the glottis to a greater extent than the trumpet players, and that the French hornists used it to a lesser extent than either the trumpet players or the trombonists.

The Glottis and Resistance—Allowing the assumption that trombones offer less blowing resistance than do trumpets, which in turn offer less resistance than French horns, the data obtained support a theory describing the glottis as a semi-automatic aperture used to provide more resistance to aid the diaphragm and its related muscu-lature in controlling the inward and upward contraction of the abdominal muscles upon exhalation.

For example, using the median figures for trombone players, the .409 glottis opening used for a very loud high note would allow the passage of the comparatively large amounts of air necessary for the production of such tones. Breath control is not a factor here so much as is pushing power in the abdominal muscles. Additional blowing resistance is neither needed nor desired.

However, the .086 glottis opening used for *soft* high notes is more or less necessary, depending upon the degree of control the player has over the muscles used for adjusting resistance to the contracting abdominal muscles. The very small amounts of air necessary for the production of such tones encountered little resistance from the large-bore trombones and large mouthpieces used exclusively in this investigation, so the glottis valve was partly closed to provide more resistance to the air stream, thus relieving the diaphragm and its related musculature of some of its responsibility in controlling the airstream.

The relative inactivity of the glottis in French horn playing is most likely due to the high degree of built-in resistance found in the French horn. The small mouthpiece, very narrow mouthpipe bore, and the lengthy and complex tubing all combine to provide a good deal of impedance to the airstream, which makes the job of the diaphragm and its controls so much easier that variation of the size of the glottis opening becomes almost unnecessary. Variation of the glottis opening for purposes of tone quality is another matter and will be discussed elsewhere.

A set of X-ray photographs was taken of a flutist to see if blowing an instrument that provides no resistance to the airstream would result in an even more active role for the glottis. The figures obtained showed the glottis to be almost completely closed under all conditions; the opening being only slightly larger for loud tones.

Implications for Teaching and Performance—The data have confirmed a statement of Philip Farkas' that "the proper use of the glottis is natural and effective and is quite likely being used by most successful brass players either consciously or subconsciously."[6]

It is at this point that extreme

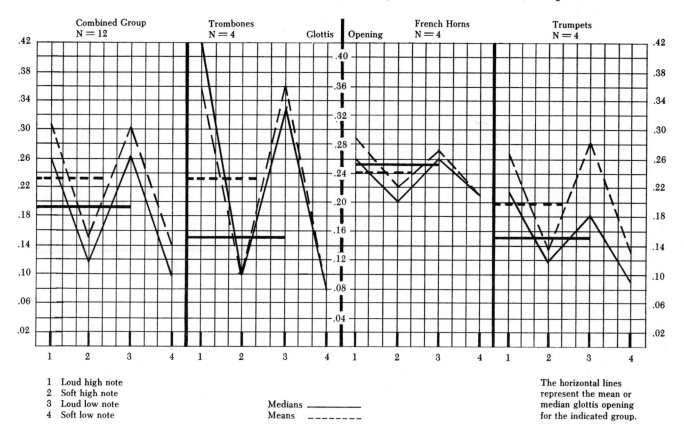

1 Loud high note
2 Soft high note
3 Loud low note
4 Soft low note

Medians ——————
Means - - - - - - -

The horizontal lines represent the mean or median glottis opening for the indicated group.

Figure 2. Changes in ratio of glottis opening with changes of loudness and pitch.

caution must be exercised in evaluating the meaning and significance of the findings. To conclude that soft notes should be played with a smaller glottis opening than loud notes would be premature, for this study has not attempted to provide that kind of an answer to the controversy over the glottis.

In a project of this sort it is rather easy to forget that the subject matter falls into the realm of *music*. With musical values as the primary consideration, a playing technique such as the use of glottis resistance for soft tones must be evaluated in large part on the basis of *tone quality*. Such an evaluation is beyond the scope of this study.

However, the fact remains that there are perceivable differences in tone quality between those tones produced with a partially closed glottis and an open glottis. These differences are large enough to provide a basis for disagreement among qualified authorities as to which sound is the best legitimate

sound. This sort of problem is perhaps best solved in the teaching studio, where the subjective judgement of the brass teacher is, quite properly, the vital element in the teaching process.

Physiology texts say that the glottis widens during quiet inhalation and narrows during exhalation. These movements are said to become more marked during *forced* respiration. *The implication here is extremely important.* Breathing while playing a brass instrument at a high loudness level must certainly be classified as "forced" breathing, in contrast to the involuntary type of breathing used when the body is at rest or in quiet activity. If there is a marked narrowing of the glottis during forced exhalation, the glottis must certainly tend to narrow during the playing of loud tones on a brass instrument! An examination of Fig. 3 will reveal that individual differences between players were much greater for loud tones than for soft

tones. Some players opened up a great deal for loud tones, and some very little. This indicates that some players have had more success than others in learning, probably unconsciously, to *overcome* the natural tendancy of the glottis to narrow during the blowing of loud tones. The glottis is subject to both involuntary and voluntary control, so such an accomplishment is quite feasible. The writer has developed a high degree of conscious control of his glottis through the practicing of various glottis exercises. This sort of awareness can eliminate some of the element of chance in brass teaching by giving teacher and pupil a tool that attacks certain aspects of the problem of tone quality and breath control directly at their source.

Fig. 4. Front sectional view of the glottis at rest. (simplified)

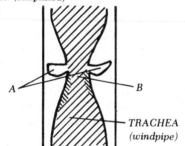

A.   Ventricles
B.   Point at which glottis opening was measured

It is the writers' contention that the forte or fortissimo sound brass teachers have in mind when they stress playing with an "open throat" is in fact the sound their students get when and if they learn to play their loud tones with an open glottis (assuming everything is normal as far as embouchure, instrument, and mouthpiece are concerned).

It is quite possible that an intensive approach, utilizing exercises designed to develop conscious control of the glottis, could significantly accelerate the development in student brass players of an acceptable, legitimate tone production; a process which can sometimes require years of effort.

Figure 3.

RATIO OF GLOTTIS OPENING TO WIDTH OF TRACHEA* OF EACH SUBJECT UNDER VARYING CONDITIONS OF PITCH AND LOUDNESS

Subject Number	Loud High Note (1)	Soft High Note (2)	Loud Low Note (3)	Soft Low Note (4)	Range
Trombones					
2	.166	.078	.208	.073	.135
7	.465	.035	.360	.139	.430
12	.354	.135	.312	.042	.312
13	.530	.095	.580	.080	.500
French Horns					
4	.171	.114	.211	.143	.100
5	.447	.255	.319	.026	.420
9	.250	.136	.250	.273	.136
10	.273	.352	.273	.386	.114
Trumpets					
3	.489	.300	.600	.255	.233
6	.138	.021	.159	.074	.138
8	.144	.100	.155	.100	.055
11	.274	.113	.208	.066	.208
Others**					
Bass Trombone					
1	.436	.141	.192	.500	.359
Flute					
14	.044	.133	.066	.044	.088

* As measured at its widest point during the blowing of a loud high note.

** Not included in the statistical analysis.

[1]Philip Farkas, *The Art of French Horn Playing* (Chicago: Clayton F. Summy Co., 1956)
[2]Philip Farkas, *The Art of Brass Playing* (Bloomington, Ind.: Brass Publications, 1963)
[3]Ibid., p. 61
[4]Ibid., p. 61
[5]Ibid., p. 61
[6]Ibid., p. 62

December, 1966

HOW TO SELECT A BRASS MOUTHPIECE

Renold Schilke

Many directors and teachers of brass, not to mention their students, have strong convictions about the brand name of the instrument used but tend to neglect the importance of the proper mouthpiece. One should bear in mind that the mouthpiece which comes with an instrument may or may not be suitable for a particular player. In truth, every player should use a mouthpiece specifically adapted to him and his instrument. Proper embouchure development, correct breath control, and a good instrument are all important, but let us not neglect a most important variable—the mouthpiece.

In selecting the best mouthpiece one needs to consider the player's teeth, jaw, size, and shape of the lips (thickness and width), as well as the strength of the embrochure, the desired tone quality, ease of playing the upper and lower range, endurance, intonation, and the type of playing done most of the time.

All teachers and players of brass instruments, both professional and amateur, will benefit much by understanding the various parts or surfaces of a brass mouthpiece and what function each has. Only then can one make intelligent and practical recommendations as to which mouthpiece will produce the desired results with a particular player.

Though a medium width cup diameter, rim thickness, rim contour, backbore, cup-depth, volume, and shape may be recommended for the average player, as a general rule it is desirable to encourage players to use larger sizes as the embouchure develops. A larger cup diameter and cup volume allows more of the lip to vibrate, which in turn produces a fuller and more resonant tone and, in addition, encourages more lip control and endurance. The location of the high point of the contour is another variable that should be kept in mind; this changes the feel of the width of the cup.

The sharpness of the edge of the rim or the "bite" affects both flexibility and precision of attack and is also important.

A small or shallow cup produces the brightest sound and aids in playing high notes, while a large, deep cup aids in producing the lower tones and produces a richer darker sound. The high note craze of some students, especially when high notes are forced or squeezed and often produced on too small a mouthpiece, is to be discouraged. The player with thick lips should choose a somewhat deeper or larger cup to compensate for the extra space his lips take up inside the cup.

A player who needs some help in the upper range should experiment using a shallower first cup with a widened second cup. The shallow first cup facilitates the playing of the upper register while the widened second cup promotes a fuller and richer tone. As the bottom of the cup becomes flatter one's attack improves, but the quality of tone becomes somewhat coarser. The

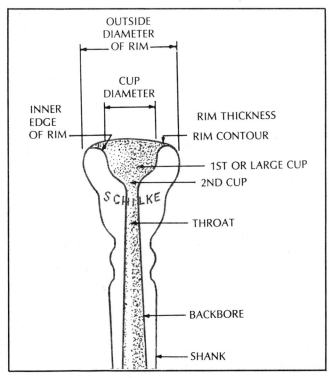

more the cup shape becomes conical the better is the quality of sound, but as this is accentuated the tone may become too dark.

A sharp rim contour permits greater lip flexibility but tends to reduce endurance. (Obviously, the amount of pressure on the lips is an important consideration too.) The flattest rim contour feels the most comfortable but tends to hold the lips somewhat immobile, thereby reducing lip flexibility. For most players a judicious compromise in rim contour is suggested using a mouthpiece which has a reasonable rim curvature to provide flexibility but with sufficient surface to improve endurance.

An average size throat (the narrowest part of the mouthpiece opening) is also preferred for the average player. However, with added embouchure development a somewhat larger throat should be tried.

Many brass teachers, students, and mouthpiece manufacturers tend to neglect the importance of the backbore. It is not unusual to find mouthpieces which are superior in every respect except the backbore. Players frequently examine the mouthpiece with great care from the top but never really examine the backbore. Part of the trouble is that the backbore is not so readily visible to the eye, but probably the more important reason is a lack of understanding of the importance of the shape of the backbore.

There is no substitute for the careful analysis of a player's needs, both physical and musical. Some experimentation in testing is encouraged. But the continuous seeking of the "perfect" mouthpiece is certain to produce only frustration.

Lack of controls in the manufacture of mouthpieces has been found through extensive testing of mouthpieces. Some manufacturers do not hold tolerances very well. It is for this reason that marked differences can be found within the same mouthpiece category of the same manufacturer, so much so that often two mouthpieces labeled differently are more alike than two which are labeled the same. This variance is often particularly noticeable when comparing the same mouthpiece made in different years. (Shapers are sharpened, and to sharpen them some metal has to be removed. Thus, a change in dimensions.) It should be mentioned that small differences in dimensions, too small to be discerned by the naked eye, *can* be discerned by a discriminating player with special measuring tools.

Since it is impossible to keep dirt from coagulating in a mouthpiece, and since any dirt especially in the throat and backbore interferes with intonation and playing ease, it is imperative to keep the mouthpiece clean. A mouthpiece brush should be used every week.

December, 1966

When a player wishes a better mouthpiece, I usually ask him several questions. What mouthpiece are you now using? What difficulty, if any, do you have with that mouthpiece? In what direction do you want to go? A change of tone color? Increased range? Better intonation? Increased endurance? The answers to these questions determine what new mouthpiece(s) should be used.

It is not unusual for a performer to be completely satisfied with a particular rim and cup he is using but wish a different tone quality. In this case it is a simple matter to duplicate the desired rim and cup exactly (regardless of make) and adjust the throat or backbone and provide him with a custom mouthpiece.

In selecting a brass mouthpiece one should strive for optimum tone quality and accurate intonation rather than ease of hitting the high notes, unless the latter is an absolute "must." Often the best possible mouthpiece is an intelligent compromise. Every teacher and player should strive for the optimum combination of the major variables. As with many things in life, there's more to a fine brass mouthpiece than meets the eye. ■

ADOLPHE SAX — INVENTOR
THE SAXHORN FAMILY

John Burnau

The saxhorn was an outgrowth of the keyed bugle of 1810. Soon after 1810 both cornets and trumpets were the recipients of piston valves. The cornet of this period was known as the Cornopienan.[1] In the middle of the nineteenth century this instrument had quite a vogue in the form of the saxhorn.

The saxhorn family was developed by Adolphe Sax in 1842. There are seven members in the family, from a high soprano in $E\flat$ to a contrabass in $B\flat$. In bore they were all conical, and their tone is especially mellow and of a song-like quality. The saxhorn mouthpiece is a deep and bell-shaped cup mouthpiece. The members of the saxhorn family are: $E\flat$ soprano, $B\flat$ soprano, $E\flat$ alto, $B\flat$ tenor, $B\flat$ baritone, $E\flat$ bass, $B\flat$ contrabass.

In 1845 Sax took out a patent for the family of saxhorns. With the invention of the saxhorn family the miscellaneous serpents, ophicleides, bombardons and other odd tenor, baritone, and bass instruments faded out of the picture. "As Haydn sounded the death knoll to the rabble of instruments through his orchestrating, so Adolphe Sax silenced the Tower of Babel through his instrument making."[2]

Besides organizing the voices of the cup-mouthpiece instruments into a logical and limited number of instruments, Sax also made a contribution to a new tonal color. Saxhorns are characterized by a conical bore of wide taper and a mouthpiece which is deep and bell-shaped. This construction results in a distinct tonal color which is round, mellow, and on the dark side of the tonal spectrum. In this country we hardly know what this tonal color is like. Our instruments have a straighter bore and are more brilliant in color. The tapered bore

is still used in Italy, France, and England. "The effect of a lot of these saxhorns playing together suggests a great pipe organ, because the tone is so full and mellow."[3]

Our so-called conical bore instruments, the cornet and the baritone horn, are more like another family of instruments invented and named by Sax the saxtrombas, than the saxhorns. The saxtromba, instead of having a conical bore, had a bore more like that of the cornet; that is they were only conical in part of their length, the rest of the bore being cylindrical. The saxtrombas used smaller tubing, about one third of which was straight, or cylindrical, the other two-thirds being conical. Adherents of the saxhorns maintained that the saxtrombas were so nearly like trumpets and trombones as to lack contrast necessary for the best musical effects.[4] American bands today seldom make any attempt to have balanced choirs of conical and cylindrical brasses.

A recent use of the saxhorn occurs in the movie, *Up from the Beach*. This production, depicting happenings in the Normandy, France area on June 6, 1944, presents the saxhorn in a town band of six amateur musicians who greet the American soldiers with sincere but abominable renditions of the "Marseillaise" and the "Star Spangled Banner." The sound track seems to have made use of an authentic saxhorn that provided the quality of tone described in this chapter. The saxhorn used in the scenes appeared to be the $E\flat$ alto. ■

1 H. S. Schwartz, *The Story of Musical Instruments* (New York: Garden City Publishing Co., Inc., 1943) p. 240
2 *Ibid.*, p. 240.
3 *Ibid.*
4 *Ibid.*, p. 180.

1967

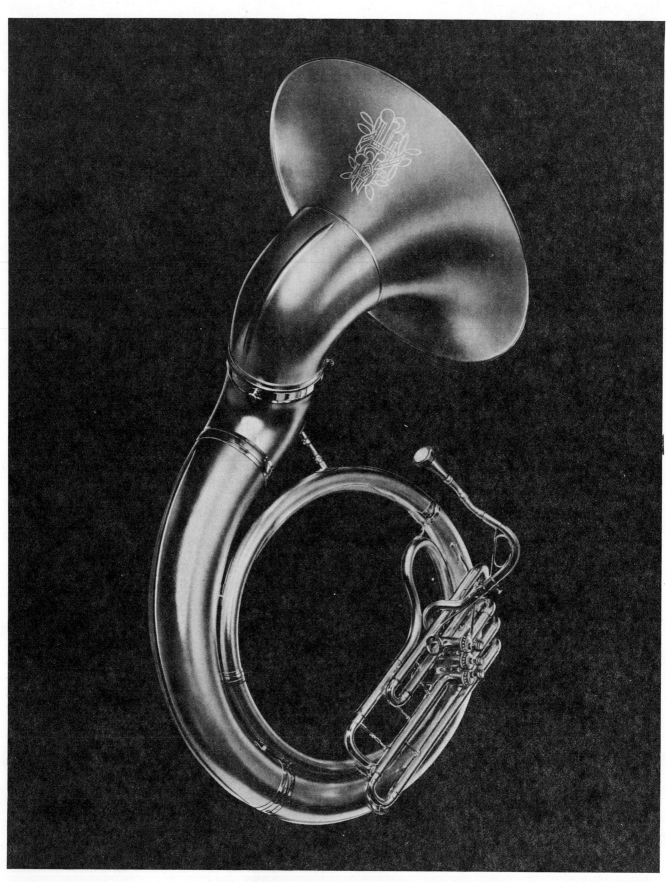

BB♭ Sousaphone (Metal)

FOR BETTER HORN PLAYERS

C. Robert Crain

The adaptability of the French horn to the diversified uses of music today is being exploited by many composers and arrangers, and this, without doubt, is one reason that the horn has become such a popular instrument among students in instrumental music classes in our schools. As professional musicians and teachers, it is our responsibility to see that beginning horn students, as well as our "experienced" high school band and orchestra members, learn and develop correct approaches to French horn playing. Following are some suggestions and observations concerning the development of solid embouchures among young horn players:

Playing Position

Before suggesting that a student begin playing the French horn, carefully consider the size of the student. He (or she) should be large enough to handle the horn comfortably without distorting the embouchure and causing an awkward playing position. Too many times one sees a junior high school or high school horn player whose embouchure has been distorted because the instrument was too large for the player as a beginner or because the student developed bad playing habits in rehearsals. In many cases this has been the fault of the director; he has not insisted on a correct playing position at all times. The following suggestions, which are concerned with the correct playing position, can help to develop a solid horn embouchure:
1. Insist that your horn players arrange their chairs in such a position that they can look directly down the mouthpipe of the horn to the music and can see the director at the same time. How important this correct chair arrangement is! Young embouchures are easily distorted simply because the player has to look to one side or the other to see the music and doesn't realize that all he needs to do is change the position of the chair to have a comfortable and correct playing position. Looking to the right or left to see the music, the player will gradually turn his head toward the music stand and will fail to make any compensation with the position of the horn. If the player has to look to the left, the mouthpiece position will gradually slip to the right of the lips, or to the left side of the lips if the music is to his right. Why not just adjust the position of the music stand in relation to the chair and develop correct and potentially strong young embouchures?

2. I have observed bad playing positions among junior high and high school horn players, caused by one of two factors. Quite often a student will begin playing the horn when he is actually not large enough to handle it comfortably, he will develop a habit of resting the bell of the instrument in his lap pointing toward the body, and will continue to play with the sound going directly into the body. In this position the mouthpipe of the horn approaches the lips at an angle that is nearly parallel to the floor (in many cases the mouthpipe extends out and upward from the lips), and the mouthpiece anchors on the top lip instead of the lower lip. Thus, a very inflexible and undependable embouchure is developed. This same bad playing position and consequent undesirable embouchure comes from another factor—girl horn players wearing straight skirts when playing! A young horn player must rest the heavy double horn on his (or her) right leg to support the instrument and quite often the right leg must be moved to the right side of the chair in order to use the leg for this needed support. If your girl horn players insist on wearing tight skirts when they practice or rehearse, it is impossible for them to assume a correct and comfortable playing position and, consequently, the horn is rested in the player's lap!

Accuracy

There are many ideas and exercises that can be used to develop accuracy and a sense of security in a student's playing—ideas that apply to all brass instruments, but in this discussion, especially to the French horn. Unless the student can "feel" the correct pitch as well as hear it, he will become unsure of his accuracy and probably will be uneasy about his ability on the instrument. The horn, by nature of the place in the overtone series where it plays most of the time, makes the matter of accuracy a real challenge to any player.

Encourage your horn players to practice long tones and lip flexibility exercises as an integral part of their daily warm-up routine. I have found that too many high school brass players are content to play through the $B\flat$ scale and a section of a march for their daily "warm-up"! Most high school band members have a few minutes between the time they enter the rehearsal room and get their instrument out of the case and the time that the rehearsal begins. If these few minutes can be used constructively, the young horn player's embouchure can undergo a continual growth. Most brass instructors will agree that long tones are a fundamental part of embouchure building, and certainly this applies to the French horn player. The following exercise, practiced daily, diligently, and with care, can make an amazing improvement in tone quality and control for the young horn player:

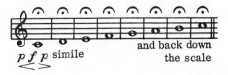

A brief sectional rehearsal with your horn section for the purpose of explaining the ideas of lip slurs will be well worth the time spent doing it. The use of lip slurs is a wonderful method of establishing a feeling for accuracy and lip control in your hornists. Young players are encouraged to use these lip slurs as a part of the daily warm-up to develop this accuracy and control. I have found that the use of the syllables *tah* and *tee* have proven to be most successful for the following lip slurs, as they are readily understandable to the student. As the player ascends in these exercises, the syllable *tee* is used to tighten the corners of the lips and helps to direct the air stream upward; the syllable *tah* during the descent helps to relax the corners and open the throat to let more air through the instrument for the low notes. The secret to flexible lip slurs is a *constant air stream*. The lip slurs must float on the stream of air!

These ideas of flexibility are certainly not new ones. They may be found in most trumpet or horn instruction books and are presented here simply as a reminder that they are fundamental to building a successful and dependable French horn embouchure. ■

February, 1967

INTONATION AND BRASS INSTRUMENTS

Doug Peterson

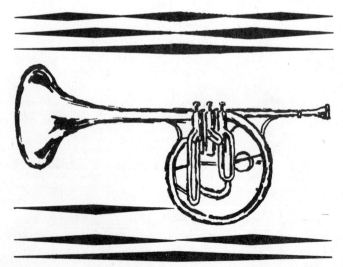

In any discussion of intonation problems on brass instruments and performance procedures that can lead to intonation improvement it should be stated at the outset that consistent performance, in tune, must be achieved first and last by listening, i.e., ear-training. The technical points to be discussed are merely aids. Brass intonation is affected by several factors common to all brass instruments—dynamics, tone quality, temperature, range, etc., and by some factors unique to the individual instruments.

Intonation and Temperature

Pitch on brass instruments definitely rises as the temperature of the vibrating air column rises; and conversely, pitch lowers as temperature lowers. Thus:
1. Tune *after* instruments have warmed to playing temperature.

2. When performing keep instrument and room temperatures as constant as possible.

3. The larger instruments are affected to a greater extent and *more slowly* by external temperature changes. Example: tubas, with more and thicker metal, take longer to absorb a temperature rise and rise in pitch to a greater extent than do trumpets. Thus, during a rehearsal or concert (often on an enclosed stage with stage lights) listen for and anticipate the need to pull main tuning slides.

Intonation and Tone Quality

Although tone quality should not be confused with intonation, a sensitive ear and correct playing procedures for a characteristic tone on each pitch can solve many intonation problems before they occur.

1. Listen for a strong characteristic tone on each instrument after listening to recordings or live performances of professionals.

2. Of paramount importance is to develop the concept of a centered or focused tone. Many players, desiring to get more edge or brilliance in their tone, favor the pitch up; or conversely, to get a mellow, blending sound, spread their tone by favoring the pitch lower. A procedure to help develop the concept of a centered tone could be to: (A) consciously favor tone up (by forming vowel sound *ee*); (B) then favor tone down *ah*); (C) then listen for a centered or focused tone in the middle. The focused tone can be achieved by forming the vowel *oh*, keeping the yawning, open feeling, then balancing the air and embouchure for a natural, ringing tone. When tuning with a mechanical tuner, tune so that you may favor the pitch *either* flat or sharp.

Intonation and Dynamics

In brass performance, the pitch has a tendency to rise when playing on louder levels; and conversely to lower or flat at softer dynamic levels.
Solutions:

1. On all tones keep the air *moving through* the instrument.

2. On full (loud) tones, pour the air through the horn. Yawn or drop the jaw and form the *oh* vowel; i.e. stretch the lips apart. Listen and practice for as round and full a tone as possible without cracking.

3. On soft tones keep the intensity, vibrancy, and life in the tone by forcing air through the instrument in a fast, pointed stream.

Intonation and Range

Low tones have a tendency to be sharp. Anticipate this by dropping the jaw, yawning, and forming the vowel *oh*.

If the student does not blow fast enough, he may have a tendency to squeeze out high notes, thus tending to be sharp. The solution would be to practice going from low to high notes by making the air move faster and by keeping the low feeling for high notes.

If student depends too much on the air for high notes before his embouchure is strong enough, the high notes may tend to sound wilted, spread, and flat. The solution would be to practice low to high, constantly listening for the focused, centered tone by balancing air intensity and embouchure firmness.

Intonation and the Overtone Series

Fundamental Overtones

Because brass instruments overblow the natural harmonic series but play in the tempered scale, some harmonics have a definite pitch discrepancy. The most used notes whose intonation is affected by this overtone series discrepancy are:

1. The 4th overtone has a definite tendency to be flat.

Listen for and anticipate the need to lip up, especially on sustained tones. Keep the air moving fast. Aim the air high.

2. The 5th overtone has a definite tendency to be sharp.

These tones are also beginning to be in the upper range and might have a tendency to be pinched and thus even more sharp. Solution:

a. Listen and anticipate the need to favor the pitch down by yawning, dropping jaw, and forming the *oh* vowel.

b. Don't pinch.

c. Keep air moving.

3. The 2nd overtone has a slight tendency to be sharp.

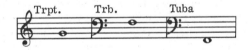

Use the same procedure as in the 5th overtone above.

Intonation and Valve Combinations

When the 1st or 2nd valves are used by themselves, the instruments are designed to sound a whole step or ½ step below the open harmonic. However, when used together or in combination with the 3rd, definite pitch problems occur.

1. The 1-2, 1-3, and 1-2-3 valve combinations have a tendency to be *progressively* sharp. Solutions:

a. Lip down, drop jaw, and form *oh* vowel.

b. In pieces with sustained tones or with no 2-3 combinations, the valve slides may be left pulled out to the necessary length (check with the tuner).

c. Some instruments have attachments to the 1st and/or 3rd valve slides that may be used quickly to adjust pitch of these combinations.

d. Some instruments have a 4th valve which can be tuned and used instead of the 1-3 combination.

2. The 2-3 valve combination has a definite tendency to be flat. Listen for and anticipate the need to lip up. Blow steadily.

Intonation and Ear Training—Listen Both Melodically And Harmonically

Melodically—Practice scales and arpeggios *slowly*, listening for a full, consistent volume, and a focused, centered tone. On *each* pitch develop the feeling of *singing*. Melodic legato playing can help to develop listening and control of air and embouchure. Harmonically, listen for:

1. The player next to you
2. The over-all pitch level of the group
3. Any other instruments that might be doubling your part.
4. Practice with a like instrument to get rid of beats (wavering sound). One player should sustain a steady tone while other player tries to match intonation exactly. The tone will be in tune when both instruments sound like *one*—one seems to disappear. This would also be a time to definitely identify to the ear the concept of flat and sharp by intentionally playing flat or sharp.

When practicing for lip and air control, the goal should be to keep lip and tongue movement to a minimum (both trending towards the big lip opening and *oh* vowel formation) and vary pitch by the intensity (speed) and volume of air. Steps to develop this control are to first play lip slurs and trills so that the tongue, saying *ah-ee*, changes the pitch. Then gradually minimize the tongue movement so that by varying the intensity of the air and thus the changing of tension of the vibrating lip the pitch changes; the flow of air is left free through the open throat, as in *oh*.

Brass instrument intonation is affected by definite acoustical factors. By knowing these influences and by constant and careful listening, brass intonation can be steadily improved. ∎

February, 1967

TEACHING CONCEPTS FOR TUBA

Donald Stanley

Webster defines a concept as "an idea, especially a generalized idea of a class of objects; a thought; general notion." Since a concept is a "generalized idea" and not necessarily a specific technique or a physical fact it is not uncommon to find brass teachers employing various, and at times opposing, concepts as a means of improving the student's playing proficiency. While these same teachers might disagree as to what particular concepts are most useful in obtaining the desired results, there would be little disagreement that concepts are of great importance, not only as teaching techniques but as a means of helping the student formulate a concept of his own, which will be of value to him in the process of improving his proficiency on his instrument.

While many of the concepts discussed in this article are applicable to other wind instruments and, in particular, to other brass instruments, there are exceptions. The concept of playing with an open throat, for example, is more applicable to tuba playing than to trumpet playing. In Volume 2, Number 2 of *The Brass World* Maurice Faulkner discusses some of the research conducted by Swiss physi-

ologists which indicates that a definite relationship exists between a closed pharynx and the ability of a trumpet player to produce the high register. Even though we would find few brass teachers who advocate playing with a tight or closed throat, there does appear to be a difference in the degree of openness required by players of the various brass instruments.*

With the foregoing thoughts in mind I should like to present the concepts which I have found useful in teaching tuba to both high school and college students. Few of these are entirely new; on the contrary, most have been acquired from former teachers or obtained from books and articles dealing with brass teaching. It is hoped that a restatement and discussion of these concepts will be helpful to others.

The inhalation process is perhaps more vital to the success of the tuba player than to the players of other wind instruments. For that reason considerable time needs to be devoted to increasing the student's air intake. Concepts such as "fill the bottom of the lungs first,"

*See "The Role of the Glottis in Brass Playing" by Wm. Carter, in *The Instrumentalist* (December, 1966, p. 75).

"make the lungs expand downward," and "inhale all the way around the body" are often effective in increasing the student's air capacity. Students need to be constantly reminded to practice this aspect of their playing if improvement is desired. Frequently it is necessary to inhale a large amount of air in a relatively short period of time. "Breathe through the corners of the mouth rather than the nose," "gulp the air," and "keep the throat open and relaxed when inhaling" are concepts which will help achieve the desired results. It is important that the student be aware of them and consciously practice this aspect of his playing.

In exhaling, the concept of blowing air "through the lips instead of at the lips" is useful. Likewise, the air must be "projected on through the instrument, not into it." Unfortunately, it is not uncommon to hear a teacher say to a student, "Put more air in the horn." This, of course, is impossible. Furthermore, it leads to incorrect playing habits and misconceptions concerning tone production. So much of the poor tuba playing which we hear today is the direct result of the player blowing air *into* the instrument rather than projecting the air stream *through* the instrument. Much of the difficulty lies in the fact that tuba parts often consist of relatively short notes. The student needs to be constantly reminded to project *all* tones, regardless of length, through the instrument and out the bell. Instead of asking the tuba player to play louder, which usually results in an uncontrolled sound referred to as "blasting" or "blatting," ask the student to project the sound.

Related to this problem of tone production is the misconception that the tone is produced when the lips start vibrating. Anyone who has heard a brass player buzz his lips will agree that this is hardly a good tone. It is only when a column of air, which has been set into vibration by the lips, is emitted from the bell of the instrument that we have tone production. For the tuba player, it is a long way from the lips to the bell.

The concept of the throat being merely a "passageway for the air" is helpful in overcoming a tight throat. Another concept which will help the tuba player to maintain this openness is "keeping the jaw relaxed." A tight or tense jaw will almost always result in tension in the throat as well. Perhaps even more fundamental to the problem of keeping the throat and jaw relaxed is the ability of the player to keep the teeth apart. The lower jaw can move independently of the lower lip so that the teeth can be kept farther apart than the lips. Ask the student to attack a pitch and while sustaining the tone to "relax and drop the lower jaw." In all probability, you will notice a big improvement in tone quality.

For developing greater facility in the upper register ask the student to "blow the air faster for high notes." It must be noted here that the student must not get the misconception that support of the air stream is required only in the upper register. It is necessary to employ breath support throughout the entire range of the instrument; however, the smaller lip aperture used in the upper register requires that the air move faster. Impress upon the student that he must "always keep an opening in the lips." In the upper register there is a tendency to contract the cheek muscles to a point where the lip aperture is flattened out and even-

tually closed. The circular band of muscles surrounding the lips must be contracted in relation to the cheek muscles so that the lip aperture remains open at all times. If air is forced out of the lips when they are closed, it is impossible to have the lips focused on the pitch to be produced. The concept of "lifting out the high notes rather than forcing them out" will help the player obtain more satisfactory results.

There is some disagreement as to proper tongue placement prior to the attack of a tone and while it not my intent to become involved in a lengthy discussion of exact tongue placement, there are several general rules to observe: Tuba players usually obtain better results with a slightly lower placement on the teeth and gums than do players of the higher brass instruments; however, the tongue must never be permitted to touch the lips. It is imperative that air be blown against the tongue prior to pulling the tongue down to release the air. It is not uncommon to find students who move the tongue and then release the air stream by relaxing the throat muscles. The concept of the tongue "releasing the air" is useful in overcoming this fault. It should be emphasized that the motion which produces the attack is a pulling motion rather than a pushing motion. This concept of "pulling the tongue down to attack the tone" is also useful in developing a lighter and more precise attack.

Another technique which will improve the tuba player's attack is that of having the student practice breath attacks using no tongue at all. This is helpful in developing the concept of blowing prior to tongue movement and also requires the student to have his embouchure focused on the pitch to be produced. Many bad attacks are the result of an incorrectly formed embouchure. Practicing breath attacks will require the student to correct the embouchure in order for the tone to sound. After the breath attack can be produced it is a relatively simple matter to employ the tongue to aid in a more precise attack and to make the necessary adjustments to produce various styles.

Unfortunately, a sound can be

produced on the tuba by forcing a large amount of air through almost any type of embouchure. This has led to a situation that finds the forming of a corrective embouchure often being neglected in the early stages of a student's experience, resulting in almost insurmountable problems as the player progresses. The exact placement of the lips on the mouthpiece is, of course, somewhat dependent on the physical characteristics of the student. Satisfactory results can usually be obtained by starting with an equal amount of both the lower and upper lip in contact with the mouthpiece of perhaps slightly more lower lip. It is absolutely necessary that the student develop, from the very beginning, the concept of the lips being held back against the teeth. Only in the extreme low register will it be necessary to permit the lips to be blown into the mouthpiece. Tone quality, intonation, response, attack, and flexibility in the low register will improve if the student lowers the jaw and keeps the teeth farther apart rather than pushing the lips forward into the mouthpiece. A certain amount of contraction of the cheek muscles is necessary to maintain control in the low register. As the student plays on up into the upper register of the instrument this contraction of the cheek muscles is, to some extent, counteracted by the contraction of the circular band of muscles surrounding the lips. This concept of "keeping the lip aperture in the same shape throughout all registers of the instrument" is necessary if the student is to develop facility in all registers.

Musically, the outlook for the tuba player is improving rapidly. Better method books, supplementary materials, and solos are now available. Contemporary works for band and wind ensemble have more demanding parts for the tuba player. It is no longer possible to "get by" with switching the poorest trumpet player to an $E\flat$ tuba and letting him struggle along on his own. If we are to develop good tuba players, who are sensitive musicians as well, we must display competence and intelligence in instructing our students in the proper techniques and concepts of tuba playing. ∎

ALTERED POSITIONS ON THE TROMBONE

Albert Stoutamire

Every school band and orchestra director, as well as every trombonist who has progressed beyond the beginning stages of instruction, should know that there are certain slide trombone tones which are played with the slide placed either shorter or longer than one of the seven normal positions. By normal positions, I mean the seven positions of the slide which can be compared with the seven combinations of valves on the standard three-valve brass instruments and which enable the player to produce a seven-step chromatic scale. These altered positions are frequently called short (or sharp) and long (or flat) positions, meaning that the player shortens or lengthens the slide from a standard position. Figure 1 gives the notes which are frequently played in these altered positions. The conventional marking for indicating the position is given above each note. These altered positions are sometimes referred to as alternate (meaning substitute) positions, but two of them (Figure 1—G and G♭) are the more frequently used positions for these notes. Therefore, these are not "alternate" positions, but are the "regular" positions for those two notes.

Figure 1

Additional altered positions include those positions used to play successive half steps, by extending the slide, below the notes given in Figure 1. For example, the B♭ (Figure 1) is played in a short fifth position, and so the A a half step lower will be played in a short sixth position. Similarly, a half step lower than F in short fourth position (Figure 1) is E, which is played in short fifth position.

Before proceeding further, it should be made clear that I do not infer that there are such things as "fixed" positions, whether they be

"standard" or "altered" positions. All slide positions on the trombone must be flexible to accommodate the physical, acoustical, and aesthetic demands prevailing at the instance of performance. Therefore allowances are made for slight deviations; basically, though, there are seven standard positions plus a number of altered positions.

How to differentiate between notes which are indicated as being played in the standard positions and notes which are indicated as being played in the altered positions has been established through conventional practice. For example, the E♭ which is a half step above D (Figure 1) is usually played in what is considered to be the standard third position even though our ears may tell us to extend the slide slightly away from third position, and, similarly, we do not refer to the tone produced a half step above the B♭ (Figure 1) as being played in a short fourth position even though it may be played slightly raised from the standard fourth position.

A basic problem which confronts students in coping with these altered positions is the fact that the amount of shortening or lengthening of the slide from the standard position is different for each tone produced. To play the G in Figure 1, the slide is made quite a bit shorter than it would be in the standard second position as contrasted with playing the B♭ in a short fifth position (Figure 1) which is, by comparison, only slightly shorter than the standard fifth position.

A teaching method I use is to say, "when going from the standard fourth position to the long fourth position to play the tone D (Figure 1), make the difference in slide length by moving only the tips of the fingers. However, the G (Figure 1) is played in a short second position which requires much more slide change, and you may need to move the wrist to

make that change."

Figure 2

The student should understand why these differences exist, and he should know which tones require greater or lesser slide alterations from the standard position locations. I try to explain this by referring to the notation given in Figure 2. Partials (fundamentals and overtones) in first position.

Brass instruments tend to have the following characteristic deficiencies, although some manufacturers modify these through design:
1. Partial 5 is slightly flat.
2. Partial 6 is slightly sharp.
3. Partial 7 is very flat and is not useable in standard positions.

From the above it will be seen that D and the F above the staff (Figure 2) may be played in tune with a slight embouchure or slide adjustment, but the A♭ cannot be played in tune in first position.

Figure 3. The Fifth Partial

Now consider the slightly flat fifth partial. If we play a series of half steps from first through seventh positions (Figure 3), it will be seen that when the tones B♭, A, and A♭ are reached, the slide must be noticeably raised from the standard fifth, sixth, and seventh position slide placements, whereas the other tones shown in Figure 3 could be raised with the embouchure alone, although most advanced players probably adjust both slide and embouchure in actual performance. In considering the sharp sixth partial we note that it would similarly call for embouchure or slide adjustments (or a combination of both) but in the opposite direction—downward.

Figure 4. The Sixth Partial

As pointed out earlier, whereas the markings as given in Figures 3 and 4 indicate that position 4 may be "long," and positions 5, 6, and 7 may be "long" or "short" when one plays fifth or sixth partial notes, the "long" and "short" markings are rarely, if ever, indicated for fifth and sixth partial notes in positions 1, 2, and 3 (F, E, and Eb) and in the fifth partial position 4 (Bb). Although performers may normally play these first through fourth position notes with the slide in a slightly shorter or longer than standard placement for those positions, conventional practice precludes the marking of these as short or long positions.

The seventh partial is not useable in first position and is useable in all other positions only when the slide is adjusted inward a good bit.

Figure 5. The Seventh Partial

(not used)

The relative distances the slide must be moved from the standard positions are not indicated by the conventional symbols such as sharp fifth position or flat fourth position, but the performer can convert these conventional symbols into more specific terms by identifying the partial to be played. That is, for fifth and sixth partial tones, flatten or sharpen very slightly (use the fingers only), and for seventh partial tones, sharpen the position quite a bit more (use the wrist).

Another factor to be considered in discussing distances between slide positions is that the distance between each of the standard positions becomes successively longer as the slide is extended. The distance from second to third position is slightly longer than the distance from first to second, and so on. Therefore, logically, the lengthening of fourth position, for example, would require more slide movement than the lengthening of first position. This helps explain why the fifth partial positions (Figure 3) become noticeably short as we reach fifth position, and the sixth partial positions (Figure 4) become noticeably long when we reach fourth position. By "notice-

ably" I mean that the common practice is to indicate the positions as long or short from those points on, as the slide is extended.

Of course, on the more elementary levels of instruction, the student can simply be told, referring again to Figure 1, that G and Gb require quite a bit of slide adjustment above the regular slide positions, but D and Bb require only a small amount of adjustment, longer or shorter respectively. The ear must tell the player how much adjustment is to be made, and eventually the player can locate the positions by "feel." But in time, the student should be led to understand why the short and long positions vary in the distance they are removed from the standard positions. The explanation should refer to the partials of the overtone series (Figure 2) and the location of the standard positions—each extension of the slide being slightly longer than the preceding one. Furthermore, fifth and sixth partial notes in all positions may be termed altered positions if the instrument being played produces these partials characteristically flat and sharp. ∎

April, 1967

THE BREATHED ATTACK

Maurice Faulkner

Last summer one of the most imaginative conductors of Europe passed on to his personal Valhalla after a lifetime of musical service. Hermann Scherchen fought for new concepts in instrumental performance just as he pioneered the contemporary music of the 20th century. He was an advocate of developing every instrument's capacity to the fullest. For instance, his discussion of "lightening" the tone of brass instruments in the performance of a variety of types of symphonic music, produced myriad examples in notation as well as in discussion.

The professionals who played under him, although they were often critical of his ideas because some of them seemed impossible to realize, admired his interpretive concepts concerning their instruments and sections. We discussed his interesting ideas with some of the European musicians and most of them agreed that they learned more from him than from other masters of the baton.

His ideas about brass attack are as illuminating as any of the other items he deals with. Anyone can consult his point of view in his *Handbook of Conducting*. And, to back up the techniques described there, one only needs turn to

the numerous recordings which he made during his lifetime. The finesse of his style is difficult to realize from electronic reproductions, but if one listens attentively he can hear the results described so meticulously in the *Handbook*.

It was better to enjoy the results in person, through attendance at the various European festivals and concerts which this great musician conducted before his death. And when one was privileged to hear orchestras which had perfected his concepts through hours of rehearsal, one could understand why the musical results were so much more impressive than from the interpretations of the lesser baton wielders.

The student of wind instrument playing should ferret out the ideas on articulation, tone extension, phrasing, etc. revealed in Scherchen's dissertation about conducting before he completes his college courses. It is essential that the young conductor examine the ideas thoroughly if he expects to compete in today's market.

This article however deals with only one phase of the imaginative background left to us by the master conductor, the "breathed attack" for brass instruments. Let us quote from Scherchen:

"There are two kinds of attack: one that takes place unnoticeably, the other is definite and sharp. 1. The unnoticeable, practically exhaled attack is used:

(a) for perfectly legato entries without accentuation or sharpness of attack, as in Beethoven's *Choral Symphony,* 3rd movement.

(b) for instrumental patterns merging into one another and intended to form an uninterrupted chain of sound.

(c) in order to introduce rest-like interruptions within the course of a soft portato."[1]

These statements lead off his discussion of woodwind playing techniques. But later in his chapter on brass-wind performance, he writes: "The points of playing, of attack, and of technique mentioned in respect of the woodwinds hold good, with slight differences, for all wind instruments—therefore, for the brass." [2]

What is Meant by "Breathed Attack"

The exhaled attack of Scherchen, or "breathed" or "diaphragmatic" tongue which other persons call the same device, is not only valuable for interpretive ideas in music, but it enhances the development of embouchure for the young student.

The principle of the "breathed attack" is nothing more than the production of the brass tone without the use of the tongue in any manner whatsoever. The syllable used to create this idea is that of *hoo, hah,* or *hee,* depending upon

[1] Herman Scherchen, *Handbook of Conducting,* trans. by M. D. Calvocoressi, London: Oxford University Press, 1933 p. 62-63.
[2] *Ibid,* p. 97.

which range one is developing. The wind is pushed from the region of the diaphragm through the focused opening of the lips. This permits the musician to obtain a pure sound without the crutch of the tongue position which often distorts the quality of the beginning of the tone and the pitch.

In order to accomplish this effectively the player must set his lips for the pitch desired and then start the breath with diaphragm pressure. As the breath passes through the tensed lips it will create an unaccented, smooth tone. At first the beginner will find that considerable breath gets through before the lips start vibrating, producing a breathy tone. But practice will overcome this problem and when the pure sound issues from the bell of the instrument the player has achieved a basis for the unaccented start of a tone. This should be practiced at all dynamic levels because each of them creates different problems in relation to the amount or volume of breath needed and the change in the size of the opening between the lips.

In addition, the musician must be able to breathe his attack in all registers. His high tones should be performed as simply and easily as his low ones. As a matter of fact, it is usually simpler to perform the medium, high range with a breathed attack than it is the extreme low range. But, if the embouchure is to be perfected so that playing a brass instrument is a pleasure, the musician must be able to breathe his tone simply and easily without using the unnecessary crutch of the tongue. So many instrumentalists use the tongue to help them obtain their high tones and thus distort all styles of interpretation into one basic, hard, accented attack that brass performance has become noted for its crudeness rather than its subtlety.

How much more finesse do our colleagues in the woodwind and string sections produce in moving from Bach, Handel, Mozart, Haydn, Beethoven, Brahms, and Wagner, to Henze, Copland, and Bernstein, than do we brass players. The woodwinds early had to accommodate their skills of tone articulation to the bow facility of the strings which were changing rapidly from the 17th century on. But,

because of the limited demands on the brasses, due to the fact that the composers could score only for the natural instruments, the brass musicians relegated themselves to playing brilliant fanfare effects and carelessly left their lyrical capacities undeveloped.

The invention of the valves changed some of this emphasis, but not enough to make a great impression on the brass specialists. Wagner, with his demands, conducted the brasses with more concern for musicality than some of his predecessors. Other imaginative conductors and composers expected more finesse from their musicians and aided in the development of brass skills. But the contemporary scene has brought about fantastic changes in brass requirements. One only needs to examine the most recent scores to see what a brass specialist must accomplish today. And contemporary conductors, following Scherchen's pattern (some of them are his students), demand a finesse and facility from their brass sections that can only be developed through long, arduous practice. The breathed attack is one of the devices which has become essential to the finely qualified, exquisite brass instrumentalist.

Where Is The Breathed Attack Used?

The quotation from Scherchen given above lists the categories in which the breathed attack should be used. One can find illustrations throughout the orchestra and concert band repertoires. I use it wherever I don't want the brass section to produce an accented attack of percussive quality. Such materials as chorales, legato slow movements, and even fast portatos, offer ideal practice opportunities for the breathed attack.

Often in private instruction when a student is having difficulty in producing a sonorous tone, I will ask him to play a passage with a breathed attack. This requires him to focus his lip tension in such a manner that the tone will develop without the aid of the tongue pressure behind the lips. This tongue pressure can often distort the lip position by pushing against the lips in order to form the beginning of the tone.

When the player has been able to form the tone easily without the tongue, he can then bring his tongue into the production of tongued attacks more easily and without using the tongue as a part of the enbouchure, which before had been necessary, at least to produce his high tones.

It does not take long to develop the breathed attack. Any young musician can learn it in a few weeks of careful practice. And when he has found it, he has greater control of his embouchure, as well as of his interpretive skills.

Any conductor is going to appreciate a brass section which can produce an unaccented, non-percussive legato sound more than he does the untrained, unskilled section that must hammer every note.

American brass instrumentalists have developed some of the finest abilities in the world. The consistency of tone, facility of range, and skill in technical matters have astonished our colleagues across the seas. We still have much to learn from them, however, concerning interpretive devices, especially in connection with the performance of their traditional works.

Herman Scherchen was one of the most imaginative conductors and stimulated some of the finest instrumentalists on the European scene. Our expert conductors have assimilated many of his ideas as well as those of his compatriots who have conducted in this country. Listen carefully to our finest bands and orchestras and you will hear the idiom of brass performance as it should be developed on all levels—including the elementary school. The breathed attack is one of the basic essentials to proper brass interpretation whether it be symphonic orchestra or concert band. ■

May, 1967

HOW TO PLAY THE "CARNIVAL OF VENICE" IN FOUR EASY LESSONS

John Haynie

While the title is an obvious oversimplification of the problems involved in performing this well known cornet solo, it is my purpose in this article to remind both student and teacher of the fundamental processes necessary to become an artistic and technically proficient cornet soloist.

Let us consider Del Staigers' version of the "Carnival of Venice" and determine what those techniques are. The opening cadenza requires a continuous lip slur and then reaches a climax on high E. It should therefore be apparent that this cadenza will necessitate a high degree of *embouchure development*. Not only is flexibility of the embouchure important but also enough strength of embouchure to be able to arrive at the high E.

In the theme of the solo the *breathing process* and the resulting tone, along with style and vibrato, become of paramount importance. Of course this is not to say that the control of the breath in playing lip slurs and high notes is of less importance. The point is that in playing melodically the student can concentrate on the more musical aspects of his abilities. Certainly

good breath control makes a more pleasing tone possible.

Finger facility is an obvious requirement of both the first and second variations while a continued effort at mastery of this embouchure and breath control must be made. It is in this area of fast finger development that a student not having the gift of a great embouchure can excel.

The Finale should give the student the inspiration and desire to develop a facile *tongue*. Triple tonguing is required and this implies a mastery of the single tongue. Double tonguing is necessary only briefly in the second variation, and should be an automatic outgrowth of a concentrated effort on single and triple tonguing.

There we have before us the four basic problems of technical and musical development necessary to play this particular solo.

Embouchure Development

Possibly the most basic factor involved in cornet playing is the preparation of the jaw position to give the mouthpiece the most solid foundation. Often the normal overbite allows the lower lip to roll too far under the upper lip. While it

is generally agreed that the upper lip is responsible for the vibration that makes the tone possible, it is important that the lower lip support the mouthpiece in order to give the upper lip freedom to vibrate with a minimum of pressure. Moist lips aid in allowing the lips to move freely, yet a solid jaw position retains the basic mouthpiece setting.

The extent to which the jaw is thrust forward can easily be determined by the following simple test. Moisten a finger and hold it near the pursed lips. Blow a column of air and locate the air stream with the finger. Now project the jaw forward and observe that the air stream goes upward. Continue to project the jaw until the air stream follows a line horizontal to the floor. This basic position would be satisfactory for tones from low F to approximately second line G. In this area the lower jaw will begin to recede ever so slightly. The ultimate range a person achieves can be largely determined by the discretion used in allowing the lower jaw to recede. The receding lower jaw causes the air stream to be directed downward, yet it is important to keep some red of the

441

lower lip visible at all times.

How high or low to place the mouthpiece on the lips has been a highly controversial subject; however all agree that the mouthpiece should be as near the center as possible, horizontally. First the lips should be closed with the corners of the mouth set firmly in a pleasant facial expression. It is this writer's opinion that the young student should be encouraged to place the mouthpiece about half on the upper lip and half on the lower lip. In time the mouthpiece will find its most natural position whether it remains half and half or adjusts itself to one-third upper, two-thirds lower, or the opposite. The object of desiring the mouthpiece to be centered is to allow an equal use of the facial and lip muscles both up and down, and side to side.

As has been mentioned, the upper lip must vibrate and possibly the lower lip vibrates sympathetically if the jaw-lower lip position is fixed as previously described. This writer recommends buzzing the lips to insure this vibration of the lips. Buzzing is especially helpful for the beginning student or for the advanced student who has some problem of embouchure which usually results in excessive mouthpiece pressure on the lips. For the cornetist who has no particular embouchure problem prolonged buzzing sessions would probably serve little purpose. Actually, too much buzzing can result in too tight a lip position and produce a pinched, forced tone.

It is obvious that merely pushing down three valves will not play all the notes in the range of the cornet. There are at least three things that we can manipulate that cause the tones to go up or down exclusive of the use of the valves. Those things are: (1) contracting or relaxing the lips, (2) arching of the tongue, and (3) pivoting the instrument and head.

For many years authorities have argued whether to use the smile system or the pucker system. Actually it is generally agreed now that it is not a matter of either-or, but a combination of both the pucker and the smile. On the other hand we could say that both systems are incorrect and avoid mentioning either term, smile or pucker. Why not simply ask the student to

contract his lips by tightening the corners of the mouth as he wishes to play a higher note? This might avoid all confusion of the controversial pucker-smile systems while in effect the student will almost automatically accomplish the desirable feat of pulling the muscles of the corners of the mouth against the muscles of the lips.

Simultaneously, as the lips contract and relax, the tongue arches, which might be described as contracting and relaxing the tongue. To understand this action of the tongue the syllables *ah* and *ee* are used. Should these syllables be meaningless to the student have him place his finger on his tongue and say *ah* and *ee*. Now he can actually feel the action of the tongue as it raises and lowers itself, *ah* position for low notes progressing toward *ee* for the high notes. It must be mentioned that pronouncing these syllables vocally is at best a rough indication of the action of the tongue. The tongue must be allowed to move in sympathy with the contracting and relaxing of the lip and facial muscles.

An interesting thing happens automatically when the jaw, lips, and tongue function as previously described. These motions encourage what is commonly known as the pivot. Observe that as the pitch ascends the bell of the cornet tilts downward and the forehead tips backward very slightly. When the pitch descends the opposite occurs, that is, the bell of the cornet tilts upward and the forehead tips forward. When this pivot occurs in reverse too much pressure is applied to the upper lip when ascending and when descending the lower lip is restricted, resulting in poor tone and attack on low notes. The person who has an abnormal occlusion of the teeth, whose lower teeth are farther forward than the upper teeth when the jaw is clamped, will be expected to pivot in reverse. This will be his natural pivot and actually is to be encouraged.

To understand all these actions of jaw, lip, placement of the mouthpiece, tongue, and pivot would be meaningless without the proper musical exercises to serve as a practice vehicle. The best exercises to practice for the development of

embouchure are lip slurs, as evidenced by the number of great cornet-trumpet players of the past and present who have written whole books of lip slurs. I recommend the following in order of difficulty:

Lowell Little, *Embouchure Builder* Pro-Art; Earl Irons, *Twenty-seven Groups of Exercises*, Southern Music Company; Charles Colin, *Lip Flexibilities*, Colin; and Max Schlossberg, *Daily Drills & Technical Studies*, Baron.

There are many other lip slur books written by equally fine performers; however these represent four distinct levels and serve their purpose very well. Unquestionably, consistent lip slur practice is the first lesson in how to play the "Carnival of Venice."

The Breathing Process

The second lesson requires a study of the breathing process and its relationship to the development of a musical tone. Much has been said about the need to practice long tones to develop tone and few teachers would disagree; however not many follow through and insist that the long tones be practiced regularly. How long is a long tone? It is this writer's opinion that a long tone is a note held as long as a person can make a sound come through the horn. It is assumed that the student will be encouraged to sit or stand with good posture in order for the breathing apparatus to function properly. The idea of "sitting tall" is sometimes helpful in an effort to sit like we stand.

Not only should the student have good posture and practice long tones, but it is also important that the volume of tone at which he plays be bold and aggressive. Nothing is accomplished practicing long tones with a weak sound. The student should work for a full, rich tone and as he gains more control of the breathing process he should reduce the dynamic level. Rarely does a young student play a "soft tone"; it is characteristically a "weak tone."

In working with students on improving breath control your writer does not concern himself too much with how the initial breath is taken. It is far more important to be concerned with those muscles that get rid of the air than those that cause the air to be taken in. In telling young students to take a big breath several things can happen that are detrimental to a good one. The inevitable problem of lifting the shoulders and the subsequent tightening of the throat and restriction of the tone are the most obvious results of too much breath. It is far better to use up more of the air we take in normally than to take too much air and try holding it back while playing the instrument. As stated before, we have a much more positive control of the muscles that expel the air than those that take it in. If a student sustains a tone for maximum length, the next breath will be a full breath through necessity, and nature will see to it that it is taken correctly. The succeeding long tone, if started immediately, will then be played with more air than the first tone. This process of long tone practice then is truly a forced expiration followed by an automatic forced inspiration. Unless we go beyond the limits of the normal breathing process the lung capacity cannot be increased nor can wind control be improved.

By this procedure the student can become artistic in his wind control without ever hearing the word "diaphragm." For those who want the whole truth a study of the breathing process from an anatomical standpoint must be made. As previously stated there are opposing muscles involved, muscles that cause air to be taken in and muscles that force the air back out. The diaphragm, the external intercostals, and sternocleidomastoids contract in such a way that a sub-atmospheric pressure is created inside the thoracic cavity. This vacuum causes air to be drawn into the lungs. Upon completion of the maximum intake of air the above mentioned muscles begin to relax and begin to return to their original position.

Now another set of muscles comes into play. The pelvic diaphragm, a pair of muscles, forms a foundation and causes all abdominal muscular force to be concentrated in an upward direction. The internal intercostal muscles contract, decreasing the size of the thoracic cavity, and when the wind is finally expelled the whole process starts all over again.

Often students say, "I can't do all that," but the truth is that they always have and always will. The breathing process is involuntary and all we can do is to *increase*, not change, the action of the muscles that take the air in and those that help us blow the instrument. Let us concentrate on getting rid of the air, and then taking air in will be both natural and effective.

A strong lip coupled with well-controlled wind is a fine beginning for a beautiful tone; however there is more. Every player must develop style and musical taste and both are usually a by-product of his musical environment. In other words, what he hears will largely determine the style he plays. Therefore it is the teacher's obligation to guide his student's listening habits just as carefully as he guides his technical development. Furthermore the student should be encouraged to play melodies, both by music and by ear. Too many students really don't know what they sound like, because they seldom use their ears. Playing by ear can be a valuable musical and training experience.

Vibrato can make the tone more musically interesting but should not be forced on the student. He may be told to move his right hand to and fro or make a chewing motion with his jaw; however he must hear what these motions do to the tone. In other words he must get the sound in his head and then the technique of either hand or lip-chin-jaw vibrato becomes a simple task.

Breath control, tone, vibrato, and style are all a part of learning to play "Carnival of Venice." It is quite possible that the greatest satisfaction in music could be found here, with practice on our second lesson.

Fingering

The third lesson, fingering, requires the greatest number of hours of practice. As a matter of fact, the practice of most students is more in the area of "finger wiggling." Unfortunately most of this practice is wasted effort rather than planned procedure.

In order to achieve the greatest control of fingering and to develop the maximum speed let us first consider hand positions. The cornet should be held firmly with the left hand, leaving the right hand completely free. This implies that the little finger of the right hand be free of the finger ring and allowed to move as the other fingers move. Furthermore, the right hand thumb must not be bent in a cramped position, but should be placed between the first and second valves and allowed to bend only slightly as required to arch the three fingers. The three fingers should be placed lightly on the valves just back of the finger tips. Caution should be observed in not pulling the valves down, not playing with the fingers straight and stiff, not allowing a double-jointed action of the first joint of the fingers, and not playing with the very tips of the fingers.

What to practice is an important factor in the development of finger execution. Scales are basic and every effort should be made to get the student to enjoy scale practice. With young students, scales can be taught with subtlety and persistence; however scales are seldom taught at this level as evidenced by the few college students who can effectively play all major and minor scales. At a young age they were never convinced that mastery of scales insures accurate and disciplined fingers as well as improving sightreading ability.

Along with scale practice there is a need for various exercises that are both fun and effective. Of course the *Arban Method* is the favorite of most teachers and its use with the *Prescott Technic System* makes it a highly reliable source for mastery of finger control. Clarke's *Technical Studies* are favorite exercises of many and are well-organized studies. Furthermore there is an endless number of exercise books available and there should be no cause for boredom. Master of scales, combined with challenging exercises, will spell success in playing Variations I and II of the "Carnival of Venice."

Tonguing

The Finale of the "Carnival of Venice" employs the use of triple tonguing, usually a fearsome thing to young players. It is by no means as difficult to accomplish as it may seem. The real problem is in the execution of the single tongue and the misconceptions regarding the placement of the tongue. The problem stems from the concept that all notes are tongued with the placement of the tongue in the identical place for every tone regardless of whether it is a high or low note. It is inconceivable to this writer that all notes could be tongued from the same position when there are so many other physical changes necessary—that is, the arching of the tongue, the dropping of the jaw, and the contraction of the lips.

It seems logical that as the lips, jaw, and teeth form a larger aperture and as the tongue flattens into the *ah* position, the tongue must come farther forward. With many fine players the tongue goes between the teeth and may even touch the lips in the extreme low range. When ascending, the teeth and lips come closer together as the tongue arches in the *ee* position; therefore the tongue placement for a clean attack would have to be behind the upper teeth, ap-

proximately where some authorities say the tongue should strike on all tones. The student must realize that there is no vocal sound made when playing the cornet; therefore to say *tu, ta,* or *tee* is pointless other than to use the syllable to describe the sound of the attack, not the position of the tongue.

As the student masters a clear, definite attack with the single tongue he already has two-thirds of triple-tonguing learned. The remaining one-third is referred to as the *ku* attack. Actually the *ku* is produced by building up the wind pressure behind the tongue, as if saying *ku* without actually making the vocal sound. The student should work on this *ku* attack until it sounds as near like the *tu* as possible. Then he can slowly work at the following combinations of *kukutu, kutuku, tukuku, tukutu,* and *tutuku.* The two accepted methods of actual performance are *tutuku* and *tukutu.* The preference is an individual matter determined by the nature of the music to be

played. In the running accented triplets of this version of the "Carnival of Venice" I would recommend the use of *tutuku.*

The four basic lessons herein described—embouchure, breathing, fingering, and tonguing—should not only prepare a person to play the "Carnival of Venice" but also any other cornet solo. Possibly a fifth requirement should be included and it would be determination. It cannot be taught, sold, or given away, but must somehow come from within the student. He must want to play the cornet well more than anything else and then he will make the effort to master these four basic techniques. ∎

Editor's Note: The Del Staigers version of the "Carnival of Venice," performed by John Haynie, may be heard on record #2, Southwest Artists' Series, Austin, Custom Records, P.O. Box 9057, Austin, Texas 78756. Other selections recorded by Mr. Haynie are: "Andante and Allegro," J. Guy Ropartz; "Capriccioso," Paul Jean; "Conversations for Cornet," Carl Grundman; "Fox Hunt," R. M. Endressen; "Norine," Herbert Clarke; and "Sonata VIII," Corelli.

June, 1967

WHY NOT CORNETS AND TRUMPETS?

Acton Ostling, Jr.

An instrument which should be in standard use by all bands is described by Percy Scholes (1877-1958), eminent English writer on music, in the **Oxford Companion to Music:**

> The cornet (in full *Cornet à Pistons*) is a metal instrument, of bore partly cylindrical (like that of the trumpet for the most part of that instrument's length) and partly conical (like that of the horn)... The tone is something between that of the horn and that of the trumpet. Unlike those two instruments, it is easy to produce from it any note, and owing to its wide bore (wider than that of the trumpet) it has great flexibility, so that passages almost like those of a clarinet or flute in its most runabout mood are within its powers. With the horn and trumpet the listener is sometimes made aware of a sense of effort on the part of the performer, with the cornet this is not so.

Perhaps the British origin of the above statements provides some insight into the stylistic description of the instrument, and one must admit that such a description of flexibility and effortlessness as characteristic of a brass instrument is certainly foreign to much of the present-day performing in bands at all levels in the United States.

The lament, often expressed by some band conductors, that cornet playing is a lost art, is certainly justi-

fied by current trends in composition as well as performance; however, as a spokesman for the cornet, one must admit that there are formidable questions as to whether this loss is indeed lamentable. The battle between the cornet and trumpet has continued for some time, and it is interesting to note that from 1880-1895 trumpets were rarely found in British orchestras—a situation which lead Walter Morrow, a great British exponent of the trumpet, to lament in 1892, "it (the cornet) has dethroned the trumpet...we rarely hear the latter now even in our finest orchestras or military bands." French composers were particularly partial to the cornet in orchestral use. The instrument gained great popularity after its introduction into the orchestra with the premiere of Rossini's **William Tell** in 1829. It is also interesting to note that in the conclusion of historical material on the cornet, the **Oxford Companion to Music** states that "the introduction of the smaller, lighter-toned, and more agile trumpets in **Bb** and **A** has been one factor in driving the cornet into the orchestral background even in France, and it now tends to disappear also from the wind band..."

Upon engaging in still another discussion on the subject of cornets and trumpets, one certainly lacks startling new revelations and must rely upon personal opinions and convictions. It is interesting, though, to review the disagreements of authorities through the years. Hector Berlioz (1803-1869) in his **Traité de l'instrumentation et d'orchestration modernes** (1843) contributed the following opinions concerning the cornet:

> Has neither the nobility of the horn nor the loftiness of the trumpet. In melodic use must play only phrases of large construction and indisputable dignity. Jocund melodies will always have to fear from this instrument the loss of a portion of their nobility, or, if they have none, an addition of triviality.

On the other hand, Frederick Corder (1852-1932), an English composer who was a professor of composition at the Royal Academy of Music and founder of the Society of British Composers, states in his book **The Orchestra and How to Write for It** (1895):

> The trumpet in the orchestra (meaning the *F* trumpet then in vogue) is an almost unmitigated nuisance...And — though I am aware that few agree with me on this point — I think the vaunted brilliancy of the trumpet its most serious drawback, because it simply kills all other instruments...I maintain that in competent hands it (the cornet) can play not only all existing trumpet parts more discreetly and bearably than the trumpet itself, but can furnish a far better upper part in the trombone harmony. A good cornet-player can do all that a trumpet-player can and nearly as brilliantly.

Ebenezer Prout (1835-1909), eminent English theorist, in his two-volume work **The Orchestra** (1898-99), says "the tone of the cornet is absolutely devoid of the nobility of the trumpet, and, unless in the hands of a very good musician, readily becomes vulgar." Charles-Marie Widor (1844-1937), distinguished French organist and composer, edited Berlioz's treatise on orchestration in 1904 adding a supplement which comments on this subject, "the timbre of the cornet and of the trumpet cannot for a moment be compared — the one being thick and vulgar, the other noble and brilliant."

In all the excerpts recorded thus far, authorities seem to be discussing the cornet **versus** the trumpet, as if one were to permanently substitute for the other, Cecil Forsyth (1870-1941), English composer and writer on music who authored a comprehensive manual, **Orchestration** (1914), provides the following refreshing statements — fully applicable to the current cornet situation in this country:

> Absurd prejudice against it, (is) based...principally on ignorance. We must not forget that the contempt which is usually bestowed on the cornet by those who have not heard it properly played is mainly a contempt because it cannot equal or beat the trumpet *in trumpet passages*. Let us accept the fact that a cornet is a cornet, not a trumpet. Then we shall be able to see what can be done with it.

Here again one witnesses a discussion of the orchestral use of the cornet rather than of its use or non-use in bands. However, all of the above comments are useful in developing a conviction concerning the return to standard use of **both** instruments in American bands. In light of Forsyth's statements it must be noted that too often in this country the cornet is **not** a cornet. It is indeed unfortunate that it was deemed necessary by some to create a supposed cornet which looks like a trumpet, but this development only completes the cycle, which started with the manufacture of trumpets which look like cornets (and are so labeled). This indeed creates an instrumenta-

tion problem. (A similar situation occurs when American instruments labeled baritones or euphoniums are neither baritones nor euphoniums.)

Performances at both the public school and college level reveal two basic approaches to developing the sound of a band. The first (and more recent approach) employs a deliberate attempt to duplicate the concept of the wind section in a symphony orchestra. Most often the sound approximates that of a doubled orchestral wind section with single performers on the non-orchestral instruments necessary to complete the instrumentation. The emphasis is constantly upon individual performers. In the finest groups of this type the listener is conscious of an organization of individual virtuosos rather than the development of sectional and group timbre.

The second approach, which in my opinion is indeed preferable, includes not only the molding of individual performers into a blended ensemble both as a total group and as separate sections, but has as its basis the development of a timbre entirely different from the orchestral wind section. One wonders whether conductors not firmly committed to the orchestral approach have really given thought to tonal concepts for the band and have selected trumpets for all occasions, or whether it has merely been more convenient to move with the popular trend rather than to develop a conviction, choose sides, and take a stand on the question.

If one is to assume a position favoring the use of true cornets, it must be acknowledged that conductors firmly committed to recreating the sound of an orchestra wind section cannot be convinced that cornets are desirable. They offer the following justifications for the exclusive use of trumpets: the difference concerns a style of playing rather than a difference in the instruments; the basic concern of the band men, historically speaking, has really been an objection to poor trumpet playing and deficient instruments; the modern trumpet, of fine quality, has sufficient stylistic flexibility to eliminate the need for the cornet; and, contemporary band music in general is composed with the sound of the modern orchestra trumpet in mind.

Bandsmen must certainly assume responsibility for the failure to create an awareness concerning the total instrumentation, including a difference between cornet and trumpet sound, and composers must somehow be educated to the fact that they are not necessarily creating music for a doubled orchestra wind section when they write for the band. One must agree that style in cornet and trumpet performance is certainly a basic problem. (Performances at contests of the cornet solos by Herbert L. Clarke now frequently sound as if written by Herbert L. Alpert!) However, given a performing concept of the cornet as being light and lyrical in style, in contrast to the trumpet's punctuation and penetration, and given a commitment to the development of a completely different timbre between orchestra wind sections and bands, the use of true cornets provides added emphasis for the light and lyrical styles, guaranteeing a **significant** difference in timbre.

Accounts of various "behind a screen" tests in which a difference between the cornet and trumpet was inaudible to the listeners are numerous, and can be quoted **ad infinitum** by the "orchestral" bandsmen. It is impossible to imagine such tests conducted with two genuine styles of playing since the person who performs **both** styles well is more than a rarity; he hardly exists. There are trumpet players who sound like cornetists, and vice versa. Given two performers, with each player musically conversant in a different style, one with a **true** cornet and the other with an orchestral trumpet, and playing **typical** parts for each instrument, the difference **will** be noticeable.

Since the cornet can be played in a brilliant fashion (as stated in the quote from Frederick Corder) and since the modern trumpet is capable of light and flexible playing, performers on both instruments can make adjustments to the style of the music. When composers utilize this tonal difference, the resources will be available for achieving definite stylistic contrasts, and in my opinion, band conductors must encourage this use. The trumpet player cannot become a cornetist by merely switching instruments. The instrument must be used steadily over a long period of time before he can adjust to its characteristics. This is also true regarding switches from cornet to trumpet.

Unfortunately, exponents of the cornet have often neglected the trumpets in bands by assigning inferior players to the trumpet parts, and by following the tradition of giving second and third parts to the trumpets when separate parts were not composed. It is suggested that a trio of trumpets functioning on **all three** cornet parts be employed with the cornet section in the absence of separate parts. It is also suggested that with the first three performers in ability, two be placed on the first cornet stand and one be assigned to first trumpet. (Of course the abilities of the performers stylistically would influence these assignments, but the intent is for fully competent performance by the trumpets.) In compositions having separate parts, the exclusive use of trumpets creates a situation in which alternating passages lack sense, and where, even if antiphonal placement in the seating arrangement is practical, only partial fulfillment of the intent of the music is possible.

Trumpet teaching at the college and university level is directly responsible for the decrease in cornet playing. Insistence upon trumpet, **and only trumpet,** as the principal instrument of study for music majors precludes the possibility of developing skillful cornet players. Those who perform on the cornet only during college band rehearsals and at all other times play the trumpet become graduates committed to the trumpet. Then, in turn, they participate in the elimination of cornet playing by students under their jurisdiction. One must state that for the student with the talent and desire for **professional** performing, the trumpet **must** be the instrument for college level study. Since few students will become professional performers, and since the cornet is well suited to the development of musicianship, I fail to comprehend the reasoning behind any prejudice against the study of cornet at the college level by students other than those who intend to play professionally.

The euphonium major, even in performance, is offered in many schools and departments of music at both the undergraduate and graduate level, and some schools allow the study of bass clarinet (including the performance of bassoon literature read in the bass clef) for music education majors at the undergraduate level. Bands need complete instrumentation, and this is a marvelous method for producing quality musicianship on all instruments. The study of the cornet at the college level should be encouraged and receive similar treatment.

Although much contemporary band music, even that composed with separate cornet and trumpet parts, is oriented to the orchestra trumpet concept, band conductors should strive for stylistic subtleties in developing the cornet and trumpet sections. The concept of brilliance for the cornet should always be tempered by its basic function as a mellow tone color. The tonal possibilities of a complete mellow brass choir **and** a complete brilliant brass choir within the band are exciting. It would indeed be unfortunate if the cornet were to fade away into extinction before this ideal becomes a reality.

June, 1967

DEVELOPING YOUR BASS TROMBONISTS

James Graham

With the increasing popularity of the bass trombone, teachers are faced with the problem of finding suitable materials for the study of this magnificent but long neglected instrument. In the past one had to do a great deal of improvising in order to provide these materials; although this is still necessary occasionally, the situation has improved a great deal.

Since John Christie's excellent article, "Teaching the Bass Trombone," appeared in the March, 1961, *Instrumentalist,* many new exercises and some adaptations of standard tenor trombone studies have appeared in print. This discussion of available materials avoids references to materials listed in the above article.

As the bass trombonist should

maintain a secure four octave range from at least high *C* down to pedal *C,*

bass trombone studies should be utilized along with many of the usual exercises for tenor trombone. It would be a serious mistake to develop one register at the expense of the other. Although the bass trombonist is primarily concerned with the lower and middle registers, an adequate upper register *must* be maintained.

Methods and studies

There are several studies available primarily for the bass trombonist. Some of their content is of great value for the large bore tenor trombone with *F* attachment—which is sometimes confused with the bass trombone as we know it in this country. These include: Bernard, *Methode Complete* (Leduc); Blume-Fink, *36 Studies for Trombone With F Attachment* (Fischer); Gillis, *20 Etudes for Bass Trombone* (Southern); Kopprasch-Fote, *Selected Studies for Trombone with F Attachment* (Kendor); Maenz, *20 Studies for Bass Trombone* (Hofmeister); Ostrander-Colin, *F Attachment and Bass Trombone* (Colin); Ostrander, *Shifting Meter Studies* (Robert King); Stefaniszn, *20 Special Etudes for Bass Trombone* (Pro Musica); Stephanovsky-Brown, *20 Studies for Bass Trombone* (International); and Williams, *Bass Trombone Method for F Attachment* (Colin).

As the bass trombone demands a very capable and mature player, one already quite proficient on tenor trombone, most of the above are somewhat difficult. The Ostrander-Colin *F Attachment and Bass Trombone* exercises and text are of great value to the person unfamiliar with the *F* attachment. Several of the Blume-Fink *36 Studies*, the Kopprasch-Fote *Selected Studies*, and the introductory section of the Williams *Bass Trombone Method* are all excellent to further the development of the novice bass trombonist. The others are perhaps best left for a later date or more advanced pupils.

In addition to the bass trombone studies, there are some tuba exercises which are well suited to the instrument: Blaezvich, *70 BBb Tuba Studies* (Robert King); Pares-Whistler, *Foundation Studies for Eb Bass* (Rubank); Tyrrell, *Advanced Studies for Eb Bass* (Boosey &

Hawkes); and Vasilev, *Etudes* (State Music Publishers Moscow).

Although the Pares-Whistler *Foundation Studies* are nothing more than scale exercises, they are of great value in developing the low register of the student new to the bass trombone. One can begin with the *F* major exercises, then *E*, *Eb*, etc., gradually descending into the lower register. When practicing these exercises, it is usually helpful to have the student crescendo as he descends. This will facilitate the "opening" of the lower notes.

The Blazevich *Studies* are essentially the well-known trombone clef studies an octave lower. They are quite valuable for bass trombone and tuba alike. The excellent Vasilev *Etudes* are not as melodic as the Blazevich and a bit more demanding technically. The Tyrrell *Advanced Studies* are not as challenging as either of the above. Although they are at times rather trite musically, they do contain passages of value.

Solo literature

Although a rather adequate supply of studies and exercises for bass trombone is available, good original solo literature for the instrument is lacking. Three of the better works are: Casterede, *Fantaise Concertante* (Leduc); Henry, *Passacaglia and Fugue* (Robert King); and McCarty, *Sonata* (Ensemble Publications).

The McCarty *Sonata* is also available with string quartet or string orchestra accompaniment on a rental basis from the publisher. From this meager listing one can easily imagine that a great deal of "borrowing" from other instruments is necessary to provide adequate recital material. The tuba repertoire, also sparse, holds some promise. Arrangements or editions of compositions originally for tuba and available specifically for bass trombone include:

Lebedev-Ostrander, *Concerto in One Movement* (Edition Musicus); Spillman, *Concerto* (Edition Musicus); and Spillman, *Two Songs* (Edition Musicus).

Suitable original literature for the tuba includes the following selections:

Boutry, *Tubacchanale* (Leduc);

Hartley, *Sonatina* (Interlochen Press); Hindemith, *Sonate* (Edition Schott); Tcherepnine, *Andante* (Boosey & Hawkes); and Vaughan-Williams, *Concerto* (Oxford).

The Tcherepnine *Andante* is an easily approachable work for the novice performer although it does demand great sustaining ability in the low register. The Vaughan-Williams *Concerto* is a very effective work for bass trombone. The middle section (Romanza) is done rather frequently on trombone recitals, but the entire work, although awkward at times for slide technique, should be of interest. The orchestral score and parts are available from the publishers.

In addition to tuba literature, certain works from the bassoon and cello literature can be utilized. As examples, the Bach *Suites* for cello (available from many publishers) with their profusion of low notes and wide skips of line make fine technical studies. If they are to be played in public, great care must be taken to insure that they are phrased properly for performance on a wind instrument. It is perhaps best to select more "trombonistic" individual movements rather than attempting to perform a particular suite in its entirety. The Hindemith *Drei Leichte Stücke* (Edition Schott) is well suited for the more inexperienced player.

In the search for suitable solo material do not overlook the repertoire of the tenor trombone as practically all of this literature is suitable for performance on the larger instrument. The main problem of bass trombonists will be in prolonged playing in the upper register, so some care must be taken when choosing literature for performance. The teacher must have a knowledge of the literature of many instruments in order to provide adequate concert fare for his bass trombonists. However, one must exercise great care in matters of musical taste and judgement. It is of no avail to "borrow" a work if it is going to sound unconvincing musically when played on the bass trombone.

Warm-up and Flexibility Exercises

The bass trombone not only requires its own studies and solo literature, but warm-up and flexibility exercises as well. When one first encounters the *F* attachment, a slower response of attacks and a "fogginess" of the tone quality is immediately apparent. It is imperative that the player quickly master the art of "matching" the tone quality of the valve notes with those on the open instrument. Also very necessary is the development of a new type of flexibility —that of switching back and forth from open and valve notes. This requires coordination of the breath, enbouchure, tongue, and thumb. Do not ignore the pedal register in this regard as it is quite difficult to move from the pedal register to the low valve notes smoothly.

To develop the balanced overall range mentioned previously, a tenor trombone warm-up routine is basic. In addition to this, certain exercises devised for the particular needs of the bass trombonist should be utilized. When coaching your students, please keep in mind the particular intonation problems of the valve notes. They should be played in the approximate positions indicated below:

It is most important that the exercises below be executed from 1st through 7th positions. Too many students fail to grasp the importance of practicing both open and valve notes in *all* slide positions. This is particularly true when one first acquires an instrument with an *F* attachment. All exercises should be done slowly at first, con-

centrating on tone quality matching and thumb valve technique. A full range of dynamics and articulations should be employed.

Exercises to develop flexibility with the trigger (Strive to attain perfect intonation):

Descend by half-steps to:

Repeat three times:

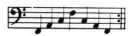

Extended:

Strive to match open and valve notes:

Exercises to develop facility between pedal and valve notes:

Devising specific exercises for specific problems is always a challenge to the instructor. The exercises above serve only as examples of what can be utilized. Most of your favorite tenor trombone exercises need only be lowered an octave. Scale studies and long tone exercises can contribute significantly to the development of the sound and technique of the low register.

In addition to actual warm-up exercises, specific studies from various publications can be quite helpful when incorporated into the daily routine. For example, exercises one and four from the Blume-Fink *36 Studies* have a great deal of value in this regard. A bit of imagination coupled with common sense can usually provide the exercise to suit the problem. By the adaptation of some of the above materials and a little ingenuity, the instructor can provide his bass trombonists with an interesting and thorough course of study. ∎

BRASS ARTICULATION

William Schmid

The most important determinant of one's musical style is articulation. Unfortunately, most brass players and teachers have only vague concepts of articulation. When compared with the string players' highly developed knowledge of articu-

lation, we brass players are still in the elementary stage of progress. Bowing on the stringed instruments has been thoroughly classified through such fine treatises as *Orchestral Bowings* by Elizabeth Green. One of the most important

advantages of this classification is its standardizing effect on notational practices.

This article will deal with two categories of brass articulation: (1) the beginning of notes and (2) the length of notes. After this discussion of fundamentals, there is an additional section on common faults and notational problems.

Beginning the Note

There are four categories of beginning articulations:
1. Slurred
2. Soft
3. Normal
4. Accented
    a. regular
    b. marcato

The normal beginning is the most common of the four. The tip of the tongue comes in contact with the juncture of the gum-line and the upper front teeth. The beginning of the note occurs when this contact is broken and the inrushing air causes the lips to vibrate, producing the tone. The function of the tongue becomes that of a vertical gate which controls the flow of air. The tongue does not *strike* the roof of the mouth. The placement of the tip of the tongue is of utmost importance. If the tongue is placed between the teeth, the resulting effect will be a fuzzy beginning, a slight dip in pitch on each note, and usually a lack of speed. These problems can be avoided by checking this action, for even a young player is able to tell his instructor where he is placing his tongue.

Accented beginnings are produced in much the same manner as the normal beginning, only the air rushes into the instrument with greater urgency. This explosion of air is caused by a build-up of greater pressure behind the tongue (gate) before the opening is created. It must be stressed that the difference between the normal and the accented beginning is not caused by the action of the tongue, but rather by the force of air behind it. The difference between the regular accent and the marcato accent is only a matter of degree, marcato being the heavier of the two.

In the soft beginning, often called legato, the top of the tongue lightly caresses the roof of the mouth, causing only a slight interruption in the flow of air. The note will seem to appear without a conscious beginning.

The slurred beginning is unlike the other three in that no interruption of the air stream takes place. Any note that is within a slur comes under this classification. The beginning of the new note is caused by a change of valve or slide, a slight lip movement, a variation in the air stream, or a combination of these.

Length of Notes

Any investigation of note lengths for brass instruments will soon reveal a marked confusion of terms. Terms such as legato, tenuto, leggiero, and staccato are rather indiscriminately used. Perhaps this confusion can be cleared up by the use of these five classifications.
1. Slur
2. Tenuto (Legato)
3. Portato
4. Staccato
5. Staccatissimo

The slur is the simplest qualification of note length, because there are no spaces between slurred notes. A slurred note must be held for its full value, since there is no interruption of the air stream between notes.

The second of the five terms, tenuto, means to hold a note for its full value. This should be the most commonly used note length. The term legato is often used interchangeably with tenuto. A phrase played tenuto or legato will have no spaces between notes other than the split-second interruption caused by the beginning of the next note. The action of the tongue here is quite simple; the beginning of the new note functions as the end of the previous note.

The third term, portato, is infrequently used by brass players, but describes exactly the next classification of length. Portato is halfway between tenuto and staccato, and indicates a slight separation between notes.

Staccato means only a separation between notes. The amount of this separation will be controlled by the value of the note, the tempo, and the style of the music. Obviously a staccato half note or quarter note would be held longer than a staccato eighth note. The staccato separation should be easily perceptible, and therefore it can be distinguished from the portato. The action of the tongue for staccato playing is also a subject of much controversy. A note can be terminated in two ways, by stopping the air flow or by touching the roof of the mouth with the tongue (closing the gate). The air-flow method should be used for slow tempi and long note values. The fast repetition of staccato notes requires the use of the tongue, because any change in the air stream would be awkward and undesirable. Two points of caution are necessary at this point. Do not constrict the throat to control the air flow. This constriction is easily detected by listening for grunting or other throat sounds. The second point is to avoid using the flat part of the tongue to stop a note. This fault is characterized by a *too-it* sound. If only the tip of the tongue is used, this sound can be avoided.

The final term, staccatissimo, is an extreme form of the staccato. It is characterized by the stopping of a note almost immediately after it is begun. The tongue must provide the stopping action here, since the breathing apparatus is too slow. The sound of a staccatissimo note will be *toot*. Once again avoid using the flat part of the tongue in stopping.

Notation

Since notational practices are certainly not standardized, the young brass player is often confused. The teacher must explain the style of the music to the student and if necessary change misleading notation. The following chart lists the types of notation that should be used in each catagory: (note that no extra signs are used to differentiate between soft and normal. The choice is left to the player. When soft articulation is desired, this may be indicated at the beginning of the section.)

Beginning of Notes

1. Slurred

2. Soft

3. Normal

3. Portato

4. Accented

    a. regular

    b. Marcato

449

Length of Notes

1. Slur

2. Tenuto

4. Staccato

5. Staccatissimo

It is very important that composers and arrangers understand the problems of articulation on brass instruments. Composers have often used the staccato sign with fast eighth or sixteenth notes, when the speed itself makes this articulation both impossible and distasteful. The young student, being unaware of this contradiction, plays in a pecky, toneless fashion. A large share of the staccato articulations now appearing in printed brass music should be crossed out or erased. Even the celebrated *Arban Method* contains an overabundance of unnecessary staccato articulations.

Common Faults

The two most common faults found among young brass players are the over-use of the staccato and the accent. Ask the average high school brass player to play the following

scale and he will invariably play it staccato.

What is the reason for this? Perhaps it is because he has never been told otherwise or has overused the staccato articulation in his practice. Two other typical errors of the same type would be the following:

written   often played

written   often played

Staccato tonguing should be used sparingly. Young players should not be introduced to the staccato until they have developed an adequate control of tenuto tonguing.

The accent is usually abused in two ways. First of all, when many young players see an accent or marcato accent, all sense of proportion seems to be lost in the frenzy of the attack. Trumpet players in particular seem to be plagued with this war-like mania. We might help this problem by deleting the word "attack" from our musical vocabulary. The second abuse is the addition of accents to the music. Too often the player will begin a note heavily with little follow up of tone.

Another common articulation fault occurs at the end of a group

of slurred notes. The last note of the slur is frequently cut short:

written   often played

Much confusion can be avoided if one only can keep beginning articulation and the length of notes separate. The use of the term tenuto is often taken to dictate also a soft beginning. This is not implied in the term. The tenuto length could be used with soft, normal, or accented beginnings.

To master articulation, one must isolate it and conscientiously practice the different types of beginnings and lengths. The student should be encouraged to make up exercises that will meet his own needs. When practicing any exercise or study, first decide on the the types of articulation to be used. Scales should be practiced using different articulations. Above all, articulations should always be chosen on the basis of the best style and taste. Brass players should be encouraged to listen to performances by woodwind and string players. When interpreting a phrase on a brass instrument, it might be worthwhile to ask ourselves and our students how a string player or a vocalist would interpret it. If such a standard were used, many of the currently accepted practices would be hard to justify and we would be on our way to a more musical use of articulation. ∎

September, 1967

THE BRASS PLAYER'S PIVOT

Douglass Smith

The subject of the brass player's pivot is one that is emphasized by some teachers and largely ignored by others. The line of pivotal disciples goes all the way from those who have heard it casually mentioned to authorities such as Dr.

Donald Reinhardt, whose *Pivot System* catalogs four embouchure types with respective sub-types, each with its own pivotal characteristics. Realizing what has been said and written, a definition such as the following may appear rather

naive, but perhaps it can be used as a point of departure: "The pivot is the tendency of a brass player's instrument to tilt slightly up or down when he changes registers."

This motion can be seen in rank beginners as well as in seasoned professionals, and many who do it well know absolutely nothing about it. One renowned trumpet virtuoso was questioned recently about the pivot in one of his clinics. He admitted to having one, but only after someone pointed it out to him did he even realize its presence. This surprised the brass teachers in the audience, but it pointed out one important thing: You don't have to understand it to do it.

Some writers claim that all the talk about the pivot is actually a waste of energy. They contend that the brass player would be much better off if he were to select a comfortable instrument angle before the first note were played, and then keep it for the rest of the piece. Actually, this is what many brass players *think they do.* Like the virtuoso mentioned above they never give the instrument angle a second thought; but close observation will nearly always point out some change in direction, even if extremely slight. The reason for this tilt, or pivot, cannot easily be observed. We usually give the "lip" credit for the majority of brass playing prowess, but the "oral machinery"—embouchure muscles, jaw, tongue—behind the scene is hard at work doing much more in the way of control and flexibility than the lip(s) could ever hope to do. If a cause for the pivot is sought, this is the area into which we must look.

In a research project directed by Texas State University, over 40 trumpet players at various stages of development were studied during actual performance by means of X-ray motion pictures. The main interest in the study was the comparison of jaw and tongue action involved in playing the trumpet, speaking, and whistling. After the first 30 subjects any hard, fast rules were most difficult to draw. One thing, though, could be said for sure: in trumpet playing, speaking, and whistling there was a definite movement of the tongue and jaw which accompanied pitch and vowel changes.

As shown in Fig. 1, the normal jaw movement in moving from a low pitch to a high pitch is slightly up and back, thus lessening the mouthpiece support by the lower

lip. If the player keeps the instrument angle the same, he will feel more pressure on the top lip than the bottom, but if he allows the mouthpiece to follow the support of the receded jaw, the instrument angle will naturally drop. That, in short, is the pivot.

Fig. 1:

Normal embouchure, low pitch:

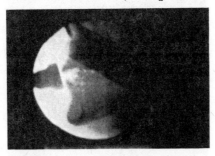

Normal embouchure, high pitch:

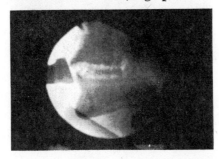

Unfortunately, these photographs are not clear enough to show the arching of the tongue, but consistent similarities appeared in the X-rays from one type of exercise to another. The spoken *ee* was always—without fail—accompanied by an extreme arching of the tongue, and the high pitch whistle showed the same extreme in a great majority of cases. In playing the trumpet, the subjects' tongues followed a similar pattern for the high tones, but the arch usually was not as pronounced while playing as it was in whistling or speaking. Even though the degree of arch varied from individual to individual, the overall pattern for the two octave slurring exercise was the same: the tongue either moved up slowly by degrees, or "bounced" from tone to tone as if it were enunciating "yah, yah, yah." In either case the slur was always accompanied by a movement of the tongue.

Several authorities, incidentally, have given the arching of the tongue as the reason, or one of the reasons, for the pivot. In spite of

the fact that the arched tongue directs the air stream downward, we cannot conclude that this directly influences the pivot, because of the tongue's separation from the mouthpiece by the teeth and lips. What we can say, though, is that since the tongue tends to direct the air downward from the *ee* or high arch position, the simultaneous downward pivot keeps the air stream relatively straight, thus helping maintain a free flow of breath. This is a convenient coincidence which enhances the value of the normal pivot.

The pivot, then, can be said to result from an unconscious effort to equalize the pressure on both lips. A. Fredrick Weldon (1862-1914), one of the outstanding teachers in the Midwest around the turn of the century, took another approach. He had his students resist undue pressure on the top lip by thrusting the jaw in the upper register. By doing this they were able to even out any necessary pressure with very little change in the instrument angle. One suggestion he often gave his students was to "blow upward," or direct the attack to the upper edge of the rim. This, of course, elicited the jaw thrust without his having to ask for it in scientific terms. Weldon's system would probably be considered a neutral, or "non-pivot," unless perhaps the jaw thrust caused a slight change in the direction of the tilt somewhere around the middle range.[1]

Another type of pivot might be thought of as a Weldon jaw thrust that got out of hand. A player with this pattern, referred to below as the "upstreamer," not only thrusts his jaw to equalize the pressure, he goes a step further and thrusts it so far forward that his lower teeth are in front of his upper teeth when he plays. The higher he goes, the further out the jaw goes, and so the higher up the bell goes! He finds that by exaggerating the jaw thrust, he can reach the upper register very easily and he builds a whole system around this premise—an underbite system.

[1]Through correspondence with James H. Winter, author of *The Brass Instruments* (Allyn & Bacon), and Leland S. Barton, a former student of Weldon.

Fig. 2:
Underbite embouchure, low pitch:

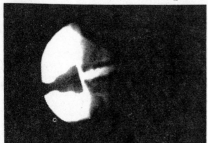

Underbite embouchure, high pitch:

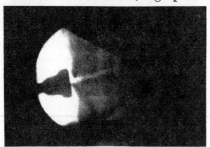

Rather than catalog a number of exercises, the discussion here will involve only one playing task: an upward slur. Before seeing what an upstreamer does to slur upward, we need first to analyze the normal downstreamer's pattern. As shown in Fig. 3, the muscles of the chin seem to be most active as they roll and "tuck in" the mouth corners, thus reducing the size of the lip aperture, yet leaving the upper lip free to vibrate.

Fig. 3:
Normal embouchure, low pitch:

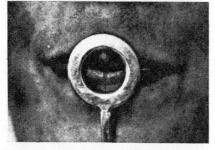

Normal embouchure, high pitch:

The upstreamer (Fig. 4) also reduces the size of the lip aperture, but instead of rolling his lower lip inward, he shoves his jaw forward. By this jaw thrust, he actually stretches the lower lip and

makes it firm without having to rely on muscular contraction alone.

This unique embouchure "crutch," not readily accessible to all players, is a kind of short cut to the upper range.

Fig. 4:
Underbite embouchure, low pitch:

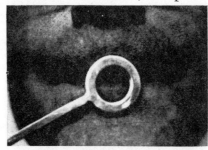

Underbite embouchure, high pitch:

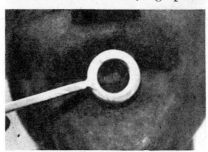

Upon close examination this embouchure would exhibit many of the qualities of the normal, "downstream" variety: flat chin, no unsightly lip flaps at the mouth corners, no puffed cheeks, and certainly a thurst jaw—if even a little too much so. One favorite stunt of the upstreamer is to lay his instrument on a case and hit a "no pressure high C," to the amazement of his friends. His background pivot understandably gives him a big advantage in that the higher the pitch goes, the higher the horn goes, so he gets extra mouthpiece pressure automatically.

Not only can he play physical "tricks," but quite possibly he can produce flexibility, range, and endurance with as much ease as his "downstream" counterpart.

Fig. 5:
Upstreamer "High C"

If all this is true, why bother

him? Most players would give their proverbial "right arms" to reduce pressure to its absolute minimum and slur from low to high with the greatest of ease.

If this were the sum total of brass playing, perhaps the upstreamer would enjoy endless bliss, but there are other things which cause him to wonder. Sometimes, for example, he feels self-conscious about his instrument; it always sticks out visually and aurally from the rest of the section. As long as he plays well this matters very little, but the first note he "cracks" seems to resound as if by high wattage amplification. At times, especially at the end of a hard playing session, his tone becomes unavoidably thin, which, coupled with a very limited "humoring range," makes accurate intonation more and more difficult. Of all his problems, perhaps the most frustrating is articulation. The higher he plays, the harder it is to tongue cleanly, and by the time he approaches the first leger line above the staff, any attempt at double, triple, or flutter tonguing is a virtual impossibility. In short, when weighed against these other difficulties, his pseudo "no pressure high C" seems insignificant indeed.

Fig. 6:
Upstreamer and downstreamer, "Low C"

Upstreamer and downstreamer, "High C"

There are several reasons, all caused by the protrusion of the jaw, contributing to the upstreamer's disadvantage as a brass player. First, it is obvious that when the jaw goes forward, the instrument must go up to equalize the pressure on the lips. If this is the only concern, a bent mouthpiece can be used to lessen the severity of the angle. Unfortunately, however, this helps appearance and projection, but other, more basic problems still remain.

Fig. 7:

Bent mouthpiece to alter instrument angle

The thin tone and weak control of intonation are caused again by the thrust jaw. To humor a pitch, the normal, downstream embouchure player ideally leaves his jaw position relatively still and adjusts the aperture evenly by a subtle "scrolling" of the lips from all sides. The upstreamer, though, shoves his jaw forward yet another notch, and in doing so makes the lower lip even thinner than it already is. As a result, the pitch may indeed rise, but as it does the tone quality will often become so thin and strange that the advantages of good intonation are all but nullified.

To understand the upstreamer's tonguing dilemma, perform this simple experiment: Shove your jaw far enough forward that the lower teeth are in front of the upper teeth. Then read the following sentence aloud: "You are probably finding that the tongue has too small and too irregular an area in which to perform adequately." Normally, people speak most clearly when the front teeth are aligned evenly, or if the jaw recedes slightly. Treatises which describe brass playing in relation to speaking (*too, dah, ah-ee, tiki,* etc.) seem to imply that the best jaw position for speaking is also ideal for brass articulation. Yet as the upstreamer approaches the more difficult upper register, his jaw goes further and further from the optimal tonguing position. Working under this handicap, his attacks are often delayed (*foo*) or hammered (*too*). The

finesse required for legato or light staccato tonguing is usually very difficult for the upstreamer to master.

Even with the foregoing background, there are still more fundamental questions left to be answered: What causes the underbite embouchure? What kind of physical features contribute to it? And what, if anything, can be done to change it?

There are authorities who claim that the pivotal pattern is inherent, and if a person plays a certain way, he just plays that way—period. Nothing could or should be done about it. After an intense preoccupation with the subject, I would have to disagree. There are a few physical characteristics which make pivoting backwards convenient, but not mandatory: an unusually long jaw bone, lower teeth which bow outward, and easy forward mobility of the jaw.

Fig. 8:

Outward bowing lower teeth

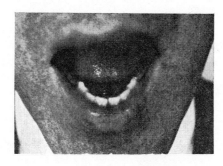

Easy forward mobility of the jaw

Those persons whose lower teeth project further forward than their upper teeth in normal bite position could possibly be the one class of "incurable upstreamers." These individuals rarely attempt to play a brass instrument, and most teachers discourage those who would. As a result, any rule about such a malocclusion as related to brass playing would be difficult to draw.

Fig. 9:

Probably an incurable upstreamer

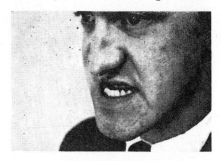

First effort at brass playing

Strangely, a few players develop the backward pivot with no apparent physical cause, possibly through compromise or convenience.

To change or reverse the backward pivot we must know basically two things: (1) what to eliminate, and (2) what to build in its place. Let me hasten to admit that some pivots have been reversed by a casual request to "tilt the horn down rather than up," requiring no understanding greater than which direction the horn should go. Sometimes a mature player, though, will need a much more thorough explanation.

The only thing that has to be eliminated in reversing an underbite pivot is the extraordinary jaw thrust, but this may not be as easy as it sounds. Realizing that the upstreamer has relied solely on his jaw for the high notes, to take away this response is to deprive him of his entire upper register in one mighty blow. Also, if he tries to pivot unnaturally without cooperation from the jaw, he may damage the lower lip, which becomes squeezed between the two opposing forces. Even after experiencing reasonable success in rebuilding the embouchure, the player will find that when fatigue sets in the jaw will instinctively "creep out" to make up for the weakness of the developing new pattern.

And what is that pattern? Overly simplified, it is the ability of the chin muscles to control the firmness of the lower lip, and the ability of both lips cooperatively to control the size of the aperture. The big differences are the chin and the mouth corners, because the brunt of the new responsibility and need for strength lies in this area.

October, 1967

Changing from an "upstreamer" to a "downstreamer" can require a week, or it can require several years, depending on the individual's physical characteristics and the rigidity of his pattern—*but it can be done!* Of course, if a player is determined to achieve perfection in performance, there is a good chance that he will play quite well no matter what method he uses. All other factors being equal, though, he will probably maintain his best control in all registers, and do it with the greatest possible ease, if his pivotal pattern follows the downstream tendencies of most brass players. These are, in the end, the goals toward which we all strive. ∎

THE BAROQUE TRUMPET

Elliot Del Borgo

In the years 1600-1750 composers used the trumpet in a manner unique to this period. Whenever one attempts to perform trumpet music of the Baroque era—whether it be solo material, brass ensemble, or orchestral parts—several factors must be considered if the performance is to be both definitive and artistically rewarding. Since there are no original recordings to listen to and very little written material, exact standards of performance are difficult to ascertain. Modern players and conductors often differ widely as to the correct performance of Baroque trumpet music. It is therefore necessary to analyze as much historical fact as possible. We may then arrive at a satisfactory solution to the problems inherent in the performance of the extremely difficult trumpet parts found in Baroque music.

The spirit that pervaded the whole of Baroque art can offer an insight into how and why the trumpet came to be so important during this period. Baroque painters, sculptors, architects, and musicians favored a means of expression that was grandiose and which was heavily laden with elaborate design. They were much concerned with nobility and splendor and it characterized their work. One need only view the paintings of Rubens, El Greco, and Rembrandt, the sculpture of Bernini, and the architecture of the great cathedrals and palaces as proof of this. The trumpet, with its commanding and brilliant tone, its ability to play extremely high and ornamental passages, thus became favored by the Baroque composers—especially Bach and Handel. Filling many different roles, the trumpet became an integral part of Baroque music. It was employed as a solo instrument (Torelli, "Concerto in *D* Major"), to play an obligato part (Handel, "The Trumpet Shall Sound" from the "Messiah"), to reenforce the higher melodic lines (J. S. Bach, "Mass in *B* Minor," "Dona Nobis Pacem"), to perform as part of a brass ensemble (Pezel, "Tower Music").

When the Baroque composer wished to obtain an air of festive brilliance and triumph he scored for the trumpets and kettledrums. The score usually called for three trumpet parts. The upper two of these, called *clarino*, (*clarini*, plural), were responsible for the high, florid passages while the third, called *principale*, fulfilled a harmonic role that was very much like the part played by the kettledrums. The distinction between the *clarino* and *principale* is an important one. During the Baroque Era, the *clarino* player was required to perform only in the very high register. He became a specialist in this range, but at the expense of playing well in the lower register of the instrument. The lower notes were then given to the regular trumpet player or the *principale*. In order to facilitate playing in this difficult register, the *clarino* used a mouthpiece that was quite different from the one used by the *principale*. The *clarino* mouthpiece was of a small cup diameter with a shallow depth, while the *principale* mouthpiece had a wider and deeper cup. These physical differences of course affected the tone quality that resulted. The *clarino* mouthpiece with its small, shallow cup produced a thin, very strident tone as opposed to the broader, more mellow tone produced by the wider and deeper cup of the *principale* mouthpiece.

There are those who contend there was another difference between the *clarino* player and the *principale*. It has been stated that in order to perform the very high register of the trumpet, the player must possess thin lips, while to play in the lower range thicker lips could function well. I would disagree with very strongly. One would have only to look at the many fine trumpet players who have thick, fleshy lips and are quite capable of playing extremely high with a great deal of flexibility. A player's ability to perform in the higher range of the instrument seems to be more a matter of muscular strength and control attained through good instruction and diligent, correct practice rather than any inherent physical characteristic. However, it is generally agreed that the *clarino* player was a specialist and trained with this goal in mind. Since the music of Bach, Handel, and other Baroque composers is not performed that frequently today, it would not be economically wise for someone to become a specialist in an area in which there is so little music literature available. This, no doubt, is one reason why the present day trumpeter has difficulty with the very high parts of the Baroque period. It is also quite evident that there are some fine players today who, with the aid of modern instruments, are capable of playing the high clarino parts, as well as the more common music written in the lower and middle range of the trumpet.

The construction of the original Baroque trumpets offers some insight into the performance of the music written for them. These were natural trumpets, that is they had no valves. The change of pitch was determined by the insertion of crooks at the mouthpiece end. Usually the instruments were pitched in *D*, sometimes in *C*, and less frequently in *F*. Since they had no valves, they were limited to sounding only the notes of the overtone series. If the trumpet player were to perform a diatonic line, this could only be done in the high register where the overtones were close together. The old trumpets therefore were much longer so as to have a low fundamental with the higher and closer overtones in a feasible playing range (e.g.—a modern *D* trumpet is 41″ long while old *D* trumpets were 82″ long). These instruments had a very small bore that flared to a bell that is also smaller than those we see on modern instruents. This, coupled with the fact that the metal used was thicker than that used for modern trumpets, gave the older instruments a darker, less piercing tone quality—a fact that should be considered for modern performance.

It has been mentioned that these old trumpets were built in *D*. The question then arises as to whether or not the *D* in Bach's time is the same as the *D* we hear today. It is in this area that there is a great deal of controversy and confusion. It is known that there did exist in Bach's time two different pitch standards—one for chamber music and one for church music. On reconstructed organs believed to have been used by Bach, the pitch of *A* is slightly lower than that which we use today. Since the human voice range has not changed significantly during the last 200 years, vocalists of today are quite capable of performing the vocal music of this period. This would indicate that the pitch must have been close to the present standard.

In light of the above, what conclusions can we arrive at concerning trumpet performance during the time of Bach and Handel? To begin with, I feel we can be sure that the parts were played by trumpets in the octave in which they were written; and most likely played by just a very few virtuoso players like Reiche, Shore, and Snow. Demanding great skill from the performer, the parts were possible on the natural trumpet—but certainly not with the same high degree of accuracy, clarity of sound, and good intonation we get from fine modern players with their much improved instruments. The Baroque audience was probably much more tolerant than our highly critical listeners who expect flawless technique, clear sound, and exact intonation. No doubt Bach himself never heard his music played with as much accuracy as we are accustomed to hearing.

Between the years 1750-1900 the art of *clarino* trumpet playing declined. The composers of the Classical period reacted against the ideals of the Baroque and sought a refinement of musical expression in place of the grandiose and florid style of Baroque composers. Mozart and Haydn, the two great composers of the Classical period, seemed to share a dislike for the trumpet and used it only sparingly in their works. Also, the addition of the clarinet to the orchestra provided Classical composers with another instrument to play in the higher register, one that was much less piercing and much more facile. Since the demand for the *clarino* player no longer existed, the trumpeters no longer worked on perfecting the extreme high register, and trumpet players, like the timpanist, became more adept at counting measures. The instrument was used very little until Berlioz and Wagner revived it during the latter part of the Romantic era.

Fortunately for trumpeters, the invention of the valve in the early part of the 19th century gave the instrument the ability to produce the full chromatic scale and thereby rescued it from the sol-do parts it had shared with the timpani for so long. With the improved instrument, virtuoso players again began to appear and the 20th century has seen a revival of fine trumpet playing. Today's dance band players began to explore the possibilities of the upper register and greater appreciation of Baroque works by the musical public has once more led to the trumpeter's interest in *clarino* playing.

In what ways do all of the above considerations affect modern attempts at the performance of the Baroque trumpet parts? First I think we should consider the relative size of the forces used by Bach and Handel as compared to those employed by modern conductors. It has been estimated that Bach employed an orchestra ranging in number from 18 to 24 players. I can not imagine anyone would think Bach such a poor musician as to allow the three trumpets to completely dominate and overpower such a relatively small group of players. Rather, I think it is more logical to assume the old trumpets were played with a smooth, almost flute-like quality, which would lend itself more towards the addition of color to the very linear style common to this period. Modern players, then should strive to produce a legato, flowing line that is free from harsh and unmusical articulations. The longer pitches (quarter and eighth notes) should be of a continuous nature with the definition supplied by a *legato* tongue stroke as well as a *slight* decrescendo on each pitch:

This will now give the trumpet line the same musical effect that is produced by fine string players when they perform Baroque music. It should be noted here that when string players perform music of the Baroque period, they generally do not use the bounding (off the string) spiccato but rather a broader, heavier bow stroke (detaché) that lends itself more readily to the style of the period. This factor is even more apparent when we consider that the bow used by the string performers at the time of Bach and Handel was convex in nature as opposed to the concave bow now in use. This convex bow easily allowed the playing of double, triple, and even quadruple stops, but did not have the high degree of spring that enables the modern string player to make use of the spiccato so frequently used later, in the music of Mozart and Haydn. Since the string community in general has arrived at what appears to be a logical style of Baroque performance, I feel the trumpeters should also perform their parts in a manner that would produce a style that is consistent with the orchestra as a whole.

The notes of shorter length (sixteenths and thirty-seconds) pose a problem of a different sort. These too must present the listener with the idea of a continuous, flowing line of sound, a melody that is spun-out and shaped in such a way as to fit with and enhance what is sounding in the other parts of the ensemble. However, the speed at which these notes are played will not allow for the slight diminuendo possible on the pitches of longer duration; the player must achieve clarity through evenness of playing. He also must refrain from overblowing—a tendency which would cause the tone to sound labored and much too ponderous to reflect the agile quality of the Baroque line. An extreme form of staccato should be avoided,

since this would detract from the melodic aspect of the line and be in opposition to the style and feeling created by the other players.

It may seem that I have avoided discussion of the most obvious question concerning performance of the *clarino* parts—how does one develop the extreme high register required to play this music? I have not written on this because it is not the purpose of this article to set forth a method for the development of trumpet players. However, I would like to mention two series of exercises which I have found helpful in the development of control and agility in the upper register. Both have to do with control of the player's aperture—that tiny opening between the lips which allows or prohibits him from attaining the desired goal of control and flexibility in the topmost range.

The first of these is a series of dominant-seventh chords to be played in all the valve combinations on B♭, C, and D trumpets.

This long slur should be effected by a closing of the aperture and increasing the lip tension (without stretching the lips out of the mouthpiece cup) to ascend and a relaxation and opening of the aperture to descend. It is also helpful to arch the rear of the tongue to pitch the air stream upwards when slurring to the top notes.

The second exercise is to be

played on the B♭ and, if possible, the C trumpet. It consists of a five tone scale, ascending and descending, to be played in all the valve combinations.

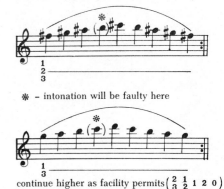

✱ - intonation will be faulty here

continue higher as facility permits ($\frac{2}{3} \frac{1}{2}$ 1 2 0)

Here again the pitch change must be effected through the use of the muscles that control the aperture and the direction of the air stream. Every effort should be made to play both of these studies as smoothly as possible, without resorting to an excessive amount of lip pressure or breath force.

The trumpet music of the Baroque era is quite unique and therefore deserves special consideration. Being aware of its inherent difficulties, we must accord a good deal of respect to the exceptional performers of the time who played under conditions which were probably much more trying than those faced by modern players. In any event, the Baroque era saw the trumpet used in a brilliant manner with such virtuosity that it will forever be a challenge to those who attempt its performance and a source of great satisfaction to those who succeed. ∎

October, 1967

THE CORNET—A DAMSEL IN DISTRESS

Harry Jenkins

In the United States today, when the word cornet is mentioned, the public immediately thinks of the concert band and the cornet soloist.

A dazzling solo is imagined with florid cadenzas, double and triple tonguing, all adding up to a superhuman display of technical ability

on the part of the performer. The cornet is not associated with any other type of music but the concert band, not the symphony orchestra, nor chamber music, nor the stage band.

There are practically no professional concert bands that operate on a year-round schedule. Full-time cornetists are few in number and the professional trumpeters rarely use the instrument. The cornet functions in professional, service, and school bands. Yet, the popularity of the instrument has fallen and the professional cornetist is more or less an anachronism. One wonders if this should be so.

Is the cornet an inferior instrument to the trumpet? Is it incapable of blending well with strings, since one rarely hears it associated with a string ensemble? Is it of little or no use in the dance band, brass or wind ensemble? Is it generally an inferior instrument to the ever popular trumpet from the standpoint of sound, construction, or intonation? After all, outside of some concert bands, conductors really do not insist upon its use and composers do not often write for it.

In comparison to the trumpet (although the actual length of tubing is the same), the cornet is shorter and has a concial, rather than cylindrical bore. The valve action is shorter too, a decided advantage in technical passages. Its tone, due to the conical bore, is mellow rather than brilliant. The trumpeter can easily switch to the cornet without any effort. Only the mouthpiece shank has to be different.

Since the cornet is more delicate in quality and construction than the trumpet, it could be considered the female counterpart of the trumpet. Due to its limited use and general neglect, it is in danger of becoming obsolete. It has become a *Damsel in Distress*.

A *Subjective View*

During World War II, I played the cornet exclusively for four years in an army band. Up until that time I had little or no acquaintance with the instrument for I had had little use for it in my professional playing. I found that it was not difficult to handle, responded easier than the trumpet, particularly in the higher register, and it took less effort to play. Endurance became a minor problem.

The greatest asset was its lyric quality. I did not have to coax a singing tone out of it, as was the case with the trumpet. While the tone was somewhat smaller than that of the trumpet, it was compact and projected well in piano and forte passages, outdoors as well as indoors. The fortissimo was not as brilliant as that of the trumpet, but it still possessed plenty of power.

After the war was over, I turned my GI cornet over to the supply sergeant and went back to civilian life and the trumpet.

In professional work I was often called upon to do ballad playing. With nostalgia, I remembered how easy and effective it had been with the cornet.

I wonder if the successful trumpeter today, who has little or no acquaintance with the instrument, is not unwittingly imitating the sound of the cornet with his trumpet when performing a lyric passage. Perhaps it would sound better if he used the cornet.

A *Future For The Cornet*

Where else can the cornet be used to good advantage besides in the concert band? There is the symphony orchestra, chamber music, stage band, wind ensemble. It can be used as a solo instrument in recital with more modern repertoire.

The truth seems to be that not enough people are fully acquainted with its full possibilities. For example, too few symphony conductors really appreciate how different and colorful the brass will sound in Tschaikovsky's *Capriccio Italien* by using the prescribed two cornets and two trumpets rather than four trumpets. Many composers in their works, among them Tschaikovsky, Franck, Berlioz, Ravel, and Dukas, have specified cornets. Yet in our symphony orchestras, it is not an uncommon sight to see trumpets substituted instead, with little or no opposition from the conductors. Evidently they do not realize the full potential of the cornet, as these composers did, since it is not heard much in the concert halls.

Composers and arrangers writing for stage or dance bands are always experimenting with "new

sounds." The flügel horn, the valve trombone, and bass trombone are being used more and more. How about the addition of cornets to the trumpets, flügel horns, and trombones?

What can be done to advertise the cornet? Perhaps the answer lies in music grants and the colleges: to turn out new music and outstanding performers, to grant full recognition of the cornet as a legitimate instrument rather than the illegitimate offspring of the ever-popular trumpet. In granting the baccalaureate degree in music education, why can't the college grant credits and honors in both trumpet *and* cornet? The graduation recital can present *both* instruments, with suitable repertoire included for the cornet, new and old alike.

Summing Up

The cornet must be heard to best advantage by all in order to be fully appreciated by conductor, composer, and arranger. At the present time, when there are few professional cornetists, its fate lies in the hands of the professional trumpeter, who upon special demand will pick it up and play it without any difficulty since it is easier to play than the trumpet.

Technically, the professional produces what is required of him, but what of the distinctive cornet sound and style? How can he match this when the characteristic trumpet quality and style still ring in his ears? Unwittingly he will duplicate the sound of the trumpet, doing full justice to neither instrument. To play the cornet well, the player must live with it awhile. With experience, he will learn that the cornet and the trumpet are two distinct instruments.

A plea has been made for the cornet: it has its present role, but it needs a new identity as a solo instrument in the orchestra, and the stage band.

The cornet, small, fragile, dainty, with its emphasis on beauty rather than strength, is the female counterpart of the trumpet. In America, only the band keeps it from becoming obsolete. Like any *Damsel in Distress*, it deserves to be rescued *now*. ∎

THE BEGINNING HORN EMBOUCHURE—
PITFALLS, PROBLEMS, AND PROGRESS

William Robinson

The importance of a valid approach and correct procedure in the development of the beginning horn student cannot be overestimated. Perhaps the most important single objective in the early stages of development is the establishment of a good embouchure. Future progress will almost certainly be limited unless the embouchure is established correctly in the beginning stages, and a faulty embouchure can keep a rather low ceiling on progress literally for years. It is a mistake to assume that the beginning horn student—even though he may be only in the fifth grade—cannot understand the details, workings, reasons, and procedures for the development of a good embouchure. Twenty years of teaching experience at all grade levels, from the fifth grade through the university years, have shown me that a very great percentage of the students *can* understand the problems without any difficulty at all. Our job as teachers is to make everything so clear to the students that they will have no problem in understanding all of the details—not only *what* should happen, but also *how* and *why*.

There are several fundamentals of embouchure formation which should be understood and at least partially set before the student is given the instrument. First of all, he should understand that the lips must remain even, or parallel (the lower lip must not slip behind the upper lip) while playing. To accomplish this most students have to move the lower jaw forward until the teeth are even; unless the teeth are even the lips will not be even. This can easily be accomplished by most students, even if the overbite is somewhat pronounced. Thus the picture of a firm, "pointed" chin is established, one which must not be "bunched up" or wrinkled.

After the student has the "picture of a horn player" in mind, he should learn to "buzz" or vibrate the lips. This will create some difficulty at first and will cause self-conscious laughter in the class, but the difficulty will quickly subside with a little careful effort on the part of both student and teacher. If the student can realize that this is something new and that the newness is the main cause of the difficulty, he will have less tendency to be discouraged. In a very few days the student should be able to vibrate the lips easily and even though he will be impatient to start playing the instrument, he can also understand that this procedure will make the road ahead a great deal easier.

When the lips are vibrating reasonably well, the student should check the air stream with his hand. Simply have him hold his hand or finger in front of the aperture and feel the air column while the lips are vibrating. If the air stream is moving straight forward, the lips are even; if it goes down toward the chin, the lower lip is back and the lower jaw should be moved forward.

After these steps are accomplished it should be relatively easy for the student to play on the mouthpiece. He should be made aware of the necessity for getting everthing set correctly when he uses the mouthpiece and he should not forget all of the carefully planned procedures which he has been practicing. He should try for a relaxed, "free" buzz, and avoid a tight, squeezed one. He should then be encouraged to play higher and lower, much like a siren—all the time maintaining ease and freedom of blowing.

Mouthpiece placement should be carefully considered in the early stages. It should be placed *over the natural aperture*. This may or may not be directly in the center of the lips. If the aperture is a little to one side of the center, the student should not hesitate to place the mouthpiece a little to one side. The important thing is that the mouthpiece should be centered over the aperture.

Generally the mouthpiece is placed approximately ⅔ on the upper lip and ⅓ on the lower. A good rule of thumb is to place the bottom edge of the mouthpiece rim just where the red part of the lip meets the white part. (However, some young students have such small lips that the mouthpiece has to be placed lower, at least until the student has grown a little.)

It is important that the upper lip be flat against the teeth (not squeezed) in such a way that not too much of the red part of the upper lip rolls out into the mouthpiece. Also, the student should be sure that enough of the red part of the lower lip is in the mouthpiece so that control of the lip muscles can be exercised. Inside the mouthpiece (a mouthpiece rim is very helpful) the position assumes more nearly a half and half appearance, while on the outside of the mouthpiece the placement appears to be more nearly ⅔ and ⅓.

The following procedure may be used for setting the mouthpiece: Set the upper edge of the mouthpiece on the white part of the upper lip, so as to hold the lip in place and not let the red part roll out into the mouthpiece; move the lower jaw forward and bring the bottom edge of the mouthpiece to the proper spot on the lower lip *with the teeth well apart;* form the embouchure by bringing the teeth a little closer together and setting the embouchure at the same time. This helps the lower lip to roll slightly into the mouthpiece if it is held firmly against the upper lip during the entire process.

An important concept for the student to learn is the relationship of range to the size of the aperture. If the student can learn to control the size of the aperture—large aperture for low tones and small aperture for high tones—his range development will be much easier and much more free from mouthpiece pressure than if he tries to develop his range without understanding the principle of controlling the size of the aperture. Also, this approach tends to keep the student from stretching the lips—a practice which hinders upper range development and produces the undesirable thin, squeezed sound mentioned above.

The student should always strive for a free, unforced sound. Without concentration on this problem, the tendency will be to use too much lip tension; few students have to be taught to use more tension. By concentrating on using a *minimum* of lip tension and mouthpiece pressure, the student should be able to produce a relaxed, free tone. This general approach to the instrument should enable the student to play easily in the middle of the treble staff. When this is accomplished, his upper range should develop easily and the low range should develop equally well when he understands that he must keep the same mouthpiece setting and lower

the jaw, thus increasing the size of the aperture adequately to gain facility in the low range.

One other problem must be considered carefully, especially for the small student. The student may learn a good mouthpiece placement, yet destroy it completely when he brings the horn to playing position. The horn is a very awkward instrument to hold at best and for the small student the difficulty is multiplied. A good procedure to follow is this:

Adjust the mouthpiece to the embrouchure before putting the mouthpiece into the horn. Then put the horn on the mouthpiece *without changing the mouthpiece position.* This may necessitate some rather strange horn positions, but the important thing is to keep the mouthpiece position right and adjust the horn accordingly. This procedure can also be used for older students, of course, but generally their position problem is not as great as that of the small child.

These painstaking procedures are well worth the effort by the teacher and student and will certainly pay large dividends in progress. It is a most gratifying feeling for us as teachers when we are able to remove technical barriers for the student so that he can progress to the fullest extent of his ability, talent, and desire. ∎

December, 1967

TOWARD BETTER BREATH CONTROL

Larry Willis

If it happens that within your band you have no brass players with an unsteady, wavering tone, an inability to play a true pianissimo, a lack of support in the upper register, or a poor crescendo or diminuendo, read no further and accept my congratulations! For those not quite so fortunate, allow me to pass along a few tips that might prove to be of

some help in solving these persistent and vexing problems.

It is assumed that, like most conscientious wind teachers, you have made certain that your students know how to breathe deeply, filling the lungs completely. Did you, however, remember to explain that breathing consists of both inhalation *and* expiration of the air, and

that controlled expiration is a key to good brass performance?

You may have done this and even urged them to practice long tones, yet the problems remain. These troubles probably can be traced to two main sources:

1. Weak and uncontrolled diaphragm muscles.

2. A lip which is not as flexible and well controlled as it might be.

To digress for just a moment, some object to the use of the term *diaphragm* in referring to the physical apparatus which controls breath support. It is recognized that the diaphragm itself is the principal muscle of inhalation and the abdominal muscles are most active in forced expiration, even though both muscle groups are active, to some extent, in both phases of breathing. Most of us understand this, so, for the sake of convenience and convention, the term diaphragm will be used here when referring to the entire breath support mechanism.

In trying to overcome these control problems, long tones, as they are commonly used, often don't seem to get the job done. It appears that many people employ long tone exercises of two basic types. The first simply is using "block" tones at a mezzo-forte level and maintaining this dynamic level throughout the length of the tone. The second is a gradual crescendo and diminuendo over eight slow counts. There seems to be no reason to quarrel with these methods except that it seems they simply do not go far enough in attacking some specific problems of control.

While a member of the faculty of the U.S. Navy School of Music, I used the following methods of long tone study and found them to be quite helpful to several of my students. Perhaps they may be of some service to you as well. These exercises will be broken into four categories:

1. block tones
2. crescendos
3. diminuendos
4. agogic accents

Throughout each of these it is imperative that the student be conscious of several factors: formation of a proper embouchure, a full breath, clean attacks and releases, and careful listening for steadiness of pitch and richness of tone. The player should spend a minimum of five minutes daily on each of these phases and perform them *in the order listed.*

1. Block tones. These should be performed first during the practice period. They are nothing more than the common block tones played at a constant dynamic level of approximately mezzo forte in the medium register of the instrument. Be aware of a firm, steady pressure from the diaphragm and listen most carefully for a steady pitch. Leonard B. Smith suggests that the student should strive to sustain the tone for at least thiry-five seconds in order to achieve the most rapid steadying of pitch. Be certain, however, that the sustained tone is full, even though the player may not be able to last thirty-five seconds.

This exercise is done simply to begin, with little strain, to loosen the vibrating surface of the lip and to provide practice in supporting and controlling the flow of air.

2. Crescendo. Begin this exercise at a piano level. Gradually increase the dynamic level until the tone begins to become uncontrollable. Stop at this point and repeat the process, trying constantly to maintain control at increasingly stronger dynamic levels.

Many students can play loudly, but with what degree of control? We are *not* merely attempting to play loudly here. Rather, we are trying to increase the *controlled* dynamic range.

The slow steady increase in pressure from the diaphragm will be an excellent source of exercise for these essential muscles. In addition, the more violent vibrations of the lip will make the tissue more flexible, much as a steak hammer tenderizes the steak. Evidence of this fact may be seen in the many professional brass players who often play a solo backstage at a very strong dynamic level so that the lip will be sensitive enough to respond at a very low dynamic level during performance.

3. Diminuendo. Having softened the tissue of the lip, begin now at a forte level and perform a slow diminuendo. The ultimate goal here is to make the lip so responsive that if *any* air passes between the lips, tone will be produced. The vast majority of students will reach a point at which the air continues to flow, but vibration ceases. When this happens, repeat the process. If carefully and persistently done, the ability to produce a tone at the level of a mere whisper will be acquired. It would be well to keep in mind that a major reason for difficulty with diminuendo comes from the fact that as the student decreases the air pressure, he forgets that the embouchure must get progressively more firm. Naturally, with the center of the embouchure too relaxed, vibration ceases due to lack of support and surface tension.

4. Agogic accent. The agogic accent is simply an accent provided by breath support alone. In performing this exercise, the selected note is attacked at a fortissimo level and immediately dropped to a pianissimo level. The tone is sustained with the accenting being done by breath support only. These pulsations should take place at measured intervals such as is diagrammed below:

Repeat several times.

When properly done, the result will sound much like two instruments; one sustaining a steady pianissimo, the other entering at regular pulsations on each beat and at a forte to fortissimo level. Notice that the forte pulsations are extremely rapid and that the pianissimo level must be regained within the space of one sixteenth note.

The first few attempts will probably be frustrating. Such a great deviation in pitch may result that a siren effect could be produced. This may be quickly eliminated if it is remembered that when the breath pressure increases the embouchure must relax in order to maintain a steady pitch. Conversely, as the air pressure lessens, the embouchure must tighten once again.

If diligently practiced, this exercise may produce a temporary soreness of the abdomen. This is excellent since this is nature's signal that a muscle is getting unaccustomed use.

By using all these exercises daily and as outlined, your students should show significant improvement in the areas mentioned at the outset of this article. This is due to the fact that they have specifically confronted the basic problems underlying all these shortcomings: control and coordination of the diaphragm and embouchure. ∎

GO HANG—
BRASS MOBILES

Dan Tetzlaff

Go hang what? Those notes you took at the brass clinic. *Why?* To improve the brass section sound. *How?* Make mobiles that float overhead, as daily reminders.
Material: 30 pieces of white cardboard, 8″ x 12″ (we used shirt boards); 2 brush writers, wide tip, different colors; a hole puncher; string loops (or opened out paper clips).
Assistance: Makes a good project for student "band-aides" who enjoy making posters.

Student Advantages
1. Short, condensed instructions are more easily understood, more readily retained;
2. Reminders are constantly *visual*—the eye sees many times what the ear could forget day to day; The repeated consideration of the "slogan" helps the concept to develop further into the reality of an actual accomplishment.

Teacher Advantages
1. Mobiles are out in the open, easy to point to for reference or reminders of the fundamental processes necessary to improve;
2. Explanation time is shortened when student attention must be held with "just words." More minutes of actual playing time allow a more efficient rehearsal;
3. Instruction becomes consistent from student to student, class to class, semester to semester.

I have already made and used the five mobiles shown on the following pages—first—for my university students, who did *not* get this instruction in high school—and then for my own band students. The idea was to use as few words as possible yet to say as much as possible. I try to use language the kids will understand—and tend to remember. These "brass mobiles" ask for involvement, not just passive reading.

1. To Emphasize the Inhale	2. How Exhale Enhances the Sound
Flat tire — Bad? ½ Flat lungs — WORSE!	Solid Tone EXHALE imitates HEAVY WHISPERING
USE ENTIRE 3/4 measure to 4/4 FILL UP!	LISTEN for an OPEN, DEEP HOOOO
for MORE inhale use BOTH NOSE and MOUTH	Keep bell HOT Warm it with Breath (like warming your hands)
LIFT ! elbows and ribs OUT→ EXPAND back & chest even 'til it hurts	LET OUT all the BREATH you can — for EVERY NOTE
learn the GULP! BIGGEST & FASTEST possible in only half a SECOND	BEAUTIFUL TONE uses MEDIUM speed breathing OUT
EVERY REST is a GAS(P) STATION "Fill 'er up"	play SOFTER by SLOW EXHALE to play louder, exhale FASTER

3. Articulation — the Simpler the Better	4. The Legato Needs 6 coordinations	5. Music Needs the Art of Correction
MOUTH CORNERS FIRM (HARD)	LUNGS STEADY PRESSURE never a let down	MUSIC is a MEMORY GAME
TEETH — APART TONGUE LEVEL floating in middle	GENEROUS EXHALE as if rolling a ball up / hill	Remember — what it FEELS LIKE in LIPS & in TIPS of tongue & fingers
LUNGS feel PRESSURE High — Firm EVEN & CONSTANT	AIM THE BREATH at the LAST NOTE use Air Energy !	REMEMBER what it SOUNDS LIKE
TIP OF THE TONGUE to tooth edge and ROOF CORNER	LIP POINTS must FEEL each different PITCH	REMEMBER what it LOOKS Like
TOUCH to same spot ALWAYS EVEN	use the LIP FLIP 1. FAST ! and 2. into BULL's EYE (tone center)	"WHITE NOTES" o are "LISTENING Places"
DART-like Action QUICK DROP and SHORT HOLD	Ear guides distance Muscles REMEMBER a tongued or gliss'ed PRE-PRACTICED Test	If you will sing or hum it first, then — test it on the mouthpiece. THE INSTRUMENT GETS EASY

1968

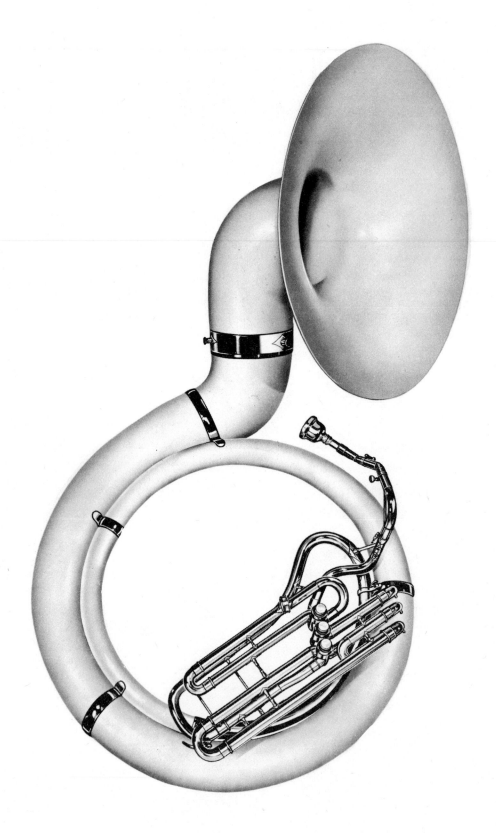

BB♭ Sousaphone (Fiberglass)

TWO IMPORTANT CONSIDERATIONS

Harry Jenkins

I. THE DAILY BALLAD

Pedagogues through the years have mentioned the fact that it is more difficult to play a piece of music slowly than rapidly. In no instance is this statement more valid than in the case of the brass player who has to contend with an unpredictable and fickle instrument.

In addition to his daily practice routine which includes long tones, intervals in slurring, staccato (single, triple, double) tonguing, scale and arpeggios, there is something invaluable that he tends to underestimate and even overlook: the benefits of ballad or song playing, the grand climax to the brass player's practice routine.

The player should choose his ballad wisely, selecting one that will give him multiple benefits. It can be any type of song, perhaps an aria, a folk song, or even a popular ballad. Here is a Bellini aria that appears on page 206 in the *Arban Conservatory Method.*

Let us study the possible benefits. What can the player gain from the daily study of this music?

1. Endurance—The first benefit would be the building up of endurance by being able to play the aria through without stopping. The nuances must be carefully observed.

2. Familiarity with various note values—There is an infinite variety of note values for familiarization. The triplet, in particular, (a much abused musical figure) is presented several ways. Daily practice will clear up any uncertainties about it.

3. Tone quality—By observing the proper nuances and not forcing the tones, the player purifies his tone and eliminates the "beard" from his sound, particularly in the middle and high registers.

4. Improvement of intonation—By playing a slow piece and listening carefully to the intervals, the player can work to improve certain notes that are out of tune.

5. Vibrato—Since the player must learn to sing into his instrument when performing a ballad, a tasteful vibrato is a must; a ballad is the best practice to perfect it.

6. Phrasing—The ultimate goal of the musician is musicianship.

7. Skill in transposition—By transposing the ballad into another key, for example a fifth higher, additional problems and challenges are presented in endurance, intonation, and control as well as in the actual skill of transposition itself.

A ballad or song serves as a general review in the practice routine, since it reinforces and sums up most of the skills. It is an ultimate test of musicianship, since its emphasis is on phrasing, the most mature aspect of performance. It also strengthens the embouchure. Here are some practical rules to follow:

1. After certain things have been perfected—rhythm, places to breathe, etc.—the ballad must be played through without stopping so the problem of endurance can be overcome. Then it must be played through once more in its entirety.

2. The nuances must be observed.

3. Faulty intonation must be corrected immediately.

4. A ballad should not be played with a tired embouchure.

BEATRICE DI TENDA

Andᵗᵉ amoroso

Bellini

con abbardono

a piacere   a tempo

poco piu lento

II. A MOUTHFUL OF CONFIDENCE

The scene is a concert which is in full swing. In the music, the orchestra is approaching a climax. Now there is a solo by the first trumpeter.

Confidently, he climbs higher and higher; his shrill, brilliant tone is penetrating and electrifying while the audience is spellbound. Suddenly he falters and breaks on a high note. The spell is suddenly shattered; it is obvious that something has gone wrong.

A look of annoyance crosses the conductor's face while the player is crestfallen—even badly shaken. Accustomed as he is to the hazards of his craft, he is aware that he will be blamed for spoiling the performance. The too frequent repetition of such mistakes can eventually cost him his position.

What can be done about broken notes, which can be as offensive to the listener as poor intonation or sloppy playing? What beneficial habits should the brass player try to acquire which will assure a good "batting average"? What things should he avoid? What routine should he follow to give himself a continuous *mouthful of confidence?*

In order to be consistent on his instrument, to keep broken notes at their absolute minimum, the brass player should strive to be a healthy individual. A good stomach, in particular, is absolutely essential. He should also guard against blisters and cold sores on the mouth.

To a brass player, proper care of the teeth, particularly the front ones, is most important. In regard to general well-being, the two people who are in the best position to help are the family dentist and physician. They should be consulted regularly *before* any mishaps occur, not afterwards.

The daily practice schedule is one of the most important activities of the player. It should be geared strictly to his daily needs. Logic will demand that he should practice less on a day when he has a performance than when there is none. Since each performance, too, will make different demands on the player, the practice routine must be geared only to the program that is to take place that day. No two players are exactly alike; no two have the exactly the same needs and therefore do not practice and prepare for a program in the same way.

How long should one practice on the day of the concert? It depends on the player and the program. Generally it is better to practice too little than too much.

Since the quest for self-improvement is a never-ending one, it is natural for players to want to experiment with new mouthpieces and instruments. A certain amount of experimentation is commendable since some improvement will be forthcoming. Caution should be exercised, though, particularly with mouthpieces. The mouthpiece is a personal thing and its value lies in the amount of confidence the player has in it. Such experimentation should take place in the slack season where broken notes will not be professionally costly.

An example of a first trumpeter in a symphony orchestra has been given. The player could just as well be in any section of a symphonic band, stage band, or ensemble.

There is no doubt that this responsible player is a talented individual who, in every way, is level-headed in respect to his craft. In his playing, he is bold in order to be at maximum effectiveness, and yet he is wary. He practices diligently but not too much. He weighs any change in mouthpiece or instrument very carefully. He does not abuse his embouchure nor his constitution. Because of this, he strives for and usually attains a *mouthful of confidence.* ∎

February 1968

TO SOUND LIKE A HORN PLAYER

Don Haddad

In order to *sound* like a horn player it is important first to *look* like a horn player and to develop a positive approach to the instrument. One of the primary prerequisites to horn playing is for the student to have correct posture and positioning of the instrument. Control and support of the horn can be maintained at two key points: the left hand and the right leg. Thus the student should pick the horn up with the left hand, swing it around to the right leg, and by adjusting the right leg find a comfortable approach to the embouchure. It is important for the beginning student to arrive at a consistent sitting position. If this position is not the same each time the student picks up the horn I find that the angle of the mouthpipe varies from day to day, thus changing the embouchure from day to day.

The following are my suggestions for "looking like a horn player":
1. Control and support the horn with the left hand and right leg.
2. Shift the body to right side of chair.
3. Lean forward slightly.
4. Place the left foot forward and the right foot back.
5. Use the appropriate right hand position in the bell.

Before it can be musical it must be muscular. Quick muscular response is important in horn playing. One should keep in mind the four muscles which are basic to performance: diaphragm, tongue, lip, and fingers.

Diaphragm. In order to make sure that a student fills up with air, I have him breathe through the mouth and immediately take two or three "sniffs" to supplement the original breath. Generally speaking, students do not take enough air for the horn, and the "sniff method" is just a check to help formulate the habit of taking full breaths.

Taking enough air is the easy part. Now we come to the problem of releasing the air. Have the student play a middle G (after loading up with air) at a soft dynamic level. While he holds this note, the teacher should give a sudden cue for a very fast breath push (use the syllable *ho*). The result should be a quick muscular response from the diaphragm.

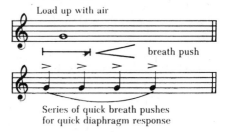

Load up with air

breath push

Series of quick breath pushes for quick diaphragm response

Once the student is aware of the fact that he has a diaphragm, he must learn when and how to use it. This response from the diaphragm is important in clear articulation. Besides the breath-push exercises I also have the students work on complete control of the release. After the student can hold a note steady for several beats (and with a good attack), he should add a long diminuendo. He should practice this several times, each time shortening the diminuendo. The result should be complete control of the end of the tone whether it be a slow or fast release. This should eliminate stopping the tone with the tongue (*tut*). See the exercise in the "Attack-Release" section.

Tongue. In horn playing we should strive for a short, quick stroke of the tongue (similar to snake's tongue). In order not to ruin the "horn sound" I also insist on a light, delicate approach to tonguing. The basic issue here is to supplement the tongue with air

(breath push) in order to avoid the use of a heavy tongue. The fundamental exercise in this case is striving for quick, short action response on one single note.

light, quick tongue response

After a student can demonstrate this "light tongue approach," he is then started on what I call "rebound tonguing." In order to avoid long strokes, I have the student tongue the second note immediately after the first as though it were on the rebound (syllables *ta-na*). The result should be quick muscular response from the tongue.

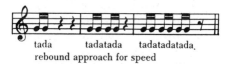

tada   tadatada   tadatadatada.
rebound approach for speed

Lip. Embouchure development is the number one concern of the horn player. My exercises for the response of the lip muscles deal with the principle of *lip tension* and *lip relaxation*. It is well to begin with lip relaxation. Thus a student can start in the middle register and *slur down* to the next mode of response.

relax

When the student *begins* to slur up an automatic "smile system" comes into play in the middle register. It is not wise to let the "smile" get carried away; therefore, at a certain point in a person's range, one must start tightening the corners of the mouth (syllable *ee*). Further in the upper register it is most helpful to add the syllable *oo*. This *ee-oo* method should develop a grip around the mouthpiece needed in the upper register.

To develop quick lip response I have the student work on the trill. Our exercise involves the use of a three note segment. To develop a quick muscular response, the first two notes are thought of as "pickups" and played as quickly as possible.

quick lip response

Fingers. I find that students can lip, blow, and tongue much better than they can manipulate their fingers. For fingering development it is important to emphasize scales, (major, minor, and chromatic). Furthermore when a student encounters coordination problems it is often helpful to press firmly with the fingers as he slowly repeats various valve combinations. The ultimate objective is again to develop quick muscular response.

First Technical—Then Musical

Attack-Release. As explained previously under "tonguing," it is important to strive for a light, quick, short action tongue. In the attack it is important to think of the tongue not as going *to* the contact point, but rather as *getting away*. (Again emphasizing quickness.)

When increased sound is needed I have the student use more air rather than more tongue so the sound will not be overpowered by the articulation.

In the release of a tone it is important to control the air stream to avoid the proverbial *tut*. For a student to gain a concept of this control he should practice executing a long diminuendo. Following this he should continually shorten the diminuendo until there is a shape to the end of the note. Depending on the musical passage, I have students practice on a *very quick* release and a slower release such as is needed for the phrase endings on the Andante Cantabile in Tchaikovsky's *Fifth Symphony*. In the exercise below the horizontal symbol designates a supported tone.

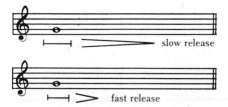

slow release

fast release

Articulations. The control of musical notation is directly related to the way one blows, lips, or tongues.

There are four symbols which describe the way in which a note should be executed or articulated: slur, legato, marcato, and staccato. I like to have the students work on these articulations in conjunction with their scales and dynamics, emphasizing *contrast* and *clarity*. Striving for a *variety* of articulations is important for the control of the musical line.

Danger Signals

If a student has a solid foundation on the horn, his future experiences could be limitless. Since the first year is the most crucial, the student and teacher should be aware of problems which might creep in. I have compiled a list of these danger signals which I use when teaching young students. These terms are remembered by the student and are meaningful to him.

1. "Pincher"—The "pincher" squeezes or tightens his lips to such an extent that the sound is not free. One simple remedy is to have the student relax his lips as much as possible. Sometimes it is helpful to have him back away from the mouthpiece slightly. Learning to "bend" notes is helpful in some cases in order to adjust the embouchure for the free sound which we are after.

2. "Tutter"—The "tutter" stops his tones with the tongue instead with the air. It is important to have the student say *tah* instead of *tah-ut*. A student can solve this problem by working on the release which is discussed above.

3. "Moaner"—The "moaner" starts the tone without sufficient air and then adds the air, producing a swelling or moaning effect. The coordination of air and tongue is very important in the attack.

4. "Firecracker attack"—The use of too much tongue in the attack, naturally will mar the tone. Working on the light tongue approach mentioned previously will help in this area.

5. "Blaster"—A "blaster" is one who thinks he is helping out the situation and plays too loudly, resulting in a brassy effect which is actually a noise instead of a musical sound. Experiment with the instrument which you are playing to determine how much air it will take before the tone becomes brassy.

6. "Ph-tu"—The "ph-tuer" begins the tone with the air and is a little late with the tongue response. Again it is important to work on a quick muscular response both from the tongue and the diaphragm.

7. "Square"—The "square" is my term designating the playing of notes in a non-musical fashion. In addition to clear articulations, rhythmic accuracy, etc., it is important to strive for some concept of phrasing and style. I always insist on playing the musical line with some character and mood.

8. "Faker"—The "faker" neglects certain notes in the musical phrase. This "fluffing off" usually occurs on the smaller notes such as eighths and sixteenths. Every note is important to the whole phrase and should be articulated clearly. Slow practice is the best method of achieving clear articulations along with *overdoing* them.

This list could be supplemented with many terms representing other problems such as "muffler," "speedster," "woofer," "sloucher," etc.

It is difficult to put down on paper what one can express in a private studio. I hope the above information is helpful in making a student look and sound more like a horn player. It is important to guide a student, especially in the first year; as problems do creep in they must be solved *simply and effectively.* I believe there is an exercise for every problem. I designed the exercises above to help my students be aware of the importance of developing muscular response. It's possible and most practical for all teachers to create similar exercises which can be employed in their own teaching approach. ∎

A GOOD BEGINNING IN FOUR EASY STEPS

Julius Erlenbach

When starting the beginning brass player it is desirable to have the first and second lessons taught privately. This is, admittedly, an idealistic situation for it is usually quite difficult to schedule private lessons for a large number of beginners. However, this should be attempted. The following four-step approach for a beginning brass player, whether taught privately or in a group, can normally be covered in the space of two 30-minute lessons.

1. The student is given the instrument and allowed to handle it. This enables him to satisfy some of his initial curiosity. The teacher shows him how to assemble and disassemble the instrument for playing purposes. Maintenance and care of instrument and mouthpiece are discussed. The student is shown how to clean lead pipes, lubricate valves and slides, etc. By allowing the player to participate actively in this discussion he is able to familierize himself with the physical structure and "feel" of his instrument while under the guidance of the teacher. This first step should take about 15 minutes. The instrument is then placed back in its case and kept by the teacher until the next lesson. Leaving the instrument with the teacher prevents the student from possibly forming any bad habits between the first two crucial lessons. It also keeps interest at a high pitch, since the student can't wait to get back to his instrument at the seond lesson.

2. Though the instrument has been put away, the mouthpiece is retained by the pupil. The child is now asked to sit up straight, fac-

ing the teacher, and to keep his feet flat on the floor. He is told that this is the best sitting position for brass playing because he can breathe to full capacity. The more insistent the teacher is about good sitting habits at the beginning the fewer problems he will have later. Further, the teacher, in facing the student, may offer a good example of the proper position.

The student is now told to hold his lips together gently and then to try to blow air between them. This may require two or three attempts with a gradual relaxation or tightening of the lips before the student will be able to create a buzzing sound. The preliminary buzzing is merely to enable the child to experience the sensation of the buzz. He is then asked to place the mouthpiece comfortably on his lips. Since there is some variation in the physical structure of each individual, the mouthpiece placement will vary somewhat. However, it is desirable to attain a mouthpiece placement which approximates the generally accepted ratio of lower lip to upper lip.

The final part of step two requires the child to combine the proper placement of the mouthpiece with the buzzing of the lips. The student is told to buzz his lips while slowly and gently placing the mouthpiece on them. He will most likely notice a difference in quality and pitch between the

open buzz and the mouthpiece buzz. This is to be expected since the buzz has now become centered in a narrower area. At this point, it is good to give a simple explanation of the workings of the embouchure muscles so that the child understands the basic principles of embouchure formation and what one must do in order to change pitches. Now have the child practice imitating buzzed pitches on the mouthpiece. This will aid in developing pitch discrimination while also furnishing necessary practice on the mouthpiece.

3. In step three the techniques of good diaphragmatic breathing should be discussed. Have a diagram of the lungs, diaphragm, and abdominal cavity at hand so that the student can see and understand the physiological process involved in good breathing. The teacher, as in all of the previous steps, must demonstrate the proper breathing method: expansion of the abdominal area upon inhalation, slight rising of the chest, shoulders steady, relaxed abdominal muscles, contraction of the abdominal area upon exhalation, relaxed throat, steady expelling of air. The student should then try this a number of times while his teacher watches for problems such as too much shoulder movement or tension in the throat area. The student may practice the breathing in conjunction with embouchure formation enabling his teacher to check for flaws here as

well. Now the breathing may be coupled with mouthpiece buzzing. Again, the teacher must be continuously alert for faults in any one of the above three steps. It is vital to spot incorrect techniques before they become habits.

4. The fourth and final step involves applying all of the experience gained thus far to the instrument. After the instrument has been assembled, the correct playing position should be demonstrated. The child must then practice this with the teacher correcting any flaws which appear. Now the student is asked to buzz a tone just as he has been accustomed to doing on the mouthpiece. It is advantageous at this stage, if the teacher also has an instrument, to play tones in the relaxed range of the instrument and to have the student match these. After the child has successfully produced his first tones on the instrument, he is ready to progress to his method book and begin class lessons.

By following this simple four-step approach, the instrumental music teacher can give his beginning brass players a solid foundation of principles and experience upon which to build. He will certainly save himself, and his students, much time and trouble at a later date if he invests the necessary time and effort at the beginning to formulate good habits among his brass students. ■

CHANGING CONCEPTS IN BRASS TONE QUALITY

Ted Kinnaman

It is, perhaps, an exercise in futility to discuss an aural sensation such as brass tone quality by verbal means only. Yet I think that it may be assumed that those who are interested in the brass instruments have enough experience and vocabulary in common so that we may communicate on concepts about which we are not in full agreement.

There is no question but that the idea of what constitutes good brass tone quality (I am referring most especially to trumpet and trombone) has been a constantly evolving one. Changes in the ma-

terial and techniques of instrument construction are bound to have had their effect upon the sound of the instruments. Besides these technological changes, the player's ideas as to the capabilities of their instruments have also been altered by the demands made upon them by composers for the traditional ensembles (orchestra and band), as well as the opportunities provided by newer groupings such as jazz combos and stage bands. Thus it would be senseless to discuss what constitutes an ideal brass sound in terms of any static concept, even if that

were possible.

Nevertheless, one wonders if it might not be worthwhile to question the direction in which much, although not all, thinking about brass tone production seems to be going. In general, based upon listening to and talking with many brass players, there seems to be an increasing tendency to judge the tone of a brass player solely in terms of volume; efforts are constantly directed towards a "bigger" tone, as if size and quantity of sound were the only components of a tone worthy of concern. Wider bores and larger bells are the natural concomitant of this desire for a larger tone with greater carrying power.

It seems to me that this development can be questioned on two counts: the first on what has usually been thought of as the traditional character of brass sound, and the second on what the increased volume from the trumpet and trombone sections is doing to the balance within the various ensembles.

In general, trumpet tone has been conceived of in terms of clarity, resonance, and brilliance. It has been a tone that could penetrate due to its color and brilliance, and not by simply overpowering the rest of the ensemble. With this type of tone, clean and precise technique was possible, as well as a wide variety of articulations. Much the same could be said for the tenor trombone; here after all, was a *tenor* voice, one which was a high, clear, and relatively small tone. In contrast to this, a good deal of present day playing is rather unpleasant to listen to.

At the same time, this emphasis on volume has, in many instances, played havoc with the balance between sections, whether it be within the symphony orchestra or the concert band. How often have we heard the trumpet section in the finale of the Beethoven *Fifth Symphony* cover up the rest of the orchestra, including the violins, who, after all, do have the melody after the first six bars. And in how many bands can the woodwinds be heard when the brasses really open up?

I am not criticizing brass instruments because they do not sound like Gabrielli's cornetts and sackbuts, or like the trumpet for which Bach and Handel wrote. I am also aware of the fact that American, German, and Russian players generally favor a wider bore and larger tone than do the French and English. What I am criticizing is the type of tone production that makes it increasingly difficult for the brass instruments to fulfill their function within the traditional instrumental ensembles which we have come to think of as standard since the time of Haydn. Since the violins replaced the gentler viols, the tonal range of the strings has changed little if at all. Some of the woodwind instruments have developed in an opposite manner from that of the brass, in that improved reed construction has resulted in greater control and sensitivity of tone, not less. Thus in comparison with the other families of instruments, there has been little need for the increased volume from the brass section.

It is possible that the marching band has played a part in the development of this type of tone production, due to the need to project tone when playing out of doors; but it is also possible that it is the result of the efforts of some performers to enhance their instrument's possibilities as a solo instrument. If this latter is the case, then it seems comparable to the situation we would have if violinists were to gear their technique and tone quality towards sheer volume, at the expense of Corelli, Mozart, and Brahms. Thus in this process, the trumpet and trombone are in danger of losing their distinctive character and taking on a lush and colorless sound of the sort that has, until recently, plagued the saxophone in its efforts to attain equal status with the other wind instruments. If we cannot agree on the pleasantness or unpleasantness of this "big" tone, it seems evident that even those who find it to their liking would have to admit that it usually restricts the versatility of the instruments concerned, and this in itself is a disservice to the fine art of brass playing. ∎

April 1968

THE COMMUNITY BRASS ENSEMBLE

Francis Marciniak

When making an objective analysis of the effectiveness of instrumental teaching one embarrassing weakness comes to the surface. We are not providing adequate opportunities for our high school and college instrumental music students to perform in ensembles *after* graduation. While it is true that there are many excellent community orchestras and bands in our country, there are still many communities which do not have their own band or orchestra or are not even situated near one.

In searching for the reasons behind this phenomenon, several factors came to light.

Economic factors are at the top of the list. To operate a large music organization involves a relatively large capital outlay. Expenditures for instruments, equipment, music, rehearsal facilities, and conductors can mount rapidly. Sustaining a group also involves a continuing financial commitment.

The administrative aspects of a large music organization often serve as a deterrent to many enthusiastic amateur musicians. One of the problems is to secure the services of a competent conductor who combines the attributes of a fine musician with those of a highly-skilled diplomat. Another problem is to provide the necessary instrumentation for a large ensemble. With the increasing mobility of today's population, the instrumentation may vary considerably from time to time.

Through diligent efforts, many communities have overcome many or all of these problems and have been successful in organizing local music organizations of the highest quality. However, for those who have not been successful, there is an alternative which might still provide an opportunity for interested amateur musicians to maintain their instrumental skills and continue to receive the aesthetic benefits of music performance. This alternative is the community brass ensemble.

Almost every community, regardless of size, has a substantial number of brass players. Many of the problems which tend to defeat the efforts of musicians to organize and maintain large community music groups can be readily surmounted through the relatively small brass ensemble.

First of all, the economic factors shrink. Most brass players own their own instruments, with the possible exception of tuba players. Music for brass ensemble is relatively inexpensive compared to scores and parts for full band or orchestra.

The smaller number of parts also eliminates some of the time-consuming library work. With the smaller groups no formally designated conductor is necessary, although, for obvious reasons, one of the performers must assume a role of leadership.

The problem of finding adequate rehearsal facilities is negligible. The average living room or family room can provide a small brass ensemble with a rehearsal room. Schools, churches, and service organizations can also supply rooms of suitable size.

The literature for brass ensembles encompasses a very wide range of periods and styles. Music from all periods can be performed without sacrificing authenticity. With the common practice of brass music publishers to print alternate parts, the instrumentation can be flexible, depending upon the availablility of personnel. For special occasions it would not be overly difficult to obtain the services of organists and/or percussionists to assist in performances of works requiring expanded instrumentation.

The possibilities for public performance by the brass ensembles are many. They can perform in large concert halls or in relatively intimate chamber music settings. The latter should be considered seriously, since many music organizations are called upon to perform for service clubs, churches, schools, and various other community groups. Transportation of the brass ensemble to a public performance can be as readily available as the family car.

The inevitable, but practical, question that arises when considering the formation of such an ensemble is: Who will undertake the task of organization? Since we, as music educators, are responsible for initiating instrumental training in the schools it is only logical to assume that it is our responsibility to provide the impetus for such a "post-graduate" program.

I am not suggesting that the brass ensemble, or any other small ensemble, should replace the community orchestra or band. I am suggesting that the small community brass ensemble will supplement the larger groups in areas where they already exist and pave the way for them in places where they do not. It would also provide the main outlet, if not the only one, for those instrumentalists who would otherwise have *no* opportunity to utilize their skills and talents after leaving our school music programs. ∎

April 1968

THE USE OF THE TROMBONE IN THE 18th CENTURY—Part I

Jay Dee Schaefer

One of the most persistent questions in regard to the use of the trombone in the 18th century is why the instrument was not included in the symphony orchestra. An answer to this question involves a discussion of the general history of the instrument and of the various musical styles and sociological attitudes of the period. It should be remembered that most of the church and opera orchestras of this period served both as concert orchestras and as accompanying groups.

The wind ensemble was the basis of the very early orchestral organizations. As the strings became the dominant instruments, the winds were pushed into supporting roles. The wind ensemble was kept alive as an entity by such organizations as the German *Stadtpfeifer* and *Türmer,* the very early military bands, and sacred performing groups. There was much music composed for wind instrument organizations during the 17th century but after 1700 much less was written. Very little of this wind literature seems to have survived.

The Stadtpfeifer and Türmer

By the beginning of the 18th century, the German tower-musicians had assumed the functions of community band masters. In this role, they supplied the musical accompaniments at church festivals, the processional music at civic pageants, and the dance music on the occasion of public holidays. Nearly every town of average size had its own band, and the rivalry between them was responsible for bringing wind instrument music to a commendable degree of perfection.

Around the second decade of the 18th century, the *Türmer* seem to have disappeared. Traces of the German *Stadtpfeifer* can be traced as far as the early 19th century. It is more than likely that terms *Türmer* and *Stadtpfeifer* simply became synonomous and the distinction between the two groups was forgotten.

A very famous *Stadtpfeifer* of the 17th and 18th centuries was Gottfried Reiche (1667-1734). This trumpet virtuoso and composer, along with Johann Pezel, formed the high point of the tower sonata literature. Reiche was a member of the *Stadtpfeifer* of Leipzig in 1691, became master violinist in 1700, and later served as first trumpeter under J. S. Bach. He was held in very high esteem, and in 1717 the Council of Leipzig had his portrait painted by Elias Gottlieb Haussmann, the famous painter of Bach.

At the close of the 17th century (1697-1699), Reiche published his *Vierundzwanzig Neue Quatricinia* for one cornett and three trombones. The manuscript of these numbers still exists, whereas Reiche's other works, *122 Abblasstücke* (small pieces for wind instruments) and five chorale books, have been lost.

Although the literature of the German tower-musician seems to have become quite scarce during the 18th century, the musicians themselves continued to be very important. We can be sure that many a German *Kantor* drew his trombonists from among the town musicians for service in the church when special occasions required a full instrumental setting of a mass, oratorio, or cantata.

It may be noted here that when J. S. Bach took over from his predecessor at Leipzig, most of his professional musicians represented "the civic office of *Stadtpfeifer*." They functioned on occasions of public ceremony, but derived their chief employment from weddings, at which they alone were privileged to perform, receiving fees according to the station of the spouses. A silver-gilt shield denoted their office. Each was proficient on the trumpet, cornett, and trombone.[1]

The practice of doubling on the brass instruments had some very direct effects on the musical literature of the century. Again, Bach may be used as an example. Charles Sanford Terry states that

471

the reason that Bach never used more than one or two cornetts with the trombone choir, and never combined the cornetts, horns, and trombones in the same composition, was that the performers of his "trumpet obbligati" were the same musicians for whom he wrote horn and trombone parts.[2] In the whole range of Bach's instrumental music, the three instruments are only once so disposed as to require separate players. The single instance to the contrary is in the secular cantata *Der zufriedengestellte Asolus,* in which three trumpets and two horns are employed. The cornett-trombone combination infrequently employed four players.

The old tutors of the German *Stadtpfeifer* organizations often recommended their brass students to learn to play string instruments. In 1757, it is recorded that Archbishop of Salzburg employed nearly 100 musicians.

> "The trombone expert, Herr Thomas Oschlatt, could acquit himself equally well on violin, cello, and horn. Most other musicians could also double."[3]

In 1784-85 Schubert wrote of the trombone in Germany as follows:

> As it is so neglected nowdays, and is played only by wretched cornett players, our musical leaders should make an effort to revive this sacred instrument. Nevertheless, there are still some good trombone players, especially in Saxony and Bohemia. Decidedly, the tone of the trombone is best suited for religious, and not for profane music.[4]

Orchestral Development

During the early decades of the 18th century, the main body of the orchestra was still in the process of formation. From the early foundations of the orchestra laid by Monteverdi in his opera *Orfeo* to the formalized classical symphony orchestra of Haydn, the instrumentation was in a constant state of flux. A study of orchestral instrumentation of this period shows the absence of the trombone in most concert groups. This leads to two questions: (1) Why was the trombone not used in the 18th century concert orchestras after much use in the earlier centuries? and (2) Why was it used in sacred music in opera orchestras but not in the concert orchestra?

During the 18th century, the foundation upon which the orchestra was built consisted of one or more keyboard instruments, to which was added a more or less complete string group, a small and rather varied woodwind group which barely supported itself harmonically, and, on some occasions, a small brass group which could not provide its own harmony. By the end of the century the original basis of the orchestra, the keyboard instrument, had been almost entirely discarded. The string group had taken its place as the main body. The still growing woodwind group had become harmonically self-supporting, while the brass group was also growing but was not yet complete harmonically. A study of the lists of 18th century orchestras show that the brass family, particularly the trombone, varied a great deal in numbers. The Vienna orchestras of 1721 and 1730 each list four trombones, while the Hamburg orchestra of 1738 lists none. The Salzburg orchestra of 1757 used three trombones with the specification that they were for church use only. The Berlin orchestra of 1787 used three trombones and the 1790 Paris concert orchestra listed only one[5]

It is evident from the orchestra lists that the trombone was present to some extent throughout the century, thus disproving the widespread belief that the trombone virtually disappeared during the mid-18th century. After observing the large number of trumpets present in many orchestra listings of the period, one wonders if these performers might not have doubled on the trombone when the need arose. It is a well documented fact that the practice of doubling was advocated at this time, as noted in the earlier discussion of the *Stadtpfeifer* and *Türmer* guilds.

THE USE OF THE TROMBONE IN THE 18th CENTURY—Part II

Jay Dee Schaefer

In the 18th century the association between the use of the voice and that of the trombone was used constantly in the performance of vocal compositions, both sacred and secular. It seemed to be the attitude of the composers that the instrument was primarily suited for choral doubling and secondarily for dramatic expression. In the majority of these compositions the alto, tenor, and bass trombone were used to double and reinforce the alto, tenor, and bass voice parts. In a few compositions the treble or discant trombone joined the rest of the family, supporting the soprano vocal line. When the trombone was allowed stand forth as a solo voice, the results were very effective. It is important to note that the sacred vocal works of Mozart provide the highest peak in all trombone literature up to that time.

When the trombone was used in the opera it oftentimes depicted a sacred subject. With this in mind, one can hardly discredit the sociological interpretation set forth by many authorities that the apparent neglect of the trombone in the symphonic concert literature of that period probably proceeded from the fact that the trombone was regarded with a sort of divinity, being confined to the church and to the king. This interpretation is also supported from the old documents listing the orchestra instrumentations, notating that the trombone was for church use only. This usage, at least in the German-speaking countries, can be linked to the Biblical use of the word *Posaune* (trombone) in the German version of "the last trumpet." The German Bible reads: *"Die letzte Posaune* (the last trombone) where our version states: "the last trumpet." Hence Mozart uses the trombone in the "Tuba mirum" of his *Requiem* and Handel uses the trumpet in his English-text *Messiah*.

Mozart's Use of the Trombone

Let us first examine Mozart's use of the instrument in his large sacred vocal compositions. Mozart utilized the trombone both as a doubling and a solo instrument. The orchestral accompaniments in Mozart's Masses were an outgrowth of the old Salzburg tradition started by Johann Ernst Eberlin, Johann Michael Haydn, and Leopold Mozart. Young Mozart held true to the tradition in the matter of reinforcing the vocal lines with the trombone; but each time he let the trombone stand forth it was to mark an important point in the composition.

Mozart's first complete Mass, the *Missa Solemnis* (K. 139) was written in typical Neapolitan style with arias, duets, and chorus accompanied by strings, two oboes, three trombones, four trumpets, and timpani. It is a curious thing that in this first complete mass, Mozart does not follow the traditional use of the trombone. In the opening of the "Kyrie" and in the adagio section of the "Credo" the trombones are used as solo instruments, accompanied by the oboes and strings. The beautiful introduction of the "Agnus Dei" is played by a trio of trombones accompanied only by the basso continuo.

Mozart makes use of the soprano trombone in the *Missa* K. 427, composed in 1782. This instrument seems to have been in *Bb*, an octave above the tenor trombone and is probably the same instrument which is found in some of Bach's scores under the names of "Tromba di tirarsi" and "Corono da tirarsi" (i.e. slide-trumpet and slide-horn). It was evidently not a true trumpet or horn as it was always treated as a non-transposing instrument. When joined by the alto, tenor, and bass trombones, a completely chromatic four voice choir was formed. In this composition, Mozart uses the soprano trombone almost exclusively to double the soprano vocal line. In the "Sanctus" of this Mass, the soprano trombone is dropped while the rest of the family plays an accompaniment figure that is very difficult technically.

In the *Messe* K. 257, composed in 1776, the *Krönungs Messe* (K. 257) composed in 1779, the *Solomnis Missa* (K. 337) composed in 1780, and the great unfinished cantata *Mass in C minor* (K. 427), Mozart makes no deviation in the use of the trombone from the pattern established earlier.

In Mozart's oratoria *Davidde Penitente* (K. 469), he employs four trombones including the soprano. In the opening chorus of this oratorio, all four trombones are used to reinforce the respective vocal lines. After the opening chorus, the soprano instrument is employed very little. The other three trombones are used continuously to double the vocal lines.

In his Requiem, K. 626, Mozart provides one of the finest examples of trombone solo literature, displaying the trombone in all its glory and splendor. Mozart remains true to the Salzburg tradition in the use of the instrument in all sections of K. 626 except the "Tuba mirum." This section contains one of the most dramatic and effective solos for the tenor trombone ever composed. (See music below)

Mozart composed several small vocal works in which he employs the trombones. In these compositions, he again follows the Salzburg tradition. In his "Litaniae de benerabili altaris sacramento," K. 243, and the "Vesperae Solennes de Confessore," K. 339, Mozart uses a chorus of three trombones to reinforce the vocal lines.

In an examination of Mozart's use of the trombone in the field of opera composition, we find that he utilized the trombone in only four of his works. However, each time the instrument was utilized, it was an important use and always associated with religious, semi-religious, or royal subject matter. In the sacred opera *Die Schuldigkeit des ersten Gebotes* (K. 35) composed in Salzburg, 1767, Mozart makes use of a single alto trombone. In its one appearance, the alto trombone is treated as a solo instrument in the aria "Jener Donnerwarte Kraft" accompanied by two violins, two violas, cello, and bass.

Mozart and Gluck appreciated the dramatic and majestic qualities of the trombone and used them with eloquent effect in their operas. In the hands of these two composers, the great dramatic possibilities of the instrument were explored.

The opera *Thamos, König in Aegypten,* (K. 336a) composed in 1788-89, contains trombone parts that are very similar to those found in the Gluck operas. In the chorus "Schon weichet dir, Sonne, des Lichtes Feindin, die Nacht" the trombones are used in a very aggressive fashion. Many times the instrument is used to state a royal fanfare figure. At other times in the chorus, Mozart uses trombones in leading the accompaniment in contrasting figures to the vocal lines.

In the sixth chorus, "Gottheit

über Alle mächtig" from *Thamos*, Mozart employs the dramatic effectiveness of the trombones. Throughout the chorus, they are used to accentuate various dramatic effects. Nearing the end of the chorus, the trombones lead in building a beautiful climax.

In *Don Giovanni* (K. 527), composed in 1787, Mozart again only uses the trombones twice but the two times still remain classic illustrations of the dramatic employment of the trombone in opera in surveying the use of the trombone in the 18th century. The first use is at the beginning of Act II, in the graveyard scene. Again, at the end of the opera when the statue of the Commandatore comes to life and drags Don Giovanni to hell to pay for his evil deeds, Mozart uses the trombones to suggest the divine or supernatural. This employment of the instrument is consistent with the use of the trombone in many of Gluck's operas, and in direct line from the early Monteverdi opera, *Orfeo*.

At the onset of the latter scene, Mozart creates a peculiar ghost-like effect by using the trombone, oboe, clarinet, bassoon, and string bass to play a series of chords de-picting the Commandatore. Later in the same scene, the trombone is again used very dramatically depicting the final duet between the Commandatore and Don Giovanni.

In the final opera in which Mozart uses the trombone, *Die Zauberflöte* (K. 620) 1791, he composed beautiful passages showing the trombone's rich and subdued harmony. In the Act II bass aria, "O Isis und Osiris" Mozart achieves a religious mood by the use of soft accompanied chords for trombones and basset horns against the solo and male chorus. The very subdued tone of the trombone was also used in the accompaniment of the "Chor der Priester" in Act II.

It is a very curious fact that Mozart waits until the finale of *Die Zauberflöte* to revert back to the Salzburg tradition of using the instrument to reinforce the vocal line. This is one of the very few times that he employs the trombones in this manner in his operas.

It is very evident, after a comparison of the compositions, that the style of trombone writing is quite different in Mozart's operatic compositions than in the large and small sacred, vocal compositions.

In Mozart's operas, the trombones almost appear to be used in the future "Beethoven style" rather than in the typical classical style that was found in the sacred compositions. However, in almost every operatic use, the trombones are still connected with religious or semi-religious themes. The trombones were used very chordally in the operas and there was very little supporting of the vocal line as found in the sacred choral compositions. As far as purely technical demands made upon the trombone performer, there is no example of operatic literature of this period to compare with some of the sacred literature.

A study of the history of the trombone shows that up to the classical era the trombone was cast in the characteristic roles of suggesting the religious or supernatural in the field of opera and of primarily supporting the vocal lines in vocal compositional forms. Mozart's compositions provided the impetus for some of the outstanding applications of the trombone in the latter part of the 18th century, and his understanding of the instrument helped pave the way for its greater usage later.

June 1968

THE USE OF THE TROMBONE IN THE 18th CENTURY — Part III

Jay Dee Schaefer

The Trombone Joins the Symphony Orchestra

Most authoritative sources state that Beethoven introduced the trombone into the symphony orchestra in the final movement of his *Fifth Symphony*. This is correct if this statement is amended to read that it was the first use of the trombone in a composition which was entitled "Symphony" by its composer. If this qualification is not added, then Johann Michael Haydn of the Salzburg school must be credited with introducing the trombone into a symphonic form of composition.

In the archive of the Benedictine monastery of Göttweig, Austria, Lothar Herbert Perger found a symphony by J. M. Haydn containing a trombone solo. The autograph manuscript is still there, contained in a codex of symphonies by the Salzburg concertmaster.

The third movement of this composition is the high point of interest; for if it is indeed a symphonic movement among a group of identifiable symphonies from the years 1763-1764, as it seems to be, it could well be the first of its kind. Since this composition was never given a title by the composer, the problem of whether this was actually a symphony or not is unresolved. The most definite proof that the work is a symphony is that the composition comes at the beginning of a codex of nine symphonies.[6] Probably the only way that this problem could be resolved is if a set of authentic parts were to be discovered.

T. Donley Thomas also mentions, in his article, "Michael Haydn's 'Trombone' Symphony," another symphony that pre-dates Beethoven in the use of the trombone. This symphony was composed by Joseph Krottendorfer. The parts of

Krottendorfer's symphony dated 1768, are also to be found in the Göttweig archive. This composition is scored for two oboes, eight trumpets, two trombones, and strings.[7]

Changes in Construction

In discussing the use of the trombone in the 18th century the construction of the instrument is another factor that must be taken into consideration. The trombone in its old "sackbut" days was designed as an instrument of medium sonority. Marin Mersenn (1588-1648) states in his *Harmonie universelle* (1636) that the trombone should not be sounded in an imitation of the trumpet, but that it should approach the softness of voices, and thus avoid spoiling the harmony of the instruments and the voices with which it is blended. This may explain why the trombone had very little flare to its bell until the late 18th century. The only major technical construction changes in the trombone since the 16th and 17th centuries were the increase in the flare of the bell in the late decades of the 18th century, and the gradual increase of the bore size. With the larger bore and increased flare of the bell, the trombones took on an entirely new character as instruments of tremendous power.

It seems, as in most innovations, that this structural change was not immediately accepted. Around 1805, Burney observes:[8]

> Tromboni and double-drums are now so frequently used at the opera, oratorios, and in symphonies that they are become a nuisance to lovers of pure harmony and refined tones; for, in fact, the vibrations of these instruments produce noise, not musical sounds.

Another important consideration that must be taken into account involves the development of the bassoon and horn, plus the changing musical styles of the century. As the new concert orchestra begin to develop, the trombone was replaced by the two instruments mentioned above. This may have been because of the attitude of the trombone's "divinity." It also might be that the bassoon and horn were considered the better suited for the musical style. The bassoon became one of the hardest working instruments in the early orchestra. It could do everything required of

the continuo-work, from doubling the bass to supplying the many notes that the horns could not provide. Both the horn and the bassoon could blend more easily with the rest of the orchestra than could the trombone. Exact replicas of the early and mid-18th century bassoon, horn, and trombone definitely prove that the first two had more penetrating power than did the trombone before its structural change.

There is some evidence that the quality of trombone performance decreased to a certain extent in the middle of the century. There are several reasons for this decline. First, it seems, from numerous accounts of the performing practice of this time, many trombone players were not hired on their trombone performing ability alone, but as often as not they were selected on the basis of how many other instruments they could play.

Probably the biggest reason for the decline of good trombone playing is concerned with the welfare of the German *Stadtpfeifer* and *Türmer*. Although the *Stadtpfeifer* survived into the 19th century, they had started to lose much of their prestige and power around the middle of the 18th century. The *Türmer* seem to have disappeared from the musical scene sometime around the 1820's.[9] With the decline of these two powerful groups of brass players, the quality of overall brass performance was sure to suffer.

The key to the revival of the trombone in the late decades of the 18th century probably is found in its structural change. With the increased bell flare, and larger bore, it could either blend with the other instruments of the orchestra or penetrate through them. This, combined with the wonderful literature composed for the instrument by Mozart and Gluck, seemed to offset the former beliefs about the instrument. With its inclusion into the French military bands in the last decades of the century, the trombone was ready for full acceptance.

The Military Bands

The development of the wind organizations known as military bands was connected with the early history of the *Stadtpfeifer* and

Türmer. The very early tower-musicians performed their duties from towers where they could keep watch and warn the people of the towns of impending attacks by the predatory feudal lords. In the 16th and 17th centuries, the trumpet was used to sound cavalry signals in the midst of battle.

The trombone was not used in the military bands of the early and middle 18th century. During the first half of the century, Germany led the way in matters of military music, and most of the European nations followed her example. The typical early and mid-18th century military band organizations consisted of no more than eight performers—two oboes, two clarinets, two horns, and two bassoons.

It was not until late in the 18th century that the trombone made its appearance in the military bands. There have been several explanations offered for this situation. One is that the instrument would prove difficult to manipulate on the march. Also, bands were often mounted on horseback, which would prove to be a very difficult position for a trombonist. Probably the best explanation is the earlier association of the trombone with the church and king. This statement is partially supported by Burney who tells us that for the Handel commemoration of 1784, the only performers on the trombone to be found in England were in the service of the king. This explanation, coupled with the strong association of the trombone with sacred vocal music, makes the strongest and most logical explanation. It must also be taken into consideration that the aforementioned major structural improvement, flaring the bell of the trombone, occurred in the late decades of the 18th century, thus making the instrument much more suitable for use in the military bands. With the increased sizes of the military organizations in the late decades of the century, the bassoon probably proved inadequate as the bass instrument because of its poor projection. With the improved bell flare of the trombones, the bass instrument of the family was the most natural replacement as the true bass voice of the organizations.

With the inordinate elevation of

military life by Napoleon at the end of the 18th century, came a fresh impulse to military music. Hence, the "modern" military band began with the French Revolution. The wind band, as an artistic unit, started with the organization of the band of the National Guard in Paris in 1789. This band was organized on the initiative of a young musician, Barnard Sarrette (1765-1858).[10] The setting was, of course, exactly right for Sarrette's enterprise: stirring music was demanded for the large popular assemblies, demonstrations, and ceremonies of the years following 1789. Other bands also came into being at this time, often as a result of the combination of small regimental or civic groups.

So long as the military band organizations had consisted of only eight performers, the bassoon was adequate in providing the bass. With the tremendous increase in the size of the organizations, though, the bassoon soon proved insufficient. When the addition of the serpent proved to be inadequate, the trombone was adopted.

There can be no doubt that the adoption of the trombone family by the military wind ensembles was the first real step towards its complete acceptance in all forms of musical composition. Most performing organizations were being increased in size at the end of the 18th century. With the forerunning trends of the Romantic period being felt, composers and orchestras were already starting to experiment and use various combinations of sound. The great dramatic possibilities of the trombone family were now ready to be fully exploited in the 19th century. ■

[1]Charles Sanford Terry, *Bach's Orchestra* (London: Oxford University Press, 1932), p. 15.
[2]*Ibid.*, p. 8.
[3]Adam Carse, *The Orchestra Of The Eighteenth Century* (Cambridge England: W. Heffer and Snos, 1940), p. 60
[4]*Ibid.*, p. 43.
[5]*Ibid.*, pp. 19-27.
[6]T. Donley Thomas, "Michael Haydn's Trombone Symphony," *Brass Quarterly*, VI, No. 1 (Fall, 1962), pp. 3-8.
[7]*Ibid.*
[8]Percy A. Scholes, *The Oxford Companion To Music* (7th ed., London: Oxford University Press, 1947), p. 956.
[9]Richard Franko Goldman, *The Wind Band* (Boston: Allyn & Bacon, Inc., 1961), p. 23.
[10]Richard Franko Goldman, *The Wind Band* (Boston: Allyn & Bacon, Inc., 1961), p. 25.

BRASS PITCH IN DEPTH

Patrick McGuffey

Music directors who are involved with bands and orchestras have asked, "How may I obtain a round, rich tone from my brass section?" As this question seems to plague many music teachers, it might be well to consider the basic factors of this "round, rich" tone: intonation, embouchure, the proper mouthpiece, and the proper instrument.

Pitch, or intonation, is the greatest factor in obtaining a rich and full tone. The general misconception is often in the actual tuning of the instrument. Although each of the brass instruments differs slightly, certain properties will, nevertheless, coincide. These differences will be discussed individually.

The French horn is probably the most flexible member of the brass family; it blends well with voices, woodwinds, strings, and tuned percussion, as well as with the other brasses. In horn playing, the secret lies in the use of the right hand for "color," and for making final adjustments in intonation. To tune the horn properly, pull all the valve slides about 3/16" to 1/4". Then tune to A 440 or a bit higher. (The area between A 440 and A 441 seems to be a better pitch frequency for obtaining the best brass sound.) Be sure to tune both the F and B♭ tuning slides to the same pitch. Avoid the practice of pulling one slide 1/2", the next pushed all the way in, the next pulled out 3/8", etc. This throws the instrument out of tune with itself and therefore the molecular structure of the vibrating instrument never settles and the student, as a result, never locks the sound in, and the quality of his tone suffers.

Trumpets and cornets are a bit easier to tune. Most trumpets and cornets of the student line, and certainly the more expensive models, are well constructed in regard to intonation. Do not, therefore, make a habit of pulling the first or second slide to correct pitch discrepancies. Rather, when one finds this necessary, the tuning slide is usually pulled out too far and this throws the instrument out of tune with itself. Pull the tuning slide about 1/4" to 1/2" for a better starting point in tuning. If the instrument is a bit sharp or flat, adjust but *do not* initiate the habit of excessive pulling out or pushing in. On most trumpets, if one must pull the tuning slide more than 1" to be in tune, the problem of pitch lies with the embouchure. On the other hand, if the instrument tunes best with the slide pushed in completely, and the embouchure is well controlled, one must have at least 1/4" removed from the tuning slide. This should be done by an experienced instrument repairman, or sent to the factory where the instrument was originally constructed.

Playing in tune on the trombone is largely dependent upon one's own ear, as the slide principle offers easy adjustment to notes that are out of tune. Generally, if one pulls the tuning slide 3/8" to 1/2", the trombone will play in tune with itself. Final adjustments must be made by the player himself, providing, of course, that his ear is so disciplined that he can adjust to the *overall* pitch.

A euphonium (or baritone) is rather like the trumpet and cornet. To tune the euphonium, follow the precepts for the trumpet and cornet. However, there are some euphoniums which have four valves. The fourth valve equals the first and third valve combination and therefore adds an alternative set of fingerings for C and B♭ in the bass staff. Rather than playing the C 1-3, use 4; and for the B♭ use 2-4 instead of the 1-2-3 combination, which is usually sharp. These combinations involving the fourth valve are well in tune. Some instruments even have compensating valve systems which allow one to play the 1-3 and 1-2-3 combinations in tune; these instruments are highly recommended.

Tubas are an enigma insofar as pitch

is concerned. Here, most successful tubists pull each valve slide about ½″ to ¾″ and then adjust the main tuning slide to the overall pitch. An instrument with four valves would be recommended if possible. In addition, some German companies manufacture a fifth valve (5 = 2-3). For example, B♮ below the staff on a BB♭ instrument, which is played 1-2-3 on a three-valve instrument, could be played 2-4 or 5-1. It is the general consensus that the extra valve is not worth the added expense, at least for students, as those pitch problems which are solved by the fifth valve, also create some difficulties which the non-professional finds insoluble.

Having discussed these factors, we now investigate the pitch affectation of the tone. Most young players have a flat quality to their sound. This generally is allied with an embouchure problem, but sometimes it is an aural one. First, the player should tune to the center of the pitch and not the bottom or top. Sometimes, in ensemble performance, it is necessary for one to adjust to the pitch of an entering instrument, or on the other hand, the note may have a high or low function within the chord. If the player tunes to the flat or sharp side of the overall pitch and the converse change is required, he has no place to go. Second, it is possible for the player to be in tune with the ensemble and "sound" sharp or flat by nature of the manner in which he tunes his instrument. Last, when tuning to the center of the pitch, the tone has a floating quality which blends with the entire ensemble and yet is flexible enough to adjust to any discrepancy which may

occur as the harmonies progress.

A final aid to the individual sound, and in turn, to the overall sound would be the cup depth of the mouthpieces used throughout the brass section. Generally, the player should try to use as deep a cup as he can control. The deeper the cup of the mouthpiece, the more Teutonic the quality; therefore the sound more closely approaches the "round, rich" tone which is desired.

Cornetists of the present day frequently choose a mouthpiece with too shallow a cup. These are usually sold with a C-cup mouthpiece; and this should not be. The cornet will never produce its true quality unless a very deep cup mouthpiece is used. This writer suggests an A-cup. The B♭ and C trumpets will sound rich and full with a B-cup and C-cup mouthpiece. However, the B-cup will give a Teutonic sound more suited to orchestra and symphonic band playing than tenor trombonist, playing the first part on a medium bore instrument, should use a slightly shallower mouthpiece than the player on the second part, playing a large bore tenor trombone. Likewise, it should go without saying that the bass trombonist should use the largest cup size he can control, and should never play on a tenor trombone mouthpiece fitted with an adapter. If one seeks a rich and full tone that will be an asset to the ensemble will the C-cup. The C-cup mouthpiece will add brilliance and edge to the sound and is generally considered better suited to the C trumpet. Deep cup mouthpieces used on the Flügelhorn, French horn, trombone, euphonium, and tuba enable the player to produce the maximum in

tonal beauty. It should be obvious that a rather than an unblending tone, at least the medium-deep cup mouthpieces are necessary.

As far as instruments are concerned, it must also be stated that the desired "round, rich" tone will not be possible on a small bore instrument. Students and directors who are seeking a large, full sound should consider only instruments of medium, medium-large, or large bore. In general, brass players would be well advised to play on as large a bore as they can handle, and still maintain the proper sound characteristics of the instrument.

The embouchure must be well controlled if the pitch is to be true and the sound "round, rich," and yet scintillating where called for. The student should endeavor to play with an embouchure which is relaxed and supple in the center and yet anchored well with firm corners. This would be analogous to a kind of "puckered-smile" often ascribed to better embouchures.

A fine embouchure also serves as a cushion for the mouthpiece and thus increases the endurance. Tone and pitch are at the mercy of the attack. The tongue should remain forward in the mouth and pronounce the syllable *tu*.

In conclusion, the pitch and general tone of a brass section, both of the individual players and the whole section as an entity in itself, are synonymical. If one tunes to the center of the *overall pitch*, possesses a *flexible embouchure*, and uses a mouthpiece in which the cup is not too shallow, that "round, rich" tone, which all brass players so desire, will be a distinctive sound "worthy of note." ∎

August 1968

SELECTING BRASS MOUTHPIECES

Marvin Rosenberg

Every band director should have knowledge of the principles guiding the selection, use, and abuse of brass instrument mouthpieces, as he is often called upon to advise students in the selection of a mouthpiece to meet individual needs. Band directors are also familiar with the young player who begins on a rented instrument and a "stock mouthpiece," (to see if he "likes music"), and who after passing the beginning stage decides to purchase a quality instrument. It is at this time that his mouthpiece needs should be thoroughly evaluated, and a change made if needed. As everyone knows, frequent changes of mouthpieces can, and do, cause more harm than good, so the *right* choice at this time is most important. Ideally, it should be for life.

In 13 years as a band director and supervisor, I've "gotten by" by recommend-

ing the equivalent of the Bach trombone 12C for the average player, and the 7C for the heavy-lipped ones. As you may have gathered, I am *not* a brass specialist.

Several months ago I started working on the trombone, not with a new career in mind, but seriously enough to put in an hour or so of practice daily and to invest in an artist quality instrument. Naturally the problem of choice of mouthpiece came up. The fruits of my struggle with this problem are the basis of this article. I feel that some of the principles that I evolved for myself, or got from others concerning the properties of mouthpieces, would help band directors who have the same 12C, 7C knowledge that I had. I have done much reading, but the opinions given here are my own, and may or may not be the opinions of the experts I

read or spoke to. I do however, have a couple of drawers full of mouthpieces, (and a pair of worn-out lips), to lend to anyone who wishes to arrive at his own conclusions about brass mouthpieces.

I began by reading articles or booklets by Vincent Bach, Renold Schilke, Dr. Jody Hall (of the Conn Corp.), Robert Giardinelli, and other mouthpiece makers. Then I started my round of buying and trying mouthpieces.

The critical parts of the mouthpiece are:

1. Cup diameter
2. Cup depth and volume
3. Shape, size and "bite" of rim
4. Throat and backbore
5. Balance of above parts.

(The numbering system used for

Bach mouthpieces is used, as this is the closest to a universal system that exists. The larger numbers refer to the *smaller* cup diameters—"A" is a deep cup depth, while "C" is medium shallow.)

1. Cup Diameter

Most authorities suggest that the player use the largest diameter he can manage. I agree. I have found that with the larger diameters, a fuller tone and more volume is possible before the sound gets unmusical. The usual drawback of a large diameter is cited as difficulty with the extreme high register. I find that the difficulty, if any, is very slight and is more than made up for by easier playing in the middle and low registers. Also, the claim is made that larger diameters mean harder blowing. I think that here most cases of harder blowing are due to an increase in throat and backbore size, (which often, but not always accompany larger diameter). Note my comments about throat and backbore later on.

I suggest that the average person use at least a No. 7 or 9 diameter mouthpiece for trombone, unless he has an unusually small mouth and lips. Heavier lipped players would probably be better off with an even larger mouthpiece. It is only when you feel that your lips are *really* "swimming" in the mouthpiece that you should go to a smaller diameter.

2. Cup Depth

Here is where your personal taste and preference in quality of sound must be your guide. The deeper cups give a darker, mellower, teutonic sound, while the shallower cups are more lively and brighter in tone, and with an edge. My preference is for the brighter sound, so I use a shallow cup, slightly shallower than a C cup of Bach. Any deeper than a C cup, to my ears, makes the tenor trombone start to sound like a baritone, (which might use an A cup for the typical round tone). However, in this instance, there is a great divergence of opinion (taste, rather), as many fine players strive for this darker, rounder sound.

One authority states that cup volume, that is the combination of diameter and depth, is what determines tone quality. He states that the shape of the cup, given equivalent cup volume, has little to do with the quality of sound. I experimented in my admittedly unscientific, subjective way by changing diameters with the same depth, and by changing depths with the same diameter. I found that within the small range of sizes and shapes that I could manage, that a shallower cup gives a brighter sound. In any case, from the practical point of view, one should choose the diameter first, based on physical make-up, and then try various depths for the desired sound.

Incidentally, this experimenting with diameters and depths was done with screw-rim mouthpieces. Anyone interested in these interchangeable rim and cup combinations can learn more about them by contacting the Giardinelli Band Instrument Company, 229 W. 52nd Street, N.Y., N.Y. 10019, who made the mouthpieces I used.

3. Rim

The point is made that the inner edge of the rim, called the bite, is important because it acts similarly to the fingers stopping a violin string, that it defines the area of lip that vibrates. In my experimenting with sharp and only slightly less sharp bites, I found little difference between the two. I imagine that one could get used to either type. However, I did not try the very curved ones that the experts warn against.

Most mouthpiece makers suggest a medium size rim. A narrow rim tends to cut into the lip, restricting blood circulation and cutting down on endurance. However, the narrower the rim, the more flexibility the lip has in moving around, changing registers, etc. A rim that is too wide does feel comfortable, and many who squeeze out high notes or use a lot of pressure use this type of rim (cushion rim). When I tried one, I felt as if I had a clamp around my lips and was unable to move around easily.

I suggest that the reputable makers experience be relied upon here to supply a medium rim that is a sensible compromise. But one could certainly try different rims to see how they feel. Just be aware that the rim must allow good lip flexibility with reasonable endurance.

4. Throat and Backbore

As with the rim, mouthpiece makers suggest a medium throat and backbore. Too tight a throat and backbore restricts the sound and causes intonation problems. Several makers provide, on special order, a larger than medium throat and backbore which does give a very dark, robust sound of great volume. However, it takes an enormous (at least to me) amount of air to feed this monster, and one must really work at filling the horn. Again, I recommend reliance on a mouthpiece maker's experience and suggest using his medium throat and backbore.

5. Balance of Parts of Mouthpiece

One cannot change the dimensions of a mouthpiece with impunity. The various parts of a mouthpiece must be in balance with each other or else it will be very difficult to play in tune. That is why I advise against "home surgery" on mouthpieces. When a good mouthpiece maker changes any dimension of a mouthpiece he knows how to adjust the rest of it to bring it back into balance. Your best bet in mouthpieces is to try the various standard models of the well-known mouthpiece and instrument makers. There is enough variety there for any possible use or taste.

As stated earlier, this is written by one who has only recently become interested in the finer points of brass mouthpieces. Perhaps it is this innocence which leads me to speak out so boldly in an area that is so very subjective, and full of "old wives tales" and half-truths. I think more open discussion is needed on proper mouthpiece choice, and I hope that this article will stimulate those who disagree with me, or those who wish to go further, to get out their pens and share their knowledge with the rest of us. ■

August 1968

WE CALLED THEM TROMBETS

Lewis Harlow

"Let's do something," said my father, "about our second and third trumpet problem!"

My father, the leader of the Aleppo Temple Shriners' Band of Boston, was a self-trained musician. Our band, limited in membership to 180 players because this was the absolute capacity of our rehearsal room, averaged 130 in attendance at Monday night rehearsals *the year round*. The time was the 1920's, a prosperous era for all the fraternal orders, and there was money to be spent on whatever would cure our "second and third trumpet problem." (We used trumpets on all the cornet parts as well as on the trumpet parts.)

My father had made possible a fine education in music for me, and

I, as assistant leader, handled the more fussy of baton assignments and also—as needed—implemented his brilliant and fearless ideas about instrumentation and scoring. His seemingly innocent "Let's do something" was actually a command for thought and action, and we went to work on both.

Bands, my father often said, must be able to *parade* or they are not true bands. Our second and third trumpets had a balance problem in marches as they were normally scored for parade use; for this reason, we felt that the problem needed major attention and deserved drastic action.

Style was changing in the writing of marches for parade use. The old instrumentally-inspired European march melody was angular, with a small range (compass), and was divided throughout into repeated sixteen-measure sections. This style was dying in America. The new thing was the vocally-inspired "popular" 32-measure refrain—plus interludes to lengthen the piece and give freshness to the second repeat of the refrain.

The greater compass of this vocal-style 32-measure refrain was the source of our trouble. The solo trumpet, of course, played the melody. When the lead tessitura was high, there was plenty of room underneath for balanced three or four part harmony supplied by the other three trumpet parts. Most arrangements in those days were scored for solo, first, second and third cornets (trumpets). When the melody went low, our second and third trumpets weezed quietly on harmony parts below the staff or played compromise and unbalancing doublings of the melody notes. Either alternative lost us the harmonic balance present in all of the other choirs of the band. Why should not the trumpets be similarly balanced? We felt that they should.

A professional trumpet player of symphony calibre can get a certain amount of power out of the extreme low range of his instrument, but he cannot do so and still make it seem to come from the same trumpet that produces the higher notes of his scale. There is a distinct change in the quality. Our second and third trumpet players were not

likely to be this gifted. Their low range was weak for reasons beyond their control, and we were asking them to play in this range almost exclusively. The mortality in this section of the band was rather high, and there was plenty of cause for their lagging interest. The music we gave them to play offered little personal satisfaction.

By our time, the glamor of the trumpet (and the advent of big woodwind sections to simulate orchestra instrumentation) had retired the cornet from almost all of its functions in most bands. The cornet, being more conical in bore, had offered a slightly more playable and listenable low range, and Sousa, in his late concertizing, went back to cornets for his second and third parts. He also tried flügelhorns, with their almost entirely conical bore.

We had also tried going back to cornets—and even flügelhorns—at our second and third desks. We even went a step further and investigated a French instrument pitched in $B\flat$, manufactured by Couturiere, who advertised that its bore was "continuously conical" *even through the valves!* (As of today, I still fail to see how such a claim could be justified). This "whatyamacallit" in $B\flat$ played and sounded like a high-quality cornet, but it did not offer a solution to our problem.

In addition to the inadequacy of any $B\flat$ instrument that we could find, there was also the matter of status. It is a little humiliating for an amateur musician to play a part marked "third," especially in the case of trumpets, where Solo and First are often not the same and what you are playing is actually Fourth. There are no Fourth Violins in the symphony orchestra. There is a Fourth Horn, maybe, but this is in the field of professionalism, and the forth hornist is often a low register specialist, with occasional solos to play—besides the pay is good.

Out of all of the above came the decision that we would have to give up the idea of a $B\flat$ instrument and go to something lower in pitch. With this first hurdle out of the way, we agreed quickly and without argument that $E\flat$ would be the key of the replacement. $E\flat$ is a

good band key, and the lowest note theortically possible to find in a third trumpet part ($F\sharp$) transposes up to $C\sharp$ on the line below the staff for an $E\flat$ instrument. This $C\sharp$ would be a relatively practical note, even for an amateur to produce with quality, volume, and musicianship. Also it would maintain most of the timbre of the other notes coming out of the same instrument.

There was of course a catch in going to an instrument pitched in $E\flat$. All of the second and third cornet (trumpet) parts in our large library (and in all new music to come) would have to be rewritten—transposed up a fifth. My father approved the general idea strongly enough so that he agreed to do this rewriting of parts.

When the new instruments materialized (which gets me a little ahead of the chronological flow of the story), he did the whole monumental rewrite job as promised, transposing literally when there was harmony to transpose and supplying harmony from horn or trombone parts when the second and third trumpet parts doubled on the melody because they couldn't reach the harmony parts present in the score.

I have touched on my father's self-education in music, and I should mention his technique in the writing of scores and/or parts. His instrument was flute, and he could "hear" anything that he saw on a printed page (or in his mind) by holding a lead pencil up to his lips flute-style and fingering it. He also had an unerring feel for the key in which any part might be written, and he never made a mistake in substituting flats for naturals or vice versa where accidentals were involved in his transposition project. All this in spite of the fact that the source material to be considered might include $B\flat$ parts, $E\flat$ parts, C parts, and bass clef parts, singly or in combination.

Now back to the principal thread of the narrative. What were to be the specifications of our new instrument? We first considered the $E\flat$ alto trumpet, still to be found, (in Janáček's *Sinfonietta,* for example) but quite rarely used in the contemporary symphony orchestra. This instrument would not do for

479

us; it had poor balance; it was too heavy to hold up and out front for the duration of a four-mile parade; the valves were too far out front; the view of the parade lyre was too remote for the possibly myopic vision of our performers.

E♭ alto horns were of course not to be considered, as their broad tone was incompatible when included in the trumpet choir.

The best idea seemed to be an E♭ alto valve trombone, an instrument that, as far as we knew, did not exist. Its over-the-shoulder bell would contribute to good balance, and the valves and lyre could be positioned at least as comfortably and usefully as they are on a B♭ trumpet.

The valve trombone in E♭ was what we wanted, and from this basic start we went on to other theoretical specifications. The bore should be cylindrical like a trumpet or trombone, not conical like a cornet, alto horn, or baritone. The gauge of the brass should be a compromise between the average gauges of band trumpets and the average gauges of band trombones —shaded perhaps toward the trumpet side. The silver content of the brass should be a little less than the silver content in top quality orchestral brass instruments. The mouthpiece? It should of course be shallow-cupped like a trumpet mouthpiece, and probably it should be an average trumpet mouthpiece scaled up about fifty percent in every dimension. Maybe forty percent. This was as far as we could go on our own.

Then we approached the late Peter Edwards, Doctor of Brass and Custom Manufacturer to Kings of Music. Peter listened to our specifications, and he agreed to the logic of them, but he was especially pleased when we told him that we were rank amateurs at instrument designing—and that we were going to tell him the results we wanted and then let him do the designing to produce these results.

We wanted a valve trombone pitched in E♭. We wanted it to sound so much like a B♭ trumpet that only an expert could tell the difference when our larger instrument was played in its middle register. We proposed to write parts for the new instrument that would go no higher than G above the staff —and very rarely lower than C below the staff. The prime consideration was our specification of tone quality, and provided that this consideration was in no way jeopardized, we wanted the instrument to be as easy to play as possible, within the playing range that we had established for it. We wanted brass finish (lacquered brass was still some years in the future), and of course we wanted a case to fit our little valve trombone—which we proposed to christen a "trombet." We would buy the sample instrument that represented his best efforts toward these objectives, and if he and we were satisfied with it, we would buy five more.

Our trombets were a complete success. Some years later I learned that we never saw the first two instruments that he built to our performance specifications; but when we were finally called in for the demonstration of the finshed product, it could not have been more right. Even I could play it effortlessly and sounding like a trumpet, and I make no pretense of being a brass man.

Our order for the other five went through without delay. You may wonder why our 130-180 piece band would be needing six musicians on second and third trumpet parts to balance the rest of the brass ensemble. Actually we didn't need all six to be played at the same time—nor expect that we would have them. We did feel that we would need four of the six to balance our rehearsal average of 130, and this was the attendance we found we could count on. Balance was pretty important at our rehearsals, because at the completion of each rehearsal session there was a *live* radio broadcast over Westinghouse Station WBZ. This of course was back in the days before the commercials dominated the broadcasting industry, and stations in those days welcomed "sustaining" weekly programs from the likes of a 130-piece band.

The players of our six trombets, having previously lived in the frustration and ineffectiveness of the second and third trumpet section, were enthusiastic to a man. Now• they were "firsts" and "seconds" on an exclusive instrument. It is true that they were still playing basically the same part that they had played before—but there was a great difference. The new instrument was right for its job. It was no longer a deterrent to its player's effective contribution to the whole. Now, if there was still a shortcoming, it was strictly up to the player to rectify, and the objective was not beyond human attainment. Gratifyingly, we observed that the trombet parts were going home after rehearsal. This had rarely been true with second and third trumpet parts, and I blame no one for the lack of ambition or even interest. There could be nothing more futile in music than solo practice at home on a third trumpet part.

The pride of playing a trombet resulted in such secondary occurances as one of the players getting a new and better-fitting upper plate, a drastic action in self-improvement which would rarely occur to an amateur player of third trumpet. This pride was most evident, of course, when we went to the annual national conventions.

No instruments were better polished than the trombets, and at parade staging areas, no trombet player ever missed the opportunity to circulate casually among players in other bands which didn't have trombets—and fish with seeming innocence for questions and conversation about his miniaturized valve trombone. This happened in Miami, and in Seattle, and in many appropriate way stations.

I wish that I could end with the comment that the trombet, having come into existence in this way, was forevermore established in the standard instrumentation of the modern band. Sadly, I must disclose that this would not be true, The depression of the 1930's dried the wellspring which had financed the thinking about trombets, the buying of them, and the writing of parts for them to play. After the depression, the Aleppo Band emerged much smaller, administered with great economy, and equipped in the old tradition of instrumentation. The torch is still smouldering, though, waiting to be picked by a new generation, still to come. ∎

September 1968

THE JUNIOR HIGH SCHOOL BRASS CHOIR

Richard Lindner

The last 30 years has witnessed a tremendous upsurge of interest in writing, arranging, and performing brass choir and brass ensemble music. Among the better known names of those closely associated with brass music are Robert King, Ernest Glover, and Roger Voisin. Mr. King has edited, arranged, and supervised the publishing of a great volume of brass music of the past and present. Mr. Glover has organized and conducted many brass choirs at the Cincinnati Conservatory of Music and has written articles in various music periodicals encouraging professional players and teachers to organize brass choirs. Roger Voisin has contributed in performance through many recordings of brass, and especially trumpet music, of all periods.

Music educators are all aware of the significant growth of public school instrumental music during the past few decades. What about brass music in the public schools? What about brass music particularly in the junior high schools? There is evidence that a brass choir or similar ensemble is a very practical and beneficial educational tool for the junior high school instrumental director. Including ensembles such as a brass choir on the junior high level allows a student an opportunity for exploration; exploration at a time when, according to educational psychologists, it is thought to give the most significant results.

One of the more important and obvious reasons to have groups such as the brass choir or clarinet choir is to help the concert band develop an ensemble sound. The old, constantly recurring problems of balance, timbre, intonation, phrasing, and attacks and releases are much more easily learned in small groups. The ever-growing importance of style and interpretation causes a real need for special work.

In addition, the aural senses are sharpened greatly in small group playing. All this and more will be carried over to the concert band which should be the focal point of sound and good concept. These all activity in the band program.

As a junior high school band director, I developed a successful brass choir program, and recognized a need for a basic list of published material for junior high brass choirs. For some time brass music has been graded and reviewed in at least two of the more popular instrumental music education periodicals. Yet it is not easy to determine from these graded reviews which

COMPOSER-ARRANGER	TITLE	PUBLISHER
Bach-Gillis	"Bach Chorales for Brass Choir"	Southern
Bach-Tote	"Chorale and Fughetta"	Barnhouse
Bach-Ostling	"Contrasts by Bach"	Belwin
Bach-Cafarella	"Five Pieces for Brass Choir"	Witmark-MPH
Bach-Johnson	"Four Chorales for Brass Sextet"	Rubank
Bach-Menhen & Baron	"Three Chorales"	Boosey & Hawkes
Bach-Uber	"Two Chorales"	Edition Musicus
Bach-Ludwig	"Three Chorales"	Ludwig
Beethoven-Holmes	"Allegro from Symphony #6"	Barnhouse
Beethoven-Ross	"Prayer"	Kendor
Bonelli	"Toccata"	King
Brahms-Wise	"Joy of Thy Salvation"	Pro Art
Christensen (arr.)	"Coventry Carol"	Kendor
Conely	"Intrada"	Kendor
Conely	"Promenade"	Kendor
Couperin-King	"Fugue"	King
Gesualdo-Freedman	"Four Madrigals"	Leeds-MCA
Gibbons, Byrd, Morely-Howe	"Three Madrigals for Brass"	Elkan-Vogel
Gounod-Ostling	"March Romaine"	Belwin
Grep	"Paduana"	King
Hilbert (arr.)	"Three Christmas Carols for Brass" (no bass part)	Concordia
Johnson	"Mood Militant"	Rubank
McKay	"Narrative Sketch"	Barnhouse
Ostransky	"Passacaglia & Scherzo"	Rubank
Palestrina-King	"Three Hymns"	King
Pelz (arr.)	"Ten Masterworks for Brass Choir"	Shawnee
Pezel	"Sonata No. 1"	King
Pezel	"Sonata No. 2"	King
Purcell-Barnes	"March and Fanfare"	Ludwig
Purcell	"Music for Queen Mary II" (optional SATB chorus)	King
Purcell-Brown	"Trumpet Voluntary"	Summy-Birchard
Scarlatti-Johnson	"Aria and Minuet"	Rubank
Schumann-Nagel	"Song, Chorale and March"	Mentor
Shelly (arr.)	"Deck the Hall"	Kendor
Tufilli	"A Prayer"	Pro Art

compositions might "fit" these young musicians.

The problem having been recognized, the task of devising a list was undertaken. In order to evaluate a large number of brass choir compositions and construct a select list of pieces for junior high school instrumentalists, a number of evaluative criteria were determined. The list was then prepared by examining many brass choir compositions in the light of these criteria.

To begin, I constructed the following brass range table:

To be sure, every band director either has or has had individuals in his music program capable of exceeding these ranges with beautiful terion is valid considering the emphasis is being placed on building ranges however, are felt to be comfortably available to the majority of junior high school brass players. All music on the list with a few exceptions complies with this table.

Secondly, the use of equal doubling of parts is possible with little or no loss of character of the piece. Some of the numbers included on the list, which are arranged as quintets or sextets, are included under this consideration. The successful performance of these will depend upon the director's care in

doubling of parts. Third, most of the music is in duple or triple meter. Fourth, there are no lengthy, exposed solos in any part. This cri-ensemble concept and sound. Finally, all of the music on the list can be performed by a brass *choir* (i.e., two or more players on a part), and all works contain parts for $B\flat$ cornet-trumpet, F horn, trombone, bass clef baritone, and tuba.

Inherent in the brass choir are many rewards and benefits for the students who comprise it, for the total band program, and for the director. It is hoped the list will be an aid to band directors interested in building a library of junior high school brass choir materials.

October 1968

THE DIFFERENCES BETWEEN THE TENOR AND BASS TROMBONES

Paul Tanner and Kenneth Sawhill

During a recent visit to Hawaii, Professor Paul Tanner and one of his students from UCLA, bass trombonist Kenneth Sawhill, presented a series of trombone clinics for the Oahu Band Directors' Association in connection with concert appearances. One of the works programmed on the concerts was the "Concert Duo for Tenor and Bass Trombone," written by Mr. Tanner and performed with the University of Hawaii Concert Band under the direction of Professor Richard Lum.

The advent of such extensive use of the bass trombone caused considerable inquiry concerning the new importance of the bass trombone. One of the clinics led to the following discussion:

Question: Professor Tanner, the performance of your composition was the first time we have witnessed such extensive use of the bass trombone. Is this a coming trend?

Tanner: The bass trombone has surely come into its own and I feel it will continue to gain in importance. When I go on a studio call in Hollywood now, if there are three trombones, one is surely a bass. I am sure that soon, wherever there are two trombones used, one will be a bass. This is not just in studio work; Ken and I see this more and more in all kinds of music around the country, and of course this includes school bands.

Sawhill: Could we put in a plea now that you don't just put your least competent player on bass trombone? Choose one of your best players; he should not only want to play the bass, but should be as talented a player as anyone else in the section.

Question: "Well, what's the difference between the tenor and the bass trombone?"

Tanner: There really is a great deal of confusion, not only among band and orchestra directors, and not only among dealers and manufacturers, but also among trombonists.

Sawhill: We honestly consider them as two separate instruments and the playing of each one is an art within itself. Some fellows, at least for a while, were doubling on both; but playing the bass trombone has become such an art of its own now; doubling isn't really very satisfactory, anyway. I am sure Paul agrees with me when I say that we have a tendency to frown on doubling.

Tanner: Yes. The approach is really quite different. I think the primary difference is the sound. One of the most important aspects affecting the quality of the sound is the size of the bore. A typical tenor bore is around .500, although you can find them as small as .464, or so. The typical bass trombone bore is around .547 and over.

Question: What is the bore size of your two trombones?

Tanner: Mine is .500.

Sawhill: Mine is .562—the biggest made by some manufacturers. Where a lot of the confusion comes is that some manufacturers call their horns tenor trombones when the bore is as large as .547; yet they will have a bass trombone the same size. Some other manufacturer may have an instrument they call a bass trombone and it could be only .545 or even smaller.

Tanner: Naturally, the larger the bore, the more tendency there is to consider the instrument a bass trombone, but there are actually instruments called tenor trombones which have larger bores than some called bass trombones.

Sawhill: Therefore, because of this overlapping, the bore size cannot be the only determining factor. This is why we say that the sound must be the main difference between the two instruments and that this is not determined by the bore size alone.

Tanner: Manufacturers have a tendency to make the larger bore horns from thicker metal.

Question: What does this do?

Tanner: Well, the thinner the metal thickness, the brighter the sound. Now, by this I don't mean the hardness or softness of the metal—but the thickness.

Sawhill: Three other important technical considerations in the production of sound are the mouthpiece, the leader pipe, and the size of the bell. Of course, on the bass trombone all three of these are larger than on the tenor trombone.

Question: Would you each comment on your mouthpiece preferences?

Sawhill: I think that as far as the bass trombone is concerned, the first consideration should be that the mouthpiece must be large enough to operate with ease between low B♭ and pedal F and even lower. It should be large enough to allow the player to have quick response and maneuverability in this area. Never sacrifice the low tones for an easier upper register. A Bach 1½G or 2G, or their equivalents, would be my suggestion.

Tanner: Even on the tenor, we don't feel that a player should sacrifice his lower register for the upper. On tenor, start a young player with a middle of the road mouthpiece—not too flat a rim so that the edge will be sharp, not too wide a rim where it will cost him flexibility, and a deep enough cup for good round sounds. I only know Bach numbers, so I can suggest a 7, 11, 12, or 15, or their equivalents, for tenor trombones.

Question: I understand that both of those trombones are the same length; would you speak then about the different ranges you should expect players to play in?

Tanner: It's true, they are the same length, and the length actually determines the pitch of an instrument. However, the larger bore and larger mouthpiece on the bass trombone make it easier to play low and harder to play high. Ken, why don't you go first?

Sawhill: Well, in the first place, we think of developing range in just the opposite way than the tenor trombone players. We think of developing range downward, we start in a comfortable area and work down. The bass trombone must operate comfortably as far down as pedal E. He should be able to sound tones all the way down to pedal B♮.

Of course it depends on the individual, but if I were going to generalize, I would say that high school players should be expected to play down to a pedal E. Also, for all practical purposes, the upper register shouldn't be ignored, the bass trombone player should be able to get up to at least a high B♭.

One of the biggest practicing fallacies is that bass trombone players don't seem to practice much in the real bass trombone register. They should spend most of their practice time from low B♭ on down, emphasizing those notes played with the trigger.

Tanner: Now that the alto trombone is almost extinct, the tenor trombonist covers not only tenor parts, but also alto parts as well. There are reference books that show you that the top of the tenor trombone is B♭ or C or D.

Actually, there really is no top, it is entirely up to the individual, and even this varies, depending upon how the individual feels at the moment. Personally, I keep a useable, workable G available. Now, nobody needs that G at all, but by having it, I then cut out the possibility of problems a fourth or a fifth lower, where I simply cannot afford to have any problems. If the C were my top note, I'd be working terribly hard most of the time.

Going the other direction, reference books will show that without the F attachment, we are not supposed to have any tones between low E and pedal B. However, we do practice in this area, it helps open up the sound all over the horn, so these notes can be sounded. Then we go on down from pedal B♭ to at least pedal E; some of us practice on down below that, I practice down to pedal C. I think you should expect your high school players to play at least up to C above middle C, higher for college players, and down to a pedal F.

Question: There has been mention about the trigger, the F attachment; is this another real difference between the tenor and bass?

Tanner: Not really, not any more. There are now plenty of trombones, called tenors by manufacturers, which have the F attachment.

Sawhill: The standard, not the only by any means, but the standard instrument today that is called a bass trombone is built in B♭ like the tenor, and it has an attachment which lowers it a fourth into F and one means or another of getting it down another half a step into E. The biggest advantage is that the area between low E and pedal B♭ is clear and strong—and this, of course, is a very important register for the bass trombone. It also helps us to go on down below pedal *E* with the feasible length of tubing for this register. There are other advantages too when you consider that anything played in sixth position can now be played in first with the trigger depressed. However, sixth and seventh positions surely should not be neglected.

Question: Mr. Tanner, with these obvious advantages, why don't you have an *F* attachment on your trombone?
Tanner: Well, I think if I had it all to do over again, I probably would. If I used it now, it would be merely to stay out of sixth and seventh positions. I have been using those positions now for over 30 years and am fairly comfortable in them. The long arms help some. I would have to also work on matching the sound with and without the trigger. This is a facet too often overlooked by players who use the trigger. But actually, I do think it is a good thing on tenors. There are plenty of advantages. The other problem is that too often a conductor sees the *F* attachment and puts the player on bass trombone parts, whereas he may not have either the sound, register, or technique for the low parts. His horn may actually be too small for the bottom parts. Of course we often see it happening the other way around too; players with pretty big horns are sometimes really laboring to play first trombone parts that go up quite high.
Sawhill: This brings us around to the only other difference I think we should mention, that is the difference in repertoire.
Tanner: Let me speak of the tenor repertoire first, Ken,

because most people know about this pretty well. The old thought of trombones just playing bravura types of parts has long ago departed. We are now expected to also play very lightly and delicately all over our horns. I would like to make one big pitch for the need for more players who can play very legato—we know that this is both possible and logical, it just takes a lot of extra work. Now, Ken, people really don't know a great deal about bass trombone literature.

Sawhill: In the past, bass trombone has been mainly an orchestral instrument playing more or less glorified tuba parts. However, this is certainly not the case at all today. Contemporary symphonic parts call for much more finesse than ever before. Certain individuals have popularized the instrument in other fields to the point where a tremendous amount of flexibility and control is expected. Not only has the aspect of maneuverability been expanded, but also we are expected to play in a melodic way and in a delicate manner beyond the previous concepts of the instrument. Bass trombonists have advanced to the point now where this instrument affords a whole new resource for composers and arrangers. It has added another unique dimension, another unique color to the whole world of music in general.

Tanner: We would like to emphasize very strongly that the people who write music should become increasingly aware of the bass trombone and of the differences between the tenor and bass trombones.

Sawhill: We would like these musicians to take advantage of this new development, realizing that the more they challenge us, the more we will extend ourselves, thereby benefiting the entire music spectrum. ■

October 1968

ROUTINE FOR ROUTINE'S SAKE?

Alvin Lowrey

As music educators, we constantly advise our students to warmup before practicing or before performing, but we often neglect to inform them *how* and *why* to warmup. They may get the mistaken idea that a warm-up is merely busy work assigned to kill time or that a warm-up is "routine for routine's sake." In a way, the warm-up is, in fact, routine for routine's sake—if you interpret routine as the *development of consistency* or as Webster's *Dictionary* states, "routine is any regular course of action adhered to through force of habit." I would like to construe this wording to state that a warm-up routine should

be a consistent and unvaried course of action *strictly* adhered to in order to *force* a habit of good performance. That is, to put it more simply, warm-ups should be designed for the purpose of *developing consistency* in performance. In order to *develop consistency, concentrate* during the warm-up routine, rather than relying on the force of habit to carry you through the warm-up. What should a person concentrate on during a warm-up? There are at least ten aspects in brass instrument performance that require constant attention. To develop consistency, concentrate on the following:

1. Breath control
2. Initial articulation
3. Lip vibration response
4. Pitch placement
5. Tone quality
6. Lip flexibility
7. Finger facility or slide technique
8. Successive or repeated articulation
9. Range
10. Endurance

The items above are not listed in order of importance but rather according to the order in which they may occur in a warm-up. Before playing the first tone of a warm-up, or of any etude or composition, breathe properly to obtain a sufficient inhalation; follow this with a controlled, steady flowing exhalation in support of the tone. Before thinking about the quality of the tone itself, get a good beginning of the sound; i.e., almost simultaneously, the initial attack must be definite and incisive (although not explosive); the lips must react by vibrating immediately as the air stream passes across them, and the pitch placement should be accurate without "scooping," "overshooting," or "splatting."

Now comes the time to think about tone quality—including the first note and every note that follows. In a warm-up, practice *with no vibrato* in order to assure a steady, unquivering, and unwavering tone; be discriminating in the tone color being produced as to whether it is dark or bright, "tubby" or brilliant, full or thin, projecting or cutting, edgy or compact.

In developing consistency in flexibility, be careful not to force upward slurs and do not allow downward slurs to slide or gliss. Once again, pitch placement is important: before slurring downward, do not allow the pitch to sag or become flat in anticipation of the lower note; and in slurring upward, do not force the lower note sharp before slurring and do not overshoot the upper note. Pitch changes in lip slurs must be smooth, unforced, and accurate.

As for finger or slide facility, the danger here is to play scale and arpeggio exercises *too rapidly* at beginning stages of the warm-up resulting in raggedness and undisciplined, spasmodic, irregularity of the fingers or slide. It is my opinion that facility exercises should be done slurred at first; then apply various articulation patterns forcing the tongue to coincide with the fingers or slide movement, which should have already attained evenness and regularity of rhythm.

The final two points listed above do not require so much mental concentration. Extension of range and endurance should be the results of a logical and sensible routine; i.e., if the warm-up routine is approached and applied properly, it should extend range (and make it consistent) and should increase endurance.

A Daily Warm-Up Routine Designed to Develop Consistency

Having discussed the *why* of routine, a discussion of a procedure to fit the purpose must follow. Oftentimes, we advise our students to use a warm-up by doing "some of this and some of that," without really prescribing any specific pattern or routine. While it may be true that not every individual needs to have exactly the same routine, it is my contention that each individual should have a consistent routine of his own, to which he religiously adheres. Some of the random exercises often suggested for a warm-up are: long tones (not too high, not too loud); scales and scale studies (usually at a certain metronomic tempi set to increase dexterity); lip slurs (usually fairly fast to prove—not improve—flexibility); pedal tones (for relaxation and to strengthen the upper register); and so on—without any indication of an

order in which to do these.

My prescription for a warm-up is simple in design, and—I think—logical in approach and direction, although it may be complicated with the amount of brain activity that must take place (conscious awareness and constant analysis of what is being done). As a starting point, in order to relax the lips and accustom them to vibrating, I advocate downward lip-slurs in the middle and low registers to be played with rather long tones at a moderate volume (Ex. 1). Then, continue with a series of downward slurs that return upward to the original starting point (Ex. 2). Exercise 3 then proceeds to add one more overtone; but notice that the lip-slurs are still primarily in the downward direction—intentionally so—to further relax the lip muscles and accustom them to vibrational response. Notice that each consecutive set of lip-slurs merely adds another overtone for range extension, but at the same time always returns to the low register to assure a low register that will respond as well as the high and to further instill relaxation in contrast to the tension brought about by the upper register.

It may be well at this time to point out that although these lip slurs may appear to be quite similar to those of Walter M. Smith, Earl D. Irons, Herbert L. Clarke, J. B. Arban, Max Schlossberg, and Charles Colin, I did not consciously "lift" any given exercise directly. Even though there are some exact duplications, I have set a prescribed order in which to play these exercises daily, rather than mastering one exercise and then moving on to master another exercise the following week. Furthermore, I have indicated that these are to be done slowly and deliberately in order to listen to accuracy

of pitch placement, tone quality, and smoothness and facility of the slur, rather than setting a fast metronome marking to be attained. It takes a lot more mental discipline to play lip-slurs slowly and deliberately than to play them rapidly and haphazardly. If these lip-slurs are done properly, they should contribute to the development of consistency in the first six items.

For development of consistency of finger (slide) facility and repeated articulation, I advocate use of Clarke's "Technical Studies," with each set of exercises to be done for approximately three to four months before moving to another set; and even after moving on to a different set of exercises, the second and fourth studies should be kept in constant review.[1] (Although these exercises are marked slurred, I advocate application of various tonguing patterns after gaining control of the fingers or slide.) Also as a procedure in going through these exercises, rather than

playing each exercise within a set, in sequence (upward chromatically), as they are presented in the book, I suggest playing them in pairs of octaves, chromatically, or in a cycle of fifths (too much low register playing without the balance of equal playing in a higher register at this point of the warm-up creates an illusion of over-relaxation which soon turns into fatigue). Another point to keep in mind is that these exercises should be used to develop *consistency* and *evenness* of facility before speed is applied; at first, speed is not of utmost concern, but rather deliberate evenness of rhythm is prime. As "Doc" Severinsen states in his article "Why Warm Up?", "Bang the valves down—hard!"[2] That is, be firm in disciplining the fingers.

In conclusion, it should be obvious that a warm-up is no better than the amount of concentration and critical evaluation that takes place simultaneously with it. ∎

November 1968

DEVELOPING FACILITY IN AUXILIARY POSITIONS

Maurice Faulkner

The astute trombonist becomes acquainted with all aspects of his instrument and is as proficient in the extended positions as he is in the close ones. The neophyte, however, attempts to perform all of his materials with the easiest and most comfortable arm movements because these are the ones he has learned first. Unfortunately, the neophyte soon turns into a first-class amateur and still continues to use the close positions for everything except when he has to extend to fifth, sixth, and seventh for the notes which can only be played in those positions.

It has been my experience as a trombone teacher that the youngest of students can learn the auxiliary

positions, both close and extended, and should study them in order to improve his ear, tone, and facility. Anyone who has played trombone for any length of time recognizes the advantages of using fourth position for D♮, second space above the bass clef, as a basic tuning asset, for we realize that it is impossible for the manufacturers to build an instrument which will play that note in tune in first position. This is only one of the many advantages of using positions for tuning purposes, and it is one that should be taught to the beginner, within the first two months of his study on the instrument.

The more complex uses of extended positions involve the player

with something more than pitch advantages. The flexibility of the performance depends upon using auxiliary positions for patterns of rapid or even slow-note passages which will facilitate slurring, fast, tongued sections, smooth legato connections, etc. Many of our contemporary composers have only a sketchy knowledge of the technical problems of the trombone. They write passages which demand auxiliary positions for facility and accuracy. They write extended legatos which can be performed either by rapid shift from close to extended positions for one or two notes and then a return to the close position for additional tones, or by a continuation of most of the notes

486

at an extended slide position area for more subtle nuance and control. If space permitted we could list the solos and excerpts which should be edited for such facilities, but any astute trombonist or teacher can search them out for himself in the materials being published today.

Transcriptions of Baroque music for trombone have become especially popular as study pieces and some of them are performed on recitals. These string (and bassoon) concertos or sonatas are filled with passages which demand such extended position editing if the trombonist is going to approach the suave character of the original. Many of our finest trombonists have been responsible for the editing and one can count upon such materials for developing the extended positions to their greatest extent. I have in mind the transcriptions of the Bach "Suites" by Robert Marsteller, Davis Shuman's editions, and those of other experts.

There are certain works in which the composer expects the shifting from close to extended positions to take place and the music will need a break between shifts to establish the characteristic created by the composer. These are few, however, and they will naturally fall into place at the first reading of the work. We are concerned here

with the intelligent understanding of style that is necessary to mark the phrasing and nuances of tongue and slur. Possessing this understanding, one can capture the essential spirit of the music of the various periods, which trombonists are playing now as study works and concert solos. It is with this material that care in use of extended and close positions needs its greatest consideration.

One of the usual situations occurs when a passage uses the 3rd space E, moving to 4th line F, to 4th line F♯, returning to E, then to 2nd space C. This can be, and is usually, played by the inexperienced player with 2nd position E, 1st position F, 5th position F♯, 2nd position E, 6th position C. If the passage is slurred throughout, the listener will be painfully aware of the roughness which the quick shifting from close to far positions will produce. A more subtle and better controlled use of auxiliary positions would set this pattern as 2nd position E, 6th position F, 5th position F♯, 7th position E, and 6th position C. One could have begun the pattern with a 7th position E, to make it even more facile, but that is only possible if the instrumentalist has developed security of pitch at this extended position for the beginning of a phrase.

usual:	2	1	5	2	6
better:	2 or 7	6	5	7	6

The reason so many of our competent young trombonists don't tackle such extended operations with their slides is because they have not developed a fine sound in those extended positions. And this is unfortunate because, when the musician has a full sonorous quality in fifth, sixth, and seventh position on all overtones of those positions, he has learned to fill his instrument properly and will carry over the magnificent masculine sonority of that area of his instrument to the shorter tubes of the close position overtones. In teaching trombonists this writer insists upon daily long tone practice at all dynamic ranges in the extended overtones in order to prepare the instrumentalist for the use of his trombone in all of its many opportunities.

The simple illustration given above can be duplicated with more complex sections of advanced works throughout the literature for the instrument. The intelligent musician will hunt them out and develop his skills for better interpretation. ∎

December 1968

LOW BRASS EMBOUCHURE CONTROL

James Robertson

The brass instrumentalist faces a unique and perplexing problem. That is, his embouchure is hidden from visual inspection. The woodwind player is not confronted with this problem, for the embouchure forms around the mouthpiece and most of the embouchure is open to view. The brass player, however, must form the embouchure within

the mouthpiece. Thus observation and control of the embouchure is made more difficult. The problem becomes more complex as the size of the mouthpiece becomes larger because more of the embouchure is hidden.

It is often advantageous to isolate one of many interrelated functions and analyze its singular duties

and how they effect the other functions. Thus the "buzz," as the center or focal point of the embouchure, becomes the springboard for this discussion.

The buzz taken by itself, that is, without any external support, serves two important ends: (1) it visualizes an otherwise hidden function, and (2) strengthens the complete embouchure when practiced. The former is of great value to the teacher and the latter to the performer. Many of us must be concerned with both.

Before continuing, the characteristics of a well-formed buzz should be discussed. The buzz should be relatively centered, say within ⅛″ of the center line of the lips. The opening must have sufficient vertical relief, that is rounded shape, as opposed to flat wide opening, as found often with smiling embouchures. This insures a soft, flexible buzz surface. Philip Farkas provides some excellent illustrations of professional embouchures in "The Art of Brass Playing."[1] It will be noticed that the larger the mouthpiece, the larger the opening required. The horizontal dimension is expanded more than the vertical.

As the buzz is adjusted for different pitches, the focusing movements of the embouchure become very important. The lip focus should be inwards as much as possible in all muscles so that the center of focus is the center of the buzz. (It is my experience that a characteristic baritone sound requires more center focus than a characteristic trombone sound.) As the pitch ascends, this consideration becomes even more important. Further, as the dynamic level decreases, focusing is necessary and, conversely, as the dynamic level increases, some expansion of the buzz opening is required, even though there may be no pitch change. With many of my students and other players whose buzz I have observed, the upper lip may protrude slightly over the lower lip in the higher range. There is often evidence of an inward horizontal focusing in the upper lip of well developed embouchures.

As a part of one's pedagogical repertoire, the unassisted buzz is invaluable. Following are some of the observations I have made in using the buzz as a diagnostic device. A stuffy tone is often caused by a closed buzz in which the lips are too close together or the tongue may be too high in the mouth. A tone that is too open or "blatty" is the result of a buzz which is too open and free. The lips may be rolled out and the buzz is in the

red of the lips, or the tongue may be too low in the mouth. A tone with ragged edges is caused by a buzz that is too wide. This tone needs more focus towards the center and the corners of the embouchure need strengthening. A breathy tone or a tone with air on or before the attack results from the lips being too far apart or from too much lip tension or stiffness. There may also be insufficient breath support behind the tongue. An embouchure which quivers and is unable to hold a stable pitch is frequently the result of uncontrolled and underdeveloped muscles. The development of a good buzz is invaluable with this problem. There may also be insufficient or incorrect breath support.

The smiling embouchure tightens the lips too much and causes a flat opening in the upper range. It is the direct opposite of the focusing embouchure. Lip tension or stiffness must not extend to the fleshy part of the lip that vibrates. The focus area of the upper lip must be especially free, as it does most of the vibrating. Pedal tones and buzzing in the low range will serve to relieve this tension, and inability to do these often indicates a tight embouchure. The foregoing are not all-inclusive, but serve rather as a comprehensive overview of the most important causes, effects, and cures.

There are three basic approaches which may be followed when developing the buzz. The first is the *mouthpiece buzz*. Edward Kleinhammer in his "The Art of Trombone Playing" provides insight to this method as well as several etudes.[2] I favor this method as being especially valuable for maintaining embouchure strength and control as well as ear training.

The second method of utilizing the buzz is with the *mouthpiece visualizer*. This device offers an accurate picture of the actual playing buzz and will reveal many problems which might otherwise go unnoticed.

However, both of these methods offer support to the embouchure. All too often a player will rely upon this support too much and will mistake an occasional good sound for a well-formed embouchure. In short, the mouthpiece is used too frequently as a crutch to

support a weak or incorrectly formed embouchure. Thus the *unassisted buzz* leaves the embouchure open to both visual and aural inspection and, since there is no longer any external support, the embouchure stands naked.

Any of the earlier mentioned illnesses may be instantly detected and diagnosed, as there is no longer any support behind which deficiencies may be hidden. And, since both the student and teacher may easily identify the problems and their causes, the eventual correction of these problems is implemented considerably.

I suggest any of the following as practice material for developing the buzz. Scales may be used to extend range in both directions. Simple melodies or tunes aid ear training, and the instructor may buzz duets or rounds with the student. Long tones which crescendo and diminuendo are helpful when working towards control of dynamic extremes while keeping the pitch constant. Tonguing exercises as the embouchure becomes stronger are of great value for endurance, control, and development of the single tongue.

One of my favorite exercises is to buzz scales while articulating 16 notes per pitch in time as I walk. Each scale is done in one breath. Thus I exercise breath support, the buzz, and the tongue for 32 steps for each scale. A little serious practice of this technique and one is surprised at how fast you must walk to keep up with your tongue.

Lip slurs provide excellent flexibility exercise and are helpful in range extension as well. All buzzing should be legato with no tongue at all in the earlier stages of development. The underdeveloped tongue will often disturb a weak embouchure.

All of the above serve as excellent maintenance and warm-up material and may be used anywhere, anytime and produce good results. However, careful attention must be paid to the buzz at all times, as incorrect practice is often more harmful than no practice at all.

Careful interpretation and practice of the foregoing will give the low brass student and teacher the information and skills necessary to meet and conquer most embouchure problems.

1969

TRUMPET AND CORNET TONE QUALITY

Lawrence Meyer

Let us assume that tone is a player's greatest asset. If an individual shows outstanding ability with his range and endurance, technique and tonguing, flexibility and style, but does not have a pure and controlled tone, we would agree that he faces a major obstacle to even moderate success with his playing. As teachers, regardless of level, we first need to be convinced that developing fine tone quality *can* be accomplished with our students, although we hope the percentage of "naturals" will continue to surprise us. Secondly, developing a good tone requires correct teaching methods on the part of the instructor, faithful practice on the part of the student, and a proper concept of tone on the part of both teacher and student.

Analyzing a problem may often be easy, but the solution many times is very difficult. For example, we might have a student who is tucking his bottom lip under the top lip. Although this would be obvious and would seriously hinder tone quality, it is not so easy to merely say "get it out" or "hold your head back." Such a problem should not have gone unnoticed early in his training.

Before discussing the technique of tone production, however, it is necessary to clarify the difference between cornet and trumpet tone quality, and its relation to the normal present usage of the instruments.

Since the tone quality of the cornet is neither superior nor inferior to the trumpet, and vice versa, the choice of instrument is determined by the purpose. A true cornet has a tone which is rich in resonance, as a result of its more conical bore.

The trumpet has upper partials which are more striking, since it is primarily cylindrical in bore, making the tone quality brighter or more brilliant. In recent years, it has become less important whether a band uses cornets or trumpets because their present-day specifications are in reality very similar. A large-bore trumpet, played correctly, can produce a very mellow sound. From a practical standpoint, in most public school and college bands, the best player now plays the solo cornet part in a band on whichever instrument he happens to own. This is becoming the policy of many outstanding all-state bands, especially in areas where orchestras and stage bands are strong. The thin, rather harsh tone quality often associated with the trumpet is not *really* characteristic of the instrument, though in many cases it seems to characterize so many young players. The cornet is an excellent instrument for the very young student. There is no doubt, however, that the professional outlets available to present-day performing musicians almost invariably demand the use of the trumpet over the cornet.

It is, of course, necessary that we have a recommended and suitable mouthpiece and an instrument and bore that is at least acceptable. An old instrument does not necessarily mean an inferior one. However, many trumpets manufactured over 20 years ago do not have a large enough bore-size to enable a player to attain the modern concept of a full tone quality. Furthermore, "hand-me-downs" (many times cornets) are worn between the valves and valve casings. Such leakage will affect both tone and pitch, as will large and numerous dents.

The mouthpiece generally found with older instruments also needs to be examined for proper diameter, depth, rim, and bore. Experiments with three or four standard mouthpieces will enable players on all levels to select and stay with a desirable mouthpiece. Thanks to healthy competition, most student-line instruments are equipped with satisfactory mouthpieces for the beginning stages of playing.

A large-bore instrument and a wide deep mouthpiece do not insure a big, full tone. In fact, very few players are able to handle this combination and keep the tone quality rich and full unless they are truly dedicated to three or four hours of serious daily practice and have the physical capabilities needed. In other words, avoid extremes and find what is best through experimentation and professional recommendations. A trumpet player who performs in a band, orchestra, and stage band, as well as playing solos, needs to find the "all-round" instrument, bore-size, and mouthpiece. Finding an outstanding instrument and the proper mouthpiece is not a problem today for the conscientious teacher or student. There are many available.

The next important determinant of tone quality is the student's own concept of tone. He must have a mental idea of the ideal tone. It is so easy today to listen to the actual sounds of our many fine performers through recordings, television, and personal appearances by outstanding clinicians and soloists. In developing a concept of desirable tone quality on cornet and trumpet, players should not be restricted to just listening to superior brass players. A cellist, vocalist, or any performer who has good tone will give students on all levels added insights into what constitutes a pleasing sound.

In developing fine tone quality, psychological concepts are as crucial as the physical aspects. Since the amount of lip tissue in the mouthpiece plays a very large role in the quality of tone, a proper embouchure and its training cannot be overemphasized. The lips must vibrate freely, although the main function of the lower lip is to control aperture size. The upper lip must act as the vibrator, and this fact puts a premium on the correct training of the embouchure so that it will respond with a rich timbre over most of three octaves.

The vertical placement of the mouthpiece is a highly individual matter, since this depends so much on the conformation of the mouth, the shape of the lips, and the length and regularity of the teeth. The red membrane of the upper lip is the primary source of vibrations. The lower lip produces changes in air compression and air velocity. Therefore, the top lip must be free to vibrate. Although a large group of professional performers use a half-and-half lip distribution on the mouthpiece, people are so different in physiological characteristics that, in the light of recent research, it still seems like good advice to encourage the "natural placement" of the mouthpiece upon the lips. For most players, the mouthpiece is placed in the center of the mouth with a slight bit more upper lip than bottom lip in use.

In explaining the formation of an embouchure, many of us find it quite successful to say that the corners of the mouth are set firmly against the teeth. At the same time, it is important to emphasize the fairly free and loose center of the lips. This "set embouchure" helps in directing the air stream directly forward and does not allow the cheeks to puff out. A setting of this type will also discourage the natural tendency to stretch the lips into an objectionable, smiling type of embouchure. Stretching results in poor resonance, intonation problems, poor range, and lack of control and endurance because the player may resort to pressure and

pinching in lieu of a proper resonating membrane.

It is necessary for the facial muscles to be properly coordinated and for the embouchure to loosen without damaging the tissues of the lip by excessive pressure. Such pressure will surely cause a breathy tone, as it restricts the normal blood circulation. The "lip-buzzing" technique as a method of warming-up does not have the wide-spread support it enjoyed a few decades ago. Many students seem to tighten the vibrating center too much when buzzing and this area needs to be free to vibrate. It can also cause a habit of bringing the lower lip in, up, or rolled under the upper lip. When the rim of the mouthpiece is set around the vibrating center, the buzz will be more natural. To buzz without the mouthpiece does not simulate normal playing conditions. To buzz with the mouthpiece (or a rim) set upon the embouchure makes sense.

We all differ as to what to use for warm-up exercises. Some advocate lip slurs, some chromatics, others long tones and scales. There are those who simply start to play without a plan at all. We all seem to agree, however, that some kind of warm-up is advantageous and that playing with a medium volume in the middle register is beneficial. Though opinions may differ concerning details, younger students do need a fairly set pattern as a guide. A combination of the above techniques would seem to be practical until the students are able to see for themselves what is needed for their own lip and tone development. Certainly faithful daily practice is a must.

Proper embouchure and conditioning could be summarized:
1. The corners of the mouth are set against the teeth, with the lips free to vibrate in the center.
2. Slightly more than half of the mouthpiece placed on the upper lip can be successful for *most* players.
3. Avoid stretching the lips back and use a mobile lower lip to determine aperture.
4. Keep the lips moist at all times.
5. Do not allow the cheeks to puff out.
6. Use the minimum possible pressure.
7. Practice should never be continued when the lips are fatigued; frequent rests are important.

8. Utilize every opportunity to relieve pressure, re-circulate the blood, and relax the muscles; be sensible and realistic in observing dynamic levels and in playing range.

Breathing

The management of air is of fundamental importance to tone quality, and the concept of proper breathing needs to be understood, developed, and practiced.

The quick, deep breaths necessary in brass performance must be expelled slowly, and such control requires training. The diaphragm, our chief respiratory muscle, consists of a pair of muscles attached to the body wall just above the stomach. Contraction of the diaphragm increases chest volume by forcing the viscera (stomach area) down, thereby drawing a corresponding amount of air into the lungs. When the diaphragm contracts, the vertical chest dimensions are increased; when the external intercostal muscles contract, the horizontal chest dimensions are increased. A discussion of this with a young student would be confusing. Merely have him keep the air coming with adequate support regardless of dynamic level and the whole concept of correct breathing should develop.

It is wise to advise the student to breathe down and out, and then up. Breathe deeply and remember to keep the abdominal muscles tight to support the air column. When these muscles relax, air will gradually escape from the lungs involuntarily. We use the diaphragm mainly to obtain a deep breath, and the abdominal muscles mainly to support and vary the air column.

To summarize:
1. Breathe deeply by opening the corners of the mouth.
2. Expand the abdomen, chest, and waistline rather than elevating the shoulders. Then contract the abdomen and lower ribs for forced expiration.
3. The amount of contraction necessary will depend upon the duration, pitch, and loudness required. It is always best to be "set," especially in meeting the demands of modern playing.
4. When firmly supporting the breath, be sure the throat is relaxed and allows the air to pass freely.

Posture

Proper body position is also a very important aspect of playing which affects a performer's tone quality. Whether standing or sitting the small of the back should be slightly curved in. In most cases the instrument is pointing slightly downward. Perhaps a better guide would be to have the trumpet at right angles to the plane of the teeth.

The chest should be lifted and held fairly high. The arms are slightly away from the body.

Do not constrict the throat by having the music stand too low or too high. The throat needs to be open; see that the head is upright, the neck straight, and the chin in a normal comfortable position. Then adjust the music stand to the proper height to maintain this good posture. Sing *ah* or *oo*. Now move the head and jaw inward toward the neck and notice how difficult the syllables are to pronounce. To enhance the tone quality in all registers, use *ah* in the low, *oo* in the middle, and *ee* in the high register. The back of the tongue has a vital function in the production of these syllables.

Vibrato

Although vibrato is not connected with pure and controlled tone, it can often destroy a basically good tone if it is poorly produced or in bad taste. Such a vibrato interferes with the important functions of the breath or embouchure. Furthermore, few teachers give enough

early instruction in correct vibrato techniques. This lack of early training may result in confused concepts, not only about whether or not to use the vibrato, but also concerning the method of producing it, how much, and when. Vibrato is a *developed*, emotional aspect of playing which definitely enhances tone quality and artistic performance in particular passages and styles.

The most commonly used vibrato on the cornet and trumpet is the hand vibrato, which is a horizontal to-and-fro movement of the right hand of about five to six pulsations per second. The thumb of the right hand is firmly based under the leader pipe, generally between the first and second valves, and is the actual cause of vibrato. All sorts of movement of the hand will not effect a vibrato unless it is tightly connected to the thumb. Therefore, it would be fitting, really, to call it *thumb vibrato*. Think of the hand and thumb as being solidly connected to the arm—down to the elbow. They all move together in a horizontal motion in the proper speed. It is hardly noticeable when mastered. It should be neither too wide nor too narrow, neither too fast nor too slow, and here again, as in the development of a tonal ideal, concepts of vibrato can be gained quickly through demonstration or by listening to the vibrato of an outstanding performer.

There are those who are able to produce a pleasant vibrato by using the jaw method. It might be ar-

gued, though, that the lower jaw would be best used to control the aperture and not to produce a vibrato. Most conscientious teachers are vehemently opposed to diaphragm vibrato for cornet and trumpet because the air stream must be continuous and consistent. Throat, tongue, lip, and head vibrato are rarely found.

Research shows the hand vibrato is the most common type used on cornet and trumpet. Furthermore, it is the easiest to learn, gives the finest control of speed and pitch variation, and minimizes the embochure problems connected with producing a vibrato.

The question of when to use the vibrato could lead to quite a lengthy discussion. Suffice it to say here that it is used primarily in lyric solo passages.

Summary of Important Points

1. A fine instrument and proper mouthpiece, kept in good, clean condition, are vital to an outstanding tone quality.
2. A good tone on any instrument requires a good tonal concept in the mind of the player.
3. Producing good tone quality requires proper embouchure and breath control, regular daily practice, and sensible intelligent pacing.
4. A systematic warm-up which includes scales, long tones, chromatics, and lip slurs is extremely helpful in developing good tone.
5. A good tone quality can be further complimented by a well-developed and properly used vibrato. ■

Basic Concepts in Trumpet Teaching

Paul Anderson

Each of us who is engaged in the pleasant occupation of teaching trumpet has his areas of special emphasis, his pet ideas, so to speak, concerning the many aspects of teaching the instrument. Since I am no exception, I herewith present a few of the concepts which I have gleaned from contact with hundreds of students, many performing associates, and several of America's finest teachers, among them Wil-

liam Thieck, formerly with the Minneapolis and Los Angeles symphonies, the renowned Herbert L. Clarke, with whom I was privileged to have only one "lesson," Clifford Lillya, professor of trumpet at the University of Michigan, and Renold Schilke of Chicago, nationally known performer, designer, consultant, trumpet manufacturer, and teacher.

Let us begin our discussion with

the most important subject—the student. A boy or girl with a reasonably good "ear," fairly even teeth, and average sized lips is usually a good prospect for trumpet study. If the lips are thinner, so much the better—for two reasons: (1) thin lips afford plenty of room for placement of the mouthpiece, and (2) thin lips are often very muscular and respond well to training.

I have always felt that it is important to place the mouthpiece in the "half and half" position on the lips. It is also important that the inside edge of the mouthpiece be above the "lip-line" of the upper lip, the lip-line meaning the line which separates the soft tissue of the lip from that area adjoining it. This placement affords a grip, allowing the mouthpiece to "stay put" without slipping down, which it might otherwise do under the inevitable pressure of high notes. Heavy lips sometimes cause a problem: how to place the mouthpiece properly, yet still allow room for maximum vibration. A mouthpiece ring is an invaluable device in placing the mouthpiece. The aperture, or opening between the lips, should appear as close to the center of the ring as possible.

The mouthpiece should be centered from left to right as well as up and down, but one should not be disturbed if it moves slightly to the side. This may occur due to the discomfort caused by a sharp or protruding tooth, or because there appears to be more muscular strength at the side than when the placement is exactly in the center.

Much as I believe in these concepts, we have only to look around a bit to find exceptions to these ideas and others. For this reason I would not turn away a prospective beginner who appears to be lacking in some of the natural attributes of trumpet playing without giving him an opportunity to try.

Another factor of at least equal importance to that of the lips is the jaw contour.

Avoid the extremely receding jaw. Induce this student to study oboe or bassoon. If he insists on trumpet then you insist (at the very first lesson) that he protrude the lower jaw forward, bringing the instrument parallel to the floor, while the head is in a normal position, not tilted back.

Remember that the average person has a slightly receding jaw—at least the lower teeth are back of the upper when the jaw is closed. This is normal and perfectly acceptable. My concern is the student whose upper teeth are far out in front of the lower. He must bring the lower jaw forward if he is to develop any

range and endurance. The player with the normally receding jaw will slant the instrument down somewhat.

Even though this is normal, I would encourage any player to hold the instrument as straight as possible. At least, do not allow him to let the horn droop lower than the jaw contour dictates. The player with the extremely receding jaw must be made to go "all the way." The horn must be straight out or it will simply fall back to the natural, impossible position.

At the first lesson I would encourage the student to "buzz" the lips alone. This gives him a concept of what causes the tone. Do not allow him to slip the lower lip up under the upper because of the incorrect impression of lip position which this might create. Next, take the mouthpiece and place it properly, using the ring and a mirror. Each student should have both available.

Have him buzz on the mouthpiece as he did with the lips alone. The student should not grasp the mouthpiece with his fist because he will invariably use too much pressure. His grip should be very light. Encourage the production of long, smooth tones with daily practice on the mouthpiece, gradually raising and lowering the pitch.

At this point a few words concerning the instrument may be helpful.

First of all select the best possible instrument for the student. This means that it will be reasonably well in tune, will have a clear tone and good response, and, finally, will have valves capable of good execution.

We know that the trumpet is not perfectly in tune because it is built on an imperfect overtone system. In addition, the production of tones using various combinations of valves creates problems in intonation. However, discriminating makers have done much to improve the basic intonation of the trumpet, and careful testing of instruments will pay off in the selection of a good horn. The inclusion of adjustable first and third valve slides is of course very important in the de-

velopment of excellent intonation on the trumpet. Naturally, this additional equipment costs money.

If you are selecting a used instrument, be sure that it has been cleaned; an accumulation of dirt in the horn can cause intonation problems. To clean the horn hold the bell under the warm water faucet —don't let the water get too hot— and allow the water to run through. Work the valves up and down so that water gets to the valve slides. This ought to be done at least once a month.

If the instrument is "stuffy," that is, has a poor response, avoid it, for it more than likely has leaky valves (too much play between the valve and the cylinder). However, the same stuffy response can result when the holes in the valves do not exactly match those in the valve slides. This partially obstructs the air passage and creates difficulty in tone production. By adjusting the thickness of pads and corks this situation can be corrected.

Now a word about the mouthpiece. Some years ago the average sized mouthpiece used by professionals and students was undoubtedly smaller than the average in use today. The modern trend is toward a larger mouthpiece, and justifiably so. While a few players with thin lips may have plenty of vibrating room on the small mouthpiece, the average player finds a mouthpiece of larger diameter more suitable in producing the big brass sound of today. The beginning student should choose a mouthpiece of medium diameter. Avoid the wide rim because it reduces flexibility, which in turn may cause fatigue. The rounded rim allows maximum flexibility but tends to reduce sureness of attack. Thus a slightly rounded edge is the best choice.

The throat of the mouthpiece is of course very effective in tone and range. The large throat produces a fine big sound, but demands more breath support to sustain it. Thus again, the "middle road" is perhaps the best.

Many a student gets carried away with the challenge of a large mouthpiece because he immediately recognizes the big sound which is produced. His enthusiasm also

allows him, temporarily at least, to maintain or even increase his upper range. Too often, after the enthusiasm wears off, the player finds that he cannot support the demands of this mouthpiece—the tone is dull and airy, the upper range has been reduced, and the tonguing action may have been impaired. A "lip reaction" sets in and the player is disillusioned. It is far better to proceed carefully, moving to a slightly larger mouthpiece one step at a time, if, indeed a larger mouthpiece seems desirable, until the player has reached his optimum size. Everyone has his limit, and it is not a disgrace to be playing on a mouthpiece smaller than that of one's colleagues. A few questions may help to determine whether the new mouthpiece is right for the student:
1. Does it improve the tone?
2. Does it decrease the range?
3. Does it affect endurance?
4. Does it adversely affect tonguing?

Unfortunately it takes days and sometimes weeks to get used to a mouthpiece. While some experimentation on the part of the student is desirable, bear in mind that too frequent mouthpiece changes will keep the embouchure in a constant state of turmoil, making it impossible for the player to do his best work. Proceed with caution.

Now let us return to the beginning student.

While it is necessary and valuable to practice buzzing on the mouthpiece alone, I believe that it is desirable to proceed with the instrument during the first lesson.

The holding position of the left hand can be very important in eliminating excessive pressure to start with or in alleviating it later on. Encourage the student to balance the instrument in the hand, not grip it tightly. You will see players grasping the horn so tightly that the ends of the fingers are white. This causes tension which will soon be felt in the arm and shoulder and will eventually create undue pressure against the lips.

The right hand should be placed so that the fingers are slightly arched, for maximum speed and positive action. A good position is as follows: Place the right thumb between the first and second valves, under the mouthpipe. This brings the fingers in line. Now

imagine that you are holding a tennis ball in your right hand. This arches the fingers nicely and allows the valves to go down straight. Sticking valves are often caused by pressing them to one side rather that straight down. I recommend that you avoid using the hook for two reasons: (1) The third finger, least agile of the three, will be curtailed still further if the little finger is not free to move with it. (2) Placing the finger in the hook often leads to a careless position of the fingers.

Now we come to the moment of truth. This is what we've been waiting for—tone production. The student has been buzzing on the mouthpiece alone. Now let him place the mouthpiece in the horn and buzz as before. Most students will begin on second line G. A few will find the low C first, and occasionally one will begin on third space C.

If you are teaching privately you can keep each student in his own "register." If, however, you have a class, encourage the students to work toward whatever notation you find in the instruction book. In most cases this will be the G.

It is not necessary at the outset to employ the tongue. A good approach is to have the student take a good breath and yell "Hoo!" as loudly as possible. Place your hand on your diaphragm and feel the action as you make the Hoo sound. Now have the student play the starting note using the Hoo approach. Encourage continued practice of this device indefinitely.

Tonguing action should begin now, if not before. In normal tonguing action, the tongue is placed back of the upper teeth, blocking the air from escaping. At the point of attack, the tip of the tongue drops down, out of the way, so that the air can strike the lips, causing them to vibrate and, in turn, setting the air in vibration.

There are of course three factors which control range on the instrument, namely lip tension, size of aperature, and velocity, or speed of air.

Lips will not vibrate without tension any more than a violin string which has become loose As the lips are tightened they must also be shaped, and the opening between the lips decreased in size

in order to provide the correct vibrating length for the higher notes. At the same time, tighter lips require more force of air to set them in motion; hence the need for greater velocity. It is the precise control of these factors which insures production of the desired pitch. They must be in proper focus to produce consistent results.

Lip tension and aperture control go hand in hand. As the tension of the lips increases, the aperture becomes smaller. Bear in mind that it is possible and even likely that the lips may close completely, thus stopping any possibility of vibration. A mouthpiece that is too small may contribute to this condition. Keep the lips as open as possible.

Breathing and breath support are of tremendous importance in trumpet playing. Shallow breathing precludes proper breath support. This in turn hinders the development of range and tone quality, and causes extreme mouthpiece pressure and tension in the throat.

Diaphragmatic breathing is very important. In working with your students check the following:

1. Have each student place his hand over the diaphragm.
2. As he inhales he should feel the abdomen (just below the rib cage) move outward.
3. As he exhales he will feel the abdomen moving inward. This is like a bellows which fills up at the bottom, and then closes, forcing the air out at the top.

It is this action of the diaphragm which develops range. Perhaps I can describe a teaching device which is the best range builder I know. Remember the Hoo exercise?

1. Hold the horn in the left hand.
2. Place the right hand on the diaphragm.
3. Using the Hoo attack, play second line G, holding it for three counts. Rest on the fourth count, relaxing the diaphragm and breathing at the same time.
4. Repeat three times.
5. Move up to third space C and repeat the process.
6. Move up to fourth space E and repeat the process. The student should go only as high as he can without undue strain. He will gradually increase to high G, high C, and higher. Keep the left hand as relaxed as possible.

No discussion of trumpet study should be terminated without a mention of the "ear" and its importance to the success of the player. Trying to play a given tone on the trumpet without a preconceived concept of the pitch is like shooting at an invisible target. Encourage your students to sing their exercises. It will help to develop "key-feeling" and pitch consciousness.

In conclusion, I hope that some of these concepts in the teaching of trumpet will help your students as they have helped mine. ■

March, 1969

DOUBLE TONGUING

David Peters

Double tonguing can be defined as a rapid type of articulation which enables the wind instrument player to play faster than with normal single tonguing. This explanation, as most given for double tonguing, does not really describe the process or technique that is involved. The following is a more complete study of double tonguing articulation.

Most instructors follow a basic pattern in teaching double tonguing. First the student is introduced to a group of syllables ranging from *tu-ku, ta-ka, du-gu, tee-kay,* to *gi-di* and *ki-tee.* Any of these syllables place the tongue in the approximate position desired. The student rehearses these sounds until he can control the tongue and then tries to adapt what he has learned to his instrument.

The second step is that of applying the syllables to the instrument without distorting the embouchure. This step is where many students give up and never attain the skill of rapid tonguing. The first mistake the younger student makes is in trying to say or speak the syllables into the instrument. This problem often occurs when the student first starts tonguing. By speaking into the instrument the student is using his voice-box and many times closing his throat. The added sound of speaking in the tone results in a poor sound. The instructor must be very careful at this point to make sure that the student does not actually speak into the horn. This can be avoided by having the student only say the *tu-ku* sound four times and then move his tongue in the same manner and blow air.

When the student picks up his horn he again is coping with all of the problems that he has had from the beginning. If the student is having trouble with the embouchure, double tonguing will not correct it. The second mistake that most students make when starting to double or triple tongue is to move the embouchure for each note. This makes rapid tonguing every bit as hard as the student thinks it should be. If there is any movement on the front of the face whatsoever, the teacher should correct this immediately. Many students with very stable embouchures start to move their lips and jaws when they start double tonguing. In some cases this is carried back to normal playing and the student has developed a bad habit, not realizing how it began.

If the student thinks each note as he plays it, he will never play rapidly. This problem can be overcome by reading beat-groupings and scale passages, rather than individual notes. In playing the rapid passages the student must not think *tu-tu-tu-,* or *tu-ku-tu-ku.* This thought alone detracts from the reading process. Too many students can play a fast passage only after they have memorized it. This problem compounds itself. The objective here is to overcome thought with a physical response.

After the student has played several notes, or groups of notes, he tries to play very fast. Some instructors try to slow their students, to be sure that they know exactly what to do. This retarding procedure usually takes the form of double tonguing groups of sixteenth notes at a slow steady tempo. Some teachers require a metronome in this practice, which makes a sound educational procedure for the speed-control of the tonguing. I am of the opinion that before this exercise is inserted, the student should attain the speed for which the tonguing was primarily designed. Just as walking is related to running, single and double tonguing are related. The manner in which we double tongue slowly is not the same as at a rapid speed. Double tonguing is easy after you have done it once. The first time is the hardest. By practicing a long string of sixteenth notes and gradually increasing the tempo, the student will increase his ability to really double tongue. There is a point that must be passed in double tonguing at which this tonguing procedure becomes more a physical response than a thought-out problem. A comparison could and should be drawn between the snare drummer and the brass player. Double tonguing should be approached with the same rehearsal techniques that the snare drummer uses to perfect his long-roll. The transition from tap to bounce stroke is very similar to the transition that the brass player must make.

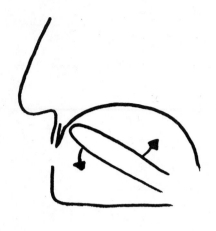

Position 1

Position 2

In spite of the many references to the tongue's movement as "back-and-forth," the tongue actually moves up and down. This movement starts a rocking action, with the tip of the tongue moving from behind the upper teeth at the gum line downward (Position I) as the middle of the tongue moves upward to touch the roof of the mouth at the soft pallet as in Position II. The faster the tongue moves, the farther up on the gum the tip of the tongue touches. This is one reason that practicing double tonguing slowly differs from the faster method of playing. Slow, deliberate practice of this type of tonguing will not increase the student's rapidity, as one might think. This slight relocation of the tongue is the reason.

If the student has started playing a brass instrument placing his tongue between his teeth while single tonguing, double tonguing will be impossible until the student corrects his single tonguing. The more movement that is needed to tongue, the slower the student will tongue. This being true, the faster the player tongues, the shorter the tonguing stroke must be. This accounts for the raising of the tongue on the gum when the student plays faster. Only after the student has attained some speed should he continue in his perfection of the double tongue. Then he should strive to control the rapidity and evenness of the double tonguing. The exercise mentioned earlier, playing measured sixteenth notes with a metronome, is a good procedure to control the speed of the tonguing. Attaining evenness is the largest problem for most students. The best way to acquire an even double tongue is to reverse the tonguing syllables and play with the *ku-tu-ku-tu* idea 50% of the practice time allotted for this type of tonguing.

Care must be taken not to give the student an exercise with a rhythmic pattern of two sixteenths and one eighth or even four sixteenths and a rest. This type of exercise is easy, but the student will develop galloping or uneven tonguing that is harder to correct than starting the student from the beginning.

Register and dynamics are two points that are rarely discussed in connection with double tonguing. The student should start his double tonguing experience in mid-range and at an *mf* to *f* dynamic level. The student will usually play much too softly when starting to double tongue, and must be encouraged to use the air to "get the notes out of the horn." As the student plays louder, another problem arises. The pupil feels he must tongue harder because of the added amount of air. By over-accenting his tonguing, the sound becomes choppy and uneven. By tonguing normally and adding more air, the volume is increased easily without the uneven side-effect. The only change that takes place here is that the tongue is moving in a stronger air column. By keeping the student in mid-register he is not bothered with the range problems of the extremities of his instrument. Only after some proficiency is gained should the upper and lower registers be approached. An $E\flat$ concert scale is a good range and key to practice double tonguing on trumpet, trombone, baritone, and tuba.

Of the syllables mentioned earlier, *tu-ku* is more staccato than *du-gu*. If a student is having trouble playing evenly, using a different set of syllables may help him to correct and smooth his tonguing.

The more of this entire process that is explained to the student, the harder the whole idea will be for him to grasp. It is up to the teacher to understand and guide the student without lecturing or belaboring the points that I have stressed. The more the student thinks about tonguing, the harder it becomes. One of the main problems the instructor has is deciding when to start the student on double tonguing. This, as in all other decisions in teaching, is not based on any one factor. The embouchure should be stable and the student should be able to single tongue well. Qualification by age or grade is hopeless. A student should, however, have started double tonguing before he reaches high school. Many grade school and junior high teachers leave this problem to the high school director. A good general rule is to start the student on double tonguing two or three years after he begins playing. By this time his embouchure and single tonguing should be adequate enough to move on to double tonguing. ■

NOTES ON THE ANCIENT OLYMPIC TRUMPET BLOWING CONTESTS

Edgar Turrentine

This past year marked the 19th Olympiad of modern times and the sporting world's attention was focused on Mexico City, site of the Summer Games. This was the third time the Olympic Summer Games had been held on the North American continent since Baron Pierre de Coubertin re-established the Games in 1896 after a period of 1500 years dormancy. In the ancient Olympics the athletes competed for the coveted olive wreath, now they compete for the coveted gold medal. In the ancient Olympics there was much pageantry and fanfare, as there is now. However, the fanfaring was a more intimate part of the ancient Games, because trumpet blowing itself was one of the contests.

The first written record of the games at Olympia is dated 776 B.C. when it was recorded that Coroebus of Elis won the olive wreath in running. Various legends are quoted concerning the origin of the games. Pindar, the poet, says the games were associated with Pelops; but Pausanias, the historian, says Heracles began them in honor of his father, Zeus. Nevertheless, they were held every four years until 394 A.D. when Emperor Theodosius of Rome abolished them because they had become so corrupt. In their greatest days, before professionalism and corruption, the right to compete was limited to freemen, of pure Hellenic blood, not guilty of crime, and who would abide by the rules of the game. The participants and spectators were limited to men, although games for women were instituted nearby in honor of the goddess Hera, and were known as the *Heraia*.

Historians state that at one time or another, during the history of the ancient Olympics, there were 24 different contests. The trumpet-blowing contest first appeared in the 96th Olympiad, that is, in 396 B.C. These were not musical contests but contests of lip and lung power; in other words, the one who could blow the loudest blast from his trumpet was awarded the olive wreath. This was not the only reward for the "windiest" trumpeter, for he was accorded the honor of starting all the other contests with a blast from his instrument. This meant that the trumpet-blowing contest, of necessity, was the first event of the Games. The afore-mentioned Pausanias describes a special altar, located at the entrance to the Olympic stadium, on which a statue of Zeus stood, from which the victorius trumpeter introduced the competitors, signalled the beginning of the events, and greeted the winner with mighty blasts.

Pausanias does not list the winners in his discussion of the introduction of the various contests of the Olympics, but Julius Africanus lists Timaios of Elis as the first winner of the trumpet-blowing contest. Strabo, Clemens Alexandria, and Paulus Silentiarius also have written of Timaios' victory.

A statue was erected at Olympia to another trumpet-blowing winner, Diogenes, son of Dionysios of Ephesos. The inscription says that he won 80 trumpet-blowing contests at Olympia, Isthmus, Nemea, and other festivals, of which five were Olympic victories. He was twice *periodonikes* — the title earned by one who won his event in the "circuit of games," that is, the Olympian, Pythian, Nemean, and Isthmian. These victories occurred during the first century A.D. The statue has not survived, but only the base with its inscription.

However, a more remarkable trumpeter was Herodorus of Megara who won the Olympic contest ten times between 328 and 292 B.C. Athenaeus of Naucratis, quoting Amarantus of Alexandria, says that this man was *periodonikes* ten times, however Pollux accords him this accomplishment only seven times. No matter, either is a remarkable feat, but then history records him as quite a remarkable man. According to Amarantus, Herodorus was three and a half cubits tall, that is, 5'3"; Pollux, though, says he was a much bigger man, four cubits tall (6'). His bigness in height may be disputed but the bigness of his appetite was not, for it has been recorded that he would consume six pints of wheat bread, 20 pounds of whatever kind of meat served him, and six quarts of wine at a single meal. (It seems that many of the Olympic contestants had enormous appetites if one is to judge from the many accounts of their eating habits. This same account by Amarantus tells of Aglais, daughter of Megacles, who wore a distinguished wig and plume. Although it is not recorded whether she participated in the *Heraia*, she was a famous Alexandrian trumpeter, and she consumed 12 pounds of meat, four pints of bread, and three quarts of wine at a meal.) At night, Herodorus slept only on a lion's skin. However, it was the loudness of his trumpet blast that was so notable; if winning the contest so many times was not enough proof, one can refer to the account of his ability to blow two trumpets at once so loudly that it inspired the soldiers to haul the immovable siege-engine up to the walls of Argos when Demetrius was besieging it.

These — Timaios, Diogenes, and Herodorus — are but

three of the winners of the trumpet-blowing contest at the Olympic games. Two of these men won at other games. Besides the other three "great" games — that is, the Pythian, Nemean, and Isthmian — games were held in all parts of Greece and were more local in character. Some of these games, which included trumpet-blowing contests, were the ones held at Orupus, Tanagra, Plataea, Thespiae, Acraephia, Coronea, Orchomenus, Mt. Ptous, Carea, Samos, Mt. Helicon, Argos, and Athens. The games held at Athens were called the Panathenaic games in honor of Athena. Trumpet-blowing contests must have been especially popular at these games because Athena was called Athena Trumpet *(Athena Salpinx)*. According to Pausanias, she was given this surname because Hegeleos built a temple in her honor and, according to legend, Hegeleos was the son of Tyrsenus who invented the trumpet.

Six different types of trumpets (salpinx) were known in Greece in Olympic times. They were named for their geographic origin and are the Egyptian, Paphlagonian, Celtic, Medean, Argive, and Tyrrhenian trumpets. (One remembers that Greece controlled all of these areas at one time or another.) Eustathios, however, describes only three types — the Egyptian, Libyan, and Tyrrhenian. From iconographic evidence, mainly from Greek vase paintings, the most popular instrument was a straight cylindrical-appearing tube with a bulbous bell rather than the flaring type of the modern instrument. From this type of evidence the instrument appears to be anywhere from two to three feet long. One writer explains that the shorter trumpet was used for military purposes and the longer one for ceremonial purposes. Only one actual Greek trumpet has survived the rogors of time and that is now the property of the Boston Museum of Fine Arts, displayed in the Department of Classical Art. This instrument is slightly over five feet long and is made of ivory except for a funnel-shaped bell of bronze. The tube is in 13 sections with bronze rings at the joints. (It should not be assumed that all Greek trumpets were made of ivory, since the writers of the time make many references to bronze instruments.) Because of the cylindrical appearance of the tube one can deduce that many or almost all of the overtones in the harmonic series were available to its blower. Aeschylus describes the sound of the trumpet in this way: "let the piercing Tyrrhene trumpet, filled with human breath, send forth its shrill blare." Euripides writes, "and shattering trumpet shrilled."

It is evident from the Greek writers that not merely blasts from the instrument were used but that regular military signals or "calls" were sounded. Xenophon lists these "calls": to rest, load your baggage, follow the van, charge, and recall. In addition, Aeneas Tacticus mentions the "assembly" and "to arms" signals. Art historians, studying the Greek vase paintings, point out that a trumpeter holding his instrument in such a position that it points to the ground, at a forty-five degree angle, is merely "warming-up" his instrument. Those pictured holding their trumpets parallel to the ground or pointed skyward are actually performing on their instruments. It can be seen from two extant statues of trumpet players that the Greeks blew their trumpets with tightly compressed lips and not with the "puffed-out-cheek" embouchure of the later Roman trumpeters.

These comments on the ancient olympic trumpet-blowing contest would not be inclusive if it were not suggested that just as present-day athletes are spurred on by the modern Olympics motto, *citius, altius, fortius* (faster, higher, stronger), contestants in ancient Greece may have been spurred on to blasts of higher and higher decibel rating with words of encouragement equivalent to *sforzando, fortissimo, energicamente.* ∎

Below: detail showing the bronze bell and one ivory section. Right: detail showing the ivory sections with the mouthpiece. Both detail photographs are of the Greek ivory trumpet from the 4-5th century B.C. Photographs courtesy of the Museum of Fine Arts, Boston. Purchased from the Frederick Brown Fund.

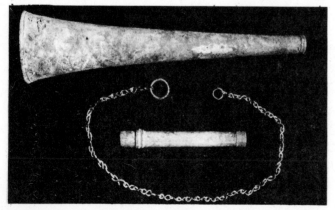

Shown below is a Greek trumpet from the 4-5th century B.C. Of particular note are the well-fitting joints, bronze bell, and carved mouthpiece. Photograph courtesy of the Museum of Fine Arts, Boston. Purchased from the Frederick Brown Fund.

April, 1969

THE PRE-ORCHESTRAL HORN

Richard Jensen

Of bras thay broughten Beemes and of boxe,
Of horne, of boon, in whiche thay blewe and powpede
And therwithal thay schrykede and thay howpede;
It semede as that hevene schulde falle.

Geoffrey Chaucer (c. 1390).

Music, it is said, "hath charms to sooth the savage breast," but the prime purpose of the earliest horns seems to have been quite the opposite. Our musical ancestors practiced the fine art of horn blowing for two principle reasons, namely, to bring them victory in war, and rain during times of drought. The idea behind these customs was the same in both cases, that is to produce fright: in battle to frighten their enemies into running away, and during rain-making to intimidate the spirits responsible for the lack of the needed showers. The customs of modern day African tribes are ample testimony to the validity of this fact.

Evidence seems to indicate that the first music instruments used by prehistoric man were the instruments of percussion — in the form of hollow logs. These were used not only in dances and ceremonials, but also as a means of signalling or warning in cases of impending danger. However, another type of instrument soon made its appearance — the horn. Animal horns were highly prized ornaments and indicative of the successful ability of the hunter. As time passed, the softer organic material comprising the center of the horn would deteriorate, leaving the hard shell which was often either polished or ornamented with carvings. Perhaps the first sound was produced by some enterprising hunter who, tired of waiting for the deterioration of the center (and perhaps not caring for the odor either), decided to hasten things along with a bit of digging and scraping, and upon blowing the residue from the horn just happened to form his lips in the correct manner necessary to produce a vibration and hence the first tone on the horn.

The horns of animals are not, however, the only material under speculation as the original lip-vibrated instrument. The following explanation is certainly as plausible as that above, although probably for different people. As for which might have come earlier, that remains a matter for conjecture.

One of the earliest forms of lip-voiced instruments is the spiral shell, found as the Cank or conch-trumpet in Asia and as the Bion in Europe. Now in order to get at the fish concealed within it, it was necessary to break off the tip of the shell and either to push it or blow it out. With the final blast that heralded the meal the vibration of the lips was discovered.

The earliest record, however, of the making of a trumpet or horn which we have been able to discover is contained in the very ancient description of the labours of the Sumerian hero, Gilgamesh, dated from the fourth or third millennium BC. In this instance the instrument was constructed of wood, in fact, made out of the hollow branch of a tree, with added refinement of a somewhat larger portion added to the end to augment the sound.[1]

Although in modern times the horn is considered to be an instrument of primarily musical function, it is not at all certain to what extent the early horns functioned as such in the lives of primitive people or, in fact, that they functioned as such at all. It *is* known, as stated, that they were used to produce fright. This was true not only in the primitive cultures, but in the more "modern" civilizations as well. Both Greek and Roman writers have referred to the fright-producing quality of the horn. Evidently even the magnificent Roman legions were not above the dire effects of the mighty horn.

As Polybius relates in the second book of his history:

The parade and tumult of the army of the Kelts terrified the Romans, for there was amongst them an infinite number of horns and trumpets which, with the shouts of the whole army in concert, make a clamour so terrible and loud that every surrounding echo was awakened, and all the adjacent country seemed to join in the horrible din.[2]

This quality was also attested to by Diordorus and Livy in their historical works.

Perhaps the oldest existing type of horn which is still used today is the Jewish shofar. It is first mentioned in the Bible as sounding when the Lord descended upon Mt. Sinai, and has been used continuously in the service from the time it was established until the present. It is sounded in the synagogue at the New Year and on the fast of the day of atonement. In the Jewish services only three notes are used, but some higher ones can be produced, depending on the player's strength of embouchure. The shofar is usually a ram's horn flattened by heat.

The first horns of metal were made by the Romans before the Christian era. The art of smelting ore and making alloys, especially those of bronze and brass, led to the construction of four horns known under the general name of *cornu*, plus two outstanding examples of which we have more information. One, the *lituus*, was carried by the Roman cavalry and was a straight pipe which curved at the end. The buccina was the first metal horn to make a complete turn and was carried by the Roman infantryman wrapped about his body much as the modern sousaphone, but consisted of a single curved tube with a slightly flaring bell.

The ancient Roman horns which have been found in the peat bogs of the British Isles, especially Ireland, are made either of wood or bronze, lost probably in tribal raids and may be seen in the National Museum in Dublin. The earliest metal ones are of cast bronze and believed to date from the fifth century BC.

With the decline of the Roman empire there was a decline of arts and crafts in general. The art of making suitable metal tubes for horns became lost until the period of rediscovery during the Middle Ages. A further set back to the development of the horn at this time was the ban on all instrumental music by the church.

During the middle ages the tendency was to revert to the actual horns of animals and new uses were found for the horn. The common bull's horn was used for military purposes in signalling, by the night watchman in cities, and by foresters and hunters. When being played this instrument had its bell pointing upward in front of the player's head and is usually represented in medieval manuscripts as a crescent-shaped instrument. Horns of other animals were also used when suitable and obtainable.

> The famous Horn of Ulphus, for instance, now in the Treasury of York Cathedral is made from an elephant's tusk curiously carved and decorated with gold." (Ulph was the son-in-law of King Canute.) "The valuable relic was lost during the Civil War," (in England), "but restored by Lord Fairfax after the Restoration and in 1675 redecorated by order of the Dean and Chapter, for whom it forms the title to several of their estates.[3]

Some other early ancestors of the horn included the Russian *rojok*, the Norwegian *luur*, the Rumanian *bucium* and the French *huchet* and *halbmond*, all used for military purposes.

Several instruments known as "Burgmote Horns" were and are still being used in England. These were used to call the people together for business of court or corporation. An excellent description of two of these instruments is given by Mr. Hipkins as follows:

> Beautiful horns of hammered and embossed bronze belonging to the corporations of Canterbury and Dover. The horn from Dover was formerly used for the calling together of the Corporations at the order of the Major. The minutes of the town proceedings were constantly headed 'At a common horn blowing' (comyne Horne Blowying). This practice continued until the year 1670 and is not yet entirely done away with as it is still blown on the occasion of certain municipal ceremonies. The motto on this horn is JOHANNES DE ALLEMAINE ME FECIT preceded by the talismanic letters A.G.L.A. — which — mean 'Thou art mighty forever, O Lord!'

> The horn is 31 3/4" long with a circumference at the larger end of 15 1/2", is of brass and is deeply chased with a spiral scrollwork of foliage chiefly on a hatched ground. The inscription is on a band that starts 4" from the mouth and continues spirally. The maker's name is now nearly effaced but the inscription shows that he was a German, and the date is assigned to the thirteenth century. —

> "The Burgmote Horn belongs to the Corporation of Canterbury, and records of its use for calling meetings of the Corporation are extant from 1376 down to the year 1835. The cord measurement of the arc of this horn is 36".[4]

Of all the ancestors of the modern day horn, one stands out as being the most influential in the development of both the horn and horn music. This is the European hunting horn. As Europe emerged from the medieval period, the hunt occupied an enormously important place in the lives of the wealthy. Kings and other noblemen often acted as hosts and were many times the most enthusiastic instigators of this form of social activity and diversion. In order that a hunt might be carried out efficiently, it had to be well organized and regulated. Therefore a variety of horn-calls were composed and used for different purposes. The hunting tunes are numerous but may be classified roughly under three headings:

> 1. Calls *(tons de chasse)* of which there were about thirty-one. These are intended to cheer on the hounds, to give warning, to call for aid and to indicate the circumstances of the hunt.
> 2. Fanfares, of which there was one for each animal, and several for the stag, according to his size and antlers.
> 3. Fancy airs performed as signs of joy or after a successful hunting.[5]

It is the third group above that indicates the purely musical use of the horn which was only a short step away from the idea of fanfares, etc., in orchestras. This accomplishment was, however, realized only after a long process of improvements in the instrument and player, as well as defeat of the prejudices against such use.

It was the French to whom the credit goes for lengthening their metal hunting horns; of necessity they became circular. This lengthening was a very important step toward introduction into the orchestra since many more notes of the harmonic series were obtainable, and, since the horn was now circular, the player was in a better position to modify the tone with his hand.

In England the shorter horn seems to have been preferred, although only rhythmic signals could be played on it. In fact it was not until the close of the 17th century that the "French-hunting-horn" (hence the misnomer "French horn") was made in England.

According to Grove's *Dictionary*, the earliest known *true* orchestral use of the horn is by a German, Reinhard Keiser (1674-1739), in his opera "Octavia" produced at Hamburg in 1705. However, this was preceded by musical calls of the hunting-horn introduced by Lully and other composers into the ballets and divertissements of the French court. It is said that Handel introduced the use of the horn as an orchestral instrument to the English in his still popular "Water Music" which was first performed in 1715.

This then, is a glance at the history and development of the pre-orchestral horn and with it, perhaps, some insight has been gained into the development of the gentle and dignified art of "horn-blowing." ∎

[1] Galpin, *Old English Instruments of Music, Their History and Character*, 3rd Edition Revised, Methuen & Co., London, 1932, p. 214.
[2] Galpin, p. 181.
[3] Galpin, p. 183.
[4] Hipkins and William Gibbs, *Musical Instruments*, A. & C. Black, London, 1921, p.1.
[5] Groves *Dictionary of Music and Musicians*, Article on horn, p. 665.

Bibliography

Apel, Willi. *Harvard Dictionary of Music*, Harvard University Press, Cambridge, Mass., 1947.

Coar, Birchard. *The French Horn*, Birchard Coar, DeKalb, Illinois, 1947.

Clappe, A.A. *The Wind Band and Its Instruments*, Wm. Reeves, London, 1912.

Galpin, Francis W. *Old English Instruments of Music Their History and Character*, 3rd Edition Revised, Methuen & Co., London, 1932. *Textbook of European Musical Instruments*, William & Norgate Ltd., London, 1937.

Gregory, Robin. *The Horn*, Faber and Faber, London, 1961.

Grove's. *Dictionary of Music and Musicians*, 5th Edition, Ed. by Eric Blom, Mac Millan & Co., Ltd., London, 1954.

Hipkins, A.J. & William Gibbs. *Musical Instruments*, A. & C. Black. London, 1921.

JUDGING THE BRASS SOLOIST IN MUSIC FESTIVALS

Maurice Faulkner

For the past 32 years it has been my privilege to rate brass instrumentalists at solo and ensemble festivals in a great variety of locations. Each time I sit behind a desk and make my evaluations, I can't help but recall the same experiences I confronted when I was one of those high school trumpeters attempting to convince a judge that my tone, technique, flexibility, and embouchure should rate the first prize in the annual contest—contests almost five decades ago.

Over the years I have analyzed the results of the many festivals and have arrived at some postulates which might be of value to the youthful artist. They are not infallible nor necessarily the best ones for a musician to follow. They are only suggestions which might aid the inexperienced instrumentalist who is beginning his career as a performer before expert critics.

First of all, a young brass specialist should not enter a festival unless he has the basic elements of good brass tone production pretty well ingrained in his skill. He should offer a good, and if possible, a lovely tone as his first ingredient for success. His range should be adequate for easy facility in the solo which he intends to perform. His ear should have been developed to the extent that he plays his diatonic and chromatic passages well in tune with themselves, as well as in tune with the accompaniment. His technical skill should reach such excellence in the work he is attempting that every problem appears to be easy for him. Tongue facility and style should reflect taste and an understanding of the music which he performs.

With these basic elements ac-

complished the youthful instrumentalist is then prepared to move into the more complex aspects of his study for the festival. His teacher will guide him in his research but cannot do the work for him. At this stage the student will want to seek beyond the notes of his piece and understand what its total purpose is. If he is performing one of our popular theme and variation solos (like any of the versions of "The Carnival of Venice") he needs to explore the theme and variation form with an insight into its history and why it evolved. If he is working with one of the French conservatory pieces he should search through several of them, compare them in difficulty to his, and attempt to analyze their structures, their technical demands, their harmonic elements. He should also be aware of their original purpose—which was a test of ability for the purposes of passing the Paris Conservatoire auditions.

If he has insisted on branching out into more involved and complex literature such as the Haydn *Concerto*, Purcell "Trumpet Voluntary," Hindemith *Sonata,* or our delightful contemporary solos for the instrument, he needs to study available information concerning his selection so that when he stands before a judge his interpretation is based upon knowledge of the why and wherefore of the music he is performing.

When he has completed this study of the immediate material of his solo he should branch out into an understanding of the epoch which brought his particular solo to the composer's mind. Research in this phase of the study is more simple than that of learning about

the specific work itself, for our greatest musicologists have established tomes of information concerning periods and styles. It is essential, though, that he broaden his scope with an emphasis on the background of his interpretation. For instance, I have found that an understanding of bowing styles and techniques has been invaluable in the interpretation of brass instrument tonguing for various periods of music history.

With the background of these two studies concerning interpretive concepts, the student is then prepared to bring his own personality into play, based upon sound ideas generated by his research. Much of the trumpet literature has been edited by specialists on the instrument. Some of it has been phrased and marked according to concepts which have been proven invalid following modern research. A competent and intelligent student who has researched his materials adequately may be able to revamp the editions so that they offer a more authentic musical experience for his auditors. As a performer and teacher, I have found it necessary to alter slurs and breath marks, cadenzas, tonguing indications, dynamics, and similar elements which are essential to a better understanding of the style.

When the young instrumentalist has achieved what he considers to be an intelligently planned and artistically conceived interpretation, he should make a recording of several of his performances and reflect upon what he hears as if he were the judge in the festival. It would not hurt if he could obtain an adjudication blank for his event and rate his recording objectively. This will give him an idea of what his judge will have to go through during the festival performance. It will aid him, too, in improving his weaknesses, as well as in understanding the problems which beset a judge who must hear a different soloist as often as every six minutes in some festivals.

A final word to the intelligent trumpeter: assume that your festival adjudicator is a knowledgeable and competent musician and interpreter. You may not always draw a brass specialist as a judge, although you should in today's world of specialization. Nevertheless, you will find that most of the judges today are capable and well-trained. They will expect certain interpretive ideas concerning style, and have been well-schooled in the skills necessary for developing such interpretation.

When you receive your rating sheet and find numerous comments which are constructive, take them seriously and attempt to correct the problems which the judge has assessed as weaknesses of your performance. Don't assume that he was wrong and you were right! Realize that he is attempting to help your future development in music and that his comments are made for the purpose of improvement.

As I noted earlier, this will be my 32nd spring of adjudication and the colleagues with which I judge each year have developed such superior stature in this business of ad-judication that I am impressed with their devotion to the evolution of improved instrumental music education in our nation. Accept them for what they are: competent musicians trained in a modern knowledge of musical style and historical accuracy, usually specialists in one or more of the instrumental families, and well-meaning persons who devote two or three days each week to hearing hundreds of soloists and ensembles for meager renumeration—for the major purpose of improving *your* performance and that of all the student musicians who pass through their auditoriums. They can err, for that is human, but their errors are miniscule in relation to their successes. Heed their advice and improve your interpretations. ■

May, 1969

IMPROVE YOUR HORN SECTION

James Parnell

How is your horn section sounding these days? Is it plagued by frequent "bloopers," sloppy technique, faulty intonation, lack of a good characteristic tone, loss of interest —any or all of these? Perhaps it is time to take stock and seek solutions to the problems. Here are a few typical symptoms and some suggested remedies.

Condition of the Instrument.

To begin, check the mechanical condition of the instrument. Has the interior of the horn been cleaned recently? If in doubt, pull a brush or swab through the mouthpipe section and take a good (though not always pleasant) look. The student should be reminded that a coating of dirt along the inside walls of the tubing will have a noticeable effect on the performance of the instrument. Dents in critical places are harmful, too. How about the mouthpiece? Not only should the mouthpiece be examined for the condition of its plat-ing, but also for dirt and a partially flattened (out-of-round) stem. What is the condition of the valve corks and strings? Are the valves properly aligned? Is the valve operation smooth enough for a fluent technique? Check the tuning slides; use a good grade of slide grease here.

Fingerings.

Once the instruments are in satisfactory playing condition, you can proceed. Do your students know the correct fingerings? Or, do they employ cornet fingerings or some set of makeshift combinations? If the double horn is employed, is it being used to good advantage or is the student playing exclusively on one side of the horn? Consult a fingering chart, as a good technique requires the proper fundamentals and patterns. Many intonation problems result from insufficient knowledge of scales and fingering patterns. As another aid to intonation, teach the student the function of all tuning slides and how to compromise slide adjustments for the best possible intonation.

Accuracy.

How about the attack problems? A simple explanation of the horn's harmonic series is in order here, with special attention to the fact that the notes become closer together in the staff—which accounts for many inaccuracies in playing on the beginning and intermediate levels. The student playing the F horn must acquire the knack of picking the third space C from a cluster of notes Bb, C, and D—all playable "open." On the Bb horn, the same written C is not quite so difficult, since the Bb horn's harmonic series is a perfect fourth higher. Conscientious daily practice in slurred and tongued arpeggio studies should help the student's ear and embouchure develop the feel or touch necessary for accurate attacks. Getting that first note is very important, for it gives the player a lift and some momentum; it is not always easy for the young player to recover his poise after he has muffed the first note or two of an important passage.

In addition to arpeggio practice, the playing of repeated notes is helpful in the development of accuracy in attacks. Try playing four or five consecutive *good*, well-centered notes on each degree of a scale, removing the mouthpiece from the lips after each note to get the feel of a new attack. Be careful of the releases, too. Stop the air stream to achieve a good release and avoid the "tut" sound.

The horn is probably only slightly more difficult for the student than the other brass instruments. However, it demands the utmost in patience and perseverance during the first few years, partly because of the aforementioned overtone clusters in that portion of the harmonic system which lie in the student's daily playing register. A look at the intervals in the educational music ranges of the other brass instruments will reveal that only near the top of the register will these players encounter similar situations. For example, a trombonist must play several ledger lines above the staff before the harmonic series intervals become seconds; even in the easier grades of school band and orchestra music, the horn student meets these same intervals *in* the staff, in his basic playing register.

Tone.

In the development of tone, suggest to your students: lip slurs and flexibility studies, long tones (properly executed), and a relaxed approach. Be sure to include some slurs which skip from one register to another. Begin some arpeggios with the lowest written *C* on the *F* horn. Encourage your students to listen to good players—both live and recorded. A good characteristic tone will require considerable time and patience (there's that word again); always keep the sound you are striving for in mind. Another aid to

tone building: play a scale or two at slow tempo using the *ha* attack. This will not only serve to improve the breath support, but it will also assist in attaining the correct release. (Of course, the syllables will change as other registers are played—i.e. *ho* in the lower and *hee* in the upper.) Then play the scale a second time, adding the tongue for a more precise attack, but continue to stress the role of the breath in both attack and release. Note the position of the right hand in the bell. The exact position will depend on the tone color desired, intonation characteristics, and the size of the hand.

Daily Drills and Warmups.

Each day's playing should begin as relaxed as possible—relaxed lips, jaw, left arm, etc. During warmup routines, take a *short* break every few minutes. Don't expect the embouchure (especially that of the student who does not play a great deal each day) to reach the ideal playing condition after a brief, strenuous warmup. How many times have you heard a student remark, "By the time I finish my warmups and daily drills, I'm too tired to continue playing right away!"? Daily drills, while employing certain traditional patterns, must be gradually adjusted to the individual student, and he must be careful to utilize them in the manner that will benefit him most. To minimize mouthpiece pressure—and it is the goal of nearly all horn players to play with an absolute minimum of pressure—it often helps to play the arpeggio lip slurs with the little finger of the left hand loose from the finger hook. In summary, help the student to adjust and improve his daily routines as necessary for his continued development. Consult a good reference such as "The Art of French Horn Playing" by Philip Farkas* for a wealth of valuable information and advice as well as excellent photographs dealing with embouchure.

Transposition.

All horn students should be able to learn and apply the E♭ transposition; the E♭ slide should *not* be used. (If this proves too difficult, the student may soon find that his days are numbered insofar as the horn is concerned, as there are other problems of a much more difficult nature than this basic transposition.) The serious student should move on to other transpositions; orchestra passages are helpful here.

Motivation.

Are your horn parts interesting? Or, is there evidence of some lack of interest because of dull, unimaginative scoring? Do you supplement band and orchestra parts with solo and ensemble material? Try to guide your students in selecting solo and ensemble music which is musically worthwhile and challenging enough to inspire work and progress. It is also desirable to play some relatively easy solos occasionally to build confidence and to permit the student to listen to his tone, pitch, and phrasing without the pressures of technical difficulties. Many solo contests are marred by students who insist on playing ("attempting" may be a better term) only those pieces which require them to play *too* far above their normal level of ability. Unless they happen to have a good day, the results are often discouraging to all concerned.

Methods and Studies.

Many young students are handicapped by the lack of a good specialized method—one written for the horn and its own unique problems. In addition, many of these (both students and methods) attempt to advance too rapidly; this usually hinders the development of tone, technique, and a relaxed style of playing. Every effort should be made to select a sequence of study which will enable the diligent student to build a solid foundation for future progress. Good luck! ∎

*Philip Farkas, *The Art of French Horn Playing*, Chicago, 1956. Summy-Birchard Co.

STUDY LITERATURE FOR THE F ATTACHMENT AND BASS TROMBONE

Leon Brown

During the past two decades, the emergence and general acceptance of the tenor trombone with *F* attachment has been particularly notable in high school, university, and professional performance. Prominent performers and teachers across the country have long realized the advantages of the *F* attachment and have strongly advocated its use. The result of their concern may be seen in the increasing number of *F* attachment users. The long waiting period required of prospective purchasers of this instrument from the manufacturers also attests to its popularity.

The technical advantages of the instrument include, first, the most obvious, the relocation of sixth and seventh positions of the standard tenor trombone to the first and second positions respectively of the *F* attachment. Logical employment of these two positions with the valve facilitates slide movement and eliminates many cumbersome intervallic situations, and, perhaps of equal importance, enables young beginners to play these tones from the very start. Even if the use of these two positions is often overemphasized, there is sufficient justification to recommend the use of the *F* attachment. Most players, unless they are interested in serious trombone study or plan to become professional trombonists, rarely advance beyond this stage in the use of the valve tones.

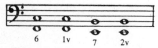

6   1v   7   2v

There is a second advantage for the advancing trombonist in the increased facility allowed by other more easily executed *F* attachment positions, embracing combinations of notes that are otherwise awkward on the standard instrument.

3v   3v   b4v   #6v   b7v

Third, the extension of the low range of the tenor trombone from low *E* to low *C* is, of course, an added advantage. (For the bass trombone, the low *B♭* is also a necessity.) Thus with both *F* and *E* attachments, a complete chromatic compass descending to pedal *B♭* becomes possible. Development of the pedal tones further extends the range of both the tenor and bass trombones.

(E valve)

1v   2v   3v   b4v | #6v | b7v   (b7v)

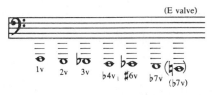

(E valve)

1v   2v   3v   b4v | #6v   b7v   (b7v)

The chief deterrent to the study of the *F* attachment and bass trombone has been the scarcity of good instructional literature. Too often, players who possess the instruments are left to their own inadequate knowledge to apply or work out this new valve technique. This problem however, is being solved with the publication of new instructional methods, authored by practicing professionals, teachers, and advocates of the instrument. In general, most of these methods presume some prior knowledge of trombone technique. Only one or

two of the methods have been designed with the beginner in mind. A few methods begin at about intermediate level, but the majority are aimed at the advanced player. Nearly all explain the differences between the positions of the standard trombone and the elongated positions of the *F* attachment and bass trombone. Charts and illustrations of the slide show these comparative positions. Most of the methods furnish extremely practical and logical suggestions and recommendations concerning the use of the valve. Careful study of this instructional material will open new vistas of technique for the student. Coupled with the excellent material now available for the tenor trombone, these *F* attachment and bass trombone studies will greatly aid the development of the complete trombonist.

It seems practical therefore, to conclude with a list of known and available methods and studies which will assist the student in developing the use of the *F* attachment to the fullest extent. The brief description and evaluation accompanying each item in the listing should be helpful in selecting suitable literature for study purposes.

The trombonist will gain further instruction from the fine literature resources of other instruments which are essentially in the same register, namely, bassoon and violoncello and to a lesser extent string bass and tuba. Listed below are a few studies frequently used.

Finally, players will find a wealth of practical study material, and a necessary requirement for prospective orchestral aspirants, in the many fine volumes of excerpts from symphonic and operatic repertoire. A partial listing includes the following:

STUDY LITERATURE FOR THE F ATTACHMENT AND BASS TROMBONE

I. Etudes, Exercises, and Studies

Bach, J. S.-
R. Marsteller

Suites for Violoncello Alone
transcribed for trombone, 2 volumes

Southern Music Co.

Musically superior, can best be
studied following thorough knowledge of thumb-valves possibilities.
Difficult.

Belke, F. A.

*Sieben Etüden für Bassposaune
und Klavier*
Excellent accompanied etudes,
only limited use of *F* attachment
required. Moderately difficult.

Hofmeister °

Bernard, Paul

*Methode Complete pour Trom-
bone Basse*
A method which encompasses
beginning to very advanced
studies. Exercises are not edited
for valve but are of exceptional
value after player has command of
F attachment possibilities.

Alphonse Leduc

Beversdorf, Thomas

The Trombone with F Valve
A concise brochure explaining the
use of *F* attachment. Valuable
information for the trombonist.
Brochure free upon request.

C. G. Conn Ltd.

Blume, O.-
R. Fink

*36 Studies for Trombone with F
Attachment*
Mr. Fink has developed these
standard studies for the *F* attachment to exploit the full range of
the trombone. Careful editing
assures that the student will
become thoroughly familiar with
the thumb-valve in all technical
possibilities. Intermediate to very
difficult.

Carl Fischer, Inc.

Colin, Charles-
B. Bower

*F Attachment Bass Trombone
Rhythms*
A study of jazz rhythms. Presumes
knowledge of *F* attachment. Intermediate to advanced.

Charles Colin

Delgiudice, Marcel

*Douze Etudes Rhythmiques et
Melodiques*
Excellent book of advanced studies.
These studies are not edited,
therefore player should know
how to use valve well.

Max Eschig

Dufresne, Gaston-
D. Schaeffer

*Sight Reading Studies for
Bass Trombone*
Carefully edited rhythmic and
melodic studies. Difficult and
challenging for the sight reader.

Charles Colin

Gillis, Lew

20 Etudes for Bass Trombone
Tuneful yet artful studies, well
edited and enjoyable to play.
Moderately difficult.

Southern Music Co.

Gillis, Lew

*70 Progressive Studies for the
Modern Bass Trombonist*
Fine intermediate to advanced
material. Logical and complete
development of the valve. Pedal
tone study. Highly recommended.

Southern Music Co.

Kleinhammer, Edward

The Art of Trombone Playing
A comprehensive treatise dealing
with all aspects of trombone
playing, with a special section on
the use of *F* attachment and bass
trombone. Excellent volume
of information.

Summy-Birchard

Knaub, Donald	*Trombone Teaching Techniques* A treatise on the essentials of trombone playing with a section devoted to *F* attachment and bass trombone. An unusually fine chart showing innumerable possibilities of the valve in all registers.	Rochester Music Publishers
Kopprasch, C.- R. Fote	*Selected Kopprasch Studies for Trombone with F Attachment* Mr. Fote has made this volume one of the most useful in literature. It includes essential material for development of the valve. Highly recommended for the advancing and advanced player.	Kendor Music Co.
Maenz, Otto	*Zwanzig Studien für Bassposaune* Difficult studies highly recommended for the advanced student. Inexpensive foreign edition.	Hofmeister °
Marsteller, Robert	*Advanced Slide Technique for Trombone, Bb Tenor and F and E Attachments* Reproduced copy of author's manuscript, highly informative and detailed. Reading is a bit tedious, but well worth the effort. Advanced material.	Southern Music Co.
McMillen, Hugh	*A Guide to Bass Trombone Playing* About the closest to a beginning method that can be found, yet it presumes prior knowledge of standard positions. Rather easy but well marked.	F. E. Olds Co.
Ostrander, Allen	*Method for Bass Trombone and F Attachment for Tenor Trombone* Mr. Ostrander, professional trombonist and teacher, has assembled in this method well organized and progressive studies logically developing the technique of the valve. Highly recommended for all students.	Carl Fischer, Inc.
Ostrander, Allen	*The F Attachment and Bass Trombone* This method is similar to the previous study. The development of the valve technique is carefully plotted. Intermediate to advanced.	Charles Colin
Ostrander, Allen	*Shifting Meter Studies for Bass Trombone or Tuba* Difficult rhythmic studies in contemporary idiom. Valve tones are clearly indicated.	Robert King
Remington, Emory	*Warm-Up Exercises for Trombone* Excellent daily drills for the trombone, with or without F attachment. Mr. Remington, eminent teacher at the Eastman School has been one of the leading advocates of the use of F attachment. Many of the volumes included in this listing are dedicated to him and his teaching. These studies should be in the library of every serious trombonist.	Pyraminx
Roberts, George and Tanner, Paul	*Let's Play Bass Trombone* A fine elementary method authored by two of the most prominent performers in America. Excellent material for the beginner and intermediate.	Belwin
Stefaniszin, Karl	*20 Spezial-Etüden für Bassposaune* Inexpensive foreign edition containing some of the finest literature available. Unedited but highly recommended to those who have a high degree of facility in the use of the valve. Difficult.	Pro Musica Verlag
Stephanovsky, Karl-K. Brown	*20 Studies for Bass Trombone or Trombone with F Attachment* American edition of preceding volume. Editor suggests maximum use of thumb-valve possibilities along with variety of articulations. Difficult.	International Music Co.

Williams, Ernest- D. Schaeffer	*Bass Trombone Method for F Attachment* A very good method filled with scale studies in all keys. The introductory portion is edited for F attachment. The latter portion allows discretionary use by player.	Charles Colin
Williams, Ernest- R. Smith	*The F Attachment on Trombone* A very good beginning to intermediate study book confined to limited use of the valve.	Charles Colin

II. Suitable Material Written for Other Instruments

Bernard, P.	*Études et Exercises pour Tuba et Saxhorn Basse*	Alphonse Leduce°
Cimera, J.	*73 Advanced Tuba Studies*	Belwin
Dotzauer, J.	*113 Selected Studies for Violoncello*	Carl Fischer, Inc.
Eby, W. M.	*Scientific Method for BB♭ Bass, E♭ Tuba and CC Bass*	Walter Jacobs
Oubradous, F.	*Enseignment Complet du Basson*	Alphonse Leduc °
Schroeder, A.	*170 Foundation Studies for Violoncello*	Carl Fischer, Inc.
Sear, W.	*Etudes for Tuba*	Walter Sear
Tyrrell, H.	*Advanced Studies for E♭ Bass*	Boosey & Hawkes
Weissenborn, J.	*Practical Method for Bassoon*	Carl Fischer, Inc.
Werner, J.	*Practical Method for Violoncello*	Carl Fischer, Inc.

III. Orchestra Studies

Brown, K.	*Orchestral Excerpts from Symphonic Repertoire for Trombone and Tuba*, 5 volumes	International
Clarke, E.	*Orchestral Studies*	Carl Fischer
Couillaud, H.	*Traites Difficules*, 2 volumes	Alphonse Leduc °
Dreyer	*Orchestral Studies from Operas*	C.F. Schmidt °
Menken, J.	*Anthology of Symphonic and Operatic Excerpts for Bass Trombone*, 2 volumes	Carl Fischer, Inc.
Mueller- Seyffarth	*Orchesterstudien für Instrumente* (Posaune), volumes 1-8, 13-17	Hofmeister
Stöneberg, A.	*Moderne Orchesterstudien für Posaune und Basstuba*, 8 volumes	Robbins Music Corp.
Strauss, R.- Berthold	*Orchestral Studies from Symphonic Works for Trombone and Tuba*	International Music Co.
Wagner, R.- Hausmann	*Orchestral Studies from Operas and Concert Works for Trombone*	International Music Co.

KEY TO PUBLISHERS

AL	Alphonse Leduc °
Bel	Belwin, Inc.
BH	Boosey and Hawkes
CC	Charles Colin
CF	Carl Fischer, Inc.
CFS	C. F. Schmidt °
CGC	C. G. Conn, Ltd.
FEO	F. E. Olds Co.
Hof	Hofmeister °
Int	International Music Co.
Ken	Kendor Music Co.
ME	Max Eschig °
PMV	Pro Musica Verlag °
Pyr	Pyraminx Publishing Co.
RDK	Robert D. King Music Co.
RMP	Rochester Music Publishers
Rob	Robbins Music Corp.
SB	Summy-Birchard
SMC	Southern Music Co.
WJ	Walter Jacobs
WS	Walter Sear

° Foreign publications are available from American publishers as follows:

Hofmeister: Associated Music Publishers Inc.; Alphonse Leduc: Chappell and Co., E.B. Marks; Max Eschig: Associated Music Publishers, Inc.

WAGNERIAN BRASS STYLE

Maurice Faulkner

Numerous brass specialists have researched the literature of that verbose composer, Richard Wagner, and those who followed him, either in conducting his music or in interpreting his words about his music, in order to learn how to perform his magnificent brass parts. The fact that this one man developed and required new brass tone colors for performances of his later operas is enough to place him in the "Brass Hall of Fame," whenever and wherever it should be established. But Wagner notwithstanding, his own descriptions of what he intended do not really place the emphasis where it belongs: namely, on the production of the brass sound on the particular instrument notated for in the score and balanced by an astute musician playing that instrument under the baton of a true Wagner conductor.

The usual German *Kapellmeister,* when he interprets Wagner, insists on loud blowing rather than a finesse of balance. Some, whom I have heard, even go so far as to permit the brasses to dominate an orchestra of one hundred men. There are moments when such domination becomes essential to the proper interpretation of the motives and the concepts of the music, but to permit such domination at practically all brass entrances is to misunderstand Wagner and spoil the performance for the true connoisseur, as well as contribute to the early damaging of the voices on the stage.

Seldom do these ordinary *Kapellmeister* earn the opportunity for conducting at the major opera houses in the world because the taste and knowledge of proper Wagner playing has become a special quality for most opera managers these days. But there were moments in history when the *"Blechbläser,"* as the brasses are called in German, meant nothing more than loud and obstinate sound, in certain quarters. I will never forget a point in my career when I was expected to overblow the climax of "Die Meistersinger" Overture and almost "blacked out" in the process. Such "windy" brass is seldom tolerated these days in the finest professional ensembles. But there is a tendency for such a thing to develop in amateur and semi-professional performances of Wagner, and brass players must guard against the tensions and stresses which generate under conductors who demand that approach.

The Proper Concept

There is no precise measurement of what is the right or proper concept except the taste of the conductor and the good judgment of the musician. I have heard fine brass sections of famous ensembles perform superbly in the first act of "Götterdämmerung" only to falter in the difficult measures of the second act. Time and again the horns measure up to the demands of the eight horn canonic materials in a Wagnerian masterpiece only to fail the conductor in the last act climaxes.

A brass musician should attempt to understand how his particular motive fits into the fabric of the orchestral accompaniment. This becomes more essential nowadays when the supply of Helden-tenors is at an all-time low and their voices need the protection of competent pit performance. When a brass figure becomes a highlight of the dramatic motion of the music and the stage action, then it must be played in the spirit of its character: a bravura solo will require a refined tongue control, not too far forward so that it doesn't become blatant, and still precise enough to give the essence of the heroic element. When the motive is more lyrical then the musician must "cuddle it," so to speak, with his tongue so that it becomes suave, velvet in color, and resonant.

Thus a concept of the dramatic materials is essential to the well-trained player. Many instrumentalists in the opera houses learn these concepts from experience in daily rehearsals under competent conductors who describe what they want and who expect the performers to produce it regardless of the technique needed. I have watched apprentice trumpeters, for instance, sit along with their teachers in the opera pits of European houses during rehearsals, listening and assisting in the climaxes, copying the sounds and the attacks of their mentors. In the United States, where we have almost no opera houses and only a limited number of opportunities for brass specialists to learn these skills, there are great varieties of sound that pass for Wagnerian style.

The Tone Quality

Basic to the Wagnerian style is the resonant, sonorous tone quality which the composer heard in his mind as he put the music on paper. Wagner has discussed these concepts in the ten volumes of his prose works, although he has not been able to define the technical skills essential to producing the results. But above all, he was acquainted with the German and Austrian version of the rotary valve trumpet which provides the musicians in those opera houses and symphony orchestras with the type of tone ingrained in their personalities and traditions. In these countries, and in most of Eastern Europe, the piston valve trumpets, such as we use, are referred to as "jazz trumpets."

The even scale of the rotary valve trumpets in the Central and Eastern European nations offers finer intonation than that of our piston models and less resistance on certain tones which speak with more body and less nasal color. Engineers will debate this with measurements and oscillograph readings that appear to be the same whatever the type of trumpet. However, all they need to do is compare, in the confines of the opera pit, the two types of instruments in a Wagnerian opera, and their ears will point up the effectiveness of the rotary valves in reproducing the Wagnerian sound in the complex environs of his scores. The same is true also for the music of Richard Strauss, although that is a topic for another article.

The instrument is not the only factor in developing the sonority of the tone. The lips must provide a smooth and full surface for the vibration of the sound. Some instrumentalists achieve this with a round opening that provides more air surface in the vibrating center than does a more tense, thin line.

The air current is also enlarged by a wider opening of the throat so that a broader volume of wind passes into the lip area. Some teachers insist upon the player forming his sound with dark syllables, such as *oh* and *awh*. This will color the tones more darkly but it also affects the pitch, and the musician must accommodate that change in order to match his colleagues in the section and throughout the orchestra.

Tongue Style

Most specialists in Wagner brass playing have emphasized a different type of staccato and legato tonguing in order to produce the broad, sonorous tone. I have analyzed a number of major brass sections including those of the Bayreuth Wagner Festival Orchestra, the Munich Opera, Vienna State Opera, Hamburg State Opera, Covent Garden Opera, Metropolitan Opera, Chicago Lyric Opera, Berlin German Opera (in the West), and the East Berlin State Opera. It appears to me in a subjective inventory of these skilled musicians that there are a variety of tongue placements essential to the total gamut of Wagner playing. These placements vary from instrument to instrument: that is, what is first-rate for a trumpet will be too forceful for a French horn, etc. I believe, though, that a competent brass specialist should be able to use the broad end of his tongue against the back of his upper or lower teeth, depending upon his needs, and produce in that fashion a full, warm, heavy attack which will not be blatant, but which will have all of the power necessary and be broad enough to match the powerful broad, string sound.

Furthermore, as the player comes upon accent marks for such a tongued note, instead of driving the tongue more forcefully into the teeth and lips, he would produce a more competent sound by using a breath accent in conjunction with the tongue rather than the hard tongue stroke so commonly used by amateurs and, unfortunately, also by some professionals.

These tongue sounds will vary as the demands and styles of the passages change, but this ability is a basic one that serves many purposes in playing Wagner. Obviously, such a skill would not be very compatible with playing Mozart or Haydn. Nevertheless, some of the finest Germanic Wagnerian playing I have heard has been accomplished with just such tongue concepts on the rotary valve instruments.

Conclusion

Space does not permit me to deal with other vital aspects of Wagner style such as transposition and alternate fingerings, so essential to proper intonation and blending. Also, the breadth of sustaining of tones in one category of playing will vary from act to act in the same opera. For instance, the quarter note with a dot or with a legato mark above it will change its character as the drama changes its intensity. Such notation in a third act climax would require a different set of values from those of the more relaxed earlier acts. The musician must measure these values against the sounds he hears evolving in the strings and woodwinds. One of the best authorities on this sort of playing was the famous Wagnerian conductor, Hermann Scherchen, whose book on conducting was a masterpiece. Unfortunately it has not been reprinted, as far as I know.

The astute section leader and section member of any orchestra or band needs to understand much more than just the requirements of the printed notes in his part. He must bring superb skills to the playing of that part, but those skills must be guided and molded by a knowledge and an understanding of what the *total* artistic idea is all about. ∎

PREVENTING LIP DAMAGE IN BRASS TEACHING

Walter Hoover

More beginning brass players fail due to the lack of proper embouchure than for any other reason. To build up a correct embouchure two things are necessary: (1) a knowledge of lip vibrations, and (2) the knack of producing vibrations with and without the aid of the mouthpiece.

Once the knack of producing a buzz on the lips has been learned, the student should practice holding the vibrations in one continuous buzz for 15 to 30 seconds. Later, he should learn to regulate the pitch of the vibrations by playing simple tunes by means of these vibrations alone. This will require persistence and experimentation, but when the student has learned to produce the vibrations on the mouthpiece, he will hear a clear and well defined buzz of "nasal" quality. It should have definite pitch, for cornet in the range between second line *G* and third space *C*—the higher the better.

The more advanced student should have a well-defined buzz, control of which can be gained to a certain extent by playing difficult tunes with the mouthpiece alone. This should be done under the supervision and guidance of a competent teacher; however, in general, the following information will help.

Explain to the student that lip vibrations are produced by forcing the breath between the gently sealed lips; the sound should resemble that made by playing a comb with a piece of paper.

The purpose of preliminary lip vibrations is (1) to insure a correct lip formation, and (2) to prepare the lips for proper mouthpiece placement. This is a very important factor. Clarinet players, for instance, after selecting the desired lay, spend much time dressing, scraping, and nursing the reeds they use on their instruments, trying to make the reeds more efficient by improving the vibration. Obviously, forcing a reed of incorrect shape, thickness, and texture will not tend to make it give better results. The analogy to the brass embouchure should be quite clear.

Place the mouthpiece in the center of the mouth, two-thirds lower and never less than one-third upper (if less, there is not enough flesh in the mouthpiece for good vibration). An equal amount on both is also good. There is no set rule. The next point, though, is a must: *never* allow the inner part of the rim to rest on the red fleshy part of the lips, this being the weak and tender surface of the lips; otherwise serious lip troubles may develop. Later on, the mouthpiece may move in one direction or another, depending upon the formation of the teeth and the jaws; but at the beginning, it should be placed in the position

described. Correct lip formation and correct mouthpiece placement determine the difference between success and failure.

There are two ways to produce tones on a brass instrument: first, by brute force, and second, by an intelligent approach. Even with the lips incorrectly formed, it is possible to produce tones in the upper register if sufficient pressure is applied to the mouthpiece and it is held against the soft, delicate, sensitive flesh of the lips, This is the strong-arm method, which brings about serious lip troubles, even lip paralysis, or if not paralysis, poor endurance. Advocate using the facial muscles instead of the arm muscles.

The young teacher of brass instruments may not have heard very much about the effects of lip paralysis; this occurs when a brass player uses too much mouthpiece pressure. We should be grateful for the scientific information we have available to avoid this condition. This information has been known and practiced for many years by great artists and teachers, but it is sometimes forgotten or ignored.

Students should be developed gradually and be properly guided through a systematic course of instruction so that the muscles and nerves in the lips will not be injured. We should remember that when the lips are damaged or injured, there is little or no help left to insure successful performance on the instrument.

Students should be warned constantly about the possibility of lip damage and advised to use as little pressure as possible. I have a nine year old cornet student who plays high C with ease, by holding the instrument with the thumb and index finger alone. Remember, *the younger the student, the more he requires professional guidance.* Without it, he may develop habits that cannot be corrected.

Many school band dirctors use grade school students to play in parades long before they are sufficiently developed to withstand such an ordeal. This is a serious mistake. Parade work is one of the roughest kinds of work, even for the professional. There is great harm done and very little benefit derived from this practice. In too many cases, students are taught to

be "windjammers" rather than intelligent and artistic performers.

If a cornet or trumpet student has serious embouchure problems, but has all of the other necessary qualifications such as good coordination or sensitive reflexes, he might do well to study trombone, baritone, or tuba.

Teachers should use a visualizer, as it will help the beginner to place the mouthpiece correctly. I put lipstick on the inner part of the mouthpiece rim in order to check on the mouthpiece placement.

Frequently you will see brass players on television, holding their instruments carelessly and with poor posture. Instead of showing how easy it can be to play the instrument, they make it appear difficult.

The ring or hook which is on most cornets and trumpets near the third valve is *not* for the performer's right hand little finger. It is there for one purpose only: as a convenience to the performer who *must* turn his music or insert a mute *while playing.* In years gone by, the solo cornetist of small bands acted as the director. He used the ring or hook to hold the instrument while directing the band with his left hand in tempo changes. As a matter of fact, the movement of the fingers is impaired if you place the little finger in the ring. The player should just allow the little finger to "ride" at will with the other fingers.

Many students, and even some mature performers, seem to think that the performer who can play the loudest has the best lip control. On the contrary, the performer who can play softly, and still control his tones, is by far the better player. Herbert L. Clarke once said, "Practice very softly. It does not tire the lips, nor the ears of those unfortunate enough to hear us."

Non-Pressure System

This term is misleading because it is impossible to perform on any brass instrument without some pressure of the mouthpiece on the lips. "Less pressure" would be a more suitable term. But regardless of what we call it, the lips must vibrate. So why not settle for "Lip Vibration"? With this system, lip slurs can be introduced to the student long before they may appear in the method book. It should be pointed out also that students should be taught and advised to warm up by buzzing with and without the mouthpiece.

At this point you are probably thinking, "He hasn't mentioned a word about breath control." That is true, but breath control is not the problem that is being so sadly neglected. Of course, breath control *is* necessary. So much so that Herbert L. Clarke spent 30 years practicing on that phase of technique.

In my years of playing and teaching, I have encountered several cases of brass players who became victims of lip paralysis and were therefore no longer able to play their instruments.

The first case was that of a young man in a theater orchestra. Being very ambitious, he played three shows daily and practiced not only every morning but also quite frequently between shows. Out of a clear blue sky something happened to his lips. He was unable to produce a tone on his instrument as a result of complete lip paralysis. Undaunted, however, he took up the study of the clarinet and became a fine professional clarinetist.

F. H. Losey, the well-known composer and arranger had the same shocking experience. Thereafter he became Thomas Edison's chief music adviser.

Bobby, a boy of eight years, started to study the cornet. His teacher was an outstanding instrumentalist, but evidently a poor teacher for such a young student. Bobby was forced to practice two hours daily. His grade school teacher was a piano major, and he really kept this boy busy playing solos, parades, and whatever else he could find to show him off. By the time he was 14, he was having all kinds of lip troubles. His parents were advised to take him to Dr. Ernest Williams, who was a nationally known teacher of cornet and trumpet. After he examined the boy, Dr. Williams informed the parents that the boy had been ruined by overwork and too much mouthpiece pressure on the lips. He diagnosed it as partial lip paralysis and advised the boy to forget his ambition to be a cornetist.

A young, matured professional trombone player of my acquaintance decided to change his mouthpiece placement from two-thirds upper to one-third. Why, I do not know, as he was already a very successful performer. However, after two weeks of experimenting with the change, which is known as the orthopedic system, he accepted a job with a circus band. Believe it or not, when he returned, he was ruined; in fact, he has never played since.

Never change the mouthpiece position unless it has been recommended by a brass teacher who understands the procedure or serious lip damage may be the result. We as teachers should also be very careful when changing mouthpieces.

Is it possible that there are a number of Herbert L. Clarkes and Arthur Pryors being ruined every day through neglect on our assembly line? It is a matter over which we should ponder long and seriously. As teachers, we can prevent such tragedies by learning more about the fundamentals of our subject and by applying our wisdom and understanding in all of these important areas of our work. ∎

WARM-UPS FOR HORN

Merton Johnson

As the performance level of school orchestras and bands throughout the country steadily increases, there is the danger that time for individual instruction may be usurped by the demands for frequent public performances. Where this happens, faults in basic playing technique may go undetected in students. Most deeply ingrained playing problems could be corrected or avoided by more individual help and more thoughtful practice.

For the serious student horn player, who cannot obtain individual attention, these suggestions might help avoid embouchure difficulties which later are most difficult to correct.

1. Examine photographs of fine horn players' embouchures and use a mirror during practice to check your own setting. *The Art of Brass Playing* by Philip Farkas (Bloomington, Ind.: Brass Publications) has excellent photos for this purpose.

2. Develop a systematic warm-up which tests and applies the embouchure setting you are trying to develop.

In regard to the second suggestion, the following ideas and examples should prove helpful.

Because warming up is a very individual matter, each player must evolve a routine practical for his own needs. Thus these exercises can only provide a starting point by illustrating a few of the possibilities. For most horn players, a through warm-up should include something from each category, together with similar patterns devised by the student himself. Having blank manuscript paper on the music stand will help encourage experimentation.

Within each group below the exercises are arranged approximately in order of difficulty. Many of the more difficult patterns can be simplified by reducing the range, tempo, amount taken on one breath, and the like. The patterns purposely have not been written out in full in order to challenge the player to think. If a student is not ready to analyze what's happening and continue the sequences "in his head," the full exercise may of course be written out.

(Note: Students or teachers may photo-copy the exercises which follow in order to make them more widely available.)

Valve Slurs:

1. a. Use normal valve patterns.
b. Try for perfectly smooth, connected slurs placed on an even, supported breath line. Do not "huff" the notes into place.

c. If other notes "fill in" your slurs it is a good indication that the slurs are well connected. This is much to be preferred to the problem of dry, unconnected attempts at slurring. Speeding up the connection slightly will smooth out the slur.

2. a. Try for extremely smooth connection. A jaw drop may be necessary for the bottom notes.

b. The exercise may be repeated on successive half steps lower (or higher).

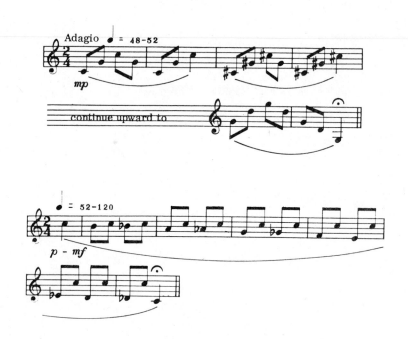

Lip Slurs:

1. a. The full pattern should be repeated downward chromatically using only the *F* horn. The fingering sequence would be: 2, 1, 1&2, 2&3, 1&3, 1&2&3. The 1&3 and 1&2&3 sequences may be too muddy to be practical.

b. For the earlier phase of warm-up or for less developed embouchures, measures 5 and 6 or measures 4, 5, and 6 can be omitted.

2. a. Play the entire pattern in one breath as rapidly as you can play it cleanly.
b. You will probably have a definite jaw drop for the bottom note of each beat. *Do not slide either lip on the mouthpiece;* jut the lower jaw downward and slightly forward so that the lower rim of the mouthpiece firmly rolls part of the red of the lower lip in over the teeth.

512

3. a. Repeat the exercise on successive half steps down to *F♯*.

b. Try for very smooth connections, slowly at first. As the exercise becomes easier, gradually pick up the tempo until you are thinking 16th notes in 2/4.

c. Maintain the same contact point between lips and mouthpiece throughout. Drop the jaw for the lower register. Don't slide either lip in or out of the mouthpiece.

4. a. This exercise is intended as preparation for lip trills and can be gradually speeded up as a trill.

b. A smooth, almost smeary, connection must be made between the two pitches. Definitely do not "huff" back and forth; play on a perfectly steady wind stream.

c. Some players find it helpful at faster tempos to alternate the vowels *oh-ee-oh-ee-oh-ee-oh-* as in saying "yoyo." This tends to cause a fluctuation in the speed of the wind stream and a slight "wiggle" in the lower jaw, both of which assist in bridging the gap between the notes.

d. Variants could include beginning on the upper note, playing sextuplets, and the like.

e. A suggested fingering pattern would be as follows:

notes:	F - G	E - F♯	E♭-F	D - E	D♭-E♭	C - D	B-C♯	B♭-C	A - B	A♭-B♭
B♭ horn:	0	2	1	1 & 2	2 & 3					
F horn:					2	0	2	1	1 & 2	2 & 3

continue chromatically

Ear Training and Initial Attacks:

1. a. As an ear training exercise and practice in clean initial attacks, the following approach is extremely useful. Using a variety of octaves and unrelated pitches, *invent* the exercise as you go along. Take the mouthpiece off the lips after each pitch.

b. If the "inventiveness" is a problem, there is an excellent exercise of this type in Philip Farkas' book, *The Art of French Horn Playing* (Evanston; Summy-Birchard Co.).

2. a. Like the above exercise, this one is to be *invented* as you go along. In addition to providing practice in initial attacks and ear training, intonation and transposition for *stopped horn* are added.

b. The stopped note will have to be transposed down a half step and will be considerably better in tune on the *F* side of the double horn. (For more discussion of the problems of hand-stopping, see the author's article "Muting the French Horn," in *The Instrumentalist* [Jan. 1965])

c. Be certain that both the open notes and the stopped notes are perfectly in tune.

d. For variety, the first note of each pair can be the stopped note, and of course different dynamic levels can be used.

Scale Patterns:

1. a. The preliminary half note is to allow the embouchure time to settle in on the pitch. During the repeated tonguing the embouchure should feel as though it is just continuing a long tone. Do *not* allow the lips to partially close prior to each attack (as though tonguing *tup, tup, tup*). Also eliminate virtually all jaw motion and motion at the corners of the lip.

b. A variety of tonguing styles may be employed, from quite legato to a firmly marked staccato.

c. Any major, minor, modal, or other scale can form the basis of the pattern.

2. a. As an early warm-up this pattern can be played higher by successive half steps to about *G* and then start again with the C chromatic scale below and work downward as far as is comfortable.

b. Speed is less important than smoothness of line.

3. a. The object is light, clean staccato tonguing with an absolute minimum of mouthpiece pressure.

b. Remove the mouthpiece slightly during the rest.

c. In addition to the downward sequence indicated below, the exercise works well progressing upward for range extension, providing the player does not force.

4. a. Play the scales on each successive half step up to *G*, then start again on *C* and continue downward to *G*.

b. For single tonguing, repeat each scale at progressively faster tempos from ♩ = 76 to ♩ = 126. As facility improves the scales can be challenging to double tongue at ♩ = 120 to ♩ = 144.

c. A variety of patterns can be introduced, of course.

5. a. Two of many possible rhythmic variants which can make scale practice more challenging are mentioned below.

Arpeggios:
1. a. Use a light, dry staccato.

b. Use minimal pressure.

c. Try for a very smooth flowing lip action as if slurring. Remove the mouthpiece after each pattern.

2. a. This pattern (taken from Haydn) and similar ones in the chamber music of Mozart and Beethoven when used regularly as warm-ups help to assure the hornist that he will be able to play this sort of thing when it comes up.

b. Repeat the passage sequentially downward by half steps using either your regular fingering or all on one valve combination in the manner of lip slur exercises for *F* horn.

3. a. As fluency develops, this exercise can be played entirely on one breath. Use a light, smooth style with supple lip action as though slurring.

Long Tones:
1. a. Along with more familiar long tone practice it is challenging to use them for developing dynamic control. Any comfortable pitch may be used. To be effective, each note must be sustained without wobble and without diminuendo.

There seem to be three ways of approaching daily brass warm-up: (1) blow at random until the "fuzz is off the lip"; (2) repeat tried and true routines while staring glassy-eyed at the wall; or (3) warm up carefully with the mind "in gear."

On the basis of the third approach, it has been the intent of this article to include general categories for warming up, illustrate them with examples, suggest a few "do's" and "don't's" for more secure technique, and put in a plea for more inventive warm-ups. The mind, too, can benefit from warm-up! ∎

November, 1969

THE BRITISH BRASS BAND

Robert Avis

It's an etymological curiosity that we always speak of a "brass band" when we're talking about a musical ensemble that may be more correctly called a "military band," or perhaps a "wind band," and is not a *brass* band at all. But the term has an authentic meaning in its place of origin.

The "brass band" (both the term and the form) came into being in England about 150 years ago, at a time when three basic developments made this possible. Two of them related to the instruments themselves. From 1800 to about 1850 a series of valve inventions and modifications gave the horns and trumpets a full chromatic scale; then Adolphe Sax devised the "saxhorn," with a complete set of valve brass instruments in matched and graduated sizes to cover the entire practical range of pitch.

The third development, also mechanical in its beginning, had

516

profound social implications. The music of the 17th and 18th centuries, all the great music of the "classical" period, was produced mainly by "working class" musicians who plied their trade for the benefit of, and in the employ of, the wealthy. There were also some wealthy "amateurs" (Frederick the Great of Prussia and Beethoven's friend Prince Rasumovsky were notable examples) but the evidence indicates that music was primarily a luxury, and there was no extensive "music for the masses." (Folk music, of course, is in another category.)

Then came the Machine Age and the Industrial Revolution—and, perhaps for the first time in history, the "working classes" found themselves with some idle time. Moreover, in the late 1800's, mass entertainment had not yet arrived to fill it. So the newly developed brass instruments came immediately into the hands of men who had *time* to play with them, and not too much else to do. Many years ago, in the West Virginia coal fields, I met an old miner who had, in his youth, played with the British brass bands (it must have been in the period just prior to the First World War), and he told me that it was their custom then to come out of the pit, wash up, eat, and go to the band room *every night!* (This is no longer true; twice a week is the rule now.)

Thus, at first, the brass bands were a "working class" diversion, and in England social conditions were particularly right for their development. Many of them were sponsored and financially supported by mills, mines, and factories. To a considerable extent this is still true. John Foster & Son's Black Dyke Mills Band has been internationally famous for a century; Munn & Felton's, Morris Motors, and Foden's are well known through recording and broadcasting. Other bands are supported by towns and communities, such as the City of Coventry, or Brighouse and Rastrick, two neighboring villages which between them maintain one of Britain's finest bands.

So, while the British military bands (that is, the bands of the armed forces) are mixed ensembles like our own, including woodwind instruments, the *brass* bands have

been traditionally the music of the British people—at least, until the Beatles! Englishmen have established them, too, in Australia and New Zealand but, interestingly, *not* in Canada, which was too strongly influenced by the United States.

The brass band is an amateur movement and has been so from its inception. In recent years mass education, mass transportation, and mass entertainment have brought changes; it is no longer limited to the "working class." Boys who grow up in the band go away to school and return later as "white-collar" workers and professional men; and to some degree the bands are losing their old "lower-middle-class" image. But they continue to fill their traditional function at sports, events, picnics, and pageants. They perform in concerts and they punctuate parades. But the most active interest of all is in contests.

The brass bands became involved in competition very early, and soon developed an elaborate, carefully thought out system of contests. Twice a year, in May and September, there are big contests in Manchester and London, and literally hundreds of smaller contests in other areas as well. A band begins at the bottom, but when it wins a prize in that section, it moves up to the next, and so on, until it reaches the top and competes with the best for the championship of England.

Not all the effects of the contests are good, especially as it applies to the socio-cultural aspects of the brass bands, but certainly one good thing has come of it: an extraordinarily high level of technical proficiency. The "second section" and "third section" bands are musically efficient, but the best bands, the bands which year after year compete for the top place, achieve a standard of playing which must be heard to be believed, especially considering their amateur status. They have a perfectly controlled dynamic range, from a pianissimmo that is a whisper of sound to a full-bodied fortissimo that is still not harsh, a faultless execution of the most intricate passages, and an exquisite precision with perfect balance throughout the whole ensemble. The "stars," the cornet, trombone, and euphonium soloists,

measure up to very high standards of playing.

In turn, this remarkable technical development has had an interesting effect on the composition of music for brass bands. In the early years the repertoire was limited to marches, waltzes, medleys, transcribed overtures and selections from operas, and popular songs of the day—much like our own band music at the turn of the century. But as brass bands matured into serious music ensembles, capable of playing first-rate music, they began to merit the attention of serious composers. Except for Gabrieli, none of the early great masters wrote much for brass. Richard Wagner was the first who was able to work with a reasonably complete and modern brass section. Because the movement was essentially British from the beginning, only British composers have heretofore written extensively for it. Holst, Bantock, Elgar, and John Ireland have all used it, and many more of great ability but less fame. In America, only the late Erik Leidzen was familiar with it and he used it with skill.

It is proper that eminent composers should now bend their talents to serve a medium that has proved its capacity to serve them well; but from its beginnings, much of the brass band literature consisted of transcriptions. It is equally as justified, I suppose, to transcribe operatic or symphonic music for brass band as it is to transcribe it for the piano, or to re-shape organ music for the symphony orchestra. But I do have some reservations about the suitability of performing, *in public*, such familiar orchestra works as Schubert's "Unfinished Symphony" or the "Rosamunde" music, although it happens and is performed well! But, suitable or not for public presentation, is there any good reason why the brass instrumentalist should not have the fun of playing them? Or should they remain in the sole possession of the symphony orchestra?

This raises a major consideration. To what extent can we make music for fun and purely for fun? We did once! Perhaps it was very bad music, but it was good fun! I remember the town band of my youth and sometimes I wonder just how very bad it was! Because at that time there were few concerts, no records, and no radio (I'm dating myself), we had no standards of comparison, but I remember that it had an important entertainment value. Now, mass entertainment has changed all our values completely. We can't go back.

It's quite certain that the phonograph, radio, and television have almost completely robbed the amateur musician of his audience. (I must except the "rock" division, where he seems to find ready acceptance.) Over the years we have become accustomed to a professional level of performance. At the flick of a switch we can hear Bernstein in New York, Ormandy in Philadelphia, and Leinsdorf in Boston, not to mention the great orchestras and conductors of Europe. We can listen to these giants every day if we like, hour after hour. So who will go to hear the town band? There's always a small audience, of course, friends and relatives, and those who will listen because of loyalty, social ties, or civic pride; but it's quite safe to assume that there is no longer a general audience for the local amateur musician. *He must play for his own personal pleasure or not at all.*

Musically, as in other areas, we are becoming a nation of spectators on the one hand, and of professional performers on the other. Recently, at a concert by the University of Florida Band, the program listed the names of all bandsmen, with their major courses; it was interesting to note that *less* than half-a-dozen were in engineering or scientific courses. All the rest were majoring in music, with an eye to a career in professional playing or teaching. This will guarantee a generous supply of professional music for the future—if we can afford it—but what about music as a *recreational* activity?

The trend is obvious in other aspects. The Little Leaguer early dreams of the big leagues; but if the dream dies, should he never again feel the satisfactory impact of a ball in his own glove? If so, how much is lost?

We will always have and enjoy professional music to the extent that we are willing (and able) to pay for it; but most of our potential musicians must play, *if at all*, with no audience and no applause, sim-

ply because there's pleasure in it. This has been perfectly stated once by a Dr. Jansen, who was then Director of Instrumental Music at the University of Ohio. It was just a casual remark dropped in the course of informal conversation, but if I had realized its full significance at the time, I would have written it down and preserved it with care. As it was 20 years ago, I must quote from memory: "The greatest pleasure that men ever enjoy is making music *together with others.*" Those last words are the key words, of course, and they have a profound implication. Later I repeated the remark to Dr. J. Henry Francis, and with his customary wit he replied, "Yes, that's true. Conversation's a great pleasure, too—*but only one can talk at a time!*

It applies equally to any form of ensemble music from jazz combo to barber-shop quartet, but we're considering particularly the brass band, which has marked advantages for the amateur. Here are some of them, presented very briefly. (Incidentally, the brass band is a separate and distinct form in its own right, and should not be confused with the brass ensemble which derives from the symphonic brass choir. Especially because the brass choir also includes the French horn, of all brass instruments the least suitable for amateur playing!)

First of all, remarkably few participants are needed to achieve satisfactory effects. The standard British contesting band includes 24 pieces, plus percussion; but 14 of them are on *doubled* parts so that seven of these players may be missing without too greatly impairing the over-all effect. There are several secondary parts which, while helpful to the ensembles, never carry anything essential. Thus it's quite possible for as few as 12-14 players to play together with complete satisfaction, needing no special arrangements and not being limited to trivial music.

Second, because all the brasses they use (except the slide trombone) are essentially different sizes of the same thing, it's practical and easily possible, in case of empty chairs, to shift the available forces around and to get both an adequate representation of parts and

a proper balance. This is a common brass band practice.

Third, while many of the standard military band arrangements are playable, with reasonably good effect, by the brass alone, many others are quite unsuitable or even impossible for small mixed combinations and special arrangements can be both troublesome and expensive. But the brass band has a great quantity and variety of suitable material readily at hand.

The instruments themselves are sturdy, weather-proof, and relatively trouble-free. (Not completely so, of course, but compare them with the strings or double reeds!) They need minimum care and little maintenance. In short, they're well adapted to the uses of amateur musicians, which are always more varied and extreme than those of the professional who usually guards his meal-ticket with punctilious care.

Next, accurate intonation is easier to achieve. This subject calls for a whole new chapter, but briefly, no wind instrument (and no instrument except the unfretted string family) can be in tune with itself in all keys. However, the brasses can be "blown" or "lipped" into tune quite easily, and competent players do it as a matter of course. This one consideration alone is of prime importance, because faulty intonation is the bugbear of nearly all amateur ensembles.

Finally in the area of public performance, the brass band clearly lacks some of the resources and tone color of the military or wind band, and because of this there is a tendency to look down on it as being of an inferior order. In point of fact, it is no more inferior than the string orchestra is inferior to the symphony orchestra. It has a different place, a more limited usefulness, and a more particular appeal. But, like the string orchestra, the male chorus, or any other limited musical form, it has an unlimited capacity for *achievement.*

It is surely not recommended that any successful wind band be discontinued and replaced by a brass band. It *is* recommended that in an area where the wind band lacks sufficient resources in flutes, oboes, clarinets bassoons, etc.—in other words, where there is not a sufficient woodwind choir to give proper balance and contrast to the brass choir—or where the available players are too few, with divided forces, to produce a virile and dynamic sound, *then* the brass band may well become a suitable

and satisfactory outlet for amateur musicianship. It is also recommended that the brass section of any amateur wind band might well try, on occasion, to go alone. (It's not unusual for string players of a symphony to play in quartets for their own enjoyment.) They would then

discover a great new world of personal satisfaction and pure fun, for no better, more practical medium has yet been devised by which *ordinary* people—with little time, limited means, and few musical resources—may enjoy the pleasures of making music together. ■

November, 1969

USING VISUAL AIDS TO TEACH THE ACOUSTICAL PRINCIPLES OF BRASS INSTRUMENTS

Robert Garofalo

As a general guide in determining basic goals and objectives for an instrumental program in the public schools, an instrumental teacher might ask himself: What do I expect from a graduating senior who has completed several years of instrumental study and performance in school ensembles? The answer should be considered in terms of musicianship, performance skills, attitudes and habits, appreciation, and general knowledge and understanding of music history, theory, acoustics, and related subject areas. When a teacher determines the end product of his instruction, he has established a set of long-range goals or instructional objectives. The next step step is to develop short-range goals or instructional objectives. Instructional objectives, sometimes referred to as tactical objectives, are of great value in determining curriculum materials and teaching techniques; they are also helpful in organizing the educative process so that meaningful learning can take place.

It is not my purpose here to discuss the process by which instrumental music objectives are established. This has been thoroughly covered by other writers. Instead, I wish to share with you a few ideas concerning the success I have had in using visual aids to facilitate the teaching of basic concepts in one area of musical knowledge—acoustics.

Since my discussion concerns the pedagogy of basic acoustical principles of brass instruments, it might be helpful to list a few of the questions most frequently asked by young instrumentalists which are relevant to that subject. What are the similarities and differences between (1) the French horn, alto horn, and mellophone: (2) the tenor trombone, tenor trombone with *F* attachment, and bass trombone with *F* and *E* attachments; (3) the trumpet, cornet, and Flügelhorn; (4) the baritone horn and euphonium; and (4) the *E♭* and *BB♭* tuba? What is the purpose of (1) the fourth valve on the double French horn, euphonium, and tuba; (2) the *F* and *E* attachments on the trombone; and (3) the compensating valves on the euphonium and tuba? Questions such as these can provide a limited basis for establishing instructional objectives. The instrumental instructor has the responsibility of seeing to it that students receive answers to their inquiries. It seems to me, however, that it is all but impossible for a conscientious teacher to give clear, logical, and well thought-out explanations to all of his students inquiries. The reason for this dilemma is simple—time, or rather, the lack of time. Consequently, it is necessary for a teacher to develop teaching aids to facilitate the process.

In my own teaching situation, I have worked out a series of charts which have proven to be valuable, time saving visual aids. The charts illustrate clearly and concisely a few fundamental acoustical characteristics of brass instruments. By using the charts as learning aids, students can more easily grasp basic acoustical similarities and differences of brass instruments. With a few words of explanation, a teacher can quickly answer the numerous questions asked by students.

When a student asked me what the differences were between the French horn in *F* and the mellophone and alto horn in *F*, I referred him to the charts. After a cursory examination of the three instruments, it was discovered that the French horn was pitched one octave lower than the alto horn and mellophone. Yet all three instruments read the same part and all sound a perfect fifth lower. From this information came the illumination which partially explains the difficulty in playing the French horn; namely, the French horn's normal playing range is much higher in its overtone series than the normal playing ranges of the other two instruments. The aphorism "a picture is worth a thousand words" contains a fundamental truth which was put to the test and not found wanting.

The question of when the charts should be introduced into the cur-

BRASS INSTRUMENT RELATIONSHIPS

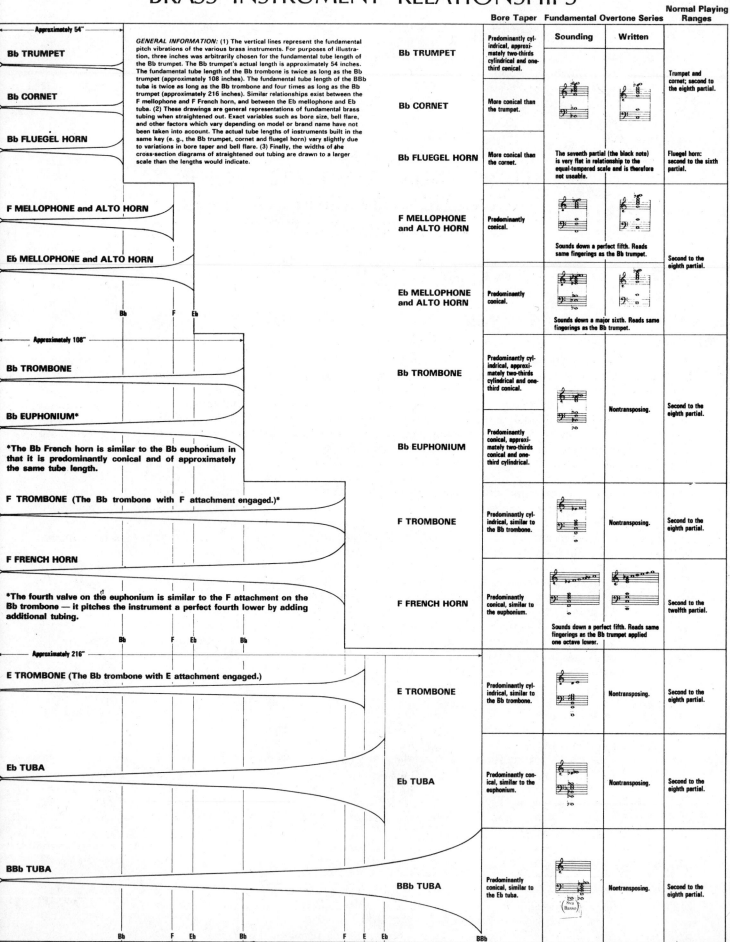

GENERAL INFORMATION: (1) The vertical lines represent the fundamental pitch vibrations of the various brass instruments. For purposes of illustration, three inches was arbitrarily chosen for the fundamental tube length of the Bb trumpet. The Bb trumpet's actual length is approximately 54 inches. The fundamental tube length of the Bb trombone is twice as long as the Bb trumpet (approximately 108 inches). The fundamental tube length of the BBb tuba is twice as long as the Bb trombone and four times as long as the Bb trumpet (approximately 216 inches). Similar relationships exist between the F mellophone and F French horn, and between the Eb mellophone and Eb tuba. (2) These drawings are general representations of fundamental brass tubing when straightened out. Exact variables such as bore size, bell flare, and other factors which vary depending on model or brand name have not been taken into account. The actual tube lengths of instruments built in the same key (e. g., the Bb trumpet, cornet and fluegel horn) vary slightly due to variations in bore taper and bell flare. (3) Finally, the widths of the cross-section diagrams of straightened out tubing are drawn to a larger scale than the lengths would indicate.

*The Bb French horn is similar to the Bb euphonium in that it is predominantly conical and of approximately the same tube length.

*The fourth valve on the euphonium is similar to the F attachment on the Bb trombone — it pitches the instrument a perfect fourth lower by adding additional tubing.

riculum and how much technical information should accompany their presentation are matters which can only be answered by individual teachers. I believe the charts can be used in beginning instrumental classes in the elementary grades. At this level they would have to be simplified and restricted. In instrumental and general music classes at the junior and senior high school levels, the charts

can be reproduced and distributed to students as supplementary learning materials. Students can make their own permanent wall posters or large portable lecture charts by using colored magic-markers and poster board.

In music education today there is a continuous need for the development and refinement of pedagogical aids, visual or otherwise,

which can be helpful in meeting instructional objectives. The chart shown in this article was developed as a result of two motivational forces: (1) a desire to meet instructional objectives which were based on student inquiries, and (2) a real need to conserve time and energy in the process. My charts have served me well; I hope they will be of some use to other music educators. ∎

LEGATO TECHNIQUE FOR TUBA

Donald Stanley

Contemporary tuba literature frequently demands that the player be able to execute a sustained and smooth legato style. This is true of both solo and ensemble literature. Unfortunately, many tuba players do not possess this ability. Too often emphasis is placed on range and facility while legato technique is neglected. The student's study should maintain a balance in all aspects of playing technique to enable him to become a more versatile performer and to make him more aware of the need to acquire correct physical processes. As an example, the breath control and support required for legato playing will probably improve tone, intonation, and range as well.

The ability to play legato on tuba, just as on the other brass instruments, depends upon the control and manipulation of the embouchure, breath, fingers, and tongue. Unless the player has control over these four factors, it is impossible to produce a satisfactory legato sound. It is equally important that the four factors be coordinated so that they interact simultaneously.

Embouchure

Provided that the embouchure is formed correctly to start with, a minimum of movement should be visible from the outward appearance as the player moves from one

pitch to another. A rather common tendency among younger players is to overemphasize the use of the cheek muscles in moving over the range of the instrument. The corners of the lips should be held firm by the cheek muscles but not so tightly that the lips are drawn into a wide smile. Perhaps even more important is the use of the circular muscles which act to draw the lips into a slight pucker formation. This balance between "smile embouchure" and "pucker embouchure" produces the elongated lip aperture through which the air passes. It is likewise important to maintain a downward pull with the chin muscles so that the lips remain separated. Many players permit the chin to "bunch up" as they play in the upper register causing poor response and a thin and pinched tone quality. This formation of the embouchure can be demonstrated to the student by holding a lighted match four or five feet in front of him and asking him to blow out the flame. As he forms his lips to focus the air stream on the flame, he will be approximating the embouchure formation desired for tuba playing.

The embouchure adjustments which are necessary to produce pitch changes consist of more firmness, both at the corners and the center of the lips as the pitch is raised, and a slight relaxation of

these muscles as the pitch lowers. The lower register also requires that the lower jaw and teeth be dropped so that the oral cavity is enlarged. It is important at this point to be aware of the fact that the player must be able to cover the entire range of the instrument with one basic embouchure setting. It is impossible to play legato if the lip has to be reset for various registers. One frequently hears players who play legato in the low register but who are unable to make a smooth change to the upper register. For this reason, it is wise to practice lip slur patterns which start in the middle register and move both above and below that pitch and return to it. In order to do this without a break in the sound requires the player to form the embouchure correctly and maintain that formation in all registers so that the lips continue their vibration.

Breath Capacity and Support

It is obvious that, if the sound is to be continuous, so must the column of air which is producing the tone. For players of the larger brass instruments, it is necessary, through practice, to acquire a considerable capacity for air so that longer phrases can be sustained. Legato style requires that the player be able to project the air in a steady stream through the instrument for the duration of the phrase. In order to do this, the player needs to feel some resistance to the air stream. This resistance is provided by the lip aperture, the mouthpiece, and the instrument itself.

To overcome this resistance, the player must use the abdominal and costal muscles to force the air out of the lungs. Ask the student to "hiss" loudly or to blow out the flame of a match, and he will be able to experience this same feeling of intensity in the air stream. Without this feeling of intensity and resistance, it is impossible to maintain a steady stream of air through the instrument. It is especially important that the player maintain this type of support in the lower register. It is not uncommon to find tuba players who do not maintain proper support in the low register, causing flatness of pitch and inconsistency in the tone.

Valve Technique

The movement of the valves creates a unique problem for the tuba player. Because of the larger tubing, the valve movement is greater than on the other brass instruments. For this reason, it is important that the valves move quickly and simultaneously. This means that valves must move together if more than one is being depressed and that all valve motion, whether up or down or a combination of both, take place at *exactly* the same time. Many players fail to push the valves all the way down or to allow the valve to come all the way up. In these cases, ask the student to slam the valves down as an aid to quickness of motion and to insure the valve moving its total distance.

Alternate fingerings can often improve legato technique. Any alternate fingering which avoids crossing a partial in the overtone series can make a pitch change smoother and cleaner. (For example, when slurring from first line G to F a whole step below and back to G, use the third valve for G and the first and third valves for F. When slurring C below the staff to B♭ a whole step below and back to C, use the fourth valve for C and

the first and fourth valves for B♭. If slurring between third space E♭ and third line D, use the first valve for E♭ and the first and second valves for D). The use of the third valve alone for bottom line G, when preceeded or followed by the F♯ a half step below, is a much easier fingering change than moving from first and second valves to second and third valves. The same is true of the D to C♯ movement below the staff. The use of these alternate fingerings will depend largely on how rapid the passage is and what intonation problems result. (The alternate fingerings quoted above are for BB♭ tuba. Tubas in other keys utilize the same fingerings at the corresponding breaks in their overtone series.)

Tonguing

The tongue is included as a factor in achieving legato technique as its movement can serve to enlarge or reduce the size of the oral cavity. The size of the oral cavity affects not only tone quality and intonation but response as well. For lower pitches, the back of the tongue should be rather low as in the syllables *tah* or *too*. For higher pitches, the back of the tongue arches upward as in the syllable *tee*. Care must be taken so that this syllable *tee* is not produced with a tight or closed throat. The *tee* syllable is a result of the upward arch of the back of the tongue.

Not all legato passages are necessarily slurred. It is possible and often necessary to articulate individual pitches within a phrase without separating the tones. This technique of legato tonguing is produced by lightly touching the tip of the tongue to the hard palate. The tongue must not create a seal so that the air is stopped. On the contrary, it is essential that the flow of air be *continuous*. The function of the tip of tongue is to create a soft articulation at the beginning of the new pitch without creating a space between the pitches. This same technique is used to articulate repeated pitches within a slurred passage.

As mentioned earlier, it is not only necessary to execute these four factors individually but to coordinate them as well. It is doubtful that any one of these, by itself, will produce a good legato sound. However, when all of the factors occur simultaneously, the result is legato technique. Therefore, a great deal of practice and concentration are required to perfect these techniques individually and collectively. The results are well worth the time and effort.

Teaching Aids

Several fine collections of studies are available which the tuba player may use to practice his legato technique. "70 Studies for Tuba" by Blazhevich contains a number of etudes requiring legato playing. Likewise the "Rubank Methods" contain a number of etudes in this style. When read an octave lower, the "Melodious Etudes for Trombone" by Bordogni-Rochut contain a wealth of literature for legato technique practice. This type of playing not only provides the student with excellent musical studies for improving legato technique and phrasing but also provides him with a welcome change from the standard band and orchestra tuba parts. These studies provide a solid background for introducing serious solo repertoire to the player.

Lip slur patterns are also helpful exercises for developing legato technique. The range of these patterns may be increased as the student becomes more advanced. By including arpeggio patterns with the lip slurs, the valve changes can also be incorporated in these studies.

It is indeed fortunate that the tuba is now being taken seriously as a solo instrument with a serious repertoire. With this new concept comes a new responsibility to interpret and perform these works in an artistic manner. As teachers, we must demand the same high level of performance from our tuba players as we expect from other instrumentalists. In this regard, a fine legato technique on the tuba becomes essential. ■

1970

DEVELOPMENT OF THE PHYSICAL ASPECTS OF BRASS PLAYING

Merlin Jenkins

There is an ever growing volume of published literature for brass instruments, consisting of a variety of excellent exercises and studies designed to develop the various techniques of brass playing. Unfortunately, little is said about the development of the physical aspects of playing and the coordination of these physical aspects, the purpose of specific exercises, or even how each exercise should be practiced.

It is my opinion that the student can progress faster by: (1) having a concept of the correct functions of four basic physical aspects; (2) practicing correctly on specific exercises designed to improve each of these four basic physical aspects; and (3) learning how, through correct teaching methods and practice procedures, to combine and coordinate the four physical aspects in order to develop more technical facility, consistency, and control.

Embouchure

It is necessary for the student to realize that the lips must vibrate freely at all times. Two things that prevent this are excessive mouthpiece pressure and squeezing the lips together too tightly. Realizing the fact that there is no such thing as "no pressure," the student should become conscious of using *as little pressure* as possible at all times. The actual amount of pressure used will vary with each individual and also within each individual, depending upon the volume and register involved. Slightly more pressure is called for when playing louder and in the upper register.

To counteract this slight increase in pressure when it is called for, the player should: (1) use moist lips so that they may vibrate freely; (2) contract lips slightly forward (in toward the mouthpiece rim) when playing higher in order to form a cushion to receive the slight increase in pressure; (3) blow air

faster through the lips instead of squeezing lips tighter in order to produce a bigger, more open sound in the upper register; (4) let the lower jaw recede slightly when ascending; (5) raise the head slightly and lower the bell of the horn when going higher (and the opposite when going lower) so that the slight increase of pressure is shifted to the bottom lip in the upper register.

Each of the five techniques above will help the player develop range, flexibility, a bigger sound, and more endurance; however, all five must be developed and coordinated in order to produce maximum results. It must be mentioned at this point that, due to individual physical characteristics, the degree to which all of these are applied will vary somewhat with each player.

Flexibility studies are excellent for concentration on the development of these techniques which lead to a more stable embouchure.

Tongue

Most younger students think of the attack or "starting the tone" as the only function of the tongue. In relation to "starting the tone," the tongue not only acts as a valve to release the air stream which causes the beginning of a tone, but also controls the styles of attack to be used. In addition to styles of attack and various types of articulation, the tongue plays an important role in controlling the velocity of the air stream through the use of various tongue levels.

With reference to attack (and release), some of the most common faults among younger students seem to be: (1) attack made with the tongue between the lips; (2) a striking motion with the tongue against the upper teeth instead of placing tongue in this position and merely withdrawing it to release

the air stream; (3) stopping the tone with the tongue, usually with a "tut" articulation; and (4) the inability to produce the various styles of attack at all dynamic levels.

The tongue should be placed at a point high enough so that it does not protrude through the lips or teeth. This placement will vary, depending upon style of attack and register, but generally it should be in such a position that the upper teeth and/or gums can be felt with the tongue. The release of the tone should be made by stopping the breath an instant before the tongue is put into position for the next attack. Tonguing through open lips and stopping tones with the tongue not only creates a very unmusical sound, but also limits the student's technical development in other areas such as flexibility, range, control, etc. This type of faulty attack and release can be corrected by making the student aware of what is being done incorrectly and how the tone should sound. The proper concept of attack and release may be developed by the student through actual demonstration on the instrument by a good teacher or student. Practicing attacks slowly and listening carefully will correct this faulty habit if the student has the proper concept of this technique.

Students would do well to devote some daily practice to styles of tonguing at various dynamic levels. An excellent text along this line is the "Celebre Method" (Vol. I, 1956 Edition) by Arban. These styles of attack are explained thoroughly and are used with various nuances throughout the method. This text is certainly more comprehensive than the old Arban Method and each of the three volumes represents a different level of difficulty.

In addition to its function of starting tones, the tongue plays the important role of controlling the air stream through the use of syllables.

The lower the tongue, the slower the air stream; the higher the tongue, the faster the air stream. The correct use of the middle and back portions of the tongue has a direct bearing on the development of range, flexibility, and overall technical facility. Syllables to be used are the vowel sounds *ah, oo,* and *ee* for the lower, middle, and upper registers, respectively. These are the vowel sounds to be used in slurring. For articulations, the placement of letter *t* in front of these vowel sounds will create the proper tongue level for attacks in these same registers (*tah, too,* and *tee*). Double and triple tonguing follow in the same manner. Examples:

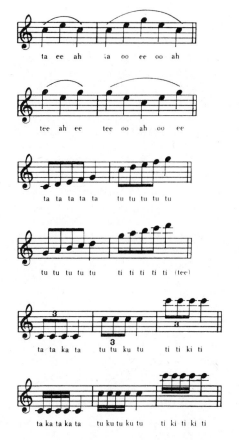

The actual degree of the tongue level will depend upon various factors such as volume, register, each individual, instrument, mouthpiece, etc. Caution must be taken that the throat is not constricted when lifting the tongue to the higher positions. Resistance is created when the tongue is raised to a higher level and this should be counteracted by a faster air stream (blowing more air through the horn) rather than by closing the throat.

Breathing

Regardless of how well-developed and coordinated the embouchure and tongue, control of the air supply is necessary to acquire control of the instrument. Range and endurance are both greatly increased by control of the air supply, and complete control of quality of sound and overall facility in all registers at various dynamic levels are not possible without the proper control of the air supply.

The concept of proper breath control is quite vague among most students. There seems to be much confusion and misunderstanding about this physical aspect. Students often hear: "Pull in with your stomach muscles," "Push out with your stomach muscles," "Lift up with your stomach muscles," "Support the air with your diaphragm," (without being told how) "Breathe from your stomach," and so on. Many students do not really know *what* the diaphragm is and *where* it is located, much less how it is used. Actually, this information is not only unnecessary to the student but more often than not, it only hampers the process of correct breathing. Usually the student becomes so confused and "tied up" while trying to think of so many things that he starts to tighten up the throat and the tone becomes choked or pinched.

Proper breathing can be taught without an explanation of the physical functions involved, and often this approach works out better (especially with younger students). The following will prove to be helpful in the development of correct breathing without having to go into a detailed discussion with the student: (1) start with correct posture (stand erect or "sit tall); (2) inhale without raising the shoulders or tightening the throat; (3) play long tones as long as possible at a good, solid dynamic level; (4) while doing these things, keep chest out in the same position but become aware of the waistline decreasing in size (front, back, and sides) as air is expelled from the lungs; (5) each long tone should be followed immediately by another to insure adequate air intake and relaxation of the throat during the inhalation process.

From an anatomical view, different sets of muscles are used during the inhalation and exhalation process. An explanation of this process is often helpful to more advanced students. The inhalation is caused by the diaphragm and not by the lungs. When taking a breath, the diaphragm descends. This creates a vacuum and air rushes into the lungs. Sometimes the instruction "breathe deeply and fill up the lower part of the stomach first" can be used to good advantage. For the most efficient action of the diaphragm, the air supply should be drawn into the bottom of the lungs so that the diaphragm can maintain continuous contact and control of the breath. During the inhalation process, expansion is created about the entire waist (front, back, and sides). Care should be taken to see that the shoulders are not lifted and that the upper chest does not expand during the inhalation process.

The exhalation process seems to be more clouded with confusion than the inhalation process. During the exhalation process, the pelvic muscles form a solid foundation which in turn causes the abdominal muscles to exert an upward force. This causes the internal intercostal muscles to contract which in turn create a decrease in size of the thoracic cavity. The same muscles we use when expecting to receive a blow in the stomach are now put into use to form this solid foundation on which it expels air from the lungs. With this solid base, the air supply is simply pushed out with any degree of velocity needed through an upward force of the abdominal muscles. During the exhalation process the reverse will be true to that of the inhalation process in that the entire waist area (front, back, and sides) will decrease in size as the air supply becomes exhausted.

The development of this physical aspect can be gained through the playing of long phrases. Since the student must (at first) concentrate on the correct physical functions rather than the difficulty of the music to be played, long tones are excellent practice. As progress is made, flexibility studies encompassing the student's range are good. After the proper breathing process becomes a habit, the student can then concentrate on more difficult exercises and further extend his breath control while at the same time developing other factors.

Technique

Correct arm and hand positions are essential to correct finger and slide technique. The instrument should be *held*—not gripped tightly. Too much of a grip often causes excessive mouthpiece pressure.

Valve instrument students should be trained to keep the fingers on the valves when playing and not to let the fingers "ride" an inch or so above the valves not being depressed. This causes many problems in finger dexterity during later technical development.

Needless to say, scales are basic to good technique. The ability to play all the scales (major, minor, chromatic, whole tone, etc.) will not only increase facility but will greatly improve sight reading ability. Too often students do not play scales (even the ones they know) —they just "wiggle fingers." Scales should be practiced slowly, both slurred and tongued, and developing speed only gradually. Playing scales *evenly* is the important thing. A good method is to establish a comfortable tempo and play chromatic scales, using two, three, four, and six notes to each beat at the same tempo. The range involved in these exercises can be adapted to the individual student.

Examples:

Tempo adjusted to the individual

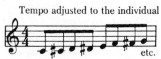

Up and down, both tongued and slurred

Same tempo as above

Same tempo as above

Same tempo as above

Daily Warm-up and Practice Procedures

Many students lack a concept of the proper way to warm up on a brass instrument. The student should understand: (1) *Why* a proper warm-up is desirable; (2) *What* material to use during a warm-up period; and (3) *How* to go about warming up.

The purpose of the warm-up is to gradually put the embouchure muscles involved into play and to get the feel of coordination between embouchure, breath control, tongue, and fingers.

The type of materials used will vary with each individual. Through the years each brass player develops his own method of warming up. The type of material used usually comes from studies and ideas gathered over a period of years from teachers and other players. These warm-up studies usually consist of both slurred and tongued exercises. Long tones and flexibility studies are very effective for good warm-up material. Also, light staccato tonguing of scales is excellent. A thorough warm-up for most players will include all of the above, and often studies containing double and triple articulations for more advanced players. Each of these types of studies or exercises can be included in a warm-up drill for younger players, and can then be extended in difficulty as the player develops. A more advanced student should always start his daily warm-up with these same easy exercises, and then continue to expand these to include more range and speed in both slurred and articulated types of playing.

The "how" of warming up is as important, if not more so, than the material used. No fast rule can be given for all to adhere to since each player has a different physical makeup. Generally, the following suggestions are helpful during the warm-up period for proper embouchure development: (1) play long tones softly in a comfortable register; (2) do not hold tones at the same volume (for warm-up only), but start softly and increase in volume and then decrease in volume; (3) avoid playing loud before the embouchure has time to feel relaxed and ready; (4) avoid playing of extreme low or high notes at be-

ginning of the warm-up period; (5) follow long tones with flexibility studies, gradually increasing range and volume; (6) include some scale studies, both slurred and tongued, for coordination.

A most important thing, and one which is often overlooked, is the "resting" periods during warm-up and practice sessions. Frequent rest periods prevent the embouchure from becoming over-tired. Playing on a tired embouchure will only tear down muscle—not build. The continued playing after fatigue has set in often leads to the development of incorrect playing habits because the student resorts to force or other incorrect compensations. Force causes a stiff embouchure the following day or so, and often leads to the use of excessive pressure.

A well-organized practice plan is most valuable in the development of basic techniques. The purpose of such a plan should be the development of *all* factors involved in the technique of playing the instrument. A well-rounded practice schedule should include daily work on warm-up, the development of all techniques such as flexibility, range, various articulations, etc., and the study of styles and repertoire. This type of practice plan will allow the student to develop in more than one area of technique. Also, all of these can be included in various lengths or numbers of practice sessions.

Each student has different problems in technique development. For some, slurring will be difficult, for others tonguing. It is at this point that the teacher must analyze the problems and correct them through proper physical adjustments and/or correct practice material and procedures.

Of course it is also the teacher's responsibility to see that the student matures *musically* as well as technically. The development of musical style and taste will come only with experience. The student should be continually exposed to good playing—through a performing teacher, concerts, recordings, etc. Only then can he develop the all-important proper concept of brass playing. ■

BASICS FOR BEGINNING FRENCH HORN STUDENTS

Nicholas Perrini

Embouchure

All statements concerning embouchure and mouthpiece position are likely to be extremely controversial. Obviously, there are many different schools of horn playing and teaching. The disciples of each school vigorously defend their own method, claiming it to be the only correct way and as proof, reference is made to certain successful students. This is a legitimate line of reasoning. After all, teaching is only a means toward an end, the end being a successful performer. It is also interesting to note that despite the controversial aspects, there are many specific similarities among these schools, especially concerning embouchure and mouthpiece position. I have used the instructions given below for the formation of the embouchure and the selection of the mouthpiece position with successful results during several years of private teaching. They evolved over a period of years spent discussing the subject with leading horn teachers and observing many young students and professional artists.

Embouchure is the formation of the lips in such a manner as to allow them to vibrate freely when air passes through. One cannot overestimate the importance of the embouchure since it has a profound effect on all phases of horn technique—especially tone quality, flexibility, and range. It is therefore amazing to find so many teachers leaving this very important phase of playing to chance. How many times has this statement been heard: "Give the youngster the instrument and let him blow. He'll find the most comfortable embouchure." I feel that this statement with its many variations may be a gross

oversimplification of the problem. Although the student may be able to produce an acceptable tone with an unorthodox embouchure and even make moderate initial progress, he may be unable to perfect advanced techniques later on. It is therefore important that the beginning student launch his playing career with a satisfactory embouchure. Changing an embouchure once the student has played any length of time is difficult, discouraging, and in most cases risky. Although it is not advisable to confuse the beginning student with elaborate explanations, an attempt should be made to explain the embouchure and its formation in simple terms.

Because of individual differences in jaw and teeth formations embouchures may differ greatly from player to player. However, it is generally agreed that the "pucker" embouchure is the most successful for horn playing. To form this embouchure, the student should first *smile* and then *pucker,* bringing the corners of the mouth in slightly to form a firm cushion of flesh in the center of the lips. The teeth should be kept apart. The student should be warned against *over-puckering* (as if to whistle); this type of embouchure may produce a large but somewhat uncentered, lifeless sound. The embouchure formed by pulling back the corners of the lips with the cheek muscles may produce a thin harsh tone, limited range, and poor endurance. It is suggested that the formation of the embouchure be practiced before a mirror until it has been perfected. The student should exercise the facial muscles daily by forming the embouchure rapidly from a relaxed lip position.

Mouthpiece Position

Mouthpiece position is not to be confused with embouchure, although both are somewhat dependent on each other. A sensible embouchure naturally favors a good mouthpiece position and vice versa.

For brass instrument instruction, one must recognize that there are three basic teeth and jaw formations: 1. upper teeth protruding beyond the lower teeth; 2. upper teeth even with the lower teeth; 3. lower teeth extending beyond the upper teeth (rare). The first two formations lend themselves well to horn playing and should be considered ideal. The third is less successful. If the student possesses a protruding lower jaw, an attempt should be made to even up the teeth by withdrawing the lower jaw slightly. Any *excessive* occlusion (an underbite or overbite in excess of one-quarter of an inch) should be corrected by moving the lower jaw in or out until the teeth mesh or a slight overbite has been achieved.

Once the student's teeth and jaw formation has been determined and corrected (correction rarely necessary except in the case of the protruding lower jaw or extreme overbite), the mouthpiece can be positioned on the lips. The mouthpiece should be placed at least *one-half* and *not more than two-thirds on the upper lip.* A setting of two-thirds upper lip and one-third lower lip usually produces successful results. The lower rim of the mouthpiece can rest just *inside* the red of the lower lip. In this type of setting the mouthpiece is anchored to the upper lip. (The upper lip usually remains stationary while the lower lip is free to accomplish the muscular change needed to play throughout the instrument's range.) While these statements may be refuted by some, it is interesting to note that virtually all successful hornists use a mouthpiece setting similar to this.

Another factor which is usually overlooked is the size of the student. It is generally accepted that the horn should be allowed to rest on the right thigh. However, if the student is of small stature this arrangement may cause the mouthpiece to strike the student in the vicinity of the forehead! This problem may be cured by a little experimentation. Try raising or lowering the thigh by moving the right foot forward or backward small distances. Notice how this action lowers the height of the mouthpiece. The student should find the correct foot placement which will allow him comfortable contact with the mouthpiece. Once this position has been found it must be adhered to religiously. Daily changes in the height of the horn may produce subtle changes in the mouthpiece position which may retard progress. If this method fails to bring the mouthpiece close to the student's lips, the horn should be held off to the right side of the body and supported by a neck strap.

An effort should be made to keep the mouthpiece near the center of the mouth. There are many sound reasons for this, three of the most important being: 1. The muscular formation of the lips tends to indicate that the muscles are strongest at a point generally in the center; 2. If the mouthpiece is placed on the right side of the mouth, the muscles on the left side may have difficulty keeping air from leaking while the muscles on the right side may not be accomplishing enough to develop strength and vice versa; 3. Since the tongue functions best where a direct stroke can be achieved, an off-center mouthpiece position can produce distortions in tonguing. As the air passes through the lips into the mouthpiece it should not be diffused in any way. Air should not be allowed to escape through the corners of the mouth. Keep the corners of the mouth firm.

Breathing

Successful performance on any wind instrument depends largely upon the correct use of the diaphragm. In spite of the existing literature explaining the use of the diaphragm in breathing, the average student is unaware of its exact function. Most students have been told at one time or another to use the diaphragm during playing. The teacher should be sure they understand the breathing process.

The horn requires a great deal of air. To produce a full tone sufficient breath must be available. The student must expand around the waist (including the small of the back) when inhaling to fill the lungs to capacity. The shoulders should remain stationary. When a breath must be taken during an extended passage, it should be taken through the corners of the mouth, not through the nose. The mouthpiece should not be removed from the lips in this situation.

The student should practice deep breathing exercises for a short period each day. Since these exercises do not require the use of the horn, they can be carried on outside the student's practice period. It is very important that these exercises be carried on for short periods of time; strenuous over-practice could cause dizziness. The technique should be tried first while the student is standing. Place the hands around the waist; note the expansion of the abdominal region during the inhaling process. Some students may actually contract the abdominal muscles while inhaling. Correct this by clasping both hands together on the front of the waist and forcing them outward while inhaling. It is important that the upper portion of the body remain in the same position. Here is a simple breathing exercise that the student can practice while walking:

1. Breath in (inhale) slowly and evenly for eight steps.
2. Hold breath for eight steps.
3. Exhale *slowly* for four steps.
4. Hold breath for four steps.
5. Repeat steps 3 and 4 until out of breath.

Improvement can be noted in the number of times steps 3 and 4 can be repeated.

Playing Position

Correct playing position is rare among beginning horn students.

Correct playing position.

The shape and weight of the instrument coupled with the size of the young player are largely responsible for this. Contrary to popular belief, the correct position may not be the most comfortable one, at least not initially. A young student must take careful stock of his playing position daily to insure correctness and eventual familiarity.

It is important to be seated while playing the horn. (If the student stands, the weight of the horn may produce unfavorable effects on the right hand position and embouchure. A seated position allows the player to make small pitch adjustments with the right hand without worrying about supporting the weight of the horn.) Sit well forward on the chair with both feet on the floor. The horn is held with the left hand while the ball rests on the right thigh. Allow the weight of the horn to rest on this leg. The student should not have the feeling that he is supporting the weight of the horn with either hand. If the student is unusually small, it is permissible to hold the horn off to the side of the body in order to insure a correct right hand position. In this case, a saxophone neck strap can be used. (Attach the strap to a strong joint on the horn, *not the tuning slide.*) Under no circumstances should the bell be faced in toward the abdomen or held away from the body parallel to the floor.

Hand Position

The position of the right hand in the bell is of paramount importance. There are about as many different hand positions as there are horn players; however, most hand positions have several basic points in common. I have been amazed to observe beginning, intermediate, and even advanced horn students who have not learned to place their right hand in the bell at all! The student should learn this very important technique at his first lesson. Young horn players usually suffer from intonation problems when performing in school music organizations as a result of incorrect right hand positions. Since a correct right hand position will *lower* the pitch of the horn somewhat, manufacturers construct the instrument slightly sharp. Therefore beginning hornists who are unaware of the right hand technique may be forced to pull the main tuning slide and all the valve slides to great lengths. Even though pulling these slides may improve general intonation, it does not aid in producing a characteristic horn tone. It is hoped that the above discussion has made the deep impression intended. The right hand should be thought of as part of the instrument.

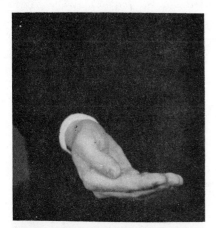

Correct right hand position.

Right hand in horn bell.

The right hand is held in a slight cup-like position as if one were trying to hold water in it. Note the straight position of the fingers. With the right hand in this position, insert it into the bell. When the horn is held in the proper playing position the fingers should rest against the bottom portion of the bell throat. The heel of the hand should be one to two inches away from the upper portion of the bell. For those students using a single Bb horn, the hand should be closed more than this. Remember to hold the fingers straight; do not allow them to curve up into the throat of the bell. The hand should open slightly for notes above written third space *C*. These higher notes on the *F* horn may have a stuffy quality and may be somewhat flat in pitch. Opening the right hand eliminates these unfavorable characteristics. This technique is not necessary when the single Bb horn is being used. Minor adjustments in pitch can be made by opening and closing the right hand. Open the hand slightly to raise pitch and close it to lower pitch.

The left hand and arm are held in a relaxed position. The left elbow should be allowed to hang freely. It should not be held up parallel to the floor. The fingers of the left hand should be held on the valves. The valves are depressed with the tips of the fingers. The student should not use excessive pressure when depressing valves. Neither should the horn be pulled toward the body with the little finger which is in the finger hook as this may result in excessive mouthpiece pressure.

Tone Production

The student should first attempt to produce an acceptable lip buzz without the mouthpiece. There are many ways to accomplish this. One method is to form the embouchure described earlier, then place the tip of the tongue behind the upper teeth and release the air into the horn by gently pulling the tongue back a short distance. Although this is recognized as being an accepted method for starting a tone, the above explanation might be confusing to the young student. Another method would be to have the student pretend he is blowing

a hair off the tip of his tongue. This usually produces a very short buzz. The next step is to have the student continue blowing after the initial buzz. If the buzz was initially obtained in this manner (by placing the tip of the tongue through the teeth), the student should now attempt to produce the same buzz by placing the tip of the tongue *behind* the upper teeth or back just slightly on the hard palate. It is interesting to note that once the lip buzz has been initially mastered, the student usually forgets about it completely. With much practice, the pitch and intensity of the lip buzz can be controlled to an amazing degree. The student should spend several minutes each day buzzing his lips. It may take several weeks or even months to develop a one octave range, but continual perseverance will pay great dividends in the long run. The student should be encouraged to buzz simple tunes and intervals.

Once the buzz can be produced freely the student is ready to buzz into the mouthpiece. The mouthpiece should be placed on the lips in the manner described earlier. After wetting the lips the student should strive to produce long sustained tones of different pitches. These tones should be produced softly with a distinct *too* sound. After obtaining the correct seated position, the student should try to produce a tone with the mouthpiece attached to the horn. The air passing through the embouchure will cause the lips to vibrate, causing a note to be produced on the horn. It doesn't matter what pitch is produced at first—just try to get a sound. Continue practicing this until a tone can be produced every time. A *too* attack sound should be used.

Once the attack has been perfected, the student should try to play second line *G* on the horn. If the pitch is too high, relax the lips slightly. Also, the student may be using too much mouthpiece pressure. If the pitch is too low, tighten the lips more. This exercise should be practiced until the *G* can be played every time. Observe the following points: (1) embouchure (wet); (2) right hand position in bell; (3) mouthpiece position and pressure; (4) general playing position.

If the tone quality is too brilliant and strident in character, close the right hand. If the tone is muffled and stuffy, open the right hand slightly and make sure the bell of the horn is not facing in toward the body.

Care and Maintenance

It is not my intention to suggest that the student memorize all the facts pertaining to care and maintenance of the horn during his first few lessons. However as the student progresses, certain specific phases of care and maintenance should be introduced.

Like any other delicate mechanism the horn needs care and maintenance. Certainly the rule "an ounce of prevention is worth a pound of cure" holds true here. Lack of preventive maintenance can result in failure of the horn to function properly, causing innumerable playing difficulties as well as the possibility of an expensive repair bill.

The Mouthpiece

The cushion of the mouthpiece (the large end which comes in contact with the lips) must be kept free from dents. An effort must be made to keep the lower edge of the mouthpiece stem (the small end) free from dents also. A small inward bend at the tip of the stem may cause many playing difficulties. The inside of the mouthpiece must be kept clean at all times.

The Mouthpipe

The inside of the mouthpipe should be cleaned every month. During playing the inside of the mouthpipe collects much residue which gradually causes the diameter of the tube to become smaller. If the student waits several months and then cleans the mouthpipe, the horn may play differently for a few days. It may seem more difficult to play than it did before the cleaning took place. The reason for this is that the diameter of the mouthpipe has actually become larger thus disturbing the player's breath support. A flexible cleaning brush is needed to clean this section of the horn's tubing. A cornet or trumpet brush should be used (do not use the trombone brush as it is much too large and may become lodged in the tube). For top performance the

mouthpipe should be kept clean *at all times*.

The Inside of the Horn

The inside of the horn should be cleaned with warm (not hot) soapy water at least every four months. The water should pass through the entire network of tubing. Remove the valve slides and depress the valves. This allows the water to flow through the valves and valve casings. Any excess water that remains on the outer portion of the valves should be dried immediately. The rest of the horn can either be dried with a soft cloth or allowed to dry naturally.

The Finish

The cleaning of the outside of the horn is optional. Some students feel that a dirty horn appears more "professional." Nothing could be farther from the truth. A good brand of instrument polish should be used. (Check first with a private teacher, band director, or knowledgable dealer before purchasing polish.) Avoid hard rubbing. A soft cloth, perhaps a chamois, should be kept in the case to wipe off finger prints and perspiration stains after each practice session.

The Bell

The bell is a very delicate section of the horn. Some instrument manufacturers take pride in constructing horns with bells that are described as being "paper thin." Regardless of its thickness, the bell is easily damaged. A great many horn students (and professional hornists!) have the habit of leaving their horns on their chairs during a rehearsal break. This is asking for trouble. Only the slightest "bump" by a careless friend could produce a dent in the bell. When the horn is not being played, it should be in the hands of the player or in the case. Avoid placing heavy pressure on the bell. Many bells have been bent by the student who placed the edge on one of his knees and attempted to remove a slide by vigorously pulling downward. Whenever difficulty is encountered removing a slide, lay the horn across both knees and pull the slide outward away from the body.

The Slides

Never allow the slides to stick within the slide casing; keep them well greased. If a commercial slide grease is not available, vaseline or cold cream are acceptable substitutes. When applying grease to a slide, be careful not to allow the grease to cake on the inner surface of the slide since this may obstruct the air column. These small particles of grease may also become loose and fall into the valve, causing it to stick. Whenever greasing a slide, remove the residue of grease from the inner portion of the slide and slide casing. Always depress the appropriate valve when pulling a slide. Note: Some single F horns are equipped with an E♭ slide. The serious horn student should be discouraged from using this slide. Virtually all of today's horn music is written for horn in F. It would therefore be superfluous to spend any length of time using the E♭ horn since the eventual change to F horn is not only practical but inevitable. Some inexperienced horn students may be unable to distinguish between the F and E♭ slides. Most E♭ slides are circular in shape. However, occasionally one finds an F slide in this shape. To distinguish between them, examine both slides; the larger (longer) is the E♭ slide.

The Valves

The valves should be oiled at least once every two weeks. This is accomplished by placing one or two drops into the valve casing through the opening of the valve slide casing. Try to drop the oil directly onto the valve. Do not allow it to run down the sides of the slide casing. The slide casing may contain foreign particles, such as dirt and grease, which the oil will pick up and carry into the valve. The inexperienced student should not disassemble the valves. If difficulty is encountered with a sluggish valve, try lubrication first. If this fails to free the valve, take the horn to an instrument repairman.

Valve Strings

Replacing a broken valve string is a technique with which every horn student should be familiar. Strong string should be used, preferably 25-pound-test fishing line. (Do not use gut violin strings. They are much too brittle and may snap after several weeks of use.) The string should be approximately six inches in length *after* it has been knotted. The student should use a small screwdriver to aid him. (A four-inch jeweler's screwdriver is ideal.) Use the five illustrations below as a guide. (1-Valve arm 2-Stop arm hub 3-Stop arm)

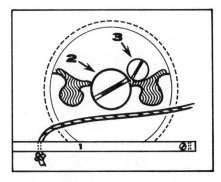

Step 1: Pull the string through the small hole in the valve arm, (make sure the knot is large enough to keep it from pulling through) and guide it between the stop arm hub and the valve arm.

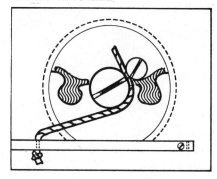

Step 2: Holding all three valve keys in a level plane, guide the string around the stop arm hub in between the stop arm and the stop arm hub.

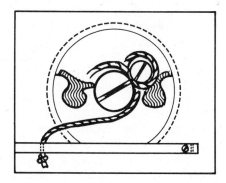

Step 3: Loop the string around the small retaining screw on the stop arm, then tighten this screw. The tightening of this screw may pull the valve key down slightly below the level of the other two keys. Compensate for this by starting with the valve key slightly above its neighbors.

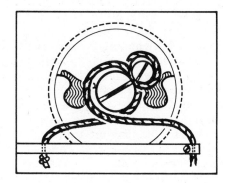

Step 4: Guide the string around the stop arm hub and through the small hole near the end of the valve arm. The string may pass over or under itself depending on the type and make of horn used. Solve this problem by inspecting the path of the string on the other two valves.

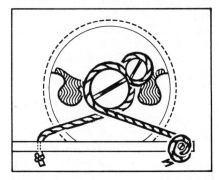

Step 5: Pull the string tight and then loop it around the small screw near the end of the valve arm. Tighten this screw.

The Case

When it comes to care and maintenance, the student usually overlooks the all important horn case. Whenever the horn is being played the case should be *closed* with the straps *inside*. When closing a case, make sure *all* the latches are fully closed. Do not keep band folders, music, books, or spare mutes in the case. A mouthpiece not properly placed in the rack may become loose and cause great damage to the horn. Therefore, keep the mouthpiece securely mounted in the rack. The case should also be tagged properly for identification purposes. ∎

March, 1970

ABOUT TROMBONE TEACHING: A NATIONAL CONSENSUS—Part I

Paul Tanner

My quarter off from UCLA in 1969 was the Spring quarter. On a research trip sponsored by UCLA Extension, I drove 15,000 miles and visited over 100 colleges and conservatories throughout the country.

Being a trombone player and teacher, one of my main interests was to find out exactly how trombone is being taught in higher education.

First, I would like to thank the trombone instructors who were gracious as well as generous with their time and information. I told each of them that the sole use of this collated material was to be of help to other trombone instructors and students. As a consequence, instead of considering their personal trombone approaches as guarded secrets, they shared their techniques willingly with me and I came home with a suitcase full of pertinent data, though sometimes diverse in opinions and directions.

I talked not only to trombone teachers, but to their students (not implying that we trombone teachers are not perennial students ourselves). I found that there are three fairly distinct categories of teachers of this instrument:

1. There is a category of teachers who have been successful over a long period of years. These gentlemen have systematized their teaching in a manner that works best for them but are also generally quite open to new and different thinking that would create the desired progress in the student.

2. On the other end of the pendulum is a group of young teachers who have not really been playing or teaching long enough to have stabilized their methods according to their required goals. These teachers are usually extremely anxious to learn of any approaches, methods, systems, concepts, or exercises that are being successfully utilized by others.

3. The middle category that I would be inclined to list are the teachers who, for the most part, have studied with a strong and influential teacher and have a tendency to hand down the "word," given to them as though it were gospel. They are in the process of finding out that even though the information and instruction that was so aptly passed down to them fitted their specific needs, it is possible that other individual students were getting different instruction pertinent to their requirements. Now that they are meeting their own varied students, they have realized the necessity to broaden their approaches.

Besides the teachers whose names most trombonists are aware of, there are also many fine teachers who are really not known outside their home area. I even came across one gentleman in New Mexico who is teaching trombone although he is not really a brass performer. Yet after visiting his school, I came away with the distinct impression that he is doing an excel-

lent job. This possibility would not have occurred to me before my trip.

Since I dislike generalizations, I was happy to find that although many of the items of information were constantly duplicated, each instructor seemed to have his own area of emphasis. Thus the teaching actually varied from school to school and from teacher to teacher. One important Midwest university has three outstanding trombone instructors. Some students try to study from all three. According to the students, each of these instructors has his own way of developing trombonists; one is much more involved in performance of literature, one is mainly preoccupied with the physiology of the player, and the third teaches very well by demonstration and imitation. All three are quite successful.

One of the first questions I asked the trombone instructors concerned the eventual direction of their students. In most cases it appeared that the majority of students who are studying trombone in college today intend to become music teachers. I did not get a feeling that the teaching was being viewed as a last resort, but that the students were conscientiously preparing themselves to teach. I did talk to some instructors, however, who said that even if a student is quite set on becoming a professional player, they do encourage him to work for a teaching credential as a security measure. Some students feel that they will be better prepared to teach music if they have actively participated as a performer. A fairly common answer was that the students would like primarily to teach and to perform some on the side. This they feel would not only add to their income, realizing that the teaching salary is sometimes not what it should be, but would also satisfy the desire to be creative and to participate. Naturally there are students whose direction is totally that of becoming a professional performer. Most of them are aware of the competitive nature of this field but are not deterred—that is it! With that type of determination, they will probably be successful. Most instructors can see the problems involved in playing trombone for a living and are honestly trying to prepare the stu-

dents to be well-rounded. With this in mind, some teachers work on exercises concerning all basics of playing while putting forth great efforts to cover a variety of styles and interpretation in a trombone choir approach. Others try to cover the multi-direction problem by encouraging their students to participate in stage band, concert band, symphony orchestra, etc. The trouble here, of course, is that the student must also study some other time-consuming courses. Some teachers say that to play well is to play well, so all the effort goes into basics and not too much concern is given to the possible differing demands of the music field outside of school. There are many teachers who say that all of their students are classically oriented, all heading toward symphony jobs. Some teachers worry because there are not enough of these jobs to go around or because some students with this in mind simply will never play well enough to work in a symphony that pays a living wage. A few teachers in this category say that they are somewhat dismayed by this limited direction of their students and would prefer more diversified possibilities.

The teaching load of these instructors varies unbelievably, but it must be understood that some trombone teachers teach other subjects, some are actually only part-time teachers, some are in big schools with many trombonists, and some just the opposite. The figures vary from two students a week to 45. The instructor who has only two students says that the rest are taught by a non-faculty instructor. In numerous cases there are only three or four trombone students on a campus. For those instrumental instructors who like to compare their teaching loads to others, it might be of interest to know that the *average* number of students taught by the teachers that I talked to was 15. It should be noted however that most teachers have many less than 15, the median being higher because of the few teachers who teach 35-45 students a week. One-third of the trombone teachers in colleges instruct from nine to 15 students a week. There are many cases where the faculty trombone instructor teaches as many students as he has time for and the rest are taught by graduate students. Some who teach trombone also teach other brass instruments. The statistics above include just trombone. In one school, only the trombonists in the symphony orchestra receive private instruction. There are schools where no undergraduate receives lessons, only graduates. In most schools though, the students take lessons for at least three years. I found very few students studying bass trombone, but many with a large bore tenor with an F attachment. In some schools, lessons are required, at least for music majors. Most of the students studying privately are working toward music degrees. Those teachers in two year schools tell me that they get quite a few students who are barely above the beginning stage.

Almost every student receives one lesson a week; however, I encountered situations where young players in the beginning stage were receiving as much as two and a half hours per week in half hour segments in order to supervise their progress more closely. Some teachers tell me that they prefer two half-hour lessons a week rather than one hour if the student is just getting started. Most students get a one hour lesson a week, some get 45 minutes, and others have a half-hour lesson. Most of the teachers who give a half-hour lesson tell me that it is terribly hard to get much accomplished in that amount of time. On the other side of the ledger, they feel that they can at least be of some help to more students. Some dedicated teachers put in a considerable number of unofficial hours, as I'm sure occurs in many aspects of the teaching profession. In some cases, an applied trombone student takes a one hour lesson, others take a half hour. I encountered a couple of situations where each student is assigned a half-hour lesson, but if he pays an extra fee, the lessons can be extended to an hour. One teacher gives many half-hour lessons a day and even carries this into Sundays. There were a few who give as many as 35 half-hour lessons a week. One well-known teacher in the East teaches privately seven hours a day, five days a week, plus his trombone ensembles, and he is in his middle 70's! I found one teacher who insists on three hours a day practice to every one hour a week lesson; he is considered more driving than others in that school.

Some teachers are so well-organized that they have a complete curriculum established for the entire time the student is in college. These instructors have specific studies and exercises, methods, etude books, and have even spelled out the solo literature to be covered each quarter or semester. Other instructors question the grading problems that occur with this type of planning when a younger player may perform better than an older player. However, the organized teachers certainly seem to know exactly where they want each student to be at every level. Most of the teachers seem to have a favorite collection of exercises and studies that they use as a point of departure. They will emphasize the studies needed most and even augment and expand according to the demands of the individual student.

Some instructors have a set routine in their weekly lessons, some do not; some say that they have a standard routine but find it impossible to follow it. I am happy to state that most trombone students are treated as individuals with their own set of assets and problems and that the lessons are tailored accordingly. How this is done varies considerably. Some lessons are split about half way between techniques and solos. Many teachers start each lesson with a portion of a Remington-type of warm-up then go into certain exercises for problems that demand the most immediate concentration. Some try to crowd a warm-up, technical studies, melodic studies, specific problems, sight-reading, and solo work into one session. Others concentrate on trying to develop the whole trombone player at once, relying greatly on assignments of multi-purpose exercises. Some consider the basics of all brass playing as a combination of air and tongue, and operate accordingly.

Most teachers make specific assignments to be heard the following week, although a few do not. One of the general attitudes by those who do make assignments is that working up specific things develops discipline in the practice. The most prevalent opinion,

though, is that the student is simply working on what the teacher wants him to work on. Some instructors go right through a book or a series of books, while others operate off the top of their heads from their own experience. One fine conservatory teacher agreed that after he has taught a student over a period of time (years), there is not a great deal left to tell him and the lessons become more like intensive coaching. There is also a small group of instructors who try to pass on exercises that can be practiced the entire length of the playing career, pointing out how each exercise can be expanded and the benefits derived from each type of expansion.

Not all trombone teachers play with or for their students as might be surmised. In one important conservatory, the student told me that they do not know of anyone who has heard their teacher play. However, most teachers do play some during the lessons; the reasons and manner vary a little. The most obvious reason is to demonstrate. Some demonstrate the way to approach an exercise, some play to demonstrate sound, or the advantages of good breathing, some are involved most of the time demonstrating different attacks; but most demonstrating seems to be in the direction of stylistic interpretation of literature. Some instructors play duets with the students for purposes of sight-reading, interpretation, balance, blend, intonation, etc. More than one instructor told me that he alternates four bars with the student. The imitation method works well here, and it also makes the student strive for flow in the music. This should work to advantage everywhere it is done. In one Midwest university, the instructor has such an excellent sound that the students simply do everything they can to emulate him.

As far as the size of the instrument that trombonists should play is concerned, the consensus of opinion goes in two different and definite directions. Many teachers are suggesting fairly large trombones, .515 bore and larger, and always with the F attachments (keep in mind that these are tenor trombones). There is a prevalent school of opinion that the larger the instrument, the larger (hence better) the sound. Granted there is an occasional teacher who has an "agreement" with a manufacturer, but this seldom influences his attitude toward the size of the trombone. One teacher says—use such and such a trombone, his mouthpiece, and relax—guaranteed success! Some fine performing teachers vary the size of their horns depending on the music they are playing. For example, somewhere around a .522 bore for symphonic work, and as small as .485 or .490 for lighter work.

There is another entire school of trombone teachers who feel that most players, especially student players, are playing on instruments that are too *large* for them. These teachers feel that students have a tendency to change to the "in" horn and suffer the illusion that their problems will all be solved. A talented man in New York suggested that there is far too much identifying with the instrument and not nearly enough with the music itself. Some instructors maintain that everyone *cannot* and actually *should not* sound alike. These teachers treat each student as an individual who is expressing himself according to his mental and physical make-up and happens to be doing it with a trombone. The teachers then work from there to escalate progress.

What I have related regarding horns also holds true for mouthpieces. There are two generalities however. There seems to be more of a liberal feeling concerning mouthpieces, in that each individual may have his own needs as far as rim shape, width and depth of the cup, and even the size of the bore of the mouthpiece are concerned. The other generality is the concern about the size being too small for a big sound or too big for adequate upper register facility. Of course, there are certain teachers who say that one specific mouthpiece is the only one to use, regardless of the student's musical thoughts or physical differences (teeth, jaw, etc.).

The previous paragraph brings up the diverse attitudes encountered concerning the embouchure itself. One of my leading questions was, "Would you change a student's embouchure?" The answers varied from an immediate "Yes" to "Not unless he simply could not play his (the student's) way." Most teachers agree that they would change a student's mouthpiece placement if: 1. the student with a radical setting is quite young; 2. if the student has gone just about as far as he can go on that embouchure; or 3. if he will progress some but will have definite long-range problems. Most teachers are not very happy about changing an embouchure. It even makes for undue mental problems unless it is handled in a most positive manner. Some teachers are concerned about the setting being too high. They prefer about half and half or even a little low. Most instructors feel that the lower lip is simply stronger. It seemed a little incongruous to me that most of those who said there is no one place for the mouthpiece also said they would move it readily to the spot they thought it "should be." I found a few who base mouthpiece placement on the sound being elicited. Some even do this to the point of disregarding any long range thinking. Most teachers agree that the lips should be even. As to whether or not the teeth should remain even, the camps are somewhat divided. If the teeth remaining even disregards the pivot system, then most teachers seem to reject it because most (not all) that I talked to do go along with the pivot system. There is worry about over-bites and under-bites (much more rare it seems) causing undue pressure on one lip. A few consider the embouchure as a combination of a "pucker" and a "smile," but the smile system of working into different registers is almost universally rejected, as is the non-pressure system.

One thing that these teachers will talk about in person but seldom in print is the aspect of shifting the mouthpiece around in extreme registers. Most of the teachers will tolerate very little mouthpiece shifting merely to make high register playing easier, but many mentioned movement of the placement when going into extreme low registers, especially pedals. The contention seems to be almost: "Do what you have to do." What it amounts to in the lower register is to drop the lower jaw and shift the pressure from even to more on the upper lip. Many fine players move the mouthpiece up toward the nose on pedals, using very little of the bottom lip. Also, there is a tendency to teach putting more of the lips into the mouthpiece in the low registers.

Two other attitudes were garnered concerning embouchure. One is that the setting is not nearly as important as strengthening the corners of the mouth by good flexibility exercises, the reasoning being that if the muscles are strong, they will do whatever you want them to with a very "normal laying of the mouthpiece on the lips" embouchure. The other attitude is one of building up the breathing apparatus and letting the embouchure take care of itself.

One teacher said that his biggest problem is that he has to do far too much remedial work, especially in the way of sight-reading. Another teacher said that his students lack sound, breath control, feasible slide control, etc., all seemingly stemming from a lack of incentive or initiative to practice. One teacher had the unique problem of having to create three "instant trombone players" out of two baritone players and a tuba player. He put the baritone players on valve trombones and taught the tuba player to operate a slide and trigger. He transposed the trombone parts to treble clef for his baritone players who only read in treble clef. Actually he had a very respectable sounding section. At one university, the students told me that the teaching there caused the unique problem of the good getting better and the bad just getting worse! A major problem that kept occuring was the lack of students playing bass trombone.

A few rather unusual teaching techniques that were introduced to me included:

1. Teaching beginners many songs by rote, concentrating on what is coming out the horn rather than what is on the sheet. The students learn by imitation.

2. Likening the upper register to the falsetto of a voice, calling it "whisper technique."

3. Making required reading of certain worthwhile articles on trombone playing.

4. Using a tape machine in the lessons, then slowing it down to hear the "wah," in the attacks.

5. Talking much more psychology than music.

6. Working with a master class where the students criticize each other.

7. Singing every note with every student.

8. Having first year students play very loudly to open up their sound.

In another article I will summarize the consensus of trombone teachers in this country regarding buzzing, breathing, tongue position, syllables, attacks, slurs, legato playing, scales, flexibility, range, vibrato, etc. ∎

A FRENCH HORN DISCOGRAPHY

Stuart Uggen

Solos

John Barrows and His French Horn
Golden Crest RE 7002
(Playing original music for horn written by Alec Wilder)

First Sonata for Horn and Piano
Suite for Horn and Piano
Second Sonata for Horn and Piano

The Art of Dennis Brain, Vol. 1
Seraphim 60040 Mono Only

Beethoven: *Sonata in F Major*
Dittersdorf-ed. Haas: *Partita in D Major*
Dukas: *Villanelle*
Haydn: *Symphony No. 31 in D Major*
Mozart: *Concerto No. 2 in E♭ Major, K. 417*
Mozart: *Divertimento in E♭ Major, K. 289*
Schumann: *Adagio and Allegro, Op. 70*

James Chambers Plays the French Horn
Award Artists Series AAS-704

Bakalinikov: *Cavatina*
Bradford-Anderson: *March, In Canon*
Clerisse: *Chant, Sans Paroles*
Heiden: *Sonata for Horn and Piano*
Hermann: *Concerto for Horn*
Mozart, L.: *Concerto*
Piatoni: *Air de Chasse*

Philip Farkas, French Horn
Coronet LP 1293

Bozza: *En Forêt*
Françaix: *Canon in Octave*
Gallay: *Unmeasured Preludes*
Glazunov: *Reverie*
Gliere: *Intermezzo*
Mozart: *Concerto No. 2*
Schumann: *Adagio and Allegro*

Roy Schaberg, French Horn
Coronet LP 1257
Corelli: *Sonata in F*
Gliere: *Concerto for Horn* (Second and Third Movements)
Mozart: *Concert Rondo*
Mozart: *Rondo* from *Quintet*
Piatoni: *Air de Chasse*
Saint-Saëns: *Morceau de Concert*
Saint-Saëns: *Romance*

French Horn Masterpieces Played by James Stagliano
Boston Records, Chamber Music Series L-200

Beethoven: *Sonata for Horn and Piano, Op. 17*
Mozart: *Concert Rondo, K. 370*
Schubert: *Auf dem Strom, Op. 119* (for horn, voice, and piano)
Schumann: *Adagio and Allegro, Op. 70*

French Horn Solos (Elementary)
Kjos—IM #22

Buchtel: *Janus*
Buchtel: *Solitude*
Buchtel: *Meditation*
Buchtel: *Arcadia*
Buchtel: *Cielito Lindo*
Chopin: *Cavatina*

French Horn Solos (Elementary)
Kjos—IM #23

Buchtel: *Caissons Go Rolling Along*
Buchtel: *Elegy*
Buchtel: *Reverie*
Buchtel: *My Buddy Waltz*
Buchtel: *Prince Rupert*
Hubay: *Träumerei*

The Art of the French Horn from Baroque to Romantic
Murray Hill Records, 419 Park Ave. So., New York, New York 10016. Stereo 2937 (4 record set)

Brahms: *Trio for Horn, Violin and Piano*
Gabrieli, A.: *Ricercar for Horn and Brass*
Gabrieli, G.: *Canzon for Horn and Brass*
Handel: *Concerto for Two Horns*
Haydn: *Horn Concerto*
Mozart: The four *Concertos*
Rosetti: *Horn Concerto in D minor*
Schumann: *Konzertstück for Four Horns*
Telemann: *Suite for Four Horns*
Vivaldi: *Concerto for Two Horns*

Solos for the Horn Player
Music Minus One MMO 6010

(Selected and edited by Mason Jones. Music minus one French horn)

Beethoven: *Scherzo from Septet, Op. 20*
Brahms: *Scherzo from Serenade in D, Op. 11*
Glazunov: *Reveries*
Handel: *I See a Huntsman*
Lefébre: *Romance*
Mendelssohn: *Andante* from *Fifth Symphony*
Purcell: *I Attempt from Love's Sickness to Fly*
Ravel: *Pavanne*
Saint-Saëns: *Romance*
Stradella: *Kirchen Arie*

Ensembles
The Hornist's Nest (Quartets)

Mark Educational Recordings, Ensemble Series MES 29088

Bach: Andante from "*Jesu, meine Freude*"
Bach: Andantino from "*Jesu, meine Freude*"
Bach: *Bourée II, English Suite No. 2*
Bach: *Fugue XI, WTC, Vol. I*
Bach: *Gigue* from *Suite for Harpsichord*

Bach: *Sarabande, English Suite No. 2*
Boismortier: *Sonata*
Shaw: *Fripperies for Four Horns, No.'s 2, 4, 5, 6, 7, 8, 9, 12*
Tchaikovsky: *Pizzicato Ostinato,* from Symphony No. 4

Berkeley: *Trio for Violin, Horn and Piano, Op. 44*
Brain, Parikian & Horsley
Seraphim 60073

Brahms: *Trio in E♭, Op. 40*
John Barrows, horn
Joseph Szigetti, violin
Mieczyslaw Horszowski, piano
Mercury MG50210; SR90210

Brahms: *Horn Trio*
Lance Productions, New York City
Frederick Vogelgesang plays all three parts

Horn Quartets, An Omnibus
Concert Disc CS-243
(Members of the Chicago Symphony Orchestra)
Bach: *Two Chorales*
Hindemith: *Sonata for Four French Horns*
Mitushin: *Concertino for Four French Horns*
Arr. Stout: *Four Short Pieces*
Tcherepnine: *The Hunt*

Beethoven: *Quintet in E♭ for Piano and Winds*
Dennis Brain
Angel 35303

Mozart: *Quintet in E♭ for Piano and Winds, K. 452*
Dennis Brain
Angel 35303

Mozart: *Quintet for Horn and Strings, K. 407*
John Barrows, horn
Concert-Disc CS-204

Music for Brass Ensemble
Music Minus One, MMO 6002
(Music minus one French horn)
Anonymous: *Sonata* from *Die Bänkelsängerlieder*
Gabrieli: *Canzona per Sonare No. 2*
Holborne: *Two Pieces*
Gabrieli, G.: *Canzona per sonare No. 1*
Pezel: *Four Pieces*
Pezel: *Sonata No. 2*
Pezel: *Sonata No. 22*
Reiche: *Sonata No. 19*
Schein: *Two Pieces*
Susato: *Three Dances*

Color Contrasts, The Horn Club of Los Angeles
Capitol SP 8525
Garcia: *Variations on a Five Note Theme*
Hyde: *Color Contrasts*
di Lasso-trans. Hyde: *Echo Song*
Mendelssohn-Steiner: *Tarantella*
Palestrina-trans. Burdick: *Stabat Mater*
Lo Presti: *Suite for Eight Horns*
Raksin: *Morning Revisited*

Concertos with Orchestra

Haydn, J.: *Concerto in D for Hunting Horn*
RCA Victrola VICS-1324;
Musical Heritage Society MHS 895
Barry Tuckwell, horn

Haydn, M: *Concerto in D Major for Horn and Orchestra*
RCA Victrola VICS-1324;
Musical Heritage Society MHS 720
Barry Tuckwell, horn

Hindemith: *Horn Concerto; Symphonia Serena*
Angel S-35491
Dennis Brain, horn
Mozart: Complete Horn Concertos
Angel 35092
Dennis Brain, horn

Mozart: The Four Horn Concertos
Vanguard SRV-173 SD
Albert Linder, horn

Mozart: Horn Concertos (with piano accompaniment)
Coronet LP 1406
Nicholas Perrini, horn

Rosetti: *Horn Concerto in D minor*
Turnabout TV 4078; TV 34078S

Strauss: The Two Concertos
Angel 35496
Dennis Brain, horn

Telemann: *Horn Concerto in D Major*
MHS 822
Georges Barboteu, horn

Telemann: *Suite in D Major for Hunting Horns and Orchestra*
MHS 822

Telemann: *Suite in F Major for Four Horns, 2 Oboes, and String Orchestra*
Turnabout TV 4078; TV 34078S

Vivaldi: *Concerto in F Major for Two Horns and String Orchestra*
Turnabout TV 4078; TV 34078S ■

MUSIC FOR MULTIPLE TUBAS

Winston Morris

This article is concerned primarily with the problems found in a large tuba ensemble (e.g., 4-6 euphoniums and 8-10 bass tubas). The published repertoire, at this time quite limited, can be expanded by the use of student arrangements and specially composed works. Most marches, for example, are easily transcribed for such a group. The literature will increase tremendously during the next few years due to the influence of various commissions and contests. The University of Miami Tuba Ensemble, under Constance Weldon, has begun an annual Tuba Ensemble Composition Contest, and the Tennessee Technological University Tuba Ensemble has been instrumental in the composition and arrangement of several works. The Tuba Ensemble at Indiana University, under the direction of Bill Bell, is responsible for a number of compositions and arrangements. Rex Conner at the University of Kentucky has inspired the composition of several such works. Undoubtedly, as the tuba ensemble becomes a more common medium, the repertoire will expand to fit the needs.

The tuba ensemble can involve itself with everything from duets to octets. However, as far as a mass ensemble (when all parts are doubled) is concerned, it seems that four-part compositions work best—specifically, compositions which involve two euphonium parts and two bass tuba parts. (The euphonium is, of course, nothing more—or less—than a tenor tuba, and since every college and high school has several euphonium players, it is simply a matter of practicality to utilize these instruments in music for tuba ensemble.) The mere nature of a mass tuba ensemble dictates to some extent the use of no more than three to five parts. Anything more causes the "line" to become lost in the "rumble." This problem is naturally more serious when performing works of a contrapuntal nature than homophonic compositions. This implies one of the important functions of the tuba ensemble as a performing medium to the student: an increased awareness of balance. This problem can best be realized by comparing a trumpet duet with a tuba duet. The balance problems involved with a trumpet duet are minimal compared with those encountered in a tuba duet. Assuming that one part has the melody and the second line the harmony, it becomes necessary to increase the dynamics of the first part *considerably* above that of the second in order to clearly distinguish the melody. This problem is compounded in proportion to the number of parts employed. The tuba ensemble demands more careful attention to balance than most tuba players ever exercise. The use of euphoniums and correct textural procedures alleviates this problem to a certain extent. With a large ensemble, the parts are doubled when playing four-part compositions; however, this does not help the balance problem. Indeed, balance be-

comes even more critical.

The tuba ensemble is the only medium in which tuba performers can experience playing an inside voice. This is another unique advantage that is offered to the student through playing in such a group. The tuba ensemble serves as a great source of encouragement and motivation to students who are too frequently relegated to "oom-pah" parts and never experience playing an extended melody or an inner voice. Any good school band library contains ensemble music for trumpets, flutes, saxophones, percussion, etc., while the most unmotivated sections of the band, the groups that needs this type of music most, the tubas and euphoniums, are neglected. As long as tuba students remain unchallenged by merely supplying "on-the-beat" parts, they will continue to remain the most consistently encountered weak section of the band. Solo work should be encouraged as much as possible, but when contest time is over, nothing will get tuba students into the practice room (or encourage a little healthy competition) faster than the availability of music for multiple tubas.

The following list of available literature for multiple tubas is not meant to be a complete list. Those compositions considered to be especially appropriate from a technical standpoint for high school students are preceded by an asterisk.

Two Tubas

Blazhevich, Vladislav: *Two Concert Duets,* high school or college, contained in *Solos for the Tuba Player* by Herbert Wekselblatt, published by G. Schirmer, $2.50.

Butterfield, Don: *7 Duets for Tubas,* high school or college, playable with euphonium on top part, published by D. B. Publishing Co., $2.50.

Catelinet, Philip: *Suite in Minature,* high school or college, playable with euphonium on top part, published by C. F. Peters, $1.50.

Corelli, A.: *Sonata da Chiesa, Op. 1, No. 10,* high school or college, two bass tubas and piano, to be published by Ludwig Music Publishing Co.

*De Jong, Conrad: *Music for Two Tubas,* high school or college, published by Elkan-Vogel, $.75.

Geib, Fred: *A Joyous Dialogue, Op. 11,* high school, two bass tubas with optional piano part, published by Mills Music, $.75.

Goldman, Richard Franko: *Duo for Tubas,* college or advanced high school, published by Mercury, $1.00.

Houston, Rudy: *Avant Garde Jazz Duets,* high school or college, tubas read down one octave, useable with euphonium, published by Charles Colin, $1.50.

*Nelhybel, Vaclav: *11 Duets for Tubas,* junior high through college, published by General Music Pub. Co., $2.00.

Saint-Jacome: *Duet,* high school or college, available in Wekselblatt book mentioned under Blazhevich above.

*Sear, Walter: *Advanced Duets,* high school or college, Cor Publishing Co., $2.50.

Stoker: *Four Dialogues,* high school or college, playable with euphonium on top part, published by C. F. Peters, $1.50.

Ryker, Robert: *Sonata for Two Bass Tubas,* college or advanced high school, available through Robert King Music Co., $1.00.

*Wadowich, James: *Two for the Tuba,* high school or college, two bass tubas with piano, published by Concert Music Pub. Co., $2.00.

*Williams, Ernest: *Easy Duets for the Bass Tuba* junior high or high school, to be published by Charles Colin.

Wilson, David: *Suite for Two Tubas (and understanding audience),* high school or college, Cleveland Chamber Music Publishers, $1.00.

Three Tubas

*Jacobson, I. D.: *Three Temperaments for Tubas,* high school or college, playable with euphonium on top part, published by Mills Music, $2.50.

*Presser, William: *Suite for Three Tubas,* high school or college, published by Tritone/Tenuto, $3.00.

Four Tubas

Ball, Eric: *Friendly Giants* and *Quartet for Tubas,* British tuba parts in treble clef (E♭ and B♭

parts—need to be transposed), available through Robert King Music Co.

Cook, Kenneth: *Introduction and Rondino,* same as above.

*De Jong, Conrad: composition in progress, commissioned by Tennessee Technological University Tuba Ensemble, two euphonium parts, two bass tuba parts, Wisconsin State University, River Falls, Wisconsin 54022.

*Hardt, Victor: *Lullaby and Dance,* high school or college (easy), best played with two euphonium and two bass tuba parts, published by Tempo Music Pub. Inc., $3.00.

Heussenstamm, George: *Tubafour, Op. 30 (1969),* college level, (Special Award—International Tuba Ensemble Composition

Contest—Univ. of Miami), published by Seesaw Music Corp., $5.00. (score only—parts on rental)

Payne, Frank Lynn: *Quartet for Tubas,* college level, (First Prize—International Tuba Ensemble Composition Contest—Univ. of Miami), to be published by Charles Colin.

Presser, William: *Serenade for Four Tubas,* college level, (Third Prize—International Tuba Ensemble Composition Contest—Univ. of Miami), to be published by Charles Colin.

Steinquest, Eugene: *Fanfare and Fuguetta,* college level, two euphonium and two bass tuba parts, composed for the Tennessee Technological University Tuba Ensemble, Northeast Louisi-

ana State College, Monroe, Louisiana.

Five Tubas

Frank, Marcel: *Lyric Poem for Five Tubas,* college level, (Second Prize—International Tuba Ensemble Composition Contest—Univ. of Miami), to be published by Charles Colin.

Six Tubas

Childs, Barney: *Music for Tubas,* college level, Wisconsin College-Conservatory, 1584, N. Prospect Ave., Milwaukee, Wisconsin 53202.

Presser, William: *Suite for Six Tubas,* college level (advanced high school), published by Tritone Tenuto, $6.00. ∎

April, 1970

FINGERING THE FOUR AND FIVE VALVE TUBAS

Rex Conner

Fingering charts for four-valve tubas have been around for some time. Yet, there is an ever-increasing demand for fingering charts for the four-valve and even five-valve tubas. There are several reasons for this: 1. concert bands throughout the country are adding German-style rotary valve tubas to their organizations, most of which are equipped with four valves; 2. we are becoming increasingly conscious of the necessity for better pitch in the bass line; and 3. a wealth of fine solo literature for tuba is beginning to emerge from excellent composers.

Even though most of the available charts are excellent, they do

need some explanation. A trumpet player or even a horn player who has never spent much time with a tuba or trombone could conceivably have difficulty in understanding these charts. For instance, how could 1&4 or 1,2&4 *both* be correct for the lowest E♭ on the piano? Or, going on down, one will find low D listed as 3&4 or 2,3&4? Are they both satisfactory? Does it depend on the make of instrument or do we expect neither to be exactly right and pick the least out of tune?

Before we get any deeper let us look at the positions on the bass trombone. The F valve lowers the instrument a perfect fourth which is precisely what a fourth valve does to a tuba.

It is commonly known that each position on the trombone corresponds to a certain fingering on a valve instrument; 1st position is open, 2nd position is 2nd valve, 3rd position is 1st valve, 4th position is 1&2, 5th position is 2&3, 6th position is 1&3 and 7th position is 1,2&3. Looking closely at the above chart, one can see that each successive position is a bit longer than the last one. Without other methods of adjustments for three-valve instruments it can readily be seen that in order to arrive at the same just intonation, which is possible on the slide trombone, it would be necessary to have not three, four, or five valves, but six. When the F valve is depressed on the trombone the positions must be made even longer. In fact, it can be seen that only six positions are possible. The 4th position of the F valve now almost coincides with what is called 5th position without the F valve and the 6th position with the F valve is even further extended than the normal 7th position. (Because a tuba is more conical these two positions do coincide quite well. On most BB♭ tubas low D is well in tune with 2,3&4.)

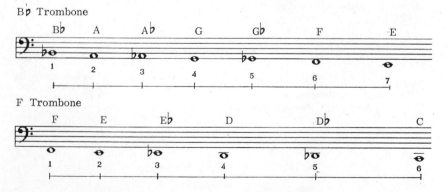

Still using the chart for the trombone F valve, let us take a look at the other tuba notes below low F. (Remember that these notes for BB♭ tuba are an octave lower than those we are referring to for bass trombone.) Most charts will show 2&4 for low E. This will be sharp unless it is lipped down or the fourth valve slide is pulled. The ear can be deceived in this range. How do we know it is in tune? Check it an octave higher by playing E with second valve only; then, play the same note with 2&4, pulling the fourth valve slide until the both fingerings match in pitch. Once this pitch matches, one can usually depend on the note an octave lower to be correct. Now, let's go on to E♭. On the trombone chart we find it falling about half way between 3rd and 4th position. What do our charts say? For the four-valve tuba —1&4 or 1,2,&4. You have reason to assume that neither is going to be correct. Remember, "a note not quite in tune is out of tune." Check again with the note one octave higher, the E♭ just below the staff. First, play the note with the first valve so that note is in tune and then add the fourth valve and pull the 1st valve slide until the pitches match. Low D has been discussed. Low D♭ is usually given as 1,3&4 but this is usually a little sharp. Pulling either the first or third valve slides will put it in tune.

On the BB♭ tuba low C, the lowest C on the piano, is extremely sharp. Pull the third valve slide almost as far as it will go. You must have a horn on which the third valve slide is readily accessible. Check the pitch with the fourth valve an octave higher. *Do not check it with 1 and 3.* This fingering is atrociously sharp and should rarely be used under any circumstances on a four-valve tuba. Incidentally, if the tuba is built correctly, the first C below the staff should be in tune when the fourth valve slide is all the way in. If this is not true, chances are it will not be possible to pull it far enough to play the 2 and 4 combinations in tune. Last but not least, we should consider the first B♮ below the staff. If low E, 2&4 is tuned correctly, one can expect B to be well in tune also with the same fingering and adjustment. It should be emphasized that low B and E on the

three-valve instruments, played 1, 2 & 3, are the two worst notes on the tuba as far as intonation is concerned. Usually they'll be about 35 hundredths of a semitone sharp. If the combinations 1, 2, 3 and 1 & 3 are in tune, the chances are that most of the rest of notes on the instrument are out of tune.

The following fingering charts have been carefully prepared. When arrows appear that point downward, the player should pull one of the slides being used because the fingering will be sharp

Note: Theoretically, by using pedal tones and the additional valves the BB♭ tuba with 4 valves could descend to a C below the piano; however, the embouchure will not vibrate this slowly.

otherwise. Where one or more fingerings are given without arrows, it may be assumed the fingerings will be in tune or very nearly so. A slight lip adjustment should suffice. It should be pointed out here that the tuba valve slides should work as quickly and easily as a trombone slide. Mechanical adjustments in pitch with tubas having slides which pull downward are almost impossible. The only alternative is adjustment with the embouchure which causes a sacrifice in tone quality and stability.

Fingering Chart for Four-Valve E♭ Tuba

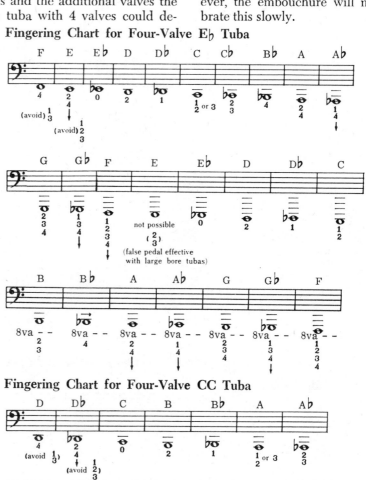

Fingering Chart for Four-Valve CC Tuba

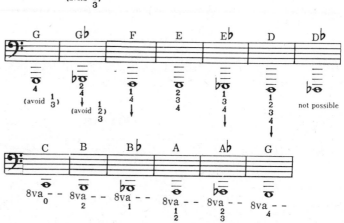

Fingering Chart for Five-Valve CC Tuba

Fingering Chart for Four-Valve BB♭ Tuba

Fingering Chart for Five-Valve BB♭ Tuba

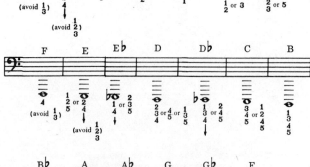

THE SOLO TUBA AND WALTER HARTLEY

Peter Popiel

Although the tubaist has had some opportunity to display his melodic and soloistic capabilities within the symphony orchestra since the time of Wagner, it has been only within the last 20 years that major figures of the stature of Hindemith and Vaughan Williams have accorded a degree of legitimacy to the tuba by writing solo works for it. The repertoire has continued to expand at a steady pace with such works as the Vincent Persichetti *Serenade No. 12 for Solo Tuba*, the Halsey Stevens *Sonatina*, Verne Reynolds' *Sonata*, Warren Benson's *Helix*, and with six compositions by the man who is the subject of this article, Walter Hartley: *Sonatina for Tuba and Piano* (Interlochen Press, 1957); *Suite for Unaccompanied Tuba* (Elkan-Vogel, 1962); *Duet for Flute and Tuba* (Tritone, 1962); *Aria for Tuba and Piano* (Elkan-Vogel, 1967); *Sonata for Tuba and Piano* (Tenuto, 1967); and the *Concertino for Tuba and Wind Ensemble* (Tenuto, 1970).

These works constitute a highly significant addition to the literature for the tuba, and they range in difficulty from a moderate level in the *Sonatina* to a rather high level in the *Sonata* and *Concertino*. Each of the six works shares high degrees of craftsmanship and musical quality. Before moving to a specific consideration of these works, some background information on the composer and on his philosophy of writing for solo tuba would be in order.

Walter Hartley studied piano at the National Music Camp, Interlochen, Michigan, and entered the Eastman School of Music in 1947. He studied piano with José Échaniz and composition with Bernard Rogers and Howard Hanson, completing B.M., M.M., and Ph.D. degrees by 1953. Currently on the faculty of the State University College, Fredonia, New York, his teaching experiences include King's College (Delaware), Longwood College (Virginia), Hope College (Michigan), the National Music Camp, and Davis and Elkins College (West Virginia), where he served as music department chairman for several years.

Hartley has written over 80 works for groups large and small, and his music is often performed on college and university programs as well as in professional music centers. His *Concerto for 23 Winds* (1957) was recorded in 1960 by the Eastman Wind Ensemble. The composer is also active as piano soloist. Hartley performed his *Concerto for Piano and Orchestra* (1952) at Interlochen in 1959 and frequently appears in recitals and on chamber music programs. His works have been published by Rochester Music Publishers, Tenuto Publications, Interlochen Press, Elkan-Vogel, Galaxy Music Corporation, and Ensemble Publications.

Hartley's ideas relating to composition for the tuba are valuable and intriguing, offering a much-needed perspective both to the player and to the potential composer.

The tuba as solo instrument, or as soloist in an ensemble, should essentially and ideally be a melodic bass. It is particularly suited to obbligato (melodic accompaniment of another melody) or other contrapuntal treatment. A good source of inspiration for tuba-writing should be the pedal parts in J. S. Bach's organ works, particularly the Trio Sonatas. The most generally useful melodic range in tubas (contrabass tubas in *CC* or in *BBb*) is *AA* to *a;* the high baritone and contrabass registers should be used sparingly, especially for younger players, although for the sake of variety they should not be avoided in serious work. Melodies conceived for higher register instruments or voices, particularly in the soprano range, tend to be unsatisfactory, for reasons of harmonic balance, when transcribed for the tuba. Spacing should always be carefully handled, especially between the tuba and other low winds, to achieve good coloristic balance. The tuba tone has fewer strong high partials than other brass instruments, particularly horn and trumpet. This must be borne in mind when associating these colors.[1]

Hartley defines his style as "freely tonal and broadly based on classical forms." This definition, which appears in the same item of correspondence as the above paragraph, can be applied to the *Suite for Unaccompanied Tuba*. Written in 1962 at the suggestion of Rex Conner, tuba instructor at the National Music Camp, the work is in four movements, each of which is cast in traditional form. The *Intrada: Alla marcia* demonstrates Hartley's free application of tonality; the first four measures pass through the keys of *G*, *Eb*, and cadence on *E* as shown in the following example:

Example 1. *Suite for Unaccompanied Tuba, Intrada: Alla marcia,* meas. 1-4

In addition to the freedom of tonality, this example typifies the somewhat angular melodic contour of Hartley's tuba writing. Many octaves, fifths and sevenths are freely used, and even the descending leap of a 14th in measure four works well on the instrument. The strong accents, sudden dynamic contrasts, and the tongue-in-cheek quotations from the typical band "oom-pah" tuba parts combine to make this a most effective movement.

The angular *Valse* opens in *B♭*, but restlessly moves to *D♭* by the fourth measure. The tonal freedom of the first movement is prominent here, particularly in the final 12 measures. As seen below, Hartley modulates rapidly through the implied keys of *A♭, D, A♭,* and very suddenly shifts into *B♭* for the final cadence.

Example 2. *Suite for Unaccompanied Tuba, Valse,* meas. 40-51

Moving now to a consideration of the accompanied works, the *Sonatina* (1957) with piano, offers a good point of departure. This work, also composed at the suggestion and inspiration of Rex Conner, is in three movements: *Allegretto, Largo maestoso* and *Allegro moderato.* When Hartley writes for tuba with accompaniment, his preference is for the piano because he feels that the percussive aspects of that instrument help the tonal distinction.[2] This percussive factor can be seen very clearly in the following passage from the *Allegretto* movement, and it would be most difficult to achieve the same effect with another accompanying medium.

Example 3. *Sonatina, Allegretto,* meas. 11-16

The following excerpt from the second movement of the same work is a further illustration of this percussive treatment of the piano which Hartley emphasizes; it is also a typical texture of which he is fond, particularly in the slow movements: the sustained melodic line supported by thick chordal structures.

Example 4. *Sonatina, Largo maestoso,* meas. 1-7

Another texture which contrasts with the one above is that involving contrapuntal writing for tuba with piano. Hartley conceives the tuba's accompaniment essentially as a partnership which should contribute musical interest of its own and not merely serve as a backdrop to the solo line. This philosophy pervades many of his works, and a clear example of this contrapuntal partnership occurs in the final movement of the *Sonatina* as seen in the excerpt quoted below, wherein the tuba opens the movement with a theme or subject which pivots between C major and Lydian mode on C via the alternation of the notes F and F♯. This relationship, with its prominent tritone, continues as the piano enters in imitation at the 12th above four measures later. The imitation is strict, however, only to measure eight, where the third voice enters, and where F and F♯ sound simultaneously after having alternated with each other in close cross-relation for two measures.

Example 5. *Sonatina, Allegro moderato,* meas. 1-12

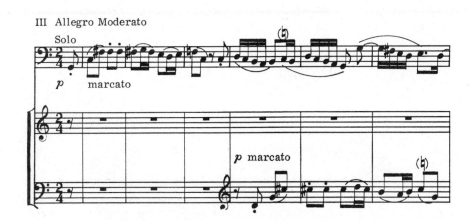

After having examined Hartley's treatment of thematic material in contrapuntal combinations, let us consider another aspect of his manipulation of themes—an aspect which occurs in his *Sonata* (1967) and in no other tuba work to date. This is the composer's most extensive work thus far for tuba and piano; it is written in four movements, the last two of which are played without pause. The work opens with a statement of a 12-tone theme by the solo tuba, a theme which is to appear in conjunction with other themes throughout the entire sonata as a cyclical force. As this theme makes its appearances, it does so in several forms: in its entirety, in truncated form, inverted, in retrograde, transposed, rhythmically transformed, and in various contrapuntal combinations.

This theme, which is presented below, is a combination of recitative and cadenza styles, and is typically chromatic; the movement unfolds with another feature of Hartley's style mentioned previously in discussing his *Unaccompanied Suite*—the disjunct, craggy melodic contour with the wide leaps between measures nine and 13, as also seen in the following example:

Example 6. *Sonata,* mvt. 1, meas. 1-13

The same contour occurs soon afterward; this time in *allegro agitato* tempo at measure 31, and the cyclic theme, or more specifically, the first nine notes of it, return transposed up a major sixth beginning in measure 41. The final two measures of the movement project notes one to four of the cyclic theme in retrograde, and these four notes foreshadow many interesting events of the next movement.

Example 7. *Sonata,* mvt. 1, thematic treatment

a. Disjunct contour, meas. 31-35

b. Transposed up a major sixth, meas. 41-43

c. Retrograde, meas. 77-78

The four notes in the above example of retrograde, c., which constitute the opening notes of the cyclic 12-tone theme from the first movement, form the "head" of a new theme which makes its appearance at the opening of the second movement in the piano. This theme is a rather extended one, with 15 measures elapsing before the entrance of the tuba with the same material. This theme, and motives taken from it, pervade the entire movement, which is an *Allegretto grazioso* of scherzo-like character. The opening of this movement also demonstrates Hartley's expert scoring of tuba with accompaniment; it is evident from the beginning that he has kept the piano left hand out of the register in which the tuba is playing, and in so doing, he has avoided the trap into which so many composers have fallen—a blurred, murky texture which results when tuba and piano articulate rapid passages in the same register.

Example 8. Sonata mvt. 2, meas. 15-19

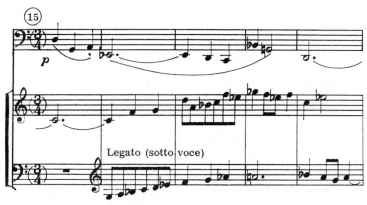

Articulation becomes a real issue as the final movement opens, and the composer's comments on it are relevant:

A solo tuba must be extremely well played to avoid untoward associations in the listener (foghorns, large ruminant animals, etc.). Perhaps the most dangerous passage I have written in this respect is the beginning of the Finale of my *Sonata* (1967) which could easily become ridiculous unless lightly and cleanly articulated.[3]

This passage, which is quoted below, can indeed justify Hartley's fears if the eighth notes in measures two and four are articulated so fast that they run together, thereby blurring the pitches. In performing this work, I have taken the liberty of beginning the movement at a slightly slower tempo and then making an accelerando reaching the ultimate tempo at the fifth measure.

Example 9. *Sonata*, mvt. 4, meas. 1-5

At the 11th measure the piano imitates the opening theme, the imitation being at the 12th above in a

Example 10. *Sonata*, mvt. 4, meas. 54-61.

texture like that of the *Sonatina* finale. The cyclic 12-tone theme returns in augmentation at the measure 54, but utilizes only one

through ten of the series, with the 11th note, G♯, appearing in the piano accompaniment, and the 12th note, C, in the tuba at measure 60.

The movement builds to an exciting *fortissimo* finish, concluding a work which makes considerable demands upon the performer, but which pays generous musical dividends to the player who masters its difficulties and understands its intricacies.

Walter Hartley's tuba works constitute a highly significant addition to the solo repertoire. Collectively

they are compositions of a high order of craftsmanship written by a man who understands the capabilities of the instrument for which he writes. Finally, and perhaps most importantly, the Hartley tuba works are most gratifying to the performer because of their musicality. Playing them gives the tubaist a musical experience which does not often occur in explorations

through much of the tuba literature. ∎

[1]Walter S. Hartley, in a letter of January 12, 1969, to the present writer.
[2]Hartley, letter of January 12, 1969.
[3]Hartley, letter of January 12, 1969.

The music examples above are used with the permission of the publishers, whose names appear with the list of works at the beginning of the article.

May, 1970

THREE IMPORTANT CONCEPTS

Harry Jenkins

I. ACCOMMODATING THE MOUTHPIECE

The importance of the mouthpiece to a brass player cannot be over-emphasized. One only needs to ask the experienced player, "Which would you rather lose, your rare impossible-to-replace mouthpiece which you have played on for many years, or that shiny, expensive instrument you bought recently?" The answer may be quite a surprising one, for the player can say, after deliberation, "The instrument, I guess." Where the mouthpiece can be easily replaced, the answer would be a different one. At any rate, everyone would agree that the proper mouthpiece is vital.

A Good Mouthpiece

The mouthpiece is a personal thing,

so it is difficult for the player to be objective about it. The scientific data: dimensions of rim, cup, bore, etc., can be objective; but the individual player's reaction to a particular mouthpiece cannot be.

The all important thing is the "feel" on the embouchure, that feeling of super-sensitivity that makes a mouthpiece almost seem glued to the lips, so naturally does it fit. If this quality is missing, the others (dimensions of cup, bore, throat, etc.) do not mean very much.

In the case of a beginner, the ideal mouthpiece can be the first one he uses. Therefore, it is important that this be purchased from a reliable manufacturer since the scientific know-how is all important. This is the one that will make

the initial impression upon the lips. Barring any outstanding abnormality in embouchure or teeth, a mouthpiece with conservative dimensions (normal diameter and medium cup) can with proper practice become the "good" mouthpiece. As he progresses, the accommodation works two ways: the mouthpiece accommodates the lips to form the embouchure, and the lips accommodate the mouthpiece. The "feel" is being acquired.

More about Mouthpiece Accommodation

No mouthpiece can solve every problem for the player, nor give him everything. A suitable mouthpiece is a compromise on several others. The one that gives the most comfort and has fewest compromises is the most suitable one. Let us take several instances.

One player has a mouthpiece which is comfortable in the middle and high registers; he practices additional drills in the low register. Thus he accommodates the mouthpiece in the low register.

Another player has a comfortable fitting mouthpiece that sounds fine in the low and middle registers; the high needs some work, therefore he will practice high notes. The accommodation will take place in the high register. After a reasonable amount of time spent in this activity, if he is still dissatisfied with his high register, he can get a similar mouthpiece with a shallower cup. Players who use a stock mouthpiece are fortunate in having a choice of several models.

In the examples above, both players had comfortably fitting mouthpieces. If a mouthpiece is not comfortable on the lips, it is unsatisfactory.

Time For A Change

A mouthpiece has ways of letting a player know that the time has come for a change.

If it is too small in diameter, the lips become bruised and swell up. An adolescent whose body is still growing (the lips included) is frequently placed in this predicament when he outgrows the mouthpiece. It suddenly feels too small. It becomes uncomfortable and the low notes are difficult to produce.

One which is too large in diameter can bind the lips. To sustain a high note fortissimo in a long passage is an ordeal leaving the player exhausted, even dizzy, afterwards. If the mouthpiece is very deep, besides, the upper register can be flat in pitch.

The change is smooth when it is made to a mouthpiece similar to the old one, especially in regard to the type of rim. Fortunate is the player who uses a reliable and tried standard make where there is an abundance of similar rims and rim sizes. He gets another from the same manufacturer, a specific number of model such and such, signifying the next size larger or smaller. The old "feel" is transferred to the new mouthpiece with more comfort forthcoming. Now accommodation will not be too much of a problem—and more improvement is yet to come. The player using a custom-made model who is forced to make a change may have a problem in selecting a new mouthpiece.

In trying a new mouthpiece for the first time, it is wise to warm up with it. Merely playing the old one and switching back and forth will not help the player in judging the new one. The routine will only confuse him. Switching to two or three during the practice session will compound the confusion even further. No judgment will be possible because the "feel," the supersensitivity, was lost somewhere along the way. If a player wants to try several mouthpieces, he should try *one* each day, on the warm up plus his regular playing. It is a slower process, but it will pay off in results, with a minimum amount of aggravation.

Some Answers from a Subjective Viewpoint

Q. What is meant by a good mouthpiece?
A. One that is comfortable and inspires confidence on the part of the player because it has stood the playing test of time under all adverse playing conditions. The player has confidence in it for its many benefits: comfort, general ease of playing, with a minimum amount of compromises.
Q. Would you say that mouthpiece accommodation is just another name for practicing?
A. Not quite, but the practice routine is greatly affected by the particular mouthpiece used. To illustrate: should the player suddenly change to a radically different one, the "what" and "how" of the practice session will be quite different.
Q. Do you claim that a beginner can do well with any mouthpiece?
A. A beginner's mouthpiece, if it is manufactured by a tried and reliable firm, can become the almost ideal one. What makes the very first impression on the lips becomes the good mouthpiece, with accommodation from the very beginning.
Q. Why do you make so much of the idea of switching mouthpieces?
A. By switching, I mean a permanent change, not experimentation; in the latter instance, the player always goes back to the old mouthpiece. A permanent change is a big move. The old mouthpiece represents almost a way of life. Some old assets just cannot be left behind but must be transferred to the new one with a promise of even better things to come. Therefore, the new one must safeguard some old benefits and promise better things. Yes, the change is a big move.
Q. Doesn't mouthpiece accommodation apply more to a new mouthpiece rather than the old one? After all, the player is already accustomed to the old one.
A. It is still a matter of mutual accommodation. Even for the player who has used the same mouthpiece over many years, there is the daily problem of embouchure accommodation to the mouthpiece. Yet, there has been mouthpiece accommodation as well. The embouchure has not remained the same over the years in spite of the fact that the same mouthpiece was used. There have been changes in the body, teeth, and gums. In this instance, mouthpiece accommodation has almost been ideal for it has been gradual, smooth, and painless. Accommodation works two ways: the mouthpiece accommodates the lips and the lips never stop accommodating the mouthpiece. It is a normal situation that brings on positive results.

II. MATCHING REGISTERS

The brass player has several registers to contend with in order to function effectively. These are usually referred to as being low, medium, and high. For my purposes, I will refer to them as being low, low-to-middle, middle-to-high, and high-to-higher. For cornet/trumpet, tenor trombone, and baritone, it shapes up this way, for trumpet:

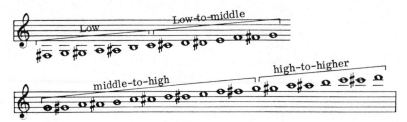

Characteristics and Faults

The middle-to-high is the "bread and butter" register. It is the most accessible, easiest to control, and presents the least intonation problems. The high-to-higher register tends to be less accessible, brilliant, and more difficult to control in soft playing. The low register seems to be the most neglected. It can be muddy and difficult to control. Extremes in pianissimo and fortissimo playing create problems as well as intonation.

Because of the characteristics of these registers, it is not uncommon to find a student who plays so unevenly that the general impression to the casual critic is that there are two, or even three players involved, rather than just the one. There is a good reason for this. The student's registers are not balanced. With **proper practice, improvement can be forthcoming.**

Matching Octaves

Studies dealing with octaves are valuable in matching registers so an equal amount of sound, rich in quality, can be produced in each.

A few sample exercises are shown below. They can be altered, if need be, to suit the individual player's needs. The first one, in particular, can produce multiple benefits. They include proper matching of registers, improvements in attack, legato, and control in general.

The general level of dynamics is mezzo forte. However, the exercise can be played piano or forte, as the player sees fit. Each octave must be uniform with no diminuendos or crescendos. False fingerings or alternate positions may be used if the intonation can be helped.

Do not play this too quickly. It can be attempted legato as well.

Try this prepared version of the "Pilgrims' Chorus" from *Tannhäuser*.

Now, match this version (an octave below). Watch the intonation.

In Conclusion

1. All the registers must be rich in quality if the player is to function well. Work on the weaker ones.
2. Practice in octaves is invaluable.
3. An equal amount of sound calls for an equal amount of good intonation. "Humoring," false fingerings, skill in the manipulation of valve slides or alternate positions on trombone can all contribute to better intonation.
4. Above all, learn to *listen*.

III. HANDLING FATIGUE

The problem of fatigue is very important to the brass player. Unless it is handled with common sense, performance on a brass instrument is poor and unpredictable.

Excessive fatigue accounts for broken notes, poor intonation, and undependable performance. The effective player, professional or otherwise, follows two courses in handling this. One way is to try to prevent it from occuring. If this is not possible, then it must be handled in such a way that there is a minimum amount.

Causes

Excessive fatigue is caused by overwork, playing almost continuously, where the player has little opportunity to take his mouthpiece off the lips. When the playing is loud, particularly in the high register, it comes about sooner.

It is little wonder that players try to avoid this fatigue like the plague since this "point of no return" makes them completely ineffectual for the rest of the day and has a negative overall effect.

One thing that makes professional players effective is their ability to handle the problem of fatigue in such a way that they function well for the entire engagement, regardless of the demands, with a minimum of negative after-effects.

Home Practice

There are precautions a person can take to ward off fatigue. He should not overpractice, particularly on the day of a performance. Practice in the high register should be held to a minimum.

In the routine, many short stops, if only for a minute or two to take the mouthpiece off the lips, refresh the embouchure and give it a new lease on life. At least 10% of the practice session should be devoted to short breaks for this purpose.

Pacing Oneself

Demands upon brass players vary according to the performance and the nature of the engagement. A player in a symphony orchestra has one group of problems, the concert band player another, and the stage band player still another. However, regardless of the type of work they do, they have one common objective: to finish the engagement satisfactorily without the ill effects of fatigue.

There are ways of pacing oneself. In a unison passage, why should all the trumpets play? Why

not alternate with one another? If a passage marked fortissimo is tutti for the entire band and the trombone section alone has the melody, why doesn't the rest of the brass section play forte instead?

Some auditoriums have very live acoustics. The brass can cut down on the volume and it will make for a graceful situation all around.

In short, the player has to size up his task *in its entirety* and to pace himself so he can get an even performance from start to finish; and he has to try to do this with a minimum amount of fatigue. By learning to "roll with the punches," pacing himself, allocating a certain amount of effort to each passage, and resting frequently, the brass player can handle fatigue gracefully.

In Conclusion

Excessive fatigue is the foe of the brass player. If it cannot be avoided, it must be handled in such a way that it constitutes a minor and only temporary problem. In order to do this:

1. He should not overpractice, especially on the day he has a performance.
2. He should rest often. He should partake of every opportunity to remove the mouthpiece from his lips, even if it is only for a moment or two.
3. He should share the burden. He should alternate in unison passages.
4. He should not overblow. In most cases it is unnecessary and does more harm than good.

One of the secrets of successful players is their ability to handle fatigue under all conditions. Any player using common sense and musical judgement should—*and must*—acquire this ability. ■

ABOUT TROMBONE TEACHING: A NATIONAL CONCENSUS—Part II

Paul Tanner

This is the second in a series of three articles on how trombone is taught in American colleges and conservatories. After taping interviews at approximately 100 of these institutions all around the country, I have been able to compile a consensus on many issues as well as to show the diversity of thinking by many scholarly and talented teachers. The first article was concerned mainly with the approach to giving lessons. This article is more involved with the varying approaches to the playing techniques. Once again, I should state that I talked with both students and teachers, and everyone gave most generously of their time and information.

It seems as though the first item to take up is that of the warm-up as that starts the lessons, practicing, or performance. About ⅔ of the trombone teachers I talked with use the Remington warm-up exercises. The only other two names with printed material that were mentioned to me were Goldman and Schlossberg. About half of the teachers write out the work to be done at this stage of practicing. The most prevalent approach is working from the middle range outward toward both ends. Most deplore students who play too high or too loud too soon. Lip slurs are called upon more than any other technique according to my findings; oddly enough, the slurs go in both directions, some up, some down. The second most used technique for a warm-up is long tones in the medium low register; those who do not use this warn that long tones are tiring. A couple of gentlemen insist on breath attacks, no tongue in the warm-up. Some take their slurs all the way to trills to make the lips pliable. Some teach-

ers have the students write out their own, whatever works for them. Some of them try to vary the warm-up to avoid a mental lock-in on a certain routine. There does seem to be one seldom discussed opinion concerning the length of time spent in warming up the muscles. There was an agreement that it varies with the individual, how much playing he has been doing, the time of day, and the temperature. At any rate, five to ten minutes should prepare a trombonist to play; most teachers felt that much longer than that showed a mental problem and that the player should be concerned about tiring himself before the actual playing gets under way.

When I asked about buzzing, the answers showed me that the consensus was that there was no consensus! The camps are actually quite evenly divided as to whether the students should practice buzzing or not. Those against point out that this is unnatural and not pertinent to making good sounds. Those for claim that the corners of the mouth are being strengthened and the lips learn to vibrate more readily. Some instructors have the students buzz both with and without the mouthpiece, some only with the mouthpiece, and partially covered at that—in order to give a semblance of natural playing conditions. Some are adamant with the opinion that it is necessary to buzz in order to produce a good sound, yet there are those who say that most players do not do anything like a buzz when they play. There are teachers who have the students buzz only for a warm-up, saying that it helps to loosen the lip tissues. Some students learn to buzz their scales as well as tunes, and seem to be practicing con-

stantly, even when away from their horns.

The one item that is more willingly discussed than any other is breathing. Most teachers claim that breathing is the single most important aspect of playing. Some state that this is 98 or 99% of performing and that proper breathing solves most range and sound problems. The semantic problem entered into this issue, as some teachers discussed breathing as breath support. Others never mentioned support but would speak of blowing through the horn and how proper concepts tend to keep the throat open. Some used words like "air pressure" or "compressed air" in place of support. There was a slight difference of opinion as to how much air to take in. Some said to fill up all the way every time, others said to learn to take quickly as much air as is needed. There certainly was great agreement about the necessity for good posture in order to breathe properly, and most said that the posture should be relaxed also, even when standing. The problem of how to go about learning to breathe properly brought vivid descriptions, most including the word "diaphragm." A method devised by Buddy Baker of Colorado has many followers. Mr. Baker is articulate and a talented player. I feel that he can be encouraged to explain his thoughts in detail, but I believe a synopsis of his attitude would be that a player breathes down, out in the middle, and up in the upper chest, slow deep breaths, expansion around the belt line or below. Another gentlemen who should be encouraged to explain his breathing approaches is Tasso Harris of Denver. Briefly, he has his students simulate getting ready to swim under water, lock in the air, then he explains two ways of controlled exhaling: 1. a "cool" breath like blowing out a match a little distance away, and 2. a "hot" breath like steaming up a window. Another talented gentleman who should certainly write about breathing is Neill Humfeld of East Texas State—a condensation of his doctoral dissertation on this matter would be of real value. One of his biggest concerns is the student's realization of proper exhalation of a supported stream of air. He uses loud whispering to demonstrate pushing down with the trunk. A resourceful Georgia teacher showed me how to use a flapping match cover to prove that the air flow can be constant and well-directed even while doing certain types of tonguing. I think that the movement of the diaphragm concerns and bewilders most people. I was told that it moves up, down, in, out, and anything else possible (and not possible). Some have students lying on the floor with books on their stomachs, yet some will not even mention breathing at all for fear of simply distracting the student's concentration on all other aspects of sound production. Several teachers did make an issue of borrowing breathing techniques from the vocal departments. One gentleman feels that you must have sufficient breath control to maintain a good sound for at least 40 seconds. A few made the point that the music determines how you breathe. Everyone says to relax and that too many young players breathe "high" or "shallow."

Some teachers put a little emphasis on what direction all this air we developed in the last paragraph is to go. There are various schools of thought. One is that trombonists should blow straight into the instrument at all times; however, the majority of teachers who speak of this have a different opinion. I will give you all three options and you can see the diversity: 1. blow straight in for low tones and up (by tilting the trombone down) for high tones; 2. blow straight in for low tones and down for high tones; 3. blow up for low tones and down for high tones. The reader may wonder about successful teachers differing like this—they most assuredly do.

Two of my stock questions concerned tongue position and the syllables used (if any). Most instructors state quickly that there is need to keep the oral cavity (or resonance chamber) as open as possible, yet some are suggesting *ee* in the upper register in order to close this cavity and thus speed the air through at a faster rate. *Ah-oo* is most often suggested for slurs down and *ah-ee* for slurs up. Most teachers approach tonguing syllables with the standard *too* and *tee*, they will also recommend *doo* for legato tonguing. When using a *t* type of attack, there is fairly general agreement about the tip of the tongue going to just about where the back of the upper teeth go into the gum. Very few recommended *th* for legato for fear it would lead to bad habits. Some teachers teach mixing *doo* with natural slurs for legato playing, others claim the attacks will match up better if *doo* is used throughout. Occasionally *dah* is taught. A fine performing teacher in Indiana varies his attacks with the repertoire: French or Italian music gets a cool dry breath with *tee*, Wagner, on the other hand gets a hot wet breath with *toe*. There simply is no arguing with his results. One teacher advocates a system that I simply do not have the capacity to handle personally—to tongue ahead of time in order to have the sound come out at the proper time. Another gentleman asserts that *tuh* gets everything started and solves a great deal of problems. Most teachers agree but seldom discuss the fact that the tongue stroke is longer on the lower pitches (consequently a much longer tongue stroke on tuba than on trumpet), and many players do actually go against approved teaching methods by tonguing between the lips in the bottom register; if they do, though, they are extremely careful to avoid a "spitting" sound. With all of this variety of opinions, I would appear timid if I did not state my own views. Clarence Sawhill taught me long ago the value of *teau, deau,* and *leau.* They start the air while keeping the oral cavity open, even in the high register. I also insist that my students attempt to be able to start sounds with no tongue, with a *sforzando,* and with everything in between. I would recom-

mend that tonguing questions be directed to Gilbert Woody in Sacramento, as he not only has made a depth study of the problems but happens to have one of the best tongues I have ever heard.

Slurs are usually studied as a separate entity with most teachers. A few only think of slurs up, but most instructors have their students practicing slurs both directions. Even though many teachers write out the slur exercises, the most commonly used are Remington's warm-ups or something fairly similar. A few instructors carry their slur warm-up on into a practice on trills. I must speak once again of the arched tongue as the most common aid to slurs going up. A few teachers have students working on slurs at almost every extended interval that the student can manipulate. They feel that it will force him to bring his diaphragm into use.

There seems to be a general agreement that legato playing is a lost art, some call this "playing with a flow," others speak of it as "singing." Many teachers use the Rochut (Bordogni) books to practice legato lines. Some like these because they combine legato work with clef studies. I talked with teachers who are more interested in legato playing than in excess technique, but they are in the minority; one gentleman said that if a student can play legato, he can usually do anything else. They all agree that legato tonguing and deep breathing must be combined with excellent slide action (there seems to be very little tolerance with faulty equipment).

I seldom found a teacher who did not agree with the value of scales one way or another. Some use scales in warm-ups, some to develop a horizontal approach to good intonation, some concentrate on matching sounds, but most use scales for developing technique. This seems to be the most standardized way of developing coordination between the slide and the tongue. The only written scale studies that were mentioned to me were Remington scales, those in Arban, and the studies by Paré. Some schools insist that certain major and minor scales be memorized depending upon the grade level of the student. I was happy to find that many teachers have students practicing scales more than one octave, realizing that the extra octave causes an entirely different feel to the study. Some work their scales from tones other than the tonic, for example, start a *C* scale on low *E*, take it as high as possible and back down again. A few teachers are using the scale studies to practice a perpetually moving slide for eventual faster technique. Even with this great emphasis, it is still quite surprising how few students know their major and minor scales.

Flexibility exercises seem to develop reputations, they are more easily recognized by ear than many other facets of practice routines. According to my survey, the most popular flexibility studies are Schlossberg, Slauma, and Colin. A word of praise is due here for the many teachers who write out the exercises for their students depending on the student's assets and debits. The most concentrated basis for these is slurring with no tongue at all, and often having to slur past some natural overtone without sounding it.

Many students are concerned about extending their high range; in fact, they seem more concerned about it than the teachers. I decided that the teachers often fear the consequences of forcing, excessive pressure, or pinching to get high notes, or that the students might sacrifice some other aspect of their playing. As a consequence, some teachers simply do not give range building exercises, feeling that each student will find his own top range and that everyone is different. There is sometimes mention of rolling back the lower lip for high notes, some say to pull down on the corners of the mouth. I was told a few times of a "grunt" concept to get out high notes. It is suggested that the playing of jazz-oriented music often helps build the upper register. Some teachers have the students write their own range builders. John Swallow of New York uses the Smith trumpet works for this phase of development. Zentner's exercise from *Practice with the Experts* emphasizes his concern for maintaining a good firm low register while expanding the high. In fact, most of the trombonists I know who have exceedingly strong upper registers also

have the most solid low registers for tenor trombones. (I often wonder why so many people ignore the fact that while tenor trombonists are building a range upward, bass trombonists must be building a range downward.)

I knew that one way I could create a controversy would be to ask about each individual teacher's attitude about vibrato—the variance is quite unbelieveable. The worry about lip or jaw vibrato is that the student may not be able to turn it off. The concern about slide vibrato is the tendency to hear all vibrato with no true center to the sound; no mention was made of use of the diaphragm. Many teachers however, inspite of their concerns about vibrato, admit difficulty conceiving a *bel canto* line being played without it. Some would mention it only if it were used and interfered with the style. Some substitute other words for vibrato, such as "warmth" or "expressiveness." The consensus of opinion is that the advantages of slide vibrato over lip (jaw) vibrato are two-fold: it can be turned off at will and it does not interfere with the embouchure setting in the upper register. However, it does seem that those trombonists who use lip vibrato successfully often also have the best flexibility. Some teachers teach both, allowing the student to adopt whichever he prefers within reason. Some teachers state that vibrato should vary not only with the repertoire, but also with the register, the upper register using a faster and more intense vibrato than the lower register. Also, some of us agree that the personality of the player enters into this expressive element. Some instructors state that the tendency toward the larger horn, hence the heavier slide, rather forces the players into jaw vibrato. Let me quote some differing adamant attitudes. One gentleman recommends jaw vibrato or none at all, as slide vibrato tends to be mechanical and too difficult (mainly because of slide condition) to manipulate. Another teaches hand vibrato—more controlled and doesn't disturb the embouchure setting. Students *must* use lip vibrato—picture what would happen with hand vibrato in sixth and seventh positions. One instructor

teaches slide, jaw, and *left hand* vibrato. Well, there you have it! Personally, my students practice sustained tones with no vibrato, with lip vibrato, and with hand vibrato—all must be controlled. When they play a legato line, I let them use whatever type they are most comfortable with. The dissention will not be decided in our time—the answers are all too personal. Maybe that is good.

There are a few other areas of special emphasis that individual teachers seem to consider extremely important. The matching of tones often gets worked into the practice routines. A few point out the advantages of resting between exercises. One gentleman was quite concerned over the need of great rhythmic discipline and recommended Baroque literature. Another said that his students seem to identify with the instrument instead of the music; this could cause two problems—faulty interpretation and looking to a change of instrument to solve all problems. A few teachers play unison with the students for ear training and some play duets for the value gleaned from imitation. One man more than others concerns himself greatly with how tones end. One instructor's grading is influenced by punctuality and attitude, explaining that these are necessary for professionalism. An analytical teacher in the South divides the problems of playing (and their resolutions) into two categories, physical and mental. Under physical he places breathing, tonguing, embouchure, and coordination. Under mental he includes pitch, rhythm, and interpretation. Most of us work terribly hard on what we seem to label "playing cleanly."

I must mention a couple of unusual exercises that I learned. One teacher has his students play quite a bit of atonal music for advanced development of the ear. I might add that this could also help the student in tone placement or developing a "feel" for where an isolated note is on his instrument, especially around high *G, A, B,* and *C.* A couple of teachers I talked with make the students invent their own warm-up and range building exercises, under supervision of course. A few are quite convinced of the value of tenor trombonists with no trigger practicing the tones between low *E* and pedal *B*. They say that it opens up the aperture and the oral cavity, strengthens the corners of the mouth, and solves the problem of an occasional inflated ego.

As you can see, the exercises handed out by the teachers across the country vary greatly; it is interesting to note that sometimes the same exercise is used but for different reasons. The approaches are occasionally so diverse that one might wonder if the same instrument were involved. Still, it is obvious that even with the many different ways of teaching and practicing, we are all merely working in our own way for better sounds and better technique.

My third article will concern itself mainly with literature. ∎

August, 1970

Twenty-five Years of Brass Instrument Playing

Maurice Faulkner

Style and Performance

Twenty-five years ago, brass instrumentalists were striving to develop the big Wagnerian tone which was so essential for symphonic orchestra and concert band artistry as depicted by the New York Philharmonic, Chicago Symphony, Boston Symphony and the Philadelphia Orchestra together with many others. The Goldman Band Mall concerts as well as those in Prospect Park, Brooklyn, gave the connoisseur of band music a treat every evening of the week. Other professional bands followed the Goldman pattern or set their own, from the east to the west coast. Herbert Clarke's Long Beach, California aggregation had lost its famous cornetist-conductor but his successors carried on the daily tourist concerts on the beach front.

Brass specialists in the big swing bands of Tommy Dorsey, Harry James, Benny Goodman, Stan Kenton and Glenn Miller filled the ballrooms throughout the nation with magnificent trumpet, trombone, saxophone, and sometimes French horn sounds which were copied by every school boy who had the price of admission. The demands of the symphony or-

chestra, band and dance band music which was being turned out by arrangers and composers on both sides of the Atlantic pushed the first stand players into the stratosphere of range and facility and developed their knowledge and artistry of style and interpretation.

Conductors became increasingly aware of proper performance skills of the wind instruments in relation to intelligent stylization. Those who played under conductors of that quality found new skills for producing old characteristics. One of the greatest trumpeters we have ever heard in the symphonic orchestral world told us one time that he "just screwed up his lips and blew!" But what divine "blowing" came out of those "screwed-up" lips. He could go into a rehearsal which called for him to perform Beethoven, Brahms, Wagner, and Aaron Copland and find the proper variety of tone qualities, tongue styles, phrase ideas, and artistry to fit his parts into the fabric of the string and woodwind colors with exact intonation in such a manner that the world's finest conductors worshipped his playing as if he were a god stemming straight from Gabriel on high.

Since this was a proper example for the young musicians who followed his every breath and performance, such musicality was catching and many of us attempted what the master could achieve so simply. Most of these apostles went out into the broad pathways of musical life in the United States and taught others the things they had discussed and learned in the metropolitan centers. Therefore, style and performance characteristics became the watchword for superb brass performers during the 25 years under discussion. Band professionals captured the ideas and made them a part of concert band performances as well. When Wagnerian operatic fare was programmed, the musicians attempted to vary the sounds from the Verdi overtures which might have opened the concerts.

Technique and Skill

Obviously, if style concepts were to be improved, the techniques and skills essential to the performances must be enhanced by greater understanding. Our colleagues in the field of university and college teaching, together with the high school and other educational instrumental teachers, have ferreted

553

out the secrets of the physical mechanism of performance on brass instruments to such an extent that seldom is there any phase of the process which hasn't been explored theoretically or experimentally. If you have a problem with any aspect of technique, look back through past issues of *The Instrumentalist* and you will find not one, but several suggestions as to solutions.

When we began this quarter of a century, the top ranges of the instruments were limited by the demands of the music and by the physical capacities of the musicians. Today every competent brass musician is able to play through the several octaves of his instrument with ease, if he has been properly trained, and if he hasn't been, he can find a well-versed teacher who will extend his top range by at least a fifth, if not another octave, within months. The pedal depths of our brasses have been brought into the mainstream of performance although they are not used very successfully by the higher instruments such as the trumpet and horn.

Analyze the facile skills of scalic and arpeggic roulades, tonguing speed, slurring of all types and all intervals, and similar problems and you will find every musician advanced in comparison to his *compadres* of 25 years ago.

Music and Teaching

As the traditional music demanded a new awareness of the great potential of our brass interpretations, the new compositions pushed our players to the ultimate of their technical abilities. Dance arrangers called on altissimo performance by brass men, new emphasis on glissandos, riffs, vibrant rhythms, new tonal centers and other similar expressive devices which had not been characteristic before. Contemporary composers followed the arrangers in developing requisite colors and skills which caused all of us to reassess our instruments and our abilities. Brass ensembles of all sizes and types evolved into top musical units demanding the best of a composer's output. We had to practice the new ideas and work up a lip for the new demands. We had to improve our ears and our expressiveness for awkward intervals and atonal melodies. We

had to sharpen our tongue styles. We were hauled out of our traditional romantic materials into a 20th century of *avant-gardism* which is pushing us ever faster into the 21st century of brass instrument performance.

Teaching materials supplemented the musical demands. New methods were developed by the performers and the competent teachers, who had found solutions to the problems of the new requirements. Range-building volumes came off the press like hotcakes from a griddle. Etudes for developing style and character followed almost as frequently. Orchestral studies preceded the other materials at an earlier date and continued to increase in numbers and types. The popular music idols had their solos written down for the embryo "take-off" boy or girl who needed to know how to play in style when his school dance band held their Friday night sessions in the gym.

Concepts of Construction

In advance of everything else and as a forerunner to many of the developments outlined above, the instrument manufacturers of the United States, as well as in other parts of the world, produced new concepts in brass instrument construction. The total form of the instrument (including special lead pipes, bores, and materials) was designed to satisfy the specific needs of the different performance areas of music: the symphony orchestra professional had requested features which were different from those desired by either the dance or concert band player.

A careful investigation of this phase of our music history needs to be undertaken in depth, for the contributions of these progressive firms have provided all of us with the vehicle for our successful musicianship and artistry. Mouthpiece manufacture, in itself an individual province, has aided all of us immensely in achieving the new goals of both contemporary and traditional music. For example, when we were all searching for a "non-pressure" system to improve our embouchure, one of the manufacturers came up with a mouthpiece which couldn't be played if the neophyte used pressure. These

benefits of an evolving technology which American ingenuity developed to serve musical needs have been brought to our readers' attention by a steady stream of advertisements and articles over the past quarter of a century.

What Lies Ahead?

With the thoroughness of the research of our musicological brass specialists we expect a great increase in the number of performances with original-type instruments. Many institutions own their clarini, cornetti, natural horns, ophicleides, etc. for proper interpretation and color in the performance of old music. We believe that this will increase to the extent that musicians will want to own the rotary valve and natural trumpets which provided the special qualities for which Beethoven, Wagner, Brahms, and other composers wrote their music in the Austria and Germany of the romantic era. We believe that those trumpeters who do not now have them, will begin to purchase the smaller bore instruments essential to the music of the French and similar styles. Alto and tenor trombones of small bore construction will become essential to certain productions of opera and concert music.

Technique and Skill

Such gains as expected above will demand new knowledge of embellishments, tone colors, tongue styles, and even finer adaptations to range. The evolution of electronic and scientific knowledge and its use in musical performance will undoubtedly affect the brass instrumentalists. Some manufacturers have produced methods of amplifying instruments for the football shows, but this is merely a hint of the ever greater developments which lie ahead. New methods of producing electronic vibrations will be invented (they may already be in production) which will be able to reproduce brass tone quality much more effectively than those in the past. There may come a day when a machine will be able to replace a complete brass section. We doubt that such an unusual phenomenon, played by one keyboard artist, will take the place of the first-rate brass specialists in a major orchestra. But with laser-beam transmission for simple uses just around the corner, no one dare predict that the unusual could not take place.

Since anything which evolves will affect our playing skills and techniques, it behooves the astute professional and ambitious amateur to keep up with the winds of change.

Evaluation of Materials

This will take on new dimensions in the future, for machines will be used to measure the success of our teaching processes and the artistry of our performances. We may not agree that such monsters can judge us adequately, but they are here and will move into our teaching studios and concert halls with multiplication in the next years. Some laboratories are ready now to measure the fatigue of musicians in rehearsals and concerts, and, when these studies are completed, new teaching materials will be developed to relieve the fatigue which is bound to be shown from such measurement. Look around you in your classrooms or concert halls and you will find overwhelming illustrations of the need for new music and worthwhile materials to accomplish the problems of our 20th-century artistic expressiveness.

Improved Construction

The program for the future outlined above will necessitate the rapid expansion of instrumental experimentation to convert present types into more encompassing equipment to meet the needs of the last decades of the 20th century. Careful studies on intonation should improve the construction of all brasses for more delicate and subtle playing. Bore changes in relation to length will make for better tone and pitch in extended positions and long tubings. I recall an Italian trombone of more than 25 years ago, in one professional band in which I played, which had a valve tubing for all seven fingerings. This was an ancient problem which they had tried to solve in the 19th century. We still have the problem, but it could be eliminated in the next three decades.

Much lies ahead, and the teacher and musician who searches his needs thoroughly and brings them to the attention of the manufacturers will aid the rest of us immeasurably.

Conclusion

This is a period in the world's history when we need music and artistic experiences to off-set the violence in our daily world. Brass instrumentalists must find their place in a world of technology which needs the stimulus of their magnificent instruments to ease emotional strains. Electronic music alone will not settle these problems. Human beings will continue to be essential as performers, but the demands upon their physical and artistic skills will become so special that the world will find new paths for superior players and new techniques for brass instrumentalists. Search out the daily environment and find a niche in it for your abilities and beneficial influences. Look into the inventions of technology, into the emotional lives of your clientele, into the inner resources of your own spirit, and come up with a plan and a brass music for the decades ahead. ∎

September, 1970

Trombone Teaching: A National Consensus *(Part III)*

Paul Tanner

This is the third and last of a series of articles explaining information gathered on a recent trip to approximately 100 American colleges and conservatories. The trombone instructors around the country were most helpful and generous. These are their opinions. Other articles appeared in March and June 1970. The first was mainly concerned with approaches to giving lessons; the second covered the techniques of practice. This concluding article investigates literature: not only for student recitals and testing, but also that which can give impetus to the students' improvement.

Arban Or Not Arban

First of all, there are pros and cons about one of the oldest books — certainly the best known in practice literature — Arban. The opinions go all the way from "Arban is a waste" to "Arban is the Bible." Many people do not use the Arban at all, some use it a little, some a lot. Most of the instructors who use it do so for one or two specific reasons only, and these vary. It is used for tonguing practice, for technique and coordination, or for scales and rhythmic exercises. Very few instructors could conceive just going straight through it; they almost all pick out isolated areas and work them into the practice routines as needed. Some bass trombonists are practicing Arban down an octave; one gentleman told me that he uses Arban only for tuba.

A question about literature for clef studies elicits one response much more than any other — that of course is Blazhevich. Some teachers do hold off on these studies until a student has progressed to a fairly advanced stage, but most like to have the players involved in tenor as well as bass clef eventually. The Blazhevich sequences are very popular and the duets give the teacher a chance to play along with the student. For the readers who are looking for a change in clef work, some instructors did recommend other authors. For trombonists who are just branching into other clefs, there are books by Fink. For the more advanced clef readers, Bitch, Maxted, Miller, and Mantia were suggested. Frankly, if a student can handle the more advanced Rochut etudes, he merely wants other books for a change of repertoire. I play duets with my students from music usually written in treble clef; we change the key signature and also practice tenor, alto, and mezzo-soprano clefs (saves transposing French horn music). Most instructors agreed that working in unusual clefs helps the student's sight-reading because he feels so comfortable when he returns to bass clef.

Sight-reading — A Problem

Speaking of sight-reading, some instructors feel that this is one of the biggest problems with younger players. They attribute this to having to "work up" a piece before performing it; however; there seems no real way out of this. The consensus of opinion is that the best way to improve sight-reading is simply to do a great deal of it. But playing in unusual clefs does help, as does the practicing of piano — after reading more than one note at a time, the return to single line trombone music makes things seem more clear. One book that was suggested to me many times was La Fosse; also, cello studies are used. Most of us try to work in some sight-reading in every lesson. One gentleman who feels that the problem is mainly one of counting has his students sight-read with a metronome. He says it makes them sensitive to other things that are happening which demand proper counting. There are two approaches to sight-reading

practice: (1) keep going at all costs, and (2) stop and correct to make everything right. Most teachers try to mix these two approaches. Those who advocate the first say· that the players must keep going because the rest of the performance group simply will not stop. Others say that playing through will develop a frame of mind in which mistakes do not matter. There is agreement that many reading mistakes can be avoided if the player examines the music carefully before he starts to play. The other consensus is that panic surely hampers reading, whereas relaxation and confidence are great aids.

There is a fair amount of material to choose from as far as etudes are concerned; however, by far the most popular is Rochut. I should hasten to add, however, that very few students ever get into Volume III. Not only is it very difficult, but by the time most players are ready, they are more involved in solo literature with performance in mind. The Rochut books are used mainly for legato playing and the development of "phrase thinking" as opposed to "note thinking." Teachers are having the students play these etudes as if they were songs, concentrating on breathing and phrasing. A couple of gentlemen told me that they felt that Rochut was dull because of too much legato work. Since most teachers agree on the advantages of practicing etudes, here is a list of other books considered extremely worthwhile: Kopprasch, Couleau, Schroeder cello works, Blazhevich sequences, Bitch, Boutry, Blume, Coulliard, Bordogni, Vobaron, Gornston, and Slama.

Method Books

Which method book to use and why to use it is a very personal preference. At first, I thought that I would end up with a long list in this category, but it seems that most of the established teachers simply do not restrict themselves to a method. Rather, they tend to be eclectic. There are some books that were mentioned to me as standard, at least in the more advanced stages of development: the advanced Rubank books, LaFosse, Fink, Practice with the Experts,

Flandrin, Slama, Blazhevich, Cimera, Cornette. Clarke, Tyrrell, and Reinhardt.

Bass Trombone

I am sorry to say that there are really not a great many situations where bass trombone is being taught. When it is, the students almost always play Rochut etudes down an octave. The method books recommended to me from the currently limited supply were Ostrander, Blume, Gillis, Roberts and Tanner, Bell's Arban, and Tyrrell's E♭ tuba book.

Trombone instructors are using works written for the cello to good advantage, especially for sight-reading. Bach cello studies have been transcribed by several people — the ones suggested to me the most were by LaFosse, Marsteller, Loeb, and Peters. Brown and Schroeder are also used. One gentleman commented that good, faithful cello transcriptions do not give a trombonist time to breathe, but they are generally used to great advantage.

The use of orchestral excerpts has its followers and dissenters. The attitudes vary from having students memorize an entire book of excerpts to not using them at all. A few teachers told me that if they taught their students well enough, excerpts could be handled as they were encountered. Some teachers restrict the study of excerpts to those who are really interested in a symphonic career. There are books by Berthold and by Menken, but the man who has published much more than anyone else in this direction is Keith Brown. A few teachers have all of his works.

Recitals and Jury Recitals

Frequency of recitals varies from none at all to one every quarter or semester. Of the schools visited, only about three percent have no student recitals; and only about six percent limit their recitals to graduate students. In some cases, the music education students who are receiving trombone instruction have slightly different requirements than those for the applied music students. The difference is that some are *encouraged* to do recitals instead of being *required,* or they can share a recital with other music education students.

Terms vary. The "jury" for a recital could be other trombone students, other brass students, any or all teachers of brass instruments, any or all performance teachers, or the entire music faculty. When the entire music faculty does the grading, the trombone instructor is on the spot as much as his student. Jury recitals may include from one to four selections, but are usually set up in such a way that the student plays a little repertoire then is asked to play certain scales or modes according to the whims of his jury. A typical situation (in case the reader wants to compare it with his own) is a one-solo jury recital each quarter, followed at the end of the year by a 2-3 solo, more public recital as a prerequisite for advancement. A final recital for graduation would be more ambitious, of course; and the final recital for a doctorate could involve four or five lengthy solos as well as participation in a couple of ensembles.

Most instructors are quite concerned that their students have a variety of solo experience, and often will let the student choose from a short list of four or five works. In some cases, at least half of the recital must be performed from memory.

The biggest problems with recitals seem to be space and time. If the object of a recital is to expose the student to the feeling of playing alone in front of a critical audience, then this is not accomplished if no one has the time to come to his recital. Some schools help solve this by requiring that all music students attend a certain number of recitals. I also spoke with trombone instructors teaching at schools where the faculty is required to give annual recitals. Incidentally, in a well-known eastern school, if a student has received his master's degree with a recital then goes out and works as a successful professional for five years, the school will then award him a DMA.

Solo Literature

There is surely no intent in this article to give a suggested list of solo literature, but there are certain works that are being used with such frequency that they must be considered standard in this field: Bach — *Suites for Cello*, Barat — *Andante et Allegro*, Berlioz — *Recitative and Prayer*, Blazhevich — *Concerto No. 2* and *Concert Piece No. 5*, Bozza — *Ballade*, Creston — *Fantasy*, Dalby — *Sonata for Trombone and Piano*, Davis — *Concertino*, Gaubert — *Morceau Symphonique*, Gillis — *Dialogue*, Grafe — *Grand Concerto for Trombone*, Guilmant — *Morceau Symphonique*, Hindemith — *Sonata*, Jacob — *Concerto*, McKay — *Sonata*, and Rimsky-Korsakov — *Concerto*. Of course, I am always extremely enthusiastic to hear of my own works being performed.

Many teachers use solo voice material, like Debussy songs, for example. Baroque literature — works by Vivaldi, Corelli, and Marcello — is recommended for rhythmic discipline. Some teachers advocate types instead of titles or composers. Occasionally I found a teacher who wants his students to perform what they can play best in spite of the grade of difficulty. One gentleman, in order for others to determine the grades for his students, had every one of them perform the Hindemith *Sonata*. A great number of teachers are keeping a running repertoire sheet on each student. It is then easier to determine the degree of difficulty of the works performed as well as the amount of variety. Some also make up a list with which the student who aspires to teach must acquaint himself.

No mention of repertoire would be complete without the suggestion that all questions should go to Leon Brown of North Texas State. Brown has been studying trombone literature on a grant and must be the world's leading authority on the subject. Readers could request his published handbook of this literature and also his sheets on literature for the bass trombone. One other important suggestion on this same line is a book on brass literature by Mary Rasmussen, published by the Brass Quarterly. Her book has been a great help to many brass instructors.

What About Jazz?

I asked each teacher if he thought that playing jazz helped or hurt his students. I think that the best way for me to show the pros and cons is to quote some actual comments, many of which were repeated over and over. Those who were opposed said, "some students get so involved with jazz bands that they neglect individual practice," "the top volume of the jazz bands causes tone distortion or a hardness in the sound," "students are not prepared for the upper register demands," "dance music interpretations are carried over into other styles," "constant loud playing of the jazz (and marching) bands costs the student some finesse and delicacy," and "jazz has too much immediate appeal that causes knowledge of the classics to suffer." Typical comments in favor of this activity include: "jazz playing helps the upper register," "the one-on-a-part situation helps independent playing," "it helps their reading," "it's the best place in the world to learn to play in time and with complicated syncopation," "it helps the bass trombonist to develop strength and mobility in his lower register," and "it builds endurance."

Some teachers are using jazz-oriented ensembles (trombone quartets, etc.) to give the students this experience. Most instructors are very concerned about whether or not the student is well-rounded, especially if he intends to play for a living. One fine symphonic player told me that he has always admired ballad players — people like J.J. Johnson and Urbie Green — and would be thrilled if one of his students were greatly talented in that direction. Several teachers said that the best players in their school played in the jazz band. I asked Phil Wilson (an extremely gifted jazz trombonist who teaches at Berklee in Boston) if he teaches his students to play jazz. His reply was, "Of course not, I just teach them trombone."

Small Ensembles

Being involved with a talented group of young players at UCLA in a trombone ensemble, I was quite interested in what other teachers were doing along this vein. Some schools do have trombone ensembles (choirs); it seemed to depend mainly upon the talent available. Some use ensembles as class lessons and the weaker players learn from the stronger players. The ones I came across seemed to fall into one of two categories — either a quarter, or a large group with two or three players on a part. They are presented with a variety of styles from pre-Gabrieli to jazz. Mark McDunn of Chicago told me that he is performing one of my quartets with 200 trombones.

This is the concluding article of three on my investigation of how trombone is taught in colleges around the country. There may be points so specific that I did not include them; if this is the case, and if any readers care to contact me with questions, I would be most happy to be of any help that I can.

Once again, a great thanks to those many teachers who gave me all of this information. I am only sorry that I was not able to talk to every individual trombone teacher in this country — these meetings were so much more than a pleasure to me. ∎

October, 1970

The Natural Trumpet in the Modern Orchestra

H. M. Lewis

Up until the past few years, trumpeters performing the works of a baroque or classical composer used without question Bb, C, or D trumpets of modern manufacture, equipped with valves, and having what is thought of as the "usual" trumpet sound. In recent years, however, certain European instrument makers, notably the performer-musicologist Edward Tarr, and Helmut Finke, have mass-produced copies of authentic natural trumpets of the type which were used in the baroque and classical period and now reside only in museums. With these instruments a new faithfulness to the composer's original intentions is now possible.

But why should the modern orchestra trumpeter consider forsaking his valve trumpet for an instrument that has not been used for over 150 years? Basically, the answer is *tone*. Over the years, due to the increased demands for agility, range, and sheer power by composers of the romantic and modern periods, the trumpet as we know it has become a very different instrument from the one Bach, Handel, Mozart, and Haydn were accustomed to hearing in performances of their own works. The length of the old instruments has been shortened by half, the bore has become much larger and much more conical, proportionally, and the thickness of metal in the instrument has been increased. All of these changes directly affect the tone of the instrument. Our modern trumpet with its large bore and bright, cutting sound is totally alien to the orchestration of the baroque and classical composers. What trumpeter has not had the experience of playing a classical mass or symphony only to be berated by the conductor for playing too loudly, even though he was doing his best to play as softly as possible? One trumpeter referred to having the conductor's "hand down my throat all the time," and others have had similar experiences. In all fairness, it is not all the player's fault. The big and bright sound of the modern trumpet was not designed for the classical and baroque orchestra, and, in the small ensemble, the problem simply becomes more acute.

Now that good copies of the natural trumpet are available, the answer to the problem of balance becomes simple. Use the trumpet for which the part was intended! The first reaction on hearing the tone of the natural trumpet in an orchestral context is one of surprise. The tone is not as loud as that of the modern trumpet, and it has a deeper, more noble quality, probably because of the greater length of the sounding tube. Rather than penetrating through the group, the tone of the natural trumpet supports the group in music of the classic period, and integrates much better with the ensemble in the polyphonic music of the baroque era. And, surprisingly, the natural trumpets are just as easy to play in the high register as are their smaller, valved descendants. The technique is tricky at first, since the trumpeter has been accustomed to relying on valves instead of lip tension variation alone to produce the different tones, but once it is mastered, the natural trumpet is as easy to play as the valve trumpet.

The new copies of the natural trumpet come in two styles: the coiled form, in which the Finke instruments are made, and the more usual long oval form, in which the Tarr instruments are made. Both instruments are

From top to bottom: Tarr model C trumpet, modern C trumpet, and modern D trumpet. The relative length of the natural instrument can be seen .

offered in a variety of pitches, and all have some sort of tone-hole nodal venting arrangement to help tune the out-of-tune partials of the overtone series. Usually the modern copies are more soundly constructed than their ancient prototypes. It was customary in the old instruments to place a block of wood between the mouthpipe and bell of the instrument, and then bind the parts together with a cord. This left the instrument free to vibrate. The modern copies are soldered in the usual manner, although a cord is wrapped around the Tarr models to preserve the illusion. Some concessions must be made in the matter of pitch and intonation (the tone-holes) if the instruments are to be used at all in public concerts. All of the copies are made to conform to modern concert pitch, although the manufacturers note that this is almost a half-tone higher than the pitch of the original instruments.

The Tarr trumpets are copies of a trumpet by Wolf Wilhelm Haas (1681-1760) which is now in the Bernoulli collection in Greifensee, Switzerland. In his famous method book on the art of trumpeting and kettledrumming, Johann Ernst Altenburg mentions the Haas trumpets as being particularly outstanding. The Finke trumpets are modeled after the trumpet held by Gottfried Reiche in his famous portrait. Unfortunately, no prototype of this instrument has survived to the present day,

It is to be hoped that trumpeters will take advantage of these fine instruments in performing baroque and classical works. Many famous musicologists, notably Robert Donington, Thurston Dart, and Nicholas Bessarbof, have bemoaned the passing of the natural trumpet with its noble tone. Now it is within the power of the trumpet playing profession to return to the nobility of the earlier instrument — and without sacrificing anything in the way of ability on the valve trumpet. In fact, practice on the natural trumpet generally makes the player far more accurate in his playing, and much keener of ear. The natural trumpet is particularly valuable to the college teacher, whose students need to be exposed to the sound of the trumpet as it was heard by the old masters.

But the natural trumpet should not be just a dusty heirloom, a reminder of bygone days before the blessings of the valve spurred the development of the brass section and started the change in the basic nature of the trumpet that has persisted until this day. It should be used! The natural trumpet is a totally different instrument from the modern valve trumpet, and pieces written for the one should not be played upon the other if there is any alternative (any more than trumpet parts should be played on a flügelhorn). Now that copies of the natural trumpets have become available, it is to be hoped that concert audiences will have the privilege of hearing the trumpet sound the old masters intended.

And maybe the conductors will stop nagging us about playing too loudly! ∎

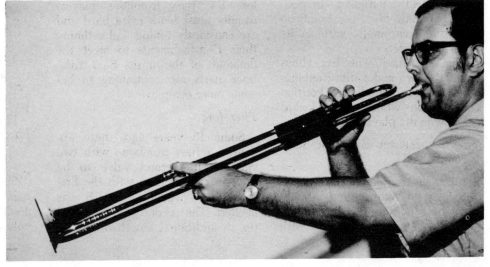

The Tarr C trumpet in playing position. Notice that the index finger of the right hand is in place over the tone hole. This position allows a free technique in covering or uncovering the tone hole. The index and middle fingers of the left hand are balanced on either side of the ornamental ball on the bell.

THE 'NOW' TROMBONE

Alan Raph

Tenor Trombone

The trombone has seven slide positions. First position (slide closed) produces a B♭ fundamental and the B♭ overtone series.

Second position produces A (fundamental and overtones); third position, A♭, etc. Combinations of slide positions and overtones make the chromatic scale of the trombone.

Whereas

There have always been two major disadvantages in playing the tenor trombone:

1. Some position combinations are very awkward to maneu-

ver.

2. The lowest register on the trombone has a five-note gap in the chromatic scale.

Therefore

The *F* Attachment trombone has evolved. With an *F* Attachment addition to the tenor trombone, the player can press a lever (trigger) with his left thumb and instantly change the 1st position *B♭* fundamental into an *F* fundamental, one fourth lower. The *F* Attachment adds additional and immediate length to the instrument.

With the thumb valve, 7th position *E* can be played in a slightly flattened 2nd position, and by extending the slide further, the player can now produce *E♭, D, D♭,* and *C* thereby narrowing the chromatic gap in the trombone's low register. Note: there are only six positions with the *F* attachment due to a greater span between each position. Most *F* Attachments have a very long tuning slide which (when extended) will tune in the missing *B* in a flattened 7th position. This now gives the trombone a complete chromatic scale in its lowest register.

The *F* Attachment has eliminated the two major disadvantages of the tenor trombone. Position combinations which were awkward are now easily playable.

The low register chromatic scale is complete.

Should the trombonist have a low *B* to play, he retunes his *F* Attachment by extending the long tuning slide . . . plays the passage with the low *B,* and at the first opportunity . . . returns the tuning slide to its normal place in order to gain back the use of 1st and 2nd position (*F* and *E*) which have been altered in the tuning slide pull for low *B.* Since low *B's* occur so infrequently in tenor trombone parts, this special tuning process becomes more academic than every-day-practical.

Now

F Attachments have become standard on tenor trombones. They increase the instrument's capabilities. Attachment-*less* trombones are on the decline as the trigger becomes more and more common.

Bass Trombone

Most bass trombones today are large bore trombones with *F* Attachments. Bass trombone music generally focuses on the low trombone register.

Whereas

Bass trombones must play *many* low *B's.* Bass trombone players usually must work extra hard and are constantly tuning and retuning their *F* attachments to meet the demands of the music. Bass trombone parts are continuing to become more complex.

Therefore

Some 15 years ago, there appeared a bass trombone with two valves! The second valve to be used in combination with the first (*F*) valve whenever a low *B* was needed. The second valve opened up an additional length of tubing and did away with the necessity of retuning the whole *F* Attachment to accommodate one note . . . low *B.* The double valve bass trombone makes life easier for the bass trombonist and offers him immediate extentions of bass trombone technique through slide, valve, and double valve position combinations.

The early double-valves merely lowered the pitch of the *F* Attachment enough to produce a low *B* (slightly more than one half-step). The set up of the double valve can add *any* additional length to the *F* Attachment.

It has been found (through much trial and error) that the most workable tuning of the double valve is to produce a *D* in first position. This makes the present bass trombone capable of producing three separate overtone series in 1st position (*B♭ F,* and *D*). The combination possibilities are enormous and have advanced bass trombone technique considerably. The double valve bass trombone (with the *D* tuning of the second valve) is an instrument capable of:

1. an extended low register (to the lowest *B♭* on the piano).

2. involved technical passages with no awkward position reaches.

3. slide and valve combinations for completely new techniques.

Now

Bass trombones are large bore double-valve trombones with great potential. ■

Long Tones For the Trumpeter

Kenneth L. Laudermilch

Long tones are an essential part of the trumpet player's foundation exercises and should be practiced daily. They develop the following:

Breath Control

The air stream never stops. Diaphragm muscles "firm-up" during inhalation and "support" during exhalation. The exact point of transition is only theoretical (as in the golfer's swing). Sound must have direction. As the volume of out-bound air decreases, diaphragmatic "support" may become ineffective if the momentum (intensity) of the air stream is not maintained.

Attacks and Releases

The tongue, pointed and arched behind the tips of the upper teeth, strikes and returns to its original position in a split second (the tongue must be withdrawn quickly so that the momentum of the air stream is not interrupted). Never allow the tongue to *grasp* the pitch by remaining against the upper teeth in preparation for the attack while air pressure builds behind it.

Dynamic Control

Develop the ability to sustain a pitch at any given dynamic level. Move smoothly from one dynamic level to another without fluctuating in pitch or tone quality.

Endurance

Both the embouchure and diaphragm muscles are developed by exposing them to periods of tension followed by equal periods of relaxation. Don't allow one muscle to do the other one's work. Find the right mixture of embouchure control and diaphragm control and guard it jealously.

Tone Quality

A good tone quality is the result of good playing habits. Improve your tone by improving all the factors involved in producing that tone.

This outline is designed to give the student and teacher a logical plan of procedure in the study of long tones. It may be modified to meet the capabilities of the beginner or adapted for the more advanced trumpet student.

Elementary Long Tones

Objectives

Duration. Increase the length of the long tones until the 30 second mark is reached. Fourth and fifth grade students are capable of playing these long tones. Achievement charts in class lessons generate interest and competitiveness.

Attack. Clean attacks result from good breathing habits and a minimum amount of tongue articulating over a well-supported (intensified) air stream. The breath is part of the attack in that the *air never stops* between inhalation and exhalation. Isolated attacks are often helpful in pinpointing difficulties.

Dynamic. Sustain the dynamic level to the release. Don't swell after the attack.

Basic Procedures

The body needs time to replenish its supply of oxygen, so rest after each long tone (a good rule of thumb is to rest as long as it took you to play the long tone).

Extended periods of long tone practice may have a tendency to deaden the response of the lips. Maintain flexibility by interspersing slurs among the long tones.

Example:

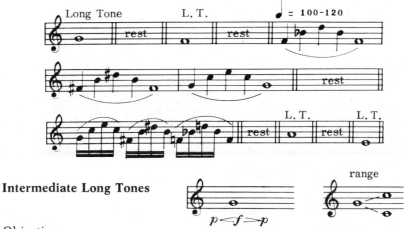

Intermediate Long Tones

Objectives

Piano attack; move smoothly from one dynamic level to another with no fluctuation in pitch or tone quality; the crescendo and diminuendo should be of equal length; return to the original dynamic level as you reach the end of the air stream.

Basic Procedures

The long tone should take the entire breath; begin the crescendo immediately after the attack; know where the *p* and *f* levels lie; practice isolated attacks at all levels.

Don't dwell on the *f* section; once it has been achieved move toward the *p* and release.

Keep the air moving toward a point in the diminuendo as well as in the crescendo.

Incorrect usage of air stream: air intensity follows dynamic curve

Result: excess lip pressure; intonation problems (pitch is not centered); tone quality changes

Correct usage of air stream: air remains intense as it moves toward release.

Advanced Long Tones

Objectives

Achieve the extreme dynamic levels of *pp* and *ff* and move smoothly from one to the other; *pp* attack; develop stamina in sustaining pitches at the *pp* level with half or more of the air stream spent.

Basic Procedures

The sustained *pp* section of the long tone should take at least one half of the total air; more advanced students may check their flexibility and control at the very end of the long tone by slurring to the next highest harmonic before releasing.

Daily Distribution

High   *Monday-Thursday-Sunday*

Middle   *Tuesday-Friday*

Low

Wednesday-Saturday

Keep the entire range "in shape" by playing long tones in a different register each day. ∎

December, 1970

Early Brass Manuscripts in Vienna

David Whitwell

The music listed here represents the complete manuscript holdings for brass instruments in two of Europe's greatest libraries of early music. In addition these libraries have large collections of published music and more recent manuscripts. As much of this latter category of music is available in other libraries, even in the United States, it was outside the concern of this researcher. There is one published composition which should be mentioned, however, as it is quite difficult to find, *Angels,* for six trumpets, by Carl Ruggels. A copy of this limited publication (London: Curiven, 1925) may be found in the Gesellschaft der Musikfreunde under the call-number: VIII 46.522.

The reader may write to the libraries, at the address below, in English. In a request for a copy the reader should give the full title, composer, and call-number (which in the list below appears before each title). Works in the Gesellschaft der Musikfreunde are so indicated by "GdMf" immediately before the call-number. All other manuscripts are in the Austrian National Library. Both libraries offer negative microfilm at 5¢ per page and positive microfilm at nearly 10¢. The Austrian National Library also offers Xerox at 10¢ per page.

Österreichische Nationalbibliothek
Musiksammlung
Josefplatz 1
Wien I, Österreich

Gesellschaft der Musikfreunde
Musik-Archiv
Bösendorferstraße 12
Wien I, Österreich

Music for Horn

Anonymous.
Sm 20470. *Quintet* for horns.
Sm 20471, 20472. (Two) *Quartets* for horns.
Bellonci von Leidesdorf.
(GdMf) XI 5983. *Sonate* for horn and piano.
Dessauer, Joseph.
(GdMf) XI 42388. *Nocturne* (1844) for horn and piano.
Haindl, Josef.
(GdMf) XI 38283. *Sonate* for horn and klavier.
Hirtl, H.
(GdMf) VIII 22526. *Concerto* for horn and orchestra.
Hoffmeister, Anton.
(GdMf) XI 10755. *Quintet* for horn and strings.
Hummel, Johann Nepomak.
Sm 4713. *Larghetto* for 4 horns and klavier.
Krause, J. H.
(GdMf) VIII 7648. *Adagio and Polonaise* for horn and orchestra.
Krenn, Franz.
Sm 13344. (Two) *Gradualien* for Bass solo, horn and orchestra.
Sm 13409. *Salve Regina* for SATB, horn solo, organ, and orchestra.
Sm 13374, 13376-13378. (Four) *Offertorium* (1859) for Soprano solo, horn solo, organ, and strings.
Sm 22487. *Offertorium* (1888) for Soprano or Tenor solo, horn solo, organ, and orchestra.
Sm 14151. *Concertino* (1841) for horn and orchestra.
Sm 14176. *Andante and Allegretto* (1841) for horn and piano.
Kreutzer, Conradin.
Sm 21133. *Das Mühlrad* for singer, horn, and piano.
Lackner, Ignaz.
Sm 20465. *Noturno* for horn and piano.
Moser, Franz (d. 1930)
Sm 21314. (Two) *Stücke*, Op. 76a and 76b, for 5 horns.
Richter, Anton.
(GdMf) VIII 38519. (Six) *Quintets and Trios* for Waldhörner.
(GdMf) VIII 38585. (Six) *Pieces* for 4 Cors de chasse.
Röllig, Carl Leopold.
Sm 18562. *Concerto* for two horns and orchestra.
Sm 18557. *Concerto* for two horns and orchestra.
Sm 18566. *Concerto* for two horns and orchestra.
Sm 18565. *Ballo* for two horns and orchestra.
Roth, Anton.
(GdMf) VIII 20055. *Concerto* for horn and orchestra.
Sperger, Johann.
(GdMf) VIII 12637. *Concerto* for horn and orchestra.
Storch, Anton.
Sm 14609. *Theme and Variations* for horn and orchestra.
Suppé, Franz von.
Sm 5358. *An Herrn von Puchruker* for voice, horn, and piano. This is the autograph.

Witt, Friedrich.
Sm 5253-5255. (Three) *Concerti* for two horns and orchestra.
Wolf, Friedrich Adolph.
Sm 13130. *Romanz* for horn, cello, and piano.
Wunderer, Anton.
Sm 9431. *Tanze und Marche* (1885) for 4 horns.

Music for Trumpet

Anonymous.
E.M. 93. *Sonata* for 2 trombe
Sm 23813. *Einige Ubungen für Maschin-Trompete.*
Baldessari, Pietro.
E.M. 97. *Sonatas* for cornetto.
Moser, Franz.
Sm 212233. *Scherzo* for 13 trumpets.
Torelli, Giuseppe.
Sm 3740. *Sonata* (1726) for 2 trombe and strings.

Music for Trombone

Collection.
Sm 15274. (10) *Stücke* for trombone (or horn) and orchestra. This apparently dates from the second half of the 19th century.
Friedl, Carl.
Sm 20462. *Solo* for trombone and strings.
Fux, Johann.
Sm 3630. *Sonatas* for trombone and 2 violins. These date from 1726 to 1739.
Van Beer, ?
Sm 1998. *Concertino* for trombone and orchestra.

Music for Mixed Ensembles of Brass Instruments

Lachner, Franz.
(GdMf) VIII 8111. *Septet* for 4 horns and 3 trombones.
(GdMf) VIII 8113. *Nonett* for 4 horns, 3 trombones and 2 trumpets.
Müller, Adolph, Jr.
Sm 14637. *Posthornklang* (1856) for singer, trumpet, horn and piano.
Weber, Bernhard.
Sm 2065. (Incidental Music for the) *Trauerspiel Klÿtemnestra* for 4 horns, 3 trombones, and 2 bassoons. The bassoons here function only as bass instruments, representing the best bass-wind choice at the time. It would be logical to rescore their parts for brass. The writer has not been able to date this work, however the manuscript paper appears to be late 18th century. If the work dates from this period, it would be an extraordinary brass ensemble work for its period and for its length.

What About That Pressure ?

G. David Peters

Perhaps one of the most discussed and argued topics in brass playing is that of pressure. There are many opinions with more articles and viewpoints than almost any other area of brass pedagogy. Most arguments stem from the amount of pressure that is required to play the instrument. The following article aims to present a workable viewpoint.

The discussions of mouthpiece-pressure, or pressure of the mouthpiece against the lip, usually divide brass instructors into two major camps: the "pressure system" and the "no-pressure system." This labeling is the first misleading point in the discussion. The term "pressure" should be changed to the word "contact" before the discussion reaches a fiery peak. This will clarify the "no-pressure" term to one of "no-contact" which is absurd. All brass instrument players will agree that the instrument must touch the lips in order to produce a sound.

With this brief change in terminology, a clear view of the real argument can be seen by the casual observer. The question or point of difference is then: "How firmly should the instrument be placed in contact with the lips of the player?;" not, "Should the player use pressure?" Every brass player must use pressure (contact) to some degree.

In arguing about the amount of pressure, many points and counter points are made.

Too Much Pressure

1. Tone becomes thin in upper register
2. Playing endurance is shortened.
3. Player is usually tense.
4. Embouchure change in various registers usually present.
5. Pressure can damage lip tissue.

Insufficient Pressure

1. Tone is "fuzzy."
2. Response is not reliable.
3. Articulation is "muddy."
4. Air leakage creates noise.
5. Lower and higher registers weak and slow to develop.

After listening to the many points and participating in these arguments, some conclusions must be reached by every brass player. Again, as in many other areas of music, there is more than one "right" answer. After trying the different embouchures and accompanying amounts of pressure, each player will usually revert to a system that is much like that with which he first started playing. This is why the initial decision of the band director is *very* important. If the brass student is started with a pro-pressure or "press-and-pray" approach, this will be the basis for his playing for years to come.

Starting the Student

Many band directors start all brass students with a buzz of the lips and secondly with a buzzing of the mouthpiece. This seems to be a very good idea at first glance because the brass students can *quietly* buzz their mouthpieces while the woodwinds are working on their embouchures. If the band director wants to start his brass section with the "minimal pressure" system, this is the way to start.

If the band director plans to use a "middle-of-the-road" system, he should move very quickly to the use of the instrument with the mouthpiece to give the proper response and use of air pressure with the buzzing lip.

The important point here is that buzzing the mouthpiece alone really does not give the student any better start at play a brass instrument than starting on the instrument in the first place. Very few brass players hold the mouthpiece to their lips as firmly when they buzz a mouthpiece as they do when they are actually playing the instrument. Buzzing the mouthpiece then, gives a false feeling of "minimal pressure."

The most popular embouchure and related amount of pressure used today is a system somewhere between extreme pressure and the minimal pressure systems. By using enough pressure to keep the air from leaking from around the mouthpiece, the student can usually accomplish a good response and good tone. Unless the student has been constantly reminded about a lack of pressure in playing, the problems usually are those of too much pressure. Very seldom must the teacher remind the student to use *more* pressure!

Guard Your Words

One or two words at the wrong moment can create lasting problems for the brass student. To play a brass instrument well, one must be as mentally confident and physically relaxed as possible. If the teacher-director of the band uses fear tactics in teaching, the students will not play as well as they would in a warm, receptive climate. DO NOT try to scare the notes out of your brass players. The key here is to avoid having the student "tense-up," especially in a high solo passage.

Even before high school, the beginning band director-teacher can start using very destructive words unintentionally. The first problems start after the student is aware that there are higher notes on the instrument that he must try. By pushing into the high register too soon, the student will start using a number of compensation devices. These devices include tucking the lower lip under the upper, the "smile-system" of pulling the corners of the lip back too far, tonguing too hard, and chiefly the use of *too much pressure*.

The Right Phrase

When a student asks how to extend his range into the upper register, do *not* use the phrases: "Pinch your lips together;"

Tighten your lips;" "Smile;" "Roll your lips in;"."Use *more* pressure on the high notes;" "Tongue harder up there;" "Spit the high notes out."

Most of these statements cause the student to use more pressure when playing because of added tension.

Equally detrimental, are the statements:

"Go home and practice!" "Just work harder on the high notes;" "Playing in the high register is hard;" "I don't care how you do it, play that high *C* next Monday — your grade depends on it;" "Any trumpet player that misses this high passage on the concert will receive a failing grade."

Try to get your message of music interpretation across to your students without using negative words. The words *hold-back, pinch, tighten, spit, pucker, draw-in, press, strain,* and *tense-up* can result in poor playing habits. If the students are in a relaxed atmosphere and are self-confident, you have achieved a major victory over pressure-related problems.

The first step in analyzing the pressure problem is to be able to recognize related problems stemming from too much pressure. One or more of the following problems usually accompany the use of too much pressure.

Problem Signs in Brass Playing

Tenseness in the arm and left side of the neck will indicate that the student is using too much pressure. Many times if the student is using an excess of pressure, the throat will be closing. Often the throat tightness is a result of the tense muscles in the left arm and neck. This has some effect on the muscles in restricting the throat. The closing of the throat is usually accompanied by added vocal noises.

The pressure ring that does not fade readily is another indication of excess pressure. Most players have a pressure ring after they finish playing but this usually fades in a few minutes and is hardly noticeable. The student who uses too much pressure will have a noticeable pressure ring for hours, not just minutes.

Complaints of a tender or sore lip are usually a direct result of excessive pressure. Too much pressure can result in a bruising or near-bruising of the lip tissue. This condition may be accompanied by a swelling of the upper lip. This swelling will occur if the student plays an unusually long time with too much pressure.

The student tires quickly. With the beginning student there are several levels of embouchure-fatigue. This makes detection of this problem hard with the beginning student. If the student is "blown-out" in rehearsal with much less endurance than his classmates, he may be using too much pressure, an incorrect embouchure, or both.

A thin high register is a result of too much tension and mouthpiece pressure, stemming from poor breath support. This thinning occurs for trumpet/cornet students on *G* or *A* above the staff. One of these notes is usually the "cut-off point" for a drastic tone thinning. Any notes above this point sound strained and anemic.

Embouchure variation usually accompanies the pressure system of playing. For signs of change watch the chin and the corners of the lips very closely. The chin will move up against the mouthpiece and cramp the embouchure in most cases. If the corners of the lips pull back, the lips are drawn into a thin line, which produces a thin tone.

The Formula

The amount of pressure needed to play a brass instrument is indirectly proportional to the amount of air used to support a given tone. In other words, the more air intensity used, the less pressure needed to produce the same pitch. "Air" indicates the amount of air intensity available at the attack, not after the note is started. This does *not* mean that your students must play *fff* in the high register. By having the student start to think about air intensity or *air* pressure, he will not be as concerned about *mouthpiece* pressure. More air pressure is needed at the attack as the student plays higher. To gain enough "air intensity" the student must have good breath support. If the student uses too little air, he will immediately compensate with added mouthpiece pressure — tension — more pressure — which results in a thin sound in the upper register.

The Solution

Prevention is the best cure for too much pressure, early detection of the problem runs a close second. By checking the *Problem Signs* (see above) frequently, you can avoid many pressure-related problems. Do not dwell on the missing of notes and a negative approach to teaching. When a student misses a high note, *he knows it!* Stopping your rehearsal or class to state the obvious will not correct his mistake. If a student comes into your classroom using too much pressure, you will do more to help him with a positive approach of air-intensity and breath control exercises than any amount of screaming about too much pressure.

Try some of the following approaches with your students who are troubled with the high register or too much pressure.

Instead of "Pinch (tighten, smile, or roll) your lips together," try "Lock the corners of the lips and *support the high tones with air.*"

Instead of "Tongue (or spit) into the horn harder on the high notes," try "Start the notes in the high register with enough air to support your pitch."

Instead of "Use more (mouthpiece) pressure for the high notes," try "Support the notes with air (intensity) at the attack."

Other references to the need for air can be substituted with good results. "Blow through the horn," "Move the air faster," "Concentrate your air on the attacks," "Think about getting the air out of the bell not just into the mouthpiece" are just a few variations.

The exercises that will help your students have been used for years. All of the breath control exercises will help relieve the pressure problem. Explain to the student that he is not trying to win a world "note-holders" record, but that he is working for good *tone* and *support.* Scale work with breath accents will give the student the idea of air on the attack. Lip slurs will help only if the student supports each tone.

Every student starts with a good embouchure. It can last for five minutes, five days, or indefinitely. By explaining how to practice the assigned exercises, you will insure the development of a self-confident, relaxed, and accurate brass player.   ∎

1971

January, 1971

Contemporary Music for

Unaccompanied Trumpet

Steven Winick

Ever since tremendous forces were employed by Mahler in the *Eighth Symphony*, the so-called "Symphony of a Thousand," and by Stravinsky in *The Rite of Spring*, which uses a minimum of 110 players, there has been a general tendency toward a reduction in the size of the performing medium. Ultimately, this trend has resulted in the appearance of contemporary music for unaccompanied instruments. The unaccompanied solo has important advantages over the accompanied solo.

The performer benefits from the unaccompanied solo by becoming, more than ever before, fully aware of all aspects of his playing. Since he cannot rely on the accompaniment to help furnish melodic, rhythmic, and dynamic contrasts, he learns to provide them himself. He also improves his interpretive skills and learns to perform the subtleties of a work effectively without overdoing them.

These benefits can also be derived from good etude material. Many of the more recent French etudes for trumpet, such as those by Bitsch, Charlier, Chaynes, Sabarich, Tomasi, and those contained in volume three of the Leduc edition of the Arban method for trumpet, are musically interesting and challenging enough to make excellent unaccompanied solos. They require a good command of technique and an understanding of style and interpretation.

André Jolivet's *Air de bravoura* is one work which might very well be found in a book of French etudes. However, it is published separately, along with an optional piano accompaniment.

Another advantage of the unaccompanied solo is its successful use in orchestra and band auditions. In these situations, the accompanied solo cannot be fully appreciated because often the accompanist is sight-reading the part poorly, or he is not even available.

An unaccompanied solo is also useful in programing because of the variety it adds to recitals of accompa-

nied works.

An accompanist is essential to complete the musical sense of accompanied solos. Unfortunately, these solos are more often than not played and studied without an accompanist. Of course, the unaccompanied solo eliminates this problem.

Since the unaccompanied solo is a complete musical entity, it is an excellent means of teaching compositional form. For example, Randell Croley's *Variazioni* for solo trumpet *con sordino* can be used to illustrate variation form. The theme of the piece is based on the semi-tonal pentatonic scale with a chromatic ornamentation which pivots around the note *B*. Each of the six variations has a single mood and explores one idea: manipulation of a certain interval, quarter tones, or ornamental flourishes which are marked *rapido* and characterize much of Croley's music.

Intrada by Otto Ketting is another unaccompanied solo which provides an excellent example of studying form. The time-line in Figure 1 shows six ways in which the structure of this piece can be observed. There are no bar lines in the piece except for double bars which are represented on the time line by short, vertical lines. Number 1 at the left of the figure indicates the number of quarter note beats in each section. By assigning a horizontal unit to each quarter note, the relative length of each section can be shown. Number 2 lists the tempo and mood indications. The third way of looking at the piece is from the standpoint of macroform — A B A C A plus the coda. Number 4 shows the subdivisions of this large form. Number 5 represents dynamic highlights and is useful as an illustration of one of the most important principles of form — that of tension and relaxation. Number 6 is concerned with the growth and treatment of the triplet figure used in the piece. A close study of these aspects, both singly and in combination, can lead to an increased knowledge and appreciation of the form and meaning of this work.

Figure 1

Some Formal Aspects in Ketting's Intrada

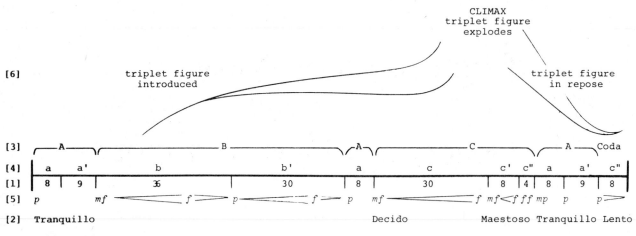

scale: 1/16th of an inch = one beat

Heinz Schröter's *Fanfarette* is cast in a *da capo* form. The melodic structure of the piece is based on the interval of a minor second. This interval is used economically and effectively to give the piece a series of constantly shifting tonal centers. Although rhythmically not very original, its cheerful, light-hearted character makes it a pleasant addition to any trumpeter's solo repertory.

A number of recent unaccompanied solos are valuable for developing a trumpeter's knowledge of contemporary techniques and effects as well as for their inherent musical worth.

Samuel Adler's *Canto #1* uses various transformations and permutations of a 12-tone set combinatorially, along with occasional repetitions of 3 or 4-note groups within a phrase. Some unusual effects employed include glissando, flutter-tongue, quarter tones, and striking the bell with the fingernails.

Equinoctial Points by this writer is based on the combination of a 12-tone set and references to *We Shall Overcome*, the unofficial hymn of the civil rights movement. This piece employs flutter-tongue, pedal tones, harmon mute, tremolo, and reverberative effects.

In John Rahn's *Counterpoints* the performer is required to use vibrato at a rate of six pulses to the beat, and to increase or decrease the rate of vibrato as a crescendo is made. One rhythmically interesting section calls on the soloist to accent every fifth note in a series of 16th notes, and every fourth note in a series of quintuplet 16th notes.

Barney Childs's *Interbalances IV* is an aleatoric work for solo trumpet and optional narrator. The performer is free to shape the total presentation as it unwinds in time. Certain sections in the trumpet part require the soloist to play pedal tones and tremolos, suck air in through the trumpet, open the water key while playing, and blow audibly through the instrument without producing any pitch.

The *Solo Piece for Trumpet* by Stefan Wolpe is built on tiny, cell-like structures which retain their basic identity through shifts of registers, rhythms, and dynamics. The phrases seem to grow out of one another, and the result is an accumulation of tensions which are never resolved. Wolpe, like Webern, is greatly concerned with the dramatic use of silence, which takes on as much importance as the sound itself.

Charles Whittenberg's *Polyphony* uses an all-combinatorial, 12-tone set which is partitioned in a cyclic manner so that dynamics, registers, and articulations are associated with particular segments of the set. Flutter-tongue, tremolo, and half-valve passages are employed.

These works represent only a fraction of an exciting, valuable, and constantly growing repertory for unaccompanied trumpet. The unaccompanied solo literature available for all instruments is really more extensive than most musicians realize. The study and performance of unaccompanied solos provides a unique and challenging musical experience which cannot be obtained from accompanied solos.

Contemporary Music For Unaccompanied Trumpet
A Selective List

Adler, Samuel. *Canto #1 Four Concert Etudes for Trumpet Solo.* (1970). Rochester, N. Y.: By the Composer, Eastman School of Music, 26 Gibbs Street. Duration 8 minutes.

Arnold, Malcolm. *Fantasy for Trumpet.* Op. 100. London: Faber Music Ltd., 1969. Duration 3 1/2 minutes.

Childs, Barney. *Interbalances IV for Trumpet and Optional Narrator.* Hattiesburg, Miss.: Tritone Press, 1962.

Croley, Randell. *Variazioni for Solo Trumpet.* Op. 44, No. 3. (1965). Hattiesburg, Miss.: Tritone Press, 1968. Duration 4 1/2 minutes.

Danburg, Russell. *Three Monologues for Solo Trumpet.* (1955). Gainesville, Fla.: By the Composer, 212 S.W. 43rd Terrace. Duration 5 minutes.

Davis, David. *Sonata for Trumpet.* (1960). Los Angeles, Calif.: By the Composer, 10501 Ashton Avenue. Duration 7 minutes

Henderson, Robert. *Variation Movements.* (1967). San Bernadino, Calif.: Roche-Thomas Music Co., 1970.

Jolivet, André. *Air de bravoure.* New York: International Music Co., 1954. Duration 1 1/2 minutes.

Ketting, Otto. *Intrada.* Amsterdam: Donemus, 1958. Duration 3 minutes.

Rahn, John. *Counterpoints for Solo Trumpet.* New York: Autograph Editions, 1970. Duration 1 minute.

Reinhardt, Bruno. *Music for Trumpet Solo.* Tel Aviv: Israeli Music Publications Ltd., 1965. Duration 5 minutes.

Schröter, Heinz. *Fanfarette pour Trompette seule.* Paris: Leduc, 1963. Duration 2 1/2 minutes.

Stein, Leon. *Sonata for Solo Trumpet.* New York: Composers Facsimile Edition, 1969. Duration 10 1/2 minutes.

Vačkář, Dalibor C. *Partita for Trumpet.* (1968). London: Ernst Eulenburg Ltd., 1969.

Whittenberg, Charles. *Polyphony for Trumpet.* (1965). New York: Josef Marx Music Co., 1970. Duration 7 minutes.

Winick, Steven. *Equinoctial Points for Solo Trumpet.* New York: Autograph Editions, 1970. Duration 3 minutes.

Wolpe, Stefan. *Solo Piece for Trumpet.* (1966). New York: Josef Marx Music Co., 1968. Duration 2 1/2 minutes.

Some Recent French Etudes
Suitable for Unaccompanied Trumpet Solos

Arban, Joseph J. B. L. *Célèbre méthode complete de trompette, cornet à pistons et saxhorn.* Edited by Jean Maire. Paris: Leduc, 1956.

Bitsch, Marcel. *Vingt études.* Paris: Leduc, 1954.

Charlier, Théo. *Trente-six études transcendantes.* Paris: Leduc, 1946.

Chaynes, Charles. *Quinze études.* Paris: Leduc, 1959.

Sabarich, Raymond, *Dix études.* Paris: Editions Selmer, 1954.

Tomasi, Henri. *Six études.* Paris: Leduc, 1955. ∎

Buying a New Trumpet

Harry Jenkins

So you are going to buy a new trumpet. Because of the expense involved, you have delayed, but now you are ready.

Which one shall it be? The model used by your favorite TV or recording star? A less expensive instrument which has made a favorable impression on you? Perhaps it will be a newer model of the one that has given you deep satisfaction over the years.

Why A New Instrument?

In most cases a player decides to buy a new trumpet because he feels that it will add to his playing.

To some extent, this decision implies dissatisfaction with the present instrument.

You may feel that one with a larger bore will help you produce that desired big symphonic sound. Or else you want a small bore that plays very easily and really "penetrates" for those long demanding engagements. Perhaps you want the new one to complement the old one: each to fill a specific need.

The Brand Name

There is little doubt that manufacturers of top brand name instruments have the most to offer . . .

but at higher prices, since research, experimentation and production costs are passed on to the customer.

The problem of choosing your ideal instrument is not solved simply by purchasing the most expensive model off the rack. A series of rigorous tests is in order.

Identical models vary considerably. No two players play exactly the same; no two instruments respond the same. The choice of instrument is a very personal one. What is "ideal" for player A will simply be "satisfactory" for player B and perhaps "unsuitable" for player C.

And that particular model used by your favorite artist? Are your needs commensurate with his? Do you do the same kind of work? If not, perhaps that manufacturer has another model more suitable for you.

For The Economy Minded

For those who cannot afford to buy the deluxe model, there is a wide choice of other models in the budget category. But take the time to do research and extensive testing.

Some manufacturers produce an economy line which is made in the same factory with the same craftsmanship and tools. The price is based on the special features (expensive case, first valve trigger, etc.) rather than that basic quality of the instrument.

Less well-known manufacturers sometimes put out instruments of excellent quality. Even the so-called "school" instrument put in the hands of a good player can sound amazingly "professional."

Intonation

We live in an imperfect world with imperfect people. No player plays perfectly in tune and no trumpet can be built with perfect intonation. However, we must try — with the best means at our disposal — to approach this perfection.

When testing the intonation of an instrument, first try the open notes.

Are all notes in tune, or are the higher notes so poor that they cannot possibly be "humored?"

On all trumpets these notes have a tendency to be flat.

When testing several instruments, here are some situations one is bound to run into:
Trumpet No. 1.

very flat   fairly good
Trumpet No. 2.

slightly flat   sharp
Trumpet No. 3.

very flat   fairly good

Trumpet No. 4.

slightly flat   sharp

My preference runs to the selection of trumpet No. 2 which has the slightly flat written D and a sharp F. The F is correctable by "lipping down" or adding a ring to the first slide, in an inexpensive trigger-like arrangement, to extend the slide. The G♭ on trumpet No. 4 can also be corrected by lipping down.

Quite often, a trumpet may combine the faults of, for example, trumpets No. 2 and No. 4 or trumpets No. 2 and No. 3.

I would definitely rule out trumpet No. 1 with the very flat D. The notes

are sharp, but this can be corrected by lengthening either the third or first valve slide.

Some trumpets come with an unusually long third valve slide, probably for the purpose of correcting these pitches. This creates problems for

An instrument built with a short third valve slide is preferable. (One can always *lengthen* the slide to correct certain notes, but those flattened because of the unusually long third slide, cannot be corrected).

Pre-Trial

The initial pre-trial occurs in the music store or factory where the player may choose from a group of trumpets, an instrument which presents the best possibilities for him.

In the pre-trial period you should watch out for several things.

1. Make sure that the tuning slide of each instrument is pulled an equal distance, so that the pitch of each is fairly uniform. In this way, you will not be unduly impressed by the alleged "brilliance" of an instrument — simply sharper in pitch because the slide happens to be in further than the others.

2. See to it that the mouthpiece fits snugly into the mouthpiece receiver. If it is loose, take a strip of paper and put it around the mouthpiece shank so it will hug

the receiver and make better contact with the instrument.

When trying the instrument: first play scales, arpeggios, octave jumps — both *piano and forte*. Questions: How does the instrument respond in general? Too hard? Are the high notes hard to reach? Does it respond too easily so you "go over" the required note? Is the low register free and open? tight and closed? or muddy?

Now play a long ballad. Questions: How are the intervals, especially the slurred ones? Does the instrument "sing?" Was the ballad particularly fatiguing? How was the intonation? What was the overall impression? Were you so pleased that you were reluctant to put the instrument down for an instant?

The Trial

A good instrument must project. Playing in an ensemble — a large one such as a symphony orchestra or large wind group with concert hall acoustics — will be an infallible check on this quality. A strenuous rehearsal with busy trumpet work will quickly bring out the strong or weak points of an instrument. The old instrument should be taken to the rehearsal as well, so that a comparison can be made.

In evaluating the new instrument, you should ask yourself the following questions: How much of an improvement is the new over the old? To what extent does it complement the present one? How well does it blend with the brass section in the *tutti* passages? How well does it speak in *pianissimo* passages as well as the *fortissimo*? How offensive are the out-of-tune notes? Are they correctable?

After the rehearsal, were your lips unusually tired and were you physically exhausted? Or were you generally in good shape in every way? Above all, were you enthusiastic about the instrument?

To summarize,

1. Do not make the final decision on a particular instrument based solely on the music store impression — the "pre-trial." Test it under actual playing conditions.

2. Be aware of the fact that so-called "identical" instruments can vary considerably. This is also true of prestigious brand names.

Try as many as you can.

3. Be philosophical about intonation and compromise on the instrument whose imperfect intonation *you* can correct.

4. Be concerned strictly with the instrument itself and not just the appearance and trimmings. Plating and engraving add little to its playing qualities.

5. Do not expect any new instrument to be a panacea for playing problems connected with embouchure or improper mouthpiece — problems that would exist regardless of the instrument used.

6. Narrow your "pre-trial" choice down to two or three instruments. Choose one and try it in ensemble.

If you have any doubts, try the other two before you make your final decision.

A new instrument is stimulating, motivating and exciting, especially when it fills a definite need. However, the choice must be a personal one. With practice and perseverance you will make it an ideal trumpet. ■

February, 1971

Tuba Recordings Might Make the Difference

R. Winston Morris

When Yuba Plays the Rumba on the Tuba is probably imbedded in the fibre of every tuba player in the country — but a lot of other pieces have been recorded since that early effort ("Bill Bell and His Tuba").

Band directors tell me about their problems with the tuba section. Recordings might make the difference.

Excellent recordings can be used in many ways — as a recruiting device, and later to provide a sample of the proper sound to be sought by beginners on the instrument. Directors can save time in the search for appropriate solos. Advanced players can get ideas for increasing their repertoire and improving their interpretation through extensive listening to recordings by fine players. A good record can even serve as a sort of "assistant teacher" for some students when contest/festival preparation time comes around. For these reasons, a complete library of recordings can be a valuable aid to the band or orchestra program. Students should be encouraged to build their own libraries as well.

Band directors frequently state that the biggest problem they have with the tuba section is how to interest students in the tuba as a music instrument in the first place. Good records can help, but the tuba has been one of the least-recorded instruments. The other brass instruments are featured in many recordings, thus most beginners start with a fairly accurate idea of how they should sound. This has not been the case with the tuba. Recently, however, many more good recordings have been made available for this instrument. After being exposed to excerpts from various albums, the potential student will be aware of the tremendous musical possibilities that the tuba offers, and the comic and "oompah" aspects of the instrument will fade to secondary importance.

Literature for the tuba has increased tremendously in the past decade. What better way of acquainting the director as well as the student with new works than through the use of recordings?

The first five albums — listed below in order of release — are solo tuba. The others are collections which include one or more works for the tuba. In addition to these albums, the tuba has had a prominent role in many jazz recordings by Bill Barber, Don Butterfield, Harvey Phillips, Red Callender, and others. Of course, all of the brass quintet recordings feature the tuba quite frequently.

Bill Bell and His Tuba, Golden Crest Records (CR 4027), Selections: When Yuba Plays the Rumba on the Tuba, Asleep in the Deep, In the Hall of the Mountain King, Tuba Man, The Elephant's Tango, Mummers, Carnival of Venice, Osis and Osiris Guide Them, Variations on the Theme of Judas Maccabeus, The Jolly Farmer Goes to Town.

Harvey Phillips — Tuba, Golden Crest Records (RE 7006), Sonata for Tuba and Piano — Alec Wilder, Air and Bourée — Bach-Bell, Andante from "Flute Sonata No. 9" — Handel, Gigue — A. Corelli, O Isis and Osiris — W. A. Mozart, Two Moods for Tuba — Donald Swann.

Tuba Solos — Rex Conner, National Contest List Recordings, Coronet Recording Co., Andante and Bouree — Handel, Menuet — Beethoven, Serenade — William Schmidt, Concert Piece No. 1 — Rodger Vaughan, Air and Bourrée — Bennie Beach, Suite for Tuba — Don Haddad, Concert Music for Bass Tuba — Florian Mueller, Lento — Paul Holmes, Suite for Unaccompanied Tuba — W. S. Hartley.

*Recital Music for the Tuba —
Peter Popiel,* Mark Educational
Recordings (MRS 28437), Air and
Bourree — Bach-Bell, Bourrée
from Sixth Flute Sonata — Handel-
Ostrander, "It is Enough" from
Elijah — Mendelssohn, Barcarolle
et Chanson Bachique — J. Semler-
Collery, Sonatina — W.S. Hart-
ley, Concerto in G Minor for Oboe
and Orchestra — Handel, Arioso —
Warren Benson, Suite for Unac-
companied Tuba — W.S. Hartley.

Roger Bobo, Tuba, Plays, Crystal
Record Co. (S 125), Sonata No.
5 — Galliard (*F* tuba), Sonata for
Basstuba and Piano — Hindemith,
Introduction and Dance — Barat
(*F* tuba), Encounters II — Wil-
liam Kraft, Effie the Elephant
Suite — Alec Wilder.

*John Barrows, Horn — Harvey
Phillips, Tuba,* Golden Crest Re-
cords (RE 7018), Sonata for French
Horn, Tuba and Piano — Alec
Wilder, Serenade No. 12 for Solo
Tuba — Persichetti.

*The Burke-Phillips All-Star Con-
cert Band,* Harvey Phillips —
Tuba, Golden Crest Records (CR
4040), The Elephant and the Fly —
H. Kling.

All-Star Concert Band, Harvey
Phillips — Tuba, Golden Crest
Records (CR 4025), Carioca —
Norman-Youmans.

Ithaca High School Band, Harvey
Phillips — Tuba, Golden Crest
Records (CR 6001), Helix — War-
ren Benson.

"Music for Young Bands" — Vol-
ume II, Peter Popiel — Tuba,
Kendor Music Inc., A Touch of
Tuba — Art Dedrick.

*Music of Morton Feldman and
Earle Brown,* Don Butterfield —
Tuba, Time Records Inc. (58007 —
stereo 8007), Durations III for
Violin, muted Tuba and Piano —
Morton Feldman.

Waukegan Grade School Band,
1969 Midwest National Band and
Orchestra Clinic, Rex Conner —
Tuba, Silver Crest Records (Gold-
en Crest Records), Fantasis di Concerto — Kent-Akers.

Tubby the Tuba (various recordings) as listed in the Schwann Long
Playing Record Catalog (Supplementary).   ■

April, 1971

Lip Vibration Characteristics
of the Trombone Embouchure in Performance

Lloyd Leno

In the last decade the physical
aspects of brass playing have been
the subject of serious investigation
by brass teachers and performers.
Studies by Fay Hanson (1968),
Joseph Meidt (1967) and John
Haynie (Tetzlaff, 1969) have provided us with photographic information concerning the function of
the jaw, tongue, throat, and breathing apparatus during performance. Unfortunately, no comparable study of the lips during performance has been available. Several investigations of lip action
under *simulated* performance conditions have been made. Dr. P. H.
Damste of the University of Ut-
recht compared the lips of a trombonist with the vocal chords by
high-speed photography of a single
player on three pitches using a

plastic mouthpiece in the shape
of a right angle prism (1966). Perhaps the most significant investigation was conducted by Robert
Weast (1963) using "square" plastic mouthpieces. The lips were observed, but not photographed,
through a stroboscopic disc as the
players produced tones on the
various brass instruments. A na-
tion-wide survey of brass teachers by Richtmeyer revealed that
"the incidence of abnormal embouchures among brass students of
college age was quite high" and he
concluded that "faulty teaching
techniques are primarily to blame
for the great majority of incorrectly developed embouchures" (Richtmeyer, 1966, pp. 157- 158).

Any attempt to develop sound
teaching procedures inevitably

must deal with problems which are
concerned with (1) the relationship
of lip vibration frequency to pitch;
(2) the relationship of the upper
lip to the lower lip; and (3) the
relationship of pitch and volume to
the aperture size. The purpose of
this research was to study these
basic vibrational characteristics
of the trombone embouchure. Four
successful trombonists, two amateur and two professional players,
were used as subjects for study.
Under carefully controlled performance conditions each subject
was photographed through a transparent mouthpiece with interior
dimensions copied from an existing performance mouthpiece. The
outer contour was designed to keep
the walls of the cup uniform in
thickness, providing for maximum

visibility and reducing distortion to a minimum. A special spray was used to prevent moisture from clouding the mouthpiece. The photography was done with two high-speed motion analysis cameras which photographed the embouchure at speeds of from 600 to 900 frames per second. Sustained tones, pitch changes and crescendo were included in the performance tasks.

Lip Vibration, General Nature

Projecting the 16 mm film at 16 frames per second provides a view of the lips moving at approximately 1/40 normal speed making detailed analysis possible. One is immediately aware that he is witnessing a vibrational motion unique in the production of sound. It is a type of motion that cannot be described. To use a well-worn phrase, it must be seen. It is a rather complex pattern that cannot be compared to double reeds or vibrating strings. Figure 1 shows two views (each by a different camera) of the lips going through various phases of the vibrating cycle. It will be noted that the lips begin the vibration cycle from a closed position drawn together by muscular contraction. Even for the lower pitches the lips are turned in somewhat, pulled toward the teeth, and this contraction intensifies with ascending pitches. The lips are blown apart by the force of the air and when they have reached the point of maximum stress they are pulled back together completing the cycle.

The lips part along the entire length of the opening established for a given pitch and for the higher pitches this vertical opening remains approximately the same size across the horizontal width of the aperture. However, during the production of the middle and lower pitches at high volume the center of the upper lip engaged in a whip-like motion in its vertical movement causing the center to open farther and close last. The front view of the subject in Figure 1 shows the center of the upper lip *opening* last; this did not occur with the other subjects.

The velocity of the lips was greatest at the beginning of the vibrating cycle, just as the lips were blown apart.

Fig. 1 Lips in various phases of the vibration cycle (B♭ 116.5)

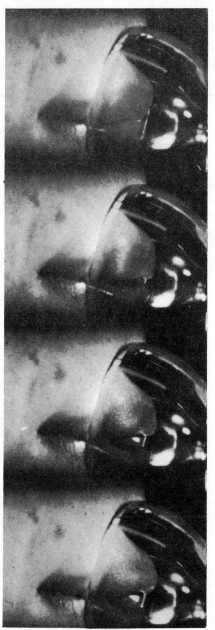

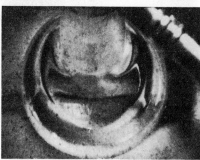
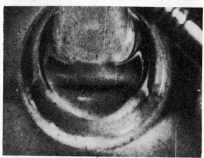
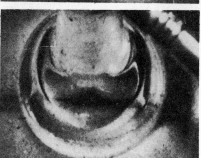

Lip Vibration, Frequency and Pitch

A definite and consistent relationship was found between the frequency of lip vibration and the pitch produced; with all subjects the vibration of the lips at a given frequency resulted in a pitch of the same frequency. While the counting of the vibrations was done over a longer period of time, the short film strips included here clearly show this relationship. The white oblong timing dots on the edge of the border of the film were automatically recorded as the film was exposed and were spaced at intervals of 1/100 of a second. Note in Figure 2 that for B♭ 116.5 the lips

went through a complete cycle just before the second dot appeared; this indicates a frequency of slightly over 100 cycles per second. Figure 3 shows another subject playing F 174.6 where it can be observed that the lips do not quite complete two cycles. This verifies a frequency of near 200 cycles per second. Lip vibration frequencies of five pitches (B♭ 116.5, F 174.6, F 349.2 and B♭ 466.2) were counted on each of the four subjects.

Lip Relationship, Upper and Lower

Distinct patterns of lip function and interaction were observed in all subjects. A significant discovery

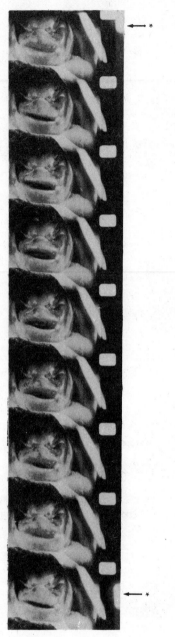

Fig. 2 B♭ 116.5   Fig. 3 F 174.6

* timing dot

was that the subjects represented two types of embouchures. In three of the subjects the air stream was directed below the mouthpiece throat, striking the lower side of the mouthpiece cup. The fourth subject consistently directed the air stream *above* the mouthpiece throat. These types are here referred to as *downstream* and *upstream* respectively. It should be noted that as here defined, the lip alignment within the mouthpiece, not the angle the instrument forms with the player's jaw, determines the type of embouchure.

It is interesting to note that the subject exhibiting the up-stream embouchure had a slightly more receding jaw than the other subjects (Figure 4). It may be that other factors such as length and texture of the lips were a deciding factor in the formation of this type of embouchure.

The down-stream types had the following characteristics: (1) a high mouthpiece placement (more than one half upper lip in the mouthpiece); (2) overlaps of upper lip over lower lip, especially in the upper register; (3) downward di-

rection of the air stream; (4) an increased amount of lower lip employed for the lower register; and (5) more active and complex vibration of the upper lip. These relationships were reversed for the up-stream type embouchure with one exception — there was no apparent overlap of the lower lip over the upper. It was also observed that in all the embouchures the air stream was directed closer to the mouthpiece throat on the lowest pitch and with ascending pitch the air stream was directed farther from the throat and against the side of the mouthpiece cup, *down* for the down-stream types and *up* for the up-stream type. Figures 5, 6, 7, and 8 show the lip alignment of the subjects in the different registers.

The photographic sequences of subject III performing an octave change revealed a shift or pivot. This was not a tilt of the instrument but a movement of the mouthpiece downward, as the pitch was descending, so that the amount of upper lip in the mouthpiece decreased while the amount of the lower lip increased. The up-stream subject exhibited a similar pivot although it was less pronounced. Like the other reverse relationships this shift or pivot was upward for descending pitch.

Figure 9 shows the shape of the lower lip of the up-stream subject playing B♭ 116.5. Compare this with the upper lip of the down-stream subject in Figures 1 and 2. The most active lip in each case opens more in the center and is drawn to a point.

While it was not the purpose of this research, nor of this article, to make a detailed study of the pivot action, a comment on the pivot

Fig. 4 Natural jaw alignment of subjects. Upstream subject is lower right.

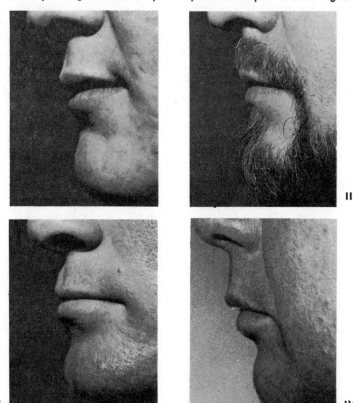

I

II

III

IV

system seems in order here. I have heard and read statements concerning the use of the pivot system as taught by Donald Reinhardt that

are misleading because they are incomplete and inaccurate. It seems quite obvious that those who define the word *pivot* simply as tilt-

Lip alignment of downstream embouchures

Fig. 5 High register B♭ 466.2

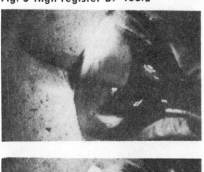

Fig. 6 Low register B♭ 116.5

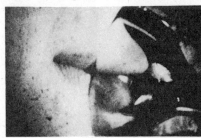
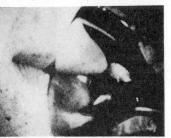

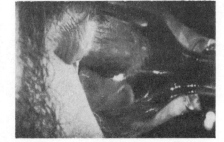

Lip alignment of upstream embouchure
Fig. 7 High register B♭ 466.2

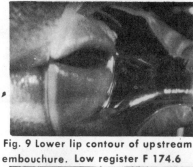

Fig. 8 Low register B♭ 116.5

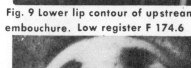

Fig. 9 Lower lip contour of upstream embouchure. Low register F 174.6

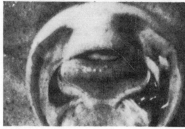

ing the instrument to transfer mouthpiece pressure from one lip to another, have not read Dr. Reinhardt's *The Encyclopedia of the Pivot System*. This book, published 22 years after his book *Pivot System,* contains a more complete explanation of what happens when a player changes registers. To quote Dr. Reinhardt, "Primarily the pivot is intended to pull or push (as the case may be) the players' lips into the path of the air column, so that the required lip vibrations for the production of sound are not hampered or impeded in any particular part of the range." He also states that "in the early stages of the pivot development, some angular motion of the instrument is often prescribed" but adds that "all exaggerated movements soon subside until they are negligible." (Reinhardt, 1964, pp. 193, 198).

In all subjects the movement of the two lips was always regular and no difference in vibration frequency could be observed. The only difference between the lips was that for the down-stream players the upper lip showed more vertical movement than the lower. In the up-stream player the upper lip was slightly more active in the upper range while in the lower range the lower lip was more active.

Lip Aperture Changes

The aperture varied in horizontal width as well as in the vertical opening with changes of pitch and volume. In all subjects the horizontal width of the aperture, as well as the vertical opening, increased as the pitch descended. The embouchure dissimilarity with vibrating strings was manifested in two ways. First, none of the players demonstrated a 1:2 relationship of horizontal width (length) of vibrating area for the change to an octave lower. Instead, the approximate ratio ranged between 1:1 and 1:1.8. Second, there was a change in vertical mass (the amount of lip area in a vertical direction) involved in vibration. For the highest pitch

(B^b 466.2), only a small area of the red portion of the lips was involved. As the pitch descended, the vibrating area spread vertically. After the change to an octave lower, there appeared to be at least twice the amount of vertical mass vibrating. The reduction in vertical mass for higher pitches was apparently achieved by a turning inward of the red portion of the lips. Figure 10 shows a comparison of apertures during the production of octaves with the volume constant. (Volume levels were verified by a Conn *Dynalevel.*)

In all subjects an increase in volume produced a corresponding increase in size of the aperture, both horizontally and vertically. The change in vertical mass which also occurred with change in volume was smaller than that which resulted from a change in pitch. Figure 11 shows examples of the embouchures at the beginning and at the end of a crescendo. No attempt was made at controlling volume levels for this musical task.

Fig. 10 Aperture size and pitch: octave relationships

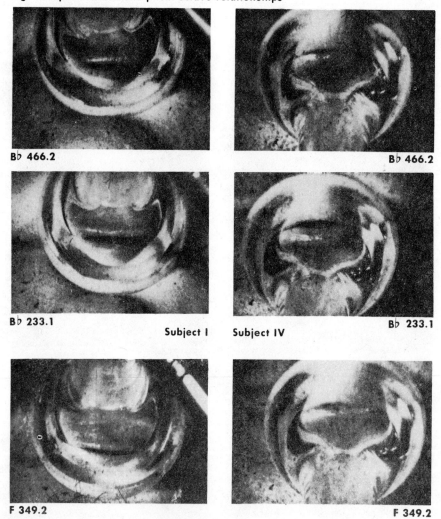

B♭ 466.2

B♭ 466.2

B♭ 233.1

Subject I   Subject IV

B♭ 233.1

F 349.2

F 349.2

Conclusions

Even though this research represents the first known photographic study of the lips of a brass player under controlled performance conditions, it must be admitted that after a study of only four subjects, conclusions must be made with caution. Nevertheless, this study does remove some speculation and doubt that has existed in certain areas. Based on the findings of this research, the following conclusions seem warranted:

1. The action of the lips is a complex one which does not invite close comparison to double reeds or vibrating strings. The vibrating lips are a unique generator of sound.

2. The knowledge that lips vibrate at the frequency of the pitch produced gives added support to the belief that buzzing the lips with and without the mouthpiece can be a helpful supplementary exercise.

3. There are at least two basic types of embouchures, classified by the direction of the air stream. It was found that jaw alignment was *not* decisive in determining embouchure type. Therefore, it would be a serious mistake for all players to use the same mouthpiece position and to attempt to direct the air stream at the same angle.

4. The findings concerning lip relationships suggest that for the down-stream types the upper lip may, in a sense, be considered the primary vibrator and that the lower lip assumes this function in up-stream types. However, inasmuch as the findings also show that in both embouchure types the lips vibrate at the same frequency and that the lip action as a whole is a very complex one, there is danger in making any statement which would oversimplify lip function.

5. Producing a tone on a brass instrument for the first time is often difficult to achieve and the explanation of this procedure can help or hinder. The position of the lips at the beginning of the vibration cycle, as observed in this study, suggests that the instructions found in some method books are inadequate and misleading. Perhaps such time-honored expressions as "spitting" and "humming" should be eliminated from the teaching vocabulary. Photographs illustrating lip position

could be substituted.

6. Because a change in pitch involves both a change in aperture width and vertical mass, teaching procedures should include exercises designed to promote the development of these adjustments.

7. It appears that as a part of the vibration cycle, complete closure of the lips is required for best tone quality. One cause of breathy tone quality and indistinct attacks might be incomplete aperture closure.

It seems obvious that more research of this type is needed to study more thoroughly the various embouchure types, pivots and abnormalities. ∎

This research was conducted under the direction of Lloyd Weldy of the University of Arizona (now of Artley West). The cameras were loaned by

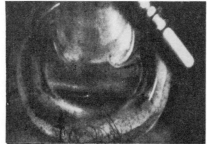

F 174.6

Subject III   Subject IV   F 174.6

Fig. 11 Aperture size and volume: crescendo

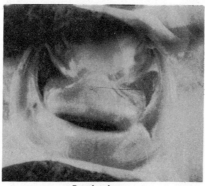
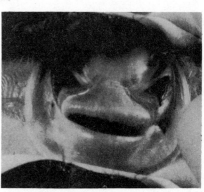

Beginning   **End**

Subject III B♭ 116.5

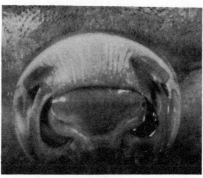
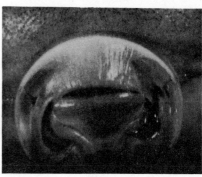

Beginning   **End**

Subject IV B♭ 233.1

the Electrical Engineering Department and the Aero Space Division of the University.

REFERENCES

Damste, P. H. "Les Vibrations Des Cordes Vocales Comparees Aux Vibrations Des Levres D'un Tromboniste," **Journal Francais-d'ot Rhino-Laryngologie,** IV:4, 1966, 395-96.

Hanson, Fay. **Brass Playing Mechanism and Technique.** New York: Carl Fischer, Inc., 1968.

Meidt, Joseph Alexis. " A Cinefluorographic Investigation of Oral Adjustments for Various Aspects of Brass Instrument Performance." Unpublished Ph. D. Dissertation, University of Iowa, 1967.

Reinhardt, Donald S. **The Encyclopedia of the Pivot System.** New York: Charles Colin, 1964.

Richtmeyer, Lorin Carol. "A Definitive Analysis of Brass Embouchure Abnormalities Including Recommended Remedial Techniques." Unpublished Ph. D. Thesis, Michigan State University. 1966.

Tetzlaff, Daniel. "The Transparent Man," **The Instrumentalist,** XXIII, No. 8 March 1969, 81.

Weast, Robert D. **Brass Performance.** New York: McGinnis & Marx, 1961.

Daily Warm-ups
for the Young Horn Student

Julius Erlenbach

Warm-up exercises are to the brass player what calisthenics are to the athlete — they help his muscles limber up for the physical activity which will follow. Without these special exercises that are executed as a daily ritual at the beginning of the playing period, he will certainly not play his best and he might damage the delicately-toned muscles involved. Professional musicians and advanced students know this. However, all too frequently the young student is forgotten. More often than not he will simply play a scale, because that is all his teacher has him do. And not to place all blame upon the teacher, there is an astonishing lack of good warm-up material in most beginning and intermediate-level method books.

Even for the young student the warm-up should serve the same basic six-fold function as for the professional: (1) it literally "wakes up" the embouchure for the playing activities of the day, (2) it helps to develop the playing range, (3) it aids in developing flexibility, (4) it assists the quality and accuracy of articulation, (5) it explores the dynamic range, and (6) it helps in the development of a desirable tone quality. With the daily use of a good warm-up by the young student it is possible to solve many playing problems early, sometimes even before they develop. In addition, we all know of instances when students complain that they do not have enough time to practice. Warm-ups need take only about ten minutes, thus there is no excuse, and at least the embouchure condition can be maintained through this minimum attention.

The following is a series of warm-ups designed for the young horn student. In all probability the student will need at least a year's experience before being able to execute these exercises with much facility. The metronome markings are to be taken as minimums — where greater speed is desired it is so indicated. Each warm-up exercise is designated by those functions it is intended to serve.

Hopefully, these warm-ups will provide a sound stepping stone for the technical and tonal development of the young horn student.

"Wake Up!", Tone ♩ = 66   or slower if desired.

1. Perform this warm-up first slurred and then tongued.
2. Begin as written (open horn). Now play it beginning on B (2nd valve), ½ step lower than written. Now begin on B♭ (1st valve) one step lower than written. Play it on A (1st and 2nd valves) now. Finally play it on A♭ (2nd and 3rd valves).
3. Breathe where and when you must.

Articulation, Tone, Low Range, and Dynamics

1. Play this exercise first slurred and with dynamics as indicated. Now play it tongued with dynamics reversed as indicated by the parenthesis.
2. Use fingerings as indicated.
3. Again, breathe when and where it is necessary.

Flexibility and Articulation

1. Play this exercise slurred and then tongued.
2. Play it as quickly and accurately as possible.
3. Now try it in other keys.

Flexibility, Articulation, and Dynamics

1. Play this warm-up first slurred and then tongued.
2. Speed is important here.
3. Gradually crescendo throughout. Now try it with a gradual decrescendo.
4. Try the exercise in different keys.
5. Breathe when necessary.

Upper Range Development

1. Practice as in Warm-up #1: first as written (open horn), then ½ step lower on 2nd valve, 1 step lower on 1st valve, etc.
2. Play the exercise at a comfortable dynamic level.
3. When the upper register becomes more highly developed option (B) may be used.

Lower Range Development

1. The exercise is written in the F clef to eliminate the necessity of numerous ledger lines.
2. Observe the suggested fingerings.
3. Play the warm-up with the best tone quality possible.

June, 1971

Cornets . . . Please! ! !

Mario F. Oneglia

Why a "dyed-in-the-wool" performer of that noble brass instrument, the trumpet, should be making this impassioned plea for greater use of the cornet, at this late date, should, perhaps give music educators and parents cause for reconsidering the "cornet vs. trumpet" controversy. I was prompted to write this article in an effort to aid students of the cup-shaped soprano of the brass family — be it cornet or trumpet — in building better foundations for performance. I feel strongly that many of the embouchure problems encountered in students' playing habits were formed rather early in their playing careers, and that a more thoughtful choice of the first instrument might have been highly beneficial in many cases. It will be advantageous for band directors, particularly those teachers who concern themselves with motivating and starting beginning players at the elementary school level, to reexamine their thinking about whether the proper instrument for youngsters is the cornet or trumpet. The recommendations of these people have a great deal to do with which instrument is rented or purchased by parents.

History

The modern trumpet and cornet have little in common with the earlier brass instruments. They both differ as to length and bore proportions. Really, the only thing they have in common with each other and their predecessors is that they are both played by vibrating the lip (reed) across a cup-shaped mouthpiece. The *cornetto*, *cornett*, or *zink* of the renaissance and early baroque periods was a wooden instrument with finger holes drilled in its body. This instrument bears no relationship to the cornet of modern times other than that the lips were vibrated across a mouthpiece carved of bone, wood, or ivory. That important element of brass playing, the harmonic series, was not used to any degree; and since the acoustical relationship of the holes and the wind column were comparable to present woodwind instruments, the tone quality of the cornetto was flute-like, and its volume soft.

The ancient trumpets, on the other hand, utilized the harmonic series, particularly the upper partials. This is evident from an examination of renaissance and baroque music. The melodies for trumpet are in a lofty tessitura where the overtone series becomes diatonic and chromatic.

With the invention of the piston valve in the early 19th century, several changes came about in the brass instruments and their uses in the orchestra. Perhaps it was because of the artistic aesthetic of the classic period which demanded restraint, that the upper register of the trumpet fell largely into disuse. The length of the instrument was shortened, and its use in the orchestra changed a a good deal. No longer a virtuoso

solo instrument, it was used mainly by classic composers for supporting the string group, emphasizing cadences, and occasionally for a martial effect. An example of this latter type of usage may be heard in Beethoven's *Leonora Overture No. 3*. The valve gave the trumpet greater flexibility by permitting it to play in many different keys without the insertion of additional tube lengths, called *crooks*. This became important for the composer as chromaticism in orchestral music increased.

At about this same time in the early 19th century, an instrument known as the *cornocopean* emerged. The invention of this valved brass instrument with a basically conical bore has been attributed to the Belgian inventor Charles Sax, father of Adolph Sax, the inventor of the saxophone. The cornocopean, a relative of the French horn because of its conical bore, soon found favor in the public ear for the mellow, lyrical qualities of its tone. This instrument, the cornocopean, of a two-thirds conical bore and one-third cylindrical bore should be conidered as the ancestor of the present-day cornet. The trumpet and the cornet differ as to tonal qualities because the bore proportions of the trumpet are reversed; it is two-thirds cylindrical and one-third conical. Because of this, perhaps, various musicologists and writers of treatises on orchestration have described the tone of the trumpet as heroic, martial, strident, and harsh. In addition to these stated differences as to tone and orchestral role, the cornet and trumpet differed in an obvious detail—the cornet was rolled up into a more compact form than the trumpet.

Napoleon to Louis

With the popularity of the military band of Napoleon Bonaparte, the cornet became the favored soprano brass instrument. It retained this position up until the 20th century, with such virtuosi as Arban, Herbert L. Clarke, and James Burke exploiting its expressive qualities. How then did the tide shift away from the cornet to the trumpet in recent years? It is my opinion that the greater communication brought about by

our mass media played a large part in this. Radio, recordings, and television have all played roles in shaping concepts and desires.

In the 1930's, the famed jazz cornetist, Louis Armstrong abandoned his cornet for the longer trumpet. Just why he did this has not been ascertained, since he started in music as a boy playing the cornet in a brass band. Mr. Armstrong's change of instruments was soon emulated by most popular cornet players, and by 1940, the cornet had all but become obsolete. The exceptions were the school band and the few remaining professional concert bands which still tended to use cornets either because they were owned by the school or were preferred by the conductor for their particular tonal qualities.

Complete Trumpet Domination

In most concert band music, parts are scored for five soprano brass instruments. The three cornet parts are assigned the dominant melodic passages and are supported by the two trumpet parts. The trumpet is also responsible for flourishes and calls because its tonal qualities are well suited for this function. Since we have had almost two generations of band directors following the shift from the cornet to the trumpet in the thirties, I would like to suggest that because of the indiscriminate mixing of either the trumpet or the cornet to play soprano parts in some bands, the whole tonal compass of the concert band has changed—and, perhaps, not for the better! The trumpet has been in the public eye and ear for so many years that students, parents, band directors and music educators in general, sometimes forget the values of the cornet. Such fine players as Harry James, Al Hirt, Doc Severinsen, Dizzy Gillespie, and Armando Ghitalla of the Boston Symphony inadvertently have furthered the movement away from the cornet by the artistry of their performances. It might be of interest to know that most of these soloists started as cornet players!

Begin on the Cornet

As a college instructor of trumpet, I have seen embouchure defects which I believe could have been avoided if the student had been started on cornet instead of trumpet.

First, let's review some fundamentals which apply to both the trumpet and cornet.

1. Hold with the left hand, with fingers gripping the valve casings *very* lightly.

2. The instrument should be horizontal with the floor, allowing the jaw, and consequently the teeth and lips, to be in a balanced relationship. The jaw, while not in a jutting or overbite position, needs to be in its forward position. The teeth should be aligned, with the lower teeth separated from the upper teeth by one-quarter to one-half inch. The lips should be touching slightly, without excess muscle pressure, so that air passing between them will send them into vibration.

The relationship of the jaw, teeth, lips, and breath is very crucial. When incorrect habits have been a part of the beginning student's playing, it has been shown that it is extremely difficult to overcome them.

The trend seems to be for elementary school children to begin the study of band and orchestra instruments in fourth or fifth grades, and sometimes earlier. The purely physical aspects of holding the instrument at this age can present difficulties. The weight of the trumpet causes a great many embouchure problems to the nine or ten year old student. It is simply too heavy to be supported horizontally, but more important, it is too long and consequently difficult to balance, even for a short four measure phrase. In spite of the exhortations of the music teacher, to "hold your horn up," the child, who is not able to do so, simply proceeds to a playing posture which, though proper for the playing of the clarinet, is completely wrong for performing acceptably on the trumpet or cornet. In addition to this, the grip of both the left and right hands becomes cramped and tends to pull the instrument into the lips in an effort to support the trumpet. This leads to poor playing habits, wherein reliance is mistakenly placed upon adding arm pressure toward the lips for playing different registers. Lip bruises, cuts, and in some cases, scars may be a result of this "strong arm" style of playing. The right hand tends also to be used as a supporting vehicle, and never develops the necessary relaxed poise which will insure technical facility.

When a youngster is started with a cornet instead of a trumpet, the hands tend to be closer to the body because of the more compact shape of the cornet. Thus, the arms themselves assist in support of the instrument. There is less strain on the wrists, arms, hands, fingers, and lips. The instructor will still need to correct postural habits, but now it will be easier for the student to comply. This is turn will allow him to develop a sound, balanced embouchure in a shorter time span.

Band directors will also be gladdened by these young cornetists feeding into the high school concert bands, since once the dark, mellow, lyric quality of the cornet is heard in the cornet section, and its lyricism exploited throughout its register and tonal compass, few conductors will wish to return to the indiscriminate mixing of cornet and trumpet tone in the color spectrum of the band. This is why I say, "Cornets...Please!!!" ∎

September, 1971

The Sackbut in the School

John R. Shoemaker

The continued success of the New York Pro Musica, the establishment of ensembles of professionals devoted to the performance of renaissance and baroque music for a livelihood, the apparent fascination of the general public with all kinds of things which are "old," the use of lutes, recorders, et al. by pop music groups, and the sound of ancient instruments on radio and television commercials, all indicate a significant rebirth in the interest of the general populace toward *compositions* from renaissance and baroque and the *sounds* created by instruments indigenous to those periods in history. Musicologists have long contemplated the sound of a composition as it was originally performed, and their persistent inquiry, along with the natural interest of instrumentalists, has led to the discovery, reconstruction, and manufacture of replicas of many instruments commonly used four centuries ago.

The reappearance of the sackbut as a viable performing instrument is due to the desire for an accurate re-creation of the technical milieu surrounding the performance of works which originally took place within another culture. Although the etymology for its name is rather uncertain, the term *sackbut* will be used when referring to the replica of the ancient instrument, and *trombone* for the instrument in normal use today.

Paintings and written documents indicate that the ancient sackbut was in use as early as the 15th century and enjoyed great popularity until approximately the middle of the 18th century. Its construction resembled that of an emaciated trombone and was available in a variety of lengths with the fundamental pitches of *Bb, C, Eb,* and *F* among the most common. The complete family included a tenor, alto, bass, and soprano — the latter being introduced near the end of the 17th century but never gaining the acceptance accorded the others. A cursory comparison of the ancient sackbut and trombone reveals that only minor visible changes have been made over the past 500 years. More stays, a water-key, and slide receiver springs have been added, and the bore and terminal bell flare enlarged. The mouthpiece, however, has been changed in almost every dimension; numerous technical adjustments of a less obvious nature have been made on the instrument.

Suave, clear, and mellow are some of the adjectives which have been used to describe the tone quality of the ancient sackbut. The volume of sound is small when compared to the trombone, enabling it to blend well with strings, voices, and recorders on a one-to-one basis. Small bore size, reduced bell diameter, and thicker metal account for this quality and volume — desirable attributes when considering the fact that the principle place of performance was in the church. Most other uses for ancient sackbuts were functional — tower music, ceremonial performances, and accompanimental music for stage plays or for soloists.

First Replicas

It was not until 1953, during the sixth Heinrich Schütz Festival in Herford, Germany, that the first steps were taken which led to the manufacturing of replicas of the ancient sackbut and to their availability at a reasonable price. Several 18th century sackbuts were obtained from a collection of ancient instruments in Greifensee bei Zurich and used in the performance of Schütz's *Psalm 136* as it had been orchestrated by the composer — the low choir using three sackbuts and one alto voice. This experiment laid the groundwork for development of suitable replicas of sackbuts. The resulting instruments were not exact copies of the original models, but modified to the extent of pitch (*Bb* instead of *C*), adding water-keys, slide springs, and solid stays. The sound produced by the "new" instruments was as close as possible to that of the ancient sackbut.

As these replicas became available through the efforts of German manufacturers such as Helmut Finke and Wilhelm Monke, in-

F alto (left) and Bb soprano (right)

terest in performance upon them increased at the professional, college, and avocational levels. Noah Greenberg, for example, formed the Pro Musica in 1958, and since that time has produced many recordings which include sackbuts along with other instruments commonly used during the renaissance and baroque periods. It would be a gross understatement of the facts to indicate that this ensemble has merely "influenced" the amateur, the educator, and the professional musician. Early music societies have sprung up throughout the country — especially in the large urban areas such as New York, St. Louis, and Chicago, to name but a few. Colleges and universities have established *collegium musicum* ensembles and have acquired a variety of replicas of ancient keyboard, wind, and string instruments.

Some of these ancient instruments are readily adaptable to performance by student instrumentalists; others prove to be considerably more complex. The instrument most compatible to the contemporary brass instrumentalist is the sackbut. It is available in several pitches and

theoretically can be played by the trombonist with little difficulty. Acquisition of a *Bb* soprano, an *F* alto, a *Bb* tenor, and a tenor with *F* attachment provides sufficient instrumentation for a variety of renaissance and baroque wind literature, e.g., selected works of Josquin, Gabrieli, Guami, Buonamente, and Reiche, among others.

A close look at the Finke #540 tenor sackbut will show that its bore is considerably smaller than that of the familiar Conn 8H, ca. .430" vis a vis .547"; the diameter of the bell, ca. 4" vis a vis 8½": the thickness of the metal, ca. .012" vis a vis .020" in the body of the bell portion of the instrument and ca. .032" vis a vis ca. .020" at the terminal flare of the bell. The mouthpiece is smaller in all dimensions and has a different shank taper than the Morse taper #1 (.050" per inch) used by American manufacturers — thereby prohibiting convenient substitution of other mouthpieces.

Performance problems on the *Bb* sackbut are multiplied rather than mitigated by a slide action which is less refined than one would expect and an overtone series which is out-of-tune within itself to an astonishing degree. Fortunately, spring stops in the slide receiver are standard, making possible adjustments in first position tones. These mechanical and acoustical problems present the contemporary performer with a new set of exigencies unknown to the user of currently manufactured "standard" trombones. In actual practice, an acceptable performance is dependent upon the ability of the performer to overcome these problems.

The *F* alto and *Bb* soprano instruments are plagued by problems created by their unique size, in addition to those mentioned above. The alto has a slide which is 17 7/8" in length, about 10" shorter than the standard *Bb* trombone, proportionally shortening each slide position. Its mouthpiece size is somewhere between that of the *Bb* tenor trombone and *Bb* trumpet — approximately that of the *Eb* alto horn. The tone quality of this instrument is simply ethereal — much lighter than that of the tenor and very clear without being harsh. The *Bb* soprano has the same range as a modern *Bb* trumpet, is fitted with a slide rather than with valves, and sounds more like its modern counterpart than do the other

sackbuts. This can be attributed to the relationships of bore and bell diameter to total length. Discovering persons capable of performing upon either the alto or soprano is an art in itself — the trumpet performer having the embouchure but lacking the slide technique, the trombonist having the slide technique but not the embouchure. The University of Hawaii Sackbut Quartet utilizes a trumpet major for the *Bb* soprano instrument, and trombone majors for the other instruments. The trombonist with the highest range normally performs upon the *F* alto instrument. The smaller mouthpiece admittedly presents an embouchure problem for that particular performer, but this arrangement has proven to be the best answer for the problem to date. A completely satisfactory solution is yet to be devised.

In attempting to overcome some of those problems, the following steps may be taken: (1) Utilize a modern mouthpiece with a rim size which is as near as possible to the rim size used by the performer on his personal instrument, but with a small cup volume and throat diameter to help match the small bore and bell: (2) Turn the shank of the mouthpiece to

fit the sackbut receiver tube. (An alternative would be to ream the sackbut receiver tube with a Morse #1 tapered reamer so that it will accept a standard mouthpiece. Mouthpiece turning and receiver reaming must be done by an expert repairman — preferably one who understands the acoustical implications involved.)

Although the aforementioned problems must be overcome, the use of the sackbut within the school instrumental music department opens a whole new world for those who participate: the literature available for performance is broadened considerably; the music itself is immediately perceived in a new light; interest is heightened in historical connotations of performance practices; a new awareness concerning the study of music history during the renaissance and baroque develops through the music; and opportunities for performance are provided with collegium and adult groups, in lecture demonstrations, and as part of formal brass concerts. Certainly, the availability of ancient instruments, particularly the sackbut, deserves serious consideration as a medium for broadening the scope of the entire school music program. ■

Tonguing

Julius Erlenbach

Correct tonguing is of paramount importance to any brass player. Poor tonguing may result in sloppy articulation, inaccurate initial pitch, and possibly, inferior tone quality. This article offers some suggestions to aid the tonguing of young brass players.

The placement of the tongue in the mouth is of prime consideration. Often young players get into the habit of tonguing between the teeth simply because their band directors require a strong attack. This is undesirable because the tongue may disrupt the embouchure setting when so placed, leading to missed notes since the em-

bouchure is constantly being upset by the tongue. In addition, the tongue has to move too great a distance to facilitate rapid tonguing. The result may be sluggish playing in fast passages.

The best tongue placement seems to be on the roof of the mouth where the upper teeth and the gums meet. From this position the tongue may be moved quickly, thereby facilitating rapid playing. Furthermore, the tongue is out of the way of the embouchure, allowing for a greater degree of accuracy. In addition, this placement enables the tongue to lie flat in the mouth after starting the tone. This

creates a larger passage through which the air column may flow. The attack itself may be varied from very light to very heavy simply by regulating the amount of air pressure which builds up behind the tongue when it is in position for the start of the tone.

Aside from applying the correct principle of tone production, the brass player's sound may be affected by the tongue. Many teachers suggest that their students pronounce certain syllables, such as *tee, too, tah*, etc., as an aid to making a correct attack. Sometimes *tee* is recommended for the upper register, *too* for the middle register, and *tah* for the lower register.

The selection of such a syllable should not be arbitrary, otherwise it might have a detrimental effect upon the sound. For example, if the student is taught to say either the syllable *tee* or *too* the problem of throat constriction may arise. Because these syllables have what might be called a "bright" sound, the chances are that the throat has to be narrowed slightly in order to say them. By constricting the throat, a certain degree of muscular tension is set up in the neck area which may lead to a tense, tight sound. Furthermore, the air passage may be narrowed, thereby inhibiting the flow of air into the instrument.

In experimenting with various syllables, I have found a sound such as *taw* to be the most helpful. When pronounced as part of an attack the sound leaves the throat free and open. This is particularly true if the student is encouraged to have the sound form deep within his throat. With no tension in the throat, the sound will be relaxed and uninhibited. Also, the *taw* syllable helps keep the tongue on the bottom of the mouth after making an attack, thus aiding the free passage of air.

Finally, tonguing with this syllabic sound, from the position described above, enables the player to develop a good staccato as well as a smooth legato tongue.

Acceptable tonguing habits should be encouraged early in the brass player's training. These are not difficult to teach and can mean the difference between a mediocre player and a polished performer. ■

October, 1971

Dental Appliances as an Aid to Brass Playing

William B. Lieberman & Robert C. Jones

In recent years large numbers of serious educators have become receptive to innovations in their area of speciality which only a few short years ago were termed radical or revolutionary. Many ideas which were rejected by those willing to remain with the status quo are now being researched, talked about, written down, and practiced. Because of the national aura of finding the better way for the better life, music educators have also begun to keep pace in a more scientific age.

Professors Matthew and Edwin Shiner of Duquesne University, Pittsburgh, Pennsylvania, have frequently remarked of their difficulty in convincing educators, musicians, and members of the dental profession that certain jaw and teeth formations could greatly alter the range, the flexibility, the tone quality, and the endurance of brass performers. Their proven techniques, developed over a lifetime, had no sympathetic audience in an earlier, less curious, less mechanized society.

In articles for the *Tri-State Digest*, published by the University of Pittsburgh in 1961, the Shiner philosophy of teeth and bone structure for maximum efficiency in brass playing was explained. These articles stated that the upper or maxillary teeth should be positioned as shown in Fig. 1 in order that the lip might vibrate freely

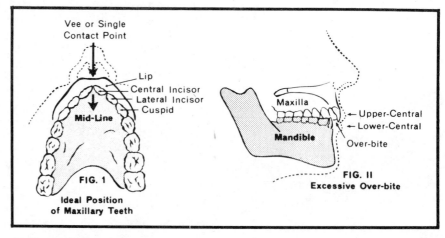

Note that the mesial labial or the "vee" formed at the midline of the two upper central incisors would bear the brunt of any mouthpiece pressure allowing the lateral portions of the lip to vibrate with more freedom than if the entire surface were flat or in some other equally poor or less comfortable position.

Equally important in this approach to brass teaching is the distance between the maxillary and the mandibular teeth (upper and lower) of the performer. Fig. 2 shows the structure of a performer with excessive overbite. In this instance there would be very little mouthpiece contact on the lower lip making flexibility difficult and greatly limiting range and endurance.

A trumpet player with this particular problem might switch to a larger mouthpiece instrument where greater contact with the lower lip would be assured. He may also try to accomplish the same end by thrusting out the lower jaw, or he may drop the bell of the instrument to an extremely low, unnatural position. A different brass instrument could merely substitute one problem for another, however, and music educators are aware that a child is not always successful when forced to play an instrument other than his first choice. Experienced teachers report too, that all students are not able to thrust out the lower jaw while playing since this "mandibular thrust" results in a forced abnormal position which can easily tire some individuals.

An orthodontist could aid the performer greatly by correcting the malocclusion, but many dentists and parents are reluctant to move healthy teeth just for the playing of a music instrument, even though the technique has been tested repeatedly and proven highly successful.

Picture 1 shows a fourth possibility in dealing with excessive overbite. This dental appliance, which fits over the lower teeth can afford maximum efficiency in the event that the above three alternatives are not suitable to the individual, the parents, or the dentist. The appliance is worn only while playing, snaps easily into place, fits tightly, and can be altered easily to meet the particular needs or idiosyncracies of the performer. In picture 2 it is clearly shown how such an appliance can eliminate excessive overbite and allow for needed comfort by distributing mouthpiece pressure over both the upper and the lower lips. This appliance should not completely eliminate the performer's overbite, however.

The brass teachers who advocate the use of the "pivot system" would notice a marked improvement in many of their students with an appliance of this kind. This would enable flexibility and the upper register to flow more easily by turning the bell of the instrument down slightly, thus turning the bottom of the mouthpiece in toward the bottom lip for additional support.

Because of the large number of performers achieving greater efficiency by wearing this type of appliance, the authors have recently begun to prescribe a similar dental apparatus which is to be worn over the upper central in-cisors. This appliance, shown in picture 3, could be tried in those circumstances where the position or structure of the teeth does not approximate that of the maxillary teeth as shown in Fig. 1, or when the individual possesses too little overbite. This problem of too little overbite is the opposite of that corrected with a lower appliance. It also inhibits an adequate pivot, and fosters minimal range, endurance and flexibility. This appliance should be consistent in contour with the natural teeth position in Fig. 1. Care should be taken in prescribing such an appliance, in the event that it be made too large; thus substituting one condition for another.

The dentition plays an important part in the overall final ability of a brass musician. The position of the teeth can limit the achievement of the serious music student if they are not ideally aligned. The relationship of the teeth of the upper and the lower jaws can also limit the total accomplishment of the brass player. This aforementioned appliance can and does alter these relationships by its design. It attempts to attain the ideal teeth formation which can improve tone and increase endurance, flexibility and range. In this era of scientific achievements, music educators should open their minds to advances in all areas which may alter difficulties of the past. ∎

Picture No. 1

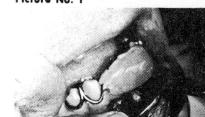

Picture No. 2

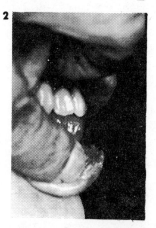

Picture No. 3 — Side

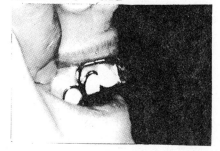

Picture No. 3 — Front

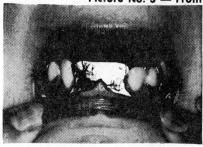

How to Care for a
Rotary-Valved Tuba

Rex Conner

There is no doubt that the rotary valved-tubas are becoming more popular with serious tuba students, and are being used in ever-increasing numbers in high school and college concert bands.

Students and directors often ask how to take the valves apart and clean them, although this is seldom necessary if the instruments are properly cared for and played regularly. All that is usually needed is to immerse the tuba in a tub full of warm water and a mild liquid detergent, and then flush it out with clear water. However, when rotary-valved tubas are left over a long period of time without playing (usually over a hot dry summer), it is quite likely that the valves will become frozen, or at least stuck. This is due to dried saliva and calcium deposited around the valve. Running water through the mouthpipe will usually loosen the valves, but if this doesn't work, you can usually take hold of the stop arm and break the rotors loose. Never force the key, as it will bend when too much pressure is applied.

Regardless of how much care a tuba is given, the time will eventually arrive when the valves must be taken apart for cleaning. It is not difficult and can be done quickly; however, it must be done correctly, and with some caution. First, remove the valve cap on the underside. If it will not loosen easily, wrap cardboard or leather around it (to protect the metal) and loosen it with a pair of vice grip pliers. There is no cap that will screw off of the *top*, although many look like they might.

The next step is the most critical one. Repair manuals and French horn players may say to loosen the stop-arm screw a few turns and then tap on it with a rawhide mallet or leave the screw driver in the slot and tap on it with a hammer. This is a dangerous procedure on some tubas. It is better to find a tool, or make one, that is the diameter of the stop-arm head screw, minus the head screw threads (so that the threads will not be damaged in the valve shaft). An old ice pick shortened and placed in the chuck of a drill and filed down to the correct diameter will work fine. It can then be put down into the place from which the screw was removed, and tapped with a hammer until the valve and bearing unit drop out. It is possible to use a small steel dowel on top of the valve shaft; however, it might damage the top of the threads. Be sure to catch the bearing unit and valve as they fall from the valve casing!

Once the valve is out of the casing it can be cleaned. Since it is solid brass, "Brasso" can be used without any appreciable amount of metal being removed. After the valve is cleaned, you can clean the casing. This is a little difficult since there is only one cap on it; but it can be cleaned by flushing or blowing all the foreign material out of it. Remember, good rotors

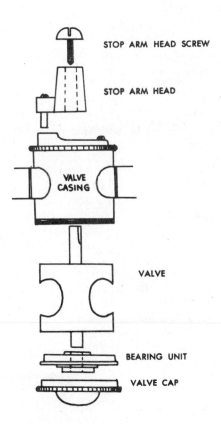

STOP ARM HEAD SCREW

STOP ARM HEAD

VALVE CASING

VALVE

BEARING UNIT

VALVE CAP

have very close tolerance and the smallest particle of dirt can cause them to stick. My own tuba will still show evidence of compression a full forty seconds after the third slide is pushed in.

Now that the valves and casings are clean, you can oil the bearing ridges, and the shafts of the valves; however, this is not necessary — even considered unwise by many. Do not oil the entire rotor. If the rotor will spin freely in the casing, you are ready to reassemble.

Most bearing units or plates, which fit over the bottom valve shaft and inside the valve casing, have a bearing mark, perhaps done with a file, and this mark must match perfectly with the continuing mark on the valve casing. After the bearing plate is in the correct position, tap it down flush with the walls of the valve casing. A small pipe (preferably of soft metal) which fits over the bearing ridge works well; otherwise, take a small, wooden dowel-rod and tap it lightly as it is rotated around the outer edge of the bearing unit. If this plate isn't down flush and at exact right angles with the bottom valve shaft it will bind, and the valve will be immobile. Quite often this is the cause of stuck rotary valves. A light tap at the correct spot on the bearing plate will often free the valve.

Check the Corks

Before putting the valve cap back on, you must now check the corks on the top side of the valve casings to see if they are the correct thickness and in good condition. These corks insure that the valves will stop precisely at the right point. If the corks need replacing, obtain some rod cork about three eighths of an inch in diameter and cut a piece off so that it is just the same height as the plate that holds the corks. Remove the old corks with a small screwdriver. Next, take the piece of rod cork that has been cut off and squeeze it between a pair of pliers *with the grain of the cork*. (Duck billed pliers are best for this work.) In its somewhat flattened state the cork can then be pushed into place quite easily. Apply some pressure and it will spread out again and remain in place.

Before replacing the stop arm head it is best to screw the valve cap on tightly to hold the bearing unit firmly in place while the stop arm head is replaced. Some heads fit the valve shaft very tightly. (They are conical.) After the stop arm head is on, remove the valve cap once more, take a strip of emery paper just wide enough to go between the stop arm and the cork, place the emery paper between the stop arm and the cork, press the stop arm lightly and pull the emery through the two until the cork is sanded enough for the marks on the valve shaft to match up with the marks on the raised portion of the bearing unit. This procedure will form a small circular seating in the rod cork for the stop arm which makes valve action just firm enough, yet not "spongy" or too hard.

String Action

Nothing has been said here about restringing keys with string action. Most French horn players can give this information. *The Practical Band Instrument Repair Manual* by Clayton H. Tiede gives an excellent description as well as drawings for this operation.* One tuba distributor is now using a 50-lb. test monofilament fishing line instead of the usual nylon or silk string and it is excellent. If you are playing a tuba with mechanical linkage and it is noisy, put a drop of 30 weight motor oil on the body of the screw and it will stop the noise if it isn't too badly worn. The wear is usually in the screw. If you are paying good money for a new tuba, buy one that will remain silent for years to come. Noisy valve action, whether piston or rotary, should not be tolerated on a tuba at any price.

One final tip — if you would like to have your lacquer finish look good for a long time, use Johnson's "Pledge" on it after cleaning with soap and water. ∎

* Tiede, Clayton H., *The Practical Band Instrument Repair Manual*, Dubuque, Iowa, Wm. C. Brown, 1962. Permission to reproduce pictures in this article granted by Mr. Tiede.

December, 1971

Solo Literature for the Bass Trombone

Thomas G. Everett

In the last 15 years the growth in awareness and interest in the bass trombone has been significant. A distinct member of the symphony orchestra for over 150 years, it has been only recently that the bass trombone sound has been taken advantage of in stage bands, concert bands, chamber music ensembles, and as a solo instrument.

The strict use of cello, string bass, and tuba materials for the bass trombone student or performer is no longer tolerable, as fine literature for the bass trombone does exist (although mostly contemporary).

The following list consists of selected works conceived for the bass trombone. It does not include arrangements or transcriptions. A large amount of French music published for bass trombone (Leduc) has been omitted because I believe that the works were originally written for tuba.

The works appearing in this selected list are representative of the most accessible and recommended literature for bass trombone. Readers interested in additional listings of works for the instrument should send a request, plus $1.50 to cover duplicating and mailing charges, to Thomas G. Everett, 9 Prescott St., Cambridge, Massachusetts 02138.

Adler, Samuel: Canto II — Four Concert Etudes for Solo Bass Trombone (1970); Oxford.

Unaccompanied in four short movements, this work exploits many facets of the bass trombone, including its lyrical and declamatory qualities. Based on a tone row freely used throughout, the piece requires great technical facility and range from pedal G to high B♭

(also requires flutter-tongue, glissandos between F and B♭ trombone, cup and velvet-tone mute). Written for Thomas Everett, this is one of the best works in the literature. Grade VI.

Andrix, George: Four Pieces for Bass Trombone and Strings (1971); Andrix.

An excellent four-movement work using strings in both accompanying and solo roles. Piece requires low B , glissandos, mute, and range from sustained pedal G to high B♭. Grade V.

Bariller, Robert: Hans De Schnokeloch — for bass trombone and piano; Leduc.

A French piece dedicated to Paul Bernard. Declamatory style with lyrical section in 5/8 alternating with 2/4, the range is from trigger C♯ to an optional high A, and requires some technique in moving triplet section (chromatic and arpeggio). Grade IV.

Bartles, Alfred: Elegy — for bass trombone and piano; Sam Fox.

Dedicated to Alan Raph, this 3½ to 4 minute work is part of the National Brass Solo Series. *Elegy* is in a slow, singing legato style ranging from pedal A up to high A. Requires good breath control. Grade IV.

Brown, James E.: Impromptu — for bass trombone and tape (1970); Brown.

Commissioned by Thomas Everett, the piece is for solo bass trombone interrupted by three sections of taped sound. The pre-recorded tape sounds are made from trombone, flute, piano and electronic sounds. The tape and trombone toy at counterpoint and at times fashion something closer in style to a recitative. The work consists of changing meter, feeling of acceleration and ritard (5 against 3 followed by 3 against 2 etc.), wide skips, requires a straight mute and a range from pedal G to high G♯. Tape operator is needed. Grade VI.

Carles-Marc: Introduction et Toccata for bass trombone and piano; Leduc.

French Conservatory piece in different tempos. Contains a trigger B♮. Grade IV.

Castérède, Jacques: Fantaisie Concertante for bass trombone and piano; Leduc.

A French contest piece dedicated to Paul Bernard, this is a major work with changing meter, turns and a range from trigger C to high G. Contains trigger B♮. Grade V.

Coker, Wilson: Concerto for Tenor-Bass Trombone — for tenor-bass trombone and symphony band; Theodore Presser.

A difficult piece in connecting sections, the work makes use of changing meter and a high tessitura (pedal B♭ to high C). Band part is also difficult. Grade V.

Cope, David: BTRB — for bass trombone performer (1970); Cope.

A theatre piece involving the "discovery" of the bass trombone. Includes producing sounds with different mouthpieces (clarinet, bassoon reed). Grade V.

Cope, David: 3 Movements for Solo Trombone with F attachment; Composer's Autograph Pub.

An unaccompanied, 6-minute work in changing meter. The three-movement piece (slow, fast, slow) requires fast mute and plunger changes. Second movement makes good use of F trigger on the staff. Shows off instrument well and requires careful articulation. Range is from low F to high B♭ (some treble clef). Grade IV.

Croley, Randell: Variazioni Piccola op. 44, no. 1 for bass trombone solo; Autograph Editions (Colombo).

A difficult unaccompanied work in cadenza style, the piece has no regular meter (no time signature). Range is from pedal G♭ to high C (tenor clef). Grade VI.

Dedrick, Chris: Inspirations — for bass trombone, winds and cello (clarinet, two B♭ trumpets, doubling flügel horns, two French horns; Kendor Music.

Written for Thomas Streeter by Chris Dedrick of the "Free Design," this three-movement work rates as one of the understanding chamber works for trombone. The piece offers a challenge for all performers and much interest through contrast. All instruments have exposed sections as well as intricate passages, and the accompanying instrumental parts are very difficult. Player needs good flexibility, agility, rhythmic independence and control. Range from pedal G♯ to high A. Grade V.

Dunn, Russell: Opus 1 for Bass Trombone — for bass trombone and concert band (1971); Dunn.

One of two works known by compiler for bass trombone and band, the piece includes varied tempos and rubatos and wavers between impressionistic (much use of 4ths and 5ths) to almost a dance style, chord structure, and voicing. No great demands are made on any of the performers. Many times trombone blends in with ensemble. Range is from trigger D to optional high G.

Everett, Thomas G.: Vietnam 70 — for bass trombone, tenor saxophone and string bass (1970); Everett.

An aleatoric and improvisational work based on the performers' reaction to war. In four sections, it requires sustained glissandos and trills with the trigger. Range from pedal B♭ to high C. Grade V.

Fulkerson, James: SDTQ — for one to four bass trombones or bass trombone, flute, string bass and percussion (1969); Fulkerson.

Instrumentation is flexible. Computer composed, the work is playable by from one to four bass trombones. The composition is not technically difficult but is in an open form (freedom within given events). Grade V.

Gay, Harry W.: Introduction and Allegro Moderato for bass trombone and piano (1969); Gay.

Commissioned by Thomas Everett and dedicated to Emory Remington, this is a fine work in basically lyrical style. A busy piano part is set against the repeated singing motif in the bass trombone. Not a difficult piece, the range is from trigger D to high F. Grade IV.

George, Thom Ritter: Concerto for Bass Trombone and Orchestra (1964); Ritter.

An outstanding major work for bass trombone and orchestra (or piano). Dedication reads "for Emory Remington and Robert Brawn, the master and his pupil." Work creates several moods and requires many short, quick glissandos and some very wide difficult skips in and out of the trigger and pedal range. Composition concludes with fugue stated by the bass trombone. Range from pedal F♯ to high F♯. Grade V.

Hartley, Walter: Arioso — for bass trombone and piano (1958); Interlochen.

An experiment in sonority designed to be playable on no other wind instrument but the trombone, *Arioso* was written for Byron McCullah. It is a short, very slow work comprising a legato statement in the bass trombone with some measured long glissandos. Piano part consists of slow moving chord clusters. Range from trigger D to high B♮ (tenor clef). Grade V.

Hartley, Walter: Sonata Breve — for bass trombone (1969); Tenuto Press (Presser).

An excellent short unaccompanied sonata in two fast movements. It requires flutter-tongue, good technical facility and range from pedal B♭ to high F♯. Commissioned by Thomas Everett and dedicated to Emory Remington. Grade V.

Hartley, Walter: Sonata da Camera for bass trombone and four winds (oboe, B♭ clarinet, A clarinet and bassoon) (1950); Ferma Music Pub. (Crescendo Music Sales).

Scored for oboe, B♭ clarinet, A clarinet, bassoon and bass trombone. This work is technically demanding and has a range from sustained pedal G (and optional pedal C♯) to high C♯. All the instruments have major roles in the work. Grade V.

Hellermann, William: Formata for bass trombone and four instruments (flute, B♭ clarinet, piano, percussion) (vibraphone, 5 temple blocks, 3 cymbals, woodblock) (1967); Hellermann.

A difficult 7-minute work in proportional notation, the parts are quite involved and all players play from the score. Has high tessitura, tenor clef, rhythmic complexities, 2 harmon mutes and range from low F to double high E♭. Grade VI.

Henry, Otto: Passacaglia and Fugue for bass trombone and piano; Robert King Music.

A 7½-minute work dedicated to John Coffey, the piece features mostly detached playing. The work needs no special technical skills but does require strict counting and slide movement in the fast, changing meter fugue. Range is from trigger D to high G. Grade V.

Kam, Dennis: Rendezvous II for bass trombone and piano; Kam.

The piece uses proportional and aleatoric notation. Interaction between players is of prime importance, and both play from the score (much work needed between performers). Requires mute, flutter tongue, humming, and range from pedal G♯ to high B♭. Grade V.

Lantier, Pierre: Introduction, Romance et Allegro pour trombone basse et piano; Lemoine c/o Elkan-Vogel.

A neo-romantic type work with introduction, slow section, and long fast section. Range is from optional pedal F to high A, and requires a technically sure performer. Grade IV.

Lassen, Edvard: Zwei Fantasiestucke for Bass Trombone and Strings 1) Devotion 2) Dance in the evening, arrangement by Ostrander of At Devotions; Edition Musicus.

Ostrander's edition of the first movement is of a slow, legato nature. Range is from trigger E♭ to high G♭. Grade IV.

Lieb, Richard: Concertino Basso for bass trombone and band; Carl Fischer.

A simple repetitious rhythm figure keeps the bass trombone in the low register. No major problems, but player should have good command of trigger and trigger register and be able to jump down to pedal register. The range is from sustained pedal G to C just above the staff. Dedicated to Alan Raph. Grade IV.

Lischka, Rainer: Drei Skizzer — for bass trombone and piano; Hofmeister.

Not technically difficult, the range is from pedal B♭ to F above the staff. A very straightforward and playable piece. Grade IV.

Margoni, Alain: Apres Une Lecture de Goldoni — for bass trombone and piano; Leduc.

French Conservatory piece in 18th century style, with scale-wise runs and arpeggios. Grade IV.

Martelli, Henri: Dialogue, op. 100, for Bass trombone and piano; Editions Max Eschig.

A major work in many varied and quick changing tempos and meters, the piece contains several low E♮'s and goes up to an F. A technically and stylistically difficult and mature work. Grade V.

Martelli, Henri: Sonate pour trombone basse et piano, op 87 (1956); Philippo (Elkan-Vogel Co.)

An easier work than the Dialogue, this similar work was composed as a Conservatory of Paris contest piece. Range is from pedal G to high A but has several low B♭'s. Grade V.

McCarty, Frank: Music for Trombone, op. 21 for bass trombone and piano; Everett.

A lyrical, difficult work with frequently changing meters and intricate piano part. In two movements, at times the bass trombone plays inside the piano. Features mute, many glissandos, tenor clef, pedal G through trigger register to high C. Grade VI.

McCarty, Patrick: Sonata for Bass Trombone—for bass trombone with string quartet or string orchestra; Ensemble Publications.

Another fine contribution to the literature, this work may be performed with string quartet, string orchestra, or piano. First movement is a legato Allegretto, second is a singing type Andante and the third is a Vivace. In general, legato flexibility into trigger register, octave jumps, and some fast slide movement in last movement are the only problems. Range is from optional pedal E and pedal register to D above the staff. Grade IV.

McCauley, William: Five Miniatures for Bass Trombone, Harp and Strings; Canadian Music Centre.

An excellent work dedicated to Emory Remington. The Five Miniatures each demonstrate a different mood (Powerful, Peaceful, Prankish, Pensive and Progressive). A difficult work that moves around and has some changing meter, it is nevertheless worthwhile and listenable. Range is from pedal E♭ (and one double pedal B♭!) to high A. Grade V.

McVey, Larry: Ballade for Trombone; Rifferendum 94; Serenade for Bass Trombone; Some Other Time — each for solo bass trombone and stage band; Regal Pub.

Written for George Roberts, these pieces show off the bass trombone excellently in a popular style. No major technical demands, the compositions, with stage band (playable by high schools), focus on the phrasing and the relaxed dark sound of the bass trombone. Rifferendum is a medium up-tempo, while the other tunes are slow. Range is from pedal G to high G. Grade IV.

Muller, J.I.: Praeludium, Chorale, Variations, Fugue — for bass trombone and piano or organ (1839); Edition Musicus.

One of the "standards" of the literature, the piece makes no great technical demands, and the range is from pedal B♭ (and a trigger B♮) to high B♭. Excellent piece from the romantic era. Grade IV.

Ostrander, Allen: Sonata in g minor — bass trombone solo (piano ad lib on rental); Edition Musicus.

An unaccompanied work (with piano part on rental) in four movements. Almost in a baroque suite style, this work makes an excellent study piece. Some changing meter and technical passages make excellent use of F attachment on staff. Range is from pedal G to high F. Grade IV.

Payne, Frank Lynn: Concert Suite for Trumpet and Bass Trombone (1970); Payne.

A four-movement suite (Rhetoric, Asymmetry, Tribute to D.S., Toccata) commissioned by Thomas Everett and dedicated to Robert Levy. Trumpet part is in C. Second movement has frequent meter changes and tenor clef. Last movement is quite fast and keeps the trombonist very active in a type of basso continuo. Piece requires range from pedal B♭ to high A♭.

Petit, Pierre: Wagenia; Leduc.

A Paris Conservatory piece in slow Wagnerian style, the work is basically in the low register with a low trigger B♮. Grade IV.

Planel, Robert: Air et Final — pour trombone basse et piano; Leduc.

This French Conservatory piece has several meter, tempo, and key changes. Range is from trigger B♮ (single F has time to pull and push E slide) to high G. Very playable work. Grade IV.

Raph, Alan: Caprice — for bass trombone solo (1963); Robert King Music Co.

An unaccompanied work making much use of the bass trombone in the upper register. Composition is based on triplet and dotted eighth and sixteenth rhythms. Some trigger notes, the range lies between pedal A♭ and high C (the last measure indicates for performer to glissando and diminuendo from high A above the bass clef to a double high A!), and demands a strong upper register. Grade V.

Riddle, Nelson: Five Pieces for Bass Trombone — with two trumpets, French horn, tuba; Dick Noel Enterprise.

A light work in dance style, the bass trombone functions within the ensemble and as soloist. The movements range from a ballad to a jazz waltz. Not difficult, but the last movement moves along and requires slide and trigger dexterity. The work is also supplied with a recording of George Roberts performing the work. The second side of the record consists of the *Five Pieces* with the bass trombone part deleted, so that one may play along. Grade V.

Somers, Paul: Two Pieces for Bass Trombone and Orchestra (full orchestra with piano) (1971); Somers.

Written for Thomas Everett, the work begins as kind of a rock piece and "regresses" to a slow '20's type jazz. The bass trombone is prominent throughout the fast first movement in a flowing lyrical style (with some call and response sections with orchestra) set off by a detached rhythmic orchestral accompaniment. Although very dissonant with several note clusters (even undetermined pitches within unison rhythms), the sparsely scored orchestra parts are not difficult. The second movement is slow and legato. Written in tenor clef, indetermined notation, the composition features high glissandos and a range from trigger C to high A.

Spillman, Robert: Concerto for Bass Trombone and Piano; Edition Musicus.

A good extended work offering many different facets of bass trombone playing. Performer needs strong trigger and pedal control, and breath control for long phrases. Range is from pedal E to optional F above the staff. Grade V.

Tanner, Paul: Concert Duet for Tenor and Bass Trombone and Band; Western Inter. Music.

This piece includes some unison work and call and response dialogue between the tenor and bass trombone, as well as an extended unaccompanied cadenza. Tenor trombone travels up to an optional double high F. No major problems in bass trombone except some extreme low sustained parts (pedal D♭). Range is from pedal D♭ to F above the staff. Grade V.

Tcherepnin, Nicolai: Une Oraison (A Prayer) for bass trombone and piano; Schirmer.

One of the earliest 20th century pieces written for bass trombone, this is a slow work with just quarter, half and whole notes. Phrasing and sound are on display. Range is from pedal B♭ to F above the staff. Grade IV.

Tomasi, Henri: Etre Ou Ne Pas Entre — pour trombone basse et piano ou trois trombones (1963); Leduc.

A subtle take-off on Hamlet's "to be or not to be," this 6-minute work may be accompanied by piano or three tenor trombones. In general, it is a very slow work with changing styles and meter in the lower bass trombone range, and can be a taxing work when played properly. Range is from pedal B♭ (trigger B♮) to D above the staff. Grade V.

Vilette, Pierre: Fantaisie Concertante pour trombone basse et orchestra de chambre; Alphonse Leduc.

A 5½ minute Andante - Vivace - Andate work with orchestra and percussion, this is a major work with technical problems and some long phrases. Requires tenor clef, mute, and some trigger B♮'s. Grade V.

Wilder, Alec: Bass Trombone Sonata for bass trombone and piano; Wilder.

Another of the outstanding works for bass trombone, this five movement piece (written for George Roberts) is as fun to listen to as it is to perform. In a third stream, pseudo-jazz style, the composition calls for meter change, much soft tongue playing, flares and drops, a trigger B♮ and some vigorous playing. Range is from pedal G to high G. Grade V.

Publishers

Andrix, George, 10715 151 St., Edmonton, Alberta, Canada

Boonin, Joseph Music Pub., 831 Main St., Hackensack, N.J. 07601

Boosey & Hawkes, Inc., Lawson Blvd., Oceanside, N.Y. 11572

Brown, James E., 100 Main St., Salem, N.Y. 12865

Canadian Music Centre, 33 Edward St., Toronto, 101 Ontario, Canada

CMP Library, University Microfilms, Ann Arbor, Michigan 48100

Colombo, Franco Pub., 16 W. 61st St., New York, N.Y. 10023

Composers Autograph Pub., Box 7103, Cleveland, Ohio 44128

Composers Facsimile Edition, 170 W. 74th St., New York, N.Y. 10023

Cope, David, 3705 Strandhill Rd., Shaker Heights, Ohio 44122

Crescendo Music Sales, 440 W. Barry, Chicago, Ill. 60657

Dunn, Russell, 179 Station St., New York, N.Y. 10002

Editions Max Eschig, 48 Rue de Rome, Paris, France

Editions Musicales, Transatlantiques, 14 Avenue Hoche, Paris (8e) France

Editions Musicus Inc., 333 W. 52nd St., New York, N.Y. 10019

Elkan-Vogel, Co., Inc., 1712 Sansom St., Philadelphia, Pa. 19103

Ensemble Publications, Box 98, Buffalo, N.Y. 14222

Everett, Thomas, 9 Prescott St., Cambridge, Mass. 02138

Fischer, Carl, 62 Cooper Square, New York, N.Y. 10003

Fox, Sam Publishing Co., 1540 Broadway, New York, N.Y. 10036

Fulkerson, James, 213 Quinbee Rd., Rochester, N.Y. 14609

Gay, Harry, W., 1677 Autumn Ave., Memphis, Tenn. 33104

Hellerman, William, 90 Morningside Dr., 4J, New York, N.Y. 10027

Hofmeister, VEB Friedrich, Musikverlag, Leipzig, Germany 7446

Kam, Dennis, 2153 Aupuni St., Honolulu, Hawaii 96817

Kendor Music, Delevan, N.Y. 14042

King, Robert Music Co., 7 Canton St., North Easton, Mass. 02356

Leduc, Alphonse et cie, 175 Rue St., Honore, Paris, France

Molenaar N.V., Wormerveer, Holland

Noel Enterprise, Dick, P.O. Box 3166, Hollywood, Ca. 90023

Oxford University Press, 200 Madison Ave., New York, N.Y. 10016

Payne, Frank Lynn, 1316 NW 21st St., Oklahoma City, Okla. 73106

Presser, Theodore Co., Bryn Mawr, Pa. 19010

Regal Publications, 7816 North Interstate, Portland, Oregon 97217

Ritter, George Thom, c/o Army Band, Washington, D.C. 20310

Schirmer, G., Inc., 609 Fifth Ave., New York, N.Y. 10017

Somers, Paul, c/o 44 Fairmont Ave., Chatham, N.J. 07928

Swing Lane Pub., Beverley, N.J. 08010

University Music Press, Ann Arbor, Michigan 48100

Western International Music, 2859 Holt Ave., Los Angeles, Ca. 90034

Wilder, Alec, c/o Hotel Algonquin, 59 W. 49th St., New York, N.Y. 10036 ∎

1972

January, 1972

A Short History
of the Trumpet

Douglas Smith

The trumpet has a rich and somewhat illustrious heritage, spanning several centuries. Coincident with its technical development, the trumpet has experienced a gradual metamorphosis from primitive signal wielder to the fine instrument we know today, prominent in many forms of music.

The Trumpet in Antiquity

The first record of trumpets in the *Bible* is found in the Book of Numbers, Chapter X, where God instructs Moses to make two trumpets for ceremonial use:

And the Lord spoke unto Moses, saying: Make thee two trumpets of silver; of beaten work shalt thou make them; and they shall be unto thee for calling of the congregation, and for causing the camps to set forward.

Aside from the rather perfunctory duty described here, these early instruments were used in battles and also in religious celebrations. According to the historian Flavius Josephus, Moses's trumpets were silver tubes about 22 inches long, ending in a flared bell.

One very well-known biblical story depicts Joshua, whose marching trumpet corps summoned Providential intervention to help destroy the wall around Jericho. Joshua's trumpets were *shofars* as were probably the instruments used by Gideon and his 300 stalwarts who terrified a numerically superior army during the night and won a battle without striking a single blow. The shofar was made from the horn of a ram or goat. The brittle appendage was steamed until soft, flattened until straight, then bent to form angles or curves. The total length of the final product ranged anywhere from seven to twenty inches.

Some musicologists feel that the conical shofar was the progenitor of our modern family of conical brasses — horns, tubas, euphoniums, and cornets — just as the hollow stem of a plant served as the ultimate ancestor of cylindrical brasses such as trumpets and trombones. Therefore, it seems entirely wrong to use the terms "trumpet" and "shofar" interchangeably; however, in the *Bible* they were, and so we are obliged to regard many references to the former as implications of the latter.

One vital question continues to puzzle those who try to ascertain the structure and use of the early trumpet. Ethnologists feel that many instruments which we would classify broadly as trumpets were not lip-energized at all, but functioned as megaphones to concentrate and/or distort the natural voice. Such a grotesque distortion would have been ideal for Gideon,

but there is no way to be sure whether Joshua's seven-day marching band marathon promoted labial callouses or glottal nodes. For all we know, every biblical trumpet was lip-energized; but then again every one might have been a megaphone type. More logical to this writer is the possibility that the two concepts co-existed during biblical times, but later, when writers attempted a description, clear distinction was not made.

Throughout history there have been many names used for what we call *trumpet*. From the 12th century we read of two instruments: the *claro*, a straight instrument roughly two or three feet long, and the *buizine*, roughly twice as long. Around 1300 the word *trompe* designated a conical brass instrument; the diminutive of *trompe*, or *trompette*, indicated a cylindrical instrument. By the early 16th century all the shorter brasses were called *trompette*, and the long brasses had adopted the name *clarion*. It is interesting to note that the 16th century word *clarion* had come to mean the exact opposite of its 12th-century root *claro*. After 1600 the semantic focus concerned the range played by a certain individual rather than the specific construction of the instrument.

Modern brass teachers often look with disdain at renaissance paintings which depict trumpeters performing with inflated cheeks. They know that such an embouchure formation produces far from satisfactory results, and they also know that painters from the renaissance were noted for the faithful portrayal of their subjects. If 15th and 16th century trumpeters actually did puff their cheeks, it has been inferred by many that they would have been able to play only the lower harmonics. Of course, had Dizzy Gillespie (a famous cheek-puffer) lived 400 years earlier, he might have taken great delight in bursting such a conjectural bubble.

Prior to the 16th century the use of the trumpet was limited primarily to realms of warfare and celebration. Trumpets were used, as were drums, simply as effect instruments. If trumpets were to be included in larger works such as secular dramas or morality plays, the players were expected to improvise fanfares appropriate to the occasion. The tone of their early signal trumpets is described to us by the writers of antiquity as being very unbeautiful, harsh, and barbarous. To what extent they were ever employed artistically we will never know, since music for them, if ever written down, unfortunately did not survive to the present time.

As early as 1494, tower-watchmen were employed at Lübeck who had among other duties "to blow and to play the whole year and every evening on the *claritte*. The expression "blow" meant perhaps a signal or fanfare, and "play" meant some form of melody. At this early date, both types were probably done on the same instrument, but later there were certain trumpets designed for fanfare playing, and others for melodies. The following paragraph, written by Altenburg in 1795, helps us to understand what made one trumpet more ideally suited than another for its specific type of music:

Our ordinary trumpet is a musical wind and military instrument, and is used more especially by the cavalry. A trumpet with a wide gauge sounds louder and is more penetrating than one with a narrow gauge, but it requires harder blowing. A trumpet made of strong, thick metal is more durable, adapted to military purposes and answers well in the low range, but on the high clarion notes it requires more wind, has an unpleasant tone, and is therefore quite unsuited as an instrument for the clarionist, or concert trumpeter. If, on the other hand, the metal be too thin, the instrument will respond very easily in the high register, and the low notes are not loud and penetrating enough for military purposes, nor is it durable.

The trumpets evidently were not very durable, considering the fact that so few are in existence today. We get some idea of a baroque trumpet's fragility by the following notations entered in the daily ledger of William Bull, a 17th century English trumpet maker.

Received Silon Pierson's trumpett, broke to pieces, weight 27 oz.

Received Thomas Barwell's trumpett, all broke to pieces, weight 16 oz. These two above-mentioned trumpetts delivered to Mr. Bull, February 20, 1685, to be made new.

The following, from an unnamed French writer, helps us to understand the difficulty early trumpeters had in being taken seriously.

Horses are always made to dance to the sound of trumpets and kettle-drums, because they are accustomed to march and move to the sound of these instruments. Trumpets are the most proper instruments for horses to dance to, as the horses like to breathe when the trumpeters do. Nor is any other instrument more agreeable to them, for it is martial, and the horse (which is naturally courageous) loves this animating sound.

In his *Harmonie Universelle* of 1636, Mersenne, another Frenchman, explained the trumpet as he saw it:

As to the compass of the trumpet, it is marvellously great if one takes all its tones from the gravest to the highest, for it supplies a 32nd so that it surpasses all the keyboards of spinets and organs. It should also be noted, though, that the tone which is ordinarily called the first or lowest on the trumpet is not that which is generally used, and which I have named ut, for it descends a whole octave below this, though some trumpeters do not believe this because they cannot do it or because they have never tried.

On most trumpets (there are some exceptions) the fundamental is unplayable. Among those harmonics which are played, there are some which are out of tune, primarily the 7th, 11th, and 13th. Bach always knew how to handle these weaknesses — by passing over them quickly on a short, unaccented part of the measure — but Handel seemed oblivious to any fault of the instrument. The famous English musicologist Carl Burney described as follows a momentous trumpet performance of June, 1784.

That favourite bass air, "The Trumpet Shall Sound," was played very well by Mr. Serjant. In the trumpet part of this air some passages occur, however, which, owing to the natural imperfections of that instrument, always produce an unpleasant effect. [Before he goes on, the tactful critic makes sure all of the strong points are covered.] Mr. Serjant's tone is most pleasing and clear, but whenever he had to sustain the note G, displeasure was depicted on every face, which grieved me sore. [1]

Dr. Burney continues:

In the Hallelujah Chorus, the fourth G is held for two bars! It is greatly to be desired that this inspiriting and brilliant instrument may be rid of its defects by some mechanical device.

Not until the advent of valves, roughly five decades after Burney's statement, did it become possible to play Handel's trumpet parts with consistency of quality and reasonably good intonation. Although he never lived to witness it, possibly Burney's voice was one of the influences toward the technical advances to follow.

Outstanding Historical Trumpet Personalities

Prior to the time of Monteverdi, trumpet and drum parts were generally left up to the discretion of the performer. However, in his opera *Orfeo* (1607), Monteverdi wrote a fanfare for five trumpets (played three times before the first act) in which he specifically designated each part, beginning from top to bottom: *clarino, quinto, alto, vulgaro, and basso.* Not long afterwards a professional hierarchy was established which separated the musicians who played high parts and those who played low parts. In Germany another distinction was made between the *Feldtrumpeter* (field trumpeter, or city musician) and the *Kammertrumpeter* (chamber, or court musician).

The absurd discrimination of one class of trumpeters against the other naturally created friction, which in turn resulted in quarrels and name-calling. The tower watchmen often suffered the indignity of being called "tame pigeons" by their chamber counterparts. However unjust the distinction might have been, each clique formed guilds ("unions") which grew quite strong. If the "tame pigeons" were caught playing notes out of their prescribed range, they were subject to severe penalties, and were even in danger of being tortured. If that sounds a bit bizarre, read on:

At the end of the 17th century in Hanover, the Elector's trumpeters once broke into the house of the chief tower-musician with whom they were at odds, took the trumpet on which he was practicing and knocked out several of his front teeth with it. And what is more, these worthy kameraden contended that they had only asserted their just right, and escaped all punishment.

The same type of rules which forced the "tame pigeons" to play only the low notes also required that the baroque "screech artists" play only in the upper range. The "Knightly Guild of Trumpetists and Kettle-drummers" forced a *clarino*, or first-part player, to specialize all his life in the highest range, without ever spoiling the taut adjustment of his lips by descending into the lower register. In such specialization, the player often availed himself of a suitable mouthpiece with a very shallow basin and a broad, lip-supporting rim. And we must assume, too, that the few very highest parts in the scores of such composers as Bach and his contemp-

---

1. The G to which Dr. Burney referred was actually G^2, or on the natural trumpet in D, the 11th harmonic, $F^\sharp$. This harmonic was so sharp when compared to equal temperament, that often composers allowed it to sound for $F^\sharp$.

oraries were probably tailored for one or two outstanding virtuosos, just as operatic arias were written in those days for the individual abilities of certain stars.

The general education then expected of the court-trumpeters was very high. They were well-paid and highly respected, so it is no wonder that the field trumpeters were envious, and were willing to risk their front teeth, if needs be, for the chance at social climbing. One of the outstanding virtuosos of the day was Johann Andreas Schachtner, the Salzburg Court Trumpeter and friend of the Mozart household. Schachtner, who had finished his academic studies at the Jesuit institution of higher learning at Ingolstadt, was also famous in his day as a poet and author.

Another interesting personage was Johann Ernst Altenburg, a cultured, most learned, highly esteemed man, lawyer, author, composer, and master of the trumpet. He also was a military man, having fought through the Seven Years' War from beginning to end. Usually these respected chamber performers were affiliated with royal courts, and the field trumpeters were servants of municipalities.

Natural Trumpet Pedagogy

Perhaps the first method book written for trumpet was by Girolamo Fantini, a Tuscan Court Trumpeter: *Modo per Imparar a Sonare di Tromba*, or roughly, Method for Teaching to Play the Trumpet, 1638. This work is understandably rather sketchy, but is important to us if for no other reason than it is the first of its kind.

The most exhaustive accounts of the use and technique of the trumpet in the 17th century are given us by Daniel Speer in his treatise, *Instruction in the Musical Art*, of 1687. Here are a few quotes taken from Speer's book:

There are but few private persons who learn this instrument. Cause: it requires great bodily exertion, difficult for an incipient to perform. With a view to learn more easily how to blow the trumpet, he should at once accustom himself to apply the mouthpiece most accurately to the upper large or hanging lip, and not so as to touch the nose; for then the flesh of the large lip is apt to gather, and fill the cup of the mouthpiece, leaving no room for tonguing; yea, it even prevents the air from getting in; and though physical strength may not be lacking, it will gradually become exhausted, as the aperture for the breath is stopped up, and the breath cannot proceed. The correct embouchure, therefore, is the chief feature of trumpet blowing.

Still on the subject of the embouchure, Speer continues: *Above all, an incipient shall accustom himself to draw in his cheeks, not blow them out, for this is not only unseemly, but hinders the breath from having its due outlet and causes a man pains at the temples, so that true teachers are accustomed to box the ears of their pupils to cure them of this bad habit.*

Speer lists five qualities which he considers indispensible to good trumpet playing: (1) healthy physical strength; (2) strong, long continuing breath; (3) a quickly moving tongue; (4) a willing industry in constant practice, whereby the embouchure is conquered and preserved; and (5) good, long trills, that are made with the chin, which must therefore be accustomed to trembling or shivering.

The outstanding trumpet treatise of the 18th century was by the above-mentioned Johann Ernst Altenburg.

Here is the full title of his work: *Attempt at an Introduction to the Heroic-Musical Art of the Trumpeters and Kettle-Drummers, Historically, Theoretically, and Practically Described and Explained with Examples, to the Better Prospering of the Same*. Altenburg compared clarino playing to the discant singing of voices, high and clear. He considered the right embouchure for the production of sound as uncommonly difficult to acquire, and did not think that it could be defined by fixed rules. On the subject of practice, he conceded that it must do the best it can, but in the final analysis, the important thing was the correct formation of the embouchure.

The Clarino Technique

It is safe to assume that trumpeters, who incidentally might have been good musicians, desired to escape from their tonic-dominant syndrome and play real tunes, as the violins or the flutes. Even though Monteverdi made a small contribution in this direction, it was left primarily to two composers to expand the use of the higher harmonics: the Italian Alessandro Scarlatti, and the Englishman Henry Purcell. Both often employed trumpets to double or imitate the violins. This forced the trumpets into a melodic style, technically possible, but heretofore unsuited to their character. Because they were now required by the music to play higher harmonics, trumpeters were obliged to cultivate what we now call the clarino register.

Other composers also experimented with the new concept. Cesti, in his opera *Il pomo d'Oro (The Golden Apple)*, produced in 1667, used trumpets of equal importance taking the top line in turn. In one chorus scene, trumpets alternated with the strings in a manner which anticipated the beginning of the 18th century.

Of course, the art of clarino playing received its greatest challenge from the works of Bach, whose *Brandenburg Concerto No. 2* stands even today as perhaps the summit of the clarino technique.

There were many other concertos written for trumpet, some of which are being resurrected for modern performances. The more well-known of these composers are Vivaldi, Stradella, Fasch, Stölzel, Telemann, Michael Haydn, and Leopold Mozart.

Before the clarino technique was fully exploited, already there was a reaction to its unusual physical demands and to its overbearing presence in every piece in which it was used. Around 1700, Buxtehude — conservative in all things musical — used paired trumpets in a rather limited manner, and never as upper voices.

Modern orchestration, as we may call it, really began in the last 40 years of the 18th century, the period of Haydn and Mozart. The working period of Gluck coincided almost exactly with these years of transition, his most important years being 1760-80. Gluck's works of this period demonstrated his conviction that instruments ought to be introduced in proportion to the degree of interest and passion in the words. He also felt that the employment of instruments should be based on the dramatic propriety of the tone, not on the dexterity of the players. Under the influence of Gluck and his contemporaries, the art of playing the demanding clarino parts died a natural death. Even Mozart, when confronted with the task of re-orchestrating Handel's *Messiah*, deleted nearly all of the trumpet parts because he considered them unplayable.

One school of thought regarded the death of the clarino technique as a step in the right direction, because it eliminated all the need for herculean strength, and all the artificial sound produced by a majority of trumpeters. On the other hand, there were those who sincerely missed hearing the trumpet play melodies, and considered it an unfortunate retrogression. These dissatisfied trumpet enthusiasts undoubtedly gave the incentive necessary for the development of the chromatic trumpet.

The Chromatic Trumpet

Even though early trumpet makers distinguished their models by means of special etching, placement of the brass ball on the pipe for holding, and patterns of bends or crooks in the tube, there was no radical change in brass instrument construction before the 19th century. The more advanced craftsmen were exacting in their handling of metal thickness, and understandably produced very satisfying natural instruments. Nevertheless, they were still *natural* trumpets, and thus incapable of playing a chromatic scale.

In 1795 Haydn wrote his concerto for clarino to be played by Anton Weidinger, virtuoso trumpeter at the Esterhazy Court. The concerto called for several chromatic scale lines which would not have been possible to play on pre-existing clarino trumpets. In the year 1801 Weidinger took out a patent on a chromatic trumpet with keys, but historians do not know how long it had been in use before the patent was granted. In fact, it is possible that Haydn wrote his concerto with the blind expectation that someone would come up with an instrument capable of playing it. If so, Haydn's influence toward technical advances in trumpet construction may have been stronger than that of any other figure in music history.

Weidinger's keyed trumpet served as a model for Joseph Halliday who, around 1810, built a similar instrument in London. In 1815 an English marching band, making a triumphal entry into Paris to celebrate Napoleon's fall, introduced the keyed trumpet into France.

Haydn's concerto was in all probability the first piece ever conceived especially for trumpet with keys, although a concerto for "chromatic trumpet" was written in 1771 by Albrechtsberger. We are reasonably sure that no *keyed* trumpet existed at such an early date, but there *was* another type of chromatic trumpet which had been in use as early as the 16th century. The *Journal of Acquisitions* at the Berlin Musical Instrument Collection lists an instrument with the name *Trombeta a tirarsi*, which is handled as a *trombone a tirarsi* (*a tirarsi* signifying "with slide"), except that instead of two sliding tubes, it has only one. Whereas the bell section on the modern trombone stays in place as the double slide moves, on the *Trombeta*, or *Tromba a tirarsi* the player presses the mouthpiece against his lips with one hand and moves the rest of the instrument back and forth with the other. The fact that the sliding part of the tube has to bear the weight of the heavy bell at the end makes the sliding intolerably difficult.

Bach often used this instrument for the performance of chorale melodies in the minor or in a key impractical for the natural trumpet. In *Cantata No. 20*, for example, Bach called for the *Tromba de tirarsi* for a diatonic chorale section, and for simply a tromba for the obbligato to a bass aria. Unlike the chorale melody, the obbligato conformed exactly to notes in the harmonic series.

Haydn's designation *clarino* in the title of his work leads us to believe that he had in mind something other than the slide trumpet, which was generally given the label *tirarsi*, or the Germanic *zug*. One other fact lends credence to the theory: certain parts of Haydn's piece have such rapid chromatic changes that they would have been virtually impossible on the *Tromba a Tirarsi*.

Not long after Haydn's concerto, Johann Nepomuk Hummel wrote a similar three-movement work for chromatic (supposedly keyed) trumpet in E Major. Hummel's music was characterized by sparkling displays of sheer virtuosity, but nevertheless its joint exclusivity with the Haydn concerto gave it great significance in early trumpet literature.

Composers of the 19th century, long since freed tonally by equal temperament, utilized a large number of keys. The standard trumpet in F was ordinarily supplied with a full complement of crooks which allowed the trumpeter to play in the keys of E, E♭, D, D♭, C, and B, and if the slides were coupled, even B♭ and A. Supposedly double coupling could provide even lower keys, but the physical bulk made it impractical.

The advent of keys was a major breakthrough for the trumpet, but there was a new problem which no one had seemed to anticipate: tonal inconsistency. Tones produced by the full length of pipe sounded differently from those involving open holes, and so further experimentation was of necessity forthcoming. Of course the answer came soon in the form of valves.

Invention of the Valve

There were two men in the early 19th century who considered themselves the inventors of the valve: the Saxon, Heinrich Stölzel; and the Silesian, Friedrich Blühmel. These two jointly took out a ten-year patent for valves in Berlin in 1818, but who was actually the first will probably never be known, for even their contemporaries were unable to agree upon it. Stölzel is known to have been a horn player in the Royal Opera Orchestra in Berlin. He also held the appointment of Royal Chamber Musician and instrument repairer to the King of Prussia. Blühmel was more obscure and the most we know of him is that he was a musician in a mine company band.

After signing with Stölzel on the original patent application, Blühmel sought to secure an exclusive patent on another valve which he had invented and, failing to do so, asserted indignantly that it was he who had originated the 1818 idea. Stölzel, Blühmel's rival in the venture, was rather highly regarded in Prussia at the time, and the Prussian patent officials were unimpressed with Blühmel's pleas. It is beyond question that Stölzel was in Berlin early in 1815 with a valve horn which he claimed as his own idea. In all probability, Stölzel was the first to *plan* a valve, while Blühmel actually *made* the first one that was satisfactory.

The horn and its offspring the cornet were the first brass instruments to benefit from the valve system. About 1825, valves were applied to the cornet, and immediately a movement was initiated to make it the soprano voice of the orchestra rather than the trumpet.

Shortly afterwards, the trumpet was also fitted with valves; however, for some time the trumpet purists refused to accept this "degenerative" innovation. They felt that the trumpet had a heritage extending hundreds of years into antiquity, and regardless of how badly out of tune certain notes sounded, they were nevertheless "noble," and for such reason, justified.

In order to satisfy both the cornet and trumpet factions, Berlioz, in his *Symphonie Fantastique* (1830), used cornets to play the high chromatic parts, and trumpets on supporting parts appearing in the harmonic series.

Trumpet Personalities

The 20th century has produced many trumpeters who can safely be categorized as idols or heroes. Such names as André, Herseth, or Severinsen elicit today much the same admiration as did Reiche, Snow, or Altenburg in the era when the natural trumpet was at the height of its prestige. During the years between 1800 and 1875, the trumpet was subjected to experimentation, and composers were understandably cautious — even anachronistic — in their use of the trumpet. Trumpet personalities during this period, with the exception of Weidinger at the Esterhazy Court, were quite difficult to find. After all, the dedication required to develop a fine embouchure was hardly worth the effort, considering parts written for trumpet in that era. The great tragedy for fine trumpeters then and now is the fact that in chamber works of Mozart, Haydn, Beethoven, and even Brahms, no trumpet parts exist. Symphonies by the same composers include trumpet figures designed to augment the percussion section, and perhaps add a prominent voice to climaxes and cadences. In short, no matter how progressive these men were in their musical concepts, they refused to allow trumpeters out of their "trumpet-and-kettledrum" role.

One champion of the modern trumpet was Oskar Boehme, who in 1870 published his *Sextet, op. 30* for brass instruments. He scored the work originally for cornet, two trumpets, bass trumpet, trombone, and tuba. He also wrote a concerto for trumpet (c. 1875) which is perhaps the outstanding contribution to solo trumpet literature of the late 19th century.

The period from about 1875 to 1925 is commonly referred to as "The Golden Age of Brass." During this period, when the professional bands of Gilmore and Sousa flourished, the cornet was at a peak of prestige. Names such as Matthew Arbuckle, Herman Bellstedt, Ernest Williams, Walter Smith, Del Staigers, Allesandro Librati, and Jules Levy were highly esteemed because of virtuosity on the cornet.

Perhaps the best-known cornetist of all time was Herbert L. Clarke, whose compositions we often avoid today in our musical sophistication, but whose performing ability on the cornet is legendary. Clarke, as soloist with Sousa's band, traveled around the world, toured Europe four times, and played to wide acclaim in the United States and Canada for the greater part of his life. He is remembered today not only for his many published solos, but also for his pedagogical volumes, *Technical Studies,* and *Characteristic Studies,* both of which have served to develop fine trumpeters as well as cornetists.

Compensating Valves

The acceptance of valves was a giant step for brass players, but soon after they came into general use, players began to find that the chromatic scale produced by the valves was not perfectly in tune. Soon came a rapid proliferation of compensating valve systems. Some of the more familiar names who designed such systems were Sax, Besson, Courtois, Arban, and Mahillon. In an attempt to promote their own mechanical systems, some of the better-known teachers — Arban, for example — required all of their students to buy instruments equipped with their own devices. After many years of experimentation and teaching, however, these mechanical pioneers decided that a sensitive student played in tune anyway, and if a student was not sensitive, all the mechanical devices in the world would not help him to achieve perfect intonation.

There are a few brass devices which have been retained even until today, such as loops or triggers on the first and third valve slides, a fourth valve which substitutes for the first and third combination, and a trigger mechanism which controls the position of the tuning slide.

Research by instrument manufacturers over the past few years has been concerned mainly with two areas: (1) the mechanical workings of the instrument — such as the tolerance of valves within their casings, and the proper fitting of the instrument to the individual; (2) the proper channeling of vibrations within the instrument, including the elimination of interference within the pipe which might adversely affect the nodal pattern.

Although the trumpet must retain its natural harmonic series, which unfortunately does not conform to man's rather ingenious system of equal temperament, perhaps some day a nearly perfect specimen will be built. Regardless of the current mechanical limitations, we in the studios will continue, as always, toward developing performers who can display every bit of the potential of the instrument, as they continue a proud tradition which spans several centuries, and which includes many outstanding practitioners. ∎

Selected Bibliography

Bate, Philip. *The Trumpet and Trombone.* New York: W.W. Norton & Company, 1966.

Bragard, Roger, and Ferdinand J. De Hen. Translated by Bill Hopkins. *Musical Instruments in Art and History.* London: Barrie and Rockliff, 1968.

Bridges, Glenn. *Pioneers in Brass.* Detroit: Sherwood Publications, 1965.

Menke, Werner. *History of the Trumpet of Bach and Handel.* Translated by Gerald Abraham. London: William Reeves Bookseller Ltd., 1934.

Pietzsch, Hermann. *Die Trompete.* Translated by John Bernhoff; revised by Clifford Lillya and Renold Schilke. Ann Arbor: University Music Press.

Three Dissertations on Ancient Instruments from Babylon to Bach: Putnam, Nathanael D. *Musical Instruments in Biblical Times;* Urban, Darrell E. *The Enigma of the Tromba Da Tirarsi;* Lewis, Horace M., Jr. *A Study of the Clarino Style.* Fullerton, Calif.: F.E. Olds & Son Music Education Library.

Terry, C.S. *Bach's Orchestra.* London: Oxford University Press, 1956.

The Trumpet in the Romantic Era

— A Forgotten Instrument

H.M. Lewis

If one element may be said to characterize the romantic era in music, that element is constant change. And nowhere is change more evident than in the orchestral wind sections — both in their make-up and in the improvements in the wind instruments themselves. But of all the instruments, the trumpet was the one most affected by change.

Whereas the trumpet of the classical and early romantic periods had been a natural (valveless) instrument, the invention of the valve around 1818 was quickly applied to all of the brass instruments, including the trumpet. The importance of this invention cannot be overrated, at least for the trumpet player, for, while the horn had achieved a degree of melodic independence under the classical composers, the trumpet was used merely to provide harmonic and rhythmic background parts, with an occasional fanfare thrown in to keep the players from outright revolt. With the invention of the valve, the trumpet was freed from the tyranny of the overtone series; it became as fully chromatic as the woodwinds or strings.

The early valve trumpets differed from their natural predecessors only in the addition of valves, retaining the internal dimensions of the natural trumpets. Thus, while the modern B♭ trumpet is slightly conical throughout, the valve trumpet of the romantic era was cylindrical up to the last section of the bell, and the bell retained the proportions of the natural trumpet bells. The mouthpiece, too, was retained from the older natural trumpets. The trumpet mouthpiece in fashion during the 19th century was larger than those in common use today, and the cup was hemispherical in shape, with a sharp corner where the throat meets the cup. By contrast, today's trumpet mouthpieces usually have a deeper, hyperbolic cup that is smaller in diameter than the old mouthpieces, and the shoulder of the throat is more rounded. All of these characteristics, both of mouthpiece and of the instrument itself, contribute to a somewhat mellower, more flexible tone in the modern instrument, coupled with a slightly shallower sound. The tone of the early valve trumpets would have been quite similar to that of the natural trumpets.

At first composers kept calling for the trumpets to be crooked in all keys, as though they were natural trumpets, but it soon became evident that the players were using one trumpet to play almost all of the parts. The trumpet in F, the highest pitched natural trumpet in common use (a perfect fifth below the modern orchestral C trumpet), became the standard instrument of the day. In the military band, the instrument was used in E♭. Evidently the composers thought that to write their trumpet parts in the key of the piece would be to follow in the footsteps of the classical masters. As time went on, however, composers bowed to the inevitable, and wrote their trumpet parts either in E or F, to be played on the deep-toned trumpet in F. When cornets were used with trumpets in the same score, the usual practice was to couple a pair of cornets in A with a pair of trumpets in E, or a pair of cornets in B♭ with a pair of trumpets in F.

Almost as soon as the composers began to recognize the fact that their parts were being played on the F trumpets, another change began to take place. As an awareness grew of the chromatic possibilities of the valve trumpet, composers began to write more difficult parts for the instrument. Where the early valve trumpet parts had been little different from the natural trumpet parts, greater range, flexibility, and dynamic contrast came to be expected of the trumpet than had ever been required before. And as the technical demands became greater, it seemed clear to most trumpeters that the long F trumpet, with its noble tone but somewhat unsure quality of attack in the higher register, was simply not the instrument for the job. Little by little, then, the trumpet in high B♭, at the same pitch as the cornet, came into accepted general use in orchestras. Richard Strauss probably was the composer most responsible for the adoption of the B♭ trumpet; his trumpet parts were the despair of even the best trumpet players of his day. A noted German opera trumpeter of the present day, whose teacher was well known as a "specialist" in Strauss operas, has said that he was told many times that even in the early part of this century a first trumpet player was not expected to last through a complete Strauss opera. If a fine performer had problems of endurance and accuracy even on the B♭ trumpet, one can imagine what performances must have been like for, say, *Symphonia Domestica* on the deep-toned F trumpets. Many musicologists, notably Robert Donington and Cecil Forsythe, have lamented the passing of the F trumpet with its nobility of tone and true trumpet sound, but in simple fact, it is the composers themselves who were responsible for its demise.

Cecil Forsythe gives some of the advantages and drawbacks to the F trumpet, from the vantage point of a listener of the early 1900's.

In the old days its business was to reiterate single notes forte and to blare out somewhat conventional flourishes and fanfares "in the tutti." On these points there was never any charge against it on the score of ineffectiveness. On the contrary, the objection was then, and is now, that to all its phrases it lends a prominence that sometimes induces almost a sense of physical pain. We must remember too that the difficulties of mastering the instrument are great. It is the undoubted heir of the classical tradition, but our regret at its restricted use is tempered by the reflection that at most one or two players in a generation can make it bearable.[1]

It is some comfort to the modern trumpeter that performers have for many years been charged with playing too loudly! Forsythe goes on to say in the same work that parts written in the classical tradition or written specifically with the deep-toned F trumpet in mind should be played on that instrument, but that more modern parts that are delicate and more closely interwoven within the fabric of the orchestra would best be played on the B♭ or C trumpet.[2]

The range of the F trumpet was

which sounded

It will be noticed that the sounding range of the instrument is, for all practical purposes, that of the modern C trumpet. The upper notes above written E were quite uncertain, and were better taken in *forte* or louder.[3]
Another point of some confusion about the deep-toned trumpet in F can be seen from the range given. The instrument was written in the notation of the natural trumpets, so that the C below the treble staff, which is the second partial of the C trumpet, was the fourth partial of the old F trumpet. In effect, then, the F trumpet parts were written an octave lower than the B♭ and C trumpet parts, although the parts for the deep-toned trumpet were played mostly in the high register.

Out of curiosity, I procured a modern F alto trumpet and, using an alto trumpet mouthpiece, set out to play some of the parts written for the deep-toned F trumpet of the nineteenth century. Basically, the F trumpet sounds like one of the natural trumpets played in the high register. The valves make a difference, allowing the player to obtain more notes than would otherwise be the case, and they also allow the player to make intonation adjustments that would have been impossible on the natural trumpet, but the overall effect is quite similar to the natural instrument. It cannot be denied that the notes in the upper range are by no means as secure as they are on the shorter B or C trumpet, and the player feels very much like a French horn player as he carefully picks out the proper note from several

partials on either side of it. On the positive side, however, the high register of the F trumpet has a darker, smoother quality than even the low registers of the B♭ and C trumpets. In works by Tchaikovsky, Franck, Goldmark, and Brahms, the F trumpet lent a distinctive color to the piece, a color quite different from the one the concert-goer is accustomed to hearing. It is my opinion that the distinctive color of the longer trumpet is important when dealing with works which require two trumpets and two cornets, because a great difference can be heard in the tonal quality of the two instruments. When the trumpet parts in such works are played on cornets (which is too often no longer the case!), the striking difference in tonal qualities is lost, and the carefully planned effects of the composer go for naught.

The foregoing is not to suggest a return to the F trumpet except, perhaps, for demonstration purposes in the classroom. Although it would be interesting to hear, for example, Franck's *Symphony in D Minor*, or Tchaikovsky's *Symphony No. 4 in F Minor* performed with the trumpeters using long F trumpets, the uncertainty of attack on these instruments puts such a performance out of the realm of the probable, exciting though it might be. Perhaps a more logical solution would be the use of German rotary-valve trumpets to play the parts originally intended for the F trumpet. The trumpet sections of both the Chicago and Cleveland orchestras already use rotary-valve instruments for the performance of many classical and romantic works. The darker, more open tone of the rotary-valve trumpet blends better with the brass section and the rest of the orchestra in general, and does not penetrate like the tone of the piston-valve B♭ and C trumpet tends to do. And the German instruments are much less expensive than domestic makes.

The important thing that must be realized about trumpet parts from the 19th century is simply that they were conceived with an entirely different instrument in mind than the one that is used today. It has been stated that the modern trumpet is really not a trumpet by definition, but a soprano trombone. Since the trumpet has changed so much in the past century and a half, the player at least owes the composer the courtesy of finding out what sound the composer originally intended. ■

1. Cecil Forsythe, *Orchestration*, 2nd edition (New York: The Macmillan Company, 1967), p. 93.
2. Forsythe, *op. cit.*, p. 94.
3. Forsythe, *op. cit.*, p. 92.

January, 1972

The Rotary Valve Trumpet and the Vienna Style

Maurice Faulkner

Vienna, Austria
Summer 1971

We have returned to our hotel from a superb concert

by a major, central-European symphony orchestra. Over the past several days in Vienna we have enjoyed performances of Schubert's Fourth Symphony in C

Minor (D 417), his Sixth in C Major (D 589), the Third in D Major (D 200), the E♭ Major Mass, Brahms's Third and Fourth Symphonies, and two piano concertos, as well as Mahler's Kindertotenlieder. As we sat enthralled in the famous concert halls of Europe's most musical city, we recalled performances of these same Romantic works by magnificent orchestras in the United States. We couldn't help but wish that our trumpet sections at home would obtain some of these rotary-valve instruments which have a different type of sound so essential to the proper performance of Viennese romanticists.

It is difficult to describe that sound in words. I began at an early age as a performer upon the piston trumpet — an instrument so dear to our American hearts that I believed it could never be improved, except for more rapid spring action and similar technical devices. But on first hearing the central Europeans with their rotary-valve instruments, I realized that a new dimension in brass sound had been introduced to my ears. After living with that European color for the past 15 summers, it has become almost a *crusade* to interest the extraordinary brass specialists in our major American symphony orchestras in performing the major romantic works on these instruments.

The Rotary-Valve Trumpet Sound

Brahms, Wagner, Mahler, Bruckner, Richard Strauss, and others from that era of great emotionalism in music, conceived their brass parts for rotary-valve trumpets. The full-ranging sonorities of trumpet sections, with bass trumpets to fill the lowest ranges, were created in the imaginations of these composers.

In the reader's ear there must be recreated the suave, velvet-like beauty of the singing strings, the piquant, dry woodwinds, and the broad brasses of the romantic symphonic orchestra. To match those sonorous strings in *tutti* the romantic composers turned to brasses which were designed for an even scale with a full, round beauty of sound throughout the necessary range. The tone seldom has the nasal and brilliant edge associated with the American and French piston-valve trumpet.

When the lyric first theme of the Brahms Fourth Symphony, first movement, sings out in the strings, the orchestral trumpets blend their accompanying chords, rhythms, and melodies into the total sound with a mellow, round color — a warm, luscious brass sound which complements the string tone, adding body to create a resonant, deep experience that touches the innermost emotions of the listener. One has to hear it to understand it!

Brief Historical Background

All brass specialists realize that for many centuries the natural trumpet, without the possibility of playing chromatic scales, ruled the orchestras and the military establishments of every nation. Pity the poor brassist who had as many as 40 key changes in a Mozart opera, scrambling among his equipment for the right crook or

shank when he had to put his natural horn into a new key so that he could play the tonic and dominant chords of the new modulation! A visit to the pits of some of those old baroque opera houses will convince the modern brass player that the life of a trumpeter in the 16th and 17th centuries was not an easy one. Along the pit walls where the trumpeters or hornists sat were shank or crook holders so that the musicians could organize their tools for the evening's work.

We cannot trace the numerous variations of pistons, rotaries, sliding mechanisms, revolving plates, etc. which were forerunners of the best of the systems. But we must point up the patent by Joseph Riedl, here in Vienna, of his *Rad-Maschine* in 1832. It did away with the awkward angles and windways which had been characteristic of the Stölzel valve, and thus eliminated many of the intonation problems and resistances which had been built-in to earlier valve systems.

The operating mechanism which he established in his patent consisted of an articulated crank, controlled by a watch spring, enclosed in a small drum. This concept with many refinements has come down to us today in our rotary-valve assemblies. The "American" version uses a string device, which connects the key to the rotor, thus eliminating some of the clanking noise that occurs when rotary valves become worn from use.

Why the Rotary-Valve Has Greater Sonority

The natural trumpet with its rather gentle curves in the bends of the tubing was fitted with the new rotary valve, which, because of the size of its mechanism, continued the easy-rounding bends of the original tube. When piston valves were developed, the necessary structure of the short pistons made it essential that the tubing be bent in such a fashion so that the long tubes would be fairly close together, in order to give strength to support the piston section.

The sharper bends of the pipe or tube, and the resultant problems with intonation, added to the somewhat more brittle and edgy tone quality, producing what we call the "French" sound. This quality of tone became a prime concept when these French piston-valve instruments emigrated to the United States. They have been a part of our musical scene since. The British also accepted the piston valve.

The central Europeans have used piston valve instruments, but seldom do they bring them into the operatic orchestras or the symphony halls. Taste and tradition in Austria, Germany, Czechoslovakia and other similar areas call for rotary valve instruments.

Although I cannot document it by research statistics, I feel the difference in sound between rotary and piston valve instruments comes from a difference in the degree to which the pipe is bent. The rotor mechanism on a rotary valve trumpet, due to its length or breadth, calls for a more gentle bending of the lead pipe tube, and consequently a more-rounded curvature in *all* of the bends on the instrument. Because of this, the partials which are being vibrated in the tube are not broken down with quite the same distortion as they are in the more narrow bends of the piston valve trumpet.

Later,
Back in the United States

As I sit in my studio and contemplate the two rotary-valve trumpets which I own and compare them to my piston-valve American instrument as well as my old-fashioned piston-valve American cornet, I believe that this difference in construction (see above) is the crux of the difference in sound and evenness of intonation which I find in the rotary-valve instruments. And when I pick up the different instruments and play them, I am convinced that the rotary-valve trumpet should be developed by our American manufacturers for those musicians who would achieve the true concept of the Viennese Style in performing the romantic music of Brahms, Mahler, Wagner, Bruckner, Strauss, and others. ∎

January, 1972

The Rotary Valve Trumpet —
An American Revival

Jack Hall

The rotary valve trumpet is enjoying a mild revival among top artists in America. Among those who are finding the instrument useful in their work are Eugene Blee of the Cincinnati Symphony Orchestra, and Leon Rapier of the Louisville Orchestra. Recently the entire Chicago Symphony Orchestra trumpet section has been using rotary valve C trumpets, and they have made their way into the Cleveland Orchestra as well.

I presently own a German rotary valve C trumpet by Monke of Köln, and I have found it to be a satisfactory instrument for orchestra, band, and chamber music performance. It certainly is an attention-getter when an audience discovers it among the instruments being used.

Because of the questions directed to me when I have performed on my rotary valve trumpet, I have explored its history and examined the testimonials of its qualities. I would like to share some of my discoveries.

Historical Background

The rotary valve trumpet and piston valve trumpet apparently arrived in the musical world about the same time — the early 19th century. Exact dates and names of inventors are open to question — but it is known that the piston valve trumpet found favor in England and France, while the rotary valve trumpet was preferred by the German and Italian musicians.

Construction Details

The rotary valve trumpet employs a different method of changing the length of the air column than the piston valve trumpet. The connection and disconnection is accomplished by a revolving cylinder triggered by a lever device, either set into motion by (1) a string or (2) a mechanical hook-up, both attached from the key-lever to the valve. The devices are equal as far as speed is concerned; however, the string method is quieter.

The horn almost exclusively used the rotary valve system to obtain the more "round" change of tone, as contrasted with the "angular" change of the piston valve.

The overall design of most trumpets is a combination of tapers, curves, and cylindrical sections.

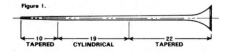

Figure 1.

| 10 TAPERED | 19 CYLINDRICAL | 22 TAPERED |

The closer a valve section is added toward the mouthpiece, the darker the sound. In the traditional construction of a rotary valve trumpet the first valve begins approximately two inches from the end of the mouthpipe, as compared to a distance of ten inches on the piston valve trumpet. This is the main reason for the characteristic dark sound of the rotary valve trumpet. Because of this darkness, a very narrow bore is employed to insure against the sound becoming too dark. Most rotary valve trumpets have very large bells of up to five and one half inches or more. However, this contributes little or nothing to the quality of sound. The thickness of the tubing of both piston and rotary valve trumpets is about the same.

One grave problem is always inherent in the construction of rotary valve instruments. The "mouthtubing enters the first valve through a decided bend, the outer edge of which comes in what would be about the middle of the tube if the latter were continued in a straight line."[1] This is probably why the scale is freer and purer on the piston valve trumpet. As of yet, no satisfactory solution has been perfected.

Employment and Playing Properties

For many years, European orchestras have been known for their deliverance of a dark "teutonic" sound from the trumpets. This tone is often described as being rich while remaining resonant and compact, without becoming shrill even during the most powerful fortissimo. Vincent Bach describes it as "a glorious, noble tone of fascinating beauty and a unique quality."[2] The rotary valve trumpet is almost synonymous with German romantic literature, displayed so effectively in the symphonies of Brahms, Mahler, Wagner, and Bruckner.

The Berlin Philharmonic Orchestra, Vienna Philharmonic Orchestra, Vienna Symphony Orchestra, and Vienna Opera Orchestra — considered to be among the world's finest — all feature rotary valve instruments in their trumpet sections.

The rotary valve trumpet has a unique and much needed character and should not be overlooked. There are unlimited possibilities for its use, not only as a fine chamber music instrument, but as a member of American symphony orchestras and bands, where it can add a timbre long missing.

Keep your eyes on the trumpet section at the next concert you attend. You may well discover that the rotary valve trumpet has found another convert. ∎

1. Menke, W., *History of the Trumpet of Bach and Handel*. London: Reeves, 1934, p. 110.
2. Bach, V., *Bach Means Quality*. New York: Vincent Bach, 1961.

January, 1972

The Trumpet Player
Who Never Missed a Note

David Whitwell

The industrial revolution which began to change the life of Europe in the 18th century created a climate for mechanical invention extending even to the arts. In music one facet of this energy was the proliferation of instrument makers and their almost unanimous desire for constant mechanical progress. Thus during a very short period in the early 19th century mechanical solutions to problems which had hampered players since antiquity were found for some instruments, e.g. Boehm's work on the flute and the addition of valves to the trumpet.

Although less well known today, an almost equal amount of effort during this period was expended in the invention of music related machines. Many of these experiments were in the cause of music education, such as the machine invented in 1739 by Lawrence Mitzler de Kolof to teach thorough-bass according to mathematical rules. Better known are the various contraptions of the 19th century designed to help the piano teacher "shape" the student's hand in a desired manner; the career of Robert Schumann, as a pianist, was ended by such a contrivance.

The musical machine most familiar to musicians is, of course, the metronome. After Galileo established the basic laws of pendulum motion, at the end of the 16th century, there were many attempts to construct a pendulum type device for measuring tempi in music. Until Maelzel, of the 19th century, all failed for one or another practical reasons.

Johann Nepomuk Maelzel (1772-1838) first attracted attention in Vienna when he exhibited a mechanical band, consisting of flutes, pipes, four trumpets, cymbals, triangle and bass drum, powered by a weight drawn wheel which ran a double bellows. From this device, which played military marches, he built more and more sophisticated mechanical ensembles, aiming for a complete symphony orchestra. It was for one of the later machines that he commissioned Beethoven to compose the *Wellington's Victory*. (Maelzel's reputation was tarnished a bit by the mechanical chessplayer he exhibited, for it was found to contain a midget.)

Maelzel's most successful machine, aside from his work on the metronome, was his mechanical trumpet player whom the inventor named, Albert. Albert contained no midget; he was spring wound (the key being on the left hip); and he played a normal trumpet of the day. A little known entry in the *Journal des Modes* (1809) gives an eyewitness account of this extraordinary machine:

From a tent Mr. Maelzel led out a fine manly-looking martial figure, in the uniform of a trumpeter of the Austrian dragoon regiment. After having pressed the figure on the left shoulder, it played not only the Austrian cavalry march, as also all the signals for the manoeuvres of that army, but also a march and an allegro by Weigl, which was accompanied by the whole orchestra. After this, the dress of the figure was completely changed into that of a French trumpeter of the guard; it then began to play the French cavalry march, also all the signals of the French cavalry manoeuvres, and lastly a march of Dussek's, and an allegro of Pleyel, accompanied again by the full orchestra. The sound of this trumpet is pure, and more agreeable than even the ablest musician could produce from that instrument, because the breath of a man gives the inside of the trumpet a moisture which is prejudicial to the purity of the tone.

It is ironic, the comment here that the machine was more agreeable than the results which might be achieved from a live musician, for this is a point much discussed today relative to the recorded and live performances of symphony orchestras. We might also point out that critics in 1809 also worried about the possibility of machines eventually replacing live musicians altogether.

And does one not hear the same fears expressed relative to "electronic music" today?

Speaking of electronic music, and those who believe music today is going to the *dogs*, we must close by describing yet another musical machine which was surely the first example of "musique concrète." It seems that after a particularly unworthy performance Louis XI once commented to his concertmeister, Abbe Debaigne, that he might as well hear a concert of pigs! Taking the king at his word, Debaigne assembled a large number of pigs, of various ages. He then constructed a machine by which, when playing upon the keyboard, sharp instruments pricked the pigs, causing a prodigious noise!

∎

January, 1972

How to Choose a Brass Instrument Mouthpiece

Vincent Bach

The most important tool and first requisite of a brass instrumentalist's success is a mouthpiece which enables him to emit a beautiful singing tone, with an easy and reliable response in all registers. The creation of such a mouthpiece is an art that can hardly be mastered by anybody but an accomplished brass instrumentalist who also enjoys sufficient mechanical training to combine both skills into a superior product; in other words, by a specialist.

The tone quality of a mouthpiece depends on various factors—the rim, the size and curvature of the cup, the funnel-like shape and size of the throat and the backbore.

The rim affects the tone-quality to the extent by which it controls the free movement of the lip muscles and response. The tone will be more metallic if the rim has a sharp inner edge, and more fuzzy, with the attack insecure, if the rim is too rounded. An extra-wide rim hampers the flexibility—only players with very thick, fleshy, soft lips can use it advantageously. A too narrow rim will dig into the muscle tissues and cut off the blood circulation, thereby paralyzing the lips, which causes slurring to become difficult. A medium-wide rim offers the greatest comfort, flexibility and endurance; however, a rim which fits most comfortably on the lips does not necessarily give the best playing results. When a mouthpiece rim cuts the lips, the instrumentalist is most likely playing with a receding lower jaw so that the lips do not rest on the flat face of the rim, but on the sharp inner edge against the teeth. The solution is for the player to raise his instrument above the horizontal position, without leaning his head back, so that the mouthpiece will press exactly perpendicularly to the face of the upper front teeth. If the jaw is pushed out so that the lower teeth are in line with the upper ones, the rim will not cut the lip.

The Cup

The cup of the mouthpiece determines the timbre (color) of tone. A shallow cup facilitates the high register, favors the higher frequencies, produces a more brilliant, bright tone, but all of this is at the expense of the low register. A medium-deep cup emits the best overall results for the high and low register and is recommended for general use. The deep cup enriches the low register causing the high tones to be more mellow and less penetrating; it is generally preferred by players performing second or fourth trumpet or French horn parts.

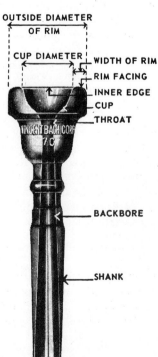

A musical tone is a composite consisting of the predominating fundamental tone (the tone we tune by) and the less intense overtones (harmonics) which are multiples of vibrations of the fundamental component. The human ear is most sensitive to frequencies above 500 vibrations. Therefore, a player whose hearing is very sensitive to high vibrations is convinced that he is playing louder by producing an excessively brilliant tone, rich in overtones, which "cuts" and sticks out like a sore thumb. While a tone rich in harmonics sounds clear and brilliant and responds well, a tone flavored with enharmonics (not being multiples of the vibrations of the fundamental element) or non-periodic vibrations, will sound nasal and displeasing, and will cause the tone to crack easily (wolf-tone). Using a mouthpiece with a deep cup (especially when playing a mellow-toned B♭ flügelhorn), an instrumentalist may complain that he can't hear himself; yet it is that kind of a rich tone that produces the greatest carrying power.

The Throat

The throat — both the funnel-shaped entrance and the size of the hole — controls the air resistance. If too small, the tone will choke and lower the high register; if too large, the mouthpiece will lack resistance, will suck the lips of the player into the cup and will tire him unduly in strenuous work. It is the medium throat, size .144", Morse drill #27, which is most desirable and which offers the average player sufficient volume of tone, excellent all-around register and maximum endurance. Symphony artists, performing in an 85 to 100 piece orchestra, may require a slightly larger "symphony throat," up to .155," Morse drill #3.9 mm, to produce that immense volume of tone required (let the manufacturer enlarge the throat — don't try to do it yourself).

The Backbore

The backbore is made in numerous sizes, generally using a few standard designs, some for special purposes to overcome deficiencies in instruments or embouchures. The choice of these should be left to the manufacturer.

In the end, *it is the skillful blend of all factors involved — the rim, cup, throat and backbore — which produces the mouthpiece of your dreams.*

The Practical Way to Select a Mouthpiece

Any brass instrument sounds best in the middle register; a mouthpiece should be selected with that in mind.

If the player tries different models of mouthpieces and obtains equally good results with both large and medium sizes, he should always give preference to the larger. A bigger cup diameter will cause a larger portion of the lip to vibrate and therefore produce more volume of tone; it will also give better lip control. If the lips should swell from too much playing, there will always be enough room to control the response. If a player splits too many tones, it is usually a sign that he is using a mouthpiece with too small a cup diameter.

By using a larger sized mouthpiece, playing with moist open lips (not pinching them tightly together so they cannot vibrate), using a minimum pressure and relaxed embouchure, a maximum volume of tone will be attained. Pinching the lips tightly together will cause the tone to be raw and fuzzy; keep the chin down. By practicing with minimum pressure on sustained tones, the lip muscles will gradually become stronger, resulting in a healthy, easy high register and a relaxed low register.

You must understand, however, that you cannot play entirely without pressure; the higher or louder you play, the more pressure you have to use; otherwise the air will escape around the outer rim of the mouthpiece. Playing a high tone *ff*, you have to contract your lip muscles, which will cause them to stiffen, and vibrate harder, requiring more air support. If you play in a full-sized concert band or in a large symphony orchestra, performing a Strauss symphony or a Wagner opera, for example, you cannot avoid using heavier pressure occasionally during a *ff* passage. The lip muscles can endure such occasional heavy pressure easily if they are not damaged by constant abuse. The idea is to do it with *restraint* — and preserve a flexible embouchure.

Famous virtuosos like Fritz Werner, Albert Couturier, Herbert Clarke, George Stellwagen (Pernet), Jules Levy, Theodore Hoch, Paris Chambers, Walter Rogers, have all used large mouthpieces with deep cups and large throats, and they have obtained fantastic results. They produced high tones just the same by diligently training their embouchures. I therefore do not hesitate to recommend that young students start on mouthpieces of a large cup diameter, playing for a while with little pressure only in the middle register, between the staves, then gradually building the range into the higher and lower compass. By using a large mouthpiece, a player can hardly force the high register, but is compelled to use his lip muscles correctly. The average trumpet player performing heavy dance work or the one who isn't keen on practicing regularly, seems to prefer a medium-sized mouthpiece; so do girls who have more delicate lip muscles.

Avoid Strain

During the initial period of becoming used to a new mouthpiece, don't get over-enthusiastic; stop playing on it *before* you tire. The secret of developing a powerful embouchure is never to abuse your lip muscles; always avoid unnecessary strain. Relax the mouthpiece pressure as often as possible by removing the mouthpiece from your lips at every opportunity. This will permit the blood to circulate. Beginners especially are in the habit of keeping the mouthpiece on the lips . . . for fear they cannot find the same place again! In so doing, they cause the lips to become numb quickly.

Many of our young people listen to so much dance music that when they play cornet, they strive to imitate the brilliant tone of jazz trumpeters by using too shallow mouthpieces or by selecting a cornet of a too small bore. The genuine cornet tone should be of dark timbre, mellow and smooth, with a voice-like quality similar to the lyric soprano in opera.

Some players imagine that if they use a mouthpiece with a small throat, they can get healthy high tones more easily, but just the reverse is true.

A Few Tips on Developing a Powerful Embouchure

The player must not permit his lips to protrude into the mouthpiece cup but should draw them back tightly against the front teeth, raising the aperture or slot between the lips a little higher so that it is exactly in line with the open space between the teeth. In other words, he should not roll the lips over the upper teeth; looking in a mirror, he should be able to see his teeth while drawing the lips back. While it is necessary to use slightly more pressure for the high tones, the additional amount of pressure is negligible; let the lip muscles do the work by *contracting* them or by *tightening* them, but not by *stretching* them.

A beginner should take it easy and avoid heavy strain. He should not attempt to force the high register but should start playing in the middle register between middle G, second line, and middle C^5, third space. Once he controls that register, he should always use C^5 as a pivot, practicing long tones *crescendo* and *decrescendo*, starting from middle C^5 up and then down:

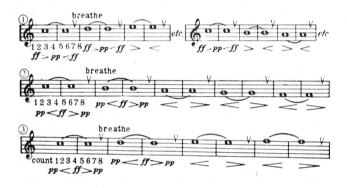

J.J. Baptiste Arban, the most successful early tutor, followed this method. When accomplishing the *crescendo,* be sure not to raise the pitch of the tone, but be sure it remains at the same level.

Line 1 should be played slowly, attacking with a pianissimo "tee," increasing the tone evenly and without vibrato up to count 4 fortissimo; at 5 start to diminish the tone, disappearing completely at the end of the eighth beat. Remove the mouthpiece from the lips for about five seconds; now proceed with the next higher tones as high as you can play without undue strain. Then stop for 15 seconds and repeat the procedure with the notes on line 2. Practicing in this manner will eventually enable one to play the high and low registers with the same embouchure by just contracting or relaxing his lip muscles. I strongly advise against starting with the lower register, which encourages the player to let his lips protrude too far forward.

A student should practice these long tones very frequently between other technical studies so that he will continue to play with a relaxed embouchure and will not neglect his tone production.

For a beginner, 20 to 25 minutes practice at a time is sufficient, but after two or three months he should be able to play 30 to 40 minutes. He should always stop before he becomes too tired, for in that way he will, after two or three hours of rest, be able to recuperate quickly and to start again with a fresh embouchure. Playing three or four sessions daily, the embouchure will gradually become stronger and stronger. An advanced player may average 40 to 60 minutes or more per session if gifted with a powerful and well-trained embouchure.

A Special Note About Beginners

A beginner should not attempt to play a horn without proper supervision. *It's the first lesson which makes or breaks a brass instrumentalist.*

Also, too many promising talents are from the beginning doomed to pass into oblivion by choosing low-quality equipment — an improperly designed mouthpiece or an inferior instrument. A student will easily become discouraged if required to play sub-standard equipment with which a professional is unable to perform.

We have today highly competent music instructors in our schools who are familiar with the results which can be obtained by pupils using quality mouthpieces and instruments. But even the best teacher cannot accomplish much if a student is poorly equipped. To purchase a cheap mouthpiece or a second-grade instrument is a very poor investment. ∎

January, 1972

The "Ideal" Mouthpiece

Robert Giardinelli

Volumes have been written about cup mouthpieces, and a great variety of ideas expressed about the various shapes and sizes which should be incorporated into the "ideal" mouthpiece. Almost every player has had an "ideal" mouthpiece. Unfortunately, too many times it was the one he lost ten years ago!

In an attempt to design or duplicate the "ideal" mouthpiece, many experiments have been performed, both practical and scientific. Mouthpieces have been cut apart, micrometered, and impressions taken. Various materials and methods of manufacture have been tried. Theories — almost as many as there are brass players — have been

formulated, developed and discarded.

After all this, we find that we can build a "perfect" mouthpiece for one player while another player will find it inadequate or even impossible to use. A good case in point:

Several years ago I developed a special mouthpiece for Maynard Ferguson. It has a small diameter cup,

V-shaped, shallow, with a rather thick, semi-flat and slightly concave rim surface and well-rounded bite. This proved to be a magnificent mouthpiece for him. His range was phenomenal ($F\sharp^3$ to D^7, 3 octaves above middle C!) but the majority of players couldn't use it.

A teacher should not recommend such an extreme model mouthpiece to young students. Most of these youngsters have not developed the endurance or embouchure necessary to withstand hours of practice on these models. A medium cup with a fairly rounded rim and balanced backbore is much easier to play, is less tiring, and gives better results in all registers.

Even so, there is no single "standard" mouthpiece. The requirements of individual players vary so much that unless a mouthpiece is tailored exactly to his needs, one can only compromise.

Dentition, lip structure, facial and throat muscles and tongue are all important factors in the selection of a mouthpiece. It could even be said that a person's entire body dictates type and style of mouthpiece. For example, lung (vital) capacity, diaphragm development, abdominal and thoracic musculature all affect the output of a mouthpiece. Fortunately, there are many mouthpieces on the market, thus the compromise need not be so great for the knowledgeable brass instrumentalist. He has to use the sensible approach of trying several mouthpieces and choosing the one that feels most comfortable and which gives the best response in all registers.

The "Desired" Sound

No one questions the fact that the mouthpiece is very important in the production of the "desired" sound. One has to decide, therefore the kind of sound desired. Many musicians come to us to try mouthpieces. Some ask for the smallest sizes; then they proceed to "screech." They never play one note in the middle or low registers. Evidently that's the type of sound they desire. Others look for quality and balance instead. Although there are notable exceptions, I have found that most symphony players use large diameters, deep cups and open backbores, while lead men for Woody Herman or Duke Ellington use very shallow cups and tight backbores.*

In my 25 years of experience in making mouthpieces I have had the pleasure — and occasionally the headache — of working with many great artists in all fields of music and from all over the world. It has been a great honor and I've learned a lot from them. Their ideas have been invaluable and have been incorporated in many of the so-called "stock" models. Our 6M mouthpiece was originally made for Billy Butterfield. The C1 horn mouthpiece was designed by Jimmy Chambers and the S15 by Joseph Singer, both famous horn artists with the New York Philharmonic for many years. The 5D trombone mouthpiece was originally the Tommy Dorsey model. Many other present models have been designed or developed in cooperation with leading instrumentalists.

Today the Screw-Rim is used to provide the advantage of using the same rim on more than one size cup, both for special momentary needs and for doublers on the various trumpets and flügelhorn, the French horn and Wagner tuba, and trombone and bass trombone. The advantage of the Screw-Rim is obvious. A player can select the rim size and contour that feels most comfortable to his lip and then he can try different cup depths and styles to suit his specific needs. Some players even change cups during a performance to facilitate certain passages.

We make a great variety of cups and rims and try to satisfy the needs and taste of most musicians, but no one could manufacture and stock all the possible combinations of shapes and sizes. Therefore, we often have requests for custom made mouthpieces and we do keep on file the forms and specifications of each custom mouthpiece we make just in case there are future calls for the same model.

Of course, after a player finds the ideal mouthpiece for his style of playing, there is still one more magic ingredient that is needed to make the player outstanding, and that is *practice*. No mouthpiece can eliminate that important activity!

*Editor's note: Herman's current lead trumpeter is using a Bach 1½C . . . and playing C^7's all night (3 octaves above middle C).

January, 1972

The Birth of a New Mouthpiece

William H. Rose

Through the past several years we have all seen enormous changes in tuba repertoire, an ever-increasing number of fine players, and the addition of excellent new tubas to the market. It seemed to me, however, that one major area had been neglected. I couldn't understand why someone had not designed and produced a new and more functional stock mouthpiece — one which would meet the demands of our modern players for more flexibility and wider range with good intonation. Concluding that perhaps the fault was with us, the players, for not making the mouthpiece manufacturers more aware of our problems, I personally began experimenting with a stock mouthpiece (Mirafone C-4). Over a period of several weeks (back and forth from my own workbench to the concert hall), I tested each mouthpiece by using it, either in rehearsal or concert, with the Houston Symphony Orchestra. I now have a mouthpiece that responds and sounds better than any other I have ever played on.

Before relating some of the highlights of my experiments, let us look back, before and after the turn of the century, when most of our problems with the tuba began.

The instrument is essentially an "infant," a little over 100 years old as we know it today, with only the serpent and ophicleide as its predecessors. These were "oddball" instruments in both looks and sound, and this new member of the brass family stood just a notch above them in its early design — so large and clumsy compared to the older and smaller brass instruments. Consequently, for many years, tuba players usually found the public (and musicians as well) looking upon the tuba as nothing more than the "ugly duckling," "oom-pah" member of the brass family.

The early tuba parts for band and small ensembles in this country were quite simple and did not require much range or technique on the part of the players. (Only the symphonic literature, band transcriptions, and opera offered any real challenge.) Therefore, most of the tuba players in earlier years were content to play on whatever mouthpiece came with the tuba they purchased, regardless of size or shape.

However, in the past few decades, the tuba has *finally emerged as a music instrument!* A tuba player can "oom-pah" on most any type or size of mouthpiece, but to play the ever-increasing amount of difficult music now being written for the instrument demands much more.

Other than a few custom-made mouthpieces found here and there (usually among professionals), most *stock* tuba mouthpieces being used today were designed *over 25 years ago!* All of these older mouthpieces met the meager demands of *those* times, but times have changed — and so has everything concerning the tuba.

Current Mouthpiece Requirements

The music, musician, and instrument of today demand the following in a mouthpiece:

1. The top octave must be in tune. As a test, play three octaves of open C's on CC tubas, or three octaves of B♭'s on BB♭ tubas — listening in particular to the top note.

2. Maximum sound needed in a symphony orchestra or band must be produced without the sound "backing up," yet not "too open" to cause an airy sound or lose too much air in loud passages.

3. Good tone quality is essential — not too loud or "blasty" in fortissimo passages. Tone must remain full even when playing softly.

4. One must be able to reach high notes, with a clean attack and clear sound, but the low register must respond equally well.

5. Double and triple tonguing must "speak" clearly, with a clean and crisp sound.

6. The rim must be as comfortable as possible, yet with enough "bite" to attack notes clearly.

At first, in my studio, I thought the C-4 mouthpiece adequate for the small bore tuba with which it came. However, I found in the concert hall that it would not produce enough sound — it had a tendency to "back up" and not blow freely in loud passages — so I decided to open up the throat a little. Four more C-4's and several drill bits were ordered. The C-4 had an 18/64th throat opening, so I went to 19/64ths first. This helped a little, but not enough; 20/64ths inch opening, with a little more taper into it worked still better, and even responded fairly well on my medium large bore tuba which I use regularly. Still, it would "back up" in fortissimo passages, and the low register would not respond well enough on either tuba. At this point I decided to enlarge the inner cup a bit, thinking it might give the sound a little more cushion, but the upper register went flat. This is the chief fault of most of the deep cup standard mouthpieces currently in use.

Since the broader cup experiment did not work, I went on to a new C-4, this time opening the throat to 21/64ths inch. Now I was not only playing in tune over three octaves, but was also producing good sound in all registers! I felt that the mouthpiece

could be perfected, so I adjusted the taper into the throat. I had to put this one aside, though, because I apparently made too much taper, which let too much air through, particularly in loud low passages. This time (my last untouched C-4) extremely small amounts were taken off in tapering, with the results tested on both size tubas. I decided the fat rounded rim needed more bite for good attacks, so, little by little, I began adjusting the inside rim (a ticklish job), and also cut down on the extremely large outside diameter which covered too much of the embouchure.

For these last few experiments, I used the mouthpiece in actual concerts. I knew it was risky, but I wanted the mouthpiece tested under the most strenuous conditions. Here I must emphasize that it not only *passed* the test, but exceeded my expectations by not only responding beautifully on the small bore tuba (which I used for *The Rite of Spring* and *Benvenuto Cellini*), but also on the medium bore instrument which I used on programs that included *1812 Overture, Till Eulenspiegel's Merry Pranks,* and *An American in Paris.* The mouthpiece was responding better than any I had ever played on (I even checked it out on a large bore instrument), but it took three or four more trips back and forth from concert to workbench to adjust the rim for good attacks as well as for comfort and endurance. Twelve University of Houston tuba students confirmed my enthusiasm.

Inasmuch as I had started all these experiments with a Mirafone C-4 mouthpiece and kept its cup size, I offered the improved version to them. The Mirafone *Rose Model* mouthpiece will soon appear on the market. ∎

The Descant Horn, Part I

Christopher Leuba

If the single F "valve horn" might be characterized as the horn of the 19th century, I would say that the double horn has been the instrument of the 20th century, and that the descant is truly the instrument of the 21st century.

The "money horn players" world-wide, are already playing

this instrument — despite its tonal shortcomings. Some of them use it exclusively.

It is important for music educators — who will hear increasing talk of the "descant horn" — to be aware of the instrument and to understand the state of its development at the present time.

The "single F" horn, commonly used by most beginning students until recently, has a fundamental tone which sounds:

The less common "single B♭" horn has a fundamental of:

The conventional "double horn" consists of the two horns, F and B♭, coupled together with a common mouthpiece and bell section. The fundamentals are:

The double horn has been generally accepted as the standard instrument of the professional performer in this country, as well as that of most advanced students. (In Europe, a considerable number of "high" players, i.e., orchestral 1st and 3rd hornists, are using the single B♭ as their basic instrument.)

The use of the B♭ horn, either as part of a double horn or by itself, is predicated by the wider spacing of the overtones in the upper register, thus enabling players to achieve greater accuracy:

During the 1930s, the "descant" horn made its first appearance, a few advanced performers in Europe experimenting with several versions of it. The first performer, of whom I am aware, who used such an instrument in the United States was the distinguished Hungarian player, Tibor Shik, who played principal horn in the Pittsburgh Symphony during most of the "Reiner Era."

Presently, descant instruments are generally available from Paxman (England), Alexander (Germany) and Mirafone (Germany); Dehmal (Vienna) has also built descant horns.

Basically, the descant horn is a single F horn, an octave higher than the traditional instrument, i.e., its fundamental sounds:

Following is a comparison of the "open tones" of the conventional F horn with those of the descant horn.

It is obvious that the chance for error in "aiming" for notes in the upper register is much less on the shorter instrument.

This "descant F horn" is often combined with a normal B♭ horn, creating a "descant double horn" with these fundamentals:

Recently, a "descant triple horn" has been devised, comprising the conventional double horn and a descant F horn; this instrument has three fundamentals:

And, in the periphery, a few less common types: the "descant G horn," which has this fundamental:

The instruments in G usually have an optional F tuning slide. As a horn in G, this instrument would seem to me to be ideal for parts of Handel's oratorio, *Judas Maccabaeus*. The "F-F descant horn" has been produced by Dehmal in Vienna: this descant double horn combines the high and low F horns, giving these fundamentals:

The "descant B♭ horn" has been used in England recently; it has this fundamental tone:

This is obviously the same fundamental as that of a normal trumpet in B♭!

Not only are there presently at least five different descant-type horns available, but there are also variants of these types, either in the method of achieving the fundamental tone (double horns), or in the mouthpipe/body/bell size ratios.

These variations reflect basic differences of concept concerning the *purpose* of using the descant — dictated, to some extent, by construction and technology.

Purpose

The player will eventually have to decide for himself whether he will use the descant as a *basic* instrument, or rather as an *adjunct* instrument reserved for particular passages which lie unusually high. This may be decided by the nature of his employment.

I was recently engaged by a major European recording company to assist a German symphony orchestra which had no qualified high horn specialist available to perform some extraordinarily high first horn parts of several middle-period Haydn symphonies, such as No. 48 ("Maria Theresa") which has numerous sounding G's and some A's as well. If this type of playing were my principal occupation, my choice of instruments would certainly be different than it is as a permanent member of a wind quintet, which requires much low horn playing, as well as occasional forays into the stratosphere. With the German orchestra, I used a descant exclusively, since the high range was of paramount importance — but, a double descant, which has the middle range available as an adjunct.

Some orchestral principal hornists are turning to the descant as an exclusive, basic instrument: these players seek a horn which produces, as much as possible, a rich quality and secure intonation in the middle range, considering the descant part as a useful adjunct.

emphasis   adjunct

or

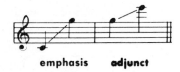

emphasis   adjunct

To decide intelligently what type of instrument is best for a specific purpose, it is helpful to understand some of the construction principles involved in creating a double horn.

Full Double and Compensating Type Horns

Two types of conventional double horns have existed for more than half a century: the more common "full double" and the "compensating double," also known as the "Wendler model." (See diagrams)

The full double system provides independent tubing and tuning slides for each horn. In the compensating system, the tubing of the higher pitched horn (B♭ horn, on a conventional instrument) is *always* in use, and the compensating slides are *added* on to bring the pitch down to the lower key. Although the higher pitched horn is usually excellent, the lower pitched horn usually has serious intonation problems as well as unevenness of tone quality, because of the extra convolutions of tubing, and because the second valve compensating tubing is not usually tunable. The same dif-

ferences exist with descants: there is a full double system and a compensating double.

Full Double Descant

The full double system, providing a completely independent tubing system for the separate horns, all other things being equal, gives the lower horn (in this case, the B♭ horn) a better tone quality and control of pitch than is to be expected on a compensating type.

However, one great difference exists between the full double descant horn and the full double conventional horn.

In order to produce a full double descant it is necessary to provide *two* change valves, rather than the one on a normal horn; these two valves are linked together to the thumb lever by various systems, depending upon the manufacturer. The resulting tubing configurations are more complicated for the shorter (descant F) horn, and as a result, the extreme high range may often be less responsive than on a compensating type horn. A serious limitation is that this complicated two-valve linkage system is not easily adjustable: *most* full double descants are built "thumb down" for F horn (an established European custom) and to change back and forth between this system and a conventional horn could be catastrophic

for some players. To have a full double with "thumb up" for F horn, the model would have to be specially ordered.

Compensating Double Descant

The compensating double descant can provide, for the higher pitched horn (descant F), a very direct air column, with only one sharp .turn at the change valve:

This gives superior response for the extreme high range; the lower range has the usual problems inherent in the compensating system. Careful engineering of mouthpipe and bell taper has improved the mid-range response of these instruments remarkably in recent years. ■

To be continued. Part II contains diagrams showing active and inactive tubing for G♯ and C♯ on various types of horns, as well as additional information on the descant.

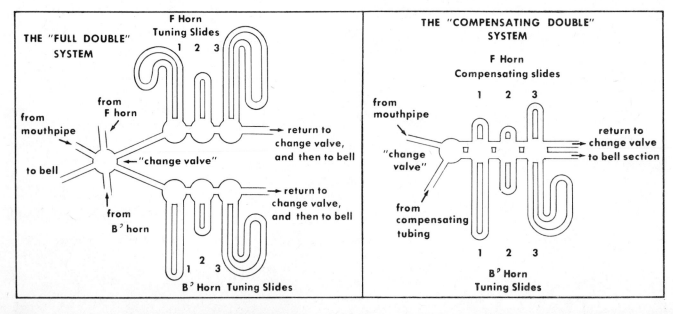

THE "FULL DOUBLE" SYSTEM

F Horn Tuning Slides
1 2 3

from mouthpipe
from F horn
to bell
"change valve"
→ return to change valve, and then to bell
from B♭ horn
→ return to change valve, and then to bell
1 2 3
B♭ Horn Tuning Slides

THE "COMPENSATING DOUBLE" SYSTEM

F Horn Compensating slides
1 2 3

from mouthpipe
"change valve"
return to change valve
to bell section
from compensating tubing
1 2 3
B♭ Horn Tuning Slides

The Descant Horn
Part II

Christopher Leuba

Bell Size

Bell size and taper has varied greatly on descants. Most of the earlier instruments had smaller bells than a conventional horn. For example, an early model Alexander, still available, has a diameter of approximately 11", as compared with over 12½' for a Conn 8D. Paxman and Mirafone have both recently produced horns with larger bells, which have noticeably improved low range response without sacrificing the true descant range. This has been achieved by careful study of the bell taper in relation to mouthpipe and body proportions.

Fingering

Fingering patterns on descant horns should be seriously considered.

The B♭ horn remains the same as upon a conventional instrument.

The F horn fingerings differ by one octave (*see comparative chart*). However, most *full double* descants have reversed thumb levers, i.e., the thumb is *down* for F and *up* for B♭. Due to the complexity of the two-change valve mechanism necessary on a full double descant, these thumb levers cannot easily be reversed. Thus, if a player is planning to use one of these instruments, he will have to accept the challenge of reversing his thumb action when changing from a conventional to a descant horn, *unless the descant has been specially built for American usage*, i.e., B♭ horn: thumb *down*. This can be done easily, but it isn't generally the case. *The compensating descant poses no such problem*: the "change valve" (thumb lever) is easily reversed.

The historic background of the development of the "reversed thumb valve" of the descant is of interest. In Europe during the present generation, most "high" horn-ists — those who would be candidates to eventually use a descant — were trained to use the single B♭ horn as their basic instrument. On single B♭ horns, the thumb lever usually operates an *alternate* fingering valve, for tuning convenience, stopping, etc., and it is not thought of as a basic "change" lever. When these European B♭ players switched to descant horns, they preferred the *thumb down* position for the high F change, since it represented, to them, an alternate fingering, and did not upset their normal "feel" of *thumb up* for B♭ horn. American players are used to *thumb down* for B♭ horn. Hence, an American player should be very careful in ordering a full double descant, *if he wishes to continue using his normal horn*. He has three alternatives:

1. Learn two sets of fingerings (difficult — but it has been done).
2. Order his full double descant thumb down for B♭ horn.
3. Rebuild his conventional horn to thumb up for B♭ horn. Two principal hornists of major United States symphonies play conventional instruments so arranged.

Mouthpieces

A horn mouthpiece places a distance of about 1½" between the vibrating lips and the point at which the mouthpiece of the instrument begins. A conventional F horn is approximately 154" in length. A descant horn is approximately 77" in length. The ratios of mouthpiece length to instrument air column length are, approximately 1:102 for the conventional F and 1:51 for the descant F.

Obviously, a mouthpiece will have a much greater effect on the intonation and tone quality of a descant horn, since the mouthpiece represents a proportionally greater part of the total vibrating column of a descant than it does on the conventional instrument.

Mouthpiece selection should be considered very carefully: using the same rim configuration (screw-on rim), a player should seek the correct combination of cup, bore and back bore to suit his individual playing style, the specific horn he is playing upon, and also the type of passage he is playing on that horn. More than upon conventional horns, players often find it advantageous to switch mouthpiece cups for specific passages.

I have observed several players "write off" very fine descant instruments because they tried them out with only their normal double horn mouthpieces. The double horn mouthpiece *may* work well; on the other hand, it may not.

It has been my experience that a more shallow cup, and smaller bore helps the descant produce its best quality and "center" in the highest range, at the expense of severe upset of the intonation and tone quality of the middle register. A shallow, small bore mouthpiece will not "take" as much air-flow, and the player must guard carefully against "over-

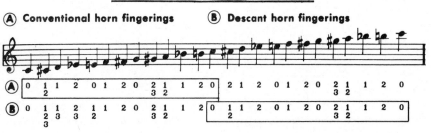

Ⓐ **Conventional horn fingerings**   Ⓑ **Descant horn fingerings**

blowing," or a very poor tone quality will result.

Instant High Register

In this time of seeking for simplistic solutions to difficult problems, is the descant really the guaranteed answer to the challenge of the high register of the horn? Do we finally have a package with the instructions, *Instant High Register*?

It is my belief that a player *will not extend his high register by the use of the descant horn.* However, whatever range the player has already acquired upon a conventional instrument will come more easily on the descant. There will be the probability of better accuracy, and greater endurance owing to the slightly lower resistance of the descant's shorter air column.

Due to the superior accuracy factor, the player's confidence in his own high register may improve greatly, and he may feel surprisingly more secure on a conventional instrument following success on a descant horn.

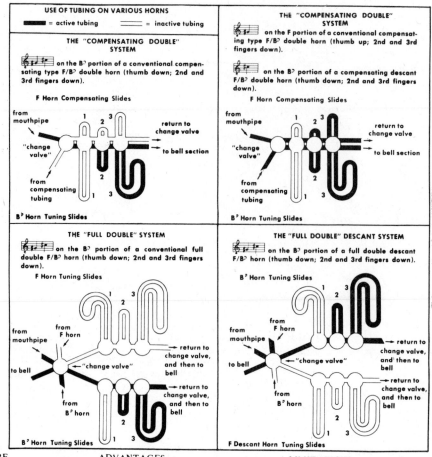

TYPE	MAKERS	BELL SIZE	BORE	ADVANTAGES	LIMITATIONS
Single F	Alexander Paxman Dehmal?	Small (app. 11")	Average or Narrow (All Alexanders are average)	Most simple tubing pattern: Superior high register	Poor intonation in middle range. Poor tone quality in middle range.
Single F	Alexander Paxman Dehmal?	Average (app. 12½ ")	Average or Narrow (All Alexanders are average.)	Most simple tubing pattern: Superior high register.	Poor intonation in middle range. Poor tone quality in middle range, but somewhat better than small bell model.
Full Double	Paxman Alexander	Average	Average	Good tuning in middle range. Generally good tone quality in middle range.	Perhaps some sacrifice of extreme high register "focus," due to complex tubing arrangement. Must be *special ordered.* Caution concerning fingering plan desired: "Thumb up" or "Thumb down" for F horn? Alexanders can be extremely variable.
Full Double	Paxman	Average	Narrow	Good tuning in middle range. Generally good tone quality in middle range.	Perhaps some sacrifice of extreme high register "focus," due to complex tubing arrangement. Must be *special ordered.* Caution concerning fingering plan desired: "Thumb up" or "Thumb down" for F horn? Perhaps less adequate tone quality in middle range. More "resistance."
Descant "Triple"	Paxman	Average	"Dual" Narrow for Descant F; Average for B-flat and Low F horns.	Superior tuning in all ranges. Generally good tone quality in middle and low ranges.	Perhaps some sacrifice of extreme high register "focus," due to complex tubing arrangement. (Very complex tubing pattern necessary.) Must be *special ordered.* Caution concerning fingering plan desired: "Thumb up" or "Thumb down" for F horn? Fingering complexity will make it difficult for a player to alternate this horn with conventional instruments. Still in development period?
Compensating Double	Mirafone Alexander Paxman?	Average	Average	Simple tubing arrangement for F horn allows for exceptionally good response in extreme high register. Thumb "change valve" can be easily adjusted. " Thumb up" or" Thumb down" for F horn. Very easy to alternate with conventional double horn.	Not generally as adequate in middle range as a "full double" horn, although Mirafone has succeeded in producing a rather well-balanced instrument in the middle range. Alexanders must be *special ordered,* and can be quite variable.
Single G (with F slide)	Alexander	Small	Average	Very simple tubing pattern: extremely good for baroque "Horn in G" music.	Very poor in middle and low range. Very specialized instrument.
Double F/ High F	Dehmal	Average	Average?	Simple tubing pattern. Good high range.	Although the low range has reasonably good tone quality, the duplication of the F harmonic series does not allow solution of some basic intonation problems.
Descant High B-flat	Paxman	Small	?	Presumably excellent range above	Lower range? Tone quality? Pitch?

The Future

If the single F "valve horn" might be characterized as the horn of the 19th century, I would say that the double horn has been the instrument of the 20th century and that the descant is truly the instrument of the 21st century. We are very close to that turning point — the 21st century — and although the descant horn has not yet been perfected, it is pointless to obstruct the progress of its acceptance. The "money horn players," world-wide, are already playing this instrument, despite its tonal shortcomings; some of them use it exclusively.

My preference, considering the present "state of the art," is to remain with the conventional double horn for the basic repertoire, and to use a compensating descant for the high passages for which it is appropriate, thus taking the best of both worlds. I have observed, however, that many educators have not yet even

arrived in the 20th century: 70 years after the acceptance of the double horn by the majority of the world's professional performers, many educators still insist that young players use a single F horn, and they still purchase these anachronisms for their school districts.

Now, when professional players are considering descants, sometimes as their *basic* instrument, I feel it is time for music educators to reconsider their philosophy behind the choice of instruments for beginners.

In what other field involving physical activity do we expect the novice to use equipment larger, heavier or more difficult to control, than that which the accomplished expert uses?

In baseball, perhaps? A *heavier* bat, for instance, for a Little Leaguer?

Why, then, any insistence on the use of the traditional single F as a starter instrument, when, *if* he survives this traumatic start, he will be switching to a double horn

anyway?

Summary

My opinion is that, at the present time, the *basic* horn is the double horn. If a school district cannot afford a full complement of double horns (4 valve), single B♭ horns are a better investment than single F horns.

The descant horn should be considered as a very useful, but "adjunct" instrument. Educators should *not* expect instant and seemingly magic improvement in the high register performance of their players by using descants. High register performance still depends upon properly developed embouchures, sufficient breath support and adequate breath flow. Nor should an educator expect a "rich" tone quality from a descant in the lower ranges: young performers should be encouraged to keep in their minds the full tone potential of the double horn, which they won't acquire unless they do play it. ∎

April, 1972

Deviled Tongue
Albert Stoutamire

The tongue can be a brass instrument performer's best friend or his worst enemy. When it is behaving properly, the tongue responds to the player's efforts as if it were charmed. When it misbehaves, it seems as if the devil himself has control of it and the performer has a *deviled tongue*.

I estimate that more than half of the private brass students I have taught have had serious articulation problems stemming from improper use of the tongue. An inferior style of tonguing produces inferior sounds. These objectionable sounds frequently heard in the tones of immature performers can be grouped into five categories, all interrelated and all associated with the use of too much tongue.

The Function of the Tongue

Before identifying the characteristic *deviled tongue* sounds, let us review the normal functions of the tongue, which are (1) to articulate the tones, (2) to help establish the pitch, and (3) to help regulate the quality or timbre of the tone.

The tongue starts virtually all non-slurred tones. It stops some. It performs these tasks in a variety of ways to effect the numerous styles of playing on the continuum between legato and staccato. The tongue assists the embouchure (or is a part of it, depending on how embouchure is defined) in establishing both pitch and tone quality. The tip of the tongue is more fre-

quently used to begin the tone, whereas the arch of the tongue is used to help control pitch and timbre.

Deviled Tongue
Sound #1 — Overblowing

The tongue is accomplice rather than villain in this first type of faulty playing. The sound is called a "blast" in its vilest form. "Overblowing" is a general term used to describe the faulty tone, and its cause is just that — too much air being released by the tongue. So much air is released that the embouchure "loses control" and does not vibrate in an acceptable manner for refined playing. An uncontrollable diaphragm, then, is the cause of the offense, but the tongue

611

is guilty of aiding and abetting.

Actually, the tongue gets more than its share of the blame for being the cause of over-accented tones. The tongue does not make the accents except in the case of sforzando. I take great delight in having a student demonstrate to himself that the tongue does very little in the way of producing an accented tone. My procedure is to tell the student to accent a certain note. Then I ask him how one goes about making an accent. The answer is almost always, "Use more tongue."

With the stage thus set, I ask him to play a series of tones — his tuning note, for example — at a *mezzo forte* level; "Tah, tah, tah, tah." Then I say, "Play the tones again, *tonguing harder* but not *blowing harder*." He will usually blow harder *and* tongue harder. When I finally get him to play with a steady and consistent air supply while articulating with varying degrees of tongue tension, he is convinced that the air is the principal ingredient for producing an accent.

Do you believe it? Try it! I have never had a student yet who was thoroughly convinced until he had tried it. Some had heard directors talking about it or had read about it, but they had not really applied the theory to their own experience.

The reason many immature players believe that forceful tonguing is necessary to produce accents relates to the principle that when we "blow harder," the tongue tends to lend support to the harder working respiratory muscles, and it too works harder. In other words, improper use of the tongue is often the result of a normal reaction — the muscles of the body tend to function in unison until they are trained otherwise. Similarly, muscular tension in arms, shoulder, back — even toes — is not necessary and can even be detrimental in the task of producing a tone on a wind instrument.

One must learn through practice to be able to "blow hard" and simultaneously "tongue easy." Of course there is a point at which increased air pressure calls for strengthening the tongue action to keep the air from escaping prematurely. But that is precisely the reason for increasing tongue effort: To retain the air, not to release it. Rather than tonguing harder to produce an accent, the proper con-

cept is to use more air pressure to prepare for an accent while sealing in the air with proper tongue resistance until time to begin the tone. The release of the air pressure is then accomplished without increasing the tension in the tongue.

Deviled Tongue
Sound #2 — Excessive Motion

The tongue is quite large and is attached to the mouth and throat over a wide area. Excessive motions in articulating can cause the throat to move unnecessarily. In addition, some players have formed the habit of allowing the jaw and lips to move when tonguing. A "tee-yaw" sound usually results. An understanding of this interaction of tongue, mouth, and throat should result from the following steps: First, set the instrument aside and say "tee-taw" repeatedly as you watch your throat and jaw in a mirror. This motion of the tongue approximates the action required to produce the highest and lowest tones of an extended range on a brass instrument, and you should notice some jaw and throat movement. Next, say "tee, tee, tee" while watching in a mirror. You should notice little or no movement in the lips, jaw, and throat because only the tip of the tongue is brought into play. Next, say "taw, taw, taw" and notice the throat and jaw movement partially resulting from larger areas of the tongue being brought into play. Finally, say "teeaw, teeaw, teeaw." Utilize these improper tongue, jaw, and throat motions in playing your instrument and you will produce deviled tongue sound number two. Use of this habit results in a tone quality which changes with each articulation and hinders rapid performance because the jaw motion shakes the instrument and is slower than the tongue acting alone.

Careful practice while using a mirror can result in eliminating the extraneous jaw and throat movement which causes *deviled tongue* sound number two.

Deviled Tongue
Sound #3 — Tongue Stop

The "back lash" or "follow through" of excessive tongue action which begins *deviled tongue* sound number two can cause *deviled tongue* sound number three. The complete cycle sounds "tee-aaaaut." This third objectionable sound is produced by stopping

the tone with excessive tonguing action. It is such a prevalent problem that the pedagogical rule, "stop the tone with the breath, not the tongue," is in general use in our schools. It works. The reason it works is that if you do not use the tongue, you do not make a noise with it.

Professional players use the tongue to stop a tone for certain styles of performance, particularly the "stage band" style. But until the student begins to reach advanced levels of playing and has complete control of his tongue actions, he will generally get the best sounds out of his instrument when he uses as little tongue as possible to terminate a tone.

Deviled Tongue
Sound #4 — Too Much Top

Another undesirable sound is caused by using too much of the top of the tongue which starts the tone with a "chee" rather than a "tee" sound. Most of the tonguing in playing a brass instrument is traditionally done with the tip of the tongue touching the gums above the teeth as in saying "tee." For lower tones, the tip of the tongue may drop down on the upper teeth, and for the lowest tones, the tip of the tongue may go between the upper and lower teeth and touch the upper lip or both lips. The latter position of the tongue is more prevalent in playing the lowest tones of the larger brass instruments. In all instances, the tip of the tongue makes and breaks the contact with gum, teeth, or lips. (The exception is noted in the extremely high registers where the player may anchor the tip of the tongue behind the bottom teeth and effectively make and break the contact between the top of the tongue and the gum.)

The following procedure will illustrate this fourth type of improper tonguing: Set the instrument aside to observe facial movement with a mirror. First, say "tee" several times. Next, while reiterating "tee," gradually lower the tip of the tongue to the upper teeth and lower the arch in the tongue at the same time. The articulation changes from 'tee' to "thee" to "tha" to "tho." Then, say "chee, chee, chee" over and over. (Notice the undesirable jaw motion as you say this.) Now, say "chee, chee, chee" and lower the tongue's arch as directed above to produce "chee, cha, cho." Finally, play a scale on a brass instrument from high to low using the articulation "chee, chee, chaa, chaa, chah, chah, cho, cho." You have now produced characteristic *deviled tongue* sound number four. Essentially, the corrective measure is to avoid using the top of the tongue and to use only the very tip of it in articulating.

Deviled Tongue Sound #5 "Quack"

This last faulty articulation is not too common except when purposely used for comic effect. However, it is heard from time to time in school bands and orchestras, where the effect is comical — but not by intention. (The trombonist on the old Spike Jones recordings frequently used this sound)

The following steps produce faulty sound number five: First, say "chur" over and over with the tongue flattened as much as possible against the roof of the mouth. Then, with the same tongue position, try playing low tones on a low brass instrument. Usually the effect is not as drastic as that described above, and it may occur only on the lowest tones produced by the player. In such a case, when a descending scale is played, satisfactory tones will gradually change to unsatisfactory sounds resembling "quack" as the lower tones are approached. The corrective measure is to flatten the tongue and open the aural cavity enough to eliminate the objectionable sound.

Conclusion

Most sounds described in this article are caused by excessive or inefficient use of the tongue in articulation. When too much movement occurs, extraneous and objectionable sounds are heard. The remedy for most of the problems discussed lies in using as little tongue as possible to get the job done effectively. For the most part, the player should articulate with the tip of the tongue, using as little of the remainder of the tongue as feasible. He should also guard against allowing the tongue to seal off excessive air pressure which, when released, will cause "overblowing."

An effective way to begin correcting articulation faults is to have the student play his instrument and watch himself in a mirror, checking for facial and throat movement. He should observe the jaw, lip, and throat and try to play repeated tones, both legato and staccato, with little or no lip and throat movement and absolutely no jaw movement. Basically, the tongue releases the air which causes the lips to vibrate and produce a tone beginning in the mouthpiece of the instrument. In this process, there is no need to move jaws, throat, or lips (except to let them vibrate).■

May, 1972

Alternate Trombone Positions
First Year of Study

Marvin Rosenberg

Most band directors, unless they have had extensive work on the trombone, do not realize how important a good functional knowlege of alternate positions is to superior trombone playing. In order for the slide trombone to compete technically with the valve brass instruments, the use of alternate positions is a must. Alternate positions not only allow faster playing, but make for cleaner slurs, smoother legato, etc.

Tones playable in more than one position (or more than one valve combination) are possible on all brass instruments, starting with some notes in the second octave of the normal range. For valved instruments, there is usually no advantage to playing the second overtone with the 1st and 3rd valves rather than open. On the trombone, however, it is very important in many passages, to be able to play middle F in the 6th position as well as in the 1st. Because alternate positions are an integral part of superior technique, beginners should use them almost from the start. In this way their correct use will become instinctive, with no need to pause and "figure out" difficult passages. Most band methods meant for group instruction do not cover this aspect of playing adequately, so the director must give his trombonists supplementary work if they are to develop a clean, musical technique.

As a general rule, the closer to first position a tone is, the better will be the sound. This is why the "normal" position for most notes is as close to the 1st position as possible. When one uses an alternate position, therefore, he must try to match *tone quality* as well as pitch.

Fourth Position D

Possibly the most used of the alternates is the 4th position middle D. When played in 1st position, this note is usually slightly flat, thus the 4th position is used as an aid to intonation, as well as technique. In the keys of Bb and Eb, or whenever passages using C, D, Eb are involved, 4th position D is generally used. G major arpeggios and many G major and D major passages also call for the 4th position D (see Ex. 1, 2, 3).

Sixth Position F

Perhaps the first alternate position a young player should use is the middle F, played in 6th position. Obviously, this is helpful in any passage involving C to F, but it will also help the student to properly locate the 6th position by trying to match F's in the 1st and 6th position. Examples 4, 5, & 6 give some use for the 6th position F. Note that Ex. 5, if played rapidly, is much smoother using the 6th position F, as the up and back "pumping" motion of the slide is broken up a little by the *extension* to F rather than a *return* for the 1st position F.

Fifth Position B♭

Another important alternate is middle B♭, played in 5th position. Arpeggios or skips involving C7 or G minor chord tones, for example, are much easier to play if one can use 5th position B♭ occasionally. (see Ex. 7, 8, 9).

I would introduce a young trombonist to these 3 alternate positions fairly early, certainly before the end of the first year of class instruction — even earlier if it were private instruction. (One other alternate position is worth considering at this early stage, middle A in 6th position. The teacher must decide whether its introduction this early will help or confuse.)

Alternate position notes are no more easy or difficult to play in

Exercises to develop alternate positions

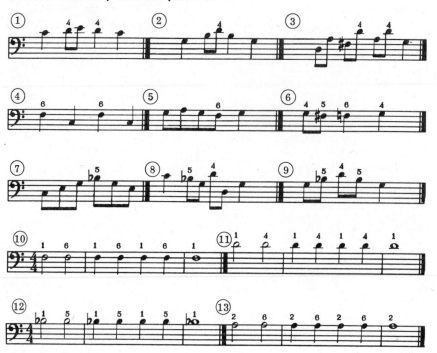

tune than are the same notes played in the "normal" position, if one is trained to listen and adjust from the beginning.

The early introduction of these key alternate positions, so important to the building of a solid playing technique, can be accomplished with a minimum of confusion by first practicing examples 10-13. Similar studies can be composed by the teacher, as the need arises.

Diligent work in this area will reward the student with the foundation for a fast, secure technique, and the teacher with a trombonist of whom he can be proud. ∎

May, 1972

The Brass Section in the Jazz Ensemble

Gene Deaton

The brass section usually consists of four trumpets and four trombones. Some of the more difficult arrangements use a fifth trumpet, a fifth trombone or tuba, and occasionally two to four French horns. French horns, although not a standard part of the jazz ensemble brass section, add a beautiful dimension if players can be found with adequate range and style.

The basic function of the brass

section is to accent figurations and create tension and excitement. This is not to imply that technically difficult or pretty melodies are the exclusive domain of the reeds, or that the reed section is incapable of tension and excitement, but to suggest that the brass section is used in this way more often than the other sections of the jazz ensemble. The drummer rarely "kicks" the reed section, for example, but often

reads directly from a trumpet part for this purpose.

The selection of personnel — a critical factor in any music organization — is especially important in a jazz ensemble because of the unique demands placed on the lead and ride players. The lead trumpet player is the workhorse in the brass section. He must play in tune, have a powerful tone, good register, a good concept of style, and a personality that is aggressive. Developing a lead player requires time and patience. Having two jazz ensembles gives a potential lead player time to develop in the second group without the pressure of the first. Two lead players can be used in both groups and allowed to alternate between the first and third parts. Endurance is a critical factor, and this arrangement affords some relief for both players.

The player who is responsible for most of the improvisation traditionally plays the second part, although solos are written for all chairs. Improvisation is quite often one of the weakest aspects of a high school or college jazz ensemble. There is absolutely no substitute for listening to major jazz artists such as Miles Davis, Clark Terry, Thad Jones, and Marvin Stamm, to name just a few fine trumpet players; but there are several books that can be very helpful to aspiring soloists on any instrument. The following list is by no means comprehensive, but represents a few of the texts that can be used.

Jazz Improvisation, by David Baker

Chord Studies for Trombone (or Saxophone) by Phil Wilson and Joseph Viola

The Lydian Chromatic Concept of Tonal Organization for Improvisation, by George Russell

A Guide to Improvisation, by John LaPorta

A New Approach to Jazz Improvisation, by Jamey Aebersold

Improvising Jazz, by Jerry Coker

These texts, when used in conjunction with extensive listening, can be a viable adjunct to any jazz program.

Brass players, a gregarious but opinionated group, seem to thoroughly enjoy discussing the merits of particular instruments, mouthpieces, or brass accessories in general. Because of the extra demands of range and endurance that a brass player in a jazz ensemble must contend with, this discussion can become an exercise in futility. I suppose that it is necessary, however, to open up this particular can of worms. What is the best combination of equipment for a brass player in a jazz ensemble? As an opinionated trombonist, I encourage our brass players to use large or medium bore horns with large to medium size mouthpieces. Eve-

ry conductor has to eventually decide upon priorities, and a full, rich sound is high on my list. It is a fallacy to assume that jazz players must use a small horn and mouthpiece in order to attain the register and endurance required to play a difficult book. I do not believe that the size of the horn or mouthpiece are factors in determining a brass player's range. It has been traditional for brass players in the jazz ensemble to use small bore horns with small mouthpieces for a variety of reasons, range supposedly one of the major ones. I believe it is more accurate to say that endurance is the prime consideration. Brass players who use large horns and mouthpieces must have a consistent practice schedule in order to build and maintain a strong embouchure. An erratic practice schedule will lead, at best, to a mediocre performance, regardless of the size of the horn or mouthpiece.

How to Choose Players

Good blend and balance start initially with available personnel. Everything else being equal, I try to choose players with similar tone quality, equipment, concept, etc. This is not always possible, but ideal if the situation permits. It is very difficult, for example, to achieve a good blend or balance if you have cornets and trumpets in the same section. The cornet sound lacks the slight edge that can be attained with the trumpet and does not carry as well.

There are other factors that effect blend and balance, as well as the over-all performance. Attacks are particularly critical, as are phrase endings. I like the analogy Leon Breeden uses of a whip cracking when the brass section hits well together. I have found it valuable to take time to make sure that all brass players are using the same kind of attack. Uniformity in this area will make a good section sound better.

It is also necessary to take time with note values and phrase endings. Like all music, jazz is written one way, but played another. Just exactly how long is a whole, half, or quarter note? In an up-tempo arrangement, the general rule-of-thumb is to cut off on the last beat of the note value. For example, a whole note would end on the down

beat of four, a dotted half note on the down beat of three, etc. Conversely, I prefer just the opposite approach to a ballad. A whole note, for example, would be off on one in the next bar.

The "jazz style," if there is such a thing, is as varied and encompasses a spectrum as diversified as Mozart to Stravinsky. There are, however, certain generalizations that can be made about most aspects of this style. A rehearsal technique that I like to use is a series of "general rules." There are exceptions to all of these, thus they should be construed only as a guide.

1. A series of eighth notes in 4/4 time should be played approximately like alternating quarters and eighths in 6/8 time. Another way to approximate the same thing would be triplets in 4/4 time:

(musical notation: 4/4 series of eighth notes = 6/8 dotted rhythm, or 4/4 triplets)

The slight accent is important and brass players can accomplish this by moving the tongue to different positions in the mouth, with the breath, and in concert with the diaphragm.

2. A tied note at the end of a series of quarter notes receives a slight accent:

(musical notation example)

3. A quarter note is usually "spaced" when it falls between two eighth notes and is on a weak part of the beat:

(musical notation example)

4. Triplets are played as written (concert style).

5. Any note that falls on the weak part of the beat should be held full value and played with a slight accent, and with "energy."

(musical notation example)

6. None of the above general rules apply to the "rock" style and only a few apply to the "jazz/rock" style. The same holds true for Latin American music. For the most part, rock and Latin American music employ even eighth notes and are generally unconcerned about the esoteric nuances of the jazz style. (This does not make them any less valid, only different.)

Intonation is a problem that all conductors must contend with, especially if the brass players are playing in the extreme registers of their horns. It is possible to have over a five octave span between the bass trombone player and the lead trumpeter in a jazz ensemble. I have found it helpful to tune two players at a time in perfect fifths, then add two more in a different octave, and so on until all eight or ten players are involved. Open fifths seem to be more readily discernible than the traditional unison and certainly

more so than a complicated chord.

Many conductors complain that their jazz ensemble doesn't "swing" because of a poor rhythm section. This is quite often true, but it is also true that a group will not "swing" unless every member in it does. It is often enlightening to have each section play without the rhythm section to see if they can maintain tempo, style, intensity, and a general sense of forward motion. I have found it valuable to occasionally dismiss the rhythm section for an entire rehearsal. This places the

responsibility to "swing" on the entire ensemble, where it justifiably belongs.

A technical analysis of the jazz style can be a valid technique, but only after the student has done extensive listening. Students learn best by emulation and should be encouraged to listen to major jazz artists as often as possible. Any other approach will result in a cursory understanding, which, in my opinion is invalid. ■

Purchasing Brass Instruments

Henry D. Zazra

Well, Mr. Band Director, you've given a "talent test" to some interested new students and you think you've found a winner or two. Assuming that you've started your students properly and that they are sufficiently interested, you are soon going to be asked about purchasing an instrument.

Before you commit yourself, you must consider price, practicality, availability . . .and the overriding factor of musical quality. Today, with mass production techniques and general mass distribution, most student-line instruments are comparable in all ways except musical quality. When it comes to this consideration, *Buy the Best Possible Horn You Can Afford!*

When recommending a horn, we should look for certain characteristics. First and foremost, a horn *must* be in tune. If it isn't, the young player is likely to get a mistaken impression of what is or is not in tune.

There must be at least an adjustable third valve slide on cornets and trumpets. An adjustable first valve slide is also desirable. If possible, baritones and tubas should be equipped with four valves. The students should be taught how to use these aids from the very start. However, the teachers must remember that adjustable slides do not guarantee an in-tune horn. Open tones must be as close as possible to exact pitch. This is the only way to assure a really good start for a student.

All valved instruments should be constructed so that both the top and bottom valve caps can be easily removed for cleaning and service. Trombone slides should have springs in the slide cups and a "super sturdy" slide lock, preferably concealed inside the slide cup. Replacement parts for valves and slides should be readily available and easily installed.

Tubing should be of the best quality and firmly braced. Care must be taken, however, that the bracing is not at a nodal point — this will greatly alter the tone quality of any horn. In the lower brass, there should be as many straight lengths of tubing as can be designed into the instrument. An epoxy finish is generally the best because it will resist all but the most corrosive hand acids.

French horns pose their own special set of problems. Standards of design and construction are to be considered only as guidelines, so a personal inspection is mandatory before buying. Be sure that the rotary valves work smoothly and that the string can be replaced quickly and easily. If at all possible, the student should start on a double horn to give him every advantage in intonation and facility.

The cornet, baritone, and tuba are basically conical and they cause great problems because of that. They respond easily — too easily, especially tuba — and they have enormous intonation

problems. For this reason, try to avoid European instruments because they are built much more conically than American horns. They have a beautiful sound, but can generally be played successfully only by mature players.

The most practical instrument is the largest instrument which the student can handle. If the choice comes down to two cornets with different bore sizes, get the one with the larger bore. Again, more air moving through the horn means more sound.

An instrument with thick, heavy metal is to be preferred over an instrument with thin, light metal. The heavier horn will have more resonance, greater projection, richer tone, and will resist denting better than a light horn.

Student grade cases are generally quite sturdy and will take much rough punishment, but they will twist and distort. Instrument makers should supply cases which do not distort and whose locks are easily fastened by young hands. All manufacturers could take a hint from luggage manufacturers and pad the undersides of the handles on their cases.

If an instrument can be found which meets the criteria outlined above, jump at the chance to purchase it. Since the perfect horn does not exist, pick and choose from among all the possibilities to secure an instrument which will give long years of satisfying musical experience. ■

Some Thoughts on Trumpet Pedal Tones

Mario F. Oneglia

It is known that many virtuoso players of the cornet and trumpet in past years, including Herbert L. Clark and Bohumir Kryl, were players of pedal tones,* as well as having been very gifted in the extreme upper registers of their instruments. A tape reproduction of Kryl playing a four octave arrangement of the "Carnival of Venice" (available from Walter S. Hoover of Connellsville, Pa.) certainly will impress the listener with the extreme flexibility of the soloist. The original recording was cut in 1908!

The use of pedal tones was considered to be, by many, a form of sensational "stunt playing" — one that could thrill audiences with the soloist's ability to leap from a trombone-like tone to the flute-like altissimo register. I am of the opinion that the ability to perform pedal tones is in itself an indication of the balanced embouchure which enhances the upper register — indeed, which makes it possible. Could the practice of pedal tones have been among the closely guarded secrets of the baroque clarinist-trumpeter?

Until fairly recently, there has been a dearth of pedal tone literature for the trumpet. The standard study books such as Arban, Gatti, Schlossberg, and Clark contain no mention of them. The St. Jacome has one or two pedal C's without any explanation as to the method of producing them or any evaluation of their use or importance.

Walter M. Eby's, *Scientific Method* contains a complete lesson on pedal tones . . . it immediately follows a lesson on extreme high tones! It would seem from all evidence that there is a correlation

between the pedal and extreme upper register of the trumpet. Yet the renowned Herbert L. Clarke (who was known to use pedal tones in his teaching and playing) makes no mention of them in either his *Studies* or the articles, "How I Became a Cornet Player."

It is probable that the demand for high register work in dance and stage bands sparked a flow of materials on pedal tones in recent years. Books which have appeared — like, *Double High C in Thirty-Seven Weeks*, *The Original Louis Maggio System for Brass*, and *Trumpet Yoga* — fall into the category of pedal tone systems. All of these methods are of value in providing advanced study material; perhaps the Maggio texts by Carleton MacBeth seem to provide the most self-explanatory textual accompaniment to the etude material. Louis Maggio, who provided the inspiration for these books, was a renowned California brass teacher whose students are in the forefront of the profession.

In recent years, Professor Kenneth Bloomquist has written a *Pedal Tone Study for Trumpet* which has added to the available information about the pedal register. This article, distributed by the Getzen Corporation, should be in every brass player's possession.

What information can the trumpet student glean from these sources? Are there areas of agreement or disagreement? Is it beneficial to practice the pedal register? None of the previously mentioned sources specifically answer all of these questions. Definite answers will probably have to await such time as scientific testing can be done and data gathered and weighed. The generalizations which follow are based upon my own work with pedal tones, and expe-

rience with students. Comment and (hopefully) discussion is invited from readers.

1. The playing of pedal tones seems to enhance ease in playing all registers, but particularly the altissimo.

2. Any fingering for pedal tones will suffice as long as the lips are kept in vibration and a sound is produced.

3. Rest periods seem a requirement of all pedal systems. One suggests "playing every other day."

4. Powerful breath support is mandatory, a requirement common to both pedal and extreme upper registers.

5. One should not attempt to play pedal tones until the embouchure is formed. Then the pedal register should be performed with as close a setting to that embouchure as possible.

6. Playing pedal tones is extremely helpful in regaining sensation in the lips when tired. They force relaxation.

7. Advanced pedal tone techniques call for moving to and from the pedal register.

8. The use of syllables seems to enhance attainment of pedals.

9. The connection between extreme registers is probably the ability to keep the lips vibrating freely away from the teeth. ∎

---

*defined as any tone below the low F# considered to be the bottom of the written range

Bloomquist, Kenneth. *Pedal Tone Study for Trumpet*. The Getzen Company, Inc., Elkhorn, Wisconsin.

Callet, Jerome. *Trumpet Yoga*. Jerome Callet Pub., Pittsburgh, Pa., 1971.

MacBeth, Carleton. *Original Louis Maggio System for Brass*. Maggio Music Press, North Hollywood, California, 1969.

Spaulding, Roger W. *Double High C in 37 Weeks*. High Note Studios, Hollywood, California, 1962.

Brass Playing on the March

Daniel B. Tetzlaff

Take it from "an old pro," there are several things brass players can do to keep up "good chops" while on the march. Those who maintain their efficiency can help out everyone in the band. Here are some suggestions for your students.

1. Give special attention to your usual lip warmup routine. You know the lip muscles will be required to do an extraordinary job, so give them more than average preparation. The purpose of the warmup is to set and control the size of the ring of muscle that must fit perfectly inside the mouthpiece ring. The term, "working up a lip" actually means allowing the muscle to swell *gradually*, while maintaining its sensitivity and feeling. The trick is to avoid an excessive swelling.

2. Check the fuel tank. Tone power requires breath power; breath power requires deep, full inhalation. Open the throat and mouth, take in as much as you can. Fill up the back and bottom of the lungs first. Inhale fast, like a gasp! Top it off by opening the nostrils and taking in even more, to fill up the top of the lungs. Fill until you feel the internal pressure that any full tank has.

3. While marching, touch the toes to the ground first, the heel almost not at all. It is sort of like walking on eggs. The idea is to keep the shock off the spine and head, and therefore, off the mouth. Legs and torso cannot be too stiff or rigid; rather, they must feel relaxed. Those who have the ability to play a good lead line should let others do the "strutting."

4. Roll the shoulders slightly and sway the instrument some from side to side. Don't be funny, corny, or exaggerated. Be cool, subtle, and smooth about it. Again, the idea is to keep the bumps off the lips. The shoulders are relaxed; the left arm and finger grip should not be tensed too much.

5. Make the breathing muscles work to save the lip. Remember the habit of filling the lungs. Let the air out generously. Out-of-doors is the place for the brass players to learn the body feelings of free and uninhibited playing. Let the air out fast. The more the lungs heave and fall, the more the chest helps the lips. Make the air stream musculature become the workhorse. Let the tone travel as free and as far as you can without feeling strained.

6. Let the tongue help the lips. The tongue helps to aim and to center each note. Tonguing also creates spacing. Each little space is another little rest for the lip. Make every "extra rest" you can by remembering, *"When in doubt, play the notes short!"* Learn when you can shorten without hurting the total sound. After all, other instrumental figures and drum beats are "filling in." Long notes bring on fatigue. Slur only when absolutely necessary. Few street or field marches depend on a sustained legato style. For brass instrumentalists this means to use neat, clean tonguing to the utmost.

7. Use the mind to save the lip. Especially on the march, the lip has only so many notes in it. Don't be wasteful. Think in terms of conserving resources (energy-sensitivity). All the notes are not equally important on the march. The better you know the music, the more you can think about playing. Favor the melodic line first; then the bugle calls, flashy runs, and any other obvious "soli" parts. Slight the insignificant fills and after-beats that sound like "arrangers' afterthoughts." In these spots the other players take their turn on the melody, so cool it and give them a chance.

8. Agree on a system of alternat-ing with a partner. Both players cover all important places, all introductions, interludes, 1st and 2nd endings. The first player is responsible for setting the example the first time through. The second player relieves, imitating the first, and covering any passage in doubt. The general idea is to keep the instrument off the lips for many short little periods that can go unnoticed in the over-all sound of the full band. Every little rest allows the blood to circulate. This is nature's way of refreshing a fatigued muscle. So we take — or make — every rest we can.

9. Reduce the swelling. In addition to taking the mouthpiece away whenever possible, increase the blood circulation by massaging the lip from the inside with the tip of the tongue. It helps just the same as when you rub any other bruise. During an intermission of some length, applying *Mentholatum* (for its liniment-like stimulation to the tissues beneath the surface) can increase comfort. So, also, will the application of either "hot" or "cold" — like ice cubes or coffee.

10. Incorporate the "stretched embouchure" technique. This is a subtle, yet invaluable aid to those who are daring enough not to reject it. The "puckered" or centered lip brings more muscle into the mouthpiece. However, lips that are lumped (from many a bump) are already too big, so until the swelling goes down to normal, they could use a thinning out — the stretched embouchure. *Stretch a little of the swelling out of the center just before placing the mouthpiece onto the lips.* The outside muscles then snap inward (as usual) to give the strength and control necessary to hold the pitch, especially against the jarring around that occurs while marching. ∎

Off-Stage Trumpet

Gerald E. Zimmerman

The off-stage trumpet parts from the orchestra literature have been a neglected part of the trumpet repertoire. While the off-stage excerpts are limited, and do not confront the performer that frequently, they nevertheless are challenging and present just as many problems as any other facet of trumpet performance.

Some Problems in Off-Stage Playing

Acoustics is an important consideration in the performance of off-stage parts. The quality of performance will be affected greatly by the acoustical properties of sound and the architectural acoustics of the auditorium. A knowledge and understanding of certain acoustical principles should improve the performance of the off-stage excerpts.

Atmospheric temperature is the largest variable in keeping instruments in tune. An increase in temperature will increase the speed of sound. It has been determined that, in the case of air, the velocity changes 1.1 feet/second/degree (Fahrenheit). (At ordinary room temperature, sound will travel in air at about 1100 feet per second.)

Ralph Pottle, in his book *Tuning the School Band and Orchestra*, states that a rise in temperature from 70° to 80° (Fahrenheit) affects the tuning of an instrument by varying degrees. In the case of the trumpet, there is a rise in pitch of 6.2 cents.[1]

The trumpet's own temperature is somewhere between body temperature and the surrounding air. Because the off-stage player usually encounters a lower temperature than on stage (lower ceiling and hot lights), his pitch will tend to be flat. The usual compensations

— adjusting the tuning slide, blowing warm air through the instrument, etc. — must almost always be made by the off-stage player.

Another problem that the off-stage trumpeter may have to face is that of distance. There are times when the off-stage and on-stage trumpets must play together. Since it will take the sound some amount of time to reach the stage (e.g. if the distance is 226 feet, it will take 1/5 second), the off-stage performers may need to play ahead of the conductor's beat.

It has usually been the practice of the off-stage trumpeter to look through a peep-hole, stage curtain, or similar observational station. As a result, the conductor's gestures were not always clear to the performer; oftentimes the conductor even had to abandon his interpretation of the excerpt and abide with that of the soloist. In recent years, the use of closed-circuit television has improved communications. A camera is focused on the conductor, with an off-stage monitor provided for the trumpeter.

This problem of timing of execution is very demanding and is not present in the solo literature. Therefore, we find one distinct challenge for the off-stage soloist not found by the recitalist.

Examples of Off-Stage Trumpet Parts

There are some general comments which apply to most off-stage trumpet literature. First, many excerpts are basically fanfares. Second, the accompaniments tend to be quite subtle — often only strings, or strings in combination with upper woodwinds. Third, the rhythmic structure is not particularly complex, but careful articulation and interpretation is required.

Composers have usually em-

ployed the off-stage trumpet to create the impression of distance, and of oncoming motion toward the auditor. Many of the works in which the off-stage trumpet is used have some connotation of program music. In Verdi's *Requiem*, the off-stage trumpets are used to announce the approach of the Great Judge in the "Dies Irae." In Mahler's *Symphony No.2*, he calls the trumpet "the voice that crieth in the wilderness." According to Mahler, the posthorn solo in his third symphony is supposed to tell the listener "what the beasts in the woods tell." In addition, the Leonore calls (probably the earliest examples of the use of an off-stage trumpet) both have programmatic elements. In the *Leonore Overture No.2* (1805), Beethoven takes the drama of *Fidelio* as far as the trumpet call which heralds liberation. The second time it occurs, it signifies that Don Fernando has arrived and that the end of Florestan's captivity has come. With the *Leonore Overture No.3* (1806), Beethoven uses the trumpet call to announce to all mankind the end of tyranny.

Both Leonore calls are essentially trumpet fanfares. While neither call is particularly demanding in technical facility, the aspect of intonation needs careful attention. Both calls are composed solely of the tonic triad, and the last pitch of both calls may tend to go sharp because of the decrescendo which occurs. In addition, the strings are sustaining a chord during the trumpet's solo, and any pitch discrepancy will be quite apparent (see Ex.1 - Leonore No.3).

By far one of the most demanding off-stage excerpts in regard to control and style is found in the second movement of Respighi's *The Pines of Rome* ("Pines of the Appian Way" - see Ex.2). Here, the

---

1. *Tuning the School Band and Orchestra* (Louisiana: Pottle, 1960), p.29.

trumpet has stepped out of its role as a fanfare instrument. This solo requires the most lyric and mellow tone possible from the performer. Furthermore, the demands made upon the soloist are comparable to any of the slow movements of the various trumpet sonatas or concerti.

A new problem confronting the soloist with the Respighi work is in trumpet selection. Either a C or B♭ trumpet may be used with equal success. Which one to employ would depend essentially on (1) the sound desired and (2) potential intonation problems. The C trumpet has more brilliance and may be capable of more delicate attacks than the B♭ trumpet. The performer will probably be more sure of himself, since the top note would be G^2 open on the C trumpet, rather than A^2 on the B♭ trumpet (which is a less secure note in response and intonation). The smoothness of attacks and releases of such notes as this concert G^2 will make the difference between an average performance and a really fine one.

Off-Stage Cornet

The cornet, which usually is associated with a more mellow and lyrical quality than the trumpet, has also been used for off-stage work. Prokofiev makes use of the cornet in *Lieutenant Kije*, although this solo is normally played on a B♭ or D trumpet. The D trumpet may be preferred, since the transposition down a major third on the D places the solo in a lower tessitura and enables the trumpeter to play mostly on open notes rather than the treacherous 2-3 combination of $G^{\#2}$ on the B♭ trumpet (see Ex.3).

Attacks and releases need the most attention in this work (though trumpet selection may help minimize or eliminate that problem). Because the off-stage soloist is not covered by a heavy instrumentation and the listener's attention is focused on his unique sound, a split attack or poorly released tone will be noticed even more than it is on stage.

Off-Stage Ensembles

The off-stage literature is not entirely limited to soloists; it may involve a choir or small ensemble of similar or mixed instruments. With any increase of performers, there

Ex. 1 — Leonore No. 3, Beethoven

Ex. 2 — Pines of Rome, Respighi (in C)

Ex. 3 — Lt. Kije, Prokofiev Andante assai (in B♭)

is a proportional increase of difficulties. Also, the aspect of distance may become crucial.

With Strauss's *Ein Heldenleben* (see Ex.4), we have 3 trumpets used off stage in the "Hero's Helpmate." In this work, the trumpets are employed in a fanfare-like display that demands a distinct balance among the 3 trumpeters. The trumpets enter alternately, but with the same rhythmic pattern. For this reason, the interpretation of this figure must be the same by all 3 performers, so that a blend of sound and style is projected to the audience.

Because the Strauss excerpt is essentially a fanfare, it will demand clean articulation and a brilliant tone from the performers. The range of the parts is such that no major problem should exist in achieving this. However, some rhythmic dif-

ficulty may be encountered, e.g., the second bar demands precise ensemble execution. The key to success is in the release of the tie in that bar and the articulation of the 16th notes in the middle of the triplet figure. These notes must be played clearly, not only for clarity's sake, but for the projection of the separate lines.

Probably the most intricate of the off-stage repertoire for an ensemble is the "Dies Irae" in Verdi's *Requiem*. The various parts themselves are not difficult; the crucial item in this work is the coordination of the two separate groups of trumpets, 4 on stage and 4 off stage. The problem increases directly as the distance between the conductor and the off-stage trumpets increases. If there is no compensation for speed of sound and temperature changes, adverse results may occur.

An excellent piece of off-stage literature is the posthorn solo in Mahler's third symphony. This solo, which has even been arranged for solo trumpet and piano (published by Edition Musicus), is as difficult and challenging as any of the repertoire in the solo literature. Range, style, tone, technic, intervals, and general musicianship all need consideration. The part includes fanfare-like passages, as well as trills and lyrical lines reminiscent of *Lieutenant Kije* and *The Pines of Rome*. The accompaniment involves strings, strings with woodwinds, and, at times, the horns are employed in a dialogue fashion with the trumpet. Thus, the trumpet soloist will need to remain in visual contact with the conductor.

The off-stage repertoire contains all of the challenges and problems of solo playing, plus the added pressures of performing in unfamiliar — often hostile — surroundings. Although this music represents a relatively small percentage of all trumpet literature, it provides formidable challenges and musically satisfying rewards, and it should be considered an important area of study for every serious player of the instrument. ∎

December, 1972

Ex. 4 — Ein Heldenleben, Strauss

Double or Nothing

How tight money in Hollywood is popularizing deskants and tubens

James Decker

Music and the movies have had a long and mutually beneficial relationship. The first true master of the celluloid art, D.W. Griffith, ordered an original score for full opera orchestra for the silent classic, *Birth of a Nation*. And who can think of silent films at all without remembering the marvelous movie-house piano?

When talkies were introduced in 1928, a musical explosion in films gave every major studio its own symphony orchestra, and Hollywood attracted as many hopeful musicians as starlets. For musicians, at least, the 30's through the early 50's were truly Hollywood's Golden Age. Copeland and Prokofiev scored for films. Oscar Levant played Chopin's fingers. Isaac Stern played someone else playing Paganini. And Heifetz... well, Heifetz played himself.

Now all that has changed. The studio symphony orchestra, along with the star system and, incidentally, most of the major studios, is gone.

Today, television is King, and music budgets are notoriously low.

A Note About Names

In the evolution of language, it is **general usage** which ultimately determines what is "correct," even though this may be in opposition to logic, desire, or "the rules." It is entirely possible that today's "error" could become tomorrow's accepted form.

The names of instruments discussed in this article are a case in point.

French horn

We are aware of the movement to drop "French," but the use of "horn" alone is not yet sufficiently clear, especially since in the vernacular of many musicians even a tenor sax is referred to as a "horn."

Tuben

Actually this instrument is the Wagner tuba in B♭. In German, the word **Tuben** is the plural form of **Tuba** (German nouns are capitalized). Tuben is now generally used in English as the singular form; thus we speak of one tuben or a quartet of tubens.

Deskant

This is the name for a single F (French) horn built an octave higher than the traditional instrument. The word is a mixture of spellings from two languages (German: Diskant; English: descant).

Consequently, to the hornists who attempt to earn their livings in Hollywood's recording studios, it is often double...or nothing. Since the musician who plays two instruments on one job earns 50% more, and the employer pays 50% *less* for a second instrument than for a second musician, the person who can play a second instrument will be called for the job in preference to a one-instrument player.

Money Not the Only Reason

Aesthetics as well as economics have popularized doubling. The more sounds a composer has to work with, the more variety he can put into the score. Even on a low budget, variety is possible with a 16-track tape recorder and the technique of overdubbing. In this way, one person can play two or more instruments literally at once, simply by re-recording.

Doubling is a new trend for hornists. It started in 1964 when an adventurous young hornist, Dave Duke, took a Wagner Tuba to a rock'n'roll recording session in Hollywood. The sound and attack of the instrument so impressed the composer that he used it in a section originally scored for the French horn. Now nearly every composer and arranger in Hollywood recognizes the value of the *tuben* (the Americanized name for a Wagner tuba) and an even closer relative of the French horn, the *deskant* (a hybrid name — see note). They are attracted to the sound variations these instruments can produce for popular recordings, television, and film. The possibilities of French horns, deskants and tubens together are truly startling — Alec Wilder's *Nonet* for two deskants, two horns, four tubens, plus tuba (*Angel S-36036* - Los Angeles Horn Club) gives ample proof of their potential.

I would estimate that during the past year, literally hundreds of calls for professional French hornists required either deskant or tuben as a double. Sometimes both were needed. Deskants and tubens can be heard almost weekly on *Mannix*, *Mission Impossible*, *Mod Squad* and several other TV shows.

Tubens

The "new" sound of tubens dates back to the latter part of the 19th century. The instrument was developed by Franz Strauss (father of Richard) and Richard Wagner, who gave it a name and a prominent role in all the operas of the Ring. In *Das Rheingold*, *Die Walküre*, *Siegfried*, and *Götterdämmerung*, a quartet of tubens is added to the orchestra and featured in no less than 16 separate motifs.

Wagner wrote for tubens with discretion, most often presenting them as a solo quartet to make sure their sound would be clearly identified. Bruckner, Mahler, Strauss and Stravinsky also wrote for the instrument, and all the world's major symphony and opera orchestras own at least one set of tubens.

There are two basic types of tubens, both with four valves, both bell-front. One is in B♭, with an F fourth valve, and the second is in low F with a C fourth valve.

The first tubens were introduced to Southern California by Sinclair Lott, 1st Horn of the Los Angeles Philharmonic and Professor of Horn at U.S.C. He acquired a set of four in Germany immediately after the collapse of the Third Reich at the end of the Second World War. Over the years, many Southern California hornists had a chance to use tubens, thanks to Sinclair Lott. In fact, Dave Duke was playing one of the four original Lott tubens the day the popular potential of the instrument was discovered.

Tubens have a number of advantages. When blown loudly, they have a devastatingly primitive sound and produce heavy rhythmic effects which are ideal in popular music. Another advantage results from the fact that the tuben's bell is in front. This makes tubens more natural to record — both for the musicians and the engineers. With French horn, the musician prefers the microphone in front of him, but the engineer insists it be placed in back. With tuben, front is the choice of both parties. Also, engineers place the microphone in front when French horns and tubens are recorded in ensemble. The instruments blend quite well and the recorded sound of the French Horn, because it is *reflected*, is most natural.

The trend to tubens spread rapidly after their popular debut in 1964. Less than a year later, Gene Page made tubens an important part of the Mo-Town Sound. In 1966, Eddie Karom introduced them on A&M Records and the *Roger Miller Show*. In 1967, George Tipton created the "Nillsson Sound" with them. Tubens helped win Mason Williams and Mike Post a Grammy in 1968 for "Classical Gas." And in 1971, a solo choir of tubens was the dramatic background for the opening scenes of *Ice Station Zebra*, a Fox release scored by Michele LeGrand.

Tubens in the Marching Band

Professional composers, arrangers and hornists on both coasts (and in between) are constantly finding new uses for this instrument. But I feel that it will ultimately be band directors throughout the nation who discover the extraordinary utility of tubens... in marching bands.

The most absurd instrument played on a football field is also the noblest: the French horn. It's an instrument designed to *reflect* sound. But in a marching band what does it reflect against? A crowd of spectators 600 feet away? The sound of the noble horn is invariably lost in the wind or bungled because the instrument is simply impossible to play on the march.

The tuben, however, similar as it is to the tenor horns used in German bands for many years, is a natural on the field. Its bell-front design produces a sound that can blend, balance and carry with the rest of the band.

The outdoor carrying power of tubens has become legendary thanks to hornist Art Maebe. Art was one of the eight hornists called for in Strauss' *Domestic Symphony*. During the Los Angeles Philharmonic's rehearsal of that work in the Hollywood Bowl, Zubin Mehta repeatedly complained that the horns weren't loud enough and demanded more sound. At length, Mr. Maebe told the conductor, "Give us tubens and we'll give you all the sound you want." (Those who were there may recall a slightly different quote.)

No discussion of marching bands would be complete without mention of the relatively new contralto horn — another splendid field replacement for French horn. The contralto horn is a 4 rotary-valved instrument with left-hand fingering. Pitched in F with auxiliary E♭ crook, the contralto has the range and fingering of an alto horn. John Paynter's Northwestern University Band, Arthur Bartner's USC Trojans and Jim Nichols' Grossmont High School Band are using contraltos for an easy-to-produce big sound, with a French horn tone quality. I predict widespread popularity for this instrument.

Deskant

The deskant horn is another instrument that has recently become popular among recording hornists. Its advantage is simple: higher register, less strain. If you've ever been aroused from a less-than-exciting television show by an extremely high French horn solo played with amazing facility and precise intonation, you've probably heard a deskant.

The deskant is strictly a specialist's horn, to be used with discretion. It's used commonly in literature that requires the first horn to play in the extreme high register for long periods. The single is a high F, the double a high F and B♭. Actually, a good hornist can play a traditional double horn in the same high register as the deskant, but accuracy is doubtful and a worry for the player. And no matter how skilled the hornist, the effort and strain can be heard.

The deskant sound is much lighter than that of the French horn; the carrying power is weaker. The deskant is ideal for small chamber ensembles and, of course, for recording. Some manufacturers have given the traditional French horn the high F deskant register.

We all realize, of course, that it's tough enough to do justice to one very difficult, very rewarding instrument: the French horn. And all this talk of alternative instruments for hornists may be disturbing to some. But as music styles change, so must we as performers. We should be willing to try something new, to introduce new sounds, to forget that hornists should never change equipment. Because when we do change, as I have learned, it can be more than profitable.

It can be fun. ∎

1973

Brass in Venice

John R. Shoemaker

There is a profusion of brass ensemble music from Venice — much of it composed by Giovanni Gabrieli (ca. 1557-1612) and his contemporaries. One important aspect of the study of this music concerns the reason for its development in Venice — or, more generally, the reason this particular city in the northeastern corner of Italy assumed such musical prominence.

Venice is located upon some 300 islands in the Adriatic Sea just off the Italian mainland. For several centuries, the location and maritime power of this influential city-state made it a safe and convenient port of entry for fleets of ships which sailed the long and dangerous route to and from the Orient. Through her portals passed many riches (such as gold and spices) on their way to kingdoms throughout Europe. The inhabitants of Venice were keenly aware of their strategic location, and allowed these goods to flow through their city only after making certain that a generous portion remained to satisfy their own needs and desires.

As a result of the accumulation of such great wealth, the city officials were able to construct huge and extremely ornate buildings to house their government and those who were responsible for keeping its wheels

in motion. One of the first buildings to be built was a sumptuous palace for the Doge — the titular head of the city. Located at the edge of the Adriatic on a bay now called the *Bacino San Marco*, it was built of shimmering pink marble and adorned with graceful, bonewhite arches, forming an impressive sight for those who visited Venice. Through the years, other buildings were added, eventually forming the complex which still stands today — essentially unchanged since the 12th century (see illustration).

The huge palace of the Doge stands on the water's edge. Next to it is the Cathedral of San Marco — originally the private chapel of the Doge. Nearby is a tall bell-tower, or Campanille. Almost 33 stories tall, it is a sight which must surely have been especially impressive to the eyes of Renaissance man. A concourse called the *Piazzetta* stretches from the bay to the *Piazza San Marco* (named after the patron saint of Venice), sometimes referred to as the "outdoor ballroom of Europe," which is surrounded by small shops and offices of government officials.

It was in this setting that dignitaries from throughout the world were entertained, and suitably impressed with the power and glory of Venice. The Doge and

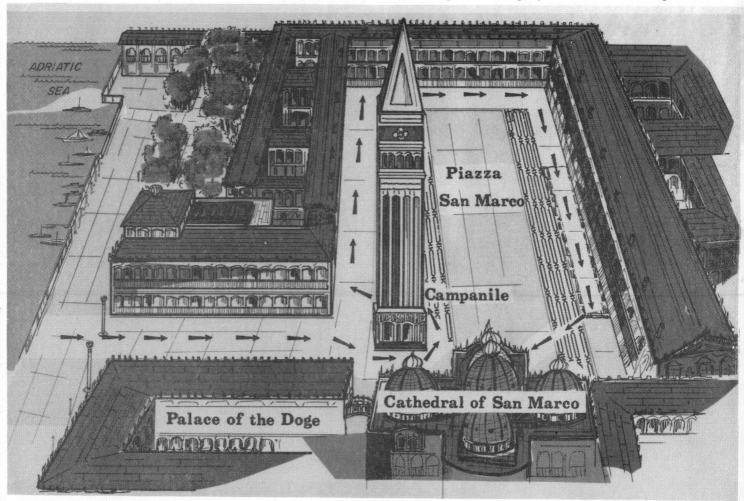

his senate (who helped to rule Venice) would greet the ships of those of the highest rank and greatest wealth, and then lead a procession through the *Piazzetta*. With musicians playing trumpets and trombones, the entire entourage would make a left turn past the Campanille and continue the stately procession around the perimeter of the Piazza. The Italian artist Gentile Bellini has left us a most impressive painting of just such a scene in his *Procession in the Piazza San Marco*. Jean Baptiste Duval, a French ambassador to Venice during the years 1607-1609, describes the sartorial splendor of the Doge as he processed in a robe of gold cloth and rode upon a golden throne with his umbrella and sword. His immediate party included musicians playing oboes and six silver trumpets.[1]

The destination of the entourage was the chapel of the Doge, better known as the Cathedral San Marco. Through the huge doors surrounded by mosaics of gold, the entourage would pass to give thanks for a safe journey and to ask blessings for the business to be transacted with the shrewd businessmen of the city-state. The music developed and nurtured in Venice could not have been supported without the cultural and financial foundation which led to the erection of San Marco and the establishment to sustain it.

Those visitors who were privileged to enter this 10th century cathedral (which took almost 100 years to construct) were treated to a church of tremendous size, spectacular architecture, and conspicuous opulence. It was built in the shape of a Greek Cross, i.e., with arms of equal length. Its uniqueness, however, lay not in the size or configuration, but in the fact that San Marco had two choir lofts facing each other in the apses of the nave, and each loft contained its own organ. Resident composers took every advantage of these unusual facilities, composing works requiring musicians to perform from both lofts simultaneously. It must have been a wondrous experience for the assemblage to hear true stereophonic music in the middle of the second millennium. There was even a period of 3 years (1588-1591) when a third organ was added — this one at the rear of the nave.

The unique combination of geographical location, cosmopolitan atmosphere, proximity of Palace, Piazza, and Cathedral, matchless performance facilities, and special government occurances in and around San Marco provided a natural setting for spectacular musical events. Those who manned the consoles of the multiple organs did their best to take advantage of this milieu.

Since San Marco was a private chapel, there were numerous occasions when its functions differed from those of most churches of the Renaissance and Baroque periods. Music was performed under a variety of circumstances — weddings, inaugurations, governmental processions, and private events for the Doge. Organs and different instruments including cornetts and trombones were frequently united with the singers for performance from the lofts. For example, on Christmas Day in 1607, Duval heard "the double organs and different instruments, such as cornettos and treble violins united with voices of the singers, and all this indeed filled the church and produced a grand harmony."[2]

Over the years the musical establishment at San Marco developed an excellent reputation, and the competition for a position there was keen. Independence of musical thinking was partly responsible for San Marco's ability to attract so many outstanding musicians. From all over Europe they came to study with and perform for such masters as Willeart, de Rore, Zarlino, Merulo, Padavano, Andrea Gabrieli, Giovanni Gabrieli, Giuseppe Guami, and Claudio Monteverdi. Sufficient numbers of performers and the quality of their performances made it possible for Venice to retain her musical prominence. Egon Kenton, in his work on Giovanni Gabrieli, indicated that the musical forces of San Marco numbered not less than 40 singers, with violinists and wind-players employed in proportionate numbers on a yearly basis.[3]

The brasses are described with particular emphasis by Ercole Bottrigari, an Italian theorist, and Thomas Coryat, a Somersetshire Englishman and world traveler. "Cornetts and trombones," writes Bottrigari in 1594 with performances in Venice especially in mind, "are played with such grace, taste and sure precision of the notes, that they are held the most excellent of the wind instruments in the profession."[4] Coryat heard a performance in 1608 at San Marco which he narrated as follows:

> ...Saturday...the sixth day of August,....I heard the best musicke that I ever did in all my life both in the morning and the afternoone, so good that I would willingly goe an hundred miles a foote at any time to heare the like.... This feast consisted principally of Musicke, which was both vocall and instrumental, so good, so delectable, so rare, so admirable, so superexcellent, that it did even ravish and stupifie all those strangers that never heard the like. But how others were affected with it I know not; for mine owne part I can say this, that I was for the time even rapt up with Saint Paul into the third heaven. Sometimes there sung sixteene or twenty men together, having their master or moderator [perhaps G. Gabrieli] to keep them in order; and when they sung, the instrumentall musitians played also. Sometimes sixteene played together upon their instruments, ten Sagbuts, foure Cornets, and two Violdegambaes of an extraordinary greatness; sometimes tenne, sixe Sagbuts and foure Cornets; sometimes two, a Cornet and a treble violl.[5]

Certainly this cosmopolitan city of Venice and her cultural heritage provided every advantage for the development of all kinds of music — including brass music. The government had many festive occasions both in- and out-of-doors, thereby creating the need. Venetian musicians — performers and composers — took their artistry seriously. The famous church of San Marco had unusual facilities, thereby providing the place for performance; and the hierarchy within the church recognized the pragmatic as well as spiritual value of music in the propagation of faith and paid her musicians more generously than did most other churches. It was within this cultural milieu that the great masters of the late Renaissance and early Baroque composed for choirs of instruments and voices. And it was here that the finest musicians in the world came to study, to teach, and to perform. There can be little wonder, then, that the quality and quantity of brass ensemble music produced in Venice in the late 16th and early 17th centuries surpassed that of any other Italian city. ∎

1. Egon Kenton, *Life and Works of Giovanni Gabrieli* (American Institute of Musicology, 1967), p. 35.

2. *Ibid.*

3. *Ibid.*, p. 34.

4. Anthony Baines, *Woodwind Instruments and Their History* (New York: Norton, 1962), p. 260.

5. Thomas Coryat, *Coryat's Crudities* (Glasglow: James MacLehose and Sons, 1905), pp. 388, 390.

Music for Brass Trio

Steven Winick

Compared to other instrument families, the brasses reached their present state of development quite recently. The most important stage of this development was the application of valves to brass instruments during the first half of the 19th century. This not only made a full chromatic scale possible for all the brass instruments, but, more importantly, enabled them to achieve musical expression comparable to that of the other instrument families. Consequently, in the last half of the 19th century, isolated works like Franz Lachner's *Nonett* (written ca. 1850) and Wilhelm Ramsöe's five brass quartets (published in 1888) appeared. It was not, however, until the twentieth century that significant brass chamber music was written.

The brass ensemble was slow to develop a standard instrumentation comparable to the string quartet or the woodwind quintet. Rasmussen writes that various instrumentations were in vogue at different times:

In the [nineteen-] thirties the most popular music was the sextet, designed for public school groups. In the forties it was the brass quartet, usually intended for college faculty and student groups. In the fifties it was the big brass ensemble piece, written for college and conservatory ensembles. In the sixties it is the trio as "pure" chamber music for skilled players of any kind, amateur and professional; and the quintet, largely written for professional groups.[1]

In addition to being an excellent medium for the expression of "pure" chamber music, the brass trio can be used successfully in situations where neither the nec-

essary players nor adequate funds are available to provide a brass quintet. Where a quintet does exist, including an occasional trio adds variety to its programs. This could also provide a rest period for the first trumpeter and tubaist, while giving the second trumpeter an opportunity to assume more of the musical responsibilities.

Most chamber music for brass tends to be relatively short in duration. This is especially true of the brass trio. Since all the instruments play almost continuously, excessively long compositions cause endurance problems.

Brass trios are written for a variety of instrumentations. There are several trios for 2 trumpets and trombone, and a few works for other combinations of 3 different brass instruments, but the largest number is for trumpet, horn, and trombone. This instrumentation gives the trio a good representation of each register, a wide variety of timbres, and a full sonority.

Among the first compositions to be published for brass trio were 2 preludes and fugues[2] by Oskar Böhme.[3] The music is scored for *trompete in B, althorn in Es* and *baryton.* The title page gives the

alternate instrumentation of cornet, waldhorn, and tenorhorn,[4] with the trombone indicated as a further substitute for the baryton. The valved brass, with their facile technique and rich timbre, are admirably suited to Böhme's romantic, flowing melodies. Long unobtainable, these trios have recently been edited and published for trumpet, horn, and trombone (see listing below).

Francis Poulenc's *Sonate* for horn, trumpet, and trombone, which was written in 1922 and revised in 1945, is remarkable for its originality and freshness. Its use of texture and timbre is more varied and interesting, and its technical demands are more challenging than previous works for brass. Furthermore, Poulenc's scoring for brass was so successfully handled that it brought to the world of music a new respect and liking for the brass trio in particular and brass chamber music in general.

The brass trios written since Poulenc's are generally rather conservative. However, trios for trumpet, horn, and trombone have shown a tendency to be somewhat more adventuresome than those for other combinations. For example, Beckwith's *Five Pieces* includes one movement in which each instrument is given a characteristic solo cadenza. Louël's *Trio* contains such features as extreme dynamic contrasts, angular melodic lines, and rapid valve technique. Roussakis' *Composition*, based on a five-note theme, utilizes flutter-tongue, glissandi, and a variety of mutes. Winick's *Con-*

1. Mary H. Rasmussen, *A Teacher's Guide to the Literature of Brass Instruments* (Durham, N.H.: Brass Quarterly, 1964), p. 35.

2. *Dreistimmiges Praludium und Fuge*, Op. 28, No.1 in C moll [sic] and *Dreistimmiges Praludium und Fuge*, Op. 28, No.2 in Es dur [sic] (Leipzig: P. Jurgenson, 1905?). Op. 28, No.1 is in Es dur and No.2 in C moll; also, the fugue of No.2 is in 3/8 meter, not 3/4.

3. The following information on Bohme has been compiled by Albert E. Wier in *The Macmillan Encyclopedia of Music and Musicians* (New York: Macmillan Co., 1938), p. 202: "German trumpet virtuoso and composer, born Potschappel, Dresden, Feb. 24, 1870. He studied with von Gurlitt, von Herzfeld and Judassohn, and became first trumpeter at the Academy Theatre, Petrograd. His compositions are chiefly for the trumpet." Best known of these are the *Konzert*, Op. 18 for trumpet and orchestra and the *Trompeten-Sextett*, Op. 30 for brass sextet.

4. Adam Carse clarifies these often inconsistent and confusing instrument names in *Musical Wind Instruments* (London: Macmillan and Co. Ltd., 1939), pp. 293-316.

frontation explores new brass textures produced by manipulating rhythms and dynamic effects.

The search for new modes of expression has resulted in a growing number of trios which use an accompaniment of taped sounds. Frohmader's *Brass Trio with Tape* utilizes "live" electronics (synthesizer). MacInnis' *Sonogram I(b)* and *Rendevous* are written for trumpet, horn, bass trombone and computer-synthesized tape. Schwartz's *Rip* deals with the interaction of taped sounds, live brass effects (especially the "rip" effect), and the word *rip* itself, which is spoken, whispered, and shouted by the performers.

It is hoped that the above remarks and the following list will attract attention to the extensive literature for brass trio. All works in the list are original music for brass; transcriptions have been omitted. The list is divided as follows: trios for trumpet, horn, and trombone; trios for 2 trumpets and trombone; and trios for miscellaneous instrumentations. Some trios have piano, orchestra, band, or taped accompaniments. The titles have frequently been shortened, since the descriptive term "for brass trio" is self-evident. Some entries include the location of annotations and reviews which have appeared since 1955 in various sources.[5]

Trumpet, Horn, and Trombone

Aschaffenburg, Walter (1927-). *Divertimento* (1952). Rochester, N.Y.: Rochester Music Photo Copy Co., Inc. [Annotation: *BW*, VI (1971), 99.] Grade V.

Avril, Edwin. *Petite Suite*. North Easton, Mass.: Robert King Music Co., 1971. Grade V.

Bassett, Leslie R. (1923-). *Trio* (1953). North Easton, Mass.: Robert King Music Co., 1968. [Annotations: Cramer. Review: *NACWPI*, XVII (Summer, 1969), 17. Shoemaker.] Grade V.

Beckwith, John (1927-). *Five Pieces* (1951). Toronto: Canadian Music Centre, 1951. Grade IV.

Bentzon, Niels Viggo (1919-). *Trio*, Opus 82 (1952). Copenhagen: Wilhelm Hansen Musik-Forlag, 1964. [Annotations: Cramer and Shoemaker.] Grade V.

Berghmans, José (1921-). *Concerto Grosso*. (String orchestra accompaniment; piano reduction available. Paris: A. Leduc, 1957. [Review: *BQ*, III (Summer, 1960), 182.] Grade V-VI.

5. For recent research which examines some aspects of form, harmony, rhythm, melody, timbre, and instrumental technique in brass trios, see Douglas M. Baer, "The Brass Trio: A Comparative Analysis of Works Published from 1924-1970." Ph.D. dissertation, Florida State University, 1970; University Microfilms [LC 71-6959].

Beyer, Frederick (1926-). *Conversations*. New York: Autograph Editions New York, 1970. [Annotation: Cramer.] Grade IV-V.

Bezanson, Philip (1916-). *Diversion*. Northampton, Mass.: New Valley Music Press, 1968.

Bialosky, Marshall (1923-). *Two Movements*. North Easton, Mass.: Robert King Music Co., 1954. [Annotations: Cramer and Shoemaker.] Grade IV.

Böhme, Oskar (1870-19??). *Prelude and Fugue*, Opus 28, No. 1 in Eb Major. New York: Autograph Editions New York, 1971. Grade IV.

Böhme, Oskar. *Prelude and Fugue*, Opus 28, No. 2 in C Minor. New York: Autograph Editions New York, 1971. Grade V.

Brandon, Sy. *Trio* (1965). Composer's MS: 3201 E. Greenlee Rd., Tucson, Arizona 85716. [Annotation: *BW*, VII, 1 (Winter, 1972), 13.] Grade IV-V.

Brehm, Alvin (1925-). *Divertimento*. New York: Edward B. Marks Music Corp., n.d. Grade V.

Bull, Edvard H. (1922-). *Concert* (1966). Paris: Editions Musicales Transatlantiques, 1967. Grade VI.

Butterworth, A. (1923-). *Trio* (1962). London: Composers' Guild of Great Britain.

Cabus, Peter (1923-). *Sonata a tre*. Brussels: Editions J. Maurer, 1962. [Review: *BQ*, VII (Winter, 1963), 105. Annotations: Cramer and Shoemaker.] Grade V.

Childs, Barney (1926-). *Brass Trio* (1959). New York: Composers Facsimile Edition, 1964. Grade V-VI.

Cowell, John. *Trio*. Massapequa, N.Y.: Cor Publishing Co., 1960. [Review: *BQ*, V (Spring, 1962), 119. Annotation: Cramer.] Grade III.

Cox, Harry (1923-). *Thème et variations* (1966). Brussels: Editions J. Maurer, 1967. Grade III.

Dedrick, Arthur (1915-). *Three To Go*. Delevan, N.Y.: Kendor Music, Inc., 1966. Grade III.

De Jong, Conrad (1934-). *Suite of Wisconsin Folk Music* (1962). Delaware Water Gap, Pa.: Shawnee Press, Inc., 1964. [Review: *BQ*, VII (Winter, 1963), 104. Annotation: Cramer.] Grade III.

Donahue, Robert L. (1931-). *Little Suite* (1968). Los Angeles: Western International Music, Inc., 1970. [Review: *INST*, XXV (Aug. 1970), 63.] Grade III.

Duckworth, William (1943-). *Transparent Interludes* (1967). Chicago, Ill.: M.M. Cole Publishing Co., 1972. Grade VI.

Everett, Thomas G. (1944-). *Fun Trio* (1965). Composer's MS: Harvard University Band, 9 Prescott St., Cambridge, Mass. Grade III.

Fink, Robert R. (1933-). *Modal Suite* (1953). New York: Edition Musicus, 1959. [Annotation: Cramer.] Grade III.

Flothius, Marius (1914-). *Sonatina*, Opus 26 (1945). Amsterdam: Donemus, 1948. [Annotation: Cramer and Husted.] Grade IV.

Frackenpohl, Arthur (1924-). *Brass Trio* (1966). Buffalo: Ensemble Publications, Inc., 1968. Grade III.

Frank, Marcel G. (1909-). *Rondo*. Berkeley, Calif.: Wynn Music, 1960. Grade II.

Frohmader, Jerold C. *Brass Trio with Tape*. (Synthesizer accompaniment.) Composer's MS: Music Dept., Glassboro State College, Glassboro, N.J. 08028. Grade V.

Gabaye, Pierre (1930-). *Récréation*. (Piano accompaniment.) Paris: A. Leduc, 1958. Grade V.

Gower, Albert E. (1935-). *Improvisations* (1970). Composer's MS: Southern Station, Box 458, Hattiesburg, Miss. 39401. Grade V.

Hansen, Einar Bech (1889-). *Trio*, Opus 8 (1953). Library of Congress MS.

Harlan, Charles L. *Trio*. Cleveland, Ohio: Composers' Autograph Publications, 1968.

Hartley, Walter S. (1927-). *Two Pastiches* (1970). New York: Autograph Editions New York, 1971. Grade V.

Hartzell, Lawrence. *Trio*. Composer's MS: Music Dept., Wisconsin State University, Eau Claire, Wisconsin 54701.

Haubiel, Charles (1892-). *Athenaeum Suite*. New York: Composers Press, Inc., 1953. [Annotation: Cramer.] Grade IV.

Hawkins, John. *Remembrances...* (1969). (Piano and harp accompaniment.) Toronto: Canadian Music Centre.

Henry, Otto. *Variations* (1961). Composer's MS: School of Music, East Carolina University, Greenville, N.C. 27834. [Review: *BQ*, IV (Summer, 1961), 176. Annotation: Cramer.] Grade IV-V.

Hogg, Merle E. (1922-). *Three Short Pieces*. New York: Autograph Editions New York, 1968. Grade V.

Hogg, Merle E. *Variations*. Cleveland, Ohio: Composers' Autograph Publications, 1969.

Hovhaness, Alan (1911-). *Fantasy No. I*, Opus 70, No. 1. New York: C.F. Peters Corp., 1969. [Review: *INST*, XXIV (Nov. 1969), 91.] Grade III.

Hovhaness, Alan. *Fantasy No. II*, Opus 70, No. 2. New York: C.F. Peters Corp., 1969. [Review: *INST*, XXIV (Nov. 1969), 92.] Grade III.

Hovhaness, Alan. *Fantasy No. III*. Opus 70, No. 3. New York: C.F. Peters Corp., 1969. [Review: *INST*, XXIV (Nov. 1969), 92.] Grade III.

Hughes, Mark (1934-1972). *Divertimento*. Hattiesburg, Miss.: Tritone Press, 1964. [Review: *BQ*, VII (Winter, 1963), 105. Annotation: Cramer.] Grade IV-V.

Hutchison, Warner (1930-). *Mini-Suite* (1972). Composer's MS: Fine Arts Dept., New Mexico State University, Las Cruces, N.M. 88001. Grade V.

Johnston, Richard. *Suite* (1972). Composer's MS: School of Music, George Peabody College, Nashville, Tenn. 37203. Grade IV.

Kaplan, Allan R. (1948-). *Scherzo and Trio* (1968). Composer's MS: 214 W. 21st St., New York, N.Y. 10011. Grade IV.

Keyes, Nelson (1928-). *Trio* (1967). Ann Arbor, Mich.: University Microfilms. Contemporary Music Project Library Edition, 034-1-02. Grade IV.

Klebe, Giselher (1925-). *Espressione liriche*. Mainz: B. Schott's Söhne, 1956.

Knight, Morris (1933-). *Cassation* (1961). Hattiesburg, Miss.: Tritone Press, 1962. [Review: *BQ*, V (Spring, 1962), 119. Annotation: Cramer.] Grade V.

Knox, Charles (1929-). *Solo for Trumpet with Brass Trio*. New York: Autograph Editions New York, 1966. [Reviews: *BWQ*, I (Winter, 1966-67), 59, and *NACWPI*, (Winter, 1969-70), 64.] Solo part - Grade IV; trio parts - Grade III.

Knox, Charles. *Solo for Tuba with Brass Trio*. Bryn Mawr, Pa.: Tenuto Publications, 1969. Solo part - Grade V; trio parts - Grade IV.

Kohs, Ellis B. (1916-). *Brass Trio* (1957). New York: Composers Facsimile Edition, 1962. Grade V.

Kox, Hans (1930-). *Concertante Muzek* (1956). (Orchestra accompaniment.) Amsterdam: Donemus, 1956. Grade V.

Kroeger, Karl (1932-). *Sonate Breve* (1937). Hattiesburg, Miss.: Tritone Press, 1962. [Review: *BQ*, V (Spring, 1962), 119. Annotation: Cramer.] Grade IV.

Krueger, T.H. *Trio*. Chicago: MS Publications, 1970.

Leclerq, Edgard (1880-1962). *Suite Classique* (1959). Brussels: Editions Musicales Brogneaux, 1959. [Annotation: Cramer.] Grade IV-V.

Lehmann, Daniel. *Five Pieces*. Composer's MS: American Music Center, Inc., 2109 Broadway, New York, N.Y. 10023.

Linke, Norbert (1933-) *Konkretionen IV*.

Cologne: Musikverlage Hans Gerig. Grade VI.

Louël, Jean (1914-). *Trio* (1951). Brussels: Centre Belge de Documentation Musicale, 1956. [Review: *BQ*, IV (Fall, 1960), 37. Annotations: Cramer and Shoemaker.] Grade VI.

Luedeke, Raymond. *Suite* (1972). Composer's MS: 1708 Strongs Ave., Stevens Point, Wis., 54481. Grade V.

Lyon, David (1938-). *Little Suite* (1965). London: Ascherberg, Hopwood & Crew Ltd., 1966. Grade III.

McBride, Robert (1911-). *Fantasy from the First Six Grades* (1968). New York: Composers Facsimile Edition, 1969.

McBride, Robert. *Lament for the Parking-Problem* (1967). New York: Composers Facsimile Edition, 1967.

MacInnis, Donald (1923-). *Sonogram I(b)*. (Computer-synthesized tape accompaniment.) Charlottesville, Va.: Wayside Press, 1966. [Review: *BW*, III(Fall, 1967), 290.] Grade V.

MacInnis, Donald. *Rendezvous* (1970). (Synthesizer and pre-recorded tape accompaniment.) New York: Edward B. Marks Music Corp., 1970. Grade V.

Maillot, Jean. *Trio*. Paris: Editions Musicales Transatlantiques, 1971. Grade V.

Maniet, René (1920-). *Trio No. 1*. Brussels: Editions J. Maurer, 1958. [Review: *BQ*, VII(Winter, 1963), 104. Annotation: Cramer.] Grade V.

Maniet, René. *A Trois* (1962). Brussels: Editions J. Maurer, 1964. Grade V.

Marek, Robert (1915-). *Trio* (1955). North Easton, Mass.: Robert King Music Co., 1959. [Review: *BQ*, III(Spring, 1960), 121. Annotations: Cramer and Shoemaker.] Grade IV.

Masso, George P. (1926-). *Trio* (1968). Providence, R.I.: Providence Music Press, 1968. Grade III.

Melillo, Peter A. *The Charioteer* (1972). (Narrator and optional tape accompaniment.) Composer's MS: 75 Bruce Ave., Yonkers, N.Y. 10705. Grade IV.

Meulemans, Arthur J. (1884-1966). *Trio* (1933). Brussels: Editions Musicales Brogneaux, 1950. [Annotations: Cramer and Shoemaker.] Grade V.

Meulemans, Arthur J. *2e Trio* (1960). Brussels: Centre Belge de Documentation Musicale, 1961. [Review: *BQ*, V(Spring, 1962), 118. Annotations: Cramer and Shoemaker.] Grade V.

Moortel, Leo van de (1919-). *Divertimento II*. Brussels: Editions J. Maurer, 1965. [Annotation: Cramer.] Grade V.

Muczynski, Robert (1929-). *Voyage*. New York: G. Schirmer, 1971. Grade V.

Mutter, Gerbert (1922-). *Kleines Trio*. Munich: Phillip Grosch-Verlag, n.d.

Nagel, Robert (1924-). *Brass Trio*. Brookfield, Conn.: Mentor Music, 1965. [Annotation: Cramer.] Grade V.

Nagel, Robert. *Brass Trio No. 2* (1966). Brookfield, Conn.: Mentor Music, 1966. [Annotation: Cramer.] Grade VI.

Nelhybel, Vaclav (1919-). *Piano-Brass Quartet*. New York: General Music Publishing Co., Inc., 1964. Grade V.

Nelhybel, Vaclav. *Trio*. New York: General Music Publishing Co., Inc., 1965. [Reviews: *BW*, IV(Winter, 1968), 324, and *BWQ*, I (Winter, 1966-67), 60. Annotation: Cramer.] Grade V.

Orval, Jules (1913-). *Piece en Re*. Brussels: Editions J. Maurer, 1970. Grade V.

Ott, Joseph (1929-). *Encore Set* (1968). Milton, Wisconsin: Claude Benny Press, 1970. [Review: *INST*, XXIV(April, 1970), 87 and *NACWPI* XX(Spring, 1972), 31.] Grade V.

Parris, Robert (1924-). *Four Pieces* (1965). New York: Composers Facsimile Edition. Grade V.

Pelemans, Willem (1901-). *Koperblazers-sonate* (1955). Brussels: Editions J. Maurer, 1956.

Peterson, Theodore (1918-). *Divertimento*. Delevan, N.Y.: Kendor Music, Inc., 1964. [Annotation: Cramer.] Grade III.

Pinkham, Daniel (1923-). *Brass Trio*. New York: C.F. Peters Corp., 1970. Grade V.

Plank, Dennis (1945-). *Three Movements* (1963). Composer's MS: Department of Music, Bishop College, Dallas, Tex. 75241. Grade V.

Poulenc, Francis (1899-1963). *Sonata* (1922, revised 1945). London: J. & W. Chester Ltd., 1924. [Annotations: Cramer, Husted, and Shoemaker.] Grade V.

Presser, William (1916-). *Prelude, Fugue, and Postlude*. New York: Autograph Editions New York, 1966. [Reviews: *BW*, V, 1(1970), 11, and *BWQ*, I(Winter, 1966-67), 59. Annotation: Cramer.] Grade V.

Quinet, Marcel (1915-). *Sonate à trois* (1961). Brussels: Centre Belge de Documentation Musicale, 1961. [Review: *BQ*, V(Spring, 1962), 118. Annotations: Cramer and Shoemaker.] Grade V.

Raphling, Sam (1910-). *Three Pieces*. New York: General Music Publishing Co., Inc., 1970. [Review: *INST*, XXV(Dec. 1970), 68.] Grade V.

Reid, Alan [Chris Dedrick] (1947-). *November Nocturn*. (Optional vibraphone or marimba accompaniment.) Delevan, N.Y.: Kendor Music, Inc., 1966. Grade III.

Roberts, Wilfred. *A Day in the Country*. Massapequa, N.Y.: Cor Publishing Co., 1963. [Annotation: Cramer.] Grade II.

Roussakis, Nicolas (1934-). *Composition* (1960). New York: Franco Colombo, Inc., 1967. Grade V.

Ruelle, Fernand (1921-). *Trio*, Opus 147. Brussels: Editions J. Maurer, 1965. [Annotation: Cramer.] Grade V.

Sanders, Robert L. (1906-). *Trio*. North Easton, Mass.: Robert King Music Co., 1961. [Review: *BQ*, V(Spring, 1962), 118. Annotations: Cramer and Shoemaker.] Grade IV.

Scharres, Charles (1888-1957). *Divertimento* (1956). Brussels: Editions Musicales Brogneaux, 1958. [Review: *BQ*, II(March, 1959), 128. Annotations: Cramer and Shoemaker.] Grade V.

Schmidt, William (1926-). *Chamber Music for Three Brass and Piano* (1969). Los Angeles: Western International Music Inc., 1969. Grade V.

Schwartz, Elliott (1936-). *Rip* (1970). (Stereo tape accompaniment.) Composer's MS: Dept. of Music, Bowdoin College, Brunswick, Maine 04011. [Annotation: *BW*, VI (1971), 103.] Grade V.

Šimai, Pavel (1930-). *Introduzione ed Allegro* (1958). Bratislava: Slovenský Hudobný Fond.

Snyder, Randall. *Dance Suite*. Los Angeles, Calif.: Western International Music, Inc., 1971. Grade V.

Stratton, Donald P. (1928-). *August, '70 Jan Trio* (1970). Composer's MS: 345 State St., Bangor, Maine 04401. Grade V.

Taranto, Vernon, Jr. *Study No. 1*. Cleveland, Ohio: Composers' Autograph Publications, 1970. Grade V.

Thielman, Ronald (1936-). *Two Moods*. Delevan, N.Y.: Kendor Music, Inc., 1962. Grade III.

Tull, Fisher (1934-). *Trio* (1967). Hollywood, Calif.: DNE Music, 1971. Grade V.

Vellère, Lucie (1896-1966). *Deux essais*. Brussels: Editions J. Maurer, 1966. [Annotation: Cramer.] Grade IV.

Volleman, Alphonse (1907-). *Trois croquis*. Brussels: Editions J. Maurer, 1961. Grade IV.

Vollrath, Carl P. *Three Movements* (1968). Composer's MS: Troy State College, Troy, Alabama 36081. Grade IV.

Walker, Richard (1912-). *Falconry Match* (1970). Delevan, N.Y.: Kendor Music, Inc., 1970. [Review: *INST*, XXV (June, 1971), 48.] Grade IV.

Werner, Jean-Jacques (1935-). *Canzoni per sonar* (1966). Paris: Editions Musicales Transatlantiques, 1966. [Review: *BWQ*, I(Spring-Winter, 1968), 173. Annotation: Cramer.] Grade V-VI.

Winick, Steven (1944-). *Confrontation* (1969). New York: Autograph Editions New York, 1970. Grade V.

Wright, James (1911-). *Trio* (1964). Far Hills, N.J.: The Horn Realm.

Young, P. (1912-). *Theme and Variations* (1961). Composer's MS: Technical College, Wulfrana St., Wolverhampton, Staffs, Great Britain.

Zbinden, Julien-Francois (1917-). *Trio*, Opus 13 (1949). Geneva: Société Intercontinentale d'Editions Musicales, 1958. [Annotation: Cramer.] Grade III.

Two Trumpets and Trombone

Amy, Gilbert (1936-). *Cuivres fanfare anniversaire*. Paris: Heugel & Cie., 1962.

Ardévol, José (1911-). *Tercera Sonata a Tres* (1942). Montevideo: Instituto Interamericano de Musicologia, 1945. [Annotation: Husted, p. 408-411.] Grade V.

Aschaffenburg, Walter (1927-). *fan-FARE for HErmAn Melville (150)* (1969). Composer's MS: Conservatory of Music, Oberlin College, Oberlin, Ohio 44074. [Annotation: *BW*, VI(1971), 99.] Grade V.

Borris, Siegfried (1906-). *Suite*, Opus 92, No. 2. Wolfenbüttel: K.H. Möseler Verlag, 1961. Grade III.

Burgon, Geoffrey. *Trio*. Surrey, Great Britain: Stainer and Bell, 1970.

Butts, Carrol M. (1924-). *Suite*. Westbury, N.Y.: Pro Art Publications, 1966. Grade II.

De Jong, Conrad (1934-). *Suite of Wisconsin Folk Music* (1962). Delaware Water Gap, Pa.: Shawnee Press, Inc., 1964. [Review: *BQ*, VII(Winter, 1963), 104. Annotation: Cramer.] Grade III.

Depelsenaire, J.M. *Concerto Grosso*. (Piano accompaniment.) New York: C.F. Peters Corp. Grade V.

Dvořáček, Jiři. *Three Miniatures*. New York: General Music Publishing Co., Inc., 1969. Grade IV-V.

Ginzburg, Dov. *The Crack: Scherzo*. Tel Aviv: Israel Publishers Agency, 1960. Grade IV.

Ginzburg, Dov. *The Ramblers: Samba*. Tel Aviv: Israel Publishers Agency, 1960. Grade IV.

Key to Annotation and Review Sources

BQ — *Brass Quarterly*

BW — *Brass World*

BWQ — *Brass and Woodwind Quarterly*

Cramer — Cramer, William F. "An Annotated List of Music for Brass Trio." *Brass World*, IV(Winter, 1968), 326-328ff.

Husted — Husted, Benjamin F. "The Brass Ensemble: Its History and Music." Unpublished Ph.D. dissertation, Eastman School of Music, 1955.

INST — *The Instrumentalist*

NACWPI — *National Association of College Wind and Percussion Instructors Journal*

Shoemaker — Shoemaker, John R. "A Selected and Annotated Listing of 20th Century Ensembles Published for Three or More Heterogeneous Brass Instruments." Ed.D. dissertation, Washington University, 1968; University Microfilms [LC 69-9009].

Ginzburg, Dov. *Trittico*. Tel Aviv: Israel Publishers Agency, 1963. [Review: *BQ*, VII(Winter, 1963), 104.] Grade IV.

Glasser, Stanley (1926-). *Trio* (1958). London: Musica Rara, 1959. [Review: *BQ*, IV(Summer, 1961), 176. Annotation: Shoemaker.] Grade V.

Gramatges, Harold (1918-). *Prelude and Invention*. Philadelphia: Henri Elkan, 1956. Grade IV.

Kocsár, Miklós. *Rézfúvós trió*. Budapest: Zeneműkiadō Vállalat, 1966.

Koepke, Paul. *Canzona*. (Piano accompaniment.) Chicago: Rubank, Inc., 1959. Grade III.

Koepke, Paul. *Fanfare Prelude*. (Piano accompaniment.) Chicago: Rubank, Inc., 1958. Grade III.

Kox, Hans (1930-). *Four Didactic Pieces*. Amsterdam: Donemus. Grade III-IV.

Kox, Hans. *Kleine Suite*. Amsterdam: Donemus, 1958. Grade IV.

Kubizek, A. (1918-). *Vier Stücke*. New York: Associated Music Publishers, 1953.

Lemmon, Douglas (1944-). *Trio* (1970). Champaign, Ill.: Media Press, Inc. 1971. Grade V.

Lessard, John (1920-). *Quodlibets*. New York: General Music Publishing Co., Inc. [Review: *INST*, XXIII (Feb. 1969), 86.] Grade VI.

Mayer, William (1925-). *Country Fair* (1962). New York: Boosey & Hawkes, 1963. [Review: *BQ*, VII(Winter, 1963), 104.] Grade IV.

Poser, Hans (1917-). *Kleine Suite*. Wolfenbüttel: K.H. Möseler Verlag, 1967.

Regner, Hermann (1928-). *Speil für drei Bläser*. Mainz: B. Schott's Söhne, 1960. [Review: *BQ*, VII(Fall, 1963), 51.] Grade III.

Riegger, Wallingford (1885-1961). *Movement*, Opus 66. (Piano accompaniment.) New York: Peer International Corp., 1960. [Review: BQ, III(Summer, 1960), 180.] Grade III.

Roberts, Wilfred. *A Day in the Country*.

Massapequa, N.Y.: Cor Publishing Co., 1963. [Annotation: Cramer.] Grade II.

Schmid, William R. (1940-). *Theme and Variations* (1969). Composer's MS: Music Education Dept., University of Kansas, Lawrence, Kansas 66044. Grade IV.

Sear, Walter E. *Brass Demonstration Piece*. Massapequa, N.Y.: Cor Publishing Co., 1958.

Searfoss, David (1947-). *Passacaglia* (1971). Composer's MS: 104 W. State Road, Hastings, Michigan 49058. Grade IV-V.

Spezzaferri, Giovanni (1888-1963). *Preludio e fuga*, Opus 81. Milan: Edizioni Suvini Zerboni, 1948. Grade V.

Šrámek, Vladimir (1923-). *Trio* (1956). Prague: Artia Verlag, 1962. [Review: *BQ*, VII(Winter, 1963), 104.] Grade V.

Thielman, Ronald (1936-). *Two Moods*. Delevan, N.Y.: Kendor Music, Inc., 1962. Grade II.

Thilman, Johannes P. (1906-). *Trio Musik*. Leipzig: Musikverlag F. Hofmeister, 1953. Grade III.

Von Kreisler, Alexander (1895-1970). *Trio*. San Antonio, Tex.: Southern Music Co., 1970. [Review: *NACWPI*, XX(Winter, 1971-72), 41-42.] Grade III.

Wigglesworth, Frank (1918-). *Trio Sonata* (1953). New York: American Composers Alliance. Grade IV-V.

Miscellaneous Combinations

Böhme, Oskar (1870-19??). *Dreistimmiges Präludium und Fuge*, Opus 28, No. 1. (Trompete in B, althorn in Es and baryton.) Leipzig: P. Jurgenson, 1905?. Grade IV.

Böhme, Oskar. *Dreistimmiges Präludium und Fuge*, Opus 28, No. 2. (Trompete in B, althorn in Es and baryton.) Leipzig: P. Jurgenson, 1905?. Grade V.

Bois, Rob du (1934-). *Trio Agitato*. (Horn, trombone, tuba.) Amsterdam: Donemus, 1969.

Brown, Rayner (1912-). *Six Fugues* (1969). (Horn, trombone, tuba.) Los Angeles: Western International Music, Inc., 1969. Grade V.

Butts, Carrol M. (1924-). *Ode for Low Brass*. (Trombone, baritone or trombone, tuba.) Westbury, N.Y.: Pro Art Publications, Inc., 1966. Grade III.

Clodomir, Pierre. *le Trio*. (Two trumpets, horn in E♭.) Wormerveer: Molenaar N.V., 1963. Grade IV.

Diercks, John H. (1927-). *Figures on China*. (Horn, trombone, tuba.) Hattiesburg, Miss.: Tenuto Publications, 1968. Grade V.

Koepke, Paul. *Canzona*. (Two trumpets, horn, piano.) Chicago: Rubank, Inc., 1959. Grade III.

Koepke, Paul. *Fanfare Prelude*. (Two trumpets, horn, piano.) Chicago: Rubank, Inc., 1958. Grade III.

Nerijnen, Jan van. *Antiqua*. (Two trumpets, baritone.) Wormerveer: Molenaar N.V., 1964. Grade II.

Nerijnen, Jan van. *2e Suite*. (Two trumpets, baritone.) Wormerveer: Molenaar N.V., 1966. Grade II.

Nerijnen, Jan van. *3e Suite*. (Two trumpets, baritone.) Wormerveer: Molenaar N.V., 1966. Grade II.

Orowan, Thomas. *Trio*, Opus I. (Two trombones, tuba.) New York: Edition Musicus, 1965. Grade IV.

Schmidt, William (1926-). *Sonatina* (1968). (Horn, trombone, tuba.) Los Angeles: Western International Music, Inc., 1968. Grade IV.

Seeger, Peter (1919-). *Kleine Spielmusik*. (Flügelhorn, tenorhorn, bariton.) Wolfenbüttel: K.H. Möseler Verlag, 1961. Grade III.

Werle, Floyd E. *Concertino*. (Trumpet, trombone, tuba with band accompaniment.) New York: Bourne Co., 1970. Grade IV.■

February, 1973

Contemporary Systems and Trends

for the Tuba

Daniel Perantoni

Nearly all of the "new music" composed for the tuba has been written especially for some outstanding artist. These compositions tend to be technically difficult and may introduce many unfamiliar notational devices. The performer must not only be well established in the traditional sense but must also be able to manage non-traditional techniques and notation. *Encounters II for Solo Tuba*[1] by William Kraft immediately comes to mind. This work was composed especially for Roger Bobo and demands incredible musicianship and technique. It encompasses a range of just about six oc-

taves 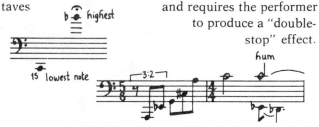 and requires the performer to produce a "double-stop" effect.

This interesting effect is brought about by humming one note while playing another simultaneously. The hummed part is usually higher in pitch than that produced by the embouchure; a reverse pattern is practically uncontrollable. The tuba seems to be very suitable for this technique because of its low range and large mouthpiece. The lower the pitch, the wider the opening has to be in the oral cavity, thus, one can more easily project the higher hummed note. (Of course, vocal range is also an important factor.) Other compositions that feature this effect are "Like a Duet" from Theodore Antoniou's *Six Likes for Solo Tuba*[2] and *Midnight Realities*[3] for solo tuba by Morgan Powell.

One of the most important works for the tuba artist is David Reck's *Five Studies for Tuba Alone*.[4] This excellent composition will enable the performer to better understand some of the newer rhythmical notation systems. (See music below and table, p. 25-27.)

notation of rhythms, dynamics and pitch. The composer's explanatory notes at the beginning are extremely valuable, since he discusses many new techniques being used by composers today.

Asleep in the Deep,[9] a fantasy by Phil Windsor for tuba and pre-recorded tape or 5 tubas plus conductor, uses a very challenging notational system. Twelve improvisational models are given in the instructions. These are numbered and numbers appearing in the score refer the player back to these models. In addition, a number appearing in the score will be accompanied by dynamics (below the staff), expression marks (on the staff), durational indications (arrows), placement of beats (perpendicular lines), etc. These should then be applied to the particular improvisational model indicated by the number. A wide variety

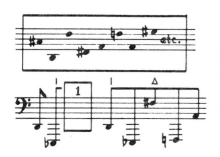 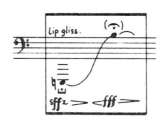 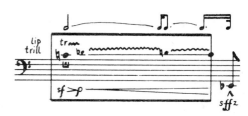

Seaview[5] for tuba and piano by Barney Childs is one necessary work for the young tubist with an interest in "new music." According to the publisher, "[Childs] has written *Seaview* to introduce young performers to contemporary compositional techniques, maintaining ease of execution for the performers without sacrificing musicality or style." This composition introduces the performer to the responsibility of improvising imaginatively on given pitches and shaping them into a musical line. In one section, the pianist and tubist are given 10 fragments and directed to play them once each, in any order.

One of the finest contemporary compositions for the tuba, Paul Zonn's *Divertimento*,[6] features a unique combination of instruments — string bass, marimba, vibraphone, xylophone, and orchestra bells — in addition to the tuba. This virtuoso composition is traditionally notated and is very challenging.

Five[7] for two tubas, by Thomas Albert, is a fairly straightforward duet, but the third movement presents an interesting treatment of so-called "proportional notation" — i.e., the pitches and pitch order are given, but the duration of each pitch is at the performer's discretion. The only stipulation is that the movement is generally slow.

George Heussenstamm's *Tubafour*[8] is one of the better works in the contemporary idiom for tuba quartet. It is written for tenor tuba, two bass tubas in F, and a contrabass tuba in C and features graphic

of effects (color-noises, talking, singing, clicks, blats, shrieks, etc.) are also included in this humorous, yet sensitive composition. The work is also important for its tremendous audience appeal, especially when performed by 5 tubas.

Walter Ross's *Midnight Variations*[10] for tuba and pre-recorded tape offers a different challenge to the performer. The composer uses consonant sounds that are pronounced through the tuba *(ch, zzz, tk,* etc.) as well as vowel sounds that are to be projected through the horn between notated sections.

Theater music may offer a new dimension to many performers. If one has interest in this area, I suggest that he become familiar with Ben Johnston's *Casta★*.[11] This work can be performed by any instrument, and I find the tuba an excellent choice. The performance requires microphones, technician, two tape recorders, mixer, typewriter (old noisy model preferred) and amplification.

1. William Kraft, *Encounters II* (Western International Music, Inc., 1970). Recording: Roger Bobo and Tuba, Crystal Records, S. 125.

2. Theodore Antoniou, *Six Likes for Solo Tuba* (Bärenreiter, 1968).

3. Morgan Powell, *Midnight Realities* (Professor Morgan Powell, School of Music, University of Illinois, Urbana, Illinois 61801, 1972).

4. David Reck, *Five Studies for Tuba Alone* (C.F. Peters, 1968).

5. Barney Childs, *Seaview* (M.M. Cole, 1971).

6. Paul Zonn, *Divertimento No. 1* (American Composer Alliance, 1967).

7. Thomas Albert, *Five* (Manuscripts for Tuba, Box 5045, Tennessee Technological University, Cookville, Tenn. 38501, 1972).

8. George Heussenstamm, *Tubafour* (Seesaw Music Corp., 1970).

Edmund Cioenek's *Lamentation of Manfred for Tuba and Narrator*[12] with the text selected from the poetry of Le Roi Jones, offers some interesting tone-painting effects.

Although these new dimensions in music are fascinating and stimulating, they are too often extremely demanding. I am aware of a feeling among many performers and educators that any music requiring new techniques and systems not found in the traditional, familiar literature is nonsense. With such a narrow view, the tuba might suffer the fate of many obsolete instruments. Today's musician must become aware of the many new techniques and devices that are necessary to understand and perform most contemporary works. The preservation of traditional performance practices is, of course, of great importance, but we must constantly re-evaluate our conception of music so that we will be able to perform and teach the techniques found in the new idiom.

Below is a table of notational systems found in many contemporary compositions. I wish to acknowledge the assistance of Professor Paul Zonn of the University of Illinois in the compilation of this list.

TEMPO FLUCTUATION

OCTAVE DISPLACEMENT

8↑ , +8 - - - - -	One octave higher
8↓ , -8 _ _ _ _ _	One octave lower
15↑	Two octaves higher
15↓	Two octaves lower

 The circled pitches are to be played one octave lower

8 bassa

DYNAMICS

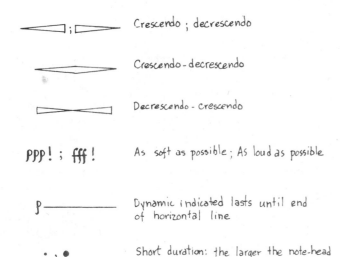

◁ ; ▷	Crescendo ; decrescendo
◁▷	Crescendo - decrescendo
▷◁	Decrescendo - crescendo
ppp! ; fff!	As soft as possible ; As loud as possible
p —————	Dynamic indicated lasts until end of horizontal line
· , ●	Short duration: the larger the note-head the louder the dynamic
⊙ , ◉	Long Duration: small dot = soft; large dot = loud

SPECIAL EFFECTS

 Play only on the mouthpiece

Enclose the mouthpiece and the mouth tightly with clenched fists, and gradually unclench them.

Blow into the instrument directly without the mouthpiece.

Remove the mouthpiece and turn it over. Holding it slightly away from the instrument, blow to create a "swoosh" sound.

Breathy tone (Blowing in effect)

(wind) Blow through tuba without producing tone

9. Phil Windsor, *Asleep In The Deep* (Phil Windsor, Dept. of Music, DePaul University, Chicago, Illinois, 1970).

10. Walter Ross, *Midnight Variations* (Walter Ross, Dept. of Music, University of Virginia, Charlottsville, Va. 22903, 1971).

11. Ben Johnston, *Casta ★* (Media Press, Box 895, Champaign, Illinois 61820, 1970).

12. Edmund Cioenek, *Lamentations of Manfred* (T.E.M.P., c/o J. Lesley Varner, School of Music, Ball State Univ., Muncie, IN 47306, 1972).

Inhale air

Exhale air

 Suck in the sound of the note (produced by kissing the mouthpiece).
A. Sound starts in and is reversed.
B. Suck air in and out.

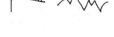 Blow through tuba, producing a rising and falling pitch.

SHH, TK, AH, CH, ZZ Produce syllable through tuba

SPOKEN WORDS Said through instrument

REMOVE TUNING SLIDE Play notes with tuning slide removed

 Sing indicated pitch through tuba

 Vocalize top pitch while playing bottom pitch

 Note played with valve ½-depressed

a, e, i, o, u Vowel sounds used to affect timbre. (Can be done on mouthpiece or while playing)

m Tone with humming noise

PITCH

▲, ◀, ▶, ▼ Highest pitch; middle to high; middle to low; lowest pitch.

△, ◁., ◁, ↑ Highest pitch possible. Duration indicated in traditional manner.

1. HIGHEST
2. MID - HIGH
3. MID - LOW
4. LOWEST   Register is shown by number

 Approximate pitch areas

 Play approximate pitch

TRILLS

 Trill between two pitches

tr⌇⌇⌇ ; tr ∿∿ Fast trill; Slow trill

VIBRATO

NV Non vibrato

SV Senza vibrato

∿∿∿ Wide, slow vibrato (may go ½ step)

∿∿∿∿ Narrow, fast vibrato

∿∿∿∿ Vary speed of vibrato

GLISSANDI

 A chromatic or articulated glissando (as opposed to the smooth glissando of a string instrument)

A half-valve glissando

A very slow glissando

Bend the pitch down to the indicated note, then back up again

A smooth-as-possible glissando

Bellowing lip glissando, following general shape and duration of outline

TONGUING

Non-rhythmic, un-even tonguing, as fast as possible

Tonguing without producing pitch

hd , td Methods of attack and release articulation ("h" or "t" at beginning and "d" at end)

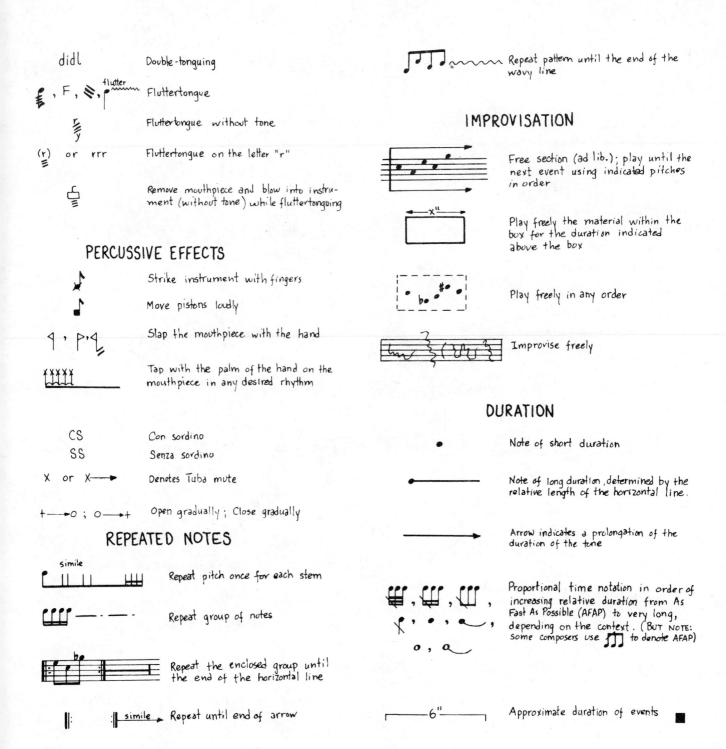

didl — Double-tonguing

♩, F, ≡, flutter — Fluttertongue

Fluttertongue without tone

(r) or rrr — Fluttertongue on the letter "r"

Remove mouthpiece and blow into instrument (without tone) while fluttertonguing

PERCUSSIVE EFFECTS

Strike instrument with fingers

Move pistons loudly

Slap the mouthpiece with the hand

Tap with the palm of the hand on the mouthpiece in any desired rhythm

CS — Con sordino
SS — Senza sordino

X or X—▶ — Denotes Tuba mute

Open gradually; Close gradually

REPEATED NOTES

Repeat pitch once for each stem

Repeat group of notes

Repeat the enclosed group until the end of the horizontal line

Repeat until end of arrow

Repeat pattern until the end of the wavy line

IMPROVISATION

Free section (ad lib.); play until the next event using indicated pitches in order

Play freely the material within the box for the duration indicated above the box

Play freely in any order

Improvise freely

DURATION

Note of short duration

Note of long duration, determined by the relative length of the horizontal line.

Arrow indicates a prolongation of the duration of the tone

Proportional time notation in order of increasing relative duration from As Fast As Possible (AFAP) to very long, depending on the context. (BUT NOTE: some composers use ♫ to denote AFAP)

Approximate duration of events

February, 1973

Tuba Design — Improvements Are Needed

Robert Pallansch:

Manufacturers, please forgive my nit-picking; I am aware of your problems with tooling, public acceptance and money, and I applaud you, for never before has the tuba player had such a variety of fine instruments to choose from. But a horn which can be made to play well can also be made comfortable to play.

The European Rotary-Valve Tuba

Many of the world's finest instruments are made in

this form. It is a fine looking instrument, but if you put it in your lap and tilt it to the left to balance it and reach everything, your right wrist bends down to such an angle that fast chromatics and trills become impossible unless you raise your elbow to an awkward position. In addition, the thumb ring may be out of reach and the mouthpiece in the wrong position. In fact, you may find yourself assuming a variety of back-breaking postures in order to play your instrument properly.

Suppose we build the horn in an oval (*Wagner Tube*) shape. Put the valves low on the horn so the slides can go mostly up. Angle the valve cluster to meet the hand in a natural, extension-of-the-arm position. Extend the spatulas to really match the fingertips, and put the thumb ring directly under and about 4 inches below the forefinger. Now angle the receiver out about 45° from the bell — and presto! Many different-sized players can play the horn comfortably.

Student Tubas

In this area professionals are a comparatively voiceless minority to most domestic manufacturers. The school band leader or music supervisor calls the shots, since he can order tubas by the dozen or gross. So it's the school band director who must see that manufacturers build instruments that students can start with comfortably and grow with, physically and musically.

First, BB♭ (or CC) tubas should have 3 front-action piston valves recessed for protection in the body of the horn, and a first valve slide that is freely extendable with a slide stop and anti-pop vent, to encourage improved intonation on 1-3 and 1-2-3 notes. It should be big enough to have a low register but without a "rain-catcher" bell. Finally, an adjustable thumb ring and a moveable leader pipe, even at some sacrifice of ideal taper, are needed — since kids vary in size even more than grown-ups.

Valves

Pistons are simpler, easier to maintain and more rugged than rotaries but tend to get sticky in horns played by several people and are not feasible for bores over .750. Rotaries are immune to variations in fingering style but hard to oil and clean (except for the magnificent old Cerveny valves), and, like pistons, they come out for service. If the rotaries begin to clatter, nylon bushings may help, and an all-nylon ball-and-socket linkage would be even better. The use of plastics for non-acoustic parts of instruments should increase. Piston valve guides, rotary horseshoes, even whole pistons and rotors would be quieter, lighter, partially self-lubricating, and longer wearing if they were made of nylon.

The detachable valve section, developed for fiberglass sousaphones, is a brilliant stroke; it makes repairs easier and cheaper. Why not adapt it to uprights also (or even contrabass trombones) so the same valve module can be snapped into sousaphone or front-action body as needed?

Finishes

Bravo for epoxy lacquer! It wears like plating (you can even buff it) and with luck soldering won't always scratch it. Satin-silver finishes wear poorly and no one polish will keep them from turning black. Bright silver is a better finish and nickel is the most durable and trouble-free plating of all.

Mutes

A tuba straight mute, to be really acceptable, must have a nice edge, even in *pp*, and cut sharply in *ff*. It must be in tune and must play all the way to the bottom of the horn without backup. (Husa's *Prague 1968* is quite a test.) Also it should be sturdy, light, roll-proof and padded. Some of these features exist now on both home-made and commercial mutes, but they are not generally available. While we're at it, won't someone develop a whisper-mute for tuba? We, too, must practice in hotel rooms.

Don Butterfield:

In the year of 1936, when I began playing the tuba in my high school band in Centralia, Washington, I had 20-20 vision in both of my eyes. Since then, I have spent countless hours playing the tuba in orchestras and varied ensembles, in many seating arrangements. About 1955 I began to notice that the vision of my left eye was no longer as good as that of my right eye. As I began to wonder why, I came to a rather chilling conclusion. Because of the traditional placement of the leadpipe (tightly up against the bell) I was often seated in such a way that as I looked past the bell of the horn I could see the conductor with my right eye only. My left eye, focusing on nothing, could see only the surface of the bell. (Up to this time I had been conscious of this vision problem, but I always dismissed it as a mild inconvenience that we tubists "had to bear.")

When I became fully convinced (after consulting several eye doctors) that damage might be occuring to my eyesight, I did something about it immediately; and I have always considered myself fortunate to have figured this out before any lasting damage was done.

To solve my vision problem, I carefully worked out some basic design changes. The instrument I was using at that time (a fine old Conn BB♭) was in need of repair and overhaul; so I decided to have the design modifications made at the same time as the repairs.

After lengthy correspondence with the manufacturer, it was decided that the work I had outlined could be done. Diagrams of my design changes, exactly as I wanted them, were sent ahead and approved. One last and very important detail remained, and could only be done with both the instrument and me together, at the factory. On June 19, 1962 I delivered the instrument to Conn for the overhaul and design changes. Very careful and precise measurements were made of me sitting with the horn in my normal and most comfortable playing position, so that the leadpipe, when re-positioned on the horn, would be at exactly the right height — for me.

The job of re-making the instrument was then begun, and a few months later it was returned to me exactly as I had wanted it. Of all the changes, the most important was that the leadpipe had been set out from the bell on braces, allowing me for the first time complete and unhampered vision of conductors and also of my music stand. Immediately that tuba became the most comfortable instrument that I ever played.

There is very little about the bass tuba that cannot be improved. While I am sympathetic with the problems of manufacturing companies, I feel that we cannot allow *all* the current research and improvements to go exclusively to better trumpet, horn and trombone design. Collectively we must pressure manufacturing companies to both recognize and solve problems in tuba construction.

Roger Bobo:

Today's tubist is more efficient than the equipment. One obvious problem involves the technical limitations caused by the size and mass of tuba valves. This is most severe with rotary valves, and the larger the bore of the tuba the worse the problem. Two obvious solutions are to make hollow valves or valves of lightweight material rather than solid brass. Although the solution is simple, it is very difficult to get a manufacturer to make the improvement. As a personal example, I recently wrote to a German factory requesting a pilot model of a set of hollow rotary valves. They replied that they had experimented with hollow valves 50 years ago and they did not hold up. However, I own an old German large bore Heizner tuba, made around the turn of the century, with hollow valves that are extremely fast, light, and free.

The other major problem with valves concerns low register intonation compensation, i.e., the capability of the instrument to play chromatically from the fundamental to the second harmonic without compromising tone quality for intonation. This situation can be improved on rotary valve instruments by tuning the fifth valve slightly sharper than a 2-3 combination, with a valve slide lever system that permits adjustments on the fifth valve slide while playing. With only 3 slide positions requiring less than 2½ inches of travel, one can play chromatically down to the fundamental with perfect intonation and without sacrifice of tone quality.

It is obvious that better cooperation between players and manufacturers is required. Players have a right to expect the best possible equipment and to speak out when it is not made available. It is time for manufacturers to use every facility available to produce a line of tubas that meets the demands of the modern player. The situation is not hopeless, but action must be taken now to change it. ∎

February, 1973

A Basic Repertoire and Studies for the Serious Tubist

R. Winston Morris

This list of materials was selected by a committee of some 20 college tuba teachers and/or professional tubists, chaired by R. Winston Morris. Most of the music requires the technical skill and musical maturity of at least an advanced high school or college student. In each listing the composer/arranger is followed by the title, publisher, and year of publication. Categories include Tuba and Piano, Solo Tuba, Study Materials, Duets, and Tuba in Mixed Ensemble.

Tuba and Piano

Bach/Bell. *Air and Bourree*. Carl Fischer, 1937.
Bartles. *Scherzo*. Sam Fox, 1970.
Beach. *Lamento*. Southern, 1961.
Bencriscutto. *Concertino*. Shawnee, 1971.
Benson. *Arioso*. Piedmont, 1954.
Bernstein. *Waltz for Mippy III*. G. Schirmer, 1950.
Beversdorf. *Sonata*. Southern, 1962.

Bottje. *Prelude and Fugue*. Composer's Facs. Ed., 1959.
Brown. *Diptych*. Western International, 1970.
Capuzzi/Catelinet. *Andante and Rondo*. Hinrichsen Ed., 1967.
Childs. *Seaview*. M.M. Cole, 1971.
Croley. *Tre Espressioni*. Autograph Editions.
Diercks. *Variations on Gottschalk*. Tenuto, 1968.
Downey. *Tabu for Tuba*. Mentor, 1965.
Frackenpohl. *Concertino*. Easton Mus., 1962.
Haddad. *Suite*. Templeton Publ. Co., 1966.
Handel/Harvey. *Honor and Arms*. Schirmer, 1940.
Handel/Morris. *Thrice Happy the Monarch*. Ludwig, 1970.
Handel-Beethoven/Bell. *Judas Maccabeus*. Carl Fischer, 1937.
Hartley. *Aria*. Elkan-Vogel, 1967.
Hartley. *Concertino*. Tenuto, 1969.
Hartley. *Sonata*. Tenuto, 1967.
Hartley. *Sonatina*. Interlochen Press, 1961.

Hindemith. *Sonate*. Schott, 1955.

Hogg. *Sonatina*. Ensemble, 1967.

Holmes. *Lento*. Shawnee Press, 1961.

Jenne. *Rondo*. Tritone/Tenuto, 1967.

Koetsier. *Sonatina*. Donemus, 1970.

Lebedev. *Concert Allegro*. University Music Press, 1962.

Lebedev/Ostrander. *Concerto in One Movement*. Edition Musicus, 1960.

Lischka. *Drei Skizzen*. Hofmeister, 1969.

Lloyd. *Three Sketches*. Tenuto, 1968.

McKay. *Suite*. University Music Press, 1958.

Mueller, Florian. *Concert Music*. University Music Press, 1961.

Muller/Ostrander. *Praeludium, Chorale, Variations, and Fugue*. Edition Musicus, 1959.

Nelhybel. *Suite*. General Music Publ., 1966.

Ostrander (arr.). *Concert Album*. Edition Musicus, 1954.

Phillips, Harry (ed.). *Eight Bel Canto Songs*. Templeton, 1967.

Presser. *Capriccio*. Tenuto, 1969.

Presser. *Concerto*. Tenuto, 1970.

Presser. *Minute Sketches*. Autograph Editions, 1967.

Reynolds. *Sonata*. Carl Fischer, 1969.

Rothgarber. *Dialogue*. Tritone, 1971.

Russell. *Suite Concertante*. Pyraminx Publ., 1963.

Sauter. *Conjectures*. Mentor Music, 1968.

Schmidt. *Serenade*. Avant, 1962.

Semler-Collery. *Bacarolle et Chanson Bachique*. Leduc, 1953.

Senaille/Catelinet. *Introduction and Allegro Spiritoso*. Hinrichsen, 1964.

Shaughnessy. *Concertino*. Peer-Southern, 1969.

Sibbing. *Sonata*. Tenuto, 1963.

Sowerby. *Chaconne*. Carl Fischer, 1938.

Spillman. *Concerto*. Edition Musicus, 1962.

Spillman. *Two Songs*. Edition Musicus, 1963.

Stabile. *Sonata*. Honour, 1970.

Stevens. *Sonatina*. Peer-Southern, 1960.

Swann. *Two Moods*. Chamber Music Library, 1961.

Takacs. *Sonata*. Ludwig-Doblinger, 1965.

Tcherepnine. *Andante*. M.P. Belaieff, 1950.

Tuthill. *Fantasia*. Ensemble, 1968.

Uber. *Pantomime*. Charles Colin, 1967.

Vaughan. *Concertpiece No. 1*. Interlochen Press, 1961.

Vaughan Williams. *Concerto*. Oxford University Press, 1955.

Vivaldi/Ostrander. *Concerto in A minor*. Edition Musicus, 1958.

Weeks. *Triptych*. Robert King, 1964.

Wekselblatt (ed.). *Solos for the Tuba Player*. Schirmer, 1964.

Wilder. *Sonata*. Mentor Music, 1963.

Wilder. *Suite No. 1*. Sam Fox, 1968.

Solo Tuba

Arnold. *Fantasy*. Faber Music, 1969.

Croley. *Variazioni*. Western International, 1968.

Fulkerson. *Patterns III*. Media Press, 1969.

Hartley. *Suite*. Elkan-Vogel, 1964.

Kraft. *Encounters II*. MCA Music, 1970.

McCarty. *Color-Etudes*. Media Press, 1970.

Persichetti. *Serenade*. Elkan-Vogel, 1963.

Presser. *Suite*. Ensemble, 1967.

Reck. *Five Studies*. C.F. Peters, 1968.

Sacco. *Tuba Mirum*. Western International, 1969.

Sear. *Sonata*. Western International, 1966.

Spillman. *Four Greek Preludes*. Edition Musicus, 1969.

Study Materials

Bell. *Tuba Warm-ups*. Charles Colin, 1954.

Blazhevich. *Seventy Etudes*. MCA, 1970.

Bordogni/Roberts. *Forty-Three Bel Canto Studies*. Robert King, 1972.

Cimera. *Seventy-Three Advanced Tuba Studies*. Belwin, 1955.

Dufresne. *Sight Reading Studies*. Charles Colin, 1964.

Fink. *Studies in Legato*. Carl Fischer, 1967.

Getchell. *Practical Studies* (Book II). Belwin, 1955.

Kopprasch. *Sixty Etudes*. Publishers: Hofmeister; King.

Kuehn (trans.). *Sixty Musical Studies* (Books I & II). Southern, 1969.

Kuehn (trans.). *Twenty-Eight Advanced Studies*. Southern, 1972.

Lachman. *Twenty-Five Etudes*. Hofmeister, 1956.

Lachman. *Twenty-Six Etudes*. Hofmeister.

Maenz. *Twelve Special Studies*. Hofmeister.

Ostrander. *Shifting Meter Studies*. Robert King, 1965.

Rusch. *Hal Leonard Advanced Band Method for Basses*. Hal Leonard, 1963.

Sear. *Etudes*. Cor, 1969.

Sear-Waldeck. *Excerpts*. Cor, 1966.

Torchinsky. *Twentieth Century Excerpts*. G. Schirmer, 1969.

Tyrrell. *Advanced Studies*. Boosey & Hawkes, 1948.

Vasiliev. *Twenty-Four Melodious Etudes*. Robert King.

Duets

Butterfield. *Seven Duets*. D.B. Publ. Co., 1960.

Catelinet. *Suite in Miniature*. Hinrichsen, 1952.

Corelli/Morris. *Sonata da Chiesa*. Ludwig, 1970.

De Jong. *Music for Two Tubas*. Elkan-Vogel, 1964.

Goldman. *Duo*. Mercury, 1948.

Luedcke. *Eight Bagatelles*. Tenuto, 1970.

Luedcke. *Wonderland Duets*. Tenuto, 1971.

Nelhybel. *Eleven Duets*. General Music Publ., 1966.

Presser. *Seven Tuba Duets*. Tenuto, 1970.

Roikjer. *Ten Inventions*. Wilhelm Hansen, 1969.

Ryker. *Sonata*. Robert King, 1959.

Sear. *Advanced Duets*. Cor, 1969.

Tuba in Mixed Ensemble

Dubensky. *Concerto Grosso* (3 trombones & tuba). Ricordi, 1950.

Feldman. *Durations III for Violin, Tuba & Piano*. C.F. Peters, 1961.

Frackenpohl. *Brass Duo* (horn/euphonium & tuba). Easton Music Co., 1972.

Gould. *Tuba Suite* (3 horns & tuba). G & C Music Corp., 1971.

Hartley. *Bivalve Suite* (euphonium & tuba). Autograph Editions, 1971.

Hartley. *Double Concerto* (tuba, alto sax, wind ensemble). Autograph Editions, 1969.

Hartley. *Duet for Flute and Tuba*. Tritone, 1963.

Knox. *Solo for Tuba with Brass Trio*. Tenuto, 1968.

Presser. *Seven Duets for Horn and Tuba*. Seesaw Music Corp., 1972.

Russell. *Suite Concertante for Tuba and Woodwind Quintet*. Pyraminx Publ., 1963.

Schmidt. *Sonatina* (horn, trombone & tuba). Western International, 1968.

Telemann/Hartley. *Three Dances* (flute & tuba). Ensemble, 1966.

Vaughan. *Quattro Bicinie* (clarinet & tuba). Autograph Editions, 1970.

Wilder. *Suite for French Horn, Tuba & Piano*. Wilder Music (Sam Fox), 1971. ∎

The Tuba Family

R. Winston Morris

Tenor Tubas

1. The *Baritone Horn*, pitched in B♭, has 3 piston valves and is built bell front.

2. The *Euphonium* is also pitched in B♭. It has a slightly larger bore than the baritone, 4 valves (rotary or piston) and is built bell up. Since the Euphonium is closest to the European concept of what a tenor tuba should be, it is best to play tenor tuba parts on the Euphonium.

3. Hybrids — such as four-valve baritones, bell-front euphoniums, etc. — are also available.

Bass Tubas

1. The *French Tuba* in C is referred to as a bass tuba by the French, but its range would place it in the tenor tuba group — it is pitched in C, a major second above the B♭ tenor tubas! It's range, however, is wider than that of tenor tubas, since it has a larger bore than the euphonium and may have as many as 6 valves. In general, if parts written for the French Tuba in C are to be played on another instrument, a tenor rather than a bass tuba should be used.

2. The *F Tuba* is *the* bass tuba in many European countries (Germany, Austria, etc.). It has 4-6 valves which give it strong upper and lower registers. This is the best instrument to use for parts originally written for ophicleide or serpent.

3. The *E♭ Tuba* is still popular in British brass bands. At one time, it was common in U.S. university and high school bands; now it can be found in school bands only occasionally. It is an easy doubling instrument for trumpet/cornet players (switch clefs and keys — use same fingerings).

4. The *CC Tuba* is the most common bass tuba in American orchestras today, and perhaps 90% of professional tubists consider this to be their major instrument. Its range is basically the same as that of the BB♭ Tuba.

5. The *BB♭ Tuba* is the most common bass tuba in American bands. Both 3 and 4 valve models are available (piston or rotary), and they are built bell front (recording bass) or in the form of a sousaphone. The great majority of high school players use a 3-valve BB♭ Tuba.

Minimum Practical Ranges for 3-Valve Tubas

In each case the range is based on a 2-octave span between open tones, with the lowest note produced by depressing all 3 valves. High school students should be able to play throughout the ranges shown here. Advanced players, with the aid of additional valves and playing experience, often develop a range of over 6 octaves.

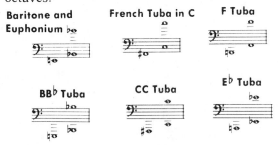

Most tubists feel that all tenor and bass tubas should be manufactured with a minimum of four valves — for reasons of both range and intonation.

February, 1973

The Tuba Ensemble

Constance Weldon

The idea of a homogeneous group of tubas playing together is not *new* — but it *has* been dormant for a long time. The rebirth of the tuba ensemble began a few years ago, and it is now earning its rightful place in the education of tuba players at the high school and college level.

In the 1940's tuba quartets were written by Eric Ball (*Quartet for Tubas* and *Friendly Giants)* and Kenneth Cook *(Introduction and Rondino)* for the standard tuba section of the English brass band, two E♭ tubas and two BB♭ tubas (all in treble clef). This was the extent of the published tuba ensemble literature available when I began thinking of organizing a performing tuba ensemble in the late 1950's. After the interest of my tuba students was aroused by the English tuba quartets, my next step was to expand our library by making tuba ensemble arrangements from literature written for other instruments.

Organizing a tuba ensemble in 1960 was not a simple project for us. In addition to having very little music to play, we had no guidelines to follow and no guarantee that what we were attempting had any long range educational value. We organized the Tuba Society of Miami and virtually went "underground" with our activities, meeting and rehearsing when and where we could. For 7 years we continued to grow under these haphazard conditions. Finally, through the foresight of the Dean of the School of Music of the University of Miami, William F. Lee, and the Chairman of the Department of Applied Music, Frederick Fennell, the tuba ensemble was assigned a course number and given 2 hours a week of scheduled rehearsal time for which students were awarded credit.

Among the many men who contributed to the steady growth of the University of Miami Tuba Ensemble were Roger P. Jones and Sam Pilafian. Dr. Jones, now Composer in Residence for several colleges in Kansas, was our "Composer in Residence" while he earned his degrees at the University of Miami; and Sam Pilafian was such a gifted tuba player that he inspired us to play beyond our abilities. Sam, now playing in New York City, made an arrangement of *Terrible T* (by D. N. Baker) which we performed at the Midwest Band and Orchestra Clinic in Chicago in 1969.

Growth of Tuba Ensemble Literature

In recent years, a repertoire for tuba ensemble has just begun to develop. William Presser, a real pioneer in this field, has produced a number of quality works for multiple tubas. His *Suite for Six Tubas* (1967), *Suite for Three Tubas* (1968), *Serenade for Four Tubas* (1969), and *Seven Tuba Duets* (1970) have not only expanded our literature but have also challenged our musicianship.

The biggest breakthrough in the growth of the literature for the tuba ensemble came when the University of Miami School of Music and the Tuba Society of Miami sponsored the International Tuba Ensemble Composition Contest (September, 1969). From the 56 compositions which were entered, the judges (William Bell, Arnold Jacobs, and I) awarded the $200 first prize to Frank Lynn Payne for "Tuba Quartet." "Lyric Poem for Five Tubas" by Marcel G. Frank received the $100 second prize. A third prize of $50 went to William Presser's "Serenade for Four Tubas," and a special award of $50 was given for "Tubafour" by George Heussenstamm. The following received honorable mention: "Tuba Quintet, Op. 1" by Guillermo Edghill; "Two Pieces for Three Tubas" by John Gessner; "Little Madrigal for Big Horns" by Ross Hastings; "Chant and Fantasie" by Roger Jones; "Prelude and Fugue" by Michael Kibble; "Suite for Six Tubas" by Joseph Ott; and "Tuba Quartet" by Mark Sassaman.

Not all the compositions entered were great contributions to tuba literature, but it was a beginning and a good one. Hopefully, as works are published and performed, more composers will be inspired to write for this medium. A chain reaction has begun all over the country. Because of the literature now available, more and more schools are organizing tuba ensembles and so the demand for music continues to increase. The University of Miami Tuba Ensemble library now holds 70 compositions written for combinations of 3-10 tubas. With our expansion to 3 ensembles (the Tuba Ensemble, the Tuba Choir, and the Reading Ensemble), our quest for more literature is still critical. We are not unique in this need. Tuba ensembles are now flourishing under the fine leadership of such men as Harvey Phillips of Indiana University, R. Winston Morris of Tennessee Technological University, David Kuehn of North Texas State University, J. Lesley Varner of Ball State University, and Daniel Perantoni of the University of Illinois.

Educational Value and Future Growth

With all the interest among tuba teachers and players for the tuba ensemble, some honest questions are certain to arise. What is the fundamental function of the tuba ensemble in the education of the tuba student? How does it help in the training of a symphony musician, a bandsman, a jazz performer, a teacher, or a composer? Will the tuba ensemble fit into the pattern necessary for all school-sponsored ensembles, that of serving the student, the school, and the community?

Through the availability of good literature, new demands are being placed on tuba players. Tuba ranges are extended, technique is challenged, learning of new notations is required, and the problem of blending of instruments is being encountered as never before. The tuba ensemble can certainly help players meet these new demands. In larger ensembles the tuba player may tend to hide behind the richness of the string bass section or become lost in a mass of sounds from 6 or more tubas; but after extensive exposure to tuba ensemble playing, he will become more aware of his individual responsibilities as a musician and respond more readily to sounds around him. This awareness of true ensemble playing will enhance his ability to perform more musically whether he be playing in a brass quintet, a jazz band, a symphonic band, or a symphony orchestra.

The tuba ensemble is even more valuable when it is handled as a democratic organization. Both teacher and students develop a feeling of responsibility to the group as a whole. Ideas are exchanged, new techniques are tried, and individual problems are mastered. All this is achieved in a spirit of working toward the common goal of constantly improving and expanding the quality of tuba playing.

Finally, as an organization greatly in need of new literature, the tuba ensemble is of great value to the student composer. He will be able to experiment with new and unusual combinations of sound and, when his works are completed, a group of performers will be eager to perform them.

If the above educational values can be achieved by playing in a tuba ensemble, this alone justifies its position as part of the general ensemble structure that serves the needs of the students. Any organization that works so diligently at its craft and encourages the expression of new ideas certainly will be an asset to the school. ∎

For a Better Brass Sound

Roger C. Heath

Does your brass section have students whose tone production indicates poor embouchure control? Pinched sounds? Poor flexibility? Limited range? If not, congratulations! Your band has to be the exception to the rule. But if these problems do persist in your brass section, here's an idea that can be used either in private lessons or section rehearsals.

First, using the mouthpiece only, show the student how to get a pinched tone on it. This is easily accomplished by pressing the lips together too tightly and using too much mouthpiece pressure on the lips. Exaggerate a bit. The characteristic sound will be one in which almost *all* of the air (tonal energy) comes out defining the pitch *too carefully*. Of course the excessive lip tension will be obvious in the tone.

Now play the same note on the mouthpiece with a normal embouchure — firm, but not tense. The more relaxed tone that results will be obvious. Curiously enough it is characterized by a "whoosh" of air that has no definition of pitch. The lips with less tension do not define the frequency of *all* of the air. The basic frequency is still obvious, but it is mixed with a generous portion of "free," non-pitched air. This is the desirable mixture for a full bodied tone.

Make certain the student hears the difference between the results of the two embouchure settings, and then let *him* try it both ways. As he plays in the relaxed style, ask him to drop the jaw until there is a finger tip distance between the upper and lower teeth and the lips just barely touch. It is usually easier to analyze the sound of the basic flow of air through the mouthpiece only, than it is to analyze the tone using the entire instrument. With the mouthpiece only, the sound is so drastically different when the tension has been completely eliminated that the student can easily feel the difference.

Next put the mouthpiece in the instrument and compare the sounds of both embouchure settings. Once the concept of a good tone has been established, both teacher and student must keep listening to make sure the old habit has been permanently replaced. Continue to check the tension frequently, again using only the mouthpiece.

Once the kinesthetics of a well controlled embouchure and the aesthetics of pleasing sound become interrelated, the other aspects of better sound production — breath control and flexibility — can be studied.

When the aperture of the lips was closed tightly, there could not be much velocity or volume in the air flow, no matter how hard the student "pushed." And it is likely that as the pressure exerted by the diaphragm increased, the lips squeezed together even more tightly. Talking about breath support was a waste of time and energy. If we can now open the passage by relaxing the embouchure, the air can flow and the player is more likely to have "breath support" and to be "filling the horn." As he develops self-confidence and a desire to express himself, this aspect of tonal control will keep improving. Require the student to demonstrate a fast flow of air through the mouthpiece now as he periodically checks to avoid excessive embouchure tension.

The next step in embouchure development is valve flexibility and range extension via lip slurs. The old "oh-ee" approach to lip slurs is still hard to beat. The "oh" formation both drops the tongue to enlarge the mouth and throat cavity and, at the same time, pulls the corners of the mouth inward to open and relax the aperture for low notes. In this position the speed of the air is relatively slow as it flows through the larger mouth cavity and lip aperture. The lips in a relaxed configuration are able to vibrate with increased amplitude.

The "ee" mouth formation for higher notes raises the tongue and creates a shallow passage within the mouth causing a greater velocity in air flow. At the same time, the corners of the mouth draw the lips outward to thin them out and provide enough firmness to support the desired frequency of vibration which is generated by air flow. Increase the flexibility by applying this concept to lip slurs in all ranges and speeds. Keep the air speed reasonably fast. The embouchure must still be firm but not ever tightly squeezed. Range extension and increased endurance will normally occur as a byproduct of this kind of exercise.

Once the student learns these concepts, it is up to him to apply them to playing clear, undistorted tones in all styles of performance. But it is still the director who must keep checking and correcting to insure that fine tone production is a reality. ∎

Trombone Articulation — Legato Style

Articulation actually means "the clear and distinct rendering of the tones;"[1] this is not necessarily synonomous with *tonguing*, although the tongue certainly plays an important part in the process. The "rendering of tones" in the legato style on the trombone is accomplished in basically the same manner as all types of articulation, i.e., the air stream remains constant and the tongue displaces the air. Because the procedure is generally the same, one may say that *staccato is short legato* and *legato is long staccato*.

To produce a good legato style, one may choose from at least three different syllables — *loo, doo,* or *roo* — experimenting with these (and others, if desired) to determine which will work best. My recommendation is the *roo* syllable, one of the movements within the multiple or rolled "r" sound.

To develop a legato style, the following technique has proven most successful for me.

1. Play F, blowing a steady air stream for 8 counts.

Air stream

2. Play F for 8 counts. While blowing a steady air stream, let the tongue gently *displace* the air — not *stop* it — in order to produce each note indicated below. Use the various syllables and decide which works best for you.

Air Stream

too roo roo roo roo
too doo doo doo doo
too loo loo loo loo

(A soft "t" sound at the beginning of a passage is suggested for security.)

3. Continue, scale-wise, to higher notes. Development of the "steady-air-stream" concept is important. A good way to demonstrate this is by

1. Willi Apel, *Harvard Dictionary of Music* (Cambridge, Mass.: Harvard University Press, 1968), p. 58.

April, 1973

turning on a water faucet and displacing the water with your hand several times. This is what the tongue does to the air stream — it *displaces* the air — it does not *stop* it! Another way one may conceptualize is to *let the new note begin at the precise moment the old one ends*. If one has difficulty in understanding the concept of a steady air stream, play any exercise without using the tongue — just blow air, move the slide and don't let the air stop — except for breath! Although this will sound bad, it will help one get the "feel" of the steady air stream.

4. As the above exercises are mastered, introduce the following:

Air Stream

too roo roo roo roo

5. Continue, scale-wise, to higher notes. For legato style playing, one must manipulate the slide quickly, but smoothly, between notes. In playing the above exercise, there is a split-second moment of stoppage on each 8th note.

The Natural Slur

The soft *roo* articulation for each note creates a secure, sustained, flowing and hopefully beautiful sounding legato style; however, the natural slur should not be overlooked entirely. Every trombonist knows that a natural slur is produced *when the note goes up and the slide goes out* or *when the note goes down and the slide comes in*. Lip slurs and trills are also natural slurs. An extraneous sound, somewhat like the "click" in valve action instruments, results from the na-

tural slurs of the trombone. Also, there are those who maintain that an over use of alternate positions to produce natural slurs will result in the destruction of the true trombone sound — or at least the performer may not be able to maintain the same characteristic sound throughout the passage. This may or may not be true, but one should analyze each passage or solo and make this decision for himself.

The following is an example of the use of natural slurs. In this passage, using the tongue will actually impair the legato sound![2]

For continuing work with the legato syle, I recommend Rochut's transcribed vocalises of Marco Bordogni's *Melodious Etudes*, Books I-III, published by Carl Fischer. These 3 books contain a total of 120 studies — progressively more difficult — edited for legato style playing.

As a continuing part of your legato studies, be sure to listen to the fine trombonists perform, either on record or in person; continue to seek out and then experiment with the ways in which the experts say they are producing legato style; finally, make your decisions according to what works best for you. ∎

2. Remarkable examples of natural slurs appear in Arthur Pryor's variation sections of "The Blue Bells of Scotland." Every slur is natural in order to allow the performer to develop and maintain a "speedy" tempo!

Improving the French Horn Section

K.R. Rumery

Faulty intonation is the greatest single cause of poor sounding band and orchestra horn sections. Yet, the intonation of most horn sections can be improved easily and dramatically by attending to a few tuning techniques including bell-hand position, consistently centered pitch placement, and accurate slide adjustment.

Bell-hand Position

The position of the bell-hand has a marked effect on both intonation and tone quality. The hand should be cupped at about a 45° angle and placed so that it covers about 25% of the bell opening. In this position, the hand is better able to open or

close the bell in order to make fine pitch adjustments or dampen raw tone quality. If the bell opening is extensively covered (50% or more), tone becomes muffled and flat; but if less than 25% is covered, some of the raw tone quality may be heard by the listener. Students should never use the bell-hand merely to grip the bell. This position has little effect on either pitch or tone quality, and the hand is in no position to move in any way to adjust intonation. The horn is quite sharp if the bell opening is not covered at all, and the extreme tuning slide pull-out required in such a situation may increase any intonation flaws present in the horn.

Pitch Placement

Consistent pitch placement in each harmonic makes all aspects of tuning the horn more successful; a group of hornists are readily coordinated as a section once these factors are under control. Pitch placement should be located near the mid-point of any given harmonic. This is done with a more relaxed embouchure, more open oral cavity, and more reliance on air flow to energize the tone. The benefits are improved tone quality, flexibility, and attack fluency. With properly centered pitch placement, the student will be able to "lip" pitches down without loss of control over timbre and intonation. If pitch placement is too high, the embouchure creates too much air resistance, squelches tone quality, becomes inflexible, less articulate, and tires more quickly. In addition, high pitches are difficult to play with such an embouchure. Regardless of range, the best results are obtained by placing pitch at about the mid-point of adjustment in each harmonic. This creates the proper balance of embouchure relaxation and air flow needed for fluency and endurance anywhere in the range of the horn. The student should experiment until he can locate this mid-point readily in any harmonic.

Slide Adjustment

The setting of valve and tuning slides is often neglected by student hornists; yet this setting is extremely important for accurate individual or sectional intonation. No pitch standard is possible among students who neglect slide settings, since one valve combination will be out of tune in a different way than another.

The adjustment of every slide on the horn should be systematically tested for accuracy with a device like the Strobotuner. This testing is generally not too time consuming; for example, a careful check of all the slides on a double horn sel-

dom takes more than ten or fifteen minutes per student. During this time, the student can learn an easy procedure for using the "Strobe" himself in later pitch checks. Although these checks are not a cure-all for intonation problems, they often result in obvious improvement in the horn section.

Tuning the Single F Horn

Review well-centered pitch placement as accurate tuning is more successful once this is under control. Also, check the octave below each pitch tested in order to see if the student's octaves are true. Now test the pitches in chromatic order:

1. Tune third space "c" by adjusting the main tuner (usually the 1st slide beyond the mouthpiece).

2. Tune "b" (2nd valve) and "bb" (1st valve). While the amount of adjustment will vary with each instrument and player, the second valve slide will probably need little or no pull-out, but the first may have to be pulled out an inch or more.

3. Tune "a" (1st and 2nd valves). This pitch is often sharp and is usually adjusted easily through playing technique. If too sharp to be adjusted easily, split the difference between "a," "b," and "bb" with more pull-out of the first and second valve slides. Although "a" will no longer be quite so sharp, all the notes played with either the second or first valves may be slightly flat.

4. Finally, tune "ab" (2nd and 3rd valves). The 3rd valve slide may have more pull-out than the 1st valve slide. Do not change any compromise adjustment made to the second valve slide.

Tuning the Double Horn

The procedure for tuning double horn slides is similar to that for single F horns. However, each valve has two slides, the upper for F tuning and the lower, shorter slide for Bb tuning (affected only when the Bb trigger is depressed). Some double horns have F tuners but no Bb tuners. Instead, these may have several main tuners which affect both the F and Bb horns. If you are unsure of the purpose of any slide, remove it and blow through the horn. Press the Bb trigger and blow once more. If no air escapes, the slide does not control the Bb horn; but if air escapes in both the F and Bb modes, the slide is a main tuner.

If the horn has no Bb tuning slide,

tune the Bb horn first with a main tuner (a slide which affects both horns), striving for minimum pull-out of main tuning slides. Begin with fifth line "f" since this is one of the octaves of the fundamental of the Bb horn and should be true. Then adjust third space "c." This note may be slightly sharp since it is the sixth harmonic. If it cannot be adjusted with a slight change of the lip, the main tuner should be pulled out a fraction of an inch. Now tune the F horn to third space "c" using F tuners only. Once "c" is in tune on both horns, tune the valve slides in the same order as on the single horn (2, 1, 1-2, 2-3). Continually compare F and Bb intonation and octaves for each valve combination.

On some makes of horn, "a" and the "d" above (1st and 2nd valves) are sharp on the Bb horn. A compromise is always required although many hornists adjust the intonation of these notes through playing technique alone. Since fourth line "d" is almost impossible to tune through slide adjustment, one should compromise only to the extent that the "a" below is tuned. This usually brings "d" down far enough to be tuned through bell-hand or lip adjustment. An attempt to tune "d" perfectly with slide adjustment may result in excessively flat pitches when either the second or first valves are used alone. Once satisfied with the compromise, tune "ab" (2nd and 3rd valves). Do not readjust the second valve slide on either horn.

A final check of accuracy is often valuable since the student may have overcompensated some of the slide adjustments. This check provides a quick review of pitch placement and octave intonation. During this check, ask the student to remember where each slide is set, especially when emptying slides. (The slides may be marked, but the mark should not be permanent since slide settings are subject to change and school owned instruments may be checked out to several students simultaneously, all of whom set their slides differently.) Finally, this check can be used to see if the student has learned the procedure for using the "strobe." Students should become more accurate with each check, and this should lead to a well-tempered and, thus, resonant horn section. ■

Trumpet Research:
A Selective Bibliography

Charles F. Decker

This list has been compiled in an effort to aid the researcher. The entries, selected from English language periodicals, are primarily concerned with 17th and 18th century historical studies and literature for the trumpet. The 65 articles have been separated into 13 categories including trumpet construction, literature, instrument makers, musicians, court and theater use, and critical reviews of reference texts. The intent is to provide a source of outstanding articles as compiled from the *Music Index, The Brass Quarterly* brass bibliography 1820-1962, and personal investigation. Selection of articles from *Brass Quarterly* (1957-1964) was difficult, as every issue contained information pertaining to the trumpet; the publication reissues are definitely a must for brass research.

Other topics (such as the cornet, cornett, and acoustics) have purposely been avoided, since they entail separate studies of their own. However, those involved in trumpet research should be aware of three outstanding sources of general interest. The *Brass Anthology* (published by The Instrumentalist Co.) is unique. This chronological presentation of brass articles from *The Instrumentalist* covers many aspects of teaching, performance, and instrument construction. Another important source is Thomas Hodstadt's "Solo Literature for the Trumpet" (F.E. Olds Company). Compiled in 1955 from suggestions of more than 90 professional players and teachers from the USA and Europe, the list is extensive and extremely valuable. Finally, the Philip Bate book, *The Trumpet and Trombone* (W.W. Norton and Company, 1966), must be mentioned as it is at present the best reference text for trumpet research.

British Trumpet Series from GSJ

Byrne, Maurice. "Goldsmith Trumpet Makers of the British Isles," XIX (April, 1966), 71-83.

Halfpenny, Eric. "Early British Trumpet Mouthpieces," XIX (March, 1967), 76-88 and XX (March, 1968), 185.

Halfpenny, Eric. "Four 17th Century British Trumpets," XXI (March, 1969), 51-57.

Halfpenny, Eric. "Notes on Two Later British Trumpets," XXIII (July, 1971), 79-83.

Halfpenny, Eric. "Two Oxford Trumpets," XVI (May, 1963), 49-62.

Halfpenny, Eric. "William Bull and the English Baroque Trumpet," XV (March, 1962), 18-24.

Halfpenny, Eric. "William Shaw's Harmonic Trumpet," XIII (July, 1960), 7-13.

Pegge, R. Morley. "Regent's Bugle," IX (June, 1956), 91-96.

Wheeler, Joseph. "Further Notes on the Classic Trumpet," XVIII (March, 1965), 14-22.

Wheeler, Joseph. "New Light on the 'Regent's Bugle' with Some Notes on the Keyed Bugle," XIX (April, 1966), 65-69.

Historical Publications

Douglas, Robert. "The First Trumpet Method: Girolamo Fantini's Modo per Impare a Sonare di Tromba (1638)," *JBR*, VII/2 (Spring, 1971), 18-22.

Lampl, Hans (trans). "Michael Praetorius on the Use of Trumpets," *BQ*, II/1 (September, 1958), 3-7.

Abbreviations	
BB	— *Brass Bulletin*
BQ	— *Brass Quarterly*
BW	— *Brass World*
D	— *Diapason*
GSJ	— *Galpin Society Journal*
Inst	— *The Instrumentalist*
JBR	— *Journal of Band Research*
MJ	— *Music Journal*
ML	— *Music and Letters*
MQ	— *Musical Quarterly*
MR	— *Music Review*

Rasmussen, Mary (trans.). "An Essay on the Instruction of the Noble Art of Trumpet and Kettledrum Playing (1795) by Johann Ernst Altenburg," *BQ*, I/3 (March, 1958), 133-145; I/4 (June, 1958), 201-213; II/1 (September, 1958), 20-30; II/2 (December, 1958), 53-62.

Instrument Makers

Byrne, Maurice. "Goldsmith Trumpet Makers . . .," Complete listing under "British Trumpet Series from *GSJ*."

Carse, Adam. "Adolphe Sax and the Distin Family," *MR*, VI (1945), 193-201.

Jaffee, Kay (ed.). "Divers Notes . . ." Complete listing under "Musicians."

Langwill, Lyndesay G. "Instrument Making in Paris in 1839," ML, XXXIX/2 (April, 1958), 135-138.

Langwill, Lyndesay G. "London Wind Instrument Makers of the 17th and 18th Centuries," *MR*, VII/2 (May, 1946), 87-102.

Montagu, Jeremy. "The Society's First Foreign Tour," *GSJ*, XXI (March, 1968), 4-23.

Smithers, Don L. "The Trumpets of J.W. Haas: A Survey of Four Generations of Nuremberg Brass Instrument Makers," *GSJ*, XVIII (March, 1965), 23-41.

Keyed Trumpet

Dahlqvist, Reine. "Johann Georg Albrechtsberger's Concertino for 'Chromatic Trumpet'," *BB*, I (October, 1971), 9-12.

Geiringer, Karl. "Haydn Trumpet Concerto," *MQ*, XLI/3 (July, 1955), 402-404.

Rasmussen, Mary. "A Concertino for Chromatic Trumpet by Johann Georg Albrechtsberger," *BQ*, V/3 (Spring, 1962), 104-108.

Literature

Berger, Jean. "Notes on Some 17th Century Compositions for Trumpets and Strings in Bologna," *MQ*, XXXVII/3 (July, 1951), 354-367.

Brofsky, Howard. "Padre Martini's Sonata for Four Trumpets and Strings," *BQ*, V/2 (Winter, 1961), 58-61.

Cherry, Norman. "A Corelli Sonata for Trumpet, Violins, and Basso Continuo," *BQ*, IV/3 (Spring, 1961), 103-113 and IV/4 (Summer, 1961), 156-158.

Conley, Philip. "The Use of the Trumpet in the Music of Henry Purcell," *BQ*, III/1 (Fall, 1959), 3-11.

Rasmussen, Mary. "English Trumpet Concertos in Some 18th Century Printed Collections," *BQ*, V/2 (Winter, 1961), 51-57.

Rasmussen, Mary. "New Light on Some Unusual 17th Century French Trumpet Parts," *BQ*, VI/1, (Fall, 1962), 9.

Smithers, Don. "17th Century English Trumpet Music," *ML*, XLVIII/4 (October, 1967), 358-365.

Tarr, Edward H. "Original Italian Baroque Compositions for Trumpet and Organ," *D*, LXI (April, 1970), 27-29.

Taylor, Thomas F. "Jeremiah Clarke's Trumpet Tunes: Another View of Origins," *MQ*, XLI/3 (July, 1970), 454-462.

Thomas, T. Donley. "Michael Haydn's Enigmatic 'Clarino' Symphony," *BQ*, VII/4 (Summer, 1964), 163-177.

Zimmerman, Franklin and Cudworth, Charles. "The Trumpet Voluntary," *ML*, XLI/4 (October, 1960), 342-348.

Musicians

"An 18th Century Directory of London Musicians," (extracted from *Mortimer's London Universal Dictionary*, 1763), *GSJ*, II (March, 1949), 27-31.

Bowles, Edmund. "Tower Musicians in the Middle Ages," *BQ*, V/3 (Spring, 1962), 91-103.

Carse, Adam. "Prince Regent's Band," *ML*, XXVII/3 (July, 1946), 147-155.

Carse, Adam. "Adolphe Sax . . ." Complete listing under "Instrument Makers."

Hoover, Cynthia. "Trumpet Battle . . ." Complete listing under "Slide Trumpet."

Jaffee, Kay (ed.). "Divers Notes on Brass Instruments in English Periodicals (1678-1719)," *BQ*, VII/4 (Summer, 1964), 178-193.

Halfpenny, Eric. "The 'Entertainment' of Charles II," *ML*, XXXVIII/1 (January, 1957), 32-44.

Halfpenny, Eric. "Musicians at James II's Coronation," *ML*, XXXII/2 (April, 1951), 103-114).

Langwill, Lyndesay G. "Two Rare 18th Century London Directories," *ML*, XXX/1 (January, 1949), 37-43.

La Rue, John and Brofsky, Howard. "Parisian Brass Players, 1751-1793," *BQ*, III/4 (Summer, 1960), 133-140.

Rasmussen, Mary. "Gottfried Reiche and His 'Vier und Zwantzig Neue Quatricinia' (1696)," *BQ*, IV/1 (Fall, 1960), 3-17.

Smithers, Don L. "The Hapsburg Imperial Trompeter and Heerpauker Privileges of 1653," *GSJ*, XXIII (July, 1971), 84-95.

Titcomb, Caldwell. "Baroque Court and Military Trumpets, Kettledrums and Music," *GSJ*, IX (June, 1956), 56-81.

Pre-Renaissance

Bowles, Edmond A. "Were Instruments Used in the Liturgical Service During the Middle Ages?" *GSJ*, X (May, 1957), 40-56.

Farmer, George H. "Crusading Martial Music," *ML*, XXX/3 (July, 1949), 243-249.

Turrentine, Edgar. "Notes on the Ancient Olympic Trumpet Blowing Contest," *Inst*, XXIII/9 (April, 1969), 42-43.

Turrentine, Edgar. "The Trumpet's Day," *Inst*, XIX/8 (March, 1965), 72-73.

Werner, Eric. "Musical Aspects of the Dead Sea Scrolls," *MQ*, XLIII/1 (January, 1957), 21-37.

Related Instruments

Hunsberger, Donald. "The Bass Trumpet: from Wagner Until Today," *Inst*, XIX/9 (April, 1965), 99-102.

Lasko, Richard. "Historical Evolution of the Flügelhorn," *BW*, I-IV (1965-1968), 128-136, 162-170, 211-215.

Smithers, Don. "The Trumpets of J.W. Haas . . ." Complete listing under "Instrument Makers."

Taylor, Lawrence. "Heyday of the Keyed Bugle," *MJ*, XI/7 (July, 1953), 16-17.

Wheeler, Joseph. "New Light on the 'Regents Bugle' . . ." Complete listing under "British Trumpet Series from *GSJ*."

Book Reviews

Fitzpatrick, Horace. "Review of *Trumpets, Horns and Music* by J. Murray Barbour," *ML*, XLVI/1 (January, 1965), 76-78.

Smithers, Don. "Review of *The Trumpet and the Trombone* by Philip

Bate," *ML*, XLVII/3 (July, 1966), 262-264.

Wheeler, Joseph. "Review of *The Trumpet and the Trombone* by Philip Bate," *GSJ*, XX (March, 1967), 106-111.

Wheeler, Joseph. "Review of *Trumpets, Horns and Music* by J. Murray Barbour," *GSJ*, XVIII (March, 1965), 137-140.

Slide Trumpet

Hoover, Cynthia A. "The Slide Trumpet of the 19th Century," *BQ*, VI/4 (Summer, 1963), 159-174.

Hoover, Cynthia A. "Trumpet Battle at Niblo's Pleasure Garden," *MQ*, XL/3 (July, 1969), 384-395.

Sachs, Curt. "Chromatic Trumpets in the Renaissance," *MQ*, XXXVI/1 (January, 1950), 62-66.

Theater Use

Bowles, Edmond A. "Musical Instruments in Medieval Sacred Drama," *MQ*, XLV/1 (January, 1959), 67-84.

Manifold, John. "Theater Music in the 16th and 17th Centuries," *ML*, XXIX/4, (October, 1948), 366-397.

Westrup, J.A. "Monteverdi and the Orchestra," *ML*, XXXI/3, (July, 1940), 230-245.

Valve Trumpet

Eliason, Robert E. "Early American Valves for Brass Instruments," *GSJ*, XXII, (August, 1970), 86-96.

Miscellaneous

Baines, Anthony. "James Talbot's Manuscripts," *GSJ*, I, (March, 1948), 9-26.

Barbour, J. Murray. "Unusual Brass Notation in the 18th Century," *BQ*, II/4 (June, 1959), 139-146.

Lewis, H.M. "The Trumpet in the Romantic Era," *Inst*, XXVI/6 (January, 1972), 26-27.

Rasmussen, Mary. "Bach Trumpet Madness: or a Plain and Easy Introduction to the Attributes, Causes and Cure of a Most Mysterious Musicological Malady," *BQ*, V/1, (Fall, 1961), 37-40.

Smith, Douglas. "A Short History of the Trumpet," *Inst*, XXVI/6 (January, 1972), 20-25. ∎

A Recommended Selected List
of French Horn Literature

Frederick Bergstone

Since one of the most difficult tasks confronting any teacher or performer is the selection of suitable repertoire, the following selected list should be of help in the search for horn literature. A rough grading is made to estimate the average level of difficulty:

E — Easy, through high school level.

M — Medium, advanced high school and average college.

D — Difficult, advanced college, graduate and professional.

Selections, made on the basis of musical worth and practical validity for development of good horn playing, represent a wide range of style and schools of playing. The intention of this list is to form a core of literature which can and should be changed as the experience and knowledge of the performer changes.

Solos for Horn and Piano

Albrechtsberger	Concerto	International	M
Bakalienikoff	Cavatina	Belwin	E
Beethoven	Sonata, Op. 17	International	D
Bozza	En Foret	Leduc	D
Chabrier	Larghetto	Costallat	M
Cherubini	Two Sonatas	International	M-D
Clerisse	Chant Sans Paroles	Leduc	E
Corelli	Sonata in g minor	Edition Musicus	M
Corelli	Sonata in F Major	Edition Musicus	M
Dukas	Villanelle	International	D
Glazounov	Reverie, Op. 24	Leeds	D
Gliere	Concerto, Op. 91	Leeds	D
Gliere	Nocturne, Op. 35, No. 10	Leeds	M
Gliere	Intermezzo, Op. 35, No. 11	Leeds	E
Goedicke	Concerto, Op. 40	Sikorsky	D
Haydn	Concerto No. 1	Breitkopf & Härtel	D
Haydn	Concerto No. 2	Breitkopf & Härtel	D
Heiden	Sonata (1939)	Associated	D
Hindemith	Concerto (1949)	Schott	D
Hindemith	Sonata (1939)	Schott	D
Hindemith	Sonata for Alto Horn (1943)	Schott	D
Jacob	Concerto	Williams	D
Mouret	Two Divertissements	Richli	E
Mozart, L.	Concerto	Carl Fischer	E
Mozart, W.A.	Concert Rondo, K. 371	Breitkopf & Härtel	M
Mozart, W.A.	Concerto No. 1, K. 412	International	M
Mozart, W.A.	Concerto No. 2, K. 417	International	D
Mozart, W.A.	Concerto No. 3, K. 447	International	M
Mozart, W.A.	Concerto No. 4, K. 495	International	D
Piatoni	Air de Chasse	Leduc	M
Poot	Sarabande	Leduc	E
Poulenc	Elegy	Chester	D
Rosetti	Concerto in E Flat	International	D
Rosetti	Concerto in d minor	Simrock	D
Saint-Saens	Concert Piece, Op. 94	International	D
Saint-Saens	Romance, Op. 36	International	M
Schmitt	Lied and Scherzo, Op. 54	Durand	D
Schumann	Adagio and Allegro	International	D
Senaille	Allegro Spirituoso	Associated	M
Stevens	Sonata	Morris	D
Strauss, F.	Concerto, Op. 8	Carl Fischer	D

Strauss, R.	Concerto No. 1, Op. 11	Universal	D
Strauss, R.	Concerto No. 2	Boosey & Hawkes	D
Telemann	Concerto in D Major	Peters	D
Telemann	Sonata in f minor	International	M
Tomasi	Concerto	Leduc	D
Weber	Concertino, Op. 45	Breitkopf & Härtel	D
Wilder	Sonata No. 3	Fox	D

Solo Collections

Boyd	Golden Melodies for French Horn	Witmark	E-M
Hauser	Modern French Horn Repertoire Album	Carl Fischer	E-M
Jones	Solos for the Horn Player	Schirmer	E-M-D
Kaufmann	Twelve Solos	Carl Fischer	E-M
Krol	Solobook for French Horn (solo part only)	Rarter	M-D
	Contemporary French Recital Pieces	International	M-D

Studies and Methods for the Horn

Bach/Hoss	Suites for Cello	Southern	M-D
Belloli	8 Etudes	International	M
Blume	36 Etudes (3 vols)	Schmidt	M-D
Franz	Complete French Horn Method	Erdmann	M
Gallay	30 Studies, Op. 13	International	M
Gallay	39 Unmeasured Preludes, Op. 27	Leduc	M
Gallay	12 Caprices, Op. 32	Leduc	D
Gallay	22 Exercises, Op. 37	Leduc	M
Gallay	12 Etudes, Op. 43	International	D
Gallay	12 Studies, Op. 57	International	M
Getchell	Practical Studies (2 vols)	Belwin	E
Gugel	12 Etudes	International	D
Horner	Primary Studies	Elkan-Vogel	E
Kling	40 Studies	International	M
Kopprasch	60 Studies (2 vols)	International	M-D
Kreutzer/Reynolds	Sixteen Studies	Schirmer	D
Maxime-Alphonse	200 Etudes Nouvelles (6 vols)	Leduc	E-M-D
Mueller	34 Etudes (2 vols)	International	M-D
Pares	Daily Exercises and Scales	Rubank	E
Pottag	French Horn Method (2 vols)	Belwin	E
Pottag (ed.)	335 Selected Studies (2 vols)	Southern	E-M-D
Reynolds	48 Etudes	Schirmer	D
Schantl	Grand Theoretical and Practical Method for the Valve Horn	Wind Music	E-M
Schuller	Studies for Unaccompanied Horn	Oxford	D
Singer	Embouchure Building	Belwin	E-M-D
Strauss, F.	16 Concert Studies	Peters	M

Orchestral Studies and Excerpts

Chambers	Orchestral Excerpts from the Symphonic Repertoire (several vols)	International	
Farkas	Orchestral Studies from the Modern French Repertoire	Elkan-Vogel	
Fontana	Passi Difficili e "a solo"	Ricordi	
Gumbert-Frehse	Orchesterstudien (12 vols)	Hofmeister	
Janetzky	Bach-Studien fur Waldhorn	Hofmeister	
Pottag	French Horn Passages (3 vols)	Belwin	
Strauss-Plotner	Orchesterstudien (3 vols)	Hofmeister	
Strauss-Chambers	Orchestral Studies	International	
Wagner-Chambers	Orchestral Studies	International	

Small Ensembles with Horn

Beethoven	Sextet (2 hns & str)	International	D
Bozza	Suite (4 hns)	Leduc	M-D
Brahms	Trio (hn, vln, pf)	International	D
Britten	Serenade for Tenor, Horn and Strings (pf)	Boosey & Hawkes	D

Duvernoy	Four Trios	Sikorski	M
Franz	100 Duets (2 vols)	Southern	E-M-D
Grass	Modern Duets and Trios	Southern	M-D
Haydn	Divertimento a Tre (hn, vln, vcl)	Doblinger	D
Heiden	Quintet (1950) (hn, str)	Associated	D
Hindemith	Sonata for Four Horns (1952)	Schott	D
Hofmeister	Concerto (2 hns & pf)	International	M
Kling	15 Duets	Southern	M
Los Angeles Horn Club	60 Selected Duets	Southern	E-M-D
Mozart, W.A.	Quintet, K. 407 (hn & str)	International	D
Mozart, W.A.	12 Duos, K. 487	Hofmeister	M-D
Mozart, W.A.	Ein Musikalische Spass, K. 522 (2 hn & str)	International	D
Pottag	60 Duets (2 vols)	Belwin	E-M-D
Pottag	Trio Album	Belwin	E-M-D
Pottag	Quartet Album	Belwin	E-M
Poulenc	Sonata (hn, tp, trb)	Chester	D
Reicha	Six Trios, Op. 82	International	M-D
Schuller	Duets for Unaccompanied Horns	Oxford	D
Schumann	Konzertstuck, Op. 86 (4 hns & orch, pf)	International	D
Tcherepnine	Six Pieces for Four Horns	Edition Musicus	M-D
Telemann	Suite in F Major (2 hns & pf)	International	D
Vivaldi	Concerto in F Major (2 hns & pf)	Editio Musica	M
Villa-Lobos	Choros No. 4 (3 hns & tb)	Eschig	D
Wilder	22 Duets	Fox	M
Wilder	4 Studies for 4 horns	Leblanc	M

■

Better Brass Articulation

Robert C. Jones

The various articulations for double and triple tonguing in brass playing have been discussed infrequently at clinics and conferences. In addition, little has appeared in print concerning the pedagogy of these skills which are vital to the maturing brass performer.

The beginning weeks of practice in learning to double or triple tongue should be spent in producing two tones of equal quality and intensity. This can best be accomplished by playing half notes very slowly, so that the student and teacher may listen carefully and compare the quality of the "T" on the first note with that of the "K" on the second. A breath is neither necessary nor desirable between the "T" and the "K," and it is important to avoid producing short staccato tones in this early period. Once an equally controlled attack is assured on each note, the tempo can be increased and the note values shortened to achieve a separated attack.

Although many brass texts advocate *too-koo* or *tu-ku* for double tonguing, *tah-kah* or *taw-kaw* will enable the performer to maintain a more natural embouchure. The *tah* or *taw* approach also permits a more open throat and assures more ease in maintaining control and exact note values.

This slow approach to either double or triple tonguing has the added advantage of enabling a student to coordinate both the fingers or slide with the tongue at early practice sessions when tempos are usually slow. And students exposed to this approach will be able to achieve cleaner playing of difficult technical passages than those who have been exposed only to an uncontrolled, fast tongue speed.

Once a controlled attack on both the "T" and the "K" syllables has been mastered, performers will encounter fewer problems with double tonguing. But dealing with the double tonguing of an odd number of notes may cause some difficulties. One fairly recent technique is to start all passages with a "T." Another (the *Arban Method*) advocates that the second, third and fourth sixteenth notes occurring after a sixteenth rest should be articulated *K-T-K*. However, beginning on K is difficult and frequently affects the clarity of the next few notes. If the performer finds it eas-

647

ier to begin such a motive with a *T*, the next two notes should not be changed, thus resulting in a rest, *T-T-K* articulation (see Ex. 1, 2).

Ex. 1

Ex. 2

Triple tonguing can be somewhat more complicated. A large percentage of teachers and students have only been exposed to the common and effective *T-T-K* method found in *Arban* and other excellent texts. This *one* approach should not and cannot be used effectively in all passages because of accents or wide intervals which (when articulated but one way) may interfere with musical sensitivity or exacting technical facility.

A fast triplet accompaniment figure should not, for example,

place the emphasis on the first note of each triplet. The second or fourth triplets occurring on the up-beats can easily be de-emphasized by using the following articulation: *T-K-T*, *K-T-K*, *T-K-T*, *K-T-K* (see Ex. 3). Notice that in this situation

Ex. 3

(Accompaniment)

the performer is merely double tonguing notes grouped rhythmically as triplets. The musical meaning might be completely altered if the performer stayed with *T-T-K* throughout and was unable to eliminate the slight, sometimes inevitable, accent that occurs on the second and fourth triplets. The above is also an excellent method of articulating scale or chromatic passages that are grouped rhythmically in triplets (see Ex. 4).

Ex. 4

(Scales)

Another seldom used method of triple tonguing — *T-K-T*, *T-K-T*, — should be used when a wide interval between the second and third notes would assure a cleaner attack than the more conventional *T-T-K* (see Ex. 5). On the other hand,

Ex. 5

T-T-K should be the performer's choice when the difficult interval lies between the first and the second notes of the triplet (see Ex. 6).

Ex. 6

Since the third note in this example is the same as the second, it is much easier to produce the 3rd note with a *K* than the second note. ∎

Mouthpieces and Wrists —
Two Tips for Trombonists

Morris Sweatt and Gregg Magnuson

The Mouthpiece

As a beginner, the typical trombone player uses whatever mouthpiece happens to be included with the purchase of the instrument. It is not until years later, usually at the urging of the band director or private teacher, that another mouthpiece is even considered.

A beginner needs a shallow cup mouthpiece to help him through the first stage of development, and most stock mouthpieces answer this description. Later he will want the added volume and horn-like quality that a deeper cup offers.

Although trial and error emerges as the final method of selection, knowing a few basic facts about the function of the separate parts of the mouthpiece will be helpful.

The parts of the mouthpiece which affect its performance are the rim, bite (the edge of the rim), cup, throat (the opening into the backbore), throat shoulder (the final curve before the backbore), and backbore (see illustration).

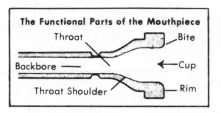

The Functional Parts of the Mouthpiece

A medium rim (standard on most stock mouthpieces) will serve most players best. A wide rim will increase endurance, but decrease flexibility and control. A narrow rim will improve flexibility, but it may

cut into the lip. A sharp bite may also cut into the lip and, although it increases the accuracy of attack, it can decrease flexibility. In contrast, a round bite offers flexibility but decreases accuracy.

The shape of the throat shoulder should be selected according to the type of tone desired. A sharp throat shoulder will give a bright, penetrating sound, while a round one gives a horn-like quality. An open throat will have little resistance and give an open, free sound, but it will make soft passages difficult to play. A narrow throat will be so hard to blow that it is not recommended for any purpose. Youngsters should use a medium throat and move to a more open throat after sufficient embouchure development.

Since a wide backbore decreases endurance and a narrow one creates resistance and a harsh, undesirable tone quality, a medium backbore is recommended. The taper of the backbore is also important. As it opens into the leadpipe (i.e., the first few inches of the instrument proper), it affects the performance of the mouthpiece to a great extent. A rapid taper results in a dark tone with little resistance; a slow taper, although it gives a bright tone and resistance, is hard to control.

Once you have found a mouthpiece that serves your purpose, *stick with it*. If one is to develop the fine points of musical performance, he must use the same equipment over an extended period of time so that the embouchure can "grow into the mouthpiece." ∎

The Wrist

The stiff right wrist is the cause of many problems of the trombonist — including the seemingly unrelated one of tone production. This is because muscular tension in the wrist travels to the upper arm, then to the shoulder, then to the neck, and eventually to the throat, thus disturbing the tone production mechanism. The key to developing the proper wrist action is to realize that the wrist was intended to move like a hinge, but only in one direction.

I have found the following procedure to be helpful in solving the problem.

1. Grip the slide with the thumb, just behind the thumb nail and fleshy pads of the first two fingers, making sure the wrist is in a "vertical" position with the palm of the hand facing "in" towards the trombone. (The common error seems to be to hold the slide with the thumb and the side of the first finger so that the palm is down and the wrist is then unable to bend sideways.)

2. Keeping the fingers gently curved and relaxed, move the slide to second position. Then *using only the wrist*, move to first position, then back to second, and then on to third. If there is any arm motion at all, it should be ever so slight so as to be almost unnoticeable when the wrist is moving.

3. Now practice etudes making extensive use of 1st, 2nd, and 3rd positions.

Make sure the bicep and tricep in the upper arm are not tense. If they are, it is an indication that the finger grip is too tight and the wrist is beginning to stiffen, if indeed, it is not already very rigid. Actually, we probably must teach muscular relaxation as much as proper grip and wrist action.

When going for 6th and 7th positions, the wrist action, in addition to the arm motion, can often mean an extra inch of reach for the young trombonist (as well as better intonation for anyone).

Once a flexible wrist is acquired (and no student is too young or inexperienced to learn proper grip), playing becomes noticeably less tiring, and in some cases much less painful. Facility increases, and often, because less bulk is moved (i.e., wrist instead of arm), the tone also improves. With the wrist relaxed, no tension can travel from it and eventually wind up in the throat. The result is better trombone playing, more pleasure and enjoyment for the trombonist, and better ensemble in the trombone section. ∎

November, 1973

A Comprehensive Bibliography of Music for Brass Quintet

Donald K. Day

The brass quintet has become the most significant performing medium in the field of brass today, and the result has been a vast increase in brass quintet literature. Many colleges and universities have formed faculty and even student quintets, and there are several fine professional performing groups. Each group has created its own literature in addition to performing works from the standard repertoire. The New York Brass Quintet, perhaps the best known performing quintet, is deluged with manuscripts dedicated to them. Other fine groups such as the Eastman Brass Quintet and The American Brass Quintet are constantly introducing new music to the literature.

In the standard brass quintet — made up of 2 trumpets, horn, trombone and tuba — each instrument of the brass family is represented. This arrangement allows for a full range of sonorities and timbres, and the use of the 2nd trumpet alleviates any endurance problems. Another popular form of brass quintet calls for 2 trumpets, horn and 2 trombones. The literature for brass quintet is not confined to one or the other arrangement, and it is quite acceptable to perform a work with either 2 trombones or trombone and tuba.

The brass quintet has served as a valuable recruiting aid for colleges and universities, and many send a faculty or student quintet on tour to give clinics and concerts in the schools throughout the area. What the prospective student foresees is a chance to participate in a small ensemble where he is sure to get individual attention and plenty of practical experience. In addition, students performing in small ensembles will have the chance to work out their own musical problems and to exchange individual ideas concerning style and performance. The many facets of music that can be learned from participation in small groups will surely manifest themselves in future teaching.

The present bibliography of literature for brass quintet will be a valuable aid to any high school or college teacher interested in adding to an established library (or in building one). One unique aspect of this list is the inclusion of music in manuscript. It is hoped that by listing such music, more performing groups will be willing to seek out and exchange quintet music written and performed in other areas of the country. It would be ideal to have a certain location where a composer could send a copy of his quintet, so that it would become available on loan to other brass quintets. (The NACWPI Manuscript Library at the University of Maryland would be a logical choice.)

This graded bibliography includes brass quintet music on every possible level and for every conceivable occasion. *Music for Queen Mary II* (Grade II) by Henry Purcell is an example that good music can exist at a simple level. Young instrumentalists are able to play the piece because of the simple rhythms and moderate range, but the demands for clean attacks and breath control can frustrate even the most polished quintet. It is a most valuable teaching piece. George Barboteu's *Astral* (Grade VI), a far more difficult piece which requires a metronome to mark the beat, is the only composition included that utilizes an additional musical instrument. Another challenging work is David Mott's *Elements II*. This work is a tour de force of the history of music and is climaxed by the sounds of Tibetan music.

Many works for brass quintet are excellent for demonstration purposes. Fisher Tull's *Exhibition* provides a good example. The introduction and finale display the quintet as a full ensemble,

while the other four movements show off each individual instrument in characteristic fashion. Another exemplary work is the *Quintet No. 2* by Thom Ritter George. The second movement is a technical display of trombone virtuosity, while the tuba predominates throughout a slow, melodic third movement. And the finale is sustained by an exciting rhythmic drive. In *Diversion* by Mark Hughes, some interesting effects are created by displaced accents within the framework of 4/2 meter. The score calls for quarter tones and out-of-tune notes, all seemingly in jest.

For a festive occasion requiring special music, David Amram's *Fanfare and Processional* would be most appropriate, although the processional is quite demanding. Jack End's *Three Salutations*, with its light-hearted variations on "Old Paint," is a popular piece to end any program.

The following list includes arrangements and transcriptions as well as original works for brass quintet. An asterisk preceding an entry designates that the work was composed for 2 trumpets, horn and 2 trombones (rather than for the standard quintet). In some instances information which was unavailable at the time of this writing has been omitted.

System of Grading

Grade I — mainly for first year instrumentalists.
Grade II — for those beyond the beginning stages.
Grade III — for those who have acquired some technique.
Grade IV — for more advanced instrumentalists.
Grade V — mostly for college players.
Grade VI — for the skilled professional.

Key to Annotation and Review Sources

BQ — Brass Quarterly
BW — Brass World
BWQ — Brass and Woodwind Quarterly
GSJ — Galpin Society Journal
INST — The Instrumentalist
ML — Music and Letters
MO — Musical Opinion
MT — Musical Times
NACWPI — National Association of College Wind and Percussion Instructors Journal
NOTES — Music Library Association Notes
Shoemaker — Shoemaker, John R. "A Selected and Annotated Listing of 20th Century Ensembles Published for Three or More Heterogeneous

Brass Instruments." Ed.D. dissertation, Washington University, 1968. University Microfilms LC 69-90091.

Adler, Samuel. *Five Movements*. North Easton, MA: Robert King Music Co., 1965. Annotation: Shoemaker, p. 123. Review: *BWQ* I/1-2(Winter, 1966-67), 57. Grade V.
Adson, John. *Consort Music*, arr. Baldwin. New York: Autograph Editions, 1971. Grade IV.
———. *Two Ayres for Cornetts and Sagbuts*, ed. King. North Easton, MA: Robert King Music Co., n.d. Grade III.
Albinoni, Tomaso. *Suite in A Major*, arr. Thilds. Paris: Editions Billaudot. Grade IV.
Alette, Carl. *Scherzo*. Composers MS. Dept. of Music, Univ. of South Alabama, Mobile, AL. Grade III.
Alexander, Josef. *Four for Five*. San Antonio, TX: Southern Music Co. Review: *INST* XXIV/6 (January, 1970), 92. Grade V.
Alford, Kenneth. *Colonel Bogey*, arr. Stratton. Oceanside, NY: Boosey and Hawkes, 1964. Grade III.
Ames, William. *Quintet*. New York: Composers Facsimile Editions.
Amram, David. *Fanfare and Processional*. New York: C.F. Peters, 1968. Grade VI.
Andrix, George. *Structures* (1971). Composers MS, 10715-151 Street, Edmonton, Alta, Canada. Review: *BW* VI/2 (1971), 98. Grade V.
Anonymous. "Sonata," from *Die Bankelsängerlieder*, ed. King. North Easton, MA: Robert King Music Co., 1958. Grade III.
———. "Sonata," from *Die Bankelsängerlieder*, arr. Sear. Massapequa, NY: Cor Publishing Co. Grade III.
———. "Sussex Mummer's" and "Angels," from *The Realms*, arr. Sear. Massapequa, NY: Cor Publishing Co. Grade IV.
Apperson, Ronald. *Fantasia* (1963). Composers MS, NACWPI Manuscript Library, Music Dept., Univ. of Maryland, College Park, MD. Grade V.
Archer, Violet. *Divertimento*. Montreal: Montreal Music Supply, 1963. Review: *BWQ* I/1-2(Winter, 1966-67), 65. Grade V.
Arnell, Richard. *Quintet*. New York: Southern Music Publishing Co. Review: *INST* XXIII/3 (October, 1968), 91. Grade IV.
———. *Variations On The Wayfaring Stranger*. New York: Southern Music Publishing Co. Grade IV.
Arnold, Malcolm. *Quintet*. London: Patersons Publications, 1961. Annotation: Shoemaker, p. 128. Review: *BQ* VII/3 (Spring, 1964), 142. *BW* I-IV (1965-68), 116. Grade V.
Ategnati, Constanzo. *Canzon XX*. London: Musica Rara. Grade IV.
Avermaa, Ovid. "Suite," on *Le Roi Renaud*. Montreal: Montreal Music Supply, 1963. Grade IV.
———. *Theme and Variations*. Montreal: Montreal Music Supply, 1967. Review: *BW* I/1 (1970), 10. Grade III.
Bach, Johann S. *Air pour Les Trompettes*, arr. Rosenthal. Los Angeles: Western International Music. Grade IV.
———. *Art of The Fugue*, trans. Sauer. Ralph Sauer, c/o Toronto Symphony Orchestra Toronto, Canada.
———. *Canzona in D Minor*, trans. Taylor. Los Angeles: Western International Music, 1971. Grade IV.
———. *Chorale and Fughetta*, arr. Fote. Delevan, NY: Kendor Music. Review: *INST* XVIII/2 (September, 1963), 70. Grade II.
———. "Contrapunctus I" from *Art of The Fugue*, ed. King. North Easton, MA: Robert King Music Co. Grade IV.
———. "Contrapunctus III" from *Art of The Fugue*, ed. King. North Easton, MA: Robert King Music Co., 1955. Grade III.
———. "Contrapunctus IV" from *Art of The Fugue*, arr. Nagel. New York: Sam Fox

Publishing Co. Review: *INST* XXIII/11 (June, 1969), 88. Grade IV.

——. "Contrapunctus V" from *Art of The Fugue*, arr. Nagel. North Easton, MA: Robert King Music Co. Review: *INST* XVI/7 (March, 1962), 84. Grade IV.

——. "Contrapunctus IX" from *Art of The Fugue*, arr. Glasel. Hempstead, NY: Mentor Music, 1959. Review: *INST* XIV/9 (May, 1960), 78. Grade IV.

——. *Fantasie*, arr. Rosenthal. Los Angeles: Western International Music, 1965. Review: *BW* I-IV (1965-68), 299. Grade IV.

——. *Fugue in D Minor*, arr. Sear. Massapequa, NY: Cor Publishing Co. Grade IV.

——. "Fugue XXII" from *Well-Tempered Clavier*, arr. Sear. Massapequa, NY: Cor Publishing Co. Grade IV.

——. *If Thou Be Near*, arr. Beeler. Miami, FL: Rubank, Inc., 1961. Review: *INST* XV/9 (May, 1961), 72. Grade III.

——. *In Dulci Jubilo*, arr. Sear. Massapequa, NY: Cor Publishing Co. Grade III.

——. *My Soul Longeth* and *March*, arr. Sear. Massapequa, NY: Cor Publishing Co. Grade III.

——. *Praeludium XXII*, arr. Sear. Massapequa, NY: Cor Publishing Co. Grade III.

——. *Prelude and Fugue in E Minor*, arr. Anderson. Los Angeles: Western International Music. Grade IV.

——. *Prelude and Fugue in G Minor*, arr. Rosenthal. Los Angeles: Western International Music. Grade IV.

°——. *Prelude and Fugue II*, trans. Taylor. Los Angeles: Western International Music, 1971. Grade IV.

——. *Prelude and Fugue XVI*, arr. Anderson. Los Angeles: Western International Music. Grade IV.

——. *Sarabande and Minuett*, ed. King. North Easton, MA: Robert King Music Co. Grade IV.

——. *Three Chorales*, arr. Menken. Oceanside, NY: Boosey and Hawkes. Grade III.

——. *Trumpet Fugue*, arr. Rosenthal. Los Angeles: Western International Music. Grade IV.

——. *Two Chorales*, arr. Uber. New York: Edition Musicus. Grade III.

——. *Wir glauben all'an einen Gott*, arr. Rosenthal. Los Angeles: Western International Music. Grade IV.

——. *Zwei Fugare*. Montreal: Montreal Music Supply, n.d. Grade II.

——. *Zwei Preludii*. Montreal: Montreal Music Supply, n.d. Grade II.

Baker, David. *Passions*. Montreal: Montreal Music Supply, n.d. Grade III.

°Balada, L. *Mosaicos*. Hastings-on-Hudson, NY: General Music Publishing Co., Inc.

Baldwin, David. *Notes*. New York: Atlantic Music Supply, 1973. Grade V.

Banchieri, Adriano. *Sinfonia*, arr. Edwards. New York: Autograph Editions, etc., 1971. Grade IV.

Banchieri, Adriano and Schutz, Heinrich. *Two Sinfonias*. Massapequa, NY: Cor Publishing Co., n.d. Grade II.

Barboteu, George. *Astral*. New York: C.F. Peters, 1970. Grade VI.

Baron, Samuel. *Impressions of a Parade*. New York: G. Schirmer, 1954. Grade III.

Bartok, Bela. *Folk Dances*, arr. Gordon. San Antonio, TX: Southern Music Co. Grade IV.

Bastien, Gilles. *Exigence*. Montreal: Montreal Music Supply, n.d. Grade IV.

°Bazelon, Irwin. *Quintet No. 2*. Oceanside NY: Boosey and Hawkes, 1965. Review: *INST* XXI/2 (September, 1966), 92. *NOTES* XXIV/1 (September, 1967), 153. Grade VI.

Beach, Bennie. *Music*. Bryn Mawr, PA: Tritone Press, 1969. Review: *INST* XXIV/10 (May, 1970), 84. Grade V.

Beckwith, John. *Taking a Stand* (1972). Composers MS, Dept. of Music, Univ. of Toronto, Toronto 5, Ontario, Canada. Grade VI.

Beethoven, Ludwig Van. *Finale, Op. 130*, arr. Sear. Massapequa, NY: Cor Publishing Co. Grade IV.

——. "Largo Appassionata" from *Sonata No. 2, Op. 2*. Montreal: Montreal Music Supply, n.d. Grade III.

——. *Prayer*. Delevan, NY: Kendor Music, Inc., 1964. Review: *INST* XIX/1 (August, 1964), 74. Grade I.

——. "Presto" from *Sonata No. 6, Op. 10*. Montreal: Montreal Music Supply, n.d. Grade III.

——. *Zwei Stücke*. Montreal: Montreal Music Supply, n.d. Grade III.

Berlioz, Hector. *Fugue*. Montreal: Montreal Music Supply, n.d. Grade III.

——. *Fugue*, arr. Homzy. New York: Autofax Publications, 1971. Grade IV.

Berman, Melvin. *Quintet*. Montreal: Montreal Music Supply, n.d. Grade IV.

Beyer, Frederick. *Overture*. Composers MS. Dept. of Music, Greensboro College, Greensboro, NC, 1966. Grade V.

Blair, Dallas. *Variations*. Composers MS. Dept. of Music, Austin Peay State Univ., Clarksville, TN. Grade V.

Blank, Alan. *Two Studies*. New York: WPN Music Co., 1970. Grade VI.

Bottje, Will. *Variations*. New York: Composers Facsimile Editions, n.d. Grade IV.

Boutry, Roger. *Prelude, Chorale and Fugue*. Paris: Alphonse Leduc. Grade IV.

Bozza, Eugene. *Bis*. Paris: Alphonse Leduc, 1963. Annotation: Shoemaker, p. 132. Review: *BQ* VII/3 (Spring, 1964), 142. *INST* XIX/4 (November, 1964), 92. Grade V.

——. *Giration*. Paris: Alphonse Leduc. Grade V.

——. *Sonatine*. Paris: Alphonse Leduc, 1951. Annotation: Shoemaker, p. 133. Grade V.

——. *Suite*. Montreal: Montreal Music Supply, 1967. Grade V.

——. *Suite Francaise*. Paris: Alphonse Leduc, 1967. Grade V.

——. *Trilogie*. Paris: Alphonse Leduc. Grade V.

Brade, William. *Four Dances*. Montreal: Montreal Music Supply, n.d. Grade III.

——. *Two Pieces*, ed. King. North Easton, MA: Robert King Music Co. Grade IV.

Bradshaw, Merrill. *Quintet* (1969). Composers MS. Dept. of Music, Brigham Young Univ., Provo, UT. Grade V.

Brahms, Johannes. *Academica: Old Student Song*, arr. Findlay. New York: Carl Fischer, Inc. Grade III.

——. *Chorale and Fugue*. New York: Atlantic Music Supply. Grade III.

——. *Chorale and Fugue*, arr. Waldeck. Massapequa, NY: Cor Publishing Co. Grade III.

——. *Es ist ein Ros' entsprungen*, arr. Niven. North Easton, MA: Robert King Music Co., n.d. Grade III.

——. *Three Choral Preludes*, arr. Rosenthal. Los Angeles: Western International Music, 1967. Grade III.

——. *Three Motets*, trans. Jolley. Los Angeles: Western International Music, 1971. Grade III.

——. *Three Songs*, arr. Lockwood. New York: Autograph Editions, 1971. Grade IV.

——. *Two Songs*, arr. Lockwood. New York: Autograph Editions, 1971. Grade III.

Broiles, Mel. *Mostly Dunes* (1965). Composers MS. Manhattan School of Music, 120 Claremont Ave., New York, NY. Grade V.

——. *Perplex Sphere* (1966). Composers MS. Manhattan School of Music, 120 Claremont Ave., New York, NY. Grade V.

Brott, Alexander. *Mutual Salvation Orgy*. Montreal: Montreal Music Supply, 1962. Review: *BWQ* I/1-2 (Winter, 1966-67), 59. Grade V.

Brown, Rayner. *Quintet No. 2*. Los Angeles: Western International Music, 1963. Review: *BQ* VII/3 (Spring, 1964), 141. *INST*

XVIII/11 (June, 1964), 79. Grade IV.

Bubalo, Ralph. *Three Pieces*. New York: Galaxy Music Corp., 1968. Review: *INST* XXIII/4 (November, 1968), 93. Grade IV.

Bury, Peter. *Down in The Deep Cellar*. Massapequa, NY: Cor Publishing Co., 1966. Grade III.

Busch, Carl. *Humoresque*. New York: Carl Fischer, Inc. Grade III.

——. *In a Happy Mood*. Boston: Cundy-Bettoney, Inc. Grade III.

——. *Quintet*. Rockville Center, NY: Belwin, Inc. Grade IV.

Byrd, William. *Alleluia, Alleluia*, ed. Wise. Los Angeles: Western International Music. Grade III.

Cabeson, A. de. *Cancion Religiosa*, trans. Sudmeier. Massapequa, NY: Cor Publishing Co., 1965. Grade III.

°Cabus, Peter. *Elegie*. Brussels: J. Maurer.

Calvert, Morely. *Occasional Suite*. Montreal: Montreal Music Supply, 1967. Grade V.

——. *Suite from the Montereggian Hills*. Montreal: Montreal Music Supply, 1962. Review: *BWQ* I/1-2 (Winter, 1966-67), 59. Grade V.

Campo, Frank. *Madrigale*. Los Angeles: Western International Music, 1971. Grade V.

Canning, Thomas. *Four Christmas Pieces*. New York: Composers Facsimile Editions. Grade IV.

Casanova, Andre. *Tre Momenti*. Paris: Editions Billaudot.

Cesti, Antonio. "Four Pieces" from *Il Pomo d'Oro*. Evanston, IL: Summy-Birchard Publishing Co., 1971. Review: *INST* XXVI/1 (August, 1971), 60. Grade III.

Chagrin, Francis. *Divertimento*. New York: Galaxy Music Corp., 1969. Review: *NOTES* XXVIII/1 (December, 1971), 317. *MT* III/1528 (June, 1970), 636. Grade VI.

Chandler, Erwin. *Quintet, Op. 21* (1968). Composers MS. 24 Pennsylvania Ave., Port Jarvis, NY. Review: *BW* VI/2 (1971), 100. Grade V.

Cheetham, John. *Scherzo*. Los Angeles: Western International Music, 1966. Annotation: Shoemaker, p. 138. Review: *BW* I-IV (1965-68), 298. Grade IV.

Childs, Barney. *Quintet*. New York: Composers Facsimile Editions, 1954. Grade V.

——. *Quintet No. 2*. New York: Pioneer Editions.

——. *Third Brass Quintet* (1965). New York: Composers Facsimile Editions. Review: *BW* VII/1 (1972), 14. Grade IV.

——. *Variations sur une chanson de canotier*. Buffalo, NY: Ensemble Publications, 1965. Review: *BWQ* I/1-2 (Winter, 1966-67), 59. *INST* XX/1 (August, 1965), 94. Grade V.

°Chilese, Bastian. *Canzon XXII*. London: Musica Rara. Grade IV.

Clark, Robert. *Concertino for Trumpet and Brass Quartet, Op. 16A*. Composers MS. Box 304, Kent, CT. Review: *BW* VI/2 (1971), 100. Grade IV.

Clark, Scotson. *Belgian March*, arr. Williams. San Antonio, TX: Southern Music Co., 1966. Grade III.

Cobine, Albert. *Trilogy*. Buffalo, NY: Ensemble Publications, 1966. Review: *INST* XXI/5 (December, 1966), 92. Grade V.

Coker, Wilson. *Quintet* (1966). Composers MS. 2948 Aulin Dr., San Jose, CA. Grade VI.

°Coleman, Charles. *Four Pieces for Sackbuts and Cornetts*, arr. Baines and Siebert. Fairlawn, NJ: Oxford University Press. Review: *GSJ* XIV (March, 1961), 98. *INST* XVII/4 (December, 1962), 45. Grade III.

Connolly, Justin. *Cinquepaces*. Fairlawn, NJ: Oxford University Press, 1971. Review: *ML* LIII/3 (July, 1972), 341. *MT* (June, 1972), 595. Grade VI.

Converse, Fred. *Two Lyric Pieces*. Miami, FL: Rubank, Inc., 1939. Grade IV.

Corelli, Arcangelo. *Adagio*, arr. Schaeffer.

Westbury, NY: Pro Art Publications, 1970. Review: INST XXV/4 (November, 1970), 72. Grade II.

———. Sonata in F Major, trans. Sudmeier. Massapequa, NY: Cor Publishing Co. Grade IV.

Corina, John. Essay for Brass (1966). Composers MS. Dept. of Music, Univ. of Georgia, Athens, GA. Grade V.

Coscia, Silvio. Madrigal and Fugue. Oyster Bay, NY: M. Baron Co., 1964. Grade IV.

———. Suite in Three Moods. Oyster Bay, NY: M. Baron Co. Grade IV.

°Cowell, Henry. Action in Brass. New York: Edition Musicus, 1943.

Croley, Randell. Concert Music (1966). Composers MS. c/o Atlantic Music Supply, New York, NY. Grade VI.

———. Disquisition. Bryn Mawr, PA: Tritone Press, 1967. Grade IV.

———. Sinfonietta. New York: Autograph Editions, 1971. Grade VI.

Cunningham, Michael. Concertant, Op. 39. New York: Composers Facsimile Editions.

Custer, Arthur. Concerto. New York: General Music Publishing Co., 1971. Grade V.

Dahl, Ingolf. Music for Brass Instruments. East Rutherford, NJ: Warner Brothers Music, 1949. Annotation: Shoemaker, p.

141. Review: BQ I/4 (June, 1958), 228. Grade V.

D'Angelo, Nicholas. Quintet No. 3 (1967). Composers MS. Dept. of Music, Hobart and Smith Colleges, Geneva, NY. Review: BW VII/1 (1972), 15. Grade VI.

———. Quintet No. 4 (1969). Composers MS. Dept. of Music, Hobart and Smith Colleges, Geneva, NY. Review: BW VII (1972), 15. Grade VI.

Daum, Ron. Suite for Young Listeners. Melville, NY: Belwin-Mills Publishing Corp. Review: INST XXIV/10 (May, 1970), 83. Grade IV.

A Comprehensive Bibliography of Music for Brass Quintet

Donald K. Day

Part II

Debussy, Claude. Golliwog's Cakewalk, arr. Rose. Massapequa, NY: Cor Publishing Co. Grade III.

Decoursey, Ralph. Sonata in Brass. Composers MS. 4708 Charleswood Dr., Calgary, Alberta, Canada.

DeJong, Conrad. Blues. Composers MS. Dept. of Music, Wisconsin State College, River Falls, WI, 1963. Grade V.

DeKruyf, Ton. Aubade. New York: C.F. Peters, 1957 (revised, 1967). Grade V.

Dela, Maurice. Divertissement. Montreal: Montreal Music Supply, 1963. Grade IV.

DePres, Josquin. Faulte d'argent. Montreal: Montreal Music Supply, n.d. Grade III.

Dering, Richard. Fantasia, arr. Cool. New York: Autograph Editions, 1971. Grade IV.

Diamond, David. Quintet. San Antonio, TX: Southern Music Co., 1962. Review: INST XVII/7 (March, 1963), 125. Grade V.

Dieterich, Milton. Horizons. Miami, FL: Rubank, Inc., 1959. Review: INST XIV/7 (March, 1960), 91. Grade II.

Dillon, Robert. Suite. Athens, OH: Accura Music, 1969. Review: INST XXIV/6 (January, 1970), 92. Grade V.

Drakeford, Richard. Tower Music. Melville, NY: Belwin-Mills Publishing Corp. Review: MT 110/1519 (September, 1969), 971.

Drew, James. Quintet D'Microtonos (1970). Composers MS. Dept. of Music, Yale Univ., New Haven, CT. Grade V.

Dutton, Brent. Small Pieces (1971). Composers MS. 295 St. Joseph St., Quebec City 2, P.Q., Canada. Grade VI.

Dvorak, Anton. Going Home, arr. Sudmeier. Massapequa, NY: Cor Publishing Co., n.d. Grade III.

———. Songs of Nature, arr. Lockwood. New York: Autograph Editions, 1971. Grade IV.

°East, Michael. Desperavi, arr. Fromme. New York: Associated Music Publishers, 1967. Review: INST XXII/10 (May, 1968), 106. Grade III.

Emmett, Daniel. Dixie, arr. Roberts. Massapequa, NY: Cor Publishing Co., 1961. Grade III.

End, Jack. Three Salutations. New York: Pyraminx Publications, 1965. Review: BW I/1 (1970), 10. Grade IV.

Etler, Alvin. Quintet. New York: Associated Music Publishers, 1957. Review: INST XV/4 (December, 1960), 53. Grade VI.

°Ewald, Victor. Quintet, ed. King. North Easton, MA: Robert King Music Co., 1957. Review: BQ I/2 (September, 1957), 120. Grade IV.

Faberman, Harold. Five Images. New York: General Music Publishing Co., Inc., 1965. Review: INST XXV/2 (September, 1970), 98. Grade VI.

Feld, Eric. Quintette. Paris: Alphonse Leduc, 1972. Grade V.

Fennelly, Brian. Prelude for Brass Quintet (1970). Composers MS. 100 Bleeker St., 23B, New York, NY. Grade V.

Ferrabosco, Alphonso II. The Hexachord. New York: Atlantic Music Supply. Grade IV.

Finck, Heinrich. Greiner Zanner, arr. Sirinek. Los Angeles: Western International Music. Grade IV.

Fischer, Jan. Bouree and Minuet, arr. Waldeck. Massapequa, NY: Cor Publishing Co. Grade III.

———. Le Journal du Printemps, arr. Waldeck. Massapequa, NY: Cor Publishing Co. Grade III.

———. Entree and Rondo, arr. Waldeck. Massapequa, NY: Cor Publishing Co. Grade III.

Flagello, Nicholas. Philos. New York: General Music Publishing Co., Inc., 1971.

Fleming, Robert. Quintet. Montreal: Montreal Music Supply, 1965. Grade V.

———. Three Miniatures. Montreal: Montreal Music Supply, 1962. Review: BWQ I/1-2 (Winter, 1966-67), 59. Grade V.

Foley, David. Cat Music I (1971). Composers MS. 117 New York Ave., Muncie, IN. Review: BW VI/2 (1971), 100. Grade V.

———. Cat Music II (1971). Composers MS. 117 New York Ave., Muncie, IN. Grade V.

Frackenpohl, Arthur. Pop Suite. Delevan, NY: Kendor Music, 1973. Grade III.

———. Quintet. Bryn Mawr, PA: Theodore Presser Co., 1966. Annotation: Shoemaker, p. 145. Review: INST XXI/7 (February,

1967), 95. Grade V.

———. Quintet No. 2. North Easton, MA: Robert King Music Co., 1972.

Franck, Melchoir. Four Intradas, trans. Singleton. Ken Singleton, 820 Orange St., New Haven, CT. Grade III.

———. Three Intradas, trans. Singleton. Ken Singleton, 820 Orange St., New Haven, CT. Grade III.

———. Two Intradas, trans. Singleton. Ken Singleton, 820 Orange St., New Haven, CT. Grade III.

Frangkiser, Carl. A Prayer. Westbury, NY: Pro Art Publications. Grade II.

Frederickson, Thomas. Quintet. Chicago: M.M. Cole Publishing Co., 1972.

Frescobaldi, Girolamo. Canzon XIII. London: Musica Rara. Grade IV.

———. Canzon XXI. London: Musica Rara. Grade IV.

Gabrieli, Andrea. Canzona, arr. Lenhert. Delevan, NY: Kendor Music. Review: BW I/1 (1970), 10. INST XXIII/6 (January, 1969), 85. Grade II.

Gabrieli, Giovanni. Canzona in Bb, arr. Waldeck. Massapequa, NY: Cor Publishing Co. Grade III.

———. Canzona prima a 5. New York: Sam Fox Publishing Co., 1961. Review: INST XV/10 (June, 1961), 65. Grade III.

———. Madrigale. Montreal: Montreal Music Supply, n.d. Grade III.

Gardner, John. Theme and Variation. London: Oxford University Press, 1970. Review: MT III/1528 (June, 1970), 636. Grade V.

Gault, George. Caledonia. East Rutherford, NJ: Warner Brothers Music, 1940.

Genzmer, Harald. Quintet. New York: C.F. Peters, 1971.

George, Thom. Quintet No. 1. Composers MS. Dept. of Music, Quincy College, Quincy, IL. Grade VI.

———. Quintet No. 2. Composers MS. Dept. of Music, Quincy College, Quincy, IL. Grade VI.

Gesualdo, Carlo. Four Madrigals, arr. Freedman. New York: MCA Music Corp., 1964. Grade III.

———. Io Tacero and Moro Lasso, trans. Singleton. Ken Singleton, 820 Orange St., New Haven, CT. Grade IV.

_____ *Three Madrigals*, trans. Upchurch. San Antonio, TX: Southern Music Co., 1965. Grade IV.

°Glasel, John (arr.). *16th Century Carmina*. New York: Sam Fox Publishing Co., 1959. Review: *BQ* IV/4 (Summer, 1961), 173. *BW* I-IV (1965-68), 202. *INST* XIV/9 (May, 1960), 80. Grade IV.

Goldberg, William. *Tower Music* (1969). Composers MS. 11 Fifth Ave., Northport, NY. Grade V.

Grant, Parks. *Lento and Allegro, Op. 49*. New York: Composers Facsimile Editions, 1954. Grade IV.

Gregson, Edward. *Quintet*. Melville, NY: Belwin-Mills Publishing Co.

Grep, Benedictus. *Paduana*, ed. King. North Easton, MA: Robert King Music Co. Grade III.

°Guami, Gioseppe. *Canzon XIX*. London: Musica Rara. Grade IV.

Guentzel, Gus. *La Fiesta*. Oskaloosa, IA: C.L. Barnhouse and Co.

Gustafson, Dwight. *Contrasts* (1966). Composers MS. Dept. of Music, Bob Jones Univ., Greenville, SC. Grade V.

°Haas, Eugene (trans.) *Two 16th Century Flemish Songs*. Delaware Water Gap, PA: Shawnee Press, 1964. Grade IV.

Haddad, Don. *Jazz Etude*. San Antonio, TX: Southern Music Co., 1969. Review: *INST* XXV/4 (November, 1970), 74. Grade IV.

_____ *Quintet* (1956). Composers MS. Dept. of Music, West Texas College, Canyon, TX. Grade IV.

Haines, Edmund. *Sonata*. North Easton, MA: Robert King Music Co., 1969. Grade IV.

_____ *Toccata*. North Easton, MA: Robert King Music Co., 1949. Annotation: Shoemaker, p. 91. Review: *BQ* I/4 (June, 1958), 164. Grade V.

Hamilton, Iain. *Quintet*. New York: Associated Music Publishers, Inc.

Hammond, Don. *Quintet*. New York: Sam Fox Publishing Co., n.d. Grade VI.

°Handel, George F. *Handel for Brass*, arr. Knight. New York: Sam Fox Publishing Co. Grade IV.

_____ *Largo*, trans. Sudmeier. Massapequa, NY: Cor Publishing Co., n.d. Grade IV.

_____ *Overture to Berenice*, trans. Glick. North Easton, MA: Robert King Music Co., n.d. Grade III.

_____ *Overture to Solomon*. New York: Atlantic Music Supply. Grade III.

_____ *Second Suite*, arr. Lockwood. New York: Autograph Editions, 1971. Grade IV.

Harder, Paul. *Quintet* (1958). Composers MS. Dept. of Music, Michigan State Univ., East Lansing, MI. Grade V.

Harris, Arthur. *Four Moods*. New York: Sam Fox Publishing Co., 1960. Review: *BQ* IV/2 (Winter, 1960), 85. *BW* I-IV (1965-68), 195. *INST* XIV/9 (May, 1960), 80. Grade IV.

Hartley, Walter. *Divertissement*. Buffalo, NY: Ensemble Publications, 1966. Review: *INST* XXI/5 (December, 1966), 92. Grade IV.

°_____ *Orpheus, Madrigal*. Naperville, IL: FEMA Music Publishers, 1960. Grade IV.

_____ *Quintet*. Bryn Mawr, PA: Theodore Presser Co., 1963. Annotation: Shoemaker, p. 148. Review: *BQ* VII/3 (Spring, 1964), 140. Grade IV.

Haufrecht, Herbert. *Conversations*. New York: Pioneer Editions, n.d. Grade IV.

_____ *Suite*. New York: Associated Music Publishers, Inc., 1965. Grade IV.

Haussman, Valentin. *Paduane mit galiarde*. Montreal: Montreal Music Supply, n.d. Grade III.

_____ *Partita*, trans. Singleton. Ken Singleton, 820 Orange St., New Haven, CT. Grade III.

_____ *Two Pieces*, trans. Singleton. Ken Singleton, 820 Orange St., New Haven, CT. Grade III.

Haydn, Joseph. *Divertimento in A♭*, arr. Sabatini. Massapequa, NY: Cor Publishing Co., 1964. Grade IV.

Heiden, Bernard. *Four Dances*. New York: A. Broude, Inc., 1968. Review: *MT* 110/1519 (September, 1969), 971. *NOTES* XXVI/1 (September, 1969), 144. Grade VI.

Hellerman, William. *Resonata* (1967). Composers MS. 90 Morningside Dr. 4J, New York, NY. Review: *BW* VI/2 (1971), 101. Grade V.

Henry, Otto. *Four Bantu Songs*. Composers MS. Dept. of Music, East Carolina Univ., Greenville, NC. Grade IV.

Hensel, Richard. *Quintet* (1966). Composers MS. Dept. of Music., Eastern Kentucky Univ., Richmond, KY. Grade II.

Hodkinson, Sydney. *Mosaic* (1964). Composers MS. Dept. of Music, Univ. of Michigan, Ann Arbor, MI. Grade V.

Hogg, Merle. *Invention*. New York: Autograph Editions.

Holborne, Anthony. *Five Pieces*, ed. King. North Easton, MA: Robert King Music Co., 1961. Review: *INST* XVI/1 (September, 1961), 94. Grade III.

°_____ *Music for Brass*. Volume I and II. London: Musica Rara, 1971. Review: *MT* (March, 1972), 291. Grade IV.

_____ *Suite*, arr. Dart and Siebert. Melville, NY: Belwin-Mills Music Co. Review: *INST* XVII/4 (December, 1962), 45. *NOTES* XXI/1-2 (1963-64), 256. Grade IV.

_____ *Three Pieces*, arr. Glasel. New York: Sam Fox Publishing Co., 1960. Review: *BQ* IV/2 (Winter, 1960), 84. *INST* XIV/9 (May, 1960), 80. Grade III.

_____ *Two Pieces*, ed. King. North Easton, MA: Robert King Music Co. Grade IV.

Homboe, Vagn. *Quintet*. Copenhagen: Wilhelm Hansen, 1965. Review: *MT* 108/1498 (December, 1967), 1138. Grade V.

Holt, Simeon. *Scenario X*. Amsterdam: Donemus, 1970. Grade VI.

Homzy, Andrew. *Sonatina*. New York: Atlantic Music Supply, 1973. Grade IV.

Horowitz, Joseph. *Music Hall Suite*. Melville, NY: Belwin-Mills Publishing Corp., 1964. Review: *MT* 108/1498 (December, 1967), 1138. Grade IV.

Horvit, Michael. *Quintet* (1970). Composers MS. 8114 Braesdale Rd., Houston, TX. Grade V.

Hovhaness, Alan. *Six Dances*. New York: C.F. Peters, 1969. Grade IV.

_____ *Suite*. New York: C.F. Peters, 1969. Review: *INST* XXIV/6 (January, 1970), 92. Grade V.

Huggler, John. *Quintet*. New York: Sam Fox Publishing Co., 1963. Review: *BQ* VII/3 (Spring, 1964), 140. Grade V.

Hughes, Mark. *Divertimento* (1969). Composers MS (composer deceased). Brass Library, Georgia State Univ., Atlanta, GA. Grade V.

Husa, Karel. *Divertimento*, n.d. Composers MS. Dept. of Music, Cornell Univ., Ithaca, NY. Review: *BW* VI/2 (1971), 101. Grade IV.

Huse, Peter. *Studies in Plane* (1963). Composers MS. 217 Glendonwynne Rd., Toronto 4, Ontario, Canada.

Isaac, Heinrich. *Canzona and Lied*. Montreal: Montreal Music Supply, n.d. Grade III.

Jackson, David. *Appalachian Folksongs*, n.d. Composers MS. Dept. of Music, Cameron State College, Lawton, OK. Grade IV.

Jenkins, John. *Newark Siege*. New York: Atlantic Music Supply, 1973. Grade IV.

Jeune, Claude le. *Deba Contre mes Debateurs*. Montreal: Montreal Music Supply, n.d. Grade III.

Johnson, Clair. *Mood Militant*. Miami, FL: Rubank, Inc., 1941. Grade IV.

Jones, Collier. *Four Movements for Five Brass*. New York: Sam Fox Publishing Co., 1965. Review: *BW* I-IV (1965-68), 196. *INST* XX/8 (March, 1966), 100. Grade IV.

Kaplan, Nathan. *Fugue on Fugue*. Woodside, NY: Chappell and Co., 1972. Grade IV.

Kersters, Willem. *Three Rondos*. Op. 48. Brussels: CeBeDem, 1970. Grade IV.

Kessel, Johann. *Sonata*, ed. King. North Easton, MA: Robert King Music Co., n.d. Grade IV.

Keves, Nelson. *Hardinsburg Joys*. New York: Autograph Editions, 1966. Review: *BW* I-IV (1965-68), 196. Grade II.

Kjell, Roikjer. *Scherzo, Op. 58*. Copenhagen: Wilhelm Hansen, 1971. Review: *MO* 95/1139 (August, 1972), 577. *MT* (November, 1972), 1114. Grade V.

Klerk, Albert de. *Preambule*. Philadelphia: Henri Elkan Music Publisher.

Knight, Morris. *Quintet No. 1* (1965). Composers MS. Dept. of Music, Ball State Univ., Muncie, IN. Grade V.

_____ *Quintet No. 2* (1968). Composers MS. Dept. of Music, Ball State Univ., Muncie, IN. Grade VI.

_____ *Quintet No. 3* (1969). Composers MS. Dept. of Music, Ball State Univ., Muncie, IN. Grade VI.

Knox, Charles. *Music*. New York: Composers Facsimile Edition, 1969. Grade V.

Korn, Peter. *Prelude and Scherzo*. Oceanside, NY: Boosey and Hawkes, 1967. Review: *INST* XXII/11 (June, 1968), 81. *NOTES* XXVI/1 (September, 1969), 144. Grade V.

Korte, Karl. *Introductions*. Philadelphia: Elkan-Vogel Co., 1968. Review: *INST* XXIII/8 (March, 1969), 115. *NOTES* XXVI/1 (September, 1969), 144. Grade V.

Kreisler, Alexander. *Andante and Allegro*. San Antonio, TX: Southern Music Co., 1968. Review: *NACWPI* XVII/4 (Summer, 1969), 36. Grade II.

_____ *Prelude*. San Antonio, TX: Southern Music Co., 1968. Grade II.

Kroeger, Karl. *Partita*. Bryn Mawr, PA: Theodore Presser Co., 1969. Review: *INST* XXIII/10 (May, 1969), 90. Grade V.

Kupferman, Meyer. *Quintet*. Boston: Frank Music Corp., 1971.

Lamb, Joseph. *Prairie Suite*. Delaware Water Gap, PA: Shawnee Press.

°Lanier, Nicolas. *Almande and Sarabande*, arr. Osborne. North Easton, MA: Robert King Music Co., 1961. Review: *INST* XVI/2 (October, 1961), 63. Grade III.

Lantz, Jack. *Quintet*. Delaware Water Gap, PA: Shawnee Press, 1972. Review: *INST* XXVII/10 (May, 1973), 78. Grade VI.

Lassus, Orlando. *Motet*. Montreal: Montreal Music Supply, n.d. Grade III.

Law, Andrew; Hewitt, James; and Billings, William. *Three New England Hymns*. North Easton, MA: Robert King Music Co., n.d. Grade II.

Lebow, Leonard. *Popular Suite*. Kenosha, WI: G. Leblanc Co., 1963. Review: *INST* XIX/1 (August, 1964), 78. Grade IV.

Leclerc, Marcel. *Par Monta et Par Vaux*. Brussels: J. Maurer, 1959. Grade V.

Lee, William. *Mosaics*. Miami, FL: Charles F. Hansen Music Corp., 1969. Review: *NOTES* XXVIII/2 (December, 1971), 317. Grade IV.

_____ *Regimentation*. New York: Sam Fox Publishing Co., 1968. Grade IV.

LeGrady, Thomas. *Divertimento*. Montreal: Montreal Music Supply, 1966. Review: *BW* I-IV (1965-68), 298. Grade V.

Suite. Montreal: Montreal Music Supply, 1963. Review: *BW I-IV* (1965-68), 298. *BWQ I/1-2* (Winter, 1966-67), 66. Grade IV.

Levin, Gregory. *Five Picasso Portraits* (1971). Composers MS. Dept. of Music, Syracuse Univ., Syracuse, NY. Grade V.

Levy, Frank. *Fanfare.* Massapequa, NY: Cor Publishing Co. Grade III.

———. *Quintet.* New York: Okra Music.

Lewis, Robert. *Music* (1966). Composers MS. Peabody Conservatory of Music, 1 East Mt. Vernon Place, Baltimore, MD. Grade VI.

Lindenfield, Harris. *Tritogenea,* n.d. Composers MS. Miller School Post Office, Charlottesville, VA. Grade V.

Locke, Matthew. *Music for His Majesty's Sackbuts and Cornetts,* trans. Baines. Massapequa, NY: Cor Publishing Co., n.d. Grade III.

Loechel, Alfred. *Weihnachtlicke Turmmusik.* Melville, NY: Belwin-Mills Publishing Corp., 1965. Grade IV.

Logan, Wendell. *Music for Brasses,* n.d. Composers MS. Dept. of Music, Western Illinois Univ., Macomb, IL. Grade V.

Lully, Jean B. *Overture to Cadmus et Hermione,* trans. King. North Easton, MA: Robert King Music Co., 1960. Grade IV.

Lunde, Ivar. *Suite* (1971). Composers MS. 3443 Riley St., Eau Claire, WI. Grade V.

Lupo, Thomas. *Fantasia.* New York: Atlantic Music Supply, 1973. Grade IV.

McCabe, John. *Rounds.* London: Novello and Co., 1969. Review: *MT 110/1519* (September, 1969), 971. Grade V.

McDaniel, William. *Quintet* (1966). Composers MS. 221 S.E. Second St., Walnut Ridge, AR. Grade IV.

McGregor, Rob Roy. *Christmas Music.* New York: Autograph Editions, 1972. Grade III.

———. *Christmas Service.* New York: Autograph Editions, 1971. Grade III.

———. *Pentahedron.* New York: Autograph Editions, 1972.

McKay, George. *Sonatina Expressiva.* San Antonio, TX: Southern Music Co., 1966. Grade IV.

McKie, Jack. *Andanta.* Buffalo, NY: Ensemble Publications, 1966. Review: *INST XXI/5* (December, 1966), 92. Grade IV.

———. *Theme for a Carousel.* Buffalo, NY: Ensemble Publications, 1966. Review: *INST XXI/5* (December, 1966), 92. Grade III.

———. *Waltz.* Buffalo, NY: Ensemble Publications, 1966. Review: *INST XXI/5* (December, 1966), 92. Grade III.

McLean, Hamilton. *Sonatina.* New York: Composers Autograph Publications, 1972. Review: *INST XXVII/10* (May, 1973), 76. Grade IV.

°Maes, Jef. *Prelude et Allegro.* Philadelphia: Henri Elkan Music Publisher, 1963. Review: *BQ VII/3* (Spring, 1964), 142. Grade V.

Marek, Robert. *Quintet* (1960). Composers MS. Dept. of Music, Univ. of South Dakota, Vermillion, SD. Grade V.

Marenzio, Luca. *La Bella.* Montreal: Montreal Music Supply, n.d. Grade III.

———. *Solo e Pensoso.* Montreal: Montreal Music Supply, n.d. Grade III.

Maschera, Florentio. *Ganzona.* New York: Autograph Editions, 1971. Grade III.

Maurer, Ludwig. *Four Songs.* New York: Sam Fox Publishing Co., 1967. Review: *INST XXI/8* (March, 1967), 99. Grade IV.

———. *Scherzo and Lied.* New York: Sam Fox Publishing Co., 1961. Review: *BQ VI/4* (Summer, 1963), 195. *INST XV/10* (June, 1961), 64. Grade III.

———. *Three Pieces.* New York: Sam Fox Publishing Co., 1960. *BQ VI/4* (Summer, 1963), 195. *INST XIV/9* (May, 1960), 80. Grade IV.

Mayer, William. *Quintet.* Philadelphia: Elkan-Vogel Co., 1964. Grade V.

Melillo, Peter. *Two Divers Pieces* (1968). Composers MS. 75 Bruce Ave., Yonkers, NY. Grade V.

Mendelssohn, Felix. *Andante Tranquillo,* arr. Moore. Los Angeles: Western International Music. Grade III.

———. "Wedding March" from *Midsummer Night's Dream,* arr. Waldeck. Massapequa, NY: Cor Publishing Co., n.d. Grade IV.

Merula, Tarquino. *Canzon La Strada.* Montreal: Montreal Music Supply, 1966. Review: *BW I-IV* (1965-68), 299. Grade III.

°Merulo, Claudio. *Canzonas 18, 23, 36.* London: Musica Rara. Grade IV.

Miller, Edward. *The Folly Stone.* New York: Composers Facsimile Editions, n.d. Grade VI.

Mills, Charles. *Quintet in Three Movements.* New York: American Composers Alliance.

Monteverdi, Claudio. *Qual 'augellin che canta si dolcemente* and *O Rosetta,* arr. Baxter. New York: Autograph Editions, 1972. Grade IV.

°———. *Sinfonia,* arr. Townsend. Melville, NY: Belwin-Mills Publishing Corp., 1968. Review: *INST XXVII/10* (May, 1973), 76. Grade IV.

Moore, Charles. *Quintet* (1961). Composers MS. Dept of Music, Concordia College, Moorehead, MN. Grade V.

Moross, Jerome. *Sonatina.* Woodside, NY: Chappell and Co., 1969. Review: *INST XXIV/10* (May, 1970), 84. *NOTES XXVIII /1* (September, 1971), 122. Grade IV.

Morel, Francois. *Quintette.* Montreal: Montreal Music Supply, 1967. Grade VI.

Moss, Lawrence. *Music for Five.* Bryn Mawr, PA: Merion Music, 1965. Review: *BW I-IV* (1965-68), 196. *BWQ I/1-2* (Winter, 1966-67), 59. Grade IV.

Mott, David. *Elements II* (1972). Composers MS. 1631 Chapel St., New Haven, CT. Grade VI.

Mouret, Jean. *Rondeau,* ed. King. North Easton, MA: Robert King Music Co., 1972. Grade IV.

Mozart, Wolfgang, A. *Church Sonata No. 6,* arr. Lockwood. New York: Autograph Editions, 1971. Grade IV.

———. *Divertimento, K. 136.* arr. Homzy. New York: Auto Publications, 1971. Grade IV.

———. *Quintet No. 8, K. 614,* arr. Lockwood. New York: Autopress Publications, 1971. Grade IV.

———. *Salzburg Sinfonia, K. 136* (first movement), arr. Lockwood. New York: Autograph Editions, 1971. Grade V.

Nagel, Robert. *This Old Man March.* New York: Sam Fox Publishing Co., 1960. Review: *INST XIV/9* (May, 1960), 77. Grade III.

Nash, Richard. *Impressions.* Hollywood, CA: Dick Noel Enterprises.

———. *Impressions for Tuba.* Hollywood, CA: Dick Noel Enterprises.

Nelhybel, Vaclav. *Quintet No. 1.* New York: General Music Publishing Co., 1968. Review: *INST XXIII/4* (November, 1968), 93. Grade V.

———. *Quintet No. 2.* New York: General Music Publishing Co., 1970. Review: *INST XXV/5* (December, 1970), 69. Grade VI.

°Nenna, Pomponio. *Apri Il Sen Alle Fiamme,* arr. Eichman. San Antonio, TX: Southern Music Co., 1971. Review: *INST XXVI/8* (March, 1972), 92. Grade IV.

°———. *Dolce Mio Voce Ardente,* arr. Eichman. San Antonio, TX: Southern Music Co., 1971. Review: *INST XXVI/8* (March, 1972), 92. Grade IV.

°———. *Ecco La Mia Dolce Pena,* arr. Eichman. San Antonio, TX: Southern Music Co., 1971. Review: *INST XXVI/8* (March, 1972), 92. Grade IV.

°———. *Itene O Miei Sospir,* arr. Eichman. San Antonio, TX: Southern Music Co., 1971. Review: *INST XXVI/8* (March, 1972), 92. Grade IV.

°———. *Occhi miei che Vedeste,* arr. Eichman. San Antonio, TX: Southern Music Co., 1971. Review: *INST XXVII/6* (January, 1973), 70. Grade III.

O'Reilly, John. *Metropolitan Quintet.* Composers MS. 29 Murray Place, Merrick, NY.

Orologio, Alexander. *Intrada Nos. 1-4.* Montreal: Montreal Music Supply, n.d. Grade II.

Orr, Buxton. *Divertimento.* London: Novello and Co., 1972. Review: *MO* (November, 1972), 77. *MT* (November, 1972), 1114. Grade V.

Ostransky, Leroy. *Character Variations on a Modal Theme.* Miami, FL: Rubank, Inc., 1959. Review: *INST XIV/5* (January, 1960), 74. Grade III.

Ott, Joseph. *Toccata.* Milton Junction, WI: Claude Benny Press, 1969. Grade V.

Palestrina, Giovanni. *Agnus Dei,* arr. Waldeck. Massapequa, NY: Cor Publishing Co. Grade III.

———. *Alleluia Tulerant,* arr. Volkmann. St Louis: Concordia Publishing House. Grade III.

°———. *Laudate Dominum,* arr. Volkmann. St. Louis: Concordia Publishing House. Grade III.

Papineau-Couture, Jean. *Canons.* Montreal: Montreal Music Supply, 1964. Grade V.

Parris, Robert. *Sinfonia.* New York: Composers Facsimile Editions.

Payne, Frank. *Quintet.* Cleveland: Composers Autograph Publications, 1968.

Pegram, Wayne. *A Short Suite,* n.d. Composers MS. Box 27A, Tennessee Tech Univ., Cookeville, TN. Grade IV.

Pellegrini, Ernesto. *Five Miniatures* (1969). Composers MS. 1143 Glade Hill Drive, Rt. 15, Knoxville, TN. Grade V.

Persichetti, Vincent. *Parable.* Bryn Mawr, PA: Theodore Presser Co.

Peruti, Carl. *Quintet* (1971). Composers MS. 1218 Hollywood Ave., Plainfield, NY. Grade IV.

Pezel, Johann. *Allemande and Courante,* arr. Sear. Massapequa, NY: Cor Publishing Co. Grade III.

———. *Bal and Sarabande,* arr. Sear. Massapequa, NY: Cor Publishing Co. Grade III.

°———. *Hora Decima.* Volumes I and II. London: Musica Rara, 1967. Grade IV.

———. *Intrada,* arr. Sear. Massapequa, NY: Cor Publishing Co. Grade III.

———. *Five Part Brass Music,* ed. Lumsden. Vol. I-III. London: Musica Rara, 1960. Review: *INST XV/6* (February, 1961), 63. *NOTES XIX/1* (December, 1961), 141. *GSJ XIV* (March, 1961), 98. Grade IV.

———. *Fünfsstimmige blasende Musik* (1685), ed. Schlegel. New York: C.F. Peters, n.d. Grade IV.

———. *Six Pieces,* ed. King. North Easton, MA: Robert King Music Co., 1955. Grade IV.

———. "Sonata No. 1" from *Hora Decima,* ed. King. North Easton, MA: Robert King Music Co., 1955. Grade III.

———. "Sonata No. 2" from *Hora Decima,* ed. King. North Easton, MA: Robert King Music Co., 1955. Grade III.

———. "Sonata No. 3" from *Hora Decima,* ed. King. North Easton, MA: Robert King Music Co., 1958. Grade IV.

———. "Sonata No. 5" from *Hora Decima,* arr. Baron and Menken. Oceanside, NY: Boosey and Hawkes, 1959. Review: *BQ III/1* (Fall, 1959), 32. *NOTES XVII/2*

(March, 1960), 307. Grade IV.

———. "Sonata No. 12" from *Hora Decima.* Melville, NY: Belwin-Mills Publishing Corp., 1959. Review: *BQ* III/3 (Spring, 1960), 120. Grade IV.

———. "Sonata No. 14" from *Hora Decima,* arr. Waldeck. Massapequa, NY: Cor Publishing Co. Grade III.

———. "Sonata No. 22" from *Hora Decima,* ed. King. North Easton, MA: Robert King Music Co. Review: *NOTES* XIV/4 (September, 1957), 618. Grade IV.

———. "Sonata No. 25" from *Hora Decima,* ed. King. North Easton, MA: Robert King Music Co. Review: *INST* XVII/2 (October, 1962), 88. Grade III.

———. "Sonata No. 27" from *Hora Decima,* arr. Brown. Miami, FL: Rubank, Inc., 1958. Review: *BQ* II/1 (September, 1958), 37. Grade IV.

———. "Sonata No. 28" from *Hora Decima,* arr. Greenberg. Melville, NY: Belwin-Mills Publishing Corp., 1948. Review: *BQ* I/3 (March, 1958), 187. Grade IV.

———. *Sixteen Dances,* arr. Miller. Buffalo, NY: Ensemble Publications, n.d. Grade IV.

———. *Suite de Danses.* Brussels: J. Maurer, n.d. Grade IV.

° ———. *Suite of Dances,* arr. Romm and Sirinek. Los Angeles: Western International Music. Grade IV.

———. *Three Pieces,* ed. King. North Easton, MA: Robert King Music Co., 1960. Grade IV.

———. *Turmmusik,* ed. Meyer. Leipzig: Breitkopf and Härtel Verlag, 1930. Grade IV.

° ———. *Twelve Sonatas,* arr. Miller. Buffalo, NY: Ensemble Publications. Grade IV.

———. *Two Pieces,* ed. King. North Easton, MA: Robert King Music Co., n.d. Grade III.

Pills, Karl. *Scherzo.* North Easton, MA: Robert King Music Co., 1972.

———. *Serenade.* Vienna: Verlag Doblinger, 1971.

Poglietti, Alessandro. *Ricercare,* arr. Hilfinger. Delevan, NY: Kendor Music, 1971. Grade IV.

Polin, Claire. *Cader Idris.* New York: G. Schirmer, 1971. Review: *INST* XXVI/10 (May, 1972), 78. *MT* (November, 1971), 1114. Grade VI.

Posch, Isaac. *Centone No. VIII,* arr. Reynolds. San Antonio, TX: Southern Music Co., 1973. Review: *INST* XXVII/11 (June, 1973), 68. Grade IV.

Praetorius, Michael. *Lo, How a Rose e'er Blooming,* arr. Uber. Charlotte, NC: Brodt Music Co., 1967. Grade III.

Presser, William. *Quintet.* New York: Autograph Editions, 1966. *BWQ* I/1-2 (Winter, 1966-67), 57. *INST* XXI/9 (April, 1967), 123. Grade V.

———. *Second Quintet.* Bryn Mawr, PA: Theodore Presser Co., 1968. Review: *NACWPI* XVIII/2 (Winter, 1969-70), 26. Grade V.

Prevost, Andre. *Mouvement.* Montreal: Montreal Music Supply, 1966. Grade VI.

° Purcell, Henry. *A Purcell Suite,* arr. Benoy. Fairlawn, NJ: Oxford University Press. Grade IV.

———. *A Purcell Suite,* arr. Lockwood. New York: Autograph Editions, 1971. Grade V.

———. *Fantasia Upon One Note,* arr. Sear. Massapequa, NY: Cor Publishing Co. Grade III.

———. *Four Part Fantasy No. 5,* arr. Sear. Massapequa, NY: Cor Publishing Co. Grade III.

———. *Four Part Fantasy No 8,* arr. Sear. Massapequa, NY: Cor Publishing Co. Grade III.

———. *Music for Queen Mary II,* ed. King. North Easton, MA: Robert King Music Co., 1956. Grade II.

———. *Suite from Bonduca,* arr. Masso. Westbury, NY: Pro Art Publications. Grade IV.

———. "Trumpet Overture" from *Indian Queen* (Act III), arr. Sear. Massapequa, NY: Cor Publishing Co. Grade IV.

———. *Trumpet Voluntary,* trans. Corley. North Easton, MA: Robert King Music Co., 1955. Grade III.

———. *Voluntary on Old 100th,* trans. Corley. North Easton, MA: Robert King Music Co., 1957. Grade IV.

Purdey, Winston. *Music for Brass.* Montreal: Montreal Music Supply, 1963. Review: *BW* I-IV (1965-68), 117. *BWQ* I/1-2 (Winter, 1966-67), 66. Grade IV.

Raph, Alan. *Call and Response.* New York: Edition Musicus.

° Rathouse, Karol. *Tower Music.* New York: Associated Music Publishers, 1960. Review: *INST* XV/6 (February, 1961), 64. Grade IV.

° Rebner, Wolfgang. *Variations.* Munich: Edition Modern, 1962. Grade IV.

Reed, Alfred. *Variations on L.B.I.F.D.* Miami, FL: Univ. of Miami Music Publications. Review: *INST* XXIV/10 (May, 1970), 84. Grade IV.

Reiche, Gottfried. *Baroque Suite,* trans. Fromme. New York: Associated Music Publishers, 1968. Review: *BW* I/1 (1970), 10. *INST* XXIII/10 (May, 1969), 89. Grade IV.

———. *Sonatina I,* arr. Homzy. New York: Autopress Publications, 1971. Grade IV.

° Reif, Paul *Quintet.* New York: Okra Music.

Reynolds, Verne (ed.). *Centone No. 1.* San Antonio, TX: Southern Music Co., n.d. Review: *NACWPI* XVIII/1 (Fall, 1969), 24. Grade IV.

——— (ed.). *Centone No. 8.* San Antonio, TX: Southern Music Co., 1972. Grade V.

———. *Quintet.* New York: MCA Music Corp., Grade V.

———. *Suite.* New York: MCA Music Corp., 1971. Review: *BW* VII/1 (1972), 10. *NOTES* XXIX/2 (December, 1972), 325. Grade VI.

Riddle, Nelson. *Five Pieces for Bass Trombone.* Hollywood, CA: Dick Noel Enterprises.

———. *Museum Piece.* Hollywood, CA: Dick Noel Enterprises.

———. *Three-Quarter Suite.* New York: MCA Music Corp., 1966. Grade IV.

° Rieti, Vittorio. *Incissioni (Engraving).* New York: General Music Publishing Co., 1969. Grade V.

Riley, James. *Etudes,* n.d. Composers MS. Dept. of Music, Wichita State Univ., Wichita, KS. Grade V.

Roberts, Wilfred. *Dixie.* Massapequa, NY: Cor Publishing Co., 1961. Grade III.

———. *Three Headlines.* Massapequa, NY: Cor Publishing Co., 1960. Review: *BQ* IV/4 (Summer, 1961), 175. Grade III.

Rolle, Wilfred. *Quintet No. 1.* Miami, FL: Rubank, Inc., 1938. Grade III.

———. *Quintet No. 6.* Miami, FL: Rubank, Inc., 1938. Grade II.

Rosenmuller, John. *Courante, Sarabande and Bal,* arr. Waldeck. Massapequa, NY: Cor Publishing Co. Grade IV.

———. *Intrada,* arr. Waldeck. Massapequa, NY: Cor Publishing Co. Grade III.

———. *Sinfonia,* arr. Waldeck. Massapequa, NY: Cor Publishing Co. Grade III.

Rosenthal, Irving. *Little Brown Jug.* Los Angeles: Western International Music, 1965. Grade IV.

——— (arr.) *Three Renaissance Madrigals.* Los Angeles: Western International Music, 1968. Grade IV.

Rossi, Salamon. *Three Pieces,* arr. Lockwood. New York: Autograph Editions, 1971. Grade III.

Sabatini, Guglielmo. *Epigram.* Massapequa, NY: Cor Publishing Co., 1967. Grade IV.

———. *Fugue in the Ancient Manner.* Massa-

pequa, NY: Cor Publishing Co. Grade IV.

———. *Homage to Bach.* Massapequa, NY: Cor Publishing Co., Grade III.

———. *Music for Curly.* Massapequa, NY: Cor Publishing Co., 1965. Grade IV.

———. *Puppet Waltz.* Massapequa, NY: Cor Publishing Co. Grade III.

———. *Three-Four for Five Brass.* Massapequa, NY: Cor Publishing Co. Grade V.

Saint-Saëns, Camille. *March Militaire Francaise,* arr. Sear. Massapequa, NY: Cor Publishing Co. Grade IV.

° Sanders, Robert. *Quintet.* Bryn Mawr, PA: Theodore Presser Co., 1948. Annotation: Shoemaker, p. 159. Review: *BQ* I/4 (June, 1958), 229. Grade V.

Sauguet, Henri. *Golden Suite.* Paris: Editions Musicales Transatlantiques, n.d

Scarlatti, Domenico. *Aria and Minuet,* arr. Johnson. Miami, FL: Rubank, Inc., 1961. Review: *INST* XV/9 (May, 1961), 72. Grade II.

° Scheidt, Samuel. *Canzon Bergamasca,* ed. Fromme. New York: Associated Music Publishers. Grade IV.

———. *Canzon Bergamasca,* arr. de Jong. Buffalo, NY: Ensemble Publications, 1966. Review: *INST* XXI/5 (December, 1966), 92. *INST* XXV/5 (December, 1970), 68. Grade IV.

———. *Canzon Super Intradem Aechiopicam.* Montreal: Montreal Music Supply, 1972. Grade IV.

———. *Centone No. 5,* trans. Reynolds. San Antonio, TX: Southern Music Co. Review: *INST* XXV/7 (February, 1971), 73. Grade IV.

———. *Suite,* arr. Green. Bryn Mawr, PA: Theodore Presser Co., 1964. Review: *BW* I-IV (1965-68), 197. *INST* XIX/9 (April, 1965), 113. Grade III.

Schein, Johann. *Centone No. VII.* San Antonio, TX: Southern Music Co. Review: *NACWPI* XX/3 (Spring, 1972), 37. Grade V.

———. *Die mit Tränen säen,* arr. Baxter. New York: Autograph Editions, 1972. Grade IV.

———. *Intrada,* arr. Sear. Massapequa, NY: Cor Publishing Co. Grade III.

———. *Suite,* ed. Magannini. New York: Edition Musicus, n.d. Grade IV.

———. *Two Pieces,* ed. King. North Easton, MA: Robert King Music Co. Grade IV.

Schmelzer, Johann. *Sonata XII,* ed. Stine. Chicago: Crown Music Press. Grade IV.

Schmidt, William. *Seven Variations on a Hexachord.* Los Angeles: Western International Music. Grade IV.

———. *Suite No. 1.* Los Angeles: Western International Music, 1967. Grade IV.

———. *Suite No. 2.* Los Angeles: Western International Music. Grade IV.

———. *Suite No. 3.* Los Angeles: Western International Music. Grade V.

———. *Variations on a Negro Folksong.* Los Angeles: Western International Music, 1959. Review: *BQ* III/2 (Winter, 1959), 85. *INST* XIV/1 (September, 1959), 114. Grade III.

° Schmutz, Albert. *Prelude and Gavotte.* Chicago: H.T. Fitzsimons Co., 1938. Grade IV.

———. *Rondo in F.* Chicago: H.T. Fitzsimons Co., 1938. Grade IV.

Schubert, Franz. *Last Waltz,* arr. Cafarella. Pittsburgh, PA: Volkwein Brothers, Inc. Grade II.

Schuller, Gunther. *Music.* New York: Associated Music Publishers, 1962. Annotation: Shoemaker, p. 164. Review: *BQ* VII/3 (Spring, 1964), 139. *INST* XVII/5 (January, 1963), 83. Grade VI.

Schumann, Robert. *Song, Chorale and March,* arr. Nagel. New York: Sam Fox Publishing Co., 1963. Review: *INST* XVIII/2 (September, 1963), 70. Grade II.

———. *Two Kinderszenen,* arr. Williams. San Antonio, TX: Southern Music Co., 1965. Grade IV.

Schwartz, Elliot. *Three Movements* (1963).

Composers MS. Dept. of Music, Bowdoin College, Brunswick, ME. Grade V.

Sear, Walter. *Two Inventions.* Massapequa, NY: Cor Publishing Co., 1965. Grade III.

Sebesky, Gerald. *Quintet No. 2* (1969). Composers MS. 584 Jacques St., Perth Amboy, NJ. Grade V.

Shelsta, Scott. *Closeness, and Other Related Things,* n.d. Composers MS. Box 1780, Augustana College, Sioux Falls, SD. Grade VI.

Shinn, Robert. *Serenade.* North Easton, MA: Robert King Music Co.

Shostakovich, Dmitri. "Satirical Dance" from *The Bolt,* arr. Raph. New York: Edition Musicus, 1968. Grade IV.

Sieg, Jerry. *Quintet* (1970). Composers MS. Dept of Music, Cumberland College, Williamsburg, KY. Grade V.

Siegner, Edward. *Invention in Brass.* Montreal: Montreal Music Supply, n.d. Grade V.

Simmes, William. *Centone No. IV,* trans. Reynolds. San Antonio, TX: Southern Music Co., 1970. Review: *INST* XXV/9 (April, 1971), 78. Grade V.

———. *Fantasia.* Montreal: Montreal Music Supply, n.d. Grade III.

Simon, Anton. *Quintet in Three Movements,* arr. Sear. Massapequa, NY: Cor Publishing Co. Grade III.

———. *Quintet, Op. 26, #2,* arr. Wilson. East Rutherford, NJ: Warner Brothers Music.

Simpson, Thomas. *Theme and Variations,* arr. Waldeck. Massapequa, NY: Cor Publishing Co.

Van Slyck, Nicholas. *Passamezzo Antico.* San Antonio, TX: Southern Music Co., 1972. Review: *INST* XXVII/10 (May, 1973), 77. Grade IV.

Snyder, Randall. *Variations on a Folk Theme.* New York: Sam Fox Publishing Co., 1968. Review: *INST* XXIII/11 (June, 1969), 89. Grade V.

Sousa, John. *Semper Fidelis,* arr. Baron and Menken. Oceanside, NY: Boosey and Hawkes, 1959. Grade III.

Spears, Jared. *Four Miniatures.* Bryn Mawr, PA: Theodore Presser Co., 1968. Review: *INST* XXIII/5 (December, 1968), 85. *NACWPI* XVIII/3 (Spring, 1970), 27. *NOTES* XXVI/2 (December, 1969), 358. Grade V.

°Speer, Daniel. *Two Sonatas.* Buffalo, NY: Ensemble Publications, 1964. Grade IV.

Spirea, Andre. *Music.* Melville, NY: Belwin-Mills Publishing Co., 1962. Review: *BW* I-IV (1965-68), 198. *INST* XVII/5 (January, 1963), 82. Grade IV.

Steinquest, Eugene. *Suite,* n.d. Composers MS. Dept. of Music, Tennessee Tech Univ., Cookesville, TN. Grade V.

Stewart, Robert. *Canzona and Ricercare.* New York: Composers Facsimile Editions.

———. *Quintet No. 2.* New York: Composers Facsimile Editions, 1967. Grade VI.

———. *Three Pieces for American Brass Quintet.* New York: Pioneer Editions, 1963. Grade VI.

Strandberg, Newton. *Music* (1966). Composers MS. Dept. of Music, Sam Houston State Univ., Huntsville, TX. Grade V.

Stratton, Donald. *Five Solo Pieces* (1964). Composers MS. Dept. of Music, Univ. of Maine, Orono, ME. Grade V.

———. *Variations on Henry VIII Theme.* Massapequa, NY: Cor Publishing Co., 1965. Grade IV.

Strauss, Joseph. *Tritsch Trasch Polka,* arr. Ligotti. Massapequa, NY: Cor Publishing Co. Grade IV.

Stroud, Richard. *The Brass Ring, Quintets 1-4,* n.d. Cleveland: Composers Autograph Publications. Review: *BW* VII/2 (1972), 109. Grade IV.

Stuessy, Joe. *Suite* (1967). Composers MS. 2028 Fordham Lane, Denton, TX. Grade V.

Sudmeier, William. *Fanfares for Brass.* Massapequa, NY: Cor Publishing Co. Grade IV.

Susato, Tilman. *Three Dances,* ed. King.

North Easton, MA: Robert King Music Co. Grade II.

Svoboda, Thomas. *Chorale and Dance.* New York: Franco Colombo, Inc., 1967.

Swanson, Howard. *Soundpiece.* New York: Weintraub Music Co., 1953. Review: *BQ* I/4 (June, 1958), 230. Grade IV.

Sydeman, William. *Quintet.* New York: Okra Music, 1967. Grade VI.

Szentkiralyi, Andras. *Variations on a Theme by Bartok.* New York: Appleton Press, 1966.

Tanenbaum, Elias. *Structures.* New York: Composers Facsimile Editions.

Tcherepnin, Alexander. *Quintet, Op. 105.* New York: C.F. Peters.

Tschaikovsky, Peter I. "Neopolitan Dance" from *Swan Lake,* arr. Waldeck. Massapequa, NY: Cor Publishing Co. Grade III.

Thomas, Alan. *Partite* (1970). Composers MS. Dept. of Music, Florida State Univ., Tallahassee, FL. Grade V.

Tillis, Frederick. *Passacaglia.* New York: Composers Facsimile Editions.

———. *Quintet.* New York: Composers Facsimile Editions.

Trythall, Gil. *Quintet, Op. 12* (1965). Composers MS. Dept. of Music, George Peabody College, Nashville, TN. Grade V.

Tull, Fisher. *Coup de Brass.* Composers MS. Dept. of Music, Sam Houston State Univ., Huntsville, TX. Grade IV.

———. *Exhibition.* Los Angeles: Western International Music, 1964. Review: *BQ* VII/3 (Spring, 1964), 141. *BW* I-IV (1965-68), 112. *INST* XIX/1 (August, 1964), 78. Grade IV.

Turner, Robert. *Four Fragments.* New York: Southern Music Publishing Co., 1972.

Turok, Paul. *Quintet, Op. 33.* Composers MS. 170 West 74th St., New York, NY. Grade V.

Tuthill, Burnet. *5 Essays for Brass 5* (1969). Composers MS. 295 Buena Vista Place, Memphis, TN. Grade IV.

°Uber, David. *A Day at the Camptown Races.* New York: Edition Musicus, 1957. Grade IV.

———. *Advanced Quintet.* Melville, NY: Belwin-Mills Publishing Corp., 1960. Grade IV.

°———. *Adventures of a Tin Horn.* New York: Edition Musicus, 1962. Grade IV.

°———. *Build a Band March.* New York: Edition Musicus, 1957. Grade III.

———. *Chinese Legend.* New York: Charles Colin.

———. *Five Short Sketches for Brass Quintet, Op. 52.* Charlotte, NC: Brodt Music Co., 1971. Grade IV.

———. *Interludes* (1968). Composers MS. Dept. of Music, Trenton State College, Trenton, NJ. Grade IV.

———. *Streets of Laredo, Op. 60.* Buffalo, NY: Ensemble Publications, 1967. Review: *NOTES* XXVIII/1 (September, 1971), 122. Grade IV.

———. "Spirituals" from *The Power and The Glory* (1958). Composers MS. Dept. of Music, Trenton State College, Trenton, NJ. Grade IV.

Valcourt, Jean. *Pentaphonie.* Montreal: Montreal Music Supply, n.d. Grade VI.

Van de Vate, Nancy. *Short Suite.* Bryn Mawr, PA: Theodore Presser Co., 1972.

Vecchi, Orazio. *Salterello Detto Trivetta.* Delevan, NY: Kendor Music, 1973. Grade IV.

Verdi, Giuseppi. "Triumphal March" from *Aida,* arr. Brower. Massapequa, NY: Cor Publishing Co. Grade IV.

Vetessy, George. *Partita.* New York: Franco Colombo Inc., 1967.

Vicentino, Nicola. *Canzon da Sonor,* arr. Upchurch. Delevan, NY: Kendor Music, 1973. Grade III.

———. *La Bella,* arr. Upchurch. Delevan, NY: Kendor Music, 1973. Grade III.

Vivaldi, Antonio. "Fugue" from *Concerto Grosso in D Minor, Op. 3, #11,* arr. Baldwin. New York: Autograph Editions, 1971. Grade V.

Wagner, Richard. *Reformation Hymn,* trans. Reisman. Massapequa, NY: Cor Publishing Co., n.d. Grade II.

Ward, John. *Fantasia,* arr. Baldwin. New York: Autograph Editions, 1971. Grade IV.

Ward-Steinman, David. *Quintet.* New York: Pioneer Editions.

Ware, John. *Quintet* (1966). Composers MS. Dept. of Music, Wisconsin State Univ., Superior, WI. Grade V.

Washburn, Robert. *Quintet.* Fairlawn, NJ: Oxford University Press, 1973. Grade V.

Weelkes, Thomas. *Centone No. VI,* trans. Reynolds. San Antonio, TX: Southern Music Co., 1970. Review: *INST* XXV/11 (June, 1971), 49. *NACWPI* XX/4 (Summer, 1972), 32. Grade IV.

Weille, Blair. *Quintet.* Massapequa, NY: Cor Publishing Co., 1958. Grade V.

———. *Suite.* Bryn Mawr, PA: Theodore Presser Co., 1969. Review: *INST* XXIV/9 (April, 1970), 87. Grade V.

Weiner, Stanley. *Suite.* Paris: Editions Billaudot, 1972. Grade V.

°Whear, Paul. *Invocation and Study.* North Easton, MA: Robert King Music Co., 1960. Review: *INST* XV/1 (September, 1960), 76. Grade III.

°Whittenberg, Charles. *Triptych.* New York: General Music Publishing Co., Inc.

Wigglesworth, Frank. *Conversations.* New York: Pioneer Editions.

———. *Quintet.* New York: American Composers Alliance, 1956.

Wilbye, John. *Two Madrigals,* arr. Baldwin. New York: Autograph Editions, 1971. Grade IV.

Wilder, Alec. *Quintet No. 2.* New York: Sam Fox Publishing Co., 1968. Review: *INST* XV/10 (June, 1961), 66. Grade V.

———. *Effie Joins the Carnival.* Massapequa, NY: Cor Publishing Co. Grade IV.

———. *Suite.* New York: Sam Fox Publishing Co., 1960. Grade V.

Williams, David. *Fanfare,* n.d. Composers MS. Eastman School of Music, Rochester, NY. Grade IV.

Wilson, David. *Tarentella.* New York: Autograph Editions, 1973.

Wilson, Donald. *Stabile II* (1965). New York: American Composers Alliance. Grade VI.

Yannatos, James. *Seven Episodes.* New York: Composers Facsimile Editions.

Young, Percy. *Music.* Montreal: Montreal Music Supply, 1963. Grade V.

°Zaninelli, Luigi. *Designs.* Delaware Water Gap, PA: Shawnee Press, 1963. Review: *BQ* VII/3 (Spring, 1964), 141. *INST* XVIII/1 (August, 1963), 77. Grade V.

Zindars, Earl. *Quintet.* North Easton, MA: Robert King Music Co., 1958. Annotation: Shoemaker, p. 170. Review: *BQ* II/3 (March, 1959), 129. *INST* XIII/6 (February, 1959), 66. Grade V.

———. *Tone Poem.* Massapequa, NY: Cor Publishing Co., 1965. Grade V.

Zuckert, Leon. *Psychedelic Suite* (1968). Composers MS. Canadian Music Centre, Toronto, Canada.

1974

Cadenzas

Christopher Leuba

Cadenzas present to the performer a challenge which is often unsuccessfully met, even by the professional. In an effort to aid the serious student in gaining insights into this problem, I have transcribed several examples of cadenzas for the Mozart Concerto No. 4 for Horn (K. 495), an especially problematic work in this regard. The transcriptions, made from 17 commercial recordings, are listed below. I would suggest that the reader listen to the actual recordings if possible, since subtle nuances are difficult to notate and the metric free-flow which is characteristic of most cadenzas can only be approximated.

The student should direct his attention to several questions which relate to the qualities of an effective cadenza.

1. A cadenza is intended to "show off" the performer. Does the cadenza do this effectively? Are there any tricks which are particularly well performed, such as rapid articulations, convincing register changes and variation of tonal sonority, appropriate use of hand stopping, effective trills, etc.? Are any of these effects unique to the individual player, or do they utilize techniques which all performers can negotiate, or at least aspire to? On the other hand, are there effects which the performer attempts unsuccessfully: trills awkwardly executed with poorly attached and unrhythmic resolutions, ugly sounding low register effects, etc.?

2. Does the cadenza utilize materials provided by the composer in the body of the concerto, or does it wander aimlessly through a series of etude-like routines, returning as if by accident to the concerto itself? There is, in fact a published cadenza "suitable for any Mozart Concerto" which is the archtype of the irrelevant cadenza.

3. Does the cadenza have a *forward motion*? By this term, I refer to a convincing harmonic progression which contains a strong rhythmic thrust. "Rhythmic thrust," that strong sense of ongoing rhythmic continuity, can easily be destroyed by too frequent use of holds and pauses. It seems to me that this is probably the most frequent shortcoming in cadenzas. Holds and pauses are most effective after really dramatic statements. Many of the banalities which are capped by a glorious hold often seem sadly out of place in the subtle interplay of a Mozart concerto.

The cadenza which Valerie Polekh plays in his performance of the Concerto by Reinhold Gliere[1] is an example of a remarkably strong cadenza by all three of the above criteria.

The use of cadenzas by other than the original composer is an accepted custom in the violin and piano repertoire. Beethoven provided a cadenza to Mozart's Piano Concerto in D, K. 466, which is preferred by the majority of performers today.

Naturally, when a well balanced cadenza, compositionally compatible with the style of the concerto, appears — whether composed by the performer or another composer — it will soon be adopted by many other performers. The "traditional" cadenza to the Mozart Concerto No. 3, K. 447, as played by Aubrey Brain[2] is an example of such a cadenza. It is brief, progresses logically through several ideas which are graceful on the instrument, and leads back to the body of the concerto with ease. Many performers use variants of this cadenza.

It was quite surprising to me, in transcribing these 17 cadenzas to the Mozart 4th, that there is so much variation in approach. However, the reasons are not difficult to understand. No one has yet come up with a classically proportioned vehicle which others can readily accept. From a purely technical standpoint, what Barry Tuckwell so effectively performs is likely to sound like fumbling under another's fingers. The problems also stem, in part, from the very nature of the thematic materials themselves: Mozart doesn't really "develop" them to any great extent, but rather depends upon the juxtaposition of one seemingly perfect idea against another, continuing on in a rather direct route. It would seem ludicrous to do *anything* to the lovely legato theme beginning at letter F. Even a partial reference to this theme is risky, as the theme's beauty lies essentially in the relationship of its parts, rather than its use as an elaboration of a germinal motive, as might have been the case in a Beethoven work.

It is my feeling that the student should be encouraged to write his own cadenza. First, he can avoid being obliged to try to do things for which he has no taste, or is not yet prepared. He will more likely incorporate ideas which uniquely exploit his own talent and abilities. Perhaps equally as important, the student, in trying to link up a sequence of ideas, can gain an unequalled opportunity to learn the "feel" and significance of harmonic modulation. If he finds himself in a bind, he can certainly look to his instrumental or theory teacher for aid in solving some of the harmonic problems encountered.

Also, in view of current compositional trends, it might be appropriate for the student to use this

---

1. This cadenza is recorded on the Classic Editions (CE 3001) label. It has also been published by International Music Publishers, New York.

2. RCA Victor (78 rpm) DM 829.

opportunity to explore such techniques as the electronic modification of the horn sonority, perhaps questionable in relationship to Mozart, but certainly not in regard to contemporary attitudes.

The 17 cadenzas have been transcribed from the following recordings of W.A. Mozart, Concerto No. 4 for Horn, K.495.

Barboteu, Georges. Monitor S 2118.
Blank, Kurt (RIAS/Ludwig, cond.). DGG Heliodor 478415.
Brain, Dennis (Halle Orchestra). Columbia ML 2088.
Brain, Dennis (Philharmonia/Susskind). Angel 35092.
Buyanovsky, Vitaly. Melodiya D 0257-97/80.
Ceccarossi, Domenico. Audio Fidelity FCS 43102.
Chiba, Kaoru (NHK/Iwaki, cond.). King SKR 1022.
Civil, Alan (RPO/Kempe). RCA LSC 2973.
Civil, Alan (Klemperer). Columbia 33CX1760.

Jones, Mason (Ormandy). Columbia ML 6185.
Linder, Albert (Vienna/Swarowsky). Vanguard VRS 1069.
Muhlbacher, Ernst (Vienna/Bauer-Theussel). Vox PL 12.630.
Penzel, Erich (Vienna/Paumgartner). Mercury 50407.
Perrini, Nicholas. Coronet S 1406.
Stagliano, James (Zimbler Sinf.). Sinequan Z4RS 1229.
Tuckwell, Barry (Maag). London BR 3102.
Tuckwell, Barry (Marriner). HMV ASD 2780.

Barboteu

Blank

Brain/Hallé

Brain/Susskind

Buyanovsky

February, 1974

Vocalization — An Introduction to Avant-Garde Trombone Techniques

Milton Stevens

Within the last 10 to 15 years, many composers and performers have been experimenting with new methods of producing sound on a trombone. To the amazement of the players, many of the things trombonists once did only backstage — as technical "tricks" or musical curiosities — have turned up in recently-composed works for the instrument!

A variety of techniques are used to produce these new sounds. Timbre or tone quality is altered by (1) a number of mutes and muting procedures, (2) various methods of producing vibrato and controlling its speed, (3) initiating sympathetic vibrations from other resonators (such as the soundboard of a piano), and (4) changing the construction of the trombone (for example, playing a pitch through the *open* F attachment pipes). Pitch can be affected in many ways. One example is the adjustment of the slide to produce quarter tones, sixth tones, and other gradations. A third group of techniques provides a variety of noises and percussive effects. A sampling of these include (1) clicking the tongue inside the mouth so that the bell and tubing of the trombone serve as an amplification unit, (2) growling from the throat, (3) popping the hand on the mouthpiece, (4) rattling the F attachment trigger, (5) slamming the slide shut, (6) pouring water into the slide and then blowing lightly to produce a gurgling effect, and (7) even striking the rim of the bell with a hard mallet! If we now add some miscellaneous techniques — such as lip trills, glissandi through the harmonic series, and shifting the main slide rapidly across alternate positions while sustaining a single pitch — a myriad of new sounds become available, some demanding entirely new systems of notation.

Singing and Playing Simultaneously

As an introduction to new sounds on brass for those who are unfamiliar with this literature, it might be instructive to speak about one performance technique quite popular in the avant-garde idiom — the use of the vocal cords to sing while simultaneously vibrating the lips in a conventional manner.[1] We are all inclined to associate this technique with the contemporary palate, but it is not really new to the mid 20th century. Gardell Simons, Simone Mantia, and Arthur Pryor were just three of the trombone virtuosi from the late nineteenth and early twentieth centuries who mastered the technique.[2] They used it to produce chords and commonly incorporated it into the cadenzas of the pyrotechnical solos they played with famous concert bands of the era. (French hornists must cope with similar chordal effects in the early nineteenth century composition *Concertino*, Op. 45 by Carl Maria von Weber.)

Singing while playing is not at all unnatural in trombone playing. In fact, the first attempts of a youngster to produce a sound from a brass instrument more often than not result in his singing into the horn. And even with instruction, a beginner frequently makes noises with his glottis or vibrates his vocal cords while simultaneously trying to buzz his lips in the mouthpiece. This sometimes happens to advanced students when playing upward slurs in an attempt to extend their high registers. These observations cause one to wonder just how early in the history of brass wind instruments the technique of vocalization while playing might have been discovered.

It is somewhat easier to learn the two functions (vibrating the lips and the vocal cords) without the instrument. First, try alternately buzzing a pitch with the lips and then singing the same pitch. Next, while sustaining the pitch with either the voice or the lips, add the other function to the first. I find it easy to hold a vocalized pitch and then lip buzz one octave higher than the sung note. Once the rudiments of vibrating the vocal cords and lips are accomplished, the trombonist can attempt to apply this concept to the instrument and expand the range above and below the middle register. Then, following a careful, logical process, the trombonist can sustain a pitch with one function, while moving the other in stepwise motion, descending and then ascending away from

---

1. This technique, although being used most extensively on the trombone, is just as effective on a French horn or trumpet and sensational on a tuba (probably because of the lower fundamentals and the amount of amplification of the voice through the enormous length of its tubing).
2. See Glenn Bridges, *Pioneers in Brass* (available from the author; 2199 Lakeview Avenue, Detroit, Michigan 48215).

the first. During some patient and not excessively long practice sessions, the trombonist should develop exercises that include playing and singing any interval desired, moving in parallel motion, moving in contrary motion, crossing registers, and then playing a tune and singing his own accompaniment!

The production of two sounds is not the only possible result of simultaneously vibrating the vocal cords and lips. Due to the phenomenon known as *acoustical combination tones* it is possible, for example, to produce complete harmonies consisting of three or maybe more tones. The reason is that any two sounds, especially if they originate from sources close to each other that are of similar intensity, will interact, producing "difference" and "summation" tones. The human ear senses these faint combination tones and adds them to the two "live" tones to yield a conglomerate sound. Combination tones will be stronger and more easily identifiable if initiating tones are consonant. The difference tone from a *harmonious* interval will form a consonance with the interval, often reinforcing one of the two louder, live sounds. And in most cases, a complete major triad will sound when only two of its members are played live.

The Use of "Vocalizing" in Avant-Garde Compositions

Larry Austin establishes a pure triadic consonance in his work *Changes* for trombone and tape written in 1965. As shown in Example 1, the difference tone has been calculated and marked in the score. In Austin's notation, white noteheads represent natural notes and black ones are used to indicate the chromatic step above the natural. Consequently, the played pitch in Example 1 is an A♯ (or, enharmonically, a B♭), the sung or hummed pitch is a D♮, and the "difference tone" (which can be heard if the major tenth interval is tuned to a pure 5:2 ratio) is an F♮.

Ex. 1. Changes by Larry Austin.
(Reprinted with permission from Composer/Performer Edition, Sacramento, California.)

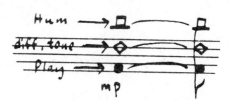

Avant-garde composers are generally more interested in producing dissonant intervals than major triads or other consonances. The second "piece" in Ernst Krenek's *Five Pieces for Trombone and Piano* (1967) (commissioned by Stuart Dempster) ends with a superb example of vocalizing to produce dissonance (Ex. 2). As the directions show, the vocalized pitches are to be sung above the played pitches. A trombonist must develop firm control of his lip vibrations in order to perform this excerpt; the dissonance of the intervals, especially the final diminished octave, produces very noticeable "beats." The last two measures of this example contain an added attraction — sympathetic vibrations that the trombonist derives by playing into the piano while the pianist silently depresses some of the keys (▮); holding down the keys raises the dampers and allows the undamped strings to vibrate freely, in sympathy with the pitches produced on the trombone.

Ex. 2. Five Pieces for Trombone and Piano by Ernst Krenek
(Reprinted with permission from Bärenreiter-Verlag, Kassel)

Sometimes consonances are used to exploit the peculiar timbres that can result when a sung sound is added to a played one. *Music for Trombone and Piano* (1966) by Barney Childs demonstrates the idea of adding a vocalized sound in unison to a played pitch, and then causing a dramatic change in this timbre (see Ex. 3). The directions imply that an F# should be played while singing the same pitch with an open "oo" vowel sound. When the vowel sound is changed to an "ee," a startling timbral change is created.

Ex. 3. *Music for Trombone and Piano* by Barney Childs.
(Copyright 1966, Barney Childs. Reprinted by permission of American Composers Alliance. New York).

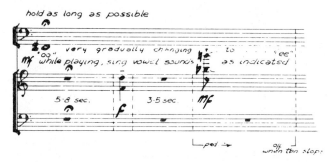

Incidentally, trombonists attempting to play compositions involving vocal technique may find that they are impaired by limitations in their vocal ranges. This is especially true for female trombonists but may affect any player. The F# in the Childs piece, for instance, may be too low even for baritone voices. However, the solution to the problem is a simple one, since the effect is not impaired if an F# an octave (or even two octaves) higher is vocalized. In some cases, however, transposing the vocalizing can result in inverted intervals, altering the total sound effect. While some works involving vocalization may be played by any trombonist, others will be restricted to those players whose vocal ranges fall within certain limits.

An article devoted to avant-garde trombone technique would not be complete without a reference to another work commissioned by Stuart Dempster, *Sequenza V* (1966) for solo trombone by Luciano Berio.

In addition to some sections which involve singing while playing, there is a line graph running below each staff which indicates positions of a metal plunger mute in front of the bell. The excerpt shown in Example 4 demonstrates the extent to which the vocalizing is calculated to match the instrumental tone of the trombone. The dark noteheads represent played pitches and the open circle with a dot in the middle illustrates a sung pitch. The first intervals shown are consonant (perfect fourth and fifth), but the major second (Eb to F#) at the end of the measure is dissonant, causing audible beats. The line beneath the staff shows that the plunger mute should gradually swing from closed to open. The vowels (u-a-i) written in brackets above the staff are added to the vocalizing in the following measure. The plunger mute helps to realize this effect by starting closed for the *u*, opening for the *a*, and closing again for the *i*. Phonetically, these vowels represent the word *why*, which at one point in the composition is actually spoken by the soloist!

Ex. 4. *Sequenza V* by Luciano Berio.
(Copyright 1968, Universal Edition. Used by permission of the publisher. Theodore Presser, Co., sole U.S. representative.)

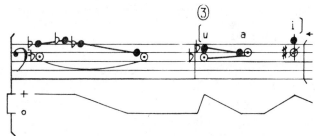

Compositions

Austin, Larry. *Changes* (1965). Composer/Performer Edition, 330 University Avenue, Davis, CA 95616.

Berio, Luciano. *Sequenza V* (1966). Universal Edition, Vienna, Austria.

Childs, Barney. *Music for Trombone and Piano* (1966). Composers Facsimile Edition, 170 W. 74th St., N.Y., NY 10023.

Krenek, Ernst. *Five Pieces for Trombone and Piano* (1967). Barenreiter, Kassel, Germany. ■

February, 1974

Principles of Trombone Legato

Richard Fote

One of the questions asked most often by music educators at clinics is, "How do you get a trombone student to play with a good legato?" After hearing many fine student players, it is evident that the area of trombone legato needs special attention. If approached methodically, however, it is my opinion that a student's ability to perform legato can be easily

developed to a degree commensurate with the other aspects of his playing.

Legato, by definition, indicates that each note of the phrase is connected. Applied to a wind instrument, it simply means that the air must "flow through the horn" continuously (keep the lips buzzing) and with a constant force until the end of the phrase. (Young players often lessen the air pressure between notes in a phrase, resulting in an unmusical "Dwah-Dwah.") In addition to proper breathing, the other essential factors in legato performance are articulation and slide movement.

Articulation in legato playing can be accomplished in two ways — with a soft stroke of the tip of the tongue or by using the lip slur method in which articulation is accomplished (without the tip of the tongue) by simply crossing the natural harmonics of the instrument.

The Tip of the Tongue Method

When articulating legato with the tip of the tongue, think of the syllable *thoo* as opposed to *too*. (Of course, the syllable *thoo* is not used in actual playing.) *Thoo* does not completely seal off the air stream as does *too*, and it allows for the continuous flow of air which is necessary to maintain continuous sound. In reality, the tip of the tongue makes contact further back in the mouth, more like the syllable *loo*. Any syllable can be suggested to the student for this legato articulation, as long as it will not make a complete seal and will allow for the continuous flow of air. Of course, this does not apply to the initial articulation of the phrase.

Ex. 1

The movement of the slide and the soft stroke of the tongue must be coordinated exactly. To develop legato, keep in mind that the student must maintain a constant air pressure, move the slide quickly and use the soft stroke of the tongue at the exact time the slide moves.

Ex. 2

Smooth slide action can best be accomplished by keeping the wrist loose as the forearm moves. To demonstrate this technique, play the following exercise in three different ways: (1) by moving the entire forearm and keeping a stiff wrist; (2) by moving the slide with the wrist alone but not moving the forearm; and (3) by combining the movements of the wrist and the elbow — the correct and obviously most efficient way. In the lower part of the slide the wrist becomes even more active.

Ex. 3

Sloppy or slow slide movement will result in a sloppy legato even though the other techniques are correct. I am not recommending that the slide be operated with

quick, jerky movements, but it must be moved quickly and efficiently — just as quickly between two whole notes as between two sixteenth notes. (Young players sometimes move the slide slowly when the rhythmic activity of the music is slow.)

In some instances, especially fast passages, the slide seems to be in continuous motion and "passes by" each position at the precise time.

Ex. 4

(Here each note would be given a soft articulation with the tip of the tongue.)

The Lip Slur Method

You can also articulate within a legato passage with the lip slur method — crossing the natural harmonics of the instrument. This can be just as effective as a soft stroke of the tongue, but it is my experience that not enough players take advantage of it. When you combine the slide movement with the lip slur concept, there are sometimes complete phrases that, after the first note, can be played without any tip-of-the-tongue articulation. For example, it is not necessary to use the tongue in this passage:

Ex. 5   1

With the appropriate shifts in the slide, the following phrase can also be played as a lip slur:

Ex. 6

Of course, there are many cases in which the pitch will change without the necessary change of harmonics to produce the articulation, and the lip slur method would only produce a glissando.

Ex. 7

In such cases, it would be necessary to use the soft stroke of the tongue with the quick slide movement. The following phrase from *Sonata No. 3* by Marcello* can be played as a lip slur with tongue articulations only on the two notes so marked

Ex. 8

Two things should be noted about the lip slur type of articulation: (1) most music will necessitate using the soft stroke of the tongue to eliminate the *gliss* at times (as in the example above); and (2) it is more

---

*Transcriptions for trombone and piano have been published by both Kendor and Associated.

effective at lower dynamic levels. In spite of this, it is my opinion that the lip slur type of articulation can be developed into a beautiful "singing" legato.

In basically scalewise legato passages of equal note values, each note should be articulated with the tongue for uniformity, but in slow sections with varied rhythms and wider intervals the lip slur approach is often more effective. It should be obvious that the method of articulation should be determined by what is most musical for a given passage. But remember that a great deal of legato playing can be done musically without the tongue — by using the lip slur method or by combining this method with the more common tip-of-the-tongue articulation. ∎

February, 1974

Improved Holding Position — Better Sound

Charles Dalkert

School band and orchestra conductors frequently ask for helpful suggestions for their trombone sections. In attempting to help these teachers, I begin by playing a major scale from F to f as I have seen student trombonists play it. In sixth position the sound is rather good, but as the slide comes up, so does the bell (and the mouthpiece!), and the sound becomes thin, tight, and generally bad. It is at this point that I usually hear, "That's the sound our section gets."

About twice a year my own playing tends to slump — sound is not quite right, playing requires effort, embouchure is uncomfortable. My first attempt at improvement is always by means of air, then embouchure. (Closing the eyes while playing makes the senses of hearing and feeling more keen . . . and aids concentration!) The problem is usually traced to the left hand. (This is not to say mouthpiece *pressure* but mouthpiece *direction* as a result of holding position.) To improve the sound, then, it must first be determined exactly how the holding position affects sound.

The first problem involves the principle of leverage. As the slide becomes longer it becomes heavier, and the instrument tends to slant downward. This is why the longer positions of the F major scale sound better than the shorter ones. The right hand cannot play a part in holding the instrument, since it can only manipulate the slide. The left hand alone **must** serve as the fulcrum and control the weight (long or short) of the instrument.

The second problem is that the slide moves near the center of the body while the arm moves from the shoulder, so that the instrument tends to move toward the right when the trombonist reaches for the long positions. The 45° slide was an attempt to correct this situation (although a curve in the lead pipe distorts sound), but a better suggestion is to reach the right hand across the body for the long positions. It is surprising how many trombonists have difficulty playing the glissandi in Stravinsky's *Firebird Suite*, because they are in effect "shooting at a moving target." Part of the daily routine should be practicing

glissandi while watching the bell of the instrument. If the bell moves with the slide, so does the mouthpiece.

The approach to holding the instrument begins with the embouchure. The left hand must accommodate the embouchure (not the reverse); and when one speaks of holding the instrument comfortably, it is the embouchure (not the left hand) that must be comfortable. To find the most natural position use the lips to hold the mouthpiece against the teeth, then place the instrument onto the mouthpiece. Another approach is to buzz, place the mouthpiece onto the buzz, and place the instrument onto the mouthpiece. In both cases adjust the instrument to the mouthpiece, not vice-versa.

The trombonist must continually study his left hand position, because carelessness here can cause embouchure problems. If fatigue occurs, it should be noticed in the arm and shoulder rather than in the embouchure. To find the proper left hand position, begin with the hand in a flat position and place the lower three fingers between the slide braces with the index finger above the upper brace (Fig. 1). This flat

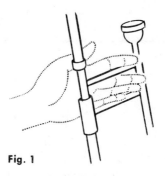

Fig. 1

hand position clearly illustrates the fact that the entire weight of the instrument is really held by the second finger. Next, close the hand with the index finger on the lead pipe or mouthpiece shank (Fig. 2).

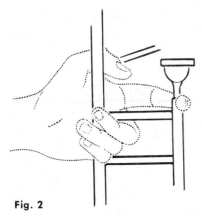

Fig. 2

The student should understand that the instrument is *suspended* from the fingers of the left hand, rather than *supported* by the arm and shoulder. As a means to show hand, arm, and wrist position, close the index finger like the other fingers but in its position above the upper slide brace (Fig. 3). This is not the actual

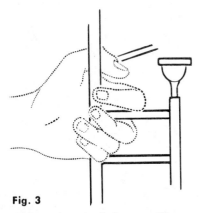

Fig. 3

playing position, but it helps to illustrate arm and wrist position.

One major problem is a falling of the left wrist. The wrist should remain straight. When it bends, not

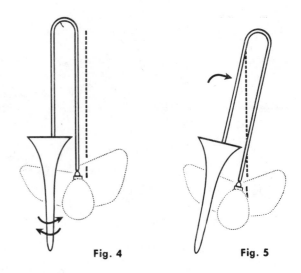

Fig. 4   **Fig. 5**

only does the instrument roll (Fig. 4), but the slide points up and to the right (Fig. 5) so that the mouthpiece rests on the right side of the embouchure. According to Donald Knaub,[1] one should be able to look straight down the slide; this will be impossible if the instrument falls.

When properly supported (suspended), the weight of the bell should be on the left slide, with the bell section in a vertical position. When the braces are not vertical, the wrist will begin to bend. It is not necessary to have the slide at a right angle to the bell, however, if the line formed by the slide braces is not horizontal (Fig. 6).

It is most important to remember that the approach to holding position should be free and effortless. Attention to the left hand can help the student achieve a more relaxed holding position and more natural tone production. ∎

1. Donald Knaub, *Trombone Teaching Techniques* (Fairport: Rochester Music Publishers, 1964), p. 4.

February, 1974

Three Great Jazz Trombone Stylists

Phil Wilson

Jack Teagarden

It was Jack Teagarden who took the jazz trombone out of the circus, off the tailgate, and placed it alongside other melodic instruments as a lyrical, flexible entity. Nobody made more of a contribution to the jazz trombone than he did.

Unfortunately, I never saw Teagarden in person. However, in an old movie ("Glass Alley" — he was a

trombone-playing bartender) there are several head-on shots of him playing. It's a typical "Class Z" flick, with the usual disregard for sound and picture coordination: while all those notes are flowing out of his trombone, it appears as though he never leaves first position. Actually, it is true that he moved his slide very sparingly, but he kept it in the vicinity of *third* position so he could use alternate positions four and five to facilitate those phenomenal lip arpeggios he played. The following are a few examples, with the probable positions marked:

Example #1: "Sunny Side of the Street"
(Satchmo at Symphony Hall;
Louis Armstrong - Decca)

** The clarity of this arpeggio leaves little doubt that these positions are correct

Example #2: "Lover"
(Satchmo at Symphony Hall;
Louis Armstrong - Decca)

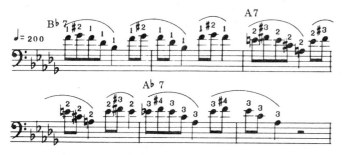

Example #3: "Muskrat Ramble"
(Coast to Coast; Bobby Hackett - Capitol)

Vic Dickenson

Vic Dickenson, who first surfaced with the Count Basie band in the thirties, has never shaken the "barrel-house player" label attached to most of the Basie trombonists of that era (including Bennie Moten and Dicky Wells). It was Vic's solo on "Sugar" in the 1946 Esquire All-Stars album (RCA 78 rpm) that first attracted my attention. Here his absolute control, sense of humor, and melodic interpretation was revealed in a brief but beautiful solo. Five years later, when he was with Bobby Hackett at a club in Boston, I had the opportunity to listen to him every Saturday night. I was 14 at the time, but Vic allowed me to sit in with the group on the first few tunes. Then I would remain in a trance listening to the group, until it was time to return home to New Hampshire. (I had to be there by eleven o'clock!) Vic would get so many colors out of the instrument — growls, whisps, pedal tones — and still maintain his relaxed, melodic sense. It would blow my mind.

Vic used to play a satire on Tommy Dorsey's theme "I'm Getting Sentimental Over You," later recorded on Blue Note (see Ex. 4). Taking it at an extremely slow tempo, and in the key of B-flat, he would shuffle the opening four notes, leaving enough daylight between tones to set up a circus. Then he would play the longest "Johnny Hodges" smear on the high A you ever heard, sauntering back down in the same manner he got up there in the first place. He followed this with a throat-growl triplet figure leading to the C7, a buzz-slur up to the D, coming down the C7 chord in an exaggerated dotted eighth and sixteenth manner. Continuing through the F7 with the same corny eighth-note feel, he would arrive at the Bb Maj.7 chord leading into the turn around with an exaggerated quarter-note triplet throat growl.

Example #4: "I'm Getting Sentimental Over You"

Carl Fontana

I first heard Carl Fontana on an old MGM ten-inch LP with the Woody Herman Band, where he played a solo on "East of the Sun." (There was no personnel listing on the album cover and most people assumed it was Urbie Green.) Woody's "Jumpin' the Line" (Mars) also featured Carl. What immediately caught my ear was Carl's melodic fluency and sense of humor. And you felt he was in control of the horn, instead of the horn controlling him, a rare trait among trombonists (or players of any other instrument, for that matter).

Perhaps Carl's biggest, yet least known, contribution to the jazz trombone is his "too-dle-ooo-dle" tonguing technique which allows him to play those beautiful semi-legato lines as if he were playing a tenor saxophone. I have been conscious of this since 1963 when Bill Watrous and I used to discuss Carl's tonguing technique. A great many trombone players have tried the "too-dle-ooo-dle" over the years, generally finding a slightly different set of syllables to fit their own needs. Carl remains the inspiration.

All three of these men have made major contributions to the art and content of playing jazz trombone: Jack Teagarden gave the trombone respectability as an equal melodic voice; Vic Dickenson continues to contribute with his feeling for colors and sense of humor; while Carl Fontana has a beautiful melodic fluency facilitated by his semi-legato tonguing technique. The influence of these great players can be heard in most trombonists on the scene today. ∎

Trombone Care and Maintenance

Robert Giardinelli

Since the tenor trombone is the simplest of all the instruments of the brass family, maintenance should also be very simple. And it is. However, since the instrument is also the most delicate of the brasses, there are a few important details which must be pointed out in order to prevent damage and deterioration.

Let us begin with a new instrument. Chances are it will be delivered to you with the slide absolutely dry. Do not start playing it — rubbing two dry surfaces together will cause scratches, especially if a little dust is present. Instead, the first thing you should do is to run clean, lukewarm water through the slides (inner and outer); then, dry the inner slides with a tissue or soft cloth. Next, apply slide cream to the inner slides and spray with water. Assemble. Only *now* are you ready to play.

After playing, it is wise to clean the outer surface and empty the trombone of all saliva. It is amazing how much damage can be caused by the perspiration and saliva of some individuals. Keeping a horn clean — inside and out — will lengthen its life tenfold. Once a week or so you should give your slides a bath. Run a few inches of lukewarm water in the tub, sprinkle in some mild soap powder, and use a flexible rod with a brush at the end (trombone cleaner) to scrub both inner and outer slides, as well as the bell section. Do one section at a time, thoroughly, yet delicately. Rinse well with fresh water, dry, lubricate, and you are ready to play again. A regular bath is necessary because even though you blow the water out after playing, a film of saliva remains on the surface of the metal inside the horn. In addition, a certain amount of slide cream will settle at the end of the stroke and into the lower crook; the bath will dissolve and clean both saliva and cream. Warning: do not use strong soap or hot water or else the lacquer will peel right off.

How to Use the Cleaning Rod

The cleaning rod can be a very dangerous weapon in the hands of a careless person. It is intended to be used somewhat like a rifle bore cleaner except that the trombone slide is 100 times more delicate than the gun barrel. This rod should be used only as follows:

1. Cut a piece of cheesecloth approximately 5 inches wide and 5 feet long.

2. Insert one end into the slot and wrap it (in spiral fashion) around the full length of the rod. Make sure the *entire* rod is covered with cloth.

3. Holding the loose end of the cloth firmly around the handle, insert the other end of the rod into the outer slide. Be sure you hold the same slide you are swabbing — do not hold one and swab the other or you may twist the slides and throw them out of alignment.

4. Swab the inner slides the same way. Do not jam the rod in too tightly, especially on the mouthpipe side. You may have to change the cloth — several times, if necessary — until it comes out clean. And if you have neglected the cleaning process for some time, you will find dirt caked in the inner slide tubes. Kerosene or benzene will loosen it.

How to Oil Rotors

If you have an instrument with either a single or a double trigger, it is necessary to oil the rotors periodically.

1. Hold the bell section with the bell flair up.

2. Put a few drops of valve oil into the slide receiver while working the trigger mechanism. This will allow the oil to flow around the rotor.

For a double trigger instrument, the best way to oil the E rotor is:

1. Pull out the E slide.

2. Put a few drops of valve oil into the slide.

3. Replace the slide while holding the bell up, then tip the horn so that the oil will run into the rotor. This method allows the oil to run into the valve without picking up slide grease and gumming up the action. ∎

Original Unaccompanied Trombone Ensemble Music

Glenn P. Smith

Even though the trombone has received considerable recognition as a solo instrument, it is probably at its best in the performance of ensemble music. This article presents a selective list of music originally written for unaccompanied trombone ensembles. Such a compilation is not known, and it is hoped that the list will be helpful to trombonists and teachers in choosing music for school festivals and college recitals. Because of problems involved in obtaining copies, no unpublished works have been included.

The duet repertory consists chiefly of nineteenth-century works. Victor Cornette's *Six Concert Duets* and O. Blume's *Duets* are recommended for high school festivals because of the contrasting movements included in each work. The collection, *24 Easy Duets*, is a reprint of an interesting old publication by the German composer, Karl Henning. William Russo's *Duets*, Op. 35, consist of short examples of contemporary techniques employed by twentieth-century composers. Although these duets are of educational value for performers, they may not be of sufficient interest to merit public performance. There are no duets listed which include notes requiring an F attachment except those of Blazhevich. His *Concert Duets* are enjoyable and useful in mastering clefs and keys.

The collection of original unaccompanied trios is limited. The Sonatas by the seventeenth-century composer Daniel Speer are historically important and of interest to both performers and audience. Anton Bruckner's *Aequale* is also a significant piece in spite of its solemnity and brevity. *Trio* by Ronald Lo Presti is an energetic work suitable for school festivals. A bass trombone is needed for Josef Alexander's *Two Essays* and Walter Skolnik's *Little Suite in F*. These two modern works, and the other more difficult pieces with tenor clef, are more appropriate for college students. Allen Chase's *Eight Trios* (which also require a bass trombone) are short, enjoyable encore pieces.

The sound of a good trombone quartet is rich, impressive and beautiful. It is the most popular trombone ensemble and naturally has the largest repertoire. The compositions of historical significance in this category are Biagio Marini's *Canzona* and Daniel Speer's *Sonata*. Both numbers are original trombone quartets from the seventeenth-century and are not transcriptions as is sometimes assumed. The nineteenth-century highlight is Beethoven's somber *Drei Equale*.

Although Philip Clapp's four pieces are published separately, they were evidently conceived as a concert suite for four trombones. A choice of two contrasting pieces by this composer is effective festival music for a junior high quartet. Several other grade II and III compositions have been listed for consideration. A bass trombone (or tenor with F attachment) is not necessary for any numbers in this classification except Raymond Premru's *In Memoriam* and Vaclav Nelhybel's *Three Organa*. Although not required, the bass instrument is advantageous and authentic in the *Canzona* by Marini.

Choice of music for the high school quartet may be limited by the number of members capable of reading tenor clef. As seen in the following list, foreign composers and publishers utilize this clef much more than their American counterparts. Leslie Bassett's *Quartet* and Robert Sander's *Scherzo & Dirge* are good concert numbers written entirely in bass clef. Tenor clef appears only in the first movement of the *Suite* by Gordon Jacob. The following quartets of intermediate difficulty include tenor clef in at least one part: André Ameller's *Chorale*, Roger Chapman's *Suite of Three Cities*, Pierre Max Dubois' *Quartet*, Jeanine Rueff's *Deux pièces brèves*, Flor Peeters' *Suite*, Op. 82 and Kazimierz Serocki's *Suite*.

The college or experienced quartet will be challenged by the following: Eugène Bozza's *Trois pièces*, Roger Boutry's *Cinq pièces*, Jean-Michel Defay's *Quarte pièces*, Désiré Dondeyne's *Suite*, George Hyde's *Suite*, Henri Tomasi's *Etre ou ne pas être* and Fisher Tull's *Concert Piece*. Thrilling indeed is the recent recording of the Bozza quartet by the trombone section of the Chicago Symphony Orchestra. The Tomasi number with Arnold Jacobs as tuba soloist (written for either tuba or bass trombone) is also featured on this recording. The piece is not demanding technically but accurate ensemble precision is difficult to achieve. A bass trombone is essential in the quartets written by Atherton, Frackenpohl, Hemel, Hornoff, Hyde, Langley, Otten (one mvt.), Orr, Peeters, Premru, Tomasi and Tull. *Comedy for Trombones* by Christensen-McDunn and *T-Bone Party* by Don Haddad are effective encore numbers.

Original serious works written for the larger ensemble or the increasingly popular trombone choir are few in number. Two compositions of significance, however, are *Pavana* by Moritz von Hessen for five trombones and *Canzon* by Tiburtio Massaino for eight trombones. These are original works of historical interest from the seventeenth century. It is advisable not to double parts in the Massaino octet because of the close scoring. The other listings are all deserving and challenging twentieth-century works.

Two Trombones

Blazhevich, V. (1881-1942). *Concert Duets*. IMC, n.d.; MCA, 1948. Grade III-V. Clefs: A-T-B.

Bleger, M. *Twelve Duets*. ed. Ostrander. IMC, 1959. Grade II-IV. Clefs: BB.

Blume, O. *Twelve Melodious Duets*. CF, 1923. Grade III-IV. Clefs: BB.

———. *Duets*. 2 vol. ed. Gibson. IMC, 1959. Clefs: BB.

Cornette, V. (1795-1868). *Six Concert Duets*. CB, 1937. Grade III-V. Clefs: BB.

Dedrick, A. (1915-). *19 Progressive Duets*. Kend, 1970. Grade I-II. Clefs: BB.

Dieppo, A. (1808-1878). *Virtuoso Studies*. ed. Ostrander. EM, 1961. Grade III-IV. Clefs: BB.

Henning, C. (1784-1867). *24 Easy Duets*. ed. Ostrander. IMC, 1960. Grade II-III. Clefs: BB.

Kahila, K. *Andante-Allegro*. EM, 1955. Grade IV. Clefs: BB.

Kreisler, A. von (1895-1970). *Andante and Presto*. SMC, 1970. Grade III. Clefs: BB.

Raphling, S. (1910-). *Sonatina*. IM, 1955. Grade III-IV. Clefs: BB.

Russo, W. (1928-). *Duets, Op. 35* (1959). Col, 1961. Grade III-IV. Clefs: BB.

Tanner, P. *Duets*. Vol. I. WIM, 1966. Grade II-III. Clefs: BB.

Uber, D. *Ten Concert Duets*. EM, 1953. Grade III-IV. Clefs: BB.

——— *Twentieth Century Duets*. Bk. 1. "Easy Duets," HA, 1960. Grade I-III. Clefs: BB; Bk. 2. "Advanced Duets," HA, 1960. Grade III-IV. Clefs: BB.

Three Trombones

Alexander, J. (1910-). *Two Essays.* Gen, 1970. Grade IV-V. Clefs: T-B, B-T, B.

Bartsch, C. *Choral, Danse nonchalante et Fanfare.* Mau, 1965. Grade IV. Clefs: BBB.

Block, R. *Incantation and Canzona.* WIM, 1972. Grade IV. Clefs: BBB.

Bruckner, A. (1824-1896). *Aequale* (1847). Ens, 1965. Grade III. Clefs: BBB.

Chase, A. *Eight Trios.* Cor, 1961. Grade IV-V. Clefs: T, T-B, B.

Conley, L. *Theme and March.* Kend, 1971. Grade II. Clefs: BBB.

Cornette, V. (1795-1868). *Trio Sonata,* Op. 1, No. 5. Ens, n.d., Grade III-IV. Clefs: B-T, B-T, B.

_____ *Trio Sonata,* Op. 1, No. 10. Ens, n.d., Grade III-IV. Clefs: T, B-T, B.

_____ *Trio Sonata,* Op. 1, No. 11. Ens, n.d., Grade III-IV. Clefs: T, T-B, B-T.

Kreisler, A. von (1895-1970). *Two Sketches.* SMC, 1969. Grade II-III. Clefs: BBB.

Lo Presti, R. (1933-). *Trio.* CF, 1968. Grade III. Clefs: BBB.

Moulaert, R. (1875-1962). *Suite* (1939). CBD, 1959. Grade III-IV. Clefs: T, B-T, B-T.

Porret, J. *Fragonard.* Mole, 1965. Grade III. Clefs: BBB.

Premru, R. (1934-). *Two Pieces* (1952). Ens, 1965. Grade IV. Clefs: BBB.

Skolnik, W. (1934-). *Little Suite in F.* Ten, 1972. Grade IV. Clefs: BBB.

Snosko-Borovsky (1889-). *Scherzo,* Op. 13. IMC, 1960. Grade IV. Clefs: B-T, B, B.

Speer, D. (1636-1707). *Two Sonatas* (1687). ed. Baines. MR, 1961. Grade III-IV. Clefs: TBB.

Tanner, P. *Imitation.* WIM, 1966. Grade III. Clefs: BBB.

_____ *Larghetto.* WIM. 1966. Grade III. Clefs: BBB.

Uber, D. *Five Concert Trios,* Op. 53. Ens, 1971. Grade III-IV. Clefs: BBB.

_____ *Modern Trios.* EM, 1948. Grade III-IV. Clefs: BBB.

Four Trombones

Ameller, A. (1912-). *Chorale.* Hin, 1960. Grade IV. Clefs: TTTB

Atherton, P. (1910-). *Suite.* SM, 1967. Grade III-IV. Clefs: BBBB.

Bark & Rabe. *Bolos* (1962). WH, 1964. avant-garde.

Bassett, L. (1923-). *Quartet* (1949). RK, 1960. Grade IV. Clefs: BBBB.

Beethoven, L. van (1770-1827). *Drei Equale* (1812). original key. B & H, n.d. Grade IV. Clefs: AATB.

_____ *Three Equali.* ed. R. King. RK, 1961. Grade III. Clefs: BBBB.

_____ *Three Equali.* ed. D. Miller. Ens, n.d. Grade III. Clefs: BBBB.

Boutry, R. (1932-). *Cinq Pièces.* Led, 1961. Grade VI. Clefs: T, T-B, B-T, B.

Bozza, E. (1905-). *Trois Pièces.* Led, 1964. Grade V. Clefs: T, B, B-T, B.

Butts, C. (1924-). *Suite.* SP, 1966. Grade II. Clefs: BBBB.

Catelinet, P. (1910-). *Divertissements.* Hin, 1953. Grade III. Clefs: TTBB.

Chapman, R. (1916-). *Suite of Three Cities.* CFP, 1960. Grade IV. Clefs: TBBB.

Charpentier, J. (1933-). *Quatuor de forme liturgique.* Led, 1960. Grade V. Clefs: BBBB.

Christensen, J. *Comedy for Trombones.* arr. McDunn. NAK, 1967. Grade III-IV. Clefs: BBBB.

Clapp, P. (1888-1954). *Chorale.* BH, 1939. Grade II. Clefs: BBBB.

_____ *Hunting Song.* BH, 1939. Grade III. Clefs: BBBB.

_____ *Nocturne.* BH, 1939. Grade II. Clefs: BBBB.

_____ *Minstrel Show.* BH, 1939. Grade III. Clefs: BBBB.

Cole, G. *Seven Impressions.* AMC, 1960. Grade III-IV. Clefs: BBBB.

Defay, J. (1932-). *Quarte Pièces.* Led, 1954. Grade V. Clefs: T, T, T, B-T.

Dondeyne, D. *Suite.* EMT, 1960. Grade IV-V. Clefs: T, T-B, T-B, B.

Dubois, P. (1930-). *Quatuor.* Led, 1962. Grade IV-V. Clefs: TTBB.

Frackenpohl, A. (1924-). *Quartet* (1948, revised 1967). Ens, 1968. Grade IV. Clefs: T-B, B-T, B, B.

Gow, D. (1924-). *Suite,* Op. 57 (1961). MR, 1967. Grade IV-V. Clefs: T-B, B-T, B-T, B.

Haddad, D. *T-Bone Party.* SP, 1972. Grade III-IV. Clefs: BBBB.

Haubiel, A. (1894-197?). *Moderni.* Bel, 1941. Grade III. Clefs: BBBB.

_____ *Recessional.* CP, 1942. Grade III. Clefs: BBBB.

Hemel, O. van (1892-). *Donquichotterie.* Don, 1962. Grade IV. Clefs: B-T, B-T, B, B.

Hornoff, A. *Suite.* Hio, 1953. Grade IV-V. Clefs: ATBB.

Hyde, G. *Suite.* WIM, 1970. Grade V. Clefs: TTTB.

Jacob, G. (1895-). *Suite.* BH, 1968. Grade III-IV. Clefs: B-T, B-T, B, B.

Johnson, W. *Prelude Solennelle.* FS, 1935. Grade IV. Clefs: BBBB.

Koepke, P. *Elégie Héröique.* Rub, 1957. Grade III. Clefs: BBBB.

_____ *Scherzo Caprice.* Rub, 1964. Grade II. Clefs: BBBB.

Langley, J. (1927-). *Suite* (1959). Hin, 1961. Grade III-IV. Clefs: T-B, B-T, B, B.

Laudenslager, H. *Three Preludes & Fugues.* Cor, 1963. Grade IV-V. Clefs: BBBB.

La Violette, W. *The Forest.* Bel, 1942. Grade II. Clefs: BBBB.

Maas, A. *Zwei Grosse Quartette* (1920). CB, 1937. Grade IV. Clefs: BBBB.

Marini, B. *Canzona* (1626). Ens, 1965. Grade III. Clefs: BBBB.

Massis, A. (1893-). *Suite.* EMT, 1964.

McCarty, P. *Recitative & Fugue.* RK, 1960. Grade III-IV. Clefs: BBBB.

McKay, F. *Festival Prelude.* Bar, 1947. Grade III. Clefs: BBBB.

_____ *Pageant March.* BH, 1963. Grade II-III. Clefs: BBBB.

McKay, G. (1899-197?). *Allegro Scherzoso.* Bar, 1965. Grade II. Clefs: BBBB.

Meulemans, A. (1884-1966). *Suite* (1942). CBD, 1958. Grade IV-V. Clefs: TTBB.

Nelhybel, V. (1919-). *Six Pieces.* Gen, 1966. Grade IV. Clefs: BBBB.

_____ *Three Organa.* FC, 1962. Grade III. Clefs: BBBB.

Olander, E. *First Suite.* ed. H. Ferguson. GS, 1951. Grade II. Clefs: BBBB.

Orr, B. *5 Sketches* (1970). RK, 1972. Grade V. Clefs: TTBB.

Ostransky, L. *Donnybrook.* Rub, 1961. Grade II. Clefs: BBBB.

_____ *Two Episodes.* Rub, 1961. Grade II-III. Clefs: BBBB.

Otten, L. (1924-). *Suite* (1951, revised 1966). Don, 1957. Grade V. Clefs: TTBB.

Peeters, F. (1903-). *Suite,* Op. 82 (1955). CFP, 1959. Grade IV. Clefs: T, B-T, B, B.

Presser, W. (1916-). *Chaconne and March.* Ten, 1973. Grade IV. Clefs: B-T, B, B, B.

Porret, J. *Hercule.* Mole, 1966. Grade III. Clefs: BBBB.

Premru, R. (1934-). *In Memoriam* (1956). Ens, 1967. Grade III. Clefs: BBBB.

_____ *Tissington Variations.* MR, 1972. Grade V. Clefs: BBBB.

Rueff, J. (1922-). *Deux Pièces brèves.* Led, 1956. Grade III-IV. Clefs: TTBB.

Sanders, R. (1906-). *Scherzo & Dirge.* AMC, 1948. Grade IV. Clefs: BBBB.

Semler-Collery, J. *Deux Pièces.* EMT, 1971. Grade III-IV. Clefs: B-T, B, B, B.

Serocki, K. (1922-   ). *Suite*. PWM, 1954. Grade IV-V. Clefs: TTBB.

Speer, D. (1636-1707). *Sonata*. ed. D. Miller. Ens, n.d. Grade III-IV. Clefs: BBBB.

_____ *Sonata*. ed. K. Brown, acc. ad lib. IMC, 1966. Clefs: TBBB.

Tanner, P. *A Study in Texture*. WIM, 1965. Grade II-III. Clefs: BBBB.

Tisné, A. *Ode*. Led, 1969. Grade III. Clefs: B-T, B-T, B, B.

Tomasi, H. (1901-   ). *Etre ou ne pas être*. Led, 1963. Grade IV. Clefs: B-T, B-T, B-T, B.

Tull, F. (1934-   ). *Concert Piece*. Educ, n.d. Grade IV-V. Clefs: BBBB.

Uber, D. *Three Miniatures*, Op. 29. Ens, 1967. Grade III-IV. Clefs: BBBB.

Walker, R. (1912-   ). *Preambule*. Pro, 1961. Grade II. Clefs: BBBB.

Five Trombones

Moritz von Hessen (1572-1632). *Pavana*. Ens, 1961. Grade III. Clefs: BBBBB.

Six Trombones

Phillips, B. (1907-   ). *Piece* (1953). RK, n.d. Grade IV. Clefs: BBBBBB.

Tull, F. (1934-   ). *Diversion*. Educ, n.d. Grade V. Clefs: T-B, B-T, B-T, B-T, B, B.

Eight Trombones

Hartley, W. *Canzona* (1969). Ens, 1972. Grade IV. Clefs: T, B-T, BBBBBB.

Massaino, T. *Canzon* (1608). RK, 1964. Grade III. Clefs: all B.

_____ *Canzona*. ed. Silliman. Ens, 1964. Grade III. Clefs: all B.

_____ *Canzona 33*. ed. Lumsden. MR, 1969. Grade III. Clefs: TTTTBBBB.

Ott, J. (1929-   ). *Suite*. CBP, 1968. Grade V. Clefs: pts. 1-5, B-T.

Twelve Trombones

Adler, S. (1928-   ). *Five Vignettes*. Oxf, 1969. Grade VI. Clefs: pts. 1-8, B-T.

Key to Publishers

AMP Associated Music Publishers, Inc., 866 Third Ave., New York, NY 10022.
Bar C.L. Barnhouse Co., Oskaloosa, Iowa 52577
Bel Belwin-Mills, 25 Deshon Dr., Melville, L.I., N.Y. 11746
BH Boosey & Hawkes, Inc., Lawson Blvd., Oceanside, NY 11572
B&H Breitkopf & Härtel — See Associated
CB Cundy-Bettoney Co., — See Carl Fischer
CBD CeBeDeM — See Henri Elkan
CBP Claude Benny Press, Box 461, Milton Jct., WI 53654
CF Carl Fischer, Inc., 62 Cooper Square, New York, NY 10003
CFP C.F. Peters, 373 Park Avenue South, New York, NY 10016
Col Charles Colin, 315 W. 53rd St., New York, NY 10019
Cor Cor Publishing Co., 67 Bell Place, Massapequa, L.I., NY 11758
Don Donemus — See Peters
EBM Edward B. Marks Corp., 136 W. 52nd St., New York, NY 10019
Educ Educulture, Inc., P.O. Box 1932, Santa Monica, CA 90406
Elk Henri Elkan, 1316 Walnut St., Philadelphia, PA 19107
EM Edition Musicus, 333 W. 52nd St., New York, NY 10019
EMT Editions Musicales Transatlantique — See Presser
Ens Ensemble Publications, Box 98, Bidwell Station, Buffalo, NY 14222
FC Franco Colombo Publications — See Belwin-Mills
FS H.T. Fitzsimons Co., 615 N. LaSalle St., Chicago, IL 60610
Gen General Music Publishing Co., c/o Frank Music Corp., 119 W. 57th St., New York, NY 10019
GS G. Schirmer, 866 Third Avenue, New York, NY 10022
HA Henry Adler — See Belwin-Mills
Hio Heinrich Hiob, c/o Verlag von Paul Zschocher, Hamburg, Germany
Hin Hinrichsen Edition — See Peters
IMC International Music Co., 511 Fifth Ave., New York, NY 10017
Kend Kendor Music, Delevan, NY 14042
Led Alphonse Leduc, 175, rue St.-Honoré, Paris, France
Mau J. Maurer, 7 Avenue du Verseau, Brussels, Belgium
MCA MCA Music Corp., 445 Park Ave., New York, NY 10022
Mole Molenaar — See Henri Elkan
MR Musica Rara, 2, Great Marlborough Street, London, W. 1
NAK Neil A. Kjos Music Co., 525 Busse Highway, Park Ridge, IL 60068
Oxf Oxford University Press, 200 Madison Ave., New York, NY 10016
Pro Pro Art Publications, 469 Union Ave., Westbury, NY 11590
PWM Polskie Wydawnictwo Nuzycne — See Marks (EBM)
RK Robert King Music Co., 112A Main St., North Easton, MA 02356
Rub Rubank, Inc., 16215 N.W. 15th Ave., Miami, FL 33159
SM Studio Music Co., 89 Vicarage Road, London, England
SMC Southern Music Co., P.O. Box 329, San Antonio, TX 78292
SP Shawnee Press Inc., Delaware Water Gap, PA 18327
Ten Tenuto Publications — See Presser
TP Theodore Presser Co., Presser Place, Bryn Mawr, PA 19010
WIM Western International Music, 2859 Holt Ave., Los Angeles, CA 90034
WH Wilhelm Hansen — See G. Schirmer

A Selected, Annotated List of Published Trombone Literature

Jim Swett

One of the basic needs of the school and/or studio teacher is a thorough knowledge of good solo literature for all playing levels. Most teachers have no problem with music for their own instrument; but since many also teach outside their area of specialization, they must depend on other sources for this information.

There are several lists of music available, but most contain no indication as to musical or pedagogical value, and thus are of little value to the teacher unfamiliar with the titles listed. It would be helpful — particularly to younger teachers — if there were lists of music selected and annotated by experienced specialists on each instrument, so that eventually a representative compilation of solo literature for all instruments would be available.

The following is my attempt to provide such a list for the trombone. The choices and comments are, of course, based on my own experience and musical taste.

Elementary

Adams/Frankiser. *Holy City*. Boosey & Hawkes. 75¢. Suitable for good first or average second year students, this sustained and lyrical work is in 4/4 meter (C). The piano is in an accompaniment role.

Arnold, J. *Everybody's Favorite Elementary Trombone Solos*, #41; *Everybody's Favorite Easy Trombone Solos*, #20 and #78; *More Easy Trombone Solos*, #32. Amsco Music Publ. Part of the large "Everybody's Favorite" series for all instruments, each of these volumes costs $3.95 and includes a large number of pieces taken from the classical repertoire. Most can be played and enjoyed by good first and second year players. They are especially good for performance and for teaching of style, tone quality, and rhythm. Some piano parts (as well as some solo parts) are harder than others but none seem to require great facility.

Buchtel. *Marines Hymn*. Southern Music Co. 40¢. This is an easy version that most kids will like to play. Unfortunately, the accompaniment is not well done.

Cook, V. *Ruby*. Rubank. 75¢. First year material incorporating sustained and detached styles, dotted and sixteenth notes and varied dynamics. It is fairly musical, with an easy piano part.

Franck/Briegel. *Panis Angelicus*. Southern Music Co. 60¢. An excellent work for teaching tone quality and musical line.

German/Smith. *Shepherd's Dance*. Belwin-Mills. 50¢. This piece is for advanced first or average second year students. It features fast 6/8 meter, a sprightly style, and is good for teaching various rhythms. The piano accompaniment is easy.

Handel/Harvey. *Where'er You Walk* from *Semele*. 35¢. This sustained aria is suitable for a second year student, although the tessitura (up to high F♯ and G) is rather high for young students. The piece moves in a slow 4 but can be subdivided into 8th-note beats. It is good for teaching song style, intonation in the upper register, and rhythmic relationships. The piano part is easy.

Kinyon, J. *Breeze-Easy Recital Pieces*; *Breeze-Easy Program Pieces*. Witmark (Warner Bros.). $3.20 each. Here are two volumes of familiar tunes that young players will want to play and perhaps perform.

Smith/Falcone. *Song Without Words*. Belwin-Mills. 50¢. The flowing style of this first year piece is good for teaching breath control. There is an easy piano part.

Smith/Falcone. *Spokane*. Belwin-Mills. 50¢. This is suitable for teaching large tone, accented notes, separation of notes, dotted eighths and sixteenths. The style is majestic but rather static in both solo and piano.

Wagner/Roberts. *Song to the Evening Star*. Cundy-Bettoney (Carl Fischer). $1.25. A flowing, sustained melody with some wide skips is featured in this piece for first or second year students.

Intermediate

Arnold, J. *Everybody's Favorite Trombone Solos*, #29. Amsco Music. $3.95. A continuation of the "Everybody's Favorite" series from the elementary levels, these solos are more mature musically and more difficult technically. Some are poorly arranged and do not fit the trombone style, but others are good. All are excerpted from operas, symphonies, etc. and are suitable for second and third year players. The piano part is not too demanding.

Bach/Kent. *Arioso* from Cantata No. 156. Carl Fischer. 90¢. This has been arranged for a great variety of instruments and combinations, but the beautiful, flowing melody is especially effective on the trombone (if the player has good lyric ability). The range goes up to high A♭, but the tessitura is generally comfortable.

Bach/Beversdorf. *Endure, Endure* from St. Matthew Passion and *Haste, Ye Shepherds* from the Christmas Oratorio. Southern Music Co. $1.50 and $1.75 (respectively). These arias are good for teaching baroque legato style to second or third year students.

Berlioz/Smith. *Recitative and Prayer* from Grand Symphony for Band, Op. 15, second movement. Merrymount Music (Presser). $1.00 Arranged for trombone and piano, this work is suitable for musically mature high school students. The wide dynamic range, high notes, and sustained playing make this somewhat tiring, but it is excellent for teaching resonance, articulation, interpretation of several styles, and expressive rubato. It is written in 3 sections — recitative followed by two progressively more lyrical sections — and comes with an accompaniment which is technically easy but requires mature musicianship. This enjoyable work is also available in a band edition.

Blazhevich, V. *Concert Piece No. 5*. Belwin-Mills. $1.00. Ranging from F on the bottom of the bass clef staff to high A, this work is suitable for high school students. It is through-composed in two large sections and features abrupt dynamic and articulation changes. It is a good pedagogical piece for nearly all technical and musical aspects of playing and an enjoyable performance piece both for listener and performer. The piano part is of medium difficulty.

Cimera/Koestner. *Andante* from Concerto for Trombone (piano reduction). Remick (Warner Bros.). $1.50. The sustained, song-like melody goes up to high A♭ unless the optional ending is used (up to double high F). Good for high school students. There are some tricky piano parts, but the accompaniment is generally not too difficult.

Guilmant/Falaguerre. *Morceau Symphonique*. Warner Bros. $1.75. This is a through-composed piece in two sections. A lyrical song-like section in G♭ is followed by a fast section with several scale-like passages in different keys. The range is from low F to high C♯ (optional) with a medium high tessitura. The piano is not too hard. A suitable performance piece for high school or college, it is also available with band accompaniment.

Handel/Beversdorf. *Ev'ry Valley* from the Messiah. Southern Music Co. $1.50. Good for teaching high school students baroque aria style and the technique of "blowing through" notes and phrases. Range to high G♯.

Hasse/Gower. *Hasse Suite*. Rubank. $1.50. This very musical work in 3 movements (fast-slow-fast), ranging from low B♭ to G above the bass staff, is good for teaching baroque forms and styles. The tonal arrangement in the third movement makes for helpful listening for intonation. The piano part is accompanimental and quite easy.

Haydn/Shuman. *Adagio* from the Cello Concerto. Warner Bros. $1.20. The 8th note is the unit of beat in this beautiful song-like work. Some of the very long phrases require good air control. It is great for style, breath control, rhythms involving small note-values, and beauty of tone and can be a convincing performance piece for high school or early college students. The piano supports in an accompaniment role.

Mullins, G. *Twelve Easy Classics* for Trombone and Piano. Summy-Birchard. $4.50. Good arrangements and tasteful pieces for developing a smooth, singing tone at the advanced junior high and early high school levels.

Ostrander. *Concert Piece in Fugal Style.* Edition Musicus. $2.00. This through-composed work in four short sections which are varied in style contains difficult octave skips and ranges from low G to high B♭. There are a few tricky fast runs and one fast tricky arpeggiated section for piano — otherwise it is not too hard. Although somewhat trite, the piece is musically acceptable for performance by high school or early college students.

Ropartz/Shapiro. *Andante et Allegro.* Cundy-Bettoney (Carl Fischer). $1.25. This two-section work is a good performance piece for high school or young college students. The slow section is easy if legato style is well developed; the fast section presents wide dynamic range and difficult fast articulation figures. Range to high A.

Smith, H. *Solos for the Trombone Player.* Schirmer. $2.50. This collection of movements from sonatas, concertos, etc. presents a variety of styles and is good for all aspects of playing. For advanced high school and early college players.

Vivaldi/Ostrander. *Sonatas 1-6.* International Music Co. $1.75 each. These four-movement sonatas (slow-fast-slow-fast), notated mostly in tenor clef, are each published separately. They are hard to bring off well on trombone but are good for teaching baroque styles and forms and tenor clef. The piano accompaniment is easy.

Weber/Laube. *Romanza Appassionata.* 60¢. This is an effective transcription for high school or freshman college performance. The sustained, subdued work features a wide dynamic range from low F to high A with some octave and twelfth skips.

Medium Advanced

Bach/Beversdorf. *Tis Thee I Would Be Praising* from the Christmas Oratorio. Southern Music Co. $1.50. There are no range problems, but the long phrases require great breath control and it is difficult to maintain the vocal style in fast passages. Both piano and trombone have technical problems. This is a good pedagogical piece for baroque style, breath control, technique, and smooth articulation, but it is difficult to bring off convincingly as a performance piece.

Barat. *Andante et Allegro.* Southern Music Co. $1.25. Characterized by beautiful harmonic and melodic writing, this piece has two main sections ranging from low F to B♭ above the bass clef staff. There is some difficult manipulation of fast triplet figures in the lyrical section and problems of clean, accurate articulations in the fast passages. In addition, both sections require a great variety of subtle articulation shadings for a musical performance. It is available with an easy piano or band accompaniment.

Bernstein, L. *Elegy for Mippy II.* Amberson Enterprises (Schirmer). 50¢. Unaccompanied. This whimsical, light piece in an easy jazz-like style uses foot tapping as an accompanying feature.

Blazhevich/LaFosse. *Concerto No. 2.* International Music Co. $2.50. Fast passages alternate with lyrical ones in this through-composed work. Constructed in three main sections with several transition and cadenza-like passages, it ranges from optional D below to B♭ above the bass clef staff and has a medium tessitura. Although musically

mediocre, it is good for technical work and performance. The piano accompaniment has several technical problems.

Boda, J. *Sonatina.* W.D. Stuart (Robert King). $2.50. This two-movement work (smooth first movement, fast and crisp second movement) has a medium tessitura and range. A very musical repertoire piece. The piano is an equal partner with the trombone and requires a mature player.

Bozza, E. *Ballade for Trombone and Orchestra* (piano reduction). Alphonse Leduc. $2.90. This work is, at the same time, a parody on several symphonic works and a serious piece. It has many difficult figures and range problems (from E below the bass clef to D♭ above the tenor clef staff), using the high tessitura typical of the "French School." It is mostly in tenor clef. A fair recital piece with some problem areas for the pianist.

Cimera. *Concerto.* Remick (Warner Bros.). Each of the three movements is published separately (Movement 1 — $2.00; Movements 2 & 3 — $1.50 each). The first and third movements are technically in the "Arthur Pryor" vein but limited musically, while the second movement is a beautiful song in the key of D♭. Good for technical development. The piano reduction is somewhat difficult.

Corelli/Ostrander. *Sonata in F Major.* $1.00. Here is an example of good music poorly transcribed for the trombone. The three baroque dances with a lyric prelude have a high tessitura, wide and difficult skips . . . and tend to be tiring.

Cowell, H. *Hymn and Fuguing Tune #13.* Associated Music Publ. $2.50. This is a fine recital piece. The two movements are very musical, ranging up to high C with medium tessitura. The piano is quite difficult in the second movement.

David/Gibson. *Concertino, Op. 4.* International Music Co. $2.00. One of the few good pieces for trombone dating from the Romantic period, this is good for teaching tone, style, and technique.

Davison, J. *Sonata.* Shawnee. $3.00. Each of the three lyrical movements is based on an English folk song. The composer has succeeded in combining the archaic sound of these tunes with a more contemporary style. The tessitura is medium high with C as top note. An excellent performance piece that is easy to listen to and enjoyable to play, this is really chamber music for trombone and piano requiring a mature pianist.

Fasch. *Sonata.* McGinnis & Marx. $3.00. Due to the embellishments, this baroque piece is perhaps better suited to the baritone. It is very musical and useful for pedagogical purposes but rather long and tiring.

Galliard/Marx. *Six Sonatas.* McGinnis & Marx. $3.00. Galliard/Brown. *Six Sonatas.* International Music. $2.50. Both editions are published in two volumes. These baroque sonatas, originally for bassoon or cello, are really better suited to baritone for performance. However, they are excellent teaching works for baroque styles and forms, and they can be convincing on trombone. Piano parts are fairly easy.

Handel/Brown. *Concerto in F Minor.* International Music. $2.00. Originally for oboe, this baroque concerto requires great breath, dynamic, technical, and wide interval control as well as good endurance. The phrases are mostly quite long and may have to be broken. Other than that, the work can be played quite convincingly by the trombonist. It is written in tenor clef with a fairly high tessitura. The piano part is fairly easy with only a few difficulties. However, for effective performance, the pianist must understand the style and be able to keep the piece moving.

Henry, Otto. *Passacaglia and Fugue for Bass Trombone.* Robert King. $3.00. This neo-baroque piece is a challenging recital work which is difficult to play well. It has many meter changes and is good for teaching marcato articulations. Range from D below to G above the bass clef staff.

Hindemith, Paul. *Sonate.* Schott & Co. (Belwin-Mills). $6.00. A staple of the repertoire, this is perhaps the earliest example of the modern trombone sonata. The piece is through-composed in 4 sections and of moderate technical difficulty — but with mature musical demands. An accomplished pianist is required, as trombone and piano act as equal partners.

Hovhaness, A. *Concerto No. 3 — Diran.* Robert King. $10.00 with string parts. This is a good recital piece for trombone and strings.

Marcello/Ostrander. *Sonata in F Major.* International Music Co. $1.75. A four-movement baroque sonata notated mostly in tenor clef. The fast parts are not too trombonistic but lay easy on the instrument, and it is not tiring due to the medium tessitura and relatively short movements. In general, this is a rather weak trombone performance piece. Aside from some tricky places, the accompaniment is not too hard.

Marcello/Ostrander. *Sonata in G Minor.* International Music Co. $1.75. This four-movement baroque sonata — mostly in tenor clef with medium tessitura — can be convincing on the trombone. The second movement has some long, fast passages. The piano part is easy.

McKay, G. *Sonata.* Remick (Warner Bros.). $3.00. This technically difficult three-movement work has many high notes but a medium tessitura. The piano part mostly supports the trombone. Although it can be used for performance, the work is not very musical and not really worth the effort needed to learn it.

Mozart/Sansone. *Concerto No. 1* for horn, transposed to Eb. $2.00. The tessitura is high and sustained in this two-movement work with moderate technical demands. It can be convincing on trombone but is best for learning Mozart style and a flowing, light, controlled upper register. The manuscript is sloppy and quite difficult to read.

Presser, W. *Sonatina for Trombone and Piano.* Tritone (Presser). $2.80. These four movements are not difficult technically or rangewise and are highly musical and enjoyable to perform. The piano has many fairly difficult and important parts of equal importance with trombone. In the third movement, for example (a parody on the *Dies Irae*), the pianist accompanies part of the time on the woodblock.

Pryor, A. *Blue Bells of Scotland.* Carl Fischer. $1.00. Pryor's pyrotechnical theme and variations on this melody requires fast tempos and several high C's. Musically very limited, it is best for technical development or for performance by pre-college students. It does sound flashy.

Pryor, A. *Thoughts of Love.* Carl Fischer. $1.00. This is very similar to the *Blue Bells of Scotland* but not quite as difficult — the tessitura is lower and no pedal tones are used.

Rimsky-Korsakov/Gibson. *Concerto for Trombone and Band.* International Music Co. $2.50. (piano reduction). The outer movements are difficult technically; the second movement is a beautiful aria. The accompaniment — whether band or piano — will have problems negotiating the opening repeated triplets. Otherwise, there will be few difficulties. This is a musically mediocre work, but it is a staple of the repertoire and worthy of performance.

Roy, K. G. *Sonata,* Opus 13 for trombone and piano. Easton Music Co. (Robert King). $3.00. The work consists of three movements, Aria, Interludio, Passacaglia: the first movement is smooth and lyrical with several wide skips; the second movement is faster and lighter but subdued; the third movement is long, fairly slow and soft. The range is not difficult, but the piece is a bit tiring. A very musical work. The piano is an equal partner with the trombone and requires a mature performer for a musical performance.

Sanders, R. *Sonata.* Remick (Warner Bros.). $4.00. These four movements of moderate technical difficulty have medium-high tessitura, never going above high Bb. The third movement is a chorale with extremes of volume and range, and the last movement is in rapid 5/8 meter. The length of 17 minutes plus sustained high playing makes the work tiring. A fine, high quality piece, it requires a mature pianist and trombonist for a musical performance.

Serocki, K. *Sonata.* Polskie Wyda Wnictwo Muz. (Belwin-Mills). $2.00. Three movements of moderate technical demands, with medium-high tessitura (range to high C) and tricky interval skips. The piano is not hard but of equal importance. This very musical piece makes for enjoyable listening.

Shostakovich/Ostrander. *Four Preludes.* Edition Musicus. $2.00. Each prelude is short and in totally different styles. The first requires good soft dynamic control, the second has some difficult interval jumps and other technical hurdles. But they are all light-hearted pieces and fun to play. The piano is easy.

Spillman, R. *Concerto for Bass Trombone.* Edition Musicus. $4.00. Control of lower register and breath are essential for performing this work. Range from pedal E to F above the bass clef staff.

Takacs, J. *Sonata, Op. 59.* Sidemton Verlag. $2.00. This single movement with four sections has some tricky technical passages. It is interesting musically and will make a fair performance piece.

Wagenseil/Janetzky. *Konzert for Trombone and Orchestra.* Willy Mueller (C.F. Peters). $6.50. Published with piano reduction. Originally for alto trombone, this two-movement work has a high tessitura with many high notes (several high C's and Bb's and even a fourth space Eb in the treble clef). The work is very tiring, but it is a musical piece that can sound very good if the player has a singing, lyrical upper register. An excellent performance work and good for teaching pre-classic style, it is in tenor clef and comes with a fairly easy piano part.

White, D. *Sonata.* Southern Music Co. $4.00. There are no particular performance problems in this three-movement sonata. A very musical and vigorous work, the third movement features an alternation of 2/4 and 3/8 meters, requiring constant alertness to underlying pulse. Piano and trombone are truly a team; neither part is interesting to work on without the other.

Advanced

Albrechtsberger. *Concerto.* Editio Musica Budapest (Boosey & Hawkes). $4.00 (piano reduction); $10.50 (with orchestra parts). One of the few extant trombone works from the classical era, this was composed for alto trombone in 1769. It is in alto trombone range with a high D and many high C's and Bb's — and if an alto trombone is available, it is a fine recital piece. Fine for teaching classic style and concerto form, it also includes cadenzas and a variety of classical ornaments.

Bach/Becker. *Six Suites for Cello Solo.* International Music Co. $1.75. This is an edition for cello. These suites are standard baroque dance movements with preludes, ranging from low C to high G (except for the sixth suite which goes completely out of the upper trombone range). Bass clef is used in all but the sixth suite. The cello edition requires trombone with trigger for all suites. There are many wide and difficult leaps, long phrases, fast technique, difficult arpeggiated patterns...plus dynamic, stylistic, and interpretive problems. Decisions regarding how chords or multiple simultaneous notes — standard cello techniques — are to be handled on the trombone confront the player. The suites do not lay easily for trombone and are difficult to play convincingly in performance. However, they are valuable as etudes to study all aspects of trombone technique as well as Bach-baroque styles and forms. They are also good for developing facility in use of the trigger. These suites are a must for the advanced trombonist's study. For trombonists with trigger, I recommend this or other cello editions for greatest authenticity — and least expense.

Bach/Marsteller. *Suites for Violoncello Alone.* Southern Music Co. Published in two volumes, $2.50 each. The same suites as above, but these have been edited for trombone either with or without trigger. There is more use of tenor clef than in the cello editions. Suites 5 and 6 are edited so they are more playable on the trombone.

Bach/LaFosse. *Suites for Violoncello Alone.* Alphonse Leduc. $3.60. Another edition of the suites but edited for trombone without trigger. Transposed to high keys with a range going up to high C, these are mostly in tenor clef. The first four suites and selected movements from 5 and 6 are included.

Beethoven. *Seven Variations on a Theme from Mozart's Magic Flute.* International Music Co. $1.25. For cello and piano, this has not been edited for trombone. Ranging from C below the bass clef staff to F on the first space treble clef, the work has a medium tessitura and is notated in bass, tenor and treble clefs. It provides good exposure to the small note-values common in Adagio writing, something the trombonist does not see too often in his literature. Chamber music for trombone and piano in the early, classic style of Beethoven, this is a beautiful piece that could be well done by a fine performer. Piano requires a mature player.

Berio, L. *Sequenza V.* Universal Edition (Presser). $3.70. This unaccompanied, aleatoric piece for the virtuoso trombonist will make an interesting program piece. It uses flutter tonguing, singing while playing, vocal sounds, flutter tonguing while singing, and other unconventional techniques. Good for teaching these particular techniques as well as a totally new notation system.

Bloch. E. *Symphony for Trombone.* Broude Bros. $6.25 (piano reduction); $9.00 (score); orchestral parts available on rental only. Almost entirely in tenor clef, this work ranges to high D with a very high tessitura. It requires mostly sustained playing, with no serious technical problems other than range and endurance. It is rather dull musically due to lack of contrast in styles. The orchestral material is important and somewhat difficult.

Casterede, J. *Sonatine.* Alphonse Leduc. $4.00. A French School work in three movements, this is an interesting and enjoyable piece to perform and hear — though somewhat on the light side. The outer movements have some shifting meter but should not present great problems; the second movement is a beautiful, subdued, smooth melody. The tessitura is high, ranging to high C in a few spots, and the piece is long and somewhat tiring. There are wide dynamic and interval ranges and a fairly frequent switching between tenor and bass clef.

Childs, B. *Sonata.* Tritone Press (Presser). $2.00. A somewhat avant-garde virtuoso piece.

Creston, P. *Fantasy for Trombone and Orchestra,* Op. 42. Schirmer. $3.00 (piano reduction); orchestral parts available on rental only. Through-composed in 4 sections, the work features high tessitura, a range to double high E♭, and difficult technical sections. It is a long piece requiring great endurance. There is much use of double sharps and flats in tenor clef, making reading difficult. The accompaniment, especially with piano, is very difficult. It

is musically mediocre but worth performing.

Croley, R. *Divertissment for Bass Trombone and Piano.* Ensemble Publications. $2.50. Difficult rhythmically and metrically, with constantly changing irregular meters. The range is from low C below the bass clef staff to A♭ above the bass staff, with a medium low tessitura. There is a wide dynamic range. The piano part is difficult.

Defay. *Two Danses for Trombone and Piano.* Alphonse Leduc. $3.20. Dance rhythms, jazz-like style, high tessitura, and range to double high F are featured. Both tenor and treble clefs are used. They are fun, light pieces, but require the strength and flexibility necessary for wide skips and upper register playing.

Gabrieli/Shuman. *Ricercar for Violoncello Solo.* Southern Music Publ. Co. 90¢. In this edition, the original has been transposed up a fifth, making the tessitura high. I suggest using the more authentic edition for cello by Schering. In any case, it will require control and endurance. This unaccompanied work will not be easy to bring off on trombone, but it can be done.

Hartley, W. *Sonata Breve.* Presser $1.00. This unaccompanied piece for bass trombone is quite disjunct and has some very wide skips. The two movements — allegro and presto — display a low tessitura with a range down to pedal A. Although there is some interesting bass trombone work in this contemporary piece, it is probably more fun to play than hear.

Hartley, W. *Sonata Concertante.* Fema Mus. Publ. $5.00. There is great dynamic contrast in this through-composed work written, essentially, in three sections with coda. Wide interval skips, fast marcato tonguing, some skips in runs, and legato runs in thirds make for problem areas. Range from pedal G♯ to high C. A fine piece for performance, requiring a mature pianist.

Jacob, G. *Concerto for Trombone and Orchestra.* Joseph Williams (Galaxy). $2.50. (piano reduction); orchestra parts available on rental only. Nearly every technical problem for the trombonist is explored in this piece: it ranges from pedal G to double high F; there is a wide range of dynamics; the second movement is very slow and sustained with a high tessitura; the third movement has a very demanding cadenza. The first movement, with a recitative-like opening and a fast ending, can stand alone effectively as a performance piece. As a whole, the work is somewhat musically lacking, but is effective in performance — though a bit showy. It is notated mostly in the bass clef with some use of tenor clef and has an easy accompaniment. The piano arrangement was made by the composer.

Larrson, Lars-Erik. *Concertino, Op. 45* for trombone and strings. Associated Music Publ. $5.60. (piano reduction); $4.50 (score). The work is composed in three movements: the cadenza-like first movement is rather free and technically demanding with fast runs that skip and long passages with six notes to the beat; the second movement is a beautiful ballad; the third movement is sprightly with several technical hurdles. Dynamic and pitch ranges are not too wide. The piano accompaniment is not too demanding. This is not the finest music, but it is acceptable and worth working on.

Milhaud. *Concertino D'Hiver* for trombone and strings. Carl Gehrmans Musikforlag. $2.50 (piano reduction); $5.50 (trombone and string arrangement). A through-composed piece in three sections written in light, French school style with no real technical problems. There is some use of flutter-tonguing, a range to high C, and medium to medium high tessitura. Both bass and tenor clefs are used. The accompaniment has an active part which is not too difficult to negotiate but which requires a mature accompanist. This is a musically interesting work that is worth performing. The piano arrangement was made by the composer. ■

Bell-Up or Bell-Front Tubas?

Ronald A. Sellers

Recently, an experiment was conducted in which several types of tubas were compared. Two were bell-front models (one a fiberglas Sousaphone) and two were bell-up models (one a German-made symphony model).

Varied seating arrangements were used for both the performing players and the observers (see illus.). And both bell positions (i.e., bell-up and bell-front) were used at each instrument location by the two instrumentalists involved — even the Sousaphone player bent over backwards to simulate a bell-up position!

The performers were music educators — one a tuba specialist, the other a clarinet major who had started a number of tuba players in school bands. Both played to the limit of their ability, without favoring any one particular instrument. Several different solo passages that used all dynamic levels and articulations were performed.

The observers were school band directors or university graduate students majoring in music education. All were instructed to set aside previous opinions, to disregard what they *saw* on the stage, and to appraise only what they actually *heard*. The observers were asked to take notes, paying particular attention to noticeable differences in tone quality, volume, fullness and focus of sound...or anything else which might be of interest.

With the instruments in the *bell-up* position, the sound produced was nondirectional, seeming to come from all over, as though the stage were one large tuba. The position of the instrument or the observer made no difference whatsoever. Attacks and articula-

tions were all heard to be precise and crisp. Tone quality in every instrument tended to be very smooth and clear in all registers. Only the most experienced ears could notice the slight differences in timbre and tone quality from instrument to instrument, despite the variance of bore size, bell size, and instrument composition.

With the instruments in the *bell-front* position, the sound produced was, as expected, quite directional. For example, sound from a tuba at playing position 3 was heard to be louder at observer position A than at

1, 2, and 3 — Instrument Positions

A, B, and C — Observer Positions

C. Poor attacks and articulations (especially those of the inexperienced player), valve clatter, and water at the water keys were all greatly amplified and rather blatantly exposed to the observers. Not even the slightest misplaced attack went unnoticed. Also, the physical differences of each instrument tended to have more of an

effect on tone quality. In the bell-front position, the symphony tuba had a more desirable tone than the fiberglas Sousaphone, whereas only a slight difference had been detected when both were in the bell-up position.

On impulse, during the experiment, all of the instruments were played at stage position 2 with the bells facing the back curtain. Except for a slight reduction in volume, the results were the same as with the bells pointed upward.

The experiment demonstrated that the bell-up instruments can produce a fine sounding, solid, non-directional bass for the band — and this is what most band directors have said they want. Though this instrument does not have the neat, tidy, and sparkling appearance of a bell-front tuba, its *musical* qualities compel me to recommend it over the bell-front type. To be sure, Sousaphones and bell-front tubas have their place in school bands — for outdoor performances; and economic considerations may force some schools to use them for all occasions. But, if possible, a school band should have two sets of tubas — Sousaphones for outdoor appearances and upright tubas for indoors. An alternative would be to buy one set of tubas with two detachable bells.

Although this was only one rather informal and loosely controlled experiment by a relatively small group of music educators, the results did confirm some widely-held convictions, as well as to suggest some other factors which should be considered when purchasing instruments for the school band. ∎

Cadenzas

Christopher Leuba

The text of this article (printed in the January, 1974 issue) contains Mr. Leuba's discussion of the qualities of an effective cadenza, along with 5 of the 17 music examples — transcriptions of the cadenzas from recordings of Concerto No. 4 for Horn by W.A. Mozart. *Those cadenzas already printed are from the following recordings:*

Barboteu, Georges. Monitor S 2118.

Blank, Kurt (RIAS/Ludwig, cond.). DGG Heliodor 478415.

Brain, Dennis (Halle Orchestra). Columbia ML 2088.

Brain, Dennis (Philharmonia/Susskind). Angel 35092.

Buyanovsky, Vitaly. Melodiya D 0257-97/80.

The following are the sources for the cadenzas which appear in this issue:

Ceccarossi, Domenico. Audio Fidelitv FCS 43102.

Chiba, Kaoru (NHK/Iwaki, cond.).

King SKR 1022.

Civil, Alan (RPO/Kempe). RCA LSC 2973.

Civil, Alan (Klemperer). Columbia 33CX1760.

Jones, Mason (Ormandy). Columbia ML 6185.

Linder, Albert (Vienna/Swarowsky). Vanguard VRS 1069.

Muhlbacher, Ernst (Vienna/Bauer-

Theussel). Vox PL 12.630.

Penzel, Erich (Vienna/Paumgartner). Mercury 50407.

Perrini, Nicholas. Coronet S 1406.

Stagliano, James (Zimbler Sinf.). Sine-quan Z4RS 1229.

Tuckwell, Barry (Maag). London BR 3102.

Tuckwell, Barry (Marriner). HMV ASD 2780.

Ceccarossi

Chiba

Civil/Kempe

Civil/Klemperer

Jones

Linder

Muhlbacher

Penzel

Perrini

Stagliano

Tuckwell/Maag

Tuckwell/Marriner

The following cadenza, by this writer, utilizes tape-loop echo effects as well as a tape-loop "drift modulation" (by altering the speed of the tape loop) from E flat to G flat major. Otherwise, it is straightforward, harmonically.

Leuba

1974

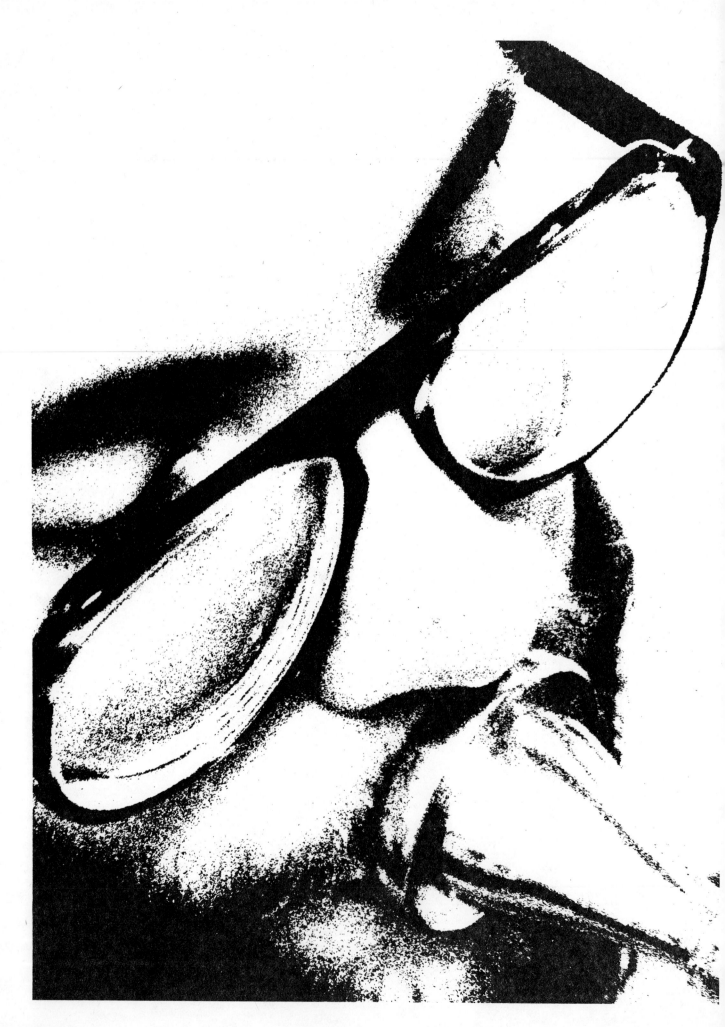

April, 1974

The Perfect Trumpet Lesson

Mario F. Oneglia

A consideration of what constitutes the "perfect" (ideal) trumpet lesson has occupied my thoughts for quite some time. Should the lesson be directed towards the increasing of skills such as technique and range, or should its focus be upon the building of balanced musicianship?

It seems to me that balance is the key here. Just as it is important in nutrition (it is unwise to overindulge in dessert at the expense of protein or carbohydrate intake), it is important for both student and teacher to use balance and moderation in their approach to the trumpet lesson.

The Warmup

A variety of warmup routines have been advocated in trumpet instruction in the past, and several new ones have developed since the inception of extreme register demands for the modern player. Most teachers and authorities agree on the need for some kind of preliminary, non-strenuous exercise that will enable the trumpet player's lips to find or "remember" the method of producing the tone. The extent of the warmup will vary — some believing that it should take as long as an hour and others suggesting just a few long tones. The form that the warmup takes will vary with different players and teachers, but most agree on the necessity for some kind of long tone or sustained and slurred warmup. My feeling is that the warmup should be essentially repetitive, so that the body can "remember the feel" more readily. The second part of the warmup ought to be calisthenic in nature, extending the physical limits of the body. These "calisthenics" might include slurred interval studies or slurred harmonic drills (such as those in the Schloss-

berg *Daily Drills*). I like to vary interval studies by adding dynamics to them. This enables the student to gain further control over that essential aspect of all wind playing: the steady, constant air stream.

Mouthpiece Buzzing

Virtuoso Maurice André has said that in France he never heard of the practice of buzzing on the mouthpiece of the trumpet. And yet, the practice of buzzing seems to be fairly common to trumpeters in this country — though some advocate "a daily half hour's practice on the mouthpiece for all serious players" (Irving Bush) while others recommend buzzing "a few notes daily" (Schlossberg). What is to be gained from the practice of buzzing the mouthpiece? My own thought is that such practice enables the player to "fix" the resistance or amount of breath pressure that is needed to play the instrument. A further advantage to buzzing is to develop greater sensitivity to pitch, since the player is forced to produce a particular pitch without the help of the instrument. I generally have my students buzz one line of a Schlossberg drill, and *then* play the same line with the trumpet.

Technical Study

A third aspect of the lesson routine is the need to develop technique. This area may be treated in a variety of ways. I have found the practice of assigning one page of etudes to be played slowly, in subdivision if possible, to work quite well. This "slow" page is then assigned to be played as quickly as it can be played correctly the second week, while a new "slow" page is assigned. Remembering the lesson of the balanced meal, it has

been my observation that it is practically impossible for the student to deal with all of his trumpet playing needs if more than this is attempted. I use the Herbert L. Clarke *Technical Studies*, but any technical method book may be utilized in this same manner.

When my students have completed the book for the first time, they go back to the beginning and repeat it using a different articulation: first the single tongue and then triple or double. It is reported that "Doc" Severinsen is on his twenty-sixth time through the Clarke studies! Quite an inspiration for the young student.

Transposition

The need for the trumpeter to transpose has existed for many years, but some young players have a tendency to neglect transposition studies if there is insufficient time for complete practice. This is the major reason I include these studies as the third item in the lesson schedule.

I have found it to be more advantageous to concentrate on one transposition, such as C trumpet, for a little while before beginning others. If the student is presented with too many, too rapidly, he is apt to become confused. By systematically including transposition in each and every lesson assignment, all are soon mastered.

Orchestral Excerpts

The judicious practice of various orchestral excerpts for trumpet is related to transposition and should be included in each lesson. I suggest that my students listen to a recording with the score in hand — in order to better understand the role of the trumpet, and as an aid to the development of all-around musicianship.

Solo Playing and Repertoire

It would be a very strange student indeed if he were not interested in playing songs, pieces, and solos — simply for enjoyment, in preparation for various auditions and recitals, or to serve as the long range building of musicianship. I believe that solo playing is a very important part of the lesson. The *Etudes de Concours* of the Paris Conservatoire are extremely useful in this area, as are *Solos for the Trumpet Player* by Walter Beeler. Other useful materials include Arban's, *The Art of Phrasing,* the Concone studies for medium high voice and various cornet solos and trumpet concerti. Since it has always seemed to me to be rather unfair to suddenly thrust "the All-State Solo" of the year at a young student, I insist that my college students (prospective teachers) study all of the solos on the state list, as well as the major concerti, such as those by Haydn, Hummel, Gianinni, and Hindemith.

Varied Etudes for Musical Development

While it is virtually impossible to play all of the studies which have been composed for the trumpet (and each teacher has his favorites), the following curriculum has been useful to me on the college level (allowing for individual differences and modes of prior study). In the freshman year it is useful to review the *Characteristic Studies* of Arban and to introduce the second and third books of the Gatti Method. The latter is a good means of provided ensem-ble experience through the playing of melodious duets with the teacher. In the event that the student has a fairly good grasp of either or both of these materials, I have used the St. Jacome studies, particularly the Bousquet Studies contained therein, with good effect.

The French school of trumpet methods is introduced during the second year. Some of these include the René Laurent Books 1, 2, and 3. These delightful studies are not only useful for technical and musical development, but are also an introduction to contemporary writing for the trumpet.

Etude studies which are assigned in the third year usually include those by H. Chavanne and A. Chavanne. Advanced students may move on to studies by Charlier, Marcel Bitsch, or Aaron Harris (although these are usually included in the fourth year curriculum). Again, in line with the theory of moderation, only one or two studies are assigned each week. In this fashion, I have found that it is possible for the student to build a solid foundation of musicianship without feeling harassed or rushed. A wise rule to follow seems to be: *give the student what he can master successfully.*

Syncopation and/or Jazz Studies

In this day of increasing interest in the jazz idiom, I have found it useful to work for a few minutes in each lesson with the problems in this area. The form that this work may take will vary from using a book for the reading of rhythms, such as Arnold's *Jazz Styles,* to an improvisation primer, such as Coker's *Improvising Jazz.*

The Warmdown

Just as athletes use a cooling off period after physical exertion, so the trumpet player should have a relaxation routine after the practice period. Pedal tone studies can be very effective here. These may take the form of descending chromatic long tones from C^1 to the double pedal two octaves below, or descending major chords. Advanced students can slur into and out of the pedal register.

The playing of pedal tones for short periods of time helps to relax tired lips and seems to lend overall tone to the embouchure. Also, the extension of the lower register seems to have a beneficial effect on the extension of the upper register. I always have students play a slurred two octave scale as a bringing-together of all playing in the termination of the practice session.

This approach to the trumpet lesson has served my students well, and I hope that it will be useful to others. High school students will benefit from the variety of means touched upon in the several areas. As a closing statement, I can think of nothing more appropriate than to quote the noted brass pedagogue, Maurice Grupp, who emphasized the need for moderation when he stated: "one must know when to put the horn in the case." ∎

French Horn Resonance

Edward Pease

Scientists consider resonance and timbre as two distinct characteristics, yet I doubt that within the practical musical situation we can ever entirely separate the two. In many situations, resonance can actually alter tone color — at least as the human ear perceives it. Consider, for example, that a musician performing in a very "live" hall is going to get a richer, fuller tone than if he plays in a small, stuffy drawing room.

Regardless of how the matter is argued, resonance is one of the really vital factors in making music. It is therefore doubly amazing that so little is said about it in the pedagogical treatises on wind playing.

Certainly, the adjustments we

make *within* our bodies, both as conscious and subconscious acts, in order to realize physically our mental image of sound are of overriding significance in tone production. But some consideration must be given to other *exterior* physiological factors as well as certain non-bodily, environmental phenomena. Here we are concerned with the effect of resonance on tone production; and this will vary according to the room or auditorium in which the hornist performs, his position in it, the instrument and its mouthpiece, and the manner in which the instrument is held (including the position of the right hand in the bell).

Unfortunately, the player rarely has control over the acoustics of the room in which he performs, yet its properties are of vital importance. The "live" room, with proper dimensions and surfaces, can in fact make the mediocre player sound much better than he deserves, but a bad hall can frustrate a first-rate artist.

As far as the actual construction of auditoriums is concerned, we are obviously dealing with a very subjective matter. Professional, ultra-scientific acousticians have built some auditoriums which are acoustical nightmares (usually not "dead" but very harsh sounding and unflattering), whereas some fine-sounding halls have come about seemingly by accident or by means of some vague trial-and-error process. Obviously, there is a discrepancy between real acoustical data and the aesthetic evaluation of the results.

There are, however, some general qualities to look for in good halls. They most often have high ceilings, rather hard surfaces, and a limited amount of curtaining or seating upholstery. Also, generous amounts of wood in the construction seem to be desirable, especially wood flooring on the stage. (The Royal Opera House in London's Covent Garden is an outstanding example of a house with flattering acoustical properties resulting from its wooden stage and orchestra pit.) Another major factor is good direction of the sound to the audience. The ideal auditorium is thus perhaps a compromise between the "dead," unflattering hall and the overly "barny" hall,

wherein the reverberation time is so long and diffused that music seems muddled (as in big cathedrals).

A few variables in auditorium acoustics can be controlled more immediately. The hard-surfaced shell or back-drop is definitely an aid to projecting the sound of the orchestral horn section; in fact, it is so successful that some hornists occasionally feel the need to put a blanket or extra coat on the chairs behind them in order not to overpower the rest of the orchestra. The clothing of the player and the hand position are also of great importance. If one has trouble projecting in a "dead" auditorium, then the rather open hand position and above all the turning of the bell away from the body are partial remedies. In very loud passages, one should by all means lift the bell off of the thigh and open up the hand position. Conversely, very delicate passages may require more closure. It is important to remember, however, that any adjustment of the hand position requires a consequent adjustment of the tuning slide.

In the orchestra, the seating of the horns is usually up to the conductor, but the now almost universal practice of placing them at the rear of the orchestra, blowing against the back-drop, is probably the best. In solo recitals and in the playing of concertos, it is quite common to see hornists position themselves in such a way that the bell faces in toward the pianist or the orchestra, almost as if they are trying to hide their wrong notes from the audience. Since this results in the loss of a great deal of clarity and projection, it is far better to sit or stand with the bell at least partially toward the audience, however unnerving this may be. Although one can achieve a bit more projection by standing rather than sitting, most players find that this makes the horn very uncomfortable to hold. In addition, one needs to experiment with various positions on the stage, seeking the ideal acoustical area. The amount that the piano lid is opened is another factor to consider.

Chamber music requires all types of subtle adjustments to a wide variety of situations. There is, for example, a striking difference between the seating position used for woodwind quintet as opposed to brass quintet. In the woodwind group, the horn tends to be too loud, so the player usually positions himself at the rear center of the ensemble, with the bell of the horn projecting back. He may also need to use a rather closed hand position to further muffle the sound, though I personally prefer developing a nice pianissimo without excessive choking of the instrument. In the all brass group, conversely, the hornist must achieve sufficient penetration to compete with trumpets and trombones; thus a seating arrangement which allows the hornist to have his bell at least partially outward is advantageous, as is a somewhat more open hand position.

Finally, a word about practice rooms. The "telephone booths" in which we are often forced to work are usually so confining and unresonant that they actually encourage a small, choked sound. Thus, they are a negative factor in developing a good tone. The best place to practice is in a large, resonant classroom or even better, an auditorium. Also, practice out-of-doors is a great aid to the large open concept.

Another important factor affecting horn resonance is the type of equipment used. Here the player has far more control over the situation. With suitable funds available, he can purchase one of innumerable horns and is deluged with mouthpieces of every size and shape.

The general trend in the United States is toward large equipment, especially the Conn-8D or large-bore Kruspe, often coupled with one of the larger Giardinelli or Horner mouthpieces (usually with a relatively thin rim). In addition, most players use considerable hand in the bell in order to develop a large, very dark "German" or "Viennese" sound. At several recent clinics, however, three of our most formidable artists had a somewhat different outlook on the matter — Barry Tuckwell uses relatively small equipment and Phillip Farkas and John Barrows both prefer equipment of moderate proportions. In a lecture, Mr. Barrows suggested that a moderate bore was important in producing a well-centered sound — one that is not so thick and dark that it fails to "sing."

While very large equipment and excessive hand in the bell may produce a thick, ultra-dark sound (which fails to carry), a very small-bore horn and shallow mouthpiece is just as objectionable, for the result is nearly always an extremely harsh sound. We need a nice core or center to the tone but without sacrificing all of the mellowness and body.

Another factor in the resonance of the instrument is the metal which is used in its manufacture. I prefer natural, unplated brass on the thin side. Lacquer can deaden the sound a little, and silver plate or alloy (German silver) can darken it (but in a way that is musically more acceptable). It will always be a subjective matter among hornists as to what material is best, just as the matter of bore, mouthpiece, and hand position will continue to be influenced by personal preferences and national considerations.

In dealing with the exterior factors of horn resonance, the performer must face a number of problems. While he does have control over some of these (such as the equipment he uses), the variables introduced by the place (auditorium, small room, etc.) and context (solo recital, orchestra, etc.) in which he performs will require a great deal of flexibility. Only when the hornist is prepared for a variety of possible adjustments in positioning, seating, and even playing techniques can he hope to perform effectively in all situations. ■

June, 1974

The Third T
of Trombone Technique

Neill H. Humfeld

Those of us who were privileged to study with Emory Remington heard this great master emphasize "the three T's of Trombone Playing" many times. Most of us understood his stressing the importance of "tonguing" and "tuning," for these two words had been in our musical vocabularies from the outset of our learning — and many articles have been written about these two "T's." The main purpose of this writing is the third "T" — *timing* — since work on this aspect of playing will do much toward helping the security of performance of any player.

The sheer technique of playing any instrument is a complex act involving skill, coordination, and general intelligence, in addition to musicianship. To sound a note, the trombonist must have the slide in the correct position, his embouchure at the correct firmness, his articulation (release of air) precisely timed, the back or center of the tongue in the correct position (ee-oo-ah), the correct air pressure to sound the note, and if he is playing on the F attachment, the thumb must engage the trigger. All this must happen at the same split second! And if it doesn't, the result is often a faulty attack or a split note.

The problem is how to develop timing, so that it becomes an automatic process — not a laborious technique. Since the main purpose is to learn how to *time* the emission of notes in order to control them completely, it is important to practice *all* excercises at the same strict tempo. Lip slurs, scales, arpeggios — the entire gamut of warm-ups — should be practiced *with a beat*. All of those faculties which are needed to obtain good timing and attack must be synchronized. This can be learned by practicing to a fixed beat.

An exceptionally fine exercise to help the timing of the slide is to play a scale starting on *do, re, do* in slow half notes. Move the slide quickly but not so fast that you shake the entire instrument. The most important thing in timing is to tongue *as you reach* the position — not *before* or you will smear, nor *after* for you will break a legato passage (or lose all sense of timing on detached passages). Next, add one note, then another, etc.

Play this exercise in all keys, giving special attention to the keys with five or six flats. (One of the most difficult slide changes is from 1 to 5 (f to g♭) and back to 1.)

Another exercise which can be very helpful is to play a note such as middle C and approach it from different areas on the slide. One need not place the slide in an exact position, just put it some place above or below the third position. Then move the slide quickly (but smoothly) and tongue just as the slide reaches the third position. Keep repeating the C from both above and below this position, each time trying to synchronize the tongue and the slide. Then repeat this exercise with different pitches throughout the range of the instrument. This should be done with both legato and staccato articulations.

An additional timing problem is present when using the F-attachment trombone. Obviously, you now have to synchronize the thumb with the tongue, slide, etc. I strongly recommend that the valve be engaged just as you reach the desired slide positions, as it will greatly facilitate your timing and

give you much more control. (If it is pushed as the slide is moving between positions, it changes the air acoustically in the instrument and articulation problems can result — particularly in legato passages.) Also, it helps the entire mental and physical process of timing to completely synchronize the thumb with the already-established timing procedures — it helps "set" the process and "locks

it in."

One can devise his own exercises, but the main thing to remember is that you are working for a quick (not fast), *timed* slide. Use scales, arpeggios, isolated notes, etc. — but always with a beat. If this point seems a bit labored, it is only because it is essential in truly understanding what Mr. Remington meant by this third "T" of trombone performance. ∎

September, 1974

An Orthodontic Aid for Young Trumpeters

Albert F. Ligotti and Eugene D. Voth

The affluence of our expanding middle class society is producing a population of young musicians wearing orthodontic appliances. Unfortunately, "braces" seem to be incompatible with wind instruments, particularly the brass. This incompatibility becomes more acute with instruments having smaller mouthpieces, because, in addition to the problems caused by the small size of the mouthpiece, greater lip pressure is required to produce musical sounds. Therefore, trumpet students constitute the largest group facing difficulty in playing their instrument while undergoing orthodontic treatment. In almost every case, the orthodontic appliances cause discomfort and pain in varying degrees, and the result is that some talented students will completely abandon the instrument during treatment.

The Basic Problem

Young trumpet players frequently exert a great deal of pressure on the lips and teeth while playing their instruments. The problem for a trumpet player wearing braces is that the pressure will cause the metal brackets, with which the wires and bands are attached, to cut the mucosa on the inside of the lips (Figure 1). This can result in

much discomfort and pain and will greatly reduce the player's endurance, playing range, hence his total playing ability. In some cases, a student may be reduced back to the level of a rank beginner. In addition to the physical handicaps, many students are so discouraged that their mental outlook is severely altered and they may abandon the instrument completely.

Finding a Solution

To aid young trumpet players, a project was undertaken with the hope of finding some solution to this growing problem. In our initial investigations, an attempt was

made to use a modified lip bumper fabricated from a pliable thermoplastic material (D-P Vangard) that is often used for mouth guards. After making these appliances for several trumpet players, it was determined that they could not be made thin enough since playing was difficult when the appliances were in place. In addition, for those in the initial stages of treatment, the movement of the teeth was great enough to require frequent readjustment of the lip guard (by the orthodontist). So this approach proved to be impractical both from the standpoint of effectiveness and expense.

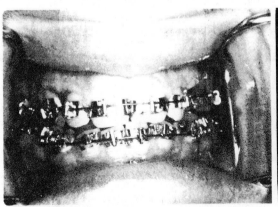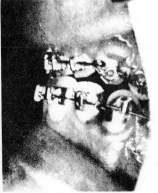

Fig. 1. An orthodontic appliance. Note the many sharp projections which tend to cut the mucosa of the lip when pressure is applied, as in playing the trumpet.

We began looking for something pliable, self-adjusting and inexpensive. We first tried beeswax, since it would be completely adaptable to almost any orthodontic situation and it is generally dispensed by the orthodontist. The wax was applied in small amounts over each bracket in the anterior portion of the mouth. The irritation was reduced, but the amount of wax needed hindered playing.

Next we tried Kerr Boxing wax sticks. (Boxing wax is packaged in thin narrow sticks.) We used a small piece stretched over the entire frontal area of the teeth, covering the brackets (Figure 2). It was thin enough to avoid the problem of unnecessary bulk, yet strong enough to reduce or eliminate the irritation. It could be inserted and molded by the student himself before each playing session. (Its bright red coloring made it easy for the student to place it exactly where he needed it.) Finally, it was economical (even though it is not re-usable) and completely adjustable to all types of orthodontic appliances.

In choosing a suitable wax, consistency was a critical factor. It must be soft enough to mold easily and yet tough enough to prevent the edges of the brackets from penetrating the wax under normal playing pressure.

After preliminary testing of several waxes, we proceeded to dispense the Kerr boxing wax sticks

to many junior high school trumpet players, either directly from the orthodontic clinic or through the local band directors. In almost every case, the student reported a vast reduction of irritation. In some instances complete elimination of discomfort and pain was reported. After a short period of adjustment, the students were able to play comfortably for longer periods of time, enabling them to continue progress on their instruments. In fact, the wax became so much a part of the braces that several students reported forgetting to remove it after a playing session — although the bright red coloring was a helpful reminder. In a few cases, students mentioned that their basic tone was actually improved with the wax — perhaps because the wax filled in the spaces between the brackets, producing a more even and solid wall of support between the teeth and the lips.

Final Results

Musically speaking, the use of this wax helped the average trumpet student to continue playing during the lengthy period required for most orthodontic treatment, since the usual irritation and soreness of the mucosa on the inside of the lips was found to be reduced or eliminated. At the same time, using the wax in no way affected the orthodontic treatment of the patients. It could be applied easily by the student and simply peeled off after each playing session, so there was no need for extra visits to the orthodontist.

Aside from the very real pain and discomfort, the major problem for brass players wearing braces seemed to be psychological. Now, however, young brass players undergoing or planning to undergo orthodontic treatment can look forward to some aid and help during this period — from both the orthodontist and the music teacher. ■

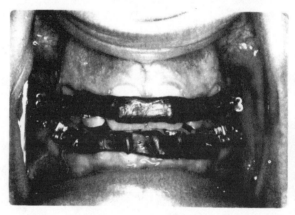

Fig. 2. Kerr boxing wax sticks are used to cover the orthodontic appliance.

A Comprehensive Bibliography
of Music for Brass Quintet
(Addendum)

Donald K. Day

Since "A Comprehensive Bibliography of Music for Brass Quintet" appeared in the November and December (1973) issues of *The Instrumentalist,* numerous additions have come to my attention. Although keeping a bibliography of this nature up to date is an impossible task, it is hoped that these additional entries will provide useful literature for brass quintets. The author welcomes information concerning brass quintets in manuscript, works to be published shortly, or corrections to existing entries.

Arnell, Richard. *Variations on "The Wayfaring Stranger."* San Antonio TX: Southern Music Company. Review: *BP* II/1 (January, 1974), p. 18. Grade V.

Bach, J.S. *Contrapunctus IX.* Delevan NY: Kendor Music, Inc., 1973. Grade IV.

———. *Sarabande and Courante*, arr. McGregor. New York: Autograph Editions, 1973. Grade IV.

Bartok, Bela. *A Little Bartok Suite*, ed. Brown. Westbury NY: Pro Art Publications, 1973. Grade IV.

Beale, David. *Spirit of St. Louis.* Boise ID: Manuscript Publications. Grade V.

Brandon, Sy. *Movements.* Boise ID: Manuscript Publications. Grade V.

Brown, Newel Kav. *Three Diverse Movements* (1968). Composers MS, School of Music, North Texas State Univ., Denton TX. Review: *BW* VIII/2 (1973), p. 103. Grade V.

Browning, Zack. *Quintet* (1973). Composers MS, 5980 River Chase Circle, Atlanta GA. Grade V.

Budd, Harold. *Jacaranda* (1971). Composers MS, 23149 Oakbridge Lane, Newhall CA. Review: *BW* VIII/2 (1973), p. 104. Grade V.

Clark, Mitch (arr.). *Two Christmas Carols.* Mitch Clark, 83 Ellis Ave., Toronto, Canada, 1973. Review: *BP* I/5 (November, 1973), p. 25. Grade III.

Fennelly, Brian. *Prelude and Elegy* (1973). Composers MS, 100 Bleeker St., New York NY. Review: *BW* VIII/2 (1973), p. 105. Grade V.

Frackenpohl, Arthur. *Three Scott Joplin Rags.* Melville NY: Belwin-Mills Publishing Corp., 1973. Grade IV.

Hannay, Roger. *Four for Five* (1973). Composers MS, Dept. of Music, Univ. of North Carolina, Chapel Hill NC. Grade V.

Holmes, Paul. *Quintet.* Boise ID: Manuscript Publications. Grade V.

Jettel, Rudolph. *Quintet No. 3.* New York: C.F. Peters Corp., 1972.

King, Robert (arr.). *Twelve Days of Christmas.* North Easton MA: Robert King Music Company, n.d. Review: *BP* I/5 (November, 1973), p. 24, Grade V.

Leichling, Alan. *Quintet.* New York: Seesaw Music Corp., 1971. Grade VI.

Levin, Gregory. *Five Picasso Portraits* (1971). Composers MS, Dept. of Music, Syracuse Univ., Syracuse NY. Grade V.

Loeillet, Jacques. *Allegro*, ed. Crown. Chicago: Crown Music Press, 1973. Grade V.

McCauley, William. *Miniature Overture.* Toronto, Canada: Canadian Music Centre, 1973. Grade V.

Mattern, James. *Sonata Breve.* Chicago: Crown Music Press, 1973. Grade V.

Maurer, Ludwig. *Twelve Little Pieces.* London: Novello and Co., 1972. Grade IV.

Molineaux, Allen. *Encounter.* Delaware Water Gap PA: Shawnee Press, 1974. Grade V.

Orr, Buxton. *Sonata* (1969). Composers MS, Scottish Music Archive, Univ. of Glasgow, Glasgow, Scotland.

Peruti, Carl Della. *Quintet.* Boise ID: Manuscript Publications. Review: *BW* VIII/1 (1973), p. 19. Grade V.

Polin, Claire. *Makimo II.* New York: Seesaw Music Corp.

Powell, Morgan. *Quintet No. 2* (1973). Composers MS, Dept. of Music, Univ. of Illinois, Urbana IL. Grade V.

Presser, William. *Folk Song Fantasy.* New York: Seesaw Music Corp., Grade V.

Raph, Alan (arr.). *Nine Christmas Carols.* New York: AR Publishing Co., 1973. Review: *BP* I/5 (November, 1973), p. 25. Grade V.

Renwick, Wilke. *Dance.* Denver CO: Tromba Publications, 1973. Grade IV.

Rice, Thomas. *Quintet.* New York: Seesaw Music Corp.

Roikjer, Kjel. *Scherzo*, Op. 58. Copenhagen: Hansen, 1971. Review: *MT* (November, 1972), p. 1114. Grade VI.

Salthouse, Graham. *Statements.* New York: Seesaw Music Corp. Grade V.

Schaeffer, Don (arr.). *Five Quintets.* Westbury NY: Pro Art Publications, 1972. Grade IV.

Schmelzer, Johann. *Sonata XII*, ed. Stine. Chicago: Crown Music Press, 1973. Grade V.

Sommer, John. *Two Dances*, ed. King. North Easton MA: Robert King Music Co., n.d. Grade IV.

Steiner, Gitta. *Quintet.* New York: Seesaw Music Corp., 1969. Grade V.

Sydeman, William. *Tower Music.* New York: Pkra Music, 1959. Grade V.

Wilder, Alec. *Brassininity.* Delevan NY: Kendor Music, Inc., 1973. Review: *BW* VIII/3 (1973), p. 108. Grade V.

———. *Quintet No. 3.* New York: Sam Fox Publishing Corp., 1970. Grade V.

System of Grading

Grade I — mainly for first year instrumentalists.

Grade II — for those beyond the beginning stages.

Grade III — for those who have acquired some technique.

Grade IV — for more advanced instrumentalists.

Grade V — mostly for college players.

Grade VI — for the skilled professional.

Key to Annotation and Review Sources

BQ — Brass Quarterly

BW — Brass World

BWQ — Brass and Woodwind Quarterly

GSJ — Galpin Society Journal

INST — The Instrumentalist

ML — Music and Letters

MO — Musical Opinion

MT — Musical Times

NACWPI — National Association of College Wind and Percussion Instructors Journal

NOTES — Music Library Association Notes

November, 1974

Improved Use of the Double Horn

Kenneth R. Rumery

The greatest asset of the double horn lies in the large number of alternate fingerings possible on the instrument. Most pitches on the double horn can be played with either F or B-flat fingerings; other alternate fingerings are available where the pitches of the several overtone series coincide. The hornist who knows these alternates can really take advantage of the double horn's assets by designing easy solutions to difficult fingering patterns. In spite of this fact, extensive use of alternate patterns is not a common feature of double horn technique.

Most student double hornists are trained to change from F horn to B-flat horn at a specific pitch or fixed pivot note. This results in a very limited fingering vocabulary with no alternates (Ex. 1). However, in teaching the student to use A or A-flat as a fixed pivot there are several advantages: it makes available to the player most of the common assets of the double horn; it provides him with an easy-to-remember point at which to change horns routinely; and it introduces him to new fingerings which can be expanded later through octave equivalents. But this approach should only be regarded as a preliminary step in training the double hornist. Once he is secure and fluent in the pivot note approach, his knowledge of fingerings can and should be extended.

Octave Equivalents

The student's initial exposure to alternate fingerings can be accomplished with octave equivalents — i.e., pitches fingered the same way on both horns in all octaves (Ex. 2).

The player can easily learn another set of alternate fingerings by knowing that, since the B-flat horn is pitched a perfect fourth above the F horn, any B-flat fingering is the same as the F fingering a perfect fourth below (Ex. 3).

It is also important to introduce students to notes which are less frequently played on the double horn (Ex. 4, 5).

To become fluent in the use of the fingerings illustrated in Examples 2-5, the student can play etudes exclusively on either the F or B-flat horn, noting which passages seem easier to handle with F or B-flat fingerings. These observations help the student to understand the logic of pattern design and may provide him with encouragement or additional incentive while laboring at a seemingly unrewarding but detailed task.

Thumb Movement

Any discussion of thumb movement and its function in finger pattern design must be based on the hornist's version of the "Rule of Thumb" — (1) the thumb should move as nature intended it, independently or in opposition to finger motion; and (2) thumb movement should be kept to a minimum.

Thumb movements should be used in such way as to duplicate the natural grasp and release functions of the hand. To engage the thumb while releasing fingers or release the thumb while engaging fingers is awkward and hard to coordinate. Thus, the B-flat horn should be engaged on repeated open or fingered notes, or against the fingerings 1, 2, or 12. The F horn should be engaged on repeated open or fingered notes, or against the release of any fingerings to open notes. (This may reveal some of the logic behind the use of the pitch "A" as a pivot note.)

Strict use of the pivot note approach sometimes encourages frequent and awkward thumb motion — especially if the range of the passage causes a great deal of traffic back and forth over the pivot note. This can be avoided, however, if the hornist adopts an expanded pivot system including all notes between A♭ and D (Ex. 6), in which

Ex. 1 - Fixed pivot note fingering chart

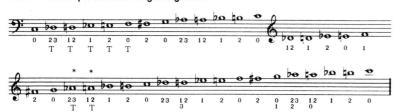

*usual position of fixed pivot, the point of change to and from B-flat horn

Ex. 5 - Less used B-flat fingerings

Ex. 6 - Optional F to B-flat pivot notes

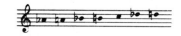

Ex. 2 - Octave equivalents: both F and B-flat fingerings

Ex. 7 - B-flat horn, isolated notes

Ex. 8 - F horn, isolated notes

Ex. 3 - Octave equivalents: B-flat fingerings

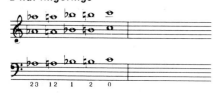

Ex. 4 - Less used F fingerings

Ex. 9 - Arpeggio fingerings, B-flat horn

Ex. 10 - Special B-flat major arpeggio fingering

the actual pivot point is allowed to fluctuate according to the nature of the passage. Thus, if the passage ranges downward from D [music notation], it should be played on the F horn; if it ranges upward from Ab [music notation], it should be played on the B-flat horn.

Disjunct passages sometimes encourage excessive use of the thumb, since isolated pitches (created by octave skips and other large intervals) may lie outside a passage which otherwise could be played entirely on one horn or the other. In general, the player should play the isolated pitch on whatever horn can be used for the entire passage (Ex. 7-8).

Arpeggios

Certain arpeggios are easier to play on a particular horn. The following example (Ex. 9) illustrates those arpeggios which are best played on the B-flat horn. The numbers in parenthesis show optional fingers, which are sometimes needed to improve pitch. For example, open A of the F major arpeggio may be very flat as it is the fifth or tenth harmonic of its series. Slow arpeggios can be more in tune if the fingering 12 is used for A.

The B-flat major arpeggio can be facilitated by a special fingering (Ex. 10). This fingering also provides a very handy solution for the

Ex. 11 - Arpeggio fingerings, F horn

Ex. 12 - Pivot note options for scale passages in most common key signatures

Ex. 13 - Pivot notes in scale context
T represents thumb engaged, assuming the note preceding T will be played with the thumb released

Ex. 14 - Pivot notes in skip-step patterns

Ex. 15 - Extended B-flat fingerings

Ex. 16 - Useful B-flat fingering patterns

Ex. 18 - Useful patterns, F fingerings

691

Cor Basse arpeggios that occur often in E-flat horn parts in most 18th century solo and chamber literature. The D minor arpeggio can be played in a similar way on the B-flat horn using the fingerings open F and 12 or 3 A and D.

F horn fingerings can be particularly useful for extremely rapid arpeggio flourishes in the mid-range of the horn (Ex. 11) and for warm-up patterns using the full range of the horn. The highest notes are of course more secure if played on the B-flat horn, but in most cases it is easy to change to the B-flat horn since the thumb movement is independent of the fingerings and easy to coordinate.

Scales

Passages based on diatonic scale materials abound in traditional literature and etudes. In mainly stepwise passages, a pivot note approach to changing horns usually works very well. The choice of pivot notes, however, depends on the key signature and range of the passage. The best pivot notes are those that involve easy to coordinate finger motions, 0-12T, 23-1T, and 0-23T. In ascending passages, the delay of thumb action until the upper pivot is sometimes advantageous; and in descending passages, the delay of thumb release until the lower pivot note has similar merit (Ex. 12).

The student should practice the above pivot notes in short scale passages in order to develop thumb facility in the various keys (Ex. 13). Later, the pivot notes can be used in longer passages in etude and solo literature.

Scale materials organized in alternating skip-step patterns (Ex. 14) occur frequently in etudes and other literature. In such cases, fingering solutions can still be based on the "rule of thumb."

Extremely rapid scale passages and flourishes are often difficult to play with conventional fingerings and may require special treatment if they are to be "tossed off" with precision. In these cases the fewer fingers used the better, and it is especially important to avoid cross-fingerings and thumb movement. The player can improve his speed and precision by extending the use of the F and B-flat horns above and below their usual limits. The extended B-flat fingerings (useful below normal pivot points) shown in Ex. 15 are best used in rapid scale flourishes containing one to four flats. The alternate fingerings for A and A-flat further minimize the number of fingers used, permitting very brisk F, B-flat, E-flat, and A-flat runs. The lowest A-flat in the example should be considered the bottom practical limit for extended B-flat passage work.

Example 16 shows a few scale segments easily played on the B-flat horn. The choice of B-flat fingerings is best if these passages are extremely rapid. This concept of fingering is similar to the principle that isolated notes should be played on the horn best suited for the entire passage.

The use of the F horn can also be extended a few notes above normal pivot points. As illustrated in Example 17, the chromatic scale (and,

Ex. 17 - Extended F fingerings

1 2 0 23 12 1 2 0 2 0 2 0

therefore, scales in most keys) can be played readily on the F horn provided the range of the passages does not exceed the top E of the example.

Example 18 shows a few scale segments which can be played easily with F fingerings. Also included are a few scale passages that can be "tossed off" on the F horn. The upper limit for F horn usage should be the top note in the examples.

Response

The previous examples reveal several possible ways to solve fingering problems through use of the assets of the double horn. Yet, the choice of F or B-flat horn is sometimes based on a preference for a particular response trait in either horn. For example, the need for light crisp attacks is best fulfilled on the B-flat horn, regardless of range. Some hornists prefer the tone quality of the F horn in lyric passages. Selection of certain alternate fingerings are made for reasons of improved intonation. But some alternate fingerings on the B-flat horn that may at first seem out of tune will improve as the player adapts to response characteristics not previously encountered. And don't forget that out-of-tune pitches are often camouflaged by rapid arpeggio and scale figures.

Solving the Technical Problems

To attain full use of the double horn, the fixed pivot system must be replaced with a more flexible approach. After all, it is the concept of alternate fingerings, movable pivot, and extended use of either horn that accounts for the great variety of keys and patterns that appear in actual literature. The student cannot begin to realize the assets of the double horn until he has learned the array of possible alternate fingerings and can choose patterns which most effectively solve the problems he sees in the music. He can gain skill in this more flexible approach by applying it regularly in practice sessions to etudes, solo, and passage literature. In this way, he can discover patterns which best agree with his strengths of manual dexterity and make them a part of his fingering vocabulary. So armed, he is well prepared to solve many of the technical problems contained in horn literature.

■

How the Professional Trumpeters
Play Double High C

Robert Gibson

In the spring of 1973 a study was begun that investigated four areas of trumpet playing — embouchure, air flow, trumpet angle to the embouchure, and facial muscle usage — to see what changes take place when playing from a low C to a double high C on a B♭ trumpet. A review of related literature and methods pertinent to the achievement of the extreme upper register revealed many points of confusion and disagreement. At this point, I felt that the best way to begin to solve these problems was to go to the players who were able to play successfully in the extreme upper register and study how they were solving the problems. Using a special portable camera with closeup lenses and positioning frames, the subjects were photographed in their own homes or studios with their own trumpets and mouthpieces. The subjects chosen to take part in the study included the following:

1. Paul Bogosian, orchestra of *Jesus Christ Superstar* (Broadway).
2. Jerry Callet, author of *Trumpet Yoga.*
3. Burt Collins, recording artist, New York City.
4. Jon Faddis, lead trumpet in the Thad Jones-Mel Lewis Band.
5. Jimmy Maxwell, Tonight Show and recording artist, New York City.
6. Bob McCoy, Tonight Show and recording artist, New York City.
7. Lloyd Michels, lead trumpet in *Jesus Christ Superstar* (Broadway).
8. Ernie Royal, recording artist, New York City.
9. Gerard Schwarz, co-principal trumpet, New York Philharmonic.
10. Joe Shepley, recording artist, New York City.
11. Roy Stevens, co-author of the *Costello-Stevens Method.*
12. Al Stewart, RCA recording artist, New York City.

Each subject was photographed 12 times. Photo 1 was of the subjects' teeth formation. Photos 2-6

Table I. Lip Placement

Pitch	Equal	More Upper	More Lower
	No. (%)	No. (%)	No. (%)
C4	0	9 (75%)	3 (25%)
C5	0	8 (67%)	4 (33%)
C6	1 (8%)	3 (25%)	8 (67%)
G6	1 (8%)	2 (17%)	9 (75%)
C7	0	4 (33%)	8 (67%)

Table II. Direction of Air Flow

Pitch	90°	Below 90°	Above 90°
C4	4 (33%)	8 (67%)	0
C5	3 (25%)	8 (67%)	1 (8%)
C6	2 (17%)	7 (58%)	3 (25%)
G6	1 (8%)	6 (50%)	5 (42%)
C7	1 (8%)	6 (50%)	5 (42%)

Table III. Angles of the Trumpet

Pitch	90°	Below 90°	Above 90°
C4	1 (8%)	11 (92%)	0
C5	1 (8%)	11 (92%)	0
C6	1 (8%)	11 (92%)	0
G6	1 (8%)	11 (92%)	0
C7	1 (8%)	11 (92%)	0

were taken through a mouthpiece ring while the subjects buzzed or positioned their lips on the following pitches:

C4   C5   C6   G6   C7

Photos 7-12 were taken while the subjects played the same pitches on their own equipment. The photos were then used for study of the four areas mentioned above. Embouchure was studied by an observation of lip placement (see Table I). Air flow direction was tested by measuring the angles from the perpendicular as the air passed through the lip aperture while the subjects played the test pitches on the mouthpiece ring (Table II). Using the parallel planes of the subjects' eyes and lower lips, the trumpet angle to the embouchure was measured in degrees from the perpendicular while the subjects played the test pitches shown in photos 7-12 (Table III). It is interesting to

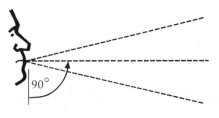

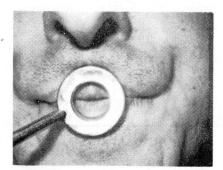

Subject 1. Paul Bogosian. Photo 2 - Low C (C4). Total lip area visible: 37/64; upper lip: 17/64; lower lip: 20/64.

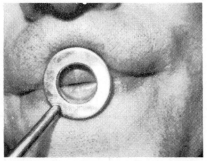

Subject 10. Joe Shepley. Photo 2 - Low C (C4). Total lip area visible: 40/64; upper lip: 22/64; lower lip: 18/64.

Subject 10. Joe Shepley. Photo 8 - Low C (C4). A very strong basic embouchure set. Lip corners are even with the lower lip. The dimple effect is created by tension of buccinator, zygomatics, and levators. Tension is also visible in the area of the risorius.

note that over 90% of the subjects stayed below a 90° angle while playing from low C to double high C.

Facial muscle usage can also be observed in photos 7-12. The facial set of a double high C is basically the same as that of a low C, but the increased muscular tension needed to achieve the extreme upper register is evident. Even more important, however, all of the subjects were able to focus this tension forward into a flow of power which could overcome the increasing resistance of the air column and metal of the mouthpiece and trumpet. Only by controlling the increasing tension and not letting it interfere with the air flow were the subjects able to achieve the upper register. The characteristic "circle of controlled power" begins with the muscles of the chin, moves through the lip corners and cheek muscles to the center of the face, and then to the lips themselves, setting up the controlled tension necessary for the correct vibrations of the lips inside the mouthpiece. This setting now needs only the increased air flow to create the power for the achievement of the extreme upper register. This feature was one of the most important findings of the study.

Also taken as supplementary information were the subjects' mouthpiece and trumpet measurements (Tables IV-V).

This study is continuing and will be expanded to include all types of trumpet embouchures — symphonic, jazz, and commercial. Hopefully, research of this nature will help to explain how the embouchure, air flow, trumpet angle and facial muscles work throughout the entire trumpet range.

Practical Applications

First, we should be aware that the changes that took place in the professional embouchures were for the most part very subtle — the movement of just 1/64th of an inch in a trumpet mouthpiece is a significant change. Second, we must realize that the most important key to successfully achieving the upper register consistently is correct air usage. Embouchure, lip vibration, mouthpiece placement, equipment, and the other factors of brass playing all depend on correct diaphragmatic breathing and speed of air flow.

Based on these two important factors, I would like to make the following recommendations to aspiring trumpeters:

1. Avoid excessive embouchure changes, retaining the same basic position from low C to high C.

2. When descending (low C to the pedal range), use slightly more upper lip. When ascending (high C to double high C), use slightly more lower lip. Always remember that 1/64th of an inch is a big change. Don't overdo it!

3. Young students should play with a 50/50 mouthpiece placement. This gives them the opportunity to make adjustments later when they are needed.

4. Allow the muscles around the mouthpiece to support the tension necessary to play in the extreme upper register, but keep the portion of the lip inside the mouthpiece ring as relaxed as possible. (If the lips become so tense that the vibrations stop, the sound will stop.) The corners of the lip should be kept firm, but not necessarily locked. Allow the corners and the facial muscles to move up and slightly forward as the air pressure

increases. Remember, the lips only set the pitch; it is the air passing through them that carries the pitch into the trumpet, where it is amplified.

5. Keep the throat open at all times, with the teeth slightly separated, and think of blowing the air towards the note you are attempting to play.

6. Hold the trumpet steady. Excessive movement destroys the em-

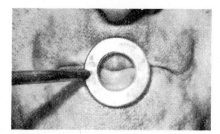

Subject 1. Paul Bogosian. Photo 6 - Double High C (C7). Total lip area visible: 37/64; upper lip: 17/64; lower lip: 20/64.

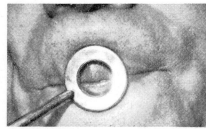

Subject 10. Joe Shepley. Photo 6 - Double High C (C7). Total lip area visible: 33/64; upper lip: 19/64; lower lip: 14/64.

Photo 9 - Middle C (C5). Lip corners are even with the lower lip. There is increased dimpling and muscle ripple in the area of the risorius and buccinator.

Photo 10 - High C (C6). Lip corners are even with the lower lip. Increased tension is indicated by further muscle rippling in all facial areas, particularly depressors and levators.

Photo 11 - High G (G6). Lip corners are even with the lower lip. There is strong facial muscle action in the zygomatic and levator areas. Increased air flow is indicated by enlargement of neck area. The slight bulge noticeable in the lower cheek area is probably due to muscle tension.

C4   C5   C6   G6   C7

Photo 12 - Double High C (C7). Shepley has an extremely consistent embouchure set throughout the entire range. The lip corners have moved slightly lower than the lower lip. There is further muscle tension in all facial areas previously noted.

bouchure set and the focus of the air as it flows into the instrument.

7. Do not sacrifice tone quality for a few high squeaky notes. Play the largest equipment you can control comfortably, and learn to fill it. Establish correct playing procedures and then carry them into the extreme range.

Practice intelligently! Do not force or push for the higher notes.

A double high C begins in the diaphragm, flows through an open throat, is focused into a compressed air stream by the tongue, passes through slightly separated teeth where it hits the lips. Then, passing through a focused aperture into the mouthpiece, it reaches the instrument and finally escapes into the room. When all those factors are working correctly then you are able to play a double high C like the professionals. ∎

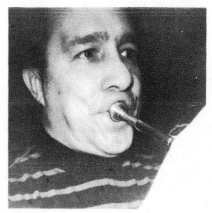

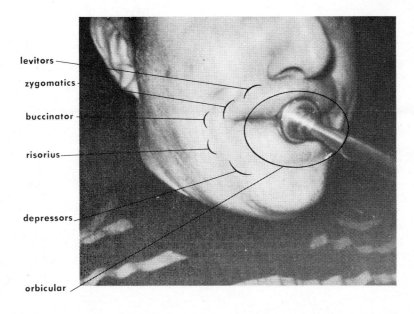

levitors
zygomatics
buccinator
risorius
depressors
orbicular

Table V. Trumpet Information

Subject	Make	Model	Bore
1. Paul Bogosian	French Besson	Brevete'	ML (460)
2. Jerry Callet	Calicchio	#3 bell, #4 pipe	ML
3. Burt Collins	Bach	72 bell	ML
4. Jon Faddis	Schilke	B♭	M
5. Jimmy Maxwell	Calicchio	—	L
6. Bob McCoy	Calicchio	—	ML (462)
7. Lloyd Michels	French Besson	Meha	LB (475)
8. Ernie Royal	Bach	#37	ML
9. Gerard Schwarz	Bach B♭	#43	M
10. Joe Shepley	Calicchio	—	L (470)
11. Roy Stevens	French Besson	Meha & Brevete'	ML
12. Al Stewart	Bach	72 bell	ML

Table IV. Mouthpiece Information

Subject	Make	Throat	Rim Thickness	Inside Cup Diameter	Model	Shank End	Cup Depth	Bite
1. Paul Bogosian	Costello	26	7/32	21.5/32	Stock	9/32	9/32	Sharp
2. Jerry Callet	Calicchio	28	13/32	21/32	3A4	10/32	11/32	Sharp
3. Burt Collins	Bach	23	6/32	21/32	6c	11.5/32	11.5/32	Medium
4. Jon Faddis	Giardinelli	29	5.5/32	21/32	Custom	11.5/32	8/32	Medium
5. Jimmy Maxwell	Bach	25	5/32	21/32	7E	10/32	11/32	Medium
6. Bob McCoy	Jet-Tone	28	5.5/32	21/32	2A	10/32	9/32	Sharp
7. Lloyd Michels	Pepi	23	8.5/32	21/32	Custom	8.5/32	9/32	Medium
8. Ernie Royal	Bach	24	6/32	21.5/32	7E	11/32	11/32	Medium
9. Gerard Schwarz	Bach	26	4.75/32	21.75/32	5C	10.5/32	11/32	Medium
10. Joe Shepley	Custom	23	6/32	22/32	—	11/32	9/32	Medium
11. Roy Stevens	Costello	26	7.5/32	22/32	Stock	10.5/32	10.5/32	Medium
12. Al Stewart	Busch	24	5.5/32	21/32	MW2	11/32	10.5/32	Medium

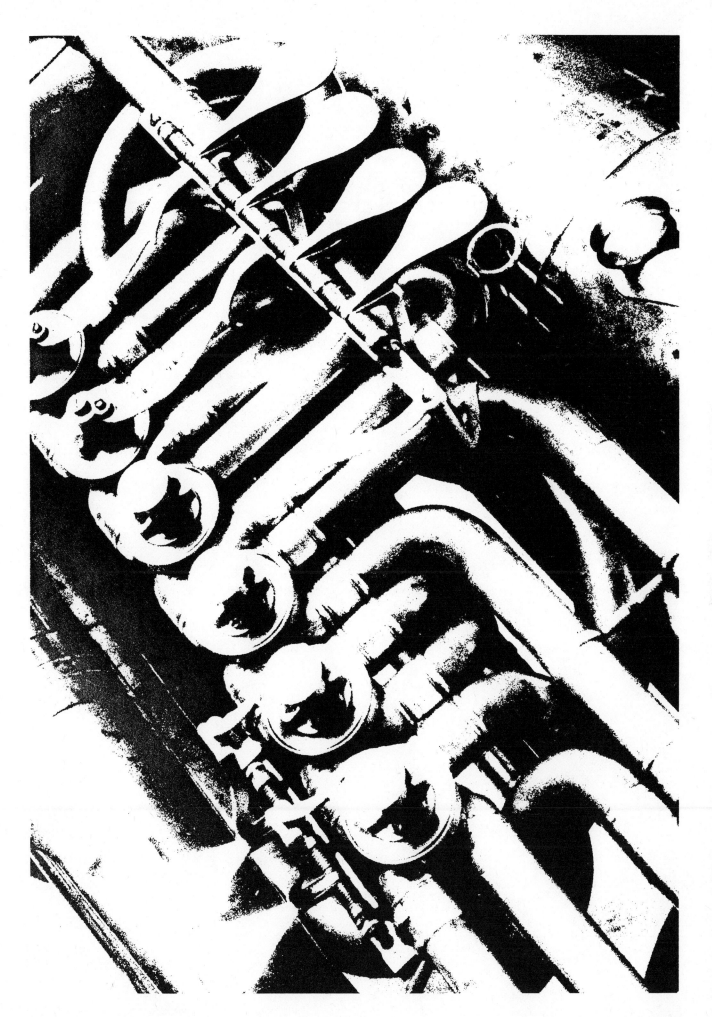

1975

A Tuba Clinic with Harvey Phillips

R. Winston Morris

This is an edited version of a "live" tuba clinic recorded in January, 1973 at the annual Tennessee Technological University Tuba/Euphonium Symposium in Cookeville, Tennessee. The audience was made up of approximately 150 tuba and euphonium students and many band directors representing a nine-state area. The central theme of the clinic revolved around fundamentals of playing the tuba, a subject which probably cannot be overly discussed with young students.

Opening Comments

As the youngest member of the brass family, the tuba has suffered for many years, primarily because master composers did not write for the instrument. Composers like Corelli, Bach, Handel, Haydn, Mozart, and Beethoven preceded the tuba and thus never knew of the instrument. I am certain these composers, given the opportunity, would have written many works for the tuba. When we have borrowed literature from such master composers, we have met with criticism from a few purists who seemingly look upon the tuba as an instrument for comical effects. Personally, I have neither patience nor time for those who would deny us this literature.

For the past twenty years, the tuba has enjoyed a renaissance which continues to grow and broaden. Important composers are writing more and more major works for the tuba recitalist. (They're even getting away from cute titles!) The level of tuba playing has risen so rapidly in the last ten years that I am convinced we will someday have tuba artists who compare very favorably with the great artists of any other instrument.

There is every reason to study

diligently and to develop your technical skills and musical artistry. The future for tuba is brighter than it has ever been.

Clinic Questions

What are the basic problems for the young tuba player — the beginner?

The most basic problem is producing a good controlled sound. I believe in an embouchure that is as close as possible to that which nature gave us. Every person, unless he is physically malformed, has a perfect embouchure for tuba. All you have to do is make the corners of your mouth firm and you have an embouchure. It is very important for the student to understand from the very beginning that we *do not* distort our facial features when we play correctly. Three bad habits to watch for and avoid are pulling back the corners of the mouth (smiling method), cheek puffing and articulating between the lips.

1. Pulling back the corners. No one, no matter how well the world is treating him, walks around with a perpetual smile on his face. If he did so, he would be pretty tired by the end of the day. And yet some tuba players will sit down for the duration of their practice session or performance and approach their instruments in just this way. They then wonder why they have so little endurance. When you pull back the corners of your mouth in a smile, you pull the skin and flesh tight against your upper gum and you reduce contact with the outer (side) edges of the mouthpiece. The temptation is to use more and more pressure, particularly in the upper register, and you end up with no cushion whatsoever. Nature provided us with a nice cushion for the mouthpiece if we will use it.

Don't pull back the corners of the mouth when playing a brass instrument in any register.

2. Puffing the cheeks. Cheek puffing is probably the worst and most common bad habit of tuba players. It generally eliminates the firm corners of the embouchure and hence control. Also, unless the cheek puffer puffs his cheeks throughout his range, he most certainly will develop at least two embouchures. I have quite often encountered student tuba players with three embouchures: one for the low register (puffed cheeks, loose corners), one for the middle register (reasonably correct), and one for the upper register (corners pulled back, much pressure). Needless to say, they sound like a different player in each register and lack both flexibility and endurance. Puffing the cheeks will also bring on the bad habit of tonguing between the lips, causing the tongue to move about 10 times further than it needs to for each articulation. Obviously, this practice will slow one's technique considerably. The worst characteristic of the player who puffs his cheeks is the uncentered "woofy" sound which is an inevitable result of cheek puffing. Do yourself — and those who hear you — a favor. Don't get in the habit of puffing your cheeks in any register.

A better way to approach the low register is to keep the corners firm and in place while dropping the lower jaw. This approach simultaneously provides more lower lip to vibrate (thicker, looser) and a larger oral cavity (resonating chamber). It enables the player to keep embouchure control and retain a centered sound, as well as achieve maximum speed of articulation in the low register.

In order for any player to do his best work, he must be comfortable (in every respect — embouchure, posture, attitude) and in control. Don't contort yourself when you play, it can be an insurmountable handicap to developing good sound and artistic control.

What approach do you take with the absolute beginner on tuba?

First, I assure myself that he or she likes music and loves the tuba. There must be commitment and there has to be desire. Hopefully, there will also be talent. I then discuss in the simplest terms important considerations for the young tuba student. Most important are the concept of sound, holding the instrument comfortably, body posture, breathing, articulation. I tell the student that some of the prerequisites for being a tuba player are the same as those for a swimmer or **singer**: being able to breathe deeply, hold the breath, and control the release of air from the lungs. I would ask the student to remember what it is like to fill his lungs with air while running, then explain that we need to breathe deeply and fill the lungs to play tuba — not in the way we do when walking down the hall but the way we do when running on the athletic field. I would then ask the student to breathe with me, to think and feel what it's like to fill the lungs with air while sitting relaxed with the tuba. It is important that the student understand both breathing and relaxation — being comfortable while playing. There must be no tension, no stiffness, no contortion. I might ask the student to practice — with me — to see how long he can hold his breath. There are many breathing exercises we can use to improve capacity and control. One of the exercises that I use takes just one minute: relax and then inhale evenly for 20 seconds; hold the breath for 20 seconds; exhale evenly for 20 seconds. This is a great exercise.

Next, I would endeavor to get across to the student my conception that the tuba is a "vocal" instrument — that once he covers his mouth with the mouthpiece the only way he has to communicate, to show how he feels, is *through* (not into) the instrument. I would point out that if you want someone to hear and understand what you are saying, whether you are speaking loudly or whispering, you must *project*, you must send the sound out.

To get the beginner to produce a sound, I ask him to relax, take a deep breath, make contact with the mouthpiece, make the corners of his mouth firm, and then project air through the lips while articulating the syllable *too*. I do not tell the student where his tongue should be positioned or where it should make contact but simply to pronounce, on the air stream, the syllable *too*. This approach should successfully lead to a pleasing sound. Quality of sound is the most important consideration for any brass player.

It is essential that a student-teacher relationship be developed that allows for maximum growth. I always try to establish a feeling of partnership and to work toward a goal that is common to both teacher and student. This goal is to have that student become the finest tuba player possible. If the teacher can develop such a partnership with each student, there will always be a free exchange of ideas and concepts — even on the beginner level. Above all else the student must know that his teacher is genuine, that he is teaching from his mind and heart and not just from a book. It is more important to inspire initiative and confidence than to relate information and methodology.

What suggestions do you have for developing the extreme registers of the tuba — the upper register especially?

Most of the difficulty in the upper register is a matter of breath support and embouchure placement. Be sure you aren't substituting muscular contraction for support. Concentrate on relaxation across the shoulders and in the arms, make the diaphragm muscles do the work, keep the throat open — don't choke off your air supply, lift your support, project the air stream, control the speed and direction of the air stream, blow through the tuba (not into it), keep the corners of the mouth firm, the lips together, let the velocity of the air stream determine the aperture of the embouchure. Project!

Let me speak of placement and why I utilize for myself a one embouchure pivot approach to playing. Imagine a tuba keyboard of four octaves and understand that, just like the piano player, the tuba player must sit in the center of his full keyboard. The center of the "tuba keyboard" (CC tuba) is the C an octave below middle C on the piano. I refer to this C as the "pivot note," the easiest most comfortable tone to produce, the center of the keyboard, with a minimum of two octaves on either side — up and down. This four octave register is the potential range for the tuba student; and it must be achieved to cover the basic orchestral and solo literature. It is possible of course for exceptional players to go beyond this basic range on both ends. I believe we should set our embouchure for the middle (pivot tone) of our full tuba keyboard (second space C for CC tuba, second line B♭ for BB♭ tubas). We must then strive to achieve — on that keyboard center — the best sound possible, the most control, the most technique. We want to retain these qualities of sound, control and technique as we ascend and as we descend. To me this demands maximum retention of the embouchure utilized in our mid-range with absolute minimum variation as we go into either the upper or lower register. In approaching the upper register, I raise the lower jaw and at the same time pitch the instrument slightly forward. This allows me to "place" my embouchure for any given note *before* it is sounded. And the note will hopefully have a centered, clear and open sound.

By thinking *placement* and keeping the integrity of the embouchure, an octave can be achieved comfortably with very little effort. Notice what happens to a sustained tone when the instrument is held free (of the body) and the bell is tipped back toward the player. With no embouchure change, the note wants to go down in pitch; tip the bell in the other direction and the pitch wants to go up. Now sustain a tone while holding the instrument rigid, drop the lower jaw and don't move the instrument. Notice now that no matter how hard you try to hold that pitch it is going to go down; raise the lower jaw and the pitch wants to go up. Specifically, the pivot approach to playing tuba means utilizing the natural hinge of the lower jaw to increase the size of the resonating chamber (oral cavity) while at the same time providing a thicker and looser string (lower lip) for the low register. To accommodate the upper register, the same hinge of the lower jaw is used to provide a smaller oral cavity with less lip to vibrate. For maximum flexibility of the lower jaw, the instrument must be free to tilt forward and back. This causes the upper rim of the mouthpiece to function like the hinge on a door, that is, it doesn't move up or down but simply opens and closes. This action alternates the amount of contact with the upper and lower rims of the mouthpiece which greatly increases comfort, endurance, and accuracy.

What about mouthpiece placement? I've noticed that you have most of your top lip in the mouthpiece.

Yes, the mouthpiece is placed more on my upper lip than lower lip when I set my embouchure. This position is most comfortable for me. However, let me get back to that imaginary beginning student we discussed earlier. I would have the beginning student place the mouthpiece exactly centered on his mouth, for his long tone studies, his first experiences playing the tuba. Depending on how much the youngster practiced and how fast he progressed, I might insist on this placement for three to six months or longer. As the student's

embouchure became stronger and as his sound improved, I would let his mouthpiece find the most comfortable position — for him. It might be more upper or lower, it might be centered, it might be more to one side or the other. But, most important is to consider the student's comfort when performing. I think a teacher can sometimes hold back the progress of a student by insisting on a specific "picture book" embouchure. There are many *perfect* embouchures, and they vary from individual to individual.

Closing Comments

No country in the world offers music education opportunities to young students equal to those offered in this country. We have tremendous music programs in our high schools, great schools of music in our colleges and universities, great conservatories. We also have some great symphony orchestras. But the mass audience that should be generated by such a system of music education is simply not there. Why? Well, we all have our own pet theories, of course, and there is no simple answer. However, I submit that the power, visibility (aural and visual), and selected fare of the recording and broadcasting industries blots out and effectively buries much of what our music education system achieves. We must all work together to improve this situation.

Every effort must be made to expand performance opportunities. New approaches must be created to attract the audiences necessary

to sustain our profession. Too many of us are content to sit back and "tsk-tsk" the situation, and wait for somebody to do something about it. Well, as far as I am concerned, each of you had better elect yourself to be that somebody who does something about it — for the sake of music and for your own well being. Earlier in this clinic session, I stated that the future for tuba is brighter than ever before. This is true because we *are* doing something about our situation. We are expanding performance opportunities for tuba players by convincing important composers to write more solo literature, better band parts, and better orchestra parts. Many arrangers and orchestrators in the commercial field of jingles, television background music, film scores, etc. are using the tuba very well. Indeed all composers, arrangers, and orchestrators are potential allies in our campaign to achieve a proper place for the tuba in every area of music. But getting music written is only the first step; we must tenaciously seek out opportunities; we must reach the general public and establish an audience for the tuba. This will be done if we convince our colleagues and music critics that we are serious about what we are doing. We must change the image of the tuba and the tuba player. Two things will do this: good music and good performance. The future for tuba will be what we make it. Each of us has much work to do in this regard, but the challenge is exciting and the goal worthwhile. ∎

February, 1975

Brass Embouchure

Burton Hardin

Application of the Lip Muscles
The Smile

Inexperienced brass players have a tendency to tense those muscles involved in smiling (the zygomatics, risorius and buccinator) in order to ascend in register — or simply to produce a note in any register. The

player may experience initial success, but because the orbicularis oris is stretched when the smile is used, endurance, range, tone quality, flexibility, and perhaps longevity of career will be affected adversely. Stretching the muscle makes it less supple and increases

the time necessary for changing the tension of the lip. When rapid movement is required, such as slurring rapidly back and forth between notes more than a major second apart, the stretched lip will not respond quickly enough. Stretching the muscle also makes it thinner;

so there is less material between the mouthpiece and the teeth to act as a cushion, making the lip more sensitive to the pressure and more liable to damage. In addition, the rim of the mouthpiece compresses the flesh against the teeth, cutting off much of the blood supply to that area and decreasing muscle strength — possibly to the extent that the brass player, at least temporarily, cannot continue to play. The stretched, more rigid lip also makes the development of an extensive high register impossible.

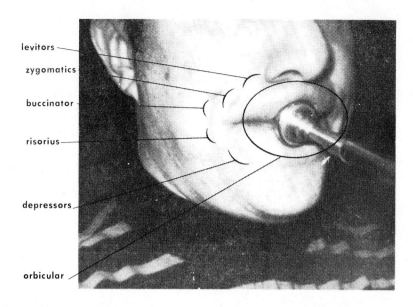

The Pucker

The other extreme is the pucker, in which the orbicularis oris is contracted, with little or no resistance from the surrounding muscles. With this conformation, the tone quality is very dark and lusterless, flexibility is impaired and range is limited, although endurance is not so likely to suffer.

Balanced Embouchure

Most authorities agree that an ideal embouchure exists somewhere between these two extremes. Both the pucker and the smile overwork *some* muscles, because they don't make adequate use of *all* the muscles of the embouchure. The muscles most closely connected to the corners of the mouth should be flexed (the degree of which depends upon the register), while those at the center of the mouth should be free to flex and relax, making greater flexibility possible. Since the muscles are all in use, there is less strain and a greater potential for range and endurance. The fixed muscles at the corner of the mouth are the "strong corners" so often mentioned as being necessary to a good embouchure.

The muscles at the center of the mouth, in conjunction with changes in air supply, tongue position and angle of mouthpiece or direction of air stream, act in such a way that the size of the aperture is changed to a small degree for each note. A low note is played with a larger opening in the lip, and a high note with a relatively smaller opening. Ideally, the corners of the mouth are the same distance apart in the high register as when relaxed. When all the muscles are functioning in this manner, they are acting in their most efficient manner, com-

plementing and supporting one another.

Mouthpiece Application

The mouthpieces of all the brass instruments should be applied to the lip, so that the mouthpiece is as near to the horizontal center as possible. In many cases perfect centering is not possible due to deviations from "perfect" in the shape of the jaws, teeth or lips. Usually the student will find the position most suited to his physical equipment without the interference of the instructor. For this reason, the instructor is wise not to attempt to correct minor deviations left or right without careful, thoughtful analysis of the makeup of the student's mouth.

This is not as true of the vertical placement. For reasons of lack of strength, a student may adopt a radical setting which impedes some aspect of his technique. The logic of settings required by some brass instruments, such as the horn, may escape the student at first. As in other aspects of brass playing, there is no "absolute" in vertical setting, and the teacher who does not make allowances for individual deviations will find some students incapable of adapting to the teacher's image of the "ideal" embouchure.

In the case of the trumpet and cornet, the mouthpiece is placed on the lips so that either an equal amount of the mouthpiece is above and below the opening, or two-thirds is on the lower lip and one-third on the upper lip.

For the horn, one-third of the mouthpiece is placed on the lower

lip and two-thirds on the upper. There are two common variations among horn players known as "Einsetzen," and "Ansetzen." In Einsetzen (setting in), the lower edge of the mouthpiece is placed within the membrane of the lip, providing more flexibility, easier production of the low register and a rich tone quality; with Ansetzen (setting on), the lower edge of the mouthpiece is slightly below the edge of the membrane on the skin of the face, giving more strength, a brighter tone quality and (sometimes) easier production of the high register. The relatively wide range required of the horn seems to be aided by the high setting. One rarely sees an extreme Einsetzen setting, where the membrane of the lower lip is rolled out and the mouthpiece is set deeply inside the membrane.

The setting of the trombone and baritone are similar to one another, and may be expected to vary from evenly divided to two-thirds upper and one-third lower lip. The same principle as with the horn seems to apply here, except that the mouthpiece is always set on the skin of the face and never within the membrane.

The size of the tuba mouthpiece dictates its setting, leaving very little room for variation.

Deviations from an ideal brass embouchure may be expected because of the relative thickness of each lip vertically and because of tooth and jaw structure. Considerations should include strength, comfort, range requirements, and flexibility.

Moistness of Lips

The relative moistness of the lips may have an effect on tone quality, flexibility, range, response and pressure. Moistness can vary between: saturated lips, dry lips, moistness of the membrane only, and moistness of one lip only.

Some persons find playing with saturated lips uncomfortable due to the feeling that the mouthpiece is insecure on the lip. However, those persons who do play that way report that flexibility and response are improved. In addition, being accustomed to the feeling of a wet lip can be an advantage when playing on a stage warm enough to produce perspiration. The person who plays with a dry lip generally uses more than a moderate amount of pressure to anchor the lip to the mouthpiece (using the surface adhesion of the dry lip). With a moist embouchure, the mouthpiece finds a more natural resting place.

Players will often moisten only the membrane of the lip, leaving the skin outside the lip dry. This results in a better response and easier production of notes, particularly soft notes. Some players, who find it necessary to move one lip in and out of the mouthpiece when changing registers, will moisten the moving lip only, so that it will slide more easily. ∎

March, 1975

Elements of Brass Intonation

Chester Roberts

It is generally conceded that acceptable intonation is a rock-bottom fundamental in good musical performance; but while we all understand in a general way what is involved, I think there are nonetheless some prevalent misconceptions concerning the problem in its many applications to brass instruments. I do not believe, for example, that intonation faults necessarily — or even usually — imply a lack of talent (a "bad ear"); many young players *hear* much better than they *play*, and they can often sing familiar sequences with very good intonation. And I don't think that out-of-tuneness occurs typically as a random aberration. What I do believe is that the most common and the most significant intonation problems of the brass player are rooted in simple and well-understood principles of physics and musical evolution, and they are to a large extent predictable.

Inherent Problems

So far as their causes lie within the instruments themselves, intonation difficulties manifest themselves in a fairly consistent manner. Anyone who has ever played a valve brass instrument knows, for example, of the pronounced sharpness in tones calling for the use of all three valves together. This is cumulative pitch error (CPE), and it becomes a serious problem in the low C♯ of the trumpet (and the corresponding note on other 3-valve instruments), as well as in the "extension register" of tubas and euphoniums equipped with one or more extra valves for playing below the normal compass of three-valve instruments.

Actually, the three-valve arrangement is a rather imperfect system in some ways and instrument-makers must resort to many compromises in order to eliminate discrepancies — or rather to distribute them as evenly and as unobtrusively as possible. The third-valve tubing is always made a little longer than the sum of the first and second in order to minimize CPE in the 1-3 and 1-2-3 combinations; as a result sharpness is usually minor in 1-3, and typically absent in 2-3. But the sharp tendency of the 1-2-3 fingering is so marked that few young players can correct it fully by embouchure alone; or if they can, such correction pulls the tone so far out of its natural placement that the stability and solidity characteristic of a truly "centered" tone are very adversely affected. The third-valve tuning slide, extended 1/2" — 3/4", can be used to correct the problem.

The 1-2 combination also has a sharp tendency. It is so slight, however, that the average player may not be aware of it; and if he has a very good natural ear, he will probably supply the required small embouchure correction more or less automatically. In some circumstances a player may want to use 3 as a flatter substitute for 1-2, although this is not a widely favored practice. A much better solution (and a virtual necessity for the serious student) is a trigger for extending the first-valve slide; this provides flexible and accurate adjustment for the 1-2 fingering, as well as an alternate means of correcting 1-2-3 and 1-3 in contexts in which the third-valve adjustment may be awkward.

There are also intonation peculiarities unrelated to CPE. In the "natural scale" of brass instruments, the fifth partial is in the simple ratio of 5:1 with the fundamental frequency, or 5:4 with the tonic note a major third below the 5th partial. And this pitch is rather noticeably lower than the corresponding tone in the equal-tempered scale. Thus, the whole *fifth-partial series* tends to be flat. While this flatness is not extreme, it occurs unfortunately at a point in the range of the trumpet, alto-horn, baritone, euphonium, and tuba in which untrained players are just beginning to experience a little difficulty in "getting the notes" with certainty. In a word, the embouchure typically doesn't quite focus, there isn't quite enough wind support, the attack isn't quite definite enough. All these factors in the instrument and in the player can concur to produce an area of pronounced (sometimes extreme) flatness. There is no effortless cure; to play these notes in tune there must be a distinctly firmer buzz formation of the lips and augmented support to balance the greater resistance in the embouchure, and there must be a sustained awareness of the problem and conscious attention to its correction for a sufficient time until it becomes habitual and automatic. In the beginning, a few sustained mouthpiece buzzes, accurately centered on the desired pitches, will help pinpoint the corrective technique.

Other intonation problems may be evident in the area of the second partial and the tones immediately below it. In the larger instruments the predominating tendency is flat; in the trumpet it is less consistent. If the embouchure is generally stiff and unresponsive, these tones will have a more or less sharp tendency; this condition seems often to be associated with under-par native pitch sense. With more flexible embouchures, especially in conjunction with relaxed or sluggish physical temperament, they often tend to be flat. In both cases the young player needs to be taught the *feeling* as well as the sound of well-centered embouchure and sufficient air flow. Long-sustained tones and mouthpiece buzzing are useful corrective approaches, especially in conjunction with some help and supervision from a capable teacher. Practice of interval exercises is also recommended for coordination of basic techniques.

Another type of discrepancy arises from the complicated proportions of the instrument's tube resulting from the introduction of a valve mechanism into what might otherwise be a much simpler ratio of expansion. This problem has occupied the attention of manufacturers for well over a century, and while it is today a minor factor in good quality instruments, it seems unlikely that it can be entirely eliminated.

Characteristic shortcomings in performing technique among young brass players tend to manifest themselves in somewhat variable ways in the several instruments, and in different parts of the range in each instrument, as well as among individual players. Although entirely separate from the instrumental peculiarities I have mentioned above, they often tend to reinforce faults resulting from these causes, making sharp tones sharper and flat tones flatter; occasionally they may act in the opposite direction to improve a situation.

So much for generalities — most of which apply to the trumpet. Let us now look at the ways in which these factors influence intonation in the other brass instruments.

The French Horn

For a variety of technical reasons, the intonation tendencies of the French horn will not be uniformly the same as those of the same written tones of the trumpet. For simplicity, let us first consider the horn as a single instrument, typically in F. An essential difference is that when the hornist is playing the scale from written middle c upwards, he is playing in the *third* octave of the instrument, not the second as on the trumpet, and the fingerings will thus be different for certain critical tones.

A good example is found in the c♯ just above the middle c. On the trumpet this is fingered 1-2-3, a notoriously sharp combination. On the horn, the fingering is 1-2 so there is only slight sharping from CPE, and this is countered by its flatness as a member of the 5th partial series. Another example is the fourth-line d which is characteristically flat on the trumpet. On the horn it is usually played *open*, as the ninth partial (which tends to be a little sharp), thus compensating for the flatness we might anticipate from technique-related causes.

Another significant factor in the horn is its flexibility. As with long, slender tubes in general, the pitch can be varied upward and especially downward more readily than with most other instruments. This characteristic was used in earlier times on the old valveless hand-horns to produce low tones as much as a fourth below the normal second partial. While this is not very practical on the modern instrument, a substantial degree of the flexibility still remains to aid in the correction of imperfect tones. Thus, the 1-2-3 fingering (which, although not encountered until nearly an octave below the middle c, shows a sharp tendency similar to other instruments) is easier to adjust by the embouchure on the horn than on other instruments.

Of course the junior player does not ordinarily have to play this low; and, by the time he does encounter this range, he is likely to have a double horn at his disposal. With the double horn, a whole new series of options throughout the compass becomes available. It is now possible, for example, to play on the B♭ side with 2-3, in which there is normally no sharp tendency. Response and centering will be easier, and the slightly brighter quality is likely to project more effectively. Due to the various special characteristics of the horn — especially the double horn — there are few really difficult intonation problems as compared with other brass instruments. It should be noted that advanced horn players generally keep all valve tuning slides pulled a little, anywhere from 1/8" - 1/2" for different valves, as determined by experience.

The Trombone

Though one might think that the trombone would be relatively free of intonation troubles, players at all stages seem to have their share of problems. A basic problem is the persistence of motor patterns learned, or mislearned, early in the game. The typical beginner learns his positions in an approximate way — first by eye, then by "feel" — and these kinetic sensations harden into habit long before there is much awareness of intonation requirements. Left to themselves, the habits tend to persist long after the musical ear has begun to develop.

While almost any faulty pattern of slide placement is possible, there are nonetheless some fairly prevalent tendencies. More often than not, the second position tends to be too low (possibly a carry-over from the intermediate "all-purpose A" (somewhere between A and A♭) used by young players at a certain stage because of split-second indecisions as to key signatures). The lowest positions usually tend to be too high. It commonly comes as a surprise, even to youngsters who can reach the seventh position without physical difficulty, how far the slide must be extended for accurate tuning of the low B. The trombone is subject to the same hazards of flatness in the 5th partial series as the valve brasses. There is the same need for live embouchure and good support. However, all tones in this series except the d just above the staff (first position) can be shaded upward by means of the slide — an adjustment of half an inch or less being sufficient. The d should be played in the fourth position when the tone occurs either as a major third or as the raised seventh in the prevailing tonality.

The trombone is the only brass instrument that can make use of the tones in the 7th partial series; f♯ and g above the staff are commonly played this way, as raised third and raised second positions respectively — and these are *substantially* raised, over an inch above the normal positions. Since these are often troublesome, the young player should also be taught to play them in the fifth and fourth positions (as in the lower octaves) to help in adjusting the tuning accurately.

Trombones equipped with the "F valve" for tones below the low E are now in wide use, even among players of high-school age. Here again, "non-standard" slide positions must be used. For the low E, the slide must be extended about an inch beyond the normal second position, and for the E♭, over two inches beyond the third. For the low D, the fourth position is extended so as to become actually a high fifth; the D♭ is taken at or a shade below the normal sixth. Low C requires maximum slide extension, and even then a little "lipping" downward. The B♮ is an impracticality for the average young player (the means by which symphonic bass trombonists produce this tone when necessary are outside the scope of our discussion). The *theory* as to the slide positions in this extension register is exceedingly simple, but it requires patient and informed practice to locate them reliably and to avoid confusion with the "normal" positions used elsewhere.

It is evident that the intonation problems of the trombone are peculiar to it; their successful resolution may require even more motivation and determination than would be necessary on the other instruments.

The Tuba

It is possible that musicians are more aware of intonation discrepancies on the tuba, because they are more conscious of the bass line as an element in harmony. Actually, the tuba is neither more nor less inherently susceptible to intonation problems than other instruments. Its tendencies are in the main similar, and it responds to the same techniques for correction; however, it does have a few problems all its own.

One of these is that, unlike trumpets and trombones, the tuba is commonly encountered in several different keys. Especially in junior bands, the E♭ may still be found beside the BB♭; and at the college level, C tubas, and an occasional F, may coexist with BB♭'s in bands and larger brass ensembles. Each of these has its own idiomatic tuning pattern. Where superlatively trained musicians are concerned, this makes no difference, but with young players, who tend to accept uncritically whatever comes out of the instrument, there will be additional problems in reconciling these patterns. This is undoubtedly a principal cause of the progressive abandonment of the E♭ tuba in bands over the past several decades.

Another hazard in the tubas is the fourth valve. If intelligently employed, it is a useful addition to the instrument's resources; however, experienced players know how imperfectly it fulfills the claim sometimes made for it that it "provides all the tones of the lowest octave." In fact, only one more semitone can be played easily in good tune; beyond this, due to CPE, serious intonation problems develop which require supplementary means for adjusting intonation, which in turn demand fairly advanced technical and musical resources in the player. Further, there is one tone at the bottom of this octave which cannot be played at all on the ordinary four-valve instrument; this is anal-

ogous to the low B♮ of the bass trombone.* School-age youngsters are not very likely to become involved with this register, as the materials they play rarely if ever descend below EE; however they are often tempted to employ the fourth valve alone as a substitute for 1-3; this is a poor idea, since it generally throws these tones flat. If the fourth valve *can* be tuned sharp enough to equate with 1-3, it will then show the same sharp tendency as 1-2-3 when used with the second valve as an alternative to that fingering. For best results, the fourth valve should be tuned perceptibly lower than 1-3, and then never used alone, except possibly for facility in very rapid passages. In any case, the tuba player who has advanced beyond the capacity of the three-valve instrument should probably consider an instrument with five valves or a fully compensating four-valve arrangement in preference to one with four uncompensated valves only.

As to the primary areas of flatness, the tones in the 5th partial series (from d on the staff down to B♮ in the case of the BB♭ tuba) show about the same behavior as in the trumpet and respond to the same corrective techniques. Flatness in the *second* partial series is, I think, somewhat more general and more evident than in the other instruments because of the greater likelihood that the wind supply will be in some degree deficient. Simple breathing exercises are indicated, with emphasis on free expansion in the abdominal area rather than in the chest. And while the lips are of course in a relatively relaxed condition in this register, they cannot be entirely slack; a definite degree of control must be maintained even in the lowest tones for good intonation and centering.

Sharpness in the 1-2 fingering seems to be a little more prevalent in the tuba than in other instruments, often coexisting with a general sharpness in the upper register. A somewhat more open jaw usually helps with this problem, and may effect a noticeable improvement in the quality of the sound as well. As a further resource in coping with this, and with CPE generally, some means of manipulating one or more tuning slides while playing is a necessary for tube as for trumpet. My experience suggests this is most usefully applied to the first valve if possible; range of adjustment should be at least an inch, and substantially more if there is no fourth valve to provide an alternative to the 1-2-3 fingering.

Euphonium and Baritone Horn

Intonation characteristics of the euphonium and baritone horn are enough like those of the trumpet and tuba that detailed discussion is unnecessary. There are the same problems of CPE in the 1-2-3 combination and in the extension register of four-valve instruments, the same primary area of flatness in the 5th partial series, and tendencies much like those of the tuba in the 2nd partial series; there is also a similar need for means of adjusting slides while playing.

Conclusion

All of the foregoing adds up to a rather complicated and perhaps seemingly forbidding picture. Doubtless the motivated individual can do much with regard to his own playing, but can the school band director hope to effect any real improvement in large groups of average youngsters? I believe he can, although certainly there are no instant solutions — after all, we are musicians, not magicians! The first and biggest step is to know *where* to look for these hazards, through an understanding of the various factors that cause them. Then the young players must be alerted. I find that most can apply the techniques for correction fairly readily once they know *where* to apply them, but this cannot be allowed to wait upon the slow growth of their own relative pitch discrimination. One picture being worth ten thousand words, I use a sprinkling of upward- and downward-pointing arrows over critical notes to show the direction in which correction will be needed. Verbal reminders can be refined to a single key word or perhaps supplanted by a gesture incorporated into the conducting technique. Even if these devices cannot be applied specifically to each and every potential hazard, they will nevertheless help to keep players more constantly aware of playing in tune and strengthen their understanding of the factors involved in intonation. ∎

April, 1975

Tuning the Double Horn

Stephen Seiffert

One of the biggest problems facing the young horn player and his non-horn playing band director is tuning the double horn. The instrument has eight or more slides which must be properly adjusted before the instrument can be played in tune. Experienced players make these adjustments by trial and error continually readjusting the slide positions until a satisfactory compromise is achieved. (A compromise is necessary because of the discrepancies between the equal tempered scale and the harmonic series, as well as the inaccuracy of the valve slide lengths when the valves are used in combinations.)

Since the experienced horn player has worked out the compromises on his own instrument, it is usually possible for him to pick up another instrument and tune it in much the same way by using his ear alone. But what about the horn student who is not in regular contact with an experienced player?

The following is a procedure for tuning the double horn which can be done by anyone who can play the horn (even in a modest way, and is simple enough for a junior high school student to understand.

1. Tune the open B♭ horn to a reliable pitch by matching the horn to the source. Use either an F on the piano, or the B♭ on a tuning bar or electric tuner. Play the appropriate note on the horn:

(piano)
(tuner)

Be sure to adjust only the main tuning slide when doing this.

2. Match the pitch of the F horn to the pitch of the B♭ horn by playing ♩ on the two horns and adjusting the F horn tuning slide until the two pitches match. (On horns with B♭ tuning slides, it may be necessary to pull out this slide before it will be possible to match the two horns. When this is necessary, step 1 should be repeated.)

3. Play ♩ open on the F horn and then with first valve on the F horn, adjusting the first F horn valve slide until the two pitches match.

4. Match the pitch of the B♭ horn first valve to the pitch of the F horn first valve by playing ♩ on the two horns and adjusting the first B♭ horn valve slide until the two pitches match.

5. Play ♩ open on the F horn and then with first and second valves on the B♭ horn, adjusting the second B♭ horn valve slide until the two pitches match.

6. Match the pitch of the F horn second valve to the pitch of the B♭ horn second valve by playing ♩ on the two horns and ad-

justing the second F horn valve slide until the two pitches match.

7. Play with second valve on the F horn and then with second and third valves on the B♭ horn, adjusting the third B♭ horn valve slide until the two pitches match.

8. Match the pitch of the F horn third valve to the pitch of the B♭ horn third valve by playing

on the two horns and adjusting the third F horn valve slide until the two pitches match.

It is important when matching pitches with two different fingerings to avoid compensating for the difference in resistance of the two tube lengths by altering the pitch when the resistance changes. The best way to do this is to play a steady tone and change the fingering back and forth about twice a second. Using this approach, any discrepancy between the resulting pitches will be due to the tube length and not tube resistance.

When the experienced horn player tries this tuning, he will no doubt find t'.... some ways it does not suit his needs. Its usefulness, however, lies in the fact that any horn player, regardless of experience, can tune his horn in a few minutes.

The compromise produced by this tuning method is quite satisfactory in relation to equal temperament except for those notes produced on the fifth partial:

These notes are all very flat, the lowest being the d which is 18 cents too low. One possible solu-

tion to this problem would be to take these notes as either fourth or sixth partials by playing them with the following fingerings (circled fingerings indicate B♭ horn):

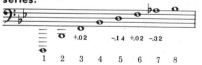

The fact remains, however, that further adjustment of the valve slides will not change the flatness of the fifth partial notes. It will always be necessary for the player to make substantial adjustments of pitch on these notes no matter where he sets his valve slides.

If you are willing to accept the necessity of raising the pitch of the fifth partial notes and the principal of compromise, this tuning system is both workable and extremely practical for many young musicians. ■

April, 1975

Using the First Valve Slide to Adjust Tuba Intonation

Larry P. Pitts

No instrument can be constructed so that it is perfectly in tune with itself. Thus, certain adjustments must be made by the performer. When the fourth valve was added to the tuba, it eliminated the necessity for many of these adjustments. For example, instead of the sharp combinations of 1-3 or 1-2-3, the fourth valve or combination of 2-4 could be used to improve the intonation. The fourth valve also made more alternate fingerings available. But because the fourth valve has not eliminated all intonation problems, the performer should take advantage of another option available for tuning — the use of the first valve slide to adjust pitches while playing. (Obviously, this method of adjustment affects only notes played when the first valve is depressed.)

The need to make adjustments with the first valve slide arises from the difference between equal temperament and the natural harmonic series. When a tone is sounded on a brass instrument, the resulting harmonic series (Figures 1 and 2) remains compatible with the equal tempered system of tuning on the first, second, fourth,

Fig. 1 — BB♭ Tuba, first valve harmonic series.

Fig. 2 — CC Tuba, first valve harmonic series.

and eighth partials; the third partial is two cents sharp, the fifth partial is fourteen cents flat, the sixth partial (an octave above the third partial) is two cents sharp, and the seventh partial is thirty-two cents flat. The seventh partial is so very flat that an alternate fingering must be used in order to play this tone in tune. The others can be adjusted by using the first valve slide: it should be pulled out for the third partial (E♭ or F) and pushed in for the fifth (c or d). It may be necessary, especially on some older instruments, to actually have the first valve slide shortened in order to bring this fifth partial up to pitch. Since this is the flattest pitch encountered in the "first valve series," the slide should be shortened so that the fifth partial is in tune when the slide is pushed all the way in. Until this can be done to the instrument, an alternate fingering of 1-3 may be necessary to raise the pitch. This is an awkward solution and should be used only as a temporary measure until the slide can be cut to the proper length.

Experimentation is necessary to discover exactly how far the slide must be pulled out or pushed in. This may vary for every performer, but there are some general guidelines that can be followed.

1. Preliminaries: the instrument should be completely warmed up to room temperature (about 70° F);

and the open horn must be tuned properly (using a Strob, if possible).

2. Tune the first valve slide to A♭ or B♭; it will probably be out 1″ to 1 1/2″.

3. Next, tune E♭ or F; the slide will probably need to be pulled out an additional 1/2″.

4. The last note is c or d and it is the easiest to tune, since the slide will have to be pushed all the way in.

Once you know how far the slide must be moved, you may have problems with compressed air "pops" that can occur when the valve is opened — although the recent advent of the "anti-pop vent" has eliminated this problem. Most "professional" line tubas are now available with "vented" valves (some players like to vent all valves whether they are pulled or not in order to help alleviate the "clicks" of compressed air encountered in normal playing), and there are competent repairmen who can vent the

valves on older horns. Without the vents it takes practice to eliminate the "pops" and make the movement smooth and co-ordinated. Of course, in very fast passages, the benefit gained from using the slide is completely nullified — the notes pass too quickly!

The first valve slide can also be used when other valves are used in combination with the first valve. As more valves are added to the first valve, the notes become sharper (e.g., 1-2, 1-3, 1-2-3). Since each added valve will require additional slide length, this length should be added by pulling the first valve slide.

Manufacturers and artists are constantly striving to perfect instrument design and eliminate intonation problems. Some day the "perfect" tuba may be designed, but until that time, each performer should use every option available to him to insure good intonation. ■

May, 1975

French Horn Maintenance

Julius E. Erlenbach

Most students need an outline of basic procedures to help them protect and maintain their instruments. Following a regular maintenance schedule offers some definite advantages: the rather large capital investment that a horn represents is protected and enhanced; small problems can be corrected before they become big problems; and the cost of expensive repairs and overhauls is noticeably diminished.

Valves

Valves must be lubricated regularly and, on occasion, cleaned. The regular use of valve oil will enable the valves to operate at their greatest rapidity and consistency. There are many fine valve oils on the market today, some of which

are designed specifically for rotary valves.

It has been my experience that the most efficient means of lubrication is to place the oil in direct contact with the inner workings of the valve (rather than simply removing the valve caps and placing a few drops of oil on the head of the rotor). This can be done by removing the valve slides for each valve and placing about 6 to 8 drops of oil down each slide. Then, reinsert the slides in their casings as far as they are able to go. Otherwise, oil will pull some of the slide lubricant presently coating the casing interior into the valves, thereby gumming them up. Tip the horn upside down and at the same time work the valves up and down,

so that the oil may run from the valve slides into the valves. This prodecure should be carried out at least once every week. If the valves appear to require more frequent oiling, by all means oil them more often.

When cleaning the valves, the same basic procedure is followed as described above. However, instead of using valve oil as a lubricant, we substitute kerosene as a cleaning agent (carried by most gasoline service stations). One-half pint of kerosene should be adequate for approximately six to eight cleanings. Apply the kerosene with an old eye dropper specifically reserved for this purpose and then follow the same procedures as for oiling the valves. The kerosene should not be left in the horn longer than 8 to 12 hours and should be removed prior to playing the instrument by emptying each slide (as for accumulation of moisture).

The fumes from kerosene can be overpowering; consequently, the cleaning of the valves should take place in a well ventilated area and the instrument should not be played while kerosene is inside the valves. As far as the valves themselves are concerned, kerosene is not a good lubricant. It is intended for cleaning only and should be removed and replaced with oil after having served its purpose. One final caution: kerosene is highly flammable; it should be kept away from all sources of heat and/or fire.

Valve Slides

Valve slides, like valves, must also be lubricated and cleaned periodically. The most important consideration is to find a good lubricant. Many materials, such as gun grease, vaseline, and cold cream, have been suggested for use on valve slides. Having experimented with all of these and a number of others, I have found that one of the better slide lubricants is anhydrous lanolin (available in most drug stores), a compound very often used as a base in cold creams and other cosmetics. It has the advantage of being practically odorless, as well as certain properties which enable a normally tight slide to be pulled very freely and a normally loose slide to be held more securely in the casing. Another advantage is the relatively inexpensive cost — about 50-75¢ per ounce, and one ounce will normally last two to three years.

Anhydrous lanolin should be applied to a clean and dry slide. Simply wipe each slide clean with cheese cloth or a clean rag. Then apply a small amount of anhydrous lanolin to each slide, rubbing it in well over the whole area. Work the slide in and out to coat both the slide and the casing, applying more lubricant if necessary. (The amount required will vary depending upon the tightness of the slide and slide casing.) Readjust each slide for intonation and the job is completed.

In cleaning the slides kerosene is, again, a very suitable cleaning agent. Wipe off the old, excess anhydrous lanolin with a rough cloth, such as terry cloth. Now apply the kerosene to each slide by dipping a piece of cheese cloth into the kerosene and rubbing each slide thoroughly. Wipe dry with a clean cloth and reapply a fresh coating of anhydrous lanolin as discussed above.

Interior Cleaning

Periodically, it will be necessary to clean out the tubing of the horn. First, a cleaning coil or snake will be needed to clean the lead pipe tubing on the body of the horn and all valve slide tubing. These coils are flexible metal springs, usually coated with a rubber or plastic material, with small bristle brushes on both ends. Though they are not usually made specifically for the horn, a coil designed for the trumpet or cornet (costing about $2.50) will serve very adequately.

A mild soap, such as Ivory Flakes, mixed in lukewarm water can serve as the basic cleaning agent. Be sure the water is lukewarm and not hot or the lacquer finish used on most horns will peel.

The mouthpiece should also be cleaned. For this, we will need a special mouthpiece brush made with short bristles of graduated length and attached to a short metal wire (which is occasionally covered with a plastic coating). As with the cleaning coil, it is difficult to find a mouthpiece brush specifically designed for the horn. A trumpet or cornet mouthpiece brush (costing about $1.50) is equally acceptable.

The best method for cleaning the tubing, and the horn body generally, is to remove all valve slides and submerge all slides and the instrument itself in the solution of lukewarm water and mild soap. (It probably will be necessary to use the bath tub or a large wash tub for relatively complete submersion.) Be sure to clean all valve slides with a terry cloth to remove excess anhydrous lanolin before placing them in the soap solution.

Allow the water to penetrate the valves by working them up and down while submerged. And be sure that the solution has penetrated all air pockets which might exist in the valve slides by holding the slides with their openings upright while under water. Each slide should now be cleaned with the cleaning coil. Be careful not to force the coil through if it seems to jam in the slides, since the curvature of some slides will make it impossible to complete a full cleaning circuit. In this case, remove the coil and insert it in the other end of the slide, cleaning as far as possible into the slide.

The coil should also be used to clean the lead pipe of the horn. This is perhaps the most important part of the cleaning process (with the exception of the mouthpiece), since it is closest to the player. If not cleaned, it can harbor bacteria. In addition, a dirt build-up in the lead pipe will negatively affect the playing quality and intonation of the instrument.

After using the cleaning coil on the slides and lead pipe, slosh the water solution around the interior of the horn body by taking the horn out of the water and allowing the solution to run back into the tub. Do this two or three times. Next the mouthpiece can be cleaned by simply submerging it in the solution and running the mouthpiece brush through it a number of times. Now discard the soap solution and use fresh lukewarm water to rinse each part of the instrument, including mouthpiece, thoroughly. Wipe dry with a soft cloth and the task of cleaning is completed. Remember that all valves should now be oiled and all slides lubricated prior to performing on the instrument.

Exterior Cleaning

Most modern horns have a lacquered finish to protect the exterior of the instrument. This finish requires little maintenance with the exception of wiping with a damp soft cloth. This should be sufficient for removing any buildup of dirt or fingerprints.

In the case of non-lacquered instruments, a high quality brass or silver polish, depending on the metal, should be applied about once every year to polish and clean the exterior. This should not be done too frequently as it can wear the metal quickly. In between polishings, wiping with a soft cloth should be sufficient to maintain the exterior of the instrument.

Replacing Valve Strings

In order to efficiently replace valve strings, much practice and the proper equipment and materials are needed. The basic equipment includes a small screw driver to loosen the stop-arm screw and the key-lever screw (see Figure 1) and a good, high-quality fish line. Use 26-30-pound test-strength linen or nylon fish line. Plastic lines will stretch and narrower lines will have a tendency to cut into the valve post.

Cut off about seven inches of fish line and double-knot it at one end. After loosening the stop-arm key-lever screws, insert the un-knotted end of string in the key-lever as illustrated in Figure 1.

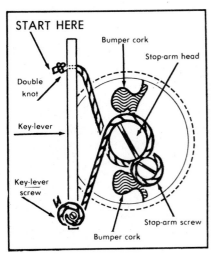

Fig. 1. Diagram for Stringing Valves

Note that the overall pattern of a strung valve is in a basic figure eight. Run the string behind the stop-arm head and loop it around the top of the stop-arm screw. Now hold the stop-arm against the valve cork (as if the valve were at rest) and adjust the height of the valve key by letting out or pulling in on the string and measuring with the fingers for valve key evenness. When the valve is level with the other two valve keys, hold the stop-arm tightly against the resting valve bumper cork and tighten the stop-arm screw. Continue in the basic figure eight pattern around the stop-arm head and push the string through the hole in the end of the key-lever. Loop the string around the key-lever screw, pull it tightly and tighten the screw. Cut the string, leaving approximately 1 - 1 1/2 inches for adjustment purposes.

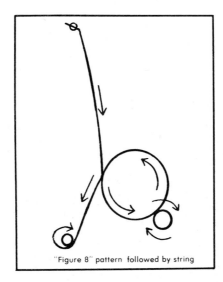

"Figure 8" pattern followed by string

If difficulties are experienced, practice the procedure a number of times, using the string of the other two valve keys as a model.

Replacing Valve Corks

When valve corks become lost or worn, the valves cease to function as accurately as they should. Consequently, it is helpful to know how to replace valve corks and re-align the valves. In order to determine the need for valve cork replacement, check the alignment of the valve by removing the valve cap. Note the marks on the rotor top and on the top valve plate (see Figure 2). These should be in alignment when the valve lever is up and when it is fully depressed.

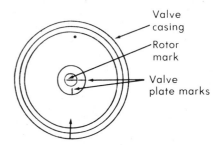

Fig. 2. Valve Alignment

If these marks do not line up, one or the other of the corks needs replacement. The cork needing replacement may be determined by comparing the marks when the valve is up and when it is down.

To replace either cork, you will need an old champagne bottle cork, a razor blade and a tweezers. After removing all remnants of the old cork, cut off a circle of cork about 1/4″ in height. Now cut this into four equal pieces. Grasp one piece with the tweezers, dip it in some water and squeeze to make it pliable. Force the cork into the jaw so that it fits tightly, slicing off any excess cork that appears above the top of the jaw area. Now check the alignment as described above. If necessary, shave down the cork carefully until the rotor and plate marks line up.

Many players prefer to use a rubber-based compound known as neoprene in lieu of ordinary cork. This material gives a bit more bounce than cork but lasts considerably longer. It is, however, somewhat more difficult to work with than cork, and more caution is advised when using it.

By way of conclusion, it should be said that basic maintenance procedures, if applied regularly, can keep the horn in good playing condition and out of the repair shop. However, should it become necessary to remove dents or perform more complicated operations than described in this article, by all means take the instrument to a competent repairman. If we stop to think about it, that, in itself, is a good basic maintenance procedure. ■

Exploring the Trumpet's Upper Register

Jay D. Zorn

Composers and arrangers are making ever increasing demands on the modern trumpet player to play higher and higher. This emphasis on the upper register has occurred in every area of trumpet playing: big band jazz, rock, symphony orchestra, studio orchestra, concert band, brass ensemble, and even solo recital. Recently, the stage band movement in the American schools has added a new impetus for trumpet players to acquire upper register proficiency at an increasingly earlier stage of development.

The jazz influence probably did more to usher in an era of upper register playing than any other. In the early 1920's jazz artists began improvising higher and higher, eventually breaking the "high C barrier" (two octaves above middle C). The big band jazz movement of the 1930's and 1940's continued this trend, as did 20th century symphonic composers, partly influenced by jazz and partly by the perfection of the modern trumpet.

Playing in the upper register requires a great deal of confidence, but mere confidence will not suffice. The confidence must be backed up with knowledge, an understanding of the mechanics involved, a great deal of patient practice, and honest personal assessment. As successful experiences are reinforced more than unsuccessful ones, confidence will begin to overbalance doubt, though doubt will

---

This article has been adapted from the introduction to *Exploring the Trumpet's Upper Register* (a systematic method for successfully attaining the upper register) by Jay D. Zorn. Delevan, New York: Kendor Music, Inc., 1975. Used by permission.

always remain to some extent. There are few artists who do not live with it, but they have learned to control their instruments so well that the doubts and fears do not interfere with their performance.

Many players have developed a strong fear of playing in the upper register, often as a result of the myth that playing in the upper register is extremely difficult and should only be attempted by a few professionals. In addition, many teachers have delayed the introduction of the upper range for too long. Young players should be encouraged to systematically explore the upper range as soon as possible. Beginning students can play a high C practically from the start, although they can't sustain it at first.

Overcoming the fear of playing in the upper register is often difficult for advanced players, as they automatically become tense as soon as ledger lines appear in their parts. Since the printed high note usually signals the old fear, practicing the upper register without music might be helpful. The player need not know to which notes he is actually climbing.

Before attempting the upper register, be sure to warm up properly. Perhaps the best time to work on the upper register is just after the first warm up of the day when the embouchure is fresh. If the embouchure is already tired, straining and excessive mouthpiece pressure is bound to occur. Rest often between upper register studies and be ready to suspend practice if the lip or throat muscles feel too tight or tensed. Any low register playing will aid in relaxing the embouchure after upper register practice.

Be careful not to overdo practice in the upper register. The actual amount of time spent practicing in the upper register will depend on each player's stage of development. For young players, 3 to 5 minutes a day will suffice. Intermediate players should try for 5 to 10 minutes of daily practice. Advanced and professional players probably should not spend more than 20 minutes each day practicing in the upper register.

Mechanics of Upper Register Playing

Adequate breath support is of great importance throughout all phases of trumpet playing, but it becomes even more important during upper register performance. As the player moves to the upper register, greater resistance is met due to the combination of many factors: the air velocity speeds up, the oral cavity becomes smaller as the throat is arched, the lip aperture gets smaller, the lips vibrate faster, the air stream is smaller, and the nodes producing the partials become shorter and more numerous. Unless the breath support is increased when moving to the upper register, the tone will get smaller, more pinched and finally cease.

The production of adequate breath support requires long, slow inhalation and controlled exhalation. As the player inhales, the diaphragm muscles should contract downward, expanding the rib cage outward and upward. To understand the full extent of his breathing capabilities, the player should try taking a double breath. This is accomplished by inhaling a long, deep breath, holding it, then inhaling some more, tucking in as much breath as possible before playing.

After the player has acquired a feeling for his inhalation capacity, the process should be accelerated, aiming for one quick, deep breath. Exhalation requires a great deal of control in the upper register in order to handle the greater volume and resistance of the air column. In exhalation, the diaphragm muscles are held firmly (never relaxed) while the abdominal muscles around the diaphragm contract, pushing the column upward.

The function of the throat arch in the oral cavity is often overlooked by developing trumpet players. As the player moves to the upper register, the back of the tongue is arched upward as if changing the vowel sounds from *ah* to *ee*. This action makes the volume of the oral cavity smaller, resulting in a more concentrated air stream that offers greater resistance to the air column. Care should be taken not to tighten the throat, neck, or chest muscles when arching the back of the tongue.

The embouchure formation for playing in the upper register is essentially the same as for the middle register. As one moves to the upper register, the corners of the mouth contract and become more firm, and the lip aperture or buzzing area becomes smaller. For most players a stretching of the lips, or smiling is less effective in the upper register than contracting the corners of the mouth.

An increase in mouthpiece pressure is normal when moving to the upper register. However, since most players have a habit of using too much pressure in the low and middle registers, they find that the added pressure in the upper register becomes intolerable. The serious trumpet student should work at using less pressure in all ranges, including the upper register.

For most embouchures, the increase of pressure used in ascending is added mainly to the lower lip and not to both lips equally. Added pressure on the lower lip tends to aid in closing the lip aperture while allowing the upper lip to continue vibrating. To demonstrate this principle the player should buzz a tone without the mouthpiece or instrument, placing one finger with pressure first on the top lip, then on the bottom lip. The pressure added to the top lip will tend to stop the buzzing, but the pressure added to the bottom lip will tend to send the pitch higher while the buzzing continues freely.

The Mouthpiece and the Upper Register

The mouthpiece usually has a direct effect on the production of the upper register and, of all the variables (breath support, throat arch, embouchure, lip aperture, mouthpiece pressure, mouthpiece, and instrument), it is the easiest to manipulate and change. The search for the ultimate in a mouthpiece usually continues throughout the entire career of most trumpet performers. Careful listening, an understanding of the mechanical functions of each of the parts of the mouthpiece, and a willingness to intelligently experiment will enable the performer to find the right combination that will make it possible for him to play up to the maximum of his potential. The following discussion of mouthpieces may provide some useful working generalizations.

Inside Rim Diameter. A larger than medium inside rim diameter (larger than a Bach 7C, for instance) will aid most players in the upper register. The larger diameter enables the lips to move more freely and to close the lip aperture without increasing mouthpiece pressure. Also, the larger inside rim diameter usually aids in the production of a bigger tone with more carrying power and affords less resistance than the smaller diameter. Of course, if the inside rim diameter is too large, the tone will spread, and the lips will get no aid from mouthpiece pressure in closing the lip aperture.

Cup Depth. A player who uses the upper register a great deal should experiment with a mouthpiece that is a little more shallow than medium. However, since depth is closely related to cup volume, the player should consider the dynamic level at which he needs to play. A mouthpiece that is too shallow will cut down on the dynamic intensity of his playing, resulting in a thin-sounding upper register.

Cup Volume. The cup volume is dependent on the combination of the inside rim diameter and the cup depth. A larger cup volume will result in a louder and fuller tone and a smaller volume in a softer and thinner tone. Cup volume also seems to affect the general control of the instrument. If cup volume is either too large or too small for a particular player, clear articulation may become difficult.

The Throat. If the throat is too small, loud playing will be more difficult, the resistance will be too great, tone quality will be thin, and the upper register will tend to block off. In contrast, if the throat is too large, then not enough resistance will be met and the tone will spread. In addition, difficulty will be experienced in sustaining long phrases, endurance will be shortened and soft playing will be more difficult.

Rim Curvature. The rim curvature is the roundness, sharpness, or bite of the inner and outer rim. The degree of roundness of the bite doesn't seem to affect the quality of sound but is more a matter of the player's comfort. How sharp a rim the player uses often depends on the shape of his teeth and amount of mouthpiece pressure he uses. If a player is in the habit of using a great deal of pressure (perhaps excessive) in the upper register, a sharp rim would be very uncomfortable. However, many players claim that they can achieve more control of their playing with a sharper rim than with a flatter or rounder rim.

Backbore. The backbore is the back end of the mouthpiece and the flare into the mouthpiece receiver of the instrument. A more closed backbore offers more resistance and makes louder playing more difficult than an open one. The amount of flare of the backbore also seems to affect the projection or carrying power of the tone. A straighter, less flared backbore that is also medium wide seems to favor resonance and projection of the upper register.

Length of Mouthpiece Shank. On every trumpet there is a mouthpiece receiver and, on the inside, the leading edge of the leadpipe. Apparently, the gap between the end of the mouthpiece shank and the leadpipe is critical to fine performance and a clear upper register. If the gap is too wide the tone will sound stuffy in both the high and low registers. If the gap is too small the upper register may sound foggy, but the middle and low registers will play well.

The Trumpet

When things go wrong, most players tend to blame the trumpet. But this is rarely the real reason for a problem. Look first to the mouthpiece, then to the other variables of breath support. Only after all other possibilities are ruled out are you justified in examining your present instrument.

There are of course dramatic differences in the playing characteristics of different trumpets, especially in the area of intonation, but tone quality, endurance, etc. rarely change radically from one instrument to another. Changing trumpets can be very costly compared to changing mouthpieces, so make sure you understand exactly what you want when doing so. The following are a few generalizations that may be of some use in selecting an instrument.

Bore. The bore is the diameter of the tubing used throughout the instrument and is usually measured at the cylindrical section around the tuning slide. Most manufacturers make their instruments with several different size bores, the large bores presenting the least resistance and the smaller ones a thinner tone and greater resistance. The medium and medium-large bores are the two sizes preferred by the majority of top professionals for both jazz and symphony work. If one has to play high and loud, the medium-large bore is probably best. If one has to play high but not too loud, the medium bore may be more comfortable.

Bell size. As with bore sizes, manufacturers usually make their best line of instruments with several bell sizes. The effect of the bell size upon volume and tone quality is similar to bore size, *i.e.,* large bells make it easier to play dark and loud, small bells thin and soft. In general, the bell size affects the volume of sound more than the quality of tone. The trend among a great many professionals

is to use a medium or medium-large bore with a large size bell.

Other Variables. There are, of course, many other variables in designing a trumpet, such as the type of brass or other metal used, the length of conical versus cylindrical tubing, the placement of braces and water keys, the type of finish (silver, gold, lacquer, unfinished), the bell reinforcement (ringing or dead bell), and the types of valves or pistons. All of these variables affect the characteristics of the trumpet to a lesser degree than bore and bell size.

High Pitched Trumpets. The Bb trumpet is the most popular, but there are trumpets manufactured in many different pitches, most of which are smaller and higher pitched than the traditional Bb trumpet. They are generally easier to play in the upper register softly but more difficult to play if greater volume is needed. Thus, the shorter, high pitched trumpets are excellent for chamber music or solo work, but for playing high and loud, the Bb trumpet is the best all-around instrument. ∎

Tips on Teaching Beginning Brass

Maurice Faulkner

The band or orchestra director who is not a specialist in brass may find that his beginning brass players are having difficulties with their instruments that he cannot easily solve. Many of these problems can be dealt with quite effectively by the non-specialist — with the help of some basic guidelines.

Selecting an Instrument

The potential brass musician will probably have decided, before he even enters the class, which brass instrument he wants to play. Do not discourage this burning desire, but analyze his physical characteristics carefully before agreeing to his choice: (1) How thick

and how short or long are his lips? (2) What type of a bite does he have? (3) What are the lengths of his arms? (4) What is the condition of his lungs? (5) What is the condition of the skin around his mouth? (Brass and metals tend to create chemical changes in the skin and will irritate a poor or unhealthy skin condition.)

While the student's preference is important, it is equally important that he choose an instrument that he has a good possibility of playing with success. Small, thin lips do not usually function as well as larger, heavier lips on the large cup instruments. Dental considerations may also be important,

and the teacher should analyze the bite of the student before assigning instruments.

A slightly built person may have inadequate lung capacity for a large bore brass instrument. To analyze the beginner's lung volume use some simple breathing exercises. For instance, have the player inhale slowly over a count of eight beats, hold the air in the lungs for eight counts, and then exhale slowly for eight counts. Most beginners won't be able to achieve this at first, but it is a good test of their potential for using the breath economically. Assign those with the most capacity to the large bore instruments — if there are no other potential problems. After all, a person with good lung capacity might have short arms that would make it difficult to reach the extended positions on the trombone or he might be too weak to handle a tuba. There are, of course, exceptions to all of these rules, and an ardent desire is much more important than a general rule in the potential for success.

It has been customary for me to let a student begin the study of whatever instrument he wishes, although I point out to him the difficulties that he might encounter. If he is not progressing as rapidly as the rest of the class by the third or fourth week of instruction, I will suggest that he try a different instrument that is more adaptable to his physical characteristics. And if, for instance, he has been struggling to play a trumpet with a thick set of lips or an improper bite, he is likely to find that switching to a larger cup mouthpiece is a delightful new experience.

Where to Start

It is best to have all beginners on brasses start their performance in a medium range, since it gives them the proper set of the lips for the majority of their first playing activities. Select a method in which the first tones to be played on the instrument are a fifth above the second overtone in the instrument's natural series (see music example). As the student improves

his accuracy in finding the pitch, he can move into higher and lower ranges by means of slurs on the various overtones above and below these initial pitches.

In the first month of instruction, it is essential that students begin to work on the pedal tones. It may be difficult to produce much sound at first, but the slow vibration relaxes the lips and permits the blood to circulate more freely (especially after it has been cut off to some degree in playing the higher notes). Many teachers emphasize the importance of buzzing on the mouthpiece or with the lips alone so that the student will develop a feeling for the tone production process without depending entirely on the pressure of the in-

strument against the lips for achieving range differences.

If you are working with a heterogeneous brass class (involving instruments in B♭, F, etc.), it will be impossible to have all instruments play in unison or octaves while remaining in their best range. To overcome this problem, I have them play at an interval of a fifth or fourth so that all can work in their better playing ranges. This procedure sounds like organum of an earlier century, but doesn't present any player group with problems of a too-relaxed or too-tight lip position. In order to control the ear training development in such situations, I have the two groups play alternately as well as together. When E♭ instruments are present, I have them play a fourth above the BB♭ tubas in concerted performance. Within four weeks they will all be able to perform in unison, octave, and harmony without difficulty, and their embouchures will have been formed at the best intermediate ranges.

Essential Exercises

Although young musicians will develop greater interest by playing little pieces from the outset, I believe it is essential to produce a series of several related good tones before attempting to form them into a tune. For this reason, I expect my students to learn a minimum of four or five notes (centered above and below the original beginning notes discussed above) before we begin the melody playing. As soon as these notes can be produced with an ability to tongue them adequately, we perform pieces in unison and octaves.

Supplemental materials based on these five notes are then formed into segments of scales and chords. Once students have learned to slur and phrase the bits and pieces of melodies and scales, they can begin to build higher and lower ranges. It is extremely important to permit the lips to strengthen themselves by lip slurs along the natural overtones of the instrument. Thus, using the open notes for lip slurs, moving upward first to the next higher overtone and then back down to the lowest tone, presents an ideal exercise in lip building.

As the range increases in both directions, scales become possible

in more complete form. At the same time, chords of the basic triads make the technical aspect of the instruction more enjoyable and also aid in the enlargement of the range. Since transposition is quite easy when you have only five notes to work with, I expect my students to transpose an interval of a whole step above and below those five or six first notes as soon as they are able to produce the note accurately.

Mechanical Aspects

Brasses are not as temperamental as the other instruments and will stand a great deal of abuse before they speak out in defense. Maintenance of valve and slide mechanisms with proper cleaning and oiling is something that both the non-brass specialist and his students can learn within a short time. Cleanliness of the instrument is a vital introductory discussion topic, and I usually over-emphasize the potential of colds, rashes, etc., which can be picked up from unclean instruments. Since the cleaning process also involves the proper replacement of valves which have been removed, slides that have been greased, etc., this aspect should be discussed thoughtfully. It is important to emphasize the fact that the brass mouthpiece can accumulate dirt inside the bore which will make tone production very difficult (if it doesn't close down the tube altogether). Lukewarm water or running water in the bathtub is best for cleaning the interior bore. Washing the exterior with mild soap and water regularly helps maintain the finish.

There are many additional problems of brass class teaching that have not been covered, but an emphasis on careful lip and mouthpiece matching, adequate breath control, proper lip exercises for forming higher and lower tones, and technical skills will enable the non-brass specialist to prepare brass instrumentalists for beginning and intermediate bands — and most will be ready within a semester or two. ∎

October, 1975

Breathing Techniques for the Tuba Player

Donald A. Stanley

The tuba makes more demands on breathing and breath support than any other wind instrument. The player must develop not only his maximum air capacity but also the muscles that will enable him to support and control the large air stream required by the instrument.

Inhalation

A relaxed and natural posture is essential for inhaling a large volume of air. It is especially important to avoid a position that requires the player to "reach" for the mouthpiece by stretching his neck forward or up or by lowering his chest or head to reach the mouthpiece. The varying sizes of instruments and players makes it necessary for each person to find his own "correct" position and manner of holding the instrument.

The chest should be held as high as possible to create the feeling of enlarging and expanding the chest cavity, since a greater amount of air can be inhaled if nothing blocks the expansion of the lungs. Avoid raising or tightening the shoulders — these are movements which do not raise the chest and thus prohibit the free flow of breath. The arms should hang loosely and naturally from the shoulders. Also essential in the correct inhalation of a large quantity of air is the proper contraction of the diaphragm, which serves to enlarge the area in which the lungs expand.

I have found it almost impossible to inhale a large amount of air through the corners of the mouth or through the nose, since the tuba mouthpiece covers too large an area of the mouth to permit enough air to enter the lungs. It is more effective to let the air rush in through the bottom of the mouth by allowing the lower jaw and lip to fall down and back, while the upper lip stays in contact with the mouthpiece. This type of breathing prevents the player from stretching his lips tighter and tighter at the corners each time he inhales. And since he is, in this sense, "breathing through the embouchure," it won't be necessary to reset the embouchure after each breath.

This whole concept of inhalation should help create a more natural and efficient means of breathing for the tuba player.

Breath Support

Breath support for the tuba player (and other brass musicians) depends on the intensity and speed of the air stream as it passes through the lips and instrument. If the tuba player relies solely on the relaxation of the diaphragm as it returns to its normal dome-shaped position during exhalation, the air stream will not have sufficient intensity and speed to produce a clear ringing quality of sound that projects well. Thus, he must also use the abdominal and intercostal muscles to push against the diaphragm, putting the air in the lungs under greater pressure. The chest should remain high and expanded during exhalation so that the lungs can quickly expand at the next point of inhalation.

Many teachers liken the experience of breath support to the feeling of "making the stomach hard." But this may be confusing, since it requires you to close the throat as in grunting. A better analogy would be that of coughing while holding your hand firmly against the stomach just under the waist-line. In this way, one can actually feel the slight lifting motion of the abdominal muscles that is necessary to support the large air stream needed by the tuba player.

A certain degree of intensity and speed must be present in the air stream when it passes through the embouchure — and it is essential that nothing inhibit the flow of the air before it reaches the embouchure. The air stream must not be controlled at the throat, since any tension in the throat or chest can interrupt the air flow. Instead it is the size of the lip opening (lip aperture) which controls the size of the air stream. Tones which are lower or louder require a larger air stream, while higher or softer tones require a smaller air stream. If the tuba player can change the size of that vibrating column of air (by varying lip aperture) without changing its speed or intensity (by maintaining sufficient breath support), he will be able to control the tone at all dynamic levels and registers. There does, however, seem to be some relationship between changes in lip aperture and amount of breath support needed. Higher pitches produced with a relatively smaller lip aperture require a greater feeling of lift, because the smaller lip aperture offers greater resistance to the air stream; lower pitches can be supported with a somewhat more relaxed feeling in the abdominal area.

Thus, an ascending pattern of intervals will call for an exaggerated lift while a descending pattern could actually call for a slight relaxation of the abdominal muscles.

Since higher tones are produced by decreasing the size of the lip aperture, players should be cautioned against trying to force too large an air stream through this small aperture. The result of "over-blowing" in attempting to force too much air through the aperture can be a feeling of "backpressure" and an extreme buildup of tension in the throat, causing real problems in developing facility, good quality, and endurance in the upper register.

Breath Control

Most tuba players find it difficult to achieve the kind of controlled air flow in long phrases that will make it possible to maintain good, consistent tone quality from beginning to end. The player should realize that due to the tremendous expansion immediately prior to inhalation, less breath support is needed at the beginning of the phrase than at the end. Initially, the player will have to control the flow of air, so that it does not escape too quickly. As the air supply decreases, a more conscious effort is necessary to support and lift out the last half of the air supply to the lips.

It should be noted that tuba players must be exposed to some type of legato and melodic material early in their training. Players exposed only to the tuba parts in most of today's band repertoire, may never be required to learn the proper habits for breathing, breath support, and breath control. For this reason, solo and small ensemble experiences are necessary for technical as well as musical achievement — and they will provide the student with an excellent opportunity to develop the kind of breathing habits that are essential in tuba performance. ■

November, 1975

The Trumpeters and Kettledrummers Art:
Book Review

H.M. Lewis

Trumpeters' and Kettledrummers' Art. Johann Ernst Altenburg. English translation by Edward H. Tarr. Nashville, Tenn.: The Brass Press, 1974. (Originally published in Halle, 1795.) 148 pp. $9.95.

Altenburg's work on the art of the trumpeter and kettledrummer is one of the few surviving documents from the 18th century which throws some light on Baroque trumpet performance. The treatise has been available in facsimile edition for some time — no fewer than five facsimile reprints have been published within the last 10 years — but the 18th century German in which it was written has been a tremendous barrier to most musicians. Even German-speaking readers have trouble with the confusingly long or incomplete sentences and pompous style characteristic of Baroque German writing.

To make this important work more accessible to modern readers, the noted trumpeter and musicologist Edward H. Tarr has prepared the first English translation of the *complete* work (a portion of the treatise was published in an English translation by Mary Rasmussen in the *Brass Quarterly*, Vol. I-II, 1958). Fortunately, Tarr has not confined himself to providing a literal translation of Altenburg's text. He has broken many long sentences into shorter ones and added words and phrases (in brackets) when necessary to make the text more understandable to the English reader. In addition, Tarr has included plates of trumpets, mouthpieces, and mutes from the Baroque period, as well as some interesting engravings from his own collection. Many added notes help clarify the text, and a very valuable translator's introduction summarizes the contents of the treatise, identifies Altenburg's sources, and provides readers with an understanding of the whole project of translation.

Altenburg's treatise is as valuable to the historian as it is to the musician, offering a fascinating insight not only into the performance practice of the 18th century, but also into the social background of the trumpeters and kettledrummers themselves. The first section of the book discusses the history of the trumpet, the trumpeters' and kettledrummers' guilds, and the duties and privileges of the court and military trumpeters of the Baroque period. Fascinating details about the lives of these 18th century musicians fill these pages. In describing the "Conditions of Field Trumpeters in General," for example, Altenburg discusses pay, uniforms, quarters, the horse and rank — and makes sure to point out that "A trumpeter shall and must live in grand style, especially when he is young and single." (p. 57)

The second part of the treatise is what we, today, would recognize as a method. This portion deals with the technical aspects of playing the trumpet and kettledrum, including the basics of music reading, performance of ornaments and certain trumpeting figures, and selection of mouthpieces and instruments. The technical discussions are all quite lucid and contain information that is still of use today — not only to historians and performers specializing in 18th century music, but to all musicians. In fact, many teachers may find some useful "gems" in the portion of Part II reprinted below. Another interesting feature in this part is the use of several musical examples, including the famous *Concerto a VII Clarini con Tymp.*

In working on the translation of this work, Tarr has managed to correct several misconceptions that have persisted for many years. He makes it quite clear in the translation that the standard trumpet of Altenburg's time was the instrument pitched in D at chamber pitch. When used in choir pitch (a full tone higher than chamber pitch), the same instrument was pitched in C. Thus, there was only one trumpet — not two — in standard use. (The *Concerto a VII Clarini con Tymp.* was actually intended for trumpets in C rather than in D.)

Edward Tarr has provided trumpeters with a valuable historical source in an easily accessible form — with additions and annotations that have made it even more valuable for the modern reader. The Brass Press has already published such previously hard-to-find sources as Fantini's trumpet method of 1638 and Hermann Eichborn's treatise on clarin playing of 1894. Here's hoping they keep up the good work. ∎

Trumpet Talk for Teachers

Clifford Lillya

When I audition an applicant, I am more interested in discovering what his basic capacities are than how much repertory he knows. During the audition I ask myself, "What's right (not what's wrong) with this student? What does he have that we can build on? How far is he from leveling off in ability? Is his temperament favorable to trumpet playing?" If you feel that you can work with the applicant and decide to accept him, then be careful to make any technical changes slowly at first — give yourself a chance to really get to know the student.

Fundamentals

In evaluating a student's tone production, I make it a point not to to handle his instrument with grace and ease, so that his imagination and musicality can function unhampered. To reach this point, the student must master certain fundamental techniques.

Tone production

Producing a sound on the trumpet is an almost mystical experience — a thrill which only trumpet players can appreciate and understand. The fascinating riddle of tone production has inspired many theories, systems, experiments, and research projects, and almost all of the resulting explanations are worthy of serious consideration. Faithfully and diligently applied, most can be expected to get results with certain students. But the individual's image of what happens when he plays is really more important to him than knowing, in scientific terms, what actually *does* happen. It is best to encourage the student to develop his own rationale.

In evaluating a student's *tone production,* I make it a point not to look directly at the embouchure — since this is only the tip of the iceberg in the whole process of tone production. However, if I do feel the need to visually check a student's embouchure, I view it indirectly through a mirror. In general, the best embouchure is the one that leaves the lips looking nearly as they do when in repose.

Moving from one pitch to another

Imagine that a trumpeter is asked to play two examples: one slurring from low C to third space C; the other from second line G to third space C. One requires a much greater leap in pitch than the other, but it should take the same amount of time to get from one note to the other in both examples — zero! In other words, there should never be a gap between the two notes. Students must learn to experience this feeling of smoothness and associate it with the desired sound. The teacher can describe the process with various analogies and similes, which will help lead the student to the brink of discovery (compare to a yodel, a harmonic, an oboe playing an octave). With sufficient repetition these mental images become woven into the fabric of the player's personality and the mechanisms will begin to function automatically.

Sustaining the long sound

To sustain a long sound in all playing, we must try to keep the sound continually even, with no narrow or frayed spots, especially when a pitch change is involved. To help the student, try using analogies such as "keep the paper on the wall" or "keep the bow on the string."

Articulating while sustaining the sound is simply a matter of blowing continuously while tonguing.

Blowing through the valve changes

Sometimes we find a young player constricting his throat unconsciously each time a valve goes down. In order to give him the feeling of blowing through the valve changes, move the valve for him while he blows. Not knowing when the valve is going to move, he doesn't make the throat constriction and he gets the point immediately.

Single tongue delivery

Here we try to create the illusion that the tones move along on a conveyor belt. Although the listener hears the tones as detached, the player knows that the effort is continuous from beginning to end. Only the first note is "from scratch." Each one thereafter relates to the one that follows it and the one that preceded it. Some students have a tendency to make a separate impulse with the blowing muscles for each tone. Instead, the student should think of a group of notes as a string of beads — the tones are the beads and the *unbroken* wind is the string that holds them together.

Another common problem among trumpet students is the pro-duction of extraneous vocal sounds in the throat each time a tone is played. This indicates a tightness in the throat. Some people can play well in spite of it, but the tone will be better if the tension is relaxed.

A Teaching Plan

In my teaching plan, I try to give my students a long series of projects by which they can gradually move to the top levels of performance. Projects should always be chosen purposefully and with special care — particularly during beginning stages — to allow the student to establish the habit of success. Often, even to the advanced player, the only difference between his getting a note or missing it is whether or not he expects to get it.

Early instruction should be in a low key — both figuratively and literally! For example, if you scream at a young student, "HOLD THAT NOTE STEADY!", he is likely to interpret this as a threatening situation and will unconsciously tighten up to forcibly straighten out the sound. Clearly the direct command does get quick results, but it also teaches the student something that he will have to unlearn later. How much better to let him experiment until he naturally comes to rest on the best tone. This method may take a little longer at first, but ultimately it saves arduous hours ironing out a deeply rooted tension problem.

Teaching on advanced levels becomes more difficult in many ways. Improvement comes more slowly and its exact nature often defies verbalization. We must deal largely with intangibles — things which involve imagination, such as style, timbre, expression, projection — and in doing so there is a tendency to use a kind of jargon made up largely of figures of speech and analogies. Unless the student learns to understand his teacher's particular language, no real communication can take place. I can remember puzzling over two seemingly opposing ideas that were advanced by two equally distinguished performers. Since they seemed completely contradictory, was one of them wrong? Of course, I know now that they were both right.

Whatever the level of the student, teach only those things that he really needs to be taught. A talented student intuitively does many things well. If he breathes properly, why talk about it? If his tone production is natural and easy, don't try to dissect and analyze it. Of course, the teacher should have the mechanics in mind, but never let the player become preoccupied with this. Keep the *music* foremost in his mind. And when problems do arise that are difficult to deal with, you can really help the student get through it all by reminding him of the satisfactions of trumpet playing...and of the importance of keeping his sense of humor! ∎

1976

Control Your Nerves
by Improving Your Playing

William C. Robinson

While slight nervous tension at a performance may create just enough excitement and "edge" to add spark and spontaneity to the performance, excessive nervousness can totally destroy it. Common symptoms of excessive nervousness are dryness in the mouth, lack of breath control, overuse of the embouchure, and lack of concentration on the music. The results are apparent immediately — not only to the player, but to the listeners as well. For example, the dryness in the mouth creates problems in articulation, tone control, and upper and lower range control. Breath instability causes the tone to quiver, lessens dynamic control, and compounds intonation problems by adversely affecting tonal focus.

Playing below the level that the player has come to expect from himself can lead to a loss in confidence. It's a vicious cycle — poor playing destroys confidence which creates poor playing which destroys confidence, and so on.

What can be done to restore the player's ability and self-confidence? Should he immediately begin a never-ending search for "the right" mouthpiece, the "perfect" instrument, better etudes, or a different hand position? Should he double his practice time? While any or all of these may be of help, it must be assumed that the basic fault lies in playing techniques, habits, and the general approach to the instrument. To find the correct solutions, the player should thoroughly evaluate every aspect of his playing. After identifying the weaknesses, practice procedures which will build a solid foundation for improvement should be instituted.

The following suggestions are given as guidelines for a systematic method of improving one's playing, for correcting faulty playing habits, and for establishing self-confidence. They are based on fundamentals of playing and should open the door for definite, consistent, and gratifying progress.

Use of the Breath

Every brass player knows the importance of using the air when playing and admonitions such as, "use the diaphragm" and "blow hard" are all too familiar. As a result, use of the breath is often taken for granted, but it should be analyzed carefully if the player is to discover and isolate his problems. Many players who *think* that they use the air correctly, in reality fail to use it as well as possible, and may depend too much on the embouchure.

When evaluating the use of the breath keep this in mind: a different sized aperture is necessary for every tone at every different dynamic level. To demonstrate aperture change, play a C major arpeggio (Example 1), slurring all the tones, using the same air speed and changing the pitch by making the aperture smaller for higher tones and larger for lower ones. The next step is to change the pitch by changing the speed of air *without changing the aperture size* (Example 2) — faster air speed for higher tones and slower air speed for lower tones.[1]

Ex. 1

Aperture smaller for higher tones; larger for lower ones.

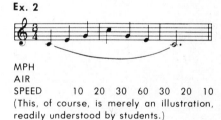

Ex. 2

MPH
AIR
SPEED   10 20 30 60 30 20 10
(This, of course, is merely an illustration, readily understood by students.)

These studies demonstrate to the player the feeling of playing "on the air" as opposed to playing "with the lip." The ultimate goal is maximum use of the air combined with minimum use of the lip. In addition, routine practice of the extremes of the musical spectrum, playing very loud and soft, fast and slow studies, will come in handy — if you can play the extremes well, you'll have no problem playing what is actually called for in a piece of music.

Proper use of the breath also depends on the way in which air is taken into the body. Note the following procedures:

1. Take a deep breath, without allowing the shoulders to rise; let the chest rise only at the last part of the inhaling procedure.

2. Maintain firmness and a fixed position in the abdominal muscles, but do not allow this to create tension in the throat.

Correct use of the breath must not be taken for granted — it requires constant concentration. When it is used properly the immediate result will be a more relaxed embouchure, a more solid tone, and better control of range and dynamics. The player's confidence will increase and the vicious cycle spoken of earlier will begin to reverse itself.

The Attack

One problem which can create a great deal of worry and nervousness is the playing of clean and accurate attacks, particularly following long rests. Frequently, the player will create too much lip tension by placing the mouthpiece on his lips and setting his embouchure too far in advance of his entrance. The following study is suggested as a guide for developing a practice routine which will combat this habit. Throughout the exercise listen for the solid core of the tone and play with firm abdominal muscles and a relaxed throat.

Ex. 3

1. All in the same instant — place the mouthpiece on the lips, set the embouchure, and start the tone.

2. Take the mouthpiece away from the lips between tones.

3. Do not use the tongue for articulation.

4. Depend entirely on the breath for tone production.

5. Play in all keys and at all dynamic levels.

6. Increase the range until three octaves are encompassed.

7. Add the use of the tongue for articulation, but do not change the method of blowing or the lip tension.

The technique of taking the mouthpiece away from the lips is also a great help in solving endurance problems. Severing contact, even for an instant, can do wonders for a tired lip. In addition, it enables the player to open the mouth freely to breathe easier, quicker, and inhale more efficiently.

Use of Scales

Practicing major and minor scales and arpeggios can provide an ideal vehicle for developing ease of playing and increasing range

control. Consider the familiar C major scale and note the following suggestions:

Ex. 4

1. Play c, d, e without any change in embouchure. To accomplish this, proper use of the breath is essential.

2. Gradually add one note at a time until the entire scale can be played *without any noticeable change in feeling or movement in the embouchure.*

3. Now that you can play all the tones in a one-octave scale with almost no change, you *know* that you can play all arpeggios and octave skips in the same manner.

4. Extend your practicing to 3-octave scales and arpeggios in all keys. Concentrate on the air speed — faster air for higher tones, slower air for lower ones.[2]

5. Listen critically for uniform quality, volume, and articulation in each tone. Be sure that the rhythm is exact and precise. Use of a tape recorder and metronome can be extremely helpful in learning to *listen* to yourself.

Use of the Tongue for Tonal Focus

Another technique which can be added to those already discussed for improvement of control, intonation and range is the proper use of the tongue for tonal focus. The *front* part of the tongue (from the tip to approximately the middle) should be considered as the focusing mechanism. Excessive movement of the back of the tongue may create tension in the throat and will negate everything positive in one's playing. Experimentation with the use of the tongue to aid in range development and tonal focus will quickly show that the tongue and breath can also relieve pressure on the lip. Needless to say, this use of the tongue will be completely ineffective without proper supporting use of air speed.

Double/Triple Tonguing

All technical facility must be based on good use of the breath, minimum movement of the embou-

chure mechanism, and minimum movement of the tip of the tongue in articulation. The following specific suggestions should prove helpful:

Double Tonguing

1. Practice repeated tones at a slow tempo, using the "k" syllable. The goal is to match this articulation with the "t" articulation.

2. Practice repeated tones using *tktk* articulations.

3. Reverse the articulations, using *ktkt*.

4. Do not create space between tones, but maintain a steady flow of air.

5. Practice at a slow tempo.

6. When a reasonable amount of control has been accomplished, practice all major and minor scales and arpeggios using double tonguing (2 octaves in all ranges). Alternate articulations: *tktk* for one scale, *ktkt* for the next.

Triple Tonguing

1. Follow the same routine used for double tonguing.

2. Practice all chromatic scales in a two-octave pattern, using triple tonguing.

3. Other articulations may also be used: *tkt, tkt,* and *tkt, ktk.*

Musical Interpretation

After mastering the techniques discussed here, the student should be closer to achieving the ideal — playing musically and knowing that technical difficulties will not hinder a performance. Here are a few suggestions, based on these techniques, for a musical performance of two well-known horn solos:

Ex. 5

Concerto for Orchestra, Bartok (4th movement).

In Example 5:

1. Play with lip change to illustrate difficulty and lack of tonal flow.

2. Play on air-speed and feel the difference in the embouchure.

3. Maintain a thread of tone between the e and the a (second measure).

4. Use air speed between b and

e (second and third measure).

5. Concentrate on air-speed between skips (third measure), leading one tone to the next and maintaining the flow of the phrase.

6. Play a slight crescendo on *c#* (fourth measure), leading to *b* and allowing dynamic contrast at *pp*.

Ex. 6

Villanelle, Dukas (opening theme)

The ability to use the technique of "playing on the air" for phrase building opens the way for flexible, free, and musical playing. To learn this type of phrase building:

1. Practice the solo with a sustained tone, a diminuendo after the beginning of the tone and a crescendo at the end, leading into the next tone. Do not let the tongue articulation interfere with the flow of tone. The arrows in Example 6 indicate this voice leading.

2. Exaggerate at first, then refine until the style is extremely subtle. Create a feeling of flow from tone to tone, providing movement within the phrase. (These subtleties should not interfere with the general rise and fall of a long phrase.)

When the player concentrates on many of the techniques discussed in this article, not only will he play better, but he will be so absorbed in the music that he will have no time to think about his nerves. ∎

1. A detailed study of this process appears in Philip Farkas, *The Art of Brass Playing* (Bloomington, Indiana: Brass Publications), 1962, pp. 40-42.

2. See scale studies in William C. Robinson, *An Advanced Illustrated Method for French Horn Playing* (Wind Music, Incorporated).

February, 1976

Teaching Trombone Legato

Stewart L. Ross

One of the most difficult and frustrating techniques for the trombonist to master is the art of legato playing — manipulating a trombone slide often proves more troublesome than pressing the valves of a trumpet. While the trombone is the only wind instrument capable of producing 1/4 tones and glissandi, these idiomatic devices, that are so helpful in some situations, do make legato playing more difficult to achieve. The student's problems are further complicated when he does not receive proper instruction.

Legato playing is not a special style to be taught only to advanced musicians who have mastered the fundamentals of good trombone playing. Because a large percentage of band music contains legato passages for the trombonist, slurring is a basic skill even for the beginner. Unnecessary delay in presenting legato playing not only deprives the student of a necessary skill but also deprives his performing group of a well-rounded player.

Legato playing should be introduced when the student has a basic understanding of the seven positions, and can find them, physically and aurally, with relative ease. Instructors should know that the beginning players will inevitably smear notes together. Watch for students who think that they are slurring but are actually using a *portamento* or a tongued style.

The following exercises and comments may be helpful in teaching legato playing.

Exercise 1 will help the student develop a controlled glissando, which is the first step towards achieving a legato style. After the initial attack, the slide should be in continuous motion until the final E♭ is reached. There should be no break in tone or sudden change in dynamics. When the student becomes accustomed to the continuous connection he is ready to work on Exercise 2.

Here the slide must be moved more quickly than when practicing the glissando, and the tongue must be used only when initiating the slur. Exercise 2 guarantees the student eventual success. Since he will be playing only "over the break" (alternating from one overtone series to another), the slur will start to lose its glissando quality and begin to resemble legato playing.

Now students should begin to learn how to slur notes within the same overtone series (the final goal). Exercise 3, more difficult than Exercise 2, will help to introduce the proper feeling; it will also prove helpful in developing the embouchure muscles.

Thus far, the tongue has been used only when initiating the slur. In order to perform a clean slur within an overtone series, the tongue must be used as part of the slur itself. In Exercise 4, the tongue should produce a light "du" articulation as the slide is moved to the slurred note. Aim at producing the same sound made when slurring notes in Exercises 2 and 3.

Larger intervals can be introduced as the slurring process is mastered. Care must now be taken to move the slide very quickly while still producing a smooth sound.

Should the student revert back to a "glissando" style of playing, have him repeat Exercise 3 and compare it to the sound of Exercise 1. Stress the need for a light "du" between the two slurred notes to do away with an otherwise "soupy" sound. All students seem to learn quickly by imitating the correct sound. If you are not able to demonstrate the legato technique yourself, enlist the aid of an advanced student, a clinician, or a quality recording. Be wary of providing lengthy explanations concerning tongue and teeth placement, embouchure shape, wrist action, etc. — they often cause more *new* problems to the young trombonist than they alleviate.

Remember, legato playing is considerably more complex for the trombonist than it is for any other instrumentalist. But it is a necessary skill that can be learned by simplifying the process and breaking it up into varying stages of difficulty. Through diligent practice by the student, and intelligent guidance by the teacher, refined legato playing can become a reality.

Exercise 1

(*mf*) glissando

Exercise 2

T = tongue

Exercise 3

Exercise 4

Exercise 5

March, 1976

Catch Those Clams

William B. Stacy

Modern technology has been unable to devise the horn player's most-desired accessory: a clam filter. In the absence of such a miraculous device, the player must assume the responsibility for keeping the clams out of the horn. The type of clams in question are not the mollusks so often found in chowders and chip dips. They are, instead, the horn player's term for the chipped notes which seem to plague so many performances. While human frailties make it virtually impossible to eliminate the clams, they can be reduced at least to the status of endangered species.

Basic Considerations

The key to accurate horn playing is proper tone production. The embouchure, breath support apparatus, and tongue must interact in a balanced manner to produce a clear, well-centered sound. If only one of these falls out of line, a clam will surely result. A brief description of each of the critical tone production factors is in order here.

Embouchure. Set the mouthpiece by having the student place the lower rim of the mouthpiece on the lower lip. Then, roll the upper rim onto the upper lip. This will give the characteristic 2/3 upper lip — 1/3 lower lip set, and should work well with most dental formations. (Young players sometimes tend to set the mouthpiece carelessly. Have them observe how carefully fine professional players set their mouthpieces.)

Using the embouchure muscles correctly results in a free dark tone, good endurance, excellent flexibility, and a relaxed high register. The key to proper usage lies in maintaining a slight pucker rather than a smile, thinking of lip compression rather than mouthpiece pressure, and keeping an open aperture between the lips rather than pinching.

Poor use of the embouchure muscles shows most clearly in the high register. Inexperienced players often try to compensate by squeezing the lips together and using an inordinate amount of mouthpiece pressure. The result is

726

a pinched sound and low endurance.

Support. Lack of support from the air column and the creation of tension often result when young players chestbreathe. The student should concentrate on expanding the abdominal muscles when taking a breath. Encourage the young player to fill the horn with a sufficient volume of air to cause the embouchure to vibrate properly.

Articulation. The horn player uses two basic types of articulation: tonguing and slurring. Most student horn players tongue too softly and fail to create the strong initial surge of air necessary to make a clean attack. Encourage your horn students to tongue much more percussively than their colleagues in the other brass sections. Not only will this produce more accurate attacks by individual horn players, but the clarity with which your horn section plays should increase.

Tongue placement varies from person to person, but I find that touching the tongue to the spot where the palate and upper teeth meet seems to work best for the majority of players. Use the syllable "duh" for the most natural tongue action.

Slurs should be made smoothly and without abrupt changes in air flow. The two most common faults in slurring are: stopping the air between notes and "pushing" each note into place — both of these produce clams.

Case Histories

I have classified the various types of clam-prone horn players. By studying these "case histories," you may find some remedies for your own students' problems.

The Quick Draw waits until the last possible second to lift the horn before playing. When he finally positions the horn, the embouchure and the notes produced seem to be a matter of chance. Encourage this student to take the time to set

carefully.

The Bush-Thwacker usually tongues between the lips, thus creating an explosion of sound on each attack. (With care, the explosion can be further developed into a resounding "splat!") Work on tongue placement and developing a continuous air stream.

The Chicken-Clucker, a cousin to "bush-thwacker," offends less because so little sound comes out of the horn. The tiny sound which he makes results from the initial surge of air behind the tongue, but no well-supported air stream follows. Have the student work on "blowing through" the sound after each attack.

The Balloon Blower has just the opposite problem from the previous two. This timid soul begins each attack with little tongue action, and swells each note into place. Work on a solid, percussive tongue action and constant air flow.

The Hooter, a highly developed "balloon blower," uses no tongue action at all. Instead, he merely blows into the horn to obtain an indistinct, delayed-action attack and a "hooty" sound. You can help this student by working on tonguing.

The Huffer pushes each note in a slur (sometimes known as the "big, bad wolf syndrome"), resulting in a "wah-wah" effect. Have the student work on keeping a steady flow of air while slurring.

The On Again-Off Again stops the air between the notes of a slur — the result — uneven slurring and frequent clams. Again, work on maintaining a steady flow of air.

The Woof-Off has problems ending notes, not beginning them. Instead of making a rounded release with the glottis, this player uses a surge of air to let everyone know exactly where the cut-off takes place. The student should practice tapering long tones, gradually making the taper and natural cut-off

happen more quickly.

The Tut-Tut, the infamous tongue cutter-offer, stops the air stream with his tongue and produces an "uht" at the end of each note. This character, like "woof-off," should concentrate on making tapered releases.

The Biter exhibits a "peach-pit chin" as he pinches for (and usually misses) high notes. Work on basic embouchure formation, keeping an open aperture, and creating a large amount of lip compression. The student should check for a flat chin, a sure sign that the embouchure muscles are working properly.

The Cud Chewer generates a large amount of chin action when attacking a note or changing pitches and extreme distortion of the embouchure results. Have the student look in a mirror as he plays, keeping in mind the necessity for firm embouchure muscles at all times.

The Half-Pint is an anemic soul, who takes little or no breath before playing and quickly runs out of air. Work on support and keep reminding him of the necessity of starting with a "full tank."

The Inflationary, a chronic chestbreather, puffs his chest like a blowfish. He develops little support, producing instead a considerable amount of physical and psychological tension. Work on abdominal action in breathing, especially during inhalation. If the student gets the knack of how to breathe properly, tone, accuracy, power, and phrase length should improve markedly.

It is important to bear in mind that secure playing results from the mastery of basic techniques. By working on the techniques of tone production and by studying the "case histories" the accuracy of your horn section should improve. Perhaps we will not need to invent a clam filter after all! ∎

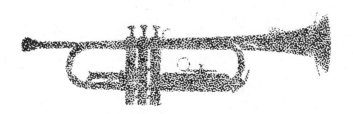

Mouthpiece Change Trauma or Triumph

Mario F. Oneglia

A trumpet teacher is often faced with difficult decisions about mouthpieces. Should the student change mouthpieces and if so, which new mouthpiece should he choose? Since the mouthpiece is a very personal item for the brass player, any change can set in motion a series of far-reaching events, either positive or detrimental for the student. Teachers must know when a change is necessary, how to choose the new mouthpiece, and what to expect from the player once the change takes place.

Reasons for Change

The principal reasons for changing mouthpieces should be physical growth in the lips, embouchure development (perhaps from a smile to a pucker), and need for more comfort. Most trumpet students do change mouthpieces at least once during their first 10 years of playing.

The noted virtuoso performer and teacher, Armando Ghitalla, told music educators, "If students practice at home, if their motor control is good, maybe they can use a larger mouthpiece, but who knows? I have to be with a student for practically a whole year before I know. In trying to decide whether it's the student or the mouthpiece, we usually try awfully hard to be sure it is the mouthpiece . . . and sometimes it is. Most of the time it isn't."[1] Teachers and students alike should profit from Ghitalla's sound advice and switch mouthpieces only as a *last* resort.

Choosing a New Mouthpiece

The casual phrase, "Here, try this mouthpiece" has become a dangerous cliche that can lead students into a state of constant turmoil. Even when a change is necessary the student and teacher often select a particular mouthpiece for the wrong reasons. Teachers

sometimes favor a mouthpiece with the reasoning that "it works well for me and other professionals, therefore it will be good for my students," without considering whether it will work for *this* student. The student or budding young professional often selects the mouthpiece currently used by a favorite player. Mouthpieces are sometimes chosen on a manufacturer's generalized descriptions such as, "suitable for players with weak lips," "produces a good high range," or "excellent for a dark, teutonic sound." Knowing more about the construction of the mouthpiece would surely help you avert disaster.

Mouthpiece Construction — Rim Size and Shape

Prospective buyers should consider the rim size and be aware that in the commonly used Bach-Selmer numbering system, larger numbers indicate small rims. The 7C trumpet rim, for example, is smaller and encompasses less lip area than the 1C.

Another consideration in buying a mouthpiece is the shape of the rim, whether rounded and sloping (as in a trumpet) or flattened (as in the French horn). Some players prefer a flattened shape and a cutting or sharp bit on the inside edge of the rim. Be sure that the size and shape of the rim you choose will be comfortable for the player.

The Cup

The depth and shape of the cup are also crucial. The term "cup" is somewhat misleading since the actual shape may vary from cup to funnel, or any combination of the two. Trumpet mouthpieces without letters have the deepest cups. (A number 7 is deeper than a 7C, while 7D and 7E become progressively more shallow). Shallower cups are often used for smaller (C, D, and Eb) trumpets and are thought to facilitate playing in the upper

register. Before switching to the shallower mouthpiece to expand the player's upper range, consider his embouchure and the amount of lip surface that enters the mouthpiece cup. Also decide whether reaching those high notes depends less on a smaller mouthpiece than on a smaller lip aperture and a more intense velocity of air.

When you look at a new mouthpiece, examine the area below the cup: the hole, the throat, and the flare or backbore (See Fig. 1).

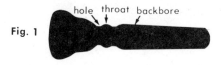
Fig. 1 hole throat backbore

The hole, through which the vibrations of the lips and air pass, is simply a drilled circle of varying dimensions which continues into the mouthpiece stem where it becomes the throat, another crucial feature. The length of the throat can also affect the sound. At the end of the throat the interior shape of the mouthpiece changes and the degree to which it flares or tapers to the bottom end of the stem can have an enormous effect on the quality of the sound.

The measurements of the hole, throat, and backbore and their relationship to each other are extremely delicate and important. Players will complain that a mouthpiece is "stuffy" or "backs up" if the drill hole is too small. A large hole can have the opposite effect. The relationship of these elements to the cup depth and shape is another variable. Larger holes and greater flares (the so-called "symphonic backbore") will generally produce a larger volume of sound from a shallow cupped mouthpiece than a smaller hole and average flare.

Always keep in mind the player's embouchure, muscular development, and method of blowing when purchasing a mouthpiece. Try to

1. Armando Ghitalla on Trumpet, (Part II, transcribed by Keith Clark). Comments to the NSOA, Tanglewood, Mass. 1974. The Instrumentalist Co., December 1974.

seek a balance among the various elements of the mouthpiece, and never stray too far from the dimensions of the present mouthpiece.

The New Mouthpiece

Players do not usually change mouthpieces unless the new mouthpiece feels, sounds, and plays better than the old one. However, after this initially favorable reaction, the student's body often revolts against the newcomer when the embouchure muscles must be retrained through a great deal of practice. During this difficult transition some players revert to their old mouthpieces, or try still another new one. As a result, neither the old nor the new feels comfortable. The muscles must be given time to accustom themselves to the new dimensions and physical demands. A series of psychological traumas or "shock waves" often accompany this period of adjustment marked by a loss of self confidence that may last days, weeks or months.

Gradually, the player adjusts to the new mouthpiece and it helps improve his playing. Folk wisdom tells us that "time is a great healer." Almost any mouthpiece may work effectively if one stays with it long enough. Too often, the teacher and the pupil expect immediate results from this physically and psychologically difficult change.

To sum up, we advise teachers and students to avoid changing mouthpieces whenever possible, not to make too radical a switch from the dimensions of the original mouthpiece when selecting a new one, and to give that new mouthpiece some time to work. ∎

May, 1976

Tunings for Double Bass Valve Trombone

Thomas G. Everett

During the past twenty years the bass trombone has come into its own as a solo and ensemble instrument. Today composers are writing for its special qualities, its dark, sonorous timbre and unique technical capabilities. We have fresh incentive to explore the potential of the bass trombone, thanks to innovations in instrument design, challenging new literature, and the proliferation of excellent young viruoso players. The study of the double valve will allow any student or performer to gain control and facility and, in fact, improve his performance. The end result is not gimmickry or technique for show, but simply a more consistent sonorous sound in all registers and a flowing musical performance.

The bass trombone is no longer as frequently confused as it once was to the large bore tenor trombone with an F attachment (sometimes called symphonic tenor or tenor-bass). Generally, a bass trombone has a bore size of .562 or larger and will probably have a 9-1/2" or 10" bell.

The F Valve

The F attachment is similar to the fourth valve on a baritone horn, euphonium, or tuba and is found on all contemporary bass trombones, as well as on many smaller sized tenor trombones. When depressed, the F attachment simply channels the air through extra tubing that changes the fundamental note of the instrument from Bb to the F a perfect fourth lower (see Ex. 1). The extra tubing approximately equals the amount of tubing present when the slide is extended to the sixth position without the valve. When the F attachment is depressed, it increases the overall length of the instrument, the total amount of tubing necessary to produce a lower note, and the distance between slide positions increases. It therefore makes fewer full positions available.

The F valve, which operates and functions exactly the same for the tenor and bass trombone, extends the range chromatically from E down to a pedal tone Bb_1 (see Ex. 2). By using the F valve for C, Bb_1, and in positions one and flat two (instead of reaching down to the sixth and seventh positions) the performer can avoid many awkward and technically difficult moves (see Ex. 3). The valve also enables the

729

Ex. 1

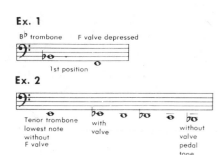

Ex. 2

Ex. 3

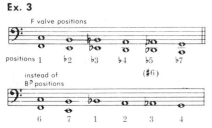

trombonist to play smooth legato and slurred passages, fast technical passages, ornaments, trills, grace notes, and special effects with greater ease.

The following system of notation is used throughout this article.

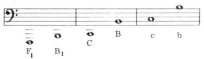

Reaching the B♮1

The F valve, which makes it possible to play a full chromatic scale on the trombone, does not allow the player to reach B1. The note may be produced in any of the three following ways.

1. Fake the pitch and flatten the C by adjusting the embouchure. Poor intonation and sound quality often result from this method.

2. Pull the F tubing and lower the pitch of the F valve to an E, a point is marked on many instruments. This point is often called the "E pull" or "E pulled." By extending the hand slide as far as it will go in the seventh, B♮1 will probably be in tune and the tone will be acceptable. Now, however, the trombonist will be unable to play the c and F in first position. B♮ and E♮ will now be found in first position with the valve depressed.

3. Use the second valve, which may be tuned to various pitches. This method is the most satisfactory one.

Most people are familiar with the proper use of the single F valve, even though some teachers and texts vary the names for positions (some relate the six F positions to the seven B♭ positions, others treat

them separately). But there is still some confusion about the double valve. What are the advantages of the double valve? How do you tune the second valve? What materials are available for study of the double valve bass trombone? The following brief discussion will answer some of these questions.

The Double Valve

The double valve (rotor) bass trombone is becoming the standard, accepted instrument for most performance situations. I cannot think of a major orchestra whose bass trombonist does not perform on a double valved instrument. Most of the studio and big band bass trombonists I surveyed recently were using the double valve with varying tunings.

The only disadvantage of the double valve is the extra weight it adds to the instrument. This should not be a major concern because, as with any other new attachment, the trombonist becomes quickly accustomed to the added weight. Likewise, the problem of "stuffiness" and added resistence can be compensated through proper adjustments.

Although there are many different designs for double valves, most work the same way. When the F valve and the second valve are depressed, air passes through the F and second valve tubing. Sometimes a rolling action of the left thumb is required to press both valves at the same time. Other instruments have a single bar, and still others have the valves placed above each other. Some manufacturers are experimenting and placing the single F in its usual position, while the second valve is controlled by the middle or ring finger of the left hand. Most designs are satisfactory, although some need the addition of a metal roller, flap, or adaptor to help make the smooth transition from one valve to another. In most cases, trombonists adapt to whatever system they learn first and then can use it successfully.

Tunings for the Second Valve: E and E♭

A new bass trombone usually comes with just the standard E tuning slide. Any other tubings must be requested, usually at extra cost, and in some cases they must be made specially by the instrument

manufacturer or local brass repair store. The single F tubing can be pulled out to create E or E♭ tuning, but then the player loses many of the advantages of the F valve — such as being able to play C and F in first position. When the second valve is tuned to E, B♮1 can be produced without sacrificing the advantages of the single F. Since the E tuning offers few advantages other than reaching B♮1, some players tune the E slide flat so that B♮1 can be produced without having to extend the arm out for the seventh position B. This tuning usually improves the pitch and tone quality, and produces a more relaxed sound. With the flat E tuning, first position is not really usable and only five positions are available.

E♭ Tuning

The E♭ tuning, a logical extension of the instrument, actually starts where E of the B♭ trombone ends. With the E♭ tuning, unlike the flat E tuning, E♭ can be played in the first position and B♮1 is still easily reached in a sharp seventh position.

D Tuning

The F-D tuning, the most advantageous for the bass trombonist, is commonly used by advanced players. Here are several advantages to the D tuning:

1. It helps avoid many wide slide movements in awkward passages and facilitates speed and accuracy. It also offers many possibilities for alternate positions to help achieve smooth legato playing.

2. It enables arpeggios from the pedal range to be played in the same slide position with only slight adjustments. It is possible to play chromatically from the upper register down to the pedal positions without reaching past fifth position (see Ex. 4).

3. It puts B♮1 within easy reach (at approximately the point of a regular fifth position).

4. It enables you to play C in the flat third position with both valves depressed. This capability is extremely helpful in technical, scale, and legato passages in avoiding the wide common movement from first to extended seventh position. It brings C position close to G with a common movement in the key of C (see Ex. 5).

Ex. 4

Playing arpeggios from pedal range

1st pos.
B♭ trom.
1st with
double
valve
depressed
1st with
single F
depressed
1st pos.
B♭ Horn

Ex. 5

D valve position
B♭ 3rd
pos.
5th pos.

5. It allows you to play the pedal tone B♭1 in the seventh position with both valves depressed.

These are just some of the advantages of the D tuning. The only real disadvantage is that on most models D in the first position is still a little flat.

G Tuning and Independent Valves

More and more trombonists are beginning to use the G tuning and independent valves, the valves that function separately from one another as well as together. Some teachers recommend the single G valve for young players — especially those with short arms — which makes it possible to play without passing the fourth position in the low staff area. The G is also used in the newer independent valves where there may be two separate valves (usually tuned to F and G). These valves are not connected (play one with the left thumb and one with the left middle finger) and work independently, so they function as a single F and single G, but when depressed together they produce the E♭ tuning.

Of course, there are other possible tunings for the double valve bass trombone (experiment yourself!) but the above discussion contains the most current uses and serves only as an introduction to the subject. For a more in-depth discussion and information on developing facility in each possible tuning consult the following list.

Methods and Studies

Methods and studies for the F attachment and double valve bass trombone still lag behind present performance practice but the following selected list of materials is quite valuable. The methods include the two main methods dealing with tunings of the double valve. The studies and etudes are useful in developing facility with the valve in the low register.

Aharoni, Eliezer. *New Method for the Modern Bass Trombone.* N. Easton, Mass.: Robert King Music Co., 1975.

This text by the bass trombonist of the Radio Symphony Orchestra of Jerusalem is the most complete book of its kind. It includes a very thorough discussion of the advantages, disadvantages, and possibilities of various tunings, along with varied etudes and exercises (all edited with use of the valve) for F, E, flat E, E♭ and D tuning. Slide comparison charts with appropriate distances between positions are also included. The independent valve (G-F-E♭) is also discussed. I strongly recommend this text for all bass trombonists.

Raph, Alan. *The Double Valve Bass Trombone.* New York: Carl Fischer, 1969.

This text, written by a studio bass trombonist, does much to present the possibilities of the "flat" E and D double valve to teachers, students and players. The method includes a slide chart, intonation graphs for the harmonic series in each position, extreme low register coordination exercise, and short discussions on other possible tunings.

Studies and Etudes

Bach, J.S. *Suites for Violoncello.* San Antonio: Southern Music Co., 1963.

There are several editions of these cello suites, all of which give the bass trombonist a chance to use the valve to solve awkward passages and problems of phrasing and breathing. The late Robert Marsteller has edited an edition for the trombone with F attachment published by Southern Music Co.

Bernard, Paul. *Method Complete pour Trombone Basse, Tuba, Saxhorns, Basses et Contrebasse.* Paris: Leduc & Cie, 1960.

More of a method for tuba than for bass trombone, this text is extremely valuable for its 10 modern unaccompanied studies at the end of the book. These diverse etudes help prepare players for the wide skips, subtle tonal shifts, and changing meters in much contemporary literature.

Blume, O. *36 Studies for Trombone with F attachment.* Edited by Reginald Fink. New York: Carl Fischer, 1962.

The author, a professor of trombone at the University of Ohio, has presented the famous Blume etudes in a lower tessitura including many low B's and wide skips. They are excellent for developing techniques in the lower register in various keys and articulations.

Bordogni-Rochut. *Melodious Studies.* New York: Carl Fischer, 1928.

Although there are some fine legato etudes on the market edited by Chester Roberts, Allan Ostrander, and Reginald Fink, I personally prefer working with the original Rochut studies for trombone and reading them down an octave. (Reading an octave above tuba parts and an octave below trombone parts must become natural for bass trombonists.)

Delgiudice, Michel. *Douze Etudes Rhythmique et Melodiques pour Trombone Basse, Saxhorn, Basse et Tuba.* Paris: Max Eschig, 1954.

Written for French tuba, these extended studies are excellent for developing a full range in both extremes within a musical setting.

Kleinhammer, Edward. *The Art of Trombone Playing.* Evanston, Ill.: Summy-Birchard Co., 1963.

This textbook by the bass trombonist of the Chicago Symphony Orchestra contains much useful information on tuning, practicing, and maintenance of the double valve.

Everett, Thomas. *Annotated Guide to Bass Trombone Literature* (2nd edition). Brass Press, 1976.

The 1976 revised edition of the *Guide* contains an annotated list of all printed and manuscript literature including solos, methods, etc. for the bass trombone, including double valve trombone.

Maenz, Otto. *Zwanzig Studien fur Bassposaune.* Frankfurt am Main, Germany: Hofmeister — currently out of print, 1962.

Hopefully this collection of excellent contemporary studies will be reprinted again. Some copies may still be found in music shops. If you are fortunate to find it, buy it! A tenor trombone version is also available.

Marsteller, Robert. *Advance Slide Technique for B♭ Tenor Slide Trombone with F and E Attachment.* New York: Southern Music Co., 1966.

The late Robert Marsteller's thesis on slide coordination, facility, and alternate positions is one of the most informative and authoritative on the subject.

Ostrander, Allen. *Method for Bass Trombone and F Attachment for Bass Trombone.* New York: Carl Fischer, 1967. *The F Attachment and Bass Trombone.*° New York: Charles Colin, 1956. *Shifting Meter Studies for Bass Trombone.* N. Easton, Mass.: Robert King Music, 1965. *Double Valve Bass Trombone Low Tone Studies.* New York: Charles Colin, 1975.

All of these books by Mr. Ostrander, the retired bass trombonist of the New York Philharmonic, are basic texts for the development of the F attachment. His *Method* was the first such text on bass trombone playing published in this country, and *The F Attachment and Bass Trombone* is still the best presentation of the F valve for a student with some experience. The *Shifting Meters Studies* and Low Tones *Studies* (based on works by Ernest Williams) are both edited for the double valve. The Ostrander works include well-written exercises incorporating the awkward and difficult movement and techniques on the bass trombone. All students should be exposed to these texts. Pederson, Tommy. *Advanced Etudes for Bass Trombone.* Minneapolis: Schmitt, Hall and McCreary, 1971.

Although these studies are not edited with the suggested valve usage, they are quite difficult and jump around in the lower register. Quite different from the usual studies, they can be played with jazz and pop phrasing. Elementary and intermediate level etudes are also available.

Supplementary Studies

Other sources of information on the F attachment are available from most instrumental companies.

Faulise, Paul and Studd, Tony. "Double Rotor Technique" and "Trombone Slide Chart" in *Connchord* XIV No. 1 (Oct. 1970). Elkhart, Ind.: Conn Corp.

Studd and Faulise are studio bass trombonists in New York City. Their sliding trombone chart shows the notes found in each position on the Bb, F, E, Eb, and D positions.

Faulise, Paul. "Trombone Conversion" in *Fourth Annual New York Brass Conference Journal.* New York: Charles Colin Co., 1976.

"Trombone Conversion" is a short but interesting article that explains the advantages of the double and independent valve systems and how Robert Giardinelli created an independent F, G or Gb, Eb or D valve system. Several useful charts, scale passages and suggestions are included.

Raph, Alan. *Double Valve Bass Trombone and How to Play It* (pamphlet). Eastlake, Ohio: King Instrument Co.

Woodson, Terry. *Exercise Book for the Olds S-24G Bass Trombone.* Fullerton, Calif.: Olds & Co.

This four-page pamphlet of exercises is the only source for suggested use of the slide for the G trombone.   ∎

°Used with permission

This slide position chart was created by Billy Robinson, a free-lance bass trombonist in the San Francisco area and director of the instrumental music program at Skyline College in San Bruno, Calif. It shows all positions on the Bb trombone in combination with F, Gb, G, Eb, and D valves.*

An Interview with Maurice André

Boris Nelson and Anne Alexander

Maurice André, *trumpeter par excellence,* has thrilled audiences worldwide with his superb intonation, brilliant upper range, and sensitive musicianship. He has enormous lung capacity, which he says he developed as a teenager while he spent four years digging in the coal mines of Southern France with his father, a professional miner. Recently he spoke with me — through an interpreter — after two breathtaking solo performances with the Toledo Symphony Orchestra under the baton of Serge Fournier.

Who were your first teachers?

My father in the South of France showed me the first steps. He was an amateur musician and often played for dances. Then Léon Bartélemy taught me basics and encouraged me. When I was 18, he told me, "Maurice, you are very talented and should go away and

study with a better teacher," Then I went to study with M. Sabarich while I was at the Conservatoire in Paris and for several years later.

Do you teach?

Yes, at the Paris Conservatoire. The students are very advanced. Many have studied seriously in the provinces. There is a very difficult competition for admission.

How do you teach the basics such as tonguing, tone quality, development of range, and endurance?

There are studies for all of these things. Each individual is different. The essential thing for any technique is to relax. The question of *l'attaque* (tonguing) is very much a matter of individual talent, but there are exercises designed to develop this. Regarding sonority, one should "vocalize" on the instrument just like a singer. There are various exercises to develop range. In all of them it is essential to relax and to support the tone with a volume of air.

To develop endurance (*la résistance*) it is important to practice often during the day, and not long at a time. Play 30 minutes and rest 15. Then play 30 minutes and rest 30. Play 30 minutes and rest an hour. The lips are a muscle and it is important to rest them frequently. In all, it is good to practice four hours per day, plus studying solfege and listening to music.

Do you recommend a certain type of mouthpiece?

The mouthpiece varies with the trumpet and with the student. The diameter depends partly upon the thickness of the player's lips. It

is really necessary for the student to try out mouthpieces and select the most suitable one for him with the help and advice of the teacher. Remember that either thick lips or thin lips can adapt well to playing the trumpet. My teacher had very thin lips and I have quite heavy lips.

How does it happen that you have made a specialty of playing Baroque music?

That idea is a mistaken one. Americans seem to think that I have made a specialty of Baroque. In Europe I play all styles of music, including at least 25 modern pieces, by composers such as Enesco.

How did this misconception come about?

I'm not really sure, I have made two tours in America. During the first, I played much Baroque. I was invited to play this because it is the trumpet music which is most popular with the public. In France I play all music including jazz.

Did you have to develop special techniques to play the various repertoires?

No. However, the Baroque requires good lips since it is the most difficult to play. The range is very high.

Have you developed any special studies to deal with the playing of this literature?

No. In my opinion, a good method is the "Arban Method" which is used all over the world. If I should write a method, I would do it at the end of my career after noting all the different types of players. I have already learned a good bit, but with the years I shall know a great deal more after working with many more students.

How can the problems of playing Baroque be overcome?

Playing Baroque frightens trumpet players. If the trumpeter has well developed lips he can play Baroque very well. Many American players handle this style quite well.

Was the 18th-century trumpet like the present day one?

No, no, no, the baroque trumpet was very large. There were two holes in the tube, but no valves. The pitch was made with the lips and the holes made certain tones easier to produce.

What is the Bach trumpet?

That is a little trumpet in "D".

Do you have any advice for stu-dents of trumpet?

Yes, I have a lot of advice, but it would take three volumes. Basically I'd say to take courage and naturally *work hard*. As with all music study, don't expect rapid progress. Another requisite is *la persévérance* — it is the same word with the same meaning in English. Many young people give up music because progress is very slow. If they will be patient the music will come.

Also, students should be aware that the fault of many trumpet players is that they don't listen to instruments such as the violin and the piano and to singers. That is the way to develop style. It is difficult to make the trumpet sing like a violin, but we must try. When music is badly played in the colleges, it is because students don't listen to enough fine music.

Once I conducted a clinic at a

university and played some beautiful music. Afterward there were students who asked me, "Why don't you play Arban's *Carnival of Venice?*" This music interests them but it is ridiculous and very ordinary.

I like band music very much when it is well played as by the band of the "Garde Républicaine." I played in a band during my youth, but in addition my father insisted that I listen to much fine music played by the best soloists. The trumpet is a noble instrument and should not sound like "pah-pah, pah-pah, pah-pah."

The great temptation, even among distinguished players and conductors, is to play too fast, which destroys the architecture of the music. It is thus brilliant but meaningless. Students must learn that every note should be spoken. ◼

Charles Schleuter on Orchestral Trumpet Playing

David Hickman

Charles Schlueter, a student of Don Lemasters, Ed Brauer, and William Vacchiano, has been principal trumpet of the American Ballet Theatre Orchestra, the Kansas City Philharmonic, the Milwaukee Symphony Orchestra, and assistant principal with the Cleveland Orchestra. He is currently principal trumpet of the Minnesota Orchestra, teaches at the University of Minnesota, and conducts master classes during the orchestra's nationwide tours.

What instruments must a trumpeter play who occupies the principal chair in a major orchestra? And what are the range, endurance, technique, and transposition requirements?

We use more instruments today than orchestral trumpeters used ten or fifteen years ago. Cornets are again being used for cornet parts and trumpets in B♭, C, D, E♭, E, F, G, and piccolo A and B♭, are used at the discretion of the player. This is due largely to the increased availability of certain instruments and improvements in instrument design. With a little ingenuity, you can even build your own instruments from other trumpet parts. I've recently put together an E♭ trumpet by using a B♭ bell and leadpipe and cutting the tubing to the correct lengths. I used a sort of "trial and error" method and had a repairman do the soldering. But with a benzene torch you could do it yourself.

The trumpet range required in the professional orchestras begins at concert E♭ below the staff (as in Bizet's *Carmen*) and extends to concert G above high C (as in Bach's Second *Brandenburg Concerto*). Endurance requirements vary. The problem in orchestral playing is that often the trumpeter doesn't play during one or two movements of a work and then he has to play difficult passages after the intonation and temperature of the instrument has changed, and the lips have lost some sensitivity. At the same time, the pitch of the orchestra has changed due to the heat of the stage lights.

Transposition is probably one of the most crucial skills required of an orchestral trumpet player. Parts are often written for trumpets in B♭, C, D, E♭, E, F, B (H), etc., and in order to play your B♭ trumpet while the part is written for an E♭ trumpet you must be able to transpose fluently at sight.

A trumpet player must also be able to suit his style and sound to the music. One must be able to switch from Mozart to Strauss, from Beethoven to Mahler, or from Gershwin to Stravinsky, and use the appropriate sound and style for each. It is necessary to have a complete palette of tonal colors, different types of vibrato, as well as different attacks and releases

to convey the correct character of each musical period and style.

What is the job market like for orchestrally oriented trumpet players? How many openings are there annually, how many applicants are there for each opening, and what are salary scales like?

There are usually three or four openings each year in the major orchestras. The competition has increased since I started playing professionally fifteen years ago and now more and better players are looking for jobs. When I auditioned for the Kansas City Philharmonic in 1962 about a dozen players competed for the position. In 1971 at the Minnesota Orchestra audition there were about 45 trumpet players, but there had been over 80 applicants before the screening.

Minimum salaries in professional orchestras have increased tremendously in the last decade. Many orchestras now have annual seasons of over 40 weeks with minimum salaries of over $200 per week. Principal chair salaries are higher and I believe that in most cases second and third chair trumpet players also receive higher than the minimum salaries, especially when the third trumpet is also an assistant principal.

Can you describe your schedule?

The average weekly schedule of a professional orchestral musician usually contains eight services. A service is either a rehearsal or a concert. (Rehearsals usually last 2½ hours.) The daily schedule varies. On some days there is one rehearsal, on some days two, and on other days we have a rehearsal and a concert. Occasionally, we play two concerts on the same day. The time between services can be used for practicing, teaching, or relaxing. One advantage of an orchestral musician's schedule is the flexibility it affords.

What is the role of the cornet in today's professional orchestras?

There are many works in the orchestral repertoire that have parts written for cornets as well as trumpets. Tchaikovsky, Berlioz, Prokofiev, and Stravinsky are some of the primary composers who utilize the sound of the cornet. Cornets should be used when called for, providing the player can employ a

true cornet mouthpiece. Most cornet mouthpieces made today are merely trumpet mouthpieces on a cornet shank (stem) that will fit the cornet properly. The cup of a cornet mouthpiece should be much deeper and more "funnel" shaped (like a French horn) than a trumpet mouthpiece. Also, the throat (bore) of the cornet mouthpiece should be at least a #20 or #18 (drill bit size) as opposed to the smaller #27 or #28 bore of a standare modern cornet or trumpet mouthpiece. Unless the cornet mouthpiece contains the correct dimensions, the difference in sound between a cornet and trumpet is too small to warrant using the cornet.

Why do many trumpet players have trouble playing offstage trumpet calls?

The biggest problem with offstage playing is intonation. The further away the player is from the orchestra, the lower his pitch will sound to the orchestra and the lower the orchestra will sound to the offstage player. The player must not tune to the orchestra when he is offstage. Pushing the tuning slide in until someone on the stage tells him that the pitch is correct is about the only way to accurately gauge correct intonation. If the player is on tour and is not familiar with the back stage area he must judge the tuning by the change in pitch from the orchestra and take his chances for the correct intonation. The beat must be anticipated by the player because the added distance will make the offstage player's sound reach the conductor later than the sound of the orchestra. In a work like *Pines of Rome* by Respighi, if the player can't see the conductor, the conductor will have to listen and accompany the offstage player during the solo.

Can one be a successful jazz player or give successful solo recitals while playing with a professional orchestra?

It would be easier to give recitals than play jazz while furthering an orchestra career. Perhaps if one used a different mouthpiece, jazz work might also be feasible. While attending Juilliard, I played lead trumpet in a jazz workshop, lead trumpet in a Latin band three nights per week, principal trumpet in the Juilliard Symphony Orchestra, and gave chamber and solo recitals. I had difficulty switching sounds from big band to orchestral until I had a shallower mouthpiece made for use in the Latin band and jazz groups.

There just aren't enough hours in the day for musicians to develop the adaptability necessary to switch style quickly. I suppose athletes have a similiar problem when trying to play professional baseball, football, tennis, and hockey at the same time.

What materials (etudes, transposition studies, etc.) would you recommend for an advanced trumpet student preparing for an orchestral playing career?

The books I recommend for my students are: Arban, *Complete Conservatory Method;* Saint-Jacome, *Grand Method;* Goldman, *Practical Studies;* Smith, *Top Tones;*

Charlier, *36 Etudes Transcendantes;* Brandt, *34 Studies* and *24 Last Studies;* Harris, *Advanced Studies;* Clarke, *Technical Studies;* Sachse, *100 Studies;* Williams, *Method for Transposition;* and all of the various orchestral excerpt books. For style, I use the books by Arban, Saint-Jacome, Goldman, Charlier, Brandt, and Harris. The *Top Tones* book by Smith is good for developing range, endurance, and fluency in the keys needed for transposition. For finesse and control, the *Technical Studies* by Clarke are excellent, provided they are approached from a lyrical rather than a mechanical standpoint. The Clarke studies can also be used to help correct excessive fortissimo playing.

How can a public school band or orchestra director help a talented student interested in a career in a professional orchestra?

Encourage talented students to

listen to recordings and attend live performances of orchestras, string quartets, woodwind quintets, singers, etc., because in orchestral playing you must be able to blend and balance with every kind of ensemble. Small ensemble playing, even at the elementary stage, is invaluable to the serious student of music.

What is the primary objective of a professional orchestral trumpet player?

The orchestral trumpet player should strive to play as musically and with as much subtlety and taste as a violinist, flutist, or singer. I sometimes feel that the trumpet is thought of as a glorified bugle, only capable of playing the correct notes, reasonably well in tune, in the right place, and at the right volume without any nuances. The ultimate goal must be to make beautiful music. ∎

October, 1976

The First International Brass Congress

An On-the-Scene Report

Harvey Phillips

Harvey Phillips was officially the "program coordinator" for the First International Brass Congress, but his involvement, influence, and dedication go far beyond the normal confines of such a title. Phillips has long worked for the tuba and tubists, and he was specially recognized for his accomplishments in *The New Yorker* magazine last December in a lengthy "Profiles" column.

In an article in *The Instrumentalist* (November 1974, p. 32), Phillips reported on the First International Brass Symposium held the previous summer, helping to generate further support for the "international" concept. From June, 1975, through this past summer, his TUBA-RANCH in Bloomington, Indiana, was an unofficial headquarters for the planning of the FIBC, and he hosted numerous meetings with the officers of the four brass organizations and IHEM. An indefatigable worker, Phillips threw himself into the FIBC project with his customary energy and zeal. In appreciation for his efforts, the presidents of the four organizations wrote Phillips a note of thanks, "for your vision, your courage, your perseverance and your patience in making this First International Brass Congress become a reality and in our opinion an inspiring and memorable success" — Lloyd Geisler (ITG), Barry Tuckwell (IHA), Buddy Baker (ITA), and R. Winston Morris (TUBA).

The First International Brass Congress was held June 13-19, 1976, in Montreux, Switzerland. The convention included worldwide attendance of four brass organizations: International Horn Society (IHS), International Trombone Association (ITA), International Trumpet Guild (ITG), and Tubists Universal Brotherhood Association (TUBA). Week-long events included lecture-demonstrations, recitals, concerts, and discussions by virtuoso artists, teachers, and scholars. Paper topics included anatomy and brass playing, acoustics of brass instruments, psychology of the brass performer, contemporary performing techniques, orchestral performance, and implications of brass pedagogy and performance in specific countries. For further information and a detailed agenda, contact the individual organizations:

IHS, c/o Nancy Fako, 337 Ridge Ave., Elmhurst, Ill. 60126
ITA, 1812 Truman Dr., Normal, Ill. 61761
ITG, c/o Lloyd Geisler, School of Music, Catholic Univ. of America, Washington, D.C. 20017
TUBA, c/o Donald C. Little, Univ. of Northern Iowa, Dept. of Music, Cedar Falls, Iowa 50613

Brass players all over the world are now united — officially. Their first meeting, the First International Brass Congress (FIBC), was held this summer in Montreux, Switzerland. It was the culmination of a 12-year-long chain of events. Between 1964 and 1974 three world-wide brass organizations had been formed: the International Horn Society, the International Trombone Association, and the Tubists International Brotherhood Association. Then the International Trumpet Guild was organized in 1975. The concept of a worldwide brass association was a natural outgrowth of these increasingly active organizations, and so the International Brass Society was born in July, 1974, at the International Brass Symposium. A 4,000-member organization, the Society represents the combined membership of the four independent brass fraternities.

Planning toward the FIBC began at the 1974 Brass Symposium, which could be considered a "dress rehearsal" for this summer's congress in Montreux. The December, 1974, Mid-West Band and Orchestra Clinic in Chicago served as further planning ground, and one year later the Clinic hosted a meeting of the newly-formed International Brass Society.

Both international brass meetings (International Brass Symposium and FIBC) were sponsored and hosted by the Institute for Advanced Musical Studies (Institut des Hautes Etudes Musicales, or IHEM) in Montreux, Switzerland. An important difference between the 1974 and 1976 brass conferences is that IHEM produced the 1974 brass symposium without the help of any outside organizations, while the 1976 FIBC was presented by IHEM in conjunction with the annual meetings of the four independent brass organizations.

Each brass organization worked hard to insure the success of the FIBC, with a list of notable contributors from all four groups which reads like a "Who's Who" of U.S. brass players. The staff of IHEM was amazing, led by Pier Talenti (president) and Richard Zellner (managing director). They somehow managed to accomplish the enormous number of details required to bring about the FIBC with courtesy, patience, and expertise. Special acknowledgement must also go to Jean-Pierre Mathez (editor/publisher of the trilingual *Brass Bulletin*) for providing coverage of the FIBC with three special issues (Prelude, Official Program, and Postlude).

A Project of Incredible Proportions

I will spare you from a full rehashing of all the logistical problems and administrative details that encumbered the FIBC. But it *is* impressive to consider the mammoth task of arranging to accommodate the hundreds of participants: booking charter flights, conference facilities, hotel rooms and meals for the visitors, arranging for the appearance of the busy international guest artists (often calling for careful and sensitive negotiation with managers and foreign officials), hiring interpreters for the several different languages, and advertising and circulating FIBC information throughout the world. How the staff members maintained their sanity is a miracle.

Raising funds, of course, was a monumental project in itself. IHEM not only hosted the FIBC but also underwrote its entire expenses — a financial investment totalling tens of thousands of dollars. The sole sources of income for the FIBC were tuition ($85-$100 per participant) and the modest fees for exhibit space rented by music industry representatives. Officers and board members of IHS, ITG, ITA, and TUBA were provided with lodging and meals, as were the 28 featured guest artists who also each received an honorarium and travel expenses. (Each of the four organizations selected seven performers from around the world.)

Congress Highlights

Each symposium session and performance was so incredible that it is difficult to single out any above the others. However, I personally have very special memories of the following:

• the outdoor reception given for all FIBC participants at the 12th-century Museum Club, and the banquet at the Montreux Casino — food, wine, Swiss bands, Shetler's Musical Puppets, beautiful scenery, and the camaraderie were all fantastic!

• the performance of Arban's *Carnival of Venice* by Danish tubist Michael Lind, prompting a spontaneous standing ovation

• the inspiring recital of the great Russian trumpet virtuoso, Timofei Dokschitzer

• the performance-demonstration of contemporary brass techniques by Vinko Globokar

• the horn recital presenting Tuckwell (England), Barboteu (France), Baumann (Germany), Bujanovsky (U.S.S.R.), Gabler (Austria), and Lansky-Otto (Sweden) all on the same program!

• the world premiere of Verne Reynolds' composition for trumpet (Thomas Stevens) and tuba (Roger Bobo) with trumpet and horn ensemble conducted by Lloyd Geisler — sensational!

• the performance of the Forefront, a great contemporary jazz ensemble from Chicago (four trumpets, bass, and drums). Impeccable!

• the Matteson-Phillips Tuba Ensemble (six tubas and four rhythm). You won't believe it until you hear it!

• the massed choirs of horns, trumpets, trombones, and tubas — each performer a great artist (language certainly was no problem here!)

• The many unscheduled social activities, the spontaneous expressions of friendship, admiration, and respect from one artist to another, crossing every language and political barrier.

• the many great lectures and performances missed because one could only be in one place at a time.

Everyone has his/her own recollections of unforgettable moments generated by mixing with over 500 artists from 26 countries. There were just too many events to relate or even comprehend.

The Second International Brass Congress is proposed for August, 1980, to be held somewhere in Eastern Europe, and the Third IBC is already planned for August, 1984, somewhere in North America. The benefits which have grown and will continue to grow out of the International Brass Congresses are priceless. . .for *all* brass players. ∎

October, 1976

Nationalistic Practices in Brass Performance

Irvin L. Wagner

I attended the First International Brass Congress in Montreux to seek answers to many questions on brass playing:

• Does the concept of tone differ from one country to another, and if so, what are the differences?

• How do various brass performers interpret the music of different nationalistic origin, both in style and in choice of instrument?

• What types of instruments are used in the different countries?

I had some preconceived ideas about possible answers to these questions, but I looked forward to the week at the FIBC in hope of gaining new information and insights. Following are some observations drawn from the week's many symposia and workshops dealing with contemporary brass performance around the world.

Differences in Tonal Concepts

I was surprised to find that some of my preconceived notions about the kinds of tone produced in various countries were not well founded. I had believed that there are different tones for different countries; that French brass players, for example, use small instruments and produce small, thin tone with an abundance of vibrato. But such was not necessarily the case. It seems now that despite some subtle lingering distinctions there is a "basic universal sound" among players of like instruments. Within each brass family subdivision, almost everyone produces a basically similar tone founded upon a fundamental universal concept.

Perhaps this uniformity has come about from the current wide distribution of recordings, or from the fact that the world's major orchestras now make regular tours to foreign countries. It is quite easy for Americans to hear such orchestras as the Berlin Philharmonic, the Moscow Symphony, or the London Symphony, on records or in live performance; and in Europe musicians can hear the symphonies of New York, Philadelphia, Chicago, Boston, and other cities.

Denis Wick, the first trombonist in the London Symphony, presented an excellent example of "sharing the sounds around the world" when he spoke of his own evolution as an orchestral trombonist. He had joined the London Symphony in the mid-1950s and played a small tenor trombone in an older traditional manner. But in 1958-59 when the New York Philharmonic toured Europe, Wick heard the larger bore trombones for the first time, played in a new style. Wick felt that this New York Philharmonic tour revolutionized the European concept of trombone tone, and that the NY Phil trombone section (Gordon Pulis, Lewis Van Haney, and Allen Ostrander at that time) became the model for European trombonists. Their rich and sonorous sound, Wick found, was flexible in its blending ability and capable at the same time of producing the forceful, heroic, and noble character so often required in orchestral literature.

Nationalistic Differences in Style

The fact that a similar, fundamental brass tonal concept has spread around the world does not necessarily mean that players from various countries sound exactly alike. Some subtle nationalistic differences in performing do exist, and these stem primarily from different methods of articulation or different musical traditions.

The articulation differences in the various countries seem to correspond to characteristics of the individual languages. For example, the French brass players use the tongue very lightly and play in a fluid style, which compares to their speaking language in which primary attention is given to flowing vowel sounds. On the other hand, the German approach to tonguing is generally more staccato and less liquid, which corresponds to the emphasis on consonants in the German language.

A vivid example of the comparison between brass articulation and language was given at a session at the FIBC when a German player and a French player discussed syllables used for tonguing. The German remarked that he uses "tat tat tat" in tonguing, and the Frenchman responded that he uses "nah nah nah."

The British have a happy combination of all extremes, and any generality about the Americans is impossible because of their many and various styles of tonguing.

This language/articulation correlation raises an interesting question. Does the language one learns while growing up shape the voice muscles and nasal cavities to such an extent that later, on taking up a brass instrument, one cannot help but articulate in the same manner that he speaks? Perhaps an interested musician-linguist can provide brass players with some valuable information on this idea.

In addition to being affected by the language/articulation relationship, national performing differences are also shaped by customs and tradition. At the FIBC the French displayed the most pronounced national style of playing. One French performer explained that until about 1974, only French citizens were allowed to audition for vacant positions in French musical organizations. But during the past two years auditions have been opened up to qualified players from European Common Market countries. Therefore, a true "national style" has been preserved in French orchestras for a longer time than in other more cosmopolitan orchestras.

Vienna has preserved a distinct sound because trumpet and horn players use the traditional instruments built in that city — Vienna horns (Wiener Waldhorn) and rotary valve trumpets.

Choice of Instruments

The sessions at Montreux provided the valuable opportunity for observing the types of instruments played in the various countries. I had wondered whether Europeans play European-made instruments and Americans play American instruments, but I found much variance on the matter.

Tubists generally play German and Swiss instruments. Trombonists nearly all play American instruments except for Denis Wick (whose British-made instrument is really just a copy of the American bore tenor trombone). Trumpet players, except the Viennese, all use American instruments.

Among horn players, much diversity was discovered. Many Americans play American instruments which produce a large, tubby sound, but many other Americans prefer the smaller German instruments with a cleaner sound. Horn players from many countries use special handmade instruments (including the already mentioned Viennese horn players). One outstanding German horn soloist, Herman Baumann, owns and regularly plays on 23 different horns.

Next came the question of changing instruments for music of different styles or historical periods. Once again there were differences in habits according to the particular brass instrument played.

Trombonists never change instruments, except in a few rare situations in classical music for which the player prefers an alto trombone. Tubists change at times, depending on the nature of the music and the necessity for blending with other instruments (with

trombones or with string basses, for example). Horn players change instruments quite frequently, usually depending on whether they're playing with a large ensemble or a smaller chamber group.

Trumpet players change very often. Knut Holvalt, the Danish virtuoso, explained to me that trumpeters use many different keys of instruments, with technical ease and intonation being the primary determinants for choice. "It is important to consider the technical facility of both fingers and lips and then to select the key of instrument which will bring the most security and clarity to the musical performance," he said. "Instruments often are selected in order to provide better overall intonation for the key of the composition, or in order to favor certain 'out-of-tune' notes on a particular instrument."

FIBC Highlights

Probably the most outstanding individual performance at the FIBC was by Timofei Dokschitzer, solo trumpet with the Bolshoi Opera Orchestra since 1945. At the beginning of his recital Dokschitzer stated that, unlike many of the trumpet players present, he plays everything on the same instrument (which happened to be a very popular American Bb trumpet), and that he is opposed to the concept of changing instruments. He said he feels it important to play on equipment with which one is familiar, and to do one's best in conveying the intentions of the composer in specific compositions by *musical* means. His performance certainly lent credibility to his philosophy; it was the most musical event during the entire week, as well as being virtually flawless and entirely from memory.

Another outstanding and well-prepared presentation was the lecture-demonstration by Don Smithers, professor at the Royal Conservatory of Music of the Netherlands at the Hague, who discussed the performance of trumpet parts of Baroque music. While most modern players choose small instruments (frequently piccolo trumpets) for the performance of these very high trumpet parts for reasons of security, Smithers suggested that this practice destroys the original character of the music. The original natural trumpets used in the Baroque period were low-pitched instruments on which the performers played very high notes. According to Smithers, these older instruments produced a mellow sound that cannot be matched by the modern small instruments.

The First International Brass Congress was a great success. The opportunity for sharing ideas about brass instruments and performance practices was golden, and I look forward to the Second International Brass Congress to continue this exchange. ■

October, 1976

Pursuing the Ideal Horn Tone

Thomas W. Murray

Horn players are constantly in pursuit of the "ideal" sound. We experiment with mouthpieces and play on every horn we meet to see if we can arrive at the "right" combination. If we want a bright, piercing sound we tend to look for a small-bore brass horn and a mouthpiece with a small- to normal-size cup and bore. If we want a darker, more mellow quality, we gravitate toward the larger bore, silver (either plate or nickel) horn. We try to avoid very small mouthpieces that limit ease in the low register and very large ones that cut off comfort in the high registers.

After all of this searching we find that we must agree with the wise words of Walter Lawson, former hornist of the Baltimore Symphony, who once said, "Give any horn player a different horn, and in two or three weeks he'll sound on it pretty much like he sounded on the last one he played." And I can say that sometimes it doesn't take even two weeks to develop the same sound. Most of my students who play on my horn sound just as they do on their own.

Better Breathing

What then, can we do to acquire the sound we want? We must start by breathing properly so that we supply that 14-odd feet of cantankerous tubing with enough air. Every breath should be a full one, taken as if the player were about to dive into the water to set the world record for underwater swimming. Imagine the lungs to be two huge elastic bags stretching from the upper chest to the groin. Fill the bottom third first, then the middle third, and finally the upper third. Have your students do this slowly at first and then try to do it rapidly, catching the air in one large gulp. To get the feel of cor-rect abdominal breathing, have them stick out their tongues and pant like dogs.

Now they are ready to blow the air into the horn. Any good horn will have a certain amount of resistance, a point at which the horn seems to say, "Whoa, I won't take any more unless you really force me to." Blowing just up against this resistance should produce a mezzo forte. If a much smaller sound results, the horn is too small and will probably refuse to play a healthy fortissimo without "cracking." If an extremely loud sound results, then the horn is too big, will require a lot of air, and will probably be hard to control at a pianissimo level. Blowing just to the point of resistance not only gives a good round sound but also makes the unpredictable monster a bit easier to control.

The Throat Chamber and the Embouchure

Next we must concentrate on the throat and mouth. The throat must be as open as possible. Have the player try to recreate the same feeling he gets when the doctor sticks that nasty tongue depressor in his mouth to view the throat while commanding him to say, "Aah." Since the vibrating air column in the horn extends past the lips back into the throat, the tone will be enhanced if this sound chamber is large. If the last statement made you raise your brow, consider this: I recently heard Fred Fox, eminent West Coast horn teacher and performer, play a pretty reasonable C scale by sucking on the horn. All the air was coming in through the horn, past the vibrating lips, and down his throat, yet the sound was clearly audible in the back of a fairly large auditorium. What better way to prove that the vibrating air column extends into the throat?

The corners of the mouth should be firm and drawn in toward a mid-point at the back of the neck, while the center of the lips is relatively relaxed and free to vibrate. Too much tension in the center of the embouchure will produce a pinched sound in the upper register, and a kazoo-like quality in the lower. Keep the lip aperture as wide open as possible in each register and supply a good strong stream of air, keeping the lips blown apart. Also, keep the jaw down as much as possible, which helps keep the lips separated and creates a larger tone. An effective but risky trick involves tuning the horn slightly sharp and then lipping it down to pitch while playing. This lipping *makes* the student pull the jaw down.

The most important factor remaining is projection — getting the tone out where the player wants it. Have the student ignore the fact that his horn is curled around, bell pointing backwards, and that his right hand is impeding the emergence of the sound from the bell. Tell him to concentrate on a point some 50 feet ahead, and try to aim the sound at that point. Imagine a large auditorium, and play to someone special seated in the back row. Blow with a thick stream of air, directing it not through the horn but straight out in front. Above all, have your students *listen*: to themselves and to other good horn players. Tell them to attend all the concerts they can and listen to records and radio broadcasts. Have them get that ideal horn sound fixed in their minds so that they can strive to achieve it through conscious imitation. Urge them to persevere, practice, and listen, and the desired sound may be theirs in very short order. ∎

The Closed-Throat Syndrome

Edward P. Sandor

Most accomplished high brass players would agree that the throat functions principally as a passageway for air. The throat should resist the flow of air as little as possible, remaining open at all times — yet many student players are constantly bothered by a *closed* throat. This problem is closely related to lack of breath support, the underlying cause of four common playing difficulties: weak sound, poor range, little endurance, and sluggish tonguing. This article points out how a closed throat may be detected, and it offers a solution for overcoming the problem.

Students who have a good and relatively strong embouchure but do not have a full sound or good range may be heard "grunting" as they attempt the upper register. This grunting is a sign that the student's throat is closing in an effort to push the air through the horn faster. While the cause may indeed be a lack of breath support, especially if his sound is weak, teaching the student how it feels to play with an open throat can only help to correct the main problem. Experiencing the benefits of playing with an open throat not only will allow the student to propel the air more efficiently from the abdomen but also will encourage him to work harder toward his goal.

On the other hand, a student with the same grunting symptom but without a strong, well-formed embouchure will want to concentrate on developing an embouchure that can afford him a good range, endurance, and a full sound. Of course, the player should check any breathing problems at the same time, and it would also be beneficial for him to experience the sensation of an open throat as his embouchure and breath support progress, so that the closed throat habit does not hinder his progress in the other closely related areas.

When the student's embouchure and breath support seem adequate, he may still have a limited range. He may display a full sound in the middle and low registers, accompanied by fluent playing within these confines, but may completely change in the upper register to a tight, bright, or even brittle sound. In this case, the problem simply may be the student's inability at his stage of development to make a small enough aperture through which to speed the air stream, but it probably indicates a closed throat (too much mouthpiece pressure may also be evident). Lip buzzing exercises will help him gain the coordination needed to make a sufficiently small aperture, but he should also be introduced to the open throat experience, so that a closed throat does not impede his otherwise correct approach to the upper register.

Occasionally, cumbersome and sluggish tonguing may be the effect of a closed throat. Tonguing problems are most often attributed to faulty tongue placement or motion. Almost always, however, the student misunderstands the function of the tongue and the throat in the performance of first notes and separated notes. If the student thinks he should start each phrase by holding the breath with the glottis (the closed throat) until he is ready to play and then release the air under pressure with the throat, he needs to be set straight. You should explain how to use the abdominal muscles both to hold the breath and put it into motion. Another mistake is using the throat instead of the tongue to separate notes. Once the student has experienced playing with an open throat, he will be able to correct this problem more easily.

Even though a player may not have any of the above malfunctions in his playing technique, he may from time to time perform with a closed throat or general tension in the throat. Since this tendency is not uncommon among high brass players, and since the tension may focus in the throat, the successful player must learn to check the devastating effects of tension before they weaken his playing.

While verbal explanations often suffice, I have found the sensory approach to problems more effective in making the student comprehend a concept and follow through with the implementation of the technique. After a student experiences the concept or technique, it seems to be much easier for him to recall it in his practicing and to maintain steady progress in attaining his goal. Therefore I suggest using the following procedure as a teaching sequence for attaining an open throat.

Furnish the student with a three-inch length carlactic (hard-wall plastic) pipe. A diameter of 1¼ inch seems to be as large as the average adult mouth can handle comfortably. Ask the student to place the pipe in his mouth, over his tongue, putting it only as far back in the mouth as is comfortable (the tube acts as an extension of the trachea while it also opens the throat as effectively as a tongue depressor does). With the tube in the mouth, the student should practice inhaling and exhaling vigorously. The student may use incorrect posture, *et al.*, at first unless the teacher instructs him otherwise, but the important matter here is that the breathing occur with minimal resistance to the air.

The types of exercises that can be used to help the individual student with his specific breathing problem are as numerous as the inventiveness of the teacher will allow, but a few possibilities are described as follows:

1. Have the student inhale slowly and deeply and then exhale in the same way, so he can concentrate on relaxation and deep, full breaths.

2. Have the student inhale rapidly, but exhale slowly, controlling the air flow with the abdominal muscles and keeping the throat open. This exercise is intended to stimulate catching a breath between phrases and continuing to play in a soft, legato style.

3. Have the student inhale rapidly and exhale very intensely in short bursts of air which have definite space between each one. The exercise simulates the air action of playing marcato passages.

4. Have the student inhale and hold his breath for a few seconds before exhaling. Watch out for an audible "clicking" noise heard as the air begins its exit through the tube; it indicates that the student is holding his breath by allowing the throat to close instead of letting his abdomen do the job.

As relaxation and openness are achieved, use the same exercises without the tube, but be sure that the student retains the open feeling. This will be difficult at first, but if the student perseveres without becoming anxious (and consequently tense), he will begin to achieve his goal. As the open throat becomes a regular occurrence, ask the student to substitute mouthpiece and/or lip buzzing for the exhalation, either on whole tones or, preferably legato tunes. This new phase is meant to help the student make the transition to actual playing.

Do not ask the student to practice the concept discussed above with his instrument until he can breathe and play openly while buzzing. This precaution is made to avoid tension-creating conflicts which may occur when the student tries to replace old, strong habits of playing with newly-formed habits. Hopefully you can avoid such conflict by strengthening the new habits, away from the horn, through buzzing. When the student realizes that the open throat is something he can make happen at will, he has reached the point when the new habit is strong and ready to challenge the old.

When the student first attempts to use the open throat in his playing, he should start with easy, legato playing in the middle register and progress gradually to more demanding playing. Be sure that the student continues to use the tube as a sensory reference in progressing toward a consistent open throat and that he moves only as fast as his development allows.

If the student is permitted to advance at his own pace, and if any problems with his breathing, breath support, embouchure, and other related areas are remedied accordingly, the student will learn to play with consistent openness. ■

December, 1976

Repertoire for Brass Soloists

Part I

Merrill Brown

This is one in a series of articles concerning repertoire most often performed by college student woodwind soloists, brass soloists, percussionists, and wind instrument ensembles. The articles are based on material published by the author in *Wind and Percussion Literature Performed in College Student Recitals (1971-1972)*, copyright 1974. We received permission to publish the following.

The selection of appropriate music literature is one of the most important responsibilities facing every performer and teacher. Many "recommended" solo and ensemble lists have been published. These lists are often of value and interest but they understandably reflect the bias and personal taste of their compilers. In addition, there are many books, catalogs, and lists that contain information about the availability of materials; while these compilations are useful to those wishing to order music, the biggest task facing the performer and teacher is knowing *what* to order. Since no one can hope to be familiar with all the literature available, the following compilation may help provide you with a means for selecting repertoire. It is the result of a survey designed to determine what music is being performed in college wind and percussion student recitals. The results seem to indicate that a basic repertoire for most instruments has become established.

Most teachers, especially those new in the field, will find in the lists below some frequently performed literature with which they are unfamiliar. These compositions, which have received the endorsement of a number of college teachers, deserve investigation for possible use in developing an expanding performance and teaching repertoire. These lists, however, should not serve to maintain the status quo. Many excellent compositions that received few performances warrant more attention. Also, new compositions are continually being published and deserve consideration.

Just because the following music has the endorsement of a number of college teachers does not mean it is appropriate for junior or senior high school or even all college students. Students should not attempt to perform music that is too far beyond them technically and/or musically. Most of the music listed below is grade IV to VI. It should be noted that those selections used in the senior and graduate recitals are generally the most difficult.

About the Survey

To collect the information for this survey, I sent a request to 701 leading college and university music departments in the United States asking that they send a copy of all student recitals performed during the 1971-72 school year. Programs were received from 273 schools representing music departments in 48 states and the District of Columbia. An estimated 4,500 printed programs were received. From these programs a total of 15,607 performances were tabulated — 10,995 solos and 4,612 ensembles. This article reports some of the findings concerning brass solo performances.

The following information concerning each solo is recorded.
1. Total number of performances
2. Number of performances on "general" recitals. These were pro-

grams which gave no indication of being either a "senior" or "graduate" recital.

3. Number of performances on recitals specified as a "senior" recital.

4. Number of performances on recitals specified as a "graduate" recital. These included both masters and doctoral recitals.

5. Unaccompanied solos have been identified with an asterisk (*)

before the name of the composer-composition.

It was so unusual for arrangers to be included on the printed programs that no attempt was made to include them in the report.

Solo Totals

Instrument	Total Performances	Number of Different Compositions	Number of Different Composers
Trumpet	1,856	453	302
French Horn	949	219	163
Trombone	994	292	202
Bass Trombone	91	51	43
Baritone	245	148	106
Tuba	501	176	120
Totals	4,636	1,339	936

Compositions are listed in order of frequency of performance.

Trumpet Solos

Number of performances	1,856
Number of different compositions	453
Number of different composers	302

Composition	Total Perf	Gen	Sen	Grad
Haydn, *Concerto in E*	86	56	24	6
Hummel, *Concerto in E*	82	53	21	8
Hindemith, *Sonata*	62	35	22	5
Kennan, *Sonata*	47	34	10	3
Goedicke, *Concert Etude*, Op. 49	46	32	11	3
Corelli, *Sonata VIII*	41	35	6	-
Riisager, *Concertino*, Op. 29	35	18	11	6
Ropartz, *Andante et Allegro*	31	24	6	1
Handel, *Aria con Variazioni*	29	22	7	-
Peeters, *Sonata*, Op. 51	26	14	8	4
Purcell, *Sonata*	24	14	8	2
Barat, *Andante et Scherzo*	23	14	8	1
Arutunian, *Concerto (Concertino)*	22	13	3	6
Giannini, *Concerto*	20	9	11	-
Handel, *Adagio and Allegro from Sonata in E*	20	15	3	2
Hovhaness, *Prayer of Saint Gregory*, Op. 62B	20	16	3	1
Latham, *Suite*	19	13	3	3
Telemann, *Concerto in D Major*	19	9	6	4
Barat, *Fantaisie en Mi Bemol*	18	14	4	-
Balay, *Petite Piéce Concertante*	17	16	1	-
Bohrnstedt, *Concerto*	16	9	5	2
Stevens, *Sonata*	16	8	3	5
Torelli, *Concerto in D Major*	15	7	3	5
Fitzgerald, *Modern Suite*	14	12	2	-
Gibbons, *Suite*	14	8	4	2
Handel, *Concerto*	14	9	4	1
Thome, *Fantaisie*	14	12	2	-
Balay, *Andante and Allegretto*	13	8	5	-
Enesco, *Legend*	13	8	1	4
Mozart, Leopold, *Concerto in D Major*	13	6	5	2
Tomasi, *Concerto*	13	6	3	4
Donato, *Prelude and Allegro*	12	6	6	-
Nelhybel, *Golden Concerto*	12	8	3	1
Robbins, *Mont-Saint-Michel*	12	9	3	-
Torelli, *Symphony with Trumpet*	12	8	1	3
Tuthill, *Sonata*, Op. 29	12	8	3	1
Bitsch, *Quatre variations sur un thème de Domenico Scarlatti*	11	5	3	3
Copland, *Quiet City*	10	4	3	3
Goeyens, *Introduction and Scherzo*	10	8	2	-
Hue, *Solo de Concert*	10	8	2	-
Persichetti, *Hollow Men*, Op. 25	10	4	6	-
Bach, J.S., *Aria from Bist du bei Mir*	9	7	1	1
Bond, *Trumpet Concerto*	9	5	3	1
Busser, *Variations in D*, Op. 53	9	6	2	1
Hubeau, *Sonate pour trompette chromatique*	9	3	3	3
Senee, *Concertino*	9	5	4	-
Vidal, *Concertino*	9	5	4	-

1977

Repertoire for Brass Soloists

Part II

Merrill Brown

The December 1976 Brass Clinic contained the first part of a listing of solo trumpet literature that is concluded here. Also in this month's list are horn, trombone, bass trombone, baritone, and tuba solos.

Bloch, *Proclamation*	8	3	3	2
Bozza, *Rustiques*	8	4	4	-
Hartley, *Sonatina*	8	6	2	-
Nelhybel, *Suite*	8	5	3	-
White, *Sonata*	8	6	1	1
Alary, *Morceau de Concours* (Concert Piece), Op. 57	7	5	2	-
Albinoni, *Sonata in C*	7	3	-	4
Bach, J.S., *Ten Preludes*	7	5	2	-
Balay, *Prélude et Ballade*	7	5	2	-
Bernstein, *Rondo for Lifey*	7	6	1	-
Bozza, *Badinage*	7	6	1	-
Delmas, *Choral and Variations*, Op. 37	7	4	2	1
Goedicke, *Concerto*, Op. 41	7	4	-	3
Goeyens, *All'Antica*	7	7	-	-
Handel, *Sonata*	7	5	2	-
Jeanjean, *Capriccioso*	7	6	1	-
Poot, *Etude de concert*	7	6	1	-
Telemann, *Concerto in D Major for Trumpet, 2 Oboes, and Continuo*	7	2	1	4
Telemann, *Heroic Music*	7	4	2	1
Wormser, *Fantaisie, Thème et Variations*	7	4	2	1

French Horn Solos

Number of performances	949			
Number of different compositions	219			
Number of different composers	163			
Mozart, *Concerto No. 3 in E♭ Major* (K447)	50	42	7	1
Strauss, R., *Concerto No. 1 in E♭ Major*, Op. 11	49	39	9	1
Mozart, *Concerto No. 4 in E♭ Major* (K495)	46	31	10	5
Beethoven, *Sonata*, Op. 17	43	27	11	5
Hindemith, *Sonata*	36	24	9	3
Dukas, *Villanelle*	35	22	13	-
Mozart, *Concerto No. 1 in D Major* (K412)	33	28	5	-
Mozart, *Concerto No. 2 in E♭ Major* (K417)	32	27	3	2
Heiden, *Sonata*	25	20	1	4
Strauss, F., *Concerto*, Op. 8	22	19	1	2
Mozart, *Concert Rondo* (K371)	20	18	1	1
Schumann, *Adagio and Allegro*, Op. 70	20	14	5	1

Mozart, *Quintet in E♭ Major for Horn and Strings* (K407) (3 with piano, 15 with strings)	18	16	2	-
Saint-Saëns, *Morceau de Concert*, Op. 94	18	13	3	2
Haydn, *Concerto No. 2 in D Major*	17	9	7	1
Francaix, *Canon in Octave*	14	10	2	2
Strauss, R., *Concerto No. 2 in E*	14	8	4	2
Poulenc, *Elégie*	13	10	2	1
Bozza, *En Foret*, Op. 40	13	9	2	2
Adler, *Sonata*	12	9	1	2
Glazounov, *Reverie*, Op. 24	10	8	1	1
Chabrier, *Larghetto*	9	7	-	2
Gliere, *Nocturne*, Op. 35, No. 10	9	5	4	-
Saint-Saëns, *Romance*, Op. 36	9	7	-	2
Corelli, *Sonata in F Major*	8	6	1	1
Rosetti (Roessler), *Concerto in d Minor*	8	4	3	1
Stevens, *Sonata*	8	2	4	2
Donato, *Sonata*	7	6	1	-
Hindemith, *Concerto*	7	3	3	1
Jacob, *Concerto*	7	7	-	-
Piantoni, *Air de chasse*	7	4	2	1
Ravel, *Pavane pour une infante défunte*	7	4	3	-
Gliere, *Intermezzo*, Op. 35, No. 11	6	5	-	1
Larsson, *Concertino*, Op. 45, No. 5	6	3	2	1
Martelli, *Waltz*	6	5	-	1
Gliere, *Concerto in B♭ Major*, Op. 91	5	4	1	-
Goedicke, *Concerto*, Op. 40	5	3	2	-
Gottwald, *Fantasie Héroique* (Sonata), Op. 25	5	3	1	1
Hindemith, *Sonata for Alto Horn and Piano*	5	3	-	2
Nelhybel, *Scherzo Concertante*	5	2	3	-
Reynolds, V., *Partita*	5	3	1	1
Rossini, *Theme and Variations*	5	4	-	1
Schoeck, *Konzert*, Op. 65	5	4	1	-

Trombone Solos

Number of performances	994
Number of different compositions	292
Number of different composers	202

Hindemith, *Sonata*	41	23	11	7
Guilmant, *Morceau Symphonique*, Op. 88	34	23	10	1
Barat, *Andante et Allegro*	26	19	7	-
Jacob, *Concerto*	22	12	8	2
Sanders, *Sonata in E*	21	10	10	1
McKay, *Sonata*	20	12	6	2
Rimsky-Korsakov, *Concerto*	19	16	3	-
Davison, *Sonata*	18	10	4	4
Galliard, *Sonata No. 3 in F Major*	17	11	5	1
Serocki, *Sonatine*	17	13	2	2
Galliard, *Sonata No. 1 in a Minor*	16	12	3	1
Blazhevich, *Concert Sketch (Piece) No. 5*	14	11	2	1
Bozza, *Ballade*, Op. 62	14	9	3	2
*Bernstein, *Elegy for Mippy II*	13	9	4	-
Telemann, *Sonata in f Minor*	13	6	3	4
Casterede, *Sonatine*	12	6	2	4
Haydn, Adagio from *Concerto for Cello*	12	9	3	-
Larsson, *Concertino*, Op. 45, No. 7	10	5	1	4
Marcello, B., *Sonata in F Major*	10	8	1	1
Saint-Saëns, *Cavatine*, Op. 144	10	6	4	-
Giffels, *Sonata*	9	1	5	3
Handel, *Concerto in Fa Mineur*	9	9	-	-
Marcello, B., *Sonata in a Minor*	9	6	3	-
Presser, *Sonatina*	9	5	4	-
Wagenseil, *Concerto*	9	4	1	4
Galliard, *Sonata No. 5 in d Minor*	8	7	1	-
Galliard, *Sonata No. 6 in C Major*	8	4	4	-
Jones, Robert W., *Sonatina*	8	5	2	1
Stevens, *Sonata*	8	3	3	2
Corelli, *Sonata in F Major*, Op. 5	7	5	2	-
Creston, *Fantasy*, Op. 42	7	4	3	-
David, F., *Concertino*, Op. 4	7	6	1	-
Marcello, B., *Sonata in g Minor*	7	3	4	-
Monaco, *Sonata*	7	4	1	2
Nelhybel, *Suite*	7	3	2	2
Vivaldi, *Sonata No. 3 in a Minor*	7	3	4	-
Weber, C.M., *Romanza Appassionata*	7	3	4	-

Whear, *Sonata*	7	4	3	-
Bassett, *Sonata*	6	2	1	3
Faure, *Après un rêve*	6	4	1	1
Galliard, *Sonata No. 4 in e Minor*	6	4	1	1
Hartley, *Sonata Concertante*	6	2	2	2
Krenek, *Five Pieces*	6	2	1	3
Marcello, B., *Sonata in e Minor*	6	2	-	4
Tomasi, *Concerto*	6	3	1	2
Vivaldi, *Sonata No. 5 in e Minor*	6	2	4	-
Vivaldi, *Sonata No. 6 in B♭ Major*	6	3	1	2

The following composition does not fall into any of the categories that appear here, but is essentially a trombone solo. Having received 4 performances, it might be of interest to trombonists:

McKenzie, Jack, *Song for Trombone and Percussion*

Bass Trombone Solos

Number of performances	91
Number of different compositions	51
Number of different composers	43

McCarty, *Sonata for Bass Trombone*	13	4	6	3
Spillman, *Concerto for Bass Trombone*	6	2	3	1
Lebedev, *Concerto in One Movement*	5	4	1	-
Bozza, *Prélude et Allegro*	4	3	1	-
Casterede, *Fantaisie Concertante*	4	3	1	-

Baritone Solos

Number of performances	245
Number of different compositions	148
Number of different composers	106

Barat, *Andante et Allegro*	7	3	3	1
Guilmant, *Morceau Symphonique*	7	4	3	-
McKay, *Sonata*	6	3	2	1
Mozart, *Concerto in B♭ Major for Bassoon* (K191)	6	2	2	2
Hutchinson, *Sonatina for Euphonium*	5	2	1	2
Blazhevich, *Concert Sketch (Piece) No. 5*	4	2	2	-
Fasch, *Sonata*	4	1	1	2
Galliard, *Sonata No. 1 in a Minor*	4	3	1	-
Galliard, *Sonata No. 3 in F Major*	4	4	-	-
Haydn, Adagio from *Concerto for Cello*	4	3	1	-
Marcello, B., *Sonata*	4	3	1	-
Sanders, *Sonata in E♭ for Trombone*	4	1	3	-
Telemann, *Sonata in f Minor*	4	2	2	-

Tuba Solos

Number of performances	501
Number of different compositions	176
Number of different composers	120

Hindemith, *Sonata for Bass Tuba*	33	12	12	9
Haddad, *Suite*	26	18	8	-
Wilder, *Suite No. 1* (Effie Suite)	22	6	11	5
Bach, J.S., *Air and Bourrée*	18	13	5	-
Beversdorf, *Sonata for Bass Tuba*	13	7	2	4
Nelhybel, *Suite*	13	9	3	1
*Hartley, *Suite*	12	5	5	2
Vaughan Williams, *Concerto for Bass Tuba*	12	4	4	4
Lebedev, *Concerto in One Movement*	10	5	3	2
Frackenpohl, *Concertino*	9	4	3	2
Galliard, *Sonata No. 5 in d Minor*	9	4	5	-
Persichetti, *Serenade No. 12 for Solo Tuba*, Op. 88	9	4	2	3
Sowerby, *Chaconne*	9	6	3	-
Stevens, *Sonatina for Bass Tuba*	8	2	2	4
Swann, *Two Moods*	8	4	4	-
Holmes, *Lento*	7	3	3	1
Kraft, *Encounters II*	7	4	2	1
Tcherepnin, *Andante pour Tuba et Piano*, Op. 64	7	3	3	1
Hartley, *Sonata*	6	4	-	2
Hartley, *Sonatina*	6	4	2	-
Wilder, *Sonata*	6	4	2	-
Beach, *Lamento*	5	2	2	1
Bernstein, *Waltz for Mippy III*	5	4	1	-
Boda, *Sonatina*	5	3	1	1
Golterman, *Concerto No. 4*, Op. 65	5	4	1	-
Lebedev, *Concert Allegro*	5	4	1	-
Mozart, *Concerto No. 3 in E♭ Major* (horn) (K477)	5	4	1	-

Tension in Brass Performance: Creative or Destructive?

Robert Gibson

Why is playing a brass instrument easier for some people and more difficult for others? Common problems such as a wavering, weak tone, missed attacks, and sloppy technique are many times caused not by a lack of practice or talent but by the incorrect use of physical and mental tension.

The use of physical tension is often discussed by brass teachers with their students, particularly regarding how to place physical tension in the abdominal walls and the corners of the mouth to play correctly and powerfully. But what about the *mental* tension needed for superior brass performance? When used constructively, "mental tension" provides the high level of concentration needed for a fine performance. But when mental tension is not properly controlled it causes nervousness which can interfere with muscular tension. Seldom are students told how to handle this tension, even though incorrect use of it can be an extremely destructive factor in such areas as air supply, technique, and embouchure control.

Air supply problems can result from destructive mental tension (nervousness), which causes the abdominal muscles to constrict and pull inward to the spine and prevents the outward and upward thrust necessary to move the air into the instrument. This tension also forces the throat muscles to constrict and the tongue to rise, thereby slowing the air movement even more.

Destructive mental tension also creates embouchure problems. It causes the facial muscles to constrict and pull apart when they should stay together and move toward the air column. The embouchure setting must be placed *upon* — not against — the freely flowing air column moving through the aperture of the lips.

Many problems in technique arise from mental tension. The valve-instrument player's fingers stiffen, and the trombonist's wrist and arm become rigid. When the muscles of the arms and hands become constricted and tense, they move *away* from their function, instead of toward it. As a result, the valves are depressed unevenly or not enough, and the trombone slide is pushed and pulled against the inner sleeve in a rough, jerky manner.

Problems caused by the destructive use of tension can be solved by learning to focus the mental tension on an outer-directed force instead of an inner one. The brass player might try the following suggestions:

1. Concentrate on keeping the air moving to a point outside the body. Blow the air into, through, and beyond the note being played.

2. Listen more closely to your own playing. Careful listening will help to focus the mind past the instrument and will automatically pull the necessary muscular functions into the proper sequence.

3. Think of the lips and corners of the embouchure as moving *toward* the air passing through them. Remember that most embouchure problems are not lip-oriented — they are caused by inadequate air support. If one would concentrate the mental tension on moving the air past the lips, 90 per cent of all embouchure problems would disappear.

4. On valve instruments, concentrate the mental tension on the inside of the finger joints, "pushing" the tension through the pads of the fingers and through the valves. The physical tension thus receives outer-directed muscular focus. Again, concentrate on placing the technique *upon* the air column. Don't work against it.

5. Play the music to be performed all the way through *mentally* — including phrasing, dynamics, nuances, articulations, etc. — before attempting to play it on the instrument. Doing so will clear the mind of all unnecessary information and will let the body completely assimilate the music to be played into the correct muscular action.

6. Relax! Too much tension will always destroy a musical performance. ∎

A New Way to Start the Day

Donald A. Hodges

One of the things that horn players (and indeed all brass players) must constantly guard against is the intrusion of tension into their playing. To counteract this, we often hear the admonition to use more breath support, but perhaps not enough is heard about the need for relaxation in the embouchure. One of the best exercises devised to combine a steady air stream with a relaxed and sensitive embouchure was designed by Wayne Barrington, a former member of the Chicago and Los Angeles Symphony Orchestras, who is now professor of horn at the University of Texas at Austin. This exercise should be practiced as early in the day as possible and should precede any other playing.

Preliminary Breath Warm-Up

1. Blow air through the horn without inserting the mouthpiece. Use full breath. Keep the flow of air steady throughout.

2. Blow through the mouthpiece only, as in Step 1. Do *not* form an embouchure.

3. Form an embouchure and blow through the mouthpiece without producing any sound. Remain as relaxed as possible.

4. While blowing as in Step 3, contract the lip just enough to make a buzz. Ease and comfort are most important. Continue buzzing as long as the breath lasts. Do not use the tongue.

5. Blow and start buzzing *simultaneously*. Do not use the tongue. The throat must be as relaxed and open as it was in the first two steps.

If if is not, repeat the initial steps.

6. Now simultaneously blow, start the buzz, and tongue. The action of the tongue must be as light as possible. The sensation should be very nearly the same as in Step 5.

7. Repeat Steps 2 through 6 with the mouthpiece on the horn.

8. Repeat Step 6 in the mid-upper and mid-lower registers.

Keep the following points in mind while doing the breath drill:

• Inhale with an *ah* rather than an *ee* breath; keep the corners of the mouth relaxed and down, not stretched.

• The breath should flow in a continuous in-out motion. There should be no hesitation between inhalation and exhalation. If you compare the breathing process to a golf swing, there should be no "hitch" between the backswing and the follow-through. You may find the following experiment helpful. Take a breath and hold it with your mouth open. Now release the air. Notice how the muscles have to let go before the air is released.

• In Step 4 of the breath drill, the air stream should remain the same before and during the buzz. If the air stream grows weaker as the buzz begins, the lips are clamping down too much. If an increase in air is necessary to start the buzz, the lips are too stiff. To illustrate this point, dangle a piece of thin paper above and in front of your head; blow a steady stream of air; and gradually lower the piece of paper. When the paper comes into contact with the air stream, it will vibrate. The paper does nothing to make itself vibrate — it simply has no choice. Repeat the process with a piece of cardboard, noticing the difference. The idea is that the lips should be so sensitive and so relaxed that they simply have to vibrate when they come into contact with a steady stream of air.

• The pitch of the buzz (and of the sounded note when Step 4 is repeated using the instrument) should be a comfortable note somewhere between middle c and the g above, such as e. The dynamic level should be a healthy *mezzo forte*.

• Some creative daydreaming may be helpful, particularly during Steps 5 and 6. Imagine that you are the principal horn player of your favorite major orchestra and the note being played is a solo from a Brahms symphony, requiring a rich, vibrant tone, light attack, and total relaxation.

• Strive to *retain* the feeling just mentioned, no matter what you are playing — regardless of the register, dynamics, or technique required.

• Any time during the practice period that you feel tension creeping in, repeat a few steps of the breath drill to recapture the feeling of relaxation.

Nothing startling may happen the first few days, but with patience a new, more relaxed embouchure should gradually emerge. Once the correct feeling is attained for the mid-range pitches, you can begin to strive for it in all registers. ■

Practical Physics for Trumpeters and Teachers

Renold O. Schilke

The designer of instruments and mouthpieces must have a thorough knowledge of physics, but it is also helpful for the player and teacher to understand some of the basic principles.

In order to produce a sound on the trumpet (or any other brass instrument), air (1) is expelled under pressure through the lips, (2) further compressed in the cup of the mouthpiece, until it reaches the throat (3) of the mouthpiece, where it sets up a pattern in the air already in the instrument.

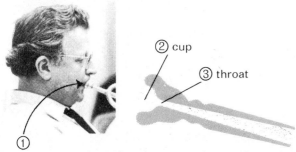

It is not necessary for the air to move *through* the instrument. I have demonstrated this at clinics by having a tuba player blow smoke into his instrument. He can play for over a minute before any smoke begins to trickle out of the bell. The pattern set up by the player in the air is more like what happens when you drop a rock in the lake — the energy impulse travels along lifting and depressing the water (making slight waves), but does not move the water to another area.

The pattern can be shown as a graph, with P= maximum pressure (like the swell of the wave in the water), and R= rarefaction, i.e. minimum pressure (like the valley of the wave).

Remember that this is a graph of *pressure*, not a picture of air movement. The pattern of air set up in the instrument concludes with a rarefaction just beyond the bell,

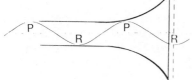

where a standing wave is formed, reflecting back through the instrument

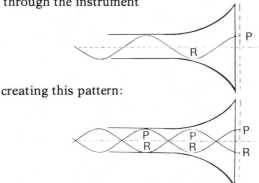

creating this pattern:

These pressure/rarefaction points are called *nodes* (places of "no movement" — as the air pulsates against the pipe there is a momentary pause in the motion).

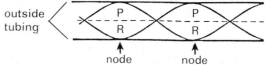

The nodal pattern is different for different notes, the number of nodes increasing with higher pitches.

Tubing is required to contain the vibrating air only at the pressure points. So it would be possible to play on a pipe full of holes — as long as those holes did not come at the pressure points...and we only had to produce one pitch.

I have often given demonstrations of this phenomenon, using a C trumpet and playing three notes, G, C, and E.

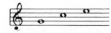

When the G is played, the nodal pattern is such that a pressure point falls exactly at the place in the tube where the water key hole is located. When this **key is**

opened, the hole in the pipe stops the tone. This fact is no surprise to anyone who has ever lost the cork on the water key.

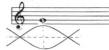

But when the C is played, the nodal pattern is different, and the water key hole in the tubing comes at the taper-off of the pressure point. This time when the water key is opened, it raises the pitch of the note a whole step (you could use it as a trill key!).

When the E is played, the pattern is once again different. This time there is absolutely no disturbance to the tone. In fact, in that area 5/8'' of tubing could be cut out of the instrument and you could play E's all day.

Once the nodes of various pitches are located, their placement — and therefore the pitch — can be changed by altering the rate of taper in the tube. It only takes .001'' to .002'', but it must be done exactly at the pressure point of the note you want to affect. And you must find a *single* pressure point in order to accomplish this. Altering the tubing at a multiple pressure point will adversely affect other notes with that same pressure point.

pressure points for note #1
pressure points for note #2
pressure points for note #3

etc. (for all notes)

multiple pressure points (places where pressure points for one or more notes coincide)

Practical Applications of Physical Principles

If the pitch of notes can be altered by changing the taper of the pipe only .001 to .002 of an inch, imagine what a little dirt can do. And then consider what effect years of accumulation will have!

I remember one of my very fine students was having terrible troubles getting a sound. One day when I left the studio for a few minutes he picked up an aluminum mouthpiece I had been experimenting with and had left on the desk. When I came back he asked if I would sell him the mouthpiece. He said, "I can play so beautifully on this." I picked up his mouthpiece and found it so full of dirt that I could hardly see a pinhole through it. A mouthpiece cleaning was all he needed — and I've never let him forget it!

I recommend oiling the valves by putting the oil into the leadpipe (rather than directly on the valves) and allowing it to work its way throughout the instrument. Because the inside is coated with oil, erosion of

752

the metal is stopped and food particles are easy to flush out once a week. Just run warm water through and every particle of dirt will come out easily. Also, the valves stay lubricated all day because the oil continues to run down into that area. I see many instruments with tiny holes starting to appear in the mouthpipe — the first sign of erosion. Anyone who uses this method of oiling can keep his instrument for a hundred years without having it wear out.

This cleaning aspect is only one rather obvious practical application of a physical principle. There are many others. For example, braces on trumpets should *not* be located at pressure points (remember the water key hole), where they can deaden the vibration of the tubing that is then in contact with the air.

Also, anything that can cause *turbulence* (interruption of the nodal pattern) will adversely affect the tone. One common turbulence trouble spot is the area where the mouthpiece fits into the receiver. Sometimes there is a gap,

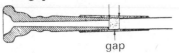

or the inside diameters of the mouthpiece backbore and the leader pipe are different.

This crucial area should look like this:

Why Change Mouthpieces

Right Reasons
    To improve sound and intonation, change tone color, increase range and endurance, add volume or flexibility, increase comfort, extend playing life

Wrong Reason
    To correct bad playing due to one's own inadequacies — such as excessive pressure, not using lips, oral cavity, and breath properly (The only exception I would make is for older players with bad habits so ingrained that they cannot change. I once made a mouthpiece for Louis Armstrong to help him play just a few more years towards the end of his career; he had learned incorrectly at the orphan's home in New Orleans and played for too many years that way to try to change.)   *R.S.*

Leaks also disturb the nodal pattern and affect intonation. Valves can be kept airtight by holding the tolerance on the pistons under .001'' (.0005'' on each side of the piston). This permits free movement of the valves and still gives good acoustical qualities. But regardless of the condition of the instrument, some players seem to be able to adjust and play beautifully. For example, when Rafael Mendez became associated with Olds, he asked them to build a new instrument that would be equal to the old Besson he had played for years. They tried everything they knew to please him, but they could not succeed. Finally one of the workmen took the valves out of the Besson, measured them, and found a surprisingly large clearance of over .008" (the result of years of wear). He then made an instrument with similarly loose valves and Mendez was thrilled with the result. He was again performing on a totally inadequate instrument, but he was happy. He had overcome the problems caused by the leaky valves through years of practice (nobody ever practiced harder than Mendez), and for him it was just right.

As physical principles are applied to the manufacture and maintenance of instruments, we gradually learn more and produce better equipment. But it continues to amaze me that people can and do adjust to almost anything. It's true with mouthpieces, too. I have some that were used by the greatest players of the past — Liberati, Arban — and they are horrible things, so far from being physically correct. Yet these people played beautifully on them.

Trumpet Mouthpieces

Three major parts of the mouthpiece affect its sound and performance qualities: rim, cup, and throat/backbore. Within each major area there are sub-categories such as width, size, shape, etc. All of these elements react with each other to affect the qualities of the mouthpiece here.

Only the most important variables are included here. In each case certain tendencies are discussed. For example, as a rim is made wider, it becomes increasingly more comfortable: as it is made narrower it provides increasingly more flexibility. In the material below, this tendency toward a specific quality is indicated by the simple entry:

> *Width*
> wider = comfort
> narrower = flexibility

Other elements are treated similarly. Obviously, there are many different measurements usable for every element, and literally millions of combinations are possible.

Joshua's Trumpet?

In Marseilles, France they are now working on a 75-foot long trumpet that will produce a "note" at 4 Hz (4 vibrations per second). No one can hear 4 Hz, of course, but with massive energy input (perhaps 350 times that of a 75-piece orchestra playing at its loudest intensity) the vibrations from this instrument could destroy an entire city the size of Chicago — just like the story of Joshua and the Battle of Jericho, where the walls came a-tumblin' down.

The people who are building this trumpet first discovered the power of highly energized low frequency sounds when they moved into a new laboratory and found that workers were getting stomach aches from ventilators that were putting out 37 Hz. They built a modified version at 17 Hz and had to shut it off instantly because the walls were cracking and everyone was doubling up on the floor.   *R.S.*

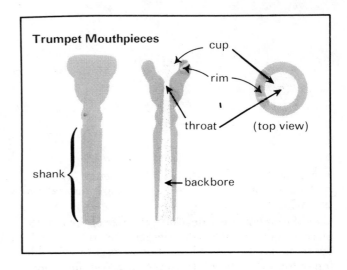

Trumpet Mouthpieces

cup

rim

throat   (top view)

shank

backbore

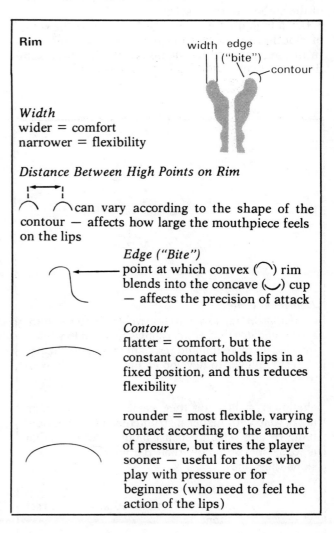

Rim

width edge
("bite")
contour

Width
wider = comfort
narrower = flexibility

Distance Between High Points on Rim

can vary according to the shape of the contour — affects how large the mouthpiece feels on the lips

Edge ("Bite")
point at which convex (⌒) rim blends into the concave (⌣) cup — affects the precision of attack

Contour
flatter = comfort, but the constant contact holds lips in a fixed position, and thus reduces flexibility

rounder = most flexible, varying contact according to the amount of pressure, but tires the player sooner — useful for those who play with pressure or for beginners (who need to feel the action of the lips)

Additional Thoughts

• The best way to test a trumpet for leaks is to play very softly in the low register.
• Continually seeking the "perfect" mouthpiece is certain to produce only frustration, but there are times when a change is desirable.
• When selecting a mouthpiece consider optimum tone quality and accurate intonation...long before range.
• Even the best mouthpiece is no substitute for proper embouchure development and no mouthpiece will sound better than the player behind it.

• A new mouthpiece should sound better *instantly*, making it easier to produce notes that are musical and in tune.

• As the embouchure develops, the size of the mouthpiece should be increased (larger cup, throat/backbore), but students should start on as large and flexible a mouthpiece as possible, so they can *feel* the actions of the embouchure muscles.

• Use a high quality tape recorder to check the sound of mouthpieces or instruments. There is a difference in the sound heard by the player and by those some distance away. "On-the-job" testing is best.

• Pick a mouthpiece according to individual characteristics. Using the same mouthpiece throughout an entire section will not necessarily produce a perfectly blended sound (unless all players have the same teeth, lips, jaws, breath control, etc.). In fact, if you want similar sounds with different players it is essential that they have *different* mouthpieces. The mouthpiece is an equalizer.

• I would rather help a person to play more correctly on his old mouthpiece than to sell him a new one that he expects to cure all his problems. ∎

Cup

diameter   depth

Depth (Volume)
deeper = better lower tones, richer darker sound, accommodates thicker lips, allows more lip to vibrate (producing more full and resonant tone) and "helps" (forces?) player to develop endurance and lip control.

shallower = brighter tone, easier to produce high notes (use with higher instruments, e.g. when doubling B♭ and D trumpets use mouthpiece for D that is .025″ more shallow than B♭, with other dimensions the same).

Shape
flatter = improved attack, coarser tone

steeper = better quality of sound, but at extreme (French horn shape) it is colorless on the trumpet

Double Cup
① shallow cup, for support in upper register
②
wider cup, for full tone

Throat/Backbore

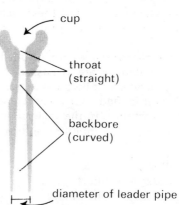

cup

throat (straight)

backbore (curved)

diameter of leader pipe

The tube leading from the cup to the end of the mouthpiece has two areas blended together. The *throat* is straight (=). The *backbore* begins when the tube begins to flare (<). The amount of taper depends on the size and length of the throat, as well as the diameter of the leader pipe (which the mouthpiece must match).

Throat Size (ranges from large to small, drill sizes of 18 to 30)
    larger = mellow sound
    smaller = brilliant sound

Length (throat length ranges from 1/8″ to 3/4″)
    longer throat (shorter backbore) = loss of tonal center, loss of resonance, increase in intonation control, sharp in high register
    shorter throat (longer backbore) = harder to control, flat in high register

Backbore shape
    flared = full tone, more difficult to control
    straight = thin tone, more easily controlled, blowing resistance increased

Timofei Dokshitzer — Russia's Greatest Trumpet Virtuoso

Donald R. Whitaker

Timofei Dokshitzer is Russia's leading trumpet virtuoso and one of the greatest musicians in the world. His unique playing style boasts an amazing variety of tonal colors, complete technical mastery, and enormous range. He is, in short, a complete musician. It is no wonder that many call him the "Oistrakh of the Trumpet."

It would seem that a musician of Dokshitzer's stature would need no introduction to the American musical world. But of the 100 or more recordings of his artistry, only a few of his albums are available in the U.S.[*]

Dokshitzer appeared last June at the International Brass Congress in Montreux, Switzerland, where he gave a recital and a lecture. His recital was very well attended, and he was one of the few performers who received a standing ovation at the conclusion of his program. Most of the selections he played, not surprisingly, were by Russians, but he started the program with his arrangement of the Albinoni *Sonata for Trumpet*. His second selection was *Concerto for Trumpet* by Aino Tamberg. He continued with the Arutunjan *Concerto for Trumpet*, once again his arrangement, as were the rest of the pieces on the program. These were Schzedrin's *Quasi Albenis*, a fragment from Shostakovich's *Phantastische Tanze*, and Tchaikovsky's *Wiegenlied*. His performance was impeccable, and it was not limited to just technical perfection; we were fascinated by his compelling musical presence and style. He had something to say musically, he knew how to say it, and he said it superbly.

At his lecture-clinic he demonstrated some of his points on the trumpet. (Since he only speaks Russian, his remarks were translated by an interpreter; the interpreter's background was in engineering, so there were some problems with the translation of musical terms, but it is my impression that most of Dokshitzer's ideas were transmitted.) He played a lacquered American-made B♭ trumpet and used a medium-sized American-made mouthpiece by a well-known maker. He stated that the B♭ trumpet is the only one used extensively in the Soviet Union.

Dokshitzer stressed the importance of studying etudes, saying that etudes connect elementary studies with music on the highest level. Memory, technic, phrasing, and interpretation can be developed through the study of etudes, he said; then he demonstrated his points using some of the Fourteen Characteristic Studies from the Arban *Method*. His emphasis on etudes reflects the Russian practice of having all trumpet students master the etudes; only the top students who are bound for a professional career are permitted to study solo repertoire.

Dokshitzer also had other advice on musicianship. He maintained that technique should be the servant to music and never an end in itself. Before playing a piece of music, he said, it is important to look ahead and see what difficulties are there before choosing a tempo, but it is imperative to capture the style of the music regardless of tempo. He emphasized that the performer must understand the mood of the music — to capture a mental image of it — before selecting the proper method of performing it.

In his lecture Dokshitzer gave a brief history of the opportunities for musical study in the Soviet Union. The first conservatory was opened in 1862 in Petersburg and the second in 1866 in Moscow, both by Anton and Nicholas Rubenstein. There are now 26 conservatories in the USSR which give training on three levels in compliance with a program drawn up by the Ministry of Education. About 6,000 students are in the program, including some 1,000 adult beginners. At the highest of these three levels in the conservatory, exams are given twice a year with quizzes at mid-semester, all from memory. They are graded from 5 to 1, corresponding to our A to F letter grades. It is a selective screening process; when a student finishes one level of study, he must have a recommendation from that school to be allowed to take entrance exams for the next higher level. Graduates of the highest level are placed in jobs as orchestra members, teachers, or soloists.

Dokshitzer was born 56 years ago in the small Ukranian town of Mezhin. He began studying trumpet at age 10, and then after moving to Moscow he attended the Central School for Gifted Children at the Moscow Conservatory. He later studied with Professors Vasilevsky and Tabokov at the Gnessin Institute and then was a conducting student a the Moscow Conservatory and the Glazunov Music School. In 1941 he was a prizewinner in an All-Soviet Competition for Young Performers, and at age 24 was appointed solo trumpeter of the famed Bolshoi Theater of Opera and Ballet in Moscow. In 1947 he won first prize at the International Competition in Prague. He is currently a trumpet professor at the Gnessin Institute, a position he has held since 1950, and is a solo artist who has appeared throughout Europe and in Canada, Cuba, and Mexico. An esteemed pedagogue, he has published numerous arrangements for trumpet. ∎

[*]Three recordings listed in the most recent Schwann catalog are: *Incredible Trumpet Virtuosity*, an album of short pieces (Odyssey/Melodiya Y-33825); Haydn and Hummel Concertos and a Biber sonata, with Barshai and the Moscow Chamber Orchestra (Melodiya/Angel S-40123); and Arutunyan, Kriukov and Vainberg Concertos, with the Bolshoi Theater Orchestra (Melodiya/Angel S-40149).

How to Test a Good Trumpet

Arthur H. Benade

A good trumpet (or other brass instrument) must have certain acoustical qualities. You can follow a fairly simple testing procedure to evaluate a trumpet once you have a basic understanding of the ideal acoustical properties.

Here are the four most important acoustical characterics:

1. A well-centered tone and stable pitch are essential; i.e., the instrument should clearly display its cleanest, most ringing tone at a particular, well-defined playing pitch. Not only does this characteristic make the instrument easy to play but it also lends variety to the player's vibrato by adding a shimmering quality to what would otherwise be a rather dull variation in pitch and/or loudness.

2. The instrument should possess an easily controlled dynamic range, with no tendency to drift sharp or flat during a crescendo.

3. It should be capable of a good clean attack with no hesitation or burble.

4. To be musically useful the ideal instrument should also be playable in tune. More precisely, when left to its own devices it should tend to produce the good sounds described above at the pitches of the equally tempered scale. The trumpet is then in a central position from which it can be moved sharp and flat by use of the valve triggers to match changing requirements of the chords in which it participates. In this way good tuning can be attained without sacrifice of the advantages gained by playing each note at its own center on the instrument.

You will notice that I have not mentioned anything about tone color in my list of virtues. This is because musical requirements for basic tone color call for differing shapes of bell, leader pipe, and mouthpiece, all of which can be adjusted by the maker to produce the desired tone while retaining the qualities that are demanded by every player regardless of his tonal needs.

The sound produced when a player blows a note on any sort of brass instrument (good or bad) is made up of a set of components whose frequencies are in a *precise* 1, 2, 3 . . . relationship, and we hear this aggregate as a single tone whose pitch is that of the lowest frequency component of the set.

The note C4 is based on the collaboration of air column resonances in 2, 4, 6, and 8, which feed the various components of the tone. To show their presence depress the keys but do not sound the notes C4, C5, and C6 on the piano, and play C4 on a C trum-

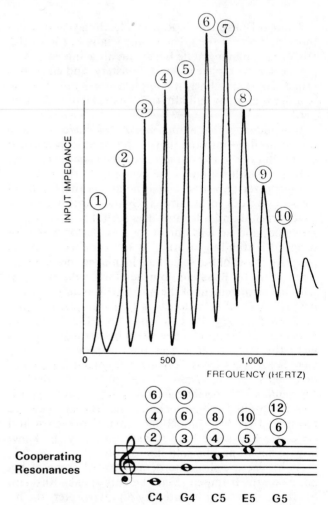

Cooperating Resonances

pet (D4 on a B♭ trumpet). You should be able to hear the components because the piano strings vibrate sympathetically with them.

In pianissimo playing, the "recipe" of components measured in the mouthpiece consists almost totally of the lowest of these components; and during a crescendo the others come in one by one. It is this fact that governs the entire question of wind instrument quality. For example, a softly-played C below the staff is the offspring of the second in the series of resonances. As a crescendo is played, the second and then the third and fourth harmonic components of the tone itself begin to develop, and if the air column's 4th, 6th and 8th resonances are properly located, a progressively more elaborate regime of oscillation is set up in which the the various air column resonances collaborate in stabilizing the oscillations of the player's lips. It is this possibility for well-organized collaboration — the proper location of resonances — that distinguishes a fine instrument from a poor one. If the resonances are not properly aligned, they work at cross purposes and make unstable compromises during a crescendo, producing pitch changes, loss of color, and a lack of steadiness at the embouchure.

The following paragraphs outline a simple test procedure (based on these ideas) that anyone can carry out.

1. Warm up the instrument and make sure that the tuning slides are at least roughly set to give a normal scale.

2. Play crescendos and diminuendos between *pp* and *ff* on the written note G4, a tone in which the 3rd, 6th, and 9th air column resonances should collaborate.

3. At each dynamic level, deliberately float the pitch up and down to seek out the fullest, clearest, and steadiest tone (like tuning in a radio station), without paying any regard whatever to the absolute correctness of its pitch.

The pitch of the played note will remain steady during the crescendo if the three natural resonances of the air column have their own frequencies in proper relationship, i.e., if it's a good instrument. You will also notice during the crescendo on a good instrument that the sound stabilizes and becomes more centered — not only in the sense of tone color, but also in the sense that at *mf* dynamic levels the loss of tone and of embouchure comfort is quite considerable if you try to play a little bit above or below the optimum pitch.

Repeat the experiment using the open C4 a fifth below, and then on to C5 a fourth above the initial G. These additional tests provide information on the relations between air column resonances (2, 4, 6, 8) and (4, 8). If once again you find no pitch drift and

the playing feel becomes more solid during a crescendo, you have confirmed by direct test that all but one of the resonances 2 through 9 on the open horn are correctly related in the way that is absolutely necessary for good response, stable pitch, and centered tone. It is also a relationship that assures accurate musical intervals between the C's and G's.

The final virtue of prompt, clean attack is also almost (but not quite) assured by test results of the sort described so far. If, on the other hand, you observe pitch drifts on the C's that are consistent with those for G2, the instrument is not quite perfect, but a tiny adjustment to the mouthpiece back-bore will suffice to remove the problem. Progressive enlargement of only .001 or .002 of an inch in the smallest part will permit you to cure a downward pitch drift and its attendant other faults, whereas tiny dabs of nail polish will serve in the opposite sense to cure the problems associated with a pitch rise during crescendo.

Inconsistent pitch changes and loss of tonal center and playing solidity during a crescendo are symptoms of more serious trouble which may arise from errors of design or construction anywhere in the system.

The basic tests need only be done on the open horn because any flaws observed in the valved notes can easily be located within the valve loops themselves.

It is often a matter of considerable subtlety to track down the causes of trouble in the main bore and to effect cures that do not at the same time produce a new set of unpleasant effects. Fortunately no one needs to put up with such a faulty instrument. Trumpets are made — at all price levels — that will pass the tests outlined here, and all of these instruments are suitable for professional music-making. ∎

April, 1977

How to Make It As a Lead Trumpet Player

Glenn Stuart

Playing lead trumpet with a big jazz band is both a mental and a physical challenge. It is no wonder that there are only a handful of really good players. The lead player must always be conscious that he is playing *music* (not just *notes*). This requirement is no different from what is expected of other musicians. But the lead player has the additional responsibility of leadership — conveying excitement and brilliance to the rest of the group and making every repeat performance of a particular piece a new and better playing experience for everyone. Without this kind of leadership, performers become complacent and lack the enthusiasm to excite an audience. The lead player is sort of a "foreman" who carries out the wishes of the band leader. This must be done with personality and vigor, tempered with tact and compassionate instruction.

The most effective leaders achieve results not by force but by first earning the respect of the section members and then transmitting to them such things as direction, interpretation, enthusiasm, and musical taste. Working closely with the drummer, the lead trumpet player can then convey phrasing, jazz concept, and interpretation to the entire band.

Prerequisites for such a career include determination, good physical health and stamina, plus guidance by a skilled teacher and lots of listening and playing experience in jazz ensembles. Extra work on range and endurance is essential, after selecting good equipment to make the upper range as comfortable as possible. Practicing exercises to develop correct air movement over the entire instrument is most important. Breathing, articulation, and phrasing must all work together.

Extended Range

Over the past 20 to 30 years, the commercial players have extended the trumpet's range far beyond its so-called "textbook" limits. They play in a register that the classical player would never attempt and with the brute force that he would never employ. It is generally agreed that today the trumpet is more physically taxing than any other commonly used instrument — especially when it is played in the upper register and at great volume.

Stressing high notes rather than musical taste has become an obsession of many school band directors. But this is not entirely their fault. Professional players and arrangers have added the pressure of playing these notes on to the shoulders of the young players, and the young high school trumpet player who has not had the proper guidance can develop bad habits that will take years to break, if they can be broken at all. The *problem* for both the student and his director is to find a competent teacher who can play in this range but at the same time will not force the young player to become just a musical acrobat. (Finding such a person may be a physical impossibility in some parts of the country.)

It takes very specific training to develop a double C that is as musically exciting as the C an octave or two octaves lower. These notes require great physical stress and put a strain on the entire body. For many years struggling trumpet players were told, "Do it correctly in the middle of the horn, over and over, and the upper notes will take of themselves." I have found that this is not the case. I do believe that the "physical" part of trumpet playing in the high register must be nurtured very carefully so as not to damage the younger muscular set up. Most younger players overadjust the embouchure to play notes in the bottom and middle part of the horn, so they pinch and squeeze to play high notes. *Air* is really the key to success, but the subject of breath support is often neglected or postponed by teachers. I believe that the proper use of the air support system is the most important single aspect of range development. Without this ingredient, the young person who tries to become a powerful lead player will surely be overtaken by frustration and disappointment — and possibly serious physical damage.

Young players, especially at the high school level, can generate ample excitement by playing good arrangements that don't take the lead player past high C. Of course, the other players in the section have to play out more on their parts. The problem is that some arrangers voice the trumpet section so high that even the 3rd player is straining to reach his notes and cannot play with the kind of solid sound that makes the group exciting. If the band uses arrangements that are written — or *re*written by the director — with voicings that are more compact and pitched a little lower, the whole brass section will have much more bite. Some players have started using the piccolo trumpet to get the high notes, but I never have used it much simply because it can't give you the big sound of a B♭ trumpet.

I cannot overemphasize the importance of watching out for the physical dangers of playing. I have seen high school trumpet players who strain so hard to play the high parts that their lips were broken open and bleeding. They may never be able to play after high school. It's also possible to rupture the face muscles — they can pop right through the skin. Musician's injuries are not talked about as much as athlete's, but the danger of injury is a serious problem for some players.

In my own teaching, I was sympathetic to the brass players and kept to a minimum the amount of time I spent going over a chart. And I always found that it was much better to have several short rehearsals per week than one long session.

One final thing that I think is essential for the lead trumpeter — and for all other brass players — is the warm-down. When you finish playing and your chops are swollen and sore, it's important to get the red corpuscles back. Most brass players, in symphonies and also now in big bands, take five or ten minutes right after their jobs to warm down. It involves just playing some long tones, going into the middle of the horn and playing down by half steps. Let the chops completely relax, and get some kind of buzz going. (The next day it helps to give yourself a relaxed warm-up early in the day and then put the horn away.) This warm-down process makes a big difference in keeping the swelling down and retaining sensitivity in the embouchure.

The lead player must be able to play constantly in the upper register, the most treacherous and tiring range of the instrument, while providing an interpretation of the arrangement that will be definitive for the rest of the brass section as well as for the whole orchestra. Not all trumpet players can achieve acceptable results, but many can come close if they *listen* carefully and try to follow common sense rules of musicianship in playing the lead part. ▪

"Child of Ecstasy" Glenn Stuart

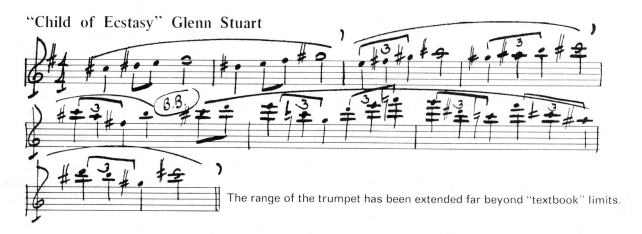

The range of the trumpet has been extended far beyond "textbook" limits.

Directory of Trumpet Players in American Symphony Orchestras

Atlanta Symphony
John Head, *Principal*
Joseph Walthall, *Assistant*
Larry Black

Baltimore Symphony
Don Tison, *Principal*
Rob Roy McGregor
Langston Fitzgerald
Gail Hutchens

Boston Symphony
Armando Ghitalla, *Principal*
Andre Come
Rolf Smedvig
Gerard Goguen

Buffalo Philharmonic
David Kuehn, *Principal*
Charles Lirette
Gerald Soffer
Charles Gleaves

Chicago Symphony
Adolph Herseth, *Principal*
Charles Geyer
William Scarlett
Philip Smith

Cincinnati Symphony
Philip Collins, *Principal*
Eugene Blee, *Second*
Marie Speziale, *Assistant*
Michael Denovchek

Cleveland Orchestra
Bernard Adelstein, *Principal*
David Zauder
Charles Couch
James Darling

Denver Symphony
Manuel S. Araujo, *Principal*
Robert Symmonds, *Assistant*
Dan Kuehn

Hartford Symphony
Ronald Kutik, *Principal*
Roger Murtha, *Assistant*
Ray Torns
Mark Hausman

Honolulu Symphony
Don Hazzard, *Principal*
Robert Fleming
Mark Schubert

Indianapolis Symphony
Marvin C. Perry, II, *Principal*
Paul Hilgeman
Robert Day

Kansas City Philharmonic
Richard Smith, *Co-Principal*
Steve Weger, *Co-Principal*
Jerrold G. Eldred
Chris Gekker

Los Angeles Philharmonic
Robert Di Vall, *Co-Principal*
Thomas Stevens, *Co-Principal*
Irving Bush
Mario Guarneri

Louisville Orchestra
Leon Rapier, *Principal*
Jerome Amend
Clifford Blackburn

Milwaukee Symphony
Richard Metzger, *Principal*
Dennis Najoom
Frederick Fuller

Minnesota Orchestra
Charles E. Schlueter, *Principal*
Ronald Hasselmann, *Assistant*
Clement Volpe
Merrimon Hipps, Jr.

National Symphony
Adel Sanchez, *Principal*
John DeWitt
David Flowers
G. Harrison Bowling

New York Philharmonic
John Ware, *Principal*
Gerard Schwarz
Carmine Fornarotto
James Smith

Oklahoma Symphony
Don Hood, *Principal*
Dan L. Francis
Bob Bogenschutz
Legh Burns

Oregon Symphony
Fred Sautter, *Principal*
Bernard Blumberg
Julian Dreyer

Philadelphia Orchestra
Frank Kaderabek, *Principal*
Donald McComas
Seymour Rosenfeld
Roger Blackburn

Pittsburgh Symphony
Charles Hois, *Principal*
John Hall, *Associate*
Jack G. McKie
Franklin H. Woodbury

Rochester Philharmonic
Richard Jones, *Principal*
John Lillard
George Vosburgh

San Francisco Symphony
Donald Reinberg, *Principal*
Laurie McGaw, *Assistant*
Chris Bogios
Edward Haug

Seattle Symphony
Carleton Whelchel, *Principal*
Jeffrey Cole
Richard Pressley

Syracuse Symphony
George Coble, *Principal*
Daniel Sapochetti
Peter Voisin

Utah Symphony
William Sullivan, *Principal*
Edmund Cord, *Associate*
Sheldon F. Hyde
Edward Gornik

Trumpet Ensemble Music

Robert Nagel

As an aspiring young trumpet student in the 1930s, I was attracted to one type of trumpet ensemble music: the cornet trio with piano or band accompaniment. It was thrilling and inspiring to hear the Goldman Band trio (Leonard Smith, Frank Elsass, and Ned Mahoney) perform such gems of cornet ensemble virtuosity as *Flirtations* by Clarke, and *The Three Kings* by Smith. Many years later I succumbed to writing some trios myself and gave them the usual fanciful titles, "Trumpets on Parade" and "Trumpets of Spain" (on occasion referred to as "Trumpets in Pain").

My involvement over several decades in the development of the brass quintet has served to increase my interest in ensemble music for trumpet on several accounts. I have found it to be a very useful medium in the teaching-learning process. The repertoire can be both challenging and enjoyable as chamber music. And it can be performed in a variety of settings.

Unfortunately, trumpeters have received a comparatively meager inheritance of trumpet music from the past. Much of it consists of rather simple military and ceremonial music. The general body of the early literature is comprised of music written for the cornetto and for the clarino trumpet, ranging from cornetto duets and trios by such composers as Fantini, Scheidt, Vierdanck to larger ensemble pieces for five or more trumpets by composers such as Biber and Altenburg. Throughout the lengthy development of the orchestra over a period of about two centuries, trumpet ensemble music was practically non-existent. It was not until the middle of the 20th century that a few original compositions and various transcriptions began to appear. Even so, horn and trombone ensemble music predominated the brass world in quality and quantity. And it has been only very recently that a contemporary body of literature for trumpets has begun to develop significantly.

Much of the current activity can be attributed in part to the high quality and increased amount of modern brass playing, especially in the U.S., and to the effective efforts of individuals and organizations in encouraging and promoting this activity. The International Horn Society, the International Trombone Association, the Tubists Universal Brotherhood Association, and more recently the International Trumpet Guild have accomplished much in this particular area. (About 50 works were submitted by composers from the U.S., Canada, Great Britain, and several European countries for consideration at a recent ITG composition contest.)

The use of trumpets in ensemble has been fairly varied. For example, there are works for multiple trumpets with orchestra, with band, with percussion, and with various types of pre-recorded tape; and there are trumpet ensembles which employ combinations of variously pitched trumpets, cornets, flugelhorns, and alto and bass trumpets. The trumpet ensemble can be used in a number of musical situations, from opening fanfares at football halftime shows to esoteric concerts of avant-garde music. Some commercial or jazz trumpet ensemble music with rhythm section is available, and publications and opportunities for performance exist in the field of church music. In addition, trumpet ensemble repertoire is useful in trumpet master classes, seminars and workshops, and in civic and ceremonial events.

I suggest the following as a basic repertoire list of published works for trumpet ensemble.

I. Three Trumpets
Bach, C.P.E. *March and Fanfare* (Belwin)
Boutry, Roger. *Fanfares pour des temps legendaires* (Leduc)
Britten, Benjamin. *Fanfare for St. Edmundsbury* (Boosey)
Dubois, Pierre Max. *Five Bagatelles* (Leduc)
Gibbons, Orlando. *The Silver Swan* (Philharmusica)
Lupo. *Fantasia* (Philharmusica)
Morrissey, John (ed.). *Trumpets 3* (Carl Fischer)
Muczynski, Robert. *Trumpet Trio* (G. Shirmer)
Nagel, Robert. *The Sound of Trumpets* (Belwin)
Nelhybel, Vaclav. *Musica Festiva* (Belwin)
Phillips, Burill. *Trio for Trumpets* (Robert King)
Schaefer. *Spielstuecke* (Barenreiter)
Stoker. *Music for Three* (Belwin)

II. Four Trumpets
Catelinet, Phillip. *Ceremonial Fanfares* (Hinrichsen)
Dillon, C. *March and Chorale* (Boosey)
Fitzgerald, Bernard. *Scherzino* (Carl Fischer)
Kay, Ulysses. *Three Fanfares* (Belwin)
Rugolo, Pete. *Four Trump* (WIM)
Scheidt, Samuel. *Canzon* (Robert King)
Schein, Johann. *Intrada* (WIM)
Tcherepnine, Alexander. *Six Pieces* (Edition Musicus)
Telemann, G.P. *Toccata* (WIM)
Tull, Fisher. *Canonical Trilogy* (WIM)
von Hessen, Moritz. *Intrada* (Ensemble)

III. Five Trumpets
Lo Presti, Ronald. *Suite* (Shawnee)
Mozart, W.A. *Divertimento No. 6* (with 2 flutes and timpani) (WIM)
Reynolds, Verne. *Music for Five Trumpets* (Robert King)
Schelokov. *Quintet for Trumpets* (Philharmusica)

IV. Six Trumpets
Biber, H.J.F. *Sonata à 7* (for six trumpets, organ, and timpani) (Musica Rara)
Cruft, Adrian. *Fanfares* (Galliard)
Rubbra, Edmund. *Fanfare* Op 142 (Alfred Lengnick & Co.)
Schmid. *Turmmusik* (Breitkopf & Haertel, Leipzig)

V. Seven Trumpets
Altenburg, Johann. *Concerto* (with timpani) (Robert King)

April, 1977

"Man Alive, What a *Kick* This Is!"

An Interview with Adolph "Bud" Herseth

Kenneth L. Neidig

Adolph "Bud" Herseth has played principal trumpet in the Chicago Symphony Orchestra ever since he became a member in 1948. He is now generally recognized as the world's greatest symphonic trumpeter. But his unpretentious nature (balanced with self-assurance) allows him to enjoy his son's idea that he is really a failure because he has been on the job for nearly 30 years and has never received a promotion. And when asked the question, "Who are you and what do you do?" he replies simply, "I'm a trumpet player in a symphony orchestra."

So many of our readers start beginners every year . . .

Yes, I'm quite familiar with *The Instrumentalist.* My son-in-law is a band director in Oconomowoc, Wisconsin and I see the magazine regularly.

I wonder if you could transpose yourself back to when you started. I believe it was at age 7.

That's right. My father was the band director at this little school in Letcher, South Dakota when I got my first trumpet and I remember very distinctly my very first time playing in the band. It was a summer band concert on the main street of that little town. I was sitting on the bandstand, way down on the 3rd or 4th part, and playing some little march. I was only 8 at the time, but I can remember it to this day. I thought, "Man alive! What a *kick* this is!" And I'll never forget my Dad looking over at me and smiling a couple of times. He could see that I really dug it.

Did you have formal lessons?

The first were with James Greco during the summer of 1937 when I went to the first high school state band camp that Gerald Prescott held at the University of Minnesota. He had heard me play at a regional contest and invited me to play solo cornet in the summer band. We had a terrific time down there. The teachers were from the symphony orchestra (Minneapolis — now the Minnesota). Jimmy Greco was the assistant first trumpeter and had come from the Roxy Theatre in New York. I had three or four lessons from him during the two or three weeks we were down there. He played some solos on concerts during the time — *Carnival of Venice* and some others, but the

one that sticks out in my mind was an encore, *The Emperor Waltz* by Strauss — with the glorious unison trumpets and trombones:

I never have played that piece without thinking of that particular scene in the Minneapolis Auditorium. It still gives me chills.

So that was my first exposure to formal, professional quality teaching. Even though it was only a short time, it was very inspiring — no doubt about it. It really lit a fire in me somewhere.

What other teachers had a similar effect?

Marcel Lafosse and Georges Mager, at the New England Conservatory in Boston when I went there for two and a half years on the GI Bill after World War II. The first year and a half I studied with Lafosse (the second trumpet player in the Boston Symphony; first trumpeter Mager's schedule was full), and with Mager for my final year. Mager was a very famous orchestral trumpet player in those days — he played in Boston under Koussevitsky, even Monteux, and must have played there 30 years or more. He was a very exciting player and a very inspiring teacher. I owe a great deal to that man.

What specific things did you get from him?

Primarily musical style, which was what I really wanted anyway. I could already play the trumpet, had played a lot of dance work, concert band, solos, and a limited amount of orchestra at Luther College in Iowa. The thing I got from him was an understanding of the different styles you need to approach the wide variety of repertoire a symphony trumpet player is faced with . . . and that was the main thing he wanted to show me. I still think that's the one thing that separates the "really good" players from the "adequate" players. I know lots of people who can play a million notes — there's always somebody who will play higher than you do, faster than you do, louder or softer than you do, and longer than you do, but it's a matter of "What can you do with the various kinds of music?"

That's where it's really at . . . in this kind of work at least.

In an informative book by Louis Davidson (Trumpet Profiles, published by Louis Davidson, 608 Kerry Dr., Bloomington, Ind. 47401) you listed a number of players you "most admired and whose playing most influenced your own playing." Can you tell us something about them? Let's start with Louis Davidson.

One of the first records we had at home — one I played a lot — was the recording of the Shostakovitch First Symphony by the Cleveland Orchestra with Artur Rodzinski conducting. I didn't know at that time who the first trumpet player was, but I was very impressed with that recording. Later I heard Louis several times in person and I always thought him a really very elegant and marvelous player. I heard many things that I liked in his playing.

When you hear something you like in someone else's playing, it eventually becomes (almost instinctively) a little part of your own equipment. That's the positive side of listening. The negative side is that sometimes you hear a player whose style or phrasing you do not like, and almost unconsciously you omit that from your style — it does not become a part of your concept.

Another name you listed is Harry Glantz.

Well, Glantz was, I suppose, the biggest name in orchestral trumpet playing for many, many years. He played in the New York Philharmonic (Mengelberg, Toscanini, others) then moved over to the NBC Orchestra a year or two after it was formed. He was a big influence on all symphonic trumpet players.

In every case was it the style you were admiring and being influenced by?

With Glantz I think I was more impressed with the solidity of his playing. To my way of thinking he was not as inspiring a player — in terms of really getting turned on when he played — as Mager was. But he was very very reliable, with an excellent sound and style of playing — one that I think probably influenced more players than any other during that period. There were three big names then — Mager, Glantz, and Saul Caston in Philadelphia. We didn't have so many Philly records around the house as we had of the Boston Orchestra — maybe that's why I always wanted to go study with that exciting guy I heard on those Boston records . . . and I was lucky enough to have the chance. Caston was a very brilliant and soloistic type of player — very exciting. Again, he influenced a lot of people.

And Maurice André.

Well, let's face it, André is . . . he's *it* in terms of solo playing. The guy sounds fabulous, that's all . . . that's all I can say. I heard him play live a couple of times, once in Amsterdam, and also in this area. I have nothing but the greatest admiration for the man's playing — fabulous.

Are there others?

Well, I've always admired Adolf Scherbaum's playing because he was the first to really go into the Baroque high trumpet playing in a big way — a very exciting player.

You've called so many of these players "exciting." What makes excitement?

It's when a guy tells a story with a piece. That's all. He gets away from the notes. It's one thing to turn a crank and get them all, but if you say something besides, that's what it's all about.

In that same book, you also listed jazz players.

Yes, I think Maynard Ferguson is the greatest brass player in this part of the century.

Brass player?

Brass player.

Not jazz player?

Just brass player — the guy is phenomenal. There are some other marvelous players, of course. I was a big Harry James fan back in the '30s and '40s, bought his records and liked his playing very much. I've enjoyed hearing Rafael Mendez on records, but have not had a chance to hear him live. There's a man in New York right now, Jon Faddis, who is a very exciting new talent in the jazz scene. There are many others, like Lew Soloff, formerly of Blood, Sweat & Tears.

You're a real jazz fan, aren't you?

Yes, I like both small combo and big band — like Kenton, Ferguson, Basie . . . .

What kind of jazz did you play?

Both. I played in a big swing band in the Navy overseas, where I split lead with a fellow named Gunnar Sorenson. I've never heard of him since, but he was very talented and knew a great deal about playing and how to lead a section. Some of that rubbed off, and it has actually been a big help to me here in the symphony.

I know you also admire a number of opera singers.

Yes, like a really marvelous Swedish tenor who died a few years ago, Jussi Bjoerling. Ahh . . . his singing was out of sight, out of sight.

Some people may wonder why an instrumentalist listens to vocalists.

You know, every instrument is in a sense an attempt by man to imitate the human voice in some way — and basically that's the ultimate goal that everybody should have in mind when they play an instrument. When you play some of the very disjointed things, especially in some of the avant-garde pieces, it's rather hard to think in terms of vocal lyricism. But nevertheless it still helps your playing . . . more phrase-wise, with a better sound, a better projection of the idea — grotesque as it might be. I think that every instrumentalist can benefit greatly from listening to fine singers, especially opera or lieder where they are telling a story. And you can learn a lot listening to a great pop singer like Frank Sinatra. The guy really puts across the lyrics of a tune.

Well, let's talk about you. You've been in that chair nearly 30 years!

Holy mackerel! That's right. This is my 29th season.

You've found a home.

You know, when I came in here Gerald Hoffman (a very nice guy in the section who had been with the Navy Band in Washington and Sousa's Band) said, "Hey, you know kid, you got to be here 25 years before you're out of the 'rookie' class." So I'm now four years out of the rookie class.

Can you remember the audition?

When I was in school in Boston I got a telegram asking if I would come to New York and play for Rodzinski, at his apartment. My understanding was that they were looking for just a section chair, somewhere down the line. I had gone to the Conservatory library and gathered up some first trumpet parts, everything that looked important, so I just put them up on the music stand, one after the other, and said, "Now I'm going to play this...and now I'm going to play that...." At the end I played a couple of solo things. After about an hour I finished, and he said, "Well, you're the next first trumpeter of the Chicago Symphony." I about went through the floor! Then he said, "Let's have some cookies and coffee...and we'll talk a little bit." He asked, "What's your experience?" And I said, "None." (Then it was his turn to go through the floor!) After that he asked, "Would you mind coming to Chicago and playing for me once more in Orchestra Hall — the hall where the orchestra plays." I said, "That's all right with me." (A very detached thought ran through my mind: obviously with a guy so green, he wants to hear him again, right? Figuring maybe once he is lucky, but if he could get through it twice, maybe he's got something going for him.) So I came out here and played for him again for about an hour or an hour and a half...whatever it was. When I had finished he said, "Well, you have passed, *summa cum laude,*" and that was it! By the time I came here to start (the summer of 1948) he was gone, and I've always been sorry. He was really a great conductor — I had gotten my "in" with him, but I never had a chance to play under him.

How do you perceive your job? Are you the leader of the section, or are you simply responsible for playing your own part as musically as possible?

Well, that first of all, of course, but there's always in your mind an awareness that yes, you are leader of the section, in the sense that unless the conductor tells you some specific way to do it, the other players in the section will naturally listen to the first player, who (by the nature of the job) sets the style. But that's not ironclad. All of us in the brass section — horn, trombone, tuba — try to listen to each other as much as possible and try to get things together. If I play a passage just after the horn, for example, and he's played it staccato, it wouldn't do for me to play it legato. But that's just the kind of sensitivity that a musician at this level should have. Basically, that's what rules all of our playing here as far as I'm concerned. Everybody tries to do his best and everybody tries to make things come together in a homogenous way.

I know you have a very strong commitment to the job. Like the other day when you said you just needed a couple days off and postponed the interview. How can you tell when you're getting to the edge?

When you lose your concentration...when it's a real *effort* to concentrate. The mind goes before the chops. The chops never quit, but once in a while the mind starts to fade a bit — it's fatigue, that's all. The schedule here is very heavy.

I'm sure that a lot of people less dedicated to their main job make a mistake in getting into so many outside activities that they eventually blow it?

Yes, I've known good players who have done that — too much outside gigging and as a result have neglected their own preparation. All I can say is that I feel sorry for them when I see it happen. That's why I have cut my teaching down and accept only a bare minimum of outside jobs. I take a few solo engagements, but that's good for my playing because it's an approach to performance that you don't get sitting in the orchestra. As a soloist you're projecting everything of your own, whereas in the orchestra you're not.

Are you completely under the will of the conductor?

Well, yes, to a certain degree. I think I can explain this best by telling you how Fritz Reiner approached the orchestra. Everybody knows that he was a tough old character, one of the last of the authoritarian era. In the first couple of seasons here he went through the orchestra with a fine-toothed comb, primarily the wind section, where everybody is responsible for a part all by himself. He knew where all the tough spots were for fourth horn, second trumpet, third bassoon, whatever, and you very soon realized that when you had something coming up you'd better be ready, because if you weren't you were going to have your month in the barrel. The interesting thing was that once you got through the test period — and we all knew we had to face it sooner or later — he didn't say much to you anymore. Because then he understood that he could get from you what he wanted and he trusted you, to the extent that unless you were noticeably away from whatever concept he was trying to project in his conducting, he didn't say anything. He just gave you a cue, you played, and that was it. Terrific. It's a good example of how that relationship can work.

Solti is very much the same way — except he never took us through the testing period. So, to me, it's not only a matter of listening and trying to get together within the orchestra, but it's also a matter of working with the conductor. The good combination of orchestra and conductor we have now is partly a result of the conductor taking the best the orchestra has to offer, and of course the orchestra doing everything they can for the conductor. If Solti were to conduct one of the Strauss pieces, a Beethoven symphony, or Brahms with another orchestra he would not get the same way of playing, because all orchestras have their own distinctive style. It just happens that our way of playing and his way of conducting seem to really hit it off.

It's a perfect marriage.

Yes, 29 years, and I'm still getting a kick out of it!

That's obvious. It really is. When you talk about those "exciting" players and about your own playing you are still excited. That's terrific.

The more you live the more you find out you don't know, the more you've still got to learn...and it *is* exciting.

What about preparation for performances?

With the schedule being what it is the last couple of years, there are times when we're not as well prepared as we would like to be. Sometimes we don't begin rehearsing for a Thursday night concert until Wednesday morning. To my mind that's shaving it a little close. For standard repertoire that's fine, but if you're going to work out some big blockbuster that hasn't been played before, you're going to have problems.

As far as the individual players are concerned, preparing for the job is just mainly keeping up with fundamentals, I guess. I practice scales, long tones, and nice broad vocalise-type studies every day.

Can you mention some specific materials?

I try to vary it quite a bit, actually, but there are several books I use, like the Charlier 36 Etudes, the Walter Smith Top Tones, the Herbert L. Clarke second and third books. And of course I practice the difficult things that are coming up. But I try not to over-practice and go stale on them. I practice to the point where I've got them, but I don't try to grind them into myself because then they become automatic, and you can lose concentration just because of that. I always like to go on the stage with the feeling that I'm doing this for the first time...and let's really go!

So the trick is to figure out when you're prepared to play it, won't miss it, but you're still not stale on it?

Right. This is an individual matter, though. Some people like to practice things over and over — maybe 20, 30, 40 times — but I like to have the excitement of just slightly improvising it. Keeps you a little freer. The other way could lock you into one exact precise way of playing — it really could.

Do you have a standard warmup routine?

No, not particularly. Here again, it's an individual matter. I do believe in warming up, and as I grow older I find that it takes a little longer to get all the brain cells and all the red corpuscles going. It's a fact of life.

You know, a warmup is just a practice session gradually approached — that's really all it is. You try to cover some of the fundamentals, first of all to get a nice freely-produced musical quality sound. And then you go through a few articulations, and gradually extend the range until your top, bottom, and middle registers, articulations, and lungs, are all there.

How long is it taking you now?

Oh, I can get ready in 15 minutes, but I don't like to. I prefer a half-hour.

Do you use any special practice techniques? I remember when someone at a clinic session asked you about

a famous Reiner incident (probably when it was your month in the barrel) when he asked you to play Also Sprach Zarathustra *over and over — 17 times was it?*

There are so many of those legends. I'm not sure where the truth is myself, I've heard them garbled up so many times.

At that particular session you described a kind of "three-baseball bat" technique where you had played the solo in every key up well beyond the one it was written in, so coming back down was easy:

Yes, because that is an interval-type thing — octaves. I practice some things in several different keys. Just transposing them around you get a better feel. You get your mind fixed a little better on the exact path this thing is taking and you also get away from that sort of stultifying effect of being locked into only one way. I sometimes transpose various etudes and find it adds another dimension to them. Or I play the etude on a different pitch trumpet and transpose that way. It works well. Otherwise I just practice what I need to cope with the job, and my needs change from week to week. I do invent a lot of exercises. It's a matter of improvising.

I know that in 1952 you were in an automobile accident that smashed up your embouchure. How were you able to come back and play again?

I was off for six weeks, then came back and played the last two weeks of the season. At home I couldn't even play out of the staff but when I got down here in the hall, with the orchestra, it all happened — Tchaikovsky 5th, everything.

That's really incredible. And when you went back home you still couldn't play out of the staff?

No. But I didn't want to waste a lot of time practicing at home anyway because I knew I had limited endurance and I wanted to save enough for just those concerts the last weeks of the season. I didn't want to sit around until Ravinia (in the summer) to know if I was going to work. And it was one of the smartest things I did, really. In fact we recorded the Tchaikovsky 5th and I played alone...without an assistant.

Amazing. Did you go through any kind of a re-training process that would be helpful to people who are just starting?

Well, I had to change the angle and the position on my lower lip because of the scar tissue and a different mouth — there were caps and crowns on rebuilt teeth and it felt very different. I had to shift around until I found a place where it worked, and I just left it there. Gradually the teeth got closer to the original contour. Two lower teeth in the middle are dead, two on one side were broken off down to the gum and rebuilt with pegs in them. Two others were just pushed back. All the tops were chipped off and all the bone was crushed away along the roots. I played with a splint anchored over my lower back teeth (to hold the teeth from rocking) for about six months.

So band directors who are telling students "you must play the trumpet in exactly the same position because that's the prescribed way" don't make any sense.

No, not at all. There are *some* rules, of course — you wouldn't want 90 percent of the upper lip in there, or 90 percent of the lower lip. There should be some equitable distribution. But it's basically a matter of getting it where it sounds the best and works the most comfortably. From that point on you just forget it. Maurice André once said that he never saw a country where people worry so much about their chops as they do in America. He asks, "Why don't you just pick it up and play?" I couldn't agree more.

Yet I'm sure some of the first questions you get at clinics are about what kind of mouthpieces you use and how much lower lip . . .

I tell them the minute I start thinking about that I can't play, so I don't think about it.

> Herseth uses a Bach 1B mouthpiece with a 22 size throat, and sometimes a 1, both on the C trumpet that he uses 99 percent of the time. On the higher pitched trumpets (piccolo for the Bach Brandenburg) he uses a shallower cup.

How about records? Can we assume that it is you who is playing first trumpet on any Chicago Symphony recording since the summer of 1948?

With only a couple of exceptions. There is one section of the Schoenberg *Variations* that my assistant William Scarlett played because it was performed in concerts when I was playing the Brandenburg Concerto and Tchaikovsky Fifth on the same program. I had told the conductor that if I could take off whatever number comes after the Brandenburg I would have time to wipe the blood off my chops and be ready for the Tchaikovsky. He said "fine" and that happened to be the Schoenberg, so Mr. Scarlett played it and did a beautiful job. He also played the "Antar" Symphony (No. 2) of Rimsky-Korsakov with Morton Gould conducting. It had been performed on a pops concert.

None of us are ready to write any epitaphs just yet, but are there any of those recordings that stand out as possible monuments?

I'm still excited when I hear the old Mercury records we did with Kubelik.

Yes, I have Pictures at an Exhibition.

You know, that was the first time I ever sat in front of a microphone.

No kidding? I've played and loved that recording for years!

It was a very exciting time for me, I'll tell you. It stands out in my mind. It's pretty hard to be specific about any others I'm especially fond of.

Unfortunately we now record for several different companies. Because no single company works with us that much, and they don't hear the orchestra that much, I don't think they are quite aware of what the characteristic sound of the orchestra is. So in many cases the record comes out sounding the way the producer thinks it should sound, not the way the orchestra actually does sound. That was not true quite so much in earlier years when we worked exclusively with Mercury, and then with RCA. Today it's a little more of a mixed bag. Records are frauds, you know . . . yes . . . to the extent that somebody other than the players and the conductor has a lot of control over how its going to sound. Musicians are really meant to play for a live audience. I know when you play for a mic, indirectly you're playing for an enormous audience. But it's not the same to sit in a hall where you have nothing but mics around and some guy yapping at you from the control room. It's a totally different feeling, like you're much more just a tool in somebody else's hand. To me live concerts are still what it's all about.

Have you done any solo recording?

No, I have not.

Any plans or interest?

It's been suggested by a number of people who've offered to set it up for me. During the season when we're working it's pretty hard to find the time and the additional energy that's necessary. And when it's vacation time . . .

Yes, I know about the golf . . .

. . . and the fishing.

Do you practice every day?

Yes, about an hour on workdays and maybe two hours on days the orchestra is not playing. It depends on the schedule. Last week I was really beat down physically with a lot of hard recording sessions and concerts. It was very hard to concentrate so I knew I was bushed. I'm 100 percent better, just from a couple days off last weekend, which we don't get too often with our schedule.

Do you play at all on those days off?

As a matter of fact last Saturday I didn't play a note. Only about once or twice during the year you get to the point that you don't want to see it. I don't like to feel that way, so I put it away. When I'm on vacation I put it away for a couple of weeks.

That long?

Yes.

You don't even touch a mouthpiece?

No. I kick it under the bed and say, "Now stay there!"

Do you have any serious problems getting back in shape?

No, as a matter of fact you come back to it better, because over the period of a long hard season there are always little things that creep into your playing that you don't want — physical or musical, sometimes a combination of the two — and you don't have the time to back away from the job to work them out, so you go along and play. When I'm on vacation, even when I'm out playing golf or fishing, once in a while something suddenly becomes very clear and I think "I must try this." And when I come back after a couple of weeks, I am renewed in mental and physical vigor. I tell you it's amazing how many little things in my playing have been improved in just that way.

After I've been off a couple of weeks I take my mouthpiece along and buzz in the car while I'm driving to the golf course. I'll stand on the tee and serenade somebody for a few seconds while they're getting ready (it's always worth a couple strokes, you know). I do that for 10 to 15 minutes two or three times a day, for about two or three days. That's before I even touch the horn. When I do, I'm already about 80 percent back in shape.

If somebody appointed you head of all music education in the United States, what would you do?

That's a pretty good order. First of all, I'd have a lot more money available for instruments, equipment, practice facilities, and I'd make many opportunities for listening to good groups. Listening is where you form your concepts. If you don't hear some good individuals or groups, you really don't know what you're shooting for.

I also think there's a need for teaching solfeggio in this country. The Europeans have long made this a basis of their musical education. We have not here. I think there should be more emphasis on as wide a variety of music as possible and less on the physical aspects of playing. Because I'm an orchestra player, I would like to see more emphasis on symphony orchestras in schools. The bulk of the great music of this world is written for symphony orchestra. I know it takes a lot of money, facilities, and trained personnel, but I would like to see it. I don't know how you go about achieving all of these things.

How would you train band directors?

With almost the same things, especially as much listening as possible to good groups. I would like to give directors a half or full year sabbatical to go study

again. Many of them would like to but can't afford either the time or the money. I see the pressure of marching band as being a little excessive. I know it's a good way of getting the community involved with the band and a good way of getting the kids themselves involved. It can be an exciting thing. I think it's overdone.

Do you see any dangers in jazz programs?

No, not at all.

No problems with range?

Occasionally, yes. If you put up a chart from one of the big bands with notes way above high C and a freshman in high school is trying to play it. Whoever's running the stage band program should have the sense not to use that kind of arrangement. It's true, kids want to sound like Maynard when they can't even get to the top of the staff, but somewhere along the way we should be realistic. As far as having students play most stage band music — I have no fears at all. Every bit of that kind of music I have played has been a benefit to me in terms of even the physical ability to cope with the job and having a much wider concept of things. I remember one time a famous jazz arranger came to one of our symphony concerts. Afterwards he said "I can tell that some of the players in the brass section have played dance work, in fact, I can tell you who they are." He named them, and he was right in every case. I thought that was very perceptive. He was saying — not in a derogatory sense at all — that he could hear certain positive things in a person's playing that had come directly from playing in that kind of group. So I think it's fine for students in school to play that kind of music. You can get turned on by a tune that you really like, and there are not so many of the really stiff disciplines imposed on you that you have playing symphony orchestra or concert band music. I think it's good for a kid to get away from having every sixteenth note crammed down his throat.

Bravo! And thanks so much. We'll all be listening to your playing with new ears. Any final word?

Practice.

■

"The Trumpet Shall Sound"

H.M. Lewis

When approaching Baroque music, trumpeters have tended to concentrate only on its range and endurance demands. But within the past few years there has been a surge of interest in the subject of performance practice, and it is no longer adequate simply to get the notes in a Baroque composition (no matter how difficult *that* may be) — they also must be played in the correct style. Musicians today are more aware that the printed notes were regarded by 17th- and 18th-century performers as just a rough guide to the re-creation of a piece of music, and that the competent performer was expected to apply certain principles of ornamentation. These principles can also be applied in the modern performance situation, as shown in the following examination of one of the most popular trumpet arias of all time, "The Trumpet Shall Sound" from G.F. Handel's *Messiah* (1743).

The trumpet aria was very popular genre during the Baroque period; composers, performers, and audiences seemed to relish the combination of trumpet, solo voice, and orchestra. Such arias were called *Arie d'imitazione* and were used in military-like situations in operas where trumpet's martial qualities could be used to advantage. In sacred music the trumpet was often used to represent the last trumpet on the day of judgement, even though it might not be specifically mentioned in the libretto.

Since "The Trumpet Shall Sound" is the one trumpet aria that trumpeters are called on most often to perform, it is an appropriate model for showing how a Baroque aria can best be interpreted in a manner that does justice both to its composer and to the performer. As in all trumpet arias the trumpet part is obbligato, an indispensable part, and the piece is actually a duet for trumpet and bass voice with accompaniment of strings and continuo. In D major, the aria is scored for trumpet in D (written at sounding pitch), violins I and II, viola, bass voice, and basso continuo. It is written in the popular da Capo form (ABA), and the trumpet plays only in the repeated and quite lengthy A section.

Choosing an Instrument

The trumpeter's first problem is choosing an instrument that can best realize the part. The valved D trumpet can be used, on which the part has a range of C4 to G5, a tessitura of C5 to G5, and a key signature of C major. The main drawback in using the D trumpet is the high tessitura which, along with the lack of rests in the extremely long passage, may present endurance problems toward the end of the piece. However, the tone of the D trumpet is similar to the brilliant tone of the modern orchestral C and B♭ trumpets, and it does provide a very pleasing effect.

Another possibility is the piccolo trumpet in high A, which would place the part in the key of F and give it a range of F3 to C5 and a tessitura of F4 to C5. While the piccolo trumpet certainly helps alleviate the problems of sustained high tessitura, its tone tends to be somewhat thin, especially in the low register, and the low notes that are so important in the opening motive tend to be very badly out of tune. Thus the piccolo is probably not the wisest choice for most trumpeters. The G trumpet might be an effective compromise.

A final possibility is the Baroque trumpet (without valves), either in D or D♭. The tone of the Baroque trumpet would certainly be more authentic, and the technical problems of playing a valveless trumpet are not insurmountable. The pitch of D♭ is suggested because, while pitch tended to vary during the Baroque period, it was generally about a half-step below our present standard pitch of A=440. (Handel's tuning fork sounded A at 422.5, which is almost exactly A♭ at our modern pitch level. Many Collegia Musica type ensembles are even using A=415 as a tuning standard.)

The tonal weight of the various trumpets described above is not a great consideration in "The Trumpet Shall Sound" because the physical distance between the bass voice and the trumpet and the singer's tonal timbre usually insure that the voice will be heard.

Working for Authenticity

For an authentic performance of this Handel aria, examine the music itself for clues. Example 1 shows the opening 28 bars of the aria, which may be considered a trumpet solo accompanied by strings and continuo because the vocalist does not enter until bar 28. The trumpet part is written at concert pitch with two sharps, as was Handel's custom in writing for the trumpet in D.

Rhythm. The first stylistic feature of the passage is the strongly marked rhythm in the first two measures, with the emphasis on the dotted-eighth and sixteenth notes. Handel was probably indulging in the Baroque convention of notating a rhythm as it was to be performed only in the first bar or so, and afterwards writing the notes as simply as possible. This convention, coupled with the Baroque tradition of playing equal notes unequally, indicates that Handel intended the trumpet to continue the dotted-eighth-sixteenth rhythm, at least through the first phrase. However, the inequality probably should not be carried past bar 7. If the dotted-eighth-sixteenth figure is overdone the effect tends to become stilted and dull. Handel does introduce this rhythmic figure at times throughout the aria, and whenever it appears, the entire phrase in which it appears should probably be treated with inequality. Many 18th-century writers mentioned the principle of inequality, and it would be difficult to find a clearer example of its intention than in "The Trumpet Shall Sound."

Ornamentation. It was also customary to ornament most long notes, whether ornamentation was indicated or not. A proficient performer during the Baroque period was expected to be able to embellish and ornament his part with taste, particularly on the repeat of the A section of a da Capo aria. Needless to say, this skill has almost vanished and seems unnatural and awkward at first to most 20th-century musicians. Like every other skill, though, it can be learned.

Most trumpeters are aware of the Baroque convention of decorating a cadence with a trill, usually starting with an anticipation note. Another commonly used ornament was the appoggiatura, which is particularly appropriate on certain of the half-notes in this section. Finally, the mordent, either normal or inverted (see Ex. 2), would also be used appropriately on many of

Ex. 2 As given by Johann Ernst Altenburg*

Inverted Mordent   Mordent

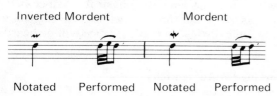

Notated   Performed   Notated   Performed

*In Altenburg's *Essay on an Introduction to the Heroic and Musical Trumpeters' and Kettledrummers' Art,* translated by Edward H. Tarr (Nashville: The Brass Press, 1974), pp. 111-112.

the half-notes. Other Baroque ornaments would have been difficult to perform on the natural trumpet and probably should not be used. A possible realization of

the trumpet part in measures 1-28, utilizing a certain amount of ornamentation and the principle of what Robert Donnington[1] calls "vigorous inequality" appears as Ex. 3.

[1] Robert Donnington, *A Performer's Guide to Baroque Music* (New York: Charles Scribner's Sons, 1973), p. 259.

[2] John Tobin, *Handel's Messiah* (New York: St. Martin's Press, 1969), p. 115.

The rest of the trumpet part (section A) can be treated in a similar manner, with one further embellishment. In measures 50-54, 78-80, and again in 91-94, the trumpet holds a sustained note against moving notes in the vocal and orchestral parts, and such a note was commonly trilled in the Baroque period, probably with a crescendo (see Ex. 4). According to

John Tobin,[2] such trills, which are intended to add intensity and interest to a sustained note, were started on the principal note of the trill and not on the auxiliary note, as is usual with Baroque trills.

Obviously, the ornamentation and inequality cannot be undertaken by the trumpeter alone. Both trumpeter and vocalist should plan their ornaments so that they are consistent and, in sections where one performer echos the other, are identical (or at least as identical as the scale of the natural trumpet would have allowed). When taking the da Capo and repeating the A section, tradition decrees even more florid ornamentation and embellishments, but both soloists must again be consistent. (John Tobin's book, *Handel's Messiah,* contains an authentic 18th-century ornamented version of the da Capo bass part and a possible cadenza for this aria, which can be an invaluable aid to the singer).

Style. Handel marked the aria "Pomposo, ma non allegro," which is as much a style indication as a tempo marking. It should be performed in a "pompous" manner at a moderate tempo, which will allow for the introduction of ornaments and embellishments, and the pomposity will be enhanced by a judicious use of inequality.

Abridging

There is often a question of whether or not to take the full da Capo since the aria is quite lengthy and may be too long for many situations, as well as presenting endurance problems both for the singer and for the trumpeter. This is particularly true for the trumpeter if the piece is to be performed as a part of the complete *Messiah*, for as soon as the aria is finished he has to be ready for the following chorus, "Worthy is the Lamb," which calls for a high D6 concert in the second measure. On the other hand, the repeat of the A section is necessary to the musical form, and it can be made more interesting to the audience with more florid embellishments. However, if the performers decide not to take the complete da Capo, the trumpeter and orchestra should close the aria by repeating the first 28 measures of A, which would give something of the feel of a da Capo.

"The Trumpet Shall Sound" has been a favorite with audiences from Handel's day to the present. Since it is an aria that everyone knows, a performance in the Baroque tradition can be a refreshing change both for the listeners and for the performers, and it can breathe new life into a familiar work. It can also give the soloists a chance to become co-creators of the music with its composer, which may improve their understanding and appreciation of Baroque music. ■

May, 1977

Trends of the Brass Ensemble

Jack Hall

Some visionary musicians are saying that we have become too comfortable with the current development of the brass ensemble. While the brass quintet and large brass ensemble are enjoying their height of popularity among students and professionals, several forward-thinking musicians believe that the brass ensemble is barely in its infancy.

Since about 1950, the brass quintet comprised of two B♭ trumpets, horn, trombone, and tuba has evolved as the most popular brass ensemble medium. At present, the bulk of the brass ensemble literature appears to be written for this quintet. The brass quintet has virtually become the string quartet of the brass world.

But the standard brass quintet is not necessarily the "ultimate" brass ensemble. Variation in instrumentation offers possibilities for change — and for improvement of acoustical problems presented by use of the horn. (While the horn emits a diffuse sonority, the trumpet, trombone, and tuba transmit entirely different sonority with a more projected, directional quality.) Some groups have excluded the horn entirely and use just a brass quartet scored for two trumpets and two trombones. Robert Nagel of the New York Brass Quintet advocates replacing the horn with a flugelhorn, and has even published a series of brass quintet music including that instrument.

Still other musicians have felt a need to enlarge the harmonic spectrum of the brass ensemble, filling out the high register beyond the range of the B♭ trumpet. We sorely need something on the top of the brass ensemble that will equal the range of the flute in the woodwind quintet or the first violin of the string quartet.

It seems rather obvious that the piccolo trumpet should be the natural choice to cope with the upper octave of the brass ensemble. However, this diminutive instrument has so far been almost completely overlooked. There is really no valid reason for this neglect. Today artists and musicians throughout the world are demonstrating that the piccolo trumpet can be played with style, beauty, blend, intonation, and endurance. Therefore, it could be just a matter of time until the piccolo trumpet becomes an honored member of the brass ensemble.

Another important brass group that should be considered is the brass trio. Since the debut of Francis Poulenc's *Trio*, this instrumentation has attracted many fine composers. The brass trio, like the quintet, has achieved a reasonably set instrumentation; most trios are for trumpet, horn, and trombone, although there are a few brass trio publications written for alternate instrumentation. But the scoring for trios should not be limited to this instrumentation.

In a group comprised of only three instruments, the available color combinations are seriously limited. One coloring device that has so far been used only rarely by composers is to vary the instrumentation from one movement to the next, as was successfully done in Virgil Thomson's *Sonata Da Chiesa* for mixed chamber ensemble; the first movement of this composition is written for trumpet in C while the third movement is for trumpet in D.

One historical ensemble that does not deserve to pass into oblivion is the brass sextet which was in the 1940s virtually the only avenue for brass chamber music participation. Admittedly, those early attempts at achieving any sort of workable brass ensemble were indeed crude. The literature was oftentimes uncharacteristic and lacking in refinement, and the instrumentation was often haphazard and nearly unworkable. Nevertheless, there were moments when some pleasant music was displayed by these pioneer ensembles. Although the instrumentation of sextets was seldom the same, it usually consisted of two B♭ trumpets, horn, trombone, baritone, and tuba. I hope that there are brass connoisseurs among us who are interested in further investigating the overall premise of the brass sextet. There just might be riches untold!

Within the last few years interest has been renewed in the large brass choir. Some controversy centers on which instruments should be included in this large ensemble. But the instrumentation does not need to be rigid; in fact, the strong point of the brass choir may be that its unspecified instrumentation lends itself to almost unlimited possibilities.

One often-discussed instrumentation problem in the brass choir is how to fill the missing range between the horn, trombone, and tuba. Fortunately, this problem can be alleviated. Several brass instrument manufacturers are now offering a new substitute — the bass trumpet. This instrument is usually pitched in the keys of B♭, C, and E♭. The bass trumpet is therefore well adapted to the tenor register in the large brass ensemble, enabling the player to develop a facile technique and a unique tone quality.

Unfortunately, the large brass ensemble — like most other brass groups — is still locked into using the traditional B♭ trumpet as the highest instrument in the group. Musicians should realize that smaller instruments are needed to extend the upper range of the whole brass chamber music domain. Since the 19th century, English brass bands have demonstrated the effectiveness of the petite brass instruments by using the E♭ cornet.

The current vogue of nostalgia has ushered in an interesting revival of a group that was popular in the post-Civil War era — the cornet band, featuring all brass instruments with a conical bore. Although the instrumentation of this ensemble for amateurs was not standardized, it usually featured B♭ cornets, tenor horns, baritones and euphoniums, E♭ helicon bass horns, and percussion. Recently in the Nashville, Tennessee, area, there has been a successful revival of the Jack Daniel's Original Silver Cornet Band. Purists who prefer the more mellow sound of a bygone era might do well to investigate the merits of the cornet band.

The greatest collaboration that has happened in many years is that of the percussionist and the brass ensemble. Brass players are at last aware of how effective the added dimension of percussion can be in the brass ensemble. With the myriad percussion instruments available, the future of the brass ensemble with percussion is limited only by our imagination.

The brass ensemble is alive and well. But as musicians we must be aware that there is great unexplored potential to be tapped in new combinations of brass instruments. ∎

May, 1977

The Brass Choir:
Suggestions for its Continued Success

David L. Kuehn

The brass choir has emerged, rather recently, as one of the most popular forms of chamber music among college and university students. Music available for this type of ensemble covers a variety of styles and periods; renaissance and Baroque transcriptions remain a staple part of the brass player's diet, while current trends in contemporary brass writing greatly expand the ensemble's technical flexibility and its range of timbres and dynamic shadings.

Although the experience of performing in large brass ensembles provides a welcome challenge to young brass players, many of us who rehearse these groups do so with a minimum of experience in rehearsal and performance techniques that are necessary for the ensemble's long-range development.

The following rehearsal and performance suggestions are obviously not original, nor do they apply strictly to the large brass ensemble. Specifically, they are *workable* suggestions based on my personal experience. The ideas found below succeed only in scratching the surface of what can be done; but, in scratching the surface, we often find a wealth of material waiting to be tried.

Warm-Up and Tuning

Ask students to warm up *before* the rehearsal. (If a rehearsal area is large enough a tuner may be placed near the door for players to check as they enter the room.) The conductor can then concentrate on *ensemble* tuning, stressing balance, blend, and proper attacks and releases.

Emphasize the importance of tuning *within* individual sections. By having each of the trumpet players, for example, tune with the section principal, attention can be given to timbre as well as proper intonation. The difference in sounding "sharp" and playing with a "pinched sound" is often hard for a young player to distinguish.

Expand the tuning process to include more than one pitch. Play and adjust perfect 4ths, 5ths, and major and minor chords. (Allow the 2nd trumpets to hold a note while the 1st trumpets play a 5th above and the 3rd trumpets a 4th below; the players may then exchange parts.)

Plan to spend time on pitches and intervals that may present problems in that particular day's rehearsal. (The euphoniums and tubas might play a scale in octaves in a difficult key, one which may appear in the first piece to be rehearsed.)

Vary the warm-up and tuning process. Try having the horns tune to the trombone section, or to the trombone section leader. The timbre of the trombone sound often helps the horn player adjust quickly to problems in pitch and timbre. Allow the principal players in each section to tune and then collectively play the tuning note for the entire ensemble. (Repeat this process at other rehearsals with different instrumentalists, including the *last* player in each section!) Consider building the pitch base from the bottom up by allowing the tuba to play the tuning note, adding, in turn, euphoniums, trombones, horns, and trumpets.

If a tuning problem occurs more than once, deal with it from the podium.

A chorale selection or tuning routine used to start every rehearsal can become dull to a performer's ear. Consider choosing the warm-up literature based on the ensemble's problems of the last rehearsal, or the potential problems that might be encountered in the music to be rehearsed that day. Balance and blend may be stressed through a chorale-type composition, whereas tuning problems might be more directly attended to by unison and octave scales.

Tuning cannot end when the first piece begins; it should be referred to and refined throughout the rehearsal. Relatively few students expect a conductor to have a "perfect" ear, but they do expect him to call their attention to problems and possible solutions. With the advent of the electronic tuner, a con-

ductor should have little difficulty in being as specific as he wants in calling problems to the attention of the performers, and offering solutions.

Rehearsal Procedures

The first rehearsal after an extended break (a weekend or vacation) normally requires a careful review of good playing habits.

When a musical section is to be rehearsed, reasons for repeating the passage should be made known to the ensemble members. Blind repetition becomes drudgery, direction is momentarily lost, and so is enthusiasm for the music.

If comments can be made briefly to one section or person without actually stopping the ensemble, time will be saved and continuity will be maintained.

Sight-reading can be a pleasant change of pace in a series of intense rehearsals, as well as a way for the ensemble members to develop and maintain this important recognition skill.

Try to see the brass choir from the player's point of view. The euphonium section that doubles trombone parts most of the time might be better off to appear only at rehearsals where actual euphonium parts are available. And it's easy to encourage a fine percussionist, for example, to join a brass ensemble and then disregard him when making long-range program selections.

Vary the instrumentation of the brass choir in relation to the type of music performed. Doubled parts add depth to certain compositions while detracting from others.

Periodic sessions should be directed toward the details of tuning, balance, and blend, while other rehearsals can be used to capture a composition's overall musical transmission.

Performances and Programming

• When in doubt, plan a shorter-than-average performance.

• If several compositions have historical data, provide program notes.

• In presenting avant-garde compositions, the inclusion of completion dates, along with program notes, is often necessary to assist the audience in enjoying — the *first* time — what it has taken *you* several weeks to discover.

• Concerts that represent a great variety of musical periods might be emphasized by including composers' dates.

• A program that presents new music could be called "A Concert of New Music" or "Musica Nova"; this label might be used to head the printed program as well as the publicity about the performance.

• Fanfares — performed in the lobby, audience seating area, or backstage — can be an effective way of opening a concert or calling the audience back after intermission.

• Performances shared with other musical ensembles (a madrigal group, string quartet, or jazz combo) can introduce the brass choir to a larger audience than it might reach by itself.

• Keep in mind the proper placement of each composition on the program. The opening selection can help set the attitude of the audience toward the remainder of the performance. The composition performed prior to intermission might very well convince those persons who normally leave at intermission to stay for the second half, while the final piece on the program often decides the fate of the entire concert and kindles the desire of the concertgoer to return.

• Examine how your group enters and leaves the performance area, and what atmosphere is maintained while on stage.

• The conductor who enters the stage with a pleasant demeanor rather than a rigid facial expression has an opportunity to establish communication with the audience from the very beginning of the performance.

Generating Public Interest

It is vital that we establish a clientele of concertgoers in our particular locale. To this end each different group has a separate set of challenges.

Advance publicity is a key to creating interest in any public performance. Campus and community radio stations are often willing to make free announcements about public concerts. A formletter, mailed enough in advance of concert dates to use the slower but less expensive bulk-mail rates, offers "directional" publicity to band directors or any other special group.

Past programs saved and sent out at the end of each semester will help stimulate interest in the ensemble for future performances.

Consideration should be given to off-campus presentations. While many small ensembles are not geared to going "on-the-road" regularly, they are quite able — in many cases *more* able than many larger groups — to present concerts within a 100-mile radius or so of the campus. A concert to open an art gallery exhibition, an open-air park performance, or a church service of antiphonal 17th-century compositions are but a few concert possibilities. High schools, junior colleges, and universities normally welcome exchange music programs.

While large ensembles often depend on parents and friends to make up a certain sizable percentage of the on-campus audience, the brass ensemble resources in this area are usually limited. College campuses do, however, offer a large number of potential concertgoers. Periodic "informals" in or around the student union building are a good start at tapping this resource.

Often a guest conductor or soloist can be a major attraction at a particular performance.

Take advantage of outstanding musicians visiting the campus or area to work with the brass choir in rehearsal and/or performance.

Additional Hints

Establish your standards for musical performance early, and *follow-through* by re-establishing these standards throughout the semester.

Plan to use the resources of your ensemble to the fullest. An unusually strong instrumentalist or percussionist might be presented as a soloist on a future program; a student who shows unusual interest and talent as a conductor could assist you with the ensemble for a semester. Students with compositional and arranging talents should be encouraged to write for brass. Encouragement, a good rehearsal tape, and possibly a public performance are often substantial rewards for the young composer or arranger. Consider the regular programming of student compositions. A trumpeter who has an interest in Baroque ornamentation could develop appropriate embellishments for a commercial brass choir transcription of that period.

Change the physical set-up of the ensemble if such a change will enhance the performance of a specific piece. (Contemporary scores often include seating suggestions.)

Most of all, develop your own rehearsal procedures and garner from others the techniques that could be applied to your ensemble. It will be a growing experience for everyone. ■

May, 1977

Breath Focus

Marden J. Pond

There are countless books, etudes, and exercises devoted to the development of both the embouchure and breath control. However, an often-overlooked aspect of playing is the physiological mechanism that exists *between* the diaphragm and the lips, i.e. the throat and the tongue. Poor control of this "forgotten" part of a brass player's anatomy can be a contributing factor to poor tone quality, bad intonation, and restricted range. Excessive tension in the throat and improper placement of the tongue cause more frustration, cracked notes, out-of-tuneness, and "mousey tone" for intermediate and advanced players than almost any other single factor. Many teachers are unaware of this fact, and attribute throat-related playing problems to other physiological or psychological factors.

The tongue and glottal area of the throat act like the nozzle on a water hose. By restricting the size of the channel through which the air stream must pass, the velocity of the air stream may be increased.

It is an acoustical reality that the faster the velocity of the air stream, the higher the pitch of the resulting tone. By learning to control precisely the velocity of the air stream with the tongue and throat, brass players may increase the ability to cause the embouchure and the *entire instrument* to resonate at the desired pitch. Conversely, if the player blows with an inconsistent (or untrained) velocity, even if the right note is produced, the instrument and/or embouchure may not respond as freely as it would with the proper wind velocity. The results may be: (1) poor intonation, (2) bad tone, and/or (3) the inability to produce notes in the extreme upper or lower ranges of the horn.

When many players try to play higher, they tighten (often unconsciously) the muscles of the throat. Although this has the tendency to increase the wind velocity, it also restricts the steady flow of the air stream, causing many of the problems mentioned above. In an analogy to the water hose and nozzle, this would be like stepping on the hose to increase the velocity of the stream flowing through it.

Following are several exercises designed to develop control of the throat, tongue, and associated muscles. Development of these exercises is dependent upon, and related to, the proper functioning of the embouchure and solid breath support from the lungs and diaphragm.

First, experiment with the back of the tongue to discover how it changes the intensity of the air stream. Anyone who has learned how to whistle should be familiar with this muscular action. Next, with the embouchure lightly set and with the lips slightly separated (so they won't buzz), try to produce regular, set pitches with the breath. Blow with the same amount of air that is used when actually playing these notes on the instrument. The following pattern (Exercise 1) should be tried with the breath only:

Ex. 1
(Trombone-8va Basso)

Now play the same pattern with the instrument, consciously controlling the breath velocity with the back of the tongue. Repeat the entire process (blow the passage first, then play), starting a half-step down. Continue the repetitions, down a half step each time, until the pedal tone is reached. Because of the wide pitch variations possible, and the open throat needed to play them, pedal tones can be of great value in developing good breath focus.

Exercise 2 may now be used to apply the breath focus concept to the middle and upper range of the instrument. Be sure to blow each arpeggio first, then play it.

Ex. 2
(Trombone-8va Basso)

After moving up by half steps to end on C5, continue up by half steps until the slightest degree of throat tension is felt. Relax. Blow and play the final arpeggio one more time, and if it is well played, (relaxed focus was achieved), move the exercise up another half step. If throat tension persists, *stop* at that point and go through the entire exercise the next day. With consistent, conscientious practice, the student should, over a longer period of time, be able to greatly expand his tone and his *relaxed, efficient range.*

Exercise 3 is a further study in increasing control over breath focus. It involves the playing of subtones (tones that lie *between* adjacent harmonics of the horn).

Ex. 3
(Trombone-8va Basso)

Blow, then play:
All open (1st position)
All 2nd valve (2nd position)
All 1st valve (3rd position)
All 1st and 2nd (4th position)
All 2nd and 3rd (5th position)
All 1st and 3rd (6th position)
All 1st, 2nd and 3rd (7th position)

Be sure to force the third note (the sub-tone) of each arpeggio into pitch by focusing the breath to that pitch. *Don't change valves or slide position during each arpeggio.*

Exercise 4 involves "bending" pitches by "bending" breath focus. Bend each note down 1/2 step with the breath as follows:

Ex. 4
(Trombone-8va Basso)

Repeat the exercise successively up or down by half steps.

Any or all of the above exercises may be incorporated into an effective warm-up routine.

To open the throat further and to gain greater control with the breath, try playing extended passages in technical, solo, or ensemble literature, with the usual fingerings or slide position but forcing all pitches down a half step with the breath.

It can be of immeasurable value to the individual player or to an entire ensemble of wind players, when rehearsing any passage or section that is difficult to play, to stop and blow the passage together, without instruments, using the breath focus principle. Then play the passage again, concentrating on velocity of the breath. I have repeatedly heard great improvements in individual *and* ensemble intonation, tone, and balance when this rehearsal technique has been applied.

By practicing the breath focus principle, a performer may more fully realize his own musical potential and the tone, range, and pitch possibilities of his instrument. ∎

Bass Trombone Jazz Styles

Stephen Pryor

The bass trombonist serves many different musical functions in the stage band, depending on the particular jazz style being played. The style determines whether the bass trombone should add mainly to the rhythm section, the trombone section, and/or the bass-line wind section. Here are some considerations for playing in four different jazz styles.

Dixieland

Bass trombones were not used in the original dixieland bands; if there is a part written specifically for the bass trombone it is probably intended either to double or replace the tuba part. Such parts combine the bouncing from tonic to dominant in most chords (used in the tuba part) with sliding arpeggios (found in the trombone part). The tonic-dominant job is done on the strong

or accented beats and the arpeggios and glissandi are negotiated on the unaccented beats.

To avoid an over-busy part some notes are omitted. Usually obvious notes, such as the tonic, are left out. It is not unusual to hear a glissando begin on the dominant and end just short of the tonic; the listener invariably infers the sound of the tonic and never misses it. This concept of supplying both a rhythmic feeling and a bass line parallels the function of today's jazz-rock trombonist.

Swing

With the advent of the string bass for the dance-oriented "big bands" the bass trombone became no more than the lowest voice of the trombone choir. Its parts were often doubled by the third trumpet and had little, if any, individuality. The problem in playing swing style is that the bass trombone must provide the bottom sound of the brass section without sticking out. This blending is achieved by being careful not to over-articulate and yet get the fullest (not the loudest) sound possible; the important thing is to achieve a smooth consistency of sound in the section. Two ways of accomplishing this goal are to breathe only in phrases with the rest of the section and to make sure all notes are held for full value.

Bop

Bop's quest for the "highest and loudest" stimulated growth in many instrumental areas. The bass trombone started to come into its own and became recognized as something more than just a "big trombone." As for parts, the style caused a shift back toward using the bass trombone for the rhythm section and for bass lines with more individualized parts (à la dixieland). In

bop pay more attention to the rhythm section and use a more aggressive type of articulation. The instrument can be played with sufficient volume to be identified within the sound texture of the entire group.

Progressive Jazz-Rock

A combination of the new, less restricted rhythm and expanded instrumental capabilities have caused a proliferation of bass-oriented wind instruments. Instead of the single baritone saxophone, many times we find parts for two. In addition, a fifth trombone or even tuba part is not uncommon. This fact, alone, calls for a more articulated and generally aggressive style of playing. The overall effect should be driving and rhythmic. To help achieve this, notes of any appreciable duration are shortened for two reasons. The beginning of the notes will be more prominent, and the player will have time to inhale sufficiently.

In addition to these considerations, the player should listen as much as possible to recordings and live performances of each period. He should also realize that musical periods do not change overnight and that there will be many "in-between" compositions.

Playing Trombone in the Stage Band

Randy Purcell

The trombone player in a stage band fulfills many purposes — that of a soloist, a trombone section member, a brass section member, and finally a part of the total ensemble. The trombone complements the power of the trumpets, mellows the edge of a band, and — with the bass trombone — extends the tonal range of the group. The section is useful as a chordal pad behind soloists and can add an organ-like beauty in chorale-style writing.

Choosing Equipment

The trombone section is usually made up of three to five players, with four parts being most common on published materials. In forming a trombone section of four players, use three tenor trombones and one bass trombone. For big band playing, because of the extra projection and edge needed to match the trumpet section, I recommend using medium-small to medium bore horns for the tenor players. Ideally, the lead player should have the smallest bore, with the second player's bore a little larger and the third player's bore larger still. This size differentiation is not necessary, but you'll be better off *not* using a medium-large bore horn constructed with orchestral playing in mind for either a stage band lead or second chair player. The sound of these horns is very beautiful, but it tends to spread too fast; this quality is appropriate for symphony orchestra work but is very undesirable for stage band playing. Eight brass players with spreading sounds (especially on high loud lead and second trombone parts) will tend to sound very blurred and will destroy the clean sound of the ensemble at high dynamic levels. The ideal is to have eight well-centered sounds, regardless of the dynamic level.

The question of what type of mouthpiece to use is very personal and it would be foolish to specify one make, size, or shape for all stage band trombonists. Teeth, jaw, and lip formations should be considered in the selection, keeping in mind the goals of projection, range, edge, sound, and endurance necessary for a big band player.

Developing the Technique

Before thinking about the special technical considerations in playing stage band music, it is very important to concentrate on first becoming a good instrumentalist and mastering the considerations of sound, flexibility, range, endurance, intonation, dynamic control, phrasing, and all the other essentials. These areas must be mastered by any trombonist hoping to become a professional, regardless of the style of music being played. When the trombonist is on solid ground in all areas of musicianship, he can begin to learn about the special aspects of playing in the stage band.

One aspect of stage band playing about which younger players tend to be very naive is the use of vibrato. The conclusion is in both how to execute a vibrato and whether or not to use it at all. My opinion is that a vibrato is still very effective in stage bands. The style of the arrangement or chart should help dictate whether vibrato is appropriate and, if so, how much should be used. In a chart from the Stan Kenton book, for example, a vibrato would be out of place except in some of the trombone ballads where a wide and slow slide vibrato could be used at the very end of the longer notes. In a chart from the Si Zentner book, it is correct to use a very fast vibrato with sforzando crescendo effects on longer tones. Trombonists should be aware that in certain styles a vibrato is entirely out of context and in others it is quite acceptable. With that knowledge, the players should attempt as much as possible to establish their own styles within the structure permitted.

When vibrato *is* used, it should be slide vibrato rather than lip vibrato. A lip vibrato takes away the intensity of the sound, whereas the slide vibrato may add to it. To get a smooth vibrato, use a loose wrist. Actually throw the slide between the thumb and index finger, to produce a fast vibrato.

It is the lead trombonist's responsibility to carry out the director's interpretation, being consistent so the rest of the section can follow him as easily as possible. It is important to remember that on full ensemble sections the lead trumpet player will be in charge of conveying the director's ideas as to phrasing, dynamics, etc. So the lead trombone player's responsibility is to follow the trumpets, not to attempt to lead the band from his chair. Differences of opinion should be worked out in rehearsals. Once articulations are marked, the lead trombonist should follow the trumpets' style as closely as possible. Remember that precise and consistent releases on note and phrase endings in stage band brass playing are extremely important. At peak volumes tongue cutoffs can help articulate a razor-sharp cutoff. Tongue cutoffs are created by placing the tongue behind the teeth at the precise cutoff point in the phrase, with no let-up in air. This move of the tongue immediately stops the sound, in marked contrast to the releases used in orchestral styles. I hold notes full value — whole note to beat one of the next bar, a dotted half to four, etc. — except where dictated otherwise by the arranger. Some bands may use other systems, but whatever is used, consistent and accurate releases will give the band a cleaner sound.

The range requirements for stage band trombonists are fairly demanding, although not usually as extreme as the trumpets. A lead trombonist with professional aspirations should have a consistent and strong F5 at his disposal. Anything above that will probably never be required except in special solos written specifically for someone with greater range. The student trombonist should strive for good sound and endurance up to C5. Very rarely will any chart, even for professional bands, be written higher than this, and then probably only to D♭ or a rare D. It is important to remember not to sacrifice sound or any other facet of playing to get extreme range. Muscles not yet developed fully or properly can be damaged, and playing in later years might suffer.

I have mentioned the word "sound" several times. To me, achieving the best sound is the single most important facet of trombone playing. Proper diaphragmatic breathing, good clean equipment, and diligent practice of long tones and slow slurs will all enhance tone quality for any style of playing. Then in the stage band specifically, trombonists must master projection — the ability to have the sound be as appealing at 50 feet from the front of your bell as it is at 3 feet. The player should think of *blowing* the air through the horn and not *squeezing* it out. When playing a concert, it helps to pick a spot on the back wall and aim the tone there. It does not necessarily mean playing louder, because projection is possible at soft dynamic levels

also. If the player concentrates on blowing the air with an open throat and oral cavity, it will do wonders for his projection. Along with projection at loud dynamic levels, the term intensity becomes important in stage band playing. When playing very loud some bands will lose their clean sound and balance. This occurs when the sounds of the players spread and become "blatty." If they can maintain an intense, centered sound the section will sound much stronger and cleaner. Remember that air support in loud and "soft" passages should be the same — with "soft" meaning not *less* air, but a slower flow of it.

Strong rhythm and a swinging feeling are essential to stage band playing. The most I can say in a short article is simply this: to achieve good time feel, be aware of the rhythm section. Relax and hear what the drummer and bass player are doing. As much as possible, be aware of their function in your band. Also be aware that the rhythm does not come only from the rhythm section but from the entire ensemble. Make sure you have all the technical requirements of your own part down, so you can then concentrate on time, rhythm, balance, intonation and the other finer points of being a stage band member.

Other Aspects

Stage band trombonists are occasionally called on to play an improvised solo. Here are a few basic suggestions to aid improvisation. The trombonists should (1) learn all scales (major, minor, blues, diminished, whole tone, and chromatic; (2) be able to name the tones of a given chord symbol; (3) listen to players such as JJ Johnson, Urbie Green, Phil Wilson, and other well-known jazz trombonists; and most importantly, (4) get up and try it. No trombonist should pass up any chance to play a chorus or two... we're all still learning.

The ability to sight-read is of

tremendous importance, especially to the trombonist aspiring to a professional gig where he'll only get one shot to play the music. To become a good reader, he should constantly challenge himself with new material. Even if a player is very accomplished in all other areas, he won't be a good sight-reader without practice. Several rules help improve sight-reading ability. When first presented a new chart, start at the upper left-hand corner and check the clef, key, and time signature. Quickly skim through the chart noting key changes, repeats, D.S., D.C., codas and other signs so they don't catch you off guard. If there is a particularly hard rhythmic passage, quietly figure it out, sub-dividing in your head, if necessary. Take any potentially rough technical passage and play it in your head, perhaps noting a good alternate position to use. These suggestions may seem very routine, but many so-called good players miss key signatures and repeats — and maybe a job — because they didn't spend a few careful seconds before playing.

As players start to develop facility in the stage band styles, they should learn all the unique rudiments of stage band trombone playing such as shakes, doinks, falls, drops, bends, etc. Talk to your teacher and director about them. Listen to different big bands on recordings and notice how some bands articulate these effects in their particular styles.

Two books which may be helpful to stage band trombonists are Paul Tanner's *Practice with the Experts* (Leeds) and *Chord Studies for Trombone* (Berklee) by Phil Wilson and Al Viola.

Finally, I recommend listening to the great trombonists on recordings and "live," talking to the players and asking questions when possible. And most important, trombonists should jump at every opportunity to play.

Singing As an Aid to Brass Performance

Derald DeYoung

The use of singing by the instrumental teacher, student, or both, can be a valuable aid to brass performance. Singing can improve breath support, tone quality, intonation, articulation, and phrasing. It will also train the ear and relax tensions. Instrumentalists need to stay closer to the original and most natural of musical instruments: the human voice. Beginning instrumentalists often sound mechanical at least somewhat because they've been divorced from any concept of how playing a brass instrument relates to using the familiar instrument of the voice.

Historically, instrumental music grew out of vocal music: instruments were used to double or replace voices in both secular and sacred polyphonic compositions in the 16th century. Indeed, most of our instrumental forms evolved from vocal prototypes: the ricercares from the motet and the canzona from the chanson. Therefore, brass instruments must have been played in a singing, vocal style which would blend with the human voice.

But how can this knowledge be used with beginning brass students? It has been my experience that a class of 10-year-old beginners on brass instruments can be persuaded to sing the tunes they are learning to play in their lesson books. If there is a group of them and the teacher is able to set an example by singing with enthusiasm, this age group will usually respond with a minimum of self-consciousness. Once the idea has been established that singing is a regular and natural part of each instrumental class lesson, it is not difficult to continue this practice through the upper grades.

Many benefits can come from singing a portion of each class lesson:

1. *Relaxation of tension.* Beginners are especially prone to develop tension in the hands and arms that easily spreads to the neck, chest, and facial muscles. Laying the instrument down while they sing a tune can serve not only to relax those tensions but also to provide a necessary rest period for embouchures which are just beginning to form. For beginners, singing is more natural than playing a brass instrument, and part of the ease of singing can be transferred to instrumental playing.

2. *Breath support.* Breathing in order to play a brass instrument is like normal breathing except it should be deeper. Shallow chest breathing seems to occur when a student is told to take a deep breath, because he is concentrating on breathing. However, when a deep breath is taken without thought, it usually goes to the right place: deep in the body. Loud, hearty singing encourages good deep breathing which can then be transferred to the brass instrument.

3. *Tone quality.* In order to produce a large sound on a brass instrument, the oral cavity of the mouth must be open. Many of the poor sounds students make on brass instruments come as a result of closed teeth and/or a closed mouth. Singing a pitch with an *ah* syllable in the mouth and then playing the pitch can make a marked improvement in tone quality. The image of a singing sound helps the student to keep the air flowing and vital, which in turn maintains a flowing, vital sound.

4. *Intonation.* Intonation problems are the result of faulty tone production, lack of breath support, poor listening, or all of the above. My experience has shown that the singing approach has had a definite positive effect on beginners' intonation. Singing improves and frees up tone production and causes the student to be more aware of pitch.

5. *Articulation.* Articulation can begin with the student singing *tah tah* in order to feel the coordination of the tongue and breath. Later, the voice can be used to demonstrate the difference between a sharp *tah* attack and a legato *dah* or *du* attack. Singing the articulations permits a student to feel how the tongue travels *on* the air column. The sensation of singing can help avoid the *tut tut* articulation so common among young brass students.

6. *Phrasing.* Musical phrasing is most easily taught through a singing approach. By singing a familiar tune, a beginner will understand where the most natural places for breathing occur. The contour of the melodic line is also more easily experienced in singing. A class that sings its music will perform it with greather sensitivity to musical nuances.

The singing approach should not be limited to beginners. Any brass student who is encouraged to develop a singing style of playing will probably have a better sound because this approach requires one to keep the air flowing through the instrument in long phrase segments; it discourages forcing the air by "hacking" or "squirting" the air out for individual notes. The singing approach encourages supporting the *phrases* rather than just the individual notes. If one sings into the horn with solid support, the breath takes on the major load of playing and allows the lips to be more relaxed and thus able to vibrate more freely.

There is nothing new about this approach. The finest brass artists (e.g., Maurice André, Adolph Herseth) are testaments to the singing style of brass playing. Master teachers such as Frank Crusafulli and the late Emory Remington have been singing for and with their students for years. From personal experience I can recommend the following advice. First, sing along occasionally with your brass students (at all levels) to relax students and help them to blow to the phrase line. Second, encourage your students to put down their horns occasionally when practicing and sing a phrase over several times to get the feeling for its contour and shape and then try to imitate this feeling on the instrument. And third, expose students to recorded examples of fine brass artists who sing on their instruments (most do!) in order for students to get this sound in their ear and to form a clear mental concept of how they want to sound. ∎

September, 1977

A Relaxed Approach to Brass Technique

Lee D. Dise

Students of brass-playing spend much of their time in what sometimes appears to be a fruitless search for the "perfect" embouchure, the "right" mouthpiece, the "secret" of breath control, or the "magic" grip for sure trombone slide control. They seek to master those physical skills that seem to be the stumbling blocks preventing them from performing as well as they believe they can.

Often the problem is that students think they are practicing enough, when in fact they are not following through with the concentration and dedication that performance success demands. But even the most conscientious student who appears to have all the mental and physical attributes necessary to advancement sometimes encounters playing problems that seem insurmountable. In this case, a short vacation from the instrument may be the best solution. After a couple of weeks of frustrationless respite, a fresh approach to playing is possible.

The following suggestions may be helpful to the student who is making a "comeback."

Mouthpiece Pressure

It is best in all types of playing to use as little mouthpiece pressure as possible. Brass players often take the conductor all too literally who tells them to "bear down." A prominent, professional performer told me that he seldom needs to do more when correcting a student's embouchure placement or function, than simply to instruct the student never to use pressure.

Too much pressure cuts off the blood supply that our lips' muscle tissue needs in order to withstand the tremendous strain imposed on it by demanding performance schedules, and can distort the performer's aperture. It is generally agreed that only a rounded, oval aperture can produce a thick, vibrant, beautiful sound throughout all registers and dynamic levels. The aperture requires the full participation of both the lips as well as of the muscles at the corners of the mouth. They should contract, not stretch, to form the aperture, so that the lips gradually become denser, stronger, and more responsive. Once these muscles are tamed, it is possible to acquire considerable finesse.

One of the most disastrous teaching methods I have ever witnessed in brass instruction is the "rubber-band" analogy in which the action of the brass player's lips is likened to the twanging of a rubber band: "You stretch the rubber band out real far, twang it, and you hear a real high note. Now do that with your lips. That's all there is to it." Though less widespread than it once was, this analogy is still used by the uninformed who think they can teach "How-to-play-great-brass-in-one-easy-lesson."

Stretching the lips to play ever higher moves the muscles at the corners of the mouth away from the mouthpiece, destroys the lip density, and thereby weakens the lip severely. Then, more and more mouthpiece pressure is needed to hold the aperture in shape. The resulting sharp, stretched aperture yields a thin, edgy sound, puts a ceiling on the high register, and causes severe pain and a lack of endurance.

A conscious effort should be made, especially at the beginning of the daily warm-up to keep the instrument "away" from the face, allowing just enough pressure to prevent air from escaping from the sides of the mouthpiece. Try to sense the physical presence of the muscles at the corners of the mouth, and "tighten" them — that is, prevent them from smiling or backing away from the lip. One of my instructors described the sensation as a "flattened pucker."

Tenseness

Sometimes, excess mouthpiece pressure is only a symptom of a much broader hindrance to good performance — tenseness and nervous anxiety. Other symptoms may be scooping up air with your throat whereby a great effort provides only a small amount of wind; trying to pull the floor up with your toes; or squeezing the trombone slide in a "Vulcan death-grip." Tenseness can adversely affect your breath capacity, the smoothness of your legato, your fast slide technique, sight-reading performance, auditioning (which I believe is a whole area of technique in itself), and that all-important sense of spontaneity which, over and above training and innate musicianship, can mean the difference between an adequate performance and an excellent one. So, after a brief vacation from your instrument, approach it with just as much looseness as possible.

Musicianship and Technical Proficiency

Music performance, unlike many academic professions, not only requires a high degree of intelligence, but also certain physical characteristics. The student musician who is confident of his intelligence and musicianship is frustrated when his performance suffers due to physical problems. But intelligence and musicianship are not enough. The student may be able to think in terms of long phrases, but without sufficient lung capacity, the audience may hear nothing but short, gasping phrases. The student may hear mentally a beautiful, lush sound, but no amount of "mental hearing" alone will transform a thin, unfocused sound into a lush sound for the listeners.

A common criticism of performers today is that they are "fine technicians, but poor musicians." Anyone who has the intelligence and perseverance to acquire a fine technique has all he needs to mature into an excellent musician. Intelligence should be perceived as a tool by which we first analyze the flaws in our technique, and which we *then* use to turn a technically sound performance into a bright musical experience. ∎

October, 1977

An Interview with Frank Crisafulli

Stewart L. Ross

What influenced you to begin playing the trombone?

That is an embarrassing question because actually I didn't make the decision. My father was a trombonist; therefore there were trombones lying around the house. Unfortunately, the grade school I attended in Chicago had no music program such as you find today. Not until I entered high school did I find a band. The bandmaster, Captain Waltz (Captain March would have been more appropriate) was a wonderful man. I remember him well. Actually, I started cold. My father supplied me with an ancient instrument. I would have preferred to have started at a much earlier age. Fortunate is he who starts an instrument when he is still "unconscious." Even more fortunate is he who has expert guidance.

When did you think music would become your career?

It was sort of a natural thing. There was not much of a question one way or the other. My father was a professional musician, my sister was, and is, a very fine pianist.

Were you expected to follow in your father's footsteps?

In effect, yes. I was not particularly ambitious in school. Nothing much appealed to me. Of course I did enjoy my music and my musical associates, and I did work with my instrument. It was really in early high school that I knew what kind of career I'd attempt.

What was the extent of your education? Didn't you attend Northwestern University?

An odd thing. As a Northwestern student I entered a liberal arts program. I did play in the band, of course. I even joined the marching band.

Who was the band director at that time?

Glenn Cliffe Bainum. That was a wonderful experience, except I couldn't continue for a number of personal reasons, finances for one. What finally decided my career was being chosen to play with the Civic Orchestra [the training orchestra of the Chicago Symphony]. At that time there were not nearly the number of talented young players in brass and woodwinds as you find today. Today people run faster, swim faster, and generally perform at a higher level.

Could you describe the circum-

stances surrounding your audition for the Chicago Symphony?

Yes, it was my first audition. I had not really thought seriously about playing in a major symphony orchestra. My father had never been in one although he had been with the Chicago Civic Opera for many years.

Are we talking about the middle 1930s?

That's right, yes. I actually got into the Chicago Symphony in 1938. There was an illness in the trombone section and they wanted an extra man. I think there were about a half a dozen of us called on to try for that position. There didn't seem to be a great deal of competition as far as I was concerned. You might say that I was a natural musician. I was selected.

I came in as an assistant to a man named Geffert, a very wonderful gentleman. Shortly thereafter the bass trombonist became very ill and I was moved to second chair and the second trombonist, David Anderson, moved to bass trombone. This was the section for the remainder of the year. The following year Geffert, who was ailing, did not want the responsibility of being first chair and actually asked that I play first and he would become the assistant. So another man was hired for the second chair.

Who was the conductor at this time?

It was Frederick Stock. I had the good fortune to enjoy my first years under him. I still have a fond recollection of that period. He was a marvelous musician; especially in directing Strauss and Beethoven. To this day I would just as soon listen to his renditions as any other. In any case there I was playing first trombone.

Within two years of joining the symphony as the assistant trombonist?

About two years. And there I stayed for many years. I don't know how much you want to know of all the dreadful things that happened after that....

We can skip over the Fritz Reiner period if you like.

He was not actually the most dreadful part of all. Not many people really know what transpired. You know, musicians are strange in the sense that our imaginations are very active and many times we make decisions that are not particularly good. I had no guidance at this time. As a matter of fact, I don't necessarily recommend studying with your father. It is a very difficult thing for a father to teach his son. My father was quite impatient with me. I think, now that I recall that period, that he rather expected that I should be able to do everything because I was his son.

In any case, I played with a very unorthodox embouchure. The setting was very peculiar and people often mentioned it to me. I was never satisfied with what I did, even though people would say that I had a beautiful sound and it seemed so easy for me. I thought I was just barely making it.

In my teaching I've come to realize that we often dwell too much on our sensations. Many times we cease listening to ourselves. The first thing you know, all you do is feel this, that, and the other thing, and you don't even hear the result of it. In any case, I made a decision which was a very unfortunate one. I thought that if I straightened out my embouchure I would gain what I was seeking.

Were you looking for perfection?

Perfection, yes. I wanted everything at my fingertips. Remember, this happened after I had been on the first stand for about fifteen years. Mind you, I was making it all this time.

At that time the orchestra worked only 28 weeks during the winter season. We were off from April until the summer season, which didn't start until July and only ran six weeks. We were off until the following October. To me, our breaks seemed like an endless length of time. I thought I could accomplish any kind of change during this period. However, making the change in my embouchure didn't quite work as I had anticipated. But I found out a great many things.

First of all, my breath control was not what it should have been. I think most of us are a little bit afraid of this anyway. Breath is subtle. Lips are physical. You can feel what you are doing and they

bother you from one day to the next.

With my attempted changes came a short circuit; in the sense of pitch, color, and releasing the breath. These things are so closely knit together that you don't know what comes first. I ran into the difficulty of breath control more than ever before. I was afraid to let the air go because I didn't know what was going to come out of the horn. Oddly enough, I was still playing well in spite of the horrors of the situation.

When I hear recordings of that period I can tell that I was producing. That is the thing that bothers me so. I was playing. Yet, anyone could have told me at the time, "you can't play anything" and I would have believed him. I was struggling and getting nowhere; at least it seemed so to me. But along came Fritz Reiner.

Here is what was my undoing. The first thing that one loses, besides the feeling of knowing exactly what is going to happen, is the loss of both ends of the register. In my case the high register disappeared. It was at this point that Mr. Reiner decided to schedule the famous undoing of many trombonists — *Bolero.* I often thought that if I had gone and spoken to him about it...who knows? I didn't. I refused to do it. When the time came at rehearsal I made the best attempt I could — it was terrible. I do admit that. The sum total of it was that I was asked if I would step down to second chair.

You were asked this by Reiner during the rehearsal?

No, no. It was all done on the side by the personnel manager.

Did you ever speak to Reiner?

Only on a few rare occasions.

So through Reiner's threats, you accepted the second chair?

Yes, I had the choice — either-or. Of course I had a family...and what difference does it make whether you play first, second, third, fourth, fifth, or sixth? If you are there and are a part of it, that is sufficient....

Years ago, when I was your student, you mentioned to me that playing second trombone was as difficult as any other part.

In a sense, yes. Consider the

problems of sitting between two other voices, the lead and the bass. If you play your own part alone it is a strange sounding thing. It is filling in the chord most of the time. It often doesn't make much sense by itself. You have to have confidence in your ear. You also have to blend with the first and third parts. If there is any discrepancy at all it is up to you to fit your part accordingly. You must realize that you do not set the pace. Who really does? It comes from the conductor. The whole group reacts immediately. No one can really sit back and follow the next fellow. If everyone did, then we would be strung out all over the place.

I know that you stress lip flexibility to your students. Can you suggest any exercises that will improve the average trombonist?

I think that these things are generally well established. In my opinion there is nothing very new in these approaches. The most important thing is to think of a long tone. The production of the tone is dependent on the flow of the breath to the lips in order to vibrate them. The flow of breath must not alter in any way the ease and positiveness of the sustained tone. That is the basis for everything we do.

Yet it is easy to forget this.

Yes, it is a funny thing. If a new pupil comes to me I will ask him first to play some of the basic things he does at the beginning of his practice day. Generally, this is called a warmup — a term I don't care for. I feel that if a person has been practicing regularly to warm up in the course of a day is a relatively short thing. It doesn't take an hour or two to warm up to play.

One should consider that warmups are really very basic. They often require the greatest finesse in the use of breath.

I think that students feel that warmups have nothing to do with later practice. From the moment you play your first sound it is music and must be thought of in that way. It is all one and the same thing. From the time I begin a practice session I am a musician. Recall the first exercise in the Remington warmups — the interval study at the beginning. So many players will go through it in a fashion that makes me feel very uneasy. It is so

uneven. They play only when they are ready. From the first breath there should be a feeling of a pulse so that there is a direction, a feeling of going somewhere. In this way, everything will fall better into place.

Is there one basic deficiency you find in your college freshmen?

In the purely physical sense, register is one of the final things to come — usually the upper later than the lower. That would be, perhaps, the greatest deficiency, but intonation is also a most disturbing problem. Students push the slide around but don't truly listen. I think we are sometimes afraid to listen. If necessary, I encourage students to play out of tune. You must get the student to play. A slow tempo should be used. Not just to get the correct notes the first time, but to be rhythmically played so that the student truly has a chance to hear what he is sounding. I stress that whenever students work on anything, no matter how simple or difficult it may be, they should apply the various articulations to it, degrees of dynamics, and work it out in intervals. If the scale pattern is heard the student will more readily control the physical sensations of the right arm. It is amazing how many times a student will move the slide in the correct direction once he has struck a note out of tune. If the teacher would only permit this to happen.

Don't you feel that many instructors fail to stress the use of the ear in finding positions?

Yes. It is up to the teacher to encourage the student to hear and be free enough to move the slide. The ear will learn to accept an out-of-tune passage. It may grate at first, but after awhile, the student resigns himself to his dilemma and soon accepts these problems. That just can't be. But if you point out something that is not beautiful in regard to intonation, it is important to encourage them not to get tight over this and try desperately to aim at the note with the slide. Rather, they must hear it.

I've discovered another interesting thing in my teaching. Let's say that I get a young student and he plays a scale. I try to get him to sing it. This isn't easy to get him to do as a general rule. For some reason or other we are so reticent about singing. Yet, the student will finally

sing. It may be quavery and hesitant, but it will be in better tune than he has just played it on the horn. These two things don't line up. There is something wrong somewhere. I sing. I sing every part I possibly can. I encourage my pupils to sing also.

How important is mouthpiece practice?

I use the mouthpiece in practicing phrases. This comes closest to singing. Vocalists have no slide positions to lean on. It must all come from within them. It must be the same for us. The mechanical method we use in helping to change pitch, other than the embouchure setting, must respond to what the ear knows it is supposed to hear.

What is it, then, that makes a good trombonist exceptional?

It is a combination of several things. The physical aspect is very important. I am convinced that not everyone adapts to an instrument as readily as another. There are some, not necessarily the most talented, who are capable almost right away of going further either into the upper or lower register. If they have that ability, then they have a lot going for them already. If coupled with some true musical talent, you will have the exceptional player. It ties in also with a natural ability to coordinate. This varies a great deal among people. Why it varies to such a degree I don't know. If a person is tense, for whatever reason, coordination will be more difficult to come by. There just seem to be some people who move everything correctly at the right place and at the right time. I envy these people. Most of us are not like that. I encourage those who don't have it immediately and think everybody else is better than they, to keep working. Don't hamper yourself mentally. It still takes only application to improve.

There are many trombone players who want to play with a major symphony orchestra yet these positions rarely open up.

Yes, I'm sure there must be at least 150 to 200 trombonists waiting for my retirement. I almost think that I shan't retire because it would be terrible to see what will happen. All joking aside, this is a painful area for me. We prepare many young people who could handle any situation in any orchestra. There are always players who can do this. Mind you, there are fine music schools across the country. I hear people from these places and they are well-coached and well-trained. I work with them, but what, really, can I promise them? Nothing. We make no false promises here at Northwestern.

What is really hurtful to me is when a young man announces that if he can't play in an orchestra then he doesn't want any part in music. He doesn't want to teach. I think this is rather sad. I point out to him that I teach and I enjoy it. I think that is a very fortunate and wonderful thing. Of course, if they don't want to or like to teach, then it is just as well that they don't.

The fact remains that in many cases they may have to settle for a job in some little orchestra, probably not even earning a living wage. Major orchestras today are looking for performers who have established themselves with another orchestra. They want someone who went out

and professionally auditioned, was accepted, and remained for some years; in effect raiding another orchestra. They reason that someone has already made a decision, which, in turn, helps them.

Oddly enough, the Chicago Symphony listens to all applicants and evaluates them. This is not done everywhere. In any case students who hope to play professionally (chances are very slight) cannot waste their time and energy worrying about this end. Their time should be spent in preparation. The tremendous discipline necessary is a marvelous thing for any human being and certainly will help them later in life.

One final question. Knowing you for the past ten years, I have often marveled at your good nature and general happiness. Do you have a special outlook or philosophy on life that you can share with us?

Well, I'm not always like that — believe me. The fact of the matter is that I found out that acting the

other way doesn't pay off any dividends at all. So what's the point? When I was in my darkest moments it always surprised me to look around outside and realize that the world was still revolving. It doesn't pay to center in on yourself. Not too many people care. I will also admit to you that I have been extremely fortunate. This I recognize. Would it be as easy for me to be happy if I had not been so fortunate? I am very grateful that I have had it this way.

With students who come in here and are debating, "should I be here or should I not," I have found that, if they end up doing very little, then really nothing happens. If they devote themselves to their work, then I think doors open for them.

I have had to go through some pretty dark moments. I must say that you find out a lot of things about yourself and other people. It is certainly interesting. I look at life as an adventure in this world of ours. ∎

November, 1977

Roger Bobo Talks Tuba

Ralph Hepola

Roger Bobo became one of the youngest professional orchestral tuba players ever when he joined the Rochester Philharmonic at age 18. He later received bachelor's and master's degrees from the Eastman School of Music. During his student years he played extra with the New York Philharmonic and gave the first tuba recital held in Carnegie Recital Hall.

In 1962 the world-renowed Concertgebouw Orchestra in Amsterdam announced a tuba vacancy. Bobo sent a tape to the orchestra and they offered to pay his airfare to Holland in order for him to audition. He got the job and stayed until 1965 when Zubin Mehta invited him to return to his native

Los Angeles as solo tubist with the Los Angeles Philharmonic.

In addition to his 1969 solo album, *Roger Bobo and Tuba Play . . .* (Crystal), Roger Bobo can be heard on recordings of the Concertgebouw Orchestra (Phillips), the Los Angeles Philharmonic (London), as a member of the Los Angeles Brass Quintet (Crystal), and with the Los Angeles Brass Quin- with the Los Angeles Philharmonic Brass Ensemble (Avant). He co-produced an album of 16th- and 17th-century Venetian brass music for members of the Los Angeles Philharmonic and the San Francisco Symphony, and performs on the Avant album with a contrabass trumpet in F — his design.

He has also recorded with jazz trumpeter Don Ellis, and recently did an extended rock-jazz work by Fred Tackett entitled *Yellow Bird* (Avant).

In recent years he has also been active as a clinician, presenting lecture-demonstrations sponsored by Mirafone.

The following interview took place earlier this year.

What do you feel is the most challenging and difficult aspect of tuba playing?

Sitting around doing nothing! That's the most difficult part. Today we took four hours to record the Bartok *Concerto for Orchestra* for television, and a good part of that, for me, was just sitting there doing nothing. I suppose the most challenging part is handling the many different aspects of tuba playing — to diversify and still maintain a good center and an equilibrium. Whether I'm playing a brass quintet concert, recording with Gerry Mulligan, playing monster music for a movie, presenting an avant-garde recital, performing in a symphony orchestra; I have to be able to handle all of those different styles, and handle them well. The age of specialization is gone. The biggest challenge and the one I enjoy dealing with the most, is maintaining a musical integrity by comparison with *all* musicians, not by comparison only with other tubists. People will accept a lower standard from the tuba than they do from other instruments.

What sort of material should a tuba student work on in his daily practice in order to develop into a well-rounded player?

Technical exercises such as Kopprasch which takes him through fingering patterns in all the major and minor keys, scales and arpeggios, and characteristic studies in Arbans. I think that a lyrical, singing style is important and also a more pesante style that we get in a lot of our orchestral music. To exemplify these things I usually use Kopprasch, Rochut, and Blazhevich as a basis and then stretch out from there in Arban's, Verne Reynold's etudes (which were originally for horn), some cello etudes and a lot of diverse trumpet etudes.

Efficient breathing is very important for a tuba player. What basic concepts should a tubist keep in mind in order to develop proper breathing habits? Can you recommend any exercises or routines useful in developing efficient breathing?

Make as little out of it as possible. As soon as breathing becomes a self-conscious function, it's becoming more important than it should be. Learn how to open your throat and breathe deeply to get all the necessary air in and then let it out in a natural way without letting anything get in the way. There are lots of exercises that I use but I don't want to take

credit for them because they belong to Arnold Jacobs [tubist of the Chicago Symphony].

What type of equipment — tuba and mouthpiece — do you recommend for all-around playing?

It's up to the individual. I happen to like the Mirafone C4 and C3 mouthpieces, and use the C4. It's a very wide-rim, shallow-cup mouthpiece. It makes for good response and without destroying too much fundamental, it keeps enough highs in the sound to keep it alive. I equate a good mouthpiece with a really good stylus on a stereo system. This really good stylus can also be an exposé for out-of-phrase components. The embouchure is the sound source. It's like the grooves in the record. The mouthpiece is sort of like the stylus which picks up these grooves and feeds them into a series of pre-amps, amplifiers, speakers, and all of that sort of thing. If all the components are functioning well I find the C4 a very efficient stylus. That's just my own metaphor.

I use a Mirafone 186 or Mirafone 184 tuba depending on the kind of work I'm doing. I also use a Mirafone F tuba and I have a *G* tuba which works very well for Berlioz, and other ophecleide parts. I have a Besson F tuba and a Besson Eb which I use occasionally. There are a lot of really excellent horns. Hirsbrunner makes the most in-tune tuba I've ever played, and he's done a lot of pathfinding work in designing lightweight valves. I would give Mirafone credit for being the best all-around horn. Czerveny, made in Czechoslovakia, has the most gorgeous, vibrant, voluptuous, warm tone that I've ever encountered. Conn has the fastest, most facile, silent and lightest valves I've ever found in my life. I feel like I've just picked up a Bach trumpet when I play that.

How does a tuba player develop a fast, clean technique?

Take it slowly and work it out with a metronome so that the functions become really steady and clear. I'm talking about just bare technique, for example a Kopprasch study that's in 16th notes or an Arban characteristic study. Find a tempo where it lays fluently, and I mean fluently, so that everything is excellent. That might be very

slow. I generally have students play with a metronome, very exactly, with a real firm attack on the notes, very slow, rather pesante, and marcato so that there's a very good impetus to each of the notes, so that the intonation, evenness of attack, and balance between the notes are all very uniform. Then move the tempo up. The shortness will take care of itself as the speed increases. The training device of playing notes a little marcato and a little tenuto more often than not helps develop a consistent technique. By consistent I mean that every note has the same characteristic and the same clarity.

How do you stabilize notes in the low register which are so often difficult to control on the tuba?

There's a certain amount of physical maturity that needs to take place before the low register is going to become real stable. I have students play long notes, maybe long quarter notes. I have them do exercises, for example the Blume exercises, so that the emphasis is not only on the attack of these low notes but also in sustaining the quality of the notes. The attack blows the embouchure open to the right proportions and usually gives an instant of good tone to model in sustaining tones. Remember that these notes have to be proportional: the hole in the embouchure and the framework behind it (the teeth and the jaw) have to be a little larger, and a larger amount of air must be used. I find it very useful, and almost universally beneficial when a player protrudes and drops his jaw somewhat in the lower register. That proportionalizes the framework behind the lips.

How about a good high register, how do you develop one?

You have to work to play high, but it can't sound difficult. You don't play relaxed up there but it should sound relaxed. Physically, you're not relaxed. The methods are well established on brass instruments to develop this. You take etudes that go progressively higher. You do a lot of Schlossberg-type trumpet studies and basic warmups that dwell up in that register.

Do you ever work with your mouthpiece alone, just buzzing it?

Yes I do. Living in Los Angeles,

I spend a lot of time on the freeway, and I usually do mouthpiece buzzing on my way to work. I don't do anything specific. I usually try to stay in the low register and get the best sound possible. If one note sounds a little foggy I'll just try to improve that one note by going up to it or by going down to it. If I find that there is a change in quality or feel over a certain point, I'll try to move back and forth over it and "erode" that change away so that it becomes imperceptible.

What great artists of the past (or present) do you imitate in your playing? Whom do you model your playing after?

I've always tried to be my own musician. However, William Bell and Arnold Jacobs have been a big influence. Those two men were my heroes when I was in junior and senior high school. I grew up with Tommy Johnson [Los Angeles area free-lancer] and we were playing duets together when I was 14 and he was 16 or 17. We still do that. He's my oldest friend on this planet. His constant friendship — and I suppose, competition (in the very most positive sense of the word) — have been a great help. So if I were to say that one tuba player has influenced me more than anyone else it would have to be Tommy Johnson. When I was at Eastman and Harvey Phillips was down in New York City playing with the New York Brass Quintet, I was always quite impressed by his facility and his really smooth technique in slurring. That made a big impression on me. After that point I really have to leave tuba players out of it.

I've listened to all the brass players. Everything that's available on record, I've heard it (Herseth, Farkas, Brain). Any knowledge that anyone has, no matter where it came from, all goes into "the computer." The influence of Tommy Stevens [co-principal trumpeter of the Los Angeles Philharmonic] is sort of a constant, day-to-day thing. These close relationships we develop with colleagues are not unlike a student/teacher relationship. There's nothing formal, we don't even talk to each other sometimes. Just hearing people play well around you makes its mark after awhile.

Who outside of brass players?

Well, I'm an Andrés Segovia fan. I've always been impressed by Dietrich Fischer-Dieskau, some of the woodwind players I dealt with in Amsterdam, Haanken Stotijn for example [principal oboe]. I'm into my 21st year of playing full-time in a symphony orchestra now, a lot more than half of my life. Whenever we have a soloist with the Philharmonic, I listen to him, and as I say, it all gets fed into "the computer." The influence is just there and I don't even know where it came from.

How do you think the tuba can be utilized most successfully in the rock and jazz idioms, by replacing the acoustic or electric bass or by being a solo voice in its own right, or by both?

I don't think it sould be used as a replacement for the bass part, that's an entity all its own. The tuba just doesn't sound as good as an electric bass. It doesn't have that impetus, or the facility.

Have you ever experimented with trying to imitate what an electric bass sound like?

I have.

Does it come out pretty successfully or can't you imitate it?

Oh it can be done real well. The way it's done is that you play real soft, real light, real clear and turn it up real loud. Use a "poppy" sort of attack. It works, but it doesn't work as well as a Fender bass. To my way of thinking it shouldn't be used to replace that instrument. You know, the market for the tuba in rock and jazz doesn't exist now, but it's just a matter of time before some guy comes along who likes that kind of music and who has tremendous facility at it, and he's going to make a market. The guy who plays in Blood, Sweat and Tears, David Bargeron, is fantastic. He's done as much as anybody to make a market for tuba in rock bands.

What are some solos that are musically valuable and well-suited to the college tuba player?...the professional?

I urge players to diversify their programs, and not be afraid to play something that's a little bit dated — 1920-type tuba solos that William

Bell might have played when he was a kid or some of the Paris Conservatory solos from the early 1950s. There's so much music for tuba now that I think it's important, especially if it's a senior recital for a college tuba player, to be fairly discriminating in the final choice for a program. One could put together 20 programs of tuba music, but I think it's very necessary now that one discriminate between what is good music and what is less than good music. Again this brings me to say that we have to compare ourselves with all other musicians and quit comparing ourselves only with other tuba players.

These tuba symposium programs are strange in that one works up something and presents it only to other tuba players. Within the past year most of my solo playing was for tuba players, instead of a general sort of public. I intend to keep going to symposiums and all that sort of thing, but it's a little euphoria that we've built for ourselves. I think we have a tendency to not deal with the real musical world.

What are the basic stylistic differences between American and European musicians? Between American and European orchestras? Between their conductors?

In a very general sort of way one could say that Europeans are more musical and perhaps creative in their approach to an instrument and that Americans stand almost above reproach technically but sometimes are a little dry. That is the end of the generalization. This difference in technical facility was much move overt about ten years ago than it is now. Now the stylistic differences between musicians are diminishing. This became very obvious at the International Brass Symposium in Montreux, Switzerland. There were enormous stylistic differences from person to person, but these were individual, not nationalistic differences. Still, one must say that generally the European orchestras are technically not up to the standards of the American orchestras. I'm talking about say, the ten best European orchestras and the ten best American orchestras. The ten best American orchestras are technically probably far superior but there's a little bit of style, a little bit of lustre, that perhaps the Berlin Philharmonic or even the Vienna Philharmonic, in certain kinds of music, would have as an advantage. It's a special flavor that they have been doing for a long time now that they know, that we haven't learned yet. But as an orchestra puts people on pension and takes on new people, the character changes. The Vienna Philharmonic is desperately trying to maintain this old character by demanding that the players use the same instruments that have been used in the orchestra for the last 100+ years. It's an interesting experiment. I don't know whether it will work or not.

How about conductors?

The conductors are individuals now, too. If a conductor stays a long time with a symphony orchestra, like ten years, his influence is going to be enormous, probably greater than the influence of the country in which the musicians are playing. The media and tourism are eroding away these nationalistic styles. It's a shame in a way, and I hate to see it go.

What are your plans for the near and distant future? Another solo album? Are you commissioning any new works for the tuba?

I'm in the process of making a solo album right now, called *BOTUBA*, which is my license plate here in California. It's going to be composed of the works I have requested or commissioned — the first piece ever written for me, *Two Songs* by Robert Spillman, and the Kraft *Encounters*. That piece was on my first album but I'm ten years further down the road now and this interpretation will be quite different. I'm also doing the Armand Russel *Suite Concertante* for woodwind quintet and tuba, a piece called *Cadenz No. 6* by Henri Lazarof for tuba and pre-recorded tape, and a short encore piece that Alec Wilder wrote for me in 1961 for my carnegie recital.

I'm also preparing a recital for the Institute of Research and Coordination of Acoustics and Music, in March. This is Pierre Boulez's institute in Paris. It's called "The Contemporary Soloist" and it's going to be made up of one person on practically every instrument playing a recital of avant-garde works. I'm playing the Kraft *Encounters*, the *Six Likes* by Theodor Antoniu, *Inconcequenza* by Mattheus Bamert, *Mirum* by Mauricio Kagel, and *Cadenz No.* 6 by Henri Lazarof. Also, Tom Stevens has written a "bon-bon" called *Encore-Bōz*. Bozo or Boze is what they call me in the orchestra here, it's my nickname in the "band." Stevens invented that name.

Also, I'm the tuba editor of the *International Brass Bulletin*. Right now I'm working on a document that all tuba players can agree on. We're trying to determine what sort of quality and specifications should be expected from tuba makers.

Zubin Mehta talked to me today about Bill Kraft's *Concerto for Tuba and Orchestra*. The premiere performance will take place in Los Angeles on January 26, 1978. ∎

December, 1977

Air Velocity

Derald DeYoung

Understanding the concept of breath support is the most fundamental aspect of learning good technique on a brass instrument because the breath affects all areas of technique (e.g., tone, articulation, tuning, and range). Yet the term breath support is not understood by most student brass players. I find that presenting the idea of breath support as compressed air or air velocity is a more graphic way of describing it. The air used to play a brass instrument comes out under pressure and speed.

When you begin working with a student, point out the need for high velocity of the air as it enters the instrument. In order to compress the air the student must first inhale a large breath into the lower cavities of his chest, push upwards with the diaphragm, and expel the air through lips formed in an embouchure. He must focus the air column into a thin bead with the lips. Show the student how fast he is able to expel the focused air by asking him to try to move a sheet of paper as it is placed further and further away.

High and Low Note Velocities

Because low notes take slower air and upper notes faster air the idea of air velocity can be further illustrated by suggesting that the air may travel at 30 mph for one note and 60 mph for a note an octave higher. Be careful not to confuse the idea of the speed of the air with that of the amount of air. Tones at all dynamic levels must be played with fast air; the difference is that notes at lower dynamic levels take less fast air than notes at higher dynamic levels. Tone quality at lower dynamic levels usually suffers because the student doesn't realize that he has reduced the air speed along with the amount of air. High velocity of the air must be maintained when less air is used for lower dynamics. The speed of the air will also change for each pitch, with more slow air for lower notes and more fast air for upper notes. Remind students that the speed of the air for the lower notes is much greater than most players use. If you hear the lack of a solid core or center to the lower tones, it is caused by air that is too slow and perhaps a quantity of air that is too little.

Air Velocity and Tone Durability

In order to produce a rich, sonorous, and vibrant tone the air must travel at the right velocity for each pitch. Each pitch has its optimum embouchure tension and velocity of air, and a student must learn how to produce the right air velocity for blowing into the resistance of the instrument. If the air is not fast enough, the point of resistance will not be reached and the tone will be undersupported. If the player blows beyond the point of resistance, the tone is overblown and blatant. Practicing long tones is a good way to discover just how fast the air needs to be for each pitch to achieve optimum resonance.

I tell my students to think of using air velocity rather than the embouchure to produce the tone, and to form the embouchure around the moving air stream. If they think of hugging the fast-moving air column with the embouchure, they will realize that the most important ingredient is fast-moving air, and an embouchure is incapable of making any sound unless the vital force of air comes first.

Air Velocity and Articulation

Articulation is also dependent on the velocity of the breath; the tongue can travel faster and easier on a fast, steady air column. Again,

concentrate on steady, aggressive air pressure and turn the attention away from the tongue. If a fast-tongued passage is a problem, blow with more steady intensity into the passage and the articulation will usually improve.

It is very important that students blow *through* articulated passages rather than *at* individual notes. If they are blowing separate breaths for separate notes, the air is not being emitted in a long, steady column and your players will not achieve a singing style in either articulated or legato passages.

Air Velocity and Intonation

Lack of sufficient breath velocity can cause pitch to go sharp in upper registers and flat in the middle and lower registers. Students will tighten their lips and pull the pitch sharp in the upper register to account for the air not moving fast enough to support the lip. If the lip is supported by blowing with adequate velocity, it is free and relaxed and the student will produce a resonant, in-tune sound.

Range in both directions is dependent on judicious use of air velocity. In the upper register one must emit the air under great compression or velocity. So important is this technique that some brass players think that increased velocity alone is responsible for causing the lips to vibrate at higher frequencies. A simple yet effective exercise for carrying air support to the upper register is an expanding scale:

When the exercise is presented, an instructor should ask his players to work for smooth connections between pitches making the increased speed of the air carry the lip to the next higher pitch. If this exercise is done with adequate air velocity, a student will get the sensation that the air is doing all the work and that his lips remain free and relaxed.

Air Velocity and Phrasing

Once a player has achieved sufficient air support on individual notes, it is a continuing challenge to maintain this support through a musical phrase. Many times a student will support quite well the pitches that fall in the middle range of the phrase but not carry that support down into the lower pitches or up into the higher pitches. Slow practice concentrating on producing the optimum tone on each note of a phrase will help achieve consistent support through the phrase.

If an instructor emphasizes the need for fast air to play a brass instrument by using terms such as velocity, speed, and compression, the elusive concept of breath support will begin to form. Then, if he insists that his students practice for tone in every aspect of playing, they will develop high-quality air velocity and produce a beautiful tone on every note no matter how short, fast, high, or low. ■

1978

Circular Breathing

Daniel Bowles

In our quest for better playing techniques, taking a breath while continuing to play is certainly not a new idea. In recent years several of the better-known American jazz players of wind instruments have begun to use circular breathing to extend phrases beyond, sometimes far beyond, the normal limits imposed by lung capacity. When Clark Terry or Bill Watrous play a chorus that goes on for two, three, or five minutes without pause, there is a wonderful ripple that goes through the audience as curiosity, disbelief, acceptance, and admiration follow one after the other.

Basically all that is necessary for circular breathing is to maintain a flow of air to the lips or past the reed while you take a breath; sniffing while pushing air out with your distended cheeks does the trick. I will use the trumpet as an example, and go through the steps:

1. Practice holding G4 while allowing the cheeks to fill up with air. Practice this until the tone stays steady and smooth while you let your cheeks fill out and then pull them back into position.

2. Without the instrument use "cheek power" to make the lips buzz.

3. Buzz with cheek power and sniff at the same time, fully closing the throat and really letting the cheeks provide the power to vibrate the lips or the reed. This is the most difficult step.

4. Using the instrument, play the tone, relax the cheeks to fill them, maintain the tone with cheek power while you sniff, and then let the air from the lungs take over again. Practice this until there is no audible sniff or "bump" in the sound as you change from cheek to lung power.

Remembering that you didn't ride a bicycle smoothly the first time you tried it should help you get over feeling badly about making strange sounds while you learn this technique. A person rarely learns how to do an action involving great coordination the first time he tries it; to gain confidence and consistency requires many repetitions. It took me a week of practice a few minutes each day to achieve smooth circular breathing as I played my instrument. During this past year, I have probably averaged only ten minutes per week working on this special technique, but I am now capable of playing two octaves while using circular breathing.

But, you might say, don't composers know that people cannot play phrases longer than their breaths will hold out; why should I learn a parlor stunt like this? If we look at an example from "legitimate" trumpet repertoire, circular breathing begins to look more practical.

Aspiring or practicing orchestral trumpeters will know the tremendous difficulty of adequately play-

Normal embouchure

Let the cheeks fill with air while doing circular breathing.

Molto Lento ($\eighthnote$ = c. 60)

(Trumpet in F) *pp* *dolcissimo* *cresc.* *sf* *p* *dim.* *p*

p *dolcissimo* *sf* *dim.* *pp*

◉ = Circular breath

ing the first two phrases in Wagner's Prelude to *Parsifal*. Circular breathing on the notes indicated ⊙ makes these treacherous phrases more manageable.

I am sure many more examples can be found by the reader in pieces of all styles for any wind instrument. This is not to suggest that we shouldn't practice controlling the air as well as we can, but that by using circular air we can keep our breath coming comfortably and eliminate in some cases the necessity of playing on the last reserves of our available air.

And even if we use tremendous effort and learn to play a long, drawn-out phrase in one breath, why not use circular breathing to lessen that effort so that we can concentrate on making the music happen for our listeners. That is really the end goal. ∎

February, 1978

Authentic Baroque Interpretation for Trumpet

H.M. Lewis

The trumpeter interested in authentic Baroque performances must be aware of three main differences between today's performance practices and those of the Baroque Era. First, the concept of playing as an ensemble composed of several different voices is essential; the music is not a trumpet solo with accompaniment. Second, in order to achieve the sound of equal and unequal stress on notes authentically, a trumpeter must use various tonguing articulations. And third, the melodic line in slow movements needs to be embellished even more than what is normally done today in order to have an authentic Baroque performance.

Although the trumpet was the loudest instrument in a Baroque ensemble of trumpet, strings, and continuo, the interplay of voices in the ensemble was the important consideration of the musicians of the Baroque period. Because of this the modern practice of performing Baroque trumpet music with piano accompaniment is not authentic although it might be an educational necessity. If a trumpeter must perform with keyboard accompaniment, the organ is a better choice than the piano because of the greater weight of tone and the possibilities of registration that can give a better impression of the interplay between ensemble voices. However, the trumpeter must still keep in mind that he is performing in an ensemble and not as a soloist with accompaniment.

The practice of stressing important tones in eighth-note and sixteenth-note passages was one of the major skills needed by Baroque musicians. It is also one of the aspects of Baroque performance practices overlooked by modern trumpeters. Johann Altenburg, noted Baroque writer, explains the concept, "Make a distinction between principal and passing notes so that the former are played somewhat louder than others."[1] It was considered inartistic to simply tongue tu, tu, tu,

as we are taught today and the distinction between principal and passing tones was made by using different syllables for tonguing. Girolamo Fantini, another noted writer of the era, gives several possibilities for tonguing a passage as in example 1.

Example 1. From Fantini's trumpet method of 1638; three possible ways of tonguing a passage.

le ra le ra li ru	li		ta te ta ta ti ta	ta
ti ri ti ri ti ri	di		la le ra la la la	la
teghe teghe teghe	di		lal de ra de ra de	ra

Altenburg also mentions the use of the alternating ti ri ti ri tonguing (example 2) especially in a fanfare or Principal register. Performers wanting an authentic sound should note that a German or French pronunciation of ri is farther back in the throat than it is in English producing more of a gutteral sound. Therefore, the ri is like a soft "ku" and the pattern is similar to double tonguing in today's practices with the difference being that the German ri is softer and therefore not as prominent.

Example 2. Giuseppe Torelli, *Sinfonia con Tromba*, G.8, third movement (Allegro), trumpet part (in D), meas. 2-3. The accents in parentheses should not be made too obvious.

di ti di di li di li di ti   di li di li di ti

1. Johann Ernst Altenburg, *Essay on an Introduction to the Herois Musical Trumpeters' and Kettledrummers' Art*, translated by Edward H. Tarr (Nashville: The Brass Press, 1974), p. 96.

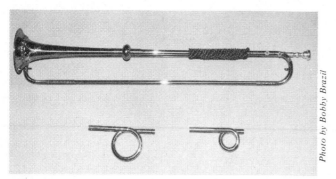

Meinl & Lauber Baroque trumpet in D, with crooks for D and C.

Ornamentation of a melodic line is not a problem in most of the trumpet music written before the 1720's because the melodic lines given the trumpet are very florid. A few ornaments were traditional including a trill on the penultimate note of a cadence and possibly an appoggiatura on the cadence note (example 5). Other ornaments included filling in triadic skips with passing tones (where the natural scale of the trumpet permits) and the addition of melismatic passages where the written part shows only a long tone.

In slow movements where a simple melodic line is given, the musician was expected to perform *divisions,* i.e., elaborate embellishments and ornaments. In most cases, it is the first violin part which contains the melodic line in a slow movement and it is this part that must be ornamented. Unfortunately, there are no hard and fast rules for this kind of embellishment. The performer is expected to use good taste in applying ornaments; over-ornamentation that obscures the original line is a sign of poor musicianship. Example 6 shows the first violin part from the second movement of Torelli's *Sinfonia,* G.8, with a possible performance version. This is just one suggestion and the performer should try his hand at writing parts (this is also valuable practice for writing concerto cadenzas). Even if a Baroque piece is to be performed with keyboard accompaniment, the upper voice of the slow movements should be ornamented in a similar manner.

The traditional method of performing sixteenth-note passages by slurring the first two notes and tonguing the third and fourth (slur two, tongue two) is not, strictly speaking, authentic although it will produce the sound of unequally stressed tones. (It would be more authentic to slur the sixteenth notes in pairs [slur two, slur two] although Baroque trumpeters would have used different tonguing syllables). Altenburg indicates, however, that ascending or descending passages on adjacent harmonics were usually slurred as in examples 3 and 4.

Example 3. Passages usually played slurred, from Altenburg, p. 97.

Example 4. Figures usually slurred, from Altenburg, p. 97.

The problem of unequal stress on tones also affects how dotted notes are treated. According to the theorists of the time, a dotted note was to be held as long as possible with the following note played as quickly as possible. The reason for holding the dotted note was to provide tension and interest that would keep the piece moving. There is little difference between this style and our modern method of performance in a fast movement, but in a slow movement or slow section of a work, using the Baroque practice will produce a totally different sound from a modern interpretation. (Some authorities have maintained that a player should double-dot all dotted note values in a slow movement, but a reliance on such a rule would be pedantic or produce a rendering not necessarily concerned with providing the needed tension for interest in the music). The trumpet was usually silent in slow movements or sections of compositions through the 1720's, however, this was not always true (see example 5).

Example 5. Archangelo Corelli, *Sonata in D* for Trumpet, 2 Violins, and Continuo, first movement (Adagio), meas. 1-2. The part as written is given above, with a possible interpretation below.

Example 6. Giuseppe Torelli, *Sinfonia con tromba,* G.8, second movement (Adagio), first violin part, meas. 1-4. The written part is given above, with a possible embellished version below.

Trumpeters, violinists, and, indeed, all musicians primarily schooled in applied music are incredulous when asked to elaborate on a given melody. Unlike their Baroque counterparts modern instrumentalists are taught to be faithful to the written note (except for jazz musicians). Worse yet, many players will use a performance by an outstanding contemporary artist to justify not using ornaments or unequal stressing of notes. A performer needs to remember, however, that concert artists who are masters of their instruments may not be knowledgeable in the field of performance practices. It is up to the musician to research and apply the knowledge needed for an authentic performance. It can be a rewarding experience for both players and audience and is an area of concern for the modern musician who wants to perform Baroque music to be heard as it was in the Baroque Era.

February, 1978

Solos and Studies for Trumpet and Horn

Maurice Faulkner

Good music for all levels of trumpet and horn performance abilities has been published by some of our more astute music companies. Original compositions with and without accompaniment proliferate. Most of them merit the attention of the finest soloists for recording and concert performances, but elementary school musicians and beginners on the trumpet and horn have not been neglected. Composers and editors knowledgeable of the young instrumentalists' problems have provided suitable materials for interpretive development. Bernard Fitzgerald has arranged a series of works for grades I-II, *Scarlatti Suite* (Belwin-Mills, 1977), that are ideal for young trumpeters. Expertly phrased and marked for proper style concepts with a range limited to G5, these three pieces, Allegro, Adagio, and Allegro, offer a combination of movements that would satisfy the most discriminating brass instrument judges in the annual solo festivals.

The French publishers have become adept at finding good quality music to publish for trumpet and horn. Gérard Billaudot, Editeur, Paris, has not neglected the beginning trumpet student. *Jour de Fête* by Claude Arrieu is a bright, short melody in concert F ranging to G5 that would be a challenge for the grade I student.

Editions Henry Lemoine, Paris, offers *Mosaique* by Nicole Philiba. A collection of four pieces for C or B♭ trumpet and piano accompaniment with both trumpet parts on one sheet, these pieces will develop a beginning student's ability in legato, staccato, and proper phrasing in ranges limited to the staff.

Trumpet Voluntary composed by Phillip Lambro for the motion picture "Mineral King" is published by Wimbledon Music Incorporated. Written at the grade II level, it is scored for C trumpet but could be played on a B♭ instrument. Its chromatic melody at a slow tempo moves from an expressive legato to a tasteful fanfare requiring a competent player capable of G# above the staff (G#5).

Oxford University Press, London, has continued its horn solo publications for young musicians with *A Second Classical and Romantic Album* as well as *A Third Classical and Romantic Album*. Both works are arranged intelligently by Watson Frobes and contain solo transcriptions from master composers including Grieg, Mozart, Weber, Handel, Beethoven, Dvorak, Schumann, Fauré, and Brahms in grades I and II.

Gérard Billaudot has published a grade II solo for horn edited by Edmond Leloir from the "Le Cor" Collection of Vincent d'Indy's *Andante pour Cor (Andante for Horn)*. Using a simple muted effect as well as bass clef notation, the piece requires fine, sustained tone quality. Martin-Joseph Mengel (1784-1851) is represented in the collection with *Solo pour Cor* for orchestra or piano, grade III. The piece is in the style of an early Richard Strauss concerto for horn.

Intermediate Solos

Vaclav Nelhybel has written a delightful contrapuntal work, *Sonata da Chiesa No. 2 (Sequence)* for B♭ trumpet (oboe) and organ or harpsichord published by Joseph Boonin. Both oboe and trumpet parts are included with the organ or harpsichord part in two staves without the pedal organ. It is a simple work in grade II-III that is musically interesting through the use of imitation between the soloist and the keyboard part in modern harmonies and tonal changes. The allegro marcato tempo ($\downarrow = 112$) and the range to an A5 will demand careful tongue and lip development.

Alphonse Leduc Editions Musicales of Paris has published four interesting volumes of Jean-Michel Defayé's *Huit Preludes pour passer le temps* for trumpet in C or B♭ and organ. The two preludes in each volume vary in difficulty ranging from grades III through V. They require a good high C (C6) in some pieces and they demand a variety of styles in tonguing and phrasing. The organ accompaniment using three manuals is expertly composed and becomes an integral part of the trumpet solo. The several volumes are expensive with difficulty varying within each volume. Volume I covers grades III-IV, volume II: grade V, volume III: grade III-IV, and volume IV: grade IV.

In their Collection for Horn Gérard Billaudot, Editeur, has published Vincenzo Bellini's *Concerto in F Majeur* for horn and orchestra with piano accompaniment. Written in two movements, Larghetto and Allegretto Brillante, the piece requires a range up to B5. In the same horn series is a piece edited by Edmond Leloir and written by J.M. Sperger (1750-1818). *Concerto* is slightly more demanding in range going up to B5 with a D6 also notated although an easier passage substitution is given. Overall, nice musical style with competent editing highlights this Collection for Horn as exemplified by these two pieces in grades III-IV.

The Maurice André Collection for Trumpet published by Gérard Billaudot, Editeur, includes works in grades III through V. One of the easier works by Johann Fischer (1670-1746) is *Suite de Danses* for trumpet and orchestra with piano adaptation. A grade III-IV piece ranging up to C6, it has excellent phrase and tonguing indications which aid the performer in capturing the Baroque mood and style. A work by Johann Christian Bach, *Sonata en Re mineur* (D minor) for trumpet and piano or organ in three movements requires nearly 18 minutes playing time and represents a fine musical addition to the trumpet solo literature. The second movement, Andante, has a delightful lyrical motive which alternates between the soloist and the pianist with an attractive recitative section for the accompaniment. The third movement, Allegro, requires a high D(D6) making it more applicable to grades IV-V capabilities.

A contemporary trumpet solo in the André Collection for piccolo B♭ trumpet and piano, *Dialogue* by Francois Zbinden, requires a specialist on the small B♭ instrument who has command of the low range as well as the top tessitura of the instrument. The rhythms are not difficult but the musicality of the accompaniment complements the piccolo trumpet part well, making this one of the more interesting publications.

Advanced Solos

Gérard Billaudot, Editeur, is also publisher of one of the latest contemporary works at the grade V level. *Héraldiques* by Antoine Tisné for C trumpet and piano is composed of five varied "Héraldiques" requiring various avant-garde trumpet techniques including "bending the tone," "two-octave glissandos," "multimetric" bars, and double and triple tonguing. The accompaniment is complex and will need considerable rehearsal. The explanation of the avant-garde notation is not comprehensive enough for the beginner, but there is a brief glossary that will help someone who is already familiar with contemporary music notation.

Alphonse Leduc Editions Musicales, Paris, has published Eugène Bozza's *Graphismes* for solo trumpet. This is a work that every advanced amateur and professional should own because it includes a description of avant-garde notation devices in a fairly comprehensive glossary as well as several movements which use the devices in an expressive manner. Here the modern trumpeter will find all of the resources of his instrument as demanded in the latest compositions of contemporary music.

For more traditionally minded in the teaching and concert fields, Warner Brothers has reissued eight of Herbert L. Clarke's most famous solos in two volumes with piano accompaniment at $2.95 for each volume. This is a real bargain that includes such favorites as "Bride of the Waves," "Carnival of Venice," "Sounds from the Hudson," "From the Shores of the Mighty Pacific," "The Debutante," and "The Southern Cross."

Solo Teaching with Tapes

Hal Leonard has recently developed a fine approach to coaching the trumpet and horn soloist at the grade II-III level. The company has published a complete package consisting of cassette performance, trumpet solo book with extensive instructions on interpretation, and practice exercises for problem areas in the music. Additional information includes material about the composer, musical style and historical period. The cassette includes performances of the solo trumpet with accompaniment and the piano accompaniment alone so that the student can play along at proper tempos. Listed as *Master Solos, Intermediate Level for Trumpet*, the pieces are effectively edited by Robert Getchell and performed by Chicago Symphony trumpeter Charles Geyer. *Master Solos, Intermediate Level for Horn* are edited with equal effectiveness by Louis Stout, Sr., of the University of Michigan and performed by his son Louis Stout, Jr. These materials, packaged in clear plastic, make an ideal teaching device for the student who needs fine professional help at home.

The explanatory materials in the solo books are well written in a simple style that covers the basic problems in each piece. The music chosen for solo performance is representative of the finest of the classic masters as well as contemporary materials composed especially for the series. In addition to the text concerning performance concepts there is a judge's comment sheet at the back of the folio which describes what is expected under each category of tone, intonation, interpretation, etc. As a long-term judge of solo and ensemble festivals this page in itself is worth the price of the book. I cannot recommend these two volumes more highly for a student at the intermediate level.

Method Books of All Levels

Thomas Stevens of the Los Angeles Philharmonic Orchestra, and a proponent of modern avant-garde trumpet music as a performer and teacher, has written *Contemporary Trumpet Studies, Number 6*, published by Gérard Billaudot, Editeur, in 1976. It is a difficult collection of studies, grade V to VI, but it should become a part of every trumpet student's and teacher's library. It deals with aleatoric (chance) elements, clock-time duration, space-time notation, quarter-tone fingerings, half-valving skills, complicated rhythms, lip slurs, tape-clock studies, modern tonguing concepts, and much more. The studies include exercises to develop contemporary playing abilities and a comprehensive explanation of avant-garde notation.

Sigmund Hering's *23 Orchestral Studies for Advanced Trumpeter*, published by Carl Fischer, is based on the idea of taking trumpet excerpts from major symphonic and operatic works and developing them into long etudes in similar style. Wagner, Beethoven, Prokofiev, Debussy, Rimsky-Korsakov, Tchaikovsky, Mahler, Richard Strauss and Shostakovitch are well-represented by this extraordinary study book in the styles which serve the orchestral palette of each composer to the best advantage.

Charles S. Peters' *Total Range* published by Neil A. Kjos Co. (Park Ridge, Illinois) is another work that every trumpeter will want to own. Written for trumpet, cornet, or baritone horn in treble clef, it has specific instructions for building range and is organized so efficiently in beginning, intermediate, advanced, and professional units of four weeks each that one could begin wherever his technique stands at the moment and progress from that point on. It uses the famous Schlossberg lip slurs as a beginning, but it adds much more based on many ideas and many sources. By the time one has completed the total volume he could have achieved a six-octave range of Cs.

An elementary French horn study, *The French Horn*, by Irving Rosenthal, published by J. Albert and Son (Sydney, Australia) offers an intelligent approach to many areas including embouchure, breathing, and tonguing but does not provide enough exercise material to develop the great variety of skills necessary in building a firm foundation. One value of the study, however, is the use of Bb and F notation for horn exposing young players to double-horn function and bass clef notation.

One of the best horn methods is William Brophy's *Technical Studies* published by Carl Fischer. It covers developing low register superbly for the young player as well as pitch-bending to open up the tone, lip trill, exercises for accurate attacks, excellent information on muting, rapid single tongue exercises giving a superior description of tongue movement, multiple articulation exercises featuring concepts of double and triple tonguing, buzzing exercises with and without the mouthpiece (including buzzed glis-

sandos with the mouthpiece off the lips and then on the lips), and new beginning exercises that are based on Arkadia Yududkin's teachings which encourage accuracy of pitch, attack, and tone.

Studio 224 of Lebanon, Indiana has published a Studio Solo Series which includes works at various grade levels for trumpet and horn with piano accompaniment. One advantage of this series is the fact that the publisher grades the solos. The prospective teacher or student has a fairly good idea of the level of difficulty.

One of the most attractive of the horn solos in the series is Robert Schumann's 1849 *Fantasy Pieces (Fantasiestücke)* originally written for piano and clarinet, violin, or cello, opus 73. Arranged by Leon Donfray for horn and piano the pieces are listed as grade V by the publisher although they can be played by a young amateur capable of grade IV-V music. The three pieces, Zart und mit Ausdruck (tender and with expression), Lebhaft (lively), and Rasch und mit Feuer (quick and with fire), provide a delightful musical experience for the sensitive performer who has a competent accompanist. A high A5 is necessary and a fine flexible lip is needed for the wide-ranging arpeggios. This new addition is a valuable

contribution to the horn repertoire. You may wish to listen to Reginald Kell's recording of the clarinet version of this work or Gregor Piatigorsky's cello disc.

The Studio Solo Series also includes an arrangement of Enrique Granados' *Orientale* for horn and piano, grade III, which will test the soloist's legato style as well as his accurate command of muted horn. R. Christian Dishinger has transcribed Camille Saint-Saens' *Allegro* for the grade I-II trumpeter in easy range (up to C5). Dishinger's transcription of a Handel *Bouree* for grade I trumpet or grade I horn were listed as grade II by the publisher. Either one would serve the first year student as good solo literature and they are marked intelligently for proper tongue and style interpretation.

This year's selection of new works offers many high points and only one low one. The more simple the music, the less musical it tends to be. But every composer, with the exception of J.S. Bach, W.A. Mozart, and Bela Bartok, have found it difficult to compose for the youthful amateur. The fact that so many of our brass composers are doing so well is encouragement for the future. ∎

Trombone and Baritone
Solo and Study Materials

William W. Richardson

The year 1977 produced literature for trombone and baritone horn in sizable quantity and varying quality. Several new works at differing grade levels will be welcomed by music educators. Be forewarned, however, that a great deal of French study and solo literature of marginal value is being imported, and at exorbitant prices. Advice for this year: buy American. The musical and educational worth is generally well above that

of the imports and it all comes at much lower prices. The following materials are noteworthy among the 1977 entries.

At the beginning level for baritone there is *Contemporary Band Course, Military March, Lazy Lullaby*, and *Aura Lee* arranged by Donald C. Little; and for trombone, *First Time Out, Outdoor Aire*, and *The Trombone Waltz* by Paul Tanner (all Belwin-Mills). This "first" solo music is easy to read, stays in

an accessible range, and has simple piano parts for young accompanists. Great music it isn't, but usable it is.

Master Solos Intermediate Level-Trombone edited and performed by Buddy Baker and *Master Solos Intermediate Level-Baritone Horn* edited and performed by Larry B. Campbell (both Hal Leonard) are well suited to junior high and first- or second-year high school students. Along with the solo and piano part are "lessons" which include work on fundamentals as well as specific preparatory work for the solos, an optional basso continuo part, and a cassette which provides a complete performance followed by performance minus the solo part. The music for both books consists mainly of transcriptions of Baroque through Romantic era pieces. If you need to choose one of the two, the trombone package would probably be preferable. The two new pieces for trombone by Robert Kehrberg deserve performances, the baritone horn package contains five duplications of the trombone book and the *Three Miniatures* for baritone horn by Don Wilson is much more advanced (college level) than the intermediate label it carries. The performances by Baker and Campbell are excellent models for young musicians, and the series is well-organized and well executed. Both are worthwhile for junior and senior high school students working toward more artistic performances.

Clef Studies for Trombone arranged by Ralph Sauer (Wimbledon Music) would be an excellent book after the trombone student has completed preliminary clef work. The 36 short, lyrical pieces from the Baroque through Romantic periods use either tenor or alto clef without mixing the two. Because they are not high register studies nor rhythmically complex, they are valuable to the student who wishes to develop clef facility without the problems of range and rhythm.

Trombone Studies in Contemporary Music by Robert Nagel (Edward B. Marks/Belwin-Mills) is an excellent book at the advanced level with which to begin the exploration of contemporary performance techniques. Mixed meter, rapid dynamic contrasts, whole tone, twelve tone, and quartal compositional techniques as well as the special effects and new notation are presented clearly and concisely. Because Nagel utilizes the middle range exclusively, he removes the high register obstacle from the student's progress, which should allay some of the fears students have acquired about the performance of contemporary music.

Although not published this year the *Annotated Guide to Trombone Solos with Band and Orchestra* by Vern Kagarice (Studio P/R) is a most valuable reference work to help you track down usable literature of all levels for trombone and band or orchestra. The annotations will give you a good idea as to the feasibility of either the solo or the band/orchestra parts. Buy it before the price catches up with the value.

The Trombonist's Handbook: A Complete Guide to Playing and Teaching the Trombone by Reginald Fink (Accura Music) is an extremely well-organized and well-presented volume. Nearly every subject that relates to trombone playing is at least touched upon. The quality of the photographs, drawings, and musical examples is superb. Because the Kagarice and particularly the Fink texts are costly to produce and appeal to an esoteric audience, they may go out of print quickly and never return. For this reason books of this quality should be added to your school or professional library as soon as possible. ∎

February, 1978

New Solos and Studies for Tuba

R. Winston Morris

It has not been very many years ago that only a few pieces for tuba would be published throughout an entire year, the result of apparent lack of interest from the tubists and assumption by the publishers that no market existed. Not only has that situation completely changed, but now music is published for solo tuba and ensembles, on a technical level that would have been thought impossible only a generation of tuba players ago. Quite a few composers and publishers have been especially active in this new atmosphere, seeming to be excited by the enthusiasm with which their new works are received and performed.

Three pieces published this year are especially interesting. The *Contemporary Band Course* series (Belwin) contains three works at Grade I level arranged for tuba and piano by Donald C. Little. Each work requires a range of approximately one octave.

For use by high school students as well as possible review by college players, there is *Master Solos, Intermediate Level, Tuba* (Hal Leonard), edited and performed by Daniel Perantoni. The package includes eight Grade III level solos in styles ranging from Bach to blues, plus a cassette tape with both a complete performance and an accompaniment-only version. The two original works and six transcriptions can be used for study, contest, or recital.

Encore: Boz (Wimbledon) is for the advanced college student or professional. It was written "for Bozo" (Roger Bobo of the Los Angeles Philharmonic) and requires a range from the highest to the lowest note now available on the tuba. The piece is avant-garde in style, involving some theatre, and intended to display the virtuosity of the performer. ∎

Beginning a Brass Quintet

Charles Decker

The brass quintet just might be the answer to a number of your problems. It is a mobile and versatile ensemble that can perform at functions where it is impossible to take an entire band or orchestra. You may be able to solve some scheduling problems by changing homogeneous lesson groupings to a mixed brass ensemble. And it's not hard on your budget, either; for the cost of only three or four concert band compositions you can purchase an entire basic library of literature for brass quintet.

Instrumentation

Flexibility of instrumentation is a unique characteristic of the brass quintet. Music is usually written for two trumpets, horn, trombone, and tuba. Most literature is more comfortably performed with the standard brass quintet instrumentation although some directors substitute bass trombone for tuba, and other variations are possible for some of the repertoire as shown below.

Usual Scoring	Possible Substitutions
1st trumpet	none
2nd trumpet	horn
horn	trumpet, trombone, euphonium
trombone	horn, euphonium
tuba	euphonium, trombone

When making substitutions, the capability of the players must be considered. For example, substituting a horn for a trombone requires a horn player with command of the lower register, just as substituting a trombone for a horn will demand good control of the upper register by the trombonist. Many Renaissance and Baroque transcriptions come with alternate parts; publications from Robert King are particularly helpful because most of his transcriptions come with as many as four substitute parts.

The upright tuba should be used exclusively in brass chamber ensembles as bell front tubas and sousaphones make it difficult to balance the sound in a group.

Seating

The standard seating arrangement for a quintet is rectangular, not semi-circular as it is with large ensembles. Music stands should be separated by two to three feet, creating a feeling of intimacy without appearing cramped. There is a variety of seating patterns, each with advantages and disadvantages.

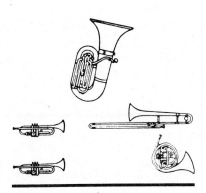

audience

This arrangement has no instrument bell directly facing the audience, therefore a very capable horn player is needed for the sound of the instrument to be heard by the audience.

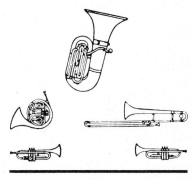

audience

In this arrangement, the sound of the horn travels directly towards the audience; also, with the trumpets facing each other the players may find it easier to hear one another.

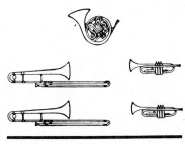

audience

This is an effective arrangement for the two trombones in the quintet (it can also be varied by having the trumpets and trombones switch sides). But, by seating the trumpets and trombones opposite each other the horn must be placed in the back position, making it difficult for him to project the sound. A balance problem can occur if he is unable to match his sound against the predominance of the more brilliant instruments. If your horn player is capable of producing a large sound, this arrangement can be very effective.

Whatever arrangement you decide to use should be flexible and can even vary within one program, according to the demands of a particular composition.

Conducting Techniques

Because the ensemble is without a conductor the responsibility for starting, stopping, establishing the pulse, and changing tempos belongs to the first trumpet player. When he is not playing, responsibility shifts to a secondary conductor either the second trumpet or the trombone (the playing position of the tuba and horn makes it difficult for players of these instruments to conduct).

Ensemble attacks and cutoffs should be indicated by lifting the bell slightly to prepare the ensemble and then bringing the horn down in a strong movement to indicate the precise moment of attack; a conductor should not use vague circling with his bell because it is difficult to follow. Tempo changes should be made by moving the instrument up and down in a steady motion with one of the members continuing this motion during long, sustained sections to help everyone feel the beat.

Repertoire

Brass quintet repertoire has developed significantly in the last decade and today includes transcriptions from every period of music history. Of the available literature, Renaissance and Baroque transcriptions, original Romantic compositions, and 20th-century works are generally the most successful for brass.

A valuable aid for locating and ordering music is the annual *Brass Player's Guide to the Literature* published by Robert King Music, North Easton, Massachusetts 02356, listing every piece of brass music in print for any combination of instruments including solo materials as well.

Recordings can be particularly beneficial in developing a concept of sound for the young quintet. I have listed here my suggestions for a training repertoire including the publisher and recordings when they are available.

Training Repertoire
Beginning Level

Bach/King	22 Chorales (King)
Glazounov/King	In Modo Religiouso (King)
King	24 Reformation Chorales (King)
Purcell/King	Music for Queen Mary (King) (RCA LSC 2938)
Rasmussen	Christmas Chorales (King) (Columbia MS 7033)

Intermediate

Adson/King	2 Ayres (King) (RCA LSC 2938)
Brana	6 Pieces for Young Brass Quintet (Galaxy)
Purcell/Corley	2 Trumpet Tunes and Ayres (King) (RCA LSC 2938)
Schein/King	2 Pieces (King)
Susato/King	3 Dances (King) (RCA LSC 2938)

Advanced Level

Bach/King	Contrapunctus I (King) (RCA LSC 2938)
Holborne/King	2 Pieces (King) (Columbia MS 6941)
Joplin/ Frackenpohl	3 Rags (Belwin) (Klavier KS 539)
Maurer/Nagel	3 Pieces (Mentor)
Nagel	This Old Man March (Mentor)
Pezel/King	6 Pieces (King) (Columbia MS 6941)

Training and Technique

Successful training of an inexperienced ensemble requires an organized approach progressing from technically simple literature to more challenging music. The basic repertoire of chorale music demands precision of attacks and releases, proper intonation, careful balance, and stable ensemble rhythm for an effective interpretation. It presents all elements on a basic level thus allowing the ensemble to concentrate on essential concepts. The four-part chorale will usually sound balanced and effective if the bass line is played in octaves by the trombone and tuba or in unison with two trombones, depending on the instrumentation of the ensemble. Important motion of non-harmonic tones in the various parts requires a slight emphasis on the moving line, while

still maintaining ensemble balance. Performing phrases at a variety of dynamic levels can help develop a wide range of dynamic control in the group, and chorale literature is especially helpful in training a quintet to start and stop together because there are many short phrases requiring good conducting-with-the-instrument skills. For practice sessions the secondary conductors should also direct the group through the chorale.

When you are ready to select more difficult literature, first consider intermediate works in which the quintet generally has similar rhythms throughout. The complexity of contrapuntal music makes it very difficult to perform, and it should be studied only after the ensemble has executed simpler music accurately and musically.

Stage Presence

Most inexperienced quintets take pride in the sound of their performance, but are embarrassed with the visual element of presenting themselves on stage. Be sure to practice stage entrances, exits, and applause recognition so the students will feel comfortable.

Some quintets prefer to have their music on the stands prior to their entrance while others will carry it with them. Entrance onto the stage or performing area should be in seating order, and performers should walk to their chairs without giving the appearance of rushing or running. After reaching the outside perimeter of their chairs, the group should accept the applause as a unit, looking to the first trumpet player in order to bow together. This bow acknowledges the applause and establishes a visual contact with the audience. After accepting the applause, the quintet should place their music on the stands; any fumbling with the music prior to accepting applause will appear very awkward, in addition to being impolite to the audience.

Following a work, the quintet should look again to the first trumpet for the signal to stand and bow together. If the members have to remove their music they should do so only after recognizing the applause with a bow, and then exit together.

Student Attitudes
Towards Performances

Most directors spend many hours developing specific skills and ensemble precision, yet little if any time on the important psychological aspects of performance. Recordings have created the impression for most young musicians that performances must be "perfect," but they should know that mistakes will occur in even the best prepared performances. Preoccupation with minor errors can destroy the major goal of playing musically; therefore, as the director, you should encourage the attitude that successful performances are based on the positive aspect of creating exciting music and not on the negative concept of trying to avoid mistakes.

Chamber music and a brass quintet experience can provide students with a genuine incentive to attain higher levels of musicianship. This, combined with the ease of mobility and a repertoire capable of fulfilling most performance situations, makes the brass quintet an attractive addition to your music program. ■

April, 1978

The Brass Connection

Joel Masser

Most brass players know something about the physical aspects of blowing the instrument, but the way these aspects are connected is often misunderstood. Any physical change, no matter how small, will require compensating changes elsewhere. For instance, it is difficult to make a long crescendo or diminuendo while keeping the pitch steady because the lips must compensate for the changing air flow.

The three most basic concerns in brass playing are embouchure aperture size, embouchure flexibility and air pressure at the embouchure; they also seem to be the ones that cause the most problems. When dealing with other functions, such as posture or finger-slide technique, we can usually spot and correct the trouble. However, the blowing and embouchure muscles are out of sight and are hard to adjust by feel. Fortunately, these functions are learned naturally and readily, just by playing the instrument. But when problems develop it is important to understand the ways they are related.

First, some observations about these three functions:

1. The embouchure aperture can be controlled naturally to produce the correct size for any note on the instrument.

2. Mouthpiece pressure can be used to reduce the size of the aperture, but this also reduces flexibility and endurance, so it is not a good procedure for general use.

3. To play higher or louder, even the beginner instinctively knows that he must blow harder; that is, he must raise the pressure in the air passages and at the embouchure.

4. Air pressure can be raised by narrowing the air passage, mainly at the throat or chest. (A smaller lip aperture will also cause higher pressure.) In other words it is possible to play somewhat higher or louder by constricting the throat or chest. However, this method of controlling air pressure does not work for large pitch or dynamic level changes, because the constriction creates down-pressure and tends to shut off the air flow. In addition the constriction adversely affects the tone quality. The correct way is to use only the abdominal muscles to support the air column. Players are especially liable to use the chest muscles when they are running out of breath at the end of a phrase.

5. Allowing air to escape from the corners of the mouth reduces air pressure and is therefore inefficient. Furthermore, it is one more variable added to an already complicated process.

One of the main obstacles in learning a brass instrument is in the coordination of these three functions. The brain must translate a mental sound image into messages sent to various muscles. If the image is vague or inaccurate, then the result is a missed note or poor intonation. Similarly, if the lips do not get the air supply they expect, a wrong or cracked note results.

An increase in air pressure must necessarily cause a change in the lips' vibration. If the lips are held firmly (less flexibly), they will have to vibrate faster and the pitch will rise. On the other hand, if the lips are allowed to vibrate widely in the direction of the air stream, then a higher dynamic level will result.

The limits of such coordination determine the limits of a player's range. The lips can always form the proper size aperture, but outside certain upper and lower bounds the system fails to produce a buzz that can be amplified by the instrument. Beyond the upper limit of a player's range, either the necessary high air pressure blows the embouchure open, or the embouchure shuts down trying to hold firm. Beyond the lower limit the player is unable to produce a steady air pressure.

Breathing and Tonguing

Proper inhalation is essential because it engages the correct abdominal blowing muscles and relaxes neck and chest muscles that should not be used. It is therefore desirable to avoid a time lag between inhaling and blowing, in order to keep the muscles from tensing. A common mistake in tonguing is to stop or slow the air stream between tongued notes. To correct this it may be helpful to think of the relationship of a water tower to a home water faucet: the force of gravity on the water in the tower creates water pressure that pushes the water out of the tap when the faucet is opened. The water pressure must remain the same regardless of the position of the faucet. In the same way the air support must remain steady when opening and closing the tongue-valve. It is sometimes helpful to practice without using the tongue, both slurring and with the "ha" articulation (but always with abdominal support, never tensing the throat or chest).

Correct tonguing is just a combination of these two ways of blowing, using the tongue for clarity.

In brass playing, everything is related. Embouchure position and air pressure are not independent of each other; modifying one will invariably cause a modification of the other. ■

May, 1978

French Horn Players, Arise!

Guy Kinney

To beginning French horn students in the fifth or sixth grade, the instrument often feels strange and cumbersome. Students sometimes place the horn on their legs in such a way that they must strain their neck upwards to reach the mouthpiece, or they lay the horn down on their laps making the lead pipe and mouthpiece almost vertical, then try to bend down to meet it, creating the worst possible posture. A natural cure for this problem is to have the child stand while playing. If the right hand is held flat on the inside top of the bell (palm up) and the left hand placed on the keys, the student should be able to stand with good posture and be in a comfortable position. The mouthpiece will thus "come to him" in a more natural manner.

In solo playing there is no reason why the student cannot stand while playing. It looks better, especially on stage with band or orchestra accompaniment, and it also allows for more freedom of movement. Following are some suggested ways to make the horn feel and sound more natural to the player who is used to being seated: remember that the right hand must support most of the weight of the instrument; do not try to lift the horn with the left hand. The left hand and arm should remain in a fairly relaxed state with the forearm at an angle going downward from the horn naturally. Do not hold the left arm out parallel to the floor as I have seen it done in marching bands. This may look sharp but does not insure a natural relaxed manner in which to perform. The thumb and fingers must control and manipulate the valve keys without muscle strain. This can be attained best if the right arm supports most of the weight of the horn.

Cup the right hand in a manner similar to that used when sitting except that the right hand should be held vertically with the fingers parallel to the floor. The right thumb and index finger should be brought side by side, helping to create a level spot on which to rest the inside top of the bell.

In most cases the player will wish to cup the hand a bit more while standing than when sitting and put it a little further into the bell. This will compensate for the brighter sound the horn will produce as a result of less body or arm being in the way to absorb some of the partials. If the right hand is cupped at an angle closer to the throat of the bell, the tone will darken. Here is where the players' tonal consideration and discretion will need to be used in order to achieve the right sound for him. Remember that intonation will change slightly when standing. Hence, the sharper sound can be compensated for by cupping the hand more, making the tone flatter. It is usually not necessary to adjust the tuning slide differently than when seated but remember to tune while standing as it may feel resonantly different to the player.

Each player will also have to decide how far out from the body the bell will be. Marching band students often play with the bell parallel to the ground. However, they are not always overly concerned with tonal quality in 35-degree weather on a muddy field. Yet I have seen a film of Dennis Brain (noted British horn player) performing the Beethoven Horn Sonata in which the horn is held out and up, parallel to the floor. Some players will want to rest the bell on the side of their body. I prefer to hold it four to six inches away from my side. My main consideration is the size, weight, and balance of my particular instrument.

Standing while soloing on the horn is impressive visually. It gives the appearance of control and confidence. It can help in tone projection, body movement, and flexibility in seeing the conductor. I strongly recommend it for teaching beginners and correcting posture problems. Remember, if a player is going to stand during a solo, there must be a great deal of practice in this position in order to make it feel natural. It is worth the effort in the freedom it gives the player. ■

May, 1978

Teaching Legato Tonguing to the Trombone Student

Michael K. Mathews

One of the most difficult problems faced by trombone teachers in dealing with the student trombonist is getting him to play in a correct legato style. Either the student will make a glissando out of every slur that the instrument won't perform for him or he will tongue every note, regardless of the indicated articulation. In either case, if he has been told anything in his previous class lessons about playing legato, it has most likely been to use a "du" tongue.

The concept of a "du" tongue is a correct one but many students seem unable to understand it. This is probably because the letter D, when used at the beginning of a word (i.e. du), has the same explosive pop as the letter T. Once we stop using the vocal chords, as for example when playing the trombone, there is practically no difference between D and T. What is meant by the "doo" tongue, and what is seldom explained, is the way the letter D is most often pronounced by English-speaking Americans when it appears in the middle of a word (e.g. "ladder").

Another way of looking at legato tonguing is that the tongue should make precisely the same motion as it does when saying the letter R as it is pronounced in Spanish. Most of us immediately think of the trilled R, that buzz saw effect so often associated with some trained singers. In conversational Spanish, however, the native speaker most often used what is referred to as a "single tap R." This single tap R is the tongue stroke that the trombonist needs for legato playing.

Unfortunately, that sound is not used in English and those few students who happen to speak some Spanish are often not adept at pronunciation. Some time ago, I reasoned that Spanish teachers must have a means of teaching the single tap R. A short conversation with a high school Spanish teacher produced the seed for the following system which I have used for a number of years. I have found this method to be successful in teaching legato tonguing to individuals and even to the whole brass section of a band.

Print the phrase "Pot of Tea" on a piece of paper. Have the student read the phrase aloud. It will probably come out something like "Pot uh Tea." What we are looking for here, however, is not the F in of, but the T as it is usually pronounced at the end of "Pot." The teacher will discover that the student slurs over that T with a sound exactly the same as the Spanish single tap R. Point out to the student his pronunciation of that particular letter, then have him say just the first two syllables, "Pot uh." Merely change this to "Tot uh" and you have the articulation for two notes, the first one tongued and the second one slurred.

The next step is to apply this articulation to the instrument. It usually works best to begin with two quarter notes of the same pitch — F3 seems to do quite well. Tell the student to pronounce the same sounds (without vocalizing them, of course) while playing those two notes. Only rarely will a student be unable to do this on the first attempt. Those few who are not immediately successful will need only two or three more tries to get the feel of the legato tongue.

Later, increase the exercise to four or five notes, saying "Tot-uh-tuh-tuh..." Then repeat this larger group on different pitches.

The young trombonist is now ready to slur between notes of different pitches. Usually two quarter notes a half step apart are sufficient for the first attempt (e.g. E3 to F3). Once this is working satisfactorily, proceed to groups of three and four chromatic pitches (e.g. E3-F3-E3-F3 or D3-Eb3-E3-F3). By this time the student should be able to play a legato scale. From then on, the sky's the limit.

The younger students will probably need to be reminded frequently to use the "pot uh tea" tongue but at least they will *know* how to play legato on the trombone. The entire teaching process takes a little over five minutes and can save literally hours of trial and tribulation in trying to get the neophyte trombonist to learn the all-important legato tongue. ∎

Research Update: Brass Performance

Harold S. Kacanek

This review provides a synopsis of research on brass performance techniques and related physical factors. Much of this research has taken place since the refinement of x-ray, electromyographic (electrical measurements of muscular action), and photographic devices. Many variables which heretofore could not be observed are now observable and measurable. Incorporating observable scientific fact into existing methodologies helps close the gap that has long existed between research results and applied use.

Some of the research cited here touches only briefly on the critical questions it attempts to explore. Some of it needs replication in order to establish reliability and some of the "facts" clearly challenge traditional beliefs.

The Embouchure

The embouchure is the critical link between mechanism and performer. Isley (1972) provides physiological evidence for a single embouchure mode which is most efficient for all brass players, on all brass instruments. Certainly the search to achieve an efficient embouchure has been the single most common denominator among brass performers. This search accounts for the great concentration of studies which focus on the problem.

Gibson (1973) observed that the quantity of upper lip which remained inside the mouthpiece decreased significantly from low to extreme high range. He also noticed a change in direction of the air flow between these ranges but no changes in trumpet position (angulation). All his observations were of professional trumpeters. However, his main observational device was a trumpet ring which, according to Martin (1942), makes these findings suspect.

Amstutz's (1970) findings regarding angulation conflict with Gibson's. His observations of "25 advanced trumpeters" revealed that the angle of instrument inclination increased as pitch ascended, and decreased as pitch descended.

In an effort to describe the action of both lips during trumpet performance, Henderson (1942) provides evidence for a "single-reed" theory. His experiments lead him to conclude that the upper lip "vibrates as a single reed against a relatively fixed body."

Using high speed photography (up to 900 frames per second) and a transparent mouthpiece, Leno (1970) observed that a definite relationship exists between the frequency of lip vibration and the pitch produced on trombone. Although he does not embrace a "double-reed" theory of lip vibration, he notes that both lips vibrate at the same frequency during performance and at the frequency of the pitch produced. Perhaps it is possible that one lip influences the other to vibrate sympathetically, the result of periodic lip closure.

Leno (1970) defines two types of players: "upstream" players who direct the air stream above the mouthpiece throat and "downstream" players who direct the air below the mouthpiece throat. In both types of players, unequal lip activity is present, the lower lips of the upstream subjects and the upper lips of the downstream subjects being the more active. He also observed that changes in pitch and/or volume involve both a change in aperture width and height. That is, the entire aperture gets larger as pitch descends and/or as volume increases.

Isley (1972), White (1972), and White and Basmajian (1974) did monumental electromyographic studies of four crucial muscles related to embouchure. Their method of observation and large sample provide one of the finest models of scientific research in this field.

Observed were the effects of register, intensity, and subjects' proficiency level on the facial muscles. Each study used indwelling fine-wire electrodes, developed by Basmajian (1967), which are sensitive to the electronic impulses emitted by muscle activity.

Their findings revealed that beginning and advanced trumpeters differ significantly in the amount of muscle activity required for various aspects of performance. Advanced trumpeters produce greater muscle activity in the muscles out-of-the-lips than those muscles directly associated with the upper and lower lips, while beginning trumpeters show no difference in the amount of use of these muscles. Beginning trumpeters show more muscle activity in the upper lip than the lower while advanced trumpeters show equal amounts of activity in both lips. This finding, according to White, et al. (1974), gives some support to a theory originally forwarded by Steven (1971) that students should attempt to concentrate more muscle activity in the lower lip.

Range

Amstutz (1970) used videofluorographic techniques to observe the action of the embouchure. Two prevailing approaches to range were observed. Where subjects did not use a lower lip pivot system, extreme overall mouthpiece pressure was necessary to facilitate performance. This conclusion seems to support Isley (1972) who recommends that mouthpiece pressure be greatest near the midline of each lip with a slightly greater distribution to the bottom lip.

Also observed (Nichols and Hanson, 1971) among professional trumpeters has been a similarity in the "dimpling" action of the modioli (the basic meeting point of embouchure musculature just slightly next to the corners of the mouth). The modioli either remain in their natural resting place horizontally or are moved towards the center (Isley, 1972).

Evidence provided by Amstutz (1970) and Nichols, et al. (1971), seems to indicate that the back of the tongue is a critical factor in extending brass range. The back of the tongue arches as the pitch ascends, creating a smaller aperture between the tongue and the palate. The motion is reversed as pitch descends. In slurring past or skipping over a partial in a harmonic series, significantly greater use of the tongue arch is required.

Embouchure fatigue

A physiological understanding of the lips' function during performance is of value in dealing with lip fatigue. Briggs (1969) states that when an airtight seal is formed between the mouthpiece and lips, the pressure from the rim causes a lack of oxygen in the lips during performance. The result is embouchure fatigue.

Most pedagogical literature recommends frequent rests during practice which allow the restoration of oxygenated blood to the embouchure.

Embouchure abnormalities

Richtmeyer (1966) indicates that the most frequent embouchure abnormalities are due to excessive mouthpiece pressure and stretching the lip corners back in an extreme smile. According to Richtmeyer's study and survey, improper teaching methods were more responsible for abnormalities than were physical malformations. Teachers of instrumental music often do not have accurate scientific information about the brass player's embouchure.

Bjurstrom (1972) observed that a large number of beginning brass players gave little thought to the possible effect that their dental abnormalities might have on their choice of instrument. This kind of disregard is often responsible for a great deal of physical discomfort (Porter, 1976). These uncomfortable playing conditions might obviously be responsible for a variety of negative musical experiences. Bjurstrom concludes that prospective brass students would benefit if there were better communication between parents, dentists, and instructors regarding proper instrument choice.

The Role of the Diaphragm

"The diaphragm is a dome-shaped muscle, roughly similar to the plane of an umbrella, the outer edge of which is attached to the bottom of the rib cage" (Smith, 1966, p. 87). Control of the diaphragm is frequently referred to as an important factor in breathing properly (Bellamah, 1976, p. 24). Berger and Hoshiko (1964) found little evidence of diaphragmatic action in tone production but considered their findings inconclusive because of the difficult nature of knowing exactly what is being measured with surface electrodes in electromyographic studies (Basmajian, 1972, p. 603). Two cinefluorographic studies (Smith, 1966 and Nichols and Hanson, 1971) indicate that virtually no control is exercised by the diaphragm in sound production on any wind instrument. Smith (1966) reports that when the diaphragm functions it moves downward, pulling the floor of the lungs with it, creating a vacuum that causes the lungs to expand and fill with air. It appears that the action of the diaphragm is by itself not controllable because it relaxes during expiration. Therefore the phrase "support from the diaphragm" might be better stated "support from the hips or intercostal or pelvic muscles." At least it is known that the contraction of the pelvic muscles gives support to the air stream.

The Larynx or Glottis

The role of the larynx has received considerably less attention in brass research than the breathing mechanism and the embouchure. Indeed some brass specialists appear to believe that the larynx plays no part in performance; others disagree. It is in the larynx that the first point of resistance to the breath can occur. Carter (1966) observed the function of the glottis while brass performers played soft and loud notes in the low and high registers. Although pitch seemed to have no effect on the glottis, a highly significant variation was noticed regarding dynamics: the glottis showed a smaller opening for soft tones than for louder ones.

One study (Nichols and Hanson, 1971) states the "control movements of the true vocal cord are the most important mechanisms for the production of sound and sound interruption in trumpet playing." The evidence of laryngeal muscles' role in the control of staccato sound production has also been investigated by Hanson (1967).

The Pharynx or Throat

Research regarding the pharynx has focused on the changes in its dimensions which occur from low to high registers. Meidt (1967) notes that the pharyngeal dimensions of French horn players are smaller for high pitched notes than for low and that the reverse was true for trumpet players. Frohrip (1973) and DeYoung (1975) report conflicting results with trombone subjects.

References

The following reference list contains full bibliographical information on the research cited in this article:

Amstutz, Allan Keith. "A Videofluorographic Study of the Teeth Aperture, Instrument Pivot and Tongue Arch and their Influence on Trumpet Performance." Unpublished Doctoral dissertation, University of Oklahoma, 1970.

_____. "The Jaw-thrust — Some Considerations," NACWPI Journal, 24:38, No. 2, 1975-1976.

Basmajian, J.V. "Electromyography Comes of Age," Science, Vol. 176, 1972, pp. 603-609.

_____. Muscles Alive, Their Functions Revealed by Electromyography, 2nd ed., Williams and Wilkins, 1967.

_____; and Stecko, G.A. "A New Bipolar Indwelling Electrode for Electromyography." Journal of Applied Physiology, Vol. 17, (1962), p. 849.

Bellamah, L.J. A Survey of Modern Brass Teaching Philosophies, Southern Music Company, 1976.

Berger, K.W. "Respiratory and Articulatory Factors in Wind Instrument Performance," Journal of Applied Physiology, Vol. 20, No. 6, (1965), pp. 1217-1221.

_____; and Hoshiko, M.S. "Respiratory Muscle Action of Trumpet Players," The Instrumentalist, October, 1964, p. 91.

Bjurstrom, N. "Orthodontic Treatment as a Factor in the Selection and Performance of Brass Musical Instruments." Unpublished Doctoral dissertation, University of Iowa, 1972.

Briggs, G.B. "Electrophysiological Examination of Labial Function in College-age Trumpet Performers." Unpublished Doctoral dissertation, University of Oklahoma, 1969.

Carter, W. "The Role of the Glottis in Brass Playing," The Instrumentalist, December, 1966, p.75.

DeYoung, D.D. "A Videofluorographic Analysis of the Pharyngeal Opening During Performance of Selected Exercises for Trombone." Unpublished Doctoral dissertation, University of Minnesota, 1975.

Duerksen, G.L. Teaching Instrumental Music, MENC, 1972.

Farkas, P. The Art of Brass Playing. Wind Music, Incorporated, 1962.

Frohrip, K.R. "A Videofluorographic Analysis of Certain Physiological Factors Involved in Performance of Selected Exercises for Trombone." Unpublished Doctoral dissertation, University of Minnesota, 1972.

Gibson, D.R. "A Photographic Study of 12 Professional Trumpet Embouchures While Playing from the Low to the Extreme Upper Register." Unpublished Doctoral dissertation, University of Minnesota, 1973.

Hanson, Fay S. "Control of Staccato Sound Production by Laryngeal Muscles," Journal of Band Research, Vol. 4, No. 1, pp. 61-64, 1967.

Haynie, J.J. "A Videofluorographic Presentation of the Physiological Phenomena of Influencing Trumpet Performance." Denton, Texas: School of Music, North Texas State University, 1967.

Henderson, H.W. "An Experimental Study of Trumpet Embouchure, *Journal of the Acoustical Society of America.*, Vol. 13, July 1942, pp. 58-64.

Hiigel, L.E. "The Relationship of Syllables to Pitch and Tonguing in Brass Instrument Playing." Unpublished Doctoral dissertation, University of California, 1967.

Isley, C.L. "A Theory of Brasswind Embouchure Based Upon Facial Anatomy Electromyographic Kinesiology, and Brasswind Embouchure Pedagogy." Unpublished Doctoral dissertation, University of Arizona, 1970.

_____. "Lip Vibration Characteristics of the Trombone Embouchure in Performance, *"The Instrumentalist,* April, 1971, p. 56.

Martin, D.W. "Lip Vibrations in a Cornet Mouthpiece," *Journal of the Acoustical Society of America,* Vol. 13, January 1942, pp.305-308.

Meidt, J.A. "A Cinefluorographic Investigation of Oral Adjustments for Various Aspects of Brass Instrument Perfor-

mance." Unpublished Doctoral dissertation, University of Iowa, 1967.

Merriman, L.C. "A Study to Explore the Possible Uses of X-Ray Motion Picture Photography for the Inprovement of Brass Instrument Teaching." USDHEW Rep. No. BR-6-8322, United States Government Printing Office, 1967.

_____; and Meidt, J.A. "A Cinefluorographic Investigation of Brass Instrument Performance," *Journal of Research in Music Education*, Vol. 16, No. 1, pp. 31-38, 1968.

Nichols, R.L.; and Others. "The Improvement of Brass Instrument Teaching Through the Use of a Profile of the Physical Aspects Involved." USDHEW Rep. No. BR-O-H-008, United States Government Printing Office, 1971.

Porter, M.M. *The Embouchure.* Boosey and Hawkes, 1976.

Richtmeyer, L.C. "A Definitive Analysis of Brass Embouchure Abnormalities Including Recommended Remedial Techniques." Unpublished Doctoral dissertation, Michigan State University, 1966.

Smith, Douglas. "The Diaphragm: Teacher's Pedagogical Pet," *The Instrumen-*

talist. March, 1966, p. 87.

Stevens, R. *Embouchure Self-Analysis and the Stevens-Costello Triple C Embouchure Technique (Complete).* The Stevens-Costello Embouchure Clinic, 1971.

Taylor, R.B. "A Study of the Concepts of Breathing as Presented in Literature Dealing with Tone Production for Orchestra Brasswind Instruments." Unpublished Doctoral dissertation, Columbia University, 1968.

Tetzlaff, D. "The Transparent Man — A Videofluorographic Presentation of the Physiological Phenomena Influencing Trumpet Performance," *The Instrumentalist,* March 1969, pp. 81-82.

Weast, R.D. "A Stroboscopic Analysis of Lip Function," *The Instrumentalist:* June, 1963, p. 44.

White, E.R. "Electromyographic Potentials of Selected Facial Muscles and Labial Mouthpiece Pressure Measurements in the Embouchure of Trumpet Players." Unpublished Doctoral dissertation, Columbia University, 1972.

_____; and Basmajian, J.V. "Electromyographic Analysis of Embouchure Muscle Function in Trumpet Playing," *Journal of Research in Music Education,* Vol. 22, No. 4, pp. 292-304, 1974. ∎

August, 1978

Playing the Horn
in a Woodwind Quintet:
Advice for Young Performers

William Brophy

An adjudicator at a recent high school solo and ensemble contest remarked to me, "What is it with horn players in woodwind quintets? They always overpower the other instruments." In many cases this is a valid criticism.

A horn player in a woodwind quintet must learn an entirely different concept of dynamics. In a band the horns are usually badly outnumbered by the other brasses, and the horn section is often asked to give more and more sound. Consequently younger players seldom play more softly than a healthy mezzo-forte. Unless someone instructs the performer otherwise he will tend to play too loudly in a woodwind quintet.

Generally speaking, woodwinds are simply not capable of the same level of forte and fortissimo as

brasses. There are exceptions of course; for example, the flute and clarinet in their upper registers at a *ff* have a good deal of power. However, the woodwinds often use the lower dynamic levels much more effectively than the young horn player.

As a consequence, the horn player needs to adjust all dynamic markings downward. For example, a tutti section marked *ff* should perhaps be played no more loudly than *mf*. Obviously the young horn player must learn a piano and pianissimo that are rarely, if ever, needed in band playing. In tutti sections and especially in accompaniment passages the horn player needs a true woodwind *mp, p,* and *pp* in order to blend with the woodwind sound. What we're looking for is good balance in the quintet.

In solo passages marked *mf, f,* or *ff,* it would be possible of course to

play these dynamics at the normal level used in large ensembles. However, there is the danger that they will sound too loud in comparison to the general dynamic level established for the entire piece. In this case the player must make a decision based on musical considerations. The important horn part in the second movement of Leclair's *Minuet and Hunting Scene,* for example, can be very effectively played at *ff* even with a "cuivré" (brassy) sound to simulate the hunting horn. On the other hand a solo passage in a Reicha quintet marked *ff* might sound absurd if played too loudly. Musical taste should be the determining factor.

Tone Quality and
Right-Hand Position

Most young horn players, who

are primarily band musicians, learn to play with a large, open tone that projects and blends with the other brasses. Because this kind of sound simply does not fit in a woodwind quintet, the young player must learn a new concept of tone quality. The best way to become familiar with a good horn sound in a woodwind quintet is to listen to live performances/recordings of fine horn players in established professional quintets.

Right-hand position must be considered in a discussion of tone quality. In band playing the wide-open hand position with the hand fairly well out of the bell may be perfectly satisfactory. In the quintet the hand position needs to be more closed and/or deeper in the bell. This will necessitate changing the tuning of the horn. The more closed the hand position or the deeper the hand goes into the bell, the more the slide must be pushed in. This slight change of hand position helps to produce a tone quality which blends best with woodwinds.

The accompanying photographs illustrate several hand positions. Figure 1 is the hand position which might work well in band, and figure 2 is the more traditional hand position for orchestral playing. Figures 3 and 4 show two alternatives for quintet work: figure 3 is more closed while figure 4 is a little more open, but the hand is narrowed so that it goes deeper into the bell.

Intonation

Chamber music playing requires more careful attention to intonation than does large group performance. In the band the use of multiple players on a part and the many doublings tend to average out minor discrepancies of pitch. In the woodwind quintet this does not happen; there is no place for the player to hide.

As mentioned earlier, the change in hand position necessary for quintet playing will require re-tuning the horn. The main, F horn slide and B♭ slide (if the instrument is so constructed) will have to be moved in a bit farther. Even the valve slides may have to be readjusted. In other words the horn will have to be tuned a littler sharper. This does not necessarily insure good intonation because the ear must be the final guide. However, it is a good way to begin.

No implication is intended that playing sharp is somehow a lesser sin than playing flat. The arguments for tuning the horn a little sharp then bringing it down to pitch with the right hand (and probably a slight relaxation of the embouchure) are based on a very practical consideration: once mastered it is by far the easiest way to play in tune.

Accuracy and Articulation

Because woodwind quintet playing is so much more exposed than large ensemble playing, accuracy becomes even more important. A slight "blurp" in the attack might not be noticed in the anonymity of the band or in the back row of the orchestra but becomes painfully obvious in the quintet. Therefore the horn player should practice for accuracy especially on initial attacks

and most especially at the softer dynamic levels.

It is also necessary to develop the ability to play a really short staccato. Woodwind players often employ a shorter staccato than brass players. The horn tone tends to ring a little longer after the release as a direct result of the horn bell being aimed toward the back wall of the room and picking up more resonance than the other instruments. In certain passages it is sometimes difficult to resist the temptation to "tut" staccato notes, depending on the echo created by the room to give the desired taper to the release. In general it is wise to avoid the "tut" sound if at all possible because it may create an unmusical effect. A player should determine the type of release he will use based on his musical sense and the acoustical properties of the room.

Figure 1

Figure 3

Figure 2

Figure 4

There are many instances in which the horn entrance should not be heard so much as felt. In this case the soft attack, a true legato (soft "d") start to the tone can be useful. This ability is especially important in an initial entrance in the middle of a tutti legato passage.

At the opposite end of the spectrum is the reinforced attack. This includes accents of all types, sforzandos, and forte-piano entrances. The woodwinds are not innately as capable of as much strength in an attack as the horn. Therefore this type of attack must be modified by the young player.

One final word of caution regarding all entrances. The tendency to be late on entrances may occur in all playing, but it is especially noticeable in the quintet. Careful listening and awareness of the rhythmic pulse of the music are absolute necessities for exact entrances.

Vibrato

Vibrato on the horn is still a controversial subject although it is becoming more common in the United States, perhaps the last bastion of the non-vibrato sound. Many of the fine European soloists use vibrato very tastefully. John Barrows, one of America's finest chamber music horn players, used a noticeable vibrato which seemed entirely appropriate in the quintet.

Whether the high school horn player should attempt to use vibrato is a difficult decision. Vibrato can be dangerous because it can easily become a habit; certainly the player does not want to lose the ability to play a straight tone. It is tempting to use some vibrato occasionally in a quintet especially when the other instruments (with the possible exception of the clarinet) are vibrating. Its use seems most appropriate in solo passages or duets with the flute, oboe, or bassoon.

The vibrato can be accomplished in a number of different ways. A player can use the lip and/or lower jaw; he can produce the sound with his right hand in the bell; or the vibrato can be produced in the wind stream, the so-called diaphragm vibrato. This last technique is perhaps more dangerous than the others because it is difficult to stop and start the vibrato as the occasion demands.

Choice of Instrument and Mouthpiece

If there is a choice of equipment I would vote for moderation in all things. Avoid the big horns which blow so freely that a true *p* and *pp* are difficult to achieve especially by the young player.

The mouthpiece is as important as the choice of horn, and it is easier and cheaper to change mouthpieces than it is to change horns. Try to avoid the overly large, deep mouthpiece with a large bore or throat. These mouthpieces produce a large quantity of sound, but the young player rarely has the embouchure and breathing apparatus sufficiently developed to control the tone, pitch, and softer dynamics.

I am not implying that a horn player should change instruments or mouthpieces in order to play in a quintet. On the contrary, a moderately sized horn and mouthpiece can work equally well in band, orchestra, solo playing, and chamber music. ∎

September, 1978

Trills and Other Frills in Brass Literature

Michael Brand

"Graces are indispensable, but if ill-chosen they may do much harm."
— *Carl Philip Emanuel Bach*

Baroque ornamentation is the result of ages of improvisation. Composers of the era traditionally omitted ornament signs or notated very few in their music, relying instead on the performer's creativity and technical facility to spontaneously complete the piece in concert.

Baroque musicians improvised freely, but modern players often require direction in interpreting ornaments. I have selected passages from brass literature to demonstrate possible translation of five commonly-used ornaments: trills, turns, mordents, appoggiaturas, and passing tones. Each example shows the original music plus my own suggested written-out version of the ornaments.

Trills

Common Baroque practice was to begin the trill on the strong beat with the upper or dissonant note resolving to the consonant harmony. From the early 17th century to the end of the 18th century the trill was usually associated with the cadence, but in the very late 18th century it was also used freely at other positions.

Examples 1 and 2 show cadential trills. As you can see, the trill in Example 2 is shorter than that in the first example. The length of a trill depends on the rhythmic value of the note marked "tr" as well as on the tempo marking of the composition. In this case both examples are to be played at approximately the same speed with the trill in Example 1 lasting longer because it is marked over a ♩ rather than over a ♪. Both examples are from Purcell's *Sonata* for trumpet, strings, and continuo. (Ed. Roger Voisin. International

Music Co., N.Y. 1962).

Example 1.

As written:

Ornamented:

Example 2.

As written:

Ornamented:

Non-cadential trills can include a turn built into the end of the trill. Jeremiah Clarke's "Trumpet Voluntary" (Example 3) contains a noncadential (*) followed by a cadential (**) trill.

Example 3. Jeremiah Clarke. From *Suite in D Major* for trumpet, 2 oboes, bassoon, strings, and continuo. Musica Rara, London 1971.

As written:

Ornamented: (with turn)

Turns

The turn (∿) consists of four or five notes revolving around the written note in a specific way. The turn begins on the note above the one written, returns to the given note, then to the note below, and ends on the written note. As shown below, the turn looks similar to the closing of a trill.

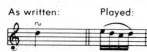

As written: Played:

During the 17th and 18th centuries it was commonly known as a short trill. The turn can last an entire beat (Example 4) or be performed on part of the beat (Example 5).

Example 4. C.F. Handel. From *Suite in D Major* for trumpet, strings, and con-

tinuo. Ed. Edward Tarr. Musica Rara, London 1969.

As written:

Ornamented:

Example 5. Giovanni Bonaventura Viviani. From *Sonata Prima Per Trombetta Sola* (Allegro-4th movement). Musica Rara, London 1969.

As written:

Ornamented:

Mordents

The mordent is performed by alternating the written note with the diatonic note below it. This ornament begins on the pulse and is indicated by either ∿ or ⚹ . The performer may choose either a single or a double alternation depending on the duration of the note. If he chooses two mordents in a row, a single should be followed by a double. A single mordent is shown below.

Example 6. G.P. Telemann. From *Twelve Heroic Marches* ("La Grace") for trumpet and organ. Ed. Gerard Billaudot. Theodore Presser, Bryn Mawr (agents) 1971.

As written:

Allegro

Ornamented:

Appoggiaturas

An appoggiatura is an accented dissonant note occurring at the interval of a second above or below the given harmonic note. The appoggiatura is played on the beat, lasting one-half as long as the original note unless the original note is dotted, in which case the appoggiatura lasts two-thirds the length of the unit (note plus dot).

Example 7. G.F. Handel. "Let the Bright Seraphim" from *Samson*, for trumpet,

soprano, strings, and continuo. Ed. Gerald Endsley. Tromba Publications, Denver 1973.

As written:

Ornamented:

Passing Tones

Passing tones are non-chordal tones which function melodically rather than harmonically. They diatonically tie together various consecutive intervals, turning the open intervals into scale passages.

Example 8. G.F. Handel. "Let the Bright Seraphim" from *Samson*, for trumpet, soprano, strings, and continuo. Ed. Gerald Endsley, Tromba Publications, Denver 1973.

As written:

Ornamented:

When using passing tones the performer must keep in mind the range and limitations of his own instrument as well as the original concept of the piece which could be spoiled by an overindulgence in ornamentation. In Example 9 the original music of Scheidt can be compared to three possible ornamentation techniques I have marked (a), (b), and (c).

Example 9. Samuel Scheidt. From *Canzona Bergamasca* for 2 trumpets, horn, trombone, and tuba. Ed. Conrad deJong. Ensemble Publications, Buffalo 1966.

As written:

Ornamented:

(a)

(b)

(c)

My suggestions for ornamentation

in these pieces are in accordance with common Baroque practices. Such improvisation is basic to performing Baroque music. Each player may choose to embellish in a different way. Learn the tools of ornamentation, then apply them according to your own musical taste. ∎

October, 1978

Reducing Pressure in the Trombone Embouchure

Donald L. Banschbach

The so-called "non-pressure embouchure theory," espoused by many teachers and performers is really a misnomer. To completely eliminate pressure would break the seal between the lips and the mouthpiece and silence the tone. But to exaggerate the pressure inhibits blood flow to the embouchure muscles and results in muscle fatigue. Players who complain of paralyzed lips have repeatedly abused their embouchures by pressing too tightly against the instrument's mouthpiece. Continual restriction of blood flow breaks down the muscles and in some cases even destroys them. The end result is muscle fiber which no longer contracts to produce the desired tone.

Pressure must be considered on a relative basis: it can be minimized but not eliminated. A player's awareness of muscle contraction and relaxation is vital to good embouchure development. He can achieve this awareness through 1) an understanding of the embouchure muscles themselves, 2) a relaxed way of holding the instrument, and 3) by practicing exercises using slurs.

Anatomically, the trombone embouchure may be defined as the muscles that surround the mouth and contract to close the lips. The lips are compressed against the teeth, and the lower lip is pressed against the upper lip. This contraction involves four sets of muscle fibers: 1) *obiscularis oris*, which act to close the lips, 2) *compressor labii*, which compress the lips against the teeth, 3) *incisivus superior and inferior*, which draw in the corners of the mouth, and 4) the *mentalis*, a triangular muscle in the chin which elevates the chin and lower lip. Pronouncing the letter "m" gives the feeling of the muscle action involved in forming the embouchure. A simple way to visualize the embouchure muscles is to imagine a central oval of heavy muscle fibers with many guide lines radiating outward from the oval. The guide lines contract to stabilize the central oval which in turn contracts to produce the desired tone.

Pitch is controlled by the contraction and relaxation of these muscles and by the proper placement of the mouthpiece on the lips. I recommend that horizontal placement be at the center of the mouth with vertical placement more toward the upper than the lower lip, moving the chin slightly upward to elevate the lower lip and push it tightly against the upper lip.

One of the best-known pedagogical techniques to demonstrate non-pressure playing is the practice of hanging a trumpet from the ceiling by strings, allowing the instrument to swing freely. The player then walks up to the instrument with his hands held behind his back and attemps to blow the horn. Naturally, it is not possible to press against the mouthpiece without also moving the instrument.

Trombonists may experiment with reduced pressure by using one of several hand positions for practicing. (These positions are not intended for regular playing.) I call the first of these positions the "left-hand 'L.'" The L is formed by the wide-open palm and thumb of the left hand. The instrument is supported on the heel of the hands and the bell tube is rested against the extended fingers. An alternate position is to rest the instrument in the left-hand thumb joint and use the extended fingers to balance the bell.

A suggested position for the right hand is one in which the slide rests on the index finger. If the slide is in good condition, it can be moved easily from one position to another by pushing or pulling the brace. Each teacher should help his students adjust their hand positions so that the trombone is held properly for purposes of pressure adjustment. All teachers are aware of the beginning student's frustrations in becoming familiar with his instrument. It is therefore advisable to wait until the student has played for a few months before starting pressure-awareness exercises. A good rule is to wait until the student can slur the interval of a fourth (say, F to B♭) in first position.

The purpose of pressure exercises is to make the player conscious of the muscle action necessary to produce tone with minimal pressure. In preparation, the player should warm up for ten to fifteen minutes to avoid practicing with a cold lip. Studies similar to those found in the *Cimera-Hovey Method* can be used. When the student can perform exercises built on the interval of a fourth, he can then progress to slurred sixths. Finally, he should practice slurring octave intervals, beginning on B♭2 and progressing chromatically upward as high as he is capable of playing with minimum pressure. Slurring broken chords and arpeggios will also increase one's flexibility.

The effects of such exercises should be carried over and applied to etudes, solos, and group perform-ances. The trombone player who re-

duces pressure has the potential for greater muscle endurance and the

prospect for a longer life of produc-tive performance. ∎

November, 1978

Accuracy for the Horn Player

Carlyle Manous

One of the most frustrating prob-lems for the beginning horn player is accuracy, the ability to produce a specific pitch in tune the very first time. The player must not only "hear" the pitch before playing it, but he must also feel it with the embouchure. At a given dynamic level there is a specific embouchure setting for every pitch. The following exercise will demonstrate the dis-crete differences in embouchure for each pitch. The four parts (a-d) of the exercise should be played slowly at first and then at increasing tempos until the limit of one's ability is reached. Several dynamic levels should be used, and the physical sensations involved in the embou-chure changes should be noted. (Play on an F horn, alternating open and first valves, and take the mouthpiece from the lips at each ∥ mark in Example 1.)

Example 1

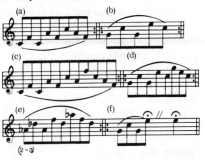

To find the best possible embou-chure setting for each pitch, begin with C5 and memorize the physical sensation of the setting and play the pitch squarely and accurately. Re-peat on each pitch as necessary (see Example 2):

Example 2

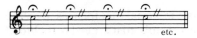

When this can be done success-fully go on to Exercise 3. Be sure that each pitch is centered and played clearly; add the settings for each new pitch to your "memory file."

Example 3

Next, try the pitches in a different context (Example 4) and see if each can be put in its memorized slot. Stop at random and hold a pitch; check and see if it is accurate. Then play the pitch again and see if the same embouchure setting is used as when the pitch was played in context (see Example 4). Play Examples 4(a), (c), and (e) on the B♭ horn [(a) and (c) through descending com-binations, (e) through ascending combinations.]

Example 4

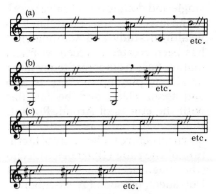

Exercise 5 adds two more prob-lems: using the tongue, and catching a quick breath between pitches. In both cases be sure that these added dimensions do not change the setting

of the embouchure. Try to do each line without missing a pitch.

Example 5

Check your embouchure memory in Example 6 by doing (a) and (b) with as short a breath as possible, thus giving less time to set the em-bouchure. For (c) flex the lips each time the mouthpiece is taken away in order to erase the embouchure setting. See how many pitches can be played in succession without a mistake.

Example 6

One must work actively on the memory part of this concept. Going through the exercises will be bene-ficial but the mind must work with the muscles to refine the memory sensations of each pitch. Since most people need to warm up anyway, these exercises provide a good core for a warm-up routine; in addition they provide the added bonus of lip conditioning. ∎

Basic Literature
for
Bass Trombone Study

Thomas Everett

Twenty years ago it was rare to see a bass trombone in public school music groups, and few players majored in bass trombone in college. Today, bass trombones are quite common in public schools and in colleges, and players are flooding the limited professional field. Manufacturers are producing quality instruments with a variety of bore and bell sizes. Such is the demand that they can hardly keep up with orders.

The bass trombone has an identifiable sonority of its own that can best be achieved by providing the student with a concept of sound to imitate. There are some excellent recorded examples of the bass trombone sound available. Equally as important, the teacher must provide study and performance literature that gives the student practice in single and double rotor (valve) work in the lower register. Fortunately, a wealth of study and solo material has been created in recent years. A mature bass trombonist today must be able to play up to C5, read alto and tenor clefs, and be familiar with the etudes of Arban, Rochut, Blazhevich (both as written and down an octave). The study of literature of the tuba (Blazhevich), cello (the magnificent Bach Suites and Dotzauer), bassoon (Weissenborn), voice, (Schubert leider are excellent for phrasing and legato), trumpet (Verne Reynolds contemporary studies), and trombone music is an absolute necessity to be a complete technician and musician. Added to this must be a core of bass trombone study material designed to develop the interpretive skills needed in contemporary bass trombone performance. Below is a selected list of basic material that focuses in on the bass trombonist's needs. Included are a few examples of outstanding solo literature that incorporate some of the ranges, techniques, and skills developed at that level. The material listed is nowhere near all that is available, but it represents a valuable sampling for a basic music library.

Elementary Level

There is very little quality literature for the bass trombone at the elementary level. Because of the size and weight of the bass trombone and the need to develop good listening and technical habits, students should start on a tenor trombone. As a young student strengthens his embouchure the teacher might introduce a slightly larger mouthpiece to help prepare the student for the bass trombone mouthpiece (but at all times the mouthpiece must fit the equipment). Development of a set embouchure, a relaxed, centered open sound, and accurate intonation, ear development through improvisation (playing simple folk-like tunes in various keys by ear), slide coordination and basic rhythmic and reading concepts are the goals that a young trombonist can master by junior high school. If students are not proficient in all the above areas they are not good candidates for the bass trombone. Available elementary trombone method/study texts fulfill the needs of the beginning trombonist.

Junior High Level

At the junior high or intermediate level a student may be switched to a bass trombone or a large bore tenor with F attachment. The introduction of some elementary tuba studies would be appropriate to focus on the lower portions of the range; slow exercises are recommended in the trigger register below E2. The student must strive to master the sound and tuning of F valve notes with regular pitches.

The F Attachment on the Trombone by Ernest Williams, edited by Roger Smith (Charles Colin). The Williams/Smith text may be the best introduction to the F valve for the young player. It avoids extreme low register and offers the student much opportunity to develop consistency of low C, F, B², E², without complicated rhythms, tonal centers, etc.

Elementary Etudes for Bass Trombone by Tommy Pederson (Schmidt Hall and McCreary). These etudes are not so elementary and actually are quite sophisticated for young players because they incorporate changing meters, wide interval shifts, unusual phrasing and varied articulations.

Junior High Level Solos. Provided the range is not consistently above an F3, a junior high student might wish to continue playing tenor solo literature. However, a few functional musical compositions are available for the more advanced trombonist at this level. *Concert Piece in Fugal Style* by Allen Ostrander (Edition Musicus) could be played by an exceptional junior high student, as could the *Lyric Etude* by Christopher Dedrick (Kendor Music).

High School Level

An abundance of material is available at this level. A bass trombonist should be playing legato studies (Rochut, Concone), beginning octave transposition (up and down), and be able to play scales slowly into the trigger register, thus extending his range. He should work toward a range of between G4 to B♭4 and down to pedal B♭ during this period.

Method Books. Let's Play Bass Trombone by George Roberts and Paul Tanner (Belwin) starts out simply but moves very quickly and is one of the few books that deals with the pedal register down to F1. A junior high student might start out in this text but probably will still be working in it in college.

The F Attachment and the Bass Trombone by Allen Ostrander (Charles Colin); *Methods for the F Attachment Trombone and Bass Trombone* by Allen Ostrander (Carl Fischer). These two texts, particularly the Ostrander, are the "bibles" for intermediate bass trombone study. The exercises are progressive, developing one position at a time. They are intentionally awkward and hard to understand and play musically because of shifting tonal centers and subtle phrasing. Orchestra excerpts are also included in these texts.

70 Progressive Studies by Lew Gillis (Southern Music Company). The Gillis studies are excellent for developing slide, valve, and tongue coordination. The exercises are repetitious but very functional in developing awareness of consistent valve use.

Intermediate Etudes for Bass Trombone by Tommy Pederson (Schmidt, Hall and McCreary). A continuation of the *Elementary Etudes*, the *Intermediate Etudes* by Pederson are fun to play for students. They incorporate double and triple tonguing, wide interval slides, and odd meters. They develop control and flexibility in the register below the staff and include jazz phrasing. These exercises do not baby the student.

Unaccompanied Solos for Bass Trombone by Tommy Pederson (Kendor). These are five volumes of material that may be played by advanced high school or college trombonists. Multiple tonguing, flexibility, articulation, and phrasing can all be developed through these studies.

36 Studies for Trombone with F Attachment by Blume, arranged by Reginald Fink (Carl Fischer). All serious tenor or bass trombone students should be exposed to this text because it really develops valve use in a variety of keys and includes articulation studies without any extremes of register.

Legato Texts: These are several studies by Chester Roberts (Robert King), Reginald Fink (Carl Fischer) and Allen Ostrander (Carl Fischer) which contain vocalises of Bordogni, Rochut, and Concone in the lower register. The Fink text is particularly well-edited.

High School Solos. Dramatique by Edward Solomon (Southern Music Company), *The Big Horn*, and *Trigger Treat* by Earl Hoffman (Southern Music Company) are similar functional solos for the high school bass trombonist. The range is from trigger C4 to G4, reasonable for a high school bass trombonist, and consist mostly of scales and arpeggios in familiar keys.

Lyric Etude by Christopher Dedrick (Kendor Music). As the title indicates, this is simply an extended legato piece that shows off a student's musicianship. There is a recording of this piece by Thomas Streeter on Kendor Records.

Sonata by Patrick McCarty (Ensemble Publications, Inc.). With its emphasis on the dorian mode, this composition has become the standard high school solo for bass trombonists. The first two movements are similar and lyrical, while the third is a technical ⅝ workout in an almost-baroque style. There is a piano reduction of the string quartet (or orchestra) version.

Postures by Newel Kay Brown (Seesaw Press). More contemporary in nature than the other works at this level, *Postures* consists of a slow movement with sustained soft pedal notes and a energetic fast section which, although technical, is very practical and reasonable in its scalewise movement.

Cameos by Gordon Jacob (Emerson Edition). The five programmatic movements are available in an easy band accompaniment or piano reduction.

Little Tune for a Big Horn by Wilfred Bob Roberts (Kendor). This is a long George Roberts-styled bass

trombone feature with stage band. It offers the student an opportunity to "sing a song."

There are also, of course, many transcriptions of baroque music (Teleman, Marcello, Frescobaldi, Bach) for tenor trombone that work well with bass trombone, especially when appropriate octave transposition is made.

College Level

Method Books. Octave transposition (8va and 8 ba), tenor and alto clefs, orchestral excerpts, tuba literature, Bach cello suites and some of the French literature should be perfected at this level.

Method for the Modern Bass Trombone by Eliezer Aharoni (Noga), *The Double Valve Bass Trombone* by Alan Raph (Carl Fischer). These two methods contain the most informative discussion and the best-edited etudes for the development of the double valve bass trombone. Various tunings are presented along with studies for the pedal register.

20 Etudes by Lewis Gillis (Southern Music Company). These etudes are intended for a bass trombone with single F valve and are technical. They are occasionally of a pop nature.

Advanced Etudes by Tommy Pederson (Schmidt, Hall and McCreary). Anyone who can play all these etudes is ready to handle big band or popular music.

Douze Etudes, Rhythmiques et Melodique by Michel Delgiudice (Max Eschig). These studies will challenge advanced students and graduate students. The trick is to play them cleanly.

College Solos. There is a wealth of original material at this level, especially in the areas of contemporary music. Some of the outstanding pieces are:

Early Music: *Canzoni per Basso Solo*, Giolamo Frescobaldi (Doblinger). The six canzoni published in two books are for any bass instrument. The range is perfect for bass trombone and could be played by technically proficient high school students.

Romantic: *Zwie Fantasiestücke*, Edward Lassen (ms - Fleisher Collection, Philadelphia Public Library), *Preludium, Chorale, Variations and Fugue*, J.I. Muller (Edition Musica). Both of these are original 19th century works. The Lassen has two movements with string orchestra. The demands are not technical but musical. The Muller is effective with organ.

20th Century: *Fantasie Concertante*, Jacques Casterade (Leduc), *Sonata*, Alec Wilder (Margun). Both of these works are for bass trombone with piano. The technical Casterade is the best of the French literature. American Alec Wilder has written a light, lyrical, bouncy, five-movement Sonata which is probably the most successful work of its kind in 20th-century literature.

Concertos: Concerto, Thom Ritter George (Rochester Music Company) The George Concerto for Bass Trombone and Orchestra loses much in the piano reduction. The work requires great flexibility and dexterity.

Unaccompanied: *Sonata Breve*, Walter Hartley (Tenuto Press), *Canto II*, Samuel Adler (Oxford University Press). Hartley's two-movement *Sonata Breve* is the shorter of these two effective unaccompanied works. It is very successful as an audition solo piece. The Adler is a four-movement, twelve-tone work exploiting various styles of the bass trombone.

Electronic Music: *Prelude, Fugue and Big Apple*, Walter Ross (Boosey and Hawkes), *Impromptu*, James Brown (Brass Press). Both of these works are on pre-recorded tape. The *Prelude, Fugue and Big Apple* is an enjoyable work in which the soloist must coordinate all notes exactly with the taped sounds (which are indicated on a graph above the trombone staff). *Impromptu* would make an excellent introduction to the tape medium as the performer does not have to play exactly with the tape.

Chamber Music: *Largo Tah* for bass trombone and marimba, Warren Benson (rental from Carl Fischer); *Concert Suite* - for bass trombone and trumpet, Frank Lynn Payne (Brass Press); *Etudes in the Form of Duos* - for tenor and bass trombones, Leslie Basset (C.F. Peters). The abstract Benson work dedicated to Emory Remington, is virtuosic for the marimba soloist. *Concert Suite* is a playful work in which the trumpet dominates; there is even a touch of Shostakovich. Pulitzer Prize-winner composer and former trombonist, Leslie Basset, has written some very practical etudes in a variety of contemporary styles that might also be performance material.

1979

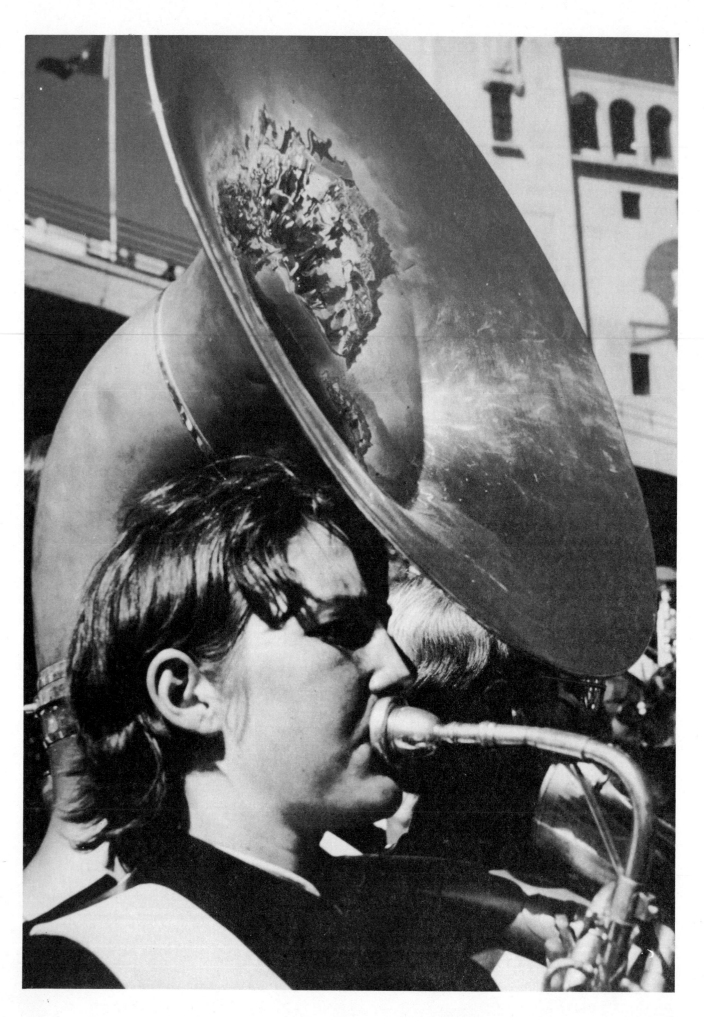

The Tuba:
Concepts in Low-Register
Tone Production

Peter Popiel

The tubist who begins to study the advanced literature for his instrument soon discovers that problems of extended range do not occur exclusively above the staff. Solo works, chamber music, and orchestral literature all require facility down through the "extension register," the register which involves additional valves beyond the basic three of the BB-flat tuba. Contemporary composers are even scoring pedals with increasing frequency. On the CC tuba, these are the notes involved:

The corresponding notes on the BB♭ tuba are these:

This article will deal only with tone production, not fingerings. As the reader knows, a BB-flat or CC tuba could be equipped with four or five valves, and the fifth valve could have various tunings. (For readers interested in specific fingerings, three sources are suggested: 1) Chester Roberts, "Coping With the Extension Register," *T.U.B.A.*

Newsletter, Winter, 1974; 2) Donald Knaub, *Progressive Techniques for Tuba,* MCA Music, 1970; and 3) Rex Conner, "Fingering the Four and Five Valve Tubas," *The Instrumentalist,* April, 1970.)

A combination of problems works against the player in this low register. Let us examine them: Unless one is playing a compensating valve tuba, considerable pitch adjustment is necessary on many of these tones. An important first step toward playing them involves choosing a fingering which provides the best combination of accurate pitch and fine tone quality. Further adjustments are then made by manipulating tuning slide settings and/or favoring the note by embouchure adjustment. I have found that the less "lipping" or bending of the note in this register, the better. Many of these tones will choke up or become very tubby and stuffy to the extent that they are bent up or down with the embouchure.

To set the embouchure in this register involves a very relaxed lip placement on the mouthpiece rim and a relaxed, slack lower jaw. Some players form the syllable "taw" in producing these low tones. Many students are amazed when shown by means of a clear plastic mouthpiece just how far open the mouth aperture really is. I have frequently demonstrated this concept to the

complete amazement of students, many of whom attempt to produce these low tones with the same sized aperture used an octave above, and who then wonder why the tone is pinched, if indeed it speaks at all. An element of caution must be exercised here: a too-open setting will result in a foggy, breathy, out-of-focus tone lacking in resonance. Let sound always be your guide.

I advocate anchoring the embouchure corners even though the jaw drops, thereby helping to prevent one problem encountered in low-register tone production, that of air leakage around one or both corners of the mouth. Should such air leakage occur, it is helpful to have the student "think in" the corners of the mouth toward the center of the mouthpiece.

The only way to develop facility in this register is to use it, practicing in a much more determined manner than many tubists are used to doing. There is ample etude literature available to the player who sets out to develop this important and often-neglected register. The musical results will be a generous compensation to the player who invests his time and energy well. ■

Calisthenics
for the Brass Player

Marden J. Pond

Ask any seasoned brass player if playing his instrument is a leisurely activity. The answer will be an emphatic, "No." Brass playing at times can be as exhausting as a marathon race and as strenuous as weight lifting. If some master performers make playing look and sound effortless, it is undoubtedly the result of long hours of practice, muscle building and toning, and reflex conditioning. It is also a fact that many excellent teachers of brass students spend a great deal of time working on calisthenics for developing the entire physical playing mechanism, including the embouchure and the muscles surrounding and supporting it, plus those muscles associated with the breathing process.

Performers who are developing proficiency learn to use body energy for only the muscular actions that are necessary to produce the desired sounds. Any extraneous muscular action is eliminated. Most teachers are familiar with the strenuous effort some beginning students display just to get a sound from the instrument. This same physical strain may even be observed in more experienced players when they attempt music that is at or beyond their limit of physical ability. These students use up great amounts of energy, not because the music or the instrument is impossibly difficult, but because their muscular or nervous responses are not developed

enough to focus on just the physical actions needed to play correctly. The proficient player, on the other hand, learns to relax the muscles not essential to playing so that he is not working against himself. This places all his required energies into the necessary neuromuscular areas needed for performing. Through this process, body energy is saved, strength and endurance are increased, and the outward appearance of the performer is one of relative relaxation and total control.

The following exercises are designed to develop and improve neuromuscular response, muscle strength, endurance, and flexibility. They are not intended to replace actual practice on the instrument; however, as part of a comprehensive routine they can augment and improve the results of practice and help develop all playing capabilities.

Exercising the Face Muscles

Without the Instrument

Facial Isometrics. Opening the mouth, eyes, and even the nose and ears as far as they will go. Hold them open briefly, about 2-5 seconds. Then do the exact opposite exercise. Pucker the mouth shut. Squint the eyes shut, and try to touch your forehead with your chin and your nose with your ears. Hold briefly. Repeat these exercises five to ten times.

The Lion. Open the eyes and mouth as wide as they will go,

extend the tongue out and down as far as possible, and hold for 15-20 seconds. Repeat 4-5 times.

The Pencil. Set your embouchure as you would for playing. Place the flat end of a pencil between the lips, against the teeth (not between the teeth), and support it with the lips so that it is held straight out from the mouth (see figure 1). Hold for 30-60 seconds.

Figure 1

Lip Corner Isometrics. Place the thumb and middle finger in the corners of the mouth against the teeth. Tighten the corners of the mouth and try to push the thumb and finger together without allowing them to move. Hold for 5-10 seconds. Repeat 5-10 times.

Lip Center Isometrics. Place the thumb and middle finger together in the center of the mouth against the teeth. Try to "bite" through the thumb and finger with the center portion of the lips. Hold for 5-10 seconds. Repeat 5-10 times.

With the Instrument

Mouthpiece Drills. Long tone or scale studies buzzed on the mouthpiece can be very effective for strengthening the embouchure. Just be sure to use as little mouthpiece pressure as possible. Holding the neck of the mouthpiece with just the thumb and middle one or two fingers will help minimize the pressure (see figure 2). Generally, mouthpiece drills should start in the middle range of the instrument and gradually progress to the extreme high and low (even the pedal tone) ranges.

Figure 2

Nose Breathing. This exercise develops the facial muscles by forcing them to remain in playing position for an extended period of time. Start with a note in the low to middle range (perhaps middle G for trumpet or horn, middle F for trombone or tuba). Play the note about mezzo piano for 5-8 seconds. Then, without allowing the embouchure to relax or the mouthpiece to leave the lips, take a large slow breath through the nose. Now play a note one half step higher than the first (5-8 seconds). Inhale again through the nose. Repeat the process, each time playing one half step higher until you have played six different pitches. Without relaxing the embouchure, return to the original pitch and repeat the entire process. This exercise should be done only once or twice each day. If the exercise is done too often it puts a tremendous strain on the facial muscles, which could be detrimental. After using the exercise for a number of weeks, move the entire series of notes up a half step or invent similar long tone passages with larger intervals or more lengthy time durations.

Lip Slurs. Brass teachers have long recognized the value of lip slurs (slurs executed from one harmonic to another without changing fingering or slide position) for developing strength and flexibility. Any organized series of lip slur studies (Arban or Clarke for ex-

ample) may be used to help develop the embouchure; or the teacher or student can create his own studies. Just remember to start in the low to middle range of the instrument and work up to the extreme high and low ranges. Also, it is important to start slowly and to gradually increase the speed of the lip slurs.

Birdcalls. Place the instrument in regular playing position. Tighten the facial muscles surrounding the embouchure so the lips are set to allow only a tiny pressurized stream of air through a very small lip aperture. With the embouchure set in this way, blow lightly but firmly into the instrument and attempt to produce high, squeaky, birdcall sounds. The sounds should be high-pitched but not loud. After training the embouchure to produce these sounds, more air can be used to create actual notes in the extreme high range.

Figure 3

Exercising the Breathing Muscles

Without The Instrument

The Cleansing Breath. The exercise helps the body take in and retain large amounts of air. Stand with the feet spread about shoulder-width apart, body bent over at the waist, and arms hanging loosely toward the floor. Begin to bring the body into an upright position (see figure 3). While raising the torso, inhale deeply and raise the arms outward and above the head. Keep the shoulders relaxed. Inhale and retain the air while holding the arms and torso up. Be sure that the air is kept in the lungs by holding all of the abdominal muscles out, not

by closing off the throat (if you can pronounce the word "who" while holding the air in, the air is being held correctly. See figure 4. After retaining the air for 5-10 seconds, exhale while returning to the first position. Repeat the exercise only once. It is easy to hyperventilate if the exercise is done too many times.

Figure 4

Regional Breath Packing. Start with a deep diaphragmatic breath. Take in as much air as you can. After holding the air briefly, and without exhaling, lean slightly to the right and try to force more air in by expanding the abdominal wall on the left front side of the body. Hold briefly. Again without exhaling, lean left and try to bring in more air with a similar expanding motion of the right front side of the abdomen. (see figure 5). Exhale. Repeat the process, this time trying to expand the abdominal wall of the right and left back portions of the lower abdomen. Leaning forward, back, and to the sides helps stretch the muscle and other tissues in each area so there is more complete muscle action. Finally, combine these separate breathing exercises into one long inhalation exercise, packing air into every available space by leaning in all directions and expanding the muscles. This exercise will strengthen the abdominal muscles and involve formerly unused muscles in the breathing and air support process. This will help the performer gain more power and control in each breath. If stretching or slight aching is felt during the exercise, this is good. It means that muscles are being used and stretched that haven't yet been contributing to full breath power and support.

Figure 5

Eye Dropper. Using the glass tube section of an eye dropper, blow into the large end of the tube. The resistance of the narrow end of the dropper will give the diaphragm and other related breathing muscles excellent exercise. Experiment to see how long one breath will last and how much air can be expelled each time.

Wind Machine. Unlike the previous exercise, this exercise works with no breath resistance. Tape an 8½ x 11 piece of paper to the bottom of the desk portion of a music stand. Allow the paper to hang freely. From a distance of one to three feet, blow against the paper. Try to keep the paper bent back for as long as you can on each breath. Keep blowing until all your air is expelled. Repeat 2-5 times. A more difficult variation of this exercise is to hold the paper against a wall. Begin blowing against the paper from one to two feet away. Let go of the paper and attempt to hold the paper against the wall with your breath. Keep blowing until the paper falls. Repeat.

With the Instrument

Resistant Mouthpiece. A rubber insulator, the kind that fits over alligator clips is required for this exercise. You can find one in an electronics store. Fit the large end of the insulator snugly over the end of your mouthpiece. The small hole in the other end of the insulator will offer considerable resistance when you buzz the mouthpiece. Play your regular mouthpiece drill. The resistance provides the extra work for developing breath control and endurance.

Pearl Diver. This exercise is designed to test and improve the players ability to play for long periods of time using the same breath. Start by playing a note in the low register (low C for trumpet and horn, low B♭ for trombone). Play about mezzo piano for as long as your breath will last. Measure the length of time you held the note. Be sure to use every last ounce of air from the lungs, even after the lips have stopped buzzing. It is not uncommon, after some practice, to approach 80-90 seconds per breath. As strength and control increase (it may take a number of weeks), play this exercise more loudly and move the exercise up one half step at a time into the higher range.

Breath Taker. This is a more advanced version of the previous exercise. Instead of using long tones, begin playing ascending arpeggios and scales at a strong, but controlled, fortissimo. Hold the top note of each arpeggio or scale until all breath is expended. If the lips stop buzzing, keep the embouchure set and continue blowing until the lungs are completely empty. As strength increases, move up one half step at a time. Naturally, the breath will be used up more quickly on these scales and arpeggios than on the Pearl Diver exercise.

Air Compressor. Choose a fast moving technical or characteristic study (such as those by Arban, Brandt, or Clarke). Play as far into each exercise as you can on one breath at a fortissimo level. When the first breath is expended, take another quick, big breath and continue. Keep going until the exercise is finished, then relax.

Intervals. Any good interval study can be used. (I prefer those in *Arban's Complete Conservatory Method*, pp. 125-131). Instead of playing in the notated rhythm, play each note *ff* for 5-10 seconds. Take another big breath and play the next notes the same way. Continue to the end of the exercise. It may take up to five minutes to play a one-line study. As your strength and endurance improve, choose exercises that move higher.

Whispa Mute. This felt-filled device (available at most music stores) is another means of playing against resistance. Practicing with this mute is like wearing leg weights in track. Strength is developed in practice that shows up when the unusal resistance is removed.

The concept of strengthening muscles to improve performance ability may be extended to other non-breathing muscles. Good posture allows the body to perform more efficiently. Proper body position while standing, the ideal playing position, can enhance and improve playing effectiveness. If the feet are spread about shoulder-width, the body is centered over the feet, the back is held in a comfortably straight position, and the shoulders and arms are relaxed, all of these muscles are then in a position to help support and aid the breathing apparatus. Using this concept of support and balance, it is actually possible to "Breath from the soles of the feet". Every body muscle serves as an integral part of breath control. Jogging, swimming, weight lifting, and other forms of physical exercise can also act as a great aid in a complete embouchure-strengthening routine. The techniques of Hatha Yoga (which deal specifically with the breath and the breathing process) are also a wonderful supplement to the wind players' routine.

The exercises presented in this article are designed to develop strength, endurance, power, and control. They must be used in combination with conscientious musical and technical study to be totally effective and worthwhile. If used alone, they tend to produce musical "animals" who have incredible range and power, but no sense of musicality or expressiveness. ∎

Trumpet Pedal Tones: The Key to an Expanded Range

Martin Berinbaum

All the current methods of learning to play high notes seem to have at least one technique in common: using pedal tones. It is my feeling, based on daily practice of pedal tones for nearly twenty years, that they help develop range, flexibility, tone quality, and endurance.

Pedal tones are notes which begin on F3 and continue downwards. They are not legitimate members of the overtone series except for C2 and C3, but they can be made to sound firm and centered.

Why Practice Pedal Tones?

Pedal tones are a means to an end. The goal is a total range of five octaves and a unified range from F3 to F6 for the orchestral player and even higher for the commercial lead player (see diagram). A player must develop this total range so that the unified range, where he does most of his playing, is flexible, centered, and has a good sound. In looking at the diagram, you can see that the unified range actually becomes the middle range relative to the total range, the low range now is the low middle range, and what some consider the high range (G5 to E5) becomes the high middle range.

Simply put, pedal tones strengthen portions of lip and facial muscles that otherwise never get a workout. Without pedal tones you are forcing a relatively small amount of lip muscle to do a great deal of work.

By practicing pedal tones you strengthen the larger muscles around the mouthpiece and make it less of a hardship on the small muscles in the lip itself.

By the way, the loose, flapping of the lips, that all players do to help relax the embouchure, is in reality a low pedal tone. If you made the same buzz into a tuba you would get a tone. I used to wonder why a good tuba player could pick up a trumpet and play a C7. I now realize that because of the constant use of a large mouthpiece their embouchure is stronger than a trumpet player's who doesn't play pedal tones. However, don't rush out to buy a tuba or trombone mouthpiece in the hopes that this will be a shortcut to strengthening your trumpet embouchure. A little practice (and I mean a little, not more than ten or twelve minutes a week) on a trombone mouthpiece probably won't hurt. But, I don't think it is necessary. The focus of the muscles in the larger mouthpiece is much different than those used in playing the trumpet, and too much practice on a larger mouthpiece could be harmful in the early stages of your pedal tone practice.

Another benefit of pedal tones is an increase in blood circulation in the facial muscle tissue. The better the circulation, the better your endurance. The less pressure used at any given moment, the better your endurance. Pressure, range, endurance, and circulation are all related. Practicing pedal tones makes you think about these four aspects of playing.

When Should You Start Practicing Pedal Tones?

One of the big mistakes teachers make with beginners is in not teaching pedal tones from the start. Quite often the beginner plays a pedal tone by accident on his way to C4, and the teacher says, "No, play a higher note". This is where the teacher should step in and teach the student to play pedal tones. But remember to have them play pedal tones only on the mouthpiece so they do not have to compensate for the trumpet. Also, it is the best basic training we can give their

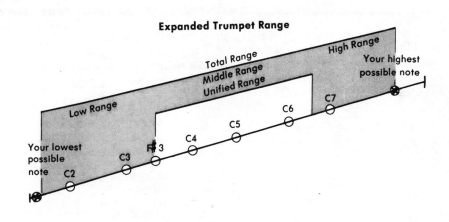

Expanded Trumpet Range

High Range
Your highest possible note

Total Range
Middle Range
Unified Range

Low Range

C7
C6
C5
C4
F#3
C3
C2
Your lowest possible note

developing muscles. But if a student can play the pedal tones on the mouthpiece but not on the trumpet, it is probably because he is opening his lips wider when he plays on the instrument than when he uses the mouthpiece. Try having the student start the note on the mouthpiece and then slide it into the trumpet as he continues to play the note. The pitch should stay the same.

How Do You Begin?

Find a teacher who is familiar with using pedal tones. If that is not possible, begin by following these instructions. Hold your trumpet without gripping the valve casings with the left hand. Keep your hand and palm flat and let the bellpipe rest on your index finger. Don't pull back with the hook and don't add any pressure until after you have your breath. Play regular easy scales while holding the trumpet in this manner. Then, try to play into the fourth octave of the total range without gripping any harder. Once you feel comfortable holding the instrument this way, begin playing the following exercises very slowly (see musical example). These exercises, used by James Stamp, are very effective in developing well-centered pedal tones.

Exercise for developing well-centered tones.

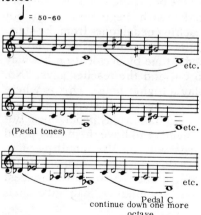

continue down one more octave

Take time to center each note, especially the note preceding the slur to the pedal tone. Finger the first octave of pedal tones as you do the octave above, then play open to produce C3 and all the notes below.

You can play them soft or loud, but if you play loudly, you will give your lips more of a workout. You will also find that arching the tongue by using a soft "who" syllable and keeping the tip of the tongue in contact with the back of the lower teeth will help focus the air and center the tones. Practice the exercises early in your daily routine; they work well as part of a warm-up.

When playing pedal tones, realize that your lowest note will be controlled by the bottom lip. The lower you play the more the bottom lip and jaw descend until the lower lip is totally out of the bottom of the mouthpiece. For me this point is G1, but I know many players who can play even lower before it happens. The lowest note is the largest lip vibration which can be focused through the mouthpiece and into the instrument without a syllable. The aperture will be very large and well past the outer rim of the mouthpiece:

As for the upper range, I don't believe anyone will ever play the highest note possible on a trumpet. It is purely a matter of how much time you wish to spend toward that end. For your highest note, however, you must use the smallest aperture you can force air through and still cause your lip to buzz. And remember, your lowest note should require almost no pressure from the left hand, and your highest note will probably require maximum pressure. The slower you are to add pressure as you ascend, the higher you will eventually be able to play.

As your lips get stronger, which pedal tones will cause them to do, you will be able to play higher, with less pressure. Pedal tones also insure that you will be playing any given note with as full an aperture as

possible, given the amount of pressure you are using on the mouthpiece.

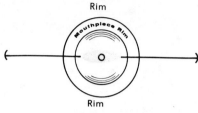

Aperture before pedal tones

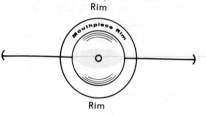

Aperture after pedal tones

The rim of the mouthpiece stops sympathetic vibrations to the buzz the way a finger on a violin stops a string from vibrating. The harder you push the mouthpiece against your lips the more the buzz is cut down and the faster or harder you have to blow in order to get the reduced lip area to vibrate at the desired pitch.

Never be satisfied with a range that just stops. You should always be able to play a half step higher than you feel you can. If you can play a firm D6, then you should be able to get a weak E♭6. If you can't, then you are not centering your notes on the way up, and your lip is out of position for the top notes. If you practice one to two hours a day and play pedal tones a total of fifteen minutes a day, you should be able to hear some positive results within three months. You should be able to add one step to your range every two months. Don't be discouraged, just keep practicing and thinking about expanding your range. ∎

Philip Farkas: Master Horn Teacher

An interview   by Kenneth L. Neidig, editor of *The Instrumentalist.*

It is almost impossible to speak with a horn player anywhere in the world and not have the name of Philip Farkas enter into the conversation. His many years of professional performance and recording, The Art of French Horn Playing *and other definitive publications, innumerable highly informative clinics, a model of horn that bears his name, and a small army of successful students have all earned him a position of the highest respect in his profession. We began by talking about his early years, about the time when he was the age of so many of the students now in our school bands and orchestras.*

Can you remember when you first discovered music?

All the kids in our neighborhood took piano lessons so I started at age 11 and hated it from the beginning. But at about the same time, I was in the Boy Scouts and they needed a bugler. I'd had my eye on a bugle in a hock shop down on 75th and Cottage Grove, so I bought it for $3. When I got home, I found out I couldn't get any sound out of it. I took the mouthpiece off, looked through, and discovered there wasn't a little brass tongue in there like the one in my Halloween horn. Finally, a neighbor, who was a jazz trumpet player, explained to me how you have to buzz your lips. So I played the bugle in the Boy Scouts for about two years, and got to like music.

In junior high school I was yelling in the swimming pool during a gym class. The teacher got mad and threw a whistle at me that left a big bruise. My folks came down the next day and told the principal I would no longer take gym because the teacher was a brute. But the principal said, "He has to. He's able-bodied and it's a required course in the Chicago schools." Suddenly his eyes lit up, and he said, "You know, he could join the marching band. That's considered physical ed." So I went down to the band department and told them, "I'm supposed to join the band. What do you have?" The answer was, "only a bass drum and a tuba." And I said, "Well, I don't think I'd like the bass drum, but I would be interested in the tuba. I'm already an experienced bugler." So at age 13, I played the tuba and enjoyed it very much, even performing "Massa's in the Cold, Cold, Ground" for a junior high assembly. Every day for about six months I carried the instrument back and forth from school on the streetcar. One day the streetcar conductor stopped me and said, "You can't bring this on board anymore, you're blocking traffic." I was crestfallen, and asked, "What would you allow me to bring on board?" He saw a group of other band kids waiting for the streetcar, and said "one of *them*," as he pointed to a horn case. So I went down to Lyon & Healy and rented "one of them." It was a fine old Schmidt horn that would now be worth $2000, but in 1927 I rented it for $3 a month. I fell in love with the instrument and soon knew that I wanted to be a professional horn player.

Was there any particular moment of discovery you remember? Any cold chills?

Yes, when I heard the horns on a Sears Roebuck *Silvertone* recording of Creatore's band playing the *William Tell Overture,* the thrilling climax we know now as "Hi-O Silver." At that moment my dad said, "Why don't you consider the horn? You like the sound of it." And I did. I was excited by it at that very moment. Up until then I'd been considering the horn only because of its size and because of what the streetcar conductor had told me.

Were your parents musicians?

No, my dad had an advertising business. Nobody in our family could even whistle a tune as far as I know. They tell me that I had a great-great aunt who was the first "Merry Widow" in the Franz Lehar production back in Vienna, but that was never substantiated.

Is the family background Austrian?

No, the name is Hungarian ("wolf") and my father was born in Budapest. At the age of four he moved to Vienna, then to America at age eight. He learned the English language so well that he put himself through a civil engineering degree at Purdue University writing short stories and novels for the old *Adventure* magazine.

Was he the one with the record collection including Creatore?

No, I bought that myself. Somebody had told me, "If you've never heard *William Tell* you haven't lived." The second record I bought was the "Nocturne" from *Midsummer Night's Dream* with the famous Bruno Jaenecke playing and Toscanini conducting. So my tastes were improving rapidly.

Who put you onto these things? The school band director?

He was the one who sparked my enthusiasm. Jimmy

Sylvester, a very fine trumpet player, was my band director at Hirsch Junior High School on the south side of Chicago. In high school I started studying privately with Louis Dufrasne, the first horn with Mary Garden's Chicago Opera Company. I was also a member of the Civic Orchestra, which is the training orchestra for the Chicago Symphony. Mr. Dufrasne was a fine teacher. With only four years of study from the time I started until I became first horn in Kansas City meant that I must have made some good progress, and I owe it all to him. Three years later the Chicago Symphony had a vacancy on first horn. Because they knew me as a student in the Civic Orchestra and they knew I had some potential, I came back to Chicago at age 21 as first horn.

Just what does it take to be a fine horn player?

I've narrowed it down to three things: (1) the technique to play any music, or any musical ideas that come to your mind, (2) the musicianship to have good things come to your mind, and (3) the courage to play in public. I know so many students who play well in their lessons and then panic when they get in front of a crowd. The one simple solution to that problem is to perform more often. Familiarity doesn't breed contempt in this case; it breeds courage. I remember my first year in the Chicago Symphony. I was only 21, playing first horn, and I remember that sea of faces frightening me so much the first year. By the second year I began to look around: there's the lady who falls asleep in the slow movements, and that's the one with the jangling bracelets, and there's the one who knits all the time.

So the fear comes from the audience more than the conductor?

Well, no, not when we got Reiner. With him, the rehearsals, strangely enough, were the hard part. In the rehearsal Reiner would stop and lay you low with epithets. On a concert you knew he was not going to stop. And since he couldn't stop, he couldn't say anything. The concerts were actually a relief after the rehearsals. I had a series of probably the most difficult conductors in the world: Artur Rodzinski, Fritz Reiner, Serge Koussevitsky, and George Szell, all notoriously tough men. On the other hand, they were great musicians; and perhaps the reason why they were great is because they were tough. Or perhaps they were tough because they were great. I don't know which it was, but they demanded a lot.

Have you figured it out since then? Which way is it?

I think it's a little of each. One time Dr. Rodzinski was asked, "Why are conductors such S.O.B.'s?" He replied "Well, show me a conductor who isn't an S.O.B., and I'll show you a man who isn't a conductor." That was his idea. I think the truth is that some of the section players need this kind of encouragement from the conductor. The soloists always want to play well. I've played with as much energy and effort and desire to succeed on a children's concert as I did on any other concert for this reason: if I had played the children's concert badly, the next night at an important concert with Claudia Cassidy [an especially tough critic] in the audience, I would be nervous because I would

remember how badly I played the day before. So it was always essential to me to play well regardless of who was there, and I think this is true of anyone on a solo part. Even practicing at home I would get quite shook up if I missed something, because there was always the thought, if this happened at the concert, what would happen to me? I always strived to do something that was not only musical, but also built up my confidence so I knew I could perform the music in public. This is also one of my basic beliefs in teaching: repetition is the only way to get a passage down well. Most musicians will agree to this, but to horn players it's particularly important because we have an instrument that's notoriously treacherous. I like to play a passage so many times that I literally feel I've put a groove in the gray matter and a groove in my lips and that if I were sitting on the back of a bouncing truck, I'd still be able to play that passage. In other words, I like to woodshed a passage so much that I feel the odds are in my favor; I want to think that it would be more difficult to miss a note than it would be to play it right. It's the same principle as putting a white rat in a maze and making him find his dinner at the other end. With enough repetitions, he'll learn the direct route. It's the same idea with the horn. Practicing actually consists of trial and error. First performances are the first trials and they have something wrong with them. Until you eliminate all of the wrong things in a musical passage, you aren't really rehearsing, you're only experimenting. It isn't until you play it well that you're ready to practice. I've often told my students, "Every time you miss a passage in preparation, that's not practicing it; when you finally get it right, then you can begin to practice it." So many students believe that after they finally perform a passage well once they can go on to the next thing. I tell them, "You've just done it five ways wrong for me; now you've done it right just once and you think you're entitled to go ahead to the next passage. The odds are 5 to 1 that you're going to miss it the next time, and even a compulsive gambler wouldn't go along with those odds."

Once you get these "grooves in the gray matter," is there any danger of becoming overconfident?

I don't think horn players get overconfident, but I suppose there is a danger. For instance on a concert sometimes I must play a very difficult passage and I have no confidence at all except for the fact that I played it 100 times yesterday and got it right every time. That gives me the courage to go ahead and play it, but not with great confidence, just with sheer grit you might say. And then, after I get it, I say, "Oh, now that difficult part of the evening is over." Then I'll have a simple note in the middle register to attack, and my overconfidence shows. I'll blurp the easiest note on the same concert that I got the most difficult things. In that way we have to be careful. I think playing the horn is very much like working with tigers or lions in the circus. You'll notice that the trainer never turns his back on the animals, even though they seem to be well-trained. It's the same with the horn, the moment you think you've got the thing mastered is when it'll turn on you and bite you. And if it happens in front of 2,000 people and a critic, then it's bad. If it happens at home, it does something to your ego, or at least to your confidence.

What about horn players' egos? Are horn players nice people?

I think so. In fact, I believe there's almost a character that goes with each instrument. Viola players are notoriously dignified. They're the ones who wear a necktie and smoke a pipe in a deliberate manner. Violinists have the wild hairdos and the T-shirts. Bass players are inclined to be a little kooky. The horn players, I think, are closer to the dignified side. If they hadn't this innate dignity, they would have taken up trumpet, trombone, or something else that would lend itself to jazz playing. Horn players, outside of a few notable exceptions, are completely oriented toward classical playing. Because of this, I think they have a certain reserve that some of the more flamboyant instruments don't have. Incidentally, I've heard some jazz played well on the horn; but it always leaves me cold because it reminds me of an elderly, white-haired lady trying to do the Charleston. There's just a certain dignity about the instrument that doesn't lend itself to jazz, whereas the same thing played on a trumpet sounds great.

But to return to the idea of confidence and ego, can you tell me when necessary self-confidence becomes the ego of a prima donna? I'm sure as a first horn player you have to know that you're going to perform well.

Yes you do. And confidence breeds on itself, doesn't it? If yesterday's concert was a good one, you can go out presuming that you'll play well today. If yesterday's concert was not a good one, you have a little temerity about this one. If you play six concerts a week, as most major orchestras do, you simply can't get nervous that many times a week for 30 weeks in a row. You can't take it physically. Not only that, but the knowledge that you played six concerts last week and they went well gives you a great deal of courage. If you think in terms of batting averages as a baseball player has to think, and you miss a little note here and there, you can say, "Well, that isn't so bad. The audience heard six good ones and now a cracked one, that isn't too shameful." As the batting average idea becomes instinctive we realize we've been doing well, and therefore have every confidence that we will continue to do well. Even if we don't, we can refer to the law of averages. Max Pottag sat beside me for a number of years in Chicago, and if I'd break a note Max would say, "Don't feel bad, we have to remind them how difficult the horn is."

Do you honestly believe that the horn is more difficult than most of the other instruments?

All you have to do is listen to a symphony orchestra for a year and jot down who makes the most mistakes. It'll be the horn player every time. But the difficulty can be proven scientifically — the horn plays regularly in the part of the harmonic series where notes are very close together, and picking one out, especially in the high register, is very treacherous.

What suggestions do you have for school band and orchestra directors who are looking for good horn players? They don't have the streetcar conductor to say, "The tuba's too big, get a horn."

Yes, my first run-in with a conductor. First of all I have the greatest admiration for American school instrumental programs and their directors, because the teaching level is so high that many graduates can go right into a major symphony orchestra, maybe not one of the big five to start with, but one of the orchestras. This was unthinkable even just 30 years ago. When I was a young man, if the major symphony orchestras wanted a brass player they invariably sent to Germany for him. Most of the woodwinds came from France, and many of the strings came from Russia. Today no one would think of importing a player from Europe for an American orchestra. As a matter of fact, the tables are turned; I have at least a half dozen students who have gone to Europe and gotten good jobs as horn players. And this situation is directly attributable to the school instrumental music programs.

Yes, I'm sure that's true, but many of us can still use a lot of help from specialists like you. You've heard many school bands and orchestras, judged plenty of solo contests through the years. What horn problems keep coming up over and over?

One of the things the band or orchestra director should be aware of is that the horn is an odd instrument for two reasons: the bell faces backward, and the hand is placed in the bell to partly muffle the tone and give it that characteristic distant sound, covered, in the woods, ethereal. If you put the horn players in the wrong position, you'll kill that effect. They should be across the middle of the group so they're facing the audience directly. Facing sideways distorts the horn tone. The stage also has a great effect. When we used to go on tour, one night we'd be on a stage with a velvet curtain all around the back. If we were right against that, it was fatal. The next day we'd be in a gymnasium playing up against a cement block wall, and then we couldn't play pianissimo. So directors should give some thought to the unique playing position of the horn and put the section where it can be heard. Sometimes when the horns cannot be heard, directors will move them further forward, when it would be more effective to move them further back so the sound would reflect off the back wall.

Should beginners be started directly on the horn?

Yes, this is the accepted way now. When I was a student, my first week on the horn was so discouraging that the band director said, "Well, forget the horn, we'll take the mellophone." So I played the mellophone for several months, switched back to the horn, and was embarrassed to find out it was no easier than it had been the first time. The mellophone is fingered with the right hand; the mouthpiece is larger than the horn mouthpiece; and the fingering is that of a trumpet. When you switch to the horn, you switch to left hand fingering, with a tiny funnel mouthpiece; your hand must be placed in the bell carefully; and presto, the fingering's all different. So what is to be gained by starting on a mellophone? I don't know. Let the student find out from the very beginning how difficult the

Philip Francis Farkas
born Chicago, Illinois, March 5, 1914
1934-36: Kansas City Philharmonic (Karl Krueger)
1936-41: Chicago Symphony Orchestra
    (Frederick Stock)
1941-45: Cleveland Orchestra (Artur Rodzinski)
1945-46: Boston Symphony (Serge Koussevitsky)
1946-47: Cleveland Orchestra (George Szell)
1947-60: Chicago Symphony Orchestra
    (Artur Rodzinski, Rafael Kubelik, Fritz Reiner)
1960-present: Indiana University

Major Publications by Philip Farkas

The Art of French Horn Playing,
Summy-Birchard, 1956.
    A 95-page treatise on all aspects of horn playing,
including warm-ups, exercises for specific playing
problems, and related etudes.

The Art of Brass Playing, Wind Music, 1962.
    A 65-page book concentrating on the formation and
use of the embouchure. Photographic studies of
virtuoso players from the Chicago Symphony are
included.

*A Photographic Study of 40 Virtuoso Horn Players'
Embouchures,* Wind Music, 1970.

The Art of Musicianship, Musical Publications, 1976.
    A 51-page publication on the skills, knowledge, and
sensitivity needed by the mature musician to perform
in an artistic and professional manner.

In the Beginning

About 1956 Traugott Rohner [founder of *The Instrumentalist*] invited me to his home because I was
going to write an article for the magazine. Two other
guests happened to be there at the same time, apparently discussing advertising. They introduced
themselves as Elliot Kaehl and Theodore Kexel,
administrators of the Holton Company in Elkhorn,
Wisconsin. About that time Traugott invited us all
to go to Fanny's Italian Restaurant for dinner. As we
sat around talking, one of them said to me, "You're a
horn player. What do you think of our Holton horn?"
And I replied very undiplomatically, "I think it's one
of the worst horns I've ever played." Instead of getting
mad they looked at each other and grinned. Then
one said, "Well, I guess that's the reason we only
sold eight last year." So they asked me, "Would you
be interested in designing horns?" I could answer
"yes" immediately because I had already thought it
out. I had planned to make a horn in 1941 with the
Buescher Company but when the war came along
they discontinued instruments and started making
submarine compasses, so the whole thing went out
the window, but not in my mind. I kept the simple
idea I had: take the good qualities of each of the
various famous horns I owned at the time and eliminate the bad qualities (I knew what they were);
then add the right bore and taper for the best blowing
horns and the added comfort in the hands, which
none of them seemed to give any consideration to. It
was actually a hybrid horn that had all the good
qualities of the Alexander, the Kruspe, the Geyer,
the Schmidt, and several others. I don't say it's a
perfect horn, but it is now the best selling horn in the
country — close to 3,000 a year — so that must
indicate something.   *P.F.*

---

horn is. The horn student has to realize that his progress is going to be slower than say, an alto saxophone
player who will have great facility in the same range.
Somebody who's going to be a horn player should
have good front teeth that are fairly smooth, lips that
are reasonably well-matched (either thick or thin).
The person must have good musical instincts because
the horn is a cranky instrument; and you have to have
somebody who is eager to play, because he will experience a lot of discouragement the first few months.
I don't know of anyone who didn't want to give it up
at first. If you can get the student over a certain psychological hump, then he'll be all right from then on.

Can other players be switched to the horn?
Yes, especially the trumpet players. But not the
good ones. Find a trumpet player who uses too much
upper lip, one who has a soggy tone, and put him on
the horn. The very thing that dulls the trumpet tone
will mellow the horn tone. On the other hand the
trumpet player who gets a brilliant sound with a
terrific high register does not make a good horn player.
Adolph Herseth [the Chicago Symphony's principal
trumpet] and I used to go fishing together in Canada,
and we took our instruments because as soon as we
got home we would have to play concerts. So just for
fun, he would play my horn and I would play his
trumpet. Great as he is as a trumpet player, he had a
cast iron sound, absolutely brittle on the horn. When
I played his trumpet, I got a foggy, thick sound like a
flugelhorn with the water key open. So if you want to
switch trumpet players to the horn, find those with
the foggy sounds. You can improve both sections in
the process.

*What equipment do you suggest for school bands and
orchestras? Should they buy double horns? B♭? F?*
I've given a lot of thought to that. If you have the
funds, by all means the double horn is the answer. If
not, I suggest 2 B♭ horns and 2 F horns. The F horn is
the basic horn for a beginner because you're playing
music that's written in F, and that puts you in the
harmonic series of the music you're playing. The F
horn has the true horn tone. Otherwise it wouldn't
have been chosen by composers as the length of horn
that has the most mellow sound without getting dull
and hard. It's the ideal horn. The beginner who starts
with that has to play a lot of lip slurs because the
nature of the harmonic series requires it. Those who
play the B♭ horn will be able to play the same passages
much easier, progress will be faster, and they will get
a more trumpet-like, open sound. So the B♭ horn will
not give them the true horn sound or really initiate
them to difficulties they'll have later. The F horns
should be used for the low horn parts, where the F
horn is in its best range, and they should be assigned
to the two least advanced players. By the time the
advanced players are able to play in a register high
enough to perform first and third horn parts, they
should have the B♭ horns. This instrument would
enhance their high register, and because they are the
more advanced players, they would be able to cope
with the B♭ horn and still get a good horn tone.

What about horns and marching bands?
I don't like them in marching bands. Horns in march-

ing bands usually play after beats, which means that invariably you're playing your note when one foot is in the air. You never have a good foundation. Our horn players at Indiana switch to upright altos, bell-front altos, or mellophoniums when they march. The horn is an awkward instrument to play when standing. As a matter of fact, most American horn players don't like to play standing, even on a solo recital when they're standing still. Also, on a football field, you need to play louder, so there's no earthly good in putting your hand in the bell. Pointing the bell up or forward without the hand in it gives a lot more resonance to the horn, but this is very awkward. It's just a double problem, and using another instrument is a better answer.

Do they have embouchure problems as a result?

Yes they do, but Fred Ebbs [the band director] has agreed with me that they can use their own horn mouthpiece on these instruments. There's a simple adapter. I think that's a much better solution.

How about concert band and orchestra literature?

Many students have quit the horn because of the uninspired music. Although I already had professional ambitions in high school, I would still have nothing to play but after beats in the school band, not only in the marches but in the concert pieces also: Out of sheer boredom I would practice octaves in my after beats, blowing one an octave higher; or play triplets, anything to help me gain some technique. That was very discouraging. Now the writers for band are so much better equipped and the horn parts are much more exciting. Still it's possible for a director to bring out some intermediate or elementary numbers which are very boring for the horn players. The director who wants to keep his horn players enthusiastic will pick music that occasionally features the horn.

When conducting a concert with an important horn solo, should the conductor throw a big cue or treat it more casually?

I always found that a big cue was never very nice. Fritz Reiner would give you the slightest nod of the head. There are three things that give you confidence when coming in: (1) you're absolutely sure of the count; (2) you'd know where to come in even if you didn't count because you've rehearsed it and you know where it comes musically; and (3) the conductor will give you a little cue. I think the conductor should avoid giving a big cue because it makes you look like an idiot: it implies that you didn't know where the place was until he told you, when the truth is you probably know the place as well or better than he does. If you're young and timid the big gesture might even scare you. Some of the best conductors look over at the strings and just give the horn a little flick of their finger. I've seen horn players fall apart completely and can't play at all when they get a double whammy from a conductor. So I think the right psychology is to cue lightly but look the other way. The moment you see you've got him started, pretend like it's not too important.

I don't want to put you on the spot with your colleagues around the world, but are there any players you particularly admire for particular reasons?

When I was growing up, most of us wanted to be or-chestra players, so people like Bruno Jaenecke (New York Philharmonic) and Anton Horner (Philadelphia Orchestra) were our idols. Now I think many of the young people consider a solo career first and the orchestra second. In that case they would certainly have to admire Barry Tuckwell, one of the leading soloists.

What do you like about his playing?

The virtuosity of it, the technique, the beautiful big tone. The fact that he can get up and play a whole recital from memory is always imposing to those of us who are orchestra players because we don't memorize. He has a patrician style, and plays with the same finesse as a good flutist, oboist, or clarinetist. That was almost unheard-of years ago. A horn player was happy to get the notes, and if he did it in tune, why, he was an expert. But now, they want finesse. And he has that. Another great name along with his is Hermann Baumann. He's very well-known nearly all over the world, but not too well-known in this country. He has the same finesse, but he has probably the most exciting aggressiveness in his playing. He takes chances, plays brilliant passages, and does them so well that you believe no one else could do it that way.

How about the orchestral players?

Well, I think you can almost say that if they're already in the big orchestras, they're already to be admired. They wouldn't be there if they couldn't play.

It's an extremely difficult league now, isn't it?

Yes. I had some talent, but I think I was extremely lucky to become first horn in Kansas City just four years after beginning on the instrument. In those days if you owned a horn you were already halfway in because it was such a rare instrument that whoever owned a horn was invited everywhere. Now that's no longer true. There were dozens studying then, today there are literally thousands of horn players and you have to be good to pass the audition. Just a few years ago there were 3 openings for the Philadelphia Orchestra and 120 people tried out. But, I'm happy to say that one who was chosen was one of my students.

What do you want to give to your students?

What they want. For example, some students want to go into the education field. I don't think they have to play like the first horn in the Boston Symphony, but they do have to play well enough to convince their students that they know what they're talking about. These education majors have to learn so many other things. The horn is my lifetime project, but for the person who is going to be a band director, I would rather see him learn to play the horn adequately, and also know fingerings on the clarinet, be able to teach trombone positions, and all of the other necessary skills. On the other hand if someone says he wants to be a symphony horn player, I don't want him to play the clarinet because it will ruin his lip for the horn. I want him to learn the orchestral literature cold so he can go up on an audition and play from memory. I think there's nothing more disconcerting to a conductor than to ask for the Tchaikovsky Fifth and see someone frantically looking through his music. You wonder what he's been doing for the last 10 years if he doesn't know that work. It's like examining a minister for the vacancy in your church and you say, "Minister number 3, please give the Lord's Prayer." And he frantically looks through the Bible. You wouldn't hire him. Well, the Tchaikovsky Fifth is our Lord's Prayer, and a horn player had better know it.

Have you developed some phrases or teaching methods through the years that make it easier to get across things that in the beginning of your teaching career were very difficult to explain?

Oh yes. I think I have quite a reputation for anecdotes or parables that illustrate what I want; but I've also tried to reduce much of my teaching to logic. First I think of myself as being similar to a tailor who alters clothing for a man who wants to dress well. I'm the tailor to a horn player who wants to play well. A person who is a perfect 42 regular can go in a store, buy a 42 regular suit, and come out without any alterations. But there are no perfect 42 regular horn players; and so I think of myself as the man who takes the student who has a lot of attributes but has a little difficulty here or there, who needs a little more in his high register, or better intonation, or improved staccato; and I alter his playing a bit. I always have graduate students who are auditors, and I beg them not to come to the same student's lesson each week, because they will think that I preach only one thing. Listening to a lesson week after week with a student who has bad intonation, they would say that all I teach is intonation. But with others I will emphasize high register or legato; the next one may have bad rhythm and I'll emphasize that. The sad truth is that the student who has a problem will have it most of his life unless he fights it right from the beginning. So I tailor the lesson to the student's needs; I don't just teach generalities.

And the second thing I believe is that the good teacher is teaching the student to be his own teacher. When I got my first job my teacher said to me, "You're ready for this job. I won't teach you another day. Your next teacher is this job." I told him I wasn't ready to cut the apron strings, but he said, "You are done. I won't teach you. I know what's best for you. You go there." So I went and when I came to a problem — a musical or a physical problem — it was almost as if Mr. Dufrasne was sitting next to me. I had studied with him for so long that when I came to a problem I knew what he would say, and I answered the question myself. He was a teacher who taught me to be my own teacher. This is the entire object. If I can teach somebody to solve his own problems, then I'm a good teacher.

What are the signs that they're ready to cut the apron strings?

It's very much like raising a child; you know when he's ready to go out into the world and when he isn't. When you get to a certain stage, you know that he still has more to learn, but the time has come when the best way to learn is in practical situations rather than through more teaching.

You spoke of reducing your teaching to logic. Can you give an example?

When a student tongues when the music says slur, or vice versa, I point out that there are only two ways you can start a note on a wind instrument: tongue it, or slur to it from a previous note. Then I say, "Play me a G and an A in that order." And so he'll play it and maybe he'll tongue it. And I say, "Bravo, that's what I was thinking of, that you would tongue it. There was only one other way you could have done it. You could have slurred it. You had a 50-50 chance of outguessing me because you could only do it one of two ways." Then I tell him, "When you're looking at the music I expect your odds to go up to 100%."

Another teaching technique is one I learned from Jerry Stowell, who was in the woodwind quintet with me in Chicago for 17 years. He was the E♭ clarinet of the Chicago Symphony, and I never heard him squeak, yet I've heard every other clarinet player in the world squeak. Furthermore, his students never squeaked. One day I asked him why. He told me that when his beginning students could hold a long tone he would tell them, "When I snap my fingers I want you to squeak that note." He said they got so they could do it at will. Then he told them, "Now you know how to squeak, never do it again." I've used this same process in my own teaching, and it works very well. One of the problems brass players have is that as you hold a middle high note and taper it off to pianissimo, sizzling noises suddenly come in. They are what we call "frying bacon sounds." I was bugged by that problem for many years, and then I decided to try Jerry Stowell's idea: first learn how to do it, then learn how to undo it. I found that by moving my lips a certain way I could bring the sizzle on immediately. So I'd hold a long note and then begin to sizzle. Then all I had to do was to reverse the process, and I've never had a sizzle since. I have one student right now who has a flutter in his tone. It's a rather common thing. He plays fortissimo and a kind of "double" sound comes out. It isn't an overtone, it's an undertone, a very rough tone sounding an octave lower. For a month or two I tried to tell him how to avoid it. I said "Try swinging the pressure on your mouthpiece a little over to the left ...then to the right...then down...then up...then move the mouthpiece up or down...drop your jaw." There are a thousand things I could tell him. Nothing seemed to help until finally one day I said, "Look, you get this sound often enough, but it's always unwillingly and you're always disappointed when it happens. What would happen if you tried to produce it? Next week come back and when I snap my fingers you get that horrible rattle that comes in." The next week he could do it. I asked him what he did to produce the sound. "Oh," he said, "I just push my jaw up a little bit." So I told him, "Well that's simple enough, never push your jaw up again and you won't have that awful rattle." It worked.

Your book, The Art of French Horn Playing (*Summy-Birchard, 1956) is so well-known, so thorough, and full of fine material. Did anything creep into the publication that is not really the way you want it?*

There may be some things I could add, but I don't want to retract anything. I found a couple of typographical errors in the first edition, and they've been corrected. I get quite a kick out of it when people like Barry Tuckwell tell me the book is the Bible for horn players. It's a nice feeling.

You've had a tremendously successful career — a quarter century of professional playing at the highest level, recordings, books; you've been teaching at Indiana University for almost 20 years. What do you believe is most significant? What really matters?

I used to wonder what I am contributing to future generations, what will I leave for posterity? And I thought, "Well, this particularly good concert is one thing." But by the time we orchestra members have changed to our street clothes, there's a man sweeping the stage, the worklight is on, and the concert is practically forgotten. The critic's review will appear in the paper the next day and from there on it goes into the dim distant past. So it's not that. That's not what you leave to posterity. And I thought, "Well, it's recordings." When Koussevitsky would make a recording he would always say, "Be very careful. We must make this well. We're not making recordings, we are making historical documents." And so I thought, "That's what

I leave to posterity." Now I'm old enough to see some of the records I made years ago arriving on the bargain counter — old 78s or mono instead of stereo. So that wasn't it. And I began to wonder, "Am I doing anything in this world that I can leave behind me?" And you know what it is? It's the students. I have students who are now at Philadelphia or the New York Philharmonic, and they in turn are teaching some of the precepts that I gave to them which my teacher gave to me, and his teacher gave to him. Who knows how far down the line it will go, but it's a nice feeling to know that some of the things I believe in that my teacher taught me are still being taught to others. That's my sole legacy to posterity, and because I can enhance the gift by writing a book, that's even better. It's the only thing I leave. The records are no good, the concerts are forgotten. What you leave is your teaching. Sometimes I meet school band and orchestra directors who say, "I missed the boat. Here I am teaching a bunch of kids — some are smart and some are dumb. But if I had really extended myself I could have been in the New York Philharmonic." The truth is that what they're doing is really more down-to-earth, practical, and self-satisfying than the playing. ∎

April, 1979

A Horn Symposium: Old Problems Re-Visited

Richard D. Bingham

In many parts of the country student horn players do not have private teachers but are solely dependent on their band or orchestra director for guidance. During the Twelfth Annual Horn Symposium held on the Tennessee Tech University campus in January of this year, I had an opportunity to observe a large number of high school horn players. I believe there are four areas of horn playing in which instrumental directors can improve on what they are teaching young horn students in the public schools: range development, playing posture, transposition, and hand stopping.

Range Development

Instrumental directors have learned what a proper horn embouchure should look like through the various college and university instrumental methods classes. Philip Farkas in *The Art of Brass Playing*[1] and *The Art of French Horn Playing*[2] has given numerous excellent photographic examples of proper horn embouchure to guide the student and director. But we have yet to clearly teach our instrumental directors what the horn student must do with the embouchure to overcome the G3 to G5 range limitation many students have (The Two Octave Syndrome). In previous years the nature of wind ensemble and orchestral

literature permitted the young horn player to get by within this limit. However, newer literature often demands extreme upper and lower register development from the student. In some instances this requires the ability to play C6 or D6 (surpassing some Baroque horn literature in upper range if not endurance) and at the same time the ability to play down to B♭2 or G2 or even lower on occasion. A proper horn embouchure formation will aid in producing these extremes but until the student supports the tone properly with the air stream the upper and lower registers will not respond well, the tone will be thin, intonation will be insecure, and the student's endurance limited.

The solution to the problem is found in the student's efficient use of the embouchure plus the air stream. Proper embouchure development has long been recognized as essential to good brass playing; however, the role of the air stream in producing the upper and lower horn registers has not been recognized by many directors as being such a significant factor. We tell our students to support the tone with the breath to achieve a "proper" horn tone; but seldom tell them to continue to use this same support for ease of tone production in the upper and lower register.

Philip Farkas in *The Art of French Horn Playing*,

pp. 57-58, and William Brophy in *Technical Studies for Solving Special Problems on the Horn*[3], pp. 11-12, discuss high range development from their respective viewpoints. The common feature found in both writers' discussions is the emphasis placed on the use of the air stream in conjunction with the embouchure for producing the upper register. Both suggest a refocusing of the aperture in the embouchure to make it smaller and an increase in the velocity and pressure of the air stream. In effect the tone is riding the air stream to a higher pitch in much the same way that a lip slur is produced in the middle register. Again, the key elements are a smaller aperture and an increase of pressure in the air stream. Farkas says the student must acquire the knack of "flicking" the notes up or down with the embouchure to give the required flexibility necessary for smooth embouchure changes. The feeling of the "flick" is described as a "mouthing" such as a goldfish makes or similar to saying a series of P's, but without completely closing the lips. Farkas then gives a slurring exercise beginning:

F horn

The drill is intended to be played on the F side of the double horn and extends up to C6 to teach the student to "flick" the upper notes into place.

Brophy's method is composed of two ways to approach the upper register: psychological and physiological. It is psychological in that if the student can play a G5 then it is a simple matter to play an A♭5 because it is only a half-step higher; it is physiological because the air stream speed and intensity are used to produce the higher tones with embouchure adjustment minimized. Brophy gives a series of six drills to develop control of the air stream that are based around:

Both of these sets of drills work well and are to be recommended to the student. But in my opinion they move a little too quickly for students who do not have the opportunity to study with a private teacher. Therefore, I would like to suggest the following exercises to directors whose students do not have this resource:

Perfect 4ths

F horn

Blow through the slur; support tone with the breath.

B♭ horn

The patterns may be reversed playing the upper note to the lower; the student should use the syllable ee-oo to make the downward slur.

Perfect 5ths

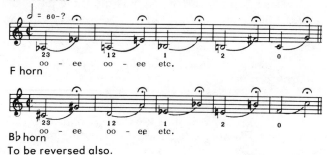

F horn
oo – ee   oo – ee   etc.

B♭ horn
oo – ee   oo – ee   etc.
To be reversed also.

Octaves   As before

F horn

B♭ horn   Reverse

Play these patterns also.

The function of these drills is to start the student working on basic embouchure aperture and air stream adjustments as preliminary study to both the Farkas and Brophy drills. When he can make the slurs easily and clearly, he may proceed to the Brophy drill and after the first two drills begin work on the Farkas drill which requires extensive use of the F side of the double horn. One important premise of the drills is to cause the student to use both the air stream and embouchure aperture as a complete unit for upper range playing. The "oo—ee" syllable will aid the production of the slur causing the additional rounding of the lip aperture necessary for the upper register and at the same time aid in refocusing the air stream and raise its intensity and pressure so that the pitch will ride it upward. Refocusing the aperture recalls a principle Gunther Schuller articulated in his book, *Horn Technique*[4] (pp. 20-21) for upper range playing. When the student refocuses and supports the tone with the breath, the air stream directed into the mouthpiece behaves as shown in the diagram.

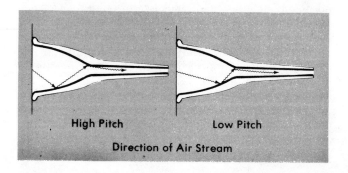

High Pitch   Low Pitch

Direction of Air Stream

To demonstrate this principle to a student, have him buzz a low tone without the mouthpiece and find the point in front of him where the air strikes his hand. Then have him buzz a high tone and find where the air hits his hand (if he can buzz high enough, the air will pass right down the front of his chin). Another check may be made to see whether the chin arches down more and whether the "U" formed by the corners of the mouth and the point of the chin becomes more clearly defined (the purpose being to keep the flesh under the mouthpiece firm and flat to balance the muscle tension in the embouchure and keep it from collapsing as the student plays in the upper register). It must be understood that the student will not achieve this objective in a matter of days or weeks. It is an on-going drill that requires months and sometimes years of concentrated effort. The reward of a free and responsive upper register is the result of continuing effort on the student's part.

Low register development requires less struggle for the student than the upper register; the chief problem being to get the student to work in this register in the first place. Once he has become accustomed to using the low range then the skill when developed will be retained for life. Farkas correctly points out that the register between C4 down to C3 is the weakest on the instrument (a fact that many directors and composers tend to forget, and one in which great flexibility is often difficult for student horn players). Farkas (p. 60) suggests a "blasting in" technique and follows this with a drill to be played slurred and tongued extending down to D3.

The drill is concentrated on strengthening the octave range of C3 to C4 but it does not go below this point. Newer literature demands that the horn players be able to play effectively and with control down at least another fifth to F2.

Brophy has developed a series of studies similar to the Farkas drills that extend all the way down to the fundamental of the F horn, C2. He then follows these drills with a series of pitch bending exercises for the Bb side of the horn using the second partials. The student is to bend the pitch by as much as a perfect fourth (pitch bending is a playing technique that was used by low horn players to obtain notes between the fundamental and the second partial by relaxing the embouchure and blowing the second partial flat during the valveless natural horn era). This in turn is followed by a similar series of drills for the F side of the instrument. The function of the drills is to strengthen the low register and to promote the development of a controlled but centered horn tone in this range. I recommend their use for low range development. I find that some students are not able to grasp the concepts in the explanations that the two authors have written and I have on occasion used a slightly different conceptual approach to deal with this problem. Since it is necessary for the student to get some of the lower lip out of the mouthpiece (only slightly though) to

allow for a larger embouchure aperture opening, which in turn facilitates the low frequency vibrations necessary for good low range playing, have him duck his head into the horn slightly. This will permit the aperture to open larger and allow the lower lip to move out of the mouthpiece the required amount. A second aid for the young student is to have him "drop" the lower jaw slightly. (Brophy describes this as a "slight forward movement" but it seems easier for students to grasp "drop".) Again, this facilitates the larger aperture opening needed for the low tones and helps pull some of the lower lip out of the mouthpiece. If the student is diligent in his practice of the low range studies, he may notice in a few days a significant improvement in the power and control he has acquired. This in turn will promote the necessary additional push to continue his work in this area.

A final low range problem for many students and some directors concerns bass clef usage. Most of us are aware that two forms of F clef notation are used in bass clef horn writing, and it is sometimes difficult to decide which one the composer has used. The *old notation* system places the notes an octave below where they really belong if written on a conventional grand staff in bass clef. This system is used in most orchestra music composed before the twentieth century when bass clef is used in the horn parts. *New notation* (predominantly a twentieth century development) puts the notes in their proper place on the grand staff. The confusion arises when the bass clef notes are playable in both systems.

R. Strauss, *Till Eulenspiegel*. In old notation; but it can be mistakenly read in new notation.

Here the sense of the line or ensemble texture may be the only guides the director has. However, if the notes are ridiculously low, such as appearing to descend past the fundamental of the F horn, then the part is definitely written in old notation.

D. Shostakovich, *Symphony No. 5*. Clearly in old notation.

Playing Posture

During the symposium I observed a number of students sitting with their backs in contact with the back of the chair. While other wind players may adopt such a playing posture, the construction of the horn requires the player to lean forward somewhat and be "over" the instrument. Indeed, this is good because of the psychological effect: the student gains confidence by being "master of the instrument." I recommend that the student sit angled to the right a bit (turn the chair slightly to the right) and turn the upper body slightly to the left in order to face front. The left leg should be in front of the chair, slightly to the right of center. The right leg should be behind and to the left of the right front chair leg. This accomplishes two purposes: (1) it permits the right leg, which supports the bell, to have a greater degree of adjustment than when it is placed in front of the chair; (2) it allows the bell to "open out" so that a channel is formed between the body and the inside of the right forearm. The right hand position within the bell itself is discussed thoroughly on pages 12-14 of *The Art of French Horn Playing*. A final advantage is gained by short or long waisted players who adopt this posture, because it becomes a simple matter for these people to bring the bell up off the leg (commonly referred to as "holding free") and adjust the instrument's position so the mouthpiece meets the lips. Otherwise those who are short waisted may find that the mouthpiece meets their forehead or those who are long waisted may find that the mouthpiece hits them in the chin or neck. This seating position also allows additional freedom of movement while playing and is more comfortable than resting the bell on the leg.

Transposition

A number of young horn students (and some directors) at the symposium did not have a clear understanding of how to read an E♭ horn part when playing the instrument in F. A simple formula will suffice: read the note down a major 2nd and add two flats to the key signature. Remember that to "add two flats" is the same as subtracting two sharps and thus an E♭ horn key signature of G (one sharp) becomes an F horn signature of F (one flat) because the one sharp cancels one of the two added flats leaving only one.

Band and orchestra directors often ask when this skill should be taught. I believe the best time is after the first year or the first method book, whichever comes first. Because a skill learned should be used, I also teach additional transpositions such as D or C after the E♭ to F. Once these have been learned by the student, the remainder of the common transpositions (low B♭, E, G, A, and high B♭) can be acquired with ease.

Both interval and clef transposition systems work well and each has its own proponents. I favor the interval system because most students and many teachers are not well enough equipped to deal with a plethora of obsolete clefs such as baritone, soprano, and mezzo-soprano to use them to transpose. A simple formula will give the proper key signature and interval for transposition: add one sharp to the key of horn that is required (other than F horn). For example, to transpose a part written for horn in D, add one sharp to that key name, resulting in a key signature of A. This also establishes the correct interval, for the distance between the D horn's written C3 and the key of A is a minor third, the correct transposition interval. Of course, the student must know his major scales and key signatures.

Transposition is a fundamental part of the horn player's equipment and should be developed early in his training. The skill is essential when reading British brass band literature, older wind ensemble music, and a large body of literature containing parts for horns with various crooks now played by many youth orchestras.

Hand Stopping

The hand stopping technique gives young players more difficulty than any other area except range development. Many directors do not understand what happens when their students are required to play stopped horn. To further complicate the matter, two different but related phenomena can take place depending on how and when the bell is closed with the right hand. For example, if the student plays C5 on the F horn and gradually closes the bell with the right hand the pitch drops until, when the bell is fully closed, it is about a half tone lower. On the other hand, if the student first tightly closes the bell of the horn with the right hand and then attempts to play C5 he will find that C♯5 is produced; the pitch has risen a half step making the F horn an F♯ horn. Much discussion and argument has taken place over the years in an effort to explain this seeming contradiction. Some writers believe that a distorted series of harmonics is produced and others believe that a new harmonic series is caused by closing the bell with the right hand.

During the natural (no valves) horn era, players took advantage of both of these phenomena to make a chromatic scale possible in the horn's middle register; today's player still uses some of this playing technique when he makes pitch and tuning corrections with the right hand in the bell. To ease confusion, the student should understand that the pitch is lowered when the right hand is placed in the bell. A quick check with a strobe tuner will convince both the student and director of this fact. Have the student play his written C5 (concert F) with his hand in the normal position within the bell and adjust the main tuning slide for correct intonation. When this is done, have him remove the right hand from the bell completely. The pitch as measured by the strobe will be much sharper, about a quarter tone. Therefore, the effect of the hand in the bell is to lower the pitch as well as to help create the characteristic horn tone. The student can use this fact to help him play better in tune.

When the bell is fully closed to begin with, the pitch rises; in effect the hand has shortened the instrument. For the student to play a stopped part on the F horn he must fully close the bell with the right hand and read (transpose) the note one half step lower. In the middle range the F horn works well, but as the notes move progressively higher the F horn harmonics become much closer together. There is no solution to the problem except for the student to listen and play as accurately as possible. The low range is also problematical but Brophy has given some assistance here by advising the student to close the bell even more tightly with the right hand and at the same time gently press down with the left.

I have not discussed hand stopping on the B♭ side of the double horn because this instrument is shorter than the F horn (about 9 feet as opposed to 12). When the bell of the B♭ horn is fully closed the pitch rises about three quarters of a tone. On a single B♭ horn with four valves no problem is encountered because the fourth valve (usually a thumb valve) is intended to overcome the problem. The thumb valve adds a length of tubing lowering the pitch by three quarters of a tone. To hand stop the instrument the student depresses the thumb valve and fingers the note normally without transposing. (The thumb valve is also useful for helping correct some intonation problems such as the flat G4 normally fingered first valve; this may be played in tune fingered thumb valve, second, and third valves.) The normal double horn does not usually have a stop valve on the B♭ side (except for some models of compensating double horns), and therefore hand stopping is only practical on the F side of the instrument. A logical fingering pattern results only on the F side of the double horn when the bell is fully closed. The B♭ side produces a stopped horn fingering pattern that is too complex for the student to use and it does not work in a logical sequence. The B♭ side may be used in a few cases to produce some useable but isolated stopped notes. An example of such use would be playing an A♭5 stopped on the B♭ horn using the alternate fingering for G5 (first valve)

instead of open. Notes which belong to partials which are by nature flat, those of the fifth, seventh, and tenth partials of the B♭ horn, may yield useable stopped notes in some circumstances. The only other solution is for American horn makers to add a stop valve to the double horn. This would be an expensive undertaking involving many acoustical and mechanical design problems that instrument makers seem little interested in. Therefore, the student must learn to cope with the F side of the instrument effectively in order to hand stop. ∎

Notes

[1]Farkas, Philip, *The Art of Brass Playing*, Wind Music, 1962.
[2]Farkas, Philip, *The Art of French Horn Playing*, Summy-Birchard, 1956.
[3]Brophy, William, *Technical Studies for Solving Special Problems on the Horn*, Carl Fischer, 1977.
[4]Schuller, Gunther, *Horn Technique*, Oxford University Press, 1962.

April, 1979

Choosing A Horn

Walter A. Lawson

Thirty years ago in this country, horn players needed to play only the standard F-B♭ double horn in order to earn a living. Pieces that called for very high, sustained playing were rarely performed and players were able to manage with their regular equipment. Seasons were shorter then, the musicians were physically fresher and missed notes were occasionally forgiven. Conductors stayed at home with their orchestras instead of guest conducting extensively and being exposed to the occasional star horn player who can negotiate extremely high parts with surety and ease. As orchestra seasons lengthened and conductors, critics, and the public became more demanding of accuracy, horn players were forced to work harder physically and were under more pressure to play the high parts without missing notes.

There were three solutions to these problems:
1. Hire more players
2. Change or modify existing equipment
3. Use different equipment

Because of longer seasons and increased numbers of services, players pressured orchestra managements to increase the number of members in the horn section. Instead of 4 players and one assistant 1st, horn sections in major orchestras began using an associate 1st player who played part of the concerts for the 1st horn leaving the assistant to spell other members of the section. Some orchestras in Europe had used six or more players for some time. Many of the large orchestras

now have a staff of six horn players and hire extras when needed. This permits occasional rest for everyone, improving performances.

Until the last decade about the only thing a horn player could do to make the equipment perform differently was to change mouthpieces. This was done to make high notes easier and to change the quality of sound. Many players now have their instruments modified in other ways. The sound and dynamic range can be altered by changing the bell; the intonation and response can be altered by changing the mouthpipe; and tubing can be cut or lengthened to change the basic key of the instrument.

Many horn players now own more than one instrument so the proper one can be selected for the part. If the music to be played is in the upper register, a horn with a shorter tube length with fewer harmonics will improve accuracy. However, tone and carrying power are often sacrificed.

Most beginning students use the single F horn because the sound of this particular instrument has long been considered the traditional sound of the horn and many teachers want to instill this concept in their students. The F horn's long tube length gives the instrument a high resistance with many close harmonics in the high register. Therefore the instrument requires precise lip control and intense mental concentration, the foundation for good musicianship. By the time the player reaches high school or college he is ready for the double horn. This instrument opens up many possibilities for a faster and more accurate technique because of its easier high register and many alternate fingerings.

Lighter instruments are also available: the compensating double F-B♭ in which the valve slides of the F horn are short extensions of the B♭ slides, and the single B♭ horn whose light weight and easy response in the upper register make things easier for the high horn player.

The B♭ and higher horns are most popular with recording artists, pit and show musicians, college instructors, and chamber music players. Recording artists are not so much concerned with sound and volume, as with accuracy and the ability to play very high parts. Pit musicians need to be able to play continuously for long periods of time and chamber music players need an instrument that makes technical passages easier.

As a result of the requirements of today's horn players, manufacturers are offering instruments in a variety of pitches, bores, and alloys. As a general rule when the basic pitch of an instrument is raised by making it shorter, the high register is more accurate due to the wider intervals between harmonics but the low register sound is less acceptable and carrying power is usually reduced.

The following modern horns are available to the player whose choice is dictated by his job requirements:

1. *Single F horn.* Still mostly used by beginning students, these instruments are made with emphasis on strength and durability rather than on playing quality. Usually this horn has three valves and sometimes an extra E♭ slide which should be discarded. A horn player should learn to transpose and can start doing this at an early age. The student also should begin to associate the harmonics with the written notes. An E♭ slide changes the harmonic series to a lower pitch causing considerable confusion.

2. *F-B♭ double horn.* By far the most-used model. Almost all horn parts can be played on these instruments but the extreme high range is precarious. They are available with a wide variety of options, some being:
   • Full double or compensating
   • Alloy — yellow brass, red brass, nickle silver.
The alloy selected affects the instrument's resistance to corrosion and the timbre of sound. The ease of response and dynamic range depends on the alloy's hardness.
   • Natural, lacquered or plated finish
   • Change valve reversible F to B♭ or B♭ to F
   • Extra stopping valve
   • Ascending 3rd valve
   • Small, medium or large bore
   • Screw bell (detachable). This is easier for travel, and also allows sound and dynamic range to be changed by using a bell of different alloy or hardness.
   • Detachable mouthpipe. Intonation and response can be changed by using a mouthpipe of a different taper.
   • Separate B♭ and F tuning slides.

3. *Single B♭.* This horn is easier to play than the full double because of its lighter weight but it still has an acceptable sound because the bell is usually the same size as a full double. Many players select a fast taper mouthpipe that favors the high register. The B♭ is mostly used by 1st and 3rd symphony players and in chamber music. The available options are nearly the same as for the full double with the following additions:
   • Extra low F crook to be used in place of the stop or A crook
   • Extra built-in low F extension operated by a 5th valve
   • Ascending valve to C (makes open notes of otherwise poor harmonics

4. *B♭-B♮ or B♭-C full double.* A rare but sometimes useful instrument which makes upward slurs easier because, as with the ascending valve, the player moves from a long to a shorter horn.

5. *B♭-High F deskant, full double or compensating model.* Usually this model has a stop valve. These instruments are now in wide use both by high and low players because of the demands of playing difficult high parts. They are also acceptable for standard orchestral high parts and are a necessary tool for the recording and chamber music artist. With a wide variety of bores and alloys available, these instruments can be modified to suit many players.

6. *Single high F deskant.* A six-foot horn, small bore, and light in weight. Usually this three-valve horn is used for chamber music and high, light passages. It is not designed for carrying power and has some intonation problems.

7. *Triple Horn in F-B♭-high F.* An attempt to put all of the qualities desired into one instrument. The mechanical parts are quite complicated. They are very expensive. There are design problems in that the horn plays best in only one register.

8. *B♭-high B♭-full double.* The recent design is, as yet, not widely used but it makes high playing even more secure.

All of these instruments are available from European factories. Most of the horns manufactured in the U.S. are full double, single F, and single B♭, in that order. American manufacturers have been slow to produce the higher pitched instruments but demands from players are being felt and some American deskants are just coming on the market.

The horn player of today has a wide variety of instruments to choose from and can perform many modifications on his own instrument. The demands are greater both physically and musically than they have ever been but instructors and manufacturers seem to be rising to the challenge. Students are better trained due to some fine teachers whose ideas have been widely published. The International Horn Society, through its clinics and journal, has exposed young people to the ideas and playing of the finest artists. And manufacturers throughout the world are exchanging ideas and striving to meet the demands of the players. All the horn player has to do is practice. ∎

April, 1979

General Maintenance of the Horn

Lawrence Kirmser

The horn has long been considered to be the aristocrat of the brass family. Rightly or wrongly, this instrument is in a number of ways unique beside the other members of this musical family. It is not unique, however, in that it, like all musical instruments, is subjected to the wear and corrosion caused by normal use. To keep the horn in top shape, and to help eliminate potential instrument failure, the responsible musician should keep their instrument on a strict general and preventive maintenance program.

General Horn Inspection

Mouthpiece. Attention should be paid to the continuity of the mouthpiece plating as well as to the condition of its rim. Is it peppered with small dents and scratches? The shaft must be straight and round so that it will fit perfectly into the instrument.

Leadpipe. After extended use, small pink spots may appear on the outside of the leadpipe. Sometimes these spots appear as small dark blemishes beneath the lacquer or epoxy coating. This symptom indicates that advanced corrosion (from the inside of the leadpipe) is working its way through to the outside surface. To correct this situation, the leadpipe should be replaced by a professional technician.

Rotor Valves. When depressing and releasing the rotor valves of an instrument, each should respond in a resilient, crisp manner. There are any number of reasons why a valve will fail to respond correctly, the most common being 1. it requires a thorough cleaning and relubrication; 2. the mechanical linkage (if present) is knocked out of alignment; 3. the valve casing has been dented or distorted or 4. a valve rotor has been distorted.

To function properly, each rotor must be in close adjustment. The valve springs should conform to the manufacturer's specifications and be balanced so that all valves possess an identical response. There should be an absence of noise when the valves are worked rapidly. The plated surface of the rotor, if present, must be without scratches, pitting or other evidence of corrosion. Deep scratches on the surface of a rotor indicate the presence of damaging foreign matter or burrs within the valve casing. Obviously, all valve caps must be present and easily unscrewed when it is necessary to remove the rotor from its casing.

Rotor mechanisms are either the *mechanical style linkage* (where a series of pivot arms activate the valves) or they use the *stringing* method to transfer the rotational motion from the key to the rotor. The rotational adjustment of the valve is checked by removing the bottom rotor cap and making sure that the mark on the bottom of the valve shaft lines up exactly with the adjacent marks on the sleeve of the rotor bearing as the key is fully depressed and released (see illustration). It is important that there is no play in the keys due to worn mechanical linkage or stretched valve string. As a final check of the rotor valves, the key levers should be adjusted to an angle that facilitates a comfortable hand position for the performer.

Tuning Slides. The tuning slides of a horn should be lubricated so that they can be easily moved with gentle finger pressure. The frequency of lubrication will depend primarily upon the amount of use and type of lubrication used. Good preventive maintenance is absolutely necessary for all brasses. This is due, for the most part, to the exposure to corrosive saliva that this family of instruments receives.

Slide tube alignment determines how easily the slide moves. The internal surface should be free from excess lubricant, saliva and corrosion. As a further check, if the slide is so equipped, examine the water key assembly (spring adjustment, lubrication, cork condition, and wobble in hinge tube).

Body Section. When all the slides and valves have been removed, check the bore of the instrument for cleanliness, residue, and any signs of corrosion. Occasionally, small objects may get lodged in the tubing of the instrument, causing it to either play very much out of tune or, in other cases, to be totally inoperable. This is a problem more common to the larger brasses, however.

Examine all of the braces for solder continuity and take special note of severe body dents that may affect the playing of the instrument. Soft soldered ferrules, slides, slide knobs, and finger hooks should also be checked for continuity. As a final step, examine the finish for surface etching where the hands touch the instrument.

Case. The importance of the instrument's case to the preventive maintenance of all instruments is often underestimated. Each case should be of a solid construction and properly fitted to its instrument with blocking and padding. It should be equipped with sturdy, dependable latches, and be devoid of loose articles that can damage the instrument.

Preventing Stuck Tuning Slides

One of the more common problems with instruments in the brass family is that of the stuck or frozen tuning slide. As with many common problems, this is usually the result of pure and simple neglect. More often than not, a slide will become frozen as the result of not being lubricated regularly enough, or by using an improper lubricating agent. Depending upon the amount of use, geographic area, etc., it is wise to pull, clean, and re-lubricate all tuning slides at least once a week. There are commercial slide greases, lanolin, or petroleum jellies available that will do this job effectively.

The slides that are most likely to become frozen are those which are exposed to saliva most. This usually means the leadpipe and the tubing up to and including the first tuning slide. Beyond this point, saliva exposure is relatively minimal, and is controlled adequately by emptying water keys frequently. It should be noted, however, that even this so-called minimal exposure is enough to cause radical damage to an instrument if not attended to regularly throughout its lifetime. Not only does saliva react chemically with the metal, causing it to pit and etch, but it also leaves grainy salt deposits that make the slide operate with even more resistance.

As a general rule the removal of frozen slides should be left to the professional technician who has the proper skills and tools at his disposal. For the professional, this is often a routine task taking only a few minutes; however if attempted by a student it usually ends up an expensive disaster.

The Rotor Valves

As with the piston-type valve, the primary function of the rotor valve is to rapidly and accurately change the length of the vibrating column of air. The development and refinement of the rotor valve was by no means a panacea for the instrument acoustically, however, it was perhaps the most significant innovation throughout its long history. The invention of the first rotor valve mechanism took place in Berlin around 1815 by Fredrich Bluhmel and/or Heinrich Stölzel (written history, unfortunately, does not address itself very clearly to this point). The rotor valve that we know today, however, is generally accredited to Joseph Riedl of Vienna, where he developed it in 1832.

For many years Europe, especially Germany, was the leader in the production of rotor-type valves. In fact, up until World War II, U.S. instrument manufacturers were importing German rotors and valve assemblies for their instrument lines. When trade with Germany ceased, manufacturers were forced to develop and manufacture their own rotor systems. C.G. Conn Corporation pioneered the development of the tapered rotor cylinder. This new design was unique in that it allowed the cylinder to settle into it's casing as it wore, thus preventing looseness. This certainly didn't eliminate the need for periodic rotor adjustment, but it did make these adjustments easier for the technician. Many other brass manufacturers have since adopted this design.

Rotor valves are also unique in that they are often unplated brass. More recently, however, rotors are commonly plated with hard nickel by manufacturers. This plating helps to increase the playing-life and durability of this valve, yet, even plated rotors must never be buffed or rubbed with abrasives unless by a qualified technician. If a cylinder does require cleaning and descaling one method is to soak it in vinegar overnight.

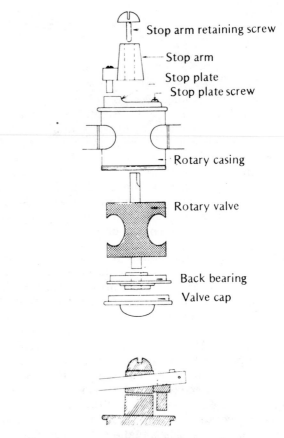

Correct angular relationship of key arm with stop arm.

Disassembly of Rotor Valve

Assembling and disassembling a rotor valve is a bit more involved than is the case with the piston type valve. It is important that the musician have a thorough knowledge and understanding of the rotor mechanism before such a task is undertaken.

1. *Remove string/disengage linkage*
   • Loosen the string retaining screws and remove the string.
   • Do not allow the key to spring free and strike adjacent slides and branches once the string is disengaged.
   • Retighten the string retaining screws to prevent them from being lost during subsequent operations.

2. *Loosen stop arm retaining screw*
   • Place the screwdriver into the stop arm retaining screw and strike a moderate blow with a leather mallet to the end of the screwdriver. This will break the metal-to-metal adhesion that may be present.

• Continue to back the retaining screw out 3 or 4 complete revolutions.

3. *Remove the valve cap*
• Turn the instrument over and remove the valve cap. An angular blow with a small leather mallet will usually loosen most stuck caps. Never use a pliers.

4. *Remove bearing and valve cylinder*
• Once again, turn the instrument over and with a leather mallet strike the top of the stop arm retaining screw (previously unscrewed 3 or 4 complete turns). This will usually result in the bottom bearing falling out, thus allowing the valve cylinder to be easily removed by completely unscrewing the stop arm retaining screw. In these two related steps, cup your free hand beneath the valve casing to catch the valve bearing and the cylinder as they drop out.
• Place all parts in a jar or medicine bottle for safe keeping.

5. *Check cylinder for residue/corrosion*
• Do not buff the rotor cylinder.
• Most residue may be removed by soaking the cylinder overnight in vinegar. This will usually remove all residue without damaging or altering the precise dimensions of the cylinder.
• If time is a factor, corrosion may be removed by immersing the cylinder in a dipping solution (such as chromic acid) for 10 seconds or so. A weak solution of Hydrochloric Acid (HCL, 20% by volume) will also work.
• Clean the cylinder with a mild detergent and warm water.

6. *Examine casing for residue/corrosion*
• To remove residue and corrosion from the casing, wrap a ½'' wooden dowel with soft gauze or cheese cloth and carefully polish the inside surfaces with a non-abrasive metal polish. Avoid scratching the interior surface of the casing.
• Flush adjacent port holes and casing with warm (not hot) water and a mild detergent. Finally, rinse all parts and tubing with clean water.

Assembly
1. *Lubricate valve casing and cylinder.* The important points of lubrication are the bearing surfaces (upper and lower). Use a low viscosity oil, specially designed for rotors.
2. *Insert valve cylinder into casing.* Both the valve and its casing must be lubricated and free of dirt and residue for it to function properly.
3. *Install the bearing into its casing.* Be sure that the notch or mark on the edge of the casing aligns exactly with the mark on its bearing. Once in place, fit the bearing snuggly into the casing by gently tapping with a leather mallet.

4. *Install the Stop Arm.* Usually the stop arm can only be placed over the valve one way. Once this is accomplished, screw in the stop arm retaining screw (lubricate the threads lightly).

5. *Adjust the stop arm corks as required.* The stop arm bumper corks are adjusted to limit the rotational movement of the valve cylinder. This movement must be adjusted so that the marks on the valve cylinder shaft (90 degrees apart) line up exactly with the central mark on the lower valve bearing as the valve cylinder is rotated fully in each direction. When installing new corks, allow for a slight amount of eventual compression.

The relationship of the shaft and bearing reference marks is shown in the diagram below.

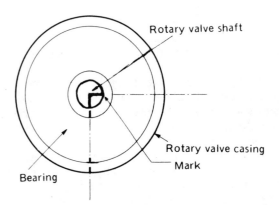

6. *Install the valve cap.* Lightly lubricate the threads of the cap with petroleum jelly.
7. *Install the valve string.* Loosen the string retaining screws. Draw the valve string through the hole located toward the center of the key arm. Secure this string with a multiple knot at the end of the string or with a retaining screw if one is provided. (30 lb. nylon fish line works well as rotor string).
Continue the operation as follows:

| Step 1 | Step 2 | Step 3 | Step 4 |

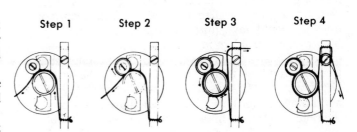

Impossible Dreams
or Great Expectations?

Douglas Hill

Have you ever heard that the horn is the most difficult instrument to play? Or have you read in orchestration books that one must be extremely careful writing anything too high, too low, too fast, or too extended (without rests) for the horn? And then have you gone to a professional orchestra concert and heard the horn players sound as if they too believed these things?

Most of us, it seems, are caught in a self-perpetuating mediocre attitude about what a horn can do. This includes teachers, students, performers, composers, and audiences.

To be realistic, the only problem which is ultimately inherent in the instrument is that the quality of its sound and attack make it virtually impossible to hide a missed note. All performers miss notes, but with the horn there is a minor explosion, a miss which destroys the musical line. This causes a tentativeness (at times even fear) in the performer, a cautious and frequently undemanding attitude from the conductor, and a general sense of uneasiness from an audience listening to an exposed horn solo. I contend that in most cases it is this factor that has perpetuated the "difficulty of the horn" attitude.

When teachers and conductors expect as much from horn players as they do from other instruments, horn players are more successful. No one can succeed where success is not expected. A number of years ago I was teaching a near beginner. He was quite intelligent and learning quickly, and asked, "How high can the horn go?" It was then I realized my answer to that common question could have quite an effect. It could make the high range a problem for him for some time to come, or I could mislead him (just a little) into a comfortable, free blowing high register. I told him that the written G (above high C) was a good note to work toward, and I played it for him. (The embouchure I used to get the note was curled inward producing somewhat of a pinched sound but he was unable to notice the difference at his age.) He took it all in stride and returned after a few weeks with a very secure high C.

My first teacher also kept his attitudes about difficulties of the horn to himself. I was learning Mozart concertos and needed to know how to play a lip trill. He demonstrated one, giving it very little fanfare, and I returned the next week performing lip trills with ease.

I've had students who were told in their early years that they had a natural set of high chops, but the low range would be difficult for them. It was, until these pre-judgements were discarded. Students have been told that trills are impossible, that stopped horn below middle C is not on the horn, and so on. And these negative attitudes have developed into walls that block out the joy of making music.

> Men are disturbed not by things, but by the views which they take of them.   *Epictetus*

Many aspects of horn playing can be made into impossible dreams by the views we take of them. Quite often the views a student takes of a specific technique have been instilled by a teacher the first time the challenge presented itself. Let's not pass on prejudices to our students; let's improve our own attitudes and thus raise the expectations of our students. In this way perhaps we can eliminate the difficulty-aura surrounding a most beautiful, yet still often misunderstood instrument.

Supplementing the Horn Player's Repertoire

Many directors have found that a great deal of the junior high and high school band and orchestra repertoire has boring horn parts, apparently the result of the belief that the horn is a difficult instrument and students should not be challenged for fear of a musical disaster. Directors can and should challenge their horn players with duet, trio, and quartet literature. The small ensemble repertoire is not flooded with masterworks, but it will allow your students to play melodic material, to work toward a good sectional sound, and to develop the technique necessary for more advanced levels.

Junior High Level

Horn Duets
Hoss, Wendell, editor. *60 Selected Duets* (Southern Music Co.)
Lasso, Orlando di. *Twelve Duets* (Ms Publications)
Niggli, Friedrich. *Acht Jagdlieder* (C.F. Peters)
Pottag, Max, editor. *60 Horn Duets* (Belwin)
Voxman, editor. *Selected Duets for French Horn* (Rubank)
Williams, Clifton. *24 Duo Studies* (Southern Music Co.)

Horn Trios
Butts, Carrol. *Ode for Horns* (Pro Art Publications)
Conley, Lloyd. *Lento and Lilt* (trio with piano) (Kendor)

Kling, H. and Wm. Teague, editors. *30 Selected Pieces* (Associated Music Publishers)

Racusen, David. *Canonic Etudes* (Shawnee Press)

Schaeffer, Don, editor. *Ancient Fugue* (16th-century) (Pro Art Publications)

Schaeffer, Don, editor. *Horn Trio Album* (Pro Art Publications)

Horn Quartets
Mayer, Rudolph. *Four Little Pieces* (Southern Music Co.)

Mueller, B.F *29 Quartets* (4 books) (Southern Music Co.)

Neuling. *Jagd Quartett* (Pro Musica Verlag)

Palestrina. *Christe Lux Vera* (Kendor)

Pottag, Max, editor. *Quartet Album* (Belwin)

Rossini. *Fanfare de Chasse* (Benjamin)

Rubank, editor. *Quartet Repertoire* (Rubank)

Stout/Lueba, editors. *Folk Song Suite* (Southern Music Co.)

Wagner. *Pilgrim's Chorus* (Sam Fox)

Wagner/Pottag. *Tannhauser* (Belwin)

Wagner/Shaw. *King's Prayer from Lohengrin* (Belwin)

Winter, James. *Suite for a Quartet of Young Horns* (Hornist's Nest Publications)

High School Level
Horn Duets
Heiden, Bernard. *Five Canons* (Associated Music)

Hill, Douglas. *Ten Pieces for Two Horns* (Hornist's Nest)

Janetzky, editor. *Waldhorn Duette-18th and 19 Centuries* (Hofmeister-Leipzig)

Kopprasch. *Eight Duets* (International)

Monkemeyer. *Masters of the 16th and 17th Centuries* (Pelikan Musikverlag-Zurich)

Mozart. *12 Duos* (MacGinnis and Marx)

Nicolai. *Duets Nos. 1-6* (Musica RaRa)

Schenk/Reynolds. *Six Sonatas* (MCA Music)

Horn Trios
Bach, J.S./Shaw. *Five Bach Trios, Bach Trios Vols. 2 & 3* (Hornist's Nest)

Beethoven. *Trio Op. 87* (Cor Publishing Co.)

Boismortier. *Sonata* (Hornist's Nest)

Dauprat. *Grand Trio No. 3* (Carl Fischer)

Hill, Douglas. *Five Pieces for Three Horns* (Hornist's Nest)

Mozart/Walshe. *Divertimento No. 2* (Hornist's Nest)

Reicha, Anton. *10 Trios Op. 82* (KaWe)

Horn Quartets
Bozza, Eugene. *Suite* (Alphonse Leduc)

LoPresti, Ronald. *Second Suite* (Shawnee Press)

Mitushin. *Concertino* (Southern Music)

Reynolds, Verne. *Short Suite* (Robert King)

Shaw, Lowell. *Fripperies* (6 vols. of 4 quartets each) (Hornist's Nest)

Snyder, Randall. *Ricecar* (Robert King)

Tcherepnine. *6 Pieces* (Edition Musicus)

May, 1979

The Mute in Contemporary Trumpet Performance

Art Brownlow

In recent years, composers of contemporary music have employed radically different performance techniques from those required in traditional literature. The most widely used special effect is muting. Although there are many different kinds of mutes, every trumpet player should be familiar with the basic mutes: straight, cup, Harmon, Solotone, plunger, whisper, and hat.

Straight Mute
The straight mute is and always has been the basic mute for trumpet. It allows for the most flexibility and freedom of execution, but like most mutes it restricts the lower register more than the upper register. The best straight mutes have a brilliant, penetrating quality that can also be pleasant on lyrical passages. However, there are no absolutes in choosing a mute. A variety of different sounds for different situations can

be found in mutes from one maker to the next. Mutes are made from plastic, fiber, cardboard, and aluminum, in both conical and pear shapes. The most popular combination seems to be the pear-shaped mute made of aluminum. This shape gives the sound power and fullness while the material gives it a metallic brilliance. The Tom Crown Company makes aluminum, pear-shaped mutes with three different types of heads for different sounds. The three heads are made from aluminum, brass, and copper for bright, medium, and dark sounds, respectively. All straight mutes have three or four strips of cork down the side to hold the mute in the bell of the trumpet. The quality of sound, as well as the response, can depend on the size of these corks. The thicker the cork, the more open the sound and more free-blowing the response.

The following chart, showing muting notation in a number of languages, refers to muting in general. Unless a composer specifies otherwise, the straight mute is to be used. He may also use the term *st. mute* or the figure ☐ to indicate the use of a straight mute.

English	Italian
with mute	con sordino. coperto
still with mute	ancore sordino
without mute	senza sordino
open	aperto
French	German
avec sourdine	mit Dämpfer gedämpft
encore la sourdine	noch Dämpfer
sans sourdine	ohne Dämpfer
ouvert	offen

Cup Mute
A cup mute is just a straight mute with a cupped resonator

835

attached to the end. This mute seems to affect normal playing less than any other mute. The cup mute is fairly versatile and a player can try a number of things to change the sound of the mute, such as trimming the corks to assure a closer fit and stuffing a piece of cloth or any soft material into the cup. The different shades of sound that can be achieved are well worth the experimentation. The Stone-Lined cup mute made by Humes and Berg is a good mute, sufficient for most cup mute playing and a popular choice by trumpet players. A cup mute can also be used for warm-ups the day after a taxing performance. It seems that either the smooth, muted sound or the added resistance has a less harsh effect on the lips. Standard notation is indicated as *with cup, cup mute,* and ◁D.

Harmon Mute

The Harmon or "wah-wah" mute, is the one with the most possibilities for producing different sounds. The metal mute looks like a thick cylinder with a partial cone on one end. This cone is the part of the mute that fits into the trumpet bell and has a solid ring of cork that allows no air to escape except through the mute. At the other end of the cylinder is the detachable stem that extends through the center of the mute. On some models, there is a detachable bell on the end of the center stem.

A number of adjustments can be made to alter the basic Harmon sound. It can be used just as is (with the center stem and bell in place) for a bright and brassy sound, with the bell on the center stem removed, with the center stem extended at different intervals from the center, and with the center stem removed completely for a darker sound.

The Harmon mute presents more problems for a player than other mutes. The response is more sluggish than with the cup or straight mutes and the intonation in the low register is unpredictable at best. Also, when the stem is out, the lowest three or four notes sound almost like an unpitched growl. However, the full range is more or less playable with the stem inserted.

The notation in a score of *Harmon mute* or *Harmon,* indicates the mute to be used with the stem removed (Harmon is not just a particular type of mute; it is a brand name and refers to the mute with the stem removed). The notation *stem in* and *stem out* calls for the stem to be placed all the way in or extended as far as possible. Composers wanting different shadings of sound may ask for the stem to be extended halfway or three-quarters.

A Harmon mute can also function as a wah-wah mute. A wah-wah sound is produced by covering and uncovering the bell with the left hand. The standard notation for this effect is as follows: + placed over a note indicates that it is to be played with the hand completely covering the bell of the mute; and ○ indicates completely removing the hand. The following notation has been endorsed by the International Conference on New Musical Notation.

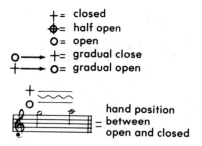

+ = closed
⊕ = half open
○ = open
○ → + = gradual close
+ → ○ = gradual open

hand position between open and closed

Other Mutes

A plunger produces a sound somewhat similar to the wah-wah. There are two types currently in use: the aluminum trumpet plunger mute and the regular rubber plumber's plunger, which seems to affect intonation and response less than the plunger mute. The notation indicating the different hand positions is the same for a plunger as it is for a Harmon mute. Composers may also write *tight* for a completely closed sound that is produced by tightly pressing the plunger against the bell of the trumpet, or *loose,* indicating that the plunger is to be angled slightly away from the bell.

The Solotone mute is a close relative of the Harmon mute in that there is a solid ring of cork to grip the bell and allow air to escape only through the mute. But it is made of fiber rather than metal and looks somewhat like a straight mute within a straight mute. The principle of air escaping only through the mute creates a lot of resistance in the Harmon and Solotone. This makes these mutes hard-blowing generally causing a performer to play sharp. The Solotone mute has a soft, dark sound without the brassy qualities of the Harmon mute.

The whisper mute is the softest of all the mutes, even the loudest volume hardly reaches a good mezzo-forte. It is made of fiber and looks somewhat like a conical straight mute. As with the Solotone and Harmon mutes, it has a solid cork band to grip the bell. The air goes through the mute and around the outer edge through a tightly fitting resonator that is stuffed with felt. The resulting sound is extremely soft and remote. Because of the resistance, a player will have to fight hard to keep from playing sharp. The whisper mute can be used effectively for inaudible offstage warm-ups.

The hat used as a mute changes the trumpet sound the least. It gives a soft, far-away quality to the sound when placed directly in front of (not touching) the trumpet bell. An ordinary hat or a metal or plastic derby can be used as is or stuffed with cloth. The indication for this type of muting is usually *in hat.* But, a player does not have to be restricted to using a hat. Experimentation is in order here. One could play into a stand, play into someone's back, play into a heavy piece of cloth, or tie a cloth bag around the end of the bell.

The mutes discussed here are by no means the final word in muting, nor are the many other types of mutes on the market. The different sounds that can be achieved by experimenting are almost limitless. Ordinary household objects such as bottles, paper bags, or cloth can be used as mutes. The player's imagination is the only limit to the variety of colors that can be produced by muting. ■

One Step at a Time

Donald Hofmeister

Three essential elements of brass instrument playing — embouchure, breathing, and tongue placement — can be isolated so students can concentrate their attention on one element at a time. When the elements are integrated once again after separate study, I have found a considerable improvement in performance. Fortunately, the principles are the same for all brass instruments, with only minor adjustments needed.

Embouchure

The mouthpiece should be centered on the lips both horizontally and vertically. Slight variations from this procedure are best handled by the teacher with consideration for the individual's instrument and facial structure.

The bottom teeth should be aligned vertically with the top teeth (usually the lower jaw must be slightly extended to accomplish this). Once this is done, the jaw is lowered the appropriate amount for the instrument being played. Aligning the teeth primarily provides support for the bottom lip and helps align the surfaces of the lips so they are about parallel. Slight variations in alignment can be tolerated and usually will not affect the sound significantly.

The corners of the lips are best left in their natural position. Generally they should not be pulled up or down, pushed forward or pulled back.

The top lip is usually the primary vibrator, moving against the bottom lip. The bottom lip adjusts the size of the aperture for pitch and volume changes. As the pitch rises, the size of the aperture decreases and the amplitude of the lip's vibrations decreases.

The pivot system is used by many players to help compress the size of the aperture. Pivoting downward as the pitch ascends moves the bottom lip up to compress the size of the aperture, at the same time allowing the top lip to vibrate at an increased speed. Although pivoting can help the embouchure function properly, I find that as the embouchure muscles improve, pivoting occurs less often.

Breathing and Tongue Placement

The speed and compression of the air column can be controlled through proper use of the breathing apparatus and the tongue. A slower, less compressed stream of air is used for low notes and a faster, more compressed stream for higher pitches.

To see how the tongue compresses the air flow, play a pitch in the middle range of any brass instrument. Then go up the interval of a fifth and feel how the tongue placement changes. By compressing the air as it approaches the lips the tongue will help speed up the air column. The position of the tongue for sustained sounds is also the proper position for repeated notes. The objective is to avoid moving the tongue farther than necessary. Practice tonguing multiple sounds after practicing the sustained note first. Then compare the tongue placement for each to see if it has changed.

Integrating the Concepts

To integrate these aspects of playing, start with this simple exercise. Play a pitch in the middle range of your instrument and hold it at a moderate volume. While you are playing, note where the tongue is placed and how it feels. Slowly play an ascending scale pattern and notice how the gradual change in the tongue position and air speed feels. Do this within the range of about a fifth.

Playing the same pattern, begin to increase the speed of the air with pulse or breath accents. This exercise will result in a more active use of the breathing muscles. As the air column moves faster on each pulse, find the tongue position where the sound is most focused.

The next step is to concentrate on the embouchure, noticing how the mouthpiece feels against the lips. The mouthpiece should feel as though it is resting on a cushion, with flexibility under the rim; the lip should not feel pinched between the teeth and the mouthpiece. Being aware of these sensations, play the same notes as before. As you go higher, the bottom lip moves up to make a smaller aperture and the horn pivots downward for most players. Both the space between the lips and the size of the vibrations become smaller. Notice how the lip and pivot change both ascending and descending. Don't forget to reverse the movements when descending. Often a player is so anxious to hit the higher notes that he forgets to reverse the process when coming back down.

There are four major variables in going from one sound on the instrument to another: the aperture, the tongue placement, the pivot of the instrument, and the speed and volume of air. The player must learn to consciously monitor these variables to be sure they are coordinated. By experimenting with them in various combinations while practicing familiar patterns you will develop more consistency, reliability, and security in your playing. ∎

Articulation and Rhythmic
Precision for the Brass Player

Guy Kinney

Although there are subtle and important muscular changes that must take place in embouchure in changing from one brass instrument to another, certain tonguing and articulation movements are universal. (By articulation is meant the rhythmic definition of the start and stop of a tone.) Certain rhythmic figures demand specific articulations of which we are not always aware, and rhythmic clarity is closely related to the syllabic tonguing used in articulating various tones.

Effective tongue-articulations are necessary to produce phrases with a sound rhythmic pattern, clean attack, and musicality. Here are some suggestions to help build solid control of the instrument.

Control of the Attack

The first step in learning articulation is to gain absolute control over one note. The note should sound clearly, evenly, and precisely when we tongue it; and achieving a clean, straight attack will require a great deal of practice. One of the best methods for achieving this control is the following exercise.

Exercise 1

mp-mf

Careful practice of this exercise will produce a solid, decisive attack. Each note should be attacked extremely cleanly with the dynamics never exceeding *mezzo forte*. The exercise should be worked chromatically up and down as far as you wish to build your range control (at

least one octave above and below the starting pitch). It is very important that each tone not waver from the initial attack to the release.

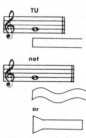

Any variation in sound other than smooth and straight should not be acceptable. Using the syllable "tu" is probably the most universally accepted practice for brass players, yet at certain dynamic levels or with accented figures other syllables such as "ta, tu, du, or tut," may be used to obtain the desired effect.

After the attack of a single note has been mastered, the next step is playing tones in an arpeggio. Negotiating the wider gap between arpeggiated tones as opposed to scalewise passages will help establish muscular and tonal memory so that the exact spot and feeling for each note will become nearly instinctive. If this exercise is done in scale passages, it is often too tempting to start with faster eighth or sixteenth notes. It is important to practice this exercise slowly; it should never be faster than quarter notes in a *moderato* tempo.

Exercise 2

mp-mf   simile

Like exercise 1, this exercise

should also be performed chromatically up and down. As greater proficiency is gained, the range can be extended.

The third exercise recommended for articulation control is an octave study.

Exercise 3

Remember to take the mouthpiece off the lips between each note (hence the rests). This will help insure that the embouchure relies on muscular memory to hit the note dead center.

The final exercise in this group is for register development, and uses scale patterns in various ranges to help develop each end of the range one note at a time.

Exercise 4

Greater speed can be used as fluency with the notes increases. Played precisely and carefully, this exercise can help establish ease of playing in all registers, tonal consistency, and greater control throughout the entire range. Few other exercises can do this as well.

These exercises should be practiced frequently either as a warm-up or as the entire practice session. Barry Tuckwell, when asked what the drawbacks were of his instrument, replied that the most discouraging thing was that he had to practice the simple basics every day in order to maintain the conditioning level necessary to play difficult and complicated solos.

Rhythmic Definition

After mastering control of the attack, the player's next challenge is to execute rhythmic passages with clarity and brilliance. Too often young performers play rhythmic passages no differently from the way they first learned them in grade school. However, in professional instrumental ensembles there is a style of articulating that is precise and clean. This doesn't happen by accident.

One concept that can help give rhythmic definition to a passage is the idea of long versus short notes (the *arsis* vs. the *thesis*). The *arsis* is that note which gives forward impetus or motion to the phrase; it is like the sprung arrow as it leaves the bow. A *thesis*, on the other hand, makes a pause or slight rest in the forward momentum of the musical phrase. More simply, the *arsis* is the accented note and the *thesis* the unaccented note.

In order to make a passage clear, certain notes need to receive more emphasis than others. For example,

would normally be played:

with the greatest emphasis on the first dotted eighth note. However, over a long extended repetition of this sequence, a fatiguing, plodding sound may develop as if the piece were gradually slowing down.

A simple solution to this problem is to define the passage this way: A slight emphasis is given to the sixteenth note. Played in this manner, the plodding effect is diminished and the rhythm still sounds clear and interesting even after several repeated measures. This is one trick that French musicians often

use, and it helps create a light, airy sound in their playing.

The Boulanger System

Nadia Boulanger, the famed teacher of composition at the Paris Conservatory, always stressed the importance of making this same slight rhythmic alteration to keep the vitality of the music. I remember performing the Poulenc *Gloria* under her direction. When I was ready to play the brass theme which rhythmically went:

she was very adamant that it be articulated:

The same principle was applied to syncopated figures. Emphasizing the short notes helped reduce the labored sound one often hears with repeated passages of this type.

Written:

Played:

The Philadelphia Orchestra System

Marcel Tabuteau, the first oboist of the Philadelphia Orchestra, helped develop a system of phrasing which was adopted by the entire orchestra. Although space here precludes an in-depth study of this system, a very simplified version which **has** much in common with Madame Boulanger's ideas is illustrated in the following examples.

A passage with sequential eighth notes would normally be counted and played as:

In order to keep this piece moving and rhythmically alive, the accents must be changed:

As a result of this shift in emphasis, the eighth-note sequences will have a feeling of continuing forward drive.

An example of a fairly well-known piece where this technique should **be used is the third movement of Mozart's horn *Concerto No. 3*. As it is so often played, the emphasis is on the first note of each group of three:**

By shifting the accents, the passage is articulated as follows:

As the tempo increases this change in emphasis becomes more subtle. Yet, if the technique is conscientiously practiced at a slow speed, there will be a light rhythmic vitality evident in the music at an allegro tempo.

Multiple Tonguing Facility

Students who are learning to double or triple tongue can run into problems at faster speeds because they fail to relax the tongue. As they gain flexibility, they may become tense. This results in a hard tonguing sound and unclear, heavy notes.

The problem can be solved by remembering that the faster the tempo, the lighter the tongue must be. And the tongue must be arched higher and placed further back in the mouth.

As you go from a slow multiple tongued passage to a faster one, there must be a gradual change from a "tu-ku" type articulation to a "du-ku." The *d* sound makes for a more relaxed tongue that you can move faster.

Clean attacks, rhythmic definition of phrases, and multiple tonguing are second only to tone quality as the most important aspects of brass playing. Practicing the exercises given above on a daily basis will improve a player's technique in these areas and lead to a more precise, clean sound. ∎

A Natural Approach to Trumpet Playing

David R. Hickman

The subconscious mind is capable of operating an extremely complex series of motor responses that occur when one swings a golf club, drives an automobile, or plays the trumpet. But the conscious mind often wants to be in control and a conflict results. Outstanding performers understand this struggle between the conscious and subconscious and have learned to separate and control their functions. Trumpet players who can become masters at this have a decided advantage.

One often hears that certain performers are "natural" trumpet players. Obviously, this can mean that the person is easily adaptable to the trumpet physically in terms of lips, teeth, or jaw, but usually a natural player is merely one who allows himself to play naturally regardless of physical adaptability to the trumpet.

Even the naturally talented player can only play correctly if exposed to correct trumpet playing. Imitation is the key to early success and a talented student can imitate bad as well as good models of playing. Correct imitation follows after a certain amount of trial and error. The natural player should be concerned only with the end product of correct tone, attack, release, etc. He should not have to think about the process he uses to achieve these goals. Through repetition, the correct overall feel will be memorized subconsciously.

I do not want to underemphasize the importance of having good embouchure, breathing, or tonguing; without physical competency, a professional level of playing will never be achieved. The student's playing should be developed pa-tiently through uninhibited trial and error with a clear concept of correct tone, articulation, and phrasing. The teacher provides the correct playing concepts and guides the student physically without making him overly aware of mechanics. The goal is to play freely and naturally with musicality being the first priority.

Tone Production

A good concept of tone is the first step in producing a beautiful trumpet sound. If one does not know what a good tone is it will be impossible to make the subconscious embouchure adjustments that will eventually attain the desired sound. In a sense the performer's ears control all playing mechanisms.

Step two is to place the mouthpiece on the lips in a position that gives the best tone, regardless of how it feels. Ideally, a mouthpiece is centered on the lips both horizontally and vertically, but individual variations due to lip shape, upper lip length, length and angle of teeth, and jaw position will almost always cause players to make minor alterations of this ideal setting. Unless the mouthpiece position is far off center, any workable position can be developed. If the tone is full and brilliant then the embouchure setting is workable.

Step three is the most crucial and unfortunately the most neglected part of embouchure development. After a workable embouchure is attained, a progressive resistance exercise program should be started to systematically develop the embouchure muscles. This is important not only for building strength but as the foundation of muscle control, consistency, and endurance. A progressive resistant exercise program gradually employs more fatiguing exercises, thus systematically encouraging the facial muscles to work together in order to preserve endurance. Even if the embouchure muscles are strong, unless they are working together — like the braces in a well-constructed bridge — the player will always be handicapped. Attempting to master the extreme upper register too early will usually be harmful. Not until the embouchure muscles throughout the face are working smoothly and effortlessly together can the upper register be developed without destroying tone, flexibility, and endurance.

There are many exercises that will help build an embouchure. Claude Gordon's *Systematic Approach To Daily Practice*, Donald Reinhardt's *Pivot System*, Carmine Caruso's *Caruso On Breath Control*, Louis Maggio's *System For Brass*, and Roger Spaulding's *Double High C In 37 Weeks* are but a few of the more popular development books. It would be impossible to outline each method here, but all of these systems will work if practiced correctly under the supervision of a qualified teacher.

Proper breathing and support are the keys to building a good tone. A workable embouchure can only be developed if the tone is full and resonant. Breathing should not be thought of as two actions, inhalation and exhalation, but as one continuous motion. If one can inhale fully in a relaxed "yawning" fashion he will also exhale in a relaxed fashion unless the air is locked, stored, and then released.

To produce a full and relaxed

tone the chest, throat, and embouchure must be as relaxed as possible yet firm enough to produce a well-centered and brilliant tone. Tension in the chest, throat, or embouchure will cause a restriction (pinching) in the tone, and if there is not enough firmness in the embouchure the tone will sound dull and tired. The mouthpiece size and instrument brand will not have any effect on sound, intonation, flexibility, or player comfort until a proper tone is produced.

Articulation

A beautiful tone can be destroyed by a poor attack. A lightening-quick tongue stroke is required for all attacks, regardless of the length of the note. If the tongue action is too slow the attack will sound like "twaa" or "thaa." Remember, the tongue should help start the note, not be part of it.

Finding the best tongue stroke can be difficult. However, using the body's natural capabilities will speed the process. For instance, most trumpet players can easily flutter tongue with the tip of the tongue. Usually this flutter stroke, which is actually an uncontrollably fast single tongue, uses only the very tip of the tongue and occurs just above the upper front teeth as if pronouncing the letter "d." The body naturally flutter tongues in that position (or whatever similar position) because it is the easiest way. By articulating in the same manner, the tongue will improve in quickness and consistency. The following exercises should be played to check that the flutter and single tongue strokes are the same. (If flutter tongue is not possible or it does not occur with the tip of the tongue, these exercises will not be useful. Some doctors say that a few people, because of heredity, cannot flutter tongue with the tip of their tongue.)

Exercise 1.

Exercise 2.

Double and triple tonguing should also be developed through the flutter tongue model. The tongue action will then be developed by allowing the body to perform naturally and efficiently.

After a fast and consistent attack is achieved, different types of attacks should be practiced. These various attacks usually require a slight adjustment in tongue placement. For example:

Exercise 3.
Marcato attack:

an accented "T" syllable

Exercise 4.
Legato attack:

quick but light "la" or "da"

Register changes also often require different tongue placements. For instance, most people release the tongue from the bottom edge of their top teeth in the extreme low register.

After proper attack is attained and speed is sought it is important that the player group multiple syllables into one basic tongue action. For example, the word "tick" requires two tongue actions. However, when pronouncing the word quickly, the mind does not concentrate on the two separate tongue actions. This same concept can be applied when articulating groups of notes. In the following exercises, concentrate on articulating a group of notes rather than separate and distinct tongue strokes.

Exercise 5. Two-note groups

Exercise 6. Three-note groups

Exercise 7. Five-note groups

Exercise 8.
Various note groups of seven and nine

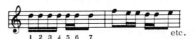

Speed will not be attained if each note is thought of as a separate stroke (even though it may actually be). A percussionist discovers this when accelerating single notes into a fast roll on the snare drum. For individual strokes to occur quickly the conscious mind must concentrate on the desired rhythm, allowing the subconscious mind to regulate the physical actions.

Building Strength

As in any physical endeavor, sufficient strength is necessary in order to do the job easily. The stronger the muscles the more efficiently they work together, the less effort is required. Without a strong, trained embouchure it would be impossible to achieve the relaxation necessary to perform well. For example, a trained weightlifter can hold a 25-pound dumbbell outstretched to his side with a relaxed arm until eventually the arm weakens and the weightlifter has to strain to hold the dumbbell. If a child of 70 pounds held the dumbbell in the same position it would be difficult from the beginning. The child could not relax for very long. In short, strength is the key to relaxation and relaxation is the key to good tone, endurance, and power.

Building strength requires two types of exercise routines. Power is improved by taxing the muscles for a relatively short period of time but while exerting full energy. On the contrary, endurance is developed over a long period of time by exerting low level energy.

Trumpet players need both power and endurance, and this requires a well-planned practice routine. Many trumpeters can play incredibly high and loudly for a few measures but are unable to play in the middle and upper registers with a good tone and endurance.

For endurance strength one should play only a few lines of low-taxing material and then rest for several seconds before continuing. One should rest even if not tired thus postponing real fatigue.

Power can best be practiced at the end of the playing day when it is possible to rest overnight. By playing a few taxing exercises (usually high or loud), the muscles will be overworked quickly. Afterward, the muscles will not only rest but will build added strength and bulk to resist future overloads. Generally, it takes 48 hours for a tired muscle to rest and build fully. This is why many trumpet range building methods advise playing only every other day (as in Spaulding's *Double High C in 37 Weeks*). The theory is sound but impractical for the working trumpet player. Daily practice will help consistency and endurance but perhaps power exercises could be used on an every-other-day basis.

Building the upper register is a slow process. Working too hard too soon may cause poor playing habits and invite excessive mouthpiece pressure. The upper register should be developed after or in conjunction with an embouchure development system such as those mentioned previously.

In order to become confident and consistent in the upper register it is necessary to have a strong, well-formed embouchure. After this, a player must acquire a "feel" for the upper range notes. Before playing high notes loudly and accurately the first step is to simply play the high notes in an easy and correct way. Scales and arpeggios played piano or mezzopiano into the upper register will need little mouthpiece pressure and the work load will be relatively light. After the notes are secure and consistent, volume can be gradually increased. Quite often students attempt to play high notes at full volume and then are discouraged because all they acquired were sore lips.

A comfortable volume and mouthpiece pressure for lip slurs and scale exercises that explore the upper register will always give best results. The following exercises will prove valueless unless played in the

prescribed manner. It's how you practice that counts.

Play exercise 9 with the same mouthpiece pressure throughout. After establishing the pressure on the first note, increase the air compression when ascending but do not allow the mouthpiece pressure to increase. Play at a volume that is comfortable and yet gives a full, brilliant tone.

Exercise 9.

Play exercise 10 as quickly as possible even though it is notated in eighth notes. Mouthpiece pressure should allow the lips to move freely without letting certain notes lock in and interrupt the continuous flow of the notes in the fast slur. Play at a comfortable and full volume.

Exercise 10.

How to Practice

A good daily practice routine should incorporate all of the ingredients of a good performance. Practice calisthenic exercises such as lip slurs, long tones, and pedal tones, as well as technical drills on scales, arpeggios, transposition, sight-reading, and multiple tonguing.

Break up the practice routine into several shorter sessions. This insures ample rest between sessions and makes each session more enjoyable and beneficial. This also provides several different physical and mental environments during each day; the player will feel slightly different during each session. Three one-hour practice sessions is

more beneficial than one three-hour session.

A suggested daily routine uses three sessions of 30-90 minutes each. The first should include warm-up fundamental exercises such as those found in Clarke's *Technical Studies*, Colin's *Lip Flexibilities*, Arban's *Method*, and the *Daily Drills*, by Schlossberg. Tone, breath control and technique should be developed in this session. In the second session (a minimum of one hour later), develop musicality through practicing solos, etudes, orchestral excerpts, transposition studies, and sight-reading. Frequent short rest periods will prolong endurance and concentration. Music to be performed in concert should be played as though the practice session were actually the concert. As you practice, visualize the auditorium, audience, and entire concert situation. With experience, the practice session and the concert become very similar and the player is more consistent and less nervous.

The third practice session of the day should be used to build strength. Use a taxing program that will train the embouchure muscles to work together and build power and endurance.

Using one's natural abilities is extremely important for rapid progress. It is easy to form poor playing habits when concentrating only on the mechanics of playing. But this physical control should be learned by striving for musical results, regardless of physical feeling or appearance. ■

Study Materials

Arban, J.B.L., *Complete Conservatory Method*, Carl Fischer.
Bush, Irving, *Advanced Range, Technique & Interval Studies*, Los Angeles, Western International Music.
Clarke, Herbert L., *Technical Studies*, Carl Fischer.
Colin, Charles, *Lip Flexibilities*, Vols. I, & II, New York, Charles Colin Music.
Gordon, Claude, *Systematic Approach To Daily Practice*, Carl Fischer.
Schlossberg, Max, *Daily Drills and Technical Studies*, Oyster Bay, New York, M. Baron Co.

Intonation Problems of Young Brass Players

Lenard Bowie

In the last several years I have done an informal study of factors affecting tuning and intonation of young brass players and have found that a significant number of intonation problems previously attributed to mechanical or acoustical factors can be traced directly to the player. I have categorized the principal causes of these problems as psychological, physiological, and mechanical.

Psychological Influences

Psychological factors are a player's concepts and perceptions of what he has learned through training and experience. Psychological influences on intonation are intangible; their symptoms cannot be heard, seen, or felt. They are difficult to pinpoint and can be easily mistaken as resulting from physical or mechanical problems.

Because students reproduce sounds consistent with preconceived pitch and tonal images which they have established in previous training and experiences, students who are consistently exposed to good training and experience tend to develop very reliable pitch references, and they play fairly well in tune. On the other hand, students who are consistently exposed to training and experience which fall considerably short of the ideals do not develop reliable pitch references for some of these reasons:

- There is an absence of detailed instruction and emphasis on tuning and playing in tune in beginning bands and orchestras.

- Many band and orchestra directors deliberately tune their groups above the standard A-440 or B♭-466.2 to accommodate inexperienced woodwind players.

- Some directors use a young clarinet or oboe player, whose embouchure and pitch may not be too reliable, to sound the tuning pitch.

In addition, brass players tend to develop high, faulty pitch references and poor intonation because of the following common practices:

- Brass players are trained to tune, match and adjust their pitch to the strings or woodwinds. They have learned to accept the pitch of these instruments as being correct.

- Brass players are taught to play under the woodwinds and strings for balance. The young

> ### Tuning and Intonation
> The terms tuning and intonation have somehow become synonomous for many musicians. The first step in solving tuning and intonation problems of young brass players is to clarify the meanings of these two words and to apply these meanings in practice.
> *Tuning* is the process of bringing tones of different timbres to a common pitch. *Intonation*, on the other hand, is the production and control of tones so they are precisely and consistently true to pitch.
> From these definitions you can see that a person's ability to play in tune is largely determined by his intonation practices and not by the way he tunes his instrument.

brass player lacking a well-developed embouchure and good breath control usually resorts to pinching of the lips, constricting the throat and oral cavity and failing to adequately support and project the tone.

- Great demands are placed on brass players in marching bands to play with more volume, range, and projection for outdoor performance. These demands are placed on brass players during a time when they are not physically prepared to meet such challenges without adverse affects on their performance. Again they resort to excessive lip and mouthpiece pressure, pinching and forcing to meet these demands.

I found that brass players who play above pitch subconsciously reject lowering their pitch because they think they will be playing flat. Secondly, they are accustomed to the embouchure settings and breathing which reinforce their higher pitch. Consequently, a student's conscious effort to lower his pitch is often negated by the physical conditioned response which maintains his original concept of the correct pitch.

Physiological Influences

Poorly developed embouchure, inconsistent embouchure setting, extreme arching of the tongue, indadequate breath support and a tight, constricted throat are perhaps the most common physiological factors which contribute to the tendency of young trumpet players to play sharp. When these physical functions are reversed the performer has a tendency to play flat.

Some physiological causes of poor intonation are directly related to psychological factors. A student hears the sound he wants to make and then finds the way to reproduce it. Through repeated practice, the various face, neck, and abdominal muscles become conditioned to automatically assume a specific shape when a specific pitch is played. Therefore, physiological and psychological causes of poor intonation practices should be considered simultaneously.

Mechanical Influences

Mechanical causes, together with acoustical problems, are perhaps the most frequently discussed and the most familiar factors of all the combined causes of poor intonation, and therefore are easier to identify and correct. Once the cause of a mechanical problem is found, it can be corrected by either mechanical adjustment, alteration of the mouthpiece or instrument, or changing fingerings. If these adjustments do not solve the problem the player may need to buy a new mouthpiece or instrument.

The following are mechanical causes of poor intonation commonly associated with trumpet playing. Many also apply to other brass instruments.

- a dirty and corroded mouthpiece or instrument
- the absence of moveable 1st or 3rd valve slides or the failure of the performer to use them in combination with regular fingerings
- water keys on both main and 3rd valve tuning slides
- defective water key corks and springs
- dents, breaks, and missing accessories
- poor alignment of valve parts with slide openings
- worn valves or valves that do not fit
- improper fit of the mouthpiece shank into the mouthpipe
- bouncy and jiggly valves
- frozen valve slides or failure to properly adjust all valve slides
- extensive welding and soldering of joints and sections
- acoustical limitations resulting in inconsistencies in the overtone series
- components of the mouthpiece which may be incompatible with each other or with the instrument
- poor choice of fingerings in various keys and registers and on specific instruments

A director should inspect and test each new student's instrument for intonation discrepancies and proper functioning.

Once a cause for poor intonation is found it can be treated by either mechanical adjustment or physical change. The following charts, compiled as an outgrowth of my study, are not intended to be complete with all possible causes and solutions of poor intonation. However, if they are used as a basis for analyzing common intonation problems, they should prove helpful. (The order of the listings on each chart does not imply frequency of occurrence as this will be different with each student.)

Pitch Problems and their Physical Causes

Sound Symptoms	Probable Causes	Results
Closed, thin, tight, sound; no body, resonance, or carrying power even with considerable effort	Tight or closed throat; high arched tongue; tight, stretched, or pinched lips	A sharp sound that's above the pitch center
Frying or sizzling sounds coming from corners of the lips	Extremely stretched lips (smile-type embouchure); tight grip at center of lips, overly relaxed corners	
Lack of a ringing, open quality; excessive highs no lows in tonal color	Extremely high arched tongue; lack of support and projection; closed throat	
Ringing, zinging sound	Firm, consistent and well-balanced embouchure (part smile, part pucker).	An in-tune sound that's on the pitch center
An open, free resonant sound rich in overtones; balanced with highs and lows	Open oral cavity and relaxed throat; well-positioned tongue	
Full-bodied sound with carrying power without force or considerable effort	Consistent, well-supported air stream; relaxed neck, shoulder, and chest muscles; physical and mechanical functions compatible	
Shallow, sagging tone	Overly relaxed embouchure; improper support	A flat sound that's below the pitch center
Hollow tone without a middle, center, or core	Extremely open aperture	
Dull and colorless sound; thick and tubby	Extremely puckered embouchure	
Airy, breathy, hoarse quality	Tongue arched too low; sagging or receding lower jaw; lips not vibrating freely	

Mechanical Tests

Tests	Negative Effect	Probable Causes	Corrective Suggestions
Place a finger under the bottom valve cap; press firmly against the air escape vent; depress the corresponding valve.	Valve can be fully depressed without pressurized resistance. (This action is normal for the 2nd valve.)	A leaky worn valve or poor tolerance in valve construction	Have valves ground or replated or install new ones (If condition is extreme, it is more practical to replace the instrument).
Fully depress a valve then cover the air escape vent as in the above test.	Valve snaps up immediately without drag or resistance. (This action is normal for the 2nd valve.)	(same as above)	(same as above)
Place mouthpiece into leader pipe without force or pressure; attempt to jiggle it from side to side.	Even the smallest amount of movement is too much.	The taper of the mouthpiece shank does not fit the leader pipe.	Have mouthpiece shank shaved down to fit leader pipe. If cornet mouthpiece is used in a trumpet, purchase a cornet mouthpiece extension.
Remove mouthpiece from leader pipe and insert a metal cleaning rod on the top side of the leader coupling joint until it makes contact with the leader pipe end. Mark the rod at the outer end of the leader coupling joint. Then remove the instrument and compare the marked length of the rod against the lodging rings on the mouthpiece shank.	If distance of rod penetration is greater than that of the mouthpiece instrument tends to play flat and sound stuffy.	Mouthpiece does not penetrate far enough to make contact with the leader pipe; collar joint is too long.	Have mouthpiece shank shaved down until it's able to penetrate far enough to meet the leader pipe end. Remove collar joint and either cut off small portions from the small end or replace it with a shorter one.
	If distance of penetration of the rod is less than that of the mouthpiece instrument tends to play sharp.	Mouthpiece shank is smaller than the leader pipe bore.	Cut off the end of the mouthpiece in small degrees and shave the shank down until it makes proper contact while maintaining at least one-half of the total length outside the leader pipe. Otherwise purchase another mouthpiece that fits properly.
Lay a light-weight index card across the valve while the instrument is in a horizontal position.	A valve, or valves, fails to make contact with the index card; index card rests at a slight angle to the instrument.	Poor valve alignment due to worn springs, corks or missing felts. Valves which stand well above the others indicates missing felts and corks.	Replace severely damaged springs, corks or felts. If springs are weak, bent, or broken, they can be stretched gently to provide a better lift.
Hold instrument at eye level. Fully depress each valve and let the finger snap off and down to the top of the valve casing.	Valve bounces or jiggles on the upstroke.	Weak, worn, or heavily damaged springs.	Replace old springs with new ones, stretching the new springs slightly before inserting.
Remove all valve slide covers; peer through the valve slide to check the alignment of the valve port openings while depressing and releasing each valve. Check the downstroke alignment of the 2nd valve slide. Check the upstroke alignment through the 3rd valve tubing with the 3rd valve depressed. Look down the bottom slide to check the alignment. The 1st and 3rd valves should be adjusted to the 2nd valve.	Portions of the valve can be seen at the bottom of the port opening on the down stroke. A small portion of the opening can be seen.	Worn or missing felts and corks, or they may be too thick or too thin.	Replace the felts or corks under the finger buttons with either thicker or thinner felts to adjust the down stroke. Replace the felts or corks above the valve springs to adjust the upstroke.
Play the chromatic scale at a slow tempo throughout the practical range of the instrument. A chromatic tuning machine should be used and several people should compare the results.	The same finger combinations produce tones consistently out-of-tune.	Inadequate slide setting. Natural acoustical discrepancy. Failure to use moveable 1st and 3rd valve slides when playing notes in 6th and 7th positions.	Sharp: pull appropriate valve slides out or adjust by pulling other valve slides in. Flat: push appropriate valve slides in or adjust by pulling other valve slides out. If flat sound persists it may be necessary to turn off small portions of the valve tubing. Make greater use of moveable 1st and 3rd valve slides when playing in 6th and 7th positions always and 4th and 5th positions if needed.

Physical Problems Contributing to Poor Intonation

Physical Symptoms	Probable Causes	Results
Thin, pinched, tight and/or outward stretched lips	Too much backward pull on the modiolus and risorius muscles (cheek muscles)	Produces a smiling type embouchure
	Failure to counter-balance the backward pull of the modiolus and risorius muscles with a forward and circular pull of the orbicularis muscle (lip muscle)	Sound is usually thin, brittle, airy, and pinched Upper register and endurance usually limited
Extreme upward arching of the tongue (cannot be detected visually)	Tendency of the tongue to float back to its natural resting position in the roof of the mouth	Produces a thin, small, closed, high-pitched sound
	Involuntary arching of the tongue due to constricting surrounding face and neck muscles	
Loose, puffy, fleshy embouchure	Lack of proper tension and control of facial muscles	Airy, breathy sound
	Air seeping into and collecting between the teeth and lips	Excessive flesh movement in and around the embouchure; puffy cheeks or air pockets in upper or lower lips
	Lack of proper seal of lip to teeth and facial bone structure	Escaping air from corners of the lips
Flesh of the chin rounded, pinched and pulling upward	Upward instead of downward pull of the chin muscle	Excessive movement of chin flesh Muscle imprint at the base of the chin dimpled — resembles peach pit
Unstable, bouncing embouchure	Moving tongue with jaw muscles	Chewing effect
	Relaxing and tightening lip muscles with each note	Wah-wah tonal effect
		Inconsistent attack
		Airy sound precedes start of tone on attacks
Swelling of the neck	Excessive tension in the throat, shoulder, and chest areas	Stiffness of neck and shoulders
	Meeting the resistance imposed by the instrument in the throat area	Upward movement of the Adam's apple
		Vocal noises in throat

October, 1979

Multiphonics
on Low Brass Instruments

Richard W. Bowles

The production of multiphonics on low brass instruments is no longer a mysterious bit of trickery. This acoustical phenomenon is increasingly important in low brass performance. Composers are notating them, and jazz artists such as Albert Mangelsdorf and Bill Watrous use them with great dramatic effect.

On brass instruments, multiphonics result when the player sounds one tone in normal fashion by buzzing the lips, and at the same time hums a tone of higher pitch (the reverse is less successful). When these two tones have the proper relationship in the harmonic series, a third tone (and sometimes a fourth tone, or even a fifth) can result. Acousticians refer to these third tones as summation tones because their pitch is the result of the sum of the frequencies of the other tones. (The term multiphonics rather than summation tones will be used here; and the terms harmonic, overtone, and partial will be used as meaning roughly the same thing.)

In general, the larger the bore of the instrument, the better the multiphonics work. They sound easily on tuba and bass trombone and are entirely practical on euphonium and trombone.

They can be produced with careful effort on the horn and only with great difficulty on cornet or trumpet.

A musical tone exists as a fundamental tone with its own series of overtones, as a part of the overtone series, and as a part of the tonal spectrum of the slide position or the fingering with which it is produced. For example, F3, played on trombone in 1st position, has all the overtones of that pitch. At the same time F is the 3rd partial of the overtone series of B♭ below the bass clef. If the player extends the slide to 6th position and produces the same pitch, the F is now the 4th partial of the series based on pedal F below the bass clef.

To understand multiphonics the player must have total familiarity with the overtone series of his instrument. In 1st position, the trombone pitched in B♭ has the following overtone series (see example 1).

With the trombone slide extended to 2nd position, the series in example 2 is created.

Extension of the slide into other positions, or the addition of triggers that lengthen the tubing obviously creates the possibility of other series.

When multiphonics are produced the resultant third tone is predictable as the sum of the relationship between the tone played and the tone sung. For example, if you play F3 and simultaneously sing middle C, the resulting multiphonic will be A4. The interval of a perfect fifth occurs between the second and third partials of the overtone series. $2+3=5$, therefore the resulting multiphonic will be the fifth partial, A. (Note, in this example and all following examples × indicates the note that sounds, □ indicates the sung note, and O is the note that is played.)

Another example would be if you played F3 and simultaneously sang D4. The resulting

multiphonic will be B♭4. The interval of a major 6th occurs between the 3rd and 5th partials. $3+5=8$, therefore the multiphonic will be the 8th partial, B♭.

One of the clearest and most ethereal multiphonics results when the player sings an augmented 4th above the note he is playing. As an illustration, if you play A♭3 and sing D4, the resulting multiphonic is a C♭5. With some instruments the player can achieve a full four-tone diminished chord with this procedure.

Perhaps the most used of all the multiphonics is that resulting from singing a major 10th above the played tone. The tone sung is in a comfortable vocal register for most male trombonists, and nearly all of the low brass instruments respond. The 3rd tone may sound although few players can make this happen.

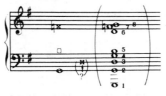

Although it is difficult for most players, a dominant 7th

chord results from singing a perfect 4th above the played tone.

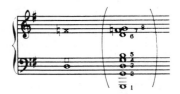

The willingness of most instruments to sound an 8th partial when even an approximation of the 3rd and 5th partials are sounded is shown by the fact that singing a minor 6th above a played tone will make the 8th partial respond.

With this background, we can now create chords deliberately. Wide individual differences exist between instruments and players, but the following chord techniques can be used in almost any register of the trombone (tubists may need to transpose).

Major Chords, root position:

Major Chords, 2nd inversion:

Example 1.

Example 2.

Minor Chords, 2nd inversion:

Seventh Chords, root position:

Seventh Chords, 2nd inversion:

Diminished Chords:

Some chorale melodies can be played in full harmony by a single brass instrument. Melodies hovering around the first step of the scale are nearly impossible to use; those grouped near the third are possible, if 7th chords offer acceptable har-

Footnotes

1. *Grove's Dictionary of Music and Musicians,* subject heading "Acoustics."
2. Helmholtz, Hermann, *On The Sensations of Tone,* Dover, New York, 1889, ed. 1954 by Ellis & Margenau.

mony; by far the best are melodies that center around the fifth scale step. Here is an example of a chorale that works well (see example 3).

A curious aspect of multiphonics is that scientists apparently have not established just what they are. Most books on the acoustics of music have some allusion to the phenomenon of tones sounding in addition to those being played, referring to them variously as combination tones, summation tones, grave harmonics, difference tones, and other terms. According to Groves,[1] the first published accounts of such things are in a text by the German organist Sorge, written in 1745. The Italian violinist, Tartini, discovered and used difference tones as a technique for tuning double stops as early perhaps as 1715. Herman Helmholtz,[2] acoustician and theorist, in 1885 referred to summation and difference tones as combinational tones, and reasoned that the tones were produced in the human ear, rather than being a physical fact.

Our own experiments with an oscilloscope show clearly, we believe, that the multiphonic is a physical reality and not merely a sensation created in the ear of the listener. Shown below are pictures of four oscilloscope sound profiles produced by a trombonist.

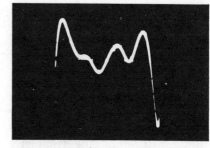

Figure 1. The profile of the tone F3 produced by buzzing the lips.

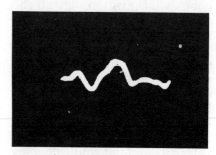

Figure 2. The profile of middle C produced by humming through the trombone.

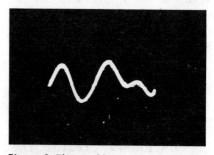

Figure 3. The profile of A4 produced by buzzing the lips.

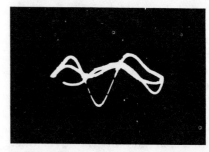

Figure 4. The profile of the multiphonic F - C - A, produced by playing F, singing C, with the resultant multiphonic, A. The profile shows three distinct patterns, clearly indicating the physical reality of the three tones.

Multiphonics today have moved out of the theoretical closet into an increasingly prominent place in low brass performance. Today's player should be aware of the acoustical principles involved in their production, and should add this dimension to the other elements of well-rounded performance technique. ∎

Example 3

Now Thank We All Our God

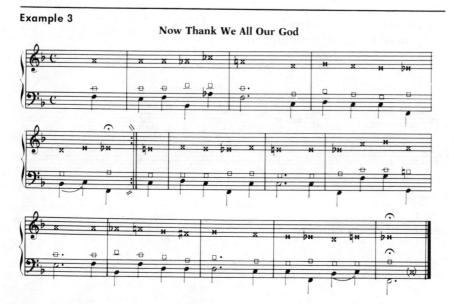

November, 1979

The British Brass Band

William V. Johnson

The British brass band movement is as much a traditional social activity as it is a musical organization. The roots of the 100-year-old movement are based on the people's gathering for camaraderie and enjoyable use of their leisure time as well as a desire to be competitive. Almost every community throughout Great Britain has a brass band, many of them sponsored by local industry. You will see names such as Foden's Motor Works Band, Fairey Engineering Band, and The Leyland Motors Band. The brass bands give regular concerts and each year participate in regional and national brass band contests.

Instrumentation

The standard size of the brass band is 25 wind players plus one or two percussionists. The score normally calls for the following:

E♭ soprano cornet	2nd trombone
Solo cornet	Bass trombone
1st cornet (3 players)	1st baritone horn
2nd cornet (2 players)	2nd baritone horn
3rd cornet (2 players)	1st euphonium
Flügelhorn	2nd euphonium
Ripieno cornet	1st E♭ tuba
Solo tenor horn	2nd E♭ tuba
1st tenor horn	1st B♭ tuba
2nd tenor horn	2nd B♭ tuba
1st trombone	Percussion

With the exception of the trombone, each instrument of the band has a conical bore capable of producing the dark, mellow tone so characteristic of the British brass band.

The smallest instrument, the E♭ soprano cornet, almost singlehandedly provides the high frequencies necessary for an overall wide harmonic range. The soprano, as it is usually called, often doubles the solo cornet one octave higher strengthening the upper partials of the solo cornet line and sometimes making the band sound as though it has a woodwind section. The solo cornet part functions as the main melody line in most brass band compositions, in addition the soprano player often has important solo passages.

The ripieno cornet line is a roving part that is used to help balance the 1st, 2nd, or 3rd cornet parts. The flügelhorn part bridges the gap between the cornet and the tenor horn and, along with the lower cornet parts, functions as an upper alto voice.

The use of the E♭ tenor horn rather than the more conventional French horn is, for us, one of the most unusual aspects of brass band instrumentation. The tenor horn serves as the middle or alto voice of the band and is used instead of the French horn because of its piston valves, upright bell, and tuba-like design. According to the British, this makes the instrument more capable of providing the desired tonal blend between the upper and lower voices of the band. Also, the fingering system for the more complex French horn is so different from the standard fingering system of all the other instruments that it would be difficult for players to switch instruments, an important factor in less-advanced ensembles. The tenor horn has a bore at its narrow end of about 3/8 inch which increases to 7/16 inch at the valves. A further expansion after the passage through the three-valve system brings the diameter to about 1¼ inches at about a foot from the bell. The final opening at the bell is about 6½ inches to 7 inches wide. A similar instrument used in some American bands is the alto horn.

Unlike concert band instrumentation where there is a part that can be played by either the baritone horn or the euphonium, the brass band instrumentation calls for both parts. Both instruments are upright and tuba-form in design but the euphonium has a full-bodied tone and is generally provided with a fourth valve and a compensating system. The baritone horn has a much smaller bore and bell and is characterized by a lighter sound and therefore is treated as a tenor voice rather than a bass voice. Because the tenor trombone is mostly cylindrical, the baritone horns are often used by composers to mellow the more strident tone of the trombones by having the baritone horns double the trombone lines. The euphonium is second only to the solo cornet as a solo instrument in the band.

The trombone plays the same role in the brass band as it does in the concert band or orchestra. This is the only instrument in the brass band that puts some edge on the tone to provide tonal contrast and excitement in the sound of the band. I was amazed to find that a couple of the bands had G trombones. I later found that the G trombone is the predecessor to the bass trombone and some of the bands still use the instrument.

The E♭ tuba is supposed to bridge the gap between the euphonium and the double B♭ tuba. This was the case in the better bands, but in the weaker bands four tubas often gave the ensemble a muddy sound. In many of the compositions the E♭ tuba was used to focus the sound of the double B♭.

The percussion section in most bands is used strictly for accompaniment. There are only one or two percussionists who play the most basic percussion instruments.

Balance, Blend and Intonation

The British brass band instrumentation is an excellent example of the concept of pyramid balance; good balance is almost automatic with the band's standard instrumentation. The contest festival rules also provide a strong incentive for organizations to meet the strict standards of instrumentation.

Exceptional blend is enhanced in many bands by the use of matched mouthpieces, matched bore sizes, and matched makes and models of instruments. This is not a new idea, but efforts to achieve blend in this manner is certainly not as common in this country.

Intonation is a critical issue with most bands and a great deal of rehearsal time is spent tuning

and correcting intonation problems. Many intonation problems are eliminated with good balance and blend; but the instruments, especially the tenor horns, baritone horns, and euphoniums, have worse than usual intonation problems which makes it difficult for less-accomplished players to play in tune. One of the most exposed problems is the octave doubling between the soprano and the solo cornet parts.

Vibrato

A distinctive aspect of British brass band performance is the prevalent use of vibrato. The extensive use of vibrato is a natural outgrowth of the performer's effort to make the playing sound as much like singing as possible. These bands have an exceptional ability to sustain a long cantabile musical line that seemingly defies the inherent mechanical problems of instrumental performance. Unfortunately, the less accomplished performers have become victims of an undisciplined, uncontrolled vibrato that causes their performance to be overly sentimental. Many of the performers have never been taught the technique of vibrato, and it is not unusual to see those in less-advanced groups shaking their heads and the instruments to achieve a vibrato. Even in the championship groups the extensive use of vibrato takes some getting used to for the typical American.

The Use of the Treble Clef

The parts for all the instruments in the brass band, with the exception of the bass trombone, are written in the treble clef. It is strange to see a tuba player, for example, reading a B♭ treble clef line as though it were a cornet part. The reason for this practice becomes obvious when you compare this system with the way in which music is written for the clarinet and saxophone families. By writing everything in the treble clef, it is possible for players to move from one instrument to another without learning a new fingering system (The baritone horn treble clef part in our instrumentation is an isolated American example of this British tradition.).

Seating Plan

There is no standard seating for the brass bands, but there are placements which most bands use. The cornet section is to the left of the conductor allowing the players to blow across the ensemble rather than straight out. The solo cornet player sits in the traditional concert master's position and, at a contest, he can often be seen with his back to the audience so that the judges will hear as little edge, noise, and distortion as possible. Because of the abundance of octave doubling, the soprano cornet players sit on the edge of the stage just in back of the solo cornet player. The flügelhorn player often sits next to him on the inside. The trombones are normally placed to the right of the conductor and in the back row so their sound will go across the ensemble. The baritone horns and the euphoniums usually sit in front of the trombones with the solo euphonium player on the edge of the stage. The tenor horns are placed in the middle, and behind them are the tubas. The object is to have the directional instruments such as the cornets and trombones blowing across the ensemble while the upright instruments play into the ceiling producing as little projective and as much reflective sound as possible — just the opposite of orchestral brass playing.

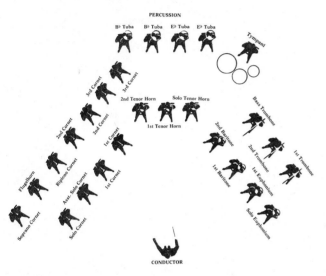

Repertoire

The brass band repertoire consists of thousands of works, many of which are not to be considered serious works, but rather functional and entertaining pieces that are composed, arranged, or transcribed for brass band. However, in recent years there has been a great effort to develop a substantial repertoire of excellent original works for brass band. The following is a list of important brass band music composers.

Arnold, Malcolm 1921
Ball, Eric 1903
Bantock, Sir Granville 1868-1946
Bath, Hubert 1883-1945
Bliss, Arthur 1891-1965
Catelinet, Philip Bramwell
Cook, Kenneth John 1926
Cundell, Edric 1893-1961

Elgar, Sir Edward 1857-1934
Fletcher, Percy 1879-1932
Geehl, Henry 1881-1961
Goffin, Dean
Golland, John 1942
Gregson, Edward
Holbrooke, Josef 1878
Holst, Gustav 1874-1934
Howarth, Elgar 1928
Howells, Herbert 1892
Hume, J. Ord 1864-1932
Ireland, John 1879-1962
Jackson, Enderby 1827-1965
Jacob, Gordon 1895
Jenkins, Cyril 1885
Keighley, Dr. Thomas
Powell, Thomas James 1897-1965
Maldwyn, Price R.
Newsome, Roy
Purcell, Henry 1658-1695
Rimmer, Drake
Rimmer, William 1862-1935
Slater, Richard 1854-1939
Wright, Denis 1895-1966
Wright, Kenneth 1899-1975
Vaughan Williams, R. 1872-1958
Vinter, Gilbert 1909-1969

The contest festival is responsible for the majority of the more substantial works for brass band. Each year numerous local and regional contests take place throughout Great Britain, all leading up to the Grand National contest held in London's Royal Albert Hall. Works are commissioned for these events with an emphasis on compositions that display the full technical and musical prowess of the bands.

One London publisher said that the brass band people place too much emphasis on technique and not enough on musicality. He referred to a piece commissioned for a contest and written for brass band by Gordon Jacob. The work had been severely criticized because it did not contain passages that would demand acrobatic displays of technical ability on each instrument. It had an abundance of half notes, quarter notes and eighth notes at a medium tempo, but at the same time it was a sensitive work, full of substance and beauty. The publisher was frustrated because it was a fine work by a well-known British composer that would probably never be fully appeciated. On the other hand, brass bands have little trouble filling concert halls or receiving financial support for their organizations and part of the reason is that their repertoire is exciting, free from pretentiousness, and has a wide performer and audience appeal. In addition there are regular broadcasts of brass band performances on both BBC radio and television.

Because of the technical ability of these bands, people are often inspired to transcribe seemingly impossible orchestral and even wind band works for brass band. The violin, flute, and clarinet parts are given to the cornets, who play them with the greatest of ease. There is even a transcription of

Sousa's *Stars and Stripes Forever* with the piccolo part played by the soprano cornet.

The following are sources for brass band music:

Richard Smith & Co. Ltd.
P.O. Box 210
Waterford
Herts
England

Studio Music
77-79 Dudden Hill Lane
London NW, 10, 1BD
England

Rosehill Music
  Publishing Co. Ltd.
The Old House
64 London End
Beaconsfield, Bucks
England

Chandos Music Ltd.
41 Charing Cross Road
London WC 2H OAR
England

The Contest Festival

Each year hundreds of bands participate in the super-organized, highly structured contest system that eventually brings the winning bands to London in October for the National Championship. Each contest is under the official auspices of the National Brass Band Championships of Great Britain. This organization provides a service to the bands including acquiring judges, keeping records, establishing and enforcing the contest rules, awarding prizes, and obtaining facilities for the various events. In any contest there are four sections of bands: the championship section, second section, third section, and fourth section. In the Northwest Region Qualifying Championship held at the Guild Hall in Preston, England, this past April there were 13 bands participating in the championship section, 17 bands in the second section, 12 bands in the third section, and 32 bands in the fourth section. First prize winners in each section received a trophy or cup and £100 (about $200). Second prize was £50 and third prize was £25.

It is not easy for a band to be chosen to participate in the championship section. If, for example, a new band were formed, it would have to win several first prizes in the fourth section before it would be allowed to participate in the third section, and so on. Each section is represented at the National Contest in October.

Each band is listed by number in the program. About 45 minutes prior to starting time, each section draws another number that establishes the order in which the bands will appear. Thus at each performance two signs are placed on the sides of the stage, one indicating which band is playing and the other giving that band's order of performance. Second, third and fourth section performances usually take place throughout the day, with the championship section beginning at about 5:00 or 6:00 p.m. and continuing into the evening.

All the bands in one section usually perform the same composition, or sometimes bands can choose between two selections. For example, 32 bands performed either *The Winter's Tale* by Reginald Heath or *Blenheim* by Arthur Butterworth in the fourth section competition at Preston, and 13 performances of Vaughan Williams' *Variation for Brass Band* were given by the championship section bands. The test pieces are normally about ten minutes long.

Great care is taken to preserve the integrity of the judging process. Adjudicators are met by contest officials upon entering the city and are then isolated from all contest participants. A few minutes prior to the contest the judge is placed in a specially constructed box that makes it impossible for him to see which band is performing. The box measures about 8 x 6 x 7 feet and has slatted windows to allow the sound in. The judge indicates that he is ready for the next band by blowing a whistle. The judges list the performances in order of excellence. There is one judge for each section, except for the championship section where there are two judges. At the conclusion of each event the judge is invited to comment about the piece and how it was performed. Judging captions cover such areas as intonation, balance, blend, rhythm, and interpretation.

Conductors

Most of Britain's 1,000 bands have regular conductors whose principal credentials are several years' experience playing in brass bands and a willingness to serve as the band's conductor. In observing many performances, I found the general level of expertise in conducting to be very low. There are, however, professional brass band conductors (not unlike old-time American itinerant ministers) who travel from band to band putting the finishing touches on imminent performances. For important events such as a contest or a recording session, the professionals will even take over as conductor. The professional conductors have studied at various colleges including the military schools of music such as the Army's Kneller Hall, the Royal Air Force School of Music, and Salford College of Technology near Manchester where a diploma in band musicianship includes such courses as Band Law and Administration, Instrumental Maintenance, and Acoustics.

School Instrumental Music

There is very little instrumental music taught as a part of the school curriculum. Young people must seek out brass players who are willing to give some lessons and then do their best to learn as much as they can on their own. There is a teenage brass band movement that has its own contest structure. This, of course, serves as a feeder system for the adult bands.

The Adult Amateur

The people in the brass bands are for the most part middle-aged and older, and they receive no financial remuneration for their time spent in rehearsals and performances. This is also true of most brass and wind bands throughout Europe. As an American music educator, I found it both strange and exciting to see people in their 40s and 50s playing band instruments as amateurs with exceptional skill and with such obvious personal satisfaction.

Brass Bands in America

There are several British type brass bands in the United States that were formed as a result of visits to Great Britain similar to mine. In the future I plan to add a brass band to our program. The fact that we do not have the traditional instruments should not be too much of a handicap. For example, I would use French horns on the tenor parts; cornet parts could be played on the trumpet; and I would use both baritone horn and euphonium. Finding E♭ tubas might be a problem. The best of the brass band literature would be an important addition to our repertoire, and the added interest in brass performance would help improve the brass section of our symphony band.

Implications for American Bands

It would be easy for the American music educator and band conductor to dismiss the British brass band movement as being amateur, provincial, trapped by its own traditions, and

Publications

The British Bandsman, The Old House, London End, Beaconsfield, Buckinghamshire, England.

The Sounding Brass and the Conductor, The Old House, London End, Beaconsfield, Buckinghamshire, England.

British Mouthpiece, The Mechanics Institute, Spring Street, Shuttleworth, Ramsbottom, Lancs, England.

Brass Band News, Parliament St., Gloucester, England.

Directory of British Brass Bands, published by The British Federation of Brass Bands, General Secretary; R.B. Kershaw, 28 Marigold Street, Rochdale OL11 1R, England.

A new book has just been published that gives a well-written history of the brass band movement. *Brass Bands* by Arthur R. Taylor is available through Wright & Round Ltd., Parliament Street, Gloucester, England.

overly motivated by the desire to win. The truth of the matter, however, is that there is much to be learned by a careful study of the activities of these highly skilled, enthusiastic, fun-loving bandsmen.

I am surprised that I can no longer accept the cylindrical sound of the "cornet" section, but desire a conical sound when the music seems to call for it. I do not advocate the over-use of vibrato but the singing approach to phrasing could make a major difference in the way our bands sound. Many of the championship bands can restore one's faith in the ability of brass players to play difficult technical passages that are normally assigned to more agile woodwind instruments in band works. I really believe that most band composers would be thrilled to be able to write brass parts with almost the same freedom of complexity as woodwind parts.

Finally, for some reason we have the idea in this country that playing in the band is strictly a school activity. Just think of the thousands of people each year who graduate from our high schools and colleges who, after having had almost 10 years of professional instruction, sell their instruments or store them in the attic. We are one of the few countries in the world where instrumental music is taught as a part of the school curriculum and yet we seem unable to create a vast amateur interest in instrumental performance beyond the age of 22. After my visit to England I am convinced that we are capable of having hundreds of adult bands that would be equal to the finest British brass bands, and these bands could even make our university and high school bands sound like the youthful organizations they really are. ■

Nine Myths of Brass Teaching

Richard E. Powell

We teachers of brass instruments often accept playing and teaching ideas without investigating and testing them. Here are nine such myths of teaching and playing brass instruments.

• *Smile to ascend the scale.* This saying was very popular in the past and still appears as gospel in many method books. Smiling to ascend does work to some degree, but it quickly limits a student's range, flexibil-

ity, and endurance. Instead, teach students to pucker and push corners of the mouth forward toward the rim of the mouthpiece.

• *Drop the jaw to play low notes.* Even though this advice lets students play notes in the low register almost immediately, the long-term effects of dropping the jaw are a lack of high range development and a gradual reduction in the high range

the student might already be able to play.

It's better to teach students to descend the scale by transferring slight mouthpiece pressure from one lip to the other. Whether it is top or bottom lip will vary with the individual. Good low playing range doesn't come as quickly this way, but when it does come, the student's high range will not suffer.

• *Tongue every note sharply.* Even though tonguing is a basic part of performance, it isn't basic to producing a sound because a student can play high, low, loud, and soft without using the tongue. First, teach a no-tongue "hoo" attack. Later, introduce the "doo" attack as a means of refining, not initiating, the attack. After the student masters these, teach him the "too" attack, but encourage the student to use the "too" attack sparingly, only for accents and sforzandi.

• *Push the diaphragm out to support the high register.* Pushing the diaphragm out doesn't support the tone adequately, and it produces a thin, high range. Instead, teach students to play with a feeling of pushing in to support the high range.

• *Always take a big breath before you play.* Following this advice can destroy a pianissimo passage. Instead, teach students to take just the amount of air they'll need for the specific phrase. Experiment with this suggestion by choosing a short phrase and playing it *pp, p, mf, f,* and *ff* in various registers. In each case try to take just the amount of air you'll need to complete the phrase. You may discover that the phrases will sound better if you end them "comfortably out of air."

• *Perfect the low register first; then work for the high register.* A much better approach is to start in the middle register and gradually work your way to both the top and the bottom. I believe this to be a better method to develop the complete range of the instrument, whether you are speaking of a daily warm-up or a long range plan.

• *Use little or no mouthpiece pressure when playing.* As you play an ascending scale, using too little pressure allows the portion of the lips inside the mouthpiece rim to move and change the embouchure setting. Using too much pressure can hurt or even damage the lip and lessen endurance. To play an ascending scale, the corners of the mouth should exert gradual forward pressure, and the left hand should exert equal pressure to the mouthpiece, keeping this balance throughout the entire scale.

• *Take the lower lip away from the mouthpiece between phrases and breathe in between the center of the lips.* Following this advice dries the vibrating points of the lip and makes it difficult to find the correct embouchure setting for the next phrase. Instead, leave the mouthpiece firmly on the lips between phrases, and open the corners of the mouth to breathe. This process is more difficult to learn — it takes concentration and perseverance — but the benefits will make it well worth the effort.

• *Place the mouthpiece in the center of the lips.* Some texts suggest that students place the mouthpiece evenly on the embouchure. Other texts urge a mouthpiece placement of two-thirds on the upper lip and one-third on the lower lip, and still other books suggest a placement of one-third on the upper lip and two-thirds on the lower lip. The author of each text may be suggesting what works best for him. Instead, help your students find a mouthpiece placement that produces a full sound and provides a solid backing for the mouthpiece. There is no single correct embouchure placement for everyone; to dispel this and other brass teaching myths, take individual differences into account. ∎

Trombone Solos, Ensemble Music, and Annotated Guides

William W. Richardson

The year 1979 was a very good one for trombonists and their teachers. First of all, beautiful sounds appear to be back in vogue; elementary-level solos are of a higher quality; and two new annotated guides to trombone literature provide information for over 650 titles, many of which were recently composed.

Elementary
Paul Tanner's *Country Cut Up, Wade in the Water, The Magnificent Seventh* and *Liebestraum,* published by Belwin-Mills, provide easy, interesting music for young players. *Country Cut Up* uses surprising silences and sophisticated harmonic shifts, and *The Magnificent Seventh* ex-

plores the cocktail ballad style of the major seventh chord.

Intermediate

David Stone's *Variations* for trombone and piano published by Boosey & Hawkes is a good, four-minute piece. The waltz of the second variation is particularly pleasing. The $\frac{5}{8}$ variation will challenge a junior high-early senior high player without defeating him.

Meditation for trombone and piano by Jim Christensen is based on Bach's *Prelude in C*. The exquisite chord progression in this Kendor publication should make working on intonation a joy. H.M. Grady's arrangment of Tchaikovsky's *Song of Praise* is a rich, 19th-century melody that lends itself to rubato treatment in a full legato style.

Advanced

To play *Fauré Melody*, arranged by Richard Fote and published by Kendor, the performer needs endurance, a free-sounding upper register, and a singing legato style. Henry Fillmore's *Lassus Trombone plus 14 Other Hot Trombone Rags* is fun to perform. One to a dozen trombone players, with a good loud accompanist, can sample the vitality of the beginning of the century as they learn about alternate positions and glissandos.

Though it is expensive, *Suite* by Atso Almila is strikingly different from most recital pieces. The first two movements contain some extraordinarily beautiful passages in a modern setting, while the third movement, a lively scherzo, has a challenging and fulfilling finish. *Suite* is a Magnamusic-Baton publication.

Concerto for Trombone and Orchestra by George Walker is published by G. Schirmer. The fine London Symphony Orchestra recording with Denis Wick has been out since 1974. Now this recital version is available. The main problem with the piano reduction is that the concerto's strength is the brilliant Benjamin Britten-like orchestration. The second movement retains its haunting moodiness in the piano reduction but the first movement seems too long and the last movement too repetitious because it lacks the changing orchestral timbres.

The Gardner Read *Invocation* for trombone and organ may have a place in the trombone literature, but its high range and disjunct thematic material will eliminate some performers. Nevertheless, the use of the cup, straight, and whisper mutes adds listener appeal to this Robert King publication.

Concerto for Bass Trombone and Strings by Karl Pilss also comes from Robert King, and has the string parts reduced for piano. This concerto has several fine movements in the late 19th-century manner, but it suffers from an overstated style that quickly wears thin. One movement would be nice for performance, but all three are too much.

Advanced Unaccompanied Solos

Panorama by Elinar Englund, an advanced unaccompanied solo published by Magnamusic-Baton, is what brass publications editor Mary Rasmussen used to call the "Quo Vadis" style of composition.

Paul Tanner's three-minute *Etude for Unaccompanied Trombone*, published by Dorabet, appears to be drawn from his *Complete Practice Book* and explores the "Rossolino turn" and "across-the-grain" ascending scales with a descending slide technic. As the title implies, the piece is better for study than for performance.

The best recent unaccompanied piece is Clinard's *Sonata* published by Shawnee Press. It works very well as a performer's first attempt at unaccompanied playing and holds the audience by its compositional strengths.

Ten Dance Studies in Jazz Idiom for Trombone Quintet by Thomas Jahn, published by G. Schirmer, is an enjoyable piece for college level players. You'll need a small bore tenor trombone on Part I and a large bore bass trombone on Part V. The beguine, cha-cha, rock, blues, and six other styles are presented as short pieces that will please your players and the audience.

As an experiment, try Mark Tezak's *Quartet for Trombones* published by Robert King. Four tenor/bass trombones are needed. A metronome and reading from the score will help an advanced quartet improve its rhythmic ensemble playing. Tenor clef plus sequence- and pitch-controlled improvisation are used.

Method Books

David R. Hickman's *Music Speed Reading for Melodic Instruments*, a Wimbledon Music publication, may become a standard method in music schools. It is such a simple approach to increased eye-movement skills, you'll wonder why you didn't think of it yourself. Remove the stems and flags and concentrate your grouping-by-pattern efforts on the note heads and their spatial patterns within each measure. Eliminate clefs and key signatures and let the performers add their own "correct" ones. The 22 lessons are tied to metronomic markings that increase as pattern-reading facility develops. The 10 etudes and 4 duets can be played as is, or new rhythmic structures can be devised by the performer.

Annotated Guides

Annotated Guide to Bass Trombone Literature by Thomas G. Everett is an indispensable resource for teacher and students. This greatly revised and enlarged second edition, with 527 concisely annotated entries, is a publication of the Brass Press. Unaccompanied solos and bass trombone music with piano, organ, strings, band, jazz ensemble, chamber music and tape are included. Duets, methods, orchestral studies, practice materials, articles, texts, recordings, and composers' and publishers' addresses are neatly catalogued and printed. The proceeds go to the International Trombone Association Scholarship Fund.

The companion volume to the Everett guide is Vern Kagarice's *Annotated Guide to Trombone Solos with Band and Orchestra* published by

Summy-Birchard. If you don't own it now, don't admit it, but get it immediately. (See the February, 1978 issue of *The Instrumentalist* for its review.)

Another indispensable volume added this year is Harry Arling's *Trombone Chamber Music: An Annotated Bibliography*. Published by the Brass Press, this volume contains 95 entries and has been edited to avoid repeating material in the Everett and Kagarice guides. The five grade levels included in Arling's book range from the college freshman to the graduate student/professional. For the price of a mouthpiece you can purchase these three annotated guides and have informed access to over 750 compositions for trombone.

December, 1979

Trumpet and Horn Solos and Studies

Maurice Faulkner

In 1979 more trumpet and horn studies were received than solos. Foreign publications are making their way to our shores, but they are very expensive.

Trumpet Studies

Robert Weast's *Keys to Natural Performance for Brass Players* (Brass World, 1979) is an unusual approach to teaching trumpet. He approaches the various aspects of playing by considering the emotional, mental, and physical requirements; and he has used other disciplines in devising his exercises. For instance, his section on "Musical Connection" refers to the concept of a musical idea having a mental state that stimulates the physical apparatus for producing a musical result. He supports his ideas with references from non-musical sources. Analogies are presented that illustrate his concept. Then he lists procedures and describes how his exercises can be used. The author treats problems like "Chromaticism," "Repetition," "Timing and Coordination," "The Pressurized Air Column," and "Mouthpiece Pressure" in intelligent, interesting style. This is a text that every teacher would want to examine.

Belwin-Mills published John Ridgeon's *How Players Do It* ($3, 1976), which contains interesting discussions and diagnoses of breathing, resistance, and embouchure. Not all brass teachers will agree with the author's ideas, but this publication gives the student a concept of what takes place physically when playing brass instruments. Lip slur exercises, similar to those which Schlossberg gave his students several decades ago, make up the practical materials. This book is a valuable addition to our teaching repertoire.

James Stamp, west coast trumpeter and teacher, offers fine technical advice on an advanced level in his *Warm-Ups and Studies* (Editions BIM, 1978, Switzerland, no price indicated). He describes the action necessary for each exercise in English, German, and French, emphasizing lip flexibility such as bending the tone, playing on the mouthpiece alone, and developing a wide range from pedal tones to the altissimo register.

In the same publications series Thomas Stevens, co-principal first trumpet player of the Los Angeles Philharmonic and trumpet teacher at the Music Academy of the West, has written *Changing Meter Studies for Trumpet, Clarinet, or Treble Clef Instruments* (Edition BIM, $7, 1978). This intermediate-level material does not require advanced technical mastery, but it is useful for developing playing ability of complex meter changes like $\frac{2}{4}$ followed immediately by $\frac{6}{8}$. The melodies are delightful, and the edition is superbly phrased and edited in three languages.

Robert King Music has published Malcolm Bennett's *14 Melodic Studies for Trumpet* ($2) with a variety of tonguing and phrasing concepts. This publication provides excellent supplemental material for the busy trumpet teacher. Instructions for performance style accmpany each exercise.

L'Arte di Suonare la Tromba (Edizioni Melodi, Milan, 1977, $12) is an interesting Italian publication with English translations by the trumpet professor of the St. Cecilia Conservatory in Rome, Reginaldo Caffarelli. This book takes the beginner from G4 through double-tongue exercises and etudes in all keys.

A well-organized new edition of Arban's *Complete Method for Trumpet or Cornet*, edited by Willard Musser and Daniel Mincarelli (Alfred, 1979, $8.95), devotes each section to a specific skill covered in the original Arban version. A feature that aids many teachers and students is the addition of articulation indications, which are specific notations for various tongue styles and accents, and a glossary of terms. The word "complete" in the title is a misnomer; major sections of the original work are missing in this adaptation.

Trumpet Solos

Belwin-Mills continues to enhance the literature for beginning trumpeters with its *Contemporary Band Course* solos. Jeremiah Clarke's *Ayre*, arranged by Howard Cable and edited by Bobby Herriot ($1.50), a grade II, empahsizes the trill and produces pleasant melodies. Bobby Herriot and Howard Cable have written *Study in Six* (1978, $1.50) emphasizing alternating meters like $\frac{6}{8}$ to $\frac{3}{4}$ with interesting sequential melodies and chromatic alterations. This selection is grade II-III.

Solos of medium difficulty dominate this year's offerings. Peter Wastall has superbly edited *Baroque Music for Trumpet* (Boosey & Hawkes, 1979, $4.50), which includes six accompanied works for trumpet, strings, and continuo (the organ or harpsichord part is included without the strings), and three unaccompanied works for two trumpets or unison instruments. Works by Telemann, Vivaldi, Torelli, Albinoni, Charpentier, and Keller are featured in this grade IV publication.

Ruth Still has arranged *Gloria 'N Cielo*, a very pleasant Christmas or Easter work that could be used as a processional. The grade IV work is for C trumpet and unison chorus (Wimbledon Music, 1978, no price). The trumpet rhythms are not difficult, and the piece has effective, Renaissance-style musicality. The final measures require the trumpeter to maintain a long, high C with the fortissimo choral phrase.

Emil Hlobil's *Intermezzo* for B♭ trumpet and piano (General Music, 1965, no price) uses large interval leaps with excellent phrase and breathing indications to create a pleasant musical experience. And David A. White's three-movement *Sonatina* for B♭ trumpet and piano creates a delightful contrast for an 8½-minute work (Shawnee Press, 1979, grade IV, no price).

Oxford University Press has published a fine edition of John Humphries' (c.1707-1730) *Concerto Opus 2, No. 12* for trumpet or horn in D with strings, harpsichord, or chamber organ accompaniment (grade IV, 1978, $13.50 with score and trumpet part; orchestral parts on rental). Richard Platt has provided the information and the style indications for this attractive, scholarly addition to trumpet literature. The first movement, Allegro, and the final Vivace are scored for the solo trumpet alone, while in the second movement, Adagio Staccato, the trumpet is tacit.

Scott Joplin's *The Easy Winner*, arranged by Howard Cable and edited by Bobby Herriot (Belwin-Mills, 1978, $1.50, grade III) is a lighter selection from the *Contemporary Band Course*. Pleasant ragtime rhythm with wide melodic leaps and tricky syncopations give the young trumpeter an experience in early Americana that is tastefully phrased and stylistically excellent.

An advanced-level *Double Crossings: A Duo for Trumpet in C and Percussion* by Irwin Bazelon (Boosey & Hawkes, 1978, grade IV, no price) takes the trumpeter from F 3 to D6. With difficult rhythms that demand a professional's lip flexibility, the piece emphasizes the great variety of tone colors of the instrument. This selection also requires a number of percussion accessories. The percussionist must also be proficient. I recommend this work for orchestra conductors and professional musicians seeking new concepts in modern sound. Fine college musicians could also handle this interesting work with success.

Trumpet Solo Collections

In *Skill Builders for Trumpet and Piano*, Stuart Isacoff has compiled a collection of simple pieces for the young musician in the categories "Folk-Rock and Folk Fun," "Bluegrass Country," and "Blues, Rags and All That Jazz." The tunes are familiar and popular (Schirmer, 1978, grades I-III, $4.95). And Willi Drath's *Klassisches Trompeten-Album* for trumpet in B♭ and piano offers attractive classical melodies by major composers with competent phrase editing (Schott, 1978, grade II-III, $10.50).

British trumpeter and teacher, Harry Mortimer, arranged a volume of old favorites like Arban's "Carnival of Venice" and Sullivan's "The Lost Chord" in *Harry Mortimer Souvenir Album*, for B♭ cornet and piano. One of the more complex pieces is for A cornet (Boosey & Hawkes, grade II-V, no price).

Horn Solos

Several easy horn solos have been published this year. Charles Forsberg's arrangement of Robert Schumann's *Romanze*, Op.138, No.5, edited by Miles Johnson, adds to the lyrical materials available (Belwin-Mills, 1978, $1.50, Grade II). But the publication has a notation error in the first measure of the horn part; the eighth notes should be sixteenths. There is also an E♭ horn part included. Forsberg's *Hornpipe and Dance* develops a pleasant melodic idea with simple range and an easy piano accompaniment (Belwin-Mills, 1978, $1.50, Grade II-III).

A third easy horn solo completes Belwin-Mills' offerings for the young hornist. Charles Forsell has arranged *Minuet and Trio* from Handel's "Water Music" in a simple style with an easy piano accompaniment. This pleasant, G minor melody lies in the treble clef for the hornist. All of these Belwin-Mills publications include an E♭ horn part (grade II, 1978, $1.50).

Medium-level horn solos are few this year. M. Bradford Anderson's *Prelude and March in Canon* for horn and piano requires an excellent low register as well as the player's skilled treble clef capacity. This piece features imitative motives played by the piano and horn in clever canonic style (Boosey & Hawkes, grade IV, 1973, $3). Universal Edition has submitted Franz Strauss' *Nocturno*, Op.7, for horn and piano in a comfortably phrased edition. Strauss, father of Richard Strauss and Wagner's solo hornist in such premieres as "Tristan," "Meistersinger," and "Parsifal," set the pattern for his son's romantic horn concertos (grade IV, $5). Richard Fote has arranged *Faure Melody* for horn and piano, which I consider a grade III. But because of its demanding long phrasing and sophisticated interpretive concept, the work might be classified as more difficult (Kendor, 1978, $1.50).

Jagdstück ("Hunting Piece") for two horns with piano by Alexander Zemlinsky, takes advantage of the classic style horn skills of the old, natural instrument, and with clever alternation between the two players, this duet provides a fine addition to the literature (Universal, grade IV, requires muting, 1977, $10).

Advanced horn solos from contemporary composers lead our list of new music submitted. Usko Meriläinen's *Grandfather Benno's Night Music* for solo horn, requires an imaginative interpreter who can play from the lowest bass clef range to an A 5 with lip flexibility and accurate pitch skills. The piece has no meter signature, and it offers a great variety of tempo changes within its short duration (Edition Fazer, Helsinki, Finland National Brass Competition piece, 1976, grade V, $2.75).

One of the finest publications of advanced horn solos this year is Novello's edition of John McCabe's three-movement *The Goddess Trilogy*, which includes "The Castle of Arianrhod," "Floraison," and "Shapeshifter." All of these require a two octave range to B♭ 5 with skills of lip flexibility and accuracy that will tax the finest professional. The pieces range from grade V to VI and the piano accompaniment is also demanding. The total performance time is about 28 minutes for the three; I takes eleven minutes, II nine minutes, III eight minutes. Each movement could be performed as a separate recital piece (1978, no price indicated for these works printed in composer's facsimile).

Barry Tuckwell has published a new version of Beethoven's *Sonata for Horn and Piano* Op.17, with excellent stylistic indications for tonguing and phrasing. The young student might not understand Tuckwell's markings in the slow movement; the notated thirty-seconds, sixteenths, and eighths have staccato dots. His purpose in this case seems to be to eliminate the usual dull and heavy interpretation common to a student performance. Those who have taught this sonata over the decades will welcome Tuckwell's edition (G. Schirmer, Grade V, 1978, $6).

An interesting new edition of Mozart's first movement, Allegro from the *Third Horn Concerto* in E♭ (KV 447), is arranged by Robert J. Bardeen. Listed as grade V with a cadenza by Micah Levy, the piece will stimulate teacher commentaries (Kendor, 1979, $4).

Rossini's *Prelude, Theme and Variation* for horn and piano, edited by Barry Tuckwell, provides a delightful treatment of this composer's style in variation form. The most difficult sections have two parts; the easier is notated, "Variation for the lazy." The difficult piano accompaniment requires a first-rate artist (G. Schirmer, grade V-VI, $6).

Horn Studies

Fifty First Exercises for Horn is designed for the beginner, and it guides him up and down the overtone series to build a fine embouchure. Intelligently paced, the youthful hornist should become adept in slurring and tonguing a variety of rhythms using this publication (Oxford, grade I-III, 1978, $8.95, 44 pages).

Tuckwell's second volume, *Playing the Horn*, contains many fine suggestions about horn skills, like "Posture," "Holding the Instrument," "The Embouchure in Detail," "Breathing in Detail"(with well-marked musical examples), "Articulation," "Lip Trills," "Muting," and "Hand-stopping." His useful suggestions for practicing difficult technical exercises and solos benefit all who perform or teach the instrument. He provides a complete fingering chart for the double horn. This volume is a fine addition to the many documents on the skill of playing the horn, and it's one which should be a part of every horn player's library (Oxford, 1978, $10, 45 pages). ∎

Tuba Solos and Studies

R. Winston Morris

The tuba music published this past year is of much higher quality than last year's disappointing collection. The majority of the better publications for tuba are linked to a fine performer or teacher, and if publishers continue to consult such experts, the quality of their publications will continue to improve. The following publications are some of the year's best.

Donald C. Little and George R. Belden have written a number of excellent transcriptions, arrangements, and compositions for tuba, euphonium, and small ensembles in Belwin-Mills' *Contemporary Band Course*. This material is primarily intended for the high school performer and it is certainly usable by college students, too. Three of these tuba solos with piano accompaniment are Handel's *Larghetto and Allegro*, Marcello's *Largo and Presto*, and *Neutron Stars*, by George Belden.

Barton Cummings has been one of the more active tubists generating new music over the past several years, and some of these works are now appearing in print. Kjos has recently released four works composed for Cummings. The two-movement *Suite for Tuba and Piano* by Carrol M. Butts is very usable for either college or advanced high school level work, and *Elegy for Tuba and Piano* by Frederick Zinos is definitely a college-level piece. *Dance Suite for Tuba and Triangle* by Bennie Beach is also a college-level piece that works well in performance and is great fun to play. *Three Abstracts for Solo Tuba* by Jae Eun Ha is played best by advanced college and professional tubists. All of these pieces are inexpensive. The Ha and Zinos works have been recently recorded by Cummings on Crystal Records.

Anyone interested in new ensemble literature should contact Whaling Music Publishers, 57 Fare Harbour Place, No. 17, New London, Connecticut. They publish materials generated by the Atlantic Tuba Quartet. Their catalog includes school through college-level material transcribed and arranged by tuba artists such as Garry Buttery, Denis Winter, David Werden, and Bill Carmody. Many of their quartet publications are featured on the ATQ recording for Golden Crest, which is also available through Whaling Music.

R. Winston Morris is associate professor of tuba/euphonium at Tennessee Technological University, Cookeville, Tennessee.

Shawnee Press has released two new excellent pieces for tuba and piano. *Concertpiece* by Lawrence I. Rappoldt is advanced high-school and college-level music and the four-movement *Sonata* by Frank Lynn Payne is a solid, college-level work.

Gordon Jacob has composed a delightful little set, *Six Little Tuba Pieces* for tuba and piano. Published by Emerson, the piece is moderately difficult and could be performed easily by the average high-school player seeking quality materials. The range is comfortable throughout except for the final high Eb above middle C. If it is faithfully executed or attempted, the work is rendered unusable by many young tubists who could otherwise play it.

Fantasia A Due for tuba and piano by Alfred Reed is a very usable work recently released by Marks Music Corporation. It was commissioned by T.U.B.A. for performance at the 3rd International Tuba/Euphonium Symposium-Workshop held in June, 1978 in Los Angeles. The work is a college-level piece. The tuba part is designated "CC tuba" but is playable on a tuba in any key.

Edition Musicus has released a very technical, three-movement *Sonata for Bass Tuba and Piano* by David Uber. It is advanced high school and college-level material.

Major Works

Sonata for Tuba and Piano by Donald H. White, commissioned for T.U.B.A. by Custom Music Company, is a three-movement work of major proportions published by Ludwig. The piece is advanced college or professional material. It involves a fairly high tessitura and would be ideal for F tuba.

Another significant composition is *Tuba Concerto* by Edward Gregson, published by Novello. This work was composed for the great English tuba artist John Fletcher. Its three movements are 18 minutes long, reminiscent of Vaughan Williams' *Concerto*. Originally composed for tuba and brass band, this arrangement with piano was prepared by the composer.

Another work, *Sonata for Tuba and Piano*, was composed for Tommy Johnson by Bruce Broughton. Tommy Johnson is quite well-known as one of the leading studio tuba artists in the world, and Broughton is active in the Los Angeles area composing for films and television. The piece is available from European American Music on rental as a tuba solo with wind ensemble accompaniment or for purchase with piano accompaniment. ∎

Cool-Down Exercises for Brass Players

James Van Develde

The practice of using low register tones to relax the brass embouchure is not new, but it is amazing how many young brass musicians are unaware of the value of low register practice and cool-down exercises, especially when so much contemporary trumpet playing focuses on the higher register.

The theory behind warm-up and cool-down studies is similar to an athlete's preparation before an event and relaxation after it is over. The muscles are brought up to peak efficiency by a gradual process, not a sudden burst from relative relaxation to great physical demand, and after a race, for example, a runner will spend time walking rather than stopping suddenly after running at top speed. In both situations the object is to reduce the possibility of muscle damage and premature fatigue.

Many times a trumpet player's time for warm-up is limited. Or perhaps the warm-up ritual was performed faithfully, but for various reasons such as insufficient practice in previous days, performance of loud, high passages, or a longer-than-usual playing session, the embouchure is very tired. It is in this situation that I recommend using the following cool-down exercises.

These low tones, played at a soft dynamic level, should rejuvenate the tired embouchure by increasing the circulation of blood to the fatigued muscles, particularly at that point where the mouthpiece rests. A player should use a minimum of mouthpiece pressure with a relaxed embouchure, and he should rest frequently.

Exercise 1

Exercise 2

Pedal tones are included for those who find them helpful, but they are not necessary to the cool-down process. The pedal tones should be played with an "oval" embouchure: the muscles in the corners of the mouth and cheeks are firmly anchored as if playing in the upper register while the embouchure aperture is widened by dropping the lower jaw. The aperture will then be more nearly oval, like an egg standing on end. If pedal tones are attempted, a player should try to produce an accurate pitch and a pleasant tone, but because pedal tones are beyond the normal trumpet range, the pitch accuracy and tone quality will not be as good. Again, brief but frequent rests are important.

The cool-down session should end with a minute or two of easy playing in the middle register (C4 to E5).

I have used the cool-down exercises with individuals, the trumpet section, and with the entire brass section. I encourage individual players to use either exercises 1 and 2 or slurred descending arpeggios into the pedal tone register (concert F4 to F3, E4 to E3, etc. down to a pedal concert Bb2). Using these exercises with the entire brass section works best during the first few weeks of the school year when embouchures are weak from summer vacation and players are trying to meet the demands of preparing marching shows. In this instance I use the first 10 measures of exercise 2.

Low register cool-down is not the panacea for all brass playing ailments, but I suggest the process to teachers whose students experience poor embouchure response the day after a demanding rehearsal, or when you overhear the comment, "I practiced two hours last night and I sound worse today instead of better." ∎

Biographies

This biographical information is current as of the date shown in parentheses.

Alexander, Anne
(June, 1976) — Public relations director of the Toledo Symphony.

Anderson, Paul
(February, 1969) — Professor of Music at the University of Wisconsin in Milwaukee, conductor of the Milwaukee Civic Symphonic Band. Active as performer with professional bands and orchestras in the community. Formerly director of bands at the University of Wisconsin.

Avis, Robert
(November, 1969) — Teacher of instrumental music in the Fort Lauderdale public schools, active in amateur bands there.

Bach, Vincent
(January, 1972) — Consultant to H & A Selmer, Inc. Former manufacturer of quality brass instruments and accessories. Education: graduate engineer. Performance: cornet soloist in Europe and the U.S.; 1st trumpet with the Boston Symphony; soloist with the Diaghilev Ballet Orchestra.

Banschbach, Donald L.
(October, 1978) — Music teacher and head of the perceptual curriculum at Lake Forest South Elementary School in Harrington, Delaware.

Benade, Arthur H.
(April, 1977) — Professor of physics at Case Western University in Cleveland. Publications: *Fundamentals of Musical Acoustics.*

Bergstone, Frederick
(June, 1973) — Faculty member at North Carolina School of the Arts; Performance: hornist with the Clarion Wind Quintet and Piedmont Chamber Orchestra.

Berinbaum, Martin
(March, 1979) — Professor of brass and conductor of the wind ensembles at the University of British Columbia in Vancouver. Education: Degrees from the University of Southern California and Julliard School of Music. Performance: recorded on Vanguard, Columbia, and Klavir labels.

Beversdorf, Thomas
(October, 1963) — Faculty member of the School of Music, Indiana University. Education: Bachelor of Music, University of Texas; Master of Music, Eastman School of Music. Performance: guest conductor, Indianapolis, Houston, and Austin Symphonies. Publications: "Sonata for Horn and Piano," "Cathedral Music" for brass choir.

Bingham, Richard
(April, 1979) — Horn teacher at Tennessee Technological University at Cookeville.

Bloomquist, Kenneth
(November, 1964) — Trumpet instructor, assistant director of bands, director of marching band and brass ensemble at the University of Kansas. Education: bachelor's and master's degrees from the University of Illinois. Teaching Experience: Illinois public schools.

Bobo, Roger
(February, 1973) — Tuba player with the Rochester Civic, Philharmonic, and Eastman-Rochester Orchestras, the Eastman Wind Ensemble, and the New York Philharmonic, the Los Angeles Philharmonic, the Hollywood Bowl Symphony Orchestra, and the Concertgebouw Orchestra of Amsterdam.

Bourdess, Jack
(June, 1958) — Teacher in the Bellevue, Nebraska public schools. Education: Bachelor of Fine Arts, Omaha University; Master of Music, University of Nebraska. Performance: 1st horn with the Omaha Symphony Orchestra.

Bowie, Lenard
(September, 1979) — Assistant professor of trumpet at Florida A & M University.

Bowles, Daniel
(January, 1978) — Assistant professor of music at the University of Tennessee at Chattanooga. Performance: trumpet player with the Chattanooga Symphony, Chattanooga Opera, Tennessee Chamber Players, and Chattanooga Brass Trio.

Bowles, Richard
(October, 1979) — Former director of bands at the University of Florida, now teacher of arranging, instrumental skills, and low brass.

Brand, Michael
(September, 1978) — Instructor of trumpet at Northwestern College, St. Paul, and at Augsburg College in Minneapolis. Performance: plays trumpet with the Minnesota Opera Orchestra, St. Paul Chamber Orchestra, Lake Harriet Orchestra, and the St. Paul Brass Trio.

Brasch, Harold
(February, 1958) — Teacher in Arlington, Virginia. Performance: Euphonium soloist with the U.S. Navy Band, and guest soloist and clinician through the U.S.

Brophy, William
(August, 1978) — Professor of brass instruments and chairman of the performance area in the School of Music at Ohio University.

Brown, Leon
(June, 1969) — Associate professor of music and director of the Brass Choir at North Texas State University; clinician and adjudicator in the Southwest. Education: Bachelor of Fine Arts in Music Education, Oklahoma State University; Master of Arts, Catholic University. Publications: more than 70 compositions or arrangements for brass or chorus.

Brown, Merrill
(December, 1976) — Professor of music at the University of Toledo. Education: PhD from the University of Iowa. Teaching Experience: Former ten-year public school teacher in Iowa.

Brownlow, Art
(May, 1979) — Holds masters degree in trumpet from Northwestern University.

Bullock, Donald
(November, 1964) — Instructor of music at Western Michigan University. Education: Bachelor of Music Education and Master of Music from Colorado University. Teaching Experience: trumpet instructor at Colorado University and director of music at the Wheatland, Wyoming public schools.

Burnau, John
(February, 1969) — Assistant professor of music at the University of South Alabama. Education: Bachelor of Music Education and Master of Music Education, University of Kansas; Doctor of Musical Arts from the University of Missouri. Teaching Experience: 14 years in elementary and high schools. Performance: clarinetist with the Central City (Colorado) Opera Association and saxophonist with the Kansas City Philharmonic Orchestra.

Butterfield, Don
(February, 1973) — Soloist and orchestral performer in New York City, and member of the faculties of three colleges in the area.

Cailliet, Lucien
(February, 1969) — Director of publications for the G. Leblanc Corporation. Education: Chalons sur Marne and the National Conservatory, France; Doctor of Music, Philadelphia Musical Academy. Performance: clarinetist and arranger for the Philadelphia Orchestra; associate conductor of the Allentown (Pennsylvania) Band. Teaching Experience: professor of music and conductor of orchestra and band at the University of Southern California; professor of composition, conductor of orchestra and band at the National Music Camp, Interlochen, Michigan. Publications: several hundred compositions, orchestrations, and band arrangements; author of a work on orchestration and band arranging.

Carnovale, Norbert
(May, 1960) — Assistant professor of music and band director at Texas Western College, teaching brass methods. Education: bachelor's degree from Louisiana State University; master's degree from Teacher's College, Columbia University.

Carter, William
(December, 1966) — Instrumental music director in the Canal Winchester (Ohio) public schools. Education: Bachelor of Science and Master of Arts, Ohio State University. Performance: trombonist with various groups in the Columbus, Ohio area.

Chase, DeForest
(March, 1957) — Instrumental music teacher in the public schools of Lakewood, Colorado. Education: Oberlin Conservatory of Music and Ohio University. Teaching Experience: faculty member of the Southwestern Louisiana Institute, Lafayette, Louisiana. Publications: "Chase Brasswind Instrument Test."

Christie, John
(February, 1969) — Editor of The Instrumentalist. Education: Bachelor of Music and Master of Music from the University of Michigan. Performance: trombonist with the Toledo, Ohio Orchestra; bass trombonist for the city of Frankfurt, Germany, the Hessen State Radio Symphony Orchestra, and the Theater of the West in Berlin. Teaching Experience: instructor of brass instruments at the University of Missouri.

Cimera, Jaroslav
(February, 1969) — Teaching Experience: Northwestern University School of Music. Performance: soloist with the Innes Band, Sousa Band, Bachman's "Million Dollar" band; soloist and assistant director of Kryl's band; director of his own band; on the staff of NBC radio for many years.

Ciurczak, Peter
(June, 1960) — Assistant professor of music at the University of Oklahoma. Education: bachelor's degree from the Oberlin Conservatory of Music; master's degree from Teacher's College of Columbia University. Performance: assistant 1st trumpet with the Baltimore Symphony Orchestra; appearances with the Boston "Pops" tour orchestra.

Conner, Rex
(November, 1971) — Assistant professor of music at the University of Kentucky. Education: bachelor's degree from the University of Kansas; master's degree from the University of Missouri. Teaching experience: Wayne State Teacher's College, Wayne, Nebraska; National Music Camp, Interlochen, Michigan; recitalist and clinician.

Crain, Robert
(January, 1967) — Assistant professor of music at Tennessee Technical College. Education: Bachelor of Music Education, Phillips University; Master of Music, Indiana University; Fulbright Scholar to the Vienna Academy of Music; Performer's Diploma in Horn, Academy of Music, Vienna, Austria. Performance: 1st hornist with the Chattanooga Opera Orchestra, Chattanooga Symphony Orchestra; hornist with chamber groups in Chattanooga area. Teaching Experience: director of high school choirs and orchestra, Chattanooga; instructor in brass instruments, Cadek Conservatory, Chattanooga.

Cramer, William
(October, 1966) — Associate professor of music at Florida State University, teaching lower brass, brass choir, and conducting. Education: Bachelor of Science in Education, Master of Arts, Ohio State University; Ed.D., Florida State University. Performance: Columbus (Ohio) Philharmonic Orchestra, Mobile (Alabama) Symphony Orchestra, Florida State Symphony. Teaching Experience: public schools in Ohio.

Cummings, Barton
(February, 1973) — Faculty member at Ball State University; active in commissioning new music for tuba, in exploring the use of tuba in the electronic studio, and in developing new techniques for the tuba. Teaching Experience: University of New Hampshire.

Dalkert, Charles
(February, 1974) — Assistant professor of trombone and tuba at the University of Western Ontario, London, Canada. Education: master's degree from the Eastman School of Music. Performance: member of London Symphony Orchestra and London Brass Quintet.

Day, Donald K.
(November, 1973) — Director of Music at the Marist School, Atlanta, Georgia. Education: master's degree from Georgia State University. Performance: solo cornetist with the Third U.S. Army Band.

Deaton, Gene
(May, 1972) — Coordinator of jazz studies at Morehead State University. Education: Murray State University; George Peabody College. Performance: lead trombone with Bob Crosby, Ralph Flannagan, Amarillo Symphony; active as an arranger.

Decker, Charles F.
(May, 1973) — Teacher of instrumental music in upstate New York public schools. Education: Eastman School of Music.

Decker, James
(December, 1972) — Professor of French horn at the University of Southern California; doubles on tuben or deskant.

Del Borgo, Elliot
(October, 1967) — Member of the brass faculty of the Crane Department of Music at the State University of New York at Potsdam. Education: Bachelor of Science, State University of New York; Master of Music, Philadelphia Conservatory of Music; Ed.M., Temple University. Teaching Experience: public schools of Philadelphia; brass instructor at the Philadelphia Conservatory, Jenkintown (Pennsylvania) School of Music, and the Haddonfield Conservatory.

Deming, Harold
(March, 1966) — Member of the faculty of Washington State University, teaching brass. Education: bachelor's and master's degrees, Eastman School of Music; further study at the University of Michigan, Oxford University (England), and Indiana University. Teaching Experience: formerly assistant professor of brass and associate director of bands at Washington State University.

Deutsch, Maury
(February, 1969) — Instrumental music teacher in the New York City public schools and educational editor of the Charles Colin Publications. Education: Bachelor of Arts, Brooklyn College; advanced degree, Musical Arts Conservatory, Amarillo, Texas. Performance: professional trumpet appearances throughout the East. Publications: twelve books on arranging, composition, ear training, and conducting.

Deye, Howard
(December, 1947) — Superintendent of Music in Pendleton, Oregon. Education: graduate work at Northwestern University and the University of Washington. Teaching Experience: instrumental music at elementary, high school, and college levels; supervisor in the Boise (Idaho) public schools.

DeYoung, Derald
(June, 1977) — Assistant professor of music at St. Olaf College in Northfield, Minnesota, teaching low brass, band, and music education. Education: MM degree from the Eastman School of Music and PhD from the University of Minnesota.

Dietz, Norman
(November, 1953) — Director of Band and Associate Professor of Music at Central Michigan College. Education: Bachelor of Science, Central Michigan; Master of Music, Michigan State. Teaching Experience: public schools of Michigan.

Dise, Lee D.
(September, 1977) — Graduate of Wichita State University. A trombonist, he has performed with the Wichita Symphony and other community orchestras and chamber ensembles.

Duerkson, George
(October, 1964) — Teaching assistant in the department of music education, University of Kansas. Education: Bachelor of Music Education and Master of Music Education, University of Kansas; Fulbright Scholar in Australia; engaged in doctoral study at the University of Kansas. Teaching Experience: instrumental music in the public high schools.

Erlenbach, Julius E.
(May, 1975) — Assistant professor of music and acting chairman of the music department at the University of Wisconsin-Stevens Point. Education: Bachelors degree from Oberlin College and MM and PhD from Northwestern University.

Evans, Ted
(December, 1952) — Instructor in French horn at the University of Michigan. Education: University of Michigan and Johns Hopkins University. Performance: Baltimore Symphony, Detroit Symphony. (Deceased).

Everett, Thomas G.
(December, 1971) — Director of Bands at Harvard University. Education: Ithaca College.

Falcone, Leonard
(February, 1969) — Now retired as director of bands and professor of music at Michigan State University. Education: bachelor's degree, University of Michigan. Teaching experience: member of the Michigan State faculty since 1927; guest teacher at universities throughout the U.S. Performance: one of the nation's noted euphonium artists; soloist with numerous bands. Publications: transcriptions for solo instruments and concert band.

Farkas, Philip
(February, 1969) — Member of the faculty of the School of Music at Indiana University. Teaching Experience: French horn instructor at Northwestern University, DePaul University (Chicago), Roosevelt University (Chicago). Performance: former 1st horn with the Chicago Symphony Orchestra; solo hornist with the Boston Symphony, Cleveland Symphony, and Kansas City Philharmonic. Publications: "The Art of French Horn Playing."

Faulkner, Maurice
(April, 1970) — Professor of music and director of the Brass Choir at the University of California at Santa Barbara. Education: bachelor's degree from Fort Hayes Kansas State College; master's degree from Columbia University; doctorate from Stanford University. Performance: conductor of the All-California High School Symphony Orchestra.

Fink, Reginald
(January, 1962) — Member of the faculty at Oklahoma City University. Education: bachelor's degree from Eastman School of Music; Master of Music Education, University of Oklahoma. Performance: principal trombonist with the Oklahoma City Symphony.

Fitzgerald, Bernard
(March, 1953) — Band director at the University of Texas. Education: bachelor's degree from Oberlin College; advanced work at Arthur Jordan Conservatory, Indianapolis, Indiana. Teaching Experience: head of wind instrument department at Arthur Jordan Conservatory; director of band and orchestra at Kansas State Teachers College; member of the faculty of the National Music Camp, Interlochen, Michigan. Performance: conductor of the Kansas All-State band and orchestra.

Fote, Richard
(February, 1974) — Trombone soloist and clinician for Kendor Music; Education: State University College of Fredonia, New York; Eastman School of Music. Teaching Experience: public schools and college. Performance: composer and arranger. Publications: music.

Garofalo, Robert J.
(November, 1969) — Director of Bands at The Catholic University of America. Education: bachelor's degree from Mansfield State College; master's degree and doctorate from The Catholic University of America.

Giardinelli, Robert
(February, 1974) — President of Giardinelli Band Instruments.

Gibson, Robert
(February, 1977) — Assistant professor of music, director of the wind ensemble, and chairman of the brass department at McGill University, Montreal, Canada.

Gihe, Osmund
(December, 1948) — Specialist in the building and repair of music instruments. Performance: noted performer on flute.

Glover, Ernest
(February, 1969) — Associate professor of music and chairman of the wind and percussion department at the University of Cincinnati College-Conservatory of Music. Education: studied in Canada and the U.S. Performance. trombonist with the Cincinnati Symphony Orchestra; assistant conductor and trombone soloist of the ARMCO Band; 1st trombonist with the Cincinnati Summer Opera and the Cincinnati May Festival Orchestra. (Deceased).

Graham, James
(June, 1967) — Instructor of lower brass and director of the brass ensemble at Southern Illinois University. Education: Bachelor of Music degree from DePauw University; Master of Arts degree from Ball State College; doctoral study at Ball State College. Teaching Experience: instructor at Ball State College; member of the staff of the Brevard Music Center. Performance: founder of the trombone choir at Southern Illinois University and member of the faculty brass quintet at the University.

Grocock, Robert
(September, 1957) — Instructor in brass and theory in the School of Music, DePauw University. Education: bachelor's and master's degrees from the Eastman School of Music. Teaching Experience: faculty member of Eastman; instructor at Syracuse University; taught in elementary schools in New York. Performance: member of the Chicago Symphony Orchestra and the Rochester Symphony Orchestra.

Haddad, Don
(February, 1968) — Professor of theory, composition, and French horn at Colorado State University. Education: Bachelor of Fine Arts and Master of Fine Arts degrees at Ohio University; engaged in doctoral study at Colorado State University. Teaching Experience: faculty member at West Texas State University, Amarillo (Texas) College, Interlochen Arts Academy. Performance: solo horn and guest artist with the Amarillo Symphony; member of the Interlochen Arts Quintet.

Hall, Jack
(January, 1972) — Trumpet instructor and assistant director of bands at Clarion State College (Pennsylvania). Education: bachelor's degree from the University of Kentucky; master's degree from Eastern Kentucky University.

Hall, Jody
(April, 1955) — Chief accoustical engineer of the Conn Corporation. Education: Bachelor of Arts, Baylor University; Master of Music Education, University of Texas; Ph.D., Indiana University. Teaching Experience: assistant in music theory, Baylor University; associate professor of music at Southwestern State College in Weatherford, Oklahoma; band director in Bastrop and San Benito, Texas; research assistant at Indiana University.

Hardin, Burton
(February, 1965) — Instructor of brass instruments at the University of South Carolina. Education: Bachelor of Music Education, University of Oklahoma; Master of Music, University of Wichita. Teaching Experience: instrumental music teacher in the Kansas schools. Performance: principal hornist of the Columbia Festival Orchestra; former member of the Wichita Symphony Orchestra. Publications: "Hunting Horns" for four horns and band.

Harlow, Lewis
(February, 1969) — Author and supervisor of instrumental music at the grade school level in New England. Education: bachelor's degree from Harvard University; further study in Paris, France. Teaching Experience: supervisor of elementary music programs.

Haynie, John
(May, 1967) — Associate professor of music at North Texas State University, teaching trumpet and brass pedagogy. Education: Bachelor of Science in Music Education and Master of Science in Music Education from the University of Illinois. Performance: recording artist with Golden Crest Records and Austin Records.

Hazelman, Herbert
(September, 1961) — Director of instrumental music in the Greensboro, North Carolina public schools.

Heath, Roger
(January, 1973) — Assistant director of bands at Purdue University; brass instructor and director of performing groups at Purdue.

Hepola, Ralph
(November, 1977) — Tubist and music education major at Northwestern University. Performance: three years with the U.S. Army Band in Washington; currently with the Minnesota Orchestra.

Hickman, David
(September, 1976) — Assistant professor of trumpet at the University of Illinois at Urbana. Performance: performances with the Denver Symphony and the University of Illinois Band.

Hill, Douglas
(May, 1979) — Associate professor of horn at the University of Wisconsin-Madison, president of the International Horn Society, and co-principal hornist with the Madison Symphony Orchestra.

Hindsley, Mark
(January, 1953) — Director of bands and professor of music at the University of Illinois. Education: Bachelor of Arts and Master of Arts, Indiana University. Teaching Experience: music director of the concert band at Indiana; director of instrumental music in the Cleveland Heights, Ohio public schools; assistant director of the University of Illinois Bands. Publications: books and articles on music education; numerous band arrangements and transcriptions.

Hodges, Donald A.
(March, 1977) — Assistant professor of music at the University of South Carolina at Columbia.

Hoffren, James
(August, 1961) — Education: master's degree from the Eastman School of Music; engaged in doctoral study in music education at the University of Illinois. Teaching Experience: trumpet instructor and director of the brass choir at the University of Wichita. Performance: 1st trumpet in the Wichita Symphony Orchestra.

Hofmeister, Donald
(June, 1979) — Elementary and junior high school instrumental music teacher in New Prague, Minnesota.

Hoover, Walter
(September, 1969) — Cornet teacher in Connellsville, Pennsylvania. Teaching Experience: instrumental music teacher and band director in the Pennsylvania public schools. Performance: cornet soloist with state bands.

Hoss, Wendell
(January, 1966) — Performer with studio orchestras in Hollywood, California. Teaching Experience: taught French horn and directed wind ensembles at Eastman School of Music. Performance: 1st horn with the Los Angeles Symphony, Chicago Symphony, Cleveland Symphony, Rochester Philharmonic, Pittsburgh Symphony, NBC Symphony Orchestra; organized the Los Angeles French Horn Club.

Hovey, Graham
(December, 1972) — Member of the editorial board of the New York Times; member of the Ridgewood, New Jersey Symphony Orchestra.

Humfeld, Neill H.
(June, 1974) — Professor of Music and chairman of the instrumental music division at East Texas State University. Education: DMA from Eastman School of Music.

Hunsberger, Donald
(April, 1965) — Co-ordinator of the instrumental ensembles at the Eastman School of Music; conductor of the Eastman Wind Ensemble and the Eastman Symphony Band. Education: bachelor's, master's, and Doctor of Musical Arts degrees from Eastman. Publications: editor of the Leeds Symphonic Wind Ensemble Series; composed and arranged numerous works for band.

Jenkins, Harry
(January, 1971) — Instrumental music teacher in the New York City public schools. Education: bachelor's and master's degrees from the Manhattan School of Music. Performance: trumpet player in the Indianapolis and New Orleans Symphony Orchestras and in the orchestras of Sigmund Romberg, Paul Whiteman, and Frank Black.

Jenkins, Merlin
(January, 1970) — Assistant professor of trumpet at Texas Christian University. Education: bachelor's and master's degrees from North Texas State University. Teaching Experience: 15 years as teacher in the public schools; clinician.

Jensen, Richard
(April, 1969) — Assistant professor of music at Central Washington State College. Education: bachelor's degree from the University of Washington; master's degree from the University of California at Los Angeles; studied with Mark Fisher, John Barrows, Sinclair Lott, and Philip Farkas. Performance: Spokane Philharmonic, Seattle Symphony Orchestra, Minneapolis Symphony, Utah Symphony Orchestra.

Johnson, Carson
(April, 1960) — Instrumental music teacher in the Carterville, Illinois public schools. Education: bachelor's degree from Indiana University; advanced work at Southern Illinois University.

Johnson, Merton
(October, 1969) — Associate professor of Music at Texas A & I University; solo horn with Corpus Christi Symphony. Education: bachelor's degree from the Curtis Institute of Music; master's degree from Illinois Wesleyan University. Teaching Experience: band director at State University College, Geneseo, New York; instructor in French horn at Wichita University; director of instrumental music at Friends University, Wichita, Kansas. Performance: played French horn with the Denver Symphony, Wichita Symphony, and the Rochester Philharmonic.

Johnson, William V.
(November, 1979) — Conductor of bands at California Polytechnic State University.

Jones, Robert C.
(September, 1973) — Assistant professor of music at Geneva College. Education: Pennsylvania State University; Duquesne University. Teaching Experience: 11 years in the public schools.

Kacanek, Harold S.
(June, 1978) — Education: Degrees from the Eastman School of Music and the University of Michigan. Currently studying for DMA at the University of Kansas.

Kinneman, Ted
(April, 1968) — Instructor in brass and instrumental music at the Rich County Campus of the University of Wisconsin Center at Janesville.

Kinney, Guy
(May, 1978) — Chairman of the music department at Candor (New York) Central School and French horn instructor at the University of Vermont summer music sessions. Performance: Former principal hornist with the Birmingham, Alabama Symphony, the Syracuse Symphony, and the Lake George Opera Festival.

Kinyon, John
(February, 1968) — Band director in the Northport, Long Island public schools. Education: Bachelor of Music, Eastman School of Music; master's degree from Ithaca College. Former educational director for music publisher. Publications: numerous band methods and band arrangements.

Kirmser, Lawrence
(April, 1979) — President of the National Association of Musical Instrument Technicians, South Bend, Indiana.

Kizer, George
(May, 1956) — Director of instrumental music in the El Reno, Oklahoma public schools. Education: bachelor's degree from Oklahoma A & M College; master's degree from the University of Michigan. Teaching Experience: over 10 years in the Oklahoma public schools.

Kosakoff, Gabriel
(October, 1959) — Director of brass and percussion instruction and band director at the High School of Music and Art in New York City. Education: bachelor's and master's degrees from New York University. Teaching Experience: director of music in the Audubon, New Jersey public schools; music instructor in the Jamaica, Long Island high schools. Performance: professional trombonist.

Kress, Victor
(March, 1960) — Teacher of brass instruments at San Francisco State College and at the Music and Arts Intitute and Peninsula Conservatory of Music in San Francisco. Performance: member of the San Francisco Symphony Orchestra and the San Francisco Opera Orchestra.

Kuehn, David
(September, 1966) — Instructor of low brass and assistant director of bands at Wisconsin State University at Eau Claire. Education: bachelor's degree from North Texas State University; master's degree from the University of Illinois; Fulbright Scholar at the Guildhall School of Music and Royal College of Music in London. Teaching Experience: faculty member of the Colorado Music Camp, Summer Youth Music Camp in Illinois, National Music Camp at Interlochen, Michigan, and summer music camps in Texas.

Laudermilch, Kenneth
(November, 1970) — Assistant professor of brass instruments at West Chester (Pennsylvania) State College. Education: bachelor's degree in applied music from the New England Conservatory of Music.

Law, Glen
(May, 1961) — Chairman of the music department at Edinboro State College in Pennsylvania. Education: bachelor's degree from the Eastman School of Music; master's and doctoral degrees from Teachers College of Columbia University. Performance: 1st trombonist with the Rochester Philharmonic, New York Symphony, Oklahoma City Symphony, and the Erie Philharmonic Orchestra.

Lawson, Walter
(April, 1979) — Horn player in the Baltimore Symphony from 1949 to 1975. Owner and operator of an instrument repair shop that specializes in horn repair and rebuilding.

Lee, Ira
(March, 1954) — Instructor of brass, assistant director of band, and director of the high school summer music session at the University of Oregon. Education: bachelor's and master's degrees from the University of Colorado; director of high school bands in Nebraska and Kansas.

Leiberman, William B.
(October, 1971) — Dentist in Beaver Falls, Pennsylvania. Education: bachelor's degree from Franklin and Marshall College; D.D.S. from the University of Pittsburgh.

Leidzen, Erik
(November, 1960) — Composer, arranger, editor, and teacher; arranger for the Goldman Band. Education: Royal Conservatory, Stockholm, Sweden. Publications: "An Invitation to Band Arranging," numerous symphonic works for orchestra and band, chamber music, songs, and instrumental solos.

Lekvold, A.D.
(November, 1953) — Associate professor of music education at Miami University, Oxford, Ohio. Education: South Dakota State College, McPhail School, and Columbia University.

Leno, H. Lloyd
(April, 1971) — Faculty member at Walla Walla College. Education: bachelor's degree from Walla Walla College; master's degree from Columbia University Teacher's College; Doctor of Musical Arts from University of Arizona.

Leuba, Christopher
(March, 1974) — Professor of French horn at the University of Washington. Performance: 1st horn with the Minneapolis and Chicago Symphony Orchestras.

Lewis, H.M.
(October, 1970) — Faculty member at the College of the Ozarks. Education: Bachelor of Arts and Bachelor of Music, Hendrix College; master's degree from Northwestern University. Teaching Experience: Arkansas public schools.

Ligotti, Albert F.
(September, 1974) — Assistant professor of music at the University of Georgia at Athens.

Lillya, Clifford
(June, 1957) — Assistant professor of brass instruments at the University of Michigan. Education: bachelor's degree from VanderCook School of Music, Chicago; master's degree from Northwestern University. Teaching Experience: instrumental music teacher and director of bands at high school and college level. Publications: band arrangements, class methods, and instructional books.

Lindner, Richard
(September, 1968) — Band director and instructor in brass at Winona State College in Minnesota. Education: Bachelor of Arts, Luther College; Master of Music, Northwestern University. Teaching Experience: instrumental music teacher in the Elgin, Illinois junior high schools.

Lindskoog, Wesley
(February, 1960) — Member of the New York Brass Ensemble; brass teacher at the Aspen Music Festival in Colorado. Education: graduate of the Eastman School of Music. Performance: member of the Utah Symphony; 1st trumpet with the Ojai Festival Orchestra, the American Ballet Theatre Orchestra, and the Little Orchestra Society of New York.

Liva, Howard
(May, 1963) — Instructor in the brass department and conductor of the brass choir at Purdue University. Education: Indiana University.

Lowrey, Alvin
(October, 1968) — Instructor of trumpet and brass ensembles at Colorado State College. Education: Bachelor of Music Education, University of Kansas; Master of Science in Music Education, University of Illinois. Teaching Experience: graduate assistant instructor of trumpet, University of Illinois. Performance: principal trumpet of Kansas University Brass Choir, University of Illinois Symphony and Wind Ensemble; member of the Champaign-Urbana Civic Orchestra and Faculty Brass Quintet at Illinois.

Lyon, Ernest
(January, 1951) — Band director and instructor of trombone, winds, orchestration, and conducting at the School of Music of the University of Kentucky. Education: bachelor's degree from Marshall College; master's degree from the Eastman School of Music. Teaching Experience: thirteen years at the University of Kentucky. Performance: 1st trombone with the North Carolina State Symphony and the Louisville Symphony Orchestra.

Mages, Samuel
(September, 1959) — Director of bands and orchestras at New Trier Township High School, Winnetka, Illinois. Education: bachelor's and master's degrees from Northwestern University. Performance: member of the Chicago Civic Orchestra and performer on trumpet in the Chicago area.

Magnell, Elmer
(February, 1968) — Director of music internships at Florida State University. Education: bachelor's degree from Gustavus Adolphus College; master's degree from the University of Iowa; doctorate from the University of Colorado. Teaching Experience: band director in Minnesota public schools; band director and instructor in methods and music education at the University of Minnesota, Duluth. Publications: "68 Paree Studies" and "29 Schantl Studies."

Magnuson, Gregg
(October, 1973) — Education: bachelor's and master's degrees from the University of Michigan.

Malek, Vincent
(February, 1969) — Head of the music department at Northeastern Illinois State University, Chicago. Former editor of The Instrumentalist. Education: bachelor's, master's, and doctoral degrees from Northwestern University. Teaching Experience: instructor at Iowa State Teachers College; band director in Woodstock, Illinois.

Manous, Carlyle
(November, 1978) — Teacher of brass instruments and conductor of the symphonic band at Pacific Union College, Angwin, California.

Marciniak, Francis
(April, 1968) — Instructor of music, director of the Concert Band and Brass Ensemble, and teacher of theory and brass at Elizabethtown College, Pennsylvania. Education: Bachelor of Science, Mansfield State College; Master of Music, Northwestern University. Teaching Experience: director of bands at St. Mary's area schools in Pennsylvania; director of bands and chairman of the music department of the schools in Dansville, New York.

Masser, Joel
(April, 1978) — Education: Degrees from Michigan State and Northwestern Universities. Currently trumpet teacher in the Chicago suburbs.

Mathews, Michael K.
(May, 1978) — Graduate of the University of Michigan who has taught instrumental music in Standish, Grand Rapids, and Kent City, Michigan.

McDunn, Mark
(January, 1966) — Member of the faculty of the DePaul University School of Music (Chicago). Education: Western Kentucky State Teachers College. Teaching Experience: instructor in applied brass instruments at Western Kentucky. Performance: free-lance recording artist with RCA Victor, Columbia, Decca, Mercury and Atlantic records; member of the CBS staff orchestra (Chicago). Publications: "Trombone Artistry"; numerous arrangements for trombone.

McGuffey, Patrick
(June, 1968) — Director of Brass Instruction and Director of the Brass-Art Chamber Quintet at Tennessee Technological University.

McKee, William
(April, 1962) — Assistant professor of music history and French horn at the University of Tulsa. Education: bachelor's degree from Syracuse University; master's degree from the Eastman School of Music; Ph.D. from North Texas State University. Performance: director of the University of Tulsa Symphony; 1st horn with the Tulsa Philharmonic Orchestra.

McMillan, Hugh
(June, 1952) — Director of bands, associate professor, and head of the wind instrument division of the College of Music at the University of Colorado. Education: bachelor's degree from Northwestern University; master's degree from the University of Colorado.

Mellon, Edward
(September, 1950) — Instructor in brass instruments at the School of Music of the University of Texas. Education: Bachelor of Music, North Texas State College. Teaching Experience: instructor at the Eastman School of Music. Performance: member of the Rochester Philharmonic Orchestra.

Meyer, Lawrence
(January, 1969) — Professor of brass and theory at the University of Arkansas; director of the university's brass choir. Education: master's degree from the University of Oregon; doctorate from Colorado State College.

Miller, Thomas
(May, 1964) — Associate professor of music and assistant to the Dean of the School of Music of East Carolina College. Education: bachelor's degree from Westchester State College; master's degree from East Carolina College. Teaching Experience: director of instrumental music in the Harrisburg, Pennsylvania high schools. Performance: trumpet performer in the Philadelphia area; solo cornetist with the Second Army Band.

Mitchell, Gilbert
(April, 1973) — Director of Northern Virginia Chamber Orchestra. Performance: solo cornet of the U.S. Army Band; member of the U.S. Army Herald Trumpets; clinician for Selmer.

Moeck, Walter
(December, 1961) — Director of music in the Catholic schools in Birmingham, Alabama; conductor of the Alabama Pops Orchestra. Education: Eastman School of Music; student of Pierre Monteux. Performance: trumpet soloist; participant in the Philadelphia Symphony Orchestra Conductor's Symposium.

Moore, E.C.
(February, 1951) — Bandmaster in the Appleton, Wisconsin high schools; education director for G. Leblanc publications.

Moore, Paul
(February, 1956) — Assistant professor of music at Minot State Teachers College in North Dakota. Education: bachelor's and master's degrees from the Colorado State College of Education. Teaching Experience: public schools in Nebraska, Texas, and Oklahoma.

Moore, Ward
(September, 1951) — Director of band at the New Jersey State Teachers College in Montclair. Education: Bachelor of Music, Illinois Wesleyan University; master's degrees from the University of Michigan and Columbia University. Performance: director of the Essex County (New Jersey) professional concert band.

Morris, R. Winston
(February, 1973) — Assistant professor of tuba/euphonium at Tennessee Technological University; director of the brass choir and tuba ensemble at the University. Education: East Carolina University; Indiana University.

Muelbe, William
(February, 1969) — 1st horn with the Minneapolis Symphony Orchestra until his retirement in 1952. Teaching Experience: instructor in French horn at the University of Minnesota; teacher of conducting and orchestration at the Minneapolis College of Music. Performance: 1st horn with the John Philip Sousa Band; conducted summer symphony concerts and operatic productions in Minneapolis; conducted radio and young people's concerts of the Minneapolis Symphony. (Deceased).

Murray, Thomas W.
(October, 1976) — Private teacher in the northern Virginia area. Education: graduate of Northwestern University. Performance: retired in 1968 as principal hornist of The United States Army Band in Washington, D.C.

Musser, Willard
(February, 1961) — Director of the wind ensemble and associate professor of music at the State University College of Education, Potsdam, New York. Education: bachelor's and master's degrees from Ithaca College.

Myers, Marceau
(February, 1963) — Director of the orchestra and assistant professor of music education at Danbury State College in Connecticut. Education: bachelor's degree from Mansfield State College: master's degree from Pennsylvania State University. Teaching Experience: public schools of New York State and Indiana.

Nagel, Robert
(March, 1961) — Faculty member of the Yale School of Music and founder-director of the New York Brass Quintet. Performance: solo trumpeter with Little Orchestra Society of New York; formerly solo cornetist with the Goldman Band.

Neidig, Kenneth L.
(April, 1979) — Editor/Advertising manager of *The Instrumentalist.*

Neilson, James
(November, 1956) — Associate professor of music at Oklahoma City University. Education: Chicago Musical College and the Juilliard School of Music. Performance: 1st trumpet with the Oklahoma Symphony Orchestra and solo cornetist with the Chicago Staff Band of the Salvation Army. Publications: co-author of a method series: "The Music Road."

Nelson, Boris
(June, 1976) — Music critic/editor of the Toledo newspaper, *The Blade.*

Olson, Dale
(September, 1964) — Engaged in research in acoustics and product development for F.E. Olds Company. Education: bachelor's and master's degrees. Teaching Experience: instrumental music in public schools. Performance: member of the Los Angeles Brass Society; performed extensively on trumpet in the California area.

Oneglia, Mario F.
(September, 1972) — Faculty member at Mon'clair State College. Education: master's degree from the Manhattan School of Music; master's degree, professional diploma, and doctor of education degrees from Columbia University. Teaching Experience: New York public schools.

Ostling Jr., Acton
(February, 1969) — Director of bands at Iowa State University. Education: Bachelor of Music and Master of Music degrees, University of Michigan. Teaching Experience: director of bands and orchestras in the Connecticut high schools; director of bands and instructor of low brass and percussion at the University of Maryland.

Owen, Herbert
(October, 1949) — Assistant professor of band instruments at Drake University in Iowa. Education: Doane College; University of Nebraska. Teaching Experience: instructor in the elementary and high schools in Nebraska and at the University of Nebraska. Performance: 1st trombone with the Drake-Des Moines Symphony.

Pallansch, Robert
(February, 1973) — Principal tubist with the U.S. Army Band.

Parnell, James
(May, 1969) — Associate professor in the School of Music at East Carolina University. Education: bachelor's degree from the Cleveland Institute of Music; master's degree from Florida State University.

Pease, Edward
(May, 1974) — Professor of music at Western Kentucky University. Education: degrees from Western Illinois University, Illinois Wesleyan University; PhD in musicology from Indiana University.

Perantoni, Daniel
(February, 1973) — Associate professor of music at the University of Illinois. Education: Eastman School of Music; Catholic University.

Perrini, Nicholas
(February, 1972) — Professor of French horn at Capital University; guest soloist and clinician.

Peters, G. David
(December, 1970) — Director of bands and brass instructor at Texas Southern University. Education: bachelor's degree from the University of Evansville; master's degree from the University of Illinois.

Peterson, Douglas
(February, 1967) — Assistant director of bands at Wheeling High School in Wheeling, Illinois. Education: Bachelor of Music Education and Master of Music Education, Drake University. Teaching Experience: brass instructor in the fine arts preparatory department at Drake University. Performance: member of the North Shore Band of Wilmette, Illinois; trombonist with the Des Moines, Iowa Symphony Orchestra.

Phillips, Harvey
(October, 1976) — Professor of music at Indiana University. Performance: Former tubist with the New York City Ballet Orchestra, Symphony of the Air, Bell Telephone Hour Orchestra. Voice of Firestone Orchestra, and the Goldman Band. Recorded on Crest, RCA Victor, United Artists, Epic, Impulse, and Mercury labels.

Phillips, June
(May, 1951) — Director of instrumental music in the public schools of LaCrosse, Wisconsin; instructor in winds at the State Teachers College in LaCrosse. Education: bachelor's degree in music education from the University of Minnesota; additional study at the Juilliard School of Music. Teaching Experience: assistant director of bands at the University of Minnesota.

Pitts, Larry P.
(April, 1975) — Graduate student in tuba performance at Northeast Louisiana University, Monroe, Louisiana.

Pond, Marden J.
(May, 1977) — Teacher at Saddleback College in Mission Viejo, California. Education: BM in music education from Brigham Young University and MM in composition from Arizona State University.

Poolos, James G.
(January, 1973) — Assistant professor of music at Pfeiffer College. Teaching Experience: Georgia public schools; Florida State University; Florida Memorial College.

Popiel, Peter
(April, 1970) — Instructor of tuba at Indiana University of Pennsylvania. Education: bachelor's degree from State University College of Fredonia, New York; master's degree from the Eastman School of Music. Performance: principal tubist with the Eastman Wind Ensemble.

Pottag, Max
(February, 1969) — Now retired, living in Indianapolis, Indiana, foremost teacher and performer on the French horn. Education: Royal Conservatory of Music in Leipzig, Germany. Teaching Experience: member of the faculty of Northwestern University. Performance: Philadelphia Orchestra; Pittsburgh Orchestra; 40 years with the Chicago Symphony Orchestra. Publications: numerous books of exercises, duets, quartets, and arrangements for the French horn.

Powell, Richard E.
(November, 1979) — Associate professor of music at West Virginia University.

Pryor, Stephen
(June, 1977) — Band director at W.A. Berry High School in Birmingham, Alabama. Education: Pursuing an MME degree at the University of Alabama.

Purcell, Randy
(June, 1977) — Education: Degree from Carnegie-Mellon University. Performance: Trombonist with Maynard Ferguson's Band. Formerly toured with the Glenn Miller and Si Zentner Bands, Fred Waring and the Pennsylvanians, and the U.S. Navy's jazz ensemble, the Commodores.

Rada, Robert
(June, 1956) — Trombonist with the Chicago Symphony Orchestra.

Raph, Alan
(October, 1970) — Studio trombonist in New York City; active clinician. Publications: method for double valve bass trombone.

Rasmussen, Mary
(January, 1954) — Student of tuba. Education: bachelor's degree from the University of New Hampshire; fellowship student in graduate work at the University of Illinois.

Richards, John
(January, 1954) — Assistant professor of music and conductor of the Symphonic Band at Lewis and Clark College (Oregon). Education: bachelor's degree from Whitman College; master's degree from the University of Southern California. Teaching Experience: instructor of brass instruments at the University of Southern California; head of instrumental music in grade schools of Walla Walla, Washington. Performance: member of the Portland Symphony Orchestra.

Richardson, William W.
(February, 1978) — Associate professor of music, trombone and low brass teacher, and supervisor of the brass chamber music program at the University of Wisconsin-Madison. Performance: Former trombonist in the United States Marine Band and St. Louis Symphony; currently member of the University of Wisconsin-Madison Brass Quintet and the Madison Symphony.

Richtmeyer, Loris
(January, 1961) — Director of bands and professor of brass instruments at Northern Michigan University. Education: bachelor's degree from the Central Michigan University; master's degree from the University of Michigan.

Righter, Charles
(February, 1969) — Now retired from his position as director of bands at the University of Iowa. Education: Bachelor of Music and Bachelor of Fine Arts degrees from the University of Nebraska. Teaching Experience: supervisor of instrumental music in the public schools of Lincoln, Nebraska; instructor of violin and school music in the School of Music at the University of Nebraska. Publications: "Success in Teaching School Orchestras and Bands," "Gridiron Pageantry," the Righter-Dasch "Tuning Method for Orchestras," and the Righter-Grabel "Tuning Method for Band."

Robbins, E.J.
(October, 1966) — Director of music for the Royal Canadian Air Force Band. Education: Royal Air Force School of Music, Uxbridge, England; holds a Licentiate Degree from the London Guildhall School of Music. Performance: soloist and assistant conductor with the RCAF Central Band in London; noted euphonium soloist in the British Commonwealth.

Roberts, Chester
(March, 1975) — Brass instrument and ensemble teacher at several Boston-area schools. Performance: principal tuba player, Pittsburgh Symphony; tubist with the Cleveland Orchestra. Teaching Experience: Oberlin Conservatory.

Robertson, James
(December, 1968) — Instructor in low brass and director of the Brass Ensemble at the University of Montana. Education: Master of Music, University of Montana. Teaching Experience: public schools in Seattle, Washington.

Robinson, William
(November, 1967) — Instructor in horn at the Florida State University. Education: bachelor's and master's degrees from Oklahoma University. Teaching Experience: instrumental music in the public schools of Oklahoma and Texas; taught French horn at Oklahoma University and Texas Western College. Performance: member of the Oklahoma City Symphony and the El Paso Symphony; member of the faculty Woodwind Quintet and Brass Trio at Florida State University.

Rohner, Traugott
(March, 1974) — Publisher of The Instrumentalist. Education: Bachelor of Arts, Central Wesleyan College; master's degree from Northwestern University; doctoral study in educational psychology at Northwestern University. Teaching Experience: band and orchestra in the high schools in Marshall, Minnesota; band, orchestra, and instrumental music in the public schools of Asheville, North Carolina and Evanston, Illinois; member of the faculty at Northwestern University. Publications: Books — "Instrumental Music Primer," "Violin Method," "Fundamentals of Music Theory," and "Basic Studies for the Instruments of the Orchestra." Arrangements — string orchestra arrangement of "Ave Maria," Menuetto from "String Quartet" by Schubert, and Adagio from "The Farewell Symphony" of Haydn.

Rose, William
(January, 1972) — Member of the Houston Symphony Orchestra; teaches tuba privately at the University of Houston.

Rosenberg, Marvin
(January, 1972) — Chairman of the music department of a junior high school in New York City. Education: Bachelor of Arts in Music and Master of Arts in Music, Manhattan School of Music. Teaching Experience: band director in Brooklyn high schools. Performance: free-lance percussionist in New York City and member of the Longines Symphonette.

Rosevear, Robert
(June, 1951) — Assistant professor of school music at the University of Toronto and a faculty member of the Royal Conservatory of Music. Education: Bachelor of Arts and Master of Arts, Cornell University; additional study at the Eastman School of Music. Teaching Experience: guest instructor at the University of Wisconsin summer program; instrumental music teacher in Missouri. Performance: 1st horn with the Royal Conservatory Opera Orchestra in Toronto; former 1st horn with the St. Louis Philharmonic Orchestra and Philharmonic Woodwind Ensemble.

Ross, Stewart L.
(February, 1976; October, 1977) — Instructor at the University of Wisconsin Center and private trombone teacher. Education: MM from Northwestern University.

Rumery, Kenneth R.
(April, 1973) — Professor of music at Northern Arizona University; member of Northern Arizona Brass and Woodwind Quintets; principal horn in the Flagstaff Symphony. Education: doctoral degree from the University of Colorado.

Sandor, Edward P.
(November, 1976) — Assistant professor of trumpet at Mansfield (Pa.) State College. Education: degrees from Ohio State University and the University of Illinois. Performance: member of the Mansfield State College Brass Quintet and the Northeast Pennsylvania Philharmonic.

Schaefer, August
(December, 1953) — Maintains a studio as a teacher of brass instruments. Teaching Experience: brass instructor at the Ohio College of Music for 30 years and instructor in instrumental music at the Cincinnati Conservatory of Music for that time. Performance: cornet soloist and 1st trumpet with numerous orchestras. Publications: composed and arranged more than 70 works.

Schaefer, Jay Dee
(May, 1968) — Director of music in the Laramie, Wyoming public schools. Education: Bachelor of Music and Master of Arts, University of Wyoming. Teaching Experience: instrumental music in the Wyoming school system; brass instructor at the University of Wyoming and director of the Brass Ensemble there. Performance: trombonist with the University of Wyoming Brass Quintet.

Schaefer, William
(September, 1965) — Professor of music and director of bands at the University of Southern California. Education: Bachelor of Science and Master of Arts, Miami University in Ohio. Teaching Experience: instructor in music education at Miami University; assistant professor of music education and director of bands at Carnegie Institute of Technology. Publications: numerous band arrangements.

Schilke, Renold
(February, 1969) — Owner of the Schilke Company, manufacturers of brass instruments and mouthpieces. Teaching Experience: former member of the faculty of Northwestern University and Roosevelt University (Chicago). Performance: former member of the Chicago Symphony Orchestra, Chicago Opera Orchestra, and the Grant Park Symphony in Chicago.

Schmid, William
(August, 1967) — Brass instructor at Winona State College, Winona, Minnesota. Education: Bachelor of Science, Luther College, Decorah, Iowa; Master of Music, Eastman School of Music; now engaged in doctoral study at Eastman.

Schmidt, Lloyd
(December, 1959) — Member of the faculty at the University of Arkansas. Education: Navy School of Music; Chicago Musical College; Northwestern University; Fulbright grant for study in Germany. Teaching Experience: public schools of Hesperia, Michigan. Performance: horn soloist with the symphony orchestras in Billings, Montana, Joplin, Missouri, and the University of Arkansas.

Schmoll, Joseph
(February, 1965) — Professor of brass instruments and theory at Texas Southern University. Education: bachelor's degree from the State University of South Dakota; Master of Music, Eastman School of Music; Ph.D., Northwestern University. Publications: books of studies for the horn.

Schulze, Robert
(April, 1950) — Member of the faculty at the Juilliard School of Music and Manhattan School of Music. Education: Juilliard School of Music. Performance: member of the New York Philharmonic Orchestra for 32 years; member of the Metropolitan Opera Orchestra, NBC Orchestra, New York Symphony, Cleveland Symphony, and the John Philip Sousa Band.

Seiffert, Stephen
(April, 1975) — Assistant professor of music at the University of Western Ontario. Education: Bachelors degree and DMA from Eastman School of Music, MA from Brown University. Performance: Rochester and Buffalo Philharmonic Orchestras, Baltimore Symphony.

Sellers, Ronald
(February, 1974) — Former band director at Brookwood, Alabama High School.

Shoemaker, John R.
(January, 1973) — Adjunct professor of music at Western Illinois University. Education: bachelor's degree from Drake University; master's degree from Northwestern University; doctoral degree from Washington University in St. Louis. Teaching Experience: faculty member at the University of Hawaii.

Silliman, Cutler
(January, 1964) — Associate professor of music at State University College, Fredonia, New York. Education: bachelor's and master's degrees from Northwestern University; Ph.D., Eastman School of Music.

Smith, Douglass
(January, 1972) — Faculty member at Dallas Baptist College; principal trumpet in the Fort Worth Symphony. Education: Master of Music Education, North Texas State; engaged in doctoral study at the University of Michigan. Teaching Experience: trumpet instructor at North Texas State University; band director in the Tennessee public high schools. Performance: played trumpet with the Knoxville (Tennessee) Symphony and the American Wind Symphony Orchestra.

Smith, Glenn P.
(February, 1974) — Professor of Music at the University of Michigan; active as adjudicator and clinician. Publications: editor of solo and ensemble literature for brass instruments.

Smith, Leonard
(February, 1969) — Noted cornetist, composer, and conductor. Education: Ernest Williams School of Music, New York City; New York University; Curtis Institute of Music. Performance: 1st trumpet with the Detroit Symphony Orchestra; cornet soloist with the Goldman Band; soloist with the U.S. Navy Band; organized the Detroit Concert Band. Publications: "Treasury of Scales" for band; cornet solos, marches, and special arrangements for cornet and band.

Snapp, Kenneth
(March, 1954) — Faculty member of the National Music Camp, Interlochen, Michigan. Education: Bachelor of Music in education, University of Miami, Florida; Master of Music, University of Michigan; Ph.D., Indiana University. Teaching Experience: summer sessions of the University of Michigan; public schools of Clayton, Missouri; band and chorus director in high schools of Cross City, Florida.

Stanley, Donald
(December, 1969) — Assistant professor of music at Mansfield State College in Pennsylvania. Education: Bachelor of Science and Master of Arts, Ohio State University. Teaching Experience: director of music in the public schools of Milan, Ohio; instructor of music at Kearney State College in Nebraska. Performance: conductor of the Marching and symphonic bands, the Brass Choir, and the Percussion Ensemble at Mansfield State College.

Stacy, William B.
(March, 1976) — Teacher at the University of Wyoming. Education: Degrees from Ohio State University, the University of North Carolina, and the University of Colorado.

Stevens, Milton
(February, 1974) — Trombone teacher and brass ensemble coach at Ohio State University; member of the Ohio Brass Quintet; 1st trombone with the Columbus Symphony Orchestra.

Stuart, Glenn
(April, 1977) — Performance: former lead trumpet player with the Stan Kenton and Don Ellis Orchestras. Publications: *The Art of Playing Lead Trumpet.*

Stoutamire, Albert
(March, 1972) — Associate professor of music at McNeese State College, Lake Charles, Louisiana. Education: Bachelor of Science, Master of Arts, and doctorate in education. Teaching Experience: instrumental music, bands, and orchestras at the elementary, junior and senior high, and college level.

Sweatt, Morris
(October, 1973) — Education: bachelor's degree from Southern Mississippi; master's degree from Northwestern University. Teaching Experience: private and secondary school teacher.

Swett, Jim
(February, 1974) — Low brass teacher at Northwestern State University of Louisiana. Education: Florida State University; George Peabody College for Teachers. Teaching Experience: instrumental music in public schools and at the college level.

Tanner, Paul
(September, 1970) — Member of the faculty of the University of California at Los Angeles and of San Fernando Valley State College. Education: bachelor's and master's degrees from the University of California, Los Angeles. Performance: 1st trombonist with the American Broadcasting Company in Los Angeles; recording artist with television and movie studio orchestras; concert soloist. Publications: six books on music for the trombone, one volume on the bass trombone, and a textbook on the study of jazz.

Tetzlaff, Daniel
(February, 1969) — Instructor of trumpet at the University of Minnesota and teacher of band in the Minneapolis high schools; editor of the Audio Visual Department of The Instrumentalist. Education: University of Minnesota. Teaching Experience: brass instructor at Augsburg College in Minneapolis and Hamline University in St. Paul. Performance: free-lance performer on trumpet in the theater-dance-show field; member of the Houston, Texas and Minneapolis Symphony Orchestras.

Thomason, Gary
(September, 1962) — Director of instrumental music in the elementary and junior high schools of Clinton, Illinois. Education: bachelor's degree from Millikin University; master's degree from Illinois State Normal University.

Torchinsky, Abe
(April, 1964) — Member of the Philadelphia Symphony and the Brass Quintet of the Philadelphia Orchestra. Education: Curtis Institute of Music. Performance: former member of the National Symphony of Washington, D.C., the NBC Symphony; member of opera companies in the Philadelphia area.

Trobian, Helen
(September, 1958) — Member of the faculty of Salem College in West Virginia. Education: bachelor's degree from Northwest Missouri State Teachers College; master's degree from Teachers College, Columbia University; Ed.D., Columbia.

Turrentine, Edgar
(April, 1969) — Associate professor of music education at the University of Minnesota. Education: Bachelor of Music Education, Wichita University; Master of Music Education, Oberlin College; Ph.D., University of Iowa. Teaching Experience: public schools of Lyons, Kansas, Wytheville, Virginia, and Fairfax, Virginia; associate professor of music education at the Conservatory of Music, Lawrence, University.

Uber, David
(April, 1963) — Assistant professor of music at Trenton State College, New Jersey. Education: bachelor's degree from Carthage College in Illinois; further study at the Curtis Institute of Music; master's degree from Teachers College, Columbia University. Teaching Experience: director of ensemble music at the National Music Camp. Performance: solo trombonist with the New York City Opera Company and the Symphony of the Air (formerly the NBC Symphony); member of the New York Brass Quintet.

Uggen, Stuart
(March, 1970) — Instructor in French horn at Appalachian State University, Education: bachelor's and master's degrees from Moorehead State College.

Van Develde, James
(December, 1979) — Director of bands at Frankenmuth (Michigan) High School.

Voth, Eugene D.
(September, 1974) — Chairman and associate professor of Orthodontics, School of Dentistry, Medical College of Georgia at Augusta.

Wagner, Irvin L.
(October, 1976) — Applied music instructor at the University of Oklahoma and freelance trombonist. Education: MA and PhD from the Eastman School of Music.

Weest, Robert
(June, 1963) — Assistant professor of brass instruments at Drake University. Publications: "Brass Performance," a text dealing with the problems of brass playing.

Weldon, Constance
(February, 1973) — Assistant professor of tuba at the University of Miami; member of the Miami Philharmonic.

Whitaker, Donald
(November, 1966) — Associate professor of brass instruments at the University of Wisconsin. Education: Bachelor of Music and Master of Music, Northwestern University; additional doctoral work at the Eastman School of Music. Teaching Experience: Wheaton College; Northwestern University. Performance: professional appearances with bands, orchestras, and quartets in the Chicago area.

Whitehill, Charles
(June, 1966) — Assistant professor and band director at Potomac State College of West Virginia University. Education: bachelor's and master's degrees in music education from West Virginia University; doctoral study at West Virginia University. Teaching Experience: band director in the junior and senior high schools in West Virginia; graduate assistant in the brass department at West Virginia University.

Whitwell, David
(January, 1972) — Conductor of the San Fernando Valley State College Wind Ensemble and Chamber Orchestra and Los Angeles Orchestra Club. Performance; has conducted major professional orchestras in Europe, the U.S.A. and South America.

Whybrew, William
(September, 1957) — Member of the faculty of Ithaca College. Education: bachelor's, master's, and Ph.D. degrees from the Eastman School of Music. Teaching Experience: band director and brass instructor in the public schools of Sodus and Rochester, New York; tuba and brass teacher at the Eastman School of Music. Performance: member of the Rochester Philharmonic Orchestra, the Rochester Civic Orchestra, and the Eastman-Rochester Orchestra.

Wilcox, Francis
(November, 1957) — Assistant professor of music at Bowling Green State University. Education: Bachelor of Arts and Master of Arts, State University of Iowa; Ph.D., Northwestern University.

Willis, Larry
(December, 1967) — Assistant director of bands and brass instructor at the University of Alabama. Education: bachelor's and master's degrees in music education from the University of Alabama. Teaching Experience: French horn instructor at the U.S. Naval School of Music. Performance: member of the U.S. Navy Academy Band at Annapolis.

Wilson, Phil
(February, 1974) — Chairman of the trombone department at Berklee College of Music in Boston; board member of the International Trombone Association. Performance: arranger and performer with the Woody Herman Band; jazz clinician.

Winick, Steven
(January, 1973) — Assistant professor of music at Georgia State University. Performance: solo trumpet with the Rochester Philharmonic; solo cornet with the Eastman Wind Ensemble and the U.S. Military Academy Band at West Point.

Winter, James
(May, 1955) — Assistant professor of brass instruments and theory and director of band at Fresno State College, California. Education: bachelor's degree from Carlton College; master's degree from Northwestern University; doctoral study at the University of Iowa.

Yanich, Milan
(April, 1959) — Instructor in French horn and ensemble at the Eastman School of Music. Education: University of Michigan; master's degree from Northwestern University. Teaching experience: faculty member at Michigan State University, Ohio State University, Baldwin-Wallace College, and Capital University. Performance: member of the Rochester Civic and Philharmonic Orchestras, the Columbus Symphony, Chicago Symphony, and Cleveland Symphony Orchestras.

Young, Raymond
(March, 1964) — Assistant professor of brass and associate director of bands at the University of Southern Mississippi. Education: bachelor's and master's degrees from the University of Michigan. Performance: soloist with the University of Michigan Symphonic Band; performer with the American Symphonic Band.

Zazra, Henry
(April, 1972) — Education: bachelor's degree from the University of Illinois at Chicago Circle; master's degree from Northwestern University.

Zimmerman, Gerald
(November, 1972) — Doctoral condidate and teaching fellow in trumpet at West Virginia University.

Zorn, Jay
(February, 1965) — Band director in the schools at Mamaroneck, New York. Education: bachelor's degrees from Oberlin Conservatory; master's degree from Columbia University.

Index of Articles by Title

(1946 - 1979)

Index of Articles by Category

(1946-1979)

ENSEMBLES

FRENCH HORN AND ALTO HORN

GENERAL ARTICLES

Index of Articles by Author
(1946-1979)